State Administrative Officials Classified by Function 1995

The Council of State Governments
Lexington, Kentucky

Headquarters — (606) 244-8000
State Leadership Directory Questions — (606) 244-8000
Publication Sales Department — (800) 800-1910
Fax — (606) 244-8001
E-mail — info@csg.org
Internet — www.csg.org

ISBN 0-87292-996-5

The Council of State Governments

The Council of State Governments is a nonpartisan organization that serves all three branches of state government through leadership, education, research and information services.

Founded more than 62 years ago, this multibranch organization of the states and U.S. territories champions excellence in state government, working with state leaders across the nation and through its regions to put the best ideas and solutions into practice.

To this end, The Council of State Governments:

- Builds leadership skills to improve decision-making;
- Advocates multistate problem-solving and partnerships;
- Interprets changing national and international conditions to prepare states for the future; and,
- Promotes the sovereignty of the states and their role in the American federal system.

Council Officers
Chair: Assemblyman Robert C. Wertz, N.Y.
Chair-Elect: Sen. Pres. Stanley J. Aronoff, Ohio
Vice Chair: Sen. Jeffrey Wells, Colo.
President: Gov. Mel Carnahan, Mo.
President-Elect: Gov. Mike Leavitt, Utah
Vice President: Gov. George Pataki, N.Y.

Council Offices
Headquarters:
Daniel M. Sprague, Executive Director
3560 Iron Works Pike
P.O. Box 11910
Lexington, KY 40578-1910
(606) 244-8000
FAX: (606) 244-8001

Shari Hendrickson, Director
Public Relations & Membership Services
(606) 244-8101

Bob Silvanik, Director
Policy & Program Development
(606) 244-8250

Phil Baughn, Director
Operations & Technology
(606) 244-8121

Washington
Abe Frank, Director
444 N. Capitol Street, NW, Suite 401
Washington, DC 20001
(202) 624-5460

Eastern:
Alan V. Sokolow, Director
5 World Trade Center, Suite 9241
New York, NY 10048
(212) 912-0128

Midwestern:
Michael H. McCabe, Director
641 E. Butterfield Road, Suite 401
Lombard, IL 60148
(708) 810-0210

Southern:
Colleen Cousineau, Director
3399 Peachtree Road, NE, Suite 810
Atlanta, GA 30326
(404) 266-1271

Western:
Andrew P. Grose, Director
121 Second Street, 4th Floor
San Francisco, CA 94105
(415) 974-6422

Manufactured in the United States of America

D024-9500
ISBN # 0-87292-996-5
Price: $45

State Leadership Directory binders are available for this publication.
Call the Publication Sales Order Department
The Council of State Governments
1-800-800-1910

CONTENTS

NOTE ON USE

Because state governments are organized in diverse ways, the functional categories and accompanying definitions presented in this volume may not apply to all states. The entries for all categories were reviewed and updated by state officials and staff. On the basis of the functional definitions, respondents identified the highest ranking officials — elected or appointed — in their respective states, who bear direct responsibility for these functions.

Other classifications, such as those employed by various national associations of state government officials, also are useful for understanding the functions performed by state administrators. However, in compiling this volume, we continue to rely on the verification of information from sources within each state.

The information for the volume was gathered and processed during a period extending from April through May 1995. Reflecting the changing nature of state government, a new category has been added to this edition: Records of Judicial Decisions.

The information in these functional categories is published yearly, and maintained on a centralized computer data base. Updated information on these entries should be directed to: Editor, State Leadership Directories, The Council of State Governments, 3560 Iron Works Pike, P.O. Box 11910, Lexington, KY 40578-1910. Please include your name, agency affiliation, address and phone number so that we may contact you for additional information, if necessary.

Please note: * means the position was not filled prior to the time of printing.
** means the updated information was not received prior to the time of printing.

ADJUTANT GENERAL

The executive or administrative head of the state's military services.

ALABAMA
James E. Moore
Acting Director
1720 Cong. Wm. Dickinson Dr.
Montgomery, AL 36130
Phone : (334) 271-7200
Fax : (334) 271-7366

ALASKA
Jake Lestenkof
Adjutant General
Dept. of Military & Vet. Affairs
P.O. Box 5800
Fort Richardson, AK 99505-5800
Phone : (907) 428-6003
Fax : (907) 428-6019

ARIZONA
Glen W. Van Dyke
Adjutant General
Arizona National Guard
5636 E. McDowell Rd.
Phoenix, AZ 85008
Phone : (602) 267-2700

ARKANSAS
Melvin C. Thrash
Adjutant General
State Military Dept.
Camp Robinson, Box 678
North Little Rock, AR 72118
Phone : (501) 791-5001
Fax : (501) 791-5009

CALIFORNIA
Tandy Bozeman
Adjutant General
Dept. of Military
9800 Goethe Rd.
Sacramento, CA 95826-9101
Phone : (916) 854-3500

COLORADO
William A. Westerdahl
Adjutant General
Dept. of Military Affairs
6848 S. Revere Pkwy.
Englewood, CO 80112
Phone : (303) 397-3000
Fax : (303) 397-3281

CONNECTICUT
David W. Gay
Adjutant General
Military Dept.
National Guard Armory
360 Broad St.
Hartford, CT 06105
Phone : (203) 524-4953

DELAWARE
G.K. Hastings
Adjutant General
Delaware National Guard
First Regiment Rd.
Wilmington, DE 19804
Phone : (302) 324-7001
Fax : (302) 324-7029

FLORIDA
Ronald O. Harrison
Adjutant General
Dept. of Military Affairs
St. Francis Barracks
P.O. Box 1008
St. Augustine, FL 32085
Phone : (904) 823-0100

GEORGIA
William P. Bland Jr.
Adjutant General
Dept. of Defense
935 Confederate Ave., SE
Atlanta, GA 30316-0965
Phone : (404) 624-6001
Fax : (404) 624-6005

HAWAII
Edward V. Richardson
Adjutant General
Dept. of Defense
3949 Diamond Head Rd.
Honolulu, HI 96816
Phone : (808) 734-2195
Fax : (808) 737-7886

IDAHO
John F. Kane
Adjutant General
Military Div.
Gowen Field
Boise, ID 83707
Phone : (208) 389-5242

ILLINOIS
Richard G. Austin
Adjutant General
Dept. of Military Affairs
Camp Lincoln
1301 N. MacArthur Blvd.
Springfield, IL 62702-2399
Phone : (217) 785-3500
Fax : (217) 785-3736

INDIANA
Charles Whitaker
Adjutant General
Off. of the Adjutant General
P.O. Box 41326
Indianapolis, IN 46241-0326
Phone : (317) 247-3274

IOWA
Warren G. Lawson
Adjutant General
Iowa National Guard
Camp Dodge
7700 NW Beaver Dr.
Johnston, IA 50131-1902
Phone : (515) 252-4211
Fax : (515) 252-4656

KANSAS
James F. Rueger
Adjutant General
2800 SW Topeka Blvd.
Topeka, KS 66601-0300
Phone : (913) 274-1001

KENTUCKY
Robert Dezarn
Adjutant General
Dept. of Military Affairs
Boone National Guard Ctr.
Frankfort, KY 40601
Phone : (502) 564-8558

LOUISIANA
Ansel M. Stroud Jr.
Adjutant General
Dept. of Military
Jackson Barracks
New Orleans, LA 70146
Phone : (504) 278-6211

MAINE
Earl L. Adams
Commissioner/Adjutant General
Dept. of Defense & Vet. Srvcs.
#33 State House Station
Augusta, ME 04333-0033
Phone : (207) 626-4225

MARYLAND
James F. Fretterd
Adjutant General
Military Dept.
Fifth Regiment Armory
Baltimore, MD 21201
Phone : (410) 576-6097
Fax : (410) 576-6191

MASSACHUSETTS
Raymond Vezina
Adjutant General
Massachusetts Army
c/o Camp Curtis Guild
Haverhill St.
Reading, MA 01867-1999
Phone : (617) 944-0500

MICHIGAN
E. Gordon Stump
Adjutant General
Dept. of Military Affairs
2500 S. Washington Ave.
Lansing, MI 48913-5101
Phone : (517) 483-5507
Fax : (517) 482-0356

MINNESOTA
Eugene R. Andreotti
Adjutant General
Dept. of Military Affairs
Veterans Service Bldg.
20 W. 12th St.
St. Paul, MN 55155-2098
Phone : (612) 282-4666

MISSISSIPPI
James H. Garner
Special Advisor for Military Affairs
Dept. of the Military
P.O. Box 5027
Jackson, MS 39216-1027
Phone : (601) 973-6232

MISSOURI
Raymond Pendergrass
Adjutant General
2302 Militia Dr.
Jefferson City, MO 65101-1203
Phone : (314) 526-9711
Fax : (314) 526-9929

MONTANA
John E. Prendergast
Adjutant General
Dept. of Military Affairs
P.O. Box 4789
Helena, MT 59604
Phone : (406) 444-6910

NEBRASKA
Stan Heng
Director
Military Dept.
National Guard Ctr.
1300 Military Rd.
Lincoln, NE 68508-1090
Phone : (402) 471-7114
Fax : (402) 471-7171

NEVADA
Drennan A. Clark
Adjutant General
Off. of the Adjutant General
2525 S. Carson St.
Carson City, NV 89701-5502
Phone : (702) 887-7302

NEW HAMPSHIRE
John E. Blair
Adjutant General
1 Airport Rd.
Concord, NH 03301
Phone : (603) 271-2331

NEW JERSEY
Paul J. Glazarto
Adjutant General
Dept. of Military & Veterans' Affairs
Eggert Crossing Rd., CN340
Trenton, NJ 08625-0340
Phone : (609) 292-3888

NEW MEXICO
Melvin S. Montano
Adjutant General
Off. of Military Affairs
National Guard Bldg.
P.O. Box 4277
Santa Fe, NM 87502-4277
Phone : (505) 474-1202
Fax : (505) 474-1289

NEW YORK*
Adjutant General
Military & Naval Affairs
330 Old Niskoyuna Rd.
Latham, NY 12110
Phone : (518) 786-4502

NORTH CAROLINA
Gerald A. Rudisill
Adjutant General
Div. of the National Guard
Crime Control & Public Safety
4105 Reedy Creek Rd.
Raleigh, NC 27607-6410
Phone : (919) 664-6101
Fax : (919) 664-6400

NORTH DAKOTA
Keith Bjerke
Adjutant General
National Guard
P.O. Box 5511
Bismarck, ND 58502-5511
Phone : (701) 224-5101
Fax : (701) 224-5180

OHIO
Richard C. Alexander
Adjutant General
Off. of Adjutant General
2825 W. Granville Rd.
Columbus, OH 43235-2789
Phone : (614) 889-7070
Fax : (614) 889-7074

OKLAHOMA
Stephen Cortright
Adjutant General
Dept. of the Military
3501 Military Cir.
Oklahoma City, OK 73111-4398
Phone : (405) 425-8000

OREGON
Raymond Fred Rees
Adjutant General
Dept. of the Military
1776 Militia Way, SE
Salem, OR 97309-5407
Phone : (503) 378-3981

PENNSYLVANIA
James MacVay
Adjutant General
Dept. of Military Affairs
Ft. Indiantown Gap
Annville, PA 17003
Phone : (717) 861-8502

RHODE ISLAND
N. Andre Trudeau
Adjutant General
National Guard
1051 N. Main St.
Providence, RI 02904
Phone : (401) 457-4100

SOUTH CAROLINA
Stan Spears
Adjutant General
1 National Guard Rd.
Columbia, SC 29201-4766
Phone : (803) 748-4217

SOUTH DAKOTA
Harold Sykora
Adjutant General
Dept. of Military & Veterans Affairs
425 E. Capitol Ave.
Pierre, SD 57501
Phone : (605) 773-3269

TENNESSEE
Dan Wood
Adjutant General
Dept. of Military
3041 Sidco Dr.
Nashville, TN 37204
Phone : (615) 532-3001
Fax : (615) 532-3419

TEXAS
Sam C. Turk
Adjutant General
P.O. Box 5218
Austin, TX 78763
Phone : (512) 465-5006

UTAH
John L. Matthews
Adjutant General
National Guard
12953 S. Minuteman Dr.
Draper, UT 84020
Phone : (801) 576-3600

VERMONT
Donald Edwards
Adjutant General
Military Dept.
Green Mountain Armory
Colchester, VT 05446
Phone : (802) 654-0124
Fax : (802) 654-0425

VIRGINIA
Carroll Thackston
Adjutant General
Dept. of Military Affairs
600 E. Broad St.
Richmond, VA 23219
Phone : (804) 775-9102
Fax : (804) 775-9338

WASHINGTON
Greg Barlow
Adjutant General
Dept. of the Military
Camp Murray
M/S: TA-20
Tacoma, WA 98430-5000
Phone : (360) 581-1950

WEST VIRGINIA
Joseph J. Skaff
Adjutant General
1707 Coonskin Dr.
Charleston, WV 25311
Phone : (304) 341-6316
Fax : (304) 341-6466

WISCONSIN
Jerald D. Slack
Adjutant General
Dept. of Military Affairs
2400 Wright St.
P.O. Box 8111
Madison, WI 53708
Phone : (608) 242-3000
Fax : (608) 242-3111

WYOMING
Ed Boenisch
Adjutant General
Dept. of the Military
P.O. Box 1709
Cheyenne, WY 82003
Phone : (307) 772-5234
Fax : (307) 772-5910

DISTRICT OF COLUMBIA
Russel C. Davis
Commanding General
DC National Guard
2001 E. Capitol St.
Washington, DC 20003-1719
Phone : (202) 433-5220

GUAM
Ramon Q. Sudo
Adjutant General
National Guard
622 E. Harmon Industrial
Park
Tamuning, GU 96911
Phone : (671) 649-0955
Fax : (671) 649-5811

PUERTO RICO
Emilio Diaz Colon
Adjutant General
National Guard
P.O. Box 3786
San Juan, PR 00902-3786
Phone : (809) 289-1400
Fax : (809) 723-6360

U.S. VIRGIN ISLANDS
Charles M. Hood
Adjutant General
VI National Guard
Alexander Hamilton
Airport
Kingshill
St. Croix, VI 00850
Phone : (809) 778-4916

ADMINISTRATION

Umbrella agency of administration that coordinates administrative services provided to state agencies.

ALABAMA
Don Drablos
Chief of Services
General Srvcs. Div.
Dept. of Finance
425 S. Union St.
Montgomery, AL 36130
Phone : (334) 242-2773
Fax : (334) 240-3402

ALASKA
Mark Boyer
Commissioner
Dept. of Administration
P.O. Box 110200
Juneau, AK 99811-0200
Phone : (907) 465-2200
Fax : (907) 465-2135

ARIZONA
Rudy Serino
Director
Dept. of Administration
Capitol Tower
1700 W. Washington
Phoenix, AZ 85007
Phone : (602) 542-1500
Fax : (602) 542-2199

ARKANSAS
Richard Weiss
Director
Dept. of Finance & Admin.
401 DFA Bldg.
1509 W. 7th St.
Little Rock, AR 17201
Phone : (501) 682-2242
Fax : (501) 682-1086

CALIFORNIA
Steve Olsen
Chief Deputy Director
Dept. of General Services
1325 J St., Ste. 1910
Sacramento, CA 95814
Phone : (916) 323-9969

Peter G. Stamison
Director
Dept. of General Services
1325 J St., Ste. 1910
Sacramento, CA 95814
Phone : (916) 445-3441

COLORADO
Andre' Pettigrew
Executive Director
Dept. of Administration
1525 Sherman St., 2nd Fl.
Denver, CO 80203
Phone : (303) 866-3221
Fax : (303) 866-6569

CONNECTICUT
Louis S. Goldberg
Commissioner
Dept. of Administrative Srvcs.
165 Capitol Ave., Rm. 491
Hartford, CT 06106
Phone : (203) 566-7528

DELAWARE
Vincent P. Meconi
Secretary
Dept. of Administrative Srvcs.
Townsend Bldg.
P.O. Box 1401
Dover, DE 19903
Phone : (302) 739-3611
Fax : (302) 739-6704

FLORIDA
Bill Linder
Secretary
Dept. of Management Services
Knight Bldg., Ste. 110
2737 Centerview Dr.
Tallahassee, FL 32399-0950
Phone : (904) 488-2786
Fax : (904) 922-6149

GEORGIA
David C. Evans
Commissioner
Dept. of Administrative Srvcs.
200 Piedmont Ave., Ste. 1520
Atlanta, GA 30334
Phone : (404) 656-5514

HAWAII
Eugene Imai
Comptroller
Dept. of Accounting & General Srvcs.
1151 Punchbowl St., Rm. 412
Honolulu, HI 96810
Phone : (808) 586-0400
Fax : (808) 586-0707

IDAHO
Pamela Ahrens
Director
Dept. of Administration
650 W. State St., Rm. 100
Boise, ID 83720
Phone : (208) 334-3382

ILLINOIS
Michael S. Schwartz
Director
Dept. of Central Mgt. Srvcs.
715 Stratton Off. Bldg.
Springfield, IL 62706
Phone : (217) 782-2141
Fax : (217) 524-1880

INDIANA
William L. Shrewsberry
Commissioner
Dept. of Administration
IGC-South, Rm. W479
402 W. Washington St.
Indianapolis, IN 46204
Phone : (317) 231-3115

IOWA
Janet E. Phipps
Director
Dept. of General Srvcs.
Hoover State Off. Bldg.
Des Moines, IA 50319
Phone : (515) 281-3196
Fax : (515) 242-5974

KANSAS
Sheila Frahm
Secretary
Dept. of Administration
State Capitol Bldg., Rm. 263E
Topeka, KS 66612-1572
Phone : (913) 296-3011
Fax : (913) 296-2702

KENTUCKY
Don Speer
Commissioner
Dept. of Administration
Finance & Admin. Cabinet
Capitol Annex, Rm. 362
Frankfort, KY 40601
Phone : (502) 564-2317

LOUISIANA
Raymond J. Laborde
Commissioner
Div. of Administration
Capitol Annex
P.O. Box 94095
Baton Rouge, LA 70804-9095
Phone : (504) 342-7000

MAINE
Janet Waldron
Commissioner
Dept. of Admin. & Financial Srvcs.
State House Station #78
Augusta, ME 04333-0078
Phone : (207) 624-7800

MARYLAND
Eugene Lynch
Acting Secretary
Dept. of General Srvcs.
301 W. Preston St., Rm. 1401
Baltimore, MD 21201
Phone : (410) 225-4960

MASSACHUSETTS
Charles Baker
Secretary
Executive Off. for Admin. & Finance
State House, Rm. 373
Boston, MA 02133
Phone : (617) 727-2040

MICHIGAN *
Director
Dept. of Management & Budget
320 S. Walnut
Lansing, MI 48909
Phone : (517) 373-1004
Fax : (517) 373-7268

MINNESOTA
Elaine Hansen
Commissioner
Dept. of Administration
200 State Admin. Bldg.
50 Sherburne Ave.
St. Paul, MN 55155
Phone : (612) 296-1424

MISSISSIPPI
Beverly Bolton
Deputy Director
Dept. of Finance & Admin.
1501 Sillers Bldg.
Jackson, MS 39201
Phone : (601) 359-3633

MISSOURI
Richard A. Hanson
Commissioner
Off. of Administration
State Capitol, Rm. 125
P.O. Box 809
Jefferson City, MO 65102
Phone : (314) 751-3311
Fax : (314) 751-1212

MONTANA
Debra Fulton
Administrator
Div. of General Services
Dept. of Administration
Capitol Annex Bldg.
Helena, MT 59620
Phone : (406) 444-3060

NEBRASKA
Lawrence S. Primeau
Director
Dept. of Administrative Srvcs.
State Capitol, Room 1315
Lincoln, NE 68509-4664
Phone : (402) 471-2331
Fax : (402) 471-4157

NEVADA
John P. Comeaux
Director
Dept. of Administration
209 E. Musser St., Rm. 200
Carson City, NV 89710
Phone : (702) 687-4065
Fax : (702) 687-3983

NEW HAMPSHIRE
Patrick Duffy
Commissioner
Dept. of Administrative Srvcs.
25 Capitol St.
Concord, NH 03301
Phone : (603) 271-3201

NEW JERSEY
George M. Gross, Jr.
Administrator
General Srvcs. Admin.
Dept. of Treasury
33 W. State St., CN039
Trenton, NJ 08625
Phone : (609) 292-4330

NEW MEXICO
Steven Beffort
Secretary
General Services Dept.
715 Alta Vista
P.O. Drawer 26110
Santa Fe, NM 87502-0110
Phone : (505) 827-2000
Fax : (505) 827-2041

NEW YORK *
Commissioner
Off. of General Srvcs.
Corning Tower Bldg., 41st Fl.
Empire State Plaza
Albany, NY 12242
Phone : (518) 474-5991

NORTH CAROLINA
Katie G. Dorsett
Secretary
Dept. of Administration
116 W. Jones St.
Raleigh, NC 27603
Phone : (919) 733-7232
Fax : (919) 733-9571

OHIO
C. James Conrad
Director
Dept. of Administrative Srvcs.
30 E. Broad St., 40th Fl.
Columbus, OH 43266
Phone : (614) 466-6511
Fax : (614) 644-8151

OKLAHOMA
Thomas Brennan
Secretary of Administration
Dept. of Central Srvcs.
State Capitol Bldg., Rm. 104
Oklahoma City, OK 73105
Phone : (405) 521-2121

OREGON
Jon Yunker
Director
Dept. of Administrative Srvcs.
155 Cottage St., NE
Salem, OR 97310
Phone : (503) 378-3104
Fax : (503) 373-7643

PENNSYLVANIA
Tom Paese
Secretary
Office of Administration
Rm. 207, Finance Bldg.
Harrisburg, PA 17120
Phone : (717) 787-9945

RHODE ISLAND
Gayl W. Doster
Director
Dept. of Administration
One Capitol Hill
Providence, RI 02908
Phone : (401) 277-2280

SOUTH CAROLINA
Richard W. Kelly
Director
Division of Operations
Budget & Control Board
Wade Hampton Bldg.
P.O. Box 12444
Columbia, SC 29211
Phone : (803) 734-2320

SOUTH DAKOTA
Tom D. Geraets
Commissioner
Bur. of Administration
500 E. Capitol Ave.
Pierre, SD 57501
Phone : (605) 773-3688

TENNESSEE
Larry Haynes
Commissioner
Dept. of General Srvcs.
Tennessee Tower, 9th Fl.
Nashville, TN 37243-0530
Phone : (615) 741-9263
Fax : (615) 741-8408

TEXAS
John Pouland
Executive Director
General Srvcs. Comm.
Capitol Station
P.O. Box 13047
Austin, TX 78711-3047
Phone : (512) 463-3035

UTAH
Raylene Ireland
Executive Director
Dept. of Administrative Srvcs.
3120 State Off. Bldg.
Salt Lake City, UT 84114
Phone : (801) 538-3010

VERMONT
William H. Sorrell
Secretary
Agency of Administration
109 State St.
Montpelier, VT 05609-0201
Phone : (802) 828-3322
Fax : (802) 828-2428

VIRGINIA
Donald C. Williams
Director
Dept. of General Services
209 9th Street Office Bldg.
Richmond, VA 23219
Phone : (804) 371-3311
Fax : (804) 786-8305

WASHINGTON
John Franklin
Director
Dept. of General Admin.
P.O. Box 41000
Olympia, WA 98504-1000
Phone : (360) 753-5439

WEST VIRGINIA
Charles Polan
Secretary
Dept. of Finance & Admin.
State Capitol, Rm. E119
1900 Kanawha Blvd., E.
Charleston, WV 25305
Phone : (304) 558-2300
Fax : (304) 558-2999

WISCONSIN
James R. Klauser
Secretary
Dept. of Administration
101 E. Wilson, 10th Fl.
P.O. Box 7864
Madison, WI 53707
Phone : (608) 266-1741
Fax : (608) 267-3842

WYOMING
Don Rolston
Director
Dept. of Admin. & Information
Emerson Bldg., Rm 104
2001 Capitol Ave.
Cheyenne, WY 82002
Phone : (307) 777-7201

DISTRICT OF COLUMBIA
James Gaston
Director
Dept. of Administrative Srvcs.
441 4th St., NW, Ste. 700
Washington, DC 20001
Phone : (202) 727-1179

AMERICAN SAMOA
Fa'i Faaita
Director
Dept. of Administrative Services
American Samoa Government
Pago Pago, AS 96799
Phone : (684) 633-4156
Fax : (684) 633-1841

GUAM
John S. Salas
Director
Dept. of Administration
P.O. Box 884
Agana, GU 96910
Phone : (671) 475-1101
Fax : (671) 477-6788

NORTHERN MARIANA ISLANDS
Joaquin I. Pangelinan
Special Assistant for Admin.
Off. of the Governor
Capitol Hill
Saipan, MP 96950
Phone : (670) 322-5091
Fax : (670) 322-5099

PUERTO RICO
Aura Gonzalez
Director
Central Office of Personnel Administration
P.O. Box 8476
San Juan, PR 00910-8476
Phone : (809) 721-4300
Fax : (809) 722-3390

U.S. VIRGIN ISLANDS
Alvin O. Davis
Commissioner
Dept. of Property & Procurement
Sub Base, Bldg. 1
St. Thomas, VI 00801
Phone : (809) 774-0828
Fax : (803) 774-9704

AERONAUTICS

Issues rules and regulations on aviation safety and prepares plans for the state's airway systems.

ALABAMA
John Eagerton
Acting Director
Dept. of Aeronautics
770 Washington Ave.
Montgomery, AL 36130
Phone: (334) 242-4480
Fax: (334) 240-3274

ALASKA
John Horn
Regional Director
Central Region
Dept. of Transportation & Public Facilities
P.O. Box 196900
Anchorage, AK 99519
Phone: (907) 266-1440
Fax: (907) 248-1573

ARIZONA
Gary Adams
Assistant Director
Aeronautics Div.
Dept. of Transportation
1841 W. Buchanan St.
Phoenix, AZ 85007
Phone: (602) 255-7691

ARKANSAS
John Knight
Director
Dept. of Aeronautics
Regional Airport Terminal
1 Airport Dr., 3rd Fl.
Little Rock, AR 72202
Phone: (501) 376-6781
Fax: (501) 378-0820

CALIFORNIA
Marlin Beckwith
Program Manager
Aeronautics Program
Dept. of Transportation
P.O. Box 942874
Sacramento, CA 94274
Phone: (809) 729-8806
Fax: (809) 722-7867

COLORADO
Dennis Roberts
Director
Aeronautics Div.
Dept. of Transportation
56 Inverness Drive East
Englewood, CO 80112-5114
Phone: (303) 792-2160
Fax: (303) 792-2180

CONNECTICUT
Robert F. Juliano
Bureau Chief
Bur. of Aviation & Ports
Dept. of Transportation
2800 Berkin Tpke.
P.O. Box 317546
Newington, CT 06131-7546
Phone: (203) 594-2529

DELAWARE
B.M. Tobey
Administrator
Aeronautics Admin.
Dept. of Transportation
Transportation Admin. Bldg.
Dover, DE 19901
Phone: (302) 739-3264

FLORIDA
Nick Serianni
Off. of Public Transportation
Dept. of Transportation
605 Suwannee St.
Tallahassee, FL 32399
Phone: (904) 488-5704

GEORGIA
Ray Fletcher
Manager
Aviation Programs
Dept. of Transportation
276 Memorial Dr., SW
Atlanta, GA 30303
Phone: (404) 651-5206

HAWAII
Owen Miyamoto
Chief
Airports Div.
Dept. of Transportation
Honolulu Intl. Airport
Honolulu, HI 96819
Phone: (808) 863-6432

IDAHO
William Cooper
Chief
Bur. of Aeronautics
P.O. Box 7129
Boise, ID 83707
Phone: (208) 334-8786

ILLINOIS
William L. Blake
Director
Div. of Aeronautics
Dept. of Transportation
Capital Airport
Springfield, IL 62706
Phone: (217) 785-8381

INDIANA
Deborah Simmons
Division Chief
Aeronautics Div.
Dept. of Transportation
100 N. Senate Ave., N901
Indianapolis, IN 46204
Phone: (317) 232-1495

IOWA
Michael Audino
Director
Air & Transit Div.
Dept. of Transportation
100 E. Euclid Ave., # 7
Des Moines, IA 50313
Phone: (515) 237-3321

KANSAS
Michael Armour
Director of Aviation
Division of Aviation
Dept. of Transportation
Docking State Off. Bldg., 7th Fl.
Topeka, KS 66612-1568
Phone: (913) 296-2553
Fax: (913) 296-3833

KENTUCKY
Bob Bodner
Director
Off. of Aeronautics
Transportation Cabinet
125 Holmes St.
Frankfort, KY 40622
Phone: (502) 564-4480

LOUISIANA
Joseph D. Levraea
Aviation Program Manager
Aviation Div.
Transportation & Dev. Dept.
P.O. Box 94245
Baton Rouge, LA 70804
Phone: (504) 379-1100

MAINE
Ron Roy
Director
Aeronautics Div.
Dept. of Transportation
State House Station # 16
Augusta, ME 04333
Phone: (207) 287-3185

MARYLAND
Theodore E. Mathison
Administrator
Aviation Admin.
Dept. of Transportation
P.O. Box 8766
Baltimore, MD 21240-0755
Phone: (410) 859-7060
Fax: (410) 859-4729

MASSACHUSETTS
Sherman W. Saltmarsh Jr.
Chairman
Aeronautics Comm.
10 Park Plz., Rm. 6620
Boston, MA 02116-3966
Phone: (617) 973-8881

MICHIGAN
William E. Gehman
Director
Bur. of Aeronautics
2700 E. Airport Service Dr.
Lansing, MI 48906
Phone: (517) 335-9943

MINNESOTA
Raymond Rought
Director
Off. of Aeronautics
Dept. of Transportation
222 East Plato Blvd.
St. Paul, MN 55107
Phone : (612) 296-8202

MISSISSIPPI
Ken Barfield
Aeronautics Director
P.O. Box 5
Jackson, MS 39205
Phone : (601) 354-6970

MISSOURI
Lloyd B. Parr
Administrator
Aviation Unit
Dept of Hwy. & Transportation
Highway Bldg., P.O. Box 270
Jefferson City, MO 65102
Phone : (314) 751-2589
Fax : (314) 526-4709

MONTANA
Michael D. Ferguson
Administrator
Aeronautics Div.
Dept. of Transportation
P.O. Box 5178
Helena, MT 59604
Phone : (406) 444-2506

NEBRASKA
Kim J. Stevens
Director
Dept. of Aeronautics
Lincoln Municipal Airport
P.O. Box 82088
Lincoln, NE 68501-2088
Phone : (402) 471-2371
Fax : (402) 471-2906

NEW HAMPSHIRE
W. Harold Buker Jr.
Director
Aeronautics Div.
Dept. of Transportation
65 Airport Road
Concord, NH 03301
Phone : (603) 271-2551

NEW JERSEY
John S. Penn
Exectutive Director
Div. of Aeronautics
Dept. of Transportation
1035 Parkway Ave., CN 610
Trenton, NJ 08625
Phone : (609) 530-2900

NEW MEXICO
Pete Alexander
Director
Aviation Div.
State Highway & Trans. Dept.
P.O. Box 1149
1550 Pacheco St.
Santa Fe, NM 87505
Phone : (505) 827-0332
Fax : (505) 827-1531

NEW YORK *
Commissioner
Dept. of Transportation
Campus, Bldg. 5
Albany, NY 12232
Phone : (518) 457-4422

NORTH CAROLINA
W.G. Plentl Jr.
Director
Div. of Aviation
Dept. of Transportation
6701 Aviation Pkwy., RDU Airport
Raleigh, NC 27623
Phone : (919) 787-9618
Fax : (919) 783-6841

NORTH DAKOTA
Gary R. Ness
Director
Aeronautics Comm.
P.O. Box 5020
Bismarck, ND 58502
Phone : (701) 328-2748
Fax : (701) 328-2780

OHIO
John Cornett
Director
Bur. of Aviation
Dept. of Transportation
2829 W. Dublin-Granville Rd.
Worthington, OH 43235
Phone : (614) 793-5042
Fax : (614) 793-8972

OKLAHOMA
Dana Batey
Director
Aeronautics Comm.
200 NE 21st St.
Oklahoma City, OK 73105
Phone : (405) 521-2377

OREGON
Betsy Johnson
Acting Manager
Aeronautics Div.
Dept. of Transportation
Salem, OR 97310
Phone : (503) 378-4882
Fax : (503) 373-1688

PENNSYLVANIA
Elizabeth Sarge Voras
Special Assistant to the Secretary
Aviation, Rail & Ports
Dept. of Transportation
1200 Transportation & Safety Bldg.
Harrisburg, PA 17120
Phone : (717) 783-2026

RHODE ISLAND
Gene Tansey
Director
Div. of Airports
Dept. of Transportation
T.F. Green Airport
Warwick, RI 02886
Phone : (401) 737-4000

SOUTH CAROLINA
Joseph J. Saleeby
Director
Aeronautics Div.
Dept. of Commerce
P.O. Box 280068
Columbia, SC 29228
Phone : (803) 822-5400
Fax : (803) 822-8002

SOUTH DAKOTA
Richard Howard
Secretary
Dept. of Transportation
700 E. Broadway
Pierre, SD 57501
Phone : (605) 773-3265

TENNESSEE
Malcolm Baird
Director
Public Trans. & Aeronautics
Dept. of Transportation
700 James K. Polk Bldg.
Nashville, TN 37243
Phone : (615) 741-2849

TEXAS
David S. Fulton
Executive Director
Aviation Division
Dept. of Transportation
P.O. Box 12607
Austin, TX 78711
Phone : (512) 476-9262

UTAH
Phillip N. Ashbaker
Director
Aeronautical Operations
Dept. of Transportation
135 N. 2400 W.
Salt Lake City, UT 84116
Phone : (801) 533-5057

VERMONT
William S. Bruzzese
Director
Air, Rail & Transit Program
Agency of Transportation
133 State St.
Montpelier, VT 05633
Phone : (802) 828-2093
Fax : (802) 828-2829

VIRGINIA
Kenneth F. Weigand
Director
Dept. of Aviation
5702 Gulfstream Rd.
Sandston, VA 23150
Phone : (804) 236-3625
Fax : (804) 236-3635

WASHINGTON
Bill Brubaker
Director
Div. of Aviation
8900 E. Marginal Way
Seattle, WA 98108
Phone : (360) 764-4131

WEST VIRGINIA
Charles Miller
Secretary
Dept. of Transportation
Bldg. 5, Rm. A109
1900 Kanawha Blvd., E.
Charleston, WV 25302
Phone : (304) 558-0444
Fax : (304) 558-1004

WISCONSIN
James Johnson
Administrator
Div. of State Agency Srvcs.
Dept. of Admininistration.
101 E. Wilson
P.O. Box 7867
Madison, WI 53707
Phone : (608) 266-1011
Fax : (608) 267-0600

WYOMING
Richard Spaeth
Administrator
Aeronautics Div.
Wyoming Transportation Dept.
P.O. Box 1708
Cheyenne, WY 82003
Phone : (307) 777-4880

AMERICAN SAMOA
Sila Poasa
Director
Dept. of Port Administration
Pago Pago, AS 96799
Phone : (684) 633-4251
Fax : (684) 633-5281

NORTHERN MARIANA ISLANDS
Carlos S. Shoda
Executive Director
Commonwealth Port Authority
P.O. Box 1055
Saipan, MP 96950
Phone : (670) 234-8315
Fax : (670) 234-5962

PUERTO RICO
Herman Sulsona
Executive Director
Port Authority
G.P.O. Box 362829
San Juan, PR 00936-2829
Phone : (809) 729-8806
Fax : (809) 722-7867

U.S. VIRGIN ISLANDS
Gordon Finch
Executive Director
Port Authority
P.O. Box 1707
St. Thomas, VI 00802
Phone : (809) 774-1629
Fax : (809) 774-8062

AGING

Develops and strengthens services for the aged and conducts or promotes research into their problems.

ALABAMA
Martha Murph Beck
Commissioner
Commission of Aging
RSA Plz., Ste. 470
770 Washington Ave.
Montgomery, AL 36130
Phone : (334) 242-5743
Fax : (334) 242-5594

ALASKA
Jane Demmert
Executive Director
Alaska Commission on Aging
Dept. of Administration
P.O. Box 110209
Juneau, AK 99811-0209
Phone : (907) 465-3250
Fax : (907) 465-4716

ARIZONA
Richard Littler
Program Administrator
Aging & Adult Administration
Dept. of Economic Security
1789 W. Jefferson
Phoenix, AZ 85007
Phone : (602) 542-4446

ARKANSAS
Herb Sanderson
Deputy Director
Aging & Adult Srvcs.
P.O. Box 1437
Little Rock, AR 72203
Phone : (501) 682-8521
Fax : (501) 682-8155

CALIFORNIA
Robert P. Martinez
Director
Dept. of Aging
1600 K St.
Sacramento, CA 95814
Phone : (916) 322-5290

COLORADO
Rita Barreras
Director
Aging & Adult Srvcs. Div.
Dept. of Human Srvcs.
110 16th St., 2nd Fl.
Denver, CO 80203
Phone : (303) 620-4127
Fax : (303) 620-4189

CONNECTICUT
Cynthia Matthews
Executive Director
Commission on Aging
25 Sigourney St., 8th Fl.
Hartford, CT 06106-5003
Phone : (203) 424-5360

DELAWARE
Eleanor Cain
Director
Div. of Aging
Health & Social Srvcs. Dept.
1901 N. DuPont Hwy.
New Castle, DE 19720
Phone : (302) 577-4660
Fax : (302) 577-4793

FLORIDA
Bentley Lipscomb
Secretary
Dept. of Elder Affairs
Bldg. E, Rm. 317
1317 Winewood Blvd.
Tallahassee, FL 32399-0700
Phone : (904) 922-5297
Fax : (904) 922-6216

GEORGIA
Judith Hagabak
Director
Div. of Aging
Dept. of Human Resources
2 Peachtree St., #18
Atlanta, GA 30303
Phone : (404) 657-5255

HAWAII
Marilyn Seely
Director
Executive Off. on Aging
Off. of the Governor
335 Merchant St., Rm. 241
Honolulu, HI 96813
Phone : (808) 586-0100
Fax : (808) 586-0185

IDAHO
Jesse S. Berain
Director
Off. on Aging
Statehouse, Rm. 108
Boise, ID 83703
Phone : (208) 334-3833

ILLINOIS
Maralee Lindley
Director
Dept. on Aging
421 E. Capitol
Springfield, IL 62701
Phone : (217) 785-2870
Fax : (217) 785-4477

INDIANA
Bobby Connor
Director
Div. of Aging & Rehabilitation
Family & Soc. Srvcs. Admn.
402 W. Washington
Indianapolis, IN 46207
Phone : (317) 232-1147

IOWA
Betty Grandquist
Executive Director
Dept. of Elder Affairs
914 Grand, 2nd Fl.
Des Moines, IA 50309
Phone : (515) 281-5188
Fax : (515) 281-4036

KANSAS
Thelma Gordon
Secretary
Dept. of Aging
Docking State Off. Bldg., Rm. 150-S
Topeka, KS 66612-1500
Phone : (913) 296-4986
Fax : (913) 296-0256

KENTUCKY
S. Jack Williams
Director
Div. of Aging Services
Dept. for Social Srvcs.
275 E. Main St.
Frankfort, KY 40621
Phone : (502) 564-6930

LOUISIANA
Bobby Fontenot
Executive Director
Off. of Elderly Affairs
4550 North Blvd.
Baton Rouge, LA 70806
Phone : (504) 925-1700

MAINE
Christine Gianopoulos
Director
Bur. of Elder & Adult Services
Dept. of Human Services
State House Station # 11
Augusta, ME 04333
Phone : (207) 624-5335

MARYLAND
Sue Ward
Director
Off. on Aging
301 W. Preston St., Rm. 1004
Baltimore, MD 21201
Phone : (410) 225-1102
Fax : (410) 333-7943

MASSACHUSETTS
Franklin Ollivierre
Secretary
Executive Off. of Elder Affairs
1 Ashburton Pl., 5th Fl.
Boston, MA 02108
Phone : (617) 727-7750

MICHIGAN
Diane Braunstein
Director
Off. of Services on Aging
611 W. Ottawa St., 3rd Fl.
Lansing, MI 48909
Phone : (517) 373-8230
Fax : (517) 373-4092

MINNESOTA
Gerald A. Bloedow
Executive Secretary
Board on Aging
Human Srvcs. Bldg., 4th Fl.
444 Lafayette Rd.
St Paul, MN 55155
Phone : (612) 296-2770

MISSISSIPPI
Eddie Anderson
Director
Council on Aging
Dept. of Human Services
P.O. Box 352
Jackson, MS 39205-0352

MISSOURI
Greg Vadner
Director
Div. of Aging
Dept. of Social Services
615 Howerton Ct.
P.O. Box 1337
Jefferson City, MO 65102
Phone : (314) 751-8535
Fax : (314) 751-8687

MONTANA
Charlie Rehbein
Aging Coordinator
Aging Division
Dept. of Family Services
48 N. Last Chance Gulch
Helena, MT 59604
Phone : (406) 444-5900

NEBRASKA
Dennis H. Loose
Director
Dept. on Aging
301 Centennial Mall S.
P.O. Box 95044
Lincoln, NE 68509-5044
Phone : (402) 471-2306
Fax : (402) 471-4619

NEVADA
Suzanne Ernst
Administrator
Div. for Aging Srvcs.
340 N. 11th St., Ste. 114
Las Vegas, NV 89101
Phone : (702) 486-3545

NEW HAMPSHIRE
Richard Chevrefils
Director
Div. of Elderly & Adult Srvcs.
Dept. of Health & Human Srvcs.
115 Pleasant St., Annex Bldg. 1
Concord, NH 03301
Phone : (603) 271-2751

NEW JERSEY
Ruth Reader
Director
Div. on Aging
Dept. of Community Affairs
101 S. Broad St., CN807
Trenton, NJ 08625
Phone : (609) 292-4833
(800) 792-8820

NEW MEXICO
Michelle Lujan Grisham
Director
State Agency on Aging
228 E. Palace Ave.
Santa Fe, NM 87501
Phone : (505) 827-7640
Fax : (505) 827-7649

NEW YORK*
Director
Off. of the Aging
Agency Bldg. 2
Empire State Plz.
Albany, NY 12223
Phone : (518) 474-4425

NORTH CAROLINA
Lynne M. Perrin
Assistant Secretary
Aging Div.
Dept. of Human Resources
101 Blair Dr.
Raleigh, NC 27603
Phone : (919) 733-3983
Fax : (919) 715-4645

NORTH DAKOTA
Linda Wright
Director
Aging Services Div.
Dept. of Human Services
P.O. Box 7070
Bismarck, ND 58507-7070
Phone : (701) 328-2577
Fax : (701) 328-5466

OHIO
Judith Y. Brachman
Director
Commission on Aging
Department of Aging
50 W. Broad St., 9th Fl.
Columbus, OH 43266
Phone : (614) 466-7246
Fax : (614) 466-5741

OKLAHOMA
George Miller
Interim Director
Health & Human Srvcs.
Dept. of Human Srvcs.
P.O. Box 25352
Oklahoma City, OK 73125
Phone : (405) 521-2778

OREGON
James C. Wilson
Administrator
Senior & Disabled Serv. Div.
Dept. of Human Resources
500 Summer St., NE
Salem, OR 97310-1015
Phone : (503) 945-5810
Fax : (503) 373-7823

PENNSYLVANIA
Richard Browdie
Secretary
Dept. of Aging
Market St. Off. Bldg., 7th Fl.
Harrisburg, PA 17120
Phone : (717) 783-1550

RHODE ISLAND
Barbara Ruffino
Director
Dept. of Elderly Affairs
160 Pine St.
Providence, RI 02903
Phone : (401) 277-2894
Fax : (401) 277-1490

SOUTH CAROLINA
Connie Rinehart
Director
Div. on Aging
202 Arbor Lake Dr.
Columbia, SC 29223
Phone : (803) 737-7500

SOUTH DAKOTA
Gail Ferris
Administrator
Div. of Adult Srvcs. & Aging
Dept. of Social Srvcs.
Kneip Bldg.
Pierre, SD 57501
Phone : (605) 773-3165

TENNESSEE
Emily Wiseman
Executive Director
Comm. on Aging
706 Church St.
Nashville, TN 37243
Phone : (615) 741-2056

TEXAS
Mary Sapp
Executive Director
Dept. on Aging
P.O. Box 12786, Capitol Station
Austin, TX 78711
Phone : (512) 444-2727

UTAH
James Quast
Director
Div. of Aging
Dept. of Social Services
120 N. 200 W., Rm. 401
Salt Lake City, UT 84103
Phone : (801) 538-3918

VERMONT
Lawrence Crist
Commissioner
Dept. of Aging & Disabilities
Agcy. of Human Services
103 S. Main St.
Waterbury, VT 05671
Phone : (802) 241-2400
Fax : (802) 241-2325

VIRGINIA
Thelma E. Bland
Commissioner
Dept. for the Aging
700 E. Franklin St., 10th Fl.
Richmond, VA 23219
Phone : (804) 225-2271

WASHINGTON
Charles Reed
Assistant Secretary
Aging & Adult Srvcs. Admin.
Dept. of Social & Health Srvcs.
P.O. Box 45050
Olympia, WA 98504
Phone : (360) 586-3768

WEST VIRGINIA
David K. Brown
Executive Director
Comm. on Aging
Holly Grove
1710 Kanawha Blvd., E.
Charleston, WV 25311
Phone : (304) 558-3317
Fax : (304) 558-0004

WISCONSIN
George Potaracke
Executive Director
Board on Aging & Long-Term Care
214 N. Hamilton, 2nd Fl.
Madison, WI 53702
Phone : (608) 266-8944

WISCONSIN — Cont.
Donna McDowell
Director
Bur. on Aging
Dept. of Health & Social Srvcs.
217 S. Hamilton, Ste. 300
P.O. Box 7851
Madison, WI 53707
Phone : (608) 266-1345
Fax : (608) 266-7882

WYOMING
Morris Gardner
Administrator
Div. on Aging
Dept. of Health
139 Hathaway Bldg.
Cheyenne, WY 82002
Phone : (307) 777-7986

DISTRICT OF COLUMBIA
Jearline Williams
Executive Director
Off. on Aging
441 4th St., NW, 9th Fl.
Washington, DC 20001-2700
Phone : (202) 724-5622

AMERICAN SAMOA
John Suisala
Director
Territorial Administration on Aging
American Samoa Government
Pago Pago, AS 96799
Phone : (684) 633-1251
Fax : (684) 633-7723

GUAM**
Leticia Espaldon
Director
Dept. of Public Health & Social Services
P.O. Box 2816
Agana, GU 96910
Phone : (671) 734-7399

NORTHERN MARIANA ISLANDS
Gregorio S. Delos Reyes
Director
Aging Off.
Community & Cultural Affairs
Lower Base
Saipan, MP 96950
Phone : (670) 234-6696
Fax : (670) 234-2565

PUERTO RICO
Rudy Rodriguez Ramirez
Executive Director
Gericulture Comm.
P.O. Box 50063
Old San Juan, PR 00910
Phone : (809) 721-5710
Fax : (809) 721-6510

U.S. VIRGIN ISLANDS
Ferrynesia Benjamin
Assistant Commissioner
Dept. of Human Services
20A Strand St. & 5BB Smith St.
Christiansted
St. Croix, VI 00820
Phone : (809) 774-0930

AGRICULTURE

Enforces agriculture laws and administers agricultural programs in the state.

ALABAMA
Jack Thompson
Commissioner
Agriculture & Industries Dept.
1445 Federal Dr.
P.O. Box 3336
Montgomery, AL 36193
Phone : (334) 242-2650
Fax : (334) 240-3414

ALASKA
John W. Cramer
Director
Div. of Agriculture
Dept. of Natural Resources
P.O. Box 949
Palmer, AK 99645
Phone : (907) 745-7200
Fax : (907) 745-7112

ARIZONA
Keith Kelly
Director
Dept. of Agriculture
1688 W. Adams
Phoenix, AZ 85007
Phone : (602) 542-0998
Fax : (602) 542-5420

ARKANSAS
Gerald King
Director
Plant Board
1 Natural Resources Dr.
Little Rock, AR 72205
Phone : (501) 225-1598
Fax : (501) 225-3590

CALIFORNIA
Ann Veneman
Secretary
Dept. of Food & Agriculture
P.O. Box 942871
Sacramento, CA 94271-0001
Phone : (916) 654-0433

COLORADO
Tom Kourlis
Commissioner
Dept. of Agriculture
700 Kipling St., # 4000
Lakewood, CO 80215
Phone : (303) 239-4100
Fax : (303) 239-4125

CONNECTICUT
Shirley Ferris
Commissioner
Dept. of Agriculture
165 Capitol Ave., Rm. 273
Hartford, CT 06106
Phone : (203) 566-4667

DELAWARE
John Tarburton
Secretary
Dept. of Agriculture
2320 S. DuPont Hwy.
Dover, DE 19901
Phone : (302) 739-4811
Fax : (302) 697-4463

FLORIDA
Bob Crawford
Commissioner
Dept. of Agriculture & Consumer Services
State Capitol, PL 10
Tallahassee, FL 32399-0810
Phone : (904) 488-3022
Fax : (904) 922-9617

GEORGIA
Thomas T. Irvin
Commissioner
Dept. of Agriculture & Consumer Services
Capitol Sq., Rm. 204
Atlanta, GA 30334
Phone : (404) 656-3600

HAWAII
James J. Nakatani
Chairman
Dept. of Agriculture
1428 S. King St.
Honolulu, HI 96814
Phone : (808) 973-9550
Fax : (808) 973-9613

IDAHO
John Hatch
Director
Dept. of Agriculture
2270 Old Penitentiary Rd.
Boise, ID 83701
Phone : (208) 334-3240

ILLINOIS
Rebecca Doyle
Director
Dept. of Agriculture
P.O. Box 19281
Springfield, IL 62794-9281
Phone : (217) 785-4789
Fax : (217) 785-4505

INDIANA
Joseph R. Pearson
Assistant Commissioner
Comm. for Agriculture & Rural Development
ISTA Ctr., Ste. 414
Indianapolis, IN 46204
Phone : (317) 232-8770

IOWA
Dale Cochran
Secretary
Dept. of Agriculture
Wallace State Off. Bldg.
Des Moines, IA 50319
Phone : (515) 281-5322

KANSAS
Allie Devine
Secretary
Dept. of Agriculture
901 S. Kansas Ave., 1st Fl.
Topeka, KS 66612-1280
Phone : (913) 296-3556
Fax : (913) 296-8389

KENTUCKY
Ed Logsdon
Commissioner
Dept. of Agriculture
Capital Plaza Tower, 5th Fl.
Frankfort, KY 40601
Phone : (502) 564-4696

LOUISIANA
Bob Odom
Commissioner
Dept. of Agriculture & Forestry
P.O. Box 631
Baton Rouge, LA 70821-0631
Phone : (504) 922-1234

MAINE
Ed McLaughlin
Commissioner
Dept. of Agriculture, Food & Rural Resources
State House Station # 28
Augusta, ME 04333-0028
Phone : (207) 287-3871

MARYLAND
Lewis R. Riley
Secretary
Dept. of Agriculture
50 Harry S. Truman Pkwy.
Annapolis, MD 21401
Phone : (410) 841-5860
Fax : (410) 333-7943

MASSACHUSETTS
John C. Phillips
Commissioner
Dept. of Food & Agriculture
Executive Off. of Environmental Affairs
100 Cambridge St., 19th Fl.
Boston, MA 02202
Phone : (617) 727-1614

MICHIGAN
Gordon Goyer
Director
Dept. of Agriculture
P.O. Box 30017
Lansing, MI 48909
Phone : (517) 373-1050
Fax : (517) 335-1423

MINNESOTA
Elton Redalen
Commissioner
Dept. of Agriculture
90 W. Plato Blvd.
St. Paul, MN 55107
Phone : (612) 297-3219

MISSISSIPPI
Jim Buck Ross
Commissioner
Dept. of Agriculture & Commerce
P.O. Box 1609
Jackson, MS 39215
Phone : (601) 354-7050

MISSOURI
John L. Saunders
Director
Dept. of Agriculture
1616 Missouri Blvd.
P.O. Box 630
Jefferson City, MO 65102
Phone : (314) 751-3359
Fax : (314) 751-1784

MONTANA
Leo A. Giacometto
Director
Dept. of Agriculture
303 N. Roberts, Rm. 220
P.O. Box 200201
Helena, MT 59620-0201
Phone : (406) 444-3144

NEBRASKA
Larry E. Sitzman
Director
Dept. of Agriculture
301 Centennial Mall S.
P.O. Box 94947
Lincoln, NE 68509-4947
Phone : (402) 471-2341
Fax : (402) 471-2759

NEVADA
Thomas W. Ballow
Administrator
Div. of Agriculture
Dept. of Business & Industry
P.O. Box 11100
Reno, NV 89510
Phone : (702) 688-1180
Fax : (702) 687-1178

NEW HAMPSHIRE
Stephen H. Taylor
Commissioner
Dept. of Agriculture
P.O. Box 2042
Concord, NH 03301
Phone : (603) 271-3551

NEW JERSEY
Arthur Brown Jr.
Secretary
Off. of the Secretary
Dept. of Agriculture
John Fitch Plz., CN330
Trenton, NJ 08625
Phone : (609) 292-3976

NEW YORK*
Commissioner
Dept. of Agriculture & Markets
Capitol Plz.
1 Winners Cir.
Albany, NY 12235
Phone : (518) 457-4188

NORTH CAROLINA
James A. Graham
Commissioner
Dept. of Agriculture
One W. Edenton St.
Raleigh, NC 27601
Phone : (919) 733-7125
Fax : (919) 733-1141

NORTH DAKOTA
Sarah Vogel
Commissioner
Dept. of Agriculture
State Capitol, 6th Fl.
600 E. Boulevard Ave.
Bismarck, ND 58505-0200
Phone : (701) 328-2231
Fax : (701) 328-4567

OHIO
Fred Dailey
Director
Dept. of Agriculture
65 S. Front St., 6th Fl.
Columbus, OH 43215
Phone : (614) 466-2737
Fax : (614) 466-6124

OKLAHOMA
Dennis Howard
Secretary of Agriculture
Dept. of Agriculture
2800 N. Lincoln Blvd.
Oklahoma City, OK 73105
Phone : (405) 521-3864

OREGON
Bruce Andrews
Director
Dept. of Agriculture
103 Agriculture Bldg.
Salem, OR 97310
Phone : (503) 378-4152
Fax : (503) 373-1947

PENNSYLVANIA
Charles C. Brosius
Secretary
Dept. of Agriculture
Rm. 211, Agriculture Bldg.
Harrisburg, PA 17120
Phone : (717) 722-2853

RHODE ISLAND
John Lawrence
Chief
Div. of Agriculture & Marketing
Dept. of Environmental Mgt.
22 Hayes St.
Providence, RI 02908
Phone : (401) 277-2781

SOUTH CAROLINA
D. Leslie Tindal
Commissioner
Dept. of Agriculture
P.O. Box 11280
Columbia, SC 29211
Phone : (803) 734-2210

SOUTH DAKOTA
Dean Anderson
Secretary
Dept. of Agriculture
Foss Bldg.
523 E. Capitol
Pierre, SD 57501-3182
Phone : (605) 773-3375

TENNESSEE
L.H. Ivy
Commissioner
Dept. of Agriculture
Ellington Agricultural Center
Nashville, TN 37204
Phone : (615) 360-0100
Fax : (675) 360-0333

TEXAS
Rick Perry
Commissioner
Dept. of Agriculture
P.O. Box 12847
Capitol Station
Austin, TX 78711
Phone : (512) 463-7476

UTAH
Cary G. Peterson
Commissioner
Dept. of Agriculture
350 N. Redwood Rd.
Salt Lake City, UT 84116
Phone: (801) 538-7101

VERMONT*
Commissioner
Dept. of Agriculture
116 State St.
Montpelier, VT 05602
Phone : (802) 828-2430
Fax : (802) 828-2361

VIRGINIA
J. Carlton Courter III
Commissioner
Dept. of Agriculture & Consumer Services
1100 Bank St., Ste. 210
Richmond, VA 23219
Phone : (804) 786-3501
Fax : (804) 371-2945

WASHINGTON
Jim Jesernig
Director
Dept. of Agriculture
111 Washington St.
P.O. Box 42560
Olympia, WA 98504-2560
Phone : (360) 902-1800

WISCONSIN
Alan Tracy
Secretary
Dept. of Agriculture, Trade & Consumer Protection
2811 Agriculture Dr.
P.O. Box 8911
Madison, WI 53708
Phone : (608) 224-5012
Fax : (608) 224-5045

WYOMING
Ron Michelt
Director
Dept. of Agriculture
2219 Carey Ave.
Cheyenne, WY 82001
Phone : (307) 777-6569

AMERICAN SAMOA
Maluia P.T. Filoitumua
Director
Dept. of Agriculture
Pago Pago, AS 96799
Phone : (684) 699-1497
Fax : (684) 699-4031

GUAM
Michael W. Kuhlman
Dept. of Agriculture
P.O. Box 2950
Agana, GU 96910
Phone : (671) 734-3942
Fax : (671) 734-6569

NORTHERN MARIANA ISLANDS
Thomas D. Dela Cruz
Director
Agriculture
Dept. of Lands and Natural Resources
Capital Hill
Saipan, MP 96950
Phone : (670) 256-3317
Fax : (670) 256-7154

PUERTO RICO
Neftali Soto Santiago
Secretary
Dept. of Agriculture
P.O. Box 10163
Santurce, PR 00908-0163
Phone : (809) 721-2120
Fax : (809) 723-9747

U.S. VIRGIN ISLANDS
Anthony Olive
Commissioner
Dept. of Economic Development & Agriculture
P.O. Box 6400
St. Thomas, VI 00803
Phone : (809) 774-8784
Fax : (809) 774-4390

AIR QUALITY

Administers the state's clean air laws.

ALABAMA
Richard E. Grusnick
Chief
Air Div.
Dept. of Environmental Mgt.
1751 Cong. Dickinson Dr.
Montgomery, AL 36130
Phone: (334) 271-7861
Fax: (334) 270-5612

ALASKA
Len Verrelli
Section Chief
Air Quality Management Section
Division of Environmental Quality
Dept. of Environmental Conservation
410 Willoughby Avenue, Suite 105
Juneau, AK 99801
Phone: (907) 465-5100
Fax: (907) 465-5274

ARIZONA
Nancy C. Wrona
Assistant Director
Off. of Air Quality
Dept. of Environmental Quality
3033 N. Central Ave.
Phoenix, AZ 85012
Phone: (602) 207-2308
Fax: (602) 207-2218

ARKANSAS
James B. Jones
Chief
Air Div.
Pollution Control & Ecology
P.O. Box 8913
Little Rock, AR 72219
Phone: (501) 562-7444
Fax: (501) 562-4632

CALIFORNIA
John Dunlap III
Chairwoman
Air Resources Bd.
Environ. Protection Agency
P.O. Box 2815
Sacramento, CA 95812
Phone: (916) 322-5840

COLORADO
Doug Lempke
Director
Air Quality Comm.
Dept. of Public Health & Env.
4300 Cherry Creek Dr. S.
Denver, CO 80222
Phone: (303) 692-2153
Fax: (303) 782-5493

CONNECTICUT
Carmen DiBattista
Bureau Chief
Air Management
Dept. of Environ. Protection
79 Elm St.
Hartford, CT 06106
Phone: (203) 424-3026

DELAWARE
Darryl D. Tyler
Program Administrator
Air Quality Mgt. Section
Dept. of Natural Resources & Environment
P.O. Box 1401
Dover, DE 19903
Phone: (302) 739-4791
Fax: (302) 739-3106

FLORIDA
Howard Rhodes
Director
Div. of Air Resources Mgt.
Dept. of Environ. Protection
2600 Blairstone Rd.
Tallahassee, FL 32399-2400
Phone: (904) 488-0114

GEORGIA
Harold Reheis
Director
Environmental Protection Div.
Dept. of Natural Resources
205 Butler St., SW
Atlanta, GA 30334
Phone: (404) 656-4317

HAWAII
Paul F. Aki
Clean Air Branch
Environ. Health Admin.
500 Ala Moana Blvd., Ste. 250 B
Honolulu, HI 96813
Phone: (808) 586-4200

IDAHO
Wally Cory
Director
Div. of Environmental Quality
Dept. of Health & Welfare
1410 N. Hilton
Boise, ID 83706
Phone: (208) 334-5840

ILLINOIS
Bharat Mathur
Manager
Div. of Air Pollution Control
Environ. Protection Agency
1340 N. Ninth St.
Springfield, IL 62702
Phone: (217) 782-9540

INDIANA
Tim Method
Assistant Commissioner
Off. of Air Mgt.
Dept. of Environ. Mgt.
P.O. Box 6015
Indianapolis, IN 46206-6015
Phone: (317) 232-8222

IOWA
Peter Hamlin
Chief, Air Quality & Solid Waste Protection
Dept. of Natural Resources
900 E. Grand
Des Moines, IA 50319
Phone: (515) 281-8852

KANSAS
John Irwin
Director
Bur. of Air & Radiation
Dept. of Health & Environment
Forbes Field, Bldg. 740
Topeka, KS 66620-0001
Phone: (913) 296-1593
Fax: (913) 296-1545

KENTUCKY
John Hornback
Director
Div. for Air Quality
Dept. for Environ. Protection
803 Schenkel Lane
Frankfort, KY 40601
Phone: (502) 564-3382

LOUISIANA
Gus Von Boudungen
Assistant Secretary
Off. of Air Quality
Dept. of Environ. Quality
P.O. Box 82178
Baton Rouge, LA 70804
Phone: (504) 765-0102

MAINE
Dennis Keschl
Director
Bur. of Air Quality Control
Dept. of Environ. Protection
State House Station # 17
Augusta, ME 04333
Phone: (207) 289-2437

MARYLAND
Merrylin Zaw-Mon
Director
Air & Radiation Mgt.
Dept. of the Environment
2500 Broening Hwy.
Baltimore, MD 21224
Phone : (301) 631-3255

MASSACHUSETTS
Thomas Powers
Acting Commissioner
Dept. of Environmental Protection
Executive Off. of Environmental Affairs
1 Winter St.
Boston, MA 02108
Phone : (617) 292-5856

MICHIGAN
Dennis Drake
Acting Chief
Air Quality Div.
Dept. of Natural Resources
P.O. Box 30028
Lansing, MI 48909
Phone : (517) 373-7023

MINNESOTA
Lisa Thorvig
Director
Div. of Air Quality
Pollution Control Agency
520 Lafayette Rd.
St. Paul, MN 55155
Phone : (612) 296-7331

MISSISSIPPI
Dwight Wylie
Chief
Air Div.
Dept. of Environmental Quality
P.O. Box 10385
Jackson, MS 39289
Phone : (601) 961-5000

MISSOURI
Roger Randolph
Director
Air Pollution Control Program
Jefferson Bldg., Rm. 125
P.O. Box 176
Jefferson City, MO 65102
Phone : (314) 751-4817
Fax : (314) 751-2706

MONTANA
Jeff T. Chaffee
Chief
Air Quality Bur.
Environmental Sciences Div.
Cogswell Bldg.
Helena, MT 59620
Phone : (406) 444-3454

NEBRASKA
Joe Francis
Assistant Director
Air & Waste Mgt. Div.
Dept. of Environmental Quality
P.O. Box 98922
Lincoln, NE 68509-8922
Phone : (402) 471-0001
Fax : (402) 471-2909

NEVADA
Lowell Shifley
Chief
Bur. of Air Quality
Div. of Environ. Protection
123 W. Nye Ln., Cap. Complex
Carson City, NV 89710
Phone : (702) 687-5065

NEW HAMPSHIRE
Ken Colburn
Director
Air Resources Div.
Dept. of Environmental Srvcs.
P.O. Box 2033
Concord, NH 03302
Phone : (603) 271-1370

NEW JERSEY
John Elston
Administrator
Air Quality Management
Dept. of Environmental Protection
401 E. State St., CN 027
Trenton, NJ 08625
Phone : (609) 292-6710

NEW MEXICO
Cecelia Williams
Chief
Air Quality Bureau
Dept. of Environment
P.O. Box 26110
Santa Fe, NM 87502
Phone : (505) 827-0031
Fax : (505) 827-0045

NEW YORK*
Director
Bur. of Abatement Planning
Div. of Air Resources
50 Wolf Rd.
Albany, NY 12233-3251
Phone : (518) 457-0631

NORTH CAROLINA
Alan Klimek
Chief
Air Quality Section
Div. of Environmental Mgt.
P.O. Box 29535
Raleigh, NC 27626
Phone : (919) 733-3340
Fax : (919) 733-2496

NORTH DAKOTA
Dana K. Mount
Director
Environ. Engineering Div.
Environ. Health Section
1200 Missouri Ave., Box 5520
Bismarck, ND 58502-5520
Phone : (701) 328-5150
Fax : (701) 328-5200

OHIO
Jennifer Till
Deputy Director
Air Pollution & Solid Waste
Environmental Protection
1800 Watermark Dr., Box 1049
Columbus, OH 43266
Phone : (614) 644-2782
Fax : (614) 644-3184

OKLAHOMA
John Drake
Chief
Air Quality Srvcs.
Dept. of Health
1000 NE 10th St., Box 53551
Oklahoma City, OK 73152
Phone : (405) 271-5220

OREGON
Gregory Green
Administrator
Div. of Air Quality
Dept. of Environmental Quality
811 SW Sixth Ave.
Portland, OR 97204
Phone : (503) 229-5397
Fax : (503) 229-5675

PENNSYLVANIA
James M. Seif
Secretary
Dept. of Environmental Resources
State Office Bldg., 16th Fl.
Market St.
Harrisburg, PA 17120
Phone : (717) 787-2814

RHODE ISLAND
Stephen Majkut
Chief
Air Quality Div.
291 Promenade St.
Providence, RI 02908
Phone : (401) 277-2797

SOUTH CAROLINA
Jim Joy
Chief
Bur. of Air Quality Control
Environ. Quality Control Off.
2600 Bull St.
Columbia, SC 29201
Phone : (803) 734-4750

SOUTH DAKOTA
Nettie Myers
Secretary
Dept. of Water & Natural Res.
523 E. Capitol, Joe Foss Bldg.
Pierre, SD 57501
Phone : (605) 773-3151

TENNESSEE
John W. Walton
Director
Div. of Air Pollution Control
Dept. of Environ. & Cons.
401 Church St., 9th Fl.
Nashville, TN 37243-1542
Phone : (615) 532-0554
Fax : (615) 532-0614

TEXAS
Doyle Pendleton
Office of Air Quality
Natural Res. Conserv. Comm.
P.O. Box 13087
Austin, TX 78711-3087
Phone : (512) 239-1602

UTAH
Richard Wayne Clark
Director
Bur. of Environmental Srvcs.
Dept. of Health
288 N. 1460 W.
P.O. Box 16690
Salt Lake City, UT 84116
Phone : (801) 533-6856

VERMONT
Richard Valentinetti
Director
Air Pollution Control Div.
Dept. of Environ. Conservation
103 S. Main St.
Waterbury, VT 05671-0402
Phone : (802) 241-3860

VIRGINIA
Peter W. Schmidt
Director
Dept. of Environmental Quality
629 E. Main St.
Richmond, VA 23219
Phone : (804) 762-4020
Fax : (804) 762-4019

WASHINGTON
Joe Williams
Program Manager
Air Quality Program
Dept. of Ecology
P.O. Box 47600
Olympia, WA 98504-7600
Phone : (360) 407-6800

WEST VIRGINIA
G. Dale Farley
Director
Air Pollution Control Comm.
1558 Washington St., E.
Charleston, WV 25311
Phone : (304) 558-2275
Fax : (304) 558-3287

WISCONSIN
Donald F. Theiler
Director
Bur. of Air Mgt.
Dept. of Natural Resources
101 S. Webster, AM/7
P.O. Box 7921
Madison, WI 53707
Phone : (608) 266-7718
Fax : (608) 267-0560

WYOMING
Chuck Collins
Administrator
Air Quality Div.
Dept. of Environmental Quality
122 W. 25th St.
Cheyenne, WY 82002
Phone : (307) 777-6923

DISTRICT OF COLUMBIA
David Wambsgans
Acting Program Manager, Air Resources
Cons. & Regulatory Affairs
2100 M.L. King, Jr. Ave., SE, Ste. 203
Washington, DC 20020
Phone : (202) 404-1180

AMERICAN SAMOA
Togipa Tausaga
Executive Secretary
Environmental Quality Comm.
Off. of the Governor
Pago Pago, AS 96799
Phone : (684) 633-2304
Fax : (684) 633-5801

GUAM
Joseph C. Cruz
Administrator
Environmental Protection Agency
D107 IT&E Harmon Plaza
130 Rojas St.
Harmon, GU 96911
Phone : (671) 646-8863
Fax : (671) 646-9402

NORTHERN MARIANA ISLANDS
Juan I. Castro
Director
Environmental Quality Div.
Public Health & Env. Srvcs.
P.O. Box 409
Saipan, MP 96950
Phone : (670) 234-1011
Fax : (670) 234-1003

PUERTO RICO
Hector Rosse
President
Environmental Quality Board
P.O. Box 11488
San Juan, PR 00910-1488
Phone : (809) 767-8056
Fax : (809) 766-2483

U.S. VIRGIN ISLANDS
Benjamin Nazario
Director
Environmental Protection Div.
Dept. of Planning & Nat. Res.
Nisky Ctr., Ste. 231
St. Thomas, VI 00802
Phone : (809) 774-3320

ALCOHOL & DRUG ABUSE

Plans, establishes and administers programs for the prevention, treatment and rehabilitation of alcohol and/or drug and other abusers.

ALABAMA
O'Neill Pollingue
Director
Substance Abuse Services
Dept. of Mental Health & Retardation
200 Interstate Park Dr.
Montgomery, AL 36193
Phone : (334) 271-9209
Fax : (334) 270-4654

ALASKA
Loren Jones
Director
Alcoholism & Drug Abuse Div.
Dept. of Health & Social Srvcs.
P.O. Box 110607
Juneau, AK 99811-0607
Phone : (907) 465-2071
Fax : (907) 465-2185

ARIZONA
Teri Geons
Manager
Off. of Substance Abuse
Behavioral Health Srvcs. Div.
2122 E. Highland, Ste. 100
Phoenix, AZ 85016
Phone : (602) 381-8999

ARKANSAS
Joe Hill
Director
Alcohol & Drug Abuse Prevention
Dept. of Health
4815 W. Markham
Little Rock, AR 72205
Phone : (501) 682-6650

CALIFORNIA
Salle Jantz
Asst. Director for Legislative Affairs
Dept. of Alcohol & Drug Programs
1700 K St.
Sacramento, CA 95814

CALIFORNIA — Cont.
Andrew M. Mecca
Director
Dept. of Alcohol & Drug Programs
1700 K St.
Sacramento, CA 95814
Phone : (916) 445-0834

COLORADO
Robert B. Aukerman
Director
Alcohol & Drug Abuse Div.
Dept. of Health
4300 Cherry Creek Dr., S.
Denver, CO 80222
Phone : (303) 692-2930

CONNECTICUT
Yvette M. Thiesfield
Acting Commissioner
Dept. of Public Health & Addiction Services
Dept. of Health Services
150 Washington St.
Hartford, CT 06106
Phone : (203) 566-2038

DELAWARE
Thomas M. Fritz
Director
Div. of Alcoholism, Drug Abuse & Mental Health
1901 N. DuPont Hwy.
New Castle, DE 19720
Phone : (302) 577-4461
Fax : (302) 577-4486

FLORIDA
Robert Constantine
Dept. of Health & Rehabilitative Services
1317 Winewood Blvd.
Tallahassee, FL 32399-0700
Phone : (904) 488-8304
Fax : (904) 922-2993

GEORGIA
Tom Hester
Acting Director
Alcoholism & Drug Abuse
Dept. of Human Resources
2 Peachtree St., 4th Fl.
Atlanta, GA 30303
Phone : (404) 657-6413

HAWAII
Elaine Wilson
Chief
Alcohol & Drug Abuse Div.
Dept. of Health
1270 Queen Emma St., Ste. 706
Honolulu, HI 96813
Phone : (808) 586-3986

IDAHO
Mike Black
Executive Director
Alcohol-Drug Abuse Comm.
Dept. of Health & Welfare
450 W. State St., 3rd Fl.
Boise, ID 83720
Phone : (208) 334-5740

ILLINOIS
Barbara A. Cimaglio
Director
Dept. of Alcoholism & Substance Abuse
222 S. College, 2nd Floor
Springfield, IL 62704
Phone : (217) 785-9067
Fax : (217) 785-0954

INDIANA
Janet Corson
Deputy Director
Off. of Public Policy
Family & Social Srvcs. Admin.
402 W. Washington, Rm. W353
Indianapolis, IN 46204
Phone : (317) 232-7387

IOWA
Janet Zwick
Director
Div. of Subs. Abuse & Health
Dept. of Public Health
Lucas State Off. Bldg.
Des Moines, IA 50319
Phone : (515) 281-4417

KANSAS
Andrew O'Donovan
Commissioner
Alcohol & Drug Abuse Srvcs.
Dept. of Social & Rehab. Srvcs.
Biddle Bldg., 2nd Fl.
300 SW Oakley
Topeka, KS 66606-1995
Phone : (913) 296-3925
Fax : (913) 296-0494

KENTUCKY
Mike Townsend
Director
Div. of Substance Abuse
Dept. of Health Srvcs.
275 E. Main St.
Frankfort, KY 40601
Phone : (502) 564-2880

LOUISIANA
Joseph R. Williams Jr.
Assistant Secretary
Alcohol & Drug Abuse
P.O. Box 2790 - BIN 18
Baton Rouge, LA 70821-2790
Phone : (504) 342-9500

MAINE
Marlene McMullen-Pelsor
Director
Off. of Substance Abuse
State House Station # 159
Augusta, ME 04333
Phone : (207) 287-6330

MARYLAND
Terry Roberts
Director
Alcoholism Control Admin.
Dept. of Health & Mental Hygiene
201 W. Preston St., 4th Fl.
Baltimore, MD 21201
Phone : (410) 225-6871

MASSACHUSETTS
David Mulligan
Commissioner
Dept. of Public Health
150 Tremont St.
Boston, MA 02111
Phone : (617) 727-0201

MICHIGAN
Robert Peterson
Director
Off. of Drug Control Policy
Michigan National Tower, Ste. 1200
Lansing, MI 48909
Phone : (517) 373-4700
Fax : (517) 373-2963

MINNESOTA
Cindy Turnure
Director
Chemical Dependency Prog. Div.
Dept. of Human Srvcs.
444 Lafayette Rd.
St. Paul, MN 55101
Phone : (612) 296-4616

MISSOURI
Michael Couty
Director
Dept. of Mental Health
1706 E. Elm St.
P.O. Box 687
Jefferson City, MO 65102
Phone : (314) 751-4942
Fax : (314) 751-7814

MONTANA
Darryl Bruno
Administrator
Alcohol & Drug Abuse Div.
Dept. of Corr. & Human Srvcs.
1539 11th Ave.
Helena, MT 59620
Phone : (406) 444-4927

NEBRASKA
Malcolm Heard
Director
Alcoholism & Drug Abuse Div.
Dept. of Public Institutions
P.O. Box 94728
Lincoln, NE 68588-0229
Phone : (402) 472-6046
Fax : (402) 471-2851

NEVADA
Elizabeth Breshears
Chief
Bur. of Alcohol & Drug Abuse
Dept. of Human Resources
505 E. King St.
Carson City, NV 89710
Phone : (702) 687-4790

NEW HAMPSHIRE
Geraldine Sylvester
Director
Off. of Alcohol & Drug Abuse
Dept. of Health & Human Srvcs.
105 Pleasant St.
Concord, NH 03301
Phone : (603) 271-6100

NEW JERSEY
Terrance O'Connor
Assistant Commissioner
Div. of Addiction Services
Dept. of Health
129 E. Hanover St., CN 362
Trenton, NJ 08625
Phone : (609) 292-5760

NEW MEXICO
Lynn Brady
Director
Behavioral Health Srvcs. Div.
Dept. of Health
P.O. Box 26110
Santa Fe, NM 87502-6110
Phone : (505) 827-2601
Fax : (505) 827-0097

NEW YORK*
Director
Off. of Alcoholism & Substance Abuse
Executive Park S.
Albany, NY 12203
Phone : (518) 457-2061

NORTH CAROLINA
Julian Keith
Director
Alcohol & Drug Abuse Srvcs.
Dept. of Human Resources
325 N. Salisbury St., Ste. 1168
Raleigh, NC 27603
Phone : (919) 733-4670
Fax : (919) 733-9455

NORTH DAKOTA
John J. Allen
Director
Alcoholism & Drug Abuse
Dept. of Human Services
1839 E. Capitol Ave.
Bismarck, ND 58501-2152
Phone : (701) 328-2769
Fax : (701) 328-3008

OHIO
Lucille Fleming
Director
Alcohol & Drug Addiction Srvcs.
280 N. High St., 12th Fl.
Columbus, OH 43215
Phone : (614) 466-3445
Fax : (614) 752-8645

OKLAHOMA
James Curry
Deputy Commissioner of Programs
Dept. of Mental Health
P.O. Box 53277, Capitol Sta.
Oklahoma City, OK 73152
Phone : (405) 271-8644

Dee Owens
Deputy Commissioner
Dept. of Mental Health & Substance Abuse Srvcs.
P.O. Box 53277
Oklahoma City, OK 73152-3277
Phone : (405) 271-7474
Fax : (405) 271-7413

OREGON
Jeffrey Kushner
Asst. Administrator
Alcohol & Drug Problems
Dept. of Human Resources
500 Summer St., NE
Salem, OR 97310
Phone : (503) 945-5763
Fax : (503) 373-8467

PENNSYLVANIA
Jeannine D. Peterson
Deputy Secretary
Drug & Alcohol Programs
Dept. of Health
809 Health & Welfare Bldg.
Harrisburg, PA 17120
Phone : (717) 787-9857

RHODE ISLAND
Peter Dennehy
Director
Dept. of Substance Abuse
P.O. Box 20363
Cranston, RI 02920
Phone : (401) 464-2091

SOUTH CAROLINA
Beverly G. Hamilton
Director
Dept. of Alcohol & Other Drug Abuse Services
3700 Forest Dr., Ste. 300
Columbia, SC 29204-4082
Phone : (803) 734-9520
Fax : (803) 734-9663

William J. McCord
Director
Dept. of Alcohol & Other Drug Abuse Services
3700 Forest Dr., # 300
Columbia, SC 29204
Phone : (803) 734-9520

SOUTH DAKOTA
Gib Sudbeck
Director
Div. of Alcohol & Drug Abuse
Human Resources
500 E. Capitol
Pierre, SD 57501
Phone : (605) 773-3123

TENNESSEE
Robbie Jackmon
Assistant Commissioner
Bur. of Alcohol & Drug Abuse
Dept. of Health
Cordell Hull Bldg., Rm. 255
Nashville, TN 37247
Phone : (615) 741-1921
Fax : (615) 532-2286

TEXAS
Bob Dickson
Executive Director
Comm. on Alcohol & Drug Abuse
720 Brazos Street
Austin, TX 78701-2576
Phone : (512) 867-8700

UTAH
Leon Povey
Director
Div. of Alcoholism & Drugs
Dept. of Social Services
120 N. 200 W., 4th Fl.
Salt Lake City, UT 84103
Phone : (801) 538-3939

VERMONT
Thomas E. Perras
Acting Director
Alcohol & Drug Programs
Agency of Human Services
103 S. Main St.
Waterbury, VT 05671-1701
Phone : (802) 241-2170
Fax : (802) 241-3095

VIRGINIA
Jerry W. Kilgore
Secretary of Public Safety
Governor's Cabinet
613 9th St. Office Bldg.
Richmond, VA 23219
Phone : (804) 786-5351
Fax : (804) 371-6381

WASHINGTON
Ken Stark
Director
Alcohol & Substance Abuse Bur.
Social & Health Srvcs. Dept.
P.O. Box 45330
Olympia, WA 98504-5330
Phone : (360) 438-8200

WEST VIRGINIA
Jack C. Clohan Jr.
Director
Div. of Alcohol & Drug Abuse
Bldg. 6, Rm. 717
1900 Kanawha Blvd., E.
Charleston, WV 25305
Phone : (304) 558-2276

WISCONSIN
Donna Bestor
Director
Alcohol & Other Drug Abuse
Dept. of Health & Social Srvcs.
1 W. Wilson
Madison, WI 53703
Phone : (608) 266-9923
Fax : (608) 266-7882

WYOMING
Jean DeFratis
Manager
Div. of Community Programs
Dept. of Health & Social Srvcs.
Hathaway Bldg., Rm. 350
Cheyenne, WY 82002
Phone : (307) 777-6494

DISTRICT OF COLUMBIA
Maude Holt
Administrator
Alcohol & Drug Abuse Srvcs. Admin.
Dept. of Human Services
1300 First St., NE
Washington, DC 20002
Phone : (202) 727-0740

AMERICAN SAMOA
Taulaga Tali
Program Manager
Alcohol & Drug Abuse
Dept. of Human Resources
Pago Pago, AS 96799
Phone : (684) 633-4211
Fax : (684) 633-7449

GUAM**
Marilyn L. Wingfield
Director
Mental Health & Substance Abuse Agency
790 Gov. Carlos G. Camacho Rd.
Tamuning, GU 96911
Phone : (671) 646-9262

NORTHERN MARIANA ISLANDS
Richard Pierce
Special Assistant for Drug & Substance Abuse
Off. of the Governor
P.O. Box 10007
Saipan, MP 96950
Phone : (670) 322-5091
Fax : (670) 322-5099

PUERTO RICO
Astrid Oyola de Benitez
Administrator
Addiction Control Service Admin.
P.O. Box 21414
San Juan, PR 00928-1414
Phone : (809) 764-3795
Fax : (809) 765-5895

U.S. VIRGIN ISLANDS
Aracelis B. Hendry
Assistant Commissioner
Dept. of Health
St. Croix Hospital
St. Croix, VI 00820
Phone : (809) 773-1311

ALCOHOLIC BEVERAGE CONTROL

Administers and enforces the laws governing the manufacturing, distribution and dispensing of alcoholic beverages.

ALABAMA
Robert B. Leavell
Director
Alcoholic Beverage Control Board
2715 Gunter Park Dr., W.
Montgomery, AL 36109
Phone: (334) 271-3840
Fax: (334) 277-2150

ALASKA
Patrick L. Sharrock
Director
Alcoholic Beverage Control Bd.
Dept. of Revenue
550 W. Seventh Ave., Ste. 350
Anchorage, AK 99501-3510
Phone: (907) 277-8638
Fax: (907) 272-9412

ARIZONA
Howard G. Adams
Superintendent
Dept. of Liquor Licenses
800 W. Washington, Ste. 500
Phoenix, AZ 85007
Phone: (602) 542-5141

ARKANSAS
Robert Moore
Director
Alcoholic Beverage Control Administration
100 Main St., Rm. 503
Little Rock, AR 72201
Phone: (501) 682-1105
Fax: (501) 682-2221

CALIFORNIA
Jay R. Stroh
Director
Dept. of Alcoholic Beverage Control
3801 Rosin Ct. #150
Sacramento, CA 95834-1633
Phone: (916) 445-3221

COLORADO
Dave Reitz
Director
Liquor Enforcement Div.
Dept. of Revenue
1375 Sherman St., Rm. 628
Denver, CO 80203
Phone: (303) 866-3741

CONNECTICUT
William Sullivan
Chairman
Liquor Control Comm.
Dept. of Liquor Control
165 Capitol Ave., Rm. 556
Hartford, CT 06106
Phone: (203) 566-4687

DELAWARE
Donald J. Bowman
Executive Secretary
Alcoholic Beverage Control Comm.
820 N. French St.
Wilmington, DE 19801
Phone: (302) 577-3200
Fax: (302) 577-3204

FLORIDA
John Harris
Director
Alcoholic Beverages & Tobacco
Dept. of Bus. & Prof. Reg.
1940 North Monroe St.
Tallahassee, FL 32399-1020
Phone: (904) 488-3227

GEORGIA
Chester Bryant
Director
Alcohol & Tobacco Tax Unit
Dept. of Revenue
270 Washington St., SW
Atlanta, GA 30334
Phone: (404) 656-4252

IDAHO
Robert Sobba
Director
Alcohol Beverage Control Div.
Dept. of Law Enforcement
P.O. Box 55
Boise, ID 83707
Phone: (208) 884-7003

ILLINOIS
Arabel A. Rosales
Executive Director
Liquor Control Comm.
100 W. Randolph, Ste. 5-300
Chicago, IL 60601
Phone: (312) 814-3930
Fax: (312) 814-2241

INDIANA
Kevin Schaefer
Chairman
Alcoholic Beverage Comm.
302 W. Washington St., Rm. E114
Indianapolis, IN 46204
Phone: (317) 232-2448

IOWA
Jack Nystrom
Director
Dept. of Commerce
1918 SE Hulsizer
Ankeny, IA 50021
Phone: (515) 281-7401
Fax: (515) 281-7372

KANSAS
Bernie Norwood
Director
Alcoholic Bev. Control Div.
Dept. of Revenue
#4 Townsite Plz., Rm. 210
200 SE 6th St.
Topeka, KS 66603-3512
Phone: (913) 296-3946
Fax: (913) 296-0922

KENTUCKY
Donald Grugin
Commissioner
Alcoholic Beverage Control
123 Walnut St.
Frankfort, KY 40601
Phone: (502) 564-4850

LOUISIANA
Terry E. Pitre
Commissioner
Off. of Alcoholic Bev. Control
Dept. of Pub. Safety & Corr.
P.O. Box 66404
Baton Rouge, LA 70896
Phone: (504) 925-4041

MAINE
David S. Campbell
Director
Bur. of Alcoholic Beverages & Lottery Operations
State House Station # 8
Augusta, ME 04333
Phone: (207) 289-3721

Eben B. Marsh
Director
Bur. of Alcoholic Beverages & Lottery Operations
State House Station #8
Augusta, ME 04333
Phone: (207) 287-3721

MARYLAND
Charles W. Ehart
Administrator
Alcohol & Tobacco Tax Unit
Comptroller of the Treasury
State Treasury Bldg., Rm. 310
Annapolis, MD 21401
Phone: (410) 974-3319

MASSACHUSETTS
Stuart Krusell
Chairman
Alcoholic Beverages Control Comm.
100 Cambridge St., Rm. 2204
Boston, MA 02202
Phone : (617) 727-3040

MICHIGAN
Phil Arthurhultz
Chairman
Liquor Control Comm.
Dept. of Commerce
7150 Harris Dr.
Lansing, MI 48909
Phone : (517) 322-1353
Fax : (517) 322-5188

MINNESOTA
Frederick C. Petersen
Director
Liquor Control Div.
Dept. of Public Safety
190 5th St., E., Rm. 105
St. Paul, MN 55101
Phone : (612) 296-6159

MISSISSIPPI
Jimmy Sullivan
Director
Alcoholic Bev. Control Div.
State Tax Comm.
P.O. Box 540
Madison, MS 39130
Phone : (601) 359-1098

MISSOURI
Ruby L. Bonner
State Supervisor
Div. of Liquor Control
Dept. of Public Safety
301 W. High St.
P.O. Box 837
Jefferson City, MO 65102
Phone : (314) 751-2333
Fax : (314) 526-4540

MONTANA
Gary Blewett
Administrator
Liquor Division
Dept. of Revenue
2517 Airport Rd.
Helena, MT 59620-2713
Phone : (406) 444-0700

NEBRASKA
Jack Crowley
Chairman
Liquor Control Comm.
301 Centennial Mall S.
P.O. Box 95046
Lincoln, NE 68509-5046
Phone : (402) 471-2571
Fax : (402) 471-2814

NEW HAMPSHIRE
Joseph J. Acorace
Chairman
Liquor Commission
P.O. Box 503
Concord, NH 03302
Phone : (603) 271-3132

NEW JERSEY
John G. Hall
Director
Alcoholic Bev. Control Div.
Dept. of Law & Public Safety
140 E. Front St., CN 087
Trenton, NJ 08625
Phone : (609) 984-2830

NEW MEXICO
Marianne Woodard
Director
Alcohol & Gaming Div.
Dept. of Reg. & Licensing
P.O. Box 25101
Santa Fe, NM 87503
Phone : (505) 827-7066
Fax : (505) 827-7168

NEW YORK*
Chairman
State Liquor Authority
250 Broadway
New York, NY 10007
Phone : (212) 417-4191

NORTH CAROLINA
Marvin L. Speight Jr.
Chairman
Alcohol Beverage Control Comm.
Dept. of Commerce
3322 Old Garner Rd.
Raleigh, NC 27610
Phone : (919) 779-0700
Fax : (919) 662-1946

NORTH DAKOTA
Laverne Reinbold
Licensing Administrator
Off. of Attorney General
State Capitol, 17th Fl.
600 E. Boulevard Ave.
Bismarck, ND 58505
Phone : (701) 328-2210
Fax : (701) 328-3535

OHIO
Michael Akrouche
Director
Dept. of Liquor Control
2323 W. Fifth Ave.
Columbus, OH 43266-0701
Phone : (614) 644-2472
Fax : (614) 644-2480

OKLAHOMA
Ron L. Willis
Director
Alcoholic Beverage Control Bd.
2501 N. Stiles
Oklahoma City, OK 73105
Phone : (405) 521-3484

OREGON
Chris Lyons
Administrator
Liquor Control
9079 SE McLoughlin Blvd.
Portland, OR 97222
Phone : (503) 653-3018

PENNSYLVANIA
James A. Goodman
Chairman
Liquor Control Board
532 Northwest Off. Bldg.
Harrisburg, PA 17124
Phone : (717) 787-2696

RHODE ISLAND
Anthony Arrico
Acting Administrator
Liquor Control
Dept. of Business Regulation
233 Richmond St.
Providence, RI 02903
Phone : (401) 277-2562

SOUTH CAROLINA
Patricia L. Stites
Supervisor
Dept. of Revenue & Taxation
Div. of Alcohol Bev. Control
301 Gervais St.
Columbia, SC 29201
Phone : (803) 734-0477

SOUTH DAKOTA
James Fry
Director
Div. of Special Taxes
Dept. of Revenue
Kneip Bldg., 3rd Fl.
Pierre, SD 57501
Phone : (605) 773-3311

TENNESSEE
Elyon Davis
Director
Alcoholic Beverage Comm.
226 Capitol Blvd., Ste. 300
Nashville, TN 37243-0775
Phone : (615) 741-1602
Fax : (615) 741-0847

TEXAS
Doyne Bailey
Administrator
Alcoholic Beverage Comm.
P.O. Box 13127
Capitol Station
Austin, TX 78711
Phone : (512) 458-2500

UTAH
Kenneth F. Wynn
Director
Liquor Control Comm.
1625 S. 900 W.
P.O. Box 30408
Salt Lake City, UT 84130
Phone : (801) 977-6800

VERMONT
Norris Hoyt
Commissioner
Dept. of Liquor Control
Green Mountain Dr.
Montpelier, VT 05602
Phone : (802) 828-2345
Fax : (802) 828-2803

VIRGINIA
Catherine H. Giordano
ABC Board Chairman
Dept. of Alcoholic
Beverage Control
2901 Hermitage Rd.
Richmond, VA 23220
Phone : (804) 367-0621
Fax : (804) 367-0622

WASHINGTON
Joe McGavick
Chair
Liquor Control Bd.
1025 E. Union St.
P.O. Box 43075
Olympia, WA 98504
Phone : (360) 753-6262

WEST VIRGINIA
Richard A. Atkinson III
Commissioner
Alcohol Beverage Control
322 70th St., SE
Charleston, WV 25304-2900
Phone : (304) 558-2481
Fax : (305) 558-0081

WISCONSIN
Jim Jenkins
Chief
Alcohol & Tobacco
Enforcement
Dept. of Revenue
4610 University Ave.
P.O. Box 8905
Madison, WI 53708
Phone : (608) 266-3969
Fax : (608) 264-6884

WYOMING
Tom Lopez
Director
Liquor Comm.
1520 E. Fifth St.
Cheyenne, WY 82002
Phone : (307) 777-6453

DISTRICT OF COLUMBIA
Paul E. Waters
Program Manager
Alcoholic Beverage
Control Div.
Dept. of Cons. & Reg.
Affairs
614 H St., NW, Rm. 807
Washington, DC 20001
Phone : (202) 727-7377

AMERICAN SAMOA
Magalei Logovii
Chairman
Alcoholic Beverage
Control Bd.
Off. of the Governor
Pago Pago, AS 96799
Phone : (684) 633-4201
Fax : (684) 633-1148

GUAM
Joaquin G. Blaz
Director
Dept. of Revenue &
Taxation
855 W. Marine Dr.
Agana, GU 96910
Phone : (671) 477-5144

NORTHERN MARIANA ISLANDS
Enrique A. Santos
Administrator
Alcoholic Beverage
Control Bd.
Garapan
Saipan, MP 96950
Phone : (670) 234-9450
Fax : (670) 322-4008

PUERTO RICO
Rafael Carraballo
Director
Bur. of Alcoholic Beverage
Taxes
Dept. of Treasury
P.O. Box S-4515
San Juan, PR 00905
Phone : (809) 721-2020
Fax : (809) 722-6749

U.S. VIRGIN ISLANDS
Vera Falu
Commissioner
Dept. of Lic. & Cons. Aff.
Property & Procurement
Bldg.
Sub Base Bldg. 1, Rm. 205
St. Thomas, VI 00802
Phone : (809) 774-3130
Fax : (809) 776-0675

ARCHIVES

Identifies, acquires, preserves and makes available state government records of continuing historical and research value.

ALABAMA
Edwin C. Bridges
Director
Dept. of Archives & History
624 Washington Ave.
Montgomery, AL 36130
Phone : (334) 242-4361
Fax : (334) 240-3433

ALASKA
John Stewart
State Archivist
Dept. of Education
141 Willoughby Ave.
Juneau, AK 99801-1720
Phone : (907) 465-2241
Fax : (907) 465-2465

ARIZONA
Arlene Bansal
Director
AZ Dept. of Library, Archives &
Public Records
Research Div./Collection Dev.
1700 W. Washington
Phoenix, AZ 85007
Phone : (602) 542-4035

ARKANSAS
John L. Ferguson
State Historian
History Comm.
One Capitol Mall
Little Rock, AR 72201
Phone : (501) 682-6900

CALIFORNIA
John F. Burns
State Archivist
State Archives
1020 O Street
Sacramento, CA 95814
Phone : (916) 653-7715

COLORADO
Terry Ketelsen
Director
Archives & Public Records Div.
Dept. of Admin.
1313 Sherman St., Rm. 1B-20
Denver, CO 80203
Phone : (303) 866-2055

CONNECTICUT
Mark Jones
State Archivist
State Library
231 Capitol Ave.
Hartford, CT 06106
Phone : (203) 566-5650
Fax : (203) 566-4460

DELAWARE
Howard P. Lowell
Administrator
Delaware State Archives
Hall of Records
Dover, DE 19901
Phone : (302) 739-5318
Fax : (502) 739-6710

FLORIDA
Jim Berberich
Chief
Bur. of Archives & Records Mgt.
Dept. of State
R.A. Gray Bldg.
500 South Bronough St.
Tallahassee, FL 32399-0250
Phone : (904) 487-2073

GEORGIA
Edward Weldon
Director
Dept. of Archives & History
330 Capitol Ave., SW
Atlanta, GA 30334
Phone : (404) 656-2358

HAWAII
Jolyn G. Tamura
State Archivist
Archives Division
Dept. of Accounting & General Srvcs.
Iolani Palace Grounds
Honolulu, HI 96816
Phone : (808) 586-0310

IDAHO
William Tydeman
State Archivist
State Historical Society
Dept. of Admin.
325 W. State
Boise, ID 83702
Phone : (208) 334-3890

ILLINOIS
John Daly
Director
State Archives & Records Div.
Archives Bldg.
Springfield, IL 62756
Phone : (217) 782-4682

INDIANA
F. Gerald Handfield Jr.
Director
Comm. on Public Records
IGC-South, Rm. W472
402 W. Washington
Indianapolis, IN 46204
Phone : (317) 232-3373

IOWA
George Hendrickson
State Archivist
Dept. of Cultural Affairs
Capitol Complex
Des Moines, IA 50319
Phone : (515) 281-3007

KANSAS
Patricia Michaelis
State Archivist
Library & Archives
State Historical Society
120 W. 10th St.
Topeka, KS 66612-1291
Phone : (913) 296-2624
Fax : (913) 296-1005

KENTUCKY
Richard N. Belding
State Archivist & Rec. Admin.
Dept. for Libraries & Archives
Public Records Division
Box 537
Frankfort, KY 40602
Phone : (502) 875-7000

LOUISIANA
W. Fox McKeithen
Secretary of State
Dept. of State
P.O. Box 94125
Baton Rouge, LA 70804
Phone : (504) 342-4479

MAINE
James Henderson
State Archivist
State House Station # 84
Augusta, ME 04333
Phone : (207) 289-5790

MARYLAND
Edward C. Papenfuse
State Archivist
350 Rowe Blvd.
Annapolis, MD 21401
Phone : (410) 974-3867
Fax : (410) 974-2525

MASSACHUSETTS
Albert H. Whitaker Jr.
Archivist
Off. of Secretary of State
220 Morrissey Blvd.
Boston, MA 02125
Phone : (617) 727-2816

MICHIGAN
David Johnson
State Archivist
Dept. of State History Bur.
717 W. Allegan
Lansing, MI 48918
Phone : (517) 373-0510

MINNESOTA
Duane Swanson
State Archivist
State Historical Society
345 Kellogg Blvd.. W.
St. Paul, MN 55102
Phone : (612) 296-6980

MISSISSIPPI
Elbert R. Hilliard
Director
Dept. of Archives & History
P.O. Box 571
Jackson, MS 39205-0571
Phone : (601) 359-6850

MISSOURI
Kenneth Winn
State Archivist
Off. of Secretary of State
600 W. Main
P.O. Box 778
Jefferson City, MO 65102
Phone : (314) 751-4717
Fax : (314) 526-3867
E-Mail: KWINN1@MAIL.MORE.NET

MONTANA
Robert M. Clark
Head
Library & Archives Program
State Historial Society
225 N. Roberts St.
Helena, MT 59620-1201
Phone : (406) 444-4787

NEBRASKA
Lawrence J. Sommer
Director
State Historial Society
P.O. Box 82554
Lincoln, NE 68501-2554
Phone : (402) 471-4745
Fax : (402) 471-3100

NEVADA
Guy Louis Rocha
Administrator
Div. of Archives & Records
State Library & Archives
100 Stewart St.
Carson City, NV 89710
Phone : (702) 687-8317

NEW HAMPSHIRE
Frank C. Mevers
Director & State Archivist
Records Mgt. & Archives
Dept. of State
71 S. Fruit St.
Concord, NH 03301
Phone : (603) 271-2236

NEW JERSEY
Karl Niederer
Director
Div. of Archives & Records Mgt.
Dept. of State
2300 Stuyvesant Ave., CN 307
Trenton, NJ 08625
Phone : (609) 530-3200

NEW MEXICO
Elaine Olah
Administrator
State Records Ctr. & Archives
404 Montezuma Ave.
Santa Fe, NM 87503
Phone : (505) 827-7332
Fax : (505) 827-7331

NEW YORK*
State Archivist
State Archives & Records Management
Dept. of Education
10D45 Cultural Education Ctr.
Albany, NY 12230
Phone: (518) 474-1195

NORTH CAROLINA
William S. Price Jr.
Director
Div. of Archives & History
Dept. of Cultural Resources
109 E. Jones St.
Raleigh, NC 27601
Phone : (919) 733-7305
Fax : (919) 733-8807

NORTH DAKOTA
Gerald G. Newborg
State Archivist
State Historical Society
North Dakota Heritage Ctr.
612 E. Boulevard Ave.
Bismarck, ND 58505
Phone : (701) 328-2668

OHIO
Gary C. Ness
Director
Historical Society
1982 Velma Ave.
Columbus, OH 43211
Phone : (614) 297-2300

OKLAHOMA
Robert L. Clark
Director
Dept. of Libraries
200 NE 18th St.
Oklahoma City, OK 73105
Phone : (405) 521-2502

OREGON
Roy C. Turnbaugh
State Archivist
Archives Div.
Off. of Secretary of State
800 Summer St., NE
Salem, OR 97310
Phone : (503) 373-0701
Fax : (503) 373-0953

PENNSYLVANIA
Brent Glass
Executive Director
State Historial & Museum Comm.
P.O. Box 1026
Harrisburg, PA 17108
Phone : (717) 787-2891

RHODE ISLAND
Timothy Slavin
State Archivist
Off. of Secretary of State
337 Westminister St.
Providence, RI 02903
Phone : (401) 277-2353

SOUTH CAROLINA
George L. Vogt
Director
Dept. of Archives & History
1430 Senate St.
P.O. Box 11669
Columbia, SC 29211
Phone : (803) 734-8577

SOUTH DAKOTA*
State Archivist
State Historical Society
900 Governors Dr.
Pierre, SD 57501
Phone : (605) 773-3804

TENNESSEE
Edwin S. Gleaves
State Librarian & Archivist
State Library & Archives
403 Seventh Ave., N.
Nashville, TN 37243-0312
Phone : (615) 741-2451
Fax : (615) 741-6471

TEXAS
Chris La Plante
State Archivist
P.O. Box 12927
Austin, TX 78711
Phone : (512) 463-5455

UTAH
Jeffery O. Johnson
Director of State Archives
State Archives & Records Srvcs.
State Capitol, Archives Bldg.
Salt Lake City, UT 84114
Phone : (801) 538-3012

VERMONT
D. Gregory Sanford
State Archivist
Off. of Secretary of State
Pavilion Off. Bldg.
109 State St.
Montpelier, VT 05609
Phone : (802) 828-2369
Fax : (802) 828-2496

VIRGINIA
Nolan T. Yelich
State Librarian
The Library of Virginia
11th St. at Capitol Sq.
Richmond, VA 23219
Phone : (804) 786-2332
Fax : (804) 786-5855

WASHINGTON
David Owens
Acting State Archivist
Archives & Records Mgt. Div.
Off. of Secretary of State
P.O. Box 40238
Olympia, WA 98504-0238
Phone : (360) 753-5485

WEST VIRGINIA
Fredrick Armstrong
Director
Archives & History Div.
Div. of Culture & History
Capitol Complex, Cultural Ctr.
Charleston, WV 25305
Phone : (304) 558-0230
Fax : (304) 558-2779

WISCONSIN
Peter Gottlieb
State Archivist
State Historical Society
816 State St., Room 421
Madison, WI 53706
Phone : (608) 264-6480
Fax : (608) 264-6404

WYOMING
Jim Donahue
Administrator
Cultural Resources Section
Dept. of Commerce
Barrett Bldg.
Cheyenne, WY 82002
Phone : (307) 777-7826

DISTRICT OF COLUMBIA
Dorothy Provine
Archivist
1300 Naylor Ct., NW
Washington, DC 20001
Phone : (202) 727-2052

AMERICAN SAMOA
James Himphill
Archivist
Dept. of Admin. Srvcs.
American Samoa Government
Pago Pago, AS 96799
Phone : (684) 633-1609
Fax : (684) 633-1010

GUAM
Christine Scott-Smith
Territorial Librarian
Nieves M. Flores Library
254 Martyr St.
Agana, GU 96910
Phone : (671) 477-6913
Fax : (671) 477-9777

NORTHERN MARIANA ISLANDS
Herbert S. Del Rosario
Archives Section
Northern Marianas College
P.O. Box 1250 CK
Saipan, MP 96950
Phone : (670) 234-6932
Fax : (670) 234-0759

PUERTO RICO
Karen Cardona
Director
General Archives
Ponce de Leon # 500
Puerta de Tierra
San Juan, PR 00902
Phone : (809) 722-0331
Fax : (809) 722-9097

U.S. VIRGIN ISLANDS
Jeannette B. Allis-Bastian
Director
Libraries, Archives & Museums
Dept. of Planning & Nat. Res.
23 Dronningens Gade
St. Thomas, VI 00802
Phone : (809) 774-5715

ARTS COUNCIL

Encourages the study and presentation of the performing and fine arts and promotes participation in and appreciation of the arts.

ALABAMA
Albert Head
Executive Director
Council on Arts & Humanities
1 Dexter Ave.
Montgomery, AL 36130
Phone : (334) 242-4076
Fax : (334) 240-3269

ALASKA
Tim Wilson
Executive Director
AK State Council on the Arts
411 W. 4th Ave., Ste. 1E
Anchorage, AK 99501-2343
Phone : (907) 269-6610
Fax : (907) 269-6601

ARIZONA
Shelley Cohn
Executive Director
Commission on the Arts
417 W. Roosevelt
Phoenix, AZ 85003
Phone : (602) 255-5882

ARKANSAS
Bill Puppione
Director
State Arts Council
323 Center St., Ste. 1500
Little Rock, AR 72201-2623
Phone : (501) 324-9150
Fax : (501) 324-9154

CALIFORNIA
Barbara Pieper
Director
Arts Council
2411 Alhambra Blvd.
Sacramento, CA 95817
Phone : (916) 227-2550

COLORADO
Fran Holden
Director
Arts & Humanities Council
Dept. of Higher Education
750 Pennsylvania St.
Denver, CO 80203
Phone : (303) 894-2617
Fax : (303) 894-2615

CONNECTICUT
John E. Ostrout
Executive Director
Comm. on the Arts
227 Lawrence St.
Hartford, CT 06106
Phone : (203) 566-4770

DELAWARE
Joan Mobley
Chair
Arts Council
Carvel State Off. Bldg.
820 N. French St.
Wilmington, DE 19801
Phone : (302) 577-3540
Fax : (302) 577-6561

FLORIDA
Peyton Fearington
Director
Cultural Affairs
Dept. of State
2475 Apalachee Parkway
Tallahassee, FL 32399-0250
Phone : (904) 487-2980

GEORGIA
Caroline Ballard
Director
Council for the Arts & Humanities
530 Means St., NW, #115
Atlanta, GA 30318-5730
Phone : (404) 651-7920

HAWAII
Wendell P.K. Silva
Executive Director
Foundation on Culture & Arts
44 Merchant St.
Honolulu, HI 96813-4311
Phone : (808) 586-0300

IDAHO
Margot H. Knight
Executive Director
Comm. on Arts
P.O. Box 83720
Boise, ID 83720-0008
Phone : (208) 334-2119

ILLINOIS
Rhonda A. Pierce
Acting Executive Director
State Arts Council
100 W. Randolph, Ste. 10-500
Chicago, IL 60601
Phone : (312) 814-6750

INDIANA
Dorothy Ilgen
Executive Director
State Arts Comm.
402 W. Washington St., Rm. 72
Indianapolis, IN 46204-2741
Phone : (317) 232-1286

IOWA
William Jackson
Director
Dept. of Cultural Affairs
State Historical Bldg.
Des Moines, IA 50319
Phone : (515) 281-7471
Fax : (515) 242-6498

KANSAS
Joan Wingerson
Executive Director
Kansas Arts Commission
700 SW Jackson St., Ste. 1004
Topeka, KS 66603-3758
Phone : (913) 296-3335
Fax : (913) 296-4989

KENTUCKY
Louis DeLuca
Director
State Arts Council
Education & Humanities Cabinet
31 Fountain Pl.
Frankfort, KY 40601
Phone : (502) 564-3757

LOUISIANA
Gerri Hobdy
Assistant Secretary
Off. of Culture, Recreation & Tourism
P.O. Box 44247
Baton Rouge, LA 70804
Phone : (504) 342-8115

MAINE
Alden C. Wilson
Executive Director
State Arts Comm.
State House Station # 25
Augusta, ME 04333
Phone : (207) 287-2724

MARYLAND
James Backas
Executive Director
State Arts Council
Dept. of Economic & Business Development
601 N. Howard St.
Baltimore, MD 21201-4582
Phone : (410) 333-8232

MASSACHUSETTS
Rose Austin
Acting Executive Director
State Cultural Council
80 Boylston St.
Boston, MA 02116
Phone : (617) 727-3668
Fax : (617) 727-0044

MICHIGAN
Judy Rapanos
Chair
Council for the Arts & Cultural Affairs
1012 W. Sugnet
Midland, MI 48640
Phone : (313) 256-3735

MINNESOTA
Sam Garbarski
Executive Director
State Arts Bd.
432 Summit Ave.
St. Paul, MN 55102
Phone : (612) 297-2603

MISSISSIPPI
Jane Hiatt
Executive Director
Arts Comm.
239 N. Lamar St., Ste. 207
Jackson, MS 39201
Phone : (601) 359-6030

MISSOURI
Anthony J. Radich
Executive Director
Missouri Arts Council
Dept. of Economic Development
111 N. Seventh St., Ste. 105
St. Louis, MO 63101-2188
Phone : (314) 340-6845
Fax : (314) 340-7215

MONTANA
Bill Pratt
Director of Organizational Srvcs.
Montana Arts Council
316 N. Park Ave., Ste. 252
Helena, MT 59620

Arlynn Fishbaugh
Executive Director
Arts Council
316 N. Park Ave., Rm. 252
Helena, MT 59620
Phone : (406) 444-6430

NEBRASKA
Jennifer Severin
Executive Director
Arts Council
Joslyn Castle Carriage House
3838 Davenport St.
Omaha, NE 68131-2329
Phone : (402) 595-2122
Fax : (402) 595-2334

NEVADA
Susan Boskoff
Executive Director
Council on the Arts
100 S. Stewart #Cap
Reno, NV 89710-0001
Phone : (702) 688-1225

NEW HAMPSHIRE
Susan Boniauto
Executive Director
Div. of the Arts
40 N. Main St.
Concord, NH 03301
Phone : (603) 271-2789

NEW JERSEY
Barbara F. Russo
Executive Director
Council on the Arts
Dept. of State
20 W. State St., CN 306
Trenton, NJ 08625
Phone : (609) 292-6130

NEW MEXICO
Laura Morrow
Director
Arts Div.
Off. of Cultural Affairs
228 E. Palace Ave.
Santa Fe, NM 87501
Phone : (505) 827-6364
Fax : (505) 827-7308

NEW YORK*
Chair
Council on Arts
915 Broadway
New York, NY 10010
Phone : (212) 387-7000

NORTH CAROLINA
Mary Regan
Director
Arts Council
Dept. of Cultural Resources
221 E. Lane St.
Raleigh, NC 27601-2807
Phone : (919) 733-2821
Fax : (919) 733-4834

NORTH DAKOTA
Patsy Thompson
Director
Council on the Arts
418 E. Broadway Ave., Ste. 70
Bismarck, ND 58501-4086
Phone : (701) 328-3954
Fax : (701) 328-3963

OHIO
Wayne P. Lawson
Executive Director
Arts Council
727 E. Main St.
Columbus, OH 43205
Phone : (614) 466-2613
Fax : (614) 466-4494

OKLAHOMA
Betty Price
Executive Director
Arts Council
2101 Jim Thorpe Bldg., Rm. 640
Oklahoma City, OK 73105
Phone : (405) 521-2931

OREGON
Leslie Tuomi
Executive Director
Arts Comm.
775 Summer St., NE
Salem, OR 97310
Phone : (503) 986-0088

PENNSYLVANIA
Philip J. Horn
Director
Council on the Arts
216 Finance Bldg.
Harrisburg, PA 17120
Phone : (717) 787-6883

RHODE ISLAND
Karolye White
Acting Executive Director
Council on the Arts
95 Cedar St., Ste. 103
Providence, RI 02903
Phone : (401) 277-3880

SOUTH CAROLINA
Suzette Surkamer
Executive Director
Arts Comm.
1800 Gervais St.
Columbia, SC 29201
Phone : (803) 734-8687

SOUTH DAKOTA
Dennis Holub
Executive Director
Arts Council
230 S. Phillips Ave., Ste. 204
Sioux Falls, SD 57102
Phone : (605) 339-6646

TENNESSEE
Bennett Tarleton
Director
Arts Commission
404 James Robertson Pkwy., Ste. 160
Nashville, TN 37243-0780
Phone : (615) 741-1701
Fax : (615) 741-8559

TEXAS
John Paul Batiste
Executive Director
Comm. on the Arts
P.O. Box 13406, Capitol Station
Austin, TX 78711
Phone : (512) 463-5535

UTAH
Bonnie H. Stephens
Director
Div. of Fine Arts
Community & Economic Development Dept.
617 E. South Temple
Salt Lake City, UT 84102
Phone : (801) 533-5895

VERMONT
Nicolette Clarke
Executive Director
Council on the Arts
133 State St.
Montpelier, VT 05633
Phone : (802) 828-3291
Fax : (802) 828-3363

VIRGINIA
Peggy J. Baggett
Executive Director
Comm. for the Arts
223 Governor St.
Richmond, VA 23219
Phone : (804) 225-3132

WASHINGTON
Karen Gose
Executive Director
Arts Comm.
234 E. 8th Ave.
Olympia, WA 98504
Phone : (360) 753-3860

WEST VIRGINIA
Lakin Ray Cook
Acting Director
Arts & Humanities Div.
Cultural Ctr.
Charleston, WV 25305
Phone : (304) 348-0240
Fax : (304) 558-2779

WISCONSIN
Dean Amhaus
Executive Director
Wisconsin Arts Board
Dept. of Administration
101 E. Wilson St., 1st Fl.
Madison, WI 53702
Phone : (608) 266-0190
Fax : (608) 267-0380

WYOMING
John Coe
Director
Council on Arts
Dept. of Commerce
2320 Capitol Ave.
Cheyenne, WY 82002
Phone : (407) 777-7473

DISTRICT OF COLUMBIA
Pamela Holt
Executive Director
Comm. on Arts & Humanities
410 8th St., N.W., Ste. 500
Washington, DC 20005
Phone : (202) 724-5613

AMERICAN SAMOA
Faailoilo Lauvao
Executive Director
Council on Arts, Culture & Humanities
Museum of American Samoa
Pago Pago, AS 96799
Phone : (684) 633-4347
Fax : (684) 633-2059

GUAM
Deborah J. Bordallo
Director
Council on the Arts & Humanities
P.O. Box 2950
Agana, GU 96910
Phone : (671) 647-2240
Fax : (671) 477-0589

NORTHERN MARIANA ISLANDS
Margarita DLG. Wonenberg
Executive Director
Commonwealth Council for Arts and Culture
P.O. Box 553 CHRB
Saipan, MP 96950
Phone : (670) 322-9982
Fax : (670) 322-9028

PUERTO RICO
Carmelo Delgado Cintron
Institute of Puerto Rican Culture
P.O. Box 4184
San Juan, PR 00905-4184
Phone : (809) 723-2115
Fax : (809) 724-8393

U.S. VIRGIN ISLANDS
John Jowers
Executive Director
Council on the Arts
41 Norre Gade
St. Thomas, VI 00802
Phone : (809) 774-5984

ATTORNEY GENERAL

The chief legal officer of the state who represents the state or its offices in all litigation.

ALABAMA
Jeff Sessions
Attorney General
Office of the Attorney General
State House
11 S. Union St.
Montgomery, AL 36130
Phone : (334) 242-7300
Fax : (334) 242-7458

ALASKA
Bruce M. Botelho
Attorney General
Department of Law
P.O. Box 110300
Juneau, AK 99811-0300
Phone : (907) 465-3600
Fax : (907) 465-2075

ARIZONA
Grant Woods
Attorney General
1275 W. Washington
Phoenix, AZ 85007
Phone : (602) 542-4266

ARKANSAS
Winston Bryant
Attorney General
323 Center St., Ste. 200
Little Rock, AR 72201
Phone : (501) 682-2007
Fax : (501) 682-8084

CALIFORNIA
Daniel E. Lungren
Attorney General
1300 I Street
Sacramento, CA 95814
Phone : (916) 324-5437

COLORADO
Gale A. Norton
Attorney General
Dept. of Law
1525 Sherman St., 5th Fl.
Denver, CO 80203-1712
Phone : (303) 866-4500
Fax : (303) 866-5691

CONNECTICUT
Richard Blumenthal
Attorney General
55 Elm St.
Hartford, CT 06106
Phone : (203) 566-2026

DELAWARE
M. Jane Brady
Office of the Attorney General
Carvel State Office Building
820 N. French St.
Wilmington, DE 19801
Phone : (302) 577-3838
Fax : (302) 577-3090

FLORIDA
Robert A. Butterworth
Attorney General
Dept. of Legal Affairs
The Capitol, PL 01
Tallahassee, FL 32399-1050
Phone : (904) 487-1963
Fax : (904) 487-2564

GEORGIA
Michael J. Bowers
Attorney General
Office of the Attorney General
40 Capitol Square, SW
Atlanta, GA 30334-1300
Phone : (404) 656-3300

HAWAII
Margery S. Bronster
Attorney General
425 Queen St.
Honolulu, HI 96813
Phone : (808) 586-1500
Fax : (808) 586-1239

IDAHO
Alan G. Lance
Attorney General of Idaho
Office of the Attorney General
Statehouse
Boise, ID 83720-1000
Phone : (208) 334-2400

ILLINOIS
Jim Ryan
Attorney General
Office of the Attorney General
State of Illinois Center
100 W. Randolph St.
Chicago, IL 60601
Phone : (312) 814-3000
Fax : (312) 814-2549

INDIANA
Pamela Fanning Carter
Attorney General
Office of the Attorney General
Indiana Government Center South
402 W. Washington St., 5th Floor
Indianapolis, IN 46204

IOWA
Tom H. Miller
Attorney General of Iowa
Off. of the Attorney General
Hoover State Off. Bldg.
Des Moines, IA 50319
Phone : (515) 281-3604
Fax : (515) 281-3604

KANSAS
Carla J. Stovall
Attorney General
Office of the Attorney General
Judicial Center, 2nd Fl.
Topeka, KS 66612-1597
Phone : (913) 296-2215
Fax : (913) 296-6296

KENTUCKY
Chris Gorman
Attorney General
Office of the Attorney General
State Capitol, Rm. 116
Frankfort, KY 40601
Phone : (502) 564-7600

LOUISIANA
Richard Ieyoub Jr.
Attorney General
Office of the Attorney General
Department of Justice
P.O. Box 94005
Baton Rouge, LA 70804-4095
Phone : (504) 342-7013

MAINE
Andrew Ketterer
Attorney General
Dept. of Attorney General
State House Station # 6
Augusta, ME 04333
Phone : (207) 626-8800

MARYLAND
J. Joseph Curran Jr.
Attorney General
Office of the Attorney General
200 Saint Paul Place
Baltimore, MD 21202-2202
Phone : (410) 576-6300
Fax : (410) 576-7003

MASSACHUSETTS
Scott Harshbarger
Attorney General
Off. of the Attorney General
1 Ashburton Pl.
Boston, MA 02108-1698
Phone : (617) 727-2200
Fax : (617) 727-3251

MICHIGAN
Frank J. Kelley
Attorney General
Law Bldg.
525 W. Ottawa
Lansing, MI 48909
Phone : (517) 373-1110

MINNESOTA
Hubert H. Humphrey III
Attorney General
Office of the Attorney General
State Capitol, Suite 102
St. Paul, MN 55155
Phone : (612) 296-6196

MISSISSIPPI
Mike Moore
Attorney General
Department of Justice
P.O. Box 220
Jackson, MS 39205-0220
Phone : (601) 359-3692

MISSOURI
Jeremiah W. Nixon
Attorney General
Office of the Attorney General
Supreme Court Bldg.
207 W. High St.
P.O. Box 899
Jefferson City, MO 65101
Phone : (314) 751-3321
Fax : (314) 751-0774

MONTANA
Joseph P. Mazurek
Attorney General
Office of the Attorney General
Justice Building
215 N. Sanders St.
Helena, MT 59620-1401
Phone : (406) 444-2026

NEBRASKA
Donald B. Stenberg
Attorney General
Office of the Attorney General
State Capitol, Rm. 2115
P.O. Box 98920
Lincoln, NE 68509-8920
Phone : (402) 471-2682
Fax : (402) 471-3297

NEVADA
Frankie Sue Del Papa
Attorney General
Office of the Attorney General
Old Supreme Court Building
198 S. Carson
Carson City, NV 89710
Phone : (702) 687-4170

NEW HAMPSHIRE
Jeffrey R. Howard
Attorney General
Office of the Attorney General
State House Annex
25 Capitol St.
Concord, NH 03301-6397
Phone : (603) 271-3655

NEW JERSEY
Deborah T. Poritz
Attorney General
Office of the Attorney General
Richard J. Hughes Justice Complex
25 Market St., CN080
Trenton, NJ 08625
Phone : (609) 292-4925

NEW MEXICO
Tim Udall
Attorney General
Office of the Attorney General
P.O. Drawer 1508
Santa Fe, NM 87504-1508
Phone : (505) 827-6000
Fax : (505) 827-5826

NEW YORK
Dennis C. Vacco
Attorney General
Office of the Attorney General
120 Broadway
New York, NY 10271

NORTH CAROLINA
Michael F. Easley
Attorney General
Office of the Attorney General
Dept. of Justice
2 E. Morgan St.
Raleigh, NC 27602
Phone : (919) 733-3377
Fax : (919) 733-7491

NORTH DAKOTA
Heidi Heitkamp
Attorney General
State Capitol, 1st Fl.
600 E. Boulevard Ave.
Bismarck, ND 58505-0040
Phone : (701) 328-2210
Fax : (701) 328-2226

OHIO
Betty D. Montgomery
Attorney General
Office of the Attorney General
State Office Tower
30 E. Broad St.
Columbus, OH 43266-0410
Phone : (614) 466-3376

OKLAHOMA
Drew Edmondson
Attorney General
Office of the Attorney General
State Capitol
2300 N. Lincoln Blvd., Rm. 112
Oklahoma City, OK 73105

OREGON
Theodore Kulongoski
Attorney General
Office of the Attorney General
Justice Building
1162 Court St., NE
Salem, OR 97310
Phone : (503) 378-6002

PENNSYLVANIA
Ernest D. Preate Jr.
Attorney General
Office of the Attorney General
Strawberry Sq., 16th Fl.
Harrisburg, PA 17120
Phone : (717) 787-3391

RHODE ISLAND
Jeffrey B. Pine
Attorney General
Office of the Attorney General
72 Pine St.
Providence, RI 02903
Phone : (401) 274-4400

SOUTH CAROLINA
Charles M. Condon
Attorney General
Office of the Attorney General
Rembert C. Dennis Office Bldg.
P.O. Box 11549
Columbia, SC 29211-1549

SOUTH DAKOTA
Mark Barnett
Attorney General
Office of the Attorney General
500 E. Capitol
Pierre, SD 57501-5070
Phone : (605) 773-3215

TENNESSEE
Charles W. Burson
Attorney General
Off. of the Attorney General
500 Charlotte Ave.
Nashville, TN 37243
Phone : (615) 741-3492

TEXAS
Dan Morales
Attorney General
Office of the Attorney General
Capitol Station
P.O. Box 12548
Austin, TX 78711-2548
Phone : (512) 463-2100

UTAH
Jan Graham
Attorney General
Office of the Attorney General
236 State Capitol
Salt Lake City, UT 84114-0810
Phone : (801) 538-1149

VERMONT
Jeffrey L. Amestoy
Attorney General
Office of the Attorney General
109 State St.
Montpelier, VT 05609-1001
Phone : (802) 828-3171
Fax : (802) 828-2154

VIRGINIA
James S. Gilmore III
Attorney General
Office of the Attorney General
Supreme Court Building
900 E. Main Street
6th Fl.
Richmond, VA 23219
Phone : (804) 786-2071
Fax : (804) 371-0200

WASHINGTON
Christine O. Gregoire
Attorney General
Office of the Attorney General
P.O. Box 40100
Olympia, WA 98504-0100
Phone : (360) 753-6200

WEST VIRGINIA
Darrell V. McGraw Jr.
Attorney General
Office of the Attorney General
State Capitol
Charleston, WV 25305
Phone : (304) 558-2021
Fax : (304) 558-0140

WISCONSIN
James E. Doyle
Attorney General
Office of the Attorney General
State Capitol, Rm. 114 E
P.O. Box 7857
Madison, WI 53707-7857
Phone : (608) 266-1221
Fax : (608) 267-2779

WYOMING
William Hill
Attorney General
Office of the Attorney General
State Capitol Building
Cheyenne, WY 82002
Phone : (307) 777-7841

DISTRICT OF COLUMBIA
Garland Pinkston
Corporate Counsel
Office of the Corporation Counsel
441 4th St., NW
Washington, DC 20001

John Payton
Corporation Counsel
Off. of Corporation Counsel
441 4th St., NW, Rm. 1060N
Washington, DC 20004
Phone : (202) 727-6248

AMERICAN SAMOA
Malaetasi Togafau
Attorney General
American Samoa Government
P.O. Box 7
Pago Pago, AS 96799
Phone : (684) 633-4163
Fax : (684) 633-1838

GUAM**
Elizabeth Barrett-Anderson
Attorney General
238 Archbishop Flores St., Ste. 701
Agana, GU 96910
Phone : (671) 475-3324

NORTHERN MARIANA ISLANDS
Richard Weil
Attorney General
Office of the Attorney General
Administration Building
Saipan, MP 96950
Phone : (670) 322-4311
Fax : (670) 322-4320

PUERTO RICO
Pedro R. Pierluisi
Attorney General
Office of the Attorney General
P.O. Box 192
San Juan, PR 00902-0192
Phone : (809) 721-7700
Fax : (809) 724-4770

U.S. VIRGIN ISLANDS
Alva A. Swan Esq.
Attorney General
Dept. of Justice
GERS Complex
48B-50C Kronprinsden Gade
St. Thomas, VI 00802
Phone : (809) 774-5666
Fax : (809) 774-9710

BANKING

Administers laws regulating the operation of banking institutions in the state.

ALABAMA
Kenneth McCartha
Acting Superintendent
Dept. of State Banking
101 S. Union St.
Montgomery, AL 36130
Phone : (334) 242-3452
Fax : (334) 242-3500

ALASKA
Willis Kirkpatrick
Director
Div. of Banking, Securities & Corps
Dept. of Commerce & Economic Development
P.O. Box 110807
Juneau, AK 99811-0807
Phone : (907) 465-2521
Fax : (907) 465-2549

ARIZONA
Richard C. Houseworth
Supertintendent
Dept. of Banking
2910 N. 44th St., Ste. 310
Phoenix, AZ 85018
Phone : (602) 255-4421

ARKANSAS
Bill Ford
Commissioner
State Bank Dept.
323 Center St., Ste. 500
Little Rock, AR 72201
Phone : (501) 324-9019
Fax : (501) 324-9028

CALIFORNIA
Conrad Hewitt
Superintendent
Dept of State Banking
111 Pine St., Ste. 1100
San Francisco, CA 94111
Phone : (415) 288-8811

COLORADO
Barbara Walker
Commissioner
Div. of Banking
1560 Broadway # 1175
Denver, CO 80202
Phone : (303) 894-7575
Fax : (303) 894-7570

CONNECTICUT
John P. Burke
Commissioner
Dept. of Banking
260 Constitution Plaza
Hartford, CT 06103
Phone : (203) 240-8100

DELAWARE
Timothy McTaggart
State Bank Commissioner
Dept. of State
P.O. Box 1401
Dover, DE 19903
Phone : (302) 739-4235
Fax : (302) 739-3609

FLORIDA
Robert F. Milligan
Comptroller
Dept. of Banking & Finance
The Capitol, PL09
Tallahassee, FL 32399-0350
Phone : (904) 488-0370
Fax : (904) 922-2442

GEORGIA
Edward D. Dunn
Commissioner
Dept. of Banking & Finance
2990 Brandywine Rd., # 200
Atlanta, GA 30341
Phone : (404) 986-1633

HAWAII
Raymond Muraoka
Commissioner
Div. of Financial Institutions
Dept. of Commerce & Consumer Affairs
250 S. King St.
Honolulu, HI 96813
Phone : (808) 586-2820

IDAHO
Gavin Gee
Director
Dept. of Finance
700 W. State St.
Boise, ID 83720
Phone : (208) 334-3319

ILLINOIS
Richard Luft
Commissioner
500 E. Monroe
Springfield, IL 62701
Phone : (217) 785-2837
Fax : (217) 524-5941

INDIANA
Charles W. Phillips
Director
Dept. of Fin. Institutions
IGC-West, Rm. 066
402 W. Washington St.
Indianapolis, IN 46204
Phone : (317) 232-0010

IOWA
Richard Buenneke
Superintendent
Banking Div.
Dept. of Commerce
200 E. Grand, Ste. 300
Des Moines, IA 50309
Phone : (515) 281-4014

KANSAS
Frank D. Dunnick
Commissioner
Off. of the State Bank Commissioner
700 Jackson, Ste. 300
Topeka, KS 66603-3796
Phone : (913) 296-2266
Fax : (913) 296-0168

KENTUCKY
Edward J. Holmes
Acting Commissioner
Dept. of Financial Inst.
Public Protection & Regulation Cabinet
477 Versailles Rd.
Frankfort, KY 40601
Phone : (502) 564-3390

LOUISIANA
Larry L. Murray
Assistant Secretary
Off. of Financial Institutions
Dept. of Economic Development
P.O. Box 94185
Baton Rouge, LA 70804-9185
Phone : (504) 925-4660

MAINE
H. Donald DeMatteis
Superintendent
Bur. of Banking
Dept. of Prof. & Fin. Reg.
State House Station # 36
Augusta, ME 04333
Phone : (207) 582-8713

MARYLAND
Margie Muller
Banking Commissioner
Dept. of Licensing & Regulation
501 St. Paul Pl., 13th Fl.
Baltimore, MD 21202
Phone : (410) 333-6812

MASSACHUSETTS
Thomas J. Curry
Acting Commissioner
Div. of Banks
100 Cambridge St., Rm. 2004
Boston, MA 02202
Phone : (617) 727-3145

MICHIGAN
Pat McQueen
Commissioner
Financial Institutions Bur.
Dept. of Commerce
P.O. Box 30224
Lansing, MI 48909
Phone : (517) 373-3460
Fax : (517) 335-0908

MINNESOTA
James Miller
Deputy Commissioner
Div. of Financial Examinations
Dept. of Commerce
133 7th St., E.
St. Paul, MN 55101
Phone : (612) 296-2715

MISSISSIPPI
Joseph H. Neely
Commissioner
Dept. of Banking & Consumer Finance
P.O. Drawer 23729
Jackson, MS 39225
Phone : (601) 359-1103

MISSOURI
Earl Manning
Commissioner of Finance
Dept. of Economic Development
Truman Bldg., Rm. 630
P.O. Box 716
Jefferson City, MO 65102
Phone : (314) 751-2545
Fax : (314) 751-9192

MONTANA
Donald W. Hutchinson
Commissioner
Financial Div.
Dept. of Commerce
1520 E. 6th Ave., Rm. 50
Helena, MT 59620
Phone : (406) 444-2091

NEBRASKA
James A. Hansen
Director
Dept. of Banking & Finance
1200 N. St. Atrium #311
P.O. Box 95006
Lincoln, NE 68508
Phone : (402) 471-2171
Fax : (402) 471-3062

NEVADA
L. Scott Walshaw
Commissioner
Div. of Financial Institutions
Dept. of Business & Industry
406 E. Second St.
Carson City, NV 89710
Phone : (702) 687-4259

NEW HAMPSHIRE
A. Roland Roberge
Commissioner
Dept. of Banking
169 Manchester St.
Concord, NH 03301
Phone : (603) 271-3561

NEW JERSEY**
Jeffrey Connor
Commissioner
Off. of the Commissioner
Dept. of Banking
20 W. State St., CN 040
Trenton, NJ 08625
Phone : (609) 292-3420

NEW MEXICO
William J. Verant
Director
Financial Institutions Div.
Dept. of Reg. & Licensing
P.O. Box 25101
725 St. Michaels Dr.
Santa Fe, NM 87504
Phone : (505) 827-7100
Fax : (505) 827-7107

NEW YORK*
Superintendent
Dept. of Banking
2 Rector St.
New York, NY 10006
Phone : (212) 618-6557

NORTH CAROLINA
William T. Graham
Commissioner
Banking Commission
Dept. of Commerce
430 N. Salisbury St.
Raleigh, NC 27603
Phone : (919) 733-3016
Fax : (919) 733-6918

NORTH DAKOTA
Gary Preszler
Commissioner
Dept. of Banking & Financial Institutions
State Capitol, 13th Fl.
600 E. Boulevard Ave.
Bismarck, ND 58505
Phone : (701) 328-2253
Fax : (701) 328-3000

OHIO
Alison Meeks
Superintendent
Div. of Banks
Dept. of Commerce
77 S. High St.
Columbus, OH 43266
Phone : (614) 466-2932
Fax : (614) 644-1631

OKLAHOMA
Mick Thompson
Commissioner
Dept. of Banking
4100 N. Lincoln Blvd.
Oklahoma City, OK 73105
Phone : (405) 521-2782

OREGON
Cecil Monroe
Deputy Administrator
Finance & Corp. Securities Div
Dept. of Consumer & Bus. Srvcs.
305 Winter St., NE
Salem, OR 97310
Phone : (503) 378-4387
Fax : (503) 378-4178

PENNSYLVANIA
Richard C. Rishel
Secretary
Dept. of Banking
Harristown 2 , 16th Fl.
Harrisburg, PA 17120
Phone : (717) 787-6991

RHODE ISLAND
Edward Pare Jr.
Associate Director
Banking Div.
Dept. of Business Regulation
233 Richmond St., Ste. 231
Providence, RI 02903
Phone : (401) 277-2405

SOUTH CAROLINA
Richard Eckstrom
State Treasurer
Wade Hampton Bldg., Rm. 120
P.O. Box 11778
Columbia, SC 29211
Phone : (803) 734-2688

SOUTH DAKOTA
Dick Duncan
Director
Div. of Banking & Finance
Dept. of Commerce & Regulation
105 N. Euclid
Pierre, SD 57501
Phone : (605) 773-3421

TENNESSEE
Talmadge Gilley
Commissioner
Dept. of Financial Institution
John Sevier Bldg., 4th Fl.
Nashville, TN 37243
Phone : (615) 741-5603
Fax : (615) 741-2883

TEXAS
Catherine A. Ghiflieri
Commissioner
Department of Banking
2601 N. Lamar Blvd.
Austin, TX 78705
Phone : (512) 475-1300

UTAH
G. Edward Leary
Commissioner
Dept. of Financial Institutions
324 S. State, Ste. 201
P.O. Box 89
Salt Lake City, UT 84110
Phone : (801) 538-8854

VERMONT
Elizabeth R. Costle
Commissioner
Dept. of Banking, Insurance & Securities
89 State St.
Montpelier, VT 05620-3101
Phone : (802) 828-3301
Fax : (802) 828-3306

VIRGINIA
Preston C. Shannon
Chair
State Corporation Comm.
Tyler Building
1300 E. Main St.
Richmond, VA 23219
Phone : (804) 371-9608
Fax : (804) 371-9376

WASHINGTON
John Bley
Director
Dept. of Financial Institutions
P.O. Box 41201
Olympia, WA 98504-1201
Phone : (360) 902-8700

WEST VIRGINIA
Sharon G. Bias
Commissioner
Div. of Banking
Bldg. 3, Rm. 311-A
1800 Washington St., E.
Charleston, WV 25305
Phone : (304) 558-2294
Fax : (304) 558-0442

WISCONSIN
Dick Dean
Commissioner
Off. of Banking
101 E. Wilson, 5th Fl.
P.O. Box 7876
Madison, WI 53707
Phone : (608) 266-1621
Fax : (608) 267-6889

WYOMING
Sue Mecca
Commissioner
Banking Div.
Dept. of Audit
Herschler Bldg., 3rd Fl.
122 W. 25th St.
Cheyenne, WY 82002
Phone : (307) 777-7797

DISTRICT OF COLUMBIA
Fe Morales Marks
Superintendent
Off. of Banking &
Financial Institutions
1250 I St., NW, Rm. 1003
Washington, DC 20005
Phone : (202) 727-1563

GUAM
Joaquin G. Blaz
Director
Dept. of Revenue & Taxation
855 W. Marine Dr.
Agana, GU 96910
Phone : (671) 477-5144

NORTHERN MARIANA ISLANDS
Enrique A. Santos
Director
Banking and Insurance
Dept. of Commerce
P.O. Box 10007
Saipan, MP 96950
Phone : (670) 322-4073
Fax : (670) 322-4008

PUERTO RICO
Hector Mayol
Commissioner
Off. Financial Institutions
1492 Ponce De Leon Centro Europa #600
San Juan, PR 00907-4022
Phone : (809) 723-3131
Fax : (809) 723-4042

U.S. VIRGIN ISLANDS
Kenneth E. Mapp
Lieutenant Governor
#18 Kongens Gade
St. Thomas, VI 00802
Phone : (809) 774-2991
Fax : (809) 774-6953

BOATING LAW ADMINISTRATION

Administers and enforces state boating laws and boating education efforts.

ALABAMA
William B. Garner
Director
Marine Police Div.
Conservation & Nat. Res. Dept.
64 N. Union St.
Montgomery, AL 36130
Phone : (334) 242-3673
Fax : (334) 242-0336

ARIZONA
Tim Wade
Boating Education/ Enforcement Coord.
Game & Fish Dept.
2221 W. Greenway Rd.
Phoenix, AZ 85023
Phone : (602) 942-3000

ARKANSAS
Mike Wilson
Boating Law Administrator
Boating Safety Section
State Game & Fish Comm.
2 Natural Resources Dr.
Little Rock, AR 72205
Phone : (501) 223-6300
Fax : (501) 223-6425

CALIFORNIA
John Banuelos
Director
Dept. of Boating & Waterways
1629 S St.
Sacramento, CA 95814
Phone : (916) 445-6281

COLORADO
Rick Storm
Boating Administrator
Div. of Parks & Outdoor Recreation
13787 S. Hwy. 85
Littleton, CO 80125
Phone : (303) 791-1954

CONNECTICUT
Timothy E. Skaates
Boating Law Administrator
Environmental Protection Dept.
333 Ferry Rd.
P.O. Box 526
Old Lyme, CT 06371
Phone : (203) 434-9840
Fax : (203) 434-3501

DELAWARE
Rodney L. Harmic
Boating Law Administrator
Dept. of Natural Resources & Environ. Control
P.O. Box 1401
Dover, DE 19903
Phone : (302) 739-3440

FLORIDA
Mickey Watson
Director
Div. of Law Enforcement
Dept. of Environmental Protection
3900 Commonwealth Blvd., MS600
Tallahassee, FL 32399-3000
Phone : (904) 488-5757

GEORGIA
David Waller
Director
Wildlife Resources Div.
Dept. of Natural Resources
2070 U.S. Hwy. 278, SE
Social Circle, GA 30279
Phone : (404) 918-6400

HAWAII
David E. Parsons
State Boating Manager
Div. of Boating & Ocean Rec.
Land & Natural Resources Dept.
79 S. Nimitz Hwy.
Honolulu, HI 96813
Phone : (808) 587-1966

IDAHO
Mark Brandt
Boating Program Supervisor
Dept. of Parks & Recreation
Statehouse Mail
Boise, ID 83720-8000
Phone : (208) 334-4199

ILLINOIS
Thomas Wakolbinger
Deputy Chief, Law Enforcement
Dept. of Conservation
524 S. Second St.
Springfield, IL 62701
Phone : (217) 782-6431

INDIANA
Larry G. Rhinehart
Boating Law Administrator/Law Enforcement
Dept. of Natural Resources
IGC-South, Rm. W255-D
402 W. Washington
Indianapolis, IN 46204
Phone : (317) 232-0614

IOWA
Larry Wilson
Director
Dept. of Natural Resouces
Wallace State Off. Bldg.
E. Ninth & Grand Ave.
Des Moines, IA 50319-0034
Phone : (515) 281-5385
Fax : (515) 281-8895

KANSAS
Jeff Gayer
Boating Safety Administrator
Dept. of Wildlife & Parks
R.R. 2, Box 54A
Pratt, KS 67124-9599
Phone : (316) 672-5911

KENTUCKY
Donovan Smith
Director
Div. of Water Patrol
107 Mero St.
Frankfort, KY 40601
Phone : (502) 564-3074

LOUISIANA
Charles Clark
Assistant Chief
Enforcement Div.
Dept. of Wildlife & Fisheries
P.O. Box 98000
Baton Rouge, LA 70898-9000
Phone : (504) 765-2346

MAINE
Parker Tripp
Chief Warden/Warden Service
Dept. of Inland Fisheries & Wildlife
State House Station # 41
Augusta, ME 04333
Phone : (207) 287-2766

MARYLAND
Bess Crandall
Director
Planning & Policy Program
Dept. of Natural Resources
580 Taylor Ave., Rm. E4
Annapolis, MD 21401
Phone : (410) 974-2939

MASSACHUSETTS
Richard A. Murray
Director
Div. of Environmental Law Enforcement
100 Nashua St., Rm. 910
Boston, MA 02114

MICHIGAN
Herbert Burns
Chief
Law Enforcement Div.
Dept. of Natural Resources
P.O. Box 30028
Lansing, MI 48909
Phone : (517) 373-1230

MINNESOTA
Kim A. Elverum
Boating & Water Safety Coordinator
Dept. of Natural Resources
500 Lafayette Rd.
St. Paul, MN 55155-4046
Phone : (612) 296-0905

MISSISSIPPI
Elizabeth Raymond
Boating Law Administrator
Dept. of Wildlife, Fisheries & Parks
P.O. Box 451
Jackson, MS 39205
Phone : (601) 362-9212

MISSOURI
Larry Whitten
Commissioner
State Water Patrol
Dept. of Public Safety
2728B Plaza Dr.
P.O. Box 1368
Jefferson City, MO 65102
Phone : (314) 751-3333
Fax : (314) 636-8428

MONTANA
Ron Aasheim
Boating Law Administrator
Dept. of Fish, Wildlife & Parks
1420 E. 6th Ave.
Helena, MT 59620
Phone : (406) 444-2452

NEBRASKA
Leroy Orvis
Boating Law Administrator
Law Enforcement Div.
Nebraska Game & Parks Comm.
2200 N. 33rd St.
P.O. Box 30370
Lincoln, NE 68503-0370
Phone : (402) 471-5579
Fax : (402) 471-5528

NEVADA
Fred Messmann
Chief Game Warden
Dept. of Wildlife
P.O. Box 10678
Reno, NV 89520-0022
Phone : (702) 688-1542

NEW HAMPSHIRE
Thomas McCabe Jr.
Chief
Marine Patrol Bur.
31 Dock Rd.
Gilford, NH 03246
Phone : (603) 271-3336

NEW JERSEY**
William J. Gronikowski
Bureau Chief
Bur. of Marine Law Enforcement
State Police Headquarters
P.O. Box 7068
West Trenton, NJ 08628-0068
Phone : (609) 882-2000

NEW MEXICO
David Skasik
Boating Administrator
Park & Recreation Div.
Energy, Min. & Nat. Res. Dept.
P.O. Box 1147
Santa Fe, NM 87504
Phone : (505) 827-7468
Fax : (505) 827-4001

NEW YORK*
Director
Bur. of Marine & Rec. Vehicles
Agency Bldg. 1
Empire State Plz.
Albany, NY 12238
Phone : (518) 474-0455

NORTH CAROLINA
Charles R. Fullwood
Executive Director
Wildlife Resources Comm.
512 N. Salisbury St.
Raleigh, NC 27604
Phone : (919) 733-3391
Fax : (919) 733-7083

NORTH DAKOTA
Wilmer Pich
Boat & Water Safety Coordinator
Dept. of Game & Fish
100 N. Bismarck Expy.
Bismarck, ND 58501
Phone : (701) 328-6327
Fax : (701) 328-6352

OHIO
Paul Gregory
Chief
Watercraft Div.
Dept. of Natural Resources
1952 Belcher Dr., #C2
Columbus, OH 43224-1386
Phone : (614) 265-6476
Fax : (614) 267-8883

OKLAHOMA
Bob Sanders
Commander
Lake Patrol Div.
Dept. of Public Safety
P.O. Box 11415
Oklahoma City, OK 73136
Phone : (405) 425-2143

OREGON
Paul Donheffner
Director
State Marine Board
435 Commercial St., NE , Ste. 400
Salem, OR 97310-0650
Phone : (503) 373-1405
Fax : (503) 378-4597

PENNSYLVANIA
John F. Simmons
Director
Fish & Boat Comm.
3532 Walnut St.
P.O. Box 67000
Harrisburg, PA 17106-7000
Phone : (717) 657-4538

RHODE ISLAND
Steven Hall
Boating Law Administrator
Dept. of Environmental Mgt.
83 Park St.
Providence, RI 02903
Phone : (401) 277-6647

SOUTH CAROLINA
Alvin A. Taylor
Boating Law Administrator
Div. of Law Enforcement & Boating
Dept. of Natural Resources
P.O. Box 12559
Charleston, SC 29422-2559
Phone : (803) 762-5034

SOUTH DAKOTA
Bill Shattuck
Boating Safety Coordinator
Div. of Wildlife
523 E. Capitol Ave.
Pierre, SD 57501-5182
Phone : (605) 773-4506

TENNESSEE
Ed Carter
Chief
Boating Div.
Wildlife Resources Agency
P.O. Box 40747
Nashville, TN 37204
Phone : (615) 781-6682

TEXAS
Howard Kidwel
Boat Registration
Dept. of Parks & Wildlife
4200 Smith School Rd.
Austin, TX 78744
Phone : (512) 389-4802

UTAH
Ted Woolley
Boating Coordinator
Div. of Parks & Recreation
1636 W. North Temple St.
Salt Lake City, UT 84116
Phone : (801) 538-7341

VERMONT
Alan F. Buck
Director
Marine Div.
State Police Headquarters
103 S. Main St.
Waterbury, VT 05676
Phone : (802) 244-8775

VIRGINIA
William L. Woodfin Jr.
Director
Game & Inland Fisheries
4010 W. Broad St.
Richmond, VA 23230
Phone : (804) 367-9231
Fax : (804) 367-0405

WASHINGTON
Jim French
Boating Programs Manager
State Parks & Recreation Comm.
P.O. Box 42650
Olympia, WA 98504-2650
Phone : (360) 902-8515

WEST VIRGINIA
Richard M. Hall
Chief
Law Enforcement Section
Dept. of Natural Resources
Capitol Complex, Bldg. 3
Charleston, WV 25305
Phone : (304) 558-2784
Fax : (304) 558-1170

WISCONSIN
William G. Engfer
Boating Law Administrator
Dept. of Natural Resources
101 S. Webster St., LE/5
P.O. Box 7921
Madison, WI 53707
Phone : (608) 266-0859
Fax : (608) 267-3579

WYOMING
Russ Pollard
Wildlife Law Enforcement Coordinator
Dept. of Game & Fish
5400 Bishop Blvd.
Cheyenne, WY 82006
Phone : (304) 777-4585

DISTRICT OF COLUMBIA
Stanley W. Hawkins
Boating Law Administrator
Metropolitan Police Dept.
Harbor Section
550 Water St., SW
Washington, DC 20024
Phone : (202) 727-4582

AMERICAN SAMOA
Richard Kasar
Commander
United States Coast Guard
P.O. Box 249
Pago Pago, AS 96799
Phone : (684) 633-2299
Fax : (684) 633-1933

GUAM
Bradley A. Hokanson
Boating Law Administrator
Police Dept.
287 W. O'Brien Dr.
Agana, GU 96910
Phone : (671) 472-8911
Fax : (671) 477-3229

NORTHERN MARIANA ISLANDS
Jose C. Sablan
Officer in Charge
Boating Safety Div.
Lower Base, Tanapag
Saipan, MP 96950
Phone : (670) 322-4037

PUERTO RICO
Jose L. Campos Avella
Commissioner of Navigation
Dept. of Natural Resources
P.O. Box 5887
San Juan, PR 00906
Phone : (809) 724-2340
Fax : (809) 724-7335

U.S. VIRGIN ISLANDS
Robert A. Danet
Director of Enforcement
Dept. of Planning & Nat. Res.
Nisky Ctr., Ste. 231
St. Thomas, VI 00802
Phone : (809) 774-3320
Fax : (809) 775-5706

BUDGET

Collects and analyzes budget requests and supporting materials and prepares the executive budget document.

ALABAMA
Jimmy Baker
Budget Officer
State Budget Office
Dept. of Finance
600 Dexter Ave., N101
Montgomery, AL 36130
Phone : (334) 242-7230
Fax : (334) 242-4488

ALASKA
Annalee McConnell
Director
Off. of Management & Budget
P.O. Box 110020
Juneau, AK 99811-0020
Phone : (907) 465-4660
Fax : (907) 465-3008

ARIZONA
Peter Burns
Director
Strategic Plan. & Budget Off.
1700 W. Washington, W. Wing
Phoenix, AZ 85007
Phone : (602) 542-5381

ARKANSAS
Mike Stormes
Administrator
Off. of Budget
Dept. of Finance & Admin.
P.O. Box 3278
Little Rock, AR 72203
Phone : (501) 682-1941
Fax : (501) 628-1086

CALIFORNIA
Russell S. Gould
Director
Dept. of Finance
State Capitol, Rm. 1145
Sacramento, CA 95814
Phone : (916) 445-4141

COLORADO
George DeLaney
Director
Off. of State Planning & Budgeting
111 State Capitol
Denver, CO 80203
Phone : (303) 866-2980
Fax : (303) 866-3044

CONNECTICUT
Carol Peterson
Assistant Executive Budget Officer
Budget & Finance Div.
Off. of Policy & Management
80 Washington St.
Hartford, CT 06106
Phone : (203) 566-3582

DELAWARE
Peter M. Ross
Director
Off. of the Budget
P.O. Box 1401
Dover, DE 19901
Phone : (302) 739-4204
Fax : (302) 739-5661

FLORIDA
Bob Bradley
Director
Off. of Planning & Budgeting
Off. of the Governor
1601 The Capitol
Tallahassee, FL 32399-0001
Phone : (904) 488-7810

GEORGIA
Henry M. Huckaby
Director
Off. of Planning & Budget
254 Washington St., SW, Ste. 614
Atlanta, GA 30334
Phone : (404) 656-3820

HAWAII
Earl I. Anzai
Director
Dept. of Budget & Finance
P.O. Box 150
Honolulu, HI 96810
Phone : (808) 586-1518
Fax : (808) 586-1976

IDAHO
Dean Van Englen
Administrator
Div. of Financial Management
Off. of the Governor
Statehouse, Rm. 122
Boise, ID 83720
Phone : (208) 334-3900

ILLINOIS
Joan Walters
Director
Bur. of the Budget
Off. of the Governor
108 State House
Springfield, IL 60706
Phone : (217) 782-4520
Fax : (217) 524-1514

INDIANA
Jean Blackwell
Director
Budget Agency
State House, Rm. 212
Indianapolis, IN 46204
Phone : (317) 232-5612

IOWA
Gretchen Tegeler
Director
Dept. of Management
State Capitol Bldg.
Des Moines, IA 50319
Phone : (515) 281-3322
Fax : (515) 242-5897

KANSAS
Gloria Timmer
Director
Div. of the Budget
Dept. of Admin.
State Capitol, 1st Fl.
Topeka, KS 66612-1504
Phone : (913) 296-2436
Fax : (913) 296-0231

KENTUCKY
Mark Guilfoyle
State Budget Director
Governor's Office
State Capitol, Rm. 106
Frankfort, KY 40601
Phone : (502) 564-2611
Fax : (502) 564-2517

LOUISIANA
Steve Winham
Budget Director
Div. of Administration
Off. of the Governor
P.O. Box 94095
Baton Rouge, LA 70804
Phone : (504) 342-7000

MAINE
John R. Nicholas
State Budget Officer
Bur. of the Budget
Dept. of Admin. & Fin. Srvcs.
State House Station # 58
Augusta, ME 04333
Phone : (207) 624-7810

MARYLAND
Marita Brown
Secretary
Dept. of Budget & Fiscal Planning
45 Calvert St.
Annapolis, MD 21404
Phone : (410) 974-2114

MASSACHUSETTS
Thomas Graf
Director
Executive Off. for Admin. & Finance
State House, Rm. 272
Boston, MA 02133
Phone : (617) 727-2081

MICHIGAN*
Director
Dept. of Mgt. & Budget
P.O. Box 30026
Lansing, MI 48909
Phone : (517) 373-1004
Fax : (517) 373-7268

MINNESOTA
Laura King
Commissioner
Dept. of Finance
400 Centennial Bldg.
658 Cedar St.
St. Paul, MN 55155
Phone : (612) 296-9721

MISSISSIPPI
Edward L. Ranck
Executive Director
Dept. of Finance & Admin.
P.O. Box 267
Jackson, MS 39205
Phone : (601) 359-3402

MISSOURI
Mark E. Ward
Deputy Commissioner
Div. of Budget & Planning
Office of Administration
State Capitol, Rm. 124
P.O. Box 809
Jefferson City, MO 65102
Phone : (314) 751-3925
Fax : (314) 526-4811

MONTANA
David Lewis
Director
Budget & Program Planning Off.
Capitol Station
Helena, MT 59620-0801
Phone : (406) 444-3616

NEBRASKA
Steve Ferris
Administrator
Budget Div.
Dept. of Administrative Srvcs.
State Capitol, Rm. 1322
P.O. Box 94664
Lincoln, NE 68509-4664
Phone : (402) 471-2526
Fax : (402) 471-4157

NEVADA
John P. Comeaux
Director
Dept. of Administration
209 E. Musser St., Rm. 200
Carson City, NV 89710
Phone : (702) 687-4065
Fax : (702) 687-3983

NEW HAMPSHIRE
Patrick Duffy
Commissioner
Dept. of Administrative Srvcs.
25 Capitol St.
Concord, NH 03301
Phone : (603) 271-3201

Donald Hill
Asst. Commissioner/ Budget Officer
Dept. of Administrative Srvcs.
25 Capitol St.
Concord, NH 03301
Phone : (603) 271-3201

NEW JERSEY
Elizabeth L. Pugh
Director
Off. of Mgt. & Budget
Dept. of Treasury
33 W. State St., CN221
Trenton, NJ 08625
Phone : (609)292-6746

NEW MEXICO
John P. Gasparich
Director
Budget Div.
Dept. of Finance & Admin.
Bataan Memorial Bldg., Rm. 190
Santa Fe, NM 87503
Phone : (505) 827-3640
Fax : (505) 827-3861

NEW YORK*
Director
Div. of Budget
Executive Dept.
State Capitol
Albany, NY 12224
Phone : (518) 474-2300

NORTH CAROLINA
Marvin K. Dorman
State Budget Officer
Off. of State Budget
116 W. Jones St.
Raleigh, NC 27603-8005
Phone : (919) 733-7061
Fax : (919) 733-0640

NORTH DAKOTA
Celeste Kubasta
Assist. Exec. Budget Analyst
Off. of Mgt. & Budget
State Capitol, 4th Fl.
600 E. Boulevard Ave.
Bismarck, ND 58505
Phone : (701) 328-4904
Fax : (701) 328-3230

Rod Brackman
Director
Off. of Mgt. & Budget
State Capitol, 4th Fl.
600 E. Boulevard Ave.
Bismarck, ND 58505
Phone : (701) 328-4904

OHIO
R. Gregory Browning
Director
Off. of Budget & Mgt.
30 E. Broad St., 34th Fl.
Columbus, OH 43266-0411
Phone : (614) 466-4034
Fax : (614) 466-5400

OKLAHOMA
Jack E. White
Director
Off. of State Finance
122 State Capitol
Oklahoma City, OK 73105
Phone : (405) 521-2141

OREGON
Theresa McHugh
Budget Director
Dept. of Administrative Srvcs.
155 Cottage St., NE
Salem, OR 97310
Phone : (503) 378-4691
Fax : (503) 373-7643

PENNSYLVANIA
Robert Bittenbender
Secretary
Budget Department
Main Capitol Bldg., Rm. 238
Harrisburg, PA 17120
Phone : (717) 787-4472

RHODE ISLAND
Michael O'Keefe
Associate Director of Finance
Budget Officer
Off. of the Budget
Dept. of Admin.
One Capitol Hill, 4th Fl.
Providence, RI 02908
Phone : (401) 277-6300

SOUTH CAROLINA
George Dorn
Director
Off. of State Budget
Budget & Control Board
1205 Pendleton St.
Columbia, SC 29201
Phone : (803) 734-1314

SOUTH DAKOTA
Curt Everson
Commissioner
Bur. of Finance & Mgt.
State Capitol, 2nd Fl.
500 E. Capitol Ave.
Pierre, SD 57501
Phone : (605) 773-3411

TENNESSEE
Jerry Lee
Assistant Commissioner
Budget Div.
Dept. of Finance & Admin.
304 State Off. Bldg.
Nashville, TN 37243
Phone : (615) 741-2401

TEXAS
Albert Hawkins
Director
Governor's Off. of Budget & Planning
P.O. Box 12428, Capitol Station
Austin, TX 78711
Phone : (512) 463-1778

UTAH
Lynne Koga
Director
Off. of Planning & Budget
116 State Capitol
Salt Lake City, UT 84114
Phone : (801) 538-1555

VERMONT
Thomas Pelham
Commissioner
Dept. of Finance & Mgt.
Agency of Administration
109 State St.
Montpelier, VT 05602
Phone : (802) 828-2376
Fax : (802) 828-2428

VIRGINIA
Robert Lauterberg
Director
Dept. of Planning & Budget
412 9th St. Office Bldg.
Richmond, VA 23219
Phone : (804) 786-7455
Fax : (804) 225-3291

WASHINGTON
Ruta Fanning
Director
Off. of Financial Mgt.
300 Insurance Bldg.
P.O. Box 43113
Olympia, WA 98504
Phone : (360) 753-5459

WEST VIRGINIA
Roger L. Smith
Director
Budget Div.
Dept. of Finance & Admin.
State Capitol
Charleston, WV 25305
Phone : (304) 558-2344
Fax : (304) 558-2999

WISCONSIN
Richard G. Chandler
Administrator
State Exec. Budget & Planning
Dept. of Admin.
101 E. Wilson, 10th Fl.
P.O. Box 7864
Madison, WI 53707
Phone : (608) 266-1035
Fax : (608) 266-7645

WYOMING
Richard B. Standiford
Administrator
Budget Div.
2001 Capitol Ave.
Cheyenne, WY 82002
Phone : (307) 777-7203

DISTRICT OF COLUMBIA
Rodney Palmer
Director
Off. of the Budget
441 4th St., NE, Ste. 350-N
Washington, DC 20001
Phone : (202) 727-6343

AMERICAN SAMOA
Iosefo K. Iuli
Director
Program Planning & Budget
Pago Pago, AS 96799
Phone : (684) 633-4201
Fax : (684) 633-1148

GUAM
Joseph E. Rivera
Director
Bur. of Budget & Mgt. Research
P.O. Box 2950
Agana, GU 96910
Phone : (671) 475-9429
Fax : (671) 472-2825

NORTHERN MARIANA ISLANDS
Eli D. Cabrera
Special Assistant for Mgt. & Budget
Off. of the Governor
P.O. Box 10007
Saipan, MP 96950
Phone : (670) 322-4313
Fax : (670) 322-4017

PUERTO RICO
Jorge Aponte Hernandez
Director
Off. of Budget & Mgt.
P.O. Box 3228
San Juan, PR 00904
Phone : (809) 725-9420
Fax : (809) 723-7308

U.S. VIRGIN ISLANDS
Nellon Bowry
Director
Off. of Mgt. & Budget
#41 Norre Gade
Emancipation Garden Sta., 2nd Fl.
St. Thomas, VI 00802
Phone : (809) 774-0750
Fax : (809) 776-0069

BUILDING CODES

Establishes and enforces standards of construction, materials and occupancy for all buildings.

ALABAMA
Stedman B. McCollough
Building Comm.
770 Washington Ave.,
Ste. 444
Montgomery, AL 36130
Phone : (334) 242-4082
Fax : (334) 242-4182

ARKANSAS
Howard Williams
Administrator
Contractor's Licensing Bd.
621 E. Capitol
Little Rock, AR 72202
Phone : (501) 372-4661
Fax : (501) 372-2247

CALIFORNIA
Travis Pitts
Deputy Director
Div. of Codes & Standards
Housing & Community
Dev. Dept.
P.O. Box 1407
Sacramento, CA 95812
Phone : (916) 445-9471

COLORADO
Lester Field
Residential Inspection
Engineer
Div. of Housing
Dept. of Local Affairs
1313 Sherman St.
Denver, CO 80203
Phone : (303) 866-2033

CONNECTICUT
Donald Vigneau
State Building Inspector
Dept. of Public Safety
P.O. Box 2794
Middleton, CT 06457-9294
Phone : (203) 685-8310

FLORIDA
Rick Dixon
Section Administrator
Codes & Standards
Section
Rhyne Bldg.
2740 Centerview Dr.
Tallahassee, FL 32399-2100
Phone : (904) 487-1824

GEORGIA
Luther C. Lewis Jr.
Acting Executive Director
Building Authority
1 M. L. King, Jr. Dr.
Atlanta, GA 30334
Phone : (404) 656-3250

IDAHO
Wayne Larsen
Administrator
Building Div.
Dept. of Labor & Ind.
Srvcs.
227 N. 6th
Boise, ID 83720
Phone : (208) 334-3896

ILLINOIS
Pamela Lenane
Acting Director
Housing Development
Authority
401 N. Michigan Ave.
Chicago, IL 60611
Phone : (312) 836-5314
Fax : (312) 836-5313

INDIANA
Gerald Dunn
State Building
Commissioner
Fire & Building Srvcs.
IGC, Rm. C246
402 W. Washington
Indianapolis, IN 46204
Phone : (317) 232-1404

IOWA
Roy Marshall
State Fire Marshal
Dept. of Public Safety
Wallace State Off. Bldg.
Des Moines, IA 50319
Phone : (515) 281-8622

KANSAS
Barry Greis
Director
Div. of Facilities Mgt.
Dept. of Administration
900 SW Jackson,
Rm. 653-S
Topeka, KS 66612-2210
Phone : (913) 296-1318
Fax : (913) 296-3456

KANSAS — Cont.
J. David DeBusman
Director
Div. of Architectural
Srvcs.
625 Polk St.
Topeka, KS 66603
Phone : (913) 233-9367

KENTUCKY
Charles A. Cotton
Commissioner
Dept. of Housing, Bldgs.
& Construction
1047 U.S. 127 S., Bay 1
Frankfort, KY 40601
Phone : (502) 564-8044

LOUISIANA
Roger Magendie
Director
Facility Planning & Ctrl.
Off.
Div. of Administration
P.O. Box 94095
Baton Rouge, LA 70804
Phone : (504) 342-7000

MARYLAND**
James Hanna
Director
Bldg. Codes Admin.
Housing & Community
Dev.
100 Community Pl.
Crownsville, MD 21032
Phone : (410) 514-7220

MASSACHUSETTS
Tom Rogers
Chief
Board of Bldg.
Regulations & Standards
1 Ashburton Pl., Rm. 1301
Boston, MA 02108
Phone : (617) 727-7532
Fax : (617) 227-1754

MICHIGAN
Henry Green
Executive Director
Bur. of Construction
Codes
Dept. of Labor
P.O. Box 30254
Lansing, MI 48909
Phone : (517) 296-4639

MINNESOTA
Thomas Joachim
State Building Inspector
Bldg. Code & Standards
Div.
Dept. of Administration
408 Metro Sq. Bldg.
St. Paul, MN 55101
Phone : (612) 296-4639

MISSISSIPPI
Julia Waggoner
Staff Architect
Div. of General Services
Dept. of Finance &
Admin.
1501 Sillers Bldg.
Jackson, MS 39201
Phone : (601) 359-3633

MISSOURI
Randall G. Allen AIA
Director
Div. of Design &
Construction
Off. of Administration
Truman Bldg., Rm. 730
P.O. Box 809
Jefferson City, MO 65102
Phone : (314) 751-3339
Fax : (314) 751-7277

MONTANA
James Brown
Chief
Building Codes Bur.
Dept. of Commerce
1218 E. 6th Ave.
Helena, MT 59620
Phone : (406) 444-3933

NEBRASKA
Ken Fougeron
Administrator
State Building Div.
Dept. of Admin. Services
State Capitol, 10th Fl.
P.O. Box 94924
Lincoln, NE 68509-4924
Phone : (402) 471-3191
Fax : (402) 471-0421

NEW JERSEY
Russsell R. Hart
Director
Div. of Bldg. & Construction
Dept. of the Treasury
50 Barrack St., CN235
Trenton, NJ 08625
Phone : (609) 292-4724

NEW MEXICO
Fred Nevarez
Chief, General Construction Bur.
Construction Industries Div.
Regulation & Licensing Dept.
P.O. Box 25101
725 St. Michaels Dr.
Santa Fe, NM 87504
Phone : (505) 827-7030
Fax : (505) 827-7045

NEW YORK*
Commissioner
Div. of Housing & Comm. Ren.
Hampton Plz.
38-40 State St.
Albany, NY 12207
Phone : (518) 486-3370

NORTH CAROLINA
Dascheil Propes
Senior Deputy Commissioner
Engineering Div.
Dept. of Insurance
430 N. Salisbury St.
Raleigh, NC 27603-5908
Phone : (919) 733-3901
Fax : (919) 733-6495

NORTH DAKOTA
Rich Gray
Intergovernmental Asst.
Off. of Mgt. & Budget
State Capitol, 14th Fl.
600 E. Boulevard Ave.
Bismarck, ND 58505-0170
Phone : (701) 328-2094
Fax : (701) 328-2308

OHIO
Elmer Waltz
Chief
Factory & Bldg. Standards Div.
Dept. of Industrial Relations
2323 W. Fifth Ave.
Columbus, OH 43266
Phone : (614) 644-2622
Fax : (614) 644-3505

OKLAHOMA
Vernon Davis
Administrator
Construction & Properties Div.
Off. of Public Affairs
50 NE 23rd
Oklahoma City, OK 73105
Phone : (405) 521-2111

OREGON
Joseph A. Brewer III
Administrator
Building Codes Agency
1535 Edgewater, NW
Salem, OR 97310
Phone : (503) 378-3176
Fax : (503) 378-2322

PENNSYLVANIA
Charles J. Sludden
Director
Occuptl. & Industrial Safety
Dept. of Labor & Industry
1529 Labor & Industry Bldg.
Harrisburg, PA 17120
Phone : (717) 787-3323

RHODE ISLAND
Daniel Varin
Associate Director
Div. of Planning
One Capitol Hill, 4th Fl.
Providence, RI 02908-5873
Phone : (401) 277-1220

SOUTH CAROLINA
Helen Zeigler
Director
Div. of General Services
State Budget & Control Board
1201 Main St., Ste. 420
Columbia, SC 29201
Phone : (803) 737-3880

SOUTH DAKOTA
Tom D. Geraets
Commissioner
Bur. of Administration
500 E. Capitol Ave.
Pierre, SD 57501
Phone : (605) 773-3688

TENNESSEE
Ken Maynard
Executive Director
Facilities Mgt.
Dept. of Finance & Admin.
Nashville City Ctr.
Nashville, TN 37243
Phone : (615) 741-6311

TEXAS
John Pouland
Executive Director
General Srvcs. Comm.
Capitol Station
P.O. Box 13047
Austin, TX 78711-3047
Phone : (512) 463-3035

UTAH
Wayne Bingham
Assistant Director
Off. of Design & Construction
Facilities Construction Mgt. Div.
4110 State Off. Bldg.
Salt Lake City, UT 84114
Phone : (801) 538-3266

VERMONT
Mary S. Hooper
Commissioner
Dept. of Labor & Industry
National Life Bldg.
Drawer 20
Montpelier, VT 05620-3401
Phone : (802) 828-2288
Fax : (802) 828-2748

VIRGINIA
David L. Caprara
Director
Dept. of Housing & Community Development
501 N. 2nd St.
Richmond, VA 23219
Phone : (804) 371-7000
Fax : (804) 371-7090

WASHINGTON
Joseph A. Brewer III
Assistant Director
Bldg. & Con. Safety Inspec.
Dept. of Labor & Industries
P.O. Box 44400
Olympia, WA 98504
Phone : (360) 902-5488

WEST VIRGINIA
Walter Smittle III
Fire Marshal
2000 Quarrier St.
Charleston, WV 25305
Phone : (304) 558-2191

WISCONSIN
Richard L. Meyer
Director
Bur. of Code Development
Indl. Labor & Human Relations
P.O. Box 7969
Madison, WI 53707
Phone : (608) 266-1542
Fax : (608) 267-9566

WYOMING
Bruce Jaspersen
Structural Safety Principle Analyst
Dept. of Fire Prevention & Electrical Safety
Herschler Bldg., Rm. 2E
Cheyenne, WY 82002
Phone : (307) 777-7960

DISTRICT OF COLUMBIA
Hampton Cross
Administrator
Bldg. & Land Regulation Admin.
Cons. & Regulatory Affairs
614 H St., N.W., Rm. 312
Washington, DC 20001
Phone : (202) 727-7340

AMERICAN SAMOA
Sam Puletasi
Director
Dept. of Public Works
American Samoa Government
Pago Pago, AS 96799
Phone : (684) 633-4141
Fax : (684) 633-5958

GUAM**
Benigno M. Palomo
Director
Dept. of Public Works
P.O. Box 2950
Agana, GU 96910
Phone : (671) 646-3131

NORTHERN MARIANA ISLANDS
Edward M. Delon Guerrero
Secretary
Dept. of Public Works
Lower Base
P.O. Box 2950
Saipan, MP 96950
Phone : (670) 322-9482
Fax : (670) 322-3547

PUERTO RICO
Sigfrido Garcia Alfonso
Administrator
Housing Codes
P.O. Box 41179, Minillas Station
Santurce, PR 00940
Phone : (809) 726-3120

U.S. VIRGIN ISLANDS
Beulah Dalmida-Smith
Commissioner
Dept. of Planning & Natural Resources
Nisky Ctr., Ste. 231
St. Thomas, VI 00802
Phone : (809) 774-3320
Fax : (809) 775-5706

CAMPAIGN FINANCE ADMINISTRATION

Administers and enforces campaign finance laws.

ALASKA
Karen Boorman
Director
Alaska Public Off. Comm.
2221 E. Northern Lights Blvd.
Anchorage, AK 99508-4149
Phone : (907) 276-4176
Fax : (907) 276-7018

ARIZONA
Jane Dee Hull
Secretary of State
1700 W. Washington St., 7th Fl.
Phoenix, AZ 85007
Phone : (602) 542-4285
Fax : (602) 542-6172

ARKANSAS
Sharon Priest
Secretary of State
256 State Capitol Bldg.
Little Rock, AR 72201
Phone : (501) 682-1010
Fax : (501) 682-3510

CALIFORNIA
Ravi Mehta
Chairman
Fair Political Practices Comm.
428 J St., Ste. 600
P.O. Box 807
Sacramento, CA 95804
Phone : (916) 322-5901

CONNECTICUT
Miles S. Rapoport
Secretary of State
State Capitol, Rm. 104
Hartford, CT 06106
Phone : (203) 566-2739
Fax : (203) 566-6318

DELAWARE
Thomas J. Cook
Commissioner
Department of Elections
32 Loockerman Square, Ste. 203
Dover, DE 19901
Phone : (302) 739-4277
Fax : (302) 739-6794

FLORIDA
David Rancourt
Director
Div. of Elections
Dept. of State
The Capitol, PL02
Tallahassee, FL 32399-0250
Phone : (904) 488-7690

GEORGIA
C. Theodore Lee
Executive Secretary
State Ethics Comm.
2082 E. Exchange Pl., Ste. 235
Tucker, GA 30084
Phone : (404) 493-5795

HAWAII
Scott Whiting
Acting Executive Director
Campaign Spending Comm.
Off. of Lt. Governor
335 Merchant St., Rm. 244B
Honolulu, HI 96813
Phone : (808) 586-0285

IDAHO
Pete T. Cenarrusa
Secretary of State
Statehouse, Rm. 203
Boise, ID 83720
Phone : (208) 334-2300

IOWA
Kay Williams
Executive Director
Ethics & Campaign Disclosure Board
514 E. Locust, Ste. 104
Des Moines, IA 50309
Phone : (515) 281-6841

KANSAS
Carol Williams
Executive Director
Kansas Commission on Governmental Standards & Conduct
109 SW 9th, 5th Fl.
Topeka, KS 66612-1287
Phone : (913) 296-4219
Fax : (913) 296-2548

KENTUCKY
George Russell
Director
Registry of Election Finance
140 Walnut St.
Frankfort, KY 40601
Phone : (502) 573-7100

LOUISIANA
W. Fox McKeithen
Secretary of State
Dept. of State
P.O. Box 94125
Baton Rouge, LA 70804
Phone : (504) 342-4479

MAINE
Marilyn Canavan
Director
Governmental Ethics & Election Practices Comm.
State House Station # 101
Augusta, ME 04333
Phone : (207) 287-4179

MASSACHUSETTS
Michael J. Sullivan
Director
Off. of Campaign & Political Finance
1 Ashburton Pl., Rm. 411
Boston, MA 02108
Phone : (617) 727-8352
Fax : (617) 727-6549

MICHIGAN
Candice Miller
Secretary of State
Treasury Bldg., 1st Fl.
430 W. Allegan St.
Lansing, MI 48918
Phone : (517) 373-2510

MINNESOTA
Joan Growe
Secretary of State
180 State Off. Bldg.
100 Constitution Ave.
St. Paul, MN 55155
Phone : (612) 296-2079

MISSISSIPPI
Dick Molpus
Secretary of State
401 Mississippi St.
P.O. Box 136
Jackson, MS 39201
Phone : (601) 359-1350

MISSOURI
Marion Sinnett
Administrative Secretary
State Ethics Comm.
221 Metro Dr.
Jefferson City, MO 65109
Phone : (314) 751-2020
Fax : (314) 526-4506

MONTANA
Ed Argenbright
Commissioner of Political Practices
1205 8th Ave.
Helena, MT 59620
Phone : (406) 444-2942

NEBRASKA
Scott Moore
Secretary of State
State Capitol, Ste. 2300
P.O. Box 94608
Lincoln, NE 68509-4608
Phone : (402) 471-2554
Fax : (402) 471-3666

NEVADA
Dean Heller
Secretary of State
Capitol Complex
Carson City, NV 89710
Phone : (702) 687-5203
Fax : (702) 687-3471

NEW MEXICO
Denise Lamb
Director
Registry of Election Finance
Off. of Secretary of State
State Capitol Bldg., Rm. 420
Santa Fe, NM 87503
Phone : (505) 827-3600
Fax : (505) 827-3634

NORTH CAROLINA
Rufus L. Edmisten
Secretary of State
300 N. Salisbury St.
Raleigh, NC 27603-5909
Phone : (919) 733-5140
Fax : (919) 733-5172

NORTH DAKOTA
Tom Mattern
Election Supervisor
Off. of Secretary of State
State Capitol, 1st Fl.
600 E. Boulevard Ave.
Bismarck, ND 58505
Phone : (701) 328-2905
Fax : (701) 328-2992

OHIO
Bob Taft
Secretary of State
30 E. Broad St., 14th Fl.
Columbus, OH 43266-0418
Phone : (614) 466-2655
Fax : (614) 644-0649

OREGON
Phil Keisling
Secretary of State
136 State Capitol
Salem, OR 97310
Phone : (503) 986-7150
Fax : (503) 373-7414

SOUTH DAKOTA
Joyce Hazeltine
Secretary of State
State Capitol, 2nd Fl.
Pierre, SD 57501
Phone : (605) 773-3537

TEXAS
John Steiner
Director
Ethics Comm.
P.O. Box 12070
Austin, TX 78711
Phone : (512) 463-5800

VERMONT
James Milne
Secretary of State
109 State St.
Montpelier, VT 05609-1101
Phone : (802) 828-2168
Fax : (802) 828-2496

WASHINGTON
Melissa Warheit
Executive Director
Public Disclosure Comm.
711 Capitol Way, Rm. 403
Olympia, WA 98504
Phone : (360) 753-1111

WEST VIRGINIA
Ken Hechler
Secretary of State
State Capitol, Rm W-157K
1900 Kanawha Blvd., E.
Charleston, WV 25305
Phone : (304) 558-6000
Fax : (304) 558-0900

WISCONSIN
Kevin J. Kennedy
Executive Secretary
State Elections Bd.
132 E Wilson, Suite 300
Madison, WI 53702
Phone : (608) 266-8005
Fax : (608) 267-0500

WYOMING
Carol Thompson
Director of Elections
Off. of Secretary of State
State Capitol
Cheyenne, WY 82002
Phone : (307) 777-5333

DISTRICT OF COLUMBIA
Robert A. Lane
Executive Director
Board of Elections & Ethics
Off. of Campaign Finance
2000 14th St., NW, Rm. 420
Washington, DC 20009
Phone : (202) 939-8710

GUAM**
Henry A. Torres
Executive Director
Election Comm.
P. O. Box BG
Agana, GU 96910
Phone: (671) 577-9791

NORTHERN MARIANA ISLANDS
Juan M. Diaz
Executive Director
Board of Elections
P.O. Box 470
Saipan, MP 96950
Phone : (670) 234-6481
Fax : (670) 233-6880

U.S. VIRGIN ISLANDS
Gwendolyn P. Adams
Commissioner
Dept. of Finance
#76 Kronprindsens Gade
St. Thomas, VI 00802
Phone : (809) 774-4750
Fax : (809) 776-4028

CASH MANAGEMENT

Manages the flow of funds deposited in the state's bank accounts for the payment of immediate obligations.

ALABAMA
Lucy Baxley
State Treasurer
Alabama State Capitol
600 Dexter Ave.
Montgomery, AL 36130
Phone : (334) 242-7500
Fax : (334) 242-7592

ALASKA
Vernon Voss
Assessment Officer
Treasury Div.
Dept. of Revenue
P.O. Box 110405
Juneau, AK 99811-0400
Phone : (907) 465-2360
Fax : (907) 465-4019

ARIZONA
Tony West
State Treasurer
106 State Capitol
1700 W. Washington
Phoenix, AZ 85007
Phone : (602) 542-5815

ARKANSAS
Tom Smith
Administrator
Office of Accounting
Dept. of Finance & Admin.
403 DFA Bldg., 1509 W. 7th St.
Little Rock, AR 72201
Phone : (501) 682-2583
Fax : (501) 682-1086

CALIFORNIA
Bruce VanHouten
Deputy Director
Cash Management Div.
915 Capitol Mall, Rm. 107
Sacramento, CA 95814
Phone : (916) 653-3601

COLORADO
George DeLaney
Director
Off. of State Planning & Budgeting
111 State Capitol
Denver, CO 80203
Phone : (303) 866-2980
Fax : (303) 866-3044

Bill Owens
State Treasurer
Dept. of Treasury
140 State Capitol Bldg.
Denver, CO 80203
Phone : (303) 866-2441

CONNECTICUT
Christopher B. Burnham
Treasurer
Off. of the Treasurer
55 Elm St.
Hartford, CT 06106-1773
Phone : (203) 566-5050

DELAWARE
Janet C. Rzewnicki
State Treasurer
Thomas Collins Building
P.O. Box 1401
Dover, DE 19903
Phone : (302) 739-3382
Fax : (302) 739-5635

FLORIDA
Bill Nelson
Treasurer/Insurance Commissioner
Dept. of Insurance
State Capitol, PL11
Tallahassee, FL 32399-0300
Phone : (904) 922-3100
Fax : (904) 488-7265

GEORGIA
Steven N. McCoy
State Treasurer
Off. of Treasury & Fiscal Srvcs.
1516 West Tower
200 Piedmont Ave., SE
Atlanta, GA 30334
Phone : (404) 656-2168

IDAHO
Lydia Justice Edwards
State Treasurer
102 State Capitol
Boise, ID 83720
Phone : (208) 334-3200

ILLINOIS
Judy Baar Topinka
State Treasurer
State House, Rm. 219
Springfield, IL 62706
Phone : (217) 782-2211
Fax : (217) 785-2777

INDIANA
Joyce Brinkman
State Treasurer
State House, Rm. 242
Indianapolis, IN 46204
Phone : (317) 232-6386

IOWA
Michael L. Fitzgerald
State Treasurer
State Capitol Bldg.
Des Moines, IA 50319
Phone : (515) 281-5368

KENTUCKY
Frances Jones Mills
State Treasurer
Capitol Annex, Rm. 183
Frankfort, KY 40601
Phone : (502) 564-4722

LOUISIANA
Mary L. Landrieu
State Treasurer
Dept. of Treasury
P.O. Box 44154
Baton Rouge, LA 70804-0154
Phone : (504) 342-0010

MARYLAND
Lucille Maurer
State Treasurer
Goldstein Treasury Bldg., Rm. 109
Annapolis, MD 21401
Phone : (301) 974-3542

MASSACHUSETTS
Joseph Malone
Treasurer & Receiver General
1 Ashburton Pl., 12th Fl.
Boston, MA 02108-1518
Phone : (617) 367-3900

MICHIGAN
Douglas B. Roberts
State Treasurer
Dept. of Treasury
430 W. Allegan St.
Lansing, MI 48922
Phone : (517) 373-3223
Fax : (517) 335-1785

MINNESOTA
Michael A. McGrath
Treasurer
303 Administration Bldg.
50 Sherburne Ave.
St. Paul, MN 55155
Phone : (612) 296-7091

MISSISSIPPI
Marshall G. Bennett
State Treasurer
Dept. of Treasury
P.O. Box 138
Jackson, MS 39205
Phone : (601) 359-3600

MISSOURI
Bob Holden
Treasurer
State Capitol, Rm. 229
P.O. Box 210
Jefferson City, MO 65102
Phone : (314) 751-2411
Fax : (314) 751-9443

MONTANA
Ray Hofland
Bureau Chief
Treasury Unit
Dept. of Admin.
Sam Mitchell Bldg., Rm. 175
Helena, MT 59620
Phone : (406) 444-2624

NEBRASKA
David E. Heineman
State Treasurer
State Capitol, Suite 2003
P.O. Box 94788
Lincoln, NE 68509-4666
Phone : (402) 471-2455
Fax : (402) 471-4390

NEVADA
Robert L. Seale
State Treasurer
Capitol Complex
Carson City, NV 89710
Phone : (702) 687-5200

NEW HAMPSHIRE
Georgie A. Thomas
State Treasurer
121 State House Annex
Concord, NH 03301
Phone : (603) 271-2621

NEW MEXICO
Lupe Sanchez
Cash Manager
Off. of State Treasurer
P.O. Box 608
Santa Fe, NM 87504
Phone : (505) 827-6400
Fax : (505) 827-6395

NEW YORK*
State Comptroller
Off. of the State Comptroller
A.E. Smith Off. Bldg., 6th Fl.
Albany, NY 12236
Phone : (518) 474-4040

NORTH CAROLINA
Harlan E. Boyles
State Treasurer
325 N. Salisbury St.
Raleigh, NC 27603-1388
Phone : (919) 733-3951
Fax : (919) 733-9586

NORTH DAKOTA
Bud Walsh
Director of Accounting
Off. of Mgt. & Budget
State Capitol, 4th Fl.
600 E. Boulevard Ave.
Bismarck, ND 58505-0400
Phone : (701) 328-2682
Fax : (701) 328-3230

OHIO
J. Kenneth Blackwell
State Treasurer
State Off. Tower, 9th Fl.
30 E. Broad St.
Columbus, OH 43215
Phone : (614) 466-2057
Fax : (614) 644-7313

OREGON
Jim Hill
State Treasurer
159 State Capitol
Salem, OR 97310
Phone : (503) 378-4329
Fax : (503) 373-7051

PENNSYLVANIA
Catherine Baker Knoll
Treasurer
Office of the Treasurer
Rm. 129, Finance Bldg.
Harrisburg, PA 17120
Phone : (717) 787-2465

RHODE ISLAND
Nancy J. Mayer
State Treasurer
State House, Rm. 102
Providence, RI 02903
Phone : (401) 277-2397

SOUTH CAROLINA
Richard Eckstrom
State Treasurer
Wade Hampton Bldg., Rm. 120
P.O. Box 11778
Columbia, SC 29211
Phone : (803) 734-2688

SOUTH DAKOTA
Richard Butler
State Treasurer
500 E. Capitol Ave.
Pierre, SD 57501
Phone : (605) 773-3378

TENNESSEE
Stephen D. Adams
State Treasurer
State Capitol
Nashville, TN 37243
Phone : (615) 741-2956
Fax : (615) 741-7328

TEXAS
Martha Whitehead
State Treasurer
Dept. of the Treasury
Capitol Station
P.O. Box 12608
Austin, TX 78711
Phone : (512) 463-6000

VERMONT
James H. Douglas
Treasurer
State Administration Bldg.
133 State St.
Montpelier, VT 05633-6200
Phone : (802) 828-2301
Fax : (802) 828-2772

VIRGINIA
Ronald L. Tillett
State Treasurer
Department of the Treasury
Monroe Bldg., 3rd Fl
101 N. 14th St.
Richmond, VA 23219
Phone : (804) 371-6013
Fax : (804) 225-3187

WASHINGTON
Daniel Grimm
State Treasurer
Legislative Bldg.
P.O. Box 40200
Olympia, WA 98504-0200
Phone : (360) 753-7130

WEST VIRGINIA
Larrie Bailey
State Treasurer
Bldg. 1, Rm. E145
1900 Kanawha Blvd., E.
Charleston, WV 25305
Phone : (304) 343-4000
Fax : (304) 346-6602

WISCONSIN
Jack C. Voight
State Treasurer
101 E Wilson St., 5th Fl.
P.O. Box 7871
Madison, WI 53707
Phone : (608) 266-1714
Fax : (608) 266-2647

WYOMING
Stan Smith
State Treasurer
State Capitol
Cheyenne, WY 82002
Phone : (307) 777-7408

DISTRICT OF COLUMBIA
Fe Morales Marks
Superintendent
Off. of Banking & Financial Institutions
1250 I St., N.W., Rm. 1003
Washington, DC 20005
Phone : (202) 727-1563

AMERICAN SAMOA
Ray Pritt
Treasurer
Dept. of the Treasury
Government of American Samoa
Pago Pago, AS 96799
Phone : (684) 633-4155
Fax : (684) 633-4100

GUAM
John S. Salas
Director
Dept. of Administration
P.O. Box 884
Agana, GU 96910
Phone : (671) 475-1101
Fax : (671) 477-6788

NORTHERN MARIANA ISLANDS
David M. Apatang
Director
Finance and Accounting
Dept. of Finance
P.O. Box 5234 CHRB
Saipan, MP 96950
Phone : (670) 664-1200
Fax : (670) 664-1215

CHIEF JUSTICE

The chief justice or judge of the state court of last resort.

ALABAMA
Sonny Hornsby Jr.
Chief Justice
Supreme Court
300 Dexter Ave.
Montgomery, AL 36104-3741
Phone : (334) 242-4599
Fax : (334) 242-4483

ALASKA
Daniel A. Moore Jr.
Chief Justice
Supreme Court
303 K St.
Anchorage, AK 99501-2084
Phone : (907) 264-0622
Fax : (907) 276-5808

ARIZONA
Stanley Feldman
Chief Justice
Supreme Court
1501 W. Washington
Phoenix, AZ 85007
Phone : (602) 542-9300
Fax : (602) 542-9480

ARKANSAS
Jack Holt Jr.
Chief Justice
Supreme Court
Justice Bldg.
Little Rock, AR 72201
Phone : (501) 682-6861
Fax : (501) 682-6877

CALIFORNIA
Malcolm M. Lucas
Chief Justice
Supreme Court
303 Second St., South Tower
San Francisco, CA 94107
Phone : (415) 396-9410

COLORADO
Anthony F. Vollack
Chief Justice
Supreme Court
State Judicial Bldg., # 435
2 E. 14th Ave.
Denver, CO 80203
Phone : (303) 861-1111
Fax : (303) 837-3702

CONNECTICUT
Ellen Ash Peters
Chief Justice
Supreme Court
P.O. Drawer N, Station A
Hartford, CT 06106
Phone : (203) 566-3054

DELAWARE
Norman Veasey
Chief Justice
Supreme Court
Carvel State Off. Bldg.
820 N. French St.
Wilmington, DE 19801
Phone : (302) 577-3700

FLORIDA
Stephen H. Grimes
Chief Justice
Supreme Court
Supreme Court Bldg.
500 South Duval St.
Tallahassee, FL 32399-1927
Phone : (904) 488-8421

GEORGIA
Harold G. Clark
Chief Justice
Supreme Court
State Judicial Bldg., Rm. 572
244 Washington St.
Atlanta, GA 30334
Phone : (404) 656-3472

HAWAII
Ronald T.Y. Moon
Chief Justice
Supreme Court
417 S. King St.
P.O. Box 2560
Honolulu, HI 96813
Phone : (808) 539-4700

IDAHO
Charles MeDevitt
Chief Justice
Supreme Court
451 W. State St.
Boise, ID 83720
Phone : (208) 334-3464

ILLINOIS
Benjamin Miller
Chief Justice
Supreme Court
First of America Ctr., Ste.560
One N. Old State Capitol Plz.
Springfield, IL 62701
Phone : (217) 782-4154

INDIANA
Randall T. Shepard
Chief Justice
Supreme Court
State House, Rm. 304
Indianapolis, IN 46204
Phone : (317) 232-2550

IOWA
Arthur A. McGiverin
Chief Justice
Supreme Court
State Capitol
Des Moines, IA 50319
Phone : (515) 281-5174

KANSAS
Richard W. Holmes
Chief Justice
Supreme Court
Kansas Judicial Center
Topeka, KS 66612-1507
Phone : (913) 296-4898

KENTUCKY
Robert F. Stephens
Chief Justice
Supreme Court
State Capitol
Frankfort, KY 40601
Phone : (502) 564-6753

LOUISIANA
Pascal F. Calogero Jr.
Chief Justice
Supreme Court
301 Loyola Ave.
New Orleans, LA 70112
Phone : (504) 568-5727

MAINE
Daniel E. Wathen
Chief Justice
Supreme Judicial Court
Kennebec County Courthouse
95 State St.
Augusta, ME 04333
Phone : (207) 623-1735

MARYLAND
Robert C. Murphy
Chief Judge
Court of Appeals
County Courts Bldg.
401 Bosley Ave., 5th Fl.
Towson, MD 21204
Phone : (410) 887-4810

MASSACHUSETTS
Paul J. Liacos
Chief Justice
Supreme Judicial Court
New Court House, 13th Fl.
Boston, MA 02108
Phone : (617) 557-1040
Fax : (617) 248-0771

MICHIGAN
James H. Brickley
Chief Justice
Supreme Court
P.O. Box 30052
Lansing, MI 48909
Phone : (517) 373-8683

MINNESOTA
Alexander Keith
Chief Justice
Supreme Court
25 Constitution Ave.
St. Paul, MN 55155
Phone : (612) 297-5454

MISSISSIPPI
Armis E. Hawkins
Chief Justice
Supreme Court
P.O. Box 117
Jackson, MS 39205
Phone : (601) 359-3702

MISSOURI
Ann K. Covington
Chief Justice
Supreme Court
207 W. High
P.O. Box 150
Jefferson City, MO 65102
Phone : (314) 751-3570
Fax : (314) 751-7161

MONTANA
Jean Turnage
Chief Justice
Supreme Court
Justice Bldg., Rm. 414
Helena, MT 59620
Phone : (406) 444-5490

NEBRASKA
C. Thomas White
Chief Justice
Supreme Court
State Capitol, Rm. 2413
P.O. Box 98910
Lincoln, NE 68509-8910
Phone : (402) 471-3736
Fax : (402) 471-3480

NEVADA
Thomas Steffen
Chief Justice
Supreme Court
Supreme Court Bldg.
Carson City, NV 89710
Phone : (702) 687-5188

NEW HAMPSHIRE
David A. Brock
Chief Justice
Supreme Court
Supreme Court Bldg.
Concord, NH 03301
Phone : (603) 271-2149

NEW JERSEY
Robert N. Wilentz
Chief Justice
Supreme Court
Judiciary Dept.
257 Monmouth Rd.
Oakhurst, NJ 07755
Phone : (908) 517-0700

NEW MEXICO
Joseph Back
Chief Justice
Supreme Court
P.O. Box 848
Santa Fe, NM 87504
Phone : (505) 827-4883
Fax : (505) 827-4837

NEW YORK*
Chief Judge
Court of Appeals
Court of Appeals Hall
20 Eagle St.
Albany, NY 12207
Phone : (518) 455-7700

NORTH CAROLINA
Burley B. Mitchell Jr.
Chief Justice
Supreme Court
2 W. Morgan St.
Raleigh, NC 27601-1400
Phone : (919) 733-3715
Fax : (919) 733-0105

NORTH DAKOTA
Gerald W. VandeWalie
Chief Justice
Supreme Court
600 E. Boulevard, 1st Fl.
Judicial Wing
Bismark, ND 58505-0530
Phone : (701) 328-2221
Fax : (701) 328-4480

OHIO
Thomas J. Moyer
Chief Justice
Supreme Court
30 E. Broad St.
Columbus, OH 43266
Phone : (614) 466-3627
Fax : (614) 752-5801

OKLAHOMA
Alma Wilson
Chief Justice
Supreme Court
State Capitol, Rm. 245
Oklahoma City, OK 73105
Phone : (405) 521-3843

OREGON
Wallace P. Carson Jr.
Chief Justice
Supreme Court
Supreme Court Bldg.
Salem, OR 97310
Phone : (503) 378-6008

PENNSYLVANIA
Robert N.C. Nix Jr.
Chief Justice
Supreme Court
Widener Bldg., Rm. 500
S. Penn Sq.
Philadelphia, PA 19107
Phone : (215) 560-3071

RHODE ISLAND
Joseph Weisberger
Chief Justice
Supreme Court
250 Benefit St.
Providence, RI 02903
Phone : (401) 277-3775

SOUTH CAROLINA
Ernest A. Finney Jr.
Chief Justice
Supreme Court
P.O. Box 11330
1231 Gervais St.
Columbia, SC 29211
Phone : (803) 734-1080

SOUTH DAKOTA
Robert A. Miller
Chief Justice
Supreme Court
500 E. Capitol Ave.
Pierre, SD 57501
Phone : (605) 773-6254

TENNESSEE
E. Riley Anderson
Chief Justice
Supreme Court
Supreme Court Bldg.,
Rm. 307
Nashville, TN 37243
Phone : (615) 741-2484

TEXAS
Thomas R. Phillips
Chief Justice
Supreme Court
P.O. Box 12248
Austin, TX 78711
Phone : (512) 463-1315

UTAH
Michael David
Zimmerman
Chief Justice
Utah Supreme Court
State Capitol
Salt Lake City, UT 84114
Phone : (801) 538-1044

VERMONT
Frederic W. Allen
Chief Justice
Supreme Court
111 State St.
Montpelier, VT 05602
Phone : (802) 828-3278

VIRGINIA
Harry L. Carrico
Chief Justice
Supreme Court
P.O. Box 1315
Richmond, VA 23210
Phone : (804) 786-2023

WASHINGTON
Barbara Durham
Chief Justice
Supreme Court
Temple of Justice
P.O. Box 40929
Olympia, WA 98504
Phone : (360) 357-2077

WEST VIRGINIA
Tom McHugh
Chief Justice
Supreme Court of Appeals
State Capitol Bldg.,
Rm. E-308
Charleston, WV 25305
Phone : (304) 558-2605
Fax : (304) 558-3815

WISCONSIN
Nathan S. Heffernan
Chief Justice
Supreme Court
State Capitol, 231 E.
P.O. Box 53702
Madison, WI 53701
Phone : (608) 266-1886
Fax : (608) 267-0640

WYOMING
Richard Macy
Chief Justice
Supreme Court
Supreme Court Bldg.
2301 Capitol Ave.
Cheyenne, WY 82002
Phone : (307) 777-7422

DISTRICT OF COLUMBIA
Annice M. Wagner
Chief Justice
Court of Appeals
500 Indiana Ave., NW
Washington, DC 20001

Chief Justice

AMERICAN SAMOA
Michael Kruse
Chief Justice
High Court of American Samoa
Courthouse
Pago Pago, AS 96799
Phone : (684) 633-1410
Fax : (684) 633-1318

GUAM
Alberto C. Lamorena III
Presiding Judge
Superior Court
Judiciary Bldg.
110 W. O'Brien Dr.
Agana, GU 96910
Phone : (671) 475-3410

NORTHERN MARIANA ISLANDS
Jose S. Dela Cruz
Chief Judge
Commonwealth Supreme Court
Nauru Bldg., 2nd Fl.
Saipan, MP 96950
Phone : (670) 234-5175
Fax : (670) 234-5183

PUERTO RICO
Jose A. Andru-Garcia
Chief Justice
Supreme Court
P.O. Box 2392
San Juan, PR 00902
Phone : (809) 724-3535
Fax : (809) 725-4910

U.S. VIRGIN ISLANDS
Thomas Moore
Chief Judge
District Court
District Court Bldg.
St. Thomas, VI 00802
Phone : (809) 773-1130

CHIEF OF STAFF (GOVERNOR'S)

ALABAMA
Bobby A. Davis
Chief of Staff
Off. of the Governor
600 Dexter Ave.
Montgomery, AL 36130
Phone : (334) 242-4655
Fax : (334) 242-2845

ALASKA
Jim Ayers
Chief of Staff
Off. of the Governor
P.O. Box 110001
Juneau, AK 99811-0001
Phone : (907) 465-3500
Fax : (907) 465-3532

ARIZONA
Wes Gullet
Chief of Staff
Off. of the Governor
1700 W. Washington
Phoenix, AZ 85007
Phone : (602) 542-1371

ARKANSAS
Neal Turner
Chief of Staff
Off. of the Governor
State Capitol, Rm. 250
Little Rock, AR 72201
Phone : (501) 682-2345
Fax : (501) 682-3597

CALIFORNIA
Bob White
Chief of Staff
Off. of the Governor
State Capitol, 1st Fl.
Sacramento, CA 95814
Phone : (916) 445-5106

COLORADO
Margaret "Meg" E. Porfido
Chief of Staff
Off. of the Governor
State Capitol, Rm. 136
Denver, CO 80203-1792
Phone : (303) 866-2471
Fax : (303) 866-2003

CONNECTICUT
John Chapin
Chief of Staff
State Capitol
210 State Capitol Ave.
Hartford, CT 06106
Phone : (203) 566-4840

DELAWARE
Jeffrey Bullock
Chief of Staff
Off. of the Governor
Legislative Hall
Wilmington, DE 19901
Phone : (302) 739-4101
Fax : (302) 739-2775

FLORIDA
John T. Herndon
Chief of Staff
Off. of the Governor
State Capitol, PL05
Tallahassee, FL 32399-0001
Phone : (904) 488-2272

GEORGIA
Steve Wrigley
Executive Secretary
Off. of the Governor
State Capitol
Atlanta, GA 30334
Phone : (404) 651-7715

HAWAII
Charles Toguchi
Administrative Director
Off. of the Governor
Executive Chambers
Honolulu, HI 96813
Phone : (808) 586-0034
Fax : (808) 586-0006

IDAHO
Jeff Malmen
Chief of Staff
Off. of the Governor
P.O. Box 83720
Boise, ID 83720-0034
Phone : (208) 334-2100

ILLINOIS
Eugene Reineke
Chief of Staff
Off. of the Governor
State House, Rm. 207
Springfield, IL 62706
Phone : (217) 782-3958
Fax : (217) 524-1675

INDIANA
Joseph H. Hogsett
Chief of Staff
Off. of the Governor
206 State House
Indianapolis, IN 46204
Phone : (317) 232-1972

IOWA
Robert L. Rafferty
Executive Assistant
Off. of the Governor
State Capitol
Des Moines, IA 50319
Phone : (515) 281-5211
Fax : (515) 281-6611

KANSAS
Joyce McGarry
Chief of Staff
Off. of the Governor
State Capitol Bldg., 2nd Fl.
Topeka, KS 66612-1590
Phone : (913) 296-3232
Fax : (913) 296-7973

KENTUCKY
Franklin Jelsma
Chief Executive Officer
Public Affairs
Office of the Governor
State Capitol, Rm. 100
Frankfort, KY 40601
Phone : (502) 564-2611

Mary Helen Miller
Chief Executive Officer of Admin.
Office of the Governor
State Capitol, Rm. 100
Frankfort, KY 40601
Phone : (502) 564-2611

LOUISIANA
Ben Jeffers
Chief of Staff
Off. of the Governor
P.O. Box 94004
Baton Rouge, LA 70804
Phone : (504) 342-1624

MAINE
Charles E. Hewett
Chief Operating Officer
Office of the Governor
State House Station # 1
Augusta, ME 04333-0001
Phone : (207) 287-3531
Fax : (207) 287-1034
E-Mail: governor@state.me.us

MARYLAND
F. Riddick
Chief of Administration
Off. of the Governor
State House
Annapolis, MD 21401
Phone : (410) 974-5024
Fax : (410) 974-5029

MASSACHUSETTS
Kevin M. Smith
Chief of Staff
Off. of the Governor
State House, Rm. 360
Boston, MA 02133
Phone : (617) 727-9173

MICHIGAN
Sharon Rothwell
Chief of Staff
Off. of the Governor
P.O. Box 30013
Lansing, MI 48909
Phone : (517) 335-7863
Fax : (517) 335-6949

MINNESOTA
Morrie Anderson
Chief of Staff
Off. of the Governor
130 State Capitol
St. Paul, MN 55155
Phone : (612) 296-3391

Chief of Staff (Governor's)

MISSISSIPPI
Mark Garriga
Chief of Staff
Off. of the Governor
P.O. Box 139
Jackson, MS 39205
Phone : (601) 359-3150

MISSOURI
Marc Farinella
Chief of Staff
Off. of the Governor
State Capitol, Rm. 218
P.O. Box 720
Jefferson City, MO 65102
Phone : (314) 751-3222
Fax : (314) 751-4458
E-Mail: MFARINEL@
SERVICES.MORE.NET

MONTANA
Judy Browing
Chief of Staff
Legal Affairs
Office of the Governor
State Capitol
Helena, MT 59620
Phone : (406) 444-3111

NEBRASKA
Tim Becker
Chief of Staff
Off. of the Governor
State Capitol, Room 2316
P.O. Box 94848
Lincoln, NE 68509
Phone : (402) 471-2244
Fax : (402) 471-6031

NEVADA
Jim Mulhall
Chief of Staff
Off. of the Governor
Capitol Complex
Carson City, NV 89710
Phone : (702) 687-5670
Fax : (702) 687-4486

NEW HAMPSHIRE
Steve Edwards
Chief of Staff
Off. of the Governor
State House
Concord, NH 03301
Phone : (603) 271-2121

NEW JERSEY
Peter Vernierd
Chief of Staff
Off. of the Governor
State House, CN001
Trenton, NJ 08625
Phone : (609) 777-2214

NEW MEXICO
Lou Gallegos
Chief of Staff
Off. of the Governor
State Capitol Bldg.,
Ste. 400
Sante Fe, NM 87503
Phone : (502) 827-3000
Fax : (502) 827-3026

NEW YORK *
Secretary to the Governor
Off. of the Governor
State Capitol
Albany, NY 12224
Phone : (518) 474-4246

NORTH CAROLINA
Ed Turlington
Chief of Staff
Off. of the Governor
State Capitol
Raleigh, NC 27603-8001
Phone : (919) 733-4240
Fax : (919) 715-3175

NORTH DAKOTA
Carol Olson
Chief of Staff
Off. of the Governor
600 E. Boulevard Ave.
Bismarck, ND 58505-0001
Phone : (701) 328-2200
Fax : (701) 328-2205

OHIO
Paul C. Mifsud
Chief of Staff
Off. of the Governor
77 S. High St., 30th Fl.
Columbus, OH 43266-0601
Phone : (614) 466-0986
Fax : (614) 466-9354

OKLAHOMA
Clinton Key
Chief of Staff
Off. of the Governor
State Capitol, Rm. 212
Oklahoma City, OK 73105
Phone : (405) 521-2342
Fax : (405) 521-3353

OREGON
Bill Wyatt
Chief of Staff
Off. of the Governor
254 State Capitol
Salem, OR 97310
Phone : (503) 378-3111
Fax : (503) 378-8970

PENNSYLVANIA
Mark Holman
Chief of Staff
Off. of the Governor
Rm. 225, Main Capitol
Bldg.
Harrisburg, PA 17120
Phone : (717) 787-2500

RHODE ISLAND
Edward M. Morabito
Chief of Staff
Off. of the Governor
State House
Providence, RI 02903
Phone : (401) 277-2080

SOUTH CAROLINA
Will McCain
Chief of Staff
Off. of the Governor
P. O. Box 11369
Columbia, SC 29211
Phone: (803) 734-9818

SOUTH DAKOTA*
Chief of Staff
Off. of the Governor
500 E. Capitol Ave.
Pierre, SD 57501
Phone : (605) 773-3661

TENNESSEE
Peaches Simpkins
Deputy to Governor for
Special Projects
Off. of the Governor
State Capitol
Nashville, TN 37243-0001
Phone : (615) 532-4630
Fax : (615) 532-8067

Tom McNamara
Deputy to the Governor
Off. of the Governor
State Capitol
Nashville, TN 37243-0001
Phone : (615) 741-2001
Fax : (615) 532-9711

TEXAS
Joe Allbaugh
Executive Assistant
Off. of the Governor
P.O. Box 12428, Capitol
Station
Austin, TX 78711
Phone : (512) 463-2000

UTAH
Charlie Johnson
Chief of Staff
Off. of the Governor
210 State Capitol
Salt Lake City, UT 84114
Phone : (801) 538-1000

VERMONT
Kathleen C. Hoyt
Chief of Staff
Off. of the Governor
109 State St.
Montpelier, VT 05609
Phone : (802) 828-3333
Fax : (802) 828-3339

VIRGINIA
Jay Timmons
Chief of Staff
Governor's Cabinet
Off. of the Governor
State Capitol Bldg., 3rd Fl.
Richmond, VA 23219
Phone : (804) 786-2211
Fax : (804) 371-6351

WASHINGTON
Lorraine Hine
Director
Off. of the Governor
P.O. Box 40002
Olympia, WA 98504-0002
Phone : (360) 753-6780

WEST VIRGINIA
David Campbell
Chief of Staff
Off. of the Governor
State Capitol
1900 Kanawha Blvd., E.
Charleston, WV 25305-
0370
Phone : (304) 558-2000
Fax : (304) 558-7025

WISCONSIN
John W. Matthews
Chief of Staff
Off. of the Governor
115 E State Captiol
P.O. Box 7863
Madison, WI 53707
Phone : (608) 266-1212
Fax : (608) 267-8983

WYOMING
Rob Wallace
Administrative Assistant
Off. of the Governor
State Capitol
Cheyenne, WY 82002
Phone : (307) 777-5930

DISTRICT OF COLUMBIA
Barry Campbell
Chief of Staff
Off. of the Mayor
441 4th St., N.W., Rm. 11105
Washington, DC 20001
Phone : (202) 727-2643

AMERICAN SAMOA
Aleni Ripine
Chief of Staff
Off. of the Governor
Pago Pago, AS 96799
Phone : (684) 633-4116
Fax : (684) 633-2269

GUAM**
Lourdes T. Pangelinan
Chief of Staff
Off. of the Governor
P.O. Box 2950
Agana, GU 96910
Phone : (671) 472-8931

NORTHERN MARIANA ISLANDS
Herman T. Guerrero
Executive Assistant to the Governor
Off. of the Governor
Capitol Hill
P.O. Box 10007
Saipan, MP 96950
Phone : (670) 322-5091
Fax : (670) 322-5096

PUERTO RICO
Alvaro Cifuentes Esq.
Secretary to the Governorship
Off. of the Governor
La Fortaleza
P.O. Box 82
San Juan, PR 00901
Phone : (809) 721-7000
Fax : (809) 724-4235

U.S. VIRGIN ISLANDS
Kevin Callwood
Executive Assistant & Chief
Off. of the Governor
21-22 Kangens Cir.
St. Thomas, VI 00802
Phone : (809) 774-0001
Fax : (809) 774-1361

CHILD LABOR

Administers and enforces child labor laws.

ALABAMA
Dottie Cieszynski
Director
Dept. of Industrial Relations
649 Monroe St.
Montgomery, AL 36131
Phone : (334) 242-8990
Fax : (334) 242-3960

ALASKA
John Abshire
Director
Div. of Labor Standards & Safety
Dept. of Labor
P.O. Box 107021
Anchorage, AK 99510
Phone : (907) 269-4914
Fax : (907) 465-3584

ARIZONA
Larry J. Etchechury
Director
Industrial Comm.
P.O. Box 19070
Phoenix, AZ 85005-9070
Phone : (602) 542-4411

ARKANSAS
Sandra King
Labor Standards Administrator
Wage & Hour Div.
Dept. of Labor
10421 W. Markham, Rm. 100
Little Rock, AR 72205
Phone : (501) 682-4500
Fax : (501) 682-4532

CALIFORNIA
Victoria L. Bradshaw
Labor Commissioner
Labor Stds. Enforcement Div.
Dept. of Industrial Relations
455 Golden Gate Ave.
San Francisco, CA 94102
Phone : (415) 703-4590

COLORADO*
Director
Div. of Labor
Dept. of Labor & Employment
1515 Arapahoe St., Tower 2
Denver, CO 80203
Phone : (303) 620-4700
Fax : (303) 620-4714

CONNECTICUT
Samuel Moore
Director
Occupational Safety & Health
Dept. of Labor
38 Wilcot Hill Rd.
Wethersfield, CT 06109
Phone : (203) 566-4550
Fax : (203) 566-6916

DELAWARE
Darrell J. Minott
Secretary
Dept. of Labor
820 N. French St., 6th Fl.
Wilmington, DE 19801
Phone : (302) 577-2710
Fax : (302) 577-2735

FLORIDA
Hayden Gray
Acting Chief
Bureau of Compliance
Dept. of Labor & Empl. Security
2661 W. Executive Center Circle
101 Clifton Bldg.
Tallahassee, FL 32399-2150
Phone : (904) 487-2536

GEORGIA
John Clark
Unit Chief
Child Labor Section
Dept. of Labor
148 International Blvd., # 276
Atlanta, GA 30303
Phone : (404) 656-3623

HAWAII
Alan Asao
Administrator
Child Labor-Wage Claims Branch
Labor & Industrial Rel. Dept.
830 Punchbowl St., Rm. 340
Honolulu, HI 96813
Phone : (808) 586-8777
Fax : (808) 586-9099

IDAHO
Bob Purcell
Director
Labor & Industrial Srvcs.
277 N. Sixth St.
Boise, ID 83720
Phone : (208) 334-3950

ILLINOIS
Shinae Chun
Director
Dept. of Labor
160 N. La Salle St., Ste. C1300
Chicago, IL 60601
Phone : (312) 793-2800
Fax : (312) 793-5257

INDIANA
Ron Wintrode
Director
Bur. of Child Labor
Dept. of Labor
402 W. Washington St., Rm. W195
Indianapolis, IN 46204
Phone : (317) 232-2676

IOWA
Olga Duran
Adm. Assistant
Div. of Labor Srvcs.
Dept. of Employment Srvcs.
2000 E. Grand
Des Moines, IA 50319
Phone : (515) 281-3606

KANSAS
Duane Guy
Acting Director
Division of Labor
Dept. of Human Resources
512 W. Sixth St.
Topeka, KS 66603
Phone : (913) 296-7475
Fax : (913) 296-4789

KENTUCKY
Denis Langford
Acting Director
Empl. Standards & Mediation
Labor Cabinet
1047 U.S. 127 S., Ste. 4
Frankfort, KY 40601
Phone : (502) 564-2784

LOUISIANA
Joseph Stone
Assistant Secretary
Dept. of Labor
P.O. Box 94094
Baton Rouge, LA 70804
Phone : (504) 342-7692

MAINE
James McGowan
Director
Bur. of Labor Standards
Dept. of Labor
State House Station # 45
Augusta, ME 04333
Phone : (207) 624-6400

MARYLAND
John O'Connor
Commissioner
Div. of Labor & Industry
Dept. of Licensing & Reg.
501 St. Paul Pl.
Baltimore, MD 21202
Phone : (410) 333-4179

MASSACHUSETTS
Virginia Melendez
Commissioner
Off. for Children
1 Ashburton Pl., Rm. 1111
Boston, MA 02108-1518
Phone : (617) 727-8900

MICHIGAN
Marsha Bowers
Program Specialist
Bur. of Employment Standards
Dept. of Labor
P.O. Box 30015
Lansing, MI 48909
Phone : (517) 322-1825

MINNESOTA
Roslyn Wade
Director
Div. of Labor Standards
Dept. of Labor & Industry
444 Lafayette Rd.
St. Paul, MN 55155
Phone : (612) 297-3349

MISSOURI
Colleen Baker
Director
Div. of Labor Standards
Dept. of Labor & Ind. Rel.
3315 W. Truman Blvd., Box 449
Jefferson City, MO 65102
Phone : (314) 751-3403
Fax : (314) 751-3721

MONTANA
John Andrew
Chief
Standards Bur.
Labor Standards Div.
Capitol Station
Helena, MT 59620
Phone : (406) 444-2723

NEBRASKA
Ray Griffin
Labor Law Compliance Program Mgr.
Safety Labor & Standards Div.
Dept. of Labor
State Off. Bldg., 1313 Farnam
Omaha, NE 68102
Phone : (402) 595-3095
Fax : (402) 595-3200

NEVADA
Frank MacDonald
Commissioner
Labor Comm.
Dept. of Business & Industry
1445 Hot Springs Rd., Ste. 108
Carson City, NV 89710
Phone : (702) 687-4850

NEW HAMPSHIRE
Diane Symonds
Commissioner
Dept. of Labor
95 Pleasant St.
Concord, NH 03301
Phone : (603) 271-3171

NEW JERSEY
Peter J. Calderone
Commissioner
Dept. of Labor
John Fitch Plz., CN110
Trenton, NJ 08625
Phone : (609) 292-2323

NEW MEXICO
Rudy J. Maestas
Director
Labor & Industrial Div.
1596 Pacheco St.
Santa Fe, NM 87501
Phone : (505) 827-6875
Fax : (505) 827-1664

NEW YORK*
Commissioner
Dept. of Labor
State Off. Bldg., State Campus
Albany, NY 12240
Phone : (518) 457-2741

NORTH CAROLINA
Thomas Harris
Director
Wage & Hour Div.
Dept. of Labor
4 W. Edenton St.
Raleigh, NC 27601-1092
Phone : (919) 733-2152
Fax : (919) 733-6197

NORTH DAKOTA
Craig Hagen
Commissioner
Dept. of Labor
State Capitol, 6th Fl.
600 E. Boulevard Ave.
Bismarck, ND 58505
Phone : (701) 328-2660
Fax : (701) 328-2031

OHIO
Michael Allen
Chief
Minimum Wage & Minors
Dept. of Industrial Relations
2323 W. Fifth Ave., Box 825
Columbus, OH 43266
Phone : (614) 644-2420
Fax : (614) 644-3417

OKLAHOMA
Don Bento
Director
Employment Standards Div.
Dept. of Labor
4001 N. Lincoln Blvd.
Oklahoma City, OK 73105
Phone : (405) 528-1500

OREGON
Paul Tiffany
Administrator
Wage & Hour Div.
Bur. of Labor & Industries
800 Oregon St., NE
Portland, OR 97232
Phone : (503) 731-4742
Fax : (503) 731-4069

PENNSYLVANIA
Helen Friedman
Director
Bur. of Labor Standards
Dept. of Labor & Industry
Labor & Industry Bd., Rm. 1305
Harrisburg, PA 17120
Phone : (717) 787-4670

RHODE ISLAND
Jacqueline Cugini
Administrator
Div. of Labor Standards
Dept. of Labor
220 Elmwood Ave.
Providence, RI 02907
Phone : (401) 457-1808

SOUTH CAROLINA
Lewis Gossett
Director
Dept. of Labor, Licensing & Regulations
P.O. Box 11329
Columbia, SC 29211
Phone : (803) 734-9600

SOUTH DAKOTA
James Marsh
Acting Director
Div. of Labor & Mgt.
Dept. of Labor
Kneip Bldg.
Pierre, SD 57501
Phone : (605) 773-3101

TENNESSEE
John Moffett
Assistant Commissioner
Labor Standards
Dept. of Labor
501 Union Bldg.
Nashville, TN 37243
Phone : (615) 741-0851

TEXAS
Jack W. Garison
Executive Director
Dept. of Licensing & Regulation
P.O. Box 12157
Austin, TX 78711
Phone : (512) 463-3173

UTAH
Anna Jenson
Director
Div. of Anti-Discrimination & Labor, Industrial Comm.
160 E. 300 S.
Salt Lake City, UT 84111
Phone : (801) 530-6921

VERMONT
Mary S. Hooper
Commissioner
Dept. of Labor & Industry
National Life Bldg.
Drawer 20
Montpelier, VT 05620-3401
Phone : (802) 828-2288
Fax : (802) 828-2748

VIRGINIA
Theron J. Bell
Commissioner
Dept. of Labor & Industry
13 S. 13th St.
Richmond, VA 23219
Phone : (804) 786-2377

WASHINGTON
Greg Mowat
Program Manager
Labor & Industries
Employ. Stds.,
Apprenticeships &
Crime Victims Div.
P.O. Box 44500
Olympia, WA 98504
Phone : (360) 902-5316

WEST VIRGINIA
Shelby Leary
Commissioner
Div. of Labor
State Capitol, Bldg. 3
Charleston, WV 25305
Phone : (304) 558-7890
Fax : (304) 558-3797

WISCONSIN
J. Sheehan Donoghue
Administrator
Div. of Equal Rights
Industrial Labor &
Human Rel.
201 E Washington,
Room 407
P.O. Box 7946
Madison, WI 53707
Phone : (608) 266-6860
Fax : (608) 267-4592

WYOMING
Mike Sullivan
Administrator
Div. of Labor Standards
Dept. of Employment
Herschler Bldg.
Cheyenne, WY 82002
Phone : (307) 777-7435

DISTRICT OF COLUMBIA**
Franklin L. Smith
Superintendent of Schools
D.C. Public Schools
415 12th St., NW,
Rm. 1209
Washington, DC 20004
Phone : (202) 724-4222

GUAM**
Edward A. Guerrero
Director
Dept. of Labor
P.O. Box 9970
Tamuning, GU 96911
Phone : (671) 646-9241

NORTHERN MARIANA ISLANDS
Herb Soll
Deputy Attorney General
Off. of the Governor
P.O. Box 10007
Saipan, MP 96950
Phone : (670) 322-4311
Fax : (670) 322-4320

PUERTO RICO
Ceasar Almodova
Machany
Secretary
Dept. of Labor & Human
Res.
Prudencio Rivera
Martinez Bldg.
Munoz Rivera 5D5
Hato Rey, PR 00918
Phone : (809) 754-2120
Fax : (809) 753-9550

U.S. VIRGIN ISLANDS
Lisa Harris-Moorhead
Commissioner
Dept. of Labor
P.O. Box 890
St. Croix, VI 00820
Phone : (809) 773-1994
Fax : (809) 773-0094

CHILD SUPPORT ENFORCEMENT

Processes child support cases and implements required provisions of the child support enforcement program.

ALASKA
Glenda Straube
Director
Child Support Enforcement Div.
Dept. of Revenue
550 W. Seventh Ave., Ste. 410
Anchorage, AK 99501
Phone : (907) 269-6800
Fax : (907) 269-6868

ARIZONA
Julie Vaughn
Assistant Director
Div. of Family Support
Dept. of Economic Security
P.O. Box 40458 (021A)
Phoenix, AZ 85007
Phone : (602) 274-7646

ARKANSAS
Judy Jones Jordan
Administrator
Child Support Enforcement
Dept. of Finance & Admin.
P.O. Box 1272
Little Rock, AR 72203
Phone : (501) 682-6169
Fax : (501) 682-6002

CALIFORNIA
Leslie Frye
Deputy Director
Child Support Program Branch
Dept. of Social Srvcs.
744 P St., MS 17-11
Sacramento, CA 95814
Phone : (916) 654-1556

COLORADO
Kathy Stumm
Director
Child Support Enforcement Div.
Dept. of Human Srvcs.
1575 Sherman St., 2nd Fl.
Denver, CO 80203
Phone : (303) 866-5994
Fax : (303) 866-4214

CONNECTICUT
Anthony DiNallo
Chief
Child Support Enforcement Bur.
Dept. of Social Services
25 Sigourney St.
Hartford, CT 06105
Phone : (203) 424-5251

DELAWARE
Barbara A. Paulin
Director
Child Support Enforcement Div.
Health & Social Srvcs. Dept.
P.O. Box 904
New Castle, DE 19720
Phone : (302) 577-4800
Fax : (302) 577-4863

FLORIDA
Joyce McGee
Director
Child Support Enforcement Program
Dept. of Revenue
Carlton Bldg.
Tallahassee, FL 32399-0100
Phone : (904) 488-6800

GEORGIA
Jerry Townsend
Director
Off. of Child Support Recovery
Dept. of Human Resources
878 Peachtree St., 15th Fl.
Atlanta, GA 30303
Phone : (404) 657-3856

HAWAII
Norma Sparks
Director
Child Support Enforcement
Dept. of the Attorney General
680 Iwilei Rd.
Honolulu, HI 96817
Phone : (808) 596-3700

IDAHO
Teresa Kaiser
Bureau Chief
Bur. of Child Support Srvcs.
Dept. of Health & Welfare
450 W. State St.
P.O. Box 83720
Boise, ID 83720-0036
Phone : (208) 334-6515
Fax : (208) 334-0666

ILLINOIS
Dianna Durham McLoud
Administrator
Div. of Child Support
Dept. of Public Aid
201 S. Grand
Springfield, IL 62763
Phone : (219) 524-4602

INDIANA
Judith Hawley
Director
Child Support Div.
IGC-South, Rm. W360
402 W. Washington
Indianapolis, IN 46204
Phone : (317) 232-4894

IOWA
Jim Hennessey
Chief
Bur. of Collections
Dept. of Human Srvcs.
Hoover State Off. Bldg.
Des Moines, IA 50319
Phone : (515) 281-5767

KANSAS
James A. Robertson
Administrator
Child Support Enforcement
Dept. of Social & Rehab. Services
300 SW Oakley Ave., West Hall
Topeka, KS 66601-1424
Phone : (913) 296-3237
Fax : (913) 296-5206

KENTUCKY
Steven P. Veno
Director
Div. of Child Support Enforcement
Human Resources Cabinet
275 E. Main St.
Frankfort, KY 40621
Phone : (502) 564-2285

LOUISIANA
Gloria Bryant-Banks
Secretary
Executive Off.
Dept. of Social Services
P.O. Box 3776
Baton Rouge, LA 70821
Phone : (504) 342-0286

MAINE
Colburn Jackson
Director
Div. of Sup. Enf. & Recovery
Dept. of Human Services
State House Station # 11
Augusta, ME 04333
Phone : (207) 287-2886

MARYLAND
Meg Sollenberger
Executive Director
Child Support Enforcement
Dept. of Human Resources
311 W. Saratoga St.
Baltimore, MD 21201
Phone : (410) 333-3979

MASSACHUSETTS
Jerry J. Fay
Deputy Commissioner
Child Support Enforcement
Dept. of Revenue
141 Portland St.
Cambridge, MA 02139
Phone : (617) 727-4200
Fax : (617) 727-4367

MICHIGAN
Marilyn Hall
State Court Administrator
State Court
Administrative Office
Supreme Court
611 W. Ottawa
Lansing, MI 48909
Phone: (517) 373-0130

MINNESOTA
Ann Damon
Director
Child Support
Enforcement Div.
Dept. of Human Srvcs.
444 Lafayette Rd.
St. Paul, MN 55155
Phone: (612) 296-2499

MISSISSIPPI
Carolyn Bridgers
Director
Div. of Child Support
Enforcement
P.O. Box 352
Jackson, MS 39205
Phone: (601) 975-5000

MISSOURI
Bill LaRue
Director
Child Support
Enforcement Div.
Dept. of Social Services
227 Metro Dr., Box 1527
Jefferson City, MO 65102
Phone: (314) 751-4301
Fax: (314) 751-8450
E-Mail: USDSSR7S@
IBMMAIL.COM

MONTANA
Mary Ann Wellbank
Administrator
Child Support
Enforcement Div.
Social & Rehab. Srvcs.
Dept.
P.O. Box 5955
Helena, MT 59604
Phone: (406) 444-4614

NEBRASKA
Ed Schulenberg
Acting Administrator
Enforcement Srvcs. Div.
Dept. of Social Srvcs.
P.O. Box 95026
Lincoln, NE 68509-5026
Phone: (402) 471-9390
Fax: (402) 471-9455

NEVADA
Myla Florence
Administrator
Welfare Div.
Dept. of Human
Resources
2527 N. Carson St.
Carson City, NV 89710
Phone: (702) 687-4128

NEW JERSEY
Marion Reitz
Director
Div. of Family
Development
Dept. of Human Services
Quakerbridge Rd., CN716
Trenton, NJ 08625
Phone: (609) 588-2361

NEW MEXICO
Ben Silva
Director
Child Support
Enforcement
Human Srvcs. Dept.
P.O. Box 25109
Santa Fe, NM 87504
Phone: (505) 827-7200
Fax: (505) 827-7285

NEW YORK *
Director
Child Support
Enforcement Off.
Dept. of Social Srvcs.
1 Commerce Plz.
P.O. Box 14
Albany, NY 12260
Phone: (518) 474-9081

NORTH CAROLINA
Michael Adams
Chief
Child Support
Enforcement
Div. of Social Srvcs.
100 E. Six Forks Rd.
Raleigh, NC 27609-7750
Phone: (919) 571-4120

NORTH DAKOTA
William Strate
Director
Child Support
Enforcement Div.
Dept. of Human Srvcs.
State Capitol, Judicial
Wing
Bismarck, ND 58505-0250
Phone: (701) 328-5493
Fax: (701) 328-5497

OHIO
Loretta Adams
Deputy Director
Office of Child Support
Enforcement
Department of Human
Services
30 E. Broad 31st
Columbus, OH 43266-0423
Phone: (614) 752-6561
Fax: (614) 752-9760

OKLAHOMA
Paula Davidson Wood
IV-D Administrator
Child Support
Enforcement Div.
P.O. Box 53552
Oklahoma City, OK 73152
Phone: (405) 521-3646

OREGON
Larry Thomson
Administrator
Support Enforcement Div.
Justice Dept.
1162 Court St. NE
Salem, OR 97310
Phone: (503) 378-4879

PENNSYLVANIA
John Stuff
Director
Child Support
Enforcement Bur.
Dept. of Public Welfare
P.O. Box 8018
Harrisburg, PA 17105
Phone: (717) 783-8729

RHODE ISLAND
Lee Grossi
Associate Director
Management Services
Dept. of Human Services
600 New Loundon Ave.
Cranston, RI 02920
Phone: (401) 464-2421

SOUTH CAROLINA
Jim Clark
Interim Commissioner
Dept. of Social Srvcs.
1535 Confederate Ave. Ext.
Columbia, SC 29202
Phone: (803) 734-5760

SOUTH DAKOTA
Terry Walter
Program Administrator
Div. of Child Support
Enforcement
Dept. of Social Srvcs.
Kneip Bldg.
Pierre, SD 57501
Phone: (605) 773-3641

TENNESSEE
Linda Rudolph
Commissioner
Dept. of Human Services
Citizens Plz., 15th Fl.
400 Deadrick St.
Nashville, TN 37248-0001
Phone: (615) 741-3241
Fax: (615) 741-4165

TEXAS
Charlie Childress
Director
Child Support
Enforcement Div.
Off. of the Attorney
General
P.O. Box 12548
Austin, TX 78711
Phone: (512) 463-2181

UTAH
Emma Chacon
Director
Off. of Recovery Srvc.
Dept. of Human Srvcs.
120 N. 200 W.
Salt Lake City, UT 84103
Phone: (801) 536-8901

VERMONT
Jeffrey Cohen
Director
Off. of Child Support
103 S. Main St.
Waterbury, VT 05671
Phone: (802) 241-2319
Fax: (802) 244-1483

VIRGINIA
Carol Brunty
Commissioner
Department of Social
Services
Theater Row Bldg.
720 E. Broad St.
Richmond, VA 23219
Phone: (804) 692-1900
Fax: (804) 692-1949

WASHINGTON
Meg Sollenberger
Director
Off. of Support Enforcement
Social & Health Srvcs. Dept.
712 Pear St., SE
Olympia, WA 98507-9162
Phone : (360) 586-3162

WEST VIRGINIA
Martha J. Hill
Director
Child Advocate Off.
Bldg. 6, Rm. 812
1900 Kanawha Blvd., E.
Charleston, WV 25305
Phone : (304) 558-3780

WISCONSIN
Jean Rogers
Administrator
Div. of Economic Support
Dept. of Health & Social Srvcs.
1 W. Wilson St., Room 358
Madison, WI 53702
Phone : (608) 266-3035
Fax : (608) 261-6376

WYOMING
Kenneth Skalitzky
Administrator
Div. of Self-Sufficiency
Dept. of Family Services
Hathaway Bldg., 3rd Fl.
Cheyenne, WY 82002
Phone : (307) 777-6849

DISTRICT OF COLUMBIA
Norris Shepherd
Chief
Child Support Enforcement
613 G St., N.W., 10th Fl.
Washington, DC 20001
Phone : (202) 727-3839

GUAM
Calvin E. Halloway
Attorney General
Attorney General's Office
120 W. O'Brien Dr., Ste. 2-200E
Agana, GU 96910
Phone : (671) 475-3324
Fax : (671) 472-2493

NORTHERN MARIANA ISLANDS
Herb Soll
Deputy Attorney General
Off. of the Attorney General
P.O. Box 10007
Saipan, MP 96950
Phone : (670) 322-4311
Fax : (670) 322-4320

U.S. VIRGIN ISLANDS
Aurjul Wilson Esq.
Director
Paternity & Child Support
Justice Dept.
GERS Complex, 2nd Fl.
St. Thomas, VI 00802
Phone : (809) 774-5666
Fax : (809) 114-9710

CHILDREN & YOUTH

Implements programs designed to protect children and youth against abuse, neglect and exploitation.

ALASKA
Diane Worley
Director
Div. of Family & Youth Srvcs.
Dept. of Health & Social Srvcs.
P.O. Box 110630
Juneau, AK 99811-0630
Phone : (907) 465-3170
Fax : (907) 465-3397

ARIZONA
Phil Bayne
Assistant Director
Children, Youth & Families
Dept. of Economic Security
1789 W. Jefferson (940A)
Phoenix, AZ 85007
Phone : (602) 542-3598

ARKANSAS
Beverly Jones
Director
Children & Family Srvcs.
Dept of Human Services
P.O. Box 1437
Little Rock, AR 72203
Phone : (501) 682-8772
Fax : (501) 682-8666

CALIFORNIA
Majorie Kelly
Deputy Director
Children & Family Services Division
Dept. of Social Srvcs.
744 P St., MS 9-100
Sacramento, CA 95814
Phone : (916) 657-2614

COLORADO
Karen Studen
Acting Director
Family & Children's Srvc. Div.
Dept. of Social Srvcs.
1575 Sherman St., 2nd Fl.
Denver, CO 80203
Phone : (303) 866-3672
Fax : (303) 866-4214

CONNECTICUT
Linda D'Amario Rossi
Commissioner
Dept. of Children & Families
505 Hudson St.
Hartford, CT 06106-7107
Phone : (203) 550-6300

DELAWARE
Thomas P. Eichler
Secretary
Dept. of Srvcs. for Children, Youth & Their Families
1825 Faulkland Rd.
Wilmington, DE 19805
Phone : (302) 633-2500
Fax : (302) 995-8290

FLORIDA
Linda Radigan
Assistant Secretary
Children & Family Srvcs.
Dept. of Health & Rehab. Srvcs
1317 Winewood Blvd., Bldg. 8
Tallahassee, FL 32399
Phone : (904) 488-8762
Fax : (904) 922-2993

GEORGIA
Eugene Walker
Commissioner
Dept. of Children & Youth Srvcs.
2 Peachtree St., 5th Fl.
Atlanta, GA 30303
Phone : (404) 657-2410

HAWAII
Deborah Lee
Program Administrator
Child Protective Srvcs.
Dept. of Human Srvcs.
810 Richards St., Ste. 400
Honolulu, HI 96813
Phone : (808) 832-5300

IDAHO
Kathryn Morris Ph.D.
Bureau Chief
Bur. of Children's Srvcs.
Dept. of Health & Welfare
450 W. State St.
P.O. Box 83720
Boise, ID 83720-0036
Phone : (208) 334-5700
Fax : (208) 334-6699

ILLINOIS
Jess McDonald
Director
Dept. of Children & Family Srvcs.
406 E. Monroe St.
Springfield, IL 62701
Phone : (217) 785-2509
Fax : (217) 785-1052

INDIANA
James Hmurovich
Director
Div. of Families & Children
Family & Soc. Srvcs. Admin.
IGC-South, Rm. W392
Indianapolis, IN 46204
Phone : (317) 232-4705

IOWA
Federico Brid
Administrator
Adult, Children & Family Srvcs
Dept. of Human Srvcs.
Hoover State Off. Bldg.
Des Moines, IA 50319
Phone : (515) 281-5521

KANSAS
Ben Coats
Acting Commissioner
Youth & Adult Srvcs.
Dept. of Social & Rehab. Srvcs.
300 SW Oakley, West Hall
Topeka, KS 66606
Phone : (913) 296-4653
Fax : (913) 296-4649

KENTUCKY
Dennis Corrigan
Director
Div. of Family Srvcs.
Dept. for Social Srvcs.
275 E. Main St.
Frankfort, KY 40601
Phone : (502) 564-6852

LOUISIANA
Brenda Kelley
Assistant Secretary
Off. of Community Services
Dept. of Social Services
P.O. Box 3776
Baton Rouge, LA 70821
Phone : (504) 342-4073

MAINE
Nancy Carlson
Director
Child & Family Srvcs.
Dept. of Human Srvcs.
State House Station # 11
Augusta, ME 04333
Phone : (207) 287-5060

MARYLAND
Linda Heisner
Director
Off. of Fam. & Child. Srvcs.
Dept. of Human Resources
311 W. Saratoga St.
Baltimore, MD 21201
Phone : (410) 333-0208

MASSACHUSETTS
Linda Carlisle
Commissioner
Dept. of Social Srvcs.
24 Farnsworth
Boston, MA 02110
Phone : (617) 727-0900

MICHIGAN
Harold Gazan
Director
Bur. of Child & Family Srvcs.
Dept. of Social Srvcs.
235 S. Grand Ave.
Lansing, MI 48909
Phone : (517) 335-6158

MINNESOTA
Denise Revels Robinson
Director
Family & Children Srvcs. Div.
Dept. of Human Srvcs.
444 Lafayette Rd.
St. Paul, MN 55155
Phone : (612) 296-5288

MISSISSIPPI
Don Taylor
Director
Div. of Family & Children's Services
P.O. Box 352
Jackson, MS 39205
Phone : (601) 354-6661

MISSOURI
Richard Matt
Deputy Director
Children's Services
Div. of Family Services
Dept. of Social Srvcs.
615 Howerton Ct.
P.O. Box 88
Jefferson City, MO 65103
Phone : (314) 751-2882
Fax : (314) 526-3971

MONTANA
Henry Hudson
Director
Dept. of Family Services
P.O. Box 8005
Helena, MT 59604
Phone : (406) 444-5900

NEBRASKA
Jessie K. Rasmussen
Administrator
Div. of Human Srvcs.
Dept. of Social Srvcs.
P.O. Box 95026
Lincoln, NE 68509
Phone : (402) 471-2932
Fax : (402) 471-2528

NEVADA
John Sarb
Administrator
Youth Services Div.
505 E. King St., Ste. 101
Carson City, NV 89710
Phone : (702) 687-6927

NEW HAMPSHIRE
Lorrie L. Lutz
Director
Children & Youth Srvcs.
Dept. of Health & Human Srvcs.
115 Pleasant St., Annex Bldg. 1
Concord, NH 03301
Phone : (603) 271-4451

NEW JERSEY
Marion Reitz
Director
Div. of Family Development
Dept. of Human Services
Quakerbridge Rd., CN716
Trenton, NJ 08625
Phone : (609) 588-2361

NEW MEXICO
Soledad Martinez
Health Program Manager
Social Srvcs. Div.
Dept. of Human Srvcs.
2491 Sawmill Rd. #1702
P.O. Drawer 5160
Santa Fe, NM 87502
Phone : (505) 827-8440
Fax : (505) 827-8480

NEW YORK *
Commissioner
Dept. of Social Srvcs.
40 N. Pearl St.
Albany, NY 12243
Phone : (518) 474-9475

NORTH CAROLINA
Kevin FitzGerald
Director of Social Services
Dept. of Human Resources
325 N. Salisbury St.
Raleigh, NC 27603-5905
Phone : (919) 733-3055
Fax : (919) 715-3581

NORTH DAKOTA
Donald L. Schmid
Director
Children & Family Srvcs.
Dept. of Human Services
600 E. Boulevard Ave.
Bismarck, ND 58505-0250
Phone : (701) 328-2316
Fax : (701) 328-2359

OHIO
Isaac R. Palmer
Deputy Director
Family & Children's Srvc. Div.
Dept. of Human Srvcs.
65 E. State St.
Columbus, OH 43215
Phone : (614) 466-1213
Fax : (614) 466-9247

OKLAHOMA
George Miller
Interim Director
Health & Human Srvcs.
Dept. of Human Srvcs.
P.O. Box 25352
Oklahoma City, OK 73125
Phone : (405) 521-2778

OREGON
Kay Toran
Administrator
Children's Services Div.
Dept. of Human Resources
500 Summer St., NE
Salem, OR 97310
Phone : (503) 945-5651
Fax : (503) 581-6198

PENNSYLVANIA
Kenneth W. Ehahart
Acting Deputy Secretary
Children, Youth & Families
Dept. of Public Welfare
P.O. Box 2675
Harrisburg, PA 17105
Phone : (717) 787-4756

RHODE ISLAND
Kenneth Fandetti
Director
Dept. of Children & Families
610 Mt. Pleasant Ave.
Providence, RI 02908
Phone : (401) 457-4750

SOUTH CAROLINA
Wilbert Lewis
Director
Child Protective & Prev. Srvcs.
Dept. of Social Srvcs.
P.O. Box 1520
Columbia, SC 29202
Phone : (803) 734-5670

SOUTH DAKOTA
Judy Hines
Administrator
Child Protection Srvcs. Div.
Dept. of Social Srvcs.
Kneip Bldg.
Pierre, SD 57501
Phone : (605) 773-3227

TENNESSEE
Betty Gayle
Assistant Commissioner
Social Services
Dept. of Human Srvcs.
400 Deaderick St.
Nashville, TN 37243
Phone : (615) 741-5924

TEXAS
Burton Raiford
Commissioner
Dept. of Human Services
P.O. Box 149030
Austin, TX 78714
Phone : (512) 450-3011

UTAH
Lynn Samsel
Director
Div. of Family Srvcs.
Dept. of Human Srvcs.
120 N. 200 W., 4th Fl.
Salt Lake City, UT 84103
Phone : (801) 538-4173

VERMONT
William Young
Director
Dept. of Social & Rehab. Srvcs.
103 S. Main St.
Waterbury, VT 05671
Phone : (802) 241-2101

VIRGINIA
Patricia L. West
Director
Dept. of Youth & Family Services
700 Centre- 4th Fl.
7th & Franklin St.
Richmond, VA 23219
Phone : (804) 371-7000
Fax : (804) 371-0773

WASHINGTON
Carol Cheatte
Director
Children & Family Srvcs. Div.
Dept. of Social & Health Srvcs.
P.O. Box 45710
Olympia, WA 98504-5710
Phone : (360) 586-8654

WEST VIRGINIA
Patricia Moore-Moss
Bureau Administrator
Social Services Bur.
Div. of Human Services
1900 Washington, E., Bldg. 6
Charleston, WV 25305
Phone : (304) 558-5388

WISCONSIN
Linda Hisgen
Acting Bureau Director
Children, Youth & Families
Dept. of Health & Social Srvcs.
1 W. Wilson, Room 465
P.O. Box 7851
Madison, WI 53707
Phone : (608) 266-3036
Fax : (608) 264-6750

WYOMING
Les Pozsgi
Probation Program Manager
Dept. of Family Services
Div. of Youth Services
2300 Capitol Ave., Hathaway Bldg., Rm. 323
Cheyenne, WY 82002
Phone : (307) 777-6089

DISTRICT OF COLUMBIA
Jan Hutchinson
Acting Administrator
Children & Youth Srvcs.
2700 M.L. King, Jr. Ave., SE, Bldg 1
Washington, DC 20032
Phone : (202) 727-5947

AMERICAN SAMOA
Fualaau Hanipale
Director & Coordinator
Child Abuse Comm.
Dept. of Human Resources
Pago Pago, AS 96799
Phone : (684) 633-4485

GUAM
Oscar E. Fortier
Director
Dept. of Youth Affairs
P.O. Box 23672
GMF, GU 96921
Phone : (671) 734-3911
Fax : (671) 734-7536

Dennis G. Rodriguez
Director
Dept. of Public Health & Social Services
P.O. Box 2816
Tamuning, GU 96911
Phone : (671) 734-7102
Fax : (671) 734-5910

NORTHERN MARIANA ISLANDS
Eloise A. Furey
Director
Div. of Youth Srvcs.
Dept. of Comm. & Cultural Aff.
P.O. Box 1000 CK
Saipan, MP 96950
Phone : (670) 233-9075
Fax : (670) 233-2221

PUERTO RICO
Carmen Rodriguez De Rivera
Secretary
Dept. of Social Srvcs.
P.O. Box 11398
San Juan, PR 00910-1398
Phone : (809) 722-7400
Fax : (809) 723-1223

U.S. VIRGIN ISLANDS
Catherine Mills
Commissioner
Dept. of Human Srvcs.
Knud Hansen Complex, Bldg. A
1303 Hospital Ground
St. Thomas, VI 00802
Phone : (809) 774-0930
Fax : (809) 774-3466

CIVIL RIGHTS

Overall responsibilities for preventing and redressing discrimination in employment, education, housing, public accommodations and credit (because of race, color, sex, age, national origin, religion or handicap).

ALASKA
Paula Haley
Executive Director
Human Rights Comm.
Off. of the Governor
800 A St., Ste. 204
Anchorage, AK 99501-3669
Phone : (907) 276-7474
Fax : (907) 278-8588

ARIZONA
H. Leslie Hall
Chief Counsel
Civil Rights Div.
Off. of the Attorney General
1275 W. Washington
Phoenix, AZ 85007
Phone : (602) 542-1401

CALIFORNIA
Nancy C. Gutierrez
Director
Fair Employment & Housing
2014 T St., Ste. 210
Sacramento, CA 95814
Phone : (916) 227-2873

COLORADO
Jack T. Langy Marquez
Director
Civil Rights Div.
Dept. of Regulatory Agencies
1560 Broadway, Rm. 1050
Denver, CO 80202
Phone : (303) 894-2997

CONNECTICUT
Louis Martin
Director
Comm. on Human Rights & Opportunities
90 Washington St.
Hartford, CT 06106
Phone : (203) 566-4895

DELAWARE
Andrew J. Turner
Chairman
Human Relations Comm.
Dept. of Community Affairs
820 N. French St., 4th Fl.
Wilmington, DE 19801
Phone : (302) 577-3485
Fax : (302) 577-3486

FLORIDA
Carolyn Franklin
Interim Director
Off. of Civil Rights
Dept. of Labor & Emp. Security
Ste. 303, Hartman Bldg.
2012 Capitol Circle, SE
Tallahassee, FL 32399-2152
Phone : (904) 488-5905
Fax : (904) 922-7119

GEORGIA
Joy Berry
Executive Director
Human Relations Comm.
225 Peachtree St., NE, # 2001
Atlanta, GA 30303-1701
Phone : (404) 651-9115

HAWAII
Linda Tseu
Executive Director
Civil Rights Comm.
Labor & Industrial Rel. Dept.
888 Mililani St., 2nd Fl.
Honolulu, HI 96813
Phone : (808) 586-8636

IDAHO
Marilyn Shuler
Director
Human Rights Comm.
Off. of the Governor
450 W. State St.
Boise, ID 83720
Phone : (208) 334-2873

ILLINOIS
Rose Mary Bombella
Director
Dept. of Human Rights
100 W. Randolph, Ste. 10-100
Chicago, IL 60601
Phone : (312) 814-6284
Fax : (312) 814-1436

INDIANA
Sandra D. Leek
Director
Civil Rights Comm.
100 N. Senate Ave., Rm. E103
Indianapolis, IN 46204
Phone : (317) 232-2600

IOWA
Don Grove
Director
Civil Rights Comm.
211 E. Maple St., 2nd Fl.
Des Moines, IA 50319
Phone : (515) 281-4121
Fax : (515) 242-5840

KANSAS
Michael J. Brungardt
Executive Director
Kansas Human Rights Commission
Landon State Off. Bldg., Ste. 851-S
Topeka, KS 66612-1258
Phone : (913) 296-3206

KENTUCKY
Beverly L. Watts
Executive Director
Comm. on Human Rights
Capital Plaza Tower, Ste. 832
500 Mero St.
Frankfort, KY 40601
Phone : (502) 564-3550

LOUISIANA
Maria Auzenne
Chairman
Off. of the Governor
300 Four United Plz.
Baton Rouge, LA 70809
Phone : (504) 342-3111

MAINE
Patricia Ryan
Executive Director
Human Rights Comm.
State House Station # 51
Augusta, ME 04333
Phone : (207) 624-6050

MARYLAND**
Jennifer Burdick
Executive Director
Human Relations Comm.
20 E. Franklin St.
Baltimore, MD 21202
Phone : (410) 333-1715

MASSACHUSETTS
Michael T. Duffy
Chairman
Comm. Against Discrimination
1 Ashburton Pl., Rm. 601
Boston, MA 02108
Phone : (617) 727-3990

MICHIGAN
Nanette Reynolds
Director
Dept. of Civil Rights
303 W. Kalamazoo
Lansing, MI 48913
Phone : (517) 335-3165
Fax : (517) 335-6790

MINNESOTA
David Beaulieu
Commissioner
Dept. of Human Rights
Bremer Tower
7th Pl. & Minnesota Streets
St. Paul, MN 55101
Phone : (612) 296-5665

MISSOURI
Alvin A. Plummer
Director
Comm. on Human Rights
Dept. of Labor & Ind. Rel.
3315 W. Truman Blvd.
P.O. Box 1129
Jefferson City, MO 65102-1129
Phone : (314) 751-3325
Fax : (314) 751-2905

MONTANA
Ann MacIntyre
Administrator
Human Rights Div.
Dept. of Labor & Industry
616 Helena Ave., Ste. 302
Steamboat Block
Helena, MT 59624-1728
Phone : (406) 444-2884

NEBRASKA
Lawrence C. Myers
Executive Director
Equal Opportunity Comm.
301 Centennial Mall S.
P.O. Box 94934
Lincoln, NE 68509-4934
Phone : (402) 471-2024
Fax : (402) 471-2597

NEVADA
Edward Johnson
Executive Director
Emplymt., Training & Rehab.
Equal Rights Comm.
1515 E. Tropicana, Ste. 590
Las Vegas, NV 89158
Phone : (702) 486-7161
Fax : (702) 486-7054

NEW HAMPSHIRE
Raymond S. Perry Jr.
Executive Director
Comm. for Human Rights
163 Loudon Rd.
Concord, NH 03301
Phone : (603) 271-2767

NEW JERSEY
C. Gregory Stewart
Director
Div. on Civil Rights
Dept. of Law & Public Safety
1100 Raymond Blvd.
Newark, NJ 07102
Phone : (201) 984-3101

NEW MEXICO
Howard Williams
Programs Div. Director
Human Rights Div.
1596 Pacheco St., Aspen Plz.
Santa Fe, NM 87503
Phone : (505) 827-6838
Fax : (505) 827-6878

NEW YORK *
Commissioner
Div. of Human Rights
Executive Dept.
55 W. 125th St.
New York, NY 10027
Phone : (217) 870-8790

NORTH CAROLINA
William J. Barber II
Director
Human Relations Council
Dept. of Administration
217 W. Jones St.
Raleigh, NC 27603-1336
Phone : (919) 733-7996
Fax : (919) 733-7940

NORTH DAKOTA
Craig Hagen
Commissioner
Dept. of Labor
State Capitol, 6th Fl.
600 E. Boulevard Ave.
Bismarck, ND 58505
Phone : (701) 328-2660
Fax : (701) 328-2031

OHIO
Joseph T. Carmichael
Director
Civil Rights Comm.
220 Parsons Ave.
Columbus, OH 43266-0543
Phone : (614) 466-2785
Fax : (614) 644-8776

OKLAHOMA
Ronald Lee Johnson
Director
Human Rights Comm.
2101 N. Lincoln Blvd., Rm. 481
Oklahoma City, OK 73105
Phone : (405) 521-3441

OREGON
Johnnie Bell
Administrator
Civil Rights Div.
Bur. of Labor & Industries
800 NE Oregon St., # 32
Portland, OR 97232
Phone : (503) 731-4873
Fax : (503) 731-4069

PENNSYLVANIA
Homer C. Floyd
Executive Director
Human Relations Comm.
P.O. Box 3145
Harrisburg, PA 17105
Phone : (717) 787-4410

RHODE ISLAND
Gene Booth
Executive Director
Human Rights Comm.
10 Abbott Park Pl.
Providence, RI 02903
Phone : (401) 277-2661

SOUTH CAROLINA
William C. Ham
Commissioner
Comm. on Human Affairs
P.O. Box 4490
Columbia, SC 29240
Phone : (803) 253-6336

SOUTH DAKOTA
Bill O'Toole
Director
Div. of Human Rights
Commerce & Regulations Dept.
910 E. Sioux
Pierre, SD 57501-5070
Phone : (605) 773-4493

TENNESSEE
Warren N. Moore
Executive Director
Human Rights Comm.
530 Church St., Ste. 400
Nashville, TN 37243
Phone : (615) 741-5825

TEXAS
William M. Hale
Executive Director
Comm. on Human Rights
P.O. Box 13493
Austin, TX 78711
Phone : (512) 837-8534

UTAH
Anna Jensen
Director
Div. of Anti-Discrimination & Labor
Industrial Comm.
160 E. 300 S.
Salt Lake City, UT 84111
Phone : (801) 530-6921

VERMONT
Susan Sussman
Executive Director
Human Rights Comm.
P.O. Box 997
Montpelier, VT 05601
Phone : (802) 828-2480
Fax : (802) 828-3522

J. Wallace Malley Jr.
Chief
Public Protection Div.
Off. of the Attorney General
109 State St.
Montpelier, VT 05602
Phone : (802) 828-3171

VIRGINIA
Roxie Raines Kornegay
Director
Council on Human Rights
1100 Bank St.
Richmond, VA 23219
Phone : (804) 225-2292
Fax : (804) 225-3294

WASHINGTON
Merritt Long
Executive Director
Human Rights Comm.
711 S. Capitol Way, Ste. 402
P.O. Box 42490
Olympia, WA 98504-2490
Phone : (360) 753-6770

WEST VIRGINIA*
Executive Director
Human Rights Comm.
East End Plz.
Morris & Lewis Sts.
Charleston, WV 25301
Phone : (304) 558-2616

WISCONSIN
J. Sheehan Donoghue
Administrator
Div. of Equal Rights
Industrial Labor & Human Rel.
201 E. Washington, Rm. 407
Madison, WI 53707
Phone : (608) 266-6860
Fax : (608) 267-4592

WYOMING
Dan Romero
EEO, Grievance & Appeals Coordinator
Personnel Div.
Dept. of Admin. & Information
Emerson Bldg.
Cheyenne, WY 82002
Phone : (307) 777-6730

DISTRICT OF COLUMBIA
Steven Jumper
Director
Off. of Human Rights
2000 14th St., N.W., 3rd Fl.
Washington, DC 20009
Phone : (202) 939-8780

GUAM**
Elizabeth Barrett-Anderson
Attorney General
238 Archbishop Flores St., Ste. 701
Agana, GU 96910
Phone : (671) 475-3324

NORTHERN MARIANA ISLANDS
Luis S. Camacho
Director of Personnel
Personnel Management Off.
Off. of the Governor
Saipan, MP 96950
Phone : (670) 234-6958
Fax : (670) 234-1013

PUERTO RICO
Jose Aulet Concepcion
Executive Director
Civil Rights Comm.
P.O. Box 192338
San Juan, PR 00919-2338
Phone : (809) 764-8779
Fax : (809) 765-9360

U.S. VIRGIN ISLANDS
Lunsford Williams
Acting Director
Civil Rights Comm.
P.O. Box 6645
St. Thomas, VI 00804
Phone : (809) 776-2485

CLERK OF STATE COURT OF LAST RESORT

Individual who keeps records of the state court of last resort.

ALABAMA
Robert Esdale
Clerk
Supreme Court
300 Dexter
Montgomery, AL 36104-3741
Phone : (334) 242-4609
Fax : (334) 242-0588

ALASKA
Jan Hansen
Clerk of the Appellate Courts
Supreme Court
303 K St.
Anchorage, AK 99501-2084
Phone : (907) 264-0607
Fax : (907) 276-5808

ARIZONA
Noel Dessaint
Clerk of Supreme Court
1501 W. Washington
Phoenix, AZ 85007
Phone : (602) 542-9396

ARKANSAS
Leslie W. Steen
Clerk
Supreme Court
Justice Bldg.
Little Rock, AR 72201
Phone : (501) 682-6841
Fax : (501) 682-6877

CALIFORNIA
Robert Wandruff
Clerk/Administrator
Supreme Court
303 Second St., 8th Fl.
San Francisco, CA 94107
Phone : (415) 396-9400

COLORADO
Mac Danford
Clerk
Supreme Court
State Judicial Bldg., # 415
2 E. 14th Ave.
Denver, CO 80203
Phone : (303) 861-1111

CONNECTICUT
Francis J. Drumm Jr.
Clerk
Supreme Court
Drawer Z, Sta. A
Hartford, CT 06106
Phone : (203) 566-8160
Fax : (203) 566-6731

DELAWARE
Cathy L. Howard
Acting Clerk
Supreme Court
55 The Green
Dover, DE 19801
Phone : (302) 739-4155
Fax : (302) 739-3751

FLORIDA
Sid J. White
Clerk
Supreme Court
Supreme Court Bldg.
500 S. Duval St.
Tallahassee, FL 32399-1927
Phone : (904) 488-0125

GEORGIA
Sheri M. Welch
Clerk
Supreme Court
State Off. Annex Bldg., Rm. 572
Atlanta, GA 30334
Phone : (404) 656-3470

HAWAII
Clement Chun
Acting Chief Clerk
Supreme Court
The Judiciary
417 S. King St.
Honolulu, HI 96813
Phone : (808) 539-4910

IDAHO
Frederick C. Lyon
Clerk
Supreme Court
451 W. State St.
Boise, ID 83720
Phone : (208) 334-2210

ILLINOIS
Juleann Hornyak
Clerk
Supreme Court
Supreme Court Bldg.
Second & Capitol St.
Springfield, IL 62706
Phone : (217) 782-2035

INDIANA
H. John Okeson
Clerk of the Court
217 State House
Indianapolis, IN 46204
Phone : (317) 232-1930
Fax : (317) 232-8365

Dwayne Brown
Clerk
Supreme Court & Court of Appeals
217 State House
Indianapolis, IN 46204
Phone : (317) 232-1930

IOWA
R.K. Richardson
Clerk
Supreme Court
Judicial Dept.
State Capitol
Des Moines, IA 50319
Phone : (515) 281-5911

KANSAS
Carol G. Green
Clerk of Appellate Courts
Supreme Court
Judicial Center
301 SW Tenth Ave.
Topeka, KS 66612-1507
Phone : (913) 296-3229

KENTUCKY
Susan Stokley-Clary
Clerk
Supreme Court
State Capitol
Frankfort, KY 40601
Phone : (502) 564-4720

LOUISIANA
Frans J. Labranche
Clerk
Supreme Court
301 Loyola Ave.
New Orleans, LA 70112
Phone : (504) 568-5707

MAINE
James C. Chute
Clerk
Supreme Judicial Court
Judicial Dept.
P.O. Box 368
Portland, ME 04112
Phone : (207) 822-4146

MARYLAND**
Alexander L. Cummings
Chief Clerk
Court of Appeals
Court of Appeals Bldg.
Annapolis, MD 21401
Phone : (410) 974-3341

MASSACHUSETTS
Richard J. Rouse
Clerk
Supreme Judicial Court
1404 New Court House
Boston, MA 02108
Phone : (617) 557-1100
Fax : (617) 523-1540

MICHIGAN
Corbin Davis
Clerk
Supreme Court
Law Bldg.
P.O. Box 30052
Lansing, MI 48909
Phone : (517) 373-0120

MINNESOTA
Fred Grittner
Clerk of Court
Supreme Court
Off. of the Appellate Court
230 State Capitol
St. Paul, MN 55155
Phone : (612) 296-2581

MISSISSIPPI
Linda Stone
Clerk
Supreme Court
P.O. Box 249
Jackson, MS 39205
Phone : (601) 359-3697

MISSOURI
Thomas F. Simon
Clerk
Supreme Court
Supreme Court Bldg.
207 W. High
P.O. Box 150
Jefferson City, MO 65102
Phone : (314) 751-4144
Fax : (314) 751-7514

MONTANA
Ed Smith
Clerk
Supreme Court
Justice Bldg.
Helena, MT 59620
Phone : (406) 444-3858

NEBRASKA
Lanet S. Asmussen
Clerk
Supreme Court
State Capitol, Rm. 2413
P.O. Box 94926
Lincoln, NE 68509-4926
Phone : (402) 471-3731
Fax : (402) 471-3480

NEVADA
Janette M. Bloom
Clerk
Supreme Court
Supreme Court Bldg.
Carson City, NV 89710
Phone : (702) 687-5180

NEW HAMPSHIRE
Howard J. Zibel
Clerk
Supreme Court
Supreme Court Bldg.
Concord, NH 03301
Phone : (603) 271-2646

NEW JERSEY
Stephen W. Townsend
Clerk
Supreme Court
CN970
Trenton, NJ 08625
Phone : (609) 984-7791

NEW MEXICO
Kathleen Jo Gibson
Chief Clerk
Supreme Court
P.O. Box 848
Santa Fe, NM 87504-0848
Phone : (505) 827-4860
Fax : (505) 827-4837

NEW YORK *
Clerk
Court of Appeals
Court of Appeals Hall
20 Eagle St.
Albany, NY 12207
Phone : (518) 455-8810

NORTH CAROLINA
Christie Speir Cameron
Clerk
Supreme Court
Justice Bldg.
2 W. Morgan St.
Raleigh, NC 27601-1400
Phone : (919) 733-3723
Fax : (919) 733-0105

NORTH DAKOTA
Penny Miller
Chief Clerk
Supreme Court
State Capitol, Judicial Wing
600 E. Boulevard Ave.
Bismarck, ND 58505-0530
Phone : (701) 328-2221
Fax : (701) 328-4480

OHIO
Marcia Mengel
Clerk
Supreme Court
30 E. Broad St., 2nd Fl.
Columbus, OH 43266-0419
Phone : (614) 466-3931
Fax : (614) 752-4418

OKLAHOMA
James Patterson
Clerk
Supreme Court & Court of Criminal Appeals
State Capitol, Rm. 1-A
Oklahoma City, OK 73105
Phone : (405) 521-2163

OREGON
R. William Linden Jr.
Administrator
Off. of Court Administrator
Supreme Court Bldg.
1163 State St.
Salem, OR 97310
Phone : (503) 378-6046

PENNSYLVANIA
Charles W. Johns
Prothonotary
Supreme Court
468 City Hall
Philadelphia, PA 19107
Phone : (215) 560-6370

RHODE ISLAND
Robert Harrell
Court Administrator
Supreme Court
250 Benefit St.
Providence, RI 02903
Phone : (401) 277-3266

SOUTH CAROLINA
Clyde N. Davis Jr.
Clerk
Supreme Court
P.O. Box 11330
Columbia, SC 29211
Phone : (803) 734-1080

SOUTH DAKOTA
Gloria J. Engel
Clerk
Supreme Court
State Capitol, 2nd Fl.
Pierre, SD 57501
Phone : (605) 773-3511

TENNESSEE
Cecil Growson Jr.
Clerk
Supreme Court
100 Supreme Court Bldg.
Nashville, TN 37243-0606
Phone : (615) 741-2681

TEXAS
John T. Adams
Clerk
Supreme Court
P.O. Box 12248, Capitol Station
Austin, TX 78711
Phone : (512) 463-1312

UTAH
Geoffrey J. Butler
Clerk
Supreme Court
332 State Capitol
Salt Lake City, UT 84114
Phone : (801) 538-1044

VERMONT
Tom Lehner
Court Administrator & Clerk
Off. of Supreme Court Administrator
111 State St.
Montpelier, VT 05602
Phone : (802) 828-3276
Fax : (802) 828-3457

VIRGINIA
Robert N. Baldwin
Executive Secretary
Supreme Court
100 N. Ninth St.
Richmond, VA 23219
Phone : (804) 786-6455
Fax : (804) 786-4542

WASHINGTON
C.J. Merritt
Clerk
Supreme Court
Temple of Justice
P.O. Box 40929
Olympia, WA 98504
Phone : (360) 357-2077

WEST VIRGINIA
Ancil G. Ramey
Clerk
Supreme Court of Appeals
State Capitol, Rm. E-317
Charleston, WV 25305
Phone : (304) 558-2601
Fax : (304) 558-3815

WISCONSIN
Marilyn L. Graves
Clerk
Supreme Court
231 E State Capitol
P.O. Box 1688
Madison, WI 53701-1688
Phone : (608) 266-1880
Fax : (608) 267-0640

Clerk of State Court of Last Resort

WYOMING
Jerrill D. Carter
Clerk of the Supreme Court
Supreme Court
Supreme Court Bldg.
Cheyenne, WY 82002
Phone : (307) 777-7316

DISTRICT OF COLUMBIA
William H. Eg
Clerk
Court of Appeals
500 Indiana Ave., NW
Washington, DC 20001
Phone : (202) 879-2725

AMERICAN SAMOA
Robert Gorniak
Clerk
High Court of American Samoa
Pago Pago, AS 96799
Phone : (684) 633-4131
Fax : (684) 633-1318

GUAM**
Alfredo M. Borlas
Clerk of Court
Superior Court
110 W. O'Brien Dr.
Agana, GU 96910
Phone : (671) 472-8956

NORTHERN MARIANA ISLANDS
John G. Moore
Recorder
Superior Court
P.O. Box 307 CK
Saipan, MP 96950
Phone : (670) 234-6401
Fax : (670) 234-8010

PUERTO RICO
Francisco R. Agrait-Llado
General Secretary
Supreme Court
P.O. Box 2392
San Juan, PR 00902-2392
Phone : (809) 723-6033
Fax : (809) 722-9177

U.S. VIRGIN ISLANDS
Orrin Arnold
Clerk
U.S. District Court
2 & 3 King St.
Christiansted
St. Croix, VI 00802
Phone : (809) 773-1130

COASTAL ZONE MANAGEMENT

Plans and implements programs for the orderly development of coastal zones.

ALABAMA
John Carlton
Chief
Coastal Section
Mobile Field Office
2204 Perimeter Rd.
Mobile, AL 36615
Phone : (334) 450-3400
Fax : (334) 479-2593

ALASKA
Susan Braley
Coordinator
Coastal Zone Mgt. Program
Dept. of Environ. Conservation
410 W. Willoughby Ave., Ste. 105
Juneau, AK 99801
Phone : (907) 465-5308
Fax : (907) 465-5274

CALIFORNIA
Peter R. Douglas
Executive Director
Coastal Comm.
Resources Agency
45 Fremont, Ste. 2000
San Francisco, CA 94105
Phone : (415) 904-5200

CONNECTICUT
Arthur J. Rocque
Senior Advisor
Long Island Sound Prog. Off.
Dept. of Environ. Protection
79 Elm St.
Hartford, CT 06106
Phone : (203) 424-3034

DELAWARE
Sarah Cooksey
Administator
Delaware Coastal Zone Mgt. Prog.
Dept. of Natural Resources & Environ.
Dover, DE 19903
Phone : (302) 739-3451
Fax : (302) 739-2048

FLORIDA
Al Devereaux
Chief
Bur. of Beaches & Costal Systems
Dept. of Environ. Protection
3900 Commonwealth Blvd., MS 300
Tallahassee, FL 32399
Phone : (904) 487-4469

GEORGIA
Duane Harris
Director
Coastal Resources Div.
Dept. of Natural Resources
One Conservation Way
Brunswick, GA 31523-8600
Phone : (912) 264-7218
Fax : (912) 262-3143

HAWAII
Douglas Tom
Program Manager
Coastal Zone Mgt. Program
Off. of State Planning
415 S. Beretania St.
Honolulu, HI 96813
Phone : (808) 587-2875
Fax : (808) 587-2848

ILLINOIS
Toby Frevert
Chief of Planning
Water Pollution Control Div.
2200 Churchill Rd.
Springfield, IL 62706
Phone : (217) 782-9540

INDIANA
John Simpson
Director
Div. of Water
Dept. of Natural Resources
402 W. Washington
Indianapolis, IN 46204

LOUISIANA
Ivar Van Heerden
Assistant Secretary
Coastal Restoration & Mgt.
Dept. of Natural Resources
P.O. Box 94396
Baton Rouge, LA 70804
Phone : (504) 342-4503

MAINE
David Keeley
Director
Coastal Program
State Planning Off.
State House Station # 38
Augusta, ME 04333
Phone : (207) 287-3261

MARYLAND
Jacob Lima
Program Director
Coastal Resources Div.
Dept. of Natural Resources
Tawes State Off. Bldg.
Annapolis, MD 21401
Phone : (410) 974-3581

MASSACHUSETTS
Peg Brady
Director
Coastal Zone Mgt.
Executive Off. of Environmental Affairs
100 Cambridge St., Rm. 2006
Boston, MA 02202
Phone : (617) 727-9530
Fax : (617) 727-2754

MICHIGAN
G. Tracy Mehan
Director
Great Lakes Off.
Dept. of Natural Resources
P.O. Box 30028
Lansing, MI 48909
Phone : (517) 335-4056
Fax : (517) 335-4242

MINNESOTA
Kent Lokkesmoe
Director
Div. of Waters
Dept. of Natural Resources
500 Lafayette Rd.
St. Paul, MN 55155
Phone : (612) 296-4810

MISSISSIPPI
Joe I. Gill
Deputy Director
Bur. of Marine Resources
2620 Beach Blvd.
Biloxi, MS 39531
Phone : (601) 385-5860

MONTANA
Steve Pilcher
Administrator
Environmental Sciences Div.
Cogswell Bldg., Rm. A107
Helena, MT 59620
Phone : (406) 444-3948

NEW HAMPSHIRE
David Hartman
Program Manager
Coastal Zone Mgt.
Off. of State Planning
2 1/2 Beacon St.
Concord, NH 03301
Phone : (603) 271-2155

NEW JERSEY
Ruth Ehinger
Bureau Chief
Bur. of Coastal Project Rev.
Dept. of Environ. Protection
501 E. State St., CN 401
Trenton, NJ 08625
Phone : (609) 633-2289

NEW YORK
Alexander F. Treadwell
Secretary of State
Dept. of State
162 Washington Ave.
Albany, NY 12231
Phone : (518) 474-0050

NORTH CAROLINA
Roger Schecter
Director
Coastal Mgt. Division
Dept. of Environment, Health & Natural Resources
225 N. McDowell St.
Raleigh, NC 27604-1148
Phone : (919) 733-2293
Fax : (919) 733-1495

OHIO
Michelle Willis
Chief
Div. of Water
Dept. of Natural Resources
Fountain Sq., Bldg. E
Columbus, OH 43224
Phone : (614) 265-6712
Fax : (614) 447-9503

OREGON
Neil Mullane
Manager
Planning & Monitoring Section
Div. of Water Quality
811 SW Sixth Ave.
Portland, OR 97204
Phone : (503) 229-5284

PENNSYLVANIA
Michael Krempasky
Director
Land & Water Conservation
Dept. of Environ. Resources
Market St. State Off. Bldg.
Harrisburg, PA 17101
Phone : (717) 783-9500

RHODE ISLAND
James Beattie
Chief
Div. of Coastal Resources
Dept. of Environmental Mgt.
22 Hayes St.
Providence, RI 02908
Phone : (401) 277-3429

SOUTH CAROLINA
H. Wayne Beam
Deputy Commissioner
Off. of Ocean & Coastal Resources Mgt.
1201 Main St., Ste. 1520
Columbia, SC 29201
Phone : (803) 737-0880

TEXAS
Sally S. Davenport
Director
Coastal Div.
General Land Off.
1700 N. Congress Ave.
Austin, TX 78701
Phone : (512) 463-5059

VIRGINIA
Peter W. Schmidt
Director
Department of Environmental Quality
629 E. Main St.
Richmond, VA 23219
Phone : (804) 762-4020
Fax : (804) 762-4019

WASHINGTON
Carol Fleskes
Program Manager
Dept. of Ecology - S/CZM
P.O. Box 47600
Olympia, WA 98504-7600
Phone : (360) 407-6602

WISCONSIN
William Lehman
Chief
Coastal Mgt. Section
Dept. of Admin.
P.O. Box 7868
Madison, WI 53707
Phone : (608) 266-8234
Fax : (608) 267-6931

AMERICAN SAMOA
Lelei Peau
Coastal Zone Manager
Off. of Economic Development Planning
Pago Pago, AS 96799
Phone : (684) 633-5155
Fax : (684) 633-4195

GUAM
Joseph C. Cruz
Administrator
Environmental Protection Agency
130 Rojas St.
Harmon, GU 96911
Phone : (671) 646-8863
Fax : (671) 646-9402

NORTHERN MARIANA ISLANDS
Manuel C. Sablan
Director
Coastal Resources Mgt. Off.
Morgen's Bldg., San Jose
P.O. Box 10007
Saipan, MP 96950
Phone : (670) 234-6623
Fax : (670) 234-0007

PUERTO RICO
Hector Russe
President
Environmental Quality Board
P.O. Box 11488
San Juan, PR 00910-1488
Phone : (809) 767-8057
Fax : (809) 766-2483

U.S. VIRGIN ISLANDS
Beulah Dalmida-Smith
Commissioner
Dept. of Planning & Natural Resources
Nisky Ctr., Ste. 231
St. Thomas, VI 00802
Phone : (809) 774-3320
Fax : (809) 775-5706

COMMERCE

Umbrella agency of commerce responsible for the overall regulation and growth of the state's economy.

ALABAMA
Charlie Snider
Interim Director
Development Off.
401 Adams Ave.
Montgomery, AL 36130
Phone : (334) 242-0400
Fax : (334) 242-5669

ARIZONA
Sara Goertzen
Director
Dept. of Commerce
3800 N. Central Ave., Ste. 1500
Phoenix, AZ 85012
Phone : (602) 280-1306

ARKANSAS
L.D. Boyette
Director
Industrial Development Comm.
1 Capitol Mall, Rm. 4C-300
Little Rock, AR 72201
Phone : (501) 682-2052
Fax : (501) 682-7394

CALIFORNIA
Julie Meier Wright
Secretary
Trade & Commerce Agency
801 K St., Ste. 1700
Sacramento, CA 95814
Phone : (916) 322-3962

CONNECTICUT
Arthur H. Diedrick
Acting Commissioner
Dept. of Economic Development
865 Brook St.
Rocky Hill, CT 06067
Phone : (203) 258-4200

DELAWARE
Edward J. Freel
Secretary of State
P.O. Box 898
Dover, DE 19903
Phone : (302) 739-4111
Fax : (302) 739-3811

FLORIDA
Charles Dusseau
Secretary of Commerce
536 Collins Bldg.
Tallahassee, FL 32399-2000
Phone : (904) 488-3104
Fax : (904) 922-9150

GEORGIA
Randolph B. Cardoza
Commissioner
Dept. of Ind., Trade & Tourism
258 Peachtree Ctr. Ave., NE, Ste. 1000
Atlanta, GA 30303
Phone : (404) 656-3556

HAWAII
Kathryn Matayoshi
Director
Dept. of Commerce & Consumer Affairs
1010 Richards St.
Honolulu, HI 96813
Phone : (808) 586-2850
Fax : (808) 586-2856

IDAHO
James V. Hawkins
Director
Dept. of Commerce
700 W. State St.
Boise, ID 83720
Phone : (208) 334-2470

ILLINOIS
Dennis R. Whetstone
Director
Dept. of Commerce & Community Affairs
620 E. Adams St., 3rd Fl.
Springfield, IL 62701
Phone : (217) 782-3233
Fax : (217) 524-0864

INDIANA
Frank L. O'Bannon
Lt. Governor
Dept. of Commerce
333 State House
Indianapolis, IN 46204
Phone : (317) 232-4545

IOWA
Jack Nystrom
Director
Dept. of Commerce
1918 SE Hulsizer
Ankeny, IA 50021
Phone : (515) 281-7401
Fax : (515) 281-7372

KANSAS
Gary Sherrer
Secretary
Dept. of Commerce & Housing
700 SW Harrison, Ste. 1300
Topeka, KS 66603-3712
Phone : (913) 296-3481
Fax : (913) 296-5055

KENTUCKY
Gene Strong
Secretary
Economic Development Cabinet
Capital Plz. Tower, 23rd Fl.
500 Mero St.
Frankfort, KY 40601
Phone : (502) 564-7670

LOUISIANA
Kevin Reilly
Secretary
Dept. of Economic Development
P.O. Box 94185
Baton Rouge, LA 70804-9185
Phone : (504) 342-5388

MAINE
Tom McBrierty
Commissioner
Dept. of Economic & Community Development
#59 State House Station
Augusta, ME 04333-0059
Phone : (207) 287-2656

MARYLAND
James D. Fielder
Director
Off. of Business & Dev.
217 E. Redwood St.
Baltimore, MD 21202
Phone : (410) 333-6985

MASSACHUSETTS
Gloria C. Larson
Secretary
Executive Off. of Economic Affairs
1 Ashburton Pl., Rm. 2101
Boston, MA 02108
Phone : (617) 727-8380

MICHIGAN
Art Ellis
Director
Dept. of Commerce
Law Bldg., 4th Fl.
P.O. Box 30004
Lansing, MI 48909
Phone : (517) 373-7230
Fax : (517) 373-3872

MINNESOTA
James Ulland
Commissioner
Dept. of Commerce
133 E. Seventh St.
St. Paul, MN 55101
Phone : (612) 296-6694

MISSISSIPPI
James B. Heidel
Executive Director
Dept. of Economic & Community Development
P.O. Box 849
Jackson, MS 39205-0849
Phone : (601) 359-3449

MISSOURI
Joseph L. Driskill
Director
Dept. of Economic Development
301 W. High St.
P.O. Box 1157
Jefferson City, MO 65102
Phone : (314) 751-3946
Fax : (314) 751-7258
E-Mail: JDRISKIL@MAIL.MORE.NET

MONTANA
John Noel
Director
Dept. of Commerce
1424 Ninth Ave.
Helena, MT 59620
Phone : (406) 444-3797

NEBRASKA
Maxine Moul
Director
Dept. of Economic Development
301 Centennial Mall S.
P.O. Box 94666
Lincoln, NE 68509-4666
Phone : (402) 471-3747
Fax : (402) 471-3778

NEVADA
Rose McKinney-James
Director
Dept. of Business & Industry
1665 Hot Springs Rd.
Carson City, NV 89710
Phone : (702) 687-4250

NEW HAMPSHIRE
William Bartlett
Commissioner
Dept. of Resources & Economic Development
P.O. Box 856
Concord, NH 03302-0856
Phone : (603) 271-2411

NEW JERSEY
Gualberto Medina
Commissioner
Dept. of Commerce & Economic Development
20 W. State St., CN820
Trenton, NJ 08625
Phone : (609) 292-2444

NEW MEXICO
Gary Bratcher
Secretary
Dept. of Economic Development
1100 St. Francis Dr.
P.O. Box 3003
Santa Fe, NM 87504
Phone : (505) 827-0380
Fax : (505) 827-0328

NEW YORK*
Commissioner
Dept. of Commerce
1 Commerce Plz.
Albany, NY 12245
Phone : (518) 474-4100

NORTH CAROLINA
S. Davis Phillips
Secretary
Dept. of Commerce
430 N. Salisbury St.
Raleigh, NC 27603-5900
Phone : (919) 733-4962
Fax : (919) 733-8356

NORTH DAKOTA
Charles W. Stroup
Director
Dept. of Economic Dev. & Finance
1833 E. Bismarck Expy.
Bismarck, ND 58504
Phone : (701) 328-5300
Fax : (701) 328-5320

OHIO
Donna Owens
Director
Dept. of Commerce
77 S. High St., 23rd Fl.
Columbus, OH 43266
Phone : (614) 644-7053
Fax : (614) 644-8292

OKLAHOMA
D. Gregory Main
Executive Director
Dept. of Commerce
6601 Broadway Ext.
Oklahoma City, OK 73116
Phone : (405) 843-9770

PENNSYLVANIA
Thomas B. Hagen
Secretary
Commerce Dept.
Rm. 433, Forum Bldg.
Harrisburg, PA 17120
Phone : (717) 783-3840

RHODE ISLAND
Marcel Valois
Director
Dept. of Economic Development
7 Jackson Walkway
Providence , RI 02903
Phone : (401) 277-2601

SOUTH CAROLINA
Bob Royall
Director
Dept. of Commerce
P.O. Box 927
Columbia, SC 29202
Phone : (803) 734-0400

SOUTH DAKOTA
David Volk
Secretary
Dept. of Commerce & Regulations
910 E. Sioux Ave.
Pierre, SD 57501
Phone : (605) 773-3178

TENNESSEE
Bill Dunavant
Commissioner
Dept. of Economic & Community Development
320 Sixth Ave., N., 8th Fl.
Nashville, TN 37243
Phone : (615) 741-1888
Fax : (615) 741-6236

TEXAS
Brenda Arnett
Executive Director
Dept. of Commerce
P.O. Box 12728, Capitol Station
Austin, TX 78711
Phone : (512) 472-5059

UTAH
Joseph Jenkins
Executive Director
Dept. of Community & Economic Development
6290 State Off. Bldg.
Salt Lake City, UT 84114
Phone : (801) 538-8708

VERMONT
William C. Shouldice
Secretary
Agency of Development & Community Affairs
109 State St.
Montpelier, VT 05609
Phone : (802) 828-3211
Fax : (802) 828-3258

VIRGINIA
Robert T. Skunda
Secretary
Governor's Cabinet
723 9th St. Office Bldg.
Richmond, VA 23219
Phone : (804) 786-7831
Fax : (804) 371-0250

WASHINGTON
Mike Fitzgerald
Director
Dept. of Trade & Econ. Dev.
101 General Admin. Bldg.
P.O. Box 42500
Olympia, WA 98504
Phone : (360) 753-7426

WEST VIRGINIA
Tom Burns
Director
Development Office
Bldg. 6, Rm. 504
1900 Kanawha Blvd., E.
Charleston, WV 25305
Phone : (304) 558-2234
Fax : (304) 558-1189

WISCONSIN
William J. McCoshen
Secretary
Dept. of Development
123 W. Washington
P.O. Box 7970
Madison, WI 53707
Phone : (608) 266-7088
Fax : (608) 264-6151

WYOMING
Celeste Colgan
Director
Dept. of Commerce
Barrett Bldg., 4th Fl.
Cheyenne, WY 82002
Phone : (307) 777-6303

DISTRICT OF COLUMBIA
George Brown
Deputy Mayor
Economic Development
Off. of the Mayor
441 4th St., NW, 11th Fl.
Washington, DC 20001
Phone : (202) 727-6365

AMERICAN SAMOA
John Fauinuina
Chairman
Commerce Comm.
Off. of Economic Development Planning
Utulei
Pago Pago, AS 96799
Phone : (684) 633-5155
Fax : (684) 633-4195

GUAM
Frank B. Aguon Jr.
Director
Dept. of Commerce
590 S. Marine Dr., Ste. 601
Tamuning, GU 96911
Phone : (671) 646-6931
Fax : (671) 646-7242

NORTHERN MARIANA ISLANDS
Pedro Q. Dela Cruz
Secretary
Dept. of Commerce
Off. of the Governor
P.O. Box 10007
Saipan, MP 96950
Phone : (670) 322-4361
Fax : (670) 322-4008

PUERTO RICO
Luis Fortuno
Secretary
Dept. of Commerce & Economic Dev.
P.O. Box 4435
San Juan, PR 00902-4436
Phone : (809) 721-2898
Fax : (809) 722-6238

U.S. VIRGIN ISLANDS
Anthony Olive
Commissioner
Dept. of Economic Develop. & Agric.
P.O. Box 6400
St. Thomas, VI 00803
Phone : (809) 774-8784
Fax : (809) 774-4390

COMMUNITY AFFAIRS

Provides a broad range of services designed to assist communities in the delivery of essential public services.

ALABAMA
Robert Lunsford
Director
Dept. of Economic & Community Affairs
P.O. Box 5690
Montgomery, AL 36103
Phone : (334) 242-8672
Fax : (334) 242-5099

ALASKA
Mike Irwin
Commissioner
Dept. of Community & Regional Affairs
P.O. Box 112100
Juneau, AK 99811-2100
Phone : (907) 465-4700
Fax : (907) 465-2948

ARIZONA
Sara Goertzen
Director
Dept. of Commerce
3800 N. Central Ave., Ste. 1500
Phoenix, AZ 85012
Phone : (602) 280-1306

ARKANSAS
Tom Dalton
Director
Dept. of Human Srvcs.
P.O. Box 1437, Slot 316
Little Rock, AR 72203
Phone : (501) 682-8650
Fax : (501) 682-6836

CALIFORNIA
Rich Nelson
Deputy Chief
Div. of Community Affairs
Dept. of Housing & Comm. Dev.
1800 Third St., Ste. 390
Sacramento, CA 95814
Phone : (916) 322-1560

COLORADO
Hal Knott
Director
Div. of Local Government
Dept. of Local Affairs
1313 Sherman St., # 521
Denver, CO 80203
Phone : (303) 866-2156
Fax : (303) 866-4819

CONNECTICUT
Don Downes
Under Secretary
Intergovernmental Policy
Off. of Policy & Mgt.
80 Washington St.
Hartford, CT 06106
Phone : (203) 566-2367

FLORIDA
Linda Loomis Shelley
Secretary
Dept. of Community Affairs
2740 Centerview Dr.
Tallahassee, FL 32399-2100
Phone : (904) 488-8466
Fax : (904) 921-0781

GEORGIA
Jim Higdon
Commissioner
Dept. of Community Affairs
Equitable Bldg., Ste. 1200
100 Peachtree St.
Atlanta, GA 30303
Phone : (404) 656-3836

HAWAII
Richard Egged
Deputy Director
Dept. of Business, Economic Development & Tourism
P.O. Box 2359
Honolulu, HI 96804
Phone : (808) 586-2362
Fax : (808) 586-2377

IDAHO
Kay Frances
Administrator
Div. of Community Development
Dept. of Commerce
700 W. State St.
Boise, ID 83720
Phone : (208) 334-2470

ILLINOIS
Dennis R. Whetstone
Director
Dept. of Commerce & Community Affairs
620 E. Adams St., 3rd Fl.
Springfield, IL 62701
Phone : (217) 782-3233
Fax : (217) 524-0864

INDIANA
Craig E. Hartzer
Director
Div. of Community Development
Dept. of Commerce
1 N. Capitol
Indianapolis, IN 46204
Phone : (317) 232-8917

IOWA
Kathleen Beery
Administrator
Div of Comm. & Rural Dev.
Dept. of Economic Development
200 E. Grand
Des Moines, IA 50309
Phone : (515) 242-4807

KANSAS
Mary LaFaver
Director
Community Development Div.
Dept. of Commerce & Housing
700 SW Harrison, Ste. 1300
Topeka, KS 66603-3712
Phone : (913) 296-3485
Fax : (913) 296-5055

KENTUCKY
Bruce Ferguson
Commissioner
Dept. of Local Government
1024 Capitol Centre Dr.
Frankfort, KY 40601
Phone : (502) 564-2382

LOUISIANA
Pat Robinson
Director
Business & Community Services
Economic Development
P.O. Box 94185
Baton Rouge, LA 70804
Phone : (504) 342-3000

MARYLAND**
Eugene P. Bartell
Executive Director
Community Srvcs. Admin.
Dept. of Human Resources
311 W. Saratoga St.
Baltimore, MD 21201
Phone : (410) 333-0053

MASSACHUSETTS
Mary L. Padula
Secretary
Executive Off. of Communities & Development
100 Cambridge St., Rm. 1804
Boston, MA 02202
Phone : (617) 727-7765

MICHIGAN
Steve Arwood
Director
Industry & Investment Relations
Michigan Jobs Commission
201 N. Washington Square
Lansing, MI 48913
Phone : (517) 373-8500
Fax : (517) 373-0314

MINNESOTA
Jennifer Engh
Deputy Commissioner
Community Development Div.
Dept. of Trade & Econ. Dev.
121 7th Pl., E.
St. Paul, MN 55101
Phone : (612) 296-5005

MISSISSIPPI
Alice Lusk
Associate Director
Community Srvcs.
Dept. of Econ. & Comm. Dev.
P.O. Box 849
Jackson, MS 39205
Phone : (601) 359-3449

MISSOURI
Garry Taylor
Director
Div. of Community & Economic Dev.
Dept. of Economic Development
Truman Bldg., Rm. 720
P.O. Box 118
Jefferson City, MO 65102
Phone : (314) 751-4241
Fax : (314) 751-7384

MONTANA
Newell Anderson
Administrator
Local Govt. Assistance Div.
Dept. of Commerce
1424 Ninth Ave.
Helena, MT 59620
Phone : (406) 444-3757

NEBRASKA
Jenne Rodriguez
Director
Div. of Community Development
Dept. of Economic Development
P.O. Box 94666
Lincoln, NE 68509
Phone : (402) 471-3111
Fax : (402) 471-3778

NEVADA
Donny Loux
Chief
Community Based Srvcs.
Dept. of Employment, Training & Rehabilitation
711 S. Stewart St.
Carson City, NV 89710
Phone : (702) 687-4452
Fax : (702) 687-3292

NEW HAMPSHIRE
Jeff Taylor
Director
Off. of State Planning
2 1/2 Beacon St.
Concord, NH 03301
Phone : (603) 271-2155

NEW JERSEY
Harriet Derman
Commissioner
Dept. of Community Affairs
101 S. Broad St., CN800
Trenton, NJ 08625
Phone : (609) 292-6420

NEW MEXICO
Roberto S. Rios
Director
Economic Development Div.
Dept. of Economic Development
1100 St. Francis Dr.
Santa Fe, NM 87503
Phone : (505) 827-0300
Fax : (505) 827-0328

NEW YORK
Alexander F. Treadwell
Secretary of State
Dept. of State
162 Washington Ave.
Albany, NY 12231
Phone : (518) 474-0050

NORTH CAROLINA
Bob Chandler
Director
Community Assistance
Dept. of Commerce
P.O. Box 12600
Raleigh, NC 27605-2600
Phone : (919) 733-2850
Fax : (919) 733-5262

NORTH DAKOTA
Shirley Dykshoorn
Director
Intergovernmental Assistance
Off. of Mgt. & Budget
600 E. Boulevard Ave.
Bismarck, ND 58505-0170
Phone : (701) 328-2094
Fax : (701) 328-2308

OHIO
Vince Lombardi
Assistant Director
Div. of Community Development
Dept. of Development
77 S. High St.
P.O. Box 1001
Columbus, OH 43266-0101
Phone : (614) 466-4588
Fax : (614) 644-0745

OKLAHOMA
D. Gregory Main
Executive Director
Dept. of Commerce
6601 Broadway Ext.
Oklahoma City, OK 73116
Phone : (405) 843-9770

OREGON
Baruti Arthare e
Director
Dept. of Housing & Community Srvcs.
1600 State St., Ste. 100
Salem, OR 97310
Phone : (503) 986-2005
Fax : (503) 986-2020

PENNSYLVANIA
William C. Bostic
Secretary
Dept. of Community Affairs
Rm. 317, Forum Bldg.
Harrisburg, PA 17120
Phone : (717) 787-7160

RHODE ISLAND
Armeather Gibbs
Director
Community Relations
Office of the Governor
State House, Rm. 111
Providence, RI 02903
Phone : (401) 277-2080

SOUTH DAKOTA
Bonnie Untereiner
Commissioner
Governor's Off. of Economic Development
Capitol Lake Plz.
Pierre, SD 57501
Phone : (605) 773-5032

TENNESSEE
Bill Dunavant
Commissioner
Dept. of Economic & Community Development
320 Sixth Ave., N., 8th Fl.
Nashville, TN 37243
Phone : (615) 741-1888
Fax : (615) 741-7306

TEXAS
Henry Flores
Executive Director
Dept. of Housing & Comm. Aff.
811 Barton Springs Rd.
P.O. Box 13166
Austin, TX 78711
Phone : (512) 475-3800

UTAH
Carol Nixon
Director
Div. of Business & Economic Dev.
Dept. of Community & Economic Dev.
324 S. State St., Ste. 300
Salt Lake City, UT 84111
Phone : (801) 538-8722

Olene S. Walker
Lt. Governor
203 State Capitol Bldg.
Salt Lake City, UT 84114
Phone : (801) 538-1520

VERMONT
William C. Shouldice
Secretary
Agency of Development & Community Affairs
109 State St.
Montpelier, VT 05609
Phone : (802) 828-3211
Fax : (802) 828-3258

VIRGINIA
Robert T. Skunda
Secretary
Governor's Cabinet
Department of Housing & Community Development
723 Ninth St. Office Bldg.
Richmond, VA 23219
Phone : (804) 786-7831
Fax : (804) 371-0250

WASHINGTON
Jean Ameluxen
Comm. Trade & Economic Dev.
906 Columbia St., SW
P.O. Box 48300
Olympia, WA 98504-8300
Phone : (360) 753-2227

WEST VIRGINIA
Tom Burns
Director
Development Office
Bldg. 6, Rm. B504
1900 Kanawha Blvd., E.
Charleston, WV 25305
Phone : (304) 558-2234
Fax : (304) 558-1189

WISCONSIN
Terry W. Grosenheider
Administrator
Div. of Economic Development
Dept. of Development
123 W Washington
P.O. Box 7970
Madison, WI 53707
Phone : (608) 266-9467
Fax : (608) 267-2829

WYOMING
George H. Gault
Director
Div. of Econ. & Comm. Dev.
Dept. of Commerce
2301 Central Ave., 4N
Cheyenne, WY 82002
Phone : (307) 777-6435

DISTRICT OF COLUMBIA
Sybil Hammond
General Assistant to the Mayor
Off. of the Mayor
441 4th St., NW
Washington, DC 20001
Phone : (202) 727-2980

AMERICAN SAMOA
Thomas Black
Territorial Planner
Community Dev. Block Grant & Dev. Srvcs. Block Grant
Utulei
Pago Pago, AS 96799
Phone : (684) 633-5155
Fax : (684) 633-4195

GUAM
Calvin E. Halloway
Attorney General
Office of the Attorney General
120 W. O'Brien Dr., Ste. 2-200E
Agana, GU 96910
Phone : (671) 475-3324
Fax : (671) 472-2493

NORTHERN MARIANA ISLANDS
Thomas A. Tebuteb
Secretary
Community & Cultural Affairs
P.O. Box 10007
Saipan, MP 96950
Phone : (670) 233-3343
Fax : (670) 233-2221

PUERTO RICO
Pedro Rosario
Administrator
Off. of Municipal Affairs
P.O. Box 70167
San Juan, PR 00936
Phone : (809) 754-8827
Fax : (809) 753-6080

U.S. VIRGIN ISLANDS
Juel T.R. Molloy
Assistant to the Governor
Dept. of Human Srvcs.
21-22 Kongens Gade
St. Thomas, VI 00802
Phone : (809) 774-0001
Fax : (809) 774-1361

COMPTROLLER

The principal accounting and disbursing officer of the state.

ALABAMA
Robert L. Childree
Comptroller
Dept. of Finance
110 Alabama State House
Montgomery, AL 36130
Phone : (334) 242-7063
Fax : (334) 242-2440

ALASKA
Betty Martin
Comptroller
Treasury Division
Dept. of Revenue
P. O. Box 110405
Juneau, AK 99811-0405
Phone : (907) 465-2350
Fax : (907) 465-2394

ARIZONA
Robert Rocha
State Comptroller
Dept. of Administration
1700 W. Washington, Rm. 290
Phoenix, AZ 85007
Phone : (602) 542-5406

ARKANSAS
Richard Weiss
Director
Dept. of Finance & Admin.
401 DFA Bldg.
1509 W. 7th St.
Little Rock, AR 77201
Phone : (501) 682-2242
Fax : (501) 682-1086

CALIFORNIA
Kathleen Connell
Controller
300 Capitol Mall, 18th Fl.
P.O. Box 942850
Sacramento, CA 94250
Phone : (916) 445-2636

COLORADO
Clifford W. Hall
State Controller
Div. of Accounts & Control
Dept. of Admininstration
1525 Sherman St., Ste. 250
Denver, CO 80203
Phone : (303) 866-3281

CONNECTICUT
Nancy Wyman
Commissioner
55 Elm St.
Hartford, CT 06106
Phone : (203) 566-5565

DELAWARE
Clifford B. Edwards
Director
Div. of Accounting
Dept. of Finance
Thomas Collins Bldg.
Dover, DE 19903
Phone : (302) 739-5454

FLORIDA
Robert F. Milligan
Comptroller
PL 09, The Capitol
Tallahassee, FL 32399-0350
Phone : (904) 488-0370
Fax : (904) 488-9818

GEORGIA
Steven N. McCoy
State Treasurer
Off. of Treasury & Fiscal Srvc
1516 West Tower
200 Piedmont Ave., SE
Atlanta, GA 30334
Phone : (404) 656-2168

HAWAII
Eugene Imai
Comptroller
Dept. of Accounting & General Srvcs.
1151 Punchbowl St., Rm. 412
Honolulu, HI 96810
Phone : (808) 586-0400
Fax : (808) 586-0707

IDAHO
J.D. Williams
State Auditor
700 W. State St., 5th Fl.
Boise, ID 83720
Phone : (208) 334-3100

ILLINOIS
Loleta A. Didrickson
Comptroller
201 State House
Springfield, IL 62706
Phone : (217) 782-6000
Fax : (217) 782-7561

INDIANA
Morris Wooden
State Auditor
Off. of the State Auditor
State House, Rm. 240
Indianapolis, IN 46204
Phone : (317) 232-3300

IOWA
Gretchen Tegeler
Director
Dept. of Mgt.
State Capitol Bldg.
Des Moines, IA 50319
Phone : (515) 281-3322
Fax : (515) 242-5897

KANSAS
Roger C. Rooker
Acting Director
Div. of Accounts & Reports
Dept. of Administration
900 SW Jackson St., Rm. 355-S
Topeka, KS 66612
Phone : (913) 296-2311
Fax : (913) 296-6841

KENTUCKY
Crit Luallen
Secretary
Finance & Admin. Cabinet
Capitol Annex, Rm. 301
Frankfort, KY 40601
Phone : (502) 564-4240

LOUISIANA
Raymond J. Laborde
Commissioner
Div. of Administration
Capitol Annex
P.O. Box 94095
Baton Rouge, LA 70804-9095
Phone : (504) 342-7000

MAINE
Carol Whitney
Controller
Bur. of Accounts & Control
Dept. of Admin. & Fin. Srvcs.
State House Station # 14
Augusta, ME 04333
Phone : (207) 626-8422

MARYLAND**
Louis L. Goldstein
Comptroller
Dept. of Budget & Fiscal Plan.
Treasury Bldg., Rm. 121
P.O. Box 466
Annapolis, MD 21404
Phone : (410) 974-3801

MASSACHUSETTS
William Kilmartin
Comptroller
Executive Off. for Administration & Finance
1 Ashburton Pl., Rm. 909
Boston, MA 02108
Phone : (617) 727-5000

MICHIGAN
Jeff Linderman
Director
Dept. of Mgt. & Budget
Office of Financial Management
Mason Bldg., 3rd Fl., Box 30026
Lansing, MI 48909
Phone : (517) 373-1010

MINNESOTA
Laura King
Commissioner
Dept. of Finance
400 Centennial Bldg.
658 Cedar St.
St. Paul, MN 55155
Phone : (612) 296-9721

MISSISSIPPI
Edward L. Ranck
Executive Director
Dept. of Finance & Admin.
P.O. Box 267
Jackson, MS 39205
Phone : (601) 359-3402

MISSOURI
James Carder
Director
Div. of Accounting
Off. of Administration
Truman Bldg., Rm. 560
P.O. Box 809
Jefferson City, MO 65102
Phone : (314) 751-2971
Fax : (314) 751-0159
E-Mail: JCARDER@MAIL.MORE.NET

MONTANA
Lois A. Menzies
Director and
Ex Officio State Treasurer
Dept. of Administration
155 Mitchell Bldg.
Helena, MT 59620
Phone : (406) 444-2032

NEBRASKA
Robert D. Luth
Administrator
Accounting Div.
Dept. of Administrative Srvcs.
1309 State Capitol, Box 94664
Lincoln, NE 68509-4664
Phone : (402) 471-2581
Fax : (402) 471-4157

NEVADA
Darrel Daines
Controller
State Capitol
Carson City, NV 89710
Phone : (702) 687-4330

NEW HAMPSHIRE
Dayle J. Carroll
Comptroller
Div. of Accounting Srvcs.
Dept. of Administrative Srvcs.
25 Capitol St., Rm. 413
Concord, NH 03301
Phone : (603) 271-3190

NEW JERSEY
Elizabeth Pugh
Director
Off. of Mgt. & Budget
Dept. of Treasury
33 W. State St., CN21
Trenton, NJ 08625
Phone : (609) 292-5258

NEW MEXICO
Michael A. Montoya
Treasurer
P.O. Box 608
Santa Fe, NM 87504
Phone : (505) 827-6400
Fax : (505) 827-6395

NEW YORK *
State Comptroller
Off. of the State Comptroller
A.E. Smith Off. Bldg., 6th Fl.
Albany, NY 12236
Phone : (518) 474-4040

NORTH CAROLINA
Ed Renfrow
State Controller
200 W. Jones St.
Raleigh, NC 27603-1380
Phone : (919) 733-0178
Fax : (919) 715-3863

NORTH DAKOTA
Rod Backman
Director
Off. of Management & Budget
State Capitol, 4th Fl.
600 E. Boulevard Ave.
Bismarck, ND 58505-0400
Phone : (701) 328-4904
Fax : (701) 328-3230

Bud Walsh
Director of Accounting
Off. of Mgt. & Budget
State Capitol, 4th Fl.
600 E. Boulevard Ave.
Bismarck, ND 58505-0400
Phone : (701) 328-2682

OHIO
J. Kenneth Blackwell
State Treasurer
State Off. Tower, 9th Fl.
30 E. Broad St.
Columbus, OH 43215
Phone : (614) 466-2057
Fax : (614) 644-7313

OKLAHOMA
Doug Enevoldsen
State Comptroller
Off. of State Finance
122 State Capitol
Oklahoma City, OK 73105
Phone : (405) 521-2141

OREGON
Jim Hill
State Treasurer
159 State Capitol
Salem, OR 97310
Phone : (503) 378-4329

PENNSYLVANIA
Harvey C. Eckert
Deputy Secretary
Comptroller Operations
Off. of the Budget
207 Finance Bldg.
Harrisburg, PA 17120
Phone : (717) 787-6496

RHODE ISLAND
Lawrence C. Franklin Jr.
State Controller
Off. of Accounts & Control
Dept. of Admin.
One Capitol Hill
Providence, RI 02908-5883
Phone : (401) 277-2271

SOUTH CAROLINA
Earle E. Morris Jr.
Comptroller General
Wade Hampton Off. Bldg.
P.O. Box 11228
Columbia, SC 29211
Phone : (803) 734-2121

SOUTH DAKOTA
Vernon L. Larson
State Auditor
500 E. Capitol Ave.
Pierre, SD 57501
Phone : (605) 773-3341
Fax : (605) 773-5929

TENNESSEE
Danny Creekmore
Chief of Accounts
Dept. of Finance & Admin.
206 John Sevier Bldg.
Nashville, TN 37243
Phone : (615) 741-0320

TEXAS
John Sharp
Comptroller
Public Accounts
P.O. Box 13528, Capitol Station
Austin, TX 78711
Phone : (512) 463-4000

UTAH
Gordon L. Crabtree
Director
Div. of Finance
Dept. of Administrative Srvcs.
2110 State Off. Bldg.
Salt Lake City, UT 84114
Phone : (801) 538-3020

VERMONT
Thomas Pelham
Commissioner
Dept. of Finance & Mgt.
Agency of Administration
109 State St.
Montpelier, VT 05602
Phone : (802) 828-2376
Fax : (802) 828-2428

VIRGINIA
William E. Landsidle
Comptroller
Dept. of Accounts
Monroe Bldg.- 2nd Floor
101 N. 14th St.
Richmond, VA 23219
Phone : (804) 225-2109
Fax : (804) 371-8587

WASHINGTON
Daniel Grimm
State Treasurer
Legislative Bldg.
P.O. Box 40200
Olympia, WA 98504-0200
Phone : (360) 753-7130

WEST VIRGINIA
Glen B. Gainer III
State Auditor
State Capitol, Rm. W-100
Charleston, WV 25305
Phone : (304) 558-2251
Fax : (304) 558-5200

WISCONSIN
William Raftery
Director
Bur. of Financial Operations
Dept. of Administration
101 E. Wilson, 8th Fl.
Madison, WI 53703
Phone : (608) 266-1694
Fax : (608) 266-7734

WYOMING
Dave Ferrari
State Auditor
State Capitol, Rm. 114
200 W. 24th St.
Cheyenne, WY 82002
Phone : (307) 777-7831

DISTRICT OF COLUMBIA
Robert Reid
Controller
Off. of Deputy Mayor for Finance
415 12th St., NW, Rm. 412
Washington, DC 20004
Phone : (202) 727-5116

AMERICAN SAMOA
Ray Pritt
Treasurer
Dept. of the Treasury
Government of American Samoa
Pago Pago, AS 96799
Phone : (684) 633-4155
Fax : (684) 633-4100

GUAM**
Wilfred G Aflague
Director
General Srvcs. Agency
Dept. of Administration
P.O. Box 884
Agana, GU 96910
Phone : (671) 475-1101

NORTHERN MARIANA ISLANDS
Maria D. Cabrera
Secretary
Dept. of Finance
P.O. Box 5234 CHRB
Saipan, MP 96950
Phone : (670) 322-9969
Fax : (670) 664-1115

PUERTO RICO
Ileana Colon Carlo
Comptroller
P.O. Box 366069
San Juan, PR 00936-6069
Phone : (809) 754-3030
Fax : (809) 751-6768

U.S. VIRGIN ISLANDS
Gwendolyn P. Adams
Commissioner
Dept. of Finance
76 Kronprindsens Gade
St. Thomas, VI 00802
Phone : (809) 774-4750
Fax : (809) 776-4028

CONSUMER AFFAIRS

Investigates and mediates consumer complaints of deceptive and fraudulent business practices.

ALASKA
James Forbes
Chief
Antitrust & Cons. Prot. Section
Dept. of Law
1031 W. Fourth Ave., Ste. 200
Anchorage, AK 99501-1994
Phone : (907) 269-5100
Fax : (907) 276-3697

ARIZONIA
Sidney K. Davis
Consumer Prot. & Anti-Trust Div.
Office of the Attorney General
1275 W. Washington
Phoenix, AZ 85007
Phone : (602) 542-3702

ARKANSAS
Winston Bryant
Attorney General
323 Center St., Ste. 200
Little Rock, AR 72201
Phone : (501) 682-2007
Fax : (501) 682-8084

CALIFORNIA
Majorie Berte
Director
Dept. of Consumer Affairs
400 R St., Rm. 1060
Sacramento, CA 95814-6213
Phone : (916) 445-4465

COLORADO
Garth Lucero
Deputy Attorney General
Consumer Protection Section
Dept. of Law
1525 Sherman St., 5th Fl.
Denver, CO 80203
Phone : (303) 866-5230

CONNECTICUT
Mark A. Shiffrin
Commissioner
Dept. of Consumer Affairs
165 Capitol Ave.
Hartford, CT 06106
Phone : (203) 566-1810

DELAWARE
Mary McDonough
Director
Div. of Consumer Affairs
Department of Justice
820 N. French St., 4th Fl.
Wilmington, DE 19801
Phone : (302) 577-3250

FLORIDA *
Director
Div. of Consumer Srvcs.
Agric. & Consumer Srvc. Dept.
Mayo Bldg.
Tallahassee, FL 32399-0800
Phone : (904) 488-2221

GEORGIA
Barry Reid
Administrator
Off. of Consumer Affairs
205 Butler St., SE, Plz.-E
Atlanta, GA 30334
Phone : (404) 656-3790

HAWAII
Russell Blair
Director
Off. of Consumer Protection
828 Fort St. Mall, Ste. 600B
Honolulu, HI 96813-4318
Phone : (808) 586-3222
Fax : (808) 586-2640

IDAHO
Alan G. Lance
Attorney General
Statehouse
Boise, ID 83720
Phone : (208) 334-2400

ILLINOIS
Jim Ryan
Attorney General
500 S. Second St.
Springfield, IL 62706
Phone : (217) 782-1090
Fax : (217) 782-1097

INDIANA
Lisa Hayes
Chief Counsel
Div. of Consumer Protection
Off. of the Attorney General
219 State House
Indianapolis, IN 46204
Phone : (317) 232-6201

IOWA
Steve St. Clair
Acting Director
Consumer Protection Div.
Off. of the Attorney General
Hoover State Off. Bldg.
Des Moines, IA 50319
Phone : (515) 281-5926

KANSAS
Theresa Nuckolls
Deputy Attorney General
Consumer Protection Div.
Off. of the Attorney General
Judicial Center, 2nd Fl.
301 W. Tenth, Judicial Ctr.
Topeka, KS 66612-1597
Phone : (913) 296-3751
Fax : (913) 296-6296

KENTUCKY
Chris Gorman
Attorney General
State Capitol, Rm. 116
Frankfort, KY 40601
Phone : (502) 564-7600

LOUISIANA
David Kimmel
Director
Public Protection Div.
Dept. of Justice
P.O. Box 94005
Baton Rouge, LA 70804-9005
Phone : (504) 342-7900

MAINE
William N. Lund
Superintendent
Bur. of Consumer Credit Protection
State House Station # 35
Augusta, ME 04333
Phone : (207) 582-8718

MARYLAND
William Leibovici
Chief
Consumer Protection Div.
Off. of the Attorney General
200 St. Paul Pl.
Baltimore, MD 21202
Phone : (410) 576-6557

MASSACHUSETTS
Priscilla H. Douglas
Secretary
Executive Off. of Consumer Affairs
1 Ashburton Pl., Rm. 1411
Boston, MA 02108
Phone : (617) 727-7755

MICHIGAN
Fredrick H. Hoffecker
Assistant in Charge
Consumer Protection Div.
Off. of Attorney General
Law Bldg., 6th Fl.
Lansing, MI 48913
Phone : (517) 335-0855

MINNESOTA
Doug Blanke
Assistant Attorney General
Consumer Div.
Off. of the Attorney General
1400 NCL Tower
St. Paul, MN 55101
Phone : (612) 296-7575

MISSISSIPPI
Tray Bobinger
Director
Consumer Protection Div.
Off. of the Attorney General
P.O. Box 220
Jackson, MS 39205
Phone : (601) 359-3835

MISSOURI
Jeremiah W. Nixon
Attorney General
Off. of the Attorney General
Supreme Court Bldg.
207 W. High St.
P.O. Box 899
Jefferson City, MO 65101
Phone : (314) 751-3321
Fax : (314) 751-0774

MONTANA
Annie Bartos
Attorney/Unit Manager
Consumer Affairs Unit
Dept. of Commerce
1424 Ninth Ave.
Helena, MT 59620
Phone : (406) 444-3553

NEBRASKA
Paul Potadle
Assistant Attorney General
Consumer Fraud Section
Off. of the Attorney General
P.O. Box 98920
Lincoln, NE 68509-4906
Phone : (402) 471-2682
Fax : (402) 471-3297

NEVADA
Patricia Morse Jarman
Commissioner
Div. of Consumer Affairs
Dept. of Business & Industry
1850 E. Sahara Ave.
Las Vegas, NV 89518
Phone : (702) 486-7352

NEW HAMPSHIRE
Jeffrey R. Howard
Attorney General
25 Capitol St.
Concord, NH 03301
Phone : (603) 271-3655

NEW JERSEY
Mark S. Herr
Director
NJ Div. of Consumer Affairs
P.O. Box 45027
Newark, NJ 07101
Phone : (201) 504-6200

NEW MEXICO
John B. Hiatt
Director
Consumer Prot. & Econ. Crimes
Off. of the Attorney General
Bataan Memorial Bldg., Rm. 236
P.O. Drawer 1508
Santa Fe, NM 87504
Phone : (505) 827-6060
Fax : (505) 827-6685

NEW YORK*
Director
Consumer Protection Bd.
Twin Towers
1 Commerce Plz.
Albany, NY 12210
Phone : (518) 474-3514

NORTH CAROLINA
Michael F. Easley
Attorney General
Dept. of Justice
2 E. Morgan St.
Raleigh, NC 27601-1497
Phone : (919) 733-7741
Fax : (919) 733-7491

NORTH DAKOTA
Tom Engelhart
Director
Consumer Fraud Div.
Off. of the Attorney General
600 E. Boulevard Ave.
Bismarck, ND 58505
Phone : (701) 328-3404
Fax : (701) 328-3535

OHIO
Robert S. Tongren
Consumers Counsel
Off. of Consumers' Counsel
77 S. High St., 15th Fl.
Columbus, OH 43266-0550
Phone : (614) 466-8574
Fax : (614) 466-9475

OKLAHOMA
John McClure
Administrator
Consumer Credit Dept.
4545 N. Lincoln Blvd., #104
Oklahoma City, OK 73105
Phone : (405) 521-3653

PENNSYLVANIA
Joseph K. Goldberg
Director
Off. of the Attorney General
Bur. of Consumer Protection
Strawberry Sq., 14th Fl.
Harrisburg, PA 17120
Phone : (717) 787-9707

RHODE ISLAND
Edwin P. Palumbo
Executive Director
Consumers' Council
100 N. Main St.
Providence, RI 02903
Phone : (401) 277-3040

SOUTH CAROLINA
Philip Porter
Administrator
Dept. of Consumer Affairs
2801 Devine St.
P.O. Box 5757
Columbia, SC 29250-5757
Phone : (803) 734-9452

SOUTH DAKOTA *
Assistant Attorney General
Div. of Consumer Affairs
Off. of the Attorney General
State Capitol
Pierre, SD 57501
Phone : (605) 773-4400

TENNESSEE
Elizabeth Owen
Director
Div. of Consumer Affairs
500 James Robertson Pkwy.
Nashville, TN 37243
Phone : (615) 741-4737
Fax : (615) 532-4994

TEXAS
Dan Morales
Attorney General
Attn: Research & Legal Support
P.O. Box 12548, Capitol Station
Austin, TX 78711-2548
Phone : (512) 463-2100

UTAH
Francine Giani
Director
Div. of Consumer Protection
Dept. of Commerce
160 E. 300 S.
Salt Lake City, UT 84114
Phone : (801) 530-7631

VERMONT
John Hafen
Chief
Public Protection Div.
Off. of the Attorney General
109 State St.
Montpelier, VT 05602
Phone : (802) 828-3171
Fax : (802) 828-2154

VIRGINIA
Betty W. Blakemore
Director
Consumer Affairs Off.
Agric. & Consumer Srvc. Dept.
1100 Bank St.
Richmond, VA 23219
Phone : (804) 786-2042

WASHINGTON
Kathleen D. Mix
Chief Deputy Attorney General
Off. of the Attorney General
P.O. Box 40100
Olympia, WA 98504-0100
Phone : (360) 753-6200

WEST VIRGINIA
Tom W. Rodd
Deputy Attorney General
Div. of Consumer Protection
Off. of the Attorney General
812 Quarrier St.
Charleston, WV 25301
Phone : (304) 558-8986

WISCONSIN
Stephen Nicks
Director
Off. of Consumer Protection
Dept. of Justice
123 W. Washington, Rm. 170
P.O. Box 7856
Madison, WI 53703
Phone : (608) 266-1852
Fax : (608) 267-2778

Patricia Allen
Administrator
Trade & Consumer Prot. Div.
Agric., Trade & Consumer Prot.
2811 Agriculture Dr.
P.O. Box 8911
Madison, WI 53708
Phone : (608) 224-4970
Fax : (608) 224-4939

WYOMING
Mark Moran
Director
Div. of Consumer Affairs
Off. of the Attorney General
State Capitol
Cheyenne, WY 82002
Phone : (307) 777-6702

DISTRICT OF COLUMBIA
Eileen Hemphill
Chief
Off. of Consumer Educ. & Info.
Cons. & Regulatory Affairs
614 H St., NW, Rm. 108
Washington, DC 20001
Phone : (202) 727-7067

Theodore Gordon
Acting Chief
Off. of Compliance
614 H St., NW, Rm. 1107
Washington, DC 20001
Phone : (202) 727-7140

AMERICAN SAMOA
Malaetasi Togafau
Attorney General
American Samoa Government
P.O. Box 7
Pago Pago, AS 96799
Phone : (684) 633-4163
Fax : (684) 633-1838

GUAM
Calvin E. Halloway
Attorney General
Off. of the Attorney General
120 W. O'Brien Dr., Ste. 2-200E
Agana, GU 96910
Phone : (671) 475-3324
Fax : (671) 472-2493

NORTHERN MARIANA ISLANDS
Elliott Sattler
Senior Counsel
Attorney General
Administration Bldg., 2nd Fl.
Capitol Hill
P.O. Box 10007
Saipan, MP 96950
Phone : (670) 322-4311
Fax : (670) 322-4320

PUERTO RICO
Ivan Ayala Cadiz
Secretary
Consumer Affairs Dept.
P.O. Box 41059, Minillas Sta.
San Juan, PR 00940-1059
Phone : (809) 721-3280

U.S. VIRGIN ISLANDS
Vera Falu
Commissioner
Dept. of Lic. & Cons. Aff.
Property & Procurement Bldg.
Sub Base Bldg. 1, Rm. 205
St. Thomas, VI 00802
Phone : (809) 774-3130
Fax : (809) 776-0675

CORPORATE RECORDS

Maintains a variety of corporate filings, records and documents.

ALABAMA
Jean Jordan
Corporate Records Supervisor
Corporation Div.
Off. of the Secretary of State
11 South Union, Rm. 207
Montgomery, AL 36104
Phone : (334) 242-5324
Fax : (334) 240-3138

ALASKA
Michael Monagle
Supervisor
Corporation Section
Dept. of Commerce & Econ. Dev.
P.O. Box 110808
Juneau, AK 99811-0808
Phone : (907) 465-2530
Fax : (907) 465-3257

ARIZONA
Renz Jennings
Commissioner
Corporation Comm.
1200 W. Washington
Phoenix, AZ 85007
Phone : (602) 542-3935

ARKANSAS
Sharon Priest
Secretary of State
256 State Capitol Bldg.
Little Rock, AR 72201
Phone : (501) 682-1010
Fax : (501) 682-3510

CALIFORNIA
Jim Clevenger
Chief
Corporate Filing Div.
Off. of Secretary of State
1230 J St.
Sacramento, CA 95814
Phone : (916) 657-5448

COLORADO
Michael Shea
Director
Div. of Commercial Recordings
Dept. of State
1560 Broadway, Ste. 200
Denver, CO 80203
Phone : (303) 894-2251

CONNECTICUT
Maria Greenslade
Assistant Deputy
Off. of Secretary of State
Commercial Recording Division
30 Trinity St.
Hartford, CT 06106
Phone : (203) 566-2448

DELAWARE
Michael Owens
Administrator
Corporation Div.
Dept. of State
Townsend Bldg.
Dover, DE 19901
Phone : (302) 739-3077
Fax : (302) 739-3815

FLORIDA
Karon Beyer
Bureau Chief
Bur. of Commercial Recording
Dept. of State
409 E. Gaines St.
Tallahassee, FL 32301
Phone : (904) 487-6900

GEORGIA
James Gullion
Director
Business Srvcs. & Regulations
Off. of Secretary of State
2 M.L. King, Jr. Dr., SE, 306
Atlanta, GA 30334
Phone : (404) 656-6478

HAWAII
Kathryn Matayoshi
Director
Dept. of Commerce & Consumer Affairs
1010 Richards St.
Honolulu, HI 96813
Phone : (808) 586-2850
Fax : (808) 586-2856

IDAHO
Pete T. Cenarrusa
Secretary of State
Statehouse, Rm. 203
Boise, ID 83720
Phone : (208) 334-2300

ILLINOIS
Philip Collins
Director of Business Services
Off. of the Secretary of State
328 Howlett Bldg.
Springfield, IL 62756
Phone : (217) 782-6961

INDIANA
Steve Rogers
Director
Corporation Section
Off. of Secretary of State
302 W. Washington, Rm. E018
Indianapolis, IN 46204
Phone : (317) 232-6587

IOWA
Allen Welsh
Corporations Director
Off. of Secretary of State
Hoover State Off. Bldg., 2nd Fl.
Des Moines, IA 50319
Phone : (515) 281-5204

KANSAS
Ron Thornburgh
Secretary of State
Corporations Division
State Capitol Bldg., 2nd Fl.
Topeka, KS 66612
Phone : (913) 296-4564
Fax : (913) 296-4570

KENTUCKY
Bob Babbage
Secretary of State
State Capitol, Rm. 150
Frankfort, KY 40601
Phone : (502) 564-3490

LOUISIANA
W. Fox McKeithen
Secretary of State
Dept. of State
P.O. Box 94125
Baton Rouge, LA 70804
Phone : (504) 342-4479

MARYLAND
Ron Wineholt
Director
Dept. of Assessments & Taxation
301 W. Preston St., Rm. 806
Baltimore, MD 21201
Phone : (410) 225-1184

MASSACHUSETTS
William F. Galvin
Secretary of the Commonwealth
State House, Rm. 337
Boston, MA 02108
Phone : (617) 727-2800
Fax : (617) 742-4722

MICHIGAN
Carl L. Tyson
Director
Corporations & Securities Bur.
Dept. of Commerce
P.O. Box 30222
Lansing, MI 48909
Phone : (517) 334-6212

MISSISSIPPI
Ray Bailey
Assistant Secretary of State
Corporations Div.
Off. of Secretary of State
P.O. Box 136
Jackson, MS 39205
Phone : (601) 359-1350

MISSOURI
Linda Oliver
Director of Corporations
Off. of Secretary of State
600 W. Main St.
P.O. Box 778
Jefferson City, MO 65102
Phone : (314) 751-3200
Fax : (314) 751-5841

MONTANA
Louise Ross
Bureau Chief
Business Srvcs. Bur.
Off. of Secretary of State
State Capitol
Helena, MT 59620
Phone : (406) 444-3665

NEBRASKA
Scott Moore
Secretary of State
P.O. Box 94608
Lincoln, NE 68509
Phone : (402) 471-2554
Fax : (402) 471-3666

NEVADA
Dean Heller
Secretary of State
Capitol Complex
Carson City, NV 89710
Phone : (702) 687-5203

NEW HAMPSHIRE
William Gardner
Secretary of State
204 State House
Concord, NH 03301
Phone : (603) 271-3242

NEW JERSEY
James Frucione
Director
Div. of Commercial Recordings
Dept. of State
820 Bear Tavern Rd., CN308
Trenton, NJ 08625
Phone : (609) 530-6400

NEW MEXICO
Pat Cleavland
Director
Dept. of Corporations
Corporation Comm.
P.O. Drawer 1269
Santa Fe, NM 87504
Phone : (505) 827-4202
Fax : (505) 827-4203

NEW YORK *
Secretary of State
Dept. of State
162 Washington Ave.
Albany, NY 12231
Phone : (518) 474-0050

NORTH CAROLINA
Billy Proctor
Director
Corporations Div.
Off. of Secretary of State
300 N. Salisbury St.
Raleigh, NC 27603-5909
Phone : (919) 733-4201
Fax : (919) 733-5172

NORTH DAKOTA
Clara Jenkins
Director
Corporation Div.
Off. of Secretary of State
600 E. Boulevard Ave.
Bismarck, ND 58505
Phone : (701) 328-4284
Fax : (701) 328-2992

OHIO
Tim Williams
Assistant Secretary of State
Off. of Secretary of State
30 E. Broad St., 14th Fl.
Columbus, OH 43266
Phone : (614) 466-3084
Fax : (614) 644-0649

OKLAHOMA
John Kennedy
Secretary of State
State Capitol, Rm. 101
Oklahoma City, OK 73105
Phone : (405) 521-3911

OREGON
Jan Sullivan
Director
Off. of Secretary of State
Public Service Bldg.
255 Capitol St., NE, Ste. 151
Salem, OR 97310
Phone : (503) 986-2205
Fax : (503) 378-4381

PENNSYLVANIA
Charles Ottaviano
Director
Corporation Bur.
Dept. of State
308 N. Off. Bldg.
Harrisburg, PA 17120
Phone : (717) 787-1379

RHODE ISLAND
Pamela Palumbo
Acting Director
Corporation Div.
Off. of Secretary of State
100 N. Main St.
Providence, RI 02903
Phone : (401) 277-3040

SOUTH CAROLINA
Jim Miles
Secretary of State
Wade Hampton Bldg.
P.O. Box 11350
Columbia, SC 29211
Phone : (803) 734-2170

TENNESSEE
Brook Thompson
Director of Services
Div. of Corporations
Off. of Secretary of State
James K. Polk Bldg.
Nashville, TN 37243
Phone : (615) 741-0584

TEXAS
Lorna Wassdorf
Director
Statutory Filings Division
Off. of Secretary of State
P.O. Box 13697, Capitol Station
Austin, TX 78711
Phone : (512) 466-3570

UTAH
Korla T. Woods
Director
Div. of Corporations
Dept. of Commerce
160 E. 300 S.
Salt Lake City, UT 84111
Phone : (801) 530-6027

VERMONT
Betty Poulin
Director
Corporations Div.
Off. of the Secretary of State
109 State St.
Montpelier, VT 05609
Phone : (802) 828-2386

VIRGINIA
Preston C. Shannon
Chair
State Corporation Commission
Tyler Bldg,
1300 E. Main St.
Richmond, VA 23219
Phone : (804) 371-9608
Fax : (804) 371-9376

WASHINGTON
Linda MacKintosh
Director
Corp., Trademark, & Ltd. Part.
Off. of Secretary of State
P.O. Box 40220
Olympia, WA 98504-0220
Phone : (360) 753-7121

WEST VIRGINIA
Ken Hechler
Secretary of State
State Capitol, Rm. W-157K
1900 Kanawha Blvd., E.
Charleston, WV 25305
Phone : (304) 558-6000

WISCONSIN
Robert J. Ritger
Administrator
Corporations Div.
Off. of Secretary of State
30 W Mifflin, 9th & 10th Fl.
P.O. Box 7846
Madison, WI 53703
Phone : (608) 266-3590
Fax : (608) 267-6813

WYOMING
Jeanne Sawyer
Director
Corporations Div.
Off. of Secretary of State
State Capitol
Cheyenne, WY 82002
Phone : (307) 777-5334

DISTRICT OF COLUMBIA
Vandy Jamison
Program Manager
Corporations Div.
Dept. of Consumer & Reg. Aff.
614 H St., NW, Rm. 407
Washington, DC 20009
Phone : (202) 727-7278

GUAM
Joseph T. Duenas
Director
Dept. of Revenue & Taxation
378 Chalan San Antonio
Tamuning, GU 96911
Phone : (671) 647-5107
Fax : (671) 632-1040

NORTHERN MARIANA ISLANDS
Soledad B. Sasamoto
Registrar of Corporations
Off. of Attorney General
Saipan, MP 96950
Phone : (670) 322-4311
Fax : (670) 322-4320

PUERTO RICO
Baltasar C. Del Rio
Secretary of State
Dept. of State
P.O. Box 3271
San Juan, PR 00904
Phone : (809) 722-2121
Fax : (809) 725-7303

U.S. VIRGIN ISLANDS
Kenneth E. Mapp
Lt. Governor
#18 Kongens Gade
St. Thomas, VI 00802
Phone : (809) 774-2991
Fax : (809) 774-6953

CORRECTIONS

Manages the state's correctional system.

ALABAMA
Ron Jones
Commissioner
Dept. of Corrections
50 N. Ripley St.
Montgomery, AL 36130
Phone : (334) 242-9400
Fax : (334) 242-9399

ALASKA
Margaret Pugh
Commissioner
Dept. of Corrections
240 Main St., Ste. 700
Juneau, AK 99801
Phone : (907) 465-4652
Fax : (907) 465-3390

ARIZONA
Samuel Lewis
Director
Dept. of Corrections
1601 W. Jefferson
Phoenix, AZ 85007
Phone : (602) 542-5536

ARKANSAS
Larry Norris
Director
Dept. of Corrections
P.O. Box 8707
Pine Bluff, AR 71611
Phone : (501) 247-1800
Fax : (501) 247-3700

CALIFORNIA
Joe Sandoval
Secretary
Youth & Adult
Corrections Agency
1100 11th St.
Sacramento, CA 95814
Phone : (916) 323-6001

COLORADO
Aristedes W. Zavares
Executive Director
Dept. of Corrections
2862 S. Circle Dr., Ste. 400
Colorado Springs, CO
80906
Phone : (303) 579-9580
Fax : (303) 540-4700

CONNECTICUT
John J. Armstrong
Commissioner
Dept. of Corrections
340 Capitol Ave.
Hartford, CT 06106
Phone : (203) 566-4457

DELAWARE
Robert J. Watson
Commissioner
Dept. of Corrections
Central Admin. Bldg.
80 Monrovia Ave.
Smyrna, DE 19977
Phone : (302) 739-5601
Fax : (302) 653-2892

FLORIDA
Harry Singletary
Secretary
Dept. of Corrections
2601 Blair Stone Rd.
Tallahassee, FL 32399-2500
Phone : (904) 488-7480
Fax : (904) 922-2848

GEORGIA
Allen L. Ault
Commissioner
Dept. of Corrections
2 M.L. King, Jr., Dr.,
Rm. 756
Atlanta, GA 30334
Phone : (404) 656-0002

HAWAII
George Ikanon
Director
Dept. of Public Safety
Div. of Community
Corrections
919 Ala Moana Blvd.,
4th Fl.
Honolulu, HI 96814
Phone : (808) 587-1288
Fax : (808) 587-1282

IDAHO
James C. Spalding
Director
Dept. of Corrections
500 S. 10th St.
Boise, ID 83702
Phone : (208) 334-2318

ILLINOIS
Odie Washington
Director
Dept. of Corrections
P.O. Box 19277
Springfield, IL 62794-9277
Phone : (217) 522-2666
Fax : (217) 522-8719

INDIANA
H. Christian DeBruyn
Commissioner
Dept. of Corrections
IGC-South, Rm. E334
Indianapolis, IN 46204
Phone : (317) 232-5569

IOWA
Sally Chandler Halford
Director
Dept. of Corrections
Capitol Annex
523 E. 12th St.
Des Moines, IA 50319
Phone : (515) 281-4811
Fax : (515) 281-7345

KANSAS
Charles Simmons
Secretary
Dept. of Corrections
Landon State Off. Bldg.
900 SW Jackson, 4th Fl.
Topeka, KS 66612
Phone : (913) 296-3317
Fax : (913) 296-0014

KENTUCKY
Jack C. Lewis
Commissioner
Dept. of Corrections
Justice Cabinet
State Off. Bldg.
Frankfort, KY 40601
Phone : (502) 564-4726

LOUISIANA
Richard Stalder
Secretary
Dept. of Public Safety &
Corrections
P.O. Box 94304
Baton Rouge, LA 70804
Phone : (504) 342-6741

MAINE
Joseph Lehamn
Commissioner
Dept. of Corrections
#111 State House Station
Augusta, ME 04333-0111
Phone : (207) 287-4360

MARYLAND
Richard A. Lanham
Commissioner
Div. of Corrections
6776 Reisterstown Rd.
Baltimore, MD 21215
Phone : (410) 764-4184

MASSACHUSETTS
Larry E. Dubois
Commissioner
Dept. of Corrections
Executive Off. of Public
Safety
100 Cambridge St.
Boston, MA 02202
Phone : (617) 727-3301

MICHIGAN
Kenneth McGinnis
Director
Dept. of Corrections
Mason Bldg., 3rd Fl.
Lansing, MI 48909
Phone : (517) 373-0720
Fax : (517) 373-3882

MINNESOTA
Frank W. Wood
Commissioner
Dept. of Corrections
300 Bigelow Bldg.
450 N. Syndicate St.
St. Paul, MN 55104
Phone : (612) 642-0282

MISSISSIPPI
Steve Puckett
Commissioner
Dept. of Corrections
723 N. President St.
Jackson, MS 39202
Phone : (601) 354-6454

MISSOURI
Dora Schriro
Director
Dept. of Corrections
2729 Plaza Dr.
P.O. Box 236
Jefferson City, MO 65102
Phone : (314) 751-2389
Fax : (314) 751-4099

MONTANA
Rick Day
Director
Dept. of Corrections & Human Srvcs.
1539 11th Ave.
Helena, MT 59620
Phone : (406) 444-3930

NEBRASKA
Harold Clarke
Director
Dept. of Correctional Services
W. Van Dorn & Folsom St.
P.O. Box 94661
Lincoln, NE 68509
Phone : (402) 471-2654
Fax : (402) 479-5119

NEVADA
Bob Bayer
Director
Dept. of Prisons
P.O. Box 7011
Carson City, NV 89702
Phone : (702) 887-3285
Fax : (702) 687-6715

NEW HAMPSHIRE
Paul Brodeur
Commissioner
Dept. of Corrections
P.O. Box 769
Concord, NH 03302
Phone : (603) 271-5600

NEW JERSEY
William H. Fauver
Commissioner
Dept. of Corrections
Whittlesey Rd., CN 863
Trenton, NJ 08625
Phone : (609) 292-4036

NEW MEXICO
Karl L. Sannicks
Secretary
Dept. of Corrections
P.O. Box 27116
Santa Fe, NM 87502-0116
Phone : (505) 827-8709
Fax : (505) 827-8801

NEW YORK *
Commissioner
Dept. of Correctional Services
Correctional Services Bldg.
State Campus
Albany, NY 12226
Phone : (518) 457-8134

NORTH CAROLINA
Franklin Freeman
Secretary
Dept. of Correction
214 W. Jones St.
Raleigh, NC 27603-1337
Phone : (919) 733-4926
Fax : (919) 733-4790

NORTH DAKOTA
Timothy Schuetzle
Warden
State Penitentiary
P.O. Box 5521
Bismarck, ND 58502
Phone : (701) 328-6100
Fax : (701) 328-6651

OHIO
Reginald A. Wilkinson
Director
Dept. of Rehabilitation & Corrections
1050 Freeway Dr., N.
Columbus, OH 43229
Phone : (614) 752-1164
Fax : (614) 752-1171

OKLAHOMA
Larry Fields
Director
Dept. of Corrections
3400 N. Eastern Ave.
Oklahoma City, OK 73111
Phone : (405) 427-6511

OREGON
John Foote
Director
Dept. of Corrections
2575 Center St., NE
Salem, OR 97310
Phone : (503) 945-0920
Fax : (503) 373-1173

PENNSYLVANIA
Martin Horn
Commissioner
Dept. of Corrections
P.O. Box 598
Camp Hill, PA 17011
Phone : (717) 975-4860

RHODE ISLAND
George A. Vose Jr.
Director
Dept. of Corrections
75 Howard Ave.
Cranston, RI 02920
Phone : (401) 464-2611

SOUTH CAROLINA
Michael Moore
Director
Dept. of Corrections
4444 Broad River Rd.
P.O. Box 21787
Columbia, SC 29221
Phone : (803) 896-8500

SOUTH DAKOTA
Jeff Bloomberg
Secretary
Dept. of Corrections
115 E. Dakota Ave.
Pierre, SD 57501
Phone : (605) 773-3478

TENNESSEE
Donal Campbell
Commissioner
Dept. of Corrections
Rachel Jackson Bldg., 4th Fl.
320 Sixth Ave., N.
Nashville, TN 37243
Phone : (615) 741-2071
Fax : (615) 532-8281

TEXAS
James A. Collins
Director
Dept. of Criminal Justice
P.O. Box 99
Huntsville, TX 77340
Phone : (409) 294-2159

UTAH
Lane McCotter
Executive Director
Dept. of Corrections
6100 S. 300 E.
Murray, UT 84107
Phone : (801) 265-5500

VERMONT
John Gorczyk
Commissioner
Dept. of Corrections
Agency of Human Services
103 S. Main St.
Waterbury, VT 05671
Phone : (802) 241-2442
Fax : (802) 241-2565

VIRGINIA
Ronald J. Angelone
Director
Dept. of Corrections
6900 Atmore Dr.
Richmond, VA 23261
Phone : (804) 674-3119
Fax : (804) 674-3509

WASHINGTON
Chase Riveland
Secretary
Dept. of Corrections
410 Capitol Center Bldg.
P.O. Box 41100
Olympia, WA 98504
Phone : (360) 753-1573

WEST VIRGINIA
Nicholas Hun
Commissioner
Div. of Corrections
112 California Ave.
Charleston, WV 25305
Phone : (304) 558-2036

WISCONSIN
Michael J. Sullivan
Secretary
Dept. of Corrections
149 E. Wilson, Rm. 1050
Madison, WI 53703
Phone : (608) 266-2471
Fax : (608) 267-3661

WYOMING
Judy Uphoff
Director
Dept. of Corrections
Herschler Bldg.
Cheyenne, WY 82002
Phone : (307) 777-7405

DISTRICT OF COLUMBIA
Maragaret Moore
Director
Dept. of Corrections
1923 Vermont Ave., NW
Washington, DC 20001
Phone : (202) 673-7316

AMERICAN SAMOA
Fonoti D. Jessop
Commissioner
Dept. of Public Safety
American Samoa Government
Pago Pago, AS 96799
Phone : (684) 633-1111
Fax : (684) 633-5111

GUAM**
Robert Klitzkie
Director
Dept. of Corrections
P.O. Box 3236
Agana, GU 96910
Phone : (671) 734-2458

NORTHERN MARIANA ISLANDS
Jose San Nicolas
Director
Corrections Div.
Dept. of Public Safety
Off. of the Governor
Saipan, MP 96950
Phone : (670) 234-8534
Fax : (670) 234-8531

PUERTO RICO
Zoraida Buxo
Secretary
Department of Correction and Rehab.
P.O. Box 71308
San Juan, PR 00902
Phone : (809) 783-0075
Fax : (809) 792-7677

U.S. VIRGIN ISLANDS
Alva A. Swan Esq.
Attorney General
Dept. of Justice
GERS Complex
48B-50C Kronprindsen Gade
St. Thomas, VI 00802
Phone : (809) 774-5666
Fax : (809) 774-9710

COURT ADMINISTRATION

Performs administrative duties for the state court of last resort.

ALABAMA
Oliver Gilmore
Administrator
Administrative Off. of the Courts
300 Dexter
Montgomery, AL 36130
Phone : (334) 242-4609
Fax : (334) 242-0588

ALASKA
Arthur H. Snowden II
Administrative Director
Court System
303 K St.
Anchorage, AK 99501-2084
Phone : (907) 264-0547
Fax : (907) 276-6985

ARIZONA
David K. Byers
Director
Admin. Off. of the Court
Supreme Court
1501 W. Washington
Phoenix, AZ 85007
Phone : (602) 542-9301

ARKANSAS
James D. Gingerich
Executive Secretary
Judicial Dept.
Justice Bldg.
Little Rock, AR 72201
Phone : (501) 376-6655
Fax : (501) 376-3520

CALIFORNIA
William C. Vickrey
Directory
Admin. Off. of the Courts
Judicial Council
S. Tower, 4th Fl., 303 Second
San Francisco, CA 94107
Phone : (415) 396-9115

COLORADO
Steven V. Berson
State Court Administrator
1301 Pennsylvania, Ste. 300
Denver, CO 80203
Phone : (303) 837-3668
Fax : (303) 831-1814

CONNECTICUT
Aaron Ment
Chief Court Admininstrator
Off. of Chief Court Administrator
Drawer N, Station A
Hartford, CT 06106
Phone : (203) 566-4461

DELAWARE
Lowell L. Groundland
Director of Administration
Court System
820 N. French St., 11th Fl.
Wilmington, DE 19801
Phone : (302) 577-2480
Fax : (302) 577-3139

FLORIDA
Ken Palmer
State Courts Administrator
Supreme Court
Supreme Court Bldg.
500 S. Duval St.
Tallahassee, FL 32399-1927
Phone : (904) 922-5081

GEORGIA
Robert L. Doss Jr.
Director
Admin. Office of the Courts
244 Washington St., Ste. 550
Atlanta, GA 30334
Phone : (404) 656-5171

HAWAII
Clyde Namuo
Acting Administrative Director
Circuit Court
P.O. Box 2560
Honolulu, HI 96804
Phone : (808) 539-4910

IDAHO
Patricia Tobias
Director
Admin. Off. of the Courts
Supreme Court
451 W. State St.
Boise, ID 83720
Phone : (208) 334-2246

ILLINOIS
Robert E. Davison
Director
Admin. Off. of the Courts
840 S. Spring
Springfield, IL 62704
Phone : (217) 785-2125

INDIANA
Bruce A. Kotzan
Executive Director
State Ct. Admin.
115 W. Washington St., Ste. 1080
Indianapolis, IN 46204-1080
Phone : (317) 232-2542

IOWA
William J. O'Brien
State Court Administrator
Judicial Dept.
State Capitol Bldg.
Des Moines, IA 50319
Phone : (515) 281-5241

KANSAS
Howard Schwartz
Judicial Administrator
Supreme Court
Kansas Judicial Center
301 W. Tenth
Topeka, KS 66612-1507
Phone : (913) 296-4873

KENTUCKY
Don Cetrulo
Director
Adm. Office of the Courts
100 Millcreek Park
Frankfort, KY 40601-9230
Phone : (502) 564-2350

LOUISIANA
Hugh M. Collins
Judicial Administrator
Supreme Court
301 Loyola Ave.
New Orleans, LA 70112-1887
Phone : (504) 568-5747

MAINE
James T. Glessner
Administrator
Admin. Off. of the Courts
Judicial Dept.
P.O. Box 4820
Portland, ME 04112
Phone : (207) 822-0793

MARYLAND
George B. Riggin Jr.
Administrator
Admin. Off. of the Courts
361 Rowe Blvd.
Annapolis, MD 21401
Phone : (410) 974-2141

MASSACHUSETTS
Arthur M. Mason
Chief Administrative Justice
Off. of the Chief Admin. Justice
2 Centre Plz., 5th Fl.
Boston, MA 02108
Phone : (617) 727-8383

MICHIGAN
Marilyn Hall
Administrator
State Court Admn. Off.
Supreme Court
P.O. Box 30048
Lansing, MI 48909
Phone : (517) 373-0130

MINNESOTA
Sue K. Dosal
Administrator
Off. of State Court Administrator
135 Minnesota Judicial Ctr.
St. Paul, MN 55155-6102
Phone : (612) 296-2474

MISSISSIPPI
Amy D. Whitten
Court Administrator
Supreme Court
P.O. Box 117
Jackson, MS 39205
Phone : (601) 359-3697

MISSOURI
Ronald L. Larkin
State Court Administrator
Off. of State Courts Administrator
1105R Southwest Blvd.
P.O. Box 104480
Jefferson City, MO 65110-4480
Phone : (314) 751-3585
Fax : (314) 751-5540

MONTANA
Patrick A. Chenovick
Administrator
Court Administration
Supreme Court
Justice Bldg., Rm. 315
Helena, MT 59620
Phone : (406) 444-2621

NEBRASKA
Joe C. Steele
Administrator
Off. of Ct. Administrator
State Capitol, Rm. 1214
P.O. Box 98910
Lincoln, NE 68509-8910
Phone : (402) 471-3730
Fax : (402) 471-2197

NEVADA
Don J. Mello
Director
Adm. Off. of the Cts.
Capitol Complex
Carson City, NV 89710
Phone : (702) 687-5076

NEW HAMPSHIRE
James F. Lynch
Director
Administrative Services
Off. of the Court
Supreme Court Bldg.
Concord, NH 03301
Phone : (603) 271-2521

NEW JERSEY
Robert D. Lipscher
Director
Adm. Off. of the Courts
Judiciary Dept.
Hughes Justice Complex, CN037
Trenton, NJ 08625
Phone : (609) 984-0275

NEW MEXICO
Deborah Kanter
Director
Admin. Off. of the Courts
Supreme Court Bldg., Rm. 25
Santa Fe, NM 87503
Phone : (505) 827-4800
Fax : (505) 827-4824

NEW YORK *
Chief Administrator
Off. of Court Admin.
Agency Bldg. 4, 20th Fl.
Empire State Plz.
Albany, NY 12223
Phone : (518) 473-6087

NORTH CAROLINA
James C. Drennan
Director
Adm. Off. of the Courts
2 W. Morgan St.
P.O. Box 2448
Raleigh, NC 27601-1400
Phone : (919) 733-7107
Fax : (919) 715-5779

NORTH DAKOTA
Keithe E. Nelson
Court Administrator
Supreme Court
State Capitol, Judicial Wing
600 E. Boulevard Ave.
Bismarck, ND 58505-0530
Phone : (701) 328-2221
Fax : (701) 328-4480

OHIO
Stephan W. Stover
Administrative Director
Supreme Court
State Off. Tower
30 E. Broad St.
Columbus, OH 43266-0419
Phone : (614) 466-2653
Fax : (614) 752-8736

OKLAHOMA
Howard W. Conyers
Administrative Director
Adm. Off. of the Courts
107 State Capitol
Oklahoma City, OK 73105
Phone : (405) 521-2318

OREGON
R. William Linden Jr.
Administrator
Off. of Court Administrator
Supreme Court Bldg.
1163 State St.
Salem, OR 97310
Phone : (503) 378-6046

PENNSYLVANIA
Nancy Sobolevitch
Administrator
Adm. Off. of the Courts
1414 Three Penn Ctr. Plz.
Philadelphia, PA 19102
Phone : (215) 560-6337

SOUTH CAROLINA
George Markert
Director
Court Admin.
P.O. Box 50447
Columbia, SC 29250
Phone : (803) 734-1800

SOUTH DAKOTA
Mike Buenger
Administrator
Supreme Court
Unified Judicial System
500 E. Capitol Ave.
Pierre, SD 57501
Phone : (605) 773-3474

TENNESSEE
Charlie Ferrell
Director
Adm. Off. of the Courts
Supreme Court
Nashville City Ctr.
Nashville, TN 37243
Phone : (615) 741-2687

TEXAS
C. Raymond Judice
Administrative Director
State Off. of Court Admin.
P.O. Box 12066
Austin, TX 78711-2066
Phone : (512) 463-1625

UTAH
Ronald Gibson
Administrator
Off. of Court Administrator
230 S. 500 E., # 300
Salt Lake City, UT 84102-2018
Phone : (801) 578-3807

VERMONT
Tom Lehner
Court Administrator & Clerk
Off. of Supreme Court Administrator
111 State St.
Montpelier, VT 05602
Phone : (802) 828-3276
Fax : (802) 828-3457

VIRGINIA
Robert N. Baldwin
Executive Secretary
Supreme Court
100 N. Ninth St., 3rd Fl.
Richmond, VA 23219
Phone : (804) 786-6455

WASHINGTON
Mary McQueen
Administrator for the Courts
P.O. Box 41170
Olympia, WA 98504-1170
Phone : (360) 753-3365

WEST VIRGINIA
Ted Philyaw
Court Administrator
Supreme Court of Appeals
State Capitol, Rm. E-400
Charleston, WV 25305
Phone : (304) 558-0145

WISCONSIN
J. Denis Moran
Director
State Courts
Supreme Court
213 Northeast, State Capitol
P.O. Box 1688
Madison, WI 53702
Phone : (608) 266-6828
Fax : (608) 267-0980

WYOMING
Robert L. Duncan
Court Coordinator
Supreme Court
Supreme Court Bldg.
Cheyenne, WY 82002
Phone : (307) 777-7581

DISTRICT OF COLUMBIA
Ulysses B. Hammond
Executive Officer
D.C. Courts
500 Indiana Ave., N.W., Rm. 1500
Washington, DC 20001
Phone : (202) 879-1700

AMERICAN SAMOA
Eliu Paopao
Administrator
High Court of American Samoa
Pago Pago, AS 96799
Phone : (684) 633-4131
Fax : (684) 633-1318

NORTHERN MARIANA ISLANDS
Margarita M. Palacios
Court Administrator
Commonwealth Superior Court
Civil Center
Saipan, MP 96950
Phone : (670) 234-6401
Fax : (670) 234-8010

PUERTO RICO
Mercedes M. Bauermeister
Admin. Director of the Courts
Off. of Courts Admin.
P.O. Box 190917
San Juan, PR 00919-0917
Phone : (809) 763-3358
Fax : (809) 250-7448

U.S. VIRGIN ISLANDS
Orrin Arnold
Clerk
U.S. District Court
2 & 3 King St.
Christiansted
St. Croix, VI 00802
Phone : (809) 773-1130

CRIME VICTIMS COMPENSATION

Provides compensation to victims of crime.

ALABAMA
Anita Armstrong-Drummond
Director
Victims of Crime Compensation
645 S. McDonough
Montgomery, AL 36130
Phone : (334) 242-4007
Fax : (334) 240-3328

ALASKA
Nola Capp
Administrator
Violent Crime Compensation Bd.
Dept. of Public Safety
P.O. Box 111200
Juneau, AK 99811-1200
Phone : (907) 465-3040
Fax : (907) 465-2379

ARKANSAS
Ginger Bailey
Deputy Director
Outreach Div.
Off. of Attorney General
323 Center St., Ste. 200
Little Rock, AR 72201
Phone : (501) 682-2007
Fax : (501) 682-8084

CALIFORNIA
Austin Eaton
Executive Officer
State Bd. of Control
P.O. Box 48
Sacramento, CA 95812-0648
Phone : (916) 323-3432

COLORADO
Bob Bush
State Victims Compensation Coordina
Div. of Criminal Justice
Dept. of Public Safety
700 Kipling St., #1000
Lakewood, CO 80215
Phone : (303) 239-4402
Fax : (303) 239-4491

CONNECTICUT
Carol Watkins
Administrator
Off. of Victim Services
1155 Silas Deane Hwy.
Wethersfield, CT 06109
Phone : (203) 529-3089

DELAWARE
Leah Betts
Chairman
Violent Crime Compensation Bd.
1500 E. Newport Pk., Ste. 10
Wilmington, DE 19802
Phone : (302) 995-8383

FLORIDA
Wanda Jackson
Chief
Bur. of Compensation
Dept. of Legal Affairs
The Capitol, PL01
Tallahassee, FL 32399
Phone : (904) 488-0848

GEORGIA
Patricia DuBose
Director
Crime Victims Compensation Bd.
503 Oak Pl.
Atlanta, GA 30349
Phone : (404) 559-4949

HAWAII
Estra Quilausing
Administrator
Criminal Injuries Comp. Comm.
Dept. of Public Safety
335 Merchant St., Rm. 244
Honolulu, HI 96813
Phone : (808) 587-1143
Fax : (808) 587-1146

IDAHO
Bill von Tagen
Special Assistant
Legislative & Public Aff. Div.
Off. of Attorney General
Statehouse
Boise, ID 83720
Phone : (208) 334-2400

ILLINOIS
Matthew Finnell
Court Administrator
Court of Claims
630 S. College
Springfield, IL 62701
Phone : (217) 782-7101

INDIANA
Rogelio Dominquez
Director
Violent Crime Compensation Div.
Workers' Compensation Bd.
402 W. Washington St., Rm. W196
Indianapolis, IN 46204
Phone : (317) 232-3808

IOWA
Marti Anderson
Administrator
Crime Victim Assistance
Off. of Attorney General
Hoover State Off. Bldg.
Des Moines, IA 50319
Phone : (515) 281-5044

KANSAS
Frank Henderson Jr.
Executive Director
Crime Victims Compensation Board
117 W. 10th St.
Topeka, KS 66612
Phone : (913) 296-2359

KENTUCKY
Jackie Howell
Executive Director
Crime Victims Compensation Bd.
Public Protection & Reg. Cab.
115 Myrtle Ave.
Frankfort, KY 40601
Phone : (502) 564-2290

LOUISIANA
Richard Ieyoub Jr.
Attorney General
Dept. of Justice
P.O. Box 94005
Baton Rouge, LA 70804
Phone : (504) 342-7013

MASSACHUSETTS
Heidi Urich
Executive Director
Victim Witness Assistance Bd.
Off. for Victim Assistance
100 Cambridge St., Rm. 1104
Boston, MA 02202
Phone : (617) 727-5200
Fax : (617) 727-6552

MICHIGAN
Michael J. Fullwood
Administrator
Crime Victims Compensation Bd.
Dept. of Mgt. & Budget
P.O. Box 30026
Lansing, MI 48909
Phone : (517) 373-7373

MINNESOTA
Michael Jordan
Commissioner
Dept. of Public Safety
211 Transportation Bldg.
395 John Ireland Blvd.
St. Paul, MN 55155
Phone : (612) 266-6642

MISSISSIPPI
Sandra Morrison
Director
Crime Victims Compensation
Dept. of Finance & Admin.
P.O. Box 267
Jackson, MS 39205
Phone : (601) 359-6766

MISSOURI
Sandy Wright
Program Manager
Crime Victims Compensation
Dept. of Labor & Ind. Rel.
3315 W. Truman
P.O. Box 58
Jefferson City, MO 65102
Phone : (314) 526-6006
Fax : (314) 526-4940

MONTANA *
Program Manager
Crime Victims Unit
Dept. of Justice
303 N. Roberts
Helena, MT 59620
Phone : (406) 444-3653

NEBRASKA
Alrtis Curtis
Executive Director
Comm. on Law Enforcement & Criminal Justice
P.O. Box 94946
Lincoln, NE 68509
Phone : (402) 471-2194
Fax : (402) 471-2837

NEVADA
Brian Nix
Coordinator
Victims of Crime Program
Dept. of Admin.
2770 Maryland Pky., Ste. 112
Las Vegas, NV 89109
Phone : (702) 486-6492

NEW HAMPSHIRE
Sandra Matheson
Director
Victim Witness Program
25 Capitol St.
Concord, NH 03301
Phone : (603) 271-3671

NEW JERSEY
Jacob Toparek
Chairman
Violent Crimes Compensation Bd.
Dept. of Law & Public Safety
60 Park Pl.
Newark, NJ 07102
Phone : (201) 648-2107

NEW MEXICO
Larry Tackman
Director
Crime Victims Reparation Comm.
8100 Mountain Rd., N.E., Ste. 106
Albuquerque, NM 87110
Phone : (505) 841-9432
Fax : (505) 841-9437

NEW YORK *
Chair
Crime Victims Bd.
270 Broadway, Rm. 200
New York, NY 10007
Phone : (212) 417-5133

NORTH CAROLINA
Gary Eichelberger
Director
Victim & Justice Srvcs.
Dept. of Crime Cont. & Public Safety
512 N. Salisbury St.
Raleigh, NC 27604-1159
Phone : (919) 733-7974
Fax : (919) 715-4209

NORTH DAKOTA
Paul Coughlin
Administrator
Crime Victims Reparations
Dept. of Corrections & Rehab.
P.O. Box 5521
Bismarck, ND 58502
Phone : (701) 328-6390
Fax : (701) 328-6651

OHIO
Mark Zemba
Acting Section Chief
Crime Victim Services
Office of Attorney General
65 E. State 8th
Columbus, OH 43215
Fax : (614) 752-2732

OKLAHOMA
Charles W. Wood
Administrator
Crime Victims Compensation Bd.
2200 Classen Blvd., Ste. 1800
Oklahoma City, OK 73106
Phone : (405) 521-5811

OREGON
Gerri Badden
Special Compensation Section
Dept. of Justice
100 Justice Bldg.
Salem, OR 97310
Phone : (503) 378-5348

PENNSYLVANIA
Mary Ann McManus
Chairman
Crime Victims Compensation Bd.
333 Market St., Lobby Level
Harrisburg, PA 17120
Phone : (717) 783-5153

RHODE ISLAND
Elaine Rendine
Director
Victim Witness Assistance
Off. of the Attorney General
72 Pine St.
Providence, RI 02903
Phone : (401) 274-4400

SOUTH CAROLINA
J. Philip Land
Director
Div. of Victims Assistance
Off. of the Governor
800 Dutch Sq. Blvd., Ste. 160
Columbia, SC 29210
Phone : (803) 737-8125

SOUTH DAKOTA
Jeff Bloomberg
Secretary
Dept. of Corrections
115 E. Dakota Ave.
Pierre, SD 57501
Phone : (605) 773-3478

TENNESSEE
Stephen D. Adams
State Treasurer
State Capitol
Nashville, TN 37243
Phone : (615) 741-2957
Fax : (615) 741-7328

TEXAS
Karen Kalergis
Director
Crime Victims Clearinghouse
Off. of the Governor
P.O. Box 12428
Austin, TX 78711
Phone : (512) 463-1886

VERMONT
Patricia Hayes
Executive Director
Center for Crime Victims
P.O. Box 991
Montpelier, VT 05601-0991
Phone : (802) 828-3374
Fax : (802) 828-3389

VIRGINIA
Bruce C. Morris
Director
Dept. of Criminal Justice Srvcs.
805 E. Broad St.
Richmond, VA 23219
Phone : (804) 786-8718
Fax : (804) 786-0588

WASHINGTON
Frank Luck
Assistant Director
Empl. Stds., App. & Crime Vic.
Dept. of Labor & Industries
P.O. Box 44000
Olympia, WA 98504-4000
Phone : (360) 902-5494

WEST VIRGINIA
Darrell V. McGraw Jr.
Attorney General
Bldg. 1, Rm. E-26
State Capitol Complex
Charleston, WV 25305
Phone : (304) 558-2021

WISCONSIN
Carol Latham
Executive Director
Crime Victims Srvcs.
Dept. of Justice
222 State St., 3rd Fl.
Madison, WI 53703
Phone : (608) 266-6470
Fax : (608) 264-6368

WYOMING
Sylvia Bagdonas
Program Manager
Crime Victims Compensation
Off. of Attorney General
Barrett Bldg.
Cheyenne, WY 82002
Phone : (307) 635-4050

DISTRICT OF COLUMBIA
Joan Watson
Chief
Crime Victims Compensation
1200 Upshur St., N.W.
Washington, DC 20011
Phone : (202) 724-2345

U.S. VIRGIN ISLANDS
Catherine Mills
Commissioner
Dept. of Human Srvcs.
Knud Hansen Complex, Bldg. A
1303 Hospital Ground
St. Thomas, VI 00802
Phone : (809) 774-0930
Fax : (809) 774-3466

CRIMINAL JUSTICE DATA

Responsible for storage and retrieval of criminal justice data.

ALABAMA
Larry Wright
Director
Criminal Justice Info. Ctr.
770 Washington Ave.
Montgomery, AL 36130
Phone : (334) 242-4900
Fax : (334) 242-0577

ARIZONA
Richard G. Carlson
Assistant Director
Service Bureau
Dept. of Public Safety
2102 W. Encanto
Phoenix, AZ 85005-6638
Phone : (602) 223-2229

ARKANSAS
David Eberdt
Director
Crime Information Ctr.
1 Capitol Mall, Rm. 4D-200
Little Rock, AR 72201
Phone : (501) 682-2222
Fax : (501) 682-7444

CALIFORNIA
Jack Scheidegger
Chief
Criminal Identification
Dept. of Justice
4949 Broadway
Sacramento, CA 95820
Phone : (916) 227-3844

COLORADO
Scott Hromas
Director
Planning & Analysis Div.
Dept. of Corrections
2862 South Cr., Ste. 400
Colorado Spring, CO 80906
Phone : (719) 579-9580

CONNECTICUT
Thomas A. Siconolfi
Director
Justice Planning Unit
Off. of Policy & Mgt.
80 Washington St.
Hartford, CT 06106
Phone : (203) 566-3020

DELAWARE
Thomas J. Quinn
Executive Director
Criminal Justice Planning Comm.
820 N. French St.
Wilmington, DE 19801
Phone : (302) 577-3431

FLORIDA
James D. Sewell
Director
Criminal Justice Information
Dept. of Law Enforcement
P.O. Box 1489
Tallahassee, FL 32302
Phone : (904) 488-3961

GEORGIA
Terry Norris
Director
Criminal Justice Coordination Council
503 Oak Pl., #540
Atlanta, GA 30349
Phone : (404) 559-4949

HAWAII
Liane M. Moriyama
Acting Administrator
Criminal Justice Data Ctr.
Dept. of Attorney General
465 S. King St.
Honolulu, HI 96813
Phone : (808) 587-3100

IDAHO
A.D. Jones
Chief
Bur. of Criminal Identification
Dept. of Law Enforcement
P.O. Box 700
Meridian, ID 83680-0700
Phone : (208) 884-7130

ILLINOIS
Thomas F. Baker
Executive Director
Criminal Justice Information Authority
120 S. Riverside Plz., # 1016
Chicago, IL 60606
Phone : (312) 793-8550
Fax : (312) 793-8422

INDIANA
Fred C. Pryor
Acting Commander
Criminal Justice Data Div.
State Police
IGC-North, Rm. W3-001
Indianapolis, IN 46204
Phone : (317) 232-8318

IOWA
Richard G. Moore
Administrator
Crim. & Juv. Justice Pl. Agcy.
Dept. of Human Rights
Executive Hills E.
Des Moines, IA 50319
Phone : (515) 282-5816

KANSAS
Lisa Moots
Executive Director
Kansas Sentencing Commission
700 SW Jackson, Ste. 501
Topeka, KS 66603-3757
Phone : (913) 296-0923
Fax : (913) 296-0927

KENTUCKY
Jerry Lovitt
Commissioner
Dept. of State Police
Justice Cabinet
919 Versailles Rd.
Frankfort, KY 40601
Phone : (502) 695-6300

LOUISIANA
Michael A. Ranatza
Director
Comm. on Law Enforcement
Off. of the Governor
1885 Wooddale Blvd., Rm. 708
Baton Rouge, LA 70806
Phone : (504) 925-1997

MAINE
Alfred Skolfield
Commissioner
Dept. of Public Safety
State House Station # 42
Augusta, ME 04333
Phone : (207) 624-7068

MARYLAND
Paul E. Leuba
Director
Div. of Data Srvcs.
6776 Reisterstown Rd.
Baltimore, MD 21215
Phone : (410) 764-4200

MASSACHUSETTS
Howard J. Lebowitz
Executive Director
Criminal Justice Training Council
41 Terrace Hall Ave.
Burlington, MA 01803-3499
Phone : (617) 727-7827
Fax : (617) 229-6054

MINNESOTA
Martin Rahinsky
Superintendent
Bur. of Criminal Apprehension
Dept. of Public Safety
1246 University Ave.
St. Paul, MN 55104
Phone : (612) 642-0600

MISSISSIPPI
Donald O'Cain
Interim Director
Div. of Public Safety Planning
P.O. Box 23039
Jackson, MS 39225-3039
Phone : (601) 949-2000

MISSOURI
Gerald E. Wethington
Director of Information Systems
State Highway Patrol
Dept. of Public Safety
1510 E. Elm
P.O. Box 568
Jefferson City, MO 65102
Phone : (314) 526-6200
Fax : (314) 751-9382

MONTANA
Ellis E. "Gene" Kiser
Executive Director
Crime Control Div.
Dept. of Justice
303 N. Roberts
Helena, MT 59620
Phone : (406) 444-3604

NEBRASKA
Al Curtis
Executive Director
Comm. on Law Enforcement & Criminal Justice
P.O. Box 94946
Lincoln, NE 68509
Phone : (402) 471-2194
Fax : (402) 471-2837

NEVADA
Dennis Debacco
Commander
Criminal Inf. Services Sect.
State Highway Patrol
555 Wright Way
Carson City, NV 89711-0525
Phone : (702) 687-5713

NEW HAMPSHIRE
Mark C. Thompson
Law Office Administrator
Off. of the Attorney General
25 Capitol St.
Concord, NH 03301
Phone : (603) 271-3654

NEW JERSEY
Terrence P. Farley
Director
Div. of Criminal Justice
Dept. of Law & Public Safety
Hughes Justice Complex, CN085
Trenton, NJ 08625
Phone : (609) 984-0029

NEW YORK*
Commissioner
Div. of Criminal Justice Srvcs.
Executive Park Tower
Stuyvesant Plz.
Albany, NY 12203
Phone : (518) 474-1260

NORTH CAROLINA
Richard P. Hawley
Assistant Director
State Bureau of Investigation
Dept. of Justice
407 N. Blount St.
Raleigh, NC 27601-1073
Phone : (919) 733-3171
Fax : (919) 715-2692

NORTH DAKOTA
Bill Broer
Director
Criminal Justice Div.
Off. of Attorney General
600 E. Boulevard Ave.
Bismarck, ND 58505
Phone : (701) 328-6180
Fax : (701) 328-5510

OHIO
Greg Berquist
Superintendent
Criminal Identification & Investigation Section
P.O. Box 365
London, OH 43140
Phone : (614) 466-8204
Fax : (614) 852-4453

OKLAHOMA
Russ Buchner
Director
Criminal Justice Resource Ctr.
Dept. of Corrections
621 N. Robinson, Ste. 445
Oklahoma City, OK 73102
Phone : (405) 232-3328

OREGON
Lloyd A. Smith
Manager
Law Enforcement Data System
Oregon State Police
400 Public Service Bldg.
Salem, OR 97310
Phone : (503) 378-3054
Fax : (503) 363-8249

PENNSYLVANIA
Paul Evanko
Commissioner
Pennsylvania State Police
1800 Elmerton Ave.
Harrisburg, PA 17110
Phone : (717) 783-5558

RHODE ISLAND*
Executive Director
Governor's Justice Comm.
275 Westminster St.
Providence, RI 02903-3434
Phone : (401) 277-2620

SOUTH CAROLINA
Lyda Glover
Director
Crim. Jus. Info. & Comm. Sys.
Dept. of Law Enforcement
P.O. Box 21398
Columbia, SC 29221
Phone : (803) 896-7051

SOUTH DAKOTA
Chuck Schamens
Director
Div. of Criminal Investigation
Off. of the Attorney General
500 E. Capitol Ave.
Pierre, SD 57501-5070
Phone : (605) 773-3332

TENNESSEE*
Project Coordinator
Criminal Justice Admin.
Dept. of Finance & Admin.
302 John Sevier Bldg.
Nashville, TN 37243
Phone : (615) 741-3784

TEXAS
Karen Greene
Executive Director
Criminal Justice Div.
Off. of the Governor
P.O. Box 12428, Capitol Station
Austin, TX 78711
Phone : (512) 463-1919

UTAH
Richard Townsend
Chief
Criminal Identification Bur.
Dept. of Public Safety
4501 S. 2700 W., 2nd Fl.
Salt Lake City, UT 84119
Phone : (801) 965-4561

VERMONT
Max Schlueter
Director
Criminal Info. Ctr.
Dept. of Public Safety
P.O. Box 189
Waterbury, VT 05676
Phone : (802) 244-8727
Fax : (802) 244-1106

VIRGINIA
Bruce C. Morris
Director
Dept. of Criminal Justice Srvcs.
805 E. Broad St., 10th Fl.
Richmond, VA 23219
Phone : (804) 786-8718
Fax : (804) 786-0588

WASHINGTON
John Broome
Division Commander
Criminal Records Div.
State Patrol
P.O. Box 42622
Tumwater, WA 98501
Phone : (360) 705-5352

WEST VIRGINIA
Thomas L. Kirk
Superintendent
Dept. of Public Safety
725 Jefferson Rd.
S. Charleston, WV 25309-1698
Phone : (304) 746-2111

WISCONSIN
Michael Roberts
Director
Crime Information Bur.
Dept. of Justice
222 State St., Room 223
Madison, WI 53703
Phone : (608) 266-7314
Fax : (608) 267-2223

WYOMING
Tom Pagel
Director
Criminal Investigation Div.
Off. of the Attorney General
316 W. 22nd
Cheyenne, WY 82002
Phone : (307) 777-7181

AMERICAN SAMOA
Laauli A. Filoiali'i
Director
Criminal Justice Agency
Pago Pago, AS 96799
Phone : (684) 633-5251
Fax : (684) 633-7552

GUAM
Lourdes T. Pangelinan
Director of
Communications
Superior Court of Guam
120 W. O'Brien Dr.
Agana, GU 96910
Phone : (671) 475-3386

NORTHERN MARIANA ISLANDS
Joaquin T. Ogumoro
Executive Director
Criminal Justice
Planning Agcy.
P.O. Box 1133 CK
Saipan, MP 96950
Phone : (670) 322-9350
Fax : (670) 322-6311

PUERTO RICO
David Gonzalez
Director
Statistics
Dept. of Justice
P.O. Box 192
San Juan, PR 00902
Phone : (809) 721-2900
Fax : (809) 725-6144

U.S. VIRGIN ISLANDS
Ramon Davila
Commissioner
Police Dept.
Nisky Ctr. #6
St. Thomas, VI 00802
Phone : (809) 774-6400
Fax : (809) 774-4057

CRIMINAL JUSTICE PLANNING

Plans improvements in crime prevention and control and criminal justice in the state.

ALABAMA
Doug Miller
Chief
Law Enforcement Planning Sec.
Dept. of Econ. & Comm. Affairs
401 Adams Ave.
P.O. Box 5670
Montgomery, AL 36103
Phone : (334) 242-5891
Fax : (334) 242-0712

ARIZONA
Rex M. Holgerson
Director
Criminal Justice Commission
1501 W. Washington St., Ste. 207
Phoenix, AZ 85007
Phone : (602) 255-1928

ARKANSAS
John Bailey
Director
State Police
P.O. Box 5901
Little Rock, AR 72215
Phone : (501) 221-8200
Fax : (501) 224-4722

CALIFORNIA
Ray Johnson
Executive Director
Criminal Justice Planning Off.
1130 K St., Ste. 300
Sacramento, CA 95814
Phone : (916) 324-9140

COLORADO
William Woodward
Director of Criminal Justice
Dept. of Public Safety
700 Kipling St., Ste. 3000
Denver, CO 80215
Phone : (303) 239-4442

CONNECTICUT
Susan Shimelman
Under Secretary
Policy Dev. & Planning Div.
Off. of Policy & Mgt.
80 Washington St.
Hartford, CT 06106
Phone : (203) 566-4298

DELAWARE
Thomas J. Quinn
Executive Director
Criminal Justice Planning Comm.
820 N. French St.
Wilmington, DE 19801
Phone : (302) 577-3431

FLORIDA
Leon Lowry
Director
Crim. Just. Standards/ Training
Dept. of Law Enforcement
P.O. Box 1489
Tallahassee, FL 32302
Phone : (904) 487-0491

GEORGIA
Terry Norris
Director
Criminal Justice Coordination Council
503 Oak Pl., #540
Atlanta, GA 30349
Phone : (404) 559-4949

HAWAII
Laraine Koga
Director
Resource Coordination Div.
Dept. of Attorney General
425 Queen St., # 221
Honolulu, HI 96813
Phone : (808) 586-1500
Fax : (808) 586-1239

IDAHO
James Benham
Chief
Criminal Justice Council
Dept. of Law Enforcement
P.O. Box 2877
Pocatello, ID 83206
Phone : (208) 234-6113

ILLINOIS
Terrence Gainer
Director
Dept. of State Police
103 State Armory
Springfield, IL 62706
Phone : (217) 782-7263
Fax : (217) 785-2821

INDIANA
Catherine O'Connor
Director
Criminal Justice Institute
302 W. Washington St., Rm.E209
Indianapolis, IN 46204
Phone : (317) 232-2561

IOWA
Richard G. Moore
Administrator
Crim. & Juv. Justice Pl. Agcy.
Dept. of Human Rights
Executive Hills E.
Des Moines, IA 50319
Phone : (515) 282-5816

KANSAS
John Bork
Deputy Attorney General
Criminal Division
Off. of the Attorney General
Judicial Center, 2nd Fl.
301 W. Tenth, Judicial Ctr.
Topeka, KS 66612-1597
Phone : (913) 296-2215
Fax : (913) 296-6296

KENTUCKY
Paul F. Isaacs
Secretary
Justice Cabinet
919 Versailles Rd.
Frankfort, KY 40601
Phone : (502) 695-6300

LOUISIANA
Michael A. Ranatza
Director
Comm. on Law Enforcement
Off. of the Governor
1885 Wooddale Blvd., Rm. 708
Baton Rouge, LA 70806
Phone : (504) 925-1997

MAINE
Alfred Skolfield
Commissioner
Dept. of Public Safety
State House Station # 42
Augusta, ME 04333
Phone : (207) 624-7068

MARYLAND
Stephen A. Bocian
Executive Director
Off. of Justice Assistance
301 W. Preston St.
Baltimore, MD 21201
Phone : (410) 225-1834

MASSACHUSETTS
Dennis Humphrey
Executive Director
Cmte. on Criminal Justice
100 Cambridge St., Rm. 2100
Boston, MA 02202
Phone : (617) 727-6300

MINNESOTA
Michael Jordan
Commissioner
Dept. of Public Safety
211 Transportation Bldg.
395 John Ireland Blvd.
St. Paul, MN 55155
Phone : (612) 266-6642

MISSISSIPPI
Donald O'Cain
Interim Director
Div. of Public Safety Planning
P.O. Box 23039
Jackson, MS 39225-3039
Phone : (601) 949-2000

MISSOURI
Gary B. Kempker
Director
Dept. of Public Safety
Truman Bldg., Rm. 870
P.O. Box 749
Jefferson City, MO 65102
Phone : (314) 751-4905
Fax : (314) 751-5399

MONTANA
Ellis E. "Gene" Kiser
Executive Director
Crime Control Div.
Dept. of Justice
303 N. Roberts
Helena, MT 59620
Phone : (406) 444-3604

NEBRASKA
Al Curtis
Executive Director
Comm. on Law Enforcement &
Criminal Justice
P.O. Box 94946
Lincoln, NE 68509
Phone : (402) 471-2194
Fax : (402) 471-2837

NEVADA
Bob Bayer
Director
Dept. of Prisons
P.O. Box 7011
Carson City, NV 89702
Phone : (702) 887-3285
Fax : (702) 687-6715

NEW HAMPSHIRE
Jeffrey R. Howard
Attorney General
25 Capitol St.
Concord, NH 03301
Phone : (603) 271-3655

NEW JERSEY
Robert T. Winter
Director
Div. of Criminal Justice
Dept. of Law & Public Safety
Hughes Justice Complex, CN085
Trenton, NJ 08625
Phone : (609) 984-0029

NEW YORK *
Commissioner
Div. of Criminal Justice Srvcs.
Executive Park Tower
Stuyvesant Plz.
Albany, NY 12203
Phone : (518) 474-1260

NORTH CAROLINA
William R. Pittman
Director
Governor's Crime Comm.
Dept. of Crime Cont. & Public Safety
3824 Barrett Dr., Ste. 100
Raleigh, NC 27609-7220
Phone : (919) 571-4736
Fax : (919) 571-4745

NORTH DAKOTA
Bill Broer
Director
Criminal Justice Div.
Off. of Attorney General
600 E. Boulevard Ave.
Bismarck, ND 58505
Phone : (701) 328-6180
Fax : (701) 328-5510

OHIO
Michael Lee
Director
Governor's Off. of Criminal
Justice Srvcs.
400 E. Town St., Ste. 120
Columbus, OH 43215
Phone : (614) 466-7782
Fax : (614) 466-0308

OREGON
Greg Peden
Director
Criminal Justice Srvcs. Div.
155 Cottage St., N.E.
Salem, OR 97310
Phone : (503) 378-4123

PENNSYLVANIA
Ernest D. Preate Jr.
Attorney General
Strawberry Sq., 16th Fl.
Harrisburg, PA 17120
Phone : (717) 787-3391

SOUTH CAROLINA
Boykin Rose
Interim Director
Dept. of Public Safety
5400 Broad River Rd.
Columbia, SC 29201
Phone : (803) 896-7844

TENNESSEE
Marsha Willis
Director
Program Assessment & Support
Criminal Justice Admin.
Dept. of Finance & Admin.
1400 Andrew Jackson Bldg.
Nashville, TN 37243-1700
Phone : (615) 741-7662
Fax : (615) 532-2989

TEXAS
Karen Greene
Director
Criminal Justice Div.
Off. of the Governor
P.O.Box 12428, Capitol Station
Austin, TX 78711
Phone : (512) 463-1919

Doyne Bailey
Executive Director
Criminal Justice Div.
Off. of the Governor
P.O.Box 12428, Capitol Station
Austin, TX 78711
Phone : (512) 463-1919

UTAH
Camille Anthony
Executive Director
Comm. on Criminal & Juvenile Justice
State Capitol, Rm. 101
Salt Lake City, UT 84114
Phone : (801) 538-1056

VERMONT
James Walton
Commissioner
Dept. of Public Safety
103 S. Main St.
Waterbury, VT 05671-2101
Phone : (802) 244-8718
Fax : (802) 244-1106

VIRGINIA
Bruce C. Morris
Director
Dept. of Criminal Justice Srvcs.
805 E. Broad St., 10th Fl.
Richmond, VA 23219
Phone : (804) 786-8718
Fax : (804) 786-0588

WASHINGTON
Annette Sandberg
Chief
State Patrol
General Administration Bldg.
P.O. Box 42601
Olympia, WA 98504-2601
Phone : (360) 753-6540

WEST VIRGINIA
James Albert
Manager
Criminal Justice & Hwy. Safety
Off. of Community & Indl. Dev.
1204 Kanawha Blvd., E.
Charleston, WV 25301
Phone : (304) 558-8814

WISCONSIN
Steven D. Sell
Executive Director
Off. of Justice Assistance
Dept. of Administration
222 State St., 2nd Fl.
Madison, WI 53702
Phone : (608) 266-3323
Fax : (608) 266-6676

AMERICAN SAMOA
Laauli A. Filoiali'i
Director
Criminal Justice Agency
Pago Pago, AS 96799
Phone : (684) 633-5251
Fax : (684) 633-7552

Criminal Justice Planning

NORTHERN MARIANA ISLANDS

Joaquin T. Ogumoro
Executive Director
Criminal Justice Planning Agcy.
P.O. Box 1133 CK
Saipan, MP 96950
Phone : (670) 322-9350
Fax : (670) 322-6311

U.S. VIRGIN ISLANDS

Ramon Davila
Commissioner
Police Dept.
Criminal Justice Complex
Nisky Ctr #6
St. Thomas, VI 00802
Phone : (809) 774-6400
Fax : (809) 774-4057

DEBT MANAGEMENT

Responsible for structuring debt issues.

ALASKA
Wilson Condon
Commissioner
Dept. of Revenue
P.O. Box 110400
Juneau, AK 99811-0400
Phone : (907) 465-2300
Fax : (907) 465-2389

Forrest Brown
Treasury Div.
Dept. of Revenue
P.O. Box 110405
Juneau, AK 99811-0405
Phone : (907) 465-2350
Fax : (907) 465-2394

ARIZONA
Tony West
State Treasurer
106 State Capitol
1700 W. Washington
Phoenix, AZ 85007
Phone : (602) 542-5815

CALIFORNIA
Bruce VanHouten
Deputy Director
Cash Management Div.
915 Capitol Mall, Rm. 107
Sacramento, CA 95814
Phone : (916) 653-2995

COLORADO
Andre' Pettigrew
Executive Director
Dept. of Admin.
1525 Sherman St., 2nd Fl.
Denver, CO 80203
Phone : (303) 866-3221
Fax : (303) 866-6569

DELAWARE
Janet C. Rzewnicki
Treasurer
Delaware State Treasurer
Thomas Collins Building
P.O. Box 1401
Dover, DE 19903
Phone : (302) 739-3382
Fax : (302) 739-5635

FLORIDA
J. Timothy Tinsley
Acting Director
Division of Bond Finance
State Board of
Administration
P.O. Drawer 5318
Tallahassee, FL 32314
Phone : (904) 488-4782

GEORGIA
Steven N. McCoy
State Treasurer
Off. of Treasury & Fiscal
Srvcs.
1516 West Tower
200 Piedmont Ave., S.E.
Atlanta, GA 30334
Phone : (404) 656-2168

HAWAII
Earl I. Anzai
Director
Dept. of Budget &
Finance
P.O. Box 150
Honolulu, HI 96810
Phone : (808) 586-1518
Fax : (808) 586-1976

IDAHO
Lydia Justice Edwards
State Treasurer
102 State Capitol
Boise, ID 83720
Phone : (208) 334-3200

ILLINOIS
Joan Walters
Director
Bur. of the Budget
Off. of the Governor
108 State House
Springfield, IL 60706
Phone : (217) 782-4520
Fax : (217) 524-1514

INDIANA
Mark Moore
Special Liaison
Public Finance
State House, Rm. 102
Indianapolis, IN 46204
Phone : (317) 233-5090

IOWA
Michael L. Fitzgerald
State Treasurer
State Capitol Bldg.
Des Moines, IA 50319
Phone : (515) 281-5368

KANSAS
Sally Thompson
State Treasurer
Landon State Office Bldg.
Rm. 201-N
Topeka, KS 66612-1235
Phone : (913) 296-3171
Fax : (913) 296-7950

KENTUCKY
Gordon Mullis
Executive Director
Office of Financial Mgt. &
Economic Analysis
Capitol Annex
Frankfort, KY 40601
Phone : (502) 564-2924

LOUISIANA
Mary L. Landrieu
State Treasurer
Dept. of Treasury
P.O. Box 44154
Baton Rouge, LA 70804-
0154
Phone : (504) 342-0010

MARYLAND
Lucille Maurer
State Treasurer
Goldstein Treasury Bldg.,
Rm. 109
Annapolis, MD 21401
Phone : (301) 974-3542

MASSACHUSETTS
Joseph Malone
Treasurer & Receiver
General
1 Ashburton Place,
12th Fl.
Boston, MA 02108-1518
Phone : (617) 369-3900

MICHIGAN
Douglas B. Roberts
Treasurer
Dept. of Treasury
Treasury Bldg.
430 W. Allegan St.
Lansing, MI 48922
Phone : (517) 373-2767
Fax : (517) 373-1785

MINNESOTA
Michael A. McGrath
Treasurer
303 Administration Bldg.
50 Sherburne Ave.
St. Paul, MN 55155
Phone : (612) 296-7091

MISSISSIPPI
Margie Fanning
Director
Investments Div.
Dept. of Treasury
P.O. Box 138
Jackson, MS 39205
Phone : (601) 359-3600

MISSOURI
Richard A. Hanson
Commissioner
Off. of Administration
State Capitol, Rm. 125
P.O. Box 809
Jefferson City, MO 65102
Phone : (314) 751-3311
Fax : (314) 751-1212

NEVADA
Robert L. Seale
State Treasurer
Capitol Complex
Carson City, NV 89710
Phone : (702) 687-5200

NEW HAMPSHIRE
Georgie A. Thomas
State Treasurer
121 State House Annex
Concord, NH 03301
Phone : (603) 271-2621

NEW MEXICO
Jimmy Joe Gonzales
Director
Debt Management
Off. of State Treasurer
130 S. Capitol
Santa Fe, NM 87501
Phone : (505) 827-6424
Fax : (505) 827-6395

NEW YORK *
State Comptroller
Off. of the State Comptroller
A.E. Smith Off. Bldg., 6th Fl.
Albany, NY 12236
Phone : (518) 474-4040

NORTH CAROLINA
Harlan E. Boyles
State Treasurer
325 N. Salisbury St.
Raleigh, NC 27603-1388
Phone : (919) 733-3951
Fax : (919) 733-9586

NORTH DAKOTA
Rod Backman
Director
Off. of Management & Budget
State Capitol, 4th Fl.
600 E. Boulevard Ave.
Bismarck, ND 58505-0400
Phone : (701) 328-4904
Fax : (701) 328-3230

OREGON
Chuck Smith
Director
Debt Management Div.
Oregon State Treasury
100 L & I Bldg.
350 Winter St., NE
Salem, OR 97310-0840
Phone : (503) 378-4930
Fax : (503) 378-2870

RHODE ISLAND
Nancy J. Mayer
State Treasurer
State House, Rm. 102
Providence, RI 02903
Phone : (401) 277-2397

SOUTH CAROLINA
Richard Eckstrom
State Treasurer
Wade Hampton Bldg., Rm. 120
P.O. Box 11778
Columbia, SC 29211
Phone : (803) 734-2688

SOUTH DAKOTA
Richard Butler
State Treasurer
500 E. Capitol Ave.
Pierre, SD 57501
Phone : (605) 773-3378

TENNESSEE
William R. Snodgrass
Comptroller of the Treasury
State Capitol, 1st Fl.
Nashville, TN 37243
Phone : (615) 741-2501
Fax : (615) 741-7328

TEXAS
Martha Whitehead
State Treasurer
Dept. of the Treasury
P.O. Box 12608, Capitol Station
Austin, TX 78711
Phone : (512) 463-6000

VERMONT
James H. Douglas
Treasurer
State Administration Bldg.
133 State St.
Montpelier, VT 05633-6200
Phone : (802) 828-2301
Fax : (802) 828-2772

VIRGINIA
Ronald L. Tillett
State Treasurer
Department of the Treasury
Monroe Bldg., 3rd Fl
101 N. 14th St.
Richmond, VA 23219
Phone : (804) 371-6013
Fax : (804) 225-3187

WASHINGTON
Daniel Grimm
State Treasurer
Legislative Bldg.
P.O. Box 40200
Olympia, WA 98504-0200
Phone : (360) 753-7130

WEST VIRGINIA
Craig Slaughter
Executive Director
Board of Investments
Bldg. 1, Rm. E122
1900 Kanawha Blvd., E.
Charleston, WV 25305
Phone : (304) 558-5000

WISCONSIN
Jack C. Voight
State Treasurer
101 E. Wilson St., 5th Fl.
P.O. Box 7871
Madison, WI 53707
Phone : (608) 266-1714
Fax : (608) 266-2647

WYOMING
Stan Smith
State Treasurer
State Capitol
Cheyenne, WY 82002
Phone : (307) 777-7408

DISTRICT OF COLUMBIA
Maria Day Marshall
Treasurer
441 4th St., NW, Ste. 360
Washington, DC 20001
Phone : (202) 727-6055

AMERICAN SAMOA
Ray Pritt
Treasurer
Dept. of the Treasury
Government of American Samoa
Pago Pago, AS 96799
Phone : (684) 633-4155
Fax : (684) 633-4100

GUAM **
Carl Taitano
Chief Financial Officer
Off. of the Governor
P.O. Box 2950
Agana, GU 96910

NORTHERN MARIANA ISLANDS
Maria D. Cabrera
Secretary of Finance
Dept. of Finance & Accounting
P.O. Box 5234, CHRB
Saipan, MP 96950
Phone : (670) 664-1100
Fax : (670) 664-1115

PUERTO RICO
Manuel Diaz Saldana
Secretary of the Treasury
Intendente Ramirez Bldg.
P.O. Box S-4515
San Juan, PR 00902
Phone : (809) 721-2020
Fax : (809) 723-6213

U.S. VIRGIN ISLANDS
Kevin Callwood
Executive Assistant & Chief
Off. of the Governor
21-22 Kongens Gade
St. Thomas, VI 00802
Phone : (809) 774-0001
Fax : (809) 774-1361

DEVELOPMENTALLY DISABLED

Oversees the care, treatment and future service needs of the developmentally disabled.

ALASKA
Mike Renfro
Director
Div. of Mental Health & Developmental Disabilities
Dept. of Health & Social Services
P.O. Box 110620
Juneau, AK 99811-0620
Phone : (907) 465-3370
Fax : (907) 465-2668

ARIZONA
Roger Deshaies
Assistant Director
Developmental Disabilities Div
Dept. of Economic Security
1789 W. Jefferson
Phoenix, AZ 85007
Phone : (602) 542-6853

ARKANSAS
Mike McCreight
Director
Dev. Disabilities Srvcs.
Human Services
5th Fl., Donaghey Plaza South
Little Rock, AR 72201
Phone : (501) 682-8662
Fax : (501) 682-8380

CALIFORNIA
Dennis G. Amundson
Director
Dept. of Developmental Srvcs.
1600 9th St., Rm. 240
Sacramento, CA 95814
Phone : (916) 654-1897

COLORADO
Charlie Allinson
Director
Dev. Disabilities Div.
Dept. of Human Srvcs.
3824 W. Princeton Cir.
Denver, CO 80236
Phone : (303) 762-4550
Fax : (303) 762-4300

DELAWARE
Nancy J. Wilson
Part H Coordinator
Div. of Management Srvcs.
Dept. of Health & Social Srvcs.
1901 N. Dupont Hwy., Main Bldg.
New Castle, DE 19720
Phone : (302) 577-5647
Fax : (302) 577-4083

FLORIDA
Charles Kimber
Assistant Secretary
Developmental Services
Dept. of Health & Rehab. Srvcs
1317 Winewood Blvd.
Tallahassee, FL 32399-0700
Phone : (904) 922-2993

GEORGIA
Zebe Schmitt
Executive Director
Governor's Council on Developmentally Disabled
2 Peachtree St., 3rd Fl.
Atlanta, GA 30303
Phone : (404) 657-2126

HAWAII
Stanley Yee
Chief
Developmentally Disabled Div.
Dept. of Health
2201 Waimano Home Rd.
Pearl City, HI 96782
Phone : (808) 453-6404
Fax : (808) 453-6317

IDAHO
Paul Swatsenbarg
Chief
Developmental Disabilities Div.
Dept. of Health & Welfare
450 W. State St.
P.O. Box 83720
Boise, ID 83720-0036
Phone : (208) 334-5512
Fax : (208) 334-6664

ILLINOIS
Audrey McCrimon
Director
Dept. of Rehabilitative Srvcs.
623 E. Adams St.
Springfield, IL 62794-9429
Phone : (217) 785-0169
Fax : (217) 785-5753

INDIANA
John Viernes
Deputy Director
Div. of Aging & Rehab. Srvcs.
Family & Social Srvcs. Admin.
IGC-South, Rm. W453
Indianapolis, IN 46204
Phone : (317) 232-3828

IOWA
Jay Brewer
Executive Director
Developmental Dis. Council
Dept. of Human Srvcs.
Hoover State Off. Bldg.
Des Moines, IA 50319
Phone : (515) 281-7635

KANSAS
Carol Rank
Director
Disability Determination Srvcs.
915 Harrison, 10th Fl.
Topeka, KS 66612-1570
Phone : (913) 296-6600
Fax : (913) 296-2545

KENTUCKY
Robin Hearn
Director
Disability Determination
Dept. for Health Srvcs.
102 Athletic Dr.
Frankfort, KY 40601
Phone : (502) 564-5028

LOUISIANA
Clarice Eichelberger
Director
Developmentally Disabled Div.
Dept. of Health & Hospitals
P.O. Box 3445
Baton Rouge, LA 70821
Phone : (504) 342-6804

MAINE
Pamela Tetley
Director
Bur. of Rehabilitation
Dept. of Human Services
State House Station # 11
Augusta, ME 04333
Phone : (207) 624-5300

MARYLAND
Diane Ebberts
Director
Off. for Individuals with Dis.
Executive Dept.
One Market Ctr., Box 10
Baltimore, MD 21201
Phone : (410) 333-3098

MASSACHUSETTS
Jody Williams
Executive Director
Developmental Disabilities Council
600 Washington St., Ste. 670
Boston, MA 02111
Phone : (617) 727-6374

MICHIGAN
James K. Hareman Jr.
Dept. of Mental Health
Lewis Cass Bldg.
Lansing, MI 48913
Phone : (517) 373-3740
Fax : (517) 335-3090

MINNESOTA
Shirley Patterson
Director
Developmental Disabilities Program
Dept. of Human Srvcs.
444 Lafayette Rd.
St. Paul, MN 55155
Phone : (612) 296-9139

MISSOURI
Greg Kramer
Director
Div. of Mental Retardation and Developmental Disabilities
1706 E. Elm St.
P.O. Box 687
Jefferson City, MO 65102
Phone : (314) 751-4054
Fax : (314) 751-9207

MONTANA
Mike Hanshew
Administrator
Developmental Disabilities Div.
Dept. of Social & Rehab. Srvcs.
111 Sanders, Rm. 305
Helena, MT 59620
Phone : (406) 444-2995

NEBRASKA
Cathy Anderson
Director
Developmental Disabilities
Dept. of Public Institutions
P.O. Box 94728
Lincoln, NE 68509-4728
Phone : (402) 471-2851
Fax : (402) 479-5145

NEVADA
Carlos Brandenburg
Administrator
Mental Hygiene & Retardation
Dept. of Human Resources
505 E. King St., Rm. 403
Carson City, NV 89710
Phone : (702) 687-5943

NEW HAMPSHIRE
Donald Shumway
Director
Div. of Mental Health & Development Srvcs.
105 Pleasant St.
Concord, NH 03301
Phone : (603) 271-5004

NEW MEXICO
Javier Acebes
Director
Developmental Disabilities Div.
Dept. of Health
1190 St. Francis, 3rd Fl.
Santa Fe, NM 87502
Phone : (505) 827-2574
Fax : (505) 827-2595

Chris Isengard
Executive Director
Developmental Disabilities Planning Council
435 St. Michael's Dr., Bldg. D
Santa Fe, NM 87501
Phone : (505) 827-7590
Fax : (505) 827-7589

NEW YORK *
Commissioner
Dept. of Mental Retardation & Developmental Disabilities
44 Holland Ave.
Albany, NY 12229
Phone : (518) 473-1997

NORTH CAROLINA
Holly Riddle
Executive Director
Council on Developmental Dis.
Dept. of Human Resources
1508 Western Blvd.
Raleigh, NC 27606-2168
Phone : (919) 733-6566
Fax : (919) 733-1863

NORTH DAKOTA
Sandi Noble
Director
Developmental Disabilities Div
Dept. of Human Srvcs.
600 E. Boulevard Ave.
Bismark, ND 58505-0250
Phone : (701) 328-2768
Fax : (701) 328-2359

OHIO
Jerome C. Manuel
Director
Dept. of Mental Retardation & Developmental Disabilities
30 E. Broad St., 12th Fl.
Columbus, OH 43266-0415
Phone : (614) 466-5214
Fax : (614) 644-5013

OREGON
James D. Toews
Assistant Administrator
Developmental Disabilities Srvcs.
Mental Health & Dev. Disibility Srvcs. Div.
2575 Bittern St., NE
Salem, OR 97310
Phone : (503) 945-9819
Fax : (503) 373-7274

RHODE ISLAND
Christie Ferguson
Director
Dept. of Human Services
600 New London Ave.
Cranston, RI 02920
Phone : (401) 464-2121

SOUTH CAROLINA
Charles Lang
Deputy Director
Div. of Human Srvcs.
Off. of the Governor
1205 Pendleton St., Rm. 372
Columbia, SC 29201
Phone : (803) 734-0465

SOUTH DAKOTA
Deb Bowman
Director
Div. of Dev. Disabilities
Dept. of Human Srvcs.
Hillsview Plz., 500 E. Capitol
Pierre, SD 57501
Phone : (605) 773-3438

TENNESSEE
Ed Davis
Assistant Commissioner
Div. of Rehabilitation Srvcs.
Dept. of Human Services
400 Deaderick St., 15th Fl.
Nashville, TN 37248
Phone : (615) 741-2019

TEXAS
Virginia Roberts
Executive Director
Cmte. on People w/ Disabilities
Off. of the Governor
P.O. Box 12428
Austin, TX 78711
Phone : (512) 463-5739

VERMONT
Charles Moseley
Director
Div. of Mental Retardation
Agency of Human Srvcs.
103 S. Main St.
Waterbury, VT 05671-1601
Phone : (802) 241-2648
Fax : (802) 241-3052

WASHINGTON
Norm Davis
Director
Developmental Disabilities Srvcs.
Dept. of Social & Health Srvcs.
P.O. Box 45310
Olympia, WA 98504-5310
Phone : (360) 753-3900

WEST VIRGINIA
Donna Heuneman
Director
Dev. Disabilities Council
Dept. of Health & Human Resources
1601 Kanawha Blvd. W., Ste. 200
Charleston, WV 25312
Phone : (304) 558-0416
Fax : (304) 558-0941

WISCONSIN
Linda Belton
Administrator
Div. of Care & Treatment Fac.
Dept. of Health & Social Srvcs.
1 W Wilson
P.O. Box 7850
Madison, WI 53703
Phone : (608) 266-8740
Fax : (608) 266-2579

WYOMING
Robert T. Clabby II
Administrator
Div. of Developmental Disability
Dept. of Health
Herschler Bldg.
Cheyenne, WY 82002
Phone : (302) 777-7115

DISTRICT OF COLUMBIA
Melvin Williams
Commissioner
Mental Health Srvcs.
Dept. of Human Srvcs.
2700 M.L. King, Jr. Ave., SE
Washington, DC 20032
Phone : (202) 673-7166

AMERICAN SAMOA
Sapini Siatu'u
Director
Dept. of Human Resources
American Samoa Government
Pago Pago, AS 96799
Phone : (684) 633-4485
Fax : (684) 633-1139

GUAM
Jess C. Torres
Executive Director
Comm. on Persons with Disabilities
Governor's Office
Executive Chambers, Adelup
Agana, GU 96910
Phone : (671) 475-9353

Joseph Artero-Cameron
Director
Dept. of Vocational Rehabilation
122 IT&E Plaza, B201
Harmon, GU 96911
Phone : (671) 646-9468
Fax : (671) 649-7672

NORTHERN MARIANA ISLANDS
Juanita S. Malone
Executive Director
Developmental Disabilities
Planning Off.
P.O. Box 2565
Saipan, MP 96950
Phone : (670) 323-3014
Fax : (670) 322-4168

U.S. VIRGIN ISLANDS
Catherine Mills
Commissioner
Dept. of Human Srvcs.
Knud Hansen Complex, Bldg. A
1303 Hospital Ground
St. Thomas, VI 00802
Phone : (809) 774-0930
Fax : (809) 774-3466

DRINKING WATER

Responsible for public drinking water supplies in the state.

ALABAMA
Joe Power
Chief
Water Supply Branch
Water Div.
1751 Cong. Dickinson Dr.
P.O. Box 301463
Montgomery, AL 36130-1463
Phone : (334) 271-7773
Fax : (334) 279-3051

ALASKA
Deena Henkins
Chief
Drinking Water & Wastewater Sec.
Div. of Environmental Quality
Dept. of Environmental Conservation
410 Willoughby Ave.
Juneau, AK 99801
Phone : (907) 465-5300
Fax : (907) 465-5274

ARIZONA
Peggy Guichard-Watters
Program Manager
Compliance Section/ Water Quality
Dept. of Environmental Quality
3033 N. Central
Phoenix, AZ 85012
Phone : (602) 207-2305

ARKANSAS
Harold Seifert
Director
Engineering Div.
Dept. of Health
4815 W. Markham St.
Little Rock, AR 72205-3867
Phone : (501) 661-2623
Fax : (501) 661-2032

CALIFORNIA
Harvey F. Collins
Chief
Div. of Drinking Water & Env.
Dept. of Health Srvcs.
601 N. 7th St.
Box 942732, MS216
Sacramento, CA 94234
Phone : (916) 322-2308

COLORADO
J. David Holm
Director
Water Quality Control Div.
Dept. of Health
4300 Cherry Crk. Dr. S.
Denver, CO 80220
Phone : (303) 692-3500
Fax : (303) 782-0390

CONNECTICUT
Gerald R. Iwan
Chief
Water Supply
Dept. of Health Srvcs.
21 Grand St.
Hartford, CT 06106
Phone : (203) 566-1253

DELAWARE
Gerald L. Esposito
Director
Division of Water Resources
Dept. on Nat. Res. & Env. Cont.
89 Kings Highway
Dover, DE 19901
Phone : (302) 739-4860
Fax : (302) 739-3491

FLORIDA
Richard M. Harvey
Director
Division of Water Facilities
Dept. of Env. Protection
2600 Blairstone Rd.
Tallahassee, FL 32399-2400
Phone : (904) 487-1855
Fax : (904) 921-4303

GEORGIA
Fred Lehman
Branch Chief
Water Protection Branch
Dept. of Natural Resources
Twin Towers East # 1362
Atlanta, GA 30334
Phone : (404) 651-5154

HAWAII
Bruce Anderson
Deputy Director
Environmental Health Admin.
Dept. of Health
1250 Punchbowl St.
Honolulu, HI 96813
Phone : (808) 586-4424
Fax : (808) 586-4444

IDAHO
Leigh Woodruff
Program Manager
Drinking Water Program
Dept. of Health & Welfare
1410 N. Hilton St.
Boise, ID 83706-1255
Phone : (208) 334-0507
Fax : (208) 334-0576

ILLINOIS
Roger Selburg
Manager
Div. of Public Water Supply
Environ. Protection Agency
1340 N. Ninth St.
Springfield, IL 62702
Phone : (217) 785-8653

INDIANA
Robert Hilton
Acting Section Chief
Off. of Water Mgt.
Dept. of Environ. Mgt.
P.O. Box 6015
Indianapolis, IN 46225
Phone : (317) 232-5084

IOWA
Dennis Alt
Supervisor
Water Supply Section
Sur. & Groundwater Prot. Bur.
Wallace State Off. Bldg.
Des Moines, IA 50319
Phone : (515) 281-8998

KANSAS
Karl Mueldener
Director
Bureau of Water
Dept. of Health & Environment
Forbes Field, Bldg. 240
Topeka, KS 66620-0001
Phone : (913) 296-5500
Fax : (913) 296-5509

KENTUCKY
Jack Wilson
Director
Div. of Water
Nat. Res. & Env. Prot. Cabinet
14 Reilly Rd.
Frankfort, KY 40601
Phone : (502) 564-3410

LOUISIANA
Russell Rader
Director
Environmental Health Services
Off. of Public Health
325 Loyola Ave., Rm. 403
New Orleans, LA 70112
Phone : (504) 568-5101

MAINE
Clough Toppan
Director
Div. of Health Engineering
Dept. of Human Services
State House Station # 11
Augusta, ME 04333
Phone : (207) 287-5338

MARYLAND
William Parrish
Administrator
Public Drinking Water Program
Dept. of the Environment
2500 Broening Hwy.
Baltimore, MD 21224
Phone : (410) 631-3702

MASSACHUSETTS
David Terry
Director
Div. of Water Supply
Dept. of Environmental Protection
1 Winter St., 9th Fl.
Boston, MA 02108
Phone : (617) 292-5770
Fax : (617) 556-1049

MICHIGAN
James Cleland
Chief
Div. of Water Supply
Dept. of Public Health
P.O. Box 30195
Lansing, MI 48909
Phone : (517) 335-9216

MINNESOTA
Milton Bellin
Supervisor
Engineering Unit
Dept. of Health
925 Delaware St., S.E.
Minneapolis, MN 55459-0040
Phone : (612) 627-5122

MISSISSIPPI
Jim McDonald
Chief
Water Supply Div.
Dept. of Health
P.O. Box 1700
Jackson, MS 39215
Phone : (601) 960-7634

MISSOURI
Jerry L. Lane
Director
Public Drinking Water Program
Dept. of Natural Resources
Jefferson Bldg., Rm. 315
P.O. Box 176
Jefferson City, MO 65102
Phone : (314) 751-5331
Fax : (314) 751-3110

MONTANA
Jim Melstad
Supervisor
Drinking Water Program
Water Quality Bur.
Cogswell Bldg.
Helena, MT 59620
Phone : (406) 444-2406

NEBRASKA
Steve Walker
Supervisor
Surface Water Section
Water Quality Div.
P.O. Box 98922
Lincoln, NE 68509
Phone : (402) 471-4700
Fax : (402) 471-2909

NEVADA
Jeff Fontaine
Supervisor
Pub. Health Eng., Health Comm.
Dept. of Human Resources
505 E. King St., Rm. 103
Carson City, NV 89710
Phone : (702) 687-4750

NEW HAMPSHIRE
Rene Pelletier
Administrator
Water Supply Engineering Bur.
Water Supply & Pol. Ctrl. Div.
6 Hazen Dr.
Concord, NH 03301
Phone : (603) 271-3503

NEW JERSEY
Thomas G. Baxter
Executive Director
Water Supply Authority
Dept. of Env. Protection Div.
P.O. Box 5196
Clinton, NJ 08809
Phone : (908) 638-6121

NEW MEXICO
Robert Gallegos
Director
Drinking Water Bureau
Dept. of Environment
2052 Galisteo
P.O. Box 968
Santa Fe, NM 87504
Phone : (505) 827-7536
Fax : (505) 827-7545

NEW YORK *
Director
Bur. of Public Water Supply
Dept. of Health
2 University Pl., Western Ave.
Albany, NY 12203
Phone : (518) 458-6731

NORTH CAROLINA
Jonathan B. Howes
Secretary
Div. of Environmental Mgt.
Dept. of Health & Nat. Res.
512 N. Salisbury St.
Raleigh, NC 27604-1148
Phone : (919) 715-4101
Fax : (919) 715-3060

NORTH DAKOTA
Jack Long
Professional Eng./Director
Div. of Municipal Facilities
Environ. Health Section
P.O. Box 5520
Bismarck, ND 58502-5520
Phone : (701) 328-5150
Fax : (701) 328-5200

OHIO
John Sadzewicz
Chief
Div. of Public Water Supply
Environmental Protection Agcy.
1800 Watermark
P.O. Box 1049
Columbus, OH 43266-1049
Phone : (614) 644-2752
Fax : (614) 644-2909

OKLAHOMA
John Craig
Chief
Water Quality Srvcs.
Environmental Health Srvcs.
1000 NE 10th St.
Oklahoma City, OK 73117
Phone : (405) 271-5205

OREGON
David Leland
Manager
Drinking Water Administrator
Div. of Health
800 NE Oregon St.
Portland, OR 97232
Phone : (503) 731-4010
Fax : (503) 731-4077

PENNSYLVANIA
Glenn E. Maurer
Director
Water Supply & Community Health
Dept. of Environmental Res.
P.O. Box 8467
Harrisburg, PA 17105
Phone : (717) 787-9035

RHODE ISLAND
June Swallow
Chief
Water Supply
Dept. of Health
3 Capitol Hill
Providence, RI 02908
Phone : (401) 277-6867

SOUTH CAROLINA
Robert Malpass
Chief
Drinking Water Program
Dept. of Health & Env. Control
2600 Bull St.
Columbia, SC 29201
Phone : (803) 734-5310

SOUTH DAKOTA
Darren Busch
Administrator
Drinking Water Program
Div. of Land & Water Quality
523 E. Capitol Ave.
Pierre, SD 57501
Phone : (605) 773-3754

TENNESSEE
W. David Draughon Jr.
Director
Div. of Water Supply
Dept. of Env. & Conservation
401 Church St.
Nashville, TN 37247
Phone : (615) 532-0191

Drinking Water

TEXAS
Laura Koesters
Deputy Director
Off. of Water Resource Mgt.
Natural Res. Conserv. Comm.
12100 Park 35 Circle
P.O. Box 13087
Austin, TX 78711-3087
Phone : (512) 239-4300
Fax : (512) 239-4303

UTAH
Kevin Brown
Director
Div. of Drinking Water
Dept. of Environmental Quality
P.O. Box 144830
Salt Lake City, UT 84114-4830
Phone : (801) 536-4208

VERMONT
Edward Leonard
Director
Water Supply Div.
Dept. of Environ. Conservation
103 S. Main St.
Waterbury, VT 05671
Phone : (802) 241-3400
Fax : (802) 241-3284

VIRGINIA
Donald R. Stern
Acting Commissioner
Department of Health
Main St. Station
1500 E. Main St., Rm. 214
Richmond, VA 23219
Phone : (804) 786-3561
Fax : (804) 786-4616

WASHINGTON
Dave Clark
Director
Div. of Drinking Water
Dept. of Health
P.O. Box 47822
Olympia, WA 98504-7822
Phone : (360) 753-1280

WEST VIRGINIA
Donald A. Kuntz
Director
Environmental Engineering Div.
Off. of Environ. Health Srvcs.
1800 Washington St., E.
Charleston, WV 25305
Phone : (304) 558-2981

WISCONSIN
Robert M. Krill
Director
Bur. of Water Supply
Dept. of Natural Resources
101 S. Webster St., WS/2
P.O. Box 7921
Madison, WI 53703
Phone : (608) 267-7651
Fax : (608) 267-3579

WYOMING
Howard Hutchings
Director
Environmental Health
Dept. of Health & Soc. Srvcs.
Hathaway Bldg., Rm. 482
Cheyenne, WY 82002
Phone : (307) 777-6017

DISTRICT OF COLUMBIA
Edward M. Scott
Administrator
Water & Sewer Utility Admin.
Dept. of Public Works
5000 Overlook Ave., SW
Washington, DC 20032
Phone : (202) 767-7651

AMERICAN SAMOA
Abe Malae
Executive Director
American Samoa Power Authority
American Samoa Government
Pago Pago, AS 96799
Phone : (684) 644-5251
Fax : (684) 644-5005

GUAM
Robert F. Kelley
Acting Chief Officer
Public Utility Agency
P.O. Box 3010
Agana, GU 96910
Phone : (671) 647-7823
Fax : (671) 649-0158

NORTHERN MARIANA ISLANDS
Timothy P. Villagomez
Executive Director
Commonwealth Utilities Corp.
Lower Base
P.O. Box 1220 CK
Saipan, MP 96950
Phone : (670) 322-4033
Fax : (670) 234-5962

PUERTO RICO
Carmen Feliciano
Secretary
Dept. of Health
P.O. Box 70184
San Juan, PR 00936-0184
Phone : (809) 766-1616
Fax : (809) 250-6547

U.S. VIRGIN ISLANDS
Alberto Bruno-Vega
Executive Director
Water & Power Authority
P.O. Box 1450
St. Thomas, VI 00804
Phone : (809) 774-3552
Fax : (809) 774-3422

ECONOMIC DEVELOPMENT

Responsible for efforts designed to encourage industry to locate, develop and expand in the state.

ALABAMA
Robert Lunsford
Dept. of Economic & Community Affairs
P.O. Box 5690
Montgomery, AL 36103
Phone : (334) 242-8672
Fax : (334) 242-5099

ALASKA
Chris Gates
Director
Economic Development
Dept. of Commerce & Eco. Dev.
P.O. Box 110804
Juneau, AK 99811
Phone : (907) 465-2017
Fax : (907) 465-3767

ARIZONA
Sara Goertzen
Director
Dept. of Commerce
3800 N. Central Ave., Ste. 1500
Phoenix, AZ 85012
Phone : (602) 280-1306

ARKANSAS
L.D. Boyette
Director
Industrial Development Comm.
1 Capitol Mall, Rm. 4C-300
Little Rock, AR 72201
Phone : (501) 682-2052
Fax : (501) 682-7394

CALIFORNIA
Julie Meier Wright
Secretary
Trade & Commerce Agency
801 K St., Ste. 1700
Sacramento, CA 95814
Phone : (916) 322-3962

COLORADO*
Off. of Business Dev.
Governor's Off.
1625 Broadway, Ste. 1710
Denver, CO 80202
Phone : (303) 892-3840
Fax : (303) 892-3848

CONNECTICUT
Arthur H. Diedrick
Commissioner
Dept. of Economic Development
865 Brook St.
Rocky Hill, CT 06067
Phone : (203) 258-4302

DELAWARE
Robert W. Coy Jr.
Director
Delaware Economic Dev. Off.
99 Kings Highway
P.O. Box 1401
Dover, DE 19903
Phone : (302) 739-4271
Fax : (302) 739-5749

FLORIDA
Steve Mayberry
Director
Div. of Econ. Dev.
Dept. of Commerce
536 Collins Bldg.
Tallahassee, FL 32399-2000
Phone : (904) 488-6300
Fax : (904) 922-9150

GEORGIA
Randolph B. Cardoza
Commissioner
Dept. of Ind., Trade & Tourism
258 Peachtree Ctr. Ave., NE, Ste. 1000
Atlanta, GA 30303
Phone : (404) 656-3556

HAWAII
Seiji Naya
Director
Dept. of Business, Economic Development & Tourism
220 S. King St., # 1100
Honolulu, HI 96813
Phone : (808) 586-2359
Fax : (808) 586-2377

IDAHO
Jay E. Engstrom
Administrator
Div. of Economic Development
Dept. of Commerce
P.O. Box 83720
Boise, ID 83720-0093
Phone : (208) 334-2470

ILLINOIS
Dennis R. Whetstone
Director
Dept. of Commerce & Community Affairs
620 E. Adams St., 3rd Fl.
Springfield, IL 62701
Phone : (217) 782-3233
Fax : (217) 524-0864

INDIANA
Frank Sabatine
Director
Bus. Dev. & Marketing Group
Dept. of Commerce
1 N. Capitol, Ste. 700
Indianapolis, IN 46204
Phone : (317) 232-0159

IOWA
Dave Lyons
Director
Dept. of Economic Development
200 E. Grand
Des Moines, IA 50309
Phone : (515) 242-4814
Fax : (515) 242-4832

KANSAS
Bob Knight
Secretary
Dept. of Commerce & Housing
700 SW Harrison, Ste. 1300
Topeka, KS 66603-3712
Phone : (913) 296-3480

KANSAS — Cont.
Steve Kelly
Director
Business Development Division
Dept. of Commerce & Housing
700 SW Harrison, Ste. 1300
Topeka, KS 66603-3712
Phone : (913) 296-5298
Fax : (913) 296-5055

Cal Lantis
Director
Div. of Existing Industry
Dept. of Commerce & Housing
700 S.W. Harrison, Ste. 1300
Topeka, KS 66603-3712
Phone : (913) 296-5298

Charles Warren
President
Kansas, Inc.
632 S.W. Van Buren St. Ste. 100
Topeka, KS 66603-3718
Phone : (913) 296-1460

KENTUCKY
Gene Strong
Secretary
Economic Development Cabinet
Capital Plz. Tower, 23rd Fl.
500 Mero St.
Frankfort, KY 40601
Phone : (502) 564-7670

LOUISIANA
Kevin Reilly
Secretary
Dept. of Economic Development
P.O. Box 94185
Baton Rouge, LA 70804-9185
Phone : (504) 342-5388

MAINE
Tom McBrierty
Commissioner
Dept. of Economic & Community Development
#59 State House Station
Augusta, ME 04333
Phone : (207) 287-2656

MARYLAND
James Brady
Secretary
Dept. of Business & Economic Development
217 E. Redwood St.
Baltimore, MD 21202
Phone : (410) 333-6901

MASSACHUSETTS
Gloria C. Larson
Secretary
Executive Off. of Economic Affairs
1 Ashburton Pl., Rm. 2101
Boston, MA 02108
Phone : (617) 727-8380

MICHIGAN
Steve Arwood
Director
Industry and Investment Relations
Michigan Jobs Commission
201 N. Washington Square
Lansing, MI 48913
Phone : (517) 373-8500
Fax : (517) 373-0314

MINNESOTA
Terrell Towers
Director
Economic Development Div.
Dept. of Business Development
500 Metro Sq., 121-9th Pl., E
St. Paul, MN 55101-2146
Phone : (612) 296-5005

MISSISSIPPI
James B. Heidel
Executive Director
Dept. of Economic & Community Development
P.O. Box 849
Jackson, MS 39205-0849
Phone : (601) 359-3449

MISSOURI
Joseph L. Driskill
Director
Dept. of Economic Development
301 W. High St.
P.O. Box 1157
Jefferson City, MO 65102
Phone : (314) 751-3946
Fax : (314) 751-7258
E-Mail: JDRISKIL@MAIL.MORE.NET

MONTANA
Andy Poole
Administrator
Business Development Div.
Dept. of Commerce
1424 Ninth Ave.
Helena, MT 59620
Phone : (406) 444-3923

NEBRASKA
Maxine Moul
Director
Dept. of Economic Development
301 Centennial Mall S.
P.O. Box 94666
Lincoln, NE 68509-4666
Phone : (402) 471-3747
Fax : (402) 471-3778

NEVADA
Tim Carlson
Executive Director
Comm. on Economic Development
5151 S. Carson St.
Carson City, NV 89710
Phone : (702) 687-4325

NEW HAMPSHIRE
William Pillsbury
Director
Off. of Bus. & Industrial Dev.
Div. of Economic Dev.
P.O. Box 856
Concord, NH 03301
Phone : (603) 271-2341

NEW JERSEY
Cy Thannikara
Director
Div. of Economic Development
Dept. of Commerce & Eco. Dev.
20 W. State St., CN823
Trenton, NJ 08625
Phone : (609) 292-7757

NEW MEXICO
Gary Bratcher
Secretary
Dept. of Economic Development
1100 St. Francis Dr.
Santa Fe, NM 87503
Phone : (505) 827-0380
Fax : (505) 827-0328

NEW YORK *
Commissioner
Dept. of Commerce
1 Commerce Plz.
Albany, NY 12245
Phone : (518) 474-4100

NORTH CAROLINA
George Watts Carr III
Director
Business/Industry Development
Dept. of Commerce
430 N. Salisbury St.
Raleigh, NC 27603-5900
Phone : (919) 733-4151
Fax : (919) 733-9205

NORTH DAKOTA
Charles W. Stroup
Director
Dept. of Economic Dev. & Finance
1833 E. Bismarck Expy.
Bismarck, ND 58504
Phone : (701) 328-5300
Fax : (701) 328-5320

OHIO
Donald Jakeway
Director
Dept. of Development
77 S. High St., 29th Fl.
Columbus, OH 43266-0101
Phone : (614) 644-9389
Fax : (614) 644-0745

OKLAHOMA
D. Gregory Main
Executive Director
Dept. of Commerce
6601 Broadway Ext.
Oklahoma City, OK 73116
Phone : (405) 843-9770

OREGON
Bill Scott
Director
Dept. of Economic Development
775 Summer St., NE
Salem, OR 97310
Phone : (503) 986-0110
Fax : (503) 581-5115

PENNSYLVANIA
Thomas B. Hagen
Secretary
Dept. of Commerce
433 Forum Bldg.
Harrisburg, PA 17120
Phone : (717) 787-3003

RHODE ISLAND
Marcel Valois
Director
Dept. of Economic Development
7 Jackson Walkway
Providence, RI 02903
Phone : (401) 277-2601

SOUTH CAROLINA
Bob Royall
Director
Dept. of Commerce
P.O. Box 927
Columbia, SC 29202
Phone : (803) 734-0400

SOUTH DAKOTA
Bonnie Untereiner
Commissioner
Governor's Off. of Economic Development
Capitol Lake Plz.
Pierre, SD 57501
Phone : (605) 773-5032

TENNESSEE
Bill Dunavant
Commissioner
Dept. of Economic & Community Development
320 Sixth Ave., N., 8th Fl.
Nashville, TN 37243
Phone : (615) 741-1888

TEXAS
Brenda Arnett
Executive Director
Dept. of Commerce
P.O. Box 12728, Capitol Station
Austin, TX 78711
Phone : (512) 472-5059

UTAH
Richard J. Mayfield
Director
Div. of Business & Economic Dev.
Dept. of Community & Economic Dev.
324 S. State St., 5th Fl.
Salt Lake City, UT 84111
Phone : (801) 538-8820
Fax : (801) 538-8889

VERMONT
Alan Davis
Commissioner
Dept. of Economic Development
109 State St.
Montpelier, VT 05602
Phone : (802) 828-3221
Fax : (802) 828-3258

VIRGINIA
Wayne L. Sterling
Director
Dept. of Economic Development
901 E. Byrd St.
Richmond, VA 23219
Phone : (804) 371-8106
Fax : (804) 371-8112

Cathleen Magennis
Secretary
Commerce & Trade
202 N. Ninth St., Rm. 723
Richmond, VA 23219
Phone : (804) 786-7831

WASHINGTON
Mike Fitzgerald
Director
Dept. of Trade & Econ. Dev.
P.O. Box 48300
Olympia, WA 98504
Phone : (360) 753-2200

WEST VIRGINIA
Tom Burns
Director
Development Office
Bldg. 6, Rm. B504
1900 Kanawha Blvd., E.
Charleston, WV 25305
Phone : (304) 558-2234
Fax : (304) 558-1189

WISCONSIN
Phil Albert
Director
Bur. of Bus. Exp. & Recrtmt.
Dept. of Development
123 W. Washington
P.O. Box 7970
Madison, WI 53703
Phone : (608) 255-9467
Fax : (608) 267-2829

WYOMING
George H. Gault
Director
Div. of Econ. & Comm. Dev.
Dept. of Commerce
2301 Central Ave., 4N
Cheyenne, WY 82002
Phone : (307) 777-6435

DISTRICT OF COLUMBIA
Merrick Malone
Chief Economic Officer
Economic Development
Off. of the Mayor
441 4th St., NW, 11th Fl.
Washington, DC 20001
Phone : (202) 727-6365

AMERICAN SAMOA
Alfonso Pete Galeai
Director
Off. of Economic Development Planning
Utulei
Pago Pago, AS 96799
Phone : (684) 633-5155
Fax : (684) 633-4195

GUAM
Gilbert E. Robles
Acting Administrator
Economic Development Authority
590 S. Marine Dr., Ste. 911
Tamuning, GU 96911
Phone : (671) 646-4141
Fax : (671) 649-4146

NORTHERN MARIANA ISLANDS
Oscar C. Camacho
Director
Economic Development
Dept. of Commerce
P.O. Box 10007
Saipan, MP 96950
Phone : (670) 322-8711
Fax : 670) 322-4008

PUERTO RICO
Jaime Morgan Stubbe
President
Industrial Development Co.
P.O. Box 362350
San Juan, PR 00936-2350
Phone : (809) 758-4747
Fax : (809) 753-6874

U.S. VIRGIN ISLANDS
Anthony Olive
Commissioner
Dept. of Economic Development & Agriculture
P.O. Box 6400
St. Thomas, VI 00804
Phone : (809) 774-8784
Fax : (809) 774-4390

EDUCATION (CHIEF STATE SCHOOL OFFICER)

Overall responsibility for public elementary and secondary school systems.

ALABAMA
Thomas E. Ingram, Jr.
Superintendent
Dept. of Education
50 N. Ripley St.
Montgomery, AL 36130
Phone : (334) 242-9700
Fax : (334) 242-9708

ALASKA
Shirley Holloway
Commissioner
Dept. of Education
801 W. 10th St., Ste. 200
Juneau, AK 99801-1894
Phone : (907) 465-2800
Fax : (907) 465-4156

ARIZONA
Lisa Graham
Supt. of Public Instruction
Dept. of Education
1535 W. Jefferson
Phoenix, AZ 85007
Phone : (602) 542-5393

ARKANSAS
Gene Wilhoit
Director
Dept. of Education
Capitol Mall, Bldg. 4
Little Rock, AR 72201-1071
Phone : (501) 682-4205
Fax : (501) 682-4466

CALIFORNIA
Delaine Eastin
Acting Superintendent
Public Instruction
Dept. of Education
721 Capitol Mall, Rm. 524
Sacramento, CA 95814
Phone : (916) 657-4766

COLORADO
William Randall
Commissioner
Dept. of Education
201 E. Colfax
Denver, CO 80203-1715
Phone : (303) 866-6600

CONNECTICUT
Theodore Sergi
Acting Commissioner
Dept. of Education
165 Capitol Ave.
Hartford, CT 06106
Phone : (203) 566-5061

DELAWARE
Pascal Forgione
Superintendent
Dept. of Public Instruction
Townsend Bldg.
P.O. Box 1402
Dover, DE 19903
Phone : (302) 739-4601
Fax : (302) 739-4654

FLORIDA
Frank Brogan
Commissioner
Dept. of Education
1702 The Capitol
Tallahassee, FL 32399
Phone : (904) 487-1785
Fax : (904) 488-1492

GEORGIA
Linda Schrenko
State School
Superintendent
Dept. of Education
205 Butler St., SE
Atlanta, GA 30334
Phone : (404) 656-2800

HAWAII
Herman M. Aizawa
Superintendent
Dept. of Education
1390 Miller St.
Honolulu, HI 96813
Phone : (808) 586-3310
Fax : (808) 586-3419

IDAHO
Anne C. Fox
Superintendent of Public
Instruction
Dept. of Education
650 W. State St.
Boise, ID 83720
Phone : (208) 334-3300

ILLINOIS
Joseph A. Spagnolo
Superintendent
State Board of Education
100 N. First St.
Springfield, IL 62777
Phone : (217) 782-2221
Fax : (217) 785-3972

INDIANA
Suellen Reed
Superintendent
Dept. of Education
State House, Rm. 227
Indianapolis, IN 46204
Phone : (317) 232-6610

IOWA
Al Ramirez
Director
Dept. of Education
Grimes State Off. Bldg.
Des Moines, IA 50319
Phone : (515) 281-5294
Fax : (515) 242-5988

KANSAS
Lee Droegemueller
Commissioner
State Board of Education
120 E. Tenth St.
Topeka, KS 66612-1182
Phone : (913) 296-3201
Fax : (913) 296-7933

KENTUCKY
Thomas C. Boysen
Commissioner
Dept. of Education
Ed. & Humanities Cabinet
Capital Plaza Tower
Frankfort, KY 40601
Phone : (502) 564-4770

LOUISIANA
Raymond Arveson
Superintendent
Dept. of Education
P.O. Box 94064
Baton Rouge, LA 70804
Phone : (504) 342-3602

MAINE
Wayne Mowatt
Commissioner
Dept. of Education
#23 State House Station
Augusta, ME 04333-0023
Phone : (207) 287-5802

MARYLAND
Nancy S. Grasmick
State Superintendent
Dept. of Education
200 W. Baltimore St.
Baltimore, MD 21201
Phone : (410) 333-2200

MASSACHUSETTS
Robert Antonucci
Commissioner
Dept. of Education
350 Main St.
Malden, MA 02148
Phone : (617) 388-3300

MICHIGAN
Robert E. Schiller
Superintendent
Dept. of Education
Ottawa Bldg. S., 4th Fl.
P.O. Box 30008
Lansing, MI 48909
Phone : (517) 373-3354
Fax : (517) 335-4565

MINNESOTA
Linda Powell
Commissioner
Dept. of Education
550 Cedar St., 8th Fl.
St. Paul, MN 55101
Phone : (612) 296-2358

MISSISSIPPI
Tom Burnham
Superintendent
Dept. of Education
P.O. Box 771
Jackson, MS 39205
Phone : (601) 359-3513

MISSOURI
Robert E. Bartman
Commissioner
Dept. of Elem. & Secon. Educ.
Jefferson Bldg., 6th Fl.
P.O. Box 480
Jefferson City, MO 65102
Phone : (314) 751-4446
Fax : (314) 751-1179
E-Mail: RBARTMAN@MAIL.ESE.STATE.MO.US

MONTANA
Nancy Keenan
Superintendent
Off. of Public Instruction
State Capitol
Helena, MT 59620
Phone : (406) 444-3680

NEBRASKA
Doug D. Christensen
Commissioner
Dept. of Education
301 Centennial Mall S.
P.O. Box 94987
Lincoln, NE 68509-4987
Phone : (402) 471-2465

NEVADA
Mary Peterson
Superintendent
Dept. of Education
400 W. King St.
Carson City, NV 89710
Phone : (702) 687-3100

NEW HAMPSHIRE
Elizabeth Twomey
Commissioner
Dept. of Education
101 Pleasant St.
Concord, NH 03301
Phone : (603) 271-3144

NEW JERSEY
Leo F. Klagholz
Commissioner
Off. of the Commissioner
Dept. of Education
225 E. State St., CN500
Trenton, NJ 08625
Phone : (609) 292-4450

NEW MEXICO
Alan Morgan
Supt. of Public Instruction
Dept. of Education
Education Bldg.
Santa Fe, NM 87501-2786
Phone : (505) 827-6635
Fax : (505) 827-6696

NEW YORK *
Commissioner
Dept. of Education
Education Bldg.
Albany, NY 12234
Phone : (518) 474-5844

NORTH CAROLINA
Bob Etheridge
Superintendent
Dept. of Public Instruction
301 N. Wilmington St.
Raleigh, NC 27601-2825
Phone : (919) 715-1000
Fax : (919) 715-1278

NORTH DAKOTA
Wayne G. Sanstead
Superintendent
Dept. of Public Instruction
State Capitol, 11th Fl.
600 E. Boulevard Ave.
Bismarck, ND 58505-0440
Phone : (701) 328-2260
Fax : (701) 328-2461

OHIO
John T. Sanders
Superintendent
Dept. of Education
65 S. Front St., Rm. 808
Columbus, OH 43266-0308
Phone : (614) 466-3304
Fax : (614) 644-5960

OKLAHOMA
Sandy Garrett
Supt. of Public Instruction
Dept. of Education
2500 N. Lincoln Blvd.
Oklahoma City, OK 73105
Phone : (405) 521-3301

OREGON
Norma Paulus
Superintendent of Public Instruction
Dept. of Education
Public Service Bldg.
255 Capitol, NE
Salem, OR 97310
Phone : (503) 378-3569
Fax : (503) 373-7968

PENNSYLVANIA
Eugene Welch Hickok Jr.
Secretary
Dept. of Education
10th Fl., Harristown 2
Harrisburg, PA 17120
Phone : (717) 787-5820

RHODE ISLAND
Peter McWalters
Commissioner
Dept. of Education
22 Hayes St.
Providence, RI 02908
Phone : (401) 277-2031

SOUTH CAROLINA
Barbara Nielsen
Superintendent
Dept. of Education
Rutledge Bldg., Rm. 1006
1429 Senate St.
Columbia, SC 29201
Phone : (803) 734-8492

SOUTH DAKOTA
John Bonaiuto
Secretary
Dept. of Education & Cultural Affairs
700 Governors Dr.
Pierre, SD 57501-2291
Phone : (605) 773-3243

TENNESSEE
Jane Walters
Commissioner
Dept. of Education
710 James Robertson Pkwy.
Nashville, TN 37243
Phone : (615) 741-2731
Fax : (615) 741-6236

TEXAS
Michael Moses
Commissioner
Education Agency
1701 N. Congress Ave.
Austin, TX 78701
Phone : (512) 463-9734

UTAH
Scott Bean
State Superintendent
Off. of Education
250 E. 500 S.
Salt Lake City, UT 84111
Phone : (801) 538-7510

VERMONT
Richard Mills
Commissioner
Dept. of Education
120 State St.
Montpelier, VT 05620
Phone : (802) 828-3135
Fax : (802) 828-3140

VIRGINIA
William C. Bosher, Jr.
Superintendent
Dept. of Education
Monroe Bldg., 25th Fl.
101 N. 14th St.
Richmond, VA 23219
Phone : (804) 225-2023
Fax : (804) 371-2099

WASHINGTON
Judith Billings
Superintendent
Public Instruction
Old Capitol Bldg.
P.O. Box 47200
Olympia, WA 98504-7200
Phone : (360) 753-6738

WEST VIRGINIA
Barbara Harmon-Schamberger
Secretary
Dept. of Education & the Arts
Bldg. 1, Rm. 151
1900 Kanawha Blvd., E.
Charleston, WV 25305
Phone : (304) 558-2440

Hank Marockie
Superintendent
Dept. of Education
1800 Washington St., E., Bldg. 6
Charleston, WV 25305
Phone : (304) 558-2681

WISCONSIN
John Benson
Superintendent
Dept. of Public Instruction
125 S. Webster St.
P.O. Box 7841
Madison, WI 53707
Phone : (608) 266-3390
Fax : (608) 267-1052

Education (Chief State School Officer)

WYOMING
Judy Catchpole
Supt. of Public Instruction
Dept. of Education
Hathaway Bldg., 2nd Fl.
2300 Capitol Ave.
Cheyenne, WY 82002-0050
Phone : (307) 777-7675

DISTRICT OF COLUMBIA
Franklin L. Smith
Superintendent of Schools
D.C. Public Schools
415 12th St., NW, Rm. 1209
Washington, DC 20004
Phone : (202) 724-4222

AMERICAN SAMOA
Tuato'o Tautalatasi
Director
Dept. of Education
Pago Pago, AS 96799
Phone : (684) 633-5237
Fax : (684) 633-4240

NORTHERN MARIANA ISLANDS
William S. Torres
Commissioner of Education
Public School System
Off. of the Governor
Saipan, MP 96950
Phone : (670) 322-6451
Fax : (670) 322-4056

PUERTO RICO
Victor Fajardo
Secretary
Dept. of Education
P.O. Box 190759
San Juan, PR 00919-0759
Phone : (809) 759-2000
Fax : (809) 250-0275

U.S. VIRGIN ISLANDS
James Cheek
Commissioner
Dept. of Education
44-46 Kongens Gade
St. Thomas, VI 00802
Phone : (809) 774-0100
Fax : (809) 774-4679

ELECTIONS ADMINISTRATION

Administers state election laws and supervises the printing and distribution of ballots.

ALASKA
Joe Swanson
Director
Div. of Elections
Off. of Lt. Governor
P.O. Box 110017
Juneau, AK 99811-0017
Phone : (907) 465-4611
Fax : (907) 465-3203

ARIZONA
Jane Dee Hull
Secretary of State
1700 W. Washington St., 7th Floor
Phoenix, AZ 85007
Phone : (602) 542-4285

ARKANSAS
Sharon Priest
Secretary of State
256 State Capitol Bldg.
Little Rock, AR 72201
Phone : (501) 682-1010
Fax : (501) 682-3510

CALIFORNIA
Bob Steele
Chief
Political Reform
Off. of the Secretary of State
1230 J St.
Sacramento,, CA 95814
Phone : (916) 657-2166

John Mott-Smith
Chief
Elections
Off. of the Secretary of State
1230 J. St.
Sacramento, CA 95814
Phone : (916) 657-2166

COLORADO
William A. Hobbs
Elections Officer
Elections Div.
Dept. of State
1560 Broadway, Ste. 200
Denver, CO 80203
Phone : (303) 894-2680
Fax : (303) 894-7732

CONNECTICUT
Thomas Ferguson
Director
Elections Div.
Off. of Secretary of State
30 Trinity St.
Hartford, CT 06106
Phone : (203) 566-3106

DELAWARE
Thomas J. Cook
Commissioner
Dept. of Elections
32 Loockerman Square, Ste. 203
Dover, DE 19901
Phone : (302) 739-4277
Fax : (302) 739-6794

FLORIDA
David Rancourt
Director
Div. of Elections
Dept. of State
PL 02, The Capitol
Tallahassee, FL 32399-0250
Phone : (904) 488-7690

GEORGIA
Max Cleland
Secretary of State
State Capitol, Rm. 214
Atlanta, GA 30334
Phone : (404) 656-2881
Fax : (404) 656-0513

HAWAII
Mazie Hirono
Lt. Governor
State Capitol, 14th Fl.
Honolulu, HI 96813
Phone : (808) 586-0255

ILLINOIS
Ronald D. Michaelson
Executive Director
State Board of Elections
1020 S. Spring St.
Springfield, IL 62708-4187
Phone : (217) 782-4141
Fax : (217) 782-5959

IOWA
Paul Pate
Secretary of State
State Capitol
Des Moines, IA 50319
Phone : (515) 281-5204

KANSAS
Ron Thornburgh
Secretary of State
Elections/Legislative Matters
State Capitol Bldg., 2nd Fl.
Topeka, KS 66612
Phone : (913) 296-4561
Fax : (913) 296-3051

KENTUCKY
George Russell
Director
Registry of Election Finance
140 Walnut St.
Frankfort, KY 40601
Phone : (502) 573-7100

LOUISIANA
Jerry M. Fowler
Commissioner
Dept. of Elections & Registration
P.O. Box 14179
Baton Rouge, LA 70898
Phone : (504) 925-7885

MARYLAND
Gene Raynor
Administrator
Adm. Board of Election Laws
Old Armory Bldg.
P.O. Box 231
Annapolis, MD 21404
Phone : (410) 974-3711

MASSACHUSETTS
John Cloonan
Director
Elections Div.
Off. of Secretary of the Commonwealth
1 Ashburton Pl., Rm. 1705
Boston, MA 02108
Phone : (617) 727-2828
Fax : (617) 742-3238

MICHIGAN
Candice Miller
Secretary of State
Treasury Bldg., 1st Fl.
430 W. Allegan St.
Lansing, MI 48918
Phone : (517) 373-2510

MINNESOTA
Joe Mansky
Director, Election Div.
Off. of Secretary of State
180 State Off. Bldg.
100 Constitution Ave.
St. Paul, MN 55155-1299
Phone : (612) 296-9218

Joan Growe
Secretary of State
180 State Off. Bldg.
100 Constitution Ave.
St. Paul, MN 55155
Phone : (612) 296-2079

MISSOURI
Joseph A. Carroll
Director
Div. of Elections
Off. of Secretary of State
600 W. Main
P.O. Box 778
Jefferson City, MO 65102
Phone : (314) 751-4875
Fax : (314) 526-3242

MONTANA
Angela Fultz
Elections Director
Elections Bur.
Elections & Leg. Srvcs. Bur.
State Capitol, Rm. 225
Helena, MT 59620
Phone : (406) 444-4732

NEBRASKA
Scott Moore
Secretary of State
P.O. Box 94608
Lincoln, NE 68509
Phone : (402) 471-2554

NEVADA
Alfredo Alonso
Deputy Secretary of State for Elections
Off. of Secretary of State
Capitol Complex
Carson City, NV 89710
Phone : (702) 687-3176

NEW HAMPSHIRE
William Gardner
Secretary of State
204 State House
Concord, NH 03301
Phone : (603) 271-3242

NEW JERSEY
Inez M. Killian
Director
Election Div.
Dept. of State
State House, CN304
Trenton, NJ 08625
Phone : (609) 292-3760

Frederick M. Herrmann
Executive Director
Election Law Enforcement Comm.
Dept. of Law & Public Safety
28 W. State St., CN 185
Trenton, NJ 08625-0185
Phone : (609) 292-8700

NEW MEXICO
Denise Lamb
Director
Registry of Election Finance
Off. of Secretary of State
State Capitol Bldg., Rm. 420
Santa Fe, NM 87503
Phone : (505) 827-3600
Fax : (505) 827-3634

NEW YORK*
Executive Director
State Board of Elections
Empire State Plz., Core I
Swan St.
Albany, NY 12223
Phone : (518) 474-8100

NORTH CAROLINA
Yvonne Sutherland
Deputy Director
NC State Board of Elections
5 W. Hargett St.
Raleigh, NC 27601-1392
Phone : (919) 733-7173
Fax : (919) 715-0135

NORTH DAKOTA
Tom Mattern
Election Supervisor
Off. of Secretary of State
State Capitol, 1st Fl.
600 E. Boulevard Ave.
Bismarck, ND 58505
Phone : (701) 328-2905
Fax : (701) 328-2992

OHIO
John R. Bender
Deputy Director
Elections Division
Office of the Secretary of State
30 E. Broad St., 14th Floor
Columbus, OH 43266
Phone : (614) 466-2585
Fax : (614) 752-4360

OKLAHOMA
Lance Ward
Secretary of the Senate
State Capitol, Rm. 3-B
Oklahoma City, OK 73105
Phone : (405) 521-2391

OREGON
Colleen Sealock
Director
Elections & Public Records
Off. of Secretary of State
141 State Capitol
Salem, OR 97310
Phone : (503) 986-1518
Fax : (503) 373-7414

PENNSYLVANIA
William Boehm
Commissioner
Bur. of Commissions, Elections & Legislation, Dept. of State
305 N. Off. Bldg.
Harrisburg, PA 17120
Phone : (717) 787-5280

RHODE ISLAND
Roger N. Begin
Chairman
Board of Elections
50 Branch Ave.
Providence, RI 02904

SOUTH CAROLINA
James Hendrix
Executive Director
State Election Comm.
2221 Devine St., Ste. 105
P.O. Box 5987
Columbia, SC 29250
Phone : (803) 734-9060

TENNESSEE
Will Burns
Coordinator of Elections
Div. of Elections
James K. Polk Bldg., Ste. 500
505 Deaderick St.
Nashville, TN 37219
Phone : (615) 741-7956

TEXAS
Tom Harrison
Director
Div. of Elections
Off. of Secretary of State
P.O. Box 12060
Austin, TX 78711
Phone : (512) 463-5701

VERMONT
James Milne
Secretary of State
26 Terrace St.
Montpelier, VT 05609-1101
Phone : (802) 828-2168
Fax : (802) 828-2496

VIRGINIA
M. Bruce Meadows
Secretary
State Bd. of Elections
101 Ninth St. Off. Bldg.
Richmond, VA 23219
Phone : (804) 786-6551
Fax : (804) 371-0194

WASHINGTON
Gary McIntosh
Supervisor
Elections Div.
Off. of Secretary of State
Legislative Bldg., Box 40229
Olympia, WA 98504-0229
Phone : (360) 753-7139

WEST VIRGINIA
Ken Hechler
Secretary of State
State Capitol, Rm W-157K
1900 Kanawha Blvd., E.
Charleston, WV 25305
Phone : (304) 558-6000

WISCONSIN
Kevin J. Kennedy
Executive Director
State Elections Bd.
132 E. Wilson St., Ste. 300
Madison, WI 53703
Phone : (608) 266-8005
Fax : (608) 267-0500

WYOMING
Carol Thompson
Director of Elections
Off. of Secretary of State
State Capitol
Cheyenne, WY 82002
Phone : (307) 777-5333

AMERICAN SAMOA
Soliai T. Fuimaono
Commissioner
Elections Comm. Off.
Pago Pago, AS 96799
Phone : (684) 633-2522
Fax : (684) 633-7116

GUAM
Henry A. Torres
Executive Director
Guam Election Comm.
P.O. Box BG
Agana, GU 96910
Phone : (671) 477-9791
Fax : (671) 477-1077

NORTHERN MARIANA ISLANDS
Juan M. Diaz
Executive Director
Board of Elections
P.O. Box 470
Saipan, MP 96950
Phone : (670) 234-6481
Fax : (670) 233-6880

PUERTO RICO

Juan R. Meleccio
President
State Election Comm.
P.O. Box 2353
San Juan, PR 00902
Phone : (809) 723-1006
Fax : (809) 721-7940

U.S. VIRGIN ISLANDS

John Abramson
Supervisor
Off. of Supvr. of Elections
Board of Elections
P.O. Box 6038
St. Thomas, VI 00801
Phone : (809) 774-3107
Fax : (809) 776-2391

EMERGENCY MANAGEMENT

Prepares, maintains and/or implements state disaster plans and coordinates emergency activities.

ALABAMA
Lee Helms
Director
Emergency Mgt. Agency
P.O. Drawer 2160
Clanton, AL 35045
Phone : (205) 280-2200
Fax : (205) 280-2410

ALASKA
Ervin P. Martin
Director
Div. of Emergency Mgt. Srvcs.
Dept. of Military & Vet. Aff.
P.O. Box 5750
Fort Richardson, AK 99505-5800
Phone : (907) 428-7000
Fax : (907) 428-7009

ARIZONA
Michael Austin
Director
Div. of Emergency Services
5636 E. McDowell Rd.
Phoenix, AZ 85008
Phone : (602) 231-6245

ARKANSAS
Joe Dillard
Director
Off. of Emergency Srvcs.
P.O. Box 758
Conway, AR 72033
Phone : (501) 329-5601
Fax : (501) 327-8047

CALIFORNIA
Richard Andrews
Director
Off. of Emergency Srvcs.
2800 Meadowview Rd.
Sacramento, CA 95832
Phone : (916) 262-1816

COLORADO
Hal Knott
Director
Off. of Emergency Mgt.
Dept. of Local Affairs
Camp George W., Bldg. 120
Golden, CO 80401
Phone : (303) 273-1622

CONNECTICUT
Robert Plant
Director
Off. of Emergency Mgt.
360 Broad St.
Hartford, CT 06105
Phone : (203) 566-3180

DELAWARE
Sean P. Mulhern
Director
Div. of Emergency Planning & Operations
P.O. Box 527
Delaware City, DE 19706
Phone : (302) 834-4531
Fax : (302) 834-7495

FLORIDA
Joseph F. Myers
Director
Div. of Emergency Mgt.
Dept. of Community Affairs
2740 Centerview Dr.
Tallahassee, FL 32399-2100
Phone : (904) 487-4918
Fax : (904) 921-0781

GEORGIA
Gary W. McConnell
Executive Director
Emergency Mgt. Agency
P.O. Box 18055
Atlanta, GA 30316
Phone : (404) 624-7002

HAWAII
Roy C. Price
Vice Director
State Civil Defense
3949 Diamond Head Rd.
Honolulu, HI 96816
Phone : (808) 734-2161

IDAHO
Darrell G. Waller
Coordinator
Bur. of Disaster Srvcs.
Military Div.
P.O. Box 83720
Boise, ID 83720-0023
Phone : (208) 334-3460

ILLINOIS
John G. Mitchell
Director
Emergency Management Agency
110 E. Adams St.
Springfield, IL 62706
Phone : (217) 782-2700
Fax : (217) 785-6043

INDIANA
Melvin Carraway
Director
State Emergency Mgt. Agency
IGC-South, Rm. 208
302 W. Washington St.
Indianapolis, IN 46204
Phone : (317) 232-3980

IOWA
Ellen Gordon
Administrator
Emergency Mgt. Div.
Dept. of Public Defense
Hoover State Off. Bldg.
Des Moines, IA 50319
Phone : (515) 281-3231

KANSAS
Lloyd E. Krase
Deputy Director
Div. of Emergency Management
Dept. of Adjutant General
2800 SW Topeka Blvd.
Topeka, KS 66601-0300
Phone : (913) 274-1400
Fax : (913) 274-1682

KENTUCKY
Ron Padgett
Acting Director
Disaster & Emergency Srvcs.
Military Affairs
Boone Ntl. Guard Ctr.
Frankfort, KY 40601
Phone : (502) 564-8682

LOUISIANA
Bill Croft
Assistant Director
Off. of Emergency Preparedness
P.O. Box 44217
Baton Rouge, LA 70804
Phone : (504) 342-5470

MAINE
David D. Brown
Director
Emergency Management Agency
State House Station #72
Augusta, ME 04333
Phone : (207) 287-4080

MARYLAND
David A. McMillion
Director
Emergency Mgt. Agency
2 Sudbrook Ln., E.
Baltimore, MD 21208
Phone : (410) 486-4422

MASSACHUSETTS
David Rodham
Director
Civil Defense Agency
P.O. Box 1496
Framingham, MA 01701
Phone : (508) 820-2000
Fax : (508) 820-2030

MICHIGAN
Sherman L. Ampey
Deputy State Director
State Police Emergency Mgt.
300 S. Washington Sq., Ste.300
Lansing, MI 48913
Phone : (517) 373-6271

MINNESOTA
James D. Franklin
Director
Div. of Emergency Mgt.
Dept. of Public Safety
Capitol Bldg., Rm. B-5
St. Paul, MN 55155
Phone : (612) 296-0449

MISSISSIPPI
James E. Maher
Director
Emergency Management Agency
P.O. Box 4501, Fondren Station
Jackson, MS 39296
Phone : (601) 352-9100

MISSOURI
Jerry Uhlmann
Director
State Emergency Mgt. Agency
Dept. of Public Safety
2302 Militia Dr.
P.O. Box 116
Jefferson City, MO 65102
Phone : (314) 526-9101
Fax : (314) 634-7966
E-Mail: MO-SEMA@SERVICES.STATE.MO.US

MONTANA
Jim Greene
Administrator
Disaster & Emergency Services Div.
1100 N. Main
Helena, MT 59620-2111
Phone : (406) 444-6911

NEBRASKA
Bill Whitney
Assistant Director
Civil Defense Agency
National Guard Ctr.
1300 Military Rd
Lincoln, NE 68508
Phone : (402) 471-7410

NEVADA
James P. Hawke
Director
Emergency Management
Motor Veh. & Pub. Safety Dept.
2525 S. Carson
Carson City, NV 89710
Phone : (702) 687-4989

NEW HAMPSHIRE
George L. Iverson
Director
Off. of Emergency Mgt.
State Off. Park S.
107 Pleasant St.
Concord, NH 03301
Phone : (603) 271-2231

NEW JERSEY
Carl A. Williams
Director
Div. of State Police
Dept. of Law & Public Safety
P.O. Box 7068
West Trenton, NJ 08625
Phone : (609) 882-2000

NEW MEXICO
Darren White
Director
Dept. of Public Safety
P.O. Box 1628
Santa Fe, NM 87504
Phone : (505) 827-3370
Fax : (505) 827-3434

NEW YORK *
Director
State Emergency Mgt. Off.
State Campus
Public Security Bldg. 22
Albany, NY 12226
Phone : (518) 457-2222

NORTH CAROLINA
Bob Bailey
Chief
Emergency Medical Services
Dept. of Human Resources
701 Barbour Dr.
Raleigh, NC 27603-2008
Phone : (919) 733-2285
Fax : (919) 733-7021

Billy Ray Cameron
Director
Div. of Emergency Mgt.
116 W. Jones St.
Raleigh, NC 27604
Phone : (919) 733-3825
Fax : (919) 733-5406

NORTH DAKOTA
Doug Friez
Director
Div. of Emergency Management
P.O. Box 5511
Bismarck, ND 58502
Phone : (701) 328-2111
Fax : (701) 328-2119

OHIO
Dale W. Shipley
Deputy Director
Emergency Mgt. Agency
Dept. of Adjutant General
2825 W. Granville Rd.
Columbus, OH 43235-2789
Phone : (614) 889-7150
Fax : (614) 889-7183

OKLAHOMA
Tom Feuerborn
Director
Dept. of Civil Emergency Mgt.
2401 N. Lincoln Blvd.
Will Rogers-Sequoyah Tunnel
Oklahoma City, OK 73105
Phone : (405) 521-2481

OREGON
Myra Thompson Lee
Director
Off. of Emergency Management
595 Cottage St., NE
Salem, OR 97310
Phone : (503) 378-2911

PENNSYLVANIA
Charles F. Wynne
Director
Emergency Management Agency
Transportation & Safety Bldg.
Rm. R-151
Harrisburg, PA 17120
Phone : (717) 783-8150

RHODE ISLAND
Joseph Carnavale
Executive Director
Emergency Management Agency
State House, Rm. 27
Providence, RI 02903
Phone : (401) 427-7333

SOUTH CAROLINA
Stan M. McKinney
Director
Div. of Emergency Preparedness
Off. of Adjutant General
1429 Senate St.
Columbia, SC 29201
Phone : (803) 734-8020

SOUTH DAKOTA
Gary N. Whitney
Director
Div. of Emergency Management
425 E. Capitol Ave.
Pierre, SD 57501
Phone : (605) 773-3231

TENNESSEE
John White
Director
Emergency Mgt. Agency
Dept. of Military
3041 Sidco Dr.
Nashville, TN 37204
Phone : (615) 741-0001

TEXAS
Tom Millwee
State Coordinator
Div. of Emergency Mgt.
Dept. of Public Safety
P.O. Box 4087
Austin, TX 78773
Phone : (512) 465-2000

UTAH
Lorayne M. Frank
Director
Comprehensive Emergency Mgt.
Emergency Mgt. Agency
State Off. Bldg., Rm. 1110
Salt Lake City, UT 84114
Phone : (801) 538-3400

VERMONT
George L. Lowe
Director
Emergency Mgt. Div.
Dept. of Public Safety
103 S. Main St.
Waterbury, VT 05671
Phone : (802) 244-8721
Fax : (802) 244-8655

VIRGINIA
Addison E. Slayton Jr.
State Coordinator
Dept. of Emergency Services
310 Turner Rd.
Richmond, VA 23225
Phone : (804) 674-2497

WASHINGTON
Ed Small
Director
Emergency Mgt. Div.
Dept. of Community Dev.
P.O. Box 48346
Olympia, WA 98504-8346
Phone : (360) 459-9191

WEST VIRGINIA
Carl L. Bradford
Director
Off. of Emergency Services
Bldg. 1, Rm. EB-80
1900 Kanawha Blvd., E.
Charleston, WV 25305
Phone : (304) 558-5380

WISCONSIN
Lee Connor
Administrator
Div. of Emergency Government
Dept. of Military Affairs
2400 Wright St.
Madison, WI 53704
Phone : (608) 242-3232
Fax : (608) 242-3247

WYOMING
Brooke Hefner
Coordinator
Emergency Manangement Agency
P.O. Box 1709
Cheyeene, WY 82002
Phone : (307) 777-7566

Robert J. Bezek
Coordinator
Emergency Management Agency
P.O. Box 1709
Cheyenne, WY 82002
Phone : (307) 777-7566

DISTRICT OF COLUMBIA
Samuel Jordon
Director
Off. of Emergency Preparedness
2000 14th St., NW, 8th Fl.
Washington, DC 20009
Phone : (202) 727-6161

AMERICAN SAMOA
Fonoti D. Jessop
Commissioner
Dept. of Public Safety
American Samoa Government
Pago Pago, AS 96799
Phone : (684) 633-1111
Fax : (684) 633-5111

GUAM
Juan B. Rosario
Director
Civil Defense
Emergency Operations Ctr.
San Ramon
P.O. Box 2877
Agana, GU 96910
Phone : (671) 477-9841
Fax : (671) 477-3727

NORTHERN MARIANA ISLANDS
Robert A. Guerrero
Director
Emergency Operations
Emergency Mgt. Off.
P.O. Box 10007
Saipan, MP 96950
Phone : (670) 322-9573
Fax : (670) 322-9500

PUERTO RICO
Epifanio Jimenez
Director
State Civil Defense Agency
P.O. Box 5127
San Juan, PR 00906-5127
Phone : (809) 724-0124
Fax : (809) 725-4244

U.S. VIRGIN ISLANDS
Kirk Grybowksi
Director
VITEMA
3-4 King St.
St. Croix, VI 00820
Phone : (809) 778-4916

EMERGENCY MEDICAL SERVICES

Administers comprehensive medical and allied programs to reduce unnecessary mortality and disability from emergency medical conditions.

ALABAMA
John W. Story
Director
Emergency Medical Srvcs. Div.
Dept. of Public Health
434 Monroe St.
Montgomery, AL 36130
Phone : (334) 613-5296
Fax : (334) 240-3061

ALASKA
Mark S. Johnson
Chief
Emergency Medical Srvcs.
Dept. of Health & Social Srvcs.
P.O. Box 110616
Juneau, AK 99811-0616
Phone : (907) 465-3027
Fax : (907) 586-1877

ARIZONA
Toni Brophy
Medical Director
Emergency Medical Srvcs. Div.
1651 E. Morten, Ste. 120
Phoenix, AZ 85020
Phone : (602) 255-1170

ARKANSAS
Doug Darr
Director
Emergency Medical Srvcs.
Dept. of Health
4815 W. Markham St.
Little Rock, AR 72205-3867
Phone : (501) 661-2262
Fax : (501) 280-4901

CALIFORNIA
Joseph Morales
Director
Emergency Medical Services Authority
1930 9th St., Ste. 100
Sacramento, CA 95814
Phone : (916) 322-4336

COLORADO
Larry L. McNatt
Director
Emergency Medical Srvc. Div.
Dept. of Public Health & Env.
4300 Cherry Creek Dr., S.
Denver, CO 80222
Phone : (303) 692-2980
Fax : (303) 782-0904

CONNECTICUT
Micheal Kleiner
Director
Off. of Emergency Medical Services
150 Washington St.
Hartford, CT 06106
Phone : (203) 566-7365

DELAWARE
Charles E. Nabb
Director
Emergency Medical Srvcs. Off.
Jesse S. Cooper Memorial Bldg.
Capitol Sq.
Dover, DE 19901
Phone : (302) 739-4710

FLORIDA
Keith Dutton
Director
Emergency Medical Srvcs.
Health & Rehab. Srvcs. Dept.
1317 Winewood Blvd.
Tallahassee, FL 32399-0700
Phone : (904) 487-1911

GEORGIA
Patrick Meehan
Acting Dir. of Emergency & Health
Div. of Public Health
Dept. of Human Resources
2 Peachtree St., 7th Fl.
Atlanta, GA 30303
Phone : (404) 657-2700

HAWAII
Donna Maiava
Chief
Emergency Medical Srvc. System
Dept. of Health
3627 Kiluaea Ave., Rm. 102
Honolulu, HI 96816
Phone : (808) 735-5270

IDAHO
Dia Gainor
Chief
Emergency Medical Srvcs. Bur.
Dept. of Health & Welfare
3092 Elder St.
P.O. Box 83720
Boise, ID 83720-0036
Phone : (208) 334-4000
Fax : (208) 334-4015

ILLINOIS
Leslee Stein-Spencer
Chief
Div. of Emergency Med. Srvcs.
Dept. of Public Health
525 W. Jefferson St., Rm. 450
Springfield, IL 62761
Phone : (217) 785-2080

INDIANA
Melvin Carraway
Director
State Emergency Mgt. Agency
IGC-South, Rm. 208
302 W. Washington St.
Indianapolis, IN 46204
Phone : (317) 232-3980

IOWA
Steve Mercer
Program Administrator
Emergency Med. Srvcs. Section
Dept. of Public Health
Lucas State Off. Bldg.
Des Moines, IA 50319-0075
Phone : (515) 281-4951

KANSAS
Bob McDaneld
Administrator
Emergency Medical Srvcs. Board
109 SW Sixth St.
Topeka, KS 66603-3826
Phone : (913) 296-7296
Fax : (913) 296-6212

KENTUCKY
Robert Calhoun
Branch Manager
Emergency Med. Srvcs. Branch
Dept. for Health Srvcs.
275 E. Main St.
Frankfort, KY 40621
Phone : (502) 564-8965

LOUISIANA
Nancy Bourgeous
Acting Director
Bur. of Emergency Med. Srvcs.
455 N. Blvd., 2nd Fl.
P.O. Box 44215
Baton Rouge, LA 70804
Phone : (504) 342-4361

MAINE
Kevin McGinnis
Director
Emergency Medical Services
353 Water Street
Augusta, ME 04333
Phone : (207) 287-3953

MARYLAND
Robert R. Bose
Director
Emergency Medical Srvcs.
636 W. Lombard St.
Baltimore, MD 21201
Phone : (410) 706-5074
Fax : (410) 706-4768

MASSACHUSETTS
Louise Goyette
Director
Off. of Emergency Medical Srvcs.
Dept. of Public Health
150 Tremont St.
Boston, MA 02111-1126
Phone : (617) 534-2367

MICHIGAN
Richard Schmidt
Division Chief
Div. of Emergency Med. Srvcs.
3423 N. Logan
P.O. Box 30195
Lansing, MI 48909
Phone : (517) 335-9502

MINNESOTA
Jennifer Deschaine
Chief
Emergency Medical Srvcs.
Dept. of Health
393 N. Dunlap St., Box 64900
St. Paul, MN 55164-0900
Phone : (612) 623-5484

MISSISSIPPI
Wade N. Spruill Jr.
Director
Emergency Medical Srvcs.
State Dept. of Health
P.O. Box 1700
Jackson, MS 39215-1700
Phone : (601) 987-3882

MISSOURI
Stephen Hise
Acting Director
Bureau of Emergency Medical Srvcs.
Dept. of Health
1738 E. Elm
P.O. Box 570
Jefferson City, MO 65102-0570
Phone : (314) 751-6356
Fax : (314) 526-4102

MONTANA
Drew Dawson
Chief
Emergency Medical Srvcs. Bur.
Health & Environ. Sciences
Cogswell Bldg.
Helena, MT 59620
Phone : (406) 444-3895

NEBRASKA
Robert Leopold
Director
Emergency Medical Services Div.
Dept. of Health
P.O. Box 95007
Lincoln, NE 68509-5007
Phone : (402) 471-2158
Fax : (402) 471-6446

NEVADA
Sheryl Yount
Supervisor
Emergency Medical Serv.
Div. of Health
505 E. King St.
Carson City, NV 89710
Phone : (702) 687-3065

NEW HAMPSHIRE
Marcia E. Houck
Bureau Chief
Emergency Medical Srvcs.
Health & Welfare Bldg.
Hazen Dr.
Concord, NH 03301
Phone : (603) 271-4569

NEW JERSEY
George Leggett
Bureau Chief
Emergency & Medical Services
Dept. of Health
300 Whitehead Rd., CN367
Trenton, NJ 08625
Phone : (609) 292-6789

NEW YORK *
Executive Deputy Commissioner
Dept. of Health
Empire State Plz., Corning Tower
Albany, NY 12237
Phone : (518) 473-0458

NORTH CAROLINA
Bob Bailey
Chief
Emergency Medical Services
Dept. of Human Resources
701 Barbour Dr.
Raleigh, NC 27603-2008
Phone : (919) 733-2285
Fax : (919) 733-7021

NORTH DAKOTA
Timothy Wiedrich
Director
Emergency Health Services
Dept. of Health
State Capitol, 600 E. Blvd. Ave.
Bismarck, ND 58505
Phone : (701) 328-2388
Fax : (701) 328-4727

OHIO
John Drstvensek
Medical Director
Emergency Medical Services Agency
P.O. Box 7167
Columbus, OH 43266-0563
Phone : (614) 466-9447
Fax : (614) 466-0433

Roger E. Glick
Administrator
Public Safety Services
Emergency Medical Srvcs. Agcy.
P.O. Box 7167
Columbus, OH 43266-0563
Phone : (614) 466-9447
Fax : (614) 466-0433

OKLAHOMA
John Manley
Director
Emergency Medical Services
P.O. Box 53551
Oklahoma City, OK 73152
Phone : (405) 271-4062

OREGON
Howard Kirkwood
Manager
Emergency Medical Services
Health Div.
Portland State Off. Bldg.
800 NE Oregon #21
Portland, OR 97232
Phone : (503) 731-4011

PENNSYLVANIA
Kum S. Ham
Director
Div. of Emergency Med. Srvcs.
Dept. of Health
Health & Welf. Bldg., Rm. 1033
Harrisburg, PA 17108
Phone : (717) 787-8741

RHODE ISLAND
Peter Leary
Chief
Emergency Medical Srvc. Div.
Dept. of Health
3 Capitol Hill
Providence, RI 02903
Phone : (401) 277-2401

SOUTH CAROLINA
Joe Fanning
Director
Emergency Medical Srvcs. Div.
Health & Environmental Control
2600 Bull St.
Columbia, SC 29201
Phone : (803) 737-7204

SOUTH DAKOTA
Robert Graff
Director
Emergency Medical Services
Div. of Health Services
445 E. Capitol Ave.
Pierre, SD 57501
Phone : (605) 773-4928

TENNESSEE
Joseph B. Phillips
Director
Emergency Medical Services
287 Plus Park Blvd.
Nashville, TN 37247-0701
Phone : (615) 367-6278

TEXAS
Pam West
Director
Emergency Medical Srvcs. Div.
Dept. of Health
1100 W. 49th St.
Austin, TX 78756
Phone : (512) 458-7111

UTAH
Jan M. Buttrey
Director
Emergency Medical Services Bur.
Dept. of Health
P.O. Box 16990
Salt Lake City, UT 84116-0990
Phone : (801) 538-6718

VERMONT
Dan Manz
Director
Emergency Medical Srvcs. Div.
Dept. of Health
131 Main St., P.O. Box 70
Burlington, VT 05402
Phone : (802) 863-7310
Fax : (802) 863-7577

VIRGINIA
Donald R. Stern
Acting Commissioner
Emergency Medical Srvc. Div.
Dept. of Health
Main St. Station, Rm. 214
1500 E. Main St.
Richmond, VA 23219
Phone : (804) 786-3561
Fax : (804) 786-4616

WASHINGTON
Janet Griffith
Program Director
Emergency Medical Srvcs.
Dept. of Health
2725 Harrison Ave., NW, Unit 500
Olympia, WA 98504
Phone : (360) 705-6745

WEST VIRGINIA
F.M. Cooley
Director
Emergency Medical Srvc. Off.
Bldg. 3, Rm. 426
1800 Washington St., E.
Charleston, WV 25305
Phone : (304) 558-3956

WISCONSIN
Mike French
Chief
Emergency Medical Srvcs.
Div. of Health
1 W Wilson, Room 94
P.O. Box 309
Madison, WI 53703
Phone : (608) 266-1568
Fax : (608) 267-2832

WYOMING
Jim Murray
Program Manager
Emergency Medical Services
Health & Medical Services Div.
Hathaway Bldg., Rm. 527
Cheyenne, WY 82002
Phone : (307) 777-6020

DISTRICT OF COLUMBIA
Robert R. Bass
Medical Director
Emergency Medical Srvc. Off.
1018 13th St., NW, 3rd Fl.
Washington, DC 20005
Phone : (202) 673-3360

AMERICAN SAMOA
Fuapopo Avegalio
EMS Coordinator
Emergency Medical Srvcs.
LBJ Tropical Medical Center
Pago Pago, AS 96799
Phone : (684) 633-1222

GUAM
Dennis G. Rodriguez
Director
Dept. of Public Health & Social Services
P.O. Box 2816
Agana, GU 96910
Phone : (671) 734-7399

PUERTO RICO
Nefer Carrillo
Assistant Secretary
Emergency Medical Services
P.O. Box 70184
San Juan, PR 00936
Phone : (809) 765-1066

NORTHERN MARIANA ISLANDS
Isamu Abraham
Secretary
Health Srvcs.
Commonwealth Health Ctr.
P.O. Box 409 Ctc
Saipan, MP 96950
Phone : (670) 234-8950
Fax : (670) 322-4336

U.S. VIRGIN ISLANDS
Thlema Watson
Director, Emergency Medical Services
Dept. of Health
St. Thomas Hospital
St. Thomas, VI 00802
Phone : (809) 776-8311

EMPLOYEE RELATIONS

Handles state employee grievances and appeals.

ALASKA
Diane Corso
Director
Div. of Labor Relations
Dept. of Administration
P.O. Box 110201
Juneau, AK 99811-0201
Phone : (907) 465-4404
Fax : (907) 465-2576

ARIZONA
William Bell
Assistant Director
Personnel Division
Dept. of Administration
1831 W. Jefferson, Rm. 100
Phoenix, AZ 85007
Phone : (602) 542-5482

ARKANSAS
Artee Williams
Administrator
Dept. of Finance & Admin.
201 DFA Bldg.
1509 W. 7th St.
Little Rock, AR 72201
Phone : (501) 682-1823
Fax : (501) 682-5094

CALIFORNIA
David J. Tirapelle
Director
Dept. of Personnel Admin.
1515 S. St., North Bldg., Ste. 400
Sacramento, CA 95814
Phone : (916) 322-5193

COLORADO
Shirley Harris
Executive Director
Dept. of Personnel
1313 Sherman St., Rm. 123
Denver, CO 80203
Phone : (303) 866-2321

CONNECTICUT
Joseph G. Wankerl
Employee Relations
Personnel & Labor Relations
Dept. of Administrative Srvcs.
165 Capitol Ave., Rm. 403
Hartford, CT 06106
Phone : (203) 566-3081

CONNECTICUT — Cont.
Barbara Waters
Department Secretary
Bureau Human Resources
165 Capitol Ave., Rm 404
Hartford, CT 06106
Phone : (203) 566-5929

DELAWARE
Harriet Smith
Director
Off. of Personnel
Townsend Bldg.
P.O. Box 1401
Dover, DE 19903
Phone : (302) 739-4195
Fax : (302) 739-3000

FLORIDA
George Haynie
Division of Administration
Dept. of Management Services
Knight Bldg., Ste. 114
Tallahassee, FL 32399-0950
Phone : (904) 448-0968
Fax : (904) 922-6149

GEORGIA
Diane Schlachter
Director
Training & Organizational Dev.
Merit System of Pers. Admin.
900 South Tower, 1 CNN Ctr.
Atlanta, GA 30303
Phone : (404) 656-2734

ILLINOIS
Michael S. Schwartz
Director
Dept. of Central Mgt. Srvcs.
715 Stratton Off. Bldg.
Springfield, IL 62706
Phone : (217) 782-2141
Fax : (217) 524-1880

INDIANA
C. Thomas Neely
Supervisor
Employee Relations Section
Personnel Dept.
IGC-South, Rm. W161
Indianapolis, IN 46204
Phone : (317) 232-3080

IOWA
Linda Hanson
Director
Dept. of Personnel
Grimes State Off. Bldg.
E. 14th & Grand
Des Moines, IA 50319
Phone : (515) 281-3351
Fax : (515) 242-6450

KANSAS
Roger Aeschliman
Deputy Secretary
Division of Staff Services
Dept. of Human Resources
401 Topeka Blvd.
Topeka, KS 66603-3182
Phone : (913) 296-5075
Fax : (913) 296-5286

KENTUCKY
Lowell W. Clark
Commissioner
Dept. of Personnel
200 Fairoaks, Suite 516
Frankfort, KY 40601
Phone : (502) 564-4460

LOUISIANA
Herbert Sumrall
Director
Civil Service Comm.
Personnel Management Div.
Dept. of Civil Service
P.O. Box 94111
Baton Rouge, LA 70804-9111
Phone : (504) 342-8272

MAINE
Kenneth A. Walo
Director
Bur. of Employee Relations
Dept. of Admin. & Fin. Srvcs.
State House Station # 79
Augusta, ME 04333
Phone : (207) 287-4447

MASSACHUSETTS
Joseph Daly
Director
Off. of Employee Relations
Executive Off. for Admin. & Finance
1 Ashburton Pl., Rm. 1002
Boston, MA 02108
Phone : (617) 727-5403

MICHIGAN
Shlomo Sperka
Director
Bur. of Employment Relations
Dept. of Labor
1200 Sixth St., 14th Fl.
Detroit, MI 48226
Phone : (313) 256-3540

MINNESOTA
Bruce E. Johnson
Commissioner
Dept. of Employee Relations
200 Centennial Bldg.
658 Cedar St.
St. Paul, MN 55101
Phone : (612) 296-8366

MISSISSIPPI
J.K. Stringer Jr.
Director
State Personnel Bd.
301 N. Lamar St., Ste. 100
Jackson, MS 39201
Phone : (601) 359-2704

MISSOURI
Judy A. Hawkins
Chair
Personnel Advisory Board
Off. of Administration
Truman Bldg., Rm. 430
P.O. Box 388
Jefferson City, MO 65102
Phone: (314) 751-4576
Fax: (314) 751-1622

MONTANA
Chuck Hunter
Administrator
Personnel Appeals Div.
Dept. of Labor & Industry
P.O. Box 1728
Helena, MT 59624
Phone: (406) 444-6530

NEBRASKA
William Wood
Director
Division of Employee Relations
Dept. of Administration Srvcs.
P.O. Box 94905
Lincoln, NE 68509-4905
Phone: (402) 471-4106
Fax: (402) 471-3754

NEVADA
Barbara Willis
Director
Dept. of Personnel
209 E. Musser St.
Carson City, NV 89710
Phone: (702) 687-3731
Fax: (702) 687-5017

NEW HAMPSHIRE
Evelyn C. LeBrun
Executive Director
Public Employees Labor Relations Bd.
163 Manchester St.
Concord, NH 03301-5142
Phone: (603) 271-2587

NEW JERSEY
James W. Mastriani
Chairman
Public Employment Relations Comm.
495 W. State St., CN 429
Trenton, NJ 08625
Phone: (609) 292-9830

NEW MEXICO
Jody Hooper
Director
State Personnel Off.
P.O. Box 26127
Santa Fe, NM 87502-6127
Phone: (505) 827-8120
Fax: (505) 827-8127

NEW YORK*
Director
Off. of Employee Relations
Agency Bldg. 2, 12th Fl.
Empire State Plz.
Albany, NY 12223-0001
Phone: (518) 474-6988

NORTH CAROLINA
Ronald G. Penny
Director
Off. of State Planning
Dept. of Administration
116 W. Jones St.
Raleigh, NC 27603-8003
Phone: (919) 733-7108

NORTH DAKOTA
Brian McClure
Director
Off. of Management & Budget
State Capitol, 1st Fl.
600 E. Boulevard Ave.
Bismarck, ND 58505-0120
Phone: (701) 328-3290
Fax: (701) 328-3000

OHIO
Patricia Hamilton
Chair
Personnel Bd. of Review
65 E. State St., 12th Fl.
Columbus, OH 43266-0319
Phone: (614) 466-7046
Fax: (614) 466-6539

OREGON
Daniel C. Ellis
Chairman
Employment Relations Bd.
528 Cottage St., NE
Salem, OR 97310
Phone: (503) 378-3807

PENNSYLVANIA
Christ J. Zervanos
Acting Director
Bur. of Labor Relations
Off. of Administration
404 Finance Bldg.
Harrisburg, PA 17105
Phone: (717) 787-5837

RHODE ISLAND
John Turano
Labor Relations Administrator
Dept. of Administration
One Capitol Hill
Providence, RI 02908
Phone: (401) 277-2154

SOUTH CAROLINA
Steve Osbourne
Director
Employee/Employer Rel. Div.
Div. of Human Resource Mgt.
1201 Main St., Ste. 1000
Columbia, SC 29201
Phone: (803) 737-0970

TENNESSEE
Marianne Batey
Director
Employee Relations
Dept. of Personnel
James K. Polk Bldg., 2nd Fl.
Nashville, TN 37243
Phone: (615) 741-1646

TEXAS
William M. Hale
Executive Director
Comm. on Human Rights
P.O. Box 13493
Austin, TX 78711
Phone: (512) 837-8534

UTAH
Robert N. White
Administrator
Career Service Review Board
1120 State Office Bldg.
Salt Lake City, UT 84114-1201
Phone: (801) 538-3047

VERMONT
Thomas D. Ball
Director of Employee Relations
Dept. of Personnel
110 State St.
Montpelier, VT 05602
Phone: (802) 828-3642
Fax: (802) 828-3409

VIRGINIA
Phyllis C. Katz
Director
Dept. of Employee Relations Counselors
700 E. Franklin St., Ste. 910
Richmond, VA 23219
Phone: (804) 786-7994

WASHINGTON
Dennis Karras
Director
Dept. of Personnel
521 Capitol Way, S.
P.O. Box 47500
Olympia, WA 98504
Phone: (360) 753-5368

WEST VIRGINIA
Robert Stevens
Director of Personnel
Civil Service System
State Capitol, Bldg. 6, Rm. 416
Charleston, WV 25305
Phone: (304) 558-3950

WISCONSIN
Jon Litscher
Secretary
Dept. of Employment Relations
137 E. Wilson St.
P.O. Box 7855
Madison, WI 53707-7855
Phone: (608) 266-9820
Fax: (608) 267-1020

WYOMING
Mike Miller
Administrator
Personnel Div.
Dept. of Admin. & Information
2001 Capitol Ave.
Cheyenne, WY 82002-0060
Phone: (307) 777-6713

DISTRICT OF COLUMBIA
Warren Cruise
Chairman
Off. of Employee Appeals
415 12th St., NW, Ste. 303
Washington, DC 20004
Phone: (202) 727-6406

DISTRICT OF COLUMBIA — Cont.
Larry King
Director
Off. of Personnel
613 G St., NW, 3rd Fl.
Washington, DC 20001
Phone : (202) 727-6406

AMERICAN SAMOA
Sapini Siatu'u
Director
Dept. of Human Resources
American Samoa Government
Pago Pago, AS 96799
Phone : (684) 633-4485
Fax : (684) 633-1139

GUAM
Edward A. Guerrero
Director
Dept. of Labor
P.O. Box 9970
Tamuning, GU 96911
Phone : (671) 646-9241

NORTHERN MARIANA ISLANDS
Eugene Santos
Board Chairman
Civil Service Comm.
Personnel Management Off.
Off. of the Governor
P.O. Box 5150 CHRB
Saipan, MP 96950
Phone : (670) 234-0829
Fax : (670) 234-2080

PUERTO RICO
Samuel De La Rosa
Director
Bur. of Employment Security
Labor & Human Resources Dept.
505 Munoz Rivera Ave.
Hato Rey, PR 00918
Phone : (809) 721-0060

U.S. VIRGIN ISLANDS
Oran C. Roebuck
Chief Negotiator
Off. of Collective Bargaining
Off. of the Governor
#8 GD Lyttons Fancy
St. Thomas, VI 00802
Phone : (809) 774-6450
Fax : (809) 779-6213

EMPLOYMENT SERVICES

Provides job counseling, testing and placement services in the state.

ALABAMA
George Register
Acting Director
Employment Services Div.
Dept. of Industrial Relations
649 Monroe St.
Montgomery, AL 36130
Phone : (334) 242-8003
Fax : (334) 242-8012

Bryan Hare
Acting Director
Employment Srvcs. Div.
Dept. of Industrial Relations
649 Monroe St.
Montgomery, AL 36130
Phone : (334) 242-8003
Fax : (334) 242-8012

ALASKA
Rebecca Nance
Director
Div. of Employment Security
Dept. of Labor
P.O. Box 25509
Juneau, AK 99802
Phone : (907) 465-2711
Fax : (907) 465-4537

ARIZONA
James B. Griffith
Assistant Director
Employment & Rehab. Srvc. Div.
Dept. of Economic Security
1789 W. Washington
Phoenix, AZ 85007
Phone : (602) 542-4910

ARKANSAS
Phil Price
Director
Employment Security Div.
Dept. of Labor
Capitol Mall
Little Rock, AR 72201
Phone : (501) 682-2121
Fax : (501) 682-3223

CALIFORNIA
Al Lee
Chief Deputy Director
Dept. of Employment Dev.
800 Capitol Mall, Rm. 5000
Sacramento, CA 95814
Phone : (916) 654-8210

COLORADO
John J. Donlon
Executive Director
Dept. of Labor & Employment
1515 Arapahoe St., Twr. 2, Ste. 400
Denver, CO 80202-2117
Phone : (303) 620-4700
Fax : (303) 620-4714

CONNECTICUT
Bennett Pudlin
Executive Director
Employment Security Div.
Dept. of Labor
38 Wolcott Hill Rd.
Wethersfield, CT 06109
Phone : (203) 566-4280

DELAWARE
Harriet Smith
Director
Off. of Personnel
Townsend Bldg.
P.O. Box 1401
Dover, DE 19903
Phone : (302) 739-4195
Fax : (302) 739-3000

FLORIDA
Martha Larson
Director
Div. of Labor, Empl. & Training
Dept. of Labor & Empl. Sec.
Atkins Bldg., Rm. 300
Tallahassee, FL 32399
Phone : (904) 488-7228
Fax : (904) 922-7119

GEORGIA
Helen Parker
Assistant Commissioner
Employment Srvcs. Div.
Dept. of Labor
148 International Blvd., Rm. 400
Atlanta, GA 30303
Phone : (404) 656-6380

HAWAII
Claudette P. Naauao
Administrator
Employment Srvc. Div.
Dept. of Labor & Ind. Rel.
830 Punchbowl St., Rm. 329
Honolulu, HI 96814
Phone : (808) 586-8812

IDAHO
Roger B. Madsen
Director
Dept. of Employment
317 Main St.
Boise, ID 83735
Phone : (208) 334-6112

ILLINOIS
Lynn Doherty
Director
Dept. of Employment Security
401 S. State St., 6th Fl.
Chicago, IL 60605
Phone : (312) 793-5700
Fax : (312) 793-9834

INDIANA
Carol Baker
Director of Field Operations
Empl. & Training Programs
Workforce Development
10 N. Senate, Ste. 331
Indianapolis, IN 46204
Phone : (317) 232-4259

IOWA
Cynthia Eisenhauser
Director
Dept. of Employment Srvcs.
1000 E. Grand
Des Moines, IA 50319
Phone : (515) 281-5365
Fax : (515) 242-5144

KANSAS
Wayne Franklin
Secretary
Dept. of Human Resources
401 SW Topeka Blvd.
Topeka, KS 66603
Phone : (913) 296-7474
Fax : (913) 296-0179

KENTUCKY
David Cooke
Director
Application Counseling & Exams
Dept. of Personnel
200 Fairoaks
Frankfort, KY 40601
Phone : (502) 564-6920

LOUISIANA
Joseph Stone
Assistant Secretary
Dept. of Labor
P.O. Box 94094
Baton Rouge, LA 70804
Phone : (504) 342-7692

MAINE
Mary Lou Dyer
Executive Director
Bur. of Employment Security
Dept. of Labor
State House Station # 55
Augusta, ME 04333
Phone : (207) 287-3377

MASSACHUSETTS
Mary O'Neil
Director
Bur. of Human Resource Dev.
Dept. of Personnel Admin.
1 Ashburton Pl., Rm. 519
Boston, MA 02108
Phone : (617) 727-7801
Fax : (617) 727-3970

MICHIGAN
F. Robert Edwards
Director
Employment Security Comm.
Dept. of Labor
7310 Woodward
Detroit, MI 48202
Phone : (313) 876-5901

MINNESOTA
Gary Sorensen
Assistant Commissioner
Job Srvc. & Unemploy. Ins. Div.
Dept. of Jobs & Training
390 N. Robert St.
St. Paul, MN 55101
Phone : (612) 296-1692

MISSISSIPPI
Tom Lord
Director
Employment Security Comm.
1520 W. Capitol
Jackson, MS 39203
Phone : (601) 354-8711

MISSOURI
Paul L. Rodgers
Director
Div. of Employment Security
Dept. of Labor & Ind. Rel.
421 E. Dunklin
P.O. Box 59
Jefferson City, MO 65104
Phone : (314) 751-3976
Fax : (314) 751-4945

MONTANA
T. Gary Curtis
Administrator
Job Service Div.
P.O. Box 1728
Helena, MT 59624
Phone : (406) 444-2648

NEBRASKA
Fernando Lecuona
Deputy Commissioner
Job Training Program
Dept. of Labor
P.O. Box 94600
Lincoln, NE 68509
Phone : (402) 471-2127

NEVADA
Stanley P. Jones
Administrator
Div. of Employment Security
Emplymt., Trng. & Rehab. Dept.
500 E. Third St.
Carson City, NV 89713
Phone : (702) 687-4635

NEW HAMPSHIRE
John J. Ratoff
Commissioner
Dept. of Employment Security
32 S. Main St.
Concord, NH 03301
Phone : (603) 224-3311

NEW JERSEY
James R. White
Director
Div. of Field Services
Dept. of Labor
John Fitch Plz., CN058
Trenton, NJ 08625
Phone : (609) 292-2400

NEW MEXICO
Clint Harder
Secretary
Dept. of Labor
P.O. Box 1928
Albuquerque, NM 87103
Phone : (505) 841-8409
Fax : (505) 841-8491

NEW YORK*
Commissioner
Dept. of Labor
State Off. Bldg., State Campus
Albany, NY 12240
Phone : (518) 457-2741

NORTH CAROLINA
Ann Duncan
Chair
Employment Security Comm.
Dept. of Commerce
700 Wade Ave.
Raleigh, NC 27605-1167
Phone : (919) 733-7546

NORTH DAKOTA
Gerald P. Balzer
Executive Director
Job Service
P.O. Box 1537
Bismarck, ND 58502
Phone : (701) 328-2836
Fax : (701) 328-4000

OHIO
Debra Bowland
Director
Bur. of Employment Srvcs.
145 S. Front St.
Columbus, OH 43216
Phone : (614) 466-8032
Fax : (614) 466-5025

OKLAHOMA
Wayne Winn
Executive Director
Employment Security Comm.
200 Will Rogers Bldg.
Oklahoma City, OK 73105
Phone : (405) 557-7200

Oscar Jackson
Secretary of Human Resources
Off. of Personnel Mgt.
Jim Thorpe Bldg., Rm. G-80
Oklahoma City, OK 73105
Phone : (405) 521-2177

OREGON
Roger Auerbach
Director
Employment Dept.
875 Union St., NE
Salem, OR 97311
Phone : (503) 378-3208
Fax : (503) 373-7298

PENNSYLVANIA
Alan Williamson
Deputy Secretary
Emp. Security & Job Training
Dept. of Labor & Industry
Rm. 1700, Labor & Industry Bldg.
Harrisburg, PA 17120
Phone : (717) 787-1745

RHODE ISLAND
Larry Fitch
Director
Dept. of Employment & Training
101 Friendship St.
Providence, RI 02903
Phone : (401) 277-3732

SOUTH CAROLINA
Robert E. David
Executive Director
Employment Security Comm.
P.O. Box 995
Columbia, SC 29202
Phone : (803) 737-2617

SOUTH DAKOTA
Bob Wagner
Office Manager
Div. of Job Services
Dept. of Labor
116 W. Missouri Ave.
Pierre, SD 57501
Phone : (605) 773-3372

TENNESSEE
Bill Stokes
Commissioner
Dept. of Employment Security
Volunteer Plz., 12th Fl.
500 James Robertson Pkwy.
Nashville, TN 37243
Phone : (615) 741-2131
Fax : (615) 741-3203

TEXAS
William Grossenbacher
Administrator
Employment Comm.
101 E. 15th St.
Austin, TX 78778
Phone : (512) 463-2222

UTAH
Floyd G. Astin
Administrator
Job Services
Dept. of Employment Security
174 Social Hall Ave.
Salt Lake City, UT 84147
Phone : (801) 536-7401

VERMONT
Susan Auld
Commissioner
Dept. of Employ. & Trng. Admin.
5 Green Mountain Dr.
Montpelier, VT 05602
Phone : (802) 828-4000
Fax : (802) 828-4022

VIRGINIA
Kenneth A. Bolles
Commissioner
Employment Commission
703 E. Main St.
Richmond, VA 23219
Phone : (804) 786-3001
Fax : (804) 225-3923

WASHINGTON
Larry Malo
Assistant Commissioner
Employment & Training Div.
Dept. of Employment Security
605 Woodview Sq.
Olympia, WA 98504-9046
Phone : (360) 438-4611

WEST VIRGINIA
Andrew N. Richardson
Commissioner
Div. of Worker's Compensation
P.O. Box 3151
Charleston, WV 25332
Phone : (304) 558-2630
Fax : (304) 558-2992

WISCONSIN
June M. Suhling
Administrator
Jobs, Empl., & Training Srvcs.
Dept. of Ind Labor & Human Rel
201 E. Washington, Rm. 201
P.O. Box 7946
Madison, WI 53703
Phone : (608) 266-0327
Fax : (608) 267-2392

WYOMING
Phil Robbins
Deputy Administrator
Job Services Div.
Employment Security Comm.
P.O. Box 2760
Casper, WY 82602
Phone : (307) 235-3611

DISTRICT OF COLUMBIA
Joseph Yeldell
Director
Dept. of Employment Services
500 C St., N.W., Rm. 600
Washington, DC 20001
Phone : (202) 724-7101

AMERICAN SAMOA
Sapini Siatu'u
Director
Dept. of Human Resources
American Samoa Government
Pago Pago, AS 96799
Phone : (684) 633-4485
Fax : (684) 633-1139

GUAM
William E. Cundiff
Director
Agency for Human Resources Devl.
P.O. Box CQ
Agana, GU 96910
Phone : (671) 646-9341
Fax : (671) 646-9339

Juan M. Taijito
Director
Dept. of Labor
P.O. Box CP
Agana, GU 96910
Phone : (671) 646-4421
Fax : (671) 646-9339

NORTHERN MARIANA ISLANDS
Jose H. Salas
Director
Employment Srvcs.
Dept. of Labor & Immigration
P.O. Box 10007
Saipan, MP 96950
Phone : (670) 234-9450
Fax : (670) 664-1020

PUERTO RICO
Ednidia Padilla
Director
Bur. of Employment Security
Dept. of Labor & Human Res.
505 Munoz Rivera Ave.
Hato Rey, PR 00918
Phone : (809) 754-5375

U.S. VIRGIN ISLANDS
Lisa Harris-Moorhead
Commissioner
Dept. of Labor
P.O. Box 208
St. Thomas, VI 00802
Phone : (809) 776-3700
Fax : (809) 773-0094

ENERGY

Develops and administers programs relating to energy conservation, alternative energy research and development, and energy information.

ALABAMA
Terry Adams
Acting Chief
Science, Tech. & Energy Div.
Dept. of Economic & Comm. Aff.
P.O. Box 5690
Montgomery, AL 36103
Phone : (334) 242-5290
Fax : (334) 242-0552

ALASKA
Percy Frisby
Director
Div. of Energy
Dept. of Community & Regional Affairs
333 West Fourth Ave., Ste. 220
Anchorage, AK 99519-2341
Phone : (907) 269-4640
Fax : (907) 269-4645

ARIZONA
Jack Haenichen
Manager
Energy Office
Dept. of Commerce
3800 N. Central Ave., Ste. 1200
Phoenix, AZ 85012
Phone : (602) 280-1402

ARKANSAS
Cherry Duckett
Deputy Director
Industrial Development Comm.
1 Capitol Mall, Rm. 4C-300
Little Rock, AR 72201
Phone : (501) 682-7350
Fax : (501) 682-7394

CALIFORNIA
Charles R. Imbrecht
Chairman
California Energy Comm.
1516 Ninth St.
Sacramento, CA 95814
Phone : (916) 654-5000

COLORADO
Wade Buchanan
Director
Off. of Energy Conservation
Off. of the Governor
1675 Broadway, # 1300
Denver, CO 80202
Phone : (303) 620-4292

CONNECTICUT
Susan Shimelman
Under Secretary
Policy Dev. & Planning Div.
Off. of Policy & Mgt.
80 Washington St.
Hartford, CT 06106
Phone : (203) 566-4287

DELAWARE
Charles Smisson
Assistant Director
Energy Off.
Dept. of Administrative Srvcs.
P.O. Box 1401
Dover, DE 19903
Phone : (302) 739-5644

FLORIDA
Jim Tait
Florida Energy Office
Dept. of Community Affairs.
2740 Centerview Dr.
Tallahassee, FL 32399-2100
Phone : (904) 488-8466
Fax : (904) 921-0781

GEORGIA
Paul Burks
Director
Off. of Energy Resources
254 Washington St., SW, Ste. 401
Atlanta, GA 30334
Phone : (404) 656-5176

HAWAII
Maurice Kaya
Division Head
Energy Div.
Planning & Econ. Dev. Dept.
335 Merchant St., Rm. 110
Honolulu, HI 96813
Phone : (808) 587-3800

IDAHO
Bob Hoppie
Administrator
Energy Div.
Dept. of Water Resources
1301 N. Orchard St.
Boise, ID 83720
Phone : (208) 327-7968

ILLINOIS
John S. Moore
Director
Dept. of Energy & Natural Resources
325 W. Adams St.
Springfield, IL 62704
Phone : (217) 785-2002
Fax : (217) 785-2618

INDIANA
Amy Lynn Stewart
Director
Div. of Energy Policy
Dept. of Commerce
1 N. Capitol, Ste. 700
Indianapolis, IN 46204
Phone : (317) 232-8939

IOWA
Larry L. Bean
Administrator
Energy & Geological Res. Div.
Dept. of Natural Resources
Wallace State Off. Bldg.
Des Moines, IA 50319
Phone : (515) 281-4308

KANSAS
Jim Polger
Director
Energy Programs
Kansas Corporation Commission
1500 SW Arrowhead Rd.
Topeka, KS 66604-4027
Phone : (913) 271-3349
Fax : (913) 271-3354

KENTUCKY
John M. Stapleton
Director
Energy Div.
Natural Resources Dept.
691 Teton Trl.
Frankfort, KY 40601
Phone : (502) 564-7192

LOUISIANA
Ernest Burguie'res
Assistant Secretary
Off. of Conservation
Dept. of Natural Resources
P.O. Box 94396
Baton Rouge, LA 70804
Phone : (504) 342-4503

MARYLAND
Fred Hoover
Director
Energy Administration
45 Calvert St., 2nd Fl.
Annapolis, MD 21401
Phone : (301) 974-2511

MASSACHUSETTS
Stephen J. Remen
Commissioner
Off. of Energy Resources
100 Cambridge St., Rm. 1500
Boston, MA 02202
Phone : (617) 727-4732

MINNESOTA
Judy Poferl
Manager
Energy Planning & Intervention
Dept. of Public Srvc.
121 7th Pl. E., #200
St. Paul, MN 55101-2115
Phone : (612) 296-0407

MISSISSIPPI
Chester Smith
Director
Div. of Energy
Dept. of Econ. & Comm. Dev.
510 George St., Ste. 301
Jackson, MS 39202
Phone : (601) 359-3449

MISSOURI
Cher Stuewe-Portnoff
Director
Div. of Energy
Dept. of Natural Resources
1500 Southridge Dr.
P.O. Box 176
Jefferson City, MO 65102
Phone : (314) 751-4000
Fax : (314) 751-6860
E-Mail: CSTUEWEP@MAIL.MORE.NET

MONTANA
Ray Beck
Administrator
Dept. of Natural Resources & Conservation
1520 E. 6th Ave.
Helena, MT 59620
Phone : (406) 444-6754

NEBRASKA
Bob Harris
Deputy Director
Energy Off.
P.O. Box 95085
Lincoln, NE 68509
Phone : (402) 471-2867

NEVADA
DeeAnn Parsons
Chief
Energy Off.
Dept. of Business & Industry
1050 E. Williams St., Ste. 401
Carson City, NV 89710
Phone : (702) 687-4910
Fax : (702) 687-4914

NEW HAMPSHIRE
Jonathan S. Osgood
Director
Governor's Off. of Energy & Community Services
57 Regional Dr.
Concord, NH 03301-8519
Phone : (603) 271-2611

NEW JERSEY
Robert Shinn
Director
Off. of Energy
Dept. of Environmental Prot.
401 E. State St., CN-402
Trenton, NJ 08625
Phone : (609) 292-2885

NEW MEXICO
Jennifer Salisbury
Director
Energy & Conservation Mgt. Div
Dept. of Energy, Min. & Natural Resources
2040 S. Pacheco St.
Santa Fe, NM 87505
Phone : (505) 827-5900
Fax : (505) 438-3855

NEW YORK*
Commissioner
Office of Energy
2 Rockefeller Plz.
Albany, NY 12223
Phone : (518) 465-6251

NORTH CAROLINA
Carson D. Culbreth
Director
Div. of Energy
Dept. of Commerce
430 N. Salisbury St.
Raleigh, NC 27603
Phone : (919) 733-2230
Fax : (919) 733-2953

NORTH DAKOTA
James Luptak
Director
Energy Dev. Impact Off.
Land Dept.
P.O. Box 5523
Bismarck, ND 58505-5523
Phone : (701) 328-3188
Fax : (701) 328-3650

OHIO
Sara Ward
Office Chief
Off. of Energy Conservation
Dept. of Development
P.O. Box 1001
Columbus, OH 43266-0101
Phone : (614) 466-8396
Fax : (614) 466-1864

OKLAHOMA
Mike Smith
Secretary of Energy
Dept. of Energy
125 NW 6th St., Ste. 416
Oklahoma City, OK 73102
Phone : (405) 840-9228

OREGON
John Savage
Director
Dept. of Energy
625 Marion St., NE
Salem, OR 97310
Phone : (503) 378-4131
Fax : (503) 373-7806

PENNSYLVANIA
Brian T. Castelli
Executive Director
Energy Off.
116 Pine St.
P.O. Box 8010
Harrisburg, PA 17101
Phone : (717) 783-9982

RHODE ISLAND
James J. Malachowski
Chairman
Public Utilities Comm.
100 Orange St.
Providence, RI 02903
Phone : (401) 277-3500

SOUTH CAROLINA
Nancy B. Wrenn
Director
Div. of Finance & Admin.
Off. of the Governor
1205 Pendleton St.
Columbia, SC 29201
Phone : (803) 734-0565

SOUTH DAKOTA
Bonnie Untereiner
Commissioner
Governor's Off. of Economic Development
Capitol Lake Plz.
Pierre, SD 57501
Phone : (605) 773-5032

TENNESSEE
Cynthia Oliphant
Director
Div. of Energy
Dept. of Econ. & Commun. Dev.
320 6th Ave., N.
Nashville, TN 37243
Phone : (615) 741-2994

TEXAS
Tobin Harvey
Director
General Srvcs. Comm.
P.O. Box 13047, Capitol Station
Austin, TX 78711-3047
Phone : (512) 463-3035

UTAH
Michael Glenn
Manager
Bldg. Conservation & Financing
Off. of Energy Services
Dept. of Community & Economic Dev.
324 S. State St., Ste. 230
Salt Lake City, UT 84111
Phone : (801) 538-8654

VERMONT
Richard Sedano
Commissioner
Dept. of Public Service
120 State St.
Montpelier, VT 05620
Phone : (802) 828-2321
Fax : (802) 828-2342

VIRGINIA
O. Gene Dishner
Director
Dept. of Mines, Minerals & Energy
202 N. 9th St., 8th Fl.
Richmond, VA 23219
Phone : (804) 692-3200
Fax : (804) 692-3237

WASHINGTON
Judith Merchant
Director
State Energy Off.
925 Plum St., SE, Bldg. 4
P.O. Box 43165
Olympia, WA 98504-3165
Phone : (360) 956-2000

WEST VIRGINIA
David Callaghan
Director
Div. of Environmental Prot.
Commerce, Labor & Env. Res.
10 McJunkin Road
Nitro, WV 25143-2506
Phone : (304) 759-0515
Fax : (304) 759-0526

WISCONSIN
Nathaniel E. Robinson
Administrator
Energy & Intergvtl. Relations
Dept. of Admin.
101 E. Wilson, 6th Fl.
P.O. Box 7868
Madison, WI 53707
Phone : (608) 266-8234
Fax : (608) 267-6931

WYOMING
John Nunley III
Director of Energy
Dept. of Commerce
Barrett Bldg.
Cheyenne, WY 82002
Phone : (307) 777-5454

DISTRICT OF COLUMBIA
Charles J. Clinton
Director
Energy Off.
613 G St., NW, Ste. 500
Washington, DC 20001
Phone : (202) 727-1800

AMERICAN SAMOA
Reupena Tagaloa
Director
Territorial Energy Off.
American Samoa Government
Pago Pago, AS 96799
Phone : (684) 699-1101
Fax : (684) 699-2835

GUAM
Fred P. Camacho
Director
Guam Energy Office
P.O. Box 2950
Agana, GU 96910
Phone : (671) 477-0538
Fax : (671) 477-0589

NORTHERN MARIANA ISLANDS
Jocelyn F. Deleon Guerrero
Director
Energy Off.
P.O. Box 10007
Saipan, MP 96950
Phone : (670) 322-9229
Fax : (670) 322-9237

PUERTO RICO
Carlos La Santa Melendez
Coordinator of Energy Program
Dept. of Consumer Affairs
Minillas Station
P.O. Box 41059
Santurce, PR 00940
Phone : (809) 722-7555

U.S. VIRGIN ISLANDS
Alicia Barnes-James
Director
Energy Office
81 Castle Coakley
Christiansted
St. Croix, VI 00820
Phone : (809) 772-2616
Fax : (809) 772-0063

ENVIRONMENTAL PROTECTION

Improves the overall quality of the environment by coordinating and managing the state's pollution control programs and planning, granting permits and regulating standards.

ALABAMA
John M. Smith
Director
Dept. of Environmental Mgt.
1751 Congressman Dickinson Dr.
Montgomery, AL 36130
Phone : (334) 271-7710
Fax : (334) 270-5612

ALASKA
Gene Burden
Commissioner
Dept. of Environmental Conser.
410 Willoughby Ave., Ste. 105
Juneau, AK 99801
Phone : (907) 465-5050
Fax : (907) 465-5070

ARIZONA
Edward Z. Fox
Director
Dept. of Environmental Quality
3033 N. Central Ave.
Phoenix, AZ 85012
Phone : (602) 207-2203
Fax : (602) 207-2218

ARKANSAS
Randall Mathis
Director
Pollution Control & Ecology
P.O. Box 8913
Little Rock, AR 72219
Phone : (501) 562-7444
Fax : (501) 562-4632

CALIFORNIA
James M. Strock
Secretary
Environmental Protection Agency
555 Capitol Mall, Ste. 525
Sacramento, CA 95814
Phone : (916) 445-3846

COLORADO
Tom Looby
Director
Off. of Environment
Dept. of Public Health & Env.
4300 Cherry Crk. Dr., S.
Denver, CO 80222-1530
Phone : (303) 692-3099
Fax : (303) 782-4969

CONNECTICUT
Sidney J. Holbrook
Commissioner
Div. of Environmental Quality
Dept. of Environmental Protection
79 Elm St.
Westbrook, CT 06498-0483
Phone : (203) 424-3001

DELAWARE
Christophe A.G. Tulou
Secretary
Dept. of Natural Resources & Environmental Control
P.O. Box 1401
Dover, DE 19903
Phone : (302) 739-4403
Fax : (302) 739-6242

FLORIDA
Virginia Wetherell
Secretary
Dept. of Env. Protection
3900 Commonwealth Bldg., MS-10
Tallahassee, FL 32399-3000
Phone : (904) 488-1554
Fax : (904) 921-4303

GEORGIA
Harold Reheis
Director
Environmental Protection Div.
Dept. of Natural Resources
205 Butler St., SW
Atlanta, GA 30334
Phone : (404) 656-4317

HAWAII
Bruce Anderson
Deputy Director
Environmental Health Admin.
Dept. of Health
1250 Punchbowl St.
Honolulu, HI 96813
Phone : (808) 586-4424
Fax : (808) 586-4444

IDAHO
Wally Cory
Administrator
Div. of Environment
Dept. of Health & Welfare
1410 N. Hilton
Boise, ID 83706-1255
Phone : (208) 334-5840
Fax : (208) 334-0417

ILLINOIS
Mary Gade
Director
Environmental Protection Agency
2200 Churchill Rd.
Springfield, IL 62706
Phone : (217) 782-9540
Fax : (217) 782-9039

INDIANA
Kathy Prosser
Commissioner
Dept. of Environmental Mgt.
P.O. Box 6015
Indianapolis, IN 46225
Phone : (317) 232-8612

IOWA
Allan Stokes
Director
Environmental Protection Div.
Dept. of Natural Resources
Wallace State Off. Bldg.
Des Moines, IA 50319
Phone : (515) 281-6284

KANSAS
Charles F. Jones
Director
Div. of the Environment
Dept. of Health & Environment
Forbes Field, Bldg. 740
Topeka, KS 66620-0001
Phone : (913) 296-1535
Fax : (913) 296-8464

KENTUCKY
Robert Logan
Commissioner
Dept. for Environ. Protection
Frankfort Off. Park
14 Reilly Rd.
Frankfort, KY 40601
Phone : (502) 564-2150

LOUISIANA
William A. Kucharski
Secretary
Dept. of Environmental Quality
7290 Bluebonnet Rd.
Baton Rouge, LA 70810
Phone : (504) 765-0741

MAINE
Ned Sullivan
Commissioner
Dept. of Environmental Protection
#17 State House Station
Augusta, ME 04333-0017
Phone : (207) 287-2812

MARYLAND
Jane Nishada
Secretary
Dept. of the Environment
2500 Broening Hwy.
Baltimore, MD 21224
Phone : (410) 631-3084

MASSACHUSETTS
Peter Webber
Commissioner
Dept. of Environmental Protection
Executive Off. of Environmental Affairs
100 Cambridge St.
Boston, MA 02202
Phone : (617) 727-3163

MICHIGAN
Roland Harmes
Director
Dept. of Natural Resources
P.O. Box 30028
Lansing, MI 48909
Phone : (517) 373-2329
Fax : (517) 335-4242

MINNESOTA
Michael Sullivan
Executive Director
Environmental Quality Bd.
Off. of Strat. & Long Range Planning
658 Cedar St., Ste. 300
St. Paul, MN 55155
Phone : (612) 296-2603

MISSISSIPPI
J.I. Palmer, Jr.
Executive Director
Dept. of Environmental Quality
P.O. Box 20305
Jackson, MS 39289
Phone : (601) 961-5000

MISSOURI
John Young
Director
Div. of Environmental Quality
Dept. of Natural Resources
Jefferson Bldg., 12th Fl.
P.O. Box 176
Jefferson City, MO 65102
Phone : (314) 751-0763
Fax : (314) 751-9277

MONTANA
Robert Robinson
Director
Environmental Sciences Div.
Cogswell Bldg.
Helena, MT 59620
Phone : (406) 444-2544

NEBRASKA
Randolph Wood
Director
Dept. of Environmental Quality
1200 N. Street, Suite #400
Lincoln, NE 68509
Phone : (402) 471-2186

NEVADA
Lew Dodgion
Administrator
Div. of Environmental Protection
123 W. Nye Ln.
Carson City, NV 89710
Phone : (702) 687-4670

NEW HAMPSHIRE
Robert Varney
Commissioner
Dept. of Environmental Srvcs.
6 Hazen Dr.
Concord, NH 03301
Phone : (603) 271-3503

NEW JERSEY
Robert Shinn
Commissioner
Dept. of Environmental Protection
401 E. State St., CN402
Trenton, NJ 08625
Phone : (609) 292-2885

NEW MEXICO
Mark Weidler
Secretary
Dept. of Environment
P.O. Box 26110
Santa Fe, NM 87502
Phone : (505) 827-2850
Fax : (505) 827-2836

NEW YORK*
Commissioner
Dept. of Environmental Conservation
50 Wolf Rd.
Albany, NY 12233
Phone : (518) 457-3446

NORTH CAROLINA
A. Preston Howard, Jr.
Director
Div. of Environmental Mgt.
Dept. of Env., Hlth. & Nat. Resources
P.O. Box 27687
Raleigh, NC 27604
Phone : (919) 733-7015

NORTH DAKOTA
Francis J. Schwindt
Chief
Environmental Health Section
Dept. of Health
P.O. Box 5520
Bismarck, ND 58502-5520
Phone : (701) 328-5150
Fax : (701) 328-5200

OHIO
Donald R. Schregardus
Director
Environmental Protection Agcy.
P.O. Box 1049
Columbus, OH 43266
Phone : (614) 644-2782
Fax : (614) 644-3184

OKLAHOMA
Mark S. Coleman
Director
Dept. of Environmental Quality
1000 NE 10th St.
Oklahoma City, OK 73117-1299
Phone : (405) 271-8056

OREGON
Langdon Marsh
Director
Dept. of Environmental Quality
811 SW Sixth Ave.
Portland, OR 97204
Phone : (503) 229-5300
Fax : (503) 229-6124

PENNSYLVANIA
Terry Fabian
Deputy Secretary
DER-Field Operations
P.O. Box 2063
Harrisburg, PA 17105-2063
Phone : (717) 787-5028

RHODE ISLAND
Timothy Keeney
Director
Dept. of Environmental Mgt.
9 Hayes St.
Providence, RI 02908-5003
Phone : (401) 277-2771

SOUTH CAROLINA
R. Lewis Shaw
Deputy Commissioner
Environ. Quality Control Off.
Dept. of Health & Envir. Cont.
2600 Bull St.
Columbia, SC 29201
Phone : (803) 734-5360

SOUTH DAKOTA
Nettie Myers
Secretary
Dept. of Water & Natural Resources
523 E. Capitol Ave.
Pierre, SD 57501
Phone : (605) 773-3151

TENNESSEE
Wayne Scharber
Asst. Commissioner
Bur. of Environment
Dept. of Environ. & Cons.
401 Church St., 15th Fl.
Nashville, TN 37247
Phone : (615) 532-0220

TEXAS
L. Don Thurman
Associate Commissioner
Environ. & Cons. Health Prot.
Dept. of Health
1100 W. 49th St.
Austin, TX 78756
Phone : (512) 458-7111

UTAH
Dianne R. Nielson
Director
Div. of Environmental Health
P.O. Box 144810
Salt Lake City, UT 84114
Phone : (801) 536-4402

VERMONT
John J. Long, Jr.
Commissioner
Dept. of Environ. Conservation
Agcy. of Natural Resources
103 S. Main St., 1 S. Bldg.
Waterbury, VT 05676
Phone : (802) 241-3808
Fax : (802) 244-5141

VIRGINIA
Peter W. Schmidt
Director
Dept. of Environmental Quality
629 E. Main St.
Richmond, VA 23219
Phone : (804) 762-4020
Fax : (804) 762-4019

WASHINGTON
Mary Riveland
Director
Dept. of Ecology
P.O. Box 47600
Olympia, WA 98504-7600
Phone : (360) 407-6000

WEST VIRGINIA
David Callaghan
Director
Div. of Environmental Prot.
Commerce, Labor & Env. Res.
10 McJunkin Road
Nitro, WV 25143-2506
Phone : (304) 759-0515
Fax : (304) 759-0526

WISCONSIN
Susan Sylvester
Administrator
Environmental Standards Div.
Dept. of Natural Resources
P.O. Box 7921
Madison, WI 53707
Phone : (608) 266-1099
Fax : (608) 266-6983

WYOMING
Dennis Hemmer
Director
Dept. of Environmental Quality
122 W. 25th St.
Cheyenne, WY 82002
Phone : (307) 777-7192

DISTRICT OF COLUMBIA
Ferial Bishop
Administrator
Env. Regulation Admin.
Dept. of Cons. & Reg. Affairs
2100 M.L. King, Jr. Ave., Ste. 203
Washington, DC 20020
Phone : (202) 404-1136

AMERICAN SAMOA
Togipa Tausaga
Executive Director
Environmental Quality Comm.
Off. of the Governor
Pago Pago, AS 96799
Phone : (684) 633-2304
Fax : (684) 633-5801

GUAM
Fred Castro
Administrator
Environmental Protection Agency
130 Rojas St.
Harmon, GU 96911
Phone : (671) 646-8863

NORTHERN MARIANA ISLANDS
Juan I. Castro
Director
Environmental Quality Div.
Public Health & Env. Srvcs.
P.O. Box 409
Saipan, MP 96950
Phone : (670) 235-1011
Fax : (670) 234-1003

PUERTO RICO
Hector Rosse
President
Environmental Quality Board
P.O. Box 11488
San Juan, PR 00910-1488
Phone : (809) 767-8057
Fax : (809) 766-2483

U.S. VIRGIN ISLANDS
Beulah Dalmida-Smith
Commissioner
Dept. of Planning & Natural Resources
Nisky Ctr., Ste. 231
St. Thomas, VI 00802
Phone : (809) 774-3320
Fax : (809) 775-7506

EQUAL EMPLOYMENT OPPORTUNITY

Enforces laws promoting equal employment opportunity in the state.

ALABAMA
Erskine Banks
Director
EEO Office
Dept. of Industrial Relations
649 Monroe St.
Montgomery, AL 36131
Phone : (334) 242-8496
Fax : (334) 242-2048

ALASKA
Phyllis Schmidt
EEO Manager
Div. of Personnel
Dept. of Administration
P.O. Box 240488
Anchorage, AK 99524-0488
Phone : (907) 562-5294
Fax : (907) 562-0470

ARIZONA
Michael Moreno
Director
Gov. Office of Equal Opportunity
1700 W. Washington, Rm. 104
Phoenix, AZ 85007
Phone : (602) 542-3711

ARKANSAS
Richard Weiss
Director
Dept. of Finance & Admin.
401 DFA Bldg.
1509 W. 7th St.
Little Rock, AR 77201
Phone : (501) 682-2242
Fax : (501) 682-1086

CALIFORNIA
Nancy C. Gutierrez
Director
Fair Employment & Housing
2014 T St., Ste. 210
Sacramento, CA 95814
Phone : (916) 227-2873

COLORADO
Jack T. Lang y Marquez
Director
Civil Rights Div.
Dept. of Regulatory Agencies
1560 Broadway, Rm. 1050
Denver, CO 80202
Phone : (303) 894-2997

CONNECTICUT
Louis Martin
Director
Comm. on Human Rights & Opportunities
90 Washington St.
Hartford, CT 06106
Phone : (203) 566-4895

DELAWARE
Gregory T. Chambers
Administrator
EEO/AA Program
State Personnel Off.
820 N. French St.
Dover, DE 19801
Phone: (302) 577-3950

FLORIDA
Ron McElrath
Executive Director
Human Relations Comm.
Dept. of Admin., Bldg. F
325 John Knox Rd., Ste. 240
Tallahassee, FL 32399-1570
Phone : (904) 488-7082
Fax : (904) 922-6149

GEORGIA
Mustafa A. Aziz
Administrator
Fair Employment Practices
229 Peachtree St., NE, Suite 710
Atlanta, GA 30303
Phone: (404) 656-1736

HAWAII
Jackie Young
Coordinator
Off. of Affirmative Action
Off. of the Governor
State Capitol
Honolulu, HI 96813
Phone : (808) 586-0073
Fax : (808) 586-0076

IDAHO
Marilyn Shuler
Director
Human Rights Comm.
Off. of the Governor
450 W. State St.
Boise, ID 83720
Phone : (208) 334-2873

ILLINOIS
Rose Mary Bombella
Director
Dept. of Human Rights
100 W. Randolph, Ste. 10-100
Chicago, IL 60601
Phone : (312) 814-6284
Fax : (312) 814-1436

INDIANA
Steven Jones
Affirmative Action Officer
Dept. of Personnel
IGC-South, Rm. W161
402 W. Washington
Indianapolis, IN 46204
Phone : (317) 232-8029

IOWA
Don Grove
Acting Director
Civil Rights Comm.
211 E. Maple St., 2nd Fl.
Des Moines, IA 50319
Phone : (515) 281-4121
Fax : (515) 242-5840

KANSAS
Wayne Franklin
Secretary
Dept. of Human Resources
401 Topeka Blvd.
Topeka, KS 66603-3182
Phone : (913) 296-5000
Fax : (913) 296-0179

KENTUCKY
Beverly L. Watts
Executive Director
Comm. on Human Rights
332 W. Broadway
Louisville, KY 40202
Phone : (502) 595-4025

LOUISIANA
Lowry Lacy
Assistant Secretary
Office of Employment Security
Dept. of Labor
P.O. Box 94094
Baton Rouge, LA 70804-9094
Phone : (504) 342-3111

MAINE
Patricia Ryan
Executive Director
Human Rights Comm.
State House Station # 51
Augusta, ME 04333
Phone : (207) 624-6050

MARYLAND
Jennifer Burdick
Executive Director
Human Relations Comm.
20 E. Franklin St.
Baltimore, MD 21202
Phone : (410) 333-1715

MASSACHUSETTS
Mark Bolling
Director
Off. of Affirmative Action
One Ashburton Pl., Rm. 213
Boston, MA 02108
Phone : (617) 727-7441

MICHIGAN
Martha Bibbs
State Personnel Director
Civil Service
400 S. Pine
Lansing, MI 48909
Phone : (517) 373-3020
Fax : (517) 373-3103

MINNESOTA
David Beaulieu
Commissioner
Dept. of Human Rights
Bremer Tower
7th Pl. & Minnesota Sts.
St. Paul, MN 55101
Phone : (612) 296-5665

MISSOURI
Alvin A. Plummer
Director
MO Commission on Human Rights
Dept. of Labor & Ind. Rel.
3315 W. Truman Blvd.
P.O. Box 1129
Jefferson City, MO 65102-1129
Phone : (314) 751-3325
Fax : (314) 751-2905

MONTANA
Ann MacIntyre
Administrator
Human Rights Div.
Dept. of Labor & Industry
616 Helena Ave., Ste. 302
Steamboat Block
Helena, MT 59624-1728
Phone : (406) 444-2884

NEBRASKA
Lawrence C. Myers
Executive Director
Equal Opportunity Comm.
301 Centennial Mall S.
P.O. Box 94934
Lincoln, NE 68509
Phone : (402) 471-2024

NEVADA
Edward Johnson
Administrator
Equal Rights Comm.
Dept. of Employment, Training & Rehabilitation
1515 E. Tropicana Ave., Ste. 590
Las Vegas, NV 89119-6522
Phone : (702) 486-7161
Fax : (702) 486-7054

NEW HAMPSHIRE
Raymond S. Perry, Jr.
Executive Director
Comm. for Human Rights
163 Loudon Rd.
Concord, NH 03301
Phone : (603) 271-2767

NEW JERSEY
Oscar Brooks
Acting Director
EEO - Affirmative Action Div.
Dept. of Personnel
3 Station Plz., CN315
Trenton, NJ 08625
Phone : (609) 777-0919

NEW MEXICO
Howard Williams
Programs Div. Director
Human Rights Div.
Aspen Plz.
1596 Pacheco St.
Santa Fe, NM 87503
Phone : (505) 827-6838
Fax : (505) 827-6878

NEW YORK*
President
Dept. of Civil Services
State Campus, Bldg. 1
Albany, NY 12239
Phone : (518) 457-3701

NORTH CAROLINA
Nellie Riley
Director
Equal Opportunity Services
Off. of State Personnel
116 W. Jones St.
Raleigh, NC 27603
Phone : (919) 733-0205

NORTH DAKOTA
Craig Hagen
Commissioner
Dept. of Labor
State Capitol, 6th Fl.
600 E. Boulevard Ave.
Bismarck, ND 58505
Phone : (701) 328-2660
Fax : (701) 328-2031

OHIO
Jack R. Marchbanks
Acting EEO Coordinator
Dept. of Admin. Srvcs.
77 S. High St., Floor 24
Columbus, OH 43266-0401
Phone : (614) 752-9271
Fax : (614) 644-1795

OKLAHOMA
Kathy Calvillo
Affirmative Action/EEO Coordinator
Off. of Personnel Mgt.
2101 N. Lincoln Blvd.
Oklahoma City, OK 73105
Phone : (405) 521-2177

OREGON
Johnnie Bell
Administrator
Civil Rights Div.
Bur. of Labor & Industries
800 NE Oregon St., # 32
Portland, OR 97232
Phone : (503) 731-4873

PENNSYLVANIA
Denise Motley-Brownlee
Director
Bur. of Affirmative Action/
Contract Compliance
508-B Finance Bldg.
Harrisburg, PA 17120
Phone : (717) 783-1130

RHODE ISLAND
Vincent Igliozzi
Administrator
Equal Opportunity Off.
Dept. of Administration
One Capitol Hill
Providence, RI 02903
Phone : (401) 227-3090

SOUTH CAROLINA
John Cummings
EEO Officer
Employment Security Comm.
P.O. Box 995
Columbia, SC 29202
Phone : (803) 737-4812

TENNESSEE
Marie Morris
Affirmative Action Officer
Equal Employment Opportunity
Dept. of Employment Security
500 James Robertson Pkwy.
Nashville, TN 37243
Phone : (615) 741-2649

TEXAS
Donna Reynolds
Director
Human Resources
Off. of the Governor
P.O. Box 12428, Capitol Station
Austin, TX 78711
Phone : (512) 463-5873

UTAH
Anna Jensen
Director
Div. of Anti-Discrimination & Labor
Industrial Comm.
160 E. 300 S.
Salt Lake City, UT 84111
Phone : (801) 530-6921

VERMONT
Avram Patt
Director
State Economic Opportunity Off.
Agency of Human Services
103 S. Main St.
Waterbury, VT 05671
Phone : (802) 241-2450

VIRGINIA
Charles E. James, Sr.
Director
Dept. of Personnel & Training
101 N. 14th St.
Richmond, VA 23219
Phone : (804) 225-2237
Fax : (804) 371-7401

WASHINGTON
Roy Standifer
Administrator
Affirmative Action Program
Dept. of Personnel
P.O. Box 47500
Olympia, WA 98504-7500
Phone : (360) 753-5368

WEST VIRGINIA
Taunja White Woods
EEO Officer
Office of the Governor
Bldg. 1
1900 Kanawha Blvd., E.
Charleston, WV 25305
Phone : (304) 558-0400
Fax : (304) 558-4983

WISCONSIN
J. Sheehan Donoghue
Administrator
Div. of Equal Rights
Industrial Labor & Human Relations
201 E Washington, Rm. 407
P.O. Box 7946
Madison, WI 53703
Phone : (608) 266-6860
Fax : (608) 267-4592

WYOMING
Dan Romero
EEO, Grievance & Appeals Coordinator
Personnel Div.
Dept. of Admin. & Information
Emerson Bldg.
Cheyenne, WY 82002
Phone : (307) 777-6730

DISTRICT OF COLUMBIA
Steven Jumper
Director
Off. of Human Rights
2000 14th St., NW, 3rd Fl.
Washington, DC 20009
Phone : (202) 939-8780

AMERICAN SAMOA
Sapini Siatu'u
Director
Dept. of Human Resources
American Samoa Government
Pago Pago, AS 96799
Phone : (684) 633-4485
Fax : (684) 633-1139

GUAM
Edward A. Guerrero
Director
Dept. of Labor
P.O. Box 9970
Tamuning, GU 96911
Phone : (671) 646-9241

NORTHERN MARIANA ISLANDS
Francisco S. Ada
Chief
Employment & Employee Relations
Personnel Mgt.
P.O. Box 5153 CHRB
Saipan, MP 96950
Phone : (670) 234-6925
Fax : (670) 234-1013

PUERTO RICO
Carmen Ana Lugo
Director
Fair Employment
Dept. of Labor & Human Resources
505 Munoz Rivera Ave.
Hato Rey, PR 00918
Phone : (809) 754-2105

U.S. VIRGIN ISLANDS
Lisa Harris-Moorhead
Commissioner
Dept. of Labor
P.O. Box 890
St. Thomas, VI 00802
Phone : (809) 773-1994
Fax : (809) 773-0094

ETHICS

Administers and enforces the state ethics laws applying to public officials.

ALASKA
Karen Boorman
Director
Public Offices Comm.
2221 E. Northern Lights Blvd., Rm. 128
Anchorage, AK 99508-4149
Phone : (907) 276-4176
Fax : (907) 276-7018

ARIZONA
Grant Woods
Attorney General
1275 W. Washington
Phoenix, AZ 85007
Phone : (602) 542-4266

ARKANSAS
Amanda Nixon White
Director
State Ethics Comm.
2020 W. Third St., Ste. 300
Little Rock, AR 72205
Phone : (501) 324-9600
Fax : (501) 324-9603

CALIFORNIA
Ravi Mehta
Chairman
Fair Political Practices Comm.
P.O. Box 807
Sacramento, CA 95804
Phone : (916) 322-5901

COLORADO
Tim Daly
Chief Legal Advisor
Off. of the Governor
136 State Capitol
Denver, CO 80203
Phone : (303) 866-2471
Fax : (303) 866-2003

J. Edgar Benton
Chairman
Board of Ethics
1700 Lincoln St., Ste. 4100
Denver, CO 80203
Phone : (303) 861-7000

CONNECTICUT
Alan S. Plofsky
Executive Director
State Ethics Comm.
20 Trinity
Hartford, CT 06106-1660
Phone : (203) 566-4472

DELAWARE
Janet Wright
Public Integrity Commission
Townsend Building
Dover, DE 19901
Phone : (302) 739-2397

FLORIDA
R. Terry Rigsby
Chairman
Commission on Ethics
P.O. Drawer 15709
Tallahassee, FL 32312-5709
Phone : (904) 488-7864
Fax : (904) 488-3077

GEORGIA
C. Theodore Lane
Executive Secretary
State Ethics Comm.
Off. of Secretary of State
2082 E. Exchange Pl., Ste. 235
Tucker, GA 30084
Phone : (404) 493-5795

HAWAII
Daniel J. Mollway
Executive Director
State Ethics Comm.
Pacific Tower, Ste. 970
1001 Bishop St.
Honolulu, HI 96813
Phone : (808) 587-0460

INDIANA
Carol Kirk
Director
State Ethics Commission
402 W. Washington St., Rm. 189
Indianapolis, IN 46204
Phone : (317) 232-3850
Fax : (317) 232-0707

IOWA
Kay Williams
Executive Director
Ethics & Campaign Disclosure Board
514 E. Locust, Ste. 104
Des Moines, IA 50309
Phone : (515) 281-6841

KANSAS
Carol Williams
Executive Director
Comm. on Governmental Standards & Conduct
109 SW Ninth St., Rm. 504
Topeka, KS 66612-1287
Phone : (913) 296-4219
Fax : (913) 296-2548

KENTUCKY
Jill LeMaster
Executive Director
Executive Branch Ethics Comm.
Capitol Annex, Rm. 273
Frankfort, KY 40601
Phone : (502) 564-7954

LOUISIANA
Robert Snyder
Chairman
Board of Ethics for Elected Officials
7434 Perkins Rd., Ste. B
Baton Rouge, LA 70808
Phone : (504) 765-2308

MAINE
Marilyn Canavan
Director
Governmental Ethics & Election Practices Comm.
State House Station # 101
Augusta, ME 04333
Phone : (207) 287-4179

MARYLAND
John O'Donnell
Executive Director
State Ethics Comm.
300 E. Joppa Rd., Ste. 301
Towson, MD 21204
Phone : (410) 321-3636

MASSACHUSETTS
Andrew B. Crane
Executive Director
State Ethics Comm.
1 Ashburton Pl., Rm. 619
Boston, MA 02108
Phone : (617) 727-0060
Fax : (617) 723-5851

MICHIGAN
Micki Czerniak
Executive Secretary
State Bd. of Ethics
Dept. of Civil Service
P.O. Box 30002
Lansing, MI 48909
Phone : (517) 373-2104

MINNESOTA
Mary Ann McCoy
Executive Director
Ethical Practices Bd.
S. Centennial Bldg., 1st Fl.
658 Cedar St.
St. Paul, MN 55155
Phone : (612) 296-1720

MISSISSIPPI
Ronald Crowe
Executive Director
Ethics Comm.
P.O. Box 22746
Jackson, MS 39225
Phone : (601) 359-1285

MONTANA
Ed Argenbright
Commissioner of Political Practices
1205 8th Ave.
Helena, MT 59620
Phone : (406) 444-2942

NEBRASKA
Dannie Trautwein
Director
Accountability & Disclosure Comm.
P.O. Box 95086
Lincoln, NE 68509
Phone : (402) 471-2522

NEVADA
Thomas R.C. Wilson
Chairman
Comm. on Ethics
Capitol Complex
Carson City, NV 89710
Phone : (702) 687-5469

NEW HAMPSHIRE
Jeffrey R. Howard
Attorney General
25 Capitol St.
Concord, NH 03301
Phone : (603) 271-3655

NEW MEXICO
Tim Udall
Attorney General
Bataan Memorial Bldg.
P.O. Drawer 1508
Santa Fe, NM 87504-1508
Phone : (505) 827-6000
Fax : (505) 827-5826

Stephanie Gonzalez
Secretary of State
State Capitol Bldg., Rm. 420
Santa Fe, NM 87503
Phone : (505) 827-3601
Fax : (505) 827-3634

NEW YORK*
Executive Director
State Ethics Comm.
39 Columbia St., # 4
Albany, NY 12007
Phone : (518) 432-8207

NORTH CAROLINA
George F. Bason
Chairman
Board of Ethics
116 W. Jones St.
Raleigh, NC 27603-8003
Phone : (919) 733-5103

OHIO
David Freel
Executive Director
Ethics Comm.
8 E. Long St., Ste. 1200
Columbus, OH 43215
Phone : (614) 466-7093
Fax : (614) 466-8368

OKLAHOMA
Marilyn Hughes
Executive Director
Ethics Comm.
State Capitol Bldg., Rm. B-2A
Oklahoma City, OK 73105
Phone : (405) 521-3451

OREGON
L. Patrick Hearn
Executive Director
Government Standards & Practices Comm.
100 High St., SE, Suite 220
Salem, OR 97310
Phone : (503) 378-5105
Fax : (503) 373-1456

PENNSYLVANIA
Daneen E. Reese
Chairman
State Ethics Comm.
P.O. Box 11470
Harrisburg, PA 17108-1470
Phone : (717) 783-1610

RHODE ISLAND
Sarah Quinn
Executive Director
State Ethics Comm.
43 Jefferson Blvd.
Warwick, RI 02888
Phone : (401) 277-3790

SOUTH CAROLINA
Gary R. Baker
Executive Director
State Ethics Comm.
P.O. Box 11926
Columbia, SC 29211
Phone : (803) 253-4192

TENNESSEE
Peggy Nance Catalano
Executive Director
Registry of Election Fin.
Off. of Secretary of State
James K. Polk Bldg.
Nashville, TN 37243
Phone : (615) 741-7959

TEXAS
John Steiner
Director
Ethics Comm.
P.O. Box 12070
Austin, TX 78711
Phone : (512) 463-5800

UTAH
Jan Graham
Attorney General
236 State Capitol
Salt Lake City, UT 84114
Phone : (801) 538-1149

VERMONT
Janet Ancel
Legal Counsel
Off. of the Governor
109 State St.
Montpelier, VT 05609
Phone : (802) 828-3333
Fax : (802) 828-3339

VIRGINIA
James S. Gilmore, III
Attorney General
900 E. Main St., 6th Fl.
Richmond, VA 23219
Phone : (804) 786-2071
Fax : (804) 371-0200

WASHINGTON
Melissa Warheit
Executive Director
Public Disclosure Comm.
711 Capitol Way, Rm. 403
Olympia, WA 98504
Phone : (360) 753-1111

WEST VIRGINIA
Richard Alker
Executive Director
State Ethics Comm.
1207 Quarrier St.
Charleston, WV 25301
Phone : (304) 558-0664
Fax : (304) 558-2169

WISCONSIN
R. Roth Judd
Executive Director
WI Ethics Board
44 E. Mifflin St., Ste. 601
Madison, WI 53703-2800
Phone : (608) 266-8123
Fax : (608) 264-9309

DISTRICT OF COLUMBIA
Robert A. Lane
Executive Director
Board of Elections & Ethics
Off. of Campaign Finance
2000 14th St., NW, Rm. 420
Washington, DC 20009
Phone : (202) 939-8710

DISTRICT OF COLUMBIA — Cont.
Garland Pinkston
Deputy Corporation Counsel
Legal Counsel Div.
Off. of Corporation Counsel
441 Fourth St., NW, Ste. 1060N
Washington, DC 20001
Phone : (202) 727-2429

GUAM
Elizabeth Barrett-Anderson
Attorney General
238 Archbishop Flores St., Ste. 701
Agana, GU 96910
Phone : (671) 475-3324

NORTHERN MARIANA ISLANDS
Leo Lawrence LaMotte
Public Auditor
P.O. Box 1399 Ctc
Saipan, MP 96950
Phone : (670) 234-6481
Fax : (670) 234-7812

PUERTO RICO
Hector Feliciano-Carreras
Executive Director
Off. of Government Ethics
P.O. Box 194629
San Juan, PR 00919-4629
Phone : (809) 766-4401
Fax : (809) 754-0977

U.S. VIRGIN ISLANDS
Paul Gimenez
Solicitor General
Dept. of Justice
GERS Bldg., 2nd Fl.
St. Thomas, VI 00802
Phone : (809) 774-5666
Fax : (809) 774-9710

FACILITIES MANAGEMENT

Maintains, constructs, designs, renovates and delivers basic services to state-owned facilities.

ALABAMA
Stedman B. McCollough
Director
Building Comm.
770 Washington Ave., Ste. 444
Montgomery, AL 36130
Phone : (334) 242-4082
Fax : (334) 242-4182

ARIZONA
Kent Bosworth
Construction & Maint. Administrator
General Services Division
Dept. of Administration
1700 W. Washington, 6th Fl.
Phoenix, AZ 85007
Phone : (602) 542-0697

ARKANSAS
Chris Burrow
Director
State Bldg. Srvcs.
1515 W. 7th St., Ste. 700
Little Rock, AR 72201
Phone : (501) 682-5558
Fax : (501) 682-5589

CALIFORNIA
Rosemand Bolden
Chief
Off. of Buildings & Grounds
Dept. of General Srvcs.
1304 O St.
Sacramento, CA 95814
Phone : (916) 327-6224

COLORADO*
Director
State Buildings Div. & State Purchasing Div.
225 E. 16th Ave.
Denver, CO 80203-1613
Phone : (303) 866-6100
Fax : (303) 894-7445

CONNECTICUT
Gary Gallucci
Administrator of Facilities Mgt.
Dept. of Public Works
165 Capitol Ave., Rm. G-39
Hartford, CT 06106
Phone : (203) 566-2815

DELAWARE
Paul Ignudo
Director
Division of Facilities Mgt.
O'Neill Building
P.O. Box 1401
Dover, DE 19903
Phone : (302) 739-3041
Fax : (302) 739-6148

FLORIDA
Phil Maher
Director
Div. of Facilities Mgt.
Dept. of Management Srvcs.
Ste. 105, Ashley Bldg.
Tallahassee, FL 32399-0950
Phone : (904) 488-2074
Fax : (904) 922-6149

GEORGIA
Luther C. Lewis, Jr.
Acting Executive Director
Building Authority
1 M. L. King, Jr. Dr.
Atlanta, GA 30334
Phone : (404) 656-3250

HAWAII
Steve Fernandes
Division Administrator
Dept. of Accounting & General Srvcs.
729 Kakoi St.
Honolulu, HI 96819
Phone : (808) 831-6730

IDAHO
Larry Osgood
Administrator
Div. of Public Works
Dept. of Administration
502 N. Fourth
Boise, ID 83720
Phone : (208) 334-3647

ILLINOIS
Carole Fox-Drury
Manager
Real Estate Div.
Bur. of Property Management
721 Stratton Off. Bldg.
Springfield, IL 62706
Phone : (217) 785-0562
Fax : (217) 524-8919

INDIANA
Patrick Carroll
Deputy Commissioner
Operations Div.
Dept. of Administration
402 W. Washington, Rm. 478
Indianapolis, IN 46204
Phone : (317) 232-3155

IOWA
Lee Hammer
Director
Facilities Management
Dept. of Transportation
800 Lincoln Way
Ames, IA 50010
Phone : (515) 239-1327

KANSAS
Thaine Hoffman
Director
Dept. of Administration
Div. of Architectural Srvcs.
625 Polk St.
Topeka, KS 66603-3288
Phone : (913) 233-9367
Fax : (913) 233-9398

KENTUCKY
R. Clark Beauchamp
Commissioner
Dept. of Facilities Mgt.
Finance & Admin. Cabinet
Capitol Annex, Rm. 76
Frankfort, KY 40601
Phone : (502) 564-3590

LOUISIANA
Roger Magendie
Director
Facility Planning & Ctrl. Off.
Div. of Administration
P.O. Box 94095
Baton Rouge, LA 70804
Phone : (504) 342-7000

MAINE
Richard A. Davis
Superintendent of Buildings
Bur. of General Services
Property Management Div.
State House Station # 76
Augusta, ME 04333
Phone : (207) 287-4151

MASSACHUSETTS
Lark Palermo
Commissioner
Div. of Planning & Dev.
Capitol Planning & Operations Dept.
1 Ashburton Pl., Rm. 1505
Boston, MA 02108
Phone : (617) 727-4050

MICHIGAN
Larry Bennett
Director
Off. of Facilities
Dept. of Mgt. & Budget
P.O. Box 30026
Lansing, MI 48909
Phone : (517) 373-3670

MINNESOTA
Dennis Spalla
Assistant Commissioner
Facilities Mgt. Bur.
Dept. of Admin.
200 Admin. Bldg., 50 Sherburne Ave.
St. Paul, MN 55155
Phone : (612) 296-6852

MISSISSIPPI
Jerry Oakes
Acting Director & Chief Architect
Bldgs., Grds. & Real Prop. Mgt.
Dept. of Finance & Admin.
1501 Walter Sillers Bldg.
Jackson, MS 39201-1198
Phone : (601) 359-3633

MISSOURI*
Director
Div. of Facilties Management
Off. of Administration
Truman Bldg., Rm. 590
P.O. Box 809
Jefferson City, MO 65102
Phone : (314) 751-1034
Fax : (314) 751-1466

MONTANA
Doug Olson
Facilities Manager
Div. of General Services
Dept. of Admin.
Annex Bldg.
Helena, MT 59620
Phone : (406) 444-3060

NEBRASKA
Ken Fougeron
Administrator
State Building Div.
Dept. of Admin. Srvcs.
State Capitol, 10th Fl.
Lincoln, NE 68509
Phone : (402) 471-3191

NEVADA
Mike Meizel
Administrator
Buildings & Grounds Div.
Dept. of Administration
406 E. Second St.
Carson City, NV 89710
Phone : (702) 687-4030

NEW HAMPSHIRE
Michael P. Connor
Administrator
Bur. of General Srvcs.
25 Capitol St.
Concord, NH 03301
Phone : (603) 271-3148

NEW JERSEY
Robert Harding
Deputy Administrator
General Services Div.
Dept. of Treasury
33 W. State St., CN039
Trenton, NJ 08625
Phone : (609) 777-4272

NEW MEXICO
Liz Raybal
Bureau Chief
Facilities Management
Property Control Div.
1100 St. Francis Dr., Montaya Bldg.
P.O. Drawer 26110
Santa Fe, NM 87502-6110
Phone : (505) 827-2150
Fax : (505) 827-2181

NEW YORK*
Deputy Commissioner
Facilties Operation Group
Off. of General Srvcs.
Corning Tower, 41st Fl.
Albany, NY 12242
Phone : (518) 474-5984

NORTH CAROLINA
Speros J. Fleggas
Director
State Construction Off.
Legis. Off. Bldg., Rm. 403
301 N. Wilmington St.
Raleigh, NC 27601-2827
Phone : (919) 733-7962
Fax : (919) 733-6609

NORTH DAKOTA
Don Mund
Admin. Officer of Operations
Facility Management Div.
State Captiol Bldg., 4th Fl.
Bismarck, ND 58505-0131
Phone : (701) 328-2471
Fax : (701) 328-3230

OHIO
Pete Langhorne
Deputy Director
Public Works Div.
Dept. of Admin. Srvcs.
30 E. Broad St., 35th Fl.
Columbus, OH 43215
Phone : (614) 466-4277
Fax : (614) 644-7982

OKLAHOMA
P. J. Falkenstein
Chief Administrator
Construction & Properties Div.
Dept. of Central Srvcs.
State Captiol Bldg., Rm. 104
Oklahoma City, OK 73105-4888
Phone : (405) 521-2111

OREGON
Mike Marsh
Administrator
Facilities Div.
Dept. of Admin. Srvcs.
1225 Ferry St., SE
Salem, OR 97310
Phone : (503) 378-4138
Fax : (503) 373-7210

PENNSYLVANIA
Charles W. Bowser
Director
Bur. of Bldgs. & Grounds
Dept. of General Srvcs.
403 North Off. Bldg.
Harrisburg, PA 17125
Phone : (717) 787-3893

RHODE ISLAND
William Tacelli
Buildings & Grounds Coordinator
Div. of Central Srvcs.
Dept. of Administration
One Capitol Hill
Providence, RI 02908-5853
Phone : (401) 277-6238

SOUTH CAROLINA
William J. Clement
Assistant Director
Div. of General Services
1201 Main St., Ste. 420
Columbia, SC 29201
Phone : (803) 734-3528

TENNESSEE
Ken Maynard
Executive Director
Facilities Mgt.
Dept. of Finance & Admin.
Nashville City Ctr.
Nashville, TN 37243
Phone : (615) 741-6311

TEXAS
Amado Ramirez
Director
Div. of Bldg. & Property Srvcs.
General Services Comm.
1711 San Jacinto
Austin, TX 78701
Phone : (512) 463-3343

UTAH
Neal P. Stowe
Director
Div. of Facilities
Construction & Mgt.
4110 State Off. Bldg.
Salt Lake City, UT 84114
Phone : (801) 538-3261

VERMONT
John J. Zampieri
Commissioner
Dept. of State Bldgs.
2 Gov. Aiken Ave.
P.O. Drawer 33
Montpelier, VT 05633
Phone : (802) 828-3314
Fax : (802) 828-3533

VIRGINIA
Donald C. Williams
Director
Dept. of General Services
209 9th St. Off. Bldg.
Richmond, VA 23219
Phone : (804) 786-3311
Fax : (804) 371-8305

WASHINGTON
Ron McQueen
Assistant Director
Div. of Capitol Facilities
Dept. of General Admin.
P.O. Box 41019
Olympia, WA 98504-1019
Phone : (360) 753-5686

WEST VIRGINIA
Douglas Koenig
Director
Div. of General Services.
Bldg. 1, Rm. MB60
1900 Kanawha Blvd., E.
Charleston, WV 25305
Phone : (304) 558-3517
Fax : (304) 558-2334

WISCONSIN
Bob Brandherm
Administrator
Div. of State Facilities Mgt.
Dept. of Admin.
101 E. Wilson, 7th Fl.
P.O. Box 7866
Madison, WI 53707
Phone : (608) 266-1031
Fax : (608) 267-2710

WYOMING
Mike Brown
Administrator
Facilities Mgt. Div.
801 W. 20th St.
Cheyenne, WY 82002
Phone : (307) 777-7767

AMERICAN SAMOA
Fa'i Faaita
Director
Dept. of Administrative Srvcs.
American Samoa Government
Pago Pago, AS 96799
Phone : (684) 633-4156
Fax : (684) 633-1841

GUAM
Gil A. Shinohara
Acting Director
Dept. of Parks
P.O. Box 2950
Agana, GU 96910
Phone : (671) 646-3101
Fax : (671) 649-6178

NORTHERN MARIANA ISLANDS
Joaquin I. Pangelinan
Special Assistant for Admin.
Off. of the Governor
P.O. Box 10007
Saipan, MP 96950
Phone : (670) 322-5091
Fax : (670) 322-5099

PUERTO RICO*
Administrator
General Services Admin.
P.O. Box 7428
San Juan, PR 00916
Phone : (809) 721-7370
Fax : (809) 722-7965

U.S. VIRGIN ISLANDS
Ann Abramson
Acting Commissioner
Dept. of Public Works
No. 8 Sub Base
St. Thomas, VI 00802
Phone : (809) 776-4844
Fax : (809) 774-5869

FEDERAL LIAISON (STATE'S WASHINGTON D.C. OFFICE)

The individual, typically based in Washington, D.C., who serves as the chief representative of state government in the nation's capital and works to promote state-federal relations.

ALASKA
John Katz
Special Counsel, State/ Federal Relations
Off. of the Governor
Hall of the States, Ste. 336
444 N. Capitol St., NW
Washington, D.C. 20001
Phone : (202) 624-5858

ARIZONA
John Kelly
Executive Assistant
Off. of the Governor
1700 W. Washington
Phoenix, AZ 85007
Phone : (602) 542-2218

CALIFORNIA
David Wetmore
Acting Director
Off. of the Governor
Hall of the States, Ste. 134
444 N. Capitol St., NW
Washington, DC 20001
Phone : (202) 624-5270
Fax : (202) 624-5280

COLORADO
Sally Vogler
Co-Director
Policy & Initiatives
Off. of the Governor
136 State Capitol
Denver, CO 80203
Phone : (303) 866-2155
Fax : (303) 866-2003

Bill Porter
Co-Director
Policy & Initiatives
Off. of the Governor
136 State Capitol
Denver, CO 80203
Phone : (303) 866-2155
Fax : (303) 866-2003

CONNECTICUT
Ruth Ravitz
Director
Washington Office
Hall of the States, Ste. 317
444 N. Capitol St., NW
Washington, DC 20001
Phone : (202) 347-4535
Fax : (202) 347-7151

DELAWARE
Elizabeth Ryan
Director
Washington Office
Off. of the Governor
Hall of the States, Ste. 230
444 N. Capitol St., NW
Washington, DC 20001
Phone : (202) 624-7724
Fax : (202) 624-5495

FLORIDA
Deborah Kilmer
Director
State/Federal Relations
Executive Off. of the Governor
Hall of the States, Ste. 349
444 N. Capitol St., NW
Washington, DC 20001
Phone : (202) 624-5885
Fax : (202) 624-5886

HAWAII
Ned Nakata
Special Assistant
Washington Off.
Hall of the States, Ste. 706
444 N. Capitol St., NW
Washington, DC 20001
Phone : (202) 508-3830

ILLINOIS
Terri Moreland
Director
Washington Office
Off. of the Governor
Hall of the States, Ste. 240
444 N. Capitol St., NW
Washington, DC 20001
Phone : (202) 624-7760
Fax : (202) 724-0689

INDIANA
Jeff Viohl
Executive Assistant
Federal Relations
c/o Cassidy & Associates
1001 G St., NW, Ste. 400 E
Wasington, DC 20001
Phone : (202) 628-3343

IOWA
Philip C. Smith
Director
Iowa Off. For State/ Federal Relations
Hall of the States, Ste. 359
444 N. Capitol St., NW
Washington, DC 20001
Phone : (202) 624-5442
Fax : (202) 624-8189

KENTUCKY
Pat Lacy Miller
Kentucky Washington Off.
Hall of the States, Ste. 351
400 N. Capitol St., NW
Washington, DC 20001
Phone : (202) 624-7741
Fax : (202) 624-7742

LOUISIANA
Ben Jeffers
Chief of Staff
Off. of the Governor
P.O. Box 94004
Baton Rouge, LA 70804
Phone : (504) 342-1624

MARYLAND
Peter Kyriacopoulos
Director
National Relations Off.
Hall of the States, Ste. 311
444 N. Capitol St., NW
Washington, DC 20001
Phone : (202) 638-2215

MASSACHUSETTS
Charlie Steele
Director
Federal Relations
Washington Office
Hall of States, Ste. 400
444 N. Capitol St., NW
Washington, DC 20001
Phone : (202) 624-7713
Fax : (202) 624-7714

MICHIGAN
LeAnne Redick
Director
Governor's Washington Off.
Hall of the States, Ste. 411
444 N. Capitol St., NW
Washington, DC 20001
Phone : (202) 624-5840
Fax : (202) 624-5841

MINNESOTA
Kathleen McCright
Director
Minnesota State Off.
Hall of the States Ste. 365S
400 N. Capitol St.
Washington, DC 20001
Phone : (202) 624-5308
Fax : (202) 624-5425

MISSISSIPPI
Thomas Phillips
Director
Off. of the Governor
Hall of the States, Ste. 367
400 N. Capitol St., NW
Washington, DC 20001
Phone : (202) 434-4871
Fax : (202) 434-4872

MISSOURI
Bradley Douglas
Director
State of MO Washington Off.
Hall of the States, Ste. 376
400 N. Capitol St., NW
Washington, DC 20001-1511
Phone : (202) 624-7720
Fax : (202) 624-5855

NEBRASKA
Tom Litjen
Government Affairs Consultant
Hall of the States, Ste. 406
444 N. Capitol St., NW
Washington, DC 20001
Phone : (202) 508-3838

NEVADA
Jim Mulhall
Chief of Staff
Off. of the Governor
Capitol Complex
Carson City, NV 89710
Phone : (702) 687-5670
Fax : (702) 687-4486

NEW HAMPSHIRE
Richard Strome
Legislative Director
Off. of the Governor
State House
Concord, NH 03301
Phone : (603) 271-2121

NEW JERSEY
Marguerite Sullivan
Director
NJ Governor's Washington Off.
Hall of the States, Ste. 201
444 N Capitol St., NW
Washington, DC 20001
Phone : (202) 638-0631

NEW YORK
Wayne Cimons
Director
Washington Office
Hall of the States, Ste. 301
444 N. Capitol St., NW
Washington, DC 20001
Phone : (202) 434-7100
Fax : (202) 434-7110

NORTH CAROLINA
Debra Bryant
Director
Washington Office
Hall of the States, Ste. 332
444 N. Capitol St., NW
Washington, DC 20001
Phone : (202) 624-5830
Fax : (202) 624-5836

OHIO
Ted Hollingsworth
Washington Off.
Ohio Governor's Off.
Hall of States, Ste. 546
444 N. Capitol St., NW
Washington, DC 20001
Phone : (202) 624-5844
Fax : (202) 624-5847

OKLAHOMA
Dan Cooney
Director
State of OK
Hall of the States, Ste. 517
444 N. Capitol St., NW
Washington, DC 20001
Phone : (202) 508-3820

PENNSYLVANIA
Becky Halokas
Director
Hall of the States, Ste. 700
400 N. Capitol St., NW
Washington, DC 20001
Phone : (202) 624-7828

RHODE ISLAND
Paul Moore
Director
Intergovernmental Relations
Off. of the Governor
1 Capitol Hill
Providence, RI 02903
Phone : (401) 277-2080
Fax : (401) 273-5301

SOUTH CAROLINA
Kelly Lineweaver
Hall of the States, Ste. 203
444 N. Capitol St., NW
Washington, DC 20001
Phone : (202) 624-7784
Fax : (202) 624-7800

TEXAS
Laurie Rich
Executive Director
Off. of Federal Relations
122 C St., NW
Washington, DC 20001
Phone : (202) 638-3927

UTAH
Joanne Neumann
Director
Washington Office
Off. of the Governor
Hall of the States, Ste. 370
400 N. Capitol St., NW
Washington, DC 20001
Phone : (202) 624-7704
Fax : (202) 624-7707

VIRGINIA
Terri Lynn Hauser
Director
Virginia Liaison Off.
Hall of the States, Ste. 214
444 N. Capitol St., NW
Washington, DC 20001
Phone : (202) 783-1769
Fax : (202) 783-7687

WASHINGTON
Stephanie Solien
Director
D.C. Office
Hall of the States, Ste. 204
444 N. Capitol St., NW
Washington, DC 20001
Phone : (202) 624-8449

WEST VIRGINIA
Judy Margolin
Senior Executive Assistant
Off. of the Governor
State Capitol
1900 Kanawha Blvd., E.
Charleston, WV 25305
Phone : (304) 558-3702
Fax : (304) 342-7025

WISCONSIN
Mary Sheehy
Director
Off. of Federal-State Relations
Dept. of Admin.
Hall of States Ste. 613
444 N. Capitol St., NW
Washington, DC 20001
Phone : (202) 624-5870
Fax : (202) 624-5871

DISTRICT OF COLUMBIA**
Steve Condrey
Off. of Intergovernmental Relations, Rm. 10105
441 4th St., NW
Washington, DC 20001
Phone : (202) 727-6265

AMERICAN SAMOA**
Fred Radewagen
Washington Representative
Pacific Island Washington Off.
1615 New Hampshire Ave., NW
Washington, DC 2009
Phone : (202) 387-8100

GUAM
Frank C. Torres III
Special Assistant
Washington Off. of the Governor of Guam
1615 New Hampshire Ave., NW
Washington, DC 20009
Phone : (202) 234-4826
Fax : (202) 797-0420

NORTHERN MARIANA ISLANDS
Juan N. Babauta
Resident Rep. to the U.S.
Commonwealth of the Northern Mariana Islands
2121 R St., NW
Washington, DC 20008
Phone : (202) 328-3847

Federal Liaison

PURERTO RICO**
Wanda Rubianes Callaso
Resident Commissioner
U.S. Congress
427 Cannon Bldg.
Washington, DC 20515
Phone : (809) 225-2615

U.S. VIRGIN ISLANDS
Carlyle Corbin
Special Asst. to the
Governor
U.S. Virgin Islands
900 17th St., NW, Ste. 500
Washington, DC 20006
Phone : (202) 293-3707

FINANCE

Responsible for multiple financial functions (budget, payroll, accounting, revenue estimation).

ALABAMA
Jimmy Baker
Acting Director
Dept. of Finance
600 Dexter Ave.
Montgomery, AL 36130
Phone : (334) 242-7160
Fax : (334) 242-4488

ALASKA
Don Wannie
Director
Div. of Finance
Dept. of Administration
P.O. Box 110204
Juneau, AK 99811-0204
Phone : (907) 465-2240
Fax : (907) 465-2169

ARIZONA
John Timko
Assistant Director, Fin. Srvcs.
Finance Division
Dept. of Administration
1700 W. Washington, Rm. 290
Phoenix, AZ 85007
Phone : (602) 542-0500

ARKANSAS
Richard Weiss
Director
Dept. of Finance & Admin.
401 DFA Bldg.
1509 W. 7th St.
Little Rock, AR 17201
Phone : (501) 682-2242
Fax : (501) 682-1086

CALIFORNIA
Russell S. Gould
Director
Dept. of Finance
State Capitol, Rm. 1145
Sacramento, CA 95814
Phone : (916) 445-4141

COLORADO
Clifford W. Hall
State Controller
Div. of Accounts & Control
Dept. of Admininstration
1525 Sherman St., Ste. 250
Denver, CO 80203
Phone : (303) 866-3281

CONNECTICUT
Reginald Jones
Secretary
Off. of Policy & Mgt.
80 Washington St.
Hartford, CT 06106
Phone : (203) 566-8070

DELAWARE
Sarah Jackson
Secretary
Dept. of Finance
540 S. DuPont Hwy.
Dover, DE 19901
Phone : (302) 739-4201
Fax : (302) 739-5000

FLORIDA
Linda G. Dilworth
Director of Finance
Dept. of Banking & Finance
PL 09 The Capitol
Tallahassee, FL 32399-0350
Phone : (904) 488-0545

GEORGIA
Steven N. McCoy
State Treasurer
Off. of Treasury & Fiscal Srvc.
1516 West Tower
200 Piedmont Ave., SE
Atlanta, GA 30334
Phone : (404) 656-2168

HAWAII
Earl I. Anzai
Director
Dept. of Budget & Finance
P.O. Box 150
Honolulu, HI 96810
Phone : (808) 586-1518
Fax : (808) 586-1518

IDAHO
Dean Van Englen
Administrator
Div. of Financial Management
Off. of the Governor
Statehouse, Rm. 122
Boise, ID 83720
Phone : (208) 334-3900

ILLINOIS
Raymond T. Wagner, Jr.
Director
Dept. of Revenue
101 W. Jefferson St., Rm. 6SW
Springfield, IL 62794
Phone : (217) 785-2602
Fax : (217) 782-6337

Joan Walters
Director
Bur. of the Budget
Off. of the Governor
108 State House
Springfield, IL 60706
Phone : (217) 782-4520
Fax : (217) 524-1514

INDIANA
Jean Blackwell
Director
Budget Agency
State House, Rm. 212
Indianapolis, IN 46204
Phone : (317) 232-5612

IOWA
Gretchen Tegeler
Director
Dept. of Management
State Capitol Bldg.
Des Moines, IA 50319
Phone : (515) 281-3322
Fax : (515) 242-5897

KANSAS
Sheila Frahm
Secretary
Dept. of Administration
State Capitol, Rm. 263-F
Topeka, KS 66612-1572
Phone : (913) 296-3011
Fax : (913) 296-2702

Susan Seltsam
Secretary
Dept. of Administration
State Capitol Bldg., Rm. 263E
Topeka, KS 66612
Phone : (913) 296-3011

KENTUCKY
Crit Luallen
Secretary
Finance & Admin. Cabinet
Capitol Annex, Rm. 301
Frankfort, KY 40601
Phone : (502) 564-4240

LOUISIANA
Raymond J. Laborde
Commissioner
Div. of Administration
Capitol Annex
P.O. Box 94095
Baton Rouge, LA 70804-9095
Phone : (504) 342-7000

MAINE
Janet Waldron
Commissioner
Dept. of Admin. & Financial Srvcs.
State House Station #78
Augusta, ME 04333
Phone : (207) 624-7800

MARYLAND
Marita Brown
Secretary
Dept. of Budget & Fiscal Planning
45 Calvert St.
Annapolis, MD 21404
Phone : (410) 974-2114

MASSACHUSETTS
Charles Baker
Secretary
Executive Off. for Admin. & Finance
State House, Rm. 373
Boston, MA 02133
Phone : (617) 727-2040

MICHIGAN
Patricia A. Woodworth
Director
Dept. of Mgt. & Budget
P.O. Box 30026
Lansing, MI 48909
Phone : (517) 373-1004
Fax : (517) 373-7268

MINNESOTA
Laura King
Commissioner
Dept. of Finance
400 Centennial Bldg.
658 Cedar St.
St. Paul, MN 55155
Phone : (612) 296-9721

MISSISSIPPI
Edward L. Ranck
Executive Director
Dept. of Finance & Admin.
P.O. Box 267
Jackson, MS 39205
Phone : (601) 359-3402

MISSOURI
Richard A. Hanson
Commissioner
Off. of Administration
State Capitol, Rm. 125
P.O. Box 809
Jefferson City, MO 65102
Phone : (314) 751-3311
Fax : (314) 751-1212

MONTANA
David Lewis
Director
Budget & Program Planning Off.
Capitol Station
Helena, MT 59620-0801
Phone : (406) 444-3616

NEBRASKA
Steve Ferris
Administrator
Budget Div.
Dept. of Administrative Srvcs.
P.O. Box 94664
Lincoln, NE 68509
Phone : (402) 471-2526

M. Berri Balka
State Tax Commissioner
Dept. of Revenue
P.O. Box 94818
Lincoln, NE 68509-4818
Phone : (402) 471-2971

John A. Breslow
Auditor of Public Accounts
State Capitol, Rm. 2303
P.O. Box 94786
Lincoln, NE 68509-4786
Phone : (402) 471-2111

NEVADA
Darrel Daines
Controller
State Capitol
Carson City, NV 89710
Phone : (702) 687-4330

NEW HAMPSHIRE
Patrick Duffy
Commissioner
Dept. of Administrative Srvcs.
25 Capitol St.
Concord, NH 03301
Phone : (603) 271-3201

NEW JERSEY
Betsy Pugh
Director
Off. of Mgt. & Budget
Dept. of Treasury
33 W. State St., CN-221
Trenton, NJ 08625
Phone : (609) 292-6746

NEW MEXICO
David Harris
Secretary
Dept. of Finance & Admin.
Bataan Memorial Bldg., Rm. 180
Santa Fe, NM 87503
Phone : (505) 827-3060
Fax : (505) 827-4984

NEW YORK*
State Comptroller
Off. of the State Comptroller
A.E. Smith Off. Bldg., 6th Fl.
Albany, NY 12236
Phone : (518) 474-4040

NORTH CAROLINA
Marvin K. Dorman
State Budget Officer
Off. of State Budget
116 W. Jones St.
Raleigh, NC 27603-8005
Phone : (919) 733-7061
Fax : (919) 733-0640

NORTH DAKOTA
Rod Backman
Director
Off. of Management & Budget
State Capitol, 4th Fl.
600 E. Boulevard Ave.
Bismarck, ND 58505-0400
Phone : (701) 328-4904
Fax : (701) 328-3230

NORTH DAKOTA — Cont.
Bud Walsh
Director of Accounting
Off. of Mgt. & Budget
State Capitol, 4th Fl.
600 E. Boulevard Ave.
Bismarck, ND 58505-0400
Phone : (701) 328-2682

OHIO
R. Gregory Browning
Director
Off. of Budget & Mgt.
30 E. Broad St., 34th Fl.
Columbus, OH 43266
Phone : (614) 752-2577
Fax : (614) 466-5400

OKLAHOMA
Tom Daxan
Secretary
Off. of State Finance
122 State Capitol
Oklahoma City, OK 73105
Phone : (405) 521-2141

OREGON
Theresa McHugh
Budget Director
Dept. of Admin. Srvcs.
155 Cottage St., NE
Salem, OR 97310
Phone : (503) 378-4691
Fax : (503) 373-7643

PENNSYLVANIA
Robert Bittenbender
Secretary
Budget Department
Rm. 238, Main Capitol Bldg.
Harrisburg, PA 17120
Phone : (717) 772-3820

RHODE ISLAND
Michael O'Keefe
Assoc. Dir. of Fin/Budget Officer
Off. of the Budget
Dept. of Admin.
One Capitol Hill, 4th Fl.
Providence, RI 02908
Phone : (401) 277-6300

SOUTH CAROLINA
L. Fred Carter
Executive Director
Budget & Control Board
P.O. Box 12444
Columbia, SC 29211
Phone : (803) 734-2320

SOUTH DAKOTA
Curt Everson
Commissioner
Bur. of Finance & Mgt.
State Capitol, 2nd Fl.
500 E. Capitol Ave.
Pierre, SD 57501
Phone : (605) 773-3411

TENNESSEE
Bob Corker
Commissioner
Dept. of Finance & Admin.
State Capitol, 1st Fl.
Nashville, TN 37243
Phone : (615) 741-2401
Fax : (615) 741-9872

TEXAS
John Sharp
Comptroller
Public Accounts
P.O. Box 13528, Capitol Station
Austin, TX 78711
Phone : (512) 463-4000

UTAH
Gordon L. Crabtree
Director
Div. of Finance
Dept. of Administrative Srvcs.
2110 State Off. Bldg.
Salt Lake City, UT 84114
Phone : (801) 538-3020

VERMONT
Thomas Pelham
Commissioner
Dept. of Finance & Mgt.
Agency of Administration
109 State St.
Montpelier, VT 05602
Phone : (802) 828-2376
Fax : (802) 828-2428

VIRGINIA
Paul W. Timmreck
Secretary of Finance
Governor's Cabinet
635 Ninth St. Off. Bldg.
Richmond, VA 23219
Phone : (804) 786-1148

WASHINGTON
Ruta Fanning
Director
Off. of Financial Mgt.
300 Insurance Bldg.
P.O. Box 43113
Olympia, WA 98504
Phone : (360) 753-5459

WEST VIRGINIA
Charles Polan
Secretary
Dept. of Finance & Admin.
State Capitol, Rm. E119
1900 Kanawha Blvd., E.
Charleston, WV 25305
Phone : (304) 558-2300
Fax : (304) 558-2999

WISCONSIN
Mark Wahl
Administrator
DOA/Div. of Tech Mgmt., 8th Fl.
101 E. Wilson St.
Madison, WI 53702
Phone : (608) 266-1651
Fax : (608) 266-2164

WYOMING
Dave Ferrari
State Auditor
State Capitol, Rm. 114
200 W. 24th St.
Cheyenne, WY 82002
Phone : (307) 777-7831

DISTRICT OF COLUMBIA
Robert Pohlman
Deputy Mayor
Financial Mgt.
441 4th St., NW, Ste. 1150
Washington, DC 20001
Phone : (202) 727-2476

AMERICAN SAMOA
Ray Pritt
Treasurer
Dept. of the Treasury
American Samoa Government
Pago Pago, AS 96799
Phone : (684) 633-4155
Fax : (684) 633-4100

GUAM
John S. Salas
Director
Dept. of Administration
P.O. Box 884
Agana, GU 96910
Phone : (671) 475-1101
Fax : (671) 477-6788

NORTHERN MARIANA ISLANDS
Maria D. Cabrera
Secretary of Finance
Dept. of Finance & Accounting
P.O. Box 5234, CHRB
Saipan, MP 96950
Phone : (670) 664-1100
Fax : (670) 664-1115

PUERTO RICO
Jorge Aponte Hernandez
Director
Off. of Budget & Mgt.
P.O. Box 3228
San Juan, PR 00904
Phone : (809) 725-9420
Fax : (809) 723-7308

U.S. VIRGIN ISLANDS
Gwendolyn P. Adams
Commissioner
Dept. of Finance
76 Kronprindsens Gade
St. Thomas, VI 00802
Phone : (809) 774-4750
Fax : (809) 776-4028

FIRE MARSHAL

Inspects businesses and public places for fire hazards.

ALABAMA
John Robinson
State Fire Marshal
135 S. Union St., Rm. 140
Montgomery, AL 36130
Phone : (334) 241-4166
Fax : (334) 269-6570

ALASKA
Craig P. Goodrich
State Fire Marshal
5700 E. Tudor Rd.
Anchorage, AK 99507-1225
Phone : (907) 269-5491
Fax : (907) 338-4375

ARIZONA
Dewayne D. Pell
State Fire Marshal
Dept. of Bldg. & Fire Safety
1540 W. Van Buren St.
Phoenix, AZ 85007
Phone : (602) 244-4964

ARKANSAS
Ray Carnahan
Commander
Off. of Fire Marshal
State Police
P.O. Box 5901
Little Rock, AR 72215
Phone : (501) 221-8200
Fax : (501) 224-4722

CALIFORNIA
Ronny J. Coleman
State Fire Marshal
7171 Bowling Dr., Ste. 600
Sacramento, CA 95823
Phone : (916) 262-1883

COLORADO
Dean Smith
Director of Fire Safety
Dept. of Public Safety
700 Kipling St.
Lakewood, CO 80215
Phone : (303) 239-4463

CONNECTICUT
Douglas Peabody
Deputy Fire Marshal
Bur. of State Fire Marshal
Dept. of Public Safety
1111 Country Club Rd.
P.O. Box 2794
Middletown, CT 06457
Phone : (203) 685-8380

DELAWARE
Daniel R. Kiley
State Fire Marshall
Fire Service Center
1537 Chestnut Grove Rd.
Dover, DE 19904-9610
Phone : (302) 739-4393
Fax : (302) 739-3696

FLORIDA
B.J. Peters
Director
Div. of State Fire Marshal
Dept. of Insurance
The Capitol
Tallahassee, FL 32399-0300
Phone : (904) 922-3170

GEORGIA
A.D. Bell
State Fire Marshal
2 M.L. King, Jr. Dr., SE, Rm. 620
Atlanta, GA 30334
Phone : (404) 656-9453

IDAHO
Lee Bright
State Fire Marshal
Dept. of Insurance
500 S. 10th St.
Boise, ID 83720
Phone : (208) 334-4371

ILLINOIS
Thomas Armstead
Fire Marshal
1035 Stevenson Dr.
Springfield, IL 62703
Phone : (217) 785-4143
Fax : (217) 782-1062

INDIANA
M. Tracy Boatwright
State Fire Marshal
Dept. of Fire & Bldg. Srvcs.
402 W. Washington St., Rm.C246
Indianapolis, IN 46204
Phone : (317) 232-2226

IOWA
Roy Marshall
State Fire Marshal
Dept. of Public Safety
Wallace State Off. Bldg.
Des Moines, IA 50319
Phone : (515) 281-8622

KANSAS
Edward Redmon
Fire Marshal
700 SW Jackson, Ste. 600
Topeka, KS 66603-3714
Phone : (913) 296-3401
Fax : (913) 296-0151

KENTUCKY
Dennis Decker
Fire Marshal
Div. of Fire Prevention
Public Protection & Reg. Cabinet
1047 U.S. 127 S.
Frankfort, KY 40601
Phone : (502) 564-3626

LOUISIANA
Charles Fredieu
Assistant Secretary
Off. of State Fire Marshal
Dept. of Pub. Safety & Corr.
P.O. Box 94304
Baton Rouge, LA 70804
Phone : (504) 925-4911

MAINE
Dennis Lundstedt
Fire Marshal
Dept. of Public Safety
State House Station # 52
Augusta, ME 04333
Phone : (207) 287-3473

MARYLAND**
Rocco J. Gabriele
Fire Marshal
106 Old Court Rd., Ste. 300
Baltimore, MD 21208-4016
Phone : (410) 764-4324

MASSACHUSETTS
Stephen Coan
Acting Fire Marshal
Div. of Fire Prevention
Exec. Off. of Public Safety
1010 Commonwealth Ave.
Boston, MA 02215
Phone : (617) 566-4500
Fax : (617) 556-2600

MICHIGAN
Wade E. Schaefer
Commanding Officer
Dept. of State Police
7150 Harris Dr.
Lansing, MI 48913
Phone : (517) 322-1924

MINNESOTA
Thomas R. Brace
State Fire Marshal
Bigelow Bldg., # 285
450 Syndicate St., N.
St. Paul, MN 55104
Phone : (612) 643-3080

MISSISSIPPI
George Dale
Commissioner
Dept. of Insurance
1804 Sillers Bldg.
Jackson, MS 39201
Phone : (601) 359-3569

MISSOURI
Edward C. Vineyard
Interim State Fire Marshal
Dept. of Public Safety
1715 Industrial Dr.
P.O. Box 844
Jefferson City, MO 65102
Phone : (314) 751-2930
Fax : (314) 751-1744

MONTANA
Bruce Suenram
Chief
Fire Prevention & Invest. Bur.
Dept. of Justice
P.O. Box 201417
Helena, MT 59620
Phone : (406) 444-2050

NEBRASKA
Michael R. Durst
Fire Marshal
246 S. 14th St.
Lincoln, NE 68508
Phone : (402) 471-2027

NEVADA*
State Fire Marshal
107 Jacobson Way
Carson City, NV 89710
Phone : (702) 687-4290

NEW HAMPSHIRE
Donald Bliss
Fire Marshal
Div. of Safety Services
Dept. of Safety
10 Hazen Dr.
Concord, NH 03305
Phone : (603) 271-3294

NEW JERSEY
William H. Cane
Director
Fire Safety Comm.
Dept. of Community Affairs
101 S. Broad St., CN809
Trenton, NJ 08625
Phone : (609) 292-9446

NEW MEXICO
George Chavez
State Fire Marshal
State Corporation Comm.
P.O. Drawer 1269
Santa Fe, NM 87504
Phone : (505) 827-3550
Fax : (505) 827-3778

NEW YORK*
State Fire Administrator
Off. of Fire Prev. & Control
Dept. of State
162 Washington Ave.
Albany, NY 12231
Phone : (518) 474-6746

NORTH CAROLINA
Jim Long
State Fire Marshal
State Fire Commission
Dept. of Insurance
430 N. Salisbury St.
Raleigh, NC 27603-1212
Phone : (919) 733-2142
Fax : (919) 733-6495

NORTH DAKOTA
Joel Boespflug
Fire Marshal
Att: General Office
P.O. Box 1054
Bismarck, ND 58502
Phone : (701) 328-5555
Fax : (701) 328-5510

OHIO
James J. McNamee
State Fire Marshal
Dept. of Commerce
P.O. Box 525
Reynoldsburg, OH 43068
Phone : (614) 752-8200
Fax : (614) 752-7213

OKLAHOMA
Byron Hollander
Fire Marshal
Fire Marshal Agcy.
4545 Lincoln Blvd.
Oklahoma City, OK 73105
Phone : (405) 524-9610
Fax : (405) 524-9810

OREGON
Robert T. Panuccio
State Fire Marshal
Oregon State Police
4760 Portland Rd., NE
Salem, OR 97305-1760
Phone : (503) 378-3473
Fax : (503) 373-1825

PENNSYLVANIA
David L. Smith
State Fire Commissioner
P.O. Box 3321
Harrisburg, PA 17105-3321
Phone : (717) 783-5061

RHODE ISLAND
Irving Owens
State Fire Marshal
272 W. Exchange St.
Providence, RI 02903-1025
Phone : (401) 277-2335

SOUTH CAROLINA
Lewis Lee
State Fire Marshal
Div. of State Fire Marshal
141 Monticello Trl.
Columbia, SC 29203
Phone : (803) 896-9800

SOUTH DAKOTA
Dan Carlson
Fire Marshal
Div. of Fire Safety
Public Safety Bldg.
Pierre, SD 57501
Phone : (605) 773-3562

TENNESSEE
Robert Frost
Assistant Commissioner
Div. of Fire Prevention
500 James Robertson Pkwy., 3rd Fl.
Nashville, TN 37243
Phone : (615) 741-2981

TEXAS
Michael E. Hines
Executive Director
Comm. on Fire Protection
12675 Research Blvd.
Austin, TX 78759-2218
Phone : (512) 873-1700

UTAH
Lynn B. Borg
Fire Marshal
Dept. of Public Safety
4501 S. 2700 W.
Salt Lake City, UT 84119
Phone : (801) 284-6358

VERMONT
Mary S. Hooper
Commissioner
Dept. of Labor & Industry
National Life Bldg.
Drawer 20
Montpelier, VT 05620-3401
Phone : (802) 828-2288
Fax : (802) 828-2748

VIRGINIA
Jack Proctor
Acting Fire Marshal
Dept. of Housing & Community Development
205 N. Fourth St.
Richmond, VA 23219
Phone : (804) 786-4751

WASHINGTON
Dick Small
Deputy Director
Fire Protecton Services
Dept. of Health
P.O. box 48350
Olympia, WA 98504-8350
Phone : (360) 493-2661

WEST VIRGINIA
Walter Smittle III
Fire Marshal
2000 Quarrier St.
Charleston, WV 25305
Phone : (304) 558-2191

WISCONSIN
Frank Meyers
State Fire Marshal
Div. of Criminal Investigation
Dept. of Justice
123 W. Washington, 7th Fl.
P.O. Box 7857
Madison, WI 53703
Phone : (608) 266-1671
Fax : (608) 624-6368

WYOMING
Gene Brooks
Director/State Fire Marshal
Dept. of Fire Prevention & Electrical Safety
Barrett Bldg.
Cheyenne, WY 82002
Phone : (307) 777-6385

DISTRICT OF COLUMBIA
Otis Latin
Fire Chief
Fire Dept.
1923 Vermont Ave., NW
Washington, DC 20001
Phone : (202) 673-3320

AMERICAN SAMOA
Fonoti D. Jessop
Commissioner
Dept. of Public Safety
American Samoa Government
Pago Pago, AS 96799
Phone : (684) 633-1111
Fax : (684) 633-5111

Fire Marshal

GUAM
Gil P. Reyes
Acting Fire Chief
Guam Fire Dept.
125 Tun Jesus Crisostomo St., Ste. 301
Tamuning, GU 96911
Phone : (671) 646-3324
Fax : (671) 646-3364

NORTHERN MARIANA ISLANDS
Jesus M. Castro
Chief
Fire Division
Dept. of Public Safety
Susupe, Civic Ctr.
Saipan, MP 96950
Phone : (670) 234-3437
Fax : (670) 234-8531

PUERTO RICO
Isaias Hernandez
Director
Fire Services
P.O. Box 13325
San Juan, PR 00908-3325
Phone : (809) 725-3444
Fax : (809) 725-3788

U.S. VIRGIN ISLANDS
Carlton Dowe
Director
Fire Srvc.
Universal Plaza, 8A E. Thomas
St. Thomas, VI 00802
Phone : (809) 774-7610
Fax : (809) 774-4718

FISH & WILDLIFE

Protects, manages and enhances fish and wildlife resources and enforces the state's fish and game laws.

ALABAMA
Charles D. Kelley
Director
Div. of Game & Fish
Dept. of Cons. & Natural Resources
64 N. Union St., Rm. 728
Montgomery, AL 36130
Phone : (334) 242-3465
Fax : (334) 242-3032

ALASKA
Frank Rue
Commissioner
Dept. of Fish & Game
P.O. Box 25526
Juneau, AK 99802-5526
Phone : (907) 465-6141
Fax : (907) 465-2332

ARIZONA
Duane L. Shroufe
Director
Dept. of Game & Fish
2222 W. Greenway Rd.
Phoenix, AZ 85023
Phone : (602) 942-3000

ARKANSAS
Steve N. Wilson
Director
Game & Fish Comm.
2 Natural Resources Dr.
Little Rock, AR 72205
Phone : (501) 223-6305
Fax : (501) 223-6425

CALIFORNIA
Chuck Raysbrook
Acting Chief Deputy Director
Dept. of Fish & Game
1416 9th St., 12th Fl.
Sacramento, CA 95814
Phone : (916) 653-7667

COLORADO*
Director
Div. of Wildlife
Dept. of Natural Resources
6060 Broadway
Denver, CO 80216
Phone : (303) 297-1192
Fax : (303) 294-0874

CONNECTICUT
George Brys
Director
Wildlife Division
79 Elm St.
Hartford, CT 06106
Phone : (203) 424-3004

Ernest Beckwith Jr.
Director
Fisheries Div.
79 Elm St.
Hartford, CT 06106
Phone : (203) 424-3004

DELAWARE
Andy Manus
Director
Div. of Fish & Wildlife
Dept. of Nat. Res. & Environ.
P.O. Box 1401
Dover, DE 19903
Phone : (302) 739-5295
Fax : (302) 739-6157

FLORIDA
Allan Egbert
Director
Game & Fresh Water Fish Comm.
620 S. Meridian St.
Tallahassee, FL 32399-1600
Phone : (904) 488-2975

GEORGIA
David Waller
Director
Wildlife Resources Div.
Dept. of Natural Resources
2070 U.S. Hwy. 278, SE
Social Circle, GA 30279
Phone : (404) 918-6400

HAWAII
Henry M. Sakuda
Director
Div. of Aquatic Resources
Dept. of Land & Natural Res.
1151 Punchbowl St.
Honolulu, HI 96801
Phone : (808) 587-0099

IDAHO
Jerry M. Conley
Director
Dept. of Fish & Game
P.O. Box 25
Boise, ID 83707
Phone : (208) 334-3771

ILLINOIS
Brent Manning
Director
Dept. of Conservation
Lincoln Towers Plz., Rm. 425
524 S. Second St.
Springfield, IL 62706
Phone : (217) 782-6302
Fax : (217) 785-9236

INDIANA
Gary L. Eldridge
Training/Personnel Officer
Fish & Wildlife Div.
402 W. Washington St., Rm. W-273
Indianapolis, IN 46204
Phone : (317) 232-4080

IOWA
Allen Farris
Administrator
Fish & Wildlife Div.
Dept. of Natural Resources
Wallace State Off. Bldg.
Des Moines, IA 50319
Phone : (515) 281-5154

KANSAS
Roger Wolfe
Supervisor
Fisheries/Wildlife Division
Dept. of Wildlife & Parks
3300 SW 29th St.
Topeka, KS 66614
Phone : (913) 273-6740
Fax : (913) 273-6757

KENTUCKY
Tom Bennett
Commissioner
Fish & Wildlife
1 Game Farm Rd.
Frankfort, KY 40601
Phone : (502) 564-3000

LOUISIANA
Joe L. Herring
Secretary
Dept. of Wildlife & Fisheries
P.O. Box 98000
Baton Rouge, LA 70898
Phone : (504) 765-2800

Edward Erxleben
Secretary
Dept. Wildlife & Fisheries
P.O. Box 98000
Baton Rouge, LA 70898-9000
Phone : (504) 765-2803

MAINE
Fred Hurley
Director
Bureau of Resource Management
Dept. of Inland Fisheries/Wildlife
#41 State House Station
Augusta, ME 04333
Phone : (207) 287-5202

MARYLAND**
Pete Jensen
Director
Fisheries Div.
Dept. of Natural Resources
Tawes State Off. Bldg.
Annapolis, MD 21401
Phone : (410) 974-3558

MASSACHUSETTS
John C. Phillips
Commissioner
Dept. of Fisheries, Wildlife & Environmental Law Enforcement
100 Cambridge St., Rm. 1902
Boston, MA 02202
Phone : (617) 727-1614

MICHIGAN
George E. Burgoyne Jr.
Chief
Wildlife Div.
Dept. of Natural Resources
P.O. Box 30028
Lansing, MI 48909
Phone : (517) 373-1280

John Robertson
Chief
Fisheries Div.
Dept. of Natural Resources
P.O. Box 30028
Lansing, MI 48909
Phone : (517) 373-1263

MINNESOTA
Roger Holmes
Director
Div. of Fish & Wildlife
Dept. of Natural Resources
500 Lafayette Rd.
St. Paul, MN 55155
Phone : (612) 296-1308

MISSISSIPPI
Sam Polles
Director
Parks & Recreation
Dept. of Wildlife, Fish & Parks
P.O. Box 451
Jackson, MS 39205
Phone : (601) 362-9212

MISSOURI
Ollie Torgerson
Chief
Div. of Wildlife
Dept. of Conservation
2901 W. Truman Blvd.
P.O. Box 180
Jefferson City, MO 65102
Phone : (314) 751-4115
Fax : (314) 526-4663

James P. Fry
Chief
Div. of Fisheries
Dept. of Conservation
2901 W. Truman Blvd.
P.O. Box 180
Jefferson City, MO 65102
Phone : (314) 751-4115
Fax : (314) 526-4047

MISSOURI — Cont.
Ronald Glover
Chief
Div. of Protection
Dept. of Conservation
2901 W. Truman Blvd.
P.O. Box 180
Jefferson City, MO 65102
Phone : (314) 751-4115
Fax : (314) 751-8971

MONTANA
Don Childress
Administrator
Wildlife Div.
Dept. of Fish, Wildlife & Parks
1420 E. 6th Ave.
Helena, MT 59620
Phone : (406) 444-2612

Larry Peterman
Administrator
Fisheries Div.
Dept. of Fish, Wildlife & Parks
1420 E. 6th Ave.
Helena, MT 59620
Phone : (406) 444-2449

NEBRASKA
James Douglas
Division Administrator
Wildlife Division
Games & Parks Commission
P.O. Box 30370
Lincoln, NE 68503
Phone : (402) 471-5435

Wesley Sheets
Assistant Director
Game & Parks Comm.
P.O. Box 30370
Lincoln, NE 68503
Phone : (402) 471-5537

NEVADA
William Molini
Administrator
Div. of Wildlife
Conservation & Nat. Res. Dept.
1100 Valley Rd.
Reno, NV 89520
Phone : (702) 789-0540

NEW HAMPSHIRE
James Distgfano
Executive Director
Dept. of Fish & Game
2 Hazen Dr.
Concord, NH 03301
Phone : (603) 271-3512

NEW JERSEY
Robert McDowell
Director
Fish, Game & Wildlife Div.
Dept. of Environ. Protection
501 E. State St., CN400
Trenton, NJ 08625
Phone : (609) 292-9410

NEW MEXICO
Gerald A. Maracchini
Director
Dept. of Game & Fish
Villagra Bldg.
408 Galisteo St.
P.O. Box 25112
Santa Fe, NM 87503
Phone : (505) 827-7899
Fax : (505) 827-7915

NEW YORK*
Director
Div. of Fish & Wildlife
Dept. of Env. Conservation
50 Wolf Rd.
Albany, NY 12233
Phone : (518) 457-5690

NORTH CAROLINA
Charles R. Fullwood
Executive Director
Wildlife Resources Comm.
512 N. Salisbury St.
Raleigh, NC 27604
Phone : (919) 733-3391
Fax : (919) 715-3060

NORTH DAKOTA
K.L. Cool
Director
Dept. of Game & Fish
100 N. Bismarck Expy.
Bismarck, ND 58501-5095
Phone : (701) 328-6300
Fax : (701) 328-6352

OHIO
Dick Pierce
Chief
Div. of Wildlife
Dept. of Natural Resources
1840 Belcher Dr., Bldg. G-3
Columbus, OH 43224
Phone : (614) 265-6305
Fax : (614) 262-1143

OKLAHOMA
Steve Lewis
Director
Dept. of Wildlife Conservation
1801 N. Lincoln Blvd.
Oklahoma City, OK 73105
Phone : (405) 521-3851

OREGON
Rudolph Rosen
Director
Dept. of Fish & Wildlife
2501 SW First Ave.
P.O. Box 59
Portland, OR 97207
Phone : (503) 229-5406
Fax : (503) 229-6134

PENNSYLVANIA
Peter A. Colangelo
Executive Director
Fish Commission
P.O. Box 67000
Harrisburg, PA 17106
Phone : (717) 657-4518

Donald C. Madl
Executive Director
Game Comm.
2001 Elmerton Ave.
Harrisburg, PA 17110
Phone : (717) 787-3633

RHODE ISLAND
David Borden
Chief
Div. of Fish & Wildlife
Dept. of Environmental Mgt.
4808 Tower Hill Rd.
Wakefield, RI 02879
Phone : (401) 789-3094

SOUTH CAROLINA
James A. Timmerman Jr.
Director
Div. of Wildlife & Marine Res.
Dept. of Natural Resources
P.O. Box 167
Columbia, SC 29203
Phone : (803) 734-3888

SOUTH DAKOTA
Doug Hansen
Director
Wildlife Div.
Dept. of Game, Fish & Parks
523 E. Capitol Ave.
Pierre, SD 57501
Phone : (605) 773-3381

TENNESSEE
Gary Myers
Executive Director
Wildlife Resources Agency
P.O. Box 40747
Nashville, TN 37204
Phone : (615) 781-6552

TEXAS
Andrew S. Sansom
Executive Director
Dept. of Parks & Wildlife
4200 Smith School Rd.
Austin, TX 78744
Phone : (512) 389-4802

UTAH
Timothy H. Provan
Director
Div. of Wildlife Resources
Dept. of Natural Resources
1596 W. North Temple
Salt Lake City, UT 84116
Phone : (801) 538-4858

VERMONT
Allen A. Elser
Commissioner
Dept. of Fish & Wildlife
Agcy. of Natural Resources
103 S. Main St.
Waterbury, VT 05676
Phone : (802) 241-3700
Fax : (802) 241-3295

VIRGINIA
William L. Woodfin, Jr.
Director
Dept. of Game & Inland Fisheries
4010 W. Broad St.
Richmond, VA 23230
Phone : (804) 367-9231
Fax : (804) 367-0405

WASHINGTON
Bob Turner
Director
Dept. of Wildlife
600 N. Capitol Way
P.O. Box 3200
Olympia, WA 98501-3200
Phone : (360) 902-2200

WEST VIRGINIA
Robert L. Miles
Chief
Div. of Wildlife Resources
Dept. of Natural Resources
Capitol Complex, Bldg. 3
Charleston, WV 25305
Phone : (304) 558-2771

WISCONSIN
Lee Kernen
Director
Bur. of Fish Mgt.
Dept. of Natural Resources
101 S. Webster, FM/4
P.O. Box 7921
Madison, WI 53707
Phone : (608) 267-0796
Fax : (608) 267-3579

WISCONSIN — Cont.
Steven W. Miller
Director
Bur. of Wildlife Mgt.
Div. of Resource Mgt.
P.O. Box 7921
Madison, WI 53707
Phone : (608) 266-2193

WYOMING
John Talbot
Acting Director
Game & Fish Comm.
5400 Bishop Blvd.
Cheyenne, WY 82006
Phone : (307) 777-4501

DISTRICT OF COLUMBIA
Ferial Bishop
Administrator
Env. Regulation Admin.
Dept. of Cons. & Reg. Affairs
2100 M.L. King, Jr. Ave., Ste. 203
Washington, DC 20020
Phone : (202) 404-1136

AMERICAN SAMOA
Ray Tulafono
Director
Marine Resources
Pago Pago, AS 96799
Phone : (684) 633-4456
Fax : (684) 633-5944

GUAM
Michael W. Kuhlman
Director
Dept. of Agriculture
P.O. Box 2950
Agana, GU 96910
Phone : (671) 734-3942
Fax : (671) 734-6569

NORTHERN MARIANA ISLANDS
Arnold I. Palacios
Chief
Fish & Wildlife Div.
Dept. of Natural Resources
Saipan, MP 96950
Phone : (670) 322-9627
Fax : (670) 322-9629

PUERTO RICO
Pedro Gelabert Marquez
Secretary
Dept. of Natural Resources
P.O. Box 5887
San Juan, PR 00906-5887
Phone : (809) 724-8774
Fax : (809) 723-4255

U.S. VIRGIN ISLANDS
Virdin C. Brown
Asst. Commissioner
Dept. of Planning & Natural Resources
Nisky Ctr., Ste. 231
St. Thomas, VI 00802
Phone : (809) 774-3320
Fax : (809) 775-5706

FLEET MANAGEMENT

Manages the state's central fleet of vehicles which are made available to other state agencies.

ALABAMA
Don Segrest
Director
Off. of Fleet Mgt.
Dept. of Finance
386 S. Ripley St.
Montgomery, AL 36130
Phone : (334) 242-4043
Fax : (334) 240-3297

ALASKA
Mal Linthwaite
Director
Div. of Engineering & Operations
Dept. of Transportation & Public Facilities
3132 Channel Dr.
Juneau, AK 99801-7898
Phone : (907) 465-2960
Fax : (907) 465-2460

ARIZONA
David St. John
Assistant Director
General Services Div.
Dept. of Administration
1700 W. Washington, Rm. 600
Phoenix, AZ 85007
Phone : (602) 542-1593

ARKANSAS
Ron Lester
Information Systems Manager
Off. of Administrative Srvcs.
Dept. of Finance & Admin.
P.O. Box 2485
Little Rock, AR 72203
Phone : (501) 324-9058
Fax : (501) 324-9070

CALIFORNIA
Timothy Bow
Chief
Off. of Fleet Administration
Dept. of General Srvcs.
802 Q St.
Sacramento, CA 95814-6422
Phone : (916) 327-2007

COLORADO
Jack Keene
Director
Central Services Div.
225 E. 16th Ave., Rm. 800
Denver, CO 80203
Phone : (303) 866-3970

CONNECTICUT
Stephen Dygus
Director
Off. of Fleet Operations
Dept. of Administrative Srvcs.
190 Huyshope Ave.
Hartford, CT 06106
Phone : (203) 566-5940

DELAWARE
Terry Barton
Fleet Administrator
Dept. of Administrative Srvcs.
Tudor Industrial Pk.
604 Otis Dr.
Dover, DE 19901
Phone : (302) 739-3039
Fax : (302) 739-5450

FLORIDA
Harrison Rivers
Fleet Manager
Div. of Motor Pool
Dept. of Mgt. Srvcs.
2737 Centerview Dr., Ste. 110
Tallahassee, FL 32399-0950
Phone : (904) 488-4099

HAWAII
Harold Sonomura
Division Head
Automotive Mgt. Div.
Accounting & Gen. Srvcs. Dept.
869-A Punchbowl St.
Honolulu, HI 96813
Phone : (808) 586-0343

IDAHO
Lloyd Howe
Director
Dept. of Administration
650 W. State St., Rm. 100
Boise, ID 83720
Phone : (208) 334-3382

ILLINOIS
Barbara Bonansinga
Manager
Div. of Vehicles
Dept. of Central Mgt. Srvcs.
200 E. Ash St.
Springfield, IL 62706
Phone : (217) 782-2535

INDIANA
Brian Renner
Superintendent
State Motor Pool
425 W. New York St.
Indianapolis, IN 46204
Phone : (317) 232-1378

IOWA
Dale Schroeder
State Vehicle Dispatcher
Vehicle Dispatcher Div.
Dept. of General Srvcs.
301 E. 7th St.
Des Moines, IA 50319
Phone : (515) 281-7702

KANSAS
Orion Jordan
Director
Central Motor Pool
Dept. of Administration
400 SW Van Buren
Topeka, KS 66603-3332
Phone : (913) 296-2245
Fax : (913) 296-8100

KENTUCKY
Joe Heady
Director
Div. of Transportation Srvcs.
Transportation Cabinet
369 Warsaw St.
Frankfort, KY 40622
Phone : (502) 564-2260

LOUISIANA
Louis Amedee
Director
Property Assistance Agency
Div. of Admin.
P.O. Box 94095
Baton Rouge, LA 70804-9095
Phone : (504) 342-6890

MAINE
William S. Pratt
Fleet Manager
Vehicle Rental Agency
Central Fleet Management
State House Station # 9
Augusta, ME 04333
Phone : (207) 287-3521

MARYLAND**
John Keavney
Fleet Administrator
Div. of Mgt. Analysis & Audits
Dept. of Budget & Fiscal Planning
45 Calvert St.
Annapolis, MD 21401
Phone : (301) 974-2310

MASSACHUSETTS
John Ewing
Fleet Administrator
Motor Vehicle Mgt. Bur.
Executive Off. of Admin. & Finance
1 Ashburton Pl., Rm. 105
Boston, MA 02108
Phone : (617) 727-8844
Fax : (617) 727-4527

MICHIGAN
Duane E. Berger
Director
Motor Transport Div.
P.O. Box 30026
Lansing, MI 48909

MINNESOTA
Tim Morse
Fleet Manager
Bur. of Field Srvcs.
Dept. of Natural Resources
500 Lafayette Rd.
St. Paul, MN 55155-4016
Phone : (612) 297-1402

Robert D. McNeil
Director
Travel Mgt. Div.
Dept. of Admin.
610 N. Robert
St. Paul, MN 55101
Phone : (612) 296-6781

MISSISSIPPI
Don Buffum
Director
Bur. of Purchasing
Off. of Purchasing & Travel
1504 Sillers Bldg.
Jackson, MS 39201
Phone : (601) 359-3409

MISSOURI
Stan Perovich
Director
Div. of General Services
Off. of Administration
Truman Bldg., Rm. 760
P.O. Box 809
Jefferson City, MO 65102
Phone : (314) 751-4656
Fax : (314) 751-7819

MONTANA
Marvin Dye
Director
Dept. of Transportation
2701 Prospect Ave.
Helena, MT 59620
Phone : (406) 444-6201

NEBRASKA
Allan L. Abbott
Director
Dept. of Roads
P.O. Box 94759
Lincoln, NE 68509-4759
Phone : (402) 479-4615
Fax : (402) 479-4325

NEVADA*
Administrator
Motor Pool Div.
Dept. of General Services
Capitol Complex
Carson City, NV 89710
Phone : (702) 885-5315

NEW JERSEY
Bud Montague
Fleet manager
Central Motor Pool
605 S. Broad St.
Trenton, NJ 08625
Phone : (609) 984-7277

NEW MEXICO
Paul Salazar
Director
Transportation Motor Pool
Dept. of General Srvcs.
2600 Cerillos Rd.
P.O. Drawer 26110
Santa Fe, NM 87502-6110
Phone : (505) 827-1950
Fax : (505) 827-2181

NEW YORK*
Director
Equipment & Inventory Mgt.
State Thruway Authority
200 Southern Blvd., Box 189
Albany, NY 12201
Phone : (518) 436-2938

NORTH CAROLINA
John T. Massey Jr.
Director
Div. of Motor Fleet Mgt.
Dept. of Administration
1915 Blue Ridge Rd.
Raleigh, NC 27607-6403
Phone : (919) 733-6540
Fax : (919) 733-2432

NORTH DAKOTA
Paul Feyereisen
Manager
State Fleet Services
Dept. of Transportation
608 E. Boulevard Ave.
Bismarck, ND 58505
Phone : (701) 328-2545
Fax : (701) 328-4623

OHIO
Leilani Napier
Fleet Administrator
Div. of Administrative Srvcs.
4200 Surface Rd.
Columbus, OH 43228-1313
Phone : (614) 466-6607
Fax : (614) 752-8883

OKLAHOMA
Steve Dwyer
Director
Div. of Fleet Mgt.
Dept. of Central Srvcs.
3301-A N. Santa Fe
Oklahoma City, OK 73118
Phone : (405) 521-2204

OREGON
Rob Cameron
Motor Fleet Manager, Fleet Admin.
Dept. of Adm. Srvcs.
100 Airport Rd., SE
Salem, OR 97310
Phone : (503) 378-3367
Fax : (503) 378-5813

PENNSYLVANIA
Ronald Thrope
Acting Manager
Fleet Management
2221 Forester St.
Harrisburg, PA 17105
Phone : (717) 787-3162

RHODE ISLAND
Stanley Jendzejec
Chief on Special Registration
Dept. of Transportation
2 Capitol Hill
Providence, RI 02903
Phone : (401) 277-2986

SOUTH CAROLINA
Gerald W. Calk
Budget & Control Board
OGS - State Fleet Management
1022 Senate Street
Columbia, SC 29201
Phone : (803) 737-0668
Fax : (803) 737-1160

Allan J. Spence
Director
Motor Vehicle Mgt. Div.
Budget & Control Board
1022 Senate St.
Columbia, SC 29201
Phone : (803) 737-1515

SOUTH DAKOTA
S.J. Axtman
Director
Fleet & Travel Management
Bur. of Administration
500 E. Capitol Ave.
Pierre, SD 57501
Phone : (605) 773-3162

TENNESSEE
Dennis Johnson
Director
Div. of Motor Vehicle Mgt.
Dept. of General Srvcs.
910 8th Ave., N.
Nashville, TN 37219
Phone : (615) 741-1637
Fax : (615) 741-2161

TEXAS
Diane Harker
Director
Administrative Services
General Services Commission
P.O. Box 13047, Capitol Station
Austin, TX 78711-3047
Phone : (512) 463-3035

Bill Workman
Manager
Off. of Transportation Srvcs.
Texas A&M University
Trans. Ctr. & Physical Plant
College Station, TX 77843
Phone : (409) 845-7121

UTAH
Steven Saltzgiver
Manager
Motor Pool
Div. of General Srvcs.
Capitol Plz.
Salt Lake City, UT 84114
Phone : (801) 535-2901

VERMONT
George S. Combes
Superintendent
Central Garage Div.
Agency of Transportation
133 State St.
Montpelier, VT 05633
Phone : (802) 828-2564
Fax : (802) 828-3576

VIRGINIA
Frank Houff
State Fleet Manager
Dept. of Transportation
1401 E. Broad St.
Richmond, VA 23219
Phone : (804) 367-6982

WASHINGTON
Tim Arnold
Assistant Director
Div. of Transportation Srvcs.
Dept. of General Admin.
1312 Fones Rd., SE, Bldg. 4
P.O. Box 41032
Olympia, WA 98504-1032
Phone : (360) 438-8247

WEST VIRGINIA
Fred Weaver
Coordinator of Travel & Fleet Mgt.
Travel Mgt. Off.
Dept. of Administration
212 California Ave.
Charleston, WV 25305
Phone : (304) 558-3259

WISCONSIN
Jeff Knight
Director
Bureau of Transportation
Dept. of Administration
201 S. Dickenson
P.O. Box 7867
Madison, WI 53703
Phone : (608) 266-9855
Fax : (608) 267-6935

WYOMING
Darrell Christensen
Vehicle Fleet Supervisor
DAFC/Central Srvcs.
723 W. 19th St.
Cheyenne, WY 82002
Phone : (307) 777-6857

DISTRICT OF COLUMBIA
Danny L. Johnson
Administrator
Fleet Mgt. Admin.
Dept. of Public Works
1725 15th St., NE
Washington, DC 20002
Phone : (202) 576-6799

AMERICAN SAMOA
Sam Puletasi
Director
Dept. of Public Works
American Samoa Government
Pago Pago, AS 96799
Phone : (684) 633-4141
Fax : (684) 633-5958

GUAM
Gil A. Shinohara
Acting Director
Dept. of Public Works
P.O. Box 2950
Agana, GU 96910
Phone : (671) 646-3101
Fax : (671) 649-6178

NORTHERN MARIANA ISLANDS
David M. Apatang
Chief
Procurement & Supply Div.
Dept. of Finance
Lower Base
Saipan, MP 96950
Phone : (670) 664-1500

PUERTO RICO*
Administrator
General Services Admin.
P.O. Box 7428
San Juan, PR 00916
Phone : (809) 721-7370
Fax : (809) 722-7965

U.S. VIRGIN ISLANDS
Joseph Farrington
Director
Div. of Transportation
Dept. of Property & Procurement
Sub Base, Bldg. 1
St. Thomas, VI 00802
Phone : (809) 774-0388
Fax : (809) 774-1163

FOOD PROTECTION

Protects the state's food supply, from the production and processing of food, through its marketing and distribution.

ALABAMA
John Block
Director
Agricultural Chemistry & Plant Industry Div.
P.O. Box 3336
Montgomery, AL 36193
Phone : (334) 242-2656
Fax : (334) 240-3103

ALASKA
Kit Ballentine
Director
Div. of Environmental Health
Dept. of Environ. Conservation
410 Willoughby Ave., Ste. 105
Juneau, AK 99801
Phone : (907) 465-5280
Fax : (907) 465-5292

ARIZONA
Norman J. Petersen
Assistant Director
Disease Control Services Div.
Dept. of Health Services
3815 N. Black Canyon Hwy.
Phoenix, AZ 85015
Phone : (602) 230-5808

ARKANSAS
Sandra Lancaster
Administrator
Food & Dairy Section
Div. of Sanitarian Srvcs.
4815 W. Markham St.
Little Rock, AR 72205
Phone : (501) 661-2171
Fax : (501) 661-2572

CALIFORNIA
Ann Veneman
Secretary
Dept. of Food & Agriculture
P.O. Box 942871
Sacramento, CA 94271-0001
Phone : (916) 654-0433

COLORADO
Tom Messenger
Director
Consumer Protection Div.
Dept. of Public Health & Env.
4300 Cherry Creek Dr., S.
Denver, CO 80222
Phone : (303) 692-3620
Fax : (303) 753-6809

CONNECTICUT
John McGuire
Director
Food Div.
Dept. of Consumer Protection
165 Capitol Ave.
Hartford, CT 06106
Phone : (203) 566-3388

DELAWARE
Teresa Crenshaw
State Chemist
Div. of Standards & Inspection
Dept. of Agriculture
2320 S. DuPont Hwy.
Dover, DE 19901
Phone : (302) 739-4811

FLORIDA
Dan S. Smyly
Director
Div. of Food Safety
Dept. of Agriculture & Consumer Srvcs.
3125 Conner Blvd.
Tallahassee, FL 32399-1650
Phone : (904) 488-0295

GEORGIA
Jim Drinnon
Director
Environmental Health Section
Dept. of Human Resources
2 Peachtree St.
Atlanta, GA 30303
Phone : (404) 657-2733

HAWAII
Bruce Anderson
Deputy Director
Environmental Health Admin.
Dept. of Health
1250 Punchbowl St.
Honolulu, HI 96813
Phone : (808) 586-4424
Fax : (808) 586-4444

IDAHO
Don Brothers
Food Program Compliance Officer
Food Section, Bur. of Health
Dept. of Health & Welfare
450 W. State St.
Boise, ID 83720
Phone : (208) 334-5938

ILLINOIS
John Lumpkin
Director
Dept. of Public Health
535 W. Jefferson St.
Springfield, IL 62761
Phone : (217) 782-4977
Fax : (217) 782-3987

INDIANA
Howard Cundiff
Director
Bur. of Consumer Services
State Bd. of Health
1330 W. Michigan St., Rm. 136
Indianapolis, IN 46206
Phone : (317) 633-0314

IOWA
Robert Haxton
Program Manager
Inspections Div.
Dept. of Inspections & Appeals
Lucas State Off. Bldg.
Des Moines, IA 50319
Phone : (515) 281-6539

KANSAS
Stephen N. Paige
Director
Food & Drug Section
Dept. of Health & Environment
Mills Bldg., 6th Fl.
Topeka, KS 66612-1274
Phone : (913) 296-5600
Fax : (913) 296-6522

KENTUCKY
Bill Patrick
Director
Div. of Food Distribution
Dept. of Agriculture
100 Fairoaks
Frankfort, KY 40601
Phone : (502) 564-4387

LOUISIANA
Eric Baumgarner
Asst. Secretary/State Health Officer
Dept. of Health & Hospitals
P.O. Box 3214
Baton Rouge, LA 70821
Phone : (504) 342-8092

MAINE
Ed McLaughlin
Commissioner
Dept. of Agriculture, Food & Rural Resources
State House Station # 28
Augusta, ME 04333
Phone : (207) 287-3871

MARYLAND*
Acting Director
Food Protection & Comm. Health
Dept. of Health & Mental Hygiene
4201 Patterson Ave.
Baltimore, MD 21215
Phone : (410) 225-6699

MASSACHUSETTS
Richard Waskiewiczi
Director
Div. of Food & Drugs
Dept. of Public Health
305 S St.
Jamaica Plain, MA 02130
Phone : (617) 727-2674
Fax : (617) 524-8062

MICHIGAN
E.C. Heffron
Director
Food Div.
Dept. of Agriculture
Ottawa Bldg., 4th Fl.
Lansing, MI 48909
Phone : (517) 373-1060

MINNESOTA
Thomas Masso
Director
Food Inspection Div.
Dept. of Agriculture
90 W. Plato Blvd.
St. Paul, MN 55107
Phone : (612) 296-2629

MISSISSIPPI
Lydia Strayer
Director
Div. of Sanitation
Dept. of Health
P.O. Box 1700
Jackson, MS 39215
Phone : (601) 960-7690

MISSOURI
Roger Gibson
Chief
Bur. of Comm. Env. Health
Dept. of Health
210 El Mercado Plaza
P.O. Box 570
Jefferson City, MO 65102
Phone : (314) 751-6095
Fax : (314) 526-6946

MONTANA
Mitzi Scwab
Chief
Food & Consumer Safety Bur.
Health & Env. Sciences
Cogswell Bldg., Rm. A113
Helena, MT 59620
Phone : (406) 444-2408

NEBRASKA
George Hanssen
Food Division Manager
Bur. of Dairies & Foods
Dept. of Agriculture
P.O. Box 95064
Lincoln, NE 68509-5064
Phone : (402) 471-2536

NEVADA
Sharon Ezell
Bureau Chief
Regulatory Health Srvc. Bur.
Dept. of Human Resources
505 E. King St.
Carson City, NV 89710
Phone : (702) 687-4475

NEW HAMPSHIRE
Charles Collins
Chief
Bur. of Food Protection
Dept. of Health & Human Srvcs.
6 Hazen Dr.
Concord, NH 03301
Phone : (603) 271-4587

NEW JERSEY
Dhun B. Patel
Director
Div. of Diary & Regulations
Dept. of Agriculture
John Fitch Plz., CN330
Trenton, NJ 08625
Phone : (609) 292-5575

NEW MEXICO
Frank Du Bois
Director
Dept. of Agriculture
New Mexico State Univ.
P.O. Box 30005, Dept. 5600
Las Cruces, NM 88003
Phone : (505) 646-4929
Fax : (505) 646-8120

NEW YORK*
Commissioner
Dept. of Ag. & Markets
Capitol Plz.
1 Winners Cir.
Albany, NY 12235
Phone : (518) 457-4188

NORTH CAROLINA
Robert L. Gordon
Director
Food & Drug Protection
Dept. of Agriculture
4000 Reedy Creek Rd.
Raleigh, NC 27607-6468
Phone : (919) 733-7366

NORTH DAKOTA
Kenan Bullinger
Director
Consolidated Laboratories Branch
P.O. Box 937
Bismarck, ND 58502
Phone : (701) 328-2392
Fax : (701) 328-4727

OHIO
Rowland Stewart
Chief
Div. of Food, Dairies & Drugs
Dept. of Agriculture
8995 E. Main St.
Reynoldsburg, OH 43068
Phone : (614) 866-6361
Fax : (614) 759-1467

OKLAHOMA
H.A. Caves
Chief
Food Protection Services
Dept. of Health
1000 NE 10th St., Box 53551
Oklahoma City, OK 73152
Phone : (405) 271-5243

OREGON
James Black
Administrator
Food Safety Div.
Dept. of Agriculture
635 Capitol St., NE
Salem, OR 97310
Phone : (503) 378-3790
Fax : (503) 378-2999

PENNSYLVANIA
Leroy Corbin
Director
Bur. of Foods & Chemistry
Dept. of Agriculture
112 Agriculture Bldg.
Harrisburg, PA 17110
Phone : (717) 787-6416

RHODE ISLAND
Ernest Julian
Chief
Food Protection & Sanitation
Dept. of Health
3 Capitol Hill
Providence, RI 02908
Phone : (401) 277-2758

SOUTH CAROLINA
Robert L. Dickinson
Director
Div. of Food Protection
Health & Environmental Control
2600 Bull St.
Columbia, SC 29201
Phone : (803) 935-7958

SOUTH DAKOTA
Barbara Smith
Secretary
Dept. of Health
445 E. Capitol Ave.
Pierre, SD 57501
Phone : (605) 773-3361

TENNESSEE
Jimmy Hopper
Director
Quality Standards
Dept. of Agriculture
Ellington Agricultural Ctr.
Nashville, TN 37204
Phone : (615) 360-0150

TEXAS
Dennis Baker
Director
Div. of Food & Drugs
Dept. of Health
1100 W. 49th St.
Austin, TX 78756
Phone : (512) 458-7111

UTAH
Kyle R. Stephens
Director
Div. of Regulatory Srvcs.
Dept. of Agriculture
350 N. Redwood Rd.
Salt Lake City, UT 84116
Phone : (801) 538-7150

VERMONT
Alfred Burns
Sanitarian Supervisor
Div. of Environmental Health
Dept. of Health
60 Main St.
Burlington, VT 05402
Phone : (802) 863-7221
Fax : (802) 863-7425

VIRGINIA
J. Carlton Courter, III
Commissioner
Dept. of Ag. & Consumer Srvc.
Washington Bldg., Ste. 210
1100 Bank St.
Richmond, VA 23219
Phone : (804) 786-3501
Fax : (804) 371-2945

WASHINGTON
John Daly
Assistant Director
Food Safety & Animal Health Div.
Dept. of Agriculture
P.O. Box 42560
Olympia, WA 98502-2581
Phone : (360) 902-1875

WEST VIRGINIA
Joseph P. Schock
Director
Environ. Health Srvcs. Off.
Div. of Health
815 Quarrier St.
Charleston, WV 25305-2616
Phone : (304) 558-2981

WISCONSIN
William D. Mathias
Administrator
Div. of Food Safety
Ag., Trade & Consumer Prot.
2811 Agriculture Dr.
P.O. Box 8911
Madison, WI 53704
Phone : (608) 224-4700
Fax : (608) 224-4710

WYOMING
John Misock
Manager
Food & Drug Section
Dept. of Agriculture
Smith Bldg.
Cheyenne, WY 82002
Phone : (307) 777-6587

DISTRICT OF COLUMBIA
Sidney Hall
Chief
Food Protection Branch
Dept. of Consumer & Reg. Aff.
614 H St., NW, Rm. 616
Washington, DC 20001
Phone : (202) 727-7250

AMERICAN SAMOA
Pasea Lafitaga
Chief
Environmental Health Branch
Dept. of Health
Pago Pago, AS 96799
Phone : (684) 633-4623
Fax : (684) 633-1869

GUAM
Dennis Rodriguez
Director
Dept. of Public Health & Social Services
P.O. Box 2816
Agana, GU 96910
Phone : (671) 734-7102
Fax : (671) 734-5910

NORTHERN MARIANA ISLANDS
Fermin M. Sakisat
Chief
Public Health Services Div.
Dept. of Public Health & Env.
P.O. Box 409
Saipan, MP 96950
Phone : (670) 234-8950

U.S. VIRGIN ISLANDS
Natalie George-McDowell
Commissioner
Dept. of Health
48 Sugar Estate
St. Thomas Hospital
St. Thomas, VI 00802
Phone : (809) 776-8311
Fax : (809) 777-4001

FORESTRY

Manages and protects the state's forest resources.

ALABAMA
Jim Martin
Commissioner
State Forestry Comm.
513 Madison Ave.
Montgomery, AL 36130
Phone : (334) 242-3486
Fax : (334) 242-3489

ALASKA
Tom Boutin
Director & State Forester
Div. of Forestry
Dept. of Natural Resources
400 Willoughby Ave., 3rd Fl.
Juneau, AK 99801-1796
Phone : (907) 465-3379
Fax : (907) 586-3113

ARIZONA
Michael Hart
Director
Forestry Division
State Land Dept.
1616 W. Adams
Phoenix, AZ 85007
Phone : (602) 542-4627

ARKANSAS
John Shannon
State Forester
Forestry Comm.
3821 W. Roosevelt Rd.
Little Rock, AR 72204-6395
Phone : (501) 664-2531
Fax : (501) 324-9096

CALIFORNIA
Richard A. Wilson
Director
Dept. of Forestry & Fire Protection
P.O. Box 944246
Sacramento, CA 94244
Phone : (916) 653-7772

COLORADO
James E. Hubbard
State Forester
Forest Service
Colorado State University
203 Forestry Bldg.
Fort Collins, CO 80523
Phone : (970) 491-6303
Fax : (970) 491-7736

CONNECTICUT
Donald H. Smith, Jr.
State Forestor
Forestry Div.
Dept. of Environmental Protection
79 Elm St.
Hartford, CT 06106
Phone : (203) 424-3630

DELAWARE
Robert T. Tjaden
State Forest Administrator
Dept. of Agriculture
2320 S. DuPont Hwy.
Dover, DE 19901
Phone : (302) 739-4811

FLORIDA
Earl Peterson
Director
Division of Forestry
Dept. of Agriculture & Consumer Services
3125 Conner Blvd.
Tallahassee, FL 32399-1650
Phone : (904) 488-4274

GEORGIA
John W. Mixon
Director
State Forestry Comm.
P.O. Box 819
Macon, GA 31298
Phone : (912) 744-3211

HAWAII
Michael Buck
Administrator
Div. of Forestry & Wildlife
Dept. of Land & Nat. Resources
1151 Punchbowl St., Rm. 325
Honolulu, HI 96813
Phone : (808) 587-0166

IDAHO
Winston Wiggins
Assistant Director
Forestry & Fire
Dept. of Lands
1215 W. 8th St.
Boise, ID 83720
Phone : (208) 334-0238

ILLINOIS
Stewart Pequignot
Chief
Forest Resources Div.
Dept. of Conservation
600 N. Grand Ave.
Springfield, IL 62701
Phone : (217) 782-2361

INDIANA
Burnell Fischer
State Forester
Forestry Div.
Dept. of Natural Resources
IGC-South, Rm. W296
Indianapolis, IN 46204
Phone : (317) 232-4107

IOWA
William Farris
State Forester
Forest & Forestry Div.
Dept. of Natural Resources
Wallace State Off. Bldg.
Des Moines, IA 50319
Phone : (515) 281-8656

KANSAS
Raymond G. Aslin
State Forester
Kansas State University & Extension Forestry
2610 Claflin Rd.
Manhattan, KS 66502-2798
Phone : (913) 537-7050

KENTUCKY
Mark Matuszews
Director
Div. of Forestry
627 Comanche Trl.
Frankfort, KY 40601
Phone : (502) 564-4496

LOUISIANA
Paul D. Frey
Assistant Commissioner
Off. of Forestry
Dept. of Agriculture
P.O. Box 631
Baton Rouge, LA 70821
Phone : (504) 925-4500

MAINE
Susan Bell
Director
Bur. of Forestry
Dept. of Conservation
State House Station # 22
Augusta, ME 04333
Phone : (207) 287-2791

MARYLAND
John Riley
State Forester
Public Lands & Forestry
Forestry Div.
Dept. of Natural Resources
Tawes State Off. Bldg.
Annapolis, MD 21401
Phone : (410) 974-3776

MASSACHUSETTS
David Struhs
Commissioner
Dept. of Environmental Protection
Executive Off. of Environmental Affairs
1 Winter St.
Boston, MA 02202
Phone : (617) 292-5500

MICHIGAN
Gerald Thiede
Chief, State Forrester
Forest Mgt. Div.
Dept. of Natural Resources
P.O. Box 30028
Lansing, MI 48909
Phone : (517) 373-1275

MINNESOTA
Gerald Rose
Director
Forestry Div.
Dept. of Natural Resources
500 Lafayette Rd.
St. Paul, MN 55155
Phone : (612) 296-4484

MISSISSIPPI
James L. Sledge
State Forester
Forestry Comm.
301 N. Lamar, Ste. 300
Jackson, MS 39201
Phone : (601) 359-2801

MISSOURI
Marvin Brown
State Forester
Div. of Forestry
Dept. of Conservation
2901 W. Truman Blvd.
P.O. Box 180
Jefferson City, MO 65102
Phone : (314) 751-4115
Fax : (314) 526-6670

MONTANA
Don Artley
Administrator
Div. of Forestry
Dept. of State Lands
2705 Spurgin Rd.
Missoula, MT 59801-3190
Phone : (406) 542-4300

NEBRASKA
Gary Hergenrader
State Forester
Forestry, Fisheries & Wildlife
Univ. of Nebraska - Lincoln
101 Plant Industry Bldg.
Lincoln, NE 68583-0814
Phone : (402) 472-2944
Fax : (402) 472-2964

NEVADA
Roy Trenoweth
State Forester
Div. of Forestry
Dept. of Cons. & Natural Res.
123 W. Nye Ln.
Carson City, NV 89710
Phone : (702) 687-4350

NEW HAMPSHIRE
John Sargent
Director
Forest & Lands Div.
Dept. of Res. & Economic Dev.
172 Pembroke Rd.
Concord, NH 03301
Phone : (603) 271-2214

NEW JERSEY
Gregory A. Marshall
Director
Div. of Parks & Forestry
Dept. of Env. Protection
501 E. State St., CN404
Trenton, NJ 08625
Phone : (609) 292-2733

NEW MEXICO
Toby Martinez
Director
Forestry & Resource Cons. Div.
Energy, Min. & Nat. Res. Dept.
P.O. Box 1948
Santa Fe, NM 87504
Phone : (505) 827-5830
Fax : (505) 827-3903

NEW YORK*
Commissioner
Dept. of Environmental Conservation
50 Wolf Rd.
Albany, NY 12233
Phone : (518) 457-3446

NORTH CAROLINA
Stan Adams
Deputy Director
Forest Resources
Dept. of Environment, Health & Natural Resources
P.O. Box 27687
Raleigh, NC 27611
Phone : (919) 733-2162
Fax : (919) 733-2835

NORTH DAKOTA
Larry Kotchman
State Forester
State Forest Service
1st & Brander
Bottineau, ND 58318
Phone : (701) 228-5490

OHIO
Ron Abraham
Chief
Div. of Forestry
Dept. of Natural Resources
Fountain Sq., Bldg. C-3
Columbus, OH 43224
Phone : (614) 265-6694
Fax : (614) 447-9231

OKLAHOMA
Roger L. Davis
Director
Div. of Forestry
Dept. of Agriculture
2800 N. Lincoln Blvd.
Oklahoma City, OK 73105
Phone : (405) 521-3864

OREGON
James E. Brown
State Forester
Dept. of Forestry
2600 State St.
Salem, OR 97310
Phone : (503) 945-7211
Fax : (503) 945-7212

PENNSYLVANIA
James R. Grace
Director
Bur. of Forestry
Dept. of Environmental Res.
P.O. Box 8552
Harrisburg, PA 17105-8552
Phone : (717) 787-2703

RHODE ISLAND
Thomas Dupree
Chief
Div. of Forest Environment
Dept. of Environmental Mgt.
1037 Hartford Pk.
P.O.Box 851
North Scituate, RI 02857
Phone : (401) 647-3367

SOUTH CAROLINA
J. Hugh Ryan
State Forester
Forestry Comm.
P.O. Box 21707
Columbia, SC 29221
Phone : (803) 896-8800

SOUTH DAKOTA
Clark Johnson
Director
Resource, Conservation & Forestry
Dept. of Agriculture
445 E. Capitol Ave.
Pierre, SD 57501
Phone : (605) 773-3623

TENNESSEE
Ken Arney
State Forester
Div. of Forestry
Dept. of Agriculture
Ellington Agricultural Ctr.
Nashville, TN 37204
Phone : (615) 360-0311

TEXAS
Bruce R. Miles
Director
Forestry Service
Texas A&M University
302 Systems Admin. Bldg.
College Station, TX 77843
Phone : (409) 845-2641

UTAH
Ed Storey
State Forester
Div. of State Lands & Forestry
Dept. of Natural Resources
355 W. North Temple
Salt Lake City, UT 84180
Phone : (801) 538-5555

VERMONT
Conrad Motyka
Commissioner
Dept. of Forests, Parks & Recreation
103 S. Main St.
Waterbury, VT 05676
Phone : (802) 241-3670
Fax : (802) 244-1481

VIRGINIA
James W. Garner Jr.
State Forester
Dept. of Forestry
P.O. Box 3758
Charlottesville, VA 22903
Phone : (804) 977-6555
Fax : (804) 296-2369

WASHINGTON
John Edwards
Div. of Forest Practices
Dept. of Natural Resources
P.O. Box 47001
Olympia, WA 98504-7001
Phone : (360) 902-1730

WEST VIRGINIA
William Maxey
Director
Div. of Forestry
1900 Kanawha Blvd., E.
Charleston, WV 25305
Phone : (304) 558-2788

WISCONSIN
Charles Higgs
Director
Bur. of Forestry
Dept. of Natural Resources
101 S. Webster, 4th Fl.
P.O. Box 7921
Madison, WI 53703
Phone : (608) 267-7494
Fax : (608) 266-8576

WYOMING
Michael Gagen
State Forester
State Forestry Div.
1100 W. 22nd St.
Cheyenne, WY 82002
Phone : (307) 777-7586

DISTRICT OF COLUMBIA
Sandra Hill
Acting Manager
Tree Maintenance Div.
Dept. of Public Works
2750 S. Capitol St., S.E.
Washington, DC 20032
Phone : (202) 767-8532

GUAM
Michael W. Kuhlman
Director
Dept. of Agriculture
P.O. Box 2950
Agana, GU 96910
Phone : (671) 734-3942
Fax : (671) 734-6569

NORTHERN MARIANA ISLANDS
Renee Tahakali
Commonwealth Forester
Dept. of Natural Resources
Capital Hill
Saipan, MP 96950
Phone : (670) 322-9830

PUERTO RICO
Pedro Gelabert Marquez
Secretary
Dept. of Natural Resources
P.O. Box 5887
San Juan, PR 00906-5887
Phone : (809) 724-8774
Fax : (809) 723-4255

GAMING OFFICIALS

Head of the entity that administers and regulates state gaming laws.

ALASKA
Dennis Poshard
Director
Charitable Gaming Div.
Dept. of Revenue
P.O. Box 110440
Juneau, AK 99811-0440
Phone : (907) 465-2229
Fax : (907) 465-3098

ARIZONA
James H. Higginbottom
Director
Dept. of Racing
800 W. Washington St.,
Ste. 515
Phoenix, AZ 85007
Phone : (602) 542-5151

CALIFORNIA
Daniel E. Lungren
Attorney General
1515 K St., Rm. 612
Sacramento, CA 95814
Phone : (916) 324-5437

COLORADO
Dan Hyatt
Chair
Gaming Comm.
P.O. Box 500
La Junta, CO 81050
Phone : (719) 384-8121

DELAWARE
Wayne Lemons
Director
State Lottery Office
Deptartment of Finance
1565 McKee Road, Ste. L
Dover, DE 19904
Phone : (302) 739-5291
Fax : (302) 739-6706

FLORIDA*
Div. of Pari-Mutuel
Wagering
Dept. of Bus. & Prof. Reg.
725 S. Bronough St.
Tallahassee, FL 32399-1000
Phone : (904) 488-9130

GEORGIA
Milton E. Nix Jr.
Director
State Bur. of Investigation
3121 Panthersville Rd.
Atlanta, GA 30034
Phone : (404) 244-2501

IDAHO
Dennis Jackson
Director
State Lottery
1199 Shoreline Ln., Ste. 100
Boise, ID 83702
Phone : (208) 334-2600

ILLINOIS
Michael Belletire
Administrator
Illinois Game Board
160 N. LaSalle, Suite 300S
Chicago, IL 60601-3103
Phone : (312) 814-4707
Fax : (312) 814-4692

INDIANA
Jack Thar
Executive Director
Gaming Comm.
N180 Gov. Ctr. N.
100 N. Senate Ave.
Indianapolis, IN 46204-2211
Phone : (317) 233-0044

IOWA
Jack Ketterer
Administrator
Racing & Gaming Comm.
Dept. of Inspections &
Appeals
Lucas State Off. Bldg.
Des Moines, IA 50319
Phone : (515) 281-7352

KANSAS
Gregory P. Ziemak
Director
Kansas Lottery
128 N. Kansas Ave.
Topeka, KS 66603-3638
Phone : (913) 296-5700
Fax : (913) 296-5712

KENTUCKY
Chris Johnson
Director
Justice Cabinet
403 Wapping St.
Frankfort, KY 40601
Phone : (502) 564-3251

LOUISIANA
Max Chastain
Chairman
Gaming Corporation
Dept. of Economic
Development
365 Canal St., Ste. 2700
New Orleans, LA 70130
Phone : (504) 568-5821

MASSACHUSETTS
Eric Turner
Executive Director
Lottery Comm.
60 Columbian St.
Braintree, MA 02184
Phone : (617) 849-5555

MINNESOTA
Harold W. Baltzer
Director
5300 1711 W. County Rd. B
Roseville, MN 55113
Phone : (612) 639-4000

MISSISSIPPI
Paul Harvey
Chairman
Mississippi Gaming
Commission
202 E. Pearl
Jackson, MS 39202
Phone : (601) 961-4400
Fax : (601) 961-4411

MISSOURI
C.E. Fisher
Deputy Director of
Enforcement
Gaming Commission
1616 Industrial Dr.
Jefferson City, MO 65109
Phone : (314) 526-4080
Fax : (314) 526-4084

MONTANA
Janet Jessup
Administrator
Gambling Control Div.
Dept. of Justice
2550 Prespect Ave.
Helena, MT 59620
Phone : (406) 444-1971

NEBRASKA
M. Berri Balka
State Tax Commissioner
Dept. of Revenue
P.O. Box 94818
Lincoln, NE 68509-4818
Phone : (402) 471-5604

NEVADA
William A. Bible
Chairman
State Gaming Control
Board
1150 E. William
Carson City, NV 89710
Phone : (702) 687-6500

NEW HAMPSHIRE
James E. Wimsatt
Executive Director
Sweepstakes Comm.
Ft. Eddy Rd.
Concord, NH 03301
Phone : (603) 271-3391

NEW JERSEY
Frank Catania
Director
Div. of Gaming
Enforcement
Law & Public Safety
140 E. State St., CN047
Trenton, NJ 08625
Phone : (609) 292-9394

NEW MEXICO
Marianne Woodard
Director
Alcohol & Gaming Div.
Dept. of Reg. & Licensing
P.O. Box 25101
Santa Fe, NM 87503
Phone : (505) 827-7066
Fax : (505) 827-7168

Gaming Officials

NEW YORK*
Chairman
Racing & Wagering Bd.
Agency Bldg. # 1
Empire State Plz.
Albany, NY 12223
Phone : (518) 473-7201

NORTH DAKOTA
Keith Lauer
Director, Gaming Section
Off. of the Attorney General
State Capitol, 17th Fl.
600 E. Boulevard Ave.
Bismarck, ND 58505
Phone : (701) 328-4848
Fax : (701) 328-3535

SOUTH DAKOTA
Tom Fahey
Executive Secretary
Div. of Gaming
118 E. Missouri
Pierre, SD 57501
Phone : (605) 773-6050

TEXAS
Nora Linares
Executive Director
Lottery Commission
6937 North IH 35
P.O. Box 13127
Austin, TX 78752-3221
Phone : (512) 323-3700

VERMONT
Fred McGibney
Director
Lottery Commission
379 South Barre Rd.
P.O. Box 420
South Barre, VT 05670-0420
Phone : (802) 479-5686
Fax : (802) 479-4294

VIRGINIA
James S. Gilmore III
Attorney General
Office of the Attorney General
900 E. Main St., 6th Fl.
Richmond, VA 23219
Phone : (804) 786-2071
Fax : (804) 371-0200

WASHINGTON
Frank L. Miller
Director
State Gambling Comm.
P.O. Box 42400
Olympia, WA 98504-2400
Phone : (360) 438-7640

WEST VIRGINIA
James H. Paige III
Secretary
Dept. of Tax & Revenue
Bldg. 1, Rm. WW-300
1900 Kanawha Blvd., E.
Charleston, WV 25305
Phone : (304) 558-0211

WISCONSIN
John Tries
Chairman
Gaming Comm.
150 E Gilman
P.O. Box 8979
Madison, WI 53703
Phone : (608) 264-6607
Fax : (608) 267-4874

WYOMING
Frank Lamb
Executive Director
Pari-Mutuel Comm.
Barrett Bldg.
Cheyenne, WY 82002
Phone : (307) 777-5928

PUERTO RICO
James McCurdy
Director
Gambling Div.
Dept. of Gaming
P.O. Box 4435
San Juan, PR 00902-4435
Phone : (809) 721-2635

U.S. VIRGIN ISLANDS
Vera Falu
Commissioner
Dept. of Lic. & Cons. Aff.
Sub Base Bldg. 1, Room 205
St. Thomas, VI 00802
Phone : (809) 774-3130
Fax : (809) 776-0675

GENERAL SERVICES

Responsible for a variety of centralized services within state government.

ALABAMA
Don Drablos
Chief of Services
General Srvcs. Div.
Dept. of Finance
432 Jefferson St.
Montgomery, AL 36130
Phone : (334) 242-2773
Fax : (334) 240-3402

ALASKA
Dugan Petty
Director
Div. of General Srvcs.
Dept. of Administration
P.O. Box 110210
Juneau, AK 99811-0210
Phone : (907) 465-2250
Fax : (907) 465-2205

ARIZONA
Ed Boot
Assistant Director
General Services Div.
Dept. of Admin.
1700 W. Washington, Rm. 600
Phoenix, AZ 85007
Phone : (602) 542-1920

ARKANSAS
Tim Leathers
Deputy Director
Dept. of Finance & Admin.
401 DFA Bldg.
1509 W. 7th St.
Little Rock, AR 72201
Phone : (501) 682-2242
Fax : (501) 682-1086

CALIFORNIA
Peter G. Stamison
Director
Dept. of General Services
1325 J St., Ste. 1910
Sacramento, CA 95814
Phone : (916) 445-3441

COLORADO
Andre' Pettigrew
Executive Director
Dept. of Admin.
1525 Sherman St., 2nd Fl.
Denver, CO 80203
Phone : (303) 620-3221
Fax : (303) 866-6569

CONNECTICUT
Peter W. Connolly
Administrative Manager
Dept. of Admin. Srvcs.
460 Silver St.
Middletown, CT 06457
Phone : (203) 638-3267

DELAWARE
Vincent P. Meconi
Secretary
Dept. of Admin. Srvcs.
Townsend Bldg.
P.O. Box 1401
Dover, DE 19903
Phone : (302) 739-3611

FLORIDA
Steve Wharton
Chief
Bureau of General Support Services
FL Public Service Commission
G-50 Fletcher Bldg.
Tallahassee, FL 32399-0864
Phone : (904) 488-4733

GEORGIA
James M. Lyle
Deputy Commissioner
General Services Div.
Dept of Administrative Srvcs.
200 Piedmont Ave., Ste. 1304
Atlanta, GA 30334
Phone : (404) 656-5753

HAWAII
Robert J. Governs
Chief
Purchasing Supply Div.
Dept. of Accounting & General Srvcs.
1151 Punchbowl St.
Honolulu, HI 96810
Phone : (808) 586-0555

IDAHO
Gerry Silvester
Administrator
Div. of General Srvcs.
Dept. of Admin.
650 W. State St.
Boise, ID 83720
Phone : (208) 327-7325

ILLINOIS
Michael S. Schwartz
Director
Dept. of Central Mgt. Srvcs.
715 Stratton Off. Bldg.
Springfield, IL 62706
Phone : (217) 782-2141
Fax : (217) 524-1880

INDIANA
William L. Shrewsberry
Commissioner
Dept. of Admin.
IGC-South, Rm. W479
402 W. Washington St.
Indianapolis, IN 46204
Phone : (317) 231-3115

IOWA
Janet E. Phipps
Director
Dept. of General Srvcs.
Hoover State Off. Bldg.
Des Moines, IA 50319
Phone : (515) 281-3196
Fax : (515) 242-5974

KANSAS
Sheila Frahm
Secretary
Dept. of Administration
Capitol Bldg., 2nd Fl.
Topeka, KS 66612-1572
Phone : (913) 296-3011
Fax : (913) 296-2702

KENTUCKY
Don Speer
Commissioner
Dept. of Administration
Finance & Admin. Cabinet
Capitol Annex, Rm. 362
Frankfort, KY 40601
Phone : (502) 564-2317

LOUISIANA
Raymond J. Laborde
Commissioner
Div. of Administration
Capitol Annex
P.O. Box 94095
Baton Rouge, LA 70804-9095
Phone : (504) 342-7000

MAINE
Dale Doughty
Acting Director
Dept. of Admin. & Financial Srvcs.
State House Station # 77
Augusta, ME 04333
Phone : (207) 287-4000

MARYLAND
Eugene Lynch
Acting Secretary
Dept. of General Srvcs.
301 W. Preston St., Rm. 1401
Baltimore, MD 21201
Phone : (410) 225-4960

MASSACHUSETTS
Charles Baker
Secretary
Executive Off. for Admin. & Finance
State House, Rm. 373
Boston, MA 02133
Phone : (617) 727-2040

MICHIGAN
Kathe Rushford Carter
Director
Off. of Support Srvcs.
Dept. of Mgt. & Budget
P.O. Box 30026
Lansing, MI 48909
Phone : (517) 335-1988

MINNESOTA
Elaine Hanson
Commissioner
Dept. of Administration
200 State Admin. Bldg.
50 Sherburne Ave.
St. Paul, MN 55155
Phone : (612) 296-1424

MISSISSIPPI
Beverly Bolton
Deputy Director
Dept. of Finance & Admin.
1501 Sillers Bldg.
Jackson, MS 39201
Phone : (601) 359-3633

MISSOURI
Stan Perovich
Director
Div. of General Srvcs.
Off. of Admin.
Truman Bldg., Rm. 760
P.O. Box 809
Jefferson City, MO 65102
Phone : (314) 751-4656
Fax : (314) 751-7819

MONTANA
Debra Fulton
Administrator
Div. of General Services
Dept. of Administration
Capitol Annex Bldg.
Helena, MT 59620
Phone : (406) 444-3060

NEBRASKA
Barbara A. Lawson
Administrator
Material Div.
Dept. of Administrative Srvcs.
301 Centennial Mall S.
Lincoln, NE 68509
Phone : (402) 471-2401

NEVADA
John P. Comeaux
Director
Dept. of Administration
209 E. Musser St., Rm. 200
Carson City, NV 89710
Phone : (702) 687-4065
Fax : (702) 687-3983

NEW HAMPSHIRE
Patrick Duffy
Commissioner
Dept. of Administrative Srvcs.
25 Capitol St.
Concord, NH 03301
Phone : (603) 271-3201

NEW JERSEY
George M. Gross
Administrator
General Srvcs. Admin.
Dept. of Treasury
33 W. State St., CN039
Trenton, NJ 08625
Phone : (609) 292-4330

NEW MEXICO
Steven Beffort
Secretary
General Services Dept.
715 Alta Vista
Santa Fe, NM 87503
Phone : (505) 827-2000
Fax : (505) 827-2041

NEW YORK*
Commissioner
Off. of General Srvcs.
Corning Tower Bldg., 41st Fl.
Empire State Plz.
Albany, NY 12242
Phone : (518) 474-5991

NORTH CAROLINA
Katie G. Dorsett
Secretary
Dept. of Administration
116 W. Jones St.
Raleigh, NC 27603
Phone : (919) 733-7232
Fax : (919) 733-9571

NORTH DAKOTA
Rod Backman
Director
Off. of Management & Budget
State Capitol, 4th Fl.
600 E. Boulevard Ave.
Bismarck, ND 58505-0400
Phone : (701) 328-4904
Fax : (701) 328-3230

OHIO
C. James Conrad
Director
Dept. of Admin. Srvcs.
30 E. Broad St., 40th Fl.
Columbus, OH 43266-0401
Phone : (614) 466-6511
Fax : (614) 644-8151

OKLAHOMA
Thomas Brennan
Secretary of Admin.
State Capitol Bldg., Rm. 104
Oklahoma City, OK 73105
Phone : (405) 521-2121

OREGON
Jon Yunker
Director
Dept. of Admin. Srvcs.
155 Cottage St., NE
Salem, OR 97310
Phone : (503) 378-3104

PENNSYLVANIA
Gary E. Crowell
Secretary
Dept. of General Services
Rm. 515, North Office Bldg.
Harrisburg, PA 17120
Phone : (717) 787-5996

RHODE ISLAND
Gayl W. Doster
Director
Dept. of Administration
One Capitol Hill
Providence, RI 02908
Phone : (401) 277-2280

SOUTH CAROLINA
Voigt Shealy
State Procurement Officer
Materials Management Div.
Dept. of General Services
1201 Main St., Ste. 600
Columbia, SC 29201
Phone : (803) 737-0600

SOUTH DAKOTA
Tom D. Geraets
Commissioner
Bur. of Administration
500 E. Capitol Ave.
Pierre, SD 57501
Phone : (605) 773-3688

TENNESSEE
Larry Haynes
Commissioner
Dept. of General Srvcs.
Tennessee Tower, 9th Fl.
Nashville, TN 37243-0530
Phone : (615) 741-9263
Fax : (615) 741-8408

TEXAS
John Pouland
General Srvcs. Comm.
P.O. Box 13047, Capitol Station
Austin, TX 78711-3047
Phone : (512) 463-3035

UTAH
Raylene Ireland
Executive Director
Dept. of Admin. Srvcs.
3120 State Off. Bldg.
Salt Lake City, UT 84114
Phone : (801) 538-3010

VERMONT
Paul F. Ohlson
Commissioner
Dept. of General Services
133 State St.
Montpelier, VT 05602
Phone : (802) 828-3331
Fax : (802) 828-2327

VIRGINIA
Donald C. Williams
Director
Dept. of General Srvcs.
209 9th St. Off. Bldg.
Richmond, VA 23219
Phone : (804) 786-3311
Fax : (804) 371-8305

WASHINGTON
John Franklin
Director
Dept. of General Admin.
P.O. Box 41000
Olympia, WA 98504-1000
Phone : (360) 753-5439

WEST VIRGINIA
Douglas Koenig
Director
Div. of General Services.
Bldg. 1, Rm. MB60
1900 Kanawha Blvd., E.
Charleston, WV 25305
Phone : (304) 558-3517

WISCONSIN
James R. Klauser
Secretary
Dept. of Administration
101 E. Wilson, 10th Fl.
P.O. Box 7869
Madison, WI 53707
Phone : (608) 266-1741
Fax : (608) 267-3848

WYOMING
Don Roulston
Director
Dept. of Admin. & Information
Emerson Bldg., Rm 104
2001 Capitol Ave.
Cheyenne, WY 82002
Phone : (307) 777-7201

DISTRICT OF COLUMBIA
James Gaston
Director
Dept. of Administrative Srvcs.
441 4th St., NW, Ste. 700
Washington, DC 20001
Phone : (202) 727-1179

AMERICAN SAMOA
Laau Seui
Director
Federal-Surplus Property Agency
Off. of Materials Mgt.
Pago Pago, AS 96799
Phone : (684) 699-1170
Fax : (684) 699-2387

GUAM
Lorenzo C. Aflague
Chief Procurement Officer
General Services Admin.
P.O. Box FG
Agana, GU 96910
Phone : (671) 477-1725
Fax : (671) 472-7538

NORTHERN MARIANA ISLANDS
Joaquin I. Pangelinan
Special Assistant for Admin.
Off. of the Governor
Capitol Hill
P.O. Box 10007
Saipan, MP 96950
Phone : (670) 322-5091
Fax : (670) 322-5099

PUERTO RICO*
Administrator
General Services Admin.
P.O. Box 7428
San Juan, PR 00916
Phone : (809) 721-7370
Fax : (809) 722-7965

U.S. VIRGIN ISLANDS
Alvin O. Davis
Commissioner
Dept. of Property & Procurement
Sub Base, Bldg. #1
St. Thomas, VI 00802
Phone : (809) 774-0828
Fax : (809) 774-9704

GEOGRAPHIC INFORMATION SYSTEMS

Coordinates geographic information systems within state government.

ALABAMA
Neil Smart
Acting Chief
Planning & Systems Analysis
Dept. of Industrial Relations
649 Monroe St., Rm. 521
Montgomery, AL 36131
Phone : (334) 242-8970
Fax : (334) 242-2042

ALASKA
Richard McMahon
Chief
Land Records Information
Dept. of Natural Resources
3601 C St., Ste 1180
Anchorage, AK 99503-5936
Phone : (907) 762-2384
Fax : (907) 563-1497

ARIZONA
Gary Irish
GIS Program Manager
Land Resources Info. System
State Land Dept.
1616 W. Adams
Phoenix, AZ 85007
Phone : (602) 542-2617

ARKANSAS
John Kennedy
Director
Dept. of Computer Srvcs.
P.O. Box 3155
Little Rock, AR 72203
Phone : (501) 682-2701
Fax : (501) 682-4310

CALIFORNIA
Randy Moory
Branch Manager
Teale Data Ctr.
P.O. Box 13436
Sacramento, CA 95813
Phone : (916) 263-1886

COLORADO
Mike Crane
Lab Manager
Rocky Mountain Mapping Center
U.S. Geological Survey
P.O. Box 25046, MS504
Denver, CO 80225
Phone : (303) 236-5838

CONNECTICUT
Edward C. Parker
Bureau Chief
Bur. of Environmental Srvcs.
Dept. of Environmental Protection
79 Elm St.
Hartford, CT 06106
Phone : (203) 424-3702

DELAWARE
Carol Webb
Manager
Div. of Water Resources
Dept. of Nat. Res & Env. Ctrl.
P.O. Box 1401
Dover, DE 19903
Phone : (302) 739-4793

FLORIDA
Mike Hale
Executive Administrator
Information Resource Comm.
112 Bloxham Bldg.
725 S. Calhoun St.
Tallahassee, FL 32399-0950
Phone : (904) 488-4574
Fax : (904) 922-5929

GEORGIA
William McLemore
State Geologist
Environmental Protection Div.
Dept. of Natural Resources
19 M.L. King, Jr. Dr., Rm. 400
Atlanta, GA 30334
Phone : (404) 656-3214

HAWAII
Craig Tasaka
Planning Program Manager
Governor's Off. of State Planning
P.O. Box 3540
Honolulu, HI 96811
Phone : (808) 587-2894

IDAHO
Dave Gruenhager
Analyst, GIS Section
Bur. of Technical Srvcs.
Dept. of Lands
1215 W. State St.
Boise, ID 83720
Phone : (208) 334-0277

ILLINOIS
Bob Liberman
Director
Off. of Research and Planning
Dept. of Energy & Nat. Res.
325 W. Adams St., Rm. 300
Springfield, IL 62704
Phone : (217) 785-3965

INDIANA
Daniel Houlihan
Director
Information Services Div.
Dept. of Admin.
100 N. Senate, #N551
Indianapolis, IN 46204
Phone : (317) 232-6750

KANSAS
Tom McClain
Section Chief
Technical Information Srvcs.
Univ. of Kansas
1930 Constant Ave., Campus W
Lawrence, KS 66047
Phone : (913) 864-3965

KENTUCKY
Belenda Holland
Manager
Natural Res. Info. System
Natural Res. & Env. Prot. Cab.
Capital Plz. Tower, 14th Fl.
Frankfort, KY 40601
Phone : (502) 564-5174

LOUISIANA
Ivar Van Heerden
Assistant Secretary
Coastal Restoration & Mgt.
Dept. of Natural Resources
P.O. Box 94396
Baton Rouge, LA 70804
Phone : (504) 342-4503

MAINE
Dan Walters
Director
Off. of Geographic Information System
Dept. of Admin. & Financial Srvcs.
#22 State House Station
Augusta, ME 04333
Phone : (207) 287-3897

MARYLAND
Ronald Kreitner
Director
Off. of Planning Data
Dept. of Planning
301 W. Preston St.
Baltimore, MD 21201
Phone : (410) 225-4510

MASSACHUSETTS
Christian Jacqz
Manager
Executive Off. of Environmental Affairs
Geographic Information Systems
20 Somerset St., 3rd Fl.
Boston, MA 02108
Phone : (617) 727-5227

MICHIGAN
Larry Folks
Resource Manager
Land & Water Mgt. Div.
Dept. of Natural Resources
P.O. Box 30028
Lansing, MI 48909
Phone : (517) 373-8000

MINNESOTA
Sue Clauve
Director
Information Systems Div.
Dept. of General Srvcs.
P.O. Drawer 26110
Santa Fe, MN 87502
Phone : (505) 277-3622

Mike Hagar
Systems Supervisor
Administration Div.
Bur. of Management Systems
500 Lafayette Rd.
St. Paul, MN 55155
Phone : (612) 296-0654

MISSISSIPPI
Paul Davis
MARIS Director
Research & Development Ctr.
3825 Ridgewood Rd.
Jackson, MS 39211
Phone : (601) 982-6354

MISSOURI
Mike Marcus
GIS Project Specialist
Div. of Geology & Land Survey
Dept. of Natural Resources
111 Fairgrounds Rd.
P.O. Box 250
Rolla, MO 65401
Phone : (314) 368-2100
Fax : (314) 368-2111

MONTANA
Allan Cox
Coordinator
Natural Resource Info. System
State Library
1515 E. 6th Ave.
Helena, MT 59620
Phone : (406) 444-5355

NEBRASKA
Don Rundquist
Office Manager
Conservation & Survey Div.
University of Nebraska
328-1 Nebraska Hall
Lincoln, NE 68588
Phone : (402) 472-3471
Fax : (402) 472-2410

NEVADA
Harold Bonham Jr.
Acting Director
State Mapping Advisory Cmte.
Bur. of Mines & Geology
Univ. of Nevada at Reno
Reno, NV 89557
Phone : (702) 784-6691

NEW HAMPSHIRE
Chris Simmons
Senior Planner
Off. of Commissioner
Dept. of Environmental Srvcs.
6 Hazen Dr.
Concord, NH 03301
Phone : (603) 271-2961

NEW JERSEY
Lewis J. Nagy
Assistant Commissioner
Policy & Planning
Dept. of Env. Protection
401 E. State St.
Trenton, NJ 08625
Phone : (609) 292-1254

NEW YORK*
Director
Planning Off.
Adirondack Park Agency
P.O. Box 99
Ray Brook, NY 12977
Phone : (518) 891-4050

NORTH CAROLINA
Charles H. Gardner
Director
Div. of Land Resources
Dept. of Environment, Health & Natural Resources
512 N. Salisbury St.
Raleigh, NC 27604-1148
Phone : (919) 733-3833
Fax : (919) 733-4407

OHIO
Thomas M. Berg
State Geologist & Chief
Geological Survey
4383 Fountain Square, Bldg. B-2
Columbus, OH 43224-1362
Phone : (614) 265-6988
Fax : (614) 447-1918

OKLAHOMA
Patricia P. Eaton
Secretary of Environment
Water Resources Board
P.O. Box 150
Oklahoma City, OK 73101
Phone : (405) 231-2500
Fax : (405) 231-2600

OREGON
Theresa Valentine
Manager
GIS Program
Dept. of Energy
625 Marion St., NE
Salem, OR 97310
Phone : (503) 378-4163

PENNSYLVANIA
William A. Gast
Chairman
Geographic Info. Sys. Cmte.
Dept. of Env. Resources
P.O. Box 8761
Harrisburg, PA 17105
Phone : (717) 541-7805

RHODE ISLAND
John Stachelhaus
GIS Coordinator
Div. of Planning
Dept. of Administration
One Capitol Hill
Providence, RI 02908
Phone : (401) 277-6483

SOUTH CAROLINA
Charles Logan
Director of Policy
Land Resources & Conservation Districts Div.
2221 Devine St., Ste. 222
Columbia, SC 29205-2474
Phone : (803) 734-9113

SOUTH DAKOTA
Kevin Dahlstad
Acting Associate Director
Engineering & Env. Resources
Box 2220, Harding Hall
South Dakota State University
Brookings, SD 57007-0199
Phone : (605) 688-4184

TENNESSEE
Clifton Whitehead
Chief Planner
Div. of Federal Aid
Wildlife Resources Agency
P.O. Box 40747, Melrose Sta.
Nashville, TN 37204
Phone : (615) 781-6599

TEXAS
Charles Palmer
Manager
Natural Resources Info. System
Water Development Board
P.O. Box 13087, Capitol Sta.
Austin, TX 78711
Phone : (512) 463-8337

UTAH
Brent Jones
Coordinator
Data Processing
Off. of Planning & Budget
Salt Lake City, UT 84114
Phone : (801) 538-3162

VERMONT
Bruce Westcott
Director
Off. of Geographic Information Srvc.
University of Vermont
Morrill Hall
Burlington, VT 05405
Phone : (802) 656-4277
Fax : (802) 656-0776

Geographic Information Systems

VIRGINIA
H. Kirby Burch
Director
Div. of Soil & Water Conservation
Dept. of Conservation & Recreation
203 Governor St.
Richmond, VA 23219
Phone : (804) 786-6124
Fax : (804) 786-6141

WASHINGTON
Al Bloomberg
Manager
Information Tech. Div.
Dept. of Natural Resources
P.O. Box 47020
Olympia, WA 98504-7020
Phone : (360) 902-1500

Bob Edwards
Manager
Div. of Information Mgt.
Dept. of Natural Resources
1111 Washington St., Box 47020
Olympia, WA 98504
Phone : (360) 902-1500

WEST VIRGINIA
Royce Chambers
Director
Information System Srvcs.
Div. of Finance & Admin.
Bldg. 6, Rm. 102
Charleston, WV 25305
Phone : (304) 558-8918

WISCONSIN
Janet Price
Director
Bur. of Information Mgt.
Dept. of Natural Resources
101 S. Webster, 8th Fl.
P.O. Box 7921
Madison, WI 53703
Phone : (608) 267-7692
Fax : (608) 267-3579

WYOMING
Rick Memmel
Software Specialist
Computer Technology Div.
Dept. of Admin. & Information
Emerson Bldg.
Cheyenne, WY 82002
Phone : (307) 777-4231

GUAM
Joseph "Tony" Martinez
Director
Dept. of Land Management
P.O. Box 2950
Agana, GU 96910
Phone : (671) 475-5263
Fax : (671) 477-0883

NORTHERN MARIANA ISLANDS
Bruce Lloyd
Public Information Officer
Off. of the Governor
Saipan, MP 96950
Phone : (670) 322-5191
Fax : (670) 322-5192

PUERTO RICO
Norma Burgos Andujar
President
Planning Board
P.O. Box 41119
San Juan, PR 00940
Phone : (809) 723-6200
Fax : (809) 724-3270

U.S. VIRGIN ISLANDS
Donald Francois
Director of Engineering
Water & Power Authority
P.O. Box 1450
St. Thomas, VI 00802
Phone : (809) 774-3552

GEOLOGICAL SURVEY

Conducts research on the state's terrain, mineral resources and possible geological hazards such as earthquakes, faults, etc.

ALABAMA
Ernest A. Mancini
State Geologist & Administrator
State Geological Survey
Oil & Gas Board
P.O. Drawer O
University, AL 35846
Phone : (334) 349-2852
Fax : (334) 349-2861

ALASKA
Thomas E. Smith
State Geologist
Geology & Geophysical Survey Div.
Dept. of Natural Resources
794 University Ave., Ste. 200
Fairbanks, AK 99707-3645
Phone : (907) 451-5037
Fax : (907) 451-5050

ARIZONA
Larry D. Fellows
Director & State Geologist
Geological Survey
845 N. Park Ave., Ste. 100
Tucson, AZ 85719
Phone : (602) 882-4795

ARKANSAS
William Bush
Acting State Geologist
Geological Comm.
3815 W. Roosevelt Rd.
Little Rock, AR 72204
Phone : (501) 324-9165
Fax : (501) 663-7360

CALIFORNIA
James F. Davis
State Geologist
Div. of Mines & Geology
Dept. of Conservation
801 K St., 12th Fl.
Sacramento, CA 95814-3533
Phone : (916) 445-1923

COLORADO
Vicki Cowart
Director/State Geologist
Geological Survey
Dept. of Natural Resources
1313 Sherman St., Rm. 715
Denver, CO 80203
Phone : (303) 866-2611

CONNECTICUT
Edward C. Parker
Bureau Chief
Bur. of Environmental Srvcs.
Dept. of Environmental Protection
79 Elm St.
Hartford, CT 06106
Phone : (203) 424-3072

DELAWARE
Robert R. Jordan
State Geologist
Geological Survey
University of Delaware
101 Penny Hall
Newark, DE 19711
Phone : (302) 451-2833

FLORIDA
Walter Schmidt
Geology, Div. of Administrative & Technical Services
Dept. of Environmental Protection
903 W. Tennessee St.
Tallahassee, FL 32304
Phone : (904) 488-4191

GEORGIA
William McLemore
State Geologist
Environmental Protection Div.
Dept. of Natural Resources
19 M.L. King, Jr. Dr., Rm. 400
Atlanta, GA 30334
Phone : (404) 656-3214

HAWAII
Charles Helsley
Director
Institute of Geophysics
University of Hawaii
2525 Correa Rd.
Honolulu, HI 96822
Phone : (808) 956-7640

IDAHO
Earl Bennett
State Geologist
Bur. of Mines & Geology
University of Idaho
332 Morrill Hall
Moscow, ID 83843
Phone : (208) 885-7991

ILLINOIS
Morris W. Leighton
Chief
Geological Survey
Natural Resources Bldg. # 121
615 E. Peabody Dr.
Champaign, IL 61820
Phone : (217) 333-4747

INDIANA
Norman C. Hester
State Geologist
Geological Survey
611 N. Walnut Grove
Bloomington, IN 47405
Phone : (812) 855-5067

IOWA
Donald L. Koch
Chief
Geological Survey Bur.
123 N. Capitol St.
Iowa City, IA 52240
Phone : (319) 335-1575

KANSAS
Lee Gerhard
Director
Geological Survey
University of Kansas
1930 Constant Ave., Campus W
Lawrence, KS 66047
Phone : (913) 864-3965

KENTUCKY
Donald C. Haney
State Geologist
Geological Survey
University of Kentucky
311 Breckenridge Hall
Lexington, KY 40506
Phone : (606) 257-5500

LOUISIANA
Rodney Jackson
Acting State Geologist
Dept. of Natural Resources
P.O. Box 94396
Baton Rouge, LA 70804-9396
Phone : (504) 342-4433

MAINE
Walter A. Anderson
State Geologist
Geological Survey
Dept. of Conservation
State House Station # 22
Augusta, ME 04333
Phone : (207) 287-2801

MARYLAND**
Emery T. Cleaves
Director
Geological Survey
Dept. of Natural Resources
2300 St. Paul St.
Baltimore, MD 21218
Phone : (301) 554-5503

MASSACHUSETTS
Richard Foster
Geologist
Environmental Quality Engineering
Executive Off. of Environmental Affairs
100 Cambridge St., 20th Fl.
Boston, MA 02202
Phone : (617) 727-9800

MICHIGAN
R. Thomas Seagull
Chief & State Geologist
Geological Survey
Dept. of Natural Resources
735 E. Hazel St.
Lansing, MI 48917
Phone : (517) 334-6907

MINNESOTA
Priscilla Grew
Director
State Geological Survey
2642 University Ave.
St. Paul, MN 55114-1057
Phone : (612) 627-4780

MISSISSIPPI
Cragin Knox
Director
Off. of Geology
Dept. of Environmental Quality
P.O. Box 20307
Jackson, MS 39289
Phone : (601) 961-5502

MISSOURI
James Williams
State Geologist
Div. of Geology & Land Survey
Dept. of Natural Resources
111 Fairgrounds Rd.
P.O. Box 250
Rolla, MO 65401
Phone : (314) 368-2100
Fax : (314) 368-2111

MONTANA
John C. Steinmetz
State Geologist and Director
Bur. of Mines & Geology
1300 W. Park St.
Butte, MT 59701-8997
Phone : (406) 496-4181

NEBRASKA
Perry B. Wigley
Director
Conservation & Survey Div.
Univ. of Nebraska
113 Nebraska Hall
Lincoln, NE 68588-0517
Phone : (402) 472-3471
Fax : (402) 472-2410

NEVADA
Harold Bonham Jr.
Acting Director
State Mapping Advisory Cmte.
Bur. of Mines & Geology
Univ. of Nevada at Reno
Reno, NV 89557
Phone : (702) 784-6691

NEW HAMPSHIRE
Eugene L. Boudette
State Geologist
Dept. of Environmental Srvcs.
P.O. Box 2008
Concord, NH 03302-2008
Phone : (603) 271-3406

NEW JERSEY
Haig Kasabach
State Geologist
Environmental Protection Dept.
29 Arctic Parkway CN427
Trenton, NJ 08625
Phone : (609) 292-1185

NEW MEXICO
Charles E. Chapin
Director
Bur. of Mines & Mineral Res.
Institute of Mining & Tech.
Campus Station
Socorro, NM 87801
Phone : (505) 835-5420
Fax : (505) 835-6333

NEW YORK*
State Geologist
State Geological Survey
Dept. of Education
Education Bldg.
Albany, NY 12234
Phone : (518) 474-5816

NORTH CAROLINA
Jeffrey C. Reid
Chief
Geological Survey
Div. of Land Resources
P.O. Box 27687
Raleigh, NC 27611
Phone : (919) 733-2423
Fax : (919) 733-2876

NORTH DAKOTA
John Bluemle
State Geologist
Geological Survey
State Industrial Comm.
600 E. Boulevard Ave.
Bismarck, ND 58505-0840
Phone : (701) 328-4109
Fax : (701) 328-3682

OHIO
Thomas M. Berg
State Geologist & Chief
Geological Survey
4383 Fountain Square, Bldg. B-2
Columbus, OH 43224-1362
Phone : (614) 265-6988
Fax : (614) 447-1918

OKLAHOMA
Charles Mankin
Director
Geological Survey
Univ. of Oklahoma
830 Van Vleet Oval, Rm. 163
Norman, OK 73019
Phone : (405) 325-3031

OREGON
Donald A. Hull
State Geologist
Dept. of Geology & Mineral Industries
800 N.E. Oregon St.
Portland, OR 97232
Phone : (503) 731-4100
Fax : (503) 731-4066

PENNSYLVANIA
Donald M. Hoskins
State Geologist
Topographic & Geol. Survey
Dept. of Env. Resources
P.O. Box 8453
Harrisburg, PA 17105-8453
Phone : (717) 787-2169

RHODE ISLAND
J. Allen Cain
State Geologist
University of Rhode Island
Dept. of Geology
Green Hall, Rm. 103
Kingston, RI 02881
Phone : (401) 792-2184

SOUTH CAROLINA
Charles Clendenin
State Geologist
SC Geological Survey
5 Geology Rd.
Columbia, SC 29210
Phone : (803) 896-7708

SOUTH DAKOTA
Cleo Christensen
State Geologist
Div. of Geological Survey
414 E. Clark St.
Vermillion, SD 57069-2390

TENNESSEE
Edward T. Luther
Director
Div. of Geology
Dept. of Environment & Conservation
401 Church St.
Nashville, TN 37243
Phone : (615) 532-1500

TEXAS
William L. Fisher
Director
Bur. of Economic Geology
Univ. of Texas
Balcomes Ctr., Bldg. 130, Box X
Austin, TX 78713
Phone : (512) 471-3434

UTAH
M. Lee Allison
Director
Geological Survey
Dept. of Natural Resources & Energy
2363 Foothill Dr.
Salt Lake City, UT 84109-1403
Phone : (801) 467-7970

VERMONT
Diane Conrad
State Geologist
Agency of Natural Resources
103 S. Main St.
Waterbury, VT 05671-0401
Phone : (802) 241-3601
Fax : (802) 241-3281

VIRGINIA
O. Gene Dishner
Director
Dept. of Mines, Minerals & Energy
202 9th St. Off. Bldg., 8th Fl.
Richmond, VA 23219
Phone : (804) 692-3200
Fax : (804) 692-3237

WASHINGTON
Ray Lasmanis
State Geologist
Div. of Geology & Earth Res.
Dept. of Natural Resources
P.O. Box 47001
Olympia, WA 98504-7001
Phone : (360) 902-1450

WEST VIRGINIA
Larry Woodfork
State Geologist
Geological & Economic Survey
P.O. Box 879
Morgantown, WV 26507
Phone : (304) 557-3170

WISCONSIN
Meredith E. Ostrom
Director & State Geologist
Geological & Natural History Survey
Univ. of Wisconsin
3817 Mineral Point Rd.
Madison, WI 53705
Phone : (608) 262-1705

WYOMING
Gary Glass
State Geologist
Geological Survey Staff
University Station
P.O. Box 3008
Laramie, WY 82071
Phone : (307) 766-2286

GUAM
Joseph "Tony" Martinez
Director
Dept. of Land Management
P.O. Box 2950
Agana, GU 96910
Phone : (671) 475-5263
Fax : (671) 477-0883

NORTHERN MARIANA ISLANDS
Nicolas M. Guerrero
Director
Dept. of Natural Resources
Off. of the Governor
Saipan, MP 96950
Phone : (670) 322-9830

PUERTO RICO
Pedro Gelabert Marquez
Secretary
Dept. of Natural Resources
P.O. Box 5887
San Juan, PR 00906-5887
Phone : (809) 724-8774
Fax : (809) 723-4255

U.S. VIRGIN ISLANDS
Beulah Dalmida-Smith
Commissioner
Dept. of Planning & Natural Resources
Nisky Ctr., Ste. 231
St. Thomas, VI 00802
Phone : (809) 774-3320
Fax : (089) 775-5706

GOVERNOR

ALABAMA
Fob James
Governor
Office of the Governor
600 Dexter Ave.
Montgomery, AL 36130-2751
Phone : (334) 242-7100
Fax : (334) 242-4541

ALASKA
Tony Knowles
Governor
Office of the Governor
P.O. Box 110001
Juneau, AK 99811-0001
Phone : (907) 465-3500
Fax : (907) 465-3532

ARIZONA
Fife Symington
Governor
Office of the Governor
1700 W. Washington St.
Phoenix, AZ 85007
Phone : (602) 542-4331
Fax : (602) 542-7601

ARKANSAS
Jim Guy Tucker
Governor
Office of the Governor
State Capitol, Rm. 250
Little Rock, AR 72201
Phone : (501) 682-2345
Fax : (501) 682-1382

CALIFORNIA
Pete Wilson
Governor
Office of the Governor
State Capitol
Sacramento, CA 95814
Phone : (916) 445-2841
Fax : (916) 445-4633

COLORADO
Roy Romer
Governor
136 State Capitol Bldg.
Denver, CO 80203
Phone : (303) 866-2471
Fax : (303) 866-2003

CONNECTICUT
John Rowland
Governor
Office of the Governor
State Capitol
Hartford, CT 06106
Phone : (203) 566-4840
Fax : (203) 566-4677

DELAWARE
Thomas R. Carper
Governor
Tatnall Bldg.
Dover, DE 19901
Phone : (302) 739-4101
Fax : (302) 739-2775

FLORIDA
Lawton Chiles
Governor
The Capitol
Tallahassee, FL 32399-0001
Phone : (904) 488-2272
Fax : (904) 487-0801

GEORGIA
Zell Miller
Governor
State Capitol, Rm. 203
Atlanta, GA 30334
Phone : (404) 656-1776
Fax : (404) 656-2612

HAWAII
Ben Cayetano
Governor
State Capitol, 15th Floor
Honolulu, HI 96813
Phone : (808) 586-0034
Fax : (808) 586-0006

IDAHO
Phil Batt
Governor
Office of the Governor
State Capitol, 2nd Fl.
Boise, ID 83720
Phone : (208) 334-2100
Fax : (208) 334-2175

ILLINOIS
Jim Edgar
Governor
207 State House
Springfield, IL 62706
Phone : (217) 782-6830
Fax : (217) 782-3560

INDIANA
Evan Bayh, III
Governor
State House, Rm. 206
Indianapolis, IN 46204
Phone : (317) 232-1048
Fax : (317) 232-3443

IOWA
Terry E. Branstad
Governor
Executive Off.
State Capitol
Des Moines, IA 50319
Phone : (515) 281-5211
Fax : (515) 281-6611

KANSAS
Bill Graves
Governor
State Capitol, 2nd Fl.
Topeka, KS 66612-1590
Phone : (913) 296-3232
Fax : (913) 296-7973

KENTUCKY
Brereton Jones
Governor
State Capitol, Rm. 100
Frankfort, KY 40601
Phone : (502) 564-2611
Fax : (502) 564-2735

LOUISIANA
Edwin Edwards
Governor
P.O. Box 94004
Baton Rouge, LA 70804-9004
Phone : (504) 342-7015
Fax : (504) 342-7099

MAINE
Angus King
Governor
Office of the Governor
State House Station #1
Augusta, ME 04333
Phone : (207) 287-3531
Fax : (207) 287-1034

MARYLAND
Parris M. Glendening
Governor
State House
Annapolis, MD 21401
Phone : (410) 974-3901
Fax : (410) 974-3275

MASSACHUSETTS
William F. Weld
Governor
State House, Rm. 360
Boston, MA 02133
Phone : (617) 727-3600

MICHIGAN
John Engler
Governor
State Capitol Bldg.
P.O. Box 30013
Lansing, MI 48909
Phone : (517) 373-3400
Fax : (517) 335-6949

MINNESOTA
Arne Carlson
Governor
130 State Capitol
Aurora Ave.
St. Paul, MN 55155
Phone : (612) 296-3391
Fax : (612) 296-2089

MISSISSIPPI
Kirk Fordice
Governor
P.O. Box 139
Jackson, MS 39205
Phone : (601) 359-3150
Fax : (601) 359-3741

MISSOURI
Mel Carnahan
Governor
State Capitol, Rm. 216
P.O. Box 720
Jefferson City, MO 65102
Phone : (314) 751-3222
Fax : (314) 751-1495

MONTANA
Marc Racicot
Governor
State Capitol, Rm. 204
Helena, MT 59620
Phone : (406) 444-3111
Fax : (406) 444-5529

NEBRASKA
Ben Nelson
Governor
State Capitol, 2nd Fl.
Lincoln, NE 68509-4848
Phone : (402) 471-2244
Fax : (402) 471-6031

NEVADA
Bob Miller
Governor
Executive Chambers
Capitol Complex
Carson City, NV 89710
Phone : (702) 885-5670
Fax : (702) 687-4486

NEW HAMPSHIRE
Stephen Merrill
Governor
State Capitol
Concord, NH 03301
Phone : (603) 271-2121

NEW JERSEY
Christine Todd Whitman
Governor
Off. of the Governor
State House, CN 001
Trenton, NJ 08625
Phone : (609) 292-6000
Fax : (609) 984-6886

NEW MEXICO
Gary E. Johnson
Governor
400 State Capitol
Santa Fe, NM 87503
Phone : (505) 827-3000
Fax : (505) 827-3026

NEW YORK
George E. Pataki
Governor
Executive Chamber
State Capitol
Albany, NY 12224
Phone : (518) 474-8390
Fax : (518) 474-1513

NORTH CAROLINA
James B. Hunt
Governor
State Capitol
116 W. Jones St.
Raleigh, NC 27603-8001
Phone : (919) 733-4240
Fax : (919) 715-3175

NORTH DAKOTA
Edward T. Schafer
Governor
State Capitol, 1st Fl.
600 E. Boulevard Ave.
Bismarck, ND 58505-0001
Phone : (701) 328-2200
Fax : (701) 328-2205

OHIO
George V. Voinovich
Governor
77 S. High St.
Columbus, OH 43266-0601
Phone : (614) 466-3555
Fax : (614) 466-9354

OKLAHOMA
Frank Keating
Governor
212 State Capitol
Oklahoma City, OK 73105
Phone : (405) 521-2342
Fax : (405) 521-3353

OREGON
John Kitzhaber
Governor
254 State Capitol Bldg.
Salem, OR 97310
Phone : (503) 378-3111
Fax : (503) 378-8970

PENNSYLVANIA
Tom Ridge
Governor
225 Main Capitol Bldg.
Harrisburg, PA 17120
Phone : (717) 787-2500
Fax : (717) 783-1396

RHODE ISLAND
Lincoln Almond
Governor
222 State House
Providence, RI 02903
Phone : (401) 277-2080
Fax : (401) 272-0860

SOUTH CAROLINA
David M. Beasley
Governor
State House
P.O. Box 11369
Columbia, SC 29211
Phone : (803) 734-9818

SOUTH DAKOTA
Bill Janklow
Governor
State Capitol
500 E. Capitol Ave.
Pierre, SD 57501
Phone : (605) 773-3212
Fax : (605) 773-4711

TENNESSEE
Don Sundquist
Governor
State Capitol Bldg.
Nashville, TN 37243
Phone : (615) 741-2001
Fax : (615) 532-9711

TEXAS
George W. Bush
Governor
P.O. Box 12428, Capitol Station
Austin, TX 78711
Phone : (512) 463-2000
Fax : (512) 475-3247

UTAH
Mike Leavitt
Governor
210 State Capitol
Salt Lake City, UT 84114
Phone : (801) 538-1000
Fax : (801) 538-1528

VERMONT
Howard Dean
Governor
Pavilion Off. Bldg.
109 State St.
Montpelier, VT 05609
Phone : (802) 828-3333
Fax : (802) 828-3339

VIRGINIA
George Allen
Governor
State Capitol, 3rd Fl.
Richmond, VA 23219
Phone : (804) 786-2211
Fax : (804) 786-3985

WASHINGTON
Mike Lowry
Governor
Legislative Bldg.
P.O. Box 40002
Olympia, WA 98504
Phone : (360) 753-6780
Fax : (360) 586-8380

WEST VIRGINIA
Gaston Caperton
Governor
Capitol Bldg.
Charleston, WV 25305
Phone : (304) 558-2000
Fax : (304) 342-7025

WISCONSIN
Tommy G. Thompson
Governor
State Capitol
115 East Ave.
P.O. Box 7863
Madison, WI 53707
Phone : (608) 266-1212
Fax : (608) 267-8983

WYOMING
Jim Geringer
Governor
State Capitol
Cheyenne, WY 82002
Phone : (307) 777-7435
Fax : (307) 777-6869

DISTRICT OF COLUMBIA
Marion Berry
Mayor
441 4th St., NW, 11th Fl.
Washington, DC 20004
Phone : (202) 727-2980

AMERICAN SOMOA
A.P. Lutali
Governor
Office of the Governor
Government House
Pago Pago, AS 96799
Phone : (684) 633-4116
Fax : (684) 633-2269

GUAM
Carl Gutierrez
Governor
Executive Chambers
P.O. Box 2950
Agana, GU 96910
Phone : (671) 475-9201
Fax : (671) 477-4826

NORTHERN MARIANA ISLANDS
Froilan C. Tenorio
Governor
Off. of the Governor
Capitol Hill
Saipan, MP 96950
Phone : (670) 322-5091

PUERTO RICO
Pedro Rossello
Governor
La Fortaleza
P.O. Box 82
San Juan, PR 00901
Phone : (809) 721-7000
Fax : (809) 729-0900

U.S. VIRGIN ISLANDS
Roy L. Schneider
Governor
Government House
21-22 Kongens Gade
Charlotte Amalie, VI 00802
Phone : (809) 774-0001
Fax : (809) 774-1361

GROUNDWATER MANAGEMENT

Manages the state's groundwater resources.

ALABAMA
James McIndoe
Chief
Water Quality Branch
Water Div.
1751 Cong. Dickinson Dr.
Montgomery, AL 36130
Phone : (334) 271-7832
Fax : (334) 271-7950

ALASKA
Jules Tileston
Director
Div. of Mining & Water Mgt.
Dept. of Natural Resources
3601 C St., Ste. 800
Anchorage, AK 99503-5935
Phone : (907) 762-2163
Fax : (907) 563-1835

ARIZONA
Edward Z. Fox
Director
Dept. of Environmental Quality
3033 N. Central Ave.
Phoenix, AZ 85012
Phone : (602) 207-2203
Fax : (602) 207-2218

ARKANSAS
William Keith
Manager
Planning Branch, Water Div.
Pollution Control & Ecology
P.O. Box 8913
Little Rock, AR 72219
Phone : (501) 562-7444
Fax : (501) 562-4632

CALIFORNIA
Raymond D. Hart
Chief
Div. of Local Assistance
Dept. of Water Resources
1020 9th St., 3rd Fl.
Sacramento, CA 95814
Phone : (916) 327-1632

COLORADO
Hal D. Simpson
State Engineer
Div. of Water Resources
Dept. of Natural Resources
1313 Sherman St., Rm. 818
Denver, CO 80203
Phone : (303) 866-3581

CONNECTICUT
Robert Smith
Chief
Bur. of Water Mgt.
Water Compliance Unit
Dept. of Environ. Protection
79 Elm St.
Hartford, CT 06106
Phone : (203) 424-3020

DELAWARE
Rodney Wyatt
Administrator
Groundwater Mgt. Branch
Natural Res. & Environ. Dept.
P.O. Box 1401
Dover, DE 19903
Phone : (302) 739-4860

FLORIDA
Richard M. Harvey
Director
Division of Water Facilities
Dept. of Env. Protection
2600 Blairstone Rd.
Tallahassee, FL 32399
Phone : (904) 487-1855

GEORGIA
William McLemore
State Geologist
Environmental Protection Div.
Dept. of Natural Resources
19 M.L. King, Jr. Dr., Rm. 400
Atlanta, GA 30334
Phone : (404) 656-3214

HAWAII
Rae M. Loui
Deputy Director
Div. of Water Resource Mgt.
Land & Natural Resources Dept.
1151 Punchbowl St.
Honolulu, HI 96813
Phone : (808) 587-0393
Fax : (808) 587-0390

IDAHO
Larry L. Koenig
Bureau Chief
Monitoring & Technical Support
Div. of Environmental Quality
1410 N. Hilton St.
Boise, ID 83706
Phone : (208) 334-5860

ILLINOIS
Don Dillenburg
Acting Chief
Groundwater
Div. of Public Water Supply
1340 N. Ninth St.
Springfield, IL 62702
Phone : (217) 782-1724

INDIANA
John Simpson
Director
Div. of Water
Dept. of Natural Resources
402 W. Washington
Indianapolis, IN 46204

IOWA
Darrell McAllister
Chief
Surface & Groundwater Prot.
Environmental Protection Div.
Wallace State Off. Bldg.
Des Moines, IA 50319
Phone : (515) 281-8869

KANSAS
Karl Mueldener
Director
Bureau of Water
Dept. of Health & Environment
Landon State Off. Bldg., 10th Fl.
Topeka, KS 66612-1290
Phone : (913) 296-5500
Fax : (913) 296-5509

KENTUCKY
David Leo
Acting Manager
Groundwater Branch
Div. of Water
14 Reilly Rd.
Frankfort, KY 40601
Phone : (502) 564-3410

LOUISIANA
Dale Givens
Assistant Secretary
Off. of Water Resources
Dept. of Environmental Quality
P.O. Box 82215
Baton Rouge, LA 70884
Phone : (504) 765-0634

MAINE
Martha Kirkpatrick
Director
Land & Water Quality Control
Dept. of Env. Protection
State House Station # 17
Augusta, ME 04333
Phone : (207) 287-3901

MARYLAND**
Jane Gottfredson
Chief
Residential Sanitation Div.
Dept. of the Environment
2500 Broening Hwy.
Baltimore, MD 21224
Phone : (301) 631-3652

MASSACHUSETTS
Dean Spencer
Acting Director
Regulatory Branch
Water Pollution Control Div.
1 Winter St., 8th Fl.
Boston, MA 02108
Phone : (617) 292-5673

MICHIGAN
Jim Sygo
Chief
Waste Mgt. Div.
Dept. of Natural Resources
P.O. Box 30028
Lansing, MI 48909
Phone : (517) 373-2730

MINNESOTA
Brian Rongitsch
Supervisor
Groundwater & Tech. Analysis
Div. of Waters
500 Lafayette Rd.
St. Paul, MN 55155-4032
Phone : (612) 296-4800

MISSISSIPPI
Bill Barnett
Chief
Groundwater Div.
Off. of Pollution Control
P.O. Box 10385
Jackson, MS 39289
Phone : (601) 961-5119

MISSOURI
Don E. Miller
Chief
Water Res. Planning Program
Div. of Geology & Land Survey
111 Fairgrounds
P.O. Box 250
Rolla, MO 65401
Phone : (314) 368-2190
Fax : (314) 368-2111

MONTANA
Fred Shewman
Supervisor
Groundwater Section
Water Quality Bur.
Cogswell Bldg.
Helena, MT 59620
Phone : (406) 444-2406

NEBRASKA
Dennis Heitmann
Supervisor
Ground Water Section
Water Quality Div.
P.O. Box 98922
Lincoln, NE 68509
Phone : (402) 471-4288

NEVADA
Dick Reavis
Deputy Administrator
Groundwater Section
Div. of Env. Protection
333 W. Nye Ln.
Carson City, NV 89710
Phone : (702) 687-5883

NEW HAMPSHIRE
Harry T. Stewart
Administrator
Groundwater Protection Bur.
Water Supply & Poll. Control
6 Hazen Dr.
Concord, NH 03301
Phone : (603) 271-3503

NEW JERSEY
James Mumman
Administrator
Water Monitoring Management
401 E. State St., CN409
Trenton, NJ 08625
Phone : (609) 292-1623

NEW MEXICO
Marcy Leavitt
Acting Bureau Chief
Groundwater Bureau
Dept. of Environment
P.O. Box 26110
Santa Fe, NM 87502
Phone : (505) 827-2918
Fax : (505) 827-2965

NEW YORK*
Commissioner
Dept. of Environmental Conservation
50 Wolf Rd.
Albany, NY 12233
Phone : (518) 457-3446

NORTH CAROLINA
Arthur Mouberry
Section Chief
Groundwater Section
Div. of Environmental Mgt.
P.O. Box 27687
Raleigh, NC 27611
Phone : (919) 733-3221
Fax : (919) 733-2496

NORTH DAKOTA
L. David Glatt
Asst. Director
Div. of Water Quality
P.O. Box 5520
Bismarck, ND 58506-5520
Phone : (701) 328-5210
Fax : (701) 328-5200

OHIO
John Sadzewicz
Chief
Div. of Public Water Supply
Environmental Protection Agency
1800 Watermark
P.O. Box 1049
Columbus, OH 43266-1049
Phone : (614) 644-2752
Fax : (614) 644-2909

OKLAHOMA
Duane Smith
Chief
Ground Water Div.
Water Resources Bd.
P.O. Box 150
Oklahoma City, OK 73101
Phone : (405) 231-2500

OREGON
Rick Kepler
Manager
Groundwater Section
Dept. of Environmental Quality
811 SW Sixth Ave.
Portland, OR 97310
Phone : (503) 229-6804

PENNSYLVANIA
Daniel B. Drawbaugh
Director
Water Quality Mgt.
Dept. of Environmental Resources
Rachel Carlson State Off. Bldg.,
P.O. Box 8465
Harrisburg, PA 17105-8465
Phone : (717) 787-2666

RHODE ISLAND
Edward Szymanski
Associate Director
Water Quality Mgt.
Div. of Groundwater
291 Promenade St.
Providence, RI 02908
Phone : (401) 277-2234

SOUTH CAROLINA
Rod W. Cherry
Director
Div. of Hydrology
Water Resources Comm.
1201 Main St., Ste. 1100
Columbia, SC 29201
Phone : (803) 737-0800

SOUTH DAKOTA
Steve Pirner
Director
Div. of Environmental Reg.
Dept. of Env. & Natural Res.
523 E. Capitol Ave.
Pierre, SD 57501
Phone : (605) 773-3296

TENNESSEE
Kent D. Taylor
Director
Div. of Groundwater Protection
Dept. of Environment & Conservation
401 Church St.
Nashville, TN 37243
Phone : (615) 532-0761

TEXAS
Laura Koesters
Deputy Director
Office of Waste Management
Natural Res. Conserv. Comm.
P.O. Box 13087
Austin, TX 78711-3087
Phone : (512) 239-4300

UTAH
Larry J. Mize
Manager
Groundwater Section
Water Pollution Control Bur.
P.O. Box 16690
Salt Lake City, UT 84114-4870
Phone : (801) 538-6835

VERMONT
Jay Rutherford
Director
Groundwater Mgt. Section
Water Supply Div.
103 S. Main St.
Waterbury, VT 05671-0403
Phone : (802) 241-3400
Fax : (802) 241-3284

VIRGINIA
Peter W. Schmidt
Director
Dept. of Environmental Quality
629 E. Main St.
Richmond, VA 23219
Phone : (804) 762-4020
Fax : (804) 762-4019

WASHINGTON
Michael T. Llewelyn
Program Manager
Water Quality Program
Dept. of Ecology
P.O. Box 47600
Olympia, WA 98504-7600
Phone : (360) 407-6400

WEST VIRGINIA
Mark A. Scott
Chief
Off. of Water Resources
Dept. of Environmental Prot.
1201 Greenbrier St.
Charleston, WV 25311
Phone : (304) 558-2107

WISCONSIN
Kevin Kessler
Chief
Groundwater Mgt. Section
Bur. of Water Resource Mgt.
Dept. of Natural Resources
101 S. Webster, 2nd Fl.
Madison, WI 53707
Phone : (608) 267-9350
Fax : (608) 267-2800

WYOMING
Richard G. Stockdale
Administrator
Ground Water Div.
Off. of State Engineer
Herschler Bldg.
Cheyenne, WY 82002
Phone : (307) 777-6160

DISTRICT OF COLUMBIA
Edward M. Scott
Administrator
Water & Sewer Utility Admin.
Dept. of Public Works
5000 Overlook Ave., SW
Washington, DC 20032
Phone : (202) 767-7651

AMERICAN SAMOA
Abe Malae
Executive Director
American Samoa Power Authority
American Samoa Government
Pago Pago, AS 96799
Phone : (684) 644-5251
Fax : (684) 644-5005

GUAM
Robert F. Kelley
Acting Chief Officer
Public Utility Agency
P.O. Box 3010
Agana, GU 96910
Phone : (671) 647-7811
Fax : (671) 649-0158

NORTHERN MARIANA ISLANDS
Timothy P. Villagomez
Executive Director
Commonwealth Utilities Corp.
Off. of the Governor
Lower Base
Saipan, MP 96950
Phone : (670) 322-4033
Fax : (670) 322-4323

PUERTO RICO
Pedro Gelabert Marquez
Secretary
Dept. of Natural Resources
P.O. Box 5887
San Juan, PR 00906-5887
Phone : (809) 724-8774
Fax : (809) 723-4255

U.S. VIRGIN ISLANDS
Beulah Dalmida-Smith
Commissioner
Dept. of Planning & Natural Resources
Nisky Ctr., Ste. 231
St. Thomas, VI 00802
Phone : (809) 774-3320
Fax : (809) 775-5706

HAZARDOUS WASTE MANAGEMENT

Develops and maintains a comprehensive hazardous waste management program in the state.

ALABAMA
Steve Jenkins
Chief
Compliance Branch, Land Div.
Dept. of Environmental Mgt.
1751 Cong. Dickinson Dr.
Montgomery, AL 36130
Phone : (334) 271-7700
Fax : (334) 270-5612

ALASKA
Heather Stockard
Chief
Solid & Hazardous Waste Mgt. Section
410 Willoughby Ave., Ste. 105
Juneau, AK 99801
Phone : (907) 465-5150
Fax : (907) 465-5164

ARIZONA
Andy Soesilo
Program Manager
Off. of Wste. Prog./Haz. Sect.
Dept. of Environmental Quality
3033 N. Central Ave.
Phoenix, AZ 85012
Phone : (602) 207-2381

ARKANSAS
Mike Bates
Chief
Hazardous Waste Div.
Pollution Control & Ecology
P.O. Box 8913
Little Rock, AR 72219
Phone : (501) 562-7444
Fax : (501) 562-4632

CALIFORNIA
Jesse Huff
Director
Toxics Substance Control
400 P St., 4th Fl.
P.O. Box 806
Sacramento, CA 95812-0806
Phone : (916) 323-9723

COLORADO
Howard Roitman
Director
Haz. Materials & Waste Mgt.
Dept. of Public Health & Env.
4300 Cherry Creek Dr., S.
Denver, CO 80222
Phone : (303) 692-3300
Fax : (303) 759-5355

CONNECTICUT
Richard Barlow
Director
Bureau of Waste Management
Dept. of Env. Protection
79 Elm St.
Hartford, CT 06106
Phone : (203) 424-3021

DELAWARE
Karen J. Anthony
Program Manager
Hazardous Waste Branch
Dept. of Nat. Res. & Env. Control
P.O. Box 1401
Dover, DE 19903
Phone : (302) 739-4781

FLORIDA
John Rudell
Director
Div. of Waste Mgt.
Dept. of Env. Protection
2600 Blairstone Rd.
Tallahassee, FL 32399
Phone : (904) 487-3299

GEORGIA
Harold Reheis
Director
Environmental Protection Div.
Dept. of Natural Resources
205 Butler St., Ste. 1152
Atlanta, GA 30334
Phone : (404) 656-4713
Fax : (404) 651-5778

HAWAII
Gracelda Simmons
Acting Manager
Solid & Hazardous Waste Branch
Dept. of Health
500 Ala Moana Blvd., Ste. 150
Honolulu, HI 96813
Phone : (808) 586-4225

IDAHO
Bryan Monson
Manager
Permitting & Enforcement
Div. of Environmental Quality
1410 N. Hilton
Boise, ID 83706
Phone : (208) 334-5898

ILLINOIS
David Thomas
Director
Hazardous Waste Ctr.
1 E. Hazelwood Dr.
Champaign, IL 61820
Phone : (217) 333-8940

INDIANA
David Wersan
Assistant Commissioner
Off. of Solid & Haz. Waste Mgt.
Dept. of Environmental Mgt.
105 S. Meridian St., Box 6015
Indianapolis, IN 46225
Phone : (317) 232-3210

IOWA
Peter Hamlin
Chief
Air Quality & Solid Waste Protection
Dept. of Natural Resources
900 E. Grand
Des Moines, IA 50319
Phone : (515) 281-8852

KANSAS
William Bider
Director
Bureau of Waste Management
Dept. of Health & Env.
Landon State Off. Bldg., 10th Fl.
Topeka, KS 66612-1290
Phone : (913) 296-1600
Fax : (913) 296-8909

KENTUCKY
Michael Welch
Branch Manager
Hazardous Waste Branch
Div. of Waste Mgt.
14 Reilly Rd.
Frankfort, KY 40601
Phone : (502) 564-6716

LOUISIANA
Glenn Miller
Assistant Secretary
Office of Solid & Haz. Waste
Dept. of Environmental Quality
7290 Bluebonnet Rd.
Baton Rouge, LA 70810
Phone : (504) 765-0741

MAINE
Alan M. Prysunka
Director
Oil & Hazardous Materials Bur.
Dept. of Env. Protection
State House Station # 17
Augusta, ME 04333
Phone : (207) 287-2651

MARYLAND**
Alvin Bowles
Administrator
Hazardous Waste Program
Haz. & Solid Waste Mgt. Admin.
2500 Broening Hwy.
Baltimore, MD 21224
Phone : (410) 631-3343

MASSACHUSETTS
Steven DeGabriel
Director
Div. of Hazardous Waste
Dept. of Environmental Protection
1 Winter St., 3rd Fl.
Boston, MA 02108
Phone : (617) 292-5574

MICHIGAN
Kenneth Burda
Chief
Hazardous Waste Program Section
Dept. of Natural Resources
P.O. Box 30028
Lansing, MI 48909
Phone : (517) 373-2730

MINNESOTA
Timothy K. Scherkenbach
Manager
Hazardous Waste Div.
Pollution Control Agency
520 Lafayette Rd.
St. Paul, MN 55155-4194
Phone : (612) 297-8502

MISSISSIPPI
Sam Mabry
Administrator
Hazardous Waste Div.
Dept. of Environmental Quality
P.O. Box 10385
Jackson, MS 39289
Phone : (601) 961-5062

MISSOURI
Ed Sadler
Director
Hazardous Waste Program
Dept. of Natural Resources
Jefferson Bldg., 13th Fl.
P.O. Box 176
Jefferson City, MO 65102
Phone : (314) 751-3176
Fax : (314) 751-7869

MONTANA
Roger Thorvilson
Supervisor
Hazardous Waste Section
Solid & Hazardous Waste Bur.
Cogswell Bldg.
Helena, MT 59620
Phone : (406) 444-1430

NEBRASKA
Bill Imig
Supervisor
Hazardous Waste Section
Dept. of Environmental Quality
P.O. Box 98922
Lincoln, NE 68509
Phone : (402) 471-4217

NEVADA
Verne Rosse
Deputy Administrator
Div. of Env. Protection
Capitol Complex
Carson City, NV 89710
Phone : (702) 687-5872

NEW HAMPSHIRE
John J. Duclos
Supervisor
Haz. Waste Compliance Section
Waste Mgt. Compliance Bur.
6 Hazen Dr.
Concord, NH 03301
Phone : (603) 271-2942

NEW JERSEY
Susan E. Boyle
Director
Div. of Responsible Party Sites Remediation
Environmental Protection Dept.
401 E. State St., CN028
Trenton, NJ 08625
Phone : (609) 633-1408

NEW MEXICO
Benito Garcia
Bureau Chief
Hazardous Waste Bur.
Dept. of Environment
P.O. Box 26110
Santa Fe, NM 87502
Phone : (505) 827-4300
Fax : (505) 827-4389

NEW YORK*
Commissioner
Dept. of Environmental Conservation
50 Wolf Rd.
Albany, NY 12233
Phone : (518) 457-3446

NORTH CAROLINA
Jerry Rhodes
Chief
Hazardous Waste Section
Div. of Solid Waste Mgt.
P.O. Box 27687
Raleigh, NC 27605-1350
Phone : (919) 733-2178

NORTH DAKOTA
Neil Knatterud
Director
Div. of Solid Waste Mgt.
Health & Consolidated Labs.
P.O. Box 5520
Bismarck, ND 58502-5520
Phone : (701) 328-5166
Fax : (701) 328-5200

OHIO
Linda Welch
Assistant Division Chief
Hazardous Waste Mgt.
Solid & Hazardous Waste Mgt.
P.O. Box 1049
Columbus, OH 43266-0149
Phone : (614) 644-2934
Fax : (614) 644-2329

OKLAHOMA
Damon Wingfield
Chief
Hazardous Waste Mgt. Srvcs.
Environmental Health Srvcs.
P.O. Box 53551
Oklahoma City, OK 73152
Phone : (405) 271-5338

OREGON
Roy Brower
Manager
Hazardous Waste Policy & Prog. Dev.
Waste & Cleanup Div.
811 SW Sixth Ave.
Portland, OR 97204
Phone : (503) 229-6585
Fax : (503) 229-6977

RHODE ISLAND
Ronald Gagnon
Acting Chief
Solid Waste Section
Air & Hazardous Materials Div.
291 Promenade St.
Providence, RI 02908
Phone : (401) 277-2797

SOUTH CAROLINA
Hartsill Truesdale
Chief
Bur. of Solid & Haz. Waste Mgt
Dept. of Health & Env. Control
2600 Bull St.
Columbia, SC 29201
Phone : (803) 896-4001

SOUTH DAKOTA
Vonnie Kallemeyn
Env. Prog. Sr. Scientist
Div. of Environmental Reg.
Waste Management Program
523 E. Capitol
Pierre, SD 57501
Phone : (605) 773-3151

TENNESSEE
Tom Tiesler
Director
Hazardous Waste Mgt. Section
Dept. of Env. & Conservation
401 Church St., 5th Fl.
Nashville, TN 37243
Phone : (615) 532-0780

TEXAS
Barry Williams
Deputy Director
Office of Waste Management
Natural Res. Conserv. Comm.
P.O. Box 13087
Austin, TX 78711-3087
Phone : (512) 239-2104

UTAH
Dennis R. Downs
Director
Div. of Solid & Hazardous Waste
Dept. of Environmental Quality
P.O. Box 14880
Salt Lake City, UT 84114-4880
Phone : (801) 538-6775

VERMONT
William Ahearn
Director
Hazardous Materials Mgt. Div.
Agency of Natural Resources
103 S. Main St.
Waterbury, VT 05671-0404
Phone : (802) 241-3888
Fax : (802) 241-3296

VIRGINIA
Peter W. Schmidt
Director
Dept. of Environmental Quality
629 E. Main St.
Richmond, VA 23219
Phone : (804) 762-4020
Fax : (804) 762-4019

WASHINGTON
Dan Silver
Assistant Director
Off. of Waste Mgt.
Dept. of Ecology
P.O. Box 47600
Olympia, WA 98504-7600
Phone : (360) 407-6000

WEST VIRGINIA
Max Robertson
Chief
Off. of Waste Mgt.
1356 Hansford St.
Charleston, WV 25301
Phone : (304) 348-5393

WISCONSIN
Barbra Zellmer
Chief
Hazardous Waste Mgt. Section
Solid & Haz. Waste Mgt. Bur.
101 S. Webster, 3rd Fl.
P.O. Box 7921
Madison, WI 53707
Phone : (608) 266-7055
Fax : (608) 267-2768

WYOMING
David Finley
Administrator
Solid & Hazardous Waste Div.
Dept. of Environmental Quality
Herschler Bldg.
Cheyenne, WY 82002
Phone : (307) 777-7753

DISTRICT OF COLUMBIA
F. Clayton Dade
Administrator
Solid Waste Mgt.
Dept. of Public Works
2750 S. Capitol St., SE
Washington, DC 20003
Phone : (202) 767-8512

AMERICAN SAMOA
Togipa Tausaga
Executive Director
Environmental Quality Comm.
Off. of the Governor
Pago Pago, AS 96799
Phone : (684) 633-2304
Fax : (684) 633-5801

GUAM
Joseph C. Cruz
Administrator
Environmental Protection Agency
130 Rojas St.
Harmon, GU 96911
Phone : (671) 646-8863
Fax : (671) 646-9402

NORTHERN MARIANA ISLANDS
Juan I. Castro
Director
Environmental Quality Div.
Public Health & Env. Srvcs.
P.O. Box 409
Saipan, MP 96950
Phone : (670) 234-1011
Fax : (670) 234-1003

PUERTO RICO
Hector Rosse
President
Environmental Quality Board
P.O. Box 11488
Santurce, PR 00910-1488
Phone : (809) 767-8057
Fax : (809) 766-2483

U.S. VIRGIN ISLANDS
Benjamin Nazario
Director
Environmental Protection Div.
Dept. of Planning & Nat. Res.
Nisky Ctr., Ste. 231
St. Thomas, VI 00802
Phone : (809) 774-3320

HEALTH

Enforces public health laws and administers health programs and services in the state.

ALABAMA
Don Williamson
State Health Officer
State Public Health Dept.
610 E. Patton
Montgomery, AL 36111
Phone : (334) 613-5200
Fax : (334) 240-3387

ALASKA
Peter Nakamura
Director
Div. of Public Health
Dept. of Health & Social Srvcs.
P.O. Box 110610
Juneau, AK 99811-0610
Phone : (907) 465-3090
Fax : (907) 586-1877

ARIZONA
Jack Dillenberg
Director
Dept. of Health Services
1740 W. Adams St.
Phoenix, AZ 85007
Phone : (602) 542-1025

ARKANSAS
Sandra Nichols
Director
Dept. of Health
4815 W. Markham St.
Little Rock, AR 72205
Phone : (501) 661-2417
Fax : (501) 661-2601

CALIFORNIA
Kim Belshe
Acting Director
Dept. of Health Services
714 P St., Rm. 1253
Sacramento, CA 95814
Phone : (916) 657-1425

COLORADO
Patti Shwayder-Coffin
Acting Executive Director
Dept. of Public Health & Environment
4300 Cherry Creek Dr., S.
Denver, CO 80222
Phone : (303) 692-2100
Fax : (303) 782-0095

CONNECTICUT
Yvette M. Thiesfield
Acting Commissioner
Dept. of Public Health & Add. Srvcs.
Dept. of Health Services
150 Washington St.
Hartford, CT 06106
Phone : (203) 566-2038

DELAWARE
Charles Konigsburg Jr.
Director
Div. of Public Health
Dept. of Health & Social Srvcs.
P.O. Box 637
Dover, DE 19903
Phone : (302) 739-4701
Fax : (302) 739-6659

FLORIDA
Charles Mahan
Deputy Secretary for Health
Health Program Off.
Dept. of Health & Rehab. Srvcs.
1317 Winewood Blvd.
Tallahassee, FL 32399-0700
Phone : (904) 487-2705
Fax : (904) 922-2993

GEORGIA
Virginia Galvin
Acting Director
Public Health Div.
Dept. of Human Resources
2 Peachtree St., 7th Fl.
Atlanta, GA 30303
Phone : (404) 657-2702

HAWAII
Lawrence Miike
Director
Dept. of Health
P.O. Box 3378
Honolulu, HI 96801
Phone : (808) 586-4410
Fax : (808) 586-4444

IDAHO
Linda Caballero
Director
Idaho Dept. of Health & Welfare
450 W. State St., 10th Fl.
P.O. Box 83720
Boise, ID 83720-0036
Phone : (208) 334-5500

ILLINOIS
John Lumpkin
Director
Dept. of Public Health
535 W. Jefferson St.
Springfield, IL 62761
Phone : (217) 782-4977
Fax : (217) 782-3987

INDIANA
John Christopher Bailey
Commissioner
State Bd. of Health
1330 W. Michigan St., # 4255
Indianapolis, IN 46206
Phone : (317) 383-6100

IOWA
Christopher Atchison
Director
Dept. of Public Health
Lucas State Off. Bldg.
Des Moines, IA 50319
Phone : (515) 281-5605
Fax : (515) 281-4958

KANSAS
James O'Connell
Secretary
Dept. of Health & Environment
Landon State Off. Bldg., 6th Fl.
Topeka, KS 66612-1290
Phone : (913) 296-1500
Fax : (913) 296-1231

KENTUCKY
Rice C. Leach
Commissioner
Dept. for Health Services
Cabinet for Human Resources
275 E. Main St.
Frankfort, KY 40601
Phone : (502) 564-3970

LOUISIANA
Eric Baumgarner
Asst. Secretary/State Health Officer
Dept. of Health & Hospitals
P.O. Box 3214
Baton Rouge, LA 70821
Phone : (504) 342-8092

MAINE
Kevin Concannon
Commissioner
Dept. of Human Services
State House Station # 11
Augusta, ME 04333
Phone : (207) 287-2736

MARYLAND
Martin Wasserman
Secretary
Dept. of Health & Mental Hygiene
201 W. Preston St., 5th Fl.
Baltimore, MD 21201
Phone : (410) 225-6505

MASSACHUSETTS
David Mulligan
Commissioner
Dept. of Public Health
150 Tremont St.
Boston, MA 02111
Phone : (617) 727-0201

MICHIGAN
Vernice Anthony-Davis
Director
Dept. of Public Health
3500 N. Logan
P.O. Box 30035
Lansing, MI 48909
Phone : (517) 335-8024
Fax : (517) 335-9476

MINNESOTA
Ann Berry
Commissioner
Dept. of Health
717 Delaware St., SE
P.O. Box 9441
Minneapolis, MN 55440
Phone : (612) 623-5460

MISSISSIPPI
Ed Thompson
State Health Officer
Dept. of Health
2423 N. State St.
Jackson, MS 39216
Phone : (601) 960-7634

MISSOURI
Coleen Kivlahan
Director
Dept. of Health
1738 E. Elm
P.O. Box 570
Jefferson City, MO 65102
Phone : (314) 751-6001
Fax : (314) 751-6041

MONTANA
J. Dale Taliaferro
Administrator
Health Services Div.
Dept. of Health & Env. Science
Cogswell Bldg.
Helena, MT 59620
Phone : (406) 444-4473

NEBRASKA
Mark B. Horton
Director
Dept. of Health
P.O Box 95007
Lincoln, NE 68509
Phone : (402) 471-2133

NEVADA
Yvonne Sylva
Administrator
Health Div.
Dept. of Human Resources
505 E. King St., Rm. 201
Carson City, NV 89710
Phone : (702) 687-4740

NEW HAMPSHIRE
Charles Danielson
Director
Div. of Public Health Srvcs.
Dept. of Health & Human Srvcs.
115 Pleasant St., Annex Bldg.1
Concord, NH 03301
Phone : (603) 271-4505

NEW JERSEY
Len Fishman
Commissioner
Dept. of Health
John Fitch Plz., CN360
Trenton, NJ 08625
Phone : (609) 292-4010

NEW MEXICO
Alex Valdez
Secretary
Dept. of Health
1190 St. Francis Dr.
Santa Fe, NM 87502
Phone : (505) 827-2613
Fax : (505) 827-2530

NEW YORK*
Commissioner
Dept. of Health
Corning Tower
Empire State Plz.
Albany, NY 12237
Phone : (518) 474-2011

NORTH CAROLINA
Dale Simmons
Director
Adult Health Promotion
Dept. of Env., Health & Natural Resources
1330 St. Mary's St.
Raleigh, NC 27611-7687
Phone : (919) 715-3158
Fax : (919) 715-3144

NORTH DAKOTA
Jon R. Rice
State Health Officer
Dept. of Health
600 E. Boulevard Ave.
Bismarck, ND 58505
Phone : (701) 328-2372
Fax : (701) 328-4727

OHIO
Peter Somani
Director
Dept. of Health
246 N. High St.
P.O. Box 118
Columbus, OH 43266-0118
Phone : (614) 466-2253
Fax : (614) 644-0085

OKLAHOMA
Jerry Nida
Commissioner
Dept. of Health
1000 NE 10th
P.O. Box 53551
Oklahoma City, OK 73152
Phone : (405) 271-4200

OREGON
Elinor C. Hall
Administrator
Health Div.
Dept. of Human Resources
800 NE Oregon St., # 21
Portland, OR 97232
Phone : (503) 731-4000
Fax : (503) 731-4078

PENNSYLVANIA
Peter J. Jannetta
Secretary
Dept. of Health
Health & Welfare Bldg., Rm. 802
Harrisburg, PA 17120
Phone : (717) 787-6436

RHODE ISLAND
Patricia A. Nolan
Director
Dept. of Health
3 Capitol Hill
Providence, RI 02908
Phone : (401) 277-2231

SOUTH CAROLINA
Doug Bryant
Commissioner
Health & Environmental Control
2600 Bull St.
Columbia, SC 29201
Phone : (803) 734-4880

SOUTH DAKOTA
Barbara Smith
Secretary
Dept. of Health
445 E. Capitol Ave.
Pierre, SD 57501
Phone : (605) 773-3361

TENNESSEE
Fredia Wadley
Commissioner
Dept. of Health
Tennessee Towers, 9th Fl.
Nashville, TN 37247
Phone : (615) 741-3111
Fax : (615) 741-2491

TEXAS
David Smith
Commissioner
Dept. of Health
1100 W. 49th St.
Austin, TX 78756
Phone : (512) 458-7111

UTAH
Rod Betit
Director
Div. of Health Care Financing
Dept. of Health
288 N. 1460 W.
Salt Lake City, UT 84116
Phone : (801) 538-6111

Patrick Johnson
Director
Government & Community Relations
288 N. 1460 W.
P.O. Box 16700
Salt Lake City, UT 84116
Phone : (801) 538-6332

VERMONT
Jan Carney
Commissioner
Dept. of Health
108 Cherry St.
P.O. Box 70
Burlington, VT 05402
Phone : (802) 863-7280
Fax : (802) 863-7425

VIRGINIA
Donald R. Stern
Acting Commissioner
Department of Health
Main St. Station
1500 E. Main St., Rm. 214
Richmond, VA 23219
Phone : (804) 786-3561
Fax : (804) 786-4616

WASHINGTON
Bruce Miyahara
Secretary
Dept. of Health
P.O. Box 47800
Olympia, WA 98504-7800
Phone : (360) 586-5846

WEST VIRGINIA
Gretchen Lewis
Secretary
Dept. of Health & Human Resources
Bldg. 3, Rm. 206
State Capitol Complex
Charleston, WV 25305
Phone : (304) 558-0684

William T. Wallace
Commissioner
Bur. of Public Health
Bldg. 3, Rm. 519
1900 Kanawha Blvd., E.
Charleston, WV 23505
Phone : (304) 558-2971

WISCONSIN
Ann Haney
Administrator
Div. of Health
Dept. of Health & Soc. Srvcs.
1 W Wilson St.
Madison, WI 53702
Phone : (608) 266-1511
Fax : (608) 267-2832

WYOMING
Kenneth C. Kamis
Director
Dept. of Health
Hathaway Bldg.
Cheyenne, WY 82002
Phone : (307) 777-7656

DISTRICT OF COLUMBIA
Mohammad N. Akhter
Commissioner
Comm. of Public Health
Dept. of Human Services
1660 L St., NW, 12th Fl.
Washington, DC 20036
Phone : (202) 673-7700

AMERICAN SAMOA
Bob E. Parks
CEO
Dept. of Health
Pago Pago, AS 96799
Phone : (684) 633-1222
Fax : (684) 633-1869

GUAM
Dennis G. Rodriguez
Director
Dept. of Public Health & Social Services
P.O. Box 2816
Agana, GU 96910
Phone : (671) 734-7102
Fax : (671) 734-5910

NORTHERN MARIANA ISLANDS
Jose L. Chong
Director
Dept. of Public Health & Environmental Srvcs.
P.O. Box 409
Saipan, MP 96950
Phone : (670) 234-8950

PUERTO RICO
Carmen Feliciano
Secretary
Dept. of Health
P.O. Box 70184
San Juan, PR 00936-0184
Phone : (809) 766-1616
Fax : (809) 250-6547

U.S. VIRGIN ISLANDS
Natalie George-McDowell
Commissioner
Dept. of Health
48 Sugar Estate
St. Thomas Hospital
St. Thomas, VI 00802
Phone : (809) 776-8311
Fax : (809) 777-4001

HIGHER EDUCATION

Serves as coordinating and planning agency for state-supported postsecondary education.

ALASKA
Joe McCormick
Executive Director
Post Secondary Education Comm.
Dept. of Education
3030 Vintage Blvd.
Juneau, AK 99801-7109
Phone : (907) 465-6740
Fax : (907) 465-3293

ARIZONA
Edward Johnson
Executive Director
Comm. for Postsecondary Educ.
2020 N. Central Ave., Ste. 275
Phoenix, AZ 85004-4503
Phone : (602) 229-2590

ARKANSAS
Diane Suitt Gilleland
Director
Dept. of Higher Education
1220 W. 3rd St.
Little Rock, AR 72201
Phone : (501) 324-9300
Fax : (501) 324-9308

CALIFORNIA
Warren H. Fox
Executive Director
Postsecondary Education Comm.
1303 J St., Ste. 500
Sacramento, CA 95814-2932
Phone : (916) 445-1000

COLORADO
Dwayne Nuzum
Executive Director
Comm. on Higher Education
1300 Broadway, 2nd Fl.
Denver, CO 80203
Phone : (303) 866-2723
Fax : (303) 860-9750

CONNECTICUT
Andrew DeRocco
Commissioner
Bd. of Higher Education
61 Woodland St.
Hartford, CT 06105
Phone : (203) 566-5766

DELAWARE
John Corrozi
Executive Director
Budget Off.
DE Higher Education Comm.
820 N. French St., 4th Fl.
Wilmington, DE 19801
Phone : (302) 577-3240
Fax : (302) 577-3862

FLORIDA
Charles B. Reed
Chancellor
Bd. of Regents
Dept. of Education
1514 Florida Education Center
Tallahassee, FL 32399
Phone : (904) 488-4234

GEORGIA
Stephen R. Portch
Chancellor
Bd. of Regents
University System of Georgia
244 Washington St., SW
Atlanta, GA 30334
Phone : (404) 656-2202

HAWAII
Kenneth P. Mortimer
President
University of Hawaii
2444 Dole St.
Honolulu, HI 96822
Phone : (808) 956-8207
Fax : (808) 956-5286

IDAHO
Rayburn Barton
Executive Director
State Bd. of Education
650 W. State St., Rm. 307
Boise, ID 83720
Phone : (208) 334-2270

ILLINOIS
Richard D. Wagner
Executive Director
Board of Higher Education
4 W. Old Capitol Sq., Rm. 500
Springfield, IL 62701
Phone : (217) 782-2551

INDIANA
Clyde R. Ingle
Commissioner
Higher Education Comm.
101 W. Ohio St., # 550
Indianapolis, IN 46204-1909
Phone : (317) 464-4400

IOWA
Al Ramirez
Director
Dept. of Education
Grimes State Off. Bldg.
Des Moines, IA 50319
Phone : (515) 281-5294
Fax : (515) 242-5988

R. Wayne Richey
Executive Secretary
Bd. of Regents
Lucas State Off. Bldg.
Des Moines, IA 50319
Phone : (515) 281-3934

KANSAS
Stephen M. Jordan
Executive Director
Board of Regents
700 SW Harrison, Ste. 1410
Topeka, KS 66603-3760
Phone : (913) 296-3421
Fax : (913) 296-0983

KENTUCKY
Gary S. Cox
Executive Director
Council on Higher Education
1050 U.S. 127 S.
Frankfort, KY 40601
Phone : (502) 564-3553

LOUISIANA
Larry Crain
Commissioner
Board of Regents
150 Third St., Ste. 129
Baton Rouge, LA 70801-1389
Phone : (504) 342-4253

MAINE
Phillip A. Dionne
Chair
State Board of Education
Dept. of Education
State House Station # 23
Augusta, ME 04333
Phone : (207) 289-2321

MARYLAND*
Secretary
Higher Education Comm.
16 Francis St.
Annapolis, MD 21401
Phone : (410) 974-2971

MASSACHUSETTS
Piedad F. Robertson
Secretary
Executive Off. of Education
1 Ashburton Pl., Rm. 1401
Boston, MA 02108
Phone : (617) 727-1313

MICHIGAN
Ronald L. Root
Director
Higher Education Mgt. Srvcs.
Dept. of Education
P.O. Box 30008
Lansing, MI 48909
Phone : (517) 373-3820

MINNESOTA
David Powers
Executive Director
Higher Education Coordinating Bd.
550 Cedar St., Rm. 400
St. Paul, MN 55101
Phone : (612) 296-9665

MISSISSIPPI
Thomas D. Layzell
Commissioner
Institutions of Higher Learning
3825 Ridgewood Rd.
Jackson, MS 39211-6611
Phone : (601) 982-6611

MISSOURI
Charles J. McClain
Commissioner
Dept. of Higher Education
3515 Amazonas Dr.
Jefferson City, MO 65109
Phone : (314) 751-2361
Fax : (314) 751-6635

MONTANA
Jeff Baker
Commissioner
Higher Education
Montana University System
2500 Broadway
Helena, MT 59620-3101
Phone : (406) 444-6570

NEBRASKA
David R. Powers
Executive Director
Coordinating Comm. for Postsecondary Education
P.O. Box 95005
Lincoln, NE 68509-5005
Phone : (402) 471-2847
Fax : (402) 471-2886

NEVADA
Richard S. Jarvis
Chancellor
University & Community College System of Nevada
2601 Enterprise Rd.
Reno, NV 89512
Phone : (702) 784-4901

NEW HAMPSHIRE
James A. Busselle
Executive Director
Postsecondary Education Comm.
2 Industrial Park Dr.
Concord, NH 03301
Phone : (603) 271-2555

NEW JERSEY
Dr. Martine Hammond-Paludin
Executive Director
Comm. on Higher Education
20 W. State St., CN 542
Trenton, NJ 08625
Phone : (609) 292-4310

NEW MEXICO
Bruce Hamlet
Director
Comm. on Higher Education
1068 Cerrillos Rd.
Santa Fe, NM 87501
Phone : (505) 827-7383
Fax : (505) 827-7392

NEW YORK*
Commissioner
Dept. of Education
Education Bldg.
Albany, NY 12234
Phone : (518) 474-5844

NORTH CAROLINA
C.D. Spangler Jr.
President
General Administration
University of North Carolina
P.O. Box 2688
Chapel Hill, NC 27515-2688
Phone : (919) 962-1000

NORTH DAKOTA
Douglas Treadway
Chancellor
ND University System
State Capitol, 10th Fl.
600 E. Boulevard Ave.
Bismarck, ND 58505-0230
Phone : (701) 328-2960
Fax : (701) 328-2961

OHIO
Elaine Hairston
Chancellor
Bd. of Regents
30 E. Broad St., 36th Fl.
Columbus, OH 43266-0417
Phone : (614) 466-0887
Fax : (614) 466-5866

OKLAHOMA
Hans Brisch
Chancellor
State Regents for Higher Education
2500 N. Lincoln, Rm. 500
Oklahoma City, OK 73105
Phone : (405) 521-2444

OREGON
Joseph W. Cox
Chancellor
Bd. of Higher Education
P.O. Box 3175
Eugene, OR 97403
Phone : (503) 346-5700
Fax : (503) 346-5764

PENNSYLVANIA*
Commissioner for Higher Educ.
Dept. of Education
333 Market St.
Harrisburg, PA 17120
Phone : (717) 787-5041

RHODE ISLAND
Americo Petrocelli
Commissioner
Off. of Higher Education
Dept. of Education
199 Promenade St.
Providence, RI 02903
Phone : (401) 277-6560

SOUTH CAROLINA
Fred R. Sheheen
Commissioner
Comm. on Higher Education
1333 Main St., Ste. 300
Columbia, SC 29201
Phone : (803) 253-6260

SOUTH DAKOTA
Tad Perry
Executive Director
Board of Regents
213 E. Capitol Ave.
Pierre, SD 57501
Phone : (605) 773-3455

TENNESSEE
Arliss Roaden
Executive Director
Higher Education Comm.
Parkway Towers, Ste. 1900
404 James Robertson Pkwy.
Nashville, TN 37243
Phone : (615) 741-3605

TEXAS
Kenneth H. Ashworth
Commissioner
Higher Edcuation Coord. Board
P.O. Box 12788, Capitol Station
Austin, TX 78711
Phone : (512) 483-6169

UTAH
Cecelia Foxley
Commissioner
Bd. of Regents
3 Triad Ctr., Ste. 550
Salt Lake City, UT 84180-1205
Phone : (801) 321-7103

VERMONT
Charles Banting
Chancellor's Office
State Colleges of VT
103 South Main St.
Waterbury, VT 05676
Phone : (802) 241-2520
Fax : (802) 241-3369

VIRGINIA
Gordon K. Davies
Director
Council of Higher Education
101 N. 14th St., 9th Fl.
Richmond, VA 23219
Phone : (804) 225-2600

WASHINGTON
Elson S. Floyd
Executive Director
Higher Educ. Coordinating Bd.
P.O. Box 43430
Olympia, WA 98504-3430
Phone : (360) 753-2210

WEST VIRGINIA
Clifford M. Trump
Chancellor
State College System
Dept. of Education
1018 Kanawha Blvd., E.
Charleston, WV 25301
Phone : (304) 558-0699

Barbara Harmon-Schamberger
Secretary
Dept. of Education & the Arts
Bldg. 1, Rm. 151
1900 Kanawha Blvd., E.
Charleston, WV 25305
Phone : (304) 558-2440

Charles Manning
University System Chancellor
Bd. of Trustees for Higher Ed.
Dept. of Education & the Arts
1018 Kanawha Blvd., E.
Charleston, WV 25301
Phone : (304) 558-0264

WISCONSIN
Katherine Lyall
President
Univ. of Wisc. System
1220 Linden Dr.
Madison, WI 53706
Phone : (608) 262-2321
Fax : (608) 267-5739

WYOMING
Clay Fechter
Executive Director
Community College
Herschler Bldg.
122 W. 25th St.
Cheyenne, WY 82002
Phone : (307) 777-7763

DISTRICT OF COLUMBIA
A. Knighton Stanley
Chairman
Bd. of Trustees
University of DC
4200 Connecticut Ave., NW
Washington, DC 20008
Phone : (202) 282-2070

Tilden J. Lemelle
President
University of DC
4200 Connecticut Ave., NW
Washington, DC 20008
Phone : (202) 727-2600

AMERICAN SAMOA
Tusi Avegalio
President
Bd. of Higher Education
American Samoa Community College
Pago Pago, AS 96799
Phone : (684) 699-9155
Fax : (684) 699-2062

GUAM
John C. Salas
President
University of Guam
UOG Station
Mangilao, GU 96923
Phone : (671) 734-9435
Fax : (671) 734-2296

NORTHERN MARIANA ISLANDS
Agnes McPhetres
President
Northern Marianas College
P.O. Box 1250
Saipan, MP 96950
Phone : (670) 234-6932

PUERTO RICO
Norman I. Maldonado
President
University of Puerto Rico
P.O. Box 364984
San Juan, PR 00936-4984
Phone : (809) 250-0000
Fax : (809) 759-6917

U.S. VIRGIN ISLANDS
Patrick N. Williams
Chairman
Board of Education
P.O. Box 11900
St. Thomas, VI 00802
Phone : (809) 774-4546

HIGHWAY SAFETY

Develops and administers a statewide traffic safety program.

ALABAMA
Jim Quinn
Chief
Highway Traffic Safety Section
Dept. of Econ. & Comm. Affairs
401 Adams Ave.
Montgomery, AL 36130-5690
Phone : (334) 242-5811
Fax : (334) 242-0712

ALASKA
Loren M. Campbell
Program Director
Highway Safety Planning Agency
Dept. of Public Safety
P.O. Box 111200
Juneau, AK 99811-1200
Phone : (907) 465-4371
Fax : (907) 463-5860

ARIZONA
Albert Gutier
Administrator
Governor's Office of Highway Safety
3010 N. Second St., Ste. 105
Phoenix, AZ 85012
Phone : (602) 255-3216

S. Duane Richens
Administrator
Governor's Off. of Highway Safety
Dept. of Public Safety
3010 N. Second St., Ste. 101
Phoenix, AZ 85012
Phone : (602) 255-3216

ARKANSAS
Dan Flowers
Director
Dept. of Highways & Transportation
P.O. Box 2261
Little Rock, AR 72203
Phone : (501) 569-2211
Fax : (501) 569-2400

CALIFORNIA
Martha Glass
Chief
Div. of Highways
Dept. of Transportation
1120 N. St., Rm. 440
Sacramento, CA 95814
Phone : (916) 654-6228

COLORADO
John Conger
Director
Off. of Transportation Safety
Dept. of Transportation
4201 E. Arkansas Ave.
Denver, CO 80222
Phone : (303) 757-9381

CONNECTICUT
Norman C. Booth
Information Systems
Dept. of Transportation
2710 Berlin Turnpike
Newington, CT 06131-7546
Phone : (203) 667-7855

DELAWARE
Trisha Roberts
Director
Off. of Highway Safety
R.R. 113 & Bay Rd.
Dover, DE 19901
Phone : (302) 739-4475
Fax : (302) 739-5995

FLORIDA
Fred O. Dickinson III
Executive Director
Dept. of Highway Safety & Motor Vehicles
Neil Kirkman Bldg.
2900 Apalachee Parkway
Tallahassee, FL 32399-0500
Phone : (904) 487-3132

GEORGIA
Thomas L. Coleman
Director
Governor's Off. of Highway Safety
100 Peachtree St., Ste. 2000
Atlanta, GA 30303
Phone : (404) 656-6996

HAWAII
Lawrence K. Hao
Administrator
Motor Vehicle Safety Off.
Dept. of Transportation
1505 Dillingham Blvd., Rm. 214
Honolulu, HI 96813
Phone : (808) 838-5820
Fax : (808) 832-5830

IDAHO
Marie Bishop
Manager
Highway Safety
Dept. of Transportation
P.O. Box 7129
Boise, ID 83707
Phone : (208) 334-8101

ILLINOIS
Gary D. March
Director
Div. of Traffic Safety
Dept. of Transportation
3215 Executive Pk. Dr.
Springfield, IL 62794
Phone : (217) 782-4972

INDIANA
Calvin Lee
Safety Manager
Operations Support Div.
Dept. of Transportation
100 N. Senate
Indianapolis, IN 46204
Phone : (317) 232-5191

IOWA
J. Michael Laski
Director
Governor's Traffic Safety Bur.
Dept. of Public Safety
Wallace State Off. Bldg.
Des Moines, IA 50319
Phone : (515) 281-8400

KANSAS
Rosalie Thornburgh
Administrator
Division of Traffic Safety
217 SE 4th, 2nd Fl.
Topeka, KS 66603
Phone : (913) 296-3756
Fax : (913) 291-3010

KENTUCKY
Jerry Lovitt
Commissioner
Dept. of State Police
Justice Cabinet
919 Versailles Rd.
Frankfort, KY 40601
Phone : (502) 695-6300

LOUISIANA
Bette Theis
Executive Director
Highway Safety Comm.
Dept. of Public Safety & Corr.
P.O. Box 66614
Baton Rouge, LA 70896
Phone : (504) 925-6991

MAINE
Richard E. Perkins
Director
Bur. of Safety
Dept. of Public Safety
36 Hospital St., Station # 42
Augusta, ME 04333
Phone : (207) 624-8756

MARYLAND
Robert L. Thomas
Chief
Field Operations Bur.
State Police
1201 Reisterstown Rd.
Baltimore, MD 21208
Phone : (410) 764-4324

MASSACHUSETTS
Jerold A. Gnazzo
Registrar
Registry of Motor Vehicles
1135 Tremont St.
Boston, MA 02120
Phone : (617) 351-2700
Fax : (617) 351-9971

MICHIGAN
Betty J. Mercer
Executive Director
Off. of Highway Safety Planning
Dept. of State Police
300 S. Washington Sq., Ste. 300
Lansing, MI 48913
Phone : (517) 373-6287

MINNESOTA
Eugene E. Ofstead
Assistant Commissioner
Technical Srvcs. Div.
Dept. of Transportation
Transportation Bldg., 4th Fl.
St. Paul, MN 55155
Phone : (612) 296-1344

MISSISSIPPI
Herbert Terry
Interim Director
Div. of Public Safety Planning
301 W. Pearl
Jackson, MS 39203
Phone : (601) 949-2228

MISSOURI
Dan Needham
Director
Div. of Highway Safety
Dept. of Public Safety
1719 Southridge Dr., Box 104808
Jefferson City, MO 65110
Phone : (314) 751-4161
Fax : (314) 634-5977

MONTANA
Albert E. Goke
Administrator
Highway Traffic Safety Div.
Dept. of Justice
310 E. Lockey
Helena, MT 59620
Phone : (406) 444-3412

NEBRASKA
Fred Zwonechek
Administrator
Off. of Highway Safety
Dept. of Motor Vehicles
P.O. Box 94612
Lincoln, NE 68509
Phone : (402) 471-2515

NEVADA
James Weller
Director
Dept. of Motor Vehicles & Public Safety
555 Wright Way
Carson City, NV 89711
Phone : (702) 687-5375
Fax : (702) 687-6798

NEW HAMPSHIRE
Peter Thomson
Coordinator
Highway Safety Agency
Dept. of Safety
117 Manchester St.
Concord, NH 03301
Phone : (603) 271-2131

NEW JERSEY
James S. Arena
Director
Div. of Highway Traffic Safety
Dept. of Law & Public Safety
Quakerbridge Plz., CN048
Trenton, NJ 08625
Phone : (609) 588-3750

NEW MEXICO
Darren White
Secretary
Dept. of Public Safety
State Police Complex
Albuquerque Hwy.
P.O. Box 1628
Santa Fe, NM 87504
Phone : (505) 827-3370
Fax : (505) 827-3434

NEW YORK*
Commissioner
Dept. of Transportation
Campus, Bldg. 5
Albany, NY 12232
Phone : (518) 457-4422

Commissioner
Dept. of Motor Vehicles
Empire State Plz.
Albany, NY 12228
Phone : (518) 474-0841

NORTH CAROLINA
Joe M. Parker
Director
Governor's Highway Safety Program
Dept. of Transportation
One S. Wilmington St.
Raleigh, NC 27611-5201
Phone : (919) 733-3083
Fax : (919) 733-0604

NORTH DAKOTA
Mylo Mehlhoff
Director
Driver's License Div.
Dept. of Highways
608 E. Boulevard Ave.
Bismarck, ND 58505-0700
Phone : (701) 328-2601
Fax : (701) 328-2435

OHIO
Charles Shipley
Director
Department of Public Safety
240 Parsons Ave.
P.O. Box 7167
Columbus, OH 43266
Phone : (614) 466-3383
Fax : (614) 466-0433

OKLAHOMA
Jack Crowley
Director
Dept. of Transportation
200 NE 21st St.
Oklahoma City, OK 73105
Phone : (405) 521-2631

OREGON
Ed Marges
Administrator
Transportation Safety
Dept. of Transportation
400 State Library Bldg.
Salem, OR 97310
Phone : (503) 378-3669
Fax : (503) 378-8445

PENNSYLVANIA
Betty Serian
Deputy Secretary
Safety Administration
Dept. of Transportation
1200 Trans. & Safety Bldg.
Harrisburg, PA 17120
Phone : (717) 787-3928

RHODE ISLAND
Edward Walsh
Coordinator
Div. of Highway Safety
Dept. of Transportation
345 Harris Ave.
Providence, RI 02909
Phone : (401) 277-3024

SOUTH CAROLINA
Burke Fitzpatrick
Administrator
Off. of Safety Grant Srvcs.
Dept. of Public Safety
5410 Broad River Rd.
Columbia, SC 29210
Phone : (803) 896-7844

SOUTH DAKOTA
David Volk
Secretary
Dept. of Commerce & Regulations
910 E. Sioux Ave.
Pierre, SD 57501
Phone : (605) 773-3178

TENNESSEE
Mike Greene
Commissioner
Dept. of Safety
1150 Foster Ave.
Nashville, TN 37249
Phone : (615) 251-5166
Fax : (615) 251-5159

TEXAS
Gary Trietsch
Director
Traffic Operations Division
Dept. of Transportation
11th & Brazos St.
Austin, TX 78701
Phone : (512) 416-3200

UTAH
K. Craig Allred
Director
Div. of Highway Safety
Dept. of Public Safety
4501 S. 2700 W., 2nd Fl.
Salt Lake City, UT 84119
Phone : (801) 255-0573

VERMONT
Jeanne Johnson
Coordinator
Governor's Highway Safety Program
Agency of Transportation
133 State St.
Montpelier, VT 05633
Phone : (802) 828-2163
Fax : (802) 828-2098

VIRGINIA
William H. Leighty
Deputy Commissioner
Transportation Safety
Dept. of Motor Vehicles
P.O. Box 27412
Richmond, VA 23269
Phone : (804) 367-6614

WASHINGTON
John Moffat
Director
Traffic Safety Comm.
1000 S. Cherry St.
P.O. Box 40944
Olympia, WA 98504
Phone : (360) 753-6197

WEST VIRGINIA
William Wilshire
Division Director
Traffic Engineering
Div. of Highways
Charleston, WV 25305
Phone : (304) 558-3722

WISCONSIN
David Manning
Director
Off. of Transportation Safety
Dept. of Transportation
P.O. Box 7916
Madison, WI 53707
Phone : (608) 266-0402
Fax : (608) 267-0441

WYOMING
Don Diller
Director
Highway Safety Div.
Dept. of Transportation
5300 Bishop Blvd.
Cheyenne, WY 82002
Phone : (307) 777-4198

DISTRICT OF COLUMBIA
Larry King
Director
Dept. of Public Works
2000 14th St., NW
Washington, DC 20009
Phone : (202) 939-8000

AMERICAN SAMOA
Fonoti D. Jessop
Commissioner
Dept. of Public Safety
American Samoa Government
Pago Pago, AS 96799
Phone : (684) 633-1111
Fax : (684) 633-5111

GUAM
Gil A. Shinohara
Acting Director
Dept. of Public Works
P.O. Box 2950
Agana, GU 96910
Phone : (671) 646-3101
Fax : (671) 649-6178

NORTHERN MARIANA ISLANDS
Claudio K. Norita
Director
Highway Safety
Dept. of Public Safety
Off. of the Governor
Saipan, MP 96950
Phone : (670) 234-6021
Fax : (670) 234-8531

PUERTO RICO
Miguel Santini Padilla
Executive Director
Traffic Safety Comm.
P.O. Box 41289, Minillas Sta.
Santurce, PR 00940
Phone : (809) 721-4142
Fax : (809) 727-0486

U.S. VIRGIN ISLANDS
Ramon Davila
Commissioner
Police Dept.
Nisky Ctr., #6
St. Thomas, VI 00802
Phone : (809) 774-6400
Fax : (809) 774-4057

HIGHWAYS

Responsible for planning, developing, designing, constructing and maintaining the state's highways.

ALABAMA
Jimmy Butts
Director
Highway Dept.
1409 Coliseum Blvd.
Montgomery, AL 36130
Phone : (334) 242-6311
Fax : (334) 262-8041

ARIZONA
Larry S. Bonine
Director
Dept. of Transportation
206 S. 17th Ave., Rm. 100A
Phoenix, AZ 85007
Phone : (602) 255-7011

ARKANSAS
Dan Flowers
Director
Dept. of Highways & Transportation
P.O. Box 2261
Little Rock, AR 72203
Phone : (501) 569-2211
Fax : (501) 569-2400

CALIFORNIA
Martha Glass
Chief
Div. of Highways
Dept. of Transportation
1120 N. St., Rm. 440
Sacramento, CA 95814
Phone : (916) 654-6228

COLORADO
Guillermo Vidal
Executive Director
Dept. of Transportation
4201 E. Arkansas Ave., Rm. 262
Denver, CO 80222
Phone : (303) 757-9011
Fax : (303) 757-9656

CONNECTICUT
Harry P. Harris
Deputy Commissioner
Engineering & Highway Operations
Dept. of Transportation
2800 Berlin Turnpike
P.O. Box 317546
Newington, CT 06131-7546
Phone : (203) 594-3000

DELAWARE
James Lutrzykowski
Director
Div. of Highway Operations
Dept. of Transportation
P.O. Box 778
Dover, DE 19903
Phone : (302) 739-4301
Fax : (302) 739-4329

FLORIDA
Ben Watts
Secretary
Dept. of Transportation
605 Suwannee St., MS 57
Tallahassee, FL 32399-0450
Phone : (904) 488-6721
Fax : (904) 488-5526

GEORGIA
Wayne Shackelford
Commissioner
Dept. of Transportation
2 Capitol Sq.
Atlanta, GA 30334
Phone : (404) 656-5206

HAWAII
Tetsuo Harano
Administrator
Highways Div.
Dept. of Transportation
869 Punchbowl St.
Honolulu, HI 96813
Phone : (808) 587-2220

IDAHO
Dwight Bower
Director
Dept. of Transportation
P.O. Box 7129
Boise, ID 83707
Phone : (208) 334-8800

ILLINOIS
Ralph C. Wehner
Director
Div. of Highways
Dept. of Transportation
2300 S. Dirksen Pkwy., Rm. 300
Springfield, IL 62764
Phone : (217) 782-2151

INDIANA
Stanley C. Smith
Commissioner
Dept. of Transportation
IGC-North, Rm. N755
Indianapolis, IN 46204
Phone : (317) 232-5525

IOWA
Tom Cackler
Director
Highway Div.
Dept. of Transportation
800 Lincoln Way
Ames, IA 50010
Phone : (515) 239-1124

KANSAS
Dean Carlson
Secretary
Dept. of Transportation
Docking State Off. Bldg.
915 Harrison, 7th Fl.
Topeka, KS 66612-1568
Phone : (913) 296-3566
Fax : (913) 296-1095

KENTUCKY
James Yowell
State Highway Engineer
Transportation Cabinet
State Off. Bldg.
Frankfort, KY 40601
Phone : (502) 564-3730

LOUISIANA
Jude W.P. Patin
Secretary
Public Transportation Section
Dept. of Transportation & Development
P.O. Box 94245
Baton Rouge, LA 70804
Phone : (504) 379-1100

MAINE
John Melrose
Commissioner
Dept. of Transportation
State House Station # 16
Augusta, ME 04333
Phone : (207) 287-2551

MARYLAND
Hal Kassoff
Administrator
Highway Admin.
Dept. of Transportation
707 N. Calvert St.
Baltimore, MD 21202
Phone : (301) 333-1111

MASSACHUSETTS
Laurinda T. Bedingfield
Commissioner
Highway Dept.
10 Park Plz., Rm. 3170
Boston, MA 02116
Phone : (617) 973-7830

MICHIGAN
Patrick Nowak
Director
Dept. of Transportation
P.O. Box 30050
Lansing, MI 48909
Phone : (517) 373-2114
Fax : (517) 373-6457

MINNESOTA
Patrick C. Hughes
Assistant Commissioner
Operations Div.
Dept. of Transportation
Transportation Bldg., 4th Fl.
St. Paul, MN 55155
Phone : (612) 296-3008

MISSISSIPPI
Bob Robinson
Director
Department of Transportation
P.O. Box 1850
Jackson, MS 39215-1850
Phone : (601) 359-1209

MISSOURI
Joe Mickes
Chief Engineer
Dept. of Highways & Transportation
Highway Bldg.
P.O. Box 270
Jefferson City, MO 65102
Phone : (314) 751-4622
Fax : (314) 526-5419

MONTANA
Marvin Dye
Director
Dept. of Transportation
2701 Prospect Ave.
Helena, MT 59620
Phone : (406) 444-6201

NEBRASKA
Allan L. Abbott
Director
Dept. of Roads
P.O. Box 94759
Lincoln, NE 68509-4759
Phone : (402) 479-4615

NEVADA
Tom Stephens
Director
Dept. of Transportation
1263 S. Stewart St.
Carson City, NV 89712
Phone : (702) 687-5440

NEW HAMPSHIRE
Charles P. O'Leary Jr.
Commissioner
Dept. of Transportation
John O. Moeton Bldg.
P.O. Box 483
Concord, NH 03302
Phone : (603) 271-3734

NEW JERSEY
Frank Wilson
Commissioner
Dept. of Transportation
1035 Parkway Ave., CN601
Trenton, NJ 08625
Phone : (609) 530-3535

NEW MEXICO
Pete Rahn
Secretary
Dept. of Highways & Transportation
1120 Cerrillos Rd.
Santa Fe, NM 87504-1149
Phone : (505) 827-5110
Fax : (505) 827-5469

NEW YORK*
Commissioner
Dept. of Transportation
Campus, Bldg. 5
Albany, NY 12232
Phone : (518) 457-4422

NORTH CAROLINA
William G. Marley Jr.
Highway Administrator
Div. of Highways
Dept. of Transportation
One S. Wilmington St.
Raleigh, NC 27601-1494
Phone : (919) 733-7384
Fax : (919) 733-9428

NORTH DAKOTA
Marshall W. Moore
Director
Dept. of Transportation
608 E. Boulevard Ave.
Bismarck, ND 58505-0700
Phone : (701) 328-2581
Fax : (701) 328-4545

OHIO
Jerry Wray
Director
Dept. of Transportation
25 S. Front St., 7th Fl.
Columbus, OH 43215
Phone : (614) 466-2335
Fax : (614) 644-0587

OKLAHOMA
Jack Crowley
Director
Dept. of Transportation
200 NE 21st St.
Oklahoma City, OK 73105
Phone : (405) 521-2631

OREGON
Don Forbes
Director
Dept. of Transportation
135 Transportation Bldg.
Salem, OR 97310
Phone : (503) 986-3200
Fax : (503) 986-3446

PENNSYLVANIA
Mike M. Ryan
Deputy Secretary
Highway Administration
Dept. of Transportation
1200 Trans. & Safety Bldg.
Harrisburg, PA 17120
Phone : (717) 787-5574

RHODE ISLAND
William Bundy
Director
Dept. of Transportation
210 State Off. Bldg.
Providence, RI 02903
Phone : (401) 277-2481

SOUTH CAROLINA
Buck Limehouse
Director
Dept. of Transportation
955 Park St.
P.O. Box 191
Columbia, SC 29202
Phone : (803) 737-1300

SOUTH DAKOTA
Larry Weiss
Chief Engineer & Director
Div. of Engineering
Dept. of Transportation
700 E. Broadway
Pierre, SD 57501-2586
Phone : (605) 773-3267

TENNESSEE
Bruce Saltsman
Commissioner
Dept. of Transportation
James K. Polk Bldg., Ste. 700
Nashville, TN 37243
Phone : (615) 741-2848
Fax : (615) 741-2508

TEXAS
William G. Burnett
Executive Director
Dept. of Transportation
11th & Brazos St.
Austin, TX 78701
Phone : (512) 463-8616

UTAH
Craig Zwick
Director
Dept. of Transportation
4501 S. 2700 W.
Salt Lake City, UT 84119
Phone : (801) 965-4113

VERMONT
Patrick Garahan
Secretary
Agency of Transportation
133 State St.
Montpelier, VT 05602
Phone : (802) 828-2657
Fax : (802) 828-3522

VIRGINIA
David R. Gehr
Commissioner
Dept. of Transportation
1401 E. Broad St.
Richmond, VA 23219
Phone : (804) 786-2701
Fax : (804) 786-2940

WASHINGTON
Sid Morrison
Secretary
Dept. of Transportation
P.O. Box 47400
Olympia, WA 98504-7400
Phone : (360) 705-7000

WEST VIRGINIA
Charles Miller
Secretary
Dept. of Transportation
Bldg. 5, Rm. A109
1900 Kanawha Blvd., E.
Charleston, WV 25302
Phone : (304) 558-0444

WISCONSIN
Frederic Ross
Administrator
Div. of Hwys. & Trans. Service
Dept. of Transportation
4802 Sheboygan Ave., Room 951
P.O. Box 7916
Madison, WI 53705
Phone : (608) 266-2910
Fax : (608) 266-7818

WYOMING
Don Diller
Director
Dept. of Transportation
5300 Bishop Blvd.
Cheyenne, WY 82002
Phone : (307) 777-4484

DISTRICT OF COLUMBIA
Gary Burch
Administrator
Design, Engineering & Construction Admin.
2000 14th St., NW
Washington, DC 20009
Phone : (202) 939-8060

AMERICAN SAMOA
Sam Puletasi
Director
Dept. of Public Works
Pago Pago, AS 96799
Phone : (684) 633-4141
Fax : (684) 633-5958

GUAM
Gil A. Shinohara
Acting Director
Dept. of Public Works
P.O. Box 2950
Agana, GU 96910
Phone : (671) 646-3101
Fax : (671) 649-6178

NORTHERN MARIANA ISLANDS
Edward M. Deleon Guerrero
Director
Dept. of Public Works
Lower Base
P.O. Box 2950
Saipan, MP 96950
Phone : (670) 322-9482
Fax : (670) 322-3547

PUERTO RICO
Sergio Gonzales Guevedo
Secretary
Highways Authority & Transportation
P.O. Box 42007
San Juan, PR 00940-2007
Phone : (809) 721-8787
Fax : (809) 727-5456

U.S. VIRGIN ISLANDS
Aloy Nielsen
Director
Highway Engineering
Dept. of Public Works
Sub Base # 8
St. Thomas, VI 00802
Phone : (809) 776-4844

HISTORIC PRESERVATION

Surveys, restores and preserves structure and/or sites of historical or architectural significance in the state.

ALABAMA
Lawrence Oaks
Executive Director
Historical Comm.
468 S. Perry St.
Montgomery, AL 36130
Phone : (334) 242-3184
Fax : (334) 240-3477

ALASKA
Judy Bittner
Alaska Historical Comm.
Dept. of Natural Resources
3601 C St., Ste. 1278
Anchorage, AK 99503-5921
Phone : (907) 762-2626
Fax : (907) 762-2622

ARIZONA
James W. Garrison
State Historic Preservation Officer
Historic Preservation Div.
State Parks Board
800 W. Washington, Ste. 415
Phoenix, AZ 85007
Phone : (602) 542-4174

ARKANSAS
Cathy Slater
Director
Historic Preservation
1500 Tower Bldg.
323 Center St.
Little Rock, AR 72201
Phone : (501) 324-9150
Fax : (501) 324-9184

CALIFORNIA
Cherilyn Widell
Historic Preservation Officer
State Historic Preservation
Dept. of Parks & Recreation
P.O. Box 942896
Sacramento, CA 94296
Phone : (916) 653-6624

COLORADO
James E. Hartman
President
Historical Society
Dept. of Higher Education
1300 Broadway, 3rd Fl.
Denver, CO 80203
Phone : (303) 866-3682
Fax : (303) 866-5739

CONNECTICUT
John W. Shannahan
Director
Historical Comm.
59 S. Prospect St.
Hartford, CT 06106
Phone : (203) 566-3005

DELAWARE
Daniel R. Griffith
Director
Historical & Cultural Affairs
Hall of Records
P.O. Box 1401
Dover, DE 19903
Phone : (302) 739-5313
Fax : (302) 739-5660

FLORIDA
George Percy
Director
Div. of Historical Resources
Dept. of State
R.A. Gray Bldg.
Tallahassee, FL 32399-0250
Phone : (904) 488-1480

GEORGIA
Elizabeth Lyon
Chief
Historic Preservation Section
Dept. of Natural Resources
205 Butler St., Ste. 1462
Atlanta, GA 30334
Phone : (404) 656-2840

HAWAII
Michael Wilson
Chairman
Dept. of Land & Natural Resources
1151 Punchbowl St.
Honolulu, HI 96813
Phone : (808) 586-0400
Fax : (808) 587-0390

IDAHO
John Hill
Director
Historical Society
State Bd. of Education
210 Main St.
Boise, ID 83702
Phone : (208) 334-2682

ILLINOIS
Susan Mogerman
Director
Historic Preservation Agency
313 S. Sixth St.
Springfield, IL 62701
Phone : (217) 785-7930
Fax : (217) 785-7937

INDIANA
James A. Glass
Director
Historic Preservation Div.
Dept. of Natural Resources
402 W. Washington St., Rm. 274
Indianapolis, IN 46204
Phone : (317) 232-1646

IOWA*
Administrator
State Historical Society
Dept. of Cultural Affairs
Historical Bldg.
Des Moines, IA 50319
Phone : (515) 281-8837

KANSAS
Ramon Powers
Executive Director
Kansas Historical Society
120 W. 10th St.
Topeka, KS 66612-1291
Phone : (913) 296-3251
Fax : (913) 296-1005

KENTUCKY
Jim Klotter
Director
Historical Society
Old Capitol Annex
P.O. Box H
Frankfort, KY 40601
Phone : (502) 564-3016

LOUISIANA
Gerri Hobdy
Assistant Secretary
Off. of Culture, Recreation & Tourism
P.O. Box 44247
Baton Rouge, LA 70804
Phone : (504) 342-8115

MAINE
Earle Shettleworth Jr.
Executive Director
Historic Preservation Comm.
State House Station # 65
Augusta, ME 04333
Phone : (207) 287-2132

MARYLAND
J. Rodney Little
Director
Historical & Cultural Programs
Dept. of Housing & Comm. Dev.
100 Community Pl.
Crownsville, MD 21032
Phone : (410) 514-7601

MASSACHUSETTS
Judith B. McDonough
Executive Director
Historical Comm.
Archives Bldg.
220 Morrissey Blvd.
Boston, MA 02125
Phone : (617) 727-8470
Fax : (617) 727-5128

MICHIGAN
Sandra Clark
Director
Bur. of History
Dept. of State
717 W. Allegan
Lansing, MI 48918
Phone : (517) 373-6362

MINNESOTA
Chuck Lawrence
Assistant Director
Historical Society
345 Kellogg Blvd., W.
St. Paul, MN 55102-1903
Phone : (612) 296-2747

MISSISSIPPI
Elbert R. Hilliard
Director
Dept. of Archives & History
P.O. Box 571
Jackson, MS 39205-0571

MISSOURI
Claire F. Blackwell
Director
Historic Preservation Program
Dept. of Natural Resources
Jefferson Bldg., 10th Fl.
P.O. Box 176
Jefferson City, MO 65102
Phone : (314) 751-7858
Fax : (314) 526-2852

MONTANA
Marcella Sherty
Administrative Officer
Historic Preservation Program
Historical Society
225 N. Roberts
Helena, MT 59620
Phone : (406) 444-7715

NEBRASKA
Lawrence J. Sommer
Director
State Historial Society
P.O. Box 82554
Lincoln, NE 68501
Phone : (402) 471-4745

NEVADA
Ronald M. James
State Historic Preservation Officer
Hist. Pres. & Archaeology Div.
Dept. of Cons. & Nat. Res.
123 W. Nye Lane, Rm. 208
Carson City, NV 89710
Phone : (702) 687-5138

NEW HAMPSHIRE
Van McLeod
Commissioner
State Library
Dept. of Cultural Affairs
20 Park St.
Concord, NH 03301
Phone : (603) 271-2540

NEW JERSEY
James F. Hall
Assistant Commissioner
Natural & Historic Resources
Dept. of Environmental Protection
501 E. State St., CN402
Trenton, NJ 08625
Phone : (609) 292-3541

NEW MEXICO
Michael Romero Taylor
Historic Preservation Officer
Div. of Cultural Affairs
228 E. Palace Ave.
P.O. Box 2087
Santa Fe, NM 87501
Phone : (505) 827-8320
Fax : (505) 827-6338

NEW YORK*
Acting Commissioner
Off. of Parks, Recreation & Historic Preservation
Empire St. Plz., Agcy. Bldg. 1
Albany, NY 12238
Phone : (518) 474-0443

NORTH CAROLINA
David Brook
Administrator
Archaeology & Historic Pres.
Dept. of Cultural Resources
507 N. Blount St.
Raleigh, NC 27604-1190
Phone : (919) 733-4763
Fax : (919) 733-8653

NORTH DAKOTA
Louis Hafermehl
Director
Archaeology & Historical Preservation Div.
612 E. Boulevard Ave.
Bismarck, ND 58505
Phone : (701) 328-2666
Fax : (701) 328-3710

OHIO
Gary C. Ness
Director
Historical Society
1982 Velma Ave.
Columbus, OH 43211
Phone : (614) 297-2300
Fax : (614) 297-2352

OKLAHOMA
J. Blake Wade
Director
Historical Society
Historical Bldg.
2100 N. Lincoln Blvd.
Oklahoma City, OK 73105
Phone : (405) 521-2491

OREGON
Chet Orloff
Executive Director
Historical Society
1230 SW Park Ave.
Portland, OR 97205
Phone : (503) 222-1741

PENNSYLVANIA
Brenda Barrett
Director
Bur. of Historic Preservation
Historical & Museum Comm.
P.O. Box 1026
Harrisburg, PA 17108
Phone : (717) 783-5321

RHODE ISLAND
Edward F. Sanderson
Executive Director
Historical Preservation & Heritage Comm.
150 Benefit St.
Providence, RI 02903
Phone : (401) 277-2678

SOUTH CAROLINA
Mary Edmonds
Deputy State Preservation Off.
Dept. of Archives & History
P.O. Box 11669
Columbia, SC 29211
Phone : (803) 734-8593

SOUTH DAKOTA
Mary B. Edelen
Director
State Historical Society
Cultural Heritage Ctr.
900 Governors Dr.
Pierre, SD 57501
Phone : (605) 773-3458

TENNESSEE
Herbert Harper
Executive Director
Historical Comm.
Dept. of Environment & Conservation
701 Broadway
Nashville, TN 37243
Phone : (615) 532-1554

TEXAS
Curtis Tunnell
Executive Director
Historical Comm.
P.O. Box 12276
Austin, TX 78711
Phone : (512) 463-6100

UTAH
Max Evans
Director
Div. of State History
Dept. of Community & Economic Dev.
300 Rio Grande
Salt Lake City, UT 84101
Phone : (801) 533-3551

VERMONT
Eric Gilbertson
Director
Div. for Historic Preservation
Agcy. of Dev. & Community Aff.
109 State St.
Montpelier, VT 05609
Phone : (802) 828-3226
Fax : (802) 828-3206

VIRGINIA
H. Alexander Wise Jr.
Director
Dept. of Historic Resources
221 Governor St.
Richmond, VA 23219
Phone : (804) 786-3143
Fax : (804) 225-4261

WASHINGTON
Mary Thompson
Assistant Director
Archaeology & Hist. Pres. Off.
Dept. of Community Development
P.O. Box 48343
Olympia, WA 98504-8343
Phone : (360) 586-7027

WEST VIRGINIA
William Farrar
Deputy Historic Pres. Off.
Historical Preservation Sect.
Div. of Culture & History
Cultural Ctr.
Charleston, WV 25305
Phone : (304) 558-0220

WISCONSIN
Jeff M. Dean
Administrator
Historic Preservation Div.
State Historical Society
816 State St., Room 300
Madison, WI 53706
Phone : (608) 264-6500
Fax : (608) 264-6404

WYOMING
David Kathka
Director
Div. of Parks & Cultural Res.
Dept. of Commerce
Barrett Bldg.
Cheyenne, WY 82002
Phone : (307) 777-7013

DISTRICT OF COLUMBIA
Stephen J. Raiche
Chief
Historic Preservation Div.
Dept. of Cons. & Reg. Affairs
614 H St., NW, Rm. 307
Washington, DC 20001
Phone : (202) 727-7360

AMERICAN SAMOA
Stan Sorensen
Chairman
Historic Preservation Comm.
Dept. of Parks & Recreation
Pago Pago, AS 96799
Phone : (684) 633-9513

GUAM
Austin J. "Sonny" Shelton
Director
Dept. of Parks & Recreation
490 Chalan Palasyo
Agana Heights, GU 96910
Phone : (671) 477-9620
Fax : (671) 472-9626

NORTHERN MARIANA ISLANDS
Micheal M. Fleming
Historic Preservation Officer
Community & Cultural Affairs
Off. of the Governor
Saipan, MP 96950
Phone : (617) 233-9722

PUERTO RICO
Arlene Pabon
Executive Director
Historic Preservation Off.
P.O. Box 82, La Fortaleza
San Juan, PR 00901
Phone : (809) 721-3737
Fax : (809) 723-0957

U.S. VIRGIN ISLANDS
Claudette Lewis
Assistant Director
Historic Preservation Div.
Dept. of Planning & Natural Resources
Nisky Ctr., Ste. 231
St. Thomas, VI 00802
Phone : (809) 774-3320

HORSE RACING

Licenses and regulates horse racing in the state.

ARIZONA
James H. Higginbottom
Director
Dept. of Racing
800 W. Washington St., Ste. 515
Phoenix, AZ 85007
Phone : (602) 542-5151

ARKANSAS
Peggy Tucker
Manager
State Racing Comm.
Finance & Administration Dept.
P.O. Box 3076
Little Rock, AR 72203
Phone : (501) 682-1467
Fax : (501) 682-5273

CALIFORNIA
Henry Chavez
Chairman
Horse Racing Bd.
1010 Hurley Way, Rm. 190
Sacramento, CA 95825
Phone : (916) 920-7178

COLORADO
Dave Reitz
Director
Div. of Racing Events
Dept. of Regulatory Agencies
1560 Broadway, Rm. 1540
Denver, CO 80202
Phone : (303) 894-2990
Fax : (303) 894-7580

CONNECTICUT
John B. Meskill
Executive Director
Div. of Special Revenue
Dept. of Revenue Srvcs.
55 Russell Rd.
Newington, CT 06111
Phone : (203) 666-7503

DELAWARE
Anthony Flynn
Chairman
State Harness Racing Comm.
Dept. of Agriculture
2320 S. DuPont Hwy.
Dover, DE 19901
Phone : (302) 739-4811

Patricia Yossick
Administrative Assistant
Div. of Resource Mgt.
Dept. of Agriculture
2320 S. DuPont Hwy.
Dover, DE 19901
Phone : (302) 734-4811
Fax : (302) 697-6287

FLORIDA*
Div. of Pari-Mutuel Wagering
Dept. of Bus. & Prof. Reg.
725 S. Bronough St.
Tallahassee, FL 32399-1000
Phone : (904) 488-9130

IDAHO
Doug Ray
Executive Director
State Racing Comm.
Dept. of Law Enforcement
P.O. Box 700
Meridian, ID 83680-0700
Phone : (208) 884-7105

ILLINOIS
Joseph Sinopoli
Executive Director
State Racing Board
100 W. Randolph, Ste. 11-100
Chicago, IL 60601
Phone : (312) 814-2600
Fax : (312) 814-5062

INDIANA
Joe Gorajec
Executive Secretary
Horse Racing Comm.
150 W. Market St., # 412
Indianapolis, IN 46204-2810
Phone : (317) 233-3121

IOWA
Jack Ketterer
Administrator
Racing & Gaming Comm.
Dept. of Inspections & Appeals
Lucas State Off. Bldg.
Des Moines, IA 50319
Phone : (515) 281-7352

KANSAS
Art J. Neubedel
Executive Director
Kansas Racing Commissioin
3400 Van Buren
Topeka, KS 66611-2228
Phone : (913) 296-5800
Fax : (913) 296-0900

KENTUCKY
Wayne Lyster
Chairman
State Racing Comm.
4063 Iron Works Pike
Lexington, KY 40511-
Phone : (606) 254-7021

LOUISIANA
Oscar Tolmas
Executive Director
State Racing Comm.
Dept. of Commerce
320 N. Carrollton., Ste. 2B
New Orleans, LA 70119
Phone : (504) 483-4000

MAINE
Philip Tarr
Executive Director
Harness Racing Comm.
Ag., Food & Rural Resources
State House Station # 28
Augusta, ME 04333
Phone : (207) 287-3221

MARYLAND
Kenneth A. Schertle
Executive Director
Racing Comm.
Licensing & Regulation Dept.
501 St. Paul Pl.
Baltimore, MD 21202-2272
Phone : (301) 333-6267

MASSACHUSETTS
Robert Hutchinson
Chairman
State Racing Comm.
1 Ashburton Pl., Rm. 1313
Boston, MA 02108
Phone : (617) 727-2581

MICHIGAN
Nelson Westrin
Racing Commissioner
Dept. of Agriculture
37650 Professional Ctr. Dr., Ste. 105A
Livonia, MI 48154-1114
Phone : (313) 462-2400

MINNESOTA
Richard Krueger
Executive Director
Racing Comm.
7825 Washington Ave., S., # 800
Minneapolis, MN 55439
Phone : (612) 341-7555

MISSOURI
Betty Weldon
Chairman
Horse Racing Comm.
P.O. Box 754
Jefferson City, MO 65102-0754

MONTANA
Steve Meloy
Chief
Prof. & Occ. Licensing Bur.
Dept. of Commerce
111 N. Jackson, Lower Level
Helena, MT 59620
Phone : (406) 444-3737

NEBRASKA
Dennis Oelschlager
Executive Secretary
Racing Comm.
P.O. Box 95014
Lincoln, NE 68509-5014
Phone : (402) 471-2577

NEVADA
Gail Horky
District Office Manager
State Gaming Control Board
4220 S. Maryland Pkwy., Bldg. D
Las Vegas, NV 89113
Phone : (702) 486-6400

NEW HAMPSHIRE
John E. Furgal
Director
Pari-Mutuel Comm.
Carringain Common, 3rd Fl.
244 N. Main St.
Concord, NH 03301
Phone : (603) 271-2158

NEW JERSEY
Frank Zanzucci
Executive Director
Racing Comm.
Dept. of Law & Public Safety
140 E. Front St., CN 088
Trenton, NJ 08625
Phone : (609) 292-0613

NEW MEXICO
Julian Luna
Executive Director
State Racing Comm.
Dept. of Tourism
P.O. Box 8576
Albuquerque, NM 87198-8576
Phone : (505) 841-6400
Fax : (505) 841-6413

NEW YORK*
Chairman
Racing & Wagering Bd.
Agency Bldg. # 1
Empire State Plz.
Albany, NY 12223
Phone : (518) 473-7201

NORTH DAKOTA
Roger Reule
Racing Commissioner
Attorney General's Off.
State Capitol, 17th Fl.
600 E. Boulevard Ave.
Bismarck, ND 58505
Phone : (701) 328-4633
Fax : (701) 328-4300

OHIO
Norman Barron
Chairman
State Racing Comm.
77 S. High St., 18th Fl.
Columbus, OH 43266-0416
Phone : (614) 466-2757
Fax : (614) 466-1900

OKLAHOMA
Gordon Hare
Executive Director
Horse Racing Comm.
6601 N. Broadway, Rm. 102
Oklahoma City, OK 73116
Phone : (405) 848-0404

OREGON
Steven W. Barham
Executive Secretary
Racing Comm.
800 NE Oregon St.
Portland, OR 97232-2109
Phone : (503) 731-4052
Fax : (503) 731-4053

PENNSYLVANIA
Kenneth E. Kirchner
Executive Director
Horse Racing Comm.
Dept. of Agriculture
Agriculture Bldg., Rm. 304
Harrisburg, PA 17110
Phone : (717) 787-1942

RHODE ISLAND
Mario R. Forte
Chief of Hearings & Investigations
Div. of Racing & Athletics
Dept. of Business Regulation
Richmond St.
Providence, RI 02903
Phone : (401) 277-6541

SOUTH DAKOTA
Tom Fahey
Executive Secretary
Div. of Gaming
118 E. Missouri
Pierre, SD 57501
Phone : (605) 773-6050

TENNESSEE
Art Giles
Executive Director
State Racing Comm.
500 James Robertson Pkwy., Ste. 635
Nashville, TN 37243
Phone : (615) 741-1952

TEXAS
David J. Freeman
Executive Secretary
Racing Comm.
P.O. Box 12080
Austin, TX 78711
Phone : (512) 794-8478

VERMONT
Harlan Sylvester
Chairman
Racing Comm.
State Off. Bldg.
120 State St.
Montpelier, VT 05620-
Phone : (802) 828-3429

VIRGINIA
Donald R. Price
Executive Secretary
Racing Comm.
Main St. Station, Ste. 301
1500 E. Main St.
Richmond, VA 23219
Phone : (804) 371-7363
Fax : (804) 371-6127

WASHINGTON
Bruce Batson
Executive Secretary
Horse Racing Comm.
7912 Martin Way, Ste. D
P.O. Box 40906
Olympia, WA 98504-0906
Phone : (360) 459-6462

WEST VIRGINIA
Robert Burke
Chairman
State Racing Comm.
P.O. Box 3327
Charleston, WV 25333-3327
Phone : (304) 558-2150

WISCONSIN
Scott Scepaniak
Div. Administrator-Racing Gaming Comm.
P.O. Box 8941
Madison, WI 53708-8941
Phone : (608) 266-3670
Fax : (608) 264-6644

WYOMING
Frank Lamb
Executive Director
Pari-Mutuel Comm.
Barrett Bldg.
Cheyenne, WY 82002-
Phone : (307) 777-5928

PUERTO RICO
Gonzalo Combas
Administrator
Horse Racing Admin.
P.O. Box 29156
San Juan, PR 00929
Phone : (809) 768-2005
Fax : (809) 762-1105

U.S. VIRGIN ISLANDS
Raymond James
Chairman
Horse Racing Comm.
P.O. Box 774
Frederickstead
St. Croix, VI 00840
Phone : (809) 773-0160

HOUSING FINANCE

Administers the state's housing assistance programs, providing low- and moderate-income housing by financing low-interest loans.

ALABAMA
Robert Strickland
Director
State Housing Finance Authority
P.O. Box 230909
Montgomery, AL 36123-0909
Phone : (205) 242-4310

ALASKA
Frank Cox
Executive Director
State Housing Finance Corp.
P.O. Box 101020
Anchorage, AK 99510
Phone : (907) 561-1900

ARIZONA
Sara Goertzen
Director
Fin. Srvcs. & Housing Dev. Div.
Dept. of Commerce
3800 N. Central
Phoenix, AZ 85012
Phone : (602) 280-1300

ARKANSAS
Vincent Tilford
President
Development Finance Authority
P.O. Box 8023
Little Rock, AR 72203
Phone : (501) 682-5900
Fax : (501) 682-7553

CALIFORNIA
Maureen Higgins
Executive Director
Housing Finance Agency
1121 L St., 7th Fl.
Sacramento, CA 95814
Phone : (916) 322-3991

COLORADO
Tom Hart
Director
Div. of Housing
Dept. of Local Affairs
1313 Sherman St., Rm. 415
Denver, CO 80203
Phone : (303) 866-2033

CONNECTICUT
Gary E. King
President-Executive Director
Housing Finance Authority
999 West Street
Rocky Hill, CT 06067
Phone : (203) 721-9501

DELAWARE
Susan W. Frank
Director
Delaware State Housing Authority
18 The Green
Dover, DE 19901
Phone : (302) 739-4263
Fax : (302) 739-6122

FLORIDA
Susan Leigh
Director
Housing Finance Agency
Dept. of Community Affairs
2740 Centerview Dr.
Tallahassee, FL 32399-2100
Phone : (904) 488-4197

GEORGIA
David Pinson
Acting Executive Director
Housing & Finance Authority
60 Executive Pkwy. S., # 250
Atlanta, GA 30329
Phone : (404) 679-4840

HAWAII
Roy Oshiro
Acting Executive Director
Housing Finance & Dev. Corp.
677 Queen St., Ste. 300
Honolulu, HI 96813
Phone : (808) 587-0640
Fax : (808) 587-0600

IDAHO
Rod Beck
Executive Director
Idaho Housing Agency
P.O. Box 7899
Boise, ID 83707-1899
Phone : (208) 331-4882

ILLINOIS
Peter Dwars
Director
Housing Development Authority
401 N. Michigan Ave.
Chicago, IL 60611
Phone : (312) 527-2509

INDIANA
Ira Peppercorn
Executive Director
Housing Finance Authority
Ste. 1350 S.
115 W. Washington St.
Indianapolis, IN 46204
Phone : (317) 232-7788

IOWA
Ted Chapler
Executive Director
State Finance Authority
Dept. of Economic Development
200 E. Grand, Ste. 222
Des Moines, IA 50309
Phone : (515) 242-4490

KANSAS
Randy Speaker
Director
Dept. of Commerce & Housing
700 SW Harrison, Ste. 1300
Topeka, KS 66603-3712
Phone : (913) 296-2686
Fax : (913) 296-3481

KENTUCKY
Robert W. Adams
Executive Director
Housing Corp.
1231 Louisville Rd.
Frankfort, KY 40601
Phone : (502) 564-7057

LOUISIANA
Jean V. Butler
President
Housing Finance Agency
200 Lafayette St., Ste. 300
Baton Rouge, LA 70801-1203
Phone : (504) 342-1320

MAINE
David Lakari
Director
State Housing Authority
State House Station # 89
Augusta, ME 04333-
Phone : (207) 626-4600

MARYLAND**
Jacqueline Rogers
Secretary
Dept. of Housing & Comm. Dev.
100 Community Pl.
Crownsville, MD 21032
Phone : (301) 514-7005

MASSACHUSETTS
Steve Pierce
Executive Director
Housing Finance Agency
1 Beacon St.
Boston, MA 02108
Phone : (617) 854-1000

MICHIGAN
Jim Logue
Director
State Housing Dev. Authority
401 S. Washington Sq.
Lansing, MI 48909
Phone : (517) 373-6022

MINNESOTA
Katherine Hadley
Commissioner
Housing Finance Agency
400 Sibley St., Ste. 300
St. Paul, MN 55101
Phone : (612) 296-5738

MISSISSIPPI
Neddie Winters
Executive Director
Home Corp.
840 E. River Pl., Ste. 605
Jackson, MS 39201-1205
Phone : (601) 354-6062

MISSOURI
Richard Grose
Executive Director
Housing Development Comm.
Dept. of Economic Development
3770 Broadway
Kansas City, MO 64111
Phone : (816) 756-3790
Fax : (816) 931-2677

MONTANA*
Director
Bd. of Housing
Dept. of Commerce
2001 11th Ave.
Helena, MT 59620
Phone : (406) 444-3040

NEBRASKA
Teresa Priefert
Housing Coordinator
Dept. of Economic Development
P.O. Box 94666
Lincoln, NE 68509-4666
Phone : (402) 471-3759

NEVADA
Charles L. Horsey III
Administrator
Housing Div.
Dept. of Commerce
1802 N. Carson St., Ste. 154
Carson City, NV 89710
Phone : (702) 885-4258

NEW HAMPSHIRE
Claira Monier
Executive Director
Housing Finance Agency
24 Constitution Dr.
Bedford, NH 03110
Phone : (603) 472-8623

NEW JERSEY
Ira Oskowsky
Executive Director
Housing & Mortgage Finance Agency
Dept. of Community Affairs
3625 Quakerbridge Rd., CN-18550
Trenton, NJ 08650-2085
Phone : (609) 890-8900

NEW MEXICO
Steve Padilla
Director
Housing Authority Div.
Economic Dev. & Tourism Dept.
810 W. San Mateo, Ste. D
Santa Fe, NM 87505
Phone : (505) 827-0258
Fax : (505) 827-9480

NEW YORK*
Executive Director
State Housing Finance Agency
3 Park Ave.
New York, NY 10016
Phone : (212) 686-9700

NORTH CAROLINA
Robert Kucab
Director
Housing Finance Agency
3300 Drake Cr., Ste. 200
Raleigh, NC 27607
Phone : (919) 781-6115

NORTH DAKOTA
Pat Fricke
Director
Housing Finance Agency
P.O. Box 1535
Bismarck, ND 58502-1535
Phone : (701) 328-3434
Fax : (701) 328-3420

OHIO
Richard Everhart
Executive Director
Housing Finance Agency
Dept. of Development
77 S. High St., 26th Fl.
Columbus, OH 43266-0101
Phone : (614) 466-7970
Fax : (614) 644-5393

OKLAHOMA
Stephen R. Weatherford
Executive Director
Housing Finance Agency
1140 NW 63rd St., Ste. 200
Oklahoma City, OK 73116
Phone : (405) 848-1144

OREGON
Baruti Artharee
Director
Dept. of Housing & Community Srvcs.
1600 State St., Ste. 100
Salem, OR 97310
Phone : (503) 986-2005
Fax : (503) 986-2020

PENNSYLVANIA
Carl Smith
Executive Director
Housing Finance Agency
P.O. Box 8029
Harrisburg, PA 17105-8029
Phone : (717) 780-3911

RHODE ISLAND
Richard H. Godfrey Jr.
Executive Director
Housing & Mortgage Finance
60 Eddy St.
Providence, RI 02903
Phone : (401) 751-5566

SOUTH CAROLINA
David M. Leopard
Executive Director
State Housing Authority
1710 Gervais St., Ste. 300
Columbia, SC 29201
Phone : (803) 734-8702

SOUTH DAKOTA
Michael J. Echols
Executive Director
Housing Development Authority
221 S. Central
P.O. Box 1237
Pierre, SD 57501-1237
Phone : (605) 773-3181

TENNESSEE
Jeff Reynolds
Director
Housing Development Agency
404 James Robertson Pkwy., Rm. 1114
Nashville, TN 37243-0900
Phone : (615) 741-2473

TEXAS
Henry Flores
Executive Director
Dept. of Housing & Comm. Aff.
811 Barton Springs Rd.
P.O. Box 13166
Austin, TX 78711
Phone : (512) 475-3800

UTAH
William H. Erickson
Director
Housing Finance Agency
177 E. First S.
Salt Lake City, UT 84111
Phone : (801) 521-6950

VERMONT
Allan Hunt
Executive Director
Housing Finance Agency
One Burlington Sq.
P.O. Box 408
Burlington, VT 05402
Phone : (802) 864-5743
Fax : (802) 864-5746

VIRGINIA
John Ritchie Jr.
Executive Director
Virginia Housing Development Authority
601 S. Belvidere St.
Richmond, VA 23220-6504
Phone : (804) 783-6700
Fax : (804) 783-6704

WASHINGTON
Kim Herman
Executive Director
Housing Finance Comm.
1000 2nd Ave., Ste. 2700
Seattle, WA 98104-1046
Phone : (360) 464-7139

WEST VIRGINIA
Joe Hatfield
Executive Director
Housing Development Fund
814 Virginia St., E.
Charleston, WV 25301
Phone : (304) 345-6475

WISCONSIN
Richard J. Longabaugh
Executive Director
Housing & Economic Development Authority
1 S. Pinckney, 500
P.O. Box 1728
Madison, WI 53703
Phone : (608) 266-7884
Fax : (608) 267-1099

WYOMING
George D. Axlund
Director
Community Development Authority
P.O. Box 634
Casper, WY 82602
Phone : (307) 265-0603

DISTRICT OF COLUMBIA
Merrick Malone
Director
Dept. of Housing & Community Dev.
51 N. St., NE, 6th Fl.
Washington, DC 20002
Phone : (202) 535-1970

AMERICAN SAMOA
Ama Fareti
Acting President
American Samoa Development Bank
Pago Pago, AS 96799
Phone : (684) 633-4031
Fax : (684) 633-1163

GUAM
James G. Sablan
President
Guam Housing Corp.
P.O. Box 3457
Agana, GU 96910
Phone : (671) 649-4421
Fax : (671) 649-4420

NORTHERN MARIANA ISLANDS
Marylou A. Sirote
Corporate Director
Northern Mariana Housing Corp.
P.O. Box 514
Saipan, MP 96950
Phone : (670) 234-7689
Fax : (670) 234-9021

PUERTO RICO
Mildres Goyer Maldonado
President
Housing Finance Bank
Housing Dept.
P.O. Box 345
Hato Rey, PR 00919
Phone : (809) 765-2537

U.S. VIRGIN ISLANDS
Jose L. George
Executive Director
Housing Finance Authority
P.O. Box 12029
St. Thomas, VI 00802
Phone : (809) 774-4481

HUMAN RESOURCES

Umbrella human resources agency that has overall responsibility for the administration of public assistance, medical care and other human services.

ALABAMA
P. L. Corley
Acting Commissoiner
Dept. of Human Resources
50 N. Ripley St.
Montgomery, AL 36130
Phone : (334) 242-8395
Fax : (334) 242-0198

ALASKA
Director
Div. of Public Assistance
Dept. of Health & Social Srvcs.
P.O. Box 110640
Juneau, AK 99811-0640
Phone : (907) 465-3347
Fax : (907) 463-5154

ARIZONA
Linda Blessing
Director
Dept. of Economic Security
1717 W. Jefferson
Phoenix, AZ 85007
Phone : (602) 542-4791

ARKANSAS
Tom Dalton
Director
Dept. of Human Srvcs.
P.O. Box 1437, Slot 316
Little Rock, AR 72203
Phone : (501) 682-8650
Fax : (501) 682-6836

CALIFORNIA
Sandra R. Smoley
Secretary
Health & Welfare Agency
1600 Ninth St., Rm. 460
Sacramento, CA 95814
Phone : (916) 445-6951

COLORADO
Karen Beye
Managing Director
Dept. of Human Srvcs.
1575 Sherman St.
Denver, CO 80203-1714
Phone : (303) 866-5700
Fax : (303) 866-4214

CONNECTICUT
Joyce Thomas
Commissioner
Dept. of Social Services
25 Sigourney St.
Hartford, CT 06106
Phone : (203) 424-5008

DELAWARE
Elaine Archangelo
Director
Div. of Social Srvcs.
P.O. Box 906
New Castle, DE 19720
Phone : (302) 421-6734
Fax : (302) 577-4405

FLORIDA
Douglas M. Cook
Executive Director
Agency for Health Care Admin.
Ste. 301, Atrium
325 John Knox Rd.
Tallahassee, FL 32303
Phone : (904) 922-5527
Fax : (904) 488-1261

GEORGIA
Tommy Olmstead
Commissioner
Dept. of Human Resources
47 Trinity Ave., SW
Atlanta, GA 30334
Phone : (404) 656-5680

HAWAII
Susan Chandler
Director
Dept. of Human Services
1390 Miller St.
Honolulu, HI 96813
Phone : (808) 586-4997
Fax : (808) 586-4890

IDAHO
Linda Caballero
Director
Idaho Dept. of Health & Welfare
450 W. State St., 10th Fl.
P.O. Box 83720
Boise, ID 83720
Phone : (208) 334-5500

ILLINOIS
Robert W. Wright
Director
Dept. of Public Aid
100 S. Grand Ave., E.
Springfield, IL 62762-
Phone : (217) 782-1200
Fax : (217) 524-7979

INDIANA
Cheryl Sullivan
Secretary
Family & Social Srvcs. Admin.
402 W. Washington St., #341
Indianapolis, IN 46204
Phone : (317) 232-4690

IOWA
Charles Palmer
Director
Dept. of Human Services
Hoover State Off. Bldg.
Des Moines, IA 50319
Phone : (515) 281-5452
Fax : (515) 281-4597

KANSAS
Wayne Franklin
Secretary
Department of Human Resources
401 Topeka Blvd.
Topeka, KS 66603-3182
Phone : (913) 296-5000
Fax : (913) 296-0179

KENTUCKY
Masten Childers
Secretary
Cabinet for Human Resources
275 E. Main St.
Frankfort, KY 40621
Phone : (502) 564-7130

LOUISIANA
Rose V. Forrest
Secretary
Dept. of Health & Hospitals
P.O. Box 629
Baton Rouge, LA 70821
Phone : (504) 342-9500

MAINE
Kevin Concannon
Commissioner
Dept. of Human Services
State House Station # 11
Augusta, ME 04333
Phone : (207) 287-2736

MARYLAND
Alvin Collins
Secretary
Dept. of Human Resources
311 W. Saratoga St.
Baltimore, MD 21201
Phone : (301) 333-0001

MASSACHUSETTS
Gerald Whitburn
Secretary
Executive Off. of Health & Human Srvcs.
1 Ashburton Pl., Rm. 1109
Boston, MA 02108
Phone : (617) 727-7600

MICHIGAN
Gerald Miller
Director
Dept. of Social Srvcs.
P.O. Box 30037
Lansing, MI 48909
Phone : (517) 373-2000
Fax : (517) 373-8471

MINNESOTA
Maria Gomez
Commissioner
Dept. of Human Srvcs.
444 Lafayette Rd.
St. Paul, MN 55155-3815
Phone : (612) 296-2701

MISSISSIPPI
Ronnie McGinnis
Director
Div. of Grants
Dept. of Human Services
P.O. Box 352
Jackson, MS 39205
Phone : (601) 359-6701

MISSOURI
Gary Stangler
Director
Dept. of Social Services
Broadway Bldg., Rm. 240
P.O. Box 1527
Jefferson City, MO 65102
Phone : (314) 751-4815
Fax : (314) 751-3203

MONTANA
Peter Blouke
Director
Dept. of Social & Rehabilitation Services
111 Sanders St.
Helena, MT 59604
Phone : (406) 444-5622

NEBRASKA
Mary Dean Harvey
Director
Dept. of Social Services
P.O. Box 95206
Nebraska State Off. Bldg.
Lincoln, NE 68509-5026
Phone : (402) 471-3121

NEVADA
Charlotte Crawford
Acting Director
Dept. of Human Resources
505 E. King St., Rm. 600
Carson City, NV 89710
Phone : (702) 687-4400

NEW HAMPSHIRE
Jonathan S. Osgood
Director
Governor's Off. of Energy & Community Services
57 Regional Dr.
Concord, NH 03301-8519
Phone : (603) 271-2611

NEW JERSEY
William Waldman
Commissioner
Dept. of Human Srvcs.
222 S. Warren St., CN700
Trenton, NJ 08625
Phone : (609) 292-5360

NEW MEXICO
Dorothy Danfeiser
Secretary
Dept. of Human Srvcs.
P.O. Box 2348
Santa Fe, NM 87504
Phone : (505) 827-7750
Fax : (505) 827-6286

NEW YORK*
Commissioner
Dept. of Social Srvcs.
40 N. Pearl St.
Albany, NY 12243
Phone : (518) 474-9475

NORTH CAROLINA
Robin Britt
Secretary
Dept. of Human Resources
101 Blair Dr.
Raleigh, NC 27603
Phone : (919) 733-4534

NORTH DAKOTA
Henry C. Wessman
Executive Director
Dept. of Human Services
State Capitol, Judicial Wing
600 E. Boulevard Ave.
Bismarck, ND 58505
Phone : (701) 328-2358
Fax : (701) 328-2359

OHIO
Arnold Tompkins
Director
Dept. of Human Services
30 E. Broad St., 32nd Fl.
Columbus, OH 43266-0423
Phone : (614) 466-6282
Fax : (614) 466-2815

OKLAHOMA
George Miller
Interim Director
Health & Human Srvcs.
Dept. of Human Srvcs.
P.O. Box 25352
Oklahoma City, OK 73125
Phone : (405) 521-2778

OREGON
Jean Thorne
Acting Director
Dept. of Human Resources
500 Summer St., NE 4th Fl.
Salem, OR 97310-1012
Phone : (503) 945-5944
Fax : (503) 378-2897

PENNSYLVANIA
Feather Houstoun
Secretary
Dept. of Public Welfare
Rm. 333, Health & Welfare Bldg.
Harrisburg, PA 17120
Phone : (717) 787-2600

RHODE ISLAND
Christie Ferguson
Director
Dept. of Human Services
600 New London Ave.
Cranston, RI 02920
Phone : (401) 464-2121

SOUTH CAROLINA
Stephen C. Osborne
Director
Office of Human Resources
1201 Main St., Ste. 1000
Columbia, SC 29201
Phone : (803) 737-0901
Fax : (803) 737-0968

Jim Clark
Commissioner
Dept. of Social Srvcs.
1535 Confederate Ave. Ext.
Columbia, SC 29202
Phone : (803) 734-5760

SOUTH DAKOTA
Bill Podradsky
Secretary
Dept. of Human Srvcs.
Hillsview Plz.
500 E. Capitol Ave.
Pierre, SD 57501
Phone : (605) 773-5990

TENNESSEE
Linda Rudolph
Commissioner
Dept. of Human Services
400 Deadrick St.
Nashville, TN 37243
Phone : (615) 741-3241
Fax : (615) 741-4165

TEXAS
Burton Raiford
Commissioner
Dept. of Human Services
P.O. Box 149030
Austin, TX 78714
Phone : (512) 450-3011

UTAH
Kerry Steadman
Executive Director
Dept. of Human Srvcs.
120 N. 200 W., # 319
Salt Lake City, UT 84103
Phone : (801) 538-3998

VERMONT
Cornelius Hogan
Secretary
Agency of Human Services
103 S. Main St.
Waterbury, VT 05671
Phone : (802) 241-2220
Fax : (802) 241-2979

VIRGINIA
Kay Coles James
Secretary
Div. of Health & Human Res.
Governor's Cabinet
622 9th St. Office Bldg.
Richmond, VA 23219
Phone : (804) 786-7765
Fax : (804) 371-6984

WASHINGTON
Jean Soliz
Secretary
Dept. of Social & Health Srvcs.
P.O. Box 45010
Olympia, WA 98504-5010
Phone : (360) 753-7039

WEST VIRGINIA
Gretchen Lewis
Secretary
Dept. of Health & Human Resources
Bldg. 3, Rm. 206
State Capitol Complex
Charleston, WV 25305
Phone : (304) 558-0684

WISCONSIN
Gerald Whitburn
Secretary
Dept. of Health & Social Srvcs.
1 W. Wilson, Room 650
P.O. Box 7850
Madison, WI 53703
Phone : (608) 266-9622
Fax : (608) 266-7882

WYOMING
Tom Pringle
Human Resources Coordinator
Planning Coordinator's Off.
Off. of the Governor
State Capitol Bldg., Rm. 124
1122 W. 25th St.
Cheyenne, WY 82002
Phone : (307) 777-7434

DISTRICT OF COLUMBIA
Vernon Hawkins
Director
Dept. of Human Services
P.O. Box 54047
Washington, DC 20032-0247
Phone : (202) 279-6002

AMERICAN SAMOA
Sapini Siatu'u
Director
Dept. of Human Resources
American Samoa Government
Pago Pago, AS 96799
Phone : (684) 633-4485
Fax : (684) 633-1139

GUAM
Dennis Rodriguez
Director
Dept of Public Health & Social Services
P.O. Box 2816
Agana, GU 96910
Phone : (671) 734-7102
Fax : (671) 734-5910

NORTHERN MARIANA ISLANDS
Isamu Abraham
Secretary
Dept. of Public Health Srvcs.
P.O. Box 409
Saipan, MP 96950
Phone : (670) 234-8950
Fax : (670) 234-8930

Thomas A. Tebuteb
Secretary
Dept. of Community & Cultural Affairs
Off. of the Governor
Saipan, MP 96950
Phone : (670) 233-3343
Fax : (670) 233-2221

PUERTO RICO
Carmen Rodriquez de Rivera
Secretary
Dept. of Social Services
P.O. Box 11398
Santurce, PR 00910
Phone : (809) 722-7400
Fax : (809) 723-1223

U.S. VIRGIN ISLANDS
Catherine Mills
Commissioner
Dept. of Human Srvcs,
Knud Hansen Complex, Bldg. A
1303 Hospital Ground
St. Thomas, VI 00802
Phone : (809) 774-0930
Fax : (809) 774-3466

INFORMATION SYSTEMS

Provides statewide computer services or coordinates the operation of various data processing systems within state government.

ALABAMA
Jacquelyn Patillo
Director
Data Systems Management Div.
Dept. of Finance
64 N. Union St.
Montgomery, AL 36130
Phone: (334) 242-3100
Fax: (334) 240-3177

ALASKA
Mark Badger
Director
Div. of Information Srvcs.
Dept. of Administration
P.O. Box 110206
Juneau, AK 99811-0206
Phone: (907) 465-2220
Fax: (907) 465-3450

ARIZONA*
Assistant Director
Information Services Div.
Dept. of Administration
1616 W. Adams St.
Phoenix, AZ 85007
Phone: (602) 542-5791

ARKANSAS
John Kennedy
Director
Dept. of Computer Srvcs.
P.O. Box 3155
Little Rock, AR 72203
Phone: (501) 682-2701
Fax: (501) 682-4310

CALIFORNIA
Lynn Wright
Deputy Chief Information Officer
Off. of Information Technology
Dept. of Finance
915 L St.
Sacramento, CA 95814-3701
Phone: (916) 445-1932

COLORADO
Jim Cleek
Director
General Government Computer Ctr.
Dept. of Administration
690 Kipling St.
Lakewood, CO 80215
Phone: (303) 239-4313
Fax: (303) 239-4383

CONNECTICUT
Robert F. Granquist
Administrator
General & Technical Srvcs.
Dept. of Administrative Srvcs.
340 Capitol Ave.
Hartford, CT 06106
Phone: (203) 566-7093

DELAWARE
John J. Nold
Director
Off. of Information Systems
P.O. Box 370
Dover, DE 19903
Phone: (302) 739-9629
Fax: (302) 739-6251

FLORIDA
Daryl Plummer
Director
Div. of Information Srvcs.
Dept. of Management Srvcs.
M-40 Carlton Bldg.
Tallahassee, FL 32399
Phone: (904) 487-2914

GEORGIA
Tom Bostick
Deputy Commissioner
Department of Administrative Srvcs.
200 Piedmont Ave.
Atlanta, GA 30334
Phone: (404) 656-5516

HAWAII
Thomas I. Yamashiro
Administrator
Information & Comm. Srvcs.
Dept. of Budget & Finance
P.O. Box 150
Honolulu, HI 96816
Phone: (808) 586-1930

IDAHO
Pamela Ahrens
Director
Dept. of Admin.
650 W. State St., Rm. 100
Boise, ID 83720
Phone: (208) 334-3382

ILLINOIS
Michael S. Schwartz
Director
Dept. of Central Mgt. Srvcs.
715 Stratton Off. Bldg.
Springfield, IL 62706
Phone: (217) 782-2141
Fax: (217) 524-1880

INDIANA
Daniel Houlihan
Director
Information Services Div.
Dept. of Admin.
100 N. Senate, #N551
Indianapolis, IN 46204
Phone: (317) 232-6750

IOWA
Dale L. Nelson
Administrator
Information Srvcs. Div.
Dept. of General Srvcs.
Hoover Bldg., Level B
Des Moines, IA 50319
Phone: (515) 281-5503

KANSAS
Don Heiman
Director
Info. Systems & Communications
Dept. of Administration
Landon Off. Bldg., Rm. 751-S
Topeka, KS 66612-1275
Phone: (913) 296-3343
Fax: (913) 296-1168

KENTUCKY
Crit Luallen
Secretary
Finance & Admin. Cabinet
Capitol Annex, Rm. 301
Frankfort, KY 40601
Phone: (502) 564-4240

LOUISIANA
Allen Doescher
Assistant Commissioner
Tech. Srvcs. & Communications
Div. of Administration
P.O. Box 94095
Baton Rouge, LA 70804-9095
Phone: (504) 342-7105

MARYLAND
Louis L. Goldstein
Comptroller
Dept. of Budget & Fiscal Planning
Treasury Bldg., Rm. 121
P.O. Box 466
Annapolis, MD 21404
Phone: (410) 974-3801

MASSACHUSETTS
John Flynn
Director
Mgt. Information Systems
Executive Off. for Admin. & Finance
1 Ashburton Pl., Rm. 801
Boston, MA 02108
Phone: (617) 973-0975

MICHIGAN
Gary Swinden
Director
Off. of Mgt. & Info. Services
320 S. Walnut
P.O. Box 30026
Lansing, MI 48909
Phone : (517) 373-8816

MINNESOTA
Bernard E. Conlin
Assistant Commissioner
Dept. of Admin.
500 Centennial Bldg.
658 Cedar St.
St. Paul, MN 55155
Phone : (612) 296-8888

Sue Clauve
Director
Information Systems Div.
Dept. of General Srvcs.
P.O. Drawer 26110
Santa Fe, MN 87502
Phone : (505) 277-3622

MISSISSIPPI
David Litchliter
Executive Director
Central Data Processing Authority
301 N. Lamar St., Ste. 508
Jackson, MS 39201
Phone : (601) 359-1395

MISSOURI
James Schutt
Director
Div. of Data Processing & Telecomm.
Off. of Administration
Truman Bldg., Rm. 280
P.O. Box 809
Jefferson City, MO 65102
Phone : (314) 751-3338
Fax : (314) 751-3299
E-Mail: JSCHUTT@MAIL.MORE.NET

MONTANA
Tony Herbert
Administrator
Information Services
Dept. of Administration
Mitchell Bldg.
Helena, MT 59620
Phone : (406) 444-2700

NEBRASKA
Steven L. Henderson
Acting Administrator
Central Data Processing
501 S. 14th St.
Lincoln, NE 68508
Phone : (402) 471-2065

NEVADA
Karen Kavanaugh
Director
Data Processing Dept.
209 E. Musser
Carson City, NV 89710
Phone : (702) 687-4090

NEW JERSEY
Linda Hibbs
Administrator
Off. of Telecommunications & Information Systems
50 W. State St., CN215
Trenton, NJ 08625
Phone : (609) 633-9070

NEW YORK*
Commissioner
Off. of General Srvcs.
Corning Tower Bldg., 41st Fl.
Empire State Plz.
Albany, NY 12242
Phone : (518) 474-5991

NORTH CAROLINA
Charles R. Williams
Chief
State Info. Processing Srvcs.
Off. of the State Controller
3700 Old Wake Forest Rd.
Raleigh, NC 27609-6860
Phone : (919) 981-5555

NORTH DAKOTA
James Heck
Director
Information Srvcs. Div.
State Capitol, Judicial Wing
600 E. Boulevard Ave.
Bismarck, ND 58505
Phone : (701) 328-3190
Fax : (701) 328-3000

OHIO
Pete McGeoch
Deputy Director
Computer & Information Systems
Dept. of Admin. Srvcs.
30 E. Broad St., 39th Fl.
Columbus, OH 43215
Phone : (614) 466-5860
Fax : (614) 644-1428

OKLAHOMA
Darrell Richardson
Director
Data Processing & Planning Div.
Dept. of Transportation
200 NE 21st St.
Oklahoma City, OK 73105
Phone : (405) 521-2528

Bill Shafer
Information Srvcs. Div. Mgt.
Off. of State Finance
State Capitol Bldg., Rm. 122
Oklahoma City, OK 73105
Phone : (405) 521-2804

OREGON
Curt Pederson
Chief Information Officer
Infor. Resources Mgt. Div.
Dept. of Adinistrative Srvcs.
155 Cottage St., NE
Salem, OR 97310
Phone : (503) 378-3161
Fax : (503) 378-4992

PENNSYLVANIA*
Special Assistant
Computer Information Systems
Off. of Administration
Finance Bldg., Rm. 207
Harrisburg, PA 17108
Phone : (717) 787-5440

RHODE ISLAND
Richard Pierson
Acting Information Processing Officer
Div. of Information Processing
Dept. of Administration
One Capitol Hill
Providence, RI 02908-5898
Phone : (401) 277-2276

SOUTH CAROLINA
Ted Lightle
Director
Div. of Info. Resource Mgt.
Budget & Control Board
1201 Main St., Ste. 930
Columbia, SC 29201
Phone : (803) 737-0077

SOUTH DAKOTA
Tom D. Geraets
Commissioner
Bur. of Administration
500 E. Capitol Ave.
Pierre, SD 57501
Phone : (605) 773-3688

TENNESSEE
Bradley Dugger
Chief
Information Systems Service
Dept. of Finance & Admin.
Nashville City Ctr., 10th Fl.
Nashville, TN 37243
Phone : (615) 741-3700

TEXAS
Carolyn Purcell
Executive Director
Dept. of Information Resources
P.O. Box 13564
Austin, TX 78711-3564
Phone : (512) 475-4700

UTAH
Brent Sanderson
Director
Div. of Data Processing
Administrative Srvcs. Dept.
5000 State Off. Bldg.
Salt Lake City, UT 84114
Phone : (801) 538-3530

VERMONT
Patricia Urban
Chief Information Officer
Administration
109 State St.
Montpelier, VT 05609
Phone : (802) 828-3322
Fax : (802) 828-2428

VIRGINIA
Charles C. Livingston
Director
Dept. of Information Technology
Richmond Plaza Bldg., 3rd Fl.
110 S. 7th St.
Richmond, VA 23219
Phone : (804) 344-5500
Fax : (804) 344-5505

WASHINGTON
George Lindamood
Director
Dept. of Information Srvcs.
1110 SE Jefferson St.
P.O. Box 42440
Olympia, WA 98504-2440
Phone : (360) 902-3560

WEST VIRGINIA
Royce Chambers
Director
Information System Srvcs.
Div. of Finance & Admin.
Bldg. 6, Rm. 102
Charleston, WV 25305
Phone : (304) 558-8918

WISCONSIN
Howard Southerland
Director
Off. of Computer Services
Dept. of Administration
101 E. Wilson, 9th Fl.
P.O. Box 7864
Madison, WI 53703
Phone : (608) 266-7627
Fax : (608) 264-9500

WYOMING
Ted Kerekes
Administrator
Computer Technology Div.
Admin. & Fiscal Control Dept.
Emerson Bldg.
Cheyenne, WY 82002
Phone : (307) 777-5000

DISTRICT OF COLUMBIA
Garu Muren
Administrator
Info. Resources Mgt. Admin.
Dept. of Admin. Srvcs.
441 4th St., NW, Rm. 750
Washington, DC 20001
Phone : (202) 727-2277

AMERICAN SAMOA
Ray Pritt
Treasurer
Dept. of Treasury
American Samoa Government
Pago Pago, AS 96799
Phone : (684) 633-4155
Fax : (684) 633-4100

GUAM
John S. Salas
Director
Dept. of Administration
P.O. Box 884
Agana, GU 96910
Phone : (671) 475-1101
Fax : (671) 477-6788

NORTHERN MARIANA ISLANDS
Robert C. Naraja
Attorney General
Administration Bldg., 2nd Fl.
Capitol Hill
Saipan, MP 96950
Phone : (670) 322-4311

Lawrence J. Laveque
Director
Data Processing Division
Dept. of Administration
Capitol Hill
Saipan, MP 96950
Phone : (670) 644-1400
Fax : (670) 664-1415

PUERTO RICO*
Administrator
General Services Admin.
P.O. Box 7428
San Juan, PR 00916
Phone : (809) 721-7370
Fax : (809) 722-7965

U.S. VIRGIN ISLANDS
Nellon Bowry
Director
Off. of Mgt. & Budget
#41 Norre Gade
Emancipation Garden Sta., 2nd Fl.
St. Thomas, VI 00802
Phone : (809) 774-0750
Fax : (809) 776-0069

INSPECTOR GENERAL

Investigates and prosecutes fraud, waste and abuse.

ALASKA
Dean Guaneli
Chief Assistant A.G.
Criminal Div.
Dept. of Law
P.O. Box 110300
Juneau, AK 99811-0300
Phone : (907) 465-3428
Fax : (907) 465-4028

ARIZONA
Douglas Norton
Auditor General
2910 N. 44th St., Ste. 410
Phoenix, AZ 85018
Phone : (602) 553-0333
Fax : (602) 553-0051

CALIFORNIA
Daniel E. Lungren
Attorney General
1515 K St., Rm. 612
Sacramento, CA 95814
Phone : (916) 324-5437

DELAWARE
R. Thomas Wagner Jr.
State Auditor
Townsend Bldg.
P.O. Box 1401
Dover, DE 19901
Phone : (302) 739-4241
Fax : (302) 739-2723

FLORIDA
Harold Lewis
Inspector General
Executive Office of the Governor
The Capitol, PL05
Tallahassee, FL 32399-0001
Phone : (904) 488-2272

IDAHO
Russ Reneau
Chief Investigator
Criminal Div.
Off. of the Attorney General
Statehouse
Boise, ID 83720
Phone : (208) 334-4529

ILLINOIS
Terrence Gainer
Director
Dept. of State Police
103 State Armory
Springfield, IL 62706
Phone : (217) 782-4593
Fax : (217) 785-2821

IOWA
Chuck Sweeney
Director
Dept. of Inspections & Appeals
Lucas State Off. Bldg.
Des Moines, IA 50319
Phone : (515) 281-5457
Fax : (515) 242-5022

KANSAS
Carla J. Stovall
Attorney General
Office of the Attorney General
Judicial Center, 2nd Fl.
Topeka, KS 66612-1597
Phone : (913) 296-2215
Fax : (913) 296-6292

KENTUCKY
William M. Gardner
Inspector General
Cabinet for Human Resources
275 E. Main St.
Frankfort, KY 40621
Phone : (502) 564-2888

LOUISIANA
Bill Lynch
Inspector General
Div. of Administration
P.O. Box 94095
Baton Rouge, LA 70804
Phone : (504) 342-4262

MAINE
Stephen L. Wessler
Chief Attorney
Public Protection Unit
Dept. of the Attorney General
State House Station # 6
Augusta, ME 04333
Phone : (207) 626-8844

MASSACHUSETTS
Robert A. Cerasoli
Inspector General
1 Ashburton Pl., Rm. 1311
Boston, MA 02108
Phone : (617) 727-9140
Fax : (617) 723-3540

MINNESOTA
Jack Tunheim
Chief Deputy Attorney General
Off. of the Attorney General
102 State Capitol
St. Paul, MN 55155
Phone : (612) 296-2351

MISSISSIPPI
Jerry Gafford
Inspector General
Off. of the Governor
119 New Capitol
Jackson, MS 39201
Phone : (601) 359-1878

MISSOURI
Jeremiah W. Nixon
Attorney General
Off. of the Attorney General
Supreme Court Bldg.
207 W. High St.
P.O. Box 899
Jefferson City, MO 65102
Phone : (314) 751-3321
Fax : (314) 751-0774

MONTANA
Scott Seacat
Legislative Auditor
Off. of Legislative Auditor
State Capitol, Rm. 135
Helena, MT 59620
Phone : (406) 444-3122

NEBRASKA
Donald B. Stenberg
Attorney General
State Capitol, Rm. 2115
P.O. Box 98920
Lincoln, NE 68509-4906
Phone : (402) 471-2682
Fax : (402) 471-3297

NEVADA
Bob Pike
Chief Investigator
Investigation Div.
Off. of the Attorney General
198 S. Carson St.
Carson City, NV 89710
Phone : (702) 687-3543

NEW HAMPSHIRE
Jeffrey R. Howard
Attorney General
25 Capitol St.
Concord, NH 03301
Phone : (603) 271-3655

NEW JERSEY
Deborah Poritz
Attorney General
Off. of the Attorney General
Dept. of Law & Public Safety
Justice Complex CN-081
Trenton, NJ 08625-081
Phone : (609) 292-8740

NEW MEXICO
Manuel Tijerina
Deputy Attorney General
Off. of the Attorney General
P.O. Drawer 1508
Santa Fe, NM 87504-1508
Phone : (505) 827-6000
Fax : (505) 827-5826

NEW YORK*
Inspector General
State Capitol, Rm. 254
Albany, NY 12224
Phone : (518) 474-1010

NORTH CAROLINA
Ralph Campbell
State Auditor
Dept. of State Auditor
300 N. Salisbury St.
Raleigh, NC 27603
Phone : (919) 733-3217
Fax : (919) 733-8443

NORTH DAKOTA
Tom Engelhart
Director
Consumer Fraud Div.
Off. of the Attorney General
600 E. Boulevard Ave.
Bismarck, ND 58505
Phone : (701) 328-3404
Fax : (701) 328-3535

OHIO
David Sturtz
Inspector General
77 S. High, Rm. 2426
Columbus, OH 43215
Phone : (614) 644-9110
Fax : (614) 644-9504

PENNSYLVANIA
Nicolette Parisi
Inspector General
Off. of Administration
Harristown 2, 9th Fl.
333 Market St.
Harrisburg, PA 17126
Phone : (717) 787-6835

SOUTH CAROLINA
Edgar A. Vaughn Jr.
State Auditor
State Auditor's Office
P.O. Box 11333
Columbia, SC 29211
Phone : (803) 253-4160

SOUTH DAKOTA
Curt Everson
Commissioner
Bur. of Finance & Mgt.
State Capitol, 2nd Fl.
500 E. Capitol Ave.
Pierre, SD 57501
Phone : (605) 773-3411

TEXAS
Barry Lovelace
Director
Ombudsman Div.
Off. of the Governor
P.O. Box 12428, Capitol Sta.
Austin, TX 78711
Phone : (512) 463-5319

UTAH
Nicholas G. Morgan III
Inspector General
Dept. of Corrections
6100 S. 300 E.
Salt Lake City, UT 84107
Phone : (801) 265-5500

VERMONT
Jeffrey L. Amestoy
Attorney General
Pavilion Off. Bldg.
109 State St.
Montpelier, VT 05602
Phone : (802) 828-3171
Fax : (802) 828-2154

WASHINGTON
Christine O. Gregoire
Attorney General
P.O. Box 40100
Olympia, WA 98504-0100
Phone : (360) 753-6200

WEST VIRGINIA
Darrell V. McGraw Jr.
Attorney General
Bldg. 1, Rm. E-26
State Capitol Complex
Charleston, WV 25305
Phone : (304) 558-2021

WISCONSIN
James E. Doyle
Attorney General
Dept. of Justice
114 E State Capitol
P.O. Box 7857
Madison, WI 53707
Phone : (608) 266-1221
Fax : (608) 267-2779

WYOMING
William Hill
Attorney General
123 State Capitol
Cheyenne, WY 82002
Phone : (307) 777-7841

DISTRICT OF COLUMBIA
Samuel McClendon
Inspector General
Off. of the Inspector General
415 12th St., NW, Rm. 804
Washington, DC 20004
Phone : (202) 727-2540

GUAM
Madeleine L. Bordallo
Quality Control Director
Off. of the Lt. Governor
Executive Chambers, Adelup
Agana, GU 96910
Phone : (671) 475-9209
Fax : (671) 477-4826

NORTHERN MARIANA ISLANDS
Scott Tan
Public Auditor
P.O. Box 1399
Saipan, MP 96950
Phone : (670) 234-6481

PUERTO RICO
Ileana Colon Carlo
Comptroller
P.O. Box 366069
San Juan, PR 00936-6069
Phone : (809) 754-3030
Fax : (809) 751-6768

U.S. VIRGIN ISLANDS
Steven G. van Beverhoudt
Inspector General
Bur. of Audit & Control
75 Kronprindsens Gade
St. Thomas, VI 00802
Phone : (809) 774-3388
Fax : (809) 774-6431

INSURANCE

Licenses and regulates insurance agents and insurance and title companies in the state.

ALABAMA
Michael Debellis
Acting Commissioner
Insurance Dept.
135 S. Union St.
Montgomery, AL 36130
Phone : (334) 269-3550
Fax : (334) 269-6570

ALASKA
Marianne Burke
Director
Div. of Insurance
Dept. of Commerce & Economic Dev.
P.O. Box 110805
Juneau, AK 99811-0805
Phone : (907) 465-2515
Fax : (907) 465-3422

ARIZONA
Chris Herstam
Director
Dept. of Insurance
2910 N. 44th St., #210
Phoenix, AZ 85018-7256
Phone : (602) 912-8456

ARKANSAS
Lee Douglass
Commissioner
Dept. of Insurance
Tower Bldg., Ste. 400
1123 S. University
Little Rock, AR 72204
Phone : (501) 686-2909
Fax : (501) 686-2913

CALIFORNIA
Charles W. Quackenbush
Commissioner
Dept. of Insurance
45 Freemont St., 23rd Fl.
Sacramento, CA 94105
Phone : (916) 904-5410

COLORADO
Jack Ehnes
Commissioner
Div. of Insurance
Dept. of Regulatory Agencies
1560 Broadway, Ste. 850
Denver, CO 80202
Phone : (303) 894-7499
Fax : (303) 894-7454

CONNECTICUT
William Gilligan
Acting Commissioner
Dept. of Insurance
P.O. Box 816
Hartford, CT 06142-0816
Phone : (203) 297-3802

DELAWARE
Donna Lee Williams
Commissioner
Dept. of Insurance
18 The Green
Dover, DE 19901
Phone : (302) 739-4251
Fax : (302) 739-5280

FLORIDA
Bill Nelson
Treasurer/Insurance Commissioner
Dept. of Insurance
State Capitol, PL11
Tallahassee, FL 32399-0300
Phone : (904) 922-3100
Fax : (904) 488-6581

GEORGIA
John Oxendine
Commissioner
Off. of Insurance Commissioner
704 West Tower
2 Martin Luther King, Jr. Dr.
Atlanta, GA 30334
Phone : (404) 656-2115

HAWAII
Wayne Metcalf
Insurance Commissioner
Div. of Insurance
Commerce & Consumer Aff. Dept.
1010 Richards St.
Honolulu, HI 96813
Phone : (808) 586-2790

IDAHO
Mike Brassey
Director
Dept. of Insurance
500 S. 10th
Boise, ID 83720
Phone : (208) 334-2255

ILLINOIS
James W. Schacht
Acting Director
Dept. of Insurance
320 W. Washington, 4th Fl.
Springfield, IL 62767
Phone : (217) 782-4515
Fax : (217) 524-6500

INDIANA
Donna Bennett
Commissioner
Dept. of Insurance
311 W. Washington St., Ste. 300
Indianapolis, IN 46204
Phone : (317) 232-2406

IOWA
Terri Vaughan
Commissioner
Insurance Div.
Dept. of Commerce
Lucas State Off. Bldg.
Des Moines, IA 50319
Phone : (515) 281-5705

KANSAS
Kathleen Sebelius
Commissioner
Department of Insurance
420 SW 9th St.
Topeka, KS 66612-1678
Phone : (913) 296-3071
Fax : (913) 296-2283

KENTUCKY
Don Stephens
Commissioner
Dept. of Insurance
Public Prot. & Regulation Cabinet
229 W. Main St.
Frankfort, KY 40601
Phone : (502) 564-6027

LOUISIANA
Jim Brown
Commissioner
Dept. of Insurance
P.O. Box 94214
Baton Rouge, LA 70804-9214
Phone : (504) 342-5423

MAINE
Brian Atchinson
Superintendent
Bur. of Insurance
Professional & Financial Regulations
State House Station # 34
Augusta, ME 04333
Phone : (207) 582-8707

MARYLAND
Dwight K. Bartlett III
Commissioner
Div. of Insurance
Licensing & Regulation Dept.
501 St. Paul St.
Baltimore, MD 21202-2272
Phone : (410) 333-6300

MASSACHUSETTS
Linda Ruthardt
Commissioner
Div. of Insurance
Executive Off. of Consumer Affairs
470 Atlantic Ave.
Boston, MA 02210-2223
Phone : (617) 521-7301

MICHIGAN
Joe Olson
Commissioner of Insurance
Licensing & Regulation Dept.
P.O. Box 30220
Lansing, MI 48909
Phone : (517) 373-9273

MINNESOTA
James Ulland
Commissioner
Dept. of Commerce
133 E. Seventh St.
St. Paul, MN 55101
Phone : (612) 296-6694

MISSISSIPPI
George Dale
Commissioner
Dept. of Insurance
1804 Sillers Bldg.
Jackson, MS 39201
Phone : (601) 359-3569

MISSOURI
Jay Angoff
Director
Dept. of Insurance
Truman Bldg., Rm. 630
P.O. Box 690
Jefferson City, MO 65102
Phone : (314) 751-1927
Fax : (314) 751-1165

MONTANA
Frank Cote
Chief Deputy
Commissioner
Insurance Div.
Off. of the State Auditor
P.O. Box 4009
Helena, MT 59620-0301
Phone : (406) 444-2997

NEBRASKA
Robert G. Lange
Director
Dept. of Insurance
The Terminal Bldg.,
Ste. 400
941 O St.
Lincoln, NE 68508
Phone : (402) 471-2201

NEVADA
Alice Molasky Esq.
Commissioner
Div. of Insurance
Dept. of Business &
Industry
1665 Hot Springs Rd.
Carson City, NV 89710
Phone : (702) 687-4270

NEW HAMPSHIRE
Sylvio Dupuis
Commissioner
Insurance Dept.
169 Manchester St.
Concord, NH 03301
Phone : (603) 271-2261

NEW JERSEY
Andrew J. Karpinski
Commissioner
Dept. of Insurance
20 W. State St., CN325
Trenton, NJ 08625
Phone : (609) 633-7667

NEW MEXICO
Christopher Krahling
Superintendent
State Corporation Comm.
Dept. of Insurance
PERA Bldg., Rm. 428
Santa Fe, NM 87503
Phone : (505) 827-4297
Fax : (505) 827-4734

NEW YORK*
Superintendent of
Insurance
Insurance Dept.
Agency Bldg. 1
Empire State Plz.
Albany, NY 12257
Phone : (518) 474-4550

NORTH CAROLINA
James E. Long
Commissioner
Dept. of Insurance
430 N. Salisbury St.
Raleigh, NC 27603-5908
Phone : (919) 733-7343
Fax : (919) 733-6495

NORTH DAKOTA
Glenn Pomoroy
Commissioner
Dept. of Insurance
State Capitol, 5th Fl.
600 E. Boulevard Ave.
Bismarck, ND 58505-0320
Phone : (701) 328-2440
Fax : (701) 328-4880

OHIO
Harold Duryee
Director
Dept. of Insurance
2100 Stella Ct.
Columbus, OH 43266-0566
Phone : (614) 644-2651
Fax : (614) 644-3743

OKLAHOMA
John P. Crawford
Insurance Commissioner
Oklahoma Insurance Dept.
1901 N. Walnut
Oklahoma City, OK 73105
Phone : (405) 521-2828
Fax : (405) 521-6635

OREGON
Kerry Barnett
Director
Dept. of Consumer &
Business Srvcs.
21 Labor & Industries Bldg.
Salem, OR 97310
Phone : (503) 378-4120
Fax : (503) 378-6444

PENNSYLVANIA
Linda S. Kaiser
Commissioner
Dept. of Insurance
Strawberry Sq., 13th Fl.
Harrisburg, PA 17120
Phone : (717) 787-5173

RHODE ISLAND
Charles Kwolek
Superintendent of
Insurance &
Associate Director
Dept. of Business
Regulation
233 Richmond St., Ste. 233
Providence, RI 02903
Phone : (401) 277-2246

SOUTH CAROLINA
Susanne Murphy
Interim Chief Insurance
Comm.
Dept. of Insurance
1612 Marion St.
Columbia, SC 29201
Phone : (803) 737-6160

SOUTH DAKOTA
David Volk
Secretary
Dept. of Commerce &
Regulations
910 E. Sioux Ave.
Pierre, SD 57501
Phone : (605) 773-3178

TENNESSEE
Doug Sizemore
Commissioner
Dept. of Commerce &
Insurance
500 James Robertson Pkwy.
Nashville, TN 37243-0565
Phone : (615) 741-2241
Fax : (615) 532-8281

TEXAS
Elton Bomer
Commissioner
Dept. of Insurance
333 Guadalupe
P.O. Box 149104
Austin, TX 78714-9104
Phone : (512) 463-6169

UTAH
Robert Wilcox
Commissioner
State Insurance Dept.
3110 State Off. Bldg.
Salt Lake City, UT 84114
Phone : (801) 538-3800

VERMONT
Elizabeth R. Costle
Commissioner
Dept. of Banking,
Insurance & Securities
89 State St.
Montpelier, VT 05620-3101
Phone : (802) 828-3301
Fax : (802) 828-3306

VIRGINIA
Preston C. Shannon
Chair
State Corporation Comm.
Tyler Bldg.
1300 E. Main St.
Richmond, VA 23219
Phone : (804) 371-9608
Fax : (804) 371-9376

WASHINGTON
Deborah Senn
Commissioner
Off. of the Insurance
Comm.
Insurance Bldg.
P.O. Box 40255
Olympia, WA 98504-0255
Phone : (360) 753-7300

WEST VIRGINIA
Hanley Clark
Commissioner
Div. of Insurance
2100 Washington St., E.
Charleston, WV 25305
Phone : (304) 558-3354

WISCONSIN
Josephine Musser
Commissioner
Off. of Comm. of Insurance
121 E. Wilson, 1st Fl.
Madison, WI 53703
Phone : (608) 266-3585
Fax : (608) 266-9935

WYOMING
John P. McBride
Commissioner
Dept. of Insurance
Herschler Bldg.
Cheyenne, WY 82002

DISTRICT OF COLUMBIA
Robert M. Willis
Administrator
Insurance Administration
Dept. of Consumer & Reg. Aff.
613 G St., N.W., Rm. 600
Washington, DC 20001
Phone : (202) 727-8000
Phone : (307) 777-6896

AMERICAN SAMOA
Tauivi Tuinei
Insurance Commissioner
Off. of the Insurance Commissioner
Governor's Off.
American Samoa Government
Pago Pago, AS 96799
Phone : (684) 633-4116
Fax : (684) 633-2269

GUAM
Joseph T. Duenas
Director
Dept. of Revenue & Taxation
378 Chalan San Antonio
Tamuning, GU 96911
Phone : (671) 647-5107
Fax : (671) 632-1040

NORTHERN MARIANA ISLANDS
Oscar C. Camacho
Special Asst. for Banking
Dept. of Commerce & Labor
Off. of the Governor
Saipan, MP 96950
Phone : (670) 322-4361

PUERTO RICO
Juan Antonio Garcia
Commissioner
Insurance Comm.
P.O. Box 8330
Santurce, PR 00910
Phone : (809) 722-8686
Fax : (809) 722-4400

U.S. VIRGIN ISLANDS
Kenneth E. Mapp
Lt. Governor
#18 Kongens Gade
St. Thomas, VI 00802
Phone : (809) 774-2991
Fax : (809) 774-6953

INTERNATIONAL TRADE

Promotes state exports, attracts overseas investments in the state and directs trade and investment missions.

ALABAMA
Fred Denton
Intl. Dev. Director
Development Off.
Center for Commerce
410 Adams Ave.
Montgomery, AL 36130
Phone : (334) 263-0048
Fax : (334) 242-0486

ALASKA*
Executive Director
Off. of Intl. Trade
Dept. of Comm. & Econ. Dev.
3601 C St., Ste. 798
Anchorage, AK 99503
Phone : (907) 561-5585
Fax : (907) 561-4577

ARIZONA
Sara Goertzen
Director
Dept. of Commerce
3800 N. Central Ave., Ste. 1500
Phoenix, AZ 85012
Phone : (602) 280-1306

ARKANSAS
Charles Sloan
Deputy Director
International Marketing Div.
Industrial Development Comm.
1 Capitol Mall, Rm. 4C-300
Little Rock, AR 72201
Phone : (501) 682-7678
Fax : (501) 324-9856

CALIFORNIA
Julie Meier Wright
Secretary
Trade & Commerce Agency
801 K St., Ste. 1700
Sacramento, CA 95814
Phone : (916) 322-3962

COLORADO
Morgan Smith
Director
International Trade Off.
Off. of the Governor
1625 Broadway, Ste. 680
Denver, CO 80202
Phone : (303) 892-3850
Fax : (303) 892-3820

CONNECTICUT
Andy Hammerl
Director
International Trade Div.
865 Brook St.
Rocky Hill, CT 06067
Phone : (203) 258-4258

DELAWARE
Robert W. Coy Jr.
Director
Development Off.
99 Kings Hwy.
P.O. Box 1401
Dover, DE 19903
Phone : (302) 739-4271
Fax : (302) 739-5749

FLORIDA
Nat M. Turnbull Jr.
Florida Intl. Affairs Comm.
Executive Off. of the Governor
The Capitol
Tallahassee, FL 32399-0001
Phone : (904) 488-2272
Fax : (904) 488-6581

GEORGIA
Randolph B. Cardoza
Commissioner
Dept. of Ind., Trade & Tourism
258 Peachtree Ctr. Ave., NE, Ste. 1000
Atlanta, GA 30303
Phone : (404) 656-3556

HAWAII
Seiji Naya
Director
Dept. of Business, Economic Development & Tourism
220 S. King St., # 1100
Honolulu, HI 96813
Phone : (808) 586-2359
Fax : (808) 586-2377

IDAHO
David P.N. Christensen
Administrator
International Trade Div.
Dept. of Commerce
700 W. State St.
Boise, ID 83720
Phone : (208) 334-2470

ILLINOIS
Dennis R. Whetstone
Director
Dept. of Commerce & Community Affairs
620 E. Adams St., 3rd Fl.
Springfield, IL 62701
Phone : (217) 782-3233
Fax : (217) 524-0864

INDIANA
Steve Condrey
International Trade Div.
Dept. of Commerce
1 N. Capitol, Ste. 700
Indianapolis, IN 46204
Phone : (317) 232-4949

IOWA
Mike Doyle
Acting Division Administrator
Bur. of International Mktg.
Dept. of Econ. Dev.
200 E. Grand
Des Moines, IA 50309
Phone : (515) 242-4729

KANSAS
Jeff Willis
Acting Director
Trade Development Division
Dept. of Commerce & Housing
700 SW Harrison, Ste. 1300
Topeka, KS 66612-3712
Phone : (913) 296-4027
Fax : (913) 296-5055

KENTUCKY
William H. Bowker
Executive Director
Coal Marketing & Exp. Council
Cabinet for Economic Dev.
302 Wilkinson Blvd, Hoge House
Frankfort, KY 40601
Phone : (502) 564-2562

LOUISIANA
Don Hayes
Assistant Secretary
Off. of International Trade
Dept. of Econ. Dev.
P.O. Box 94185
Baton Rouge, LA 70804
Phone : (504) 342-3000

MAINE
Tom McBrierty
Commissioner
Dept. of Economic & Community Development
State House Station # 59
Augusta, ME 04333
Phone : (207) 287-2656

MARYLAND
Scott M. Blacklin
Director, International Div.
Dept. of Econ. & Comm. Dev.
World Trade Ctr., 7th Fl.
401 E. Pratt St.
Baltimore, MD 21202
Phone : (410) 333-8180

MASSACHUSETTS
Nicholas Rostow
Director
Off. of International Trade
100 Cambridge St., 13th Fl.
Boston, MA 02202
Phone : (617) 367-1830

MICHIGAN
Kathy Reid-Kleckner
Acting Executive Director
Michigan Int'l Trade Authority
Dept. of Commerce
P.O. Box 30225
Lansing, MI 48909
Phone : (517) 373-6390

MINNESOTA
George Crolick
Director
Trade Office
1000 World Trade Ctr.
30 E. Seventh St.
St. Paul, MN 55101
Phone : (612) 297-4222

MISSISSIPPI
Jay Moon
Deputy Director
Dept. of Economic & Community Dev.
P.O. Box 849
Jackson, MS 39205
Phone : (601) 359-3448

MISSOURI
Chris Gutierrez
Acting Director
International Trade & Dev.
Comm. & Economic Dev.
Truman Bldg., Rm. 720
P.O. Box 118
Jefferson City, MO 65102
Phone : (314) 751-4855
Fax : (314) 751-7384

MONTANA
Mark Bisom
International Affairs Coordinator
Dept. of Commerce
1424 Ninth Ave.
Helena, MT 59620
Phone : (406) 444-4380

NEBRASKA
Maxine Moul
Director
Dept. of Economic Development
301 Centennial Mall S.
P.O. Box 94666
Lincoln, NE 68509-4666
Phone : (402) 471-3747

NEVADA
Tim Carlson
Executive Director
Comm. on Economic Development
5151 S. Carson St.
Carson City, NV 89710
Phone : (702) 687-4325

NEW HAMPSHIRE
Dawn Wivell
Director
International Commerce
Dept. of Resources & Econ. Dev.
601 Spaulding Tpke., Ste. 29
Portsmouth, NH 03801
Phone : (603) 334-6074

NEW JERSEY
Carlos Kearns
Director
Div. of International Trade
Dept. of Commerce & Econ. Dev.
28 W. State St., 8th Fl.
CN-836
Trenton, NJ 08625
Phone : (609) 633-3606

NEW MEXICO
Roberto Castillo
Director
International Trade Div.
Dept. of Economic Dev.
1100 St. Francis Dr.
Santa Fe, NM 87503
Phone : (505) 827-0309
Fax : (505) 827-0263

NEW YORK*
Commissioner
Dept. of Commerce
1 Commerce Plz.
Albany, NY 12245
Phone : (518) 474-4100

NORTH CAROLINA
Dick Quinlan
Director
International Div.
Dept. of Commerce
430 N. Salisbury St.
Raleigh, NC 27603
Phone : (919) 733-7193
Fax : (919) 733-8356

NORTH DAKOTA
Charles W. Stroup
Director
Dept. of Economic Dev. & Finance
1833 E. Bismarck Expy.
Bismarck, ND 58504
Phone : (701) 328-5300
Fax : (701) 328-5320

OHIO
James E.P. Sisto
Deputy Director
Div. of International Trade
Dept. of Development
P.O. Box 1001
Columbus, OH 43266
Phone : (614) 466-5017
Fax : (614) 463-1540

OKLAHOMA
Gary H. Miller
Director
International Trade Div.
Dept. of Econ. Dev.
6601 Broadway Ext.
Oklahoma City, OK 73116
Phone : (405) 843-9770

OREGON
Glenn Ford
Manager
Economic Development Dept.
1 World Trade Ctr.
121 SW Salmon, Ste. 300
Portland, OR 97204
Phone : (503) 229-5625

PENNSYLVANIA
Ronald Anderson
Director
Off. of International Dev.
Dept. of Commerce
464 Forum Bldg.
Harrisburg, PA 17120-
Phone : (717) 787-7190

RHODE ISLAND
Marcel Valois
Director
Dept. of Economic Development
7 Jackson Walkway
Providence, RI 02903
Phone : (401) 277-2601

SOUTH CAROLINA
Will Lacey
Manager
Trade Promotion
Dept. of Commerce
1201 Main St.
Columbia, SC 29201
Phone : (803) 737-0437

SOUTH DAKOTA
Bonnie Untereiner
Commissioner
Governor's Off. of Economic Development
Capitol Lake Plz.
Pierre, SD 57501
Phone : (605) 773-5032

TENNESSEE
Michael Sadler
Assistant Commissioner
International Marketing
Dept. of Econ. & Community Dev.
320 Sixth Ave., N.
Nashville, TN 37243
Phone : (615) 741-2549

TEXAS
Brenda Arnett
Executive Director
Dept. of Commerce
P.O. Box 12728, Capitol Station
Austin, TX 78711
Phone : (512) 472-5059

UTAH
Richard J. Mayfield
Director
Div. of Business & Economic Dev.
Dept. of Community & Economic Dev.
324 S. State St., Ste. 200
Salt Lake City, UT 84111
Phone : (801) 538-8820

VERMONT
Tom Myers
Director
International Business
Dept. of Economic Development
109 State St.
Montpelier, VT 05609
Phone : (802) 828-3221
Fax : (802) 828-3258

VIRGINIA
Wayne L. Sterling
Director
Dept. of Economic Development
West Tower-19th Fl.
901 E. Byrd St.
Richmond, VA 23219
Phone : (804) 371-8106
Fax : (804) 371-8112

WASHINGTON
Bob Randolph
State Trade Rep.
Off. of WA State Trade Rep.
2001 Sixth Ave., Ste. 2600
Seattle, WA 98121
Phone : (360) 464-7143

WEST VIRGINIA
Tom Burns
Director
Development Office
Bldg. 6, Rm. B504
1900 Kanawha Blvd., E.
Charleston, WV 25305
Phone : (304) 558-2234

WISCONSIN
Mary Regel
Director
Bur. of International Dev.
Dept. of Development
123 W. Washington Ave.
P.O. Box 7970
Madison, WI 53707
Phone : (608) 267-9227
Fax : (608) 266-5551

WYOMING
George H. Gault
Director
Div. of Econ. & Comm. Dev.
Dept. of Commerce
2301 Central Ave., 4N
Cheyenne, WY 82002
Phone : (307) 777-6435

DISTRICT OF COLUMBIA
Bill Byrd
Executive Director
Off. of International Business
717 14th St. NW #1100
Washington, DC 20005-3206
Phone : (202) 727-1576

AMERICAN SAMOA
Alfonso Pete Galeai
Director
Off. Of Economic Development Planning
Utulei
Pago Pago, AS 96799
Phone : (684) 633-5155
Fax : (684) 633-4195

GUAM
Frank B. Aguon Jr.
Director
Dept. of Commerce
590 S. Marine Dr., Ste. 601
Tamuning, GU 96911
Phone : (671) 646-6931
Fax : (671) 646-7242

NORTHERN MARIANA ISLANDS
Joaquin S. Torres
Director
Dept. of Commerce & Labor
Off. of the Governor
Saipan, MP 96950
Phone : (670) 322-4361

PUERTO RICO
Lissette Dias De Rivera
Director
Dept. of Commerce
P.O. Box S-4275
San Juan, PR 00905
Phone : (809) 724-1451

U.S. VIRGIN ISLANDS
Anthony Olive
Commissioner
Dept. of Economic Development & Agriculture
P.O. Box 6400
St. Thomas, VI 00803
Phone : (809) 774-8784
Fax : (809) 774-4390

JOB TRAINING

Administers job training and services for the unemployed, under-employed and economically disadvantaged in the state.

ALABAMA
Ray Clenney
Bureau of Job Training
Econ. & Community Aff. Dept.
401 Adams Ave., Suite 370
Montgomery, AL 36031
Phone : (334) 242-8672
Fax : (334) 242-5515

Mary Louise Sims
Bur. of Job Training
401 Adams Ave., Ste. 424
Montgomery, AL 36031
Phone : (334) 242-8672
Fax : (334) 242-5515

ALASKA
Tom Cashen
Commissioner
Dept. of Labor
P.O. Box 21149
Juneau, AK 99802-1149
Phone : (907) 465-2700
Fax : (907) 465-2784

ARIZONA
James B. Griffith
Assistant Director
Employment & Rehab. Srvc. Div.
Dept. of Economic Security
1789 W. Washington
Phoenix, AZ 85007
Phone : (602) 542-4910

ARKANSAS
Phil Price
Director
Employment Security Div.
Dept. of Labor
Capitol Mall
Little Rock, AR 72201
Phone : (501) 682-2121
Fax : (501) 682-3713

CALIFORNIA
Al Lee
Chief Deputy Director
Dept. of Employment Dev.
800 Capitol Mall, Rm. 5000
Sacramento, CA 95814
Phone : (916) 654-8210

COLORADO
Les Franklin
Director
Governor's Job Training Off.
Off. of the Governor
720 S. Colorado Blvd., # 550
Denver, CO 80222
Phone : (303) 758-5020

CONNECTICUT
Joseph E. Arborio
Chairman
JTPA Administration
Dept. of Labor
200 Folly Brook Blvd.
Wethersfield, CT 06109
Phone : (203) 566-7550

DELAWARE
John Modica
Director
Div. of Employment & Training
Dept. of Labor
Univ. Plz., Stockton Bldg.
Newark, DE 19702
Phone : (302) 368-6810

FLORIDA
Martha Larson
Director
Div. of Labor, Empl. & Train.
Dept. of Labor & Empl. Sec.
Atkins Bldg., Rm. 300
Tallahassee, FL 32399
Phone : (904) 488-7228

GEORGIA
Richard Botters
Assistant Commissioner
Job Training
Dept. of Labor
148 International Blvd., Rm. 222
Atlanta, GA 30303
Phone : (404) 656-5810

HAWAII
Lorraine Akiba
Director
Dept. of Labor & Industrial Relations
830 Punchbowl St.
Honolulu, HI 96813
Phone : (808) 586-8844
Fax : (808) 586-9099

IDAHO
Cheryl Brush
Bureau Chief
Bur. of Planning & Training Programs
Dept. of Employment
317 Main St.
Boise, ID 83735
Phone : (208) 334-6303

ILLINOIS
Dennis R. Whetstone
Director
Dept. of Commerce & Community Affairs
620 E. Adams St., 3rd Fl.
Springfield, IL 62701
Phone : (217) 782-3233
Fax : (217) 524-0864

INDIANA
Carol Baker
Director of Field Operations
Empl. & Training Programs
Workforce Development
10 N. Senate, Ste. 331
Indianapolis, IN 46204
Phone : (317) 232-4259

IOWA
Jeff Nall
Administrator
Div. of Job Training
Dept. of Economic Dev.
200 E. Grand
Des Moines, IA 50309
Phone : (515) 281-4219

KANSAS
Peter Latessa
Director
Div. of Employment & Training
Dept. of Human Resources
1321 SW Topeka Blvd.
Topeka, KS 66612-1894
Phone : (913) 296-7874
Fax : (913) 296-5112

KENTUCKY
Treva B. Wright-Donnell
Commissioner
Dept. for Employment Srvcs.
Cabinet for Human Resources
275 E. Main St.
Frankfort, KY 40621
Phone : (502) 564-5331

LOUISIANA
Gayle Truly
Secretary
Dept. of Labor
P.O. Box 94094
Baton Rouge, LA 70804
Phone : (504) 342-3011

MAINE
James Nimon
Director
Occupational Info. Coord. Cmte.
State House Station #71
Augusta, ME 04333
Phone : (207) 287-2411

MARYLAND
Charles Middlebrooks
Assistant Secretary
Employment & Training
Dept. of Economic & Empl. Dev.
1100 N. Eutaw St.
Baltimore, MD 21201
Phone : (301) 333-5070

MASSACHUSETTS
Nils L. Nordberg
Commissioner
Dept. of Employment & Training
Charles F. Hurley Bldg.
19 Staniford St., 3rd Fl.
Boston, MA 02114
Phone : (617) 626-6600

MICHIGAN
Douglas Stites
Vice President
Workforce Development
Jobs Comm.
201 N. Washington
Lansing, MI 48913
Phone : (517) 373-8500

MINNESOTA
R. Jane Brown
Commissioner
Dept. of Jobs & Training
390 N. Robert St.
St. Paul, MN 55101
Phone : (612) 296-3711

MISSISSIPPI
Jean Denson
Director
Employment & Training Div.
Dept. of Econ. & Comm. Dev.
301 W. Pearl St.
Jackson, MS 39203
Phone : (601) 949-2000

MISSOURI
Irvin Whitehead
Acting Director
Div. of Job Dev. & Training
Dept. of Economic Development
2023 St. Mary's Blvd.
P.O. Box 1087
Jefferson City, MO 65102-1087
Phone : (314) 751-4750
Fax : (314) 751-6765

MONTANA
T. Gary Curtis
Administrator
Job Service Div.
P.O. Box 1728
Helena, MT 59624
Phone : (406) 444-2648

NEBRASKA
Fernando Lecuona
Deputy Commissioner
Job Training Program
Dept. of Labor
P.O. Box 94600
Lincoln, NE 68509
Phone : (402) 471-2127

NEVADA
Barbara Weinberg
Director
State Job Training Off.
Dept. of Employment Training & Rehabilitation
400 W. King St.
Carson City, NV 89710
Phone : (702) 687-4310

NEW HAMPSHIRE
Ray Worden
Executive Director
Jobs Training Council
64 Old Suncook Rd.
Concord, NH 03301
Phone : (603) 228-9500

NEW JERSEY
Paulette Laubsch
Asstistant Commissioner
Employment Security & Job Training
Dept. of Labor
John Fitch Plaza, CN-058
Trenton, NJ 08625
Phone : (609) 984-5666

NEW MEXICO
Howard Williams
Director
Training Div.
Dept. of Labor
1596 Pacheco St., Box 4218
Santa Fe, NM 87502
Phone : (505) 827-6827
Fax : (505) 827-6812

NEW YORK*
Commissioner
Dept. of Labor
State Off. Bldg., State Campus
Albany, NY 12240
Phone : (518) 457-2741

NORTH CAROLINA
Joel C. New
Director
Employment & Training
Env., Health & Nat. Res. Dept.
111 Seaboard Ave.
Raleigh, NC 27604
Phone : (919) 733-6383

NORTH DAKOTA
James Hirsch
Director
Employment & Training Program
Job Service
P.O. Box 1537
Bismarck, ND 58502
Phone : (701) 328-2825
Fax : (701) 328-4000

OHIO
Evelyn Bissonett
Director
Job Training Partnership Act
Bur. of Employment Srvcs.
145 S. Front St., 4th Fl.
Columbus, OH 43266-0556
Phone : (614) 466-3817
Fax : (614) 752-6582

OKLAHOMA
Wayne Winn
Executive Director
Employment Security Comm.
200 Will Rogers Bldg.
Oklahoma City, OK 73105
Phone : (405) 557-7200

OREGON
Bill Easly
Manager
Job Training Partnership Admin.
Dept. of Economic Development
777 Summer St., NE
Salem, OR 97310
Phone : (503) 373-1995

PENNSYLVANIA
Alan Williamson
Deputy Secretary
Emp. Security & Job Training
Dept. of Labor & Industry
Rm. 1700, Labor & Industry Bldg.
Harrisburg, PA 17120
Phone : (717) 787-1745

RHODE ISLAND
Larry Fitch
Director
Dept. of Employment & Training
101 Friendship St.
Providence, RI 02903
Phone : (401) 277-3732

SOUTH CAROLINA
Robert E. David
Executive Director
Employment Security Comm.
P.O. Box 995
Columbia, SC 29202
Phone : (803) 737-2617

SOUTH DAKOTA
Mike Ryan
JTPA Administrator
Dept. of Labor
Kneip Bldg.
Pierre, SD 57501
Phone : (605) 773-3101

TENNESSEE
Bob L. Morris
Assistant Commissioner
Dept. of Labor
501 Union Bldg., Ste. 600
Nashville, TN 37243
Phone : (615) 741-1031

TEXAS
Sunny Alexander
Director
Job Services
Texas Employment Comm.
101 E. 15th St.
Austin, TX 78701
Phone : (512) 463-2659

UTAH
Greg Gardner
Director
Off. of Job Training for Economic Development
6136 State Off. Bldg.
Salt Lake City, UT 84114
Phone : (801) 538-8750

VERMONT
Bob Ware
Director
Jobs & Training Div.
Dept. of Employment & Training
P.O. Box 488
Montpelier, VT 05601-0488
Phone : (802) 828-4151
Fax : (802) 828-4022

VIRGINIA
Clarence H. Carter
Executive Director
Governor's Employment & Training Dept.
4615 W. Broad St.
Richmond, VA 23230
Phone : (804) 367-9803
Fax : (804) 367-6172

WASHINGTON
Larry Malo
Assistant Commissioner
Employment & Training Div.
Dept. of Employment Security
212 Maple Park, 6000
P.O. Box 9046
Olympia, WA 98504-9046
Phone : (360) 753-5116

WEST VIRGINIA
Quetta Muzzle
Director
Job Training Program Division
Bldg. 4, Rm. 610
612 California Ave.
Charleston, WV 25305
Phone : (304) 558-5920

WISCONSIN
June M. Suhling
Administrator
Jobs, Empl., & Training Srvcs.
Dept. of Ind. Labor & Human Rel.
201 E. Washington, Rm. 201
P.O. Box 7946
Madison, WI 53703
Phone : (608) 266-0327
Fax : (608) 267-2392

WYOMING
Matt Johnson
Administrator
Job Training Program
Dept. of Employment
P.O. Box 2760
Casper, WY 82602
Phone : (307) 235-3601

DISTRICT OF COLUMBIA
Joseph Yeldell
Director
Dept. of Employment Services
500 C St., NW, Rm. 600
Washington, DC 20001
Phone : (202) 724-7101

AMERICAN SAMOA
Sapini Siatu'u
Director
Dept. of Human Resources
American Samoa Government
Pago Pago, AS 96799
Phone : (684) 633-4485
Fax : (684) 633-1139

GUAM
William E. Cundiff
Director
Agency for Human Resources Development
P.O. Box CQ
Agana, GU 96910
Phone : (671) 646-9341
Fax : (671) 646-9339

NORTHERN MARIANA ISLANDS
Felix Nogis
Director
Job Training Partnership Admn.
Dept. of Labor
Saipan, MP 96950
Phone : (670) 664-1700
Fax : (670) 322-7333

PUERTO RICO
Ceasar Almodova Machany
Secretary
Dept. of Labor & Human Resources
505 Munoz Rivera Ave.
Hato Rey, PR 00918
Phone : (809) 754-5353
Fax : (809) 753-9550

U.S. VIRGIN ISLANDS
Lisa Harris-Moorhead
Commissioner
Dept. of Labor
P.O. Box 208
St. Thomas, VI 00802
Phone : (809) 776-3700
Fax : (809) 773-0094

JUDICIAL CONDUCT ORGANIZATIONS

Oversees the investigation and hearings of judges charged with misconduct.

ALASKA
Marla Greenstein
Executive Director
Comm. on Judicial Conduct
310 K St., Ste. 301
Anchorage, AK 99501
Phone : (907) 272-1033
Fax : (907) 272-9309

ARIZONA
E. Keith Stott
Executive Director
Comm. on Judicial Conduct
1501 W. Washington St.
Phoenix, AZ 85007
Phone : (602) 542-5200

CALIFORNIA
William C. Vickrey
Director
Judicial Council of California
South Tower, 4th Fl.
303 Second St.
San Francisco, CA 94107
Phone : (415) 904-3650

DELAWARE
Cathy L. Howard
Acting Clerk
State Supreme Court
55 The Green
Dover, DE 19901
Phone : (302) 739-4155
Fax : (302) 739-3751

FLORIDA
Brook S. Kennerly
Executive Director
Judicial Qualifications Comm.
The Historic Capitol, Ste. 102
Tallahassee, FL 32399-6000
Phone : (904) 488-1581

GEORGIA
Norman Underwood
Judicial Qualifications Comm.
600 Peachtree St., NE, Ste. 5200
Atlanta, GA 30308-2216
Phone : (404) 885-3228

HAWAII
Gerald Sekiya
Chair
Comm. on Judicial Conduct
The Judiciary/Supreme Court
P.O. Box 2560
Honolulu, HI 96804-2560
Phone : (808) 539-4790

IDAHO
Robert G. Hamlin
Executive Director
Judicial Council
P.O. Box 16488
Boise, ID 83715-6488
Phone : (208) 344-8474

ILLINOIS
Ray Breen
Executive Director
Judicial Inquiry Bd.
100 W. Randolph St., Ste. 14-500
Chicago, IL 60601
Phone : (312) 814-5554

INDIANA
Meg W. Babcock
Counsel
Comm. on Judicial Qualifications
115 W. Washington St., Ste. 1080
Indianapolis, IN 46204-3417
Phone : (317) 232-4706

KANSAS
Carol G. Green
Clerk of Appellate Courts
Judicial Branch
Judicial Center
301 SW Tenth Ave.
Topeka, KS 66612-1507
Phone : (913) 296-3229

KENTUCKY
James D. Lawson
Secretary
Judicial Retirement & Removal Comm.
P.O. Box 2168
Lexington, KY 40522
Phone : (606) 233-4128

LOUISIANA
Pascal F. Calogero, Jr.
Chief Justice
Supreme Court
301 Loyola Ave.
New Orleans, LA 70112
Phone : (504) 568-5727

MAINE
Merle Loper
Executive Secretary
Cmte. on Judicial Responsibility & Disability
P.O. Box 8058
Portland, ME 04104
Phone : (207) 780-4364

MARYLAND
Howard E. Wallin
Executive Secretary
University of Baltimore
1420 N. Charles St.
Baltimore, MD 21201
Phone : (410) 837-4628

MASSACHUSETTS
Barbara Morgan Fauth
Executive Director
Comm. on Judicial Conduct
14 Beacon St.
Boston, MA 02108
Phone : (617) 725-8050

MICHIGAN
Joseph Resnier
Exec. Dir. & General Counsel
Judicial Tenure Commission
211 W. Fort St.
Detroit, MI 48226
Phone : (313) 256-9104

MISSOURI
James M. Smith
Commissioner
Comm. on Retirement, Removal and Discipline of Judges
6933 Hampton Ave.
St. Louis, MO 63109
Phone : (314) 352-6944
Fax : (314) 832-0754

MONTANA
Patrick A. Chenovick
Administrator
Court Administration
Supreme Court
Justice Bldg., Rm. 315
Helena, MT 59620
Phone : (406) 444-2621

NEVADA
Eve Miceli King
Administrator
Comm. on Judicial Discipline
P.O. Box 48
Carson City, NV 89702
Phone : (702) 687-4017

NEW JERSEY
Patrick J. Monahan
Chief
Judiciary Dept.
Hughes Justice Complex
CN-037
Trenton, NJ 08625
Phone : (609) 292-2552

NEW MEXICO
Donald Perkins
Chairman
Judicial Standards Comm.
2539 Wyoming NE, Ste. A
Albuquerque, NM 87112
Phone : (505) 841-9438
Fax : (505) 841-9439

NEW YORK*
Administrator
State Comm. on Judicial Conduct
801 Second St.
New York, NY 10017
Phone : (212) 949-8860

NORTH CAROLINA
Sidney S. Eagles Jr.
Chair
Judicial Standards Comm.
P.O. Box 1122
Raleigh, NC 27602
Phone : (919) 733-2690

NORTH DAKOTA
Vivian E. Berg
Staff Counsel
Supreme Court
State Capitol, Judiciary Wing
600 E. Boulevard Ave.
Bismarck, ND 58505
Phone : (701) 328-3927
Fax : (701) 328-4480

OHIO
Jonathon W. Marshall
Director
Board of Commissions on Grievances & Discipline
Ohio Supreme Court
41 S. High St., Ste. 3370
Columbus, OH 43215
Phone : (614) 644-5800
Fax : (614) 644-5804

RHODE ISLAND
Thomas H. Needham
Chairman
Comm. on Judicial Tenure & Discipline, Superior Court
250 Benefit St.
Providence, RI 02903
Phone : (401) 277-3239

SOUTH CAROLINA
Sally Speth
Director
Judicial Standards Comm.
Judicial Dept.
P.O. Box 50487
Columbia, SC 29205
Phone : (803) 734-1965

SOUTH DAKOTA
Robert Hofer
Chair
Judicial Qualifications Comm.
319 S. Cotau
P.O. Box 280
Pierre, SD 57501-0280
Phone : (605) 224-5826

TENNESSEE
Joe G. Riley Jr.
Presiding Judge
Court of the Judiciary
111 Lake St.
Ridgely, TN 38080
Phone : (901) 264-5671

TEXAS
Robert Flowers
Executive Director
State Comm. on Judicial Conduct
P.O. Box 12265
Austin, TX 78711
Phone : (512) 463-5533

VERMONT
Leslie Blake
Chair
Judicial Conduct Board
P.O. Box 796
White River Jct, VT 05001
Phone : (802) 295-5631

VIRGINIA
Philip A. Leone
Director
Jt. Legis. Audit & Review Comm.
General Assembly Bldg.
910 Capitol St., Ste. 1100
Richmond, VA 23219
Phone : (804) 786-1258
Fax : (804) 371-0101

WASHINGTON
David Akana
Executive Director
Comm. on Judicial Conduct
P.O. Box 1817
Olympia, WA 98507-1817
Phone : (360) 753-4585

WEST VIRGINIA
Betty L. Lambert
Executive Secretary
Judicial Investigation Comm.
Bldg. 1, Rm. E400
1900 Kanawha Blvd., E.
Charleston, WV 25304
Phone : (304) 558-0169

WYOMING
Maxwell E. Osborn
Chairman
Judicial Supervisory Comm.
Supreme Court Bldg.
Cheyenne, WY 82002
Phone : (307) 777-7581

U.S. VIRGIN ISLANDS
Thomas Moore
Chief Judge
District Court
District Court Bldg.
St. Thomas, VI 00802
Phone : (809) 773-1130

JUVENILE REHABILITATION

Administers rehabilitative facilities and programs for delinquent youth committed by the courts.

ALABAMA
Teresa Smiley
Executive Director
Dept. of Youth Affairs
Alabama State House
P.O. Box 66
Mt. Meigs, AL 36057
Phone : (205) 242-7193

ALASKA
Diane Worley
Director
Div. of Family & Youth Srvcs.
Dept. of Health & Social Srvcs.
P.O. Box 110630
Juneau, AK 99811-0630
Phone : (907) 465-3170
Fax : (907) 465-3397

ARIZONA
Eugene R. Moore
Director
Dept. of Youth Treatment & Rehabilitation
1624 W. Adams St.
Phoenix, AZ 85007
Phone : (602) 542-3987

ARKANSAS
Beverly Jones
Director
Children & Family Srvcs.
Dept of Human Services
P.O. Box 1437
Little Rock, AR 72203
Phone : (501) 682-8772
Fax : (501) 682-8666

CALIFORNIA
Francisco J. Alarcon
Chief Deputy Director
Dept. of Youth Authority
4241 Williamsborough Dr., Ste. 201
Sacramento, CA 95823
Phone : (916) 262-1467

COLORADO
Jerry Adamek
Director
Div. of Youth Srvcs. & Families
Dept. of Human Srvcs.
4255 S. Knox Ct.
Denver, CO 80236
Phone : (303) 762-4695
Fax : (303) 762-1418

CONNECTICUT
Joseph D'Alesio
Director
Div. of Court Operation
75 Elm St.
Hartford, CT 06106
Phone : (203) 722-5897

DELAWARE
Guy Sapp
Director
Youth Rehab. Srvcs. Div.
Children, Youth & Families
1825 Faulkland Rd.
Wilmington, DE 19805
Phone : (302) 633-2620

FLORIDA
Calvin Ross
Dept. of Juvenile Justice
2737 Centerview Dr.
Tallahassee, FL 32399-3100
Phone : (904) 488-1850
Fax : (904) 921-4159

GEORGIA
Eugene Walker
Commissioner
Dept. of Children & Youth Srvcs.
2 Peachtree St., 5th Fl.
Atlanta, GA 30303
Phone : (404) 657-2410

HAWAII
Wayne Matsuo
Executive Director
Off. of Youth Srvcs.
Dept. of Human Srvcs.
1481 S. King St., Rm. 223
Honolulu, HI 96814
Phone : (808) 973-9494

IDAHO
George Neumayer
Acting Director
Dept. of Juvenile Corrections
Statehouse, DFM
Boise, ID 83720
Phone : (208) 334-3900

ILLINOIS
Odie Washington
Director
Dept. of Corrections
P.O. Box 19277
Springfield, IL 62794-9277
Phone : (217) 522-2666
Fax : (217) 522-8719

INDIANA
Pam Cline
Director
Juvenile Srvcs.
Dept. of Corrections
IGC-South, Rm. E 334
Indianapolis, IN 46204
Phone : (317) 232-1746

IOWA
Federico Brid
Administrator
Adult, Children & Family Srvcs.
Dept. of Human Srvcs.
Hoover State Off. Bldg.
Des Moines, IA 50319
Phone : (515) 281-5521

KANSAS
Ben Coats
Acting Commissioner
Youth & Adult Services
Dept. of Social & Rehab. Srvcs.
300 SW Oakley, West Hall
Topeka, KS 66606-2807
Phone : (913) 296-4653
Fax : (913) 296-4649

KENTUCKY
Peggy Wallace
Commissioner
Dept. for Social Srvcs.
Cabinet for Human Resources
275 E. Main St.
Frankfort, KY 40621
Phone : (502) 564-4650

LOUISIANA
Reginald Grace
Assistant Secretary
Off. of Juvenile Services
Pub. Safety & Corrections Dept.
P.O. Box 94304
Baton Rouge, LA 70804-9304
Phone : (504) 342-6001

MAINE
Richard J. Wyse
Superintendent
Maine Youth Center
Dept. of Corrections
675 Westbrook St.
South Portland, ME 04106
Phone : (207) 822-0000

MARYLAND
Stuart Simms
Secretary
Juvenile Srvcs. Admin.
321 Fallsway
Baltimore, MD 21202
Phone : (301) 333-6751

MASSACHUSETTS
William O'Leary
Commissioner
Dept. of Youth Srvcs.
27-43 Wormwood St., Ste. 400
Boston, MA 02210
Phone : (617) 727-7575

MICHIGAN
Harold Gazan
Director
Off. of Children & Family Srvcs.
Dept. of Social Srvcs.
235 S. Grand Ave.
Lansing, MI 48909
Phone: (517) 335-6158

MINNESOTA
Richard Quick
Executive Officer
Juvenile Release Div.
Dept. of Corrections
450 N. Syndicate
St. Paul, MN 55104
Phone: (612) 642-0274

MISSISSIPPI
Don Taylor
Director
Off. of Youth Services
Dept. of Human Services
P.O. Box 352
Jackson, MS 39205
Phone: (601) 960-4250

MISSOURI
Mark Steward
Director
Div. of Youth Services
Dept. of Social Services
Broadway Bldg., Rm. 540
P.O. Box 447
Jefferson City, MO 65102
Phone: (314) 751-3324
Fax: (314) 526-4494

MONTANA*
Administrator
Corrections Div.
Dept. of Corr. & Human Srvcs.
1539 11th Ave.
Helena, MT 59620
Phone: (406) 444-3902

NEBRASKA
Christine Hanus-Schulenberg
Administrator
Div. of Human Srvcs.
Dept. of Social Srvcs.
P.O. Box 95026
Lincoln, NE 68509
Phone: (402) 471-9308

NEBRASKA — Cont.
Harold Clarke
Director
Dept. of Correctional Services
W. Van Dorn & Folsom St.
P.O. Box 94661
Lincoln, NE 68509
Phone: (402) 471-2654

NEVADA
John Sarb
Administrator
Youth Services Div.
505 E. King St., Ste. 101
Carson City, NV 89710
Phone: (702) 687-6927

NEW HAMPSHIRE
Ronald Adams
Superintendent
Youth Development Ctr.
Children & Youth Services
1056 N. River Rd.
Manchester, NH 03104
Phone: (603) 625-5471

NEW JERSEY
Frank Gripp
Director
Div. of Operations/ Juvenile Complex
Dept. of Corrections
Whittlesey Rd., CN863
Trenton, NJ 08625
Phone: (609) 292-4640

NEW MEXICO
Loretta Henry
Director
Juvenile Justice Srvcs. Div.
Dept. of Children, Youth & Families
P.O. Drawer 5160
Santa Fe, NM 87502-5160
Phone: (505) 827-7629
Fax: (505) 827-8408

NEW YORK*
Director
Div. for Youth
84 Holland Ave.
Albany, NY 12208
Phone: (518) 473-8437

NORTH CAROLINA
Gwen Chunn
Director
Div. of Youth Services
Dept. of Human Resources
705 Palmer Dr.
Raleigh, NC 27603-2266
Phone: (919) 733-3011

NORTH DAKOTA
Al Lick
Director
Div. of Juvenile Services
Dept. of Corrections
P.O. Box 1898
Bismarck, ND 58502-1898
Phone: (701) 328-6390
Fax: (701) 328-6651

OHIO
Isaac R. Palmer
Deputy Director
Family & Children's Srvc. Div.
Dept. of Human Srvcs.
65 E. State St.
Columbus, OH 43215
Phone: (614) 466-1213
Fax: (614) 466-9247

OKLAHOMA
George Miller
Interim Director
Health & Human Srvcs.
Dept. of Human Srvcs.
P.O. Box 25352
Oklahoma City, OK 73125
Phone: (405) 521-2778

OREGON
Diane Walton
Executive Director
State Comm. on Children & Families
530 Center St., NE, Ste. 300
Salem, OR 97310
Phone: (503) 373-1570
Fax: (503) 378-8395

PENNSYLVANIA
George B. Taylor
Deputy Secretary
Children, Youth & Families
Dept. of Public Welfare
P.O. Box 2675
Harrisburg, PA 17105
Phone: (717) 787-4756

RHODE ISLAND
Kenneth Fandetti
Acting Director
Dept. of Children & Families
610 Mt. Pleasant Ave.
Providence, RI 02908
Phone: (401) 457-4750

SOUTH DAKOTA
Judy Hines
Administrator
Child Protection Srvcs. Div.
Dept. of Social Srvcs.
Kneip Bldg.
Pierre, SD 57501
Phone: (605) 773-3227

SOUTH CAROLINA
Flora Boyd
Director
Dept. of Juvenile Justice
P.O. Box 21069
Columbia, SC 29221-1069
Phone: (803) 896-9359

TENNESSEE
George Hathaway
Commissioner
Dept. of Youth Development
710 James Robertson Pkwy.
Nashville, TN 37243-1290
Phone: (615) 741-9701
Fax: (615) 532-8079

TEXAS
Steve Robinson
Director
Youth Comm.
P.O. Box 4260
Austin, TX 78765-4260
Phone: (512) 483-5000

UTAH
Gary Dalton
Director
Div. of Youth Corrections
Dept. of Human Srvcs.
120 N. 200 W., Rm. 422
Salt Lake City, UT 84103
Phone: (801) 538-4328

VERMONT
William Young
Director
Dept. of Social & Rehab. Srvcs.
103 S. Main St.
Waterbury, VT 05671
Phone : (802) 241-2101
Fax : (802) 241-2980

VIRGINIA
Patricia L. West
Director
Dept. of Youth & Family Srvcs.
700 Centre, 4th Fl.
7th & Franklin Streets
Richmond, VA 23219
Phone : (804) 371-0700
Fax : (804) 371-0773

WASHINGTON
Jerome M. Wasson
Director
Juvenile Rehabilitation Div.
Social & Health Srvcs. Dept.
P.O. Box 45720
Olympia, WA 98504
Phone : (360) 753-7402

WEST VIRGINIA
Susan Salmons
Director
Youth Srvcs.
Dept. of Health & Human Resources
3135 16th St.
Huntington, WV 25705
Phone : (304) 528-5800

WISCONSIN
Michael J. Sullivan
Secretary
Dept. of Corrections
149 E. Wilson, Rm. 1050
Madison, WI 53703
Phone : (608) 266-2471

WYOMING
Judy Uphoff
Director
Dept. of Corrections
Herschler Bldg.
Cheyenne, WY 82002
Phone : (307) 777-7405

DISTRICT OF COLUMBIA**
Dorothy Chambers
Acting Administrator
Receiving Home for Children
Dept. of Human Services
1000 Mt. Olivet Rd., NE
Washington, DC 20002
Phone : (402) 576-7250

AMERICAN SAMOA
Sapini Siatu'u
Director
Dept. of Human Resources
American Samoa Government
Pago Pago, AS 96799
Phone : (684) 633-4485
Fax : (684) 633-1139

GUAM
Oscar E. Fortier
Director
Dept. of Youth Affairs
P.O. Box 23672
GMF, GU 96921
Phone : (671) 734-3911
Fax : (671) 734-7536

NORTHERN MARIANA ISLANDS
Margarita O. Taitano
Administrator
Div. of Youth Srvcs.
Dept. of Comm. & Cultural Aff.
P.O. Box 1000 CK
Saipan, MP 96950
Phone : (670) 233-9075

PUERTO RICO
Ceasar Almodova Machany
Secretary
Dept. of Labor & Human Resources
505 Munoz Rivera Ave.
Hato Rey, PR 00918
Phone : (809) 754-5353
Fax : (809) 753-9550

U.S. VIRGIN ISLANDS
Catherine Mills
Assistant Commissioner
Dept. of Human Services
Barbel Plz., S.
St. Thomas, VI 00802
Phone : (809) 774-0930

LABOR

Overall responsibility for administering and enforcing the state's labor law.

ALABAMA
Jerry Ray
Commissioner
Dept. of Labor
1789 Congressman Dickinson Dr., 2nd Fl.
Montgomery, AL 36130
Phone: (334) 242-3460
Fax: (334) 240-3417

ALASKA
Tom Cashen
Commissioner
Dept. of Labor
P.O. Box 21149
Juneau, AK 99802-1149
Phone: (907) 465-2700
Fax: (907) 465-2784

ARIZONA
Larry J. Etchechury
Director
Industrial Comm.
P.O. Box 19070
Phoenix, AZ 85005-9070
Phone: (602) 542-4411

ARKANSAS
James Salkeld
Director
Dept. of Labor
10421 W. Markham, Ste. 100
Little Rock, AR 72205
Phone: (501) 682-4500
Fax: (501) 682-4532

CALIFORNIA
Lloyd W. Aubry, Jr.
Director
Dept. of Industrial Relations
455 Golden Gate Ave.
San Francisco, CA 94102
Phone: (415) 703-4590

COLORADO
John J. Donlon
Executive Director
Dept. of Labor & Employment
1515 Arapahoe St., Twr. 2, Ste. 400
Denver, CO 80202-2117
Phone: (303) 620-4717
Fax: (303) 620-4714

CONNECTICUT
John Saunders
Acting Commissioner
Dept. of Labor
200 Folly Brook Blvd.
Wethersfield, CT 06109
Phone: (203) 566-4384

DELAWARE
Darrell J. Minott
Secretary
Dept. of Labor
820 N. French St., 6th Fl.
Wilmington, DE 19801
Phone: (302) 577-2710
Fax: (302) 577-2735

FLORIDA
Doug Jamerson
Secretary
Dept. of Labor & Empl. Security
Hartman Bldg., Ste. 303
2012 Capitol Circle SE
Tallahassee, FL 32399-2152
Phone: (904) 922-7021
Fax: (904) 922-7119

GEORGIA
David Poythress
Commissioner
Dept. of Labor
148 International Blvd.
Atlanta, GA 30303
Phone: (404) 656-3011

HAWAII
Lorraine Akiba
Director
Dept. of Labor & Industrial Relations
830 Punchbowl St.
Honolulu, HI 96813
Phone: (808) 586-8844
Fax: (808) 586-9099

IDAHO
Bob Purcell
Director
Labor & Industrial Srvcs.
277 N. Sixth St.
Boise, ID 83720
Phone: (208) 334-3950

ILLINOIS
Shinae Chun
Director
Dept. of Labor
160 N. La Salle St., Ste. C1300
Chicago, IL 60601
Phone: (312) 793-2800
Fax: (312) 793-5257

INDIANA
Kenneth Zeller
Commissioner
Dept. of Labor
IGC-South, Rm. W195
402 W. Washington
Indianapolis, IN 46204
Phone: (317) 232-2663

IOWA
Al Meier
Commissioner
Labor Div.
Dept. Of Employment Srvcs.
Employment Service Bldg.
Des Moines, IA 50319
Phone: (515) 281-8067
Fax: (515) 242-5144

KANSAS
Duane Guy
Acting Director
Division of Labor
Dept. of Human Resources
401 Topeka Blvd.
Topeka, KS 66603-3182
Phone: (913) 296-7475
Fax: (913) 296-8177

KENTUCKY
Bill Riggs
Secretary
Labor Cabinet
1049 U.S. 127 S.
Frankfort, KY 40601
Phone: (502) 564-3070

LOUISIANA
Gayle Truly
Secretary
Dept. of Labor
P.O. Box 94094
Baton Rouge, LA 70804
Phone: (504) 342-3011

MAINE
Val Landry
Commissioner
Dept. of Labor
State House Station # 54
Augusta, ME 04333
Phone: (207) 287-3788

MARYLAND
John O'Connor
Commissioner
Div. of Labor & Industry
Dept. of Licensing & Reg.
501 St. Paul Pl.
Baltimore, MD 21202
Phone: (410) 333-4179

MASSACHUSETTS
Christine E. Morris
Commissioner
Dept. of Labor & Industries
Executive Off. of Labor
100 Cambridge St.
Boston, MA 02202
Phone: (617) 727-3455

MICHIGAN
Lowell Perry
Director
Dept. of Labor
P.O. Box 30015
Lansing, MI 48909
Phone: (517) 373-9600
Fax: (517) 373-3728

MINNESOTA
Gary Bastien
Commissioner
Dept. of Labor & Industry
443 Lafayette Rd.
St. Paul, MN 55101
Phone: (612) 296-2342

MISSOURI
Sandra M. Moore
Director
Dept. of Labor & Industrial Relations
3315 W. Truman Blvd.
P.O. Box 504
Jefferson City, MO 65102-0504
Phone: (314) 751-4091
Fax: (314) 751-4135

MONTANA
Laurie Ekanger
Commissioner
Dept. of Labor & Industry
P.O. Box 1728
Helena, MT 59624-1728
Phone : (406) 444-3555

NEBRASKA
Dan Dolan
Commissioner
Dept. of Labor
P.O. Box 94600
Lincoln, NE 68509
Phone : (402) 471-9000

NEVADA
Carol Jackson
Director
Dept. of Employment, Training & Rehabilitation
1830 E. Sahara Ave., Ste. 225
Las Vegas, NV 89104
Phone : (702) 486-7923
Fax : (702) 687-7924

NEW HAMPSHIRE
Diane Symonds
Commissioner
Dept. of Labor
95 Pleasant St.
Concord, NH 03301
Phone : (603) 271-3171

NEW JERSEY
Peter Calderone
Commissioner
Dept. of Labor
CN 110
Trenton, NJ 08625-0312
Phone : (609) 292-2323

NEW MEXICO
Clint Hardin
Secretary
Dept. of Labor
P.O. Box 1928
Albuquerque, NM 87103
Phone : (505) 841-8409
Fax : (505) 841-8491

NEW YORK*
Commissioner
Dept. of Labor
State Off. Bldg., State Campus
Albany, NY 12240
Phone : (518) 457-2741

NORTH CAROLINA
Harry E. Payne, Jr.
Commissioner
Dept. of Labor
4 W. Edenton St.
Raleigh, NC 27601-1092
Phone : (919) 733-7166
Fax : (919) 733-6197

NORTH DAKOTA
Craig Hagen
Commissioner
Dept. of Labor
State Capitol, 6th Fl.
600 E. Boulevard Ave.
Bismarck, ND 58505
Phone : (701) 328-2660
Fax : (701) 328-2031

OHIO
Andy Lyles
Director
Dept. of Industrial Relations
2323 W. Fifth Ave.
P.O. Box 825
Columbus, OH 43266-0567
Phone : (614) 644-2223
Fax : (614) 644-2618

OKLAHOMA
Brenda Reneau
Commissioner
Dept. of Labor
1315 Broadway Pl.
Oklahoma City, OK 73103
Phone : (405) 521-2461

OREGON
Jack Roberts
Commissioner
Bur. of Labor & Industries
800 NE Oregon St.
Portland, OR 97232
Phone : (503) 731-4070
Fax : (503) 731-4103

PENNSYLVANIA
Johnny J. Butler
Secretary
Dept. of Labor & Industry
Rm. 1700, Labor & Industry Bldg.
Harrisburg, PA 17120
Phone : (717) 787-3756

RHODE ISLAND
William F. Tammelleo
Director
Workers Compensation Div.
Dept. of Labor
220 Elmwood Ave.
Providence, RI 02907
Phone : (401) 272-0700

SOUTH CAROLINA
Virgil W. Duffie, Jr.
Director
Dept. of Labor, Licensing & Regulations
P.O. Box 11329
Columbia, SC 29211
Phone : (803) 734-9600

SOUTH DAKOTA
Craig Johnson
Secretary
Dept. of Labor
700 Governors Dr.
Pierre, SD 57501
Phone : (605) 773-3101

TENNESSEE
Alphonso R. Bodie
Commissioner
Dept. of Labor
Gateway Plaza, 2nd Floor
Nashville, TN 37243
Phone : (615) 741-2582
Fax : (615) 741-5078

TEXAS
Jim Grametbauer
Director
Dept. of Labor Laws
Employment Comm.
3520 Executive Ctr. Dr., # 320
Austin, TX 78731
Phone : (512) 463-2222

UTAH
Stephen M. Hadley
Chairman
State Industrial Comm.
State of Utah
Salt Lake City, UT 84114
Phone : (801) 530-6880

VERMONT
Mary S. Hooper
Commissioner
Dept. of Labor & Industry
National Life Bldg.
Drawer 20
Montpelier, VT 05620-3401
Phone : (802) 828-2288
Fax : (802) 828-2748

VIRGINIA
Theron J. Bell
Commissioner
Dept. of Labor & Industry
13 S. 13th St.
Richmond, VA 23219
Phone : (804) 786-2377

WASHINGTON
Mark Brown
Director
Dept. of Labor & Industries
P.O. Box 44000
Olympia, WA 98504
Phone : (360) 902-4200

WEST VIRGINIA
Shelby Leary
Commissioner
Div. of Labor
State Capitol Complex, Bldg. 3
Charleston, WV 25305
Phone : (304) 558-7890

WISCONSIN
Carol Skornicka
Secretary
Dept. of Ind. Labor & Hum. Rel
201 E. Washington Ave.
P.O. Box 7946
Madison, WI 53707
Phone : (608) 266-7552
Fax : (608) 266-1784

WYOMING
Mike Sullivan
Administrator
Div. of Labor Standards
Dept. of Employment
Herschler Bldg.
Cheyenne, WY 82002
Phone : (307) 777-7435

DISTRICT OF COLUMBIA**
Maria G. Borrero
Director
Dept. of Employment Services
500 C St., NW, Rm. 600
Washington, DC 20001
Phone : (202) 724-7101

GUAM
Juan M. Taijito
Director
Dept. of Labor
P.O. Box 9970
Tamuning, GU 96911
Phone : (671) 646-4142
Fax : (671) 646-9004

NORTHERN MARIANA ISLANDS
Joaquin S. Torres
Director
Dept. of Commerce & Labor
Off. of the Governor
Saipan, MP 96950
Phone : (670) 322-4361

PUERTO RICO
Ceasar Almodova Machany
Secretary
Dept. of Labor & Human Resources
505 Munoz Rivera Ave.
Hato Rey, PR 00918
Phone : (809) 754-5353
Fax : (809) 753-9550

U.S. VIRGIN ISLANDS
Lisa Harris-Moorhead
Commissioner
Dept. of Labor
P.O. Box 208
St. Thomas, VI 00802
Phone : (809) 776-3700
Fax : (809) 773-0094

LABOR – ARBITRATION & MEDIATION

Promotes voluntary and peaceful settlement of labor disputes.

ALABAMA
Jerry Ray
Commissioner
Dept. of Labor
1789 Congressman Dickinson Dr., 2nd Fl.
Montgomery, AL 36130
Phone : (334) 242-3460
Fax : (334) 240-3417

ALASKA
Diane Corso
Labor Relations Mgr.
Div. of Personnel
Dept. of Administration
P.O. Box 110201
Juneau, AK 99811-0201
Phone : (907) 465-4404
Fax : (907) 465-2576

ARKANSAS
Edward L. House
Mediator
Mediation & Conciliation Div.
Dept. of Labor
10421 W. Markham St., Ste. 100
Little Rock, AR 72205
Phone : (501) 682-4511
Fax : (501) 682-4508

CALIFORNIA
Lloyd W. Aubry Jr.
Director
Dept. of Industrial Relations
455 Golden Gate Ave.
San Francisco, CA 94102
Phone : (415) 703-4590

COLORADO
John J. Donlon
Executive Director
Dept. of Labor & Employment
1515 Arapahoe St., Twr. 2, Ste. 400
Denver, CO 80202-2117
Phone : (303) 620-4717
Fax : (303) 620-4714

CONNECTICUT
Peter R. Blum
Chair
Mediation & Arbitration Bd.
Dept. of Labor
38 Wolcott Hill Rd.
Wethersfield, CT 06109
Phone : (203) 566-4394

DELAWARE
Charles D. Long
Executive Director
Pub. Employment Relations Bd.
Dept. of Administrative Srvcs.
Carvel State Off. Bldg.
Wilmington, DE 19801
Phone : (302) 577-2959

FLORIDA
Martha Larson
Director
Div. of Labor, Empl. & Training
Dept. of Labor & Empl. Sec.
Atkins Bldg., Rm. 300
Tallahassee, FL 32399
Phone : (904) 488-7228

GEORGIA
David Poythress
Commissioner
Dept. of Labor
148 International Blvd.
Atlanta, GA 30303
Phone : (404) 656-3011

HAWAII
Bert Tomasu
Chairman
State Labor Relations Board
Dept. of Labor & Ind. Rel.
550 Halekauwila St., 2nd Fl.
Honolulu, HI 96813
Phone : (808) 586-8610

IDAHO
Bob Purcell
Director
Labor & Industrial Srvcs.
277 N. Sixth St.
Boise, ID 83720
Phone : (208) 334-3950

ILLINOIS
Shinae Chun
Director
Dept. of Labor
160 N. La Salle St., Ste. C1300
Chicago, IL 60601
Phone : (312) 793-2800
Fax : (312) 793-5257

INDIANA
Kenneth Zeller
Commissioner
Dept. of Labor
IGC-South, Rm. W195
402 W. Washington
Indianapolis, IN 46204
Phone : (317) 232-2663

IOWA
Richard R. Ramsey
Chairman
Public Employment Relations Bd.
515 E. Locust, Ste. 202
Des Moines, IA 50309
Phone : (515) 281-4414

KANSAS
Duane Guy
Acting Director
Division of Labor
Dept. of Human Resources
401 Topeka Blvd.
Topeka, KS 66603-3182
Phone : (913) 296-7475
Fax : (913) 296-8177

KENTUCKY
Gary Moberly
Office Head
Labor-Management Relations
Labor Cabinet
1047 U.S. Highway 127 S., Ste. 4
Frankfort, KY 40601
Phone : (502) 564-3070

LOUISIANA
Joseph Stone
Assistant Secretary
Dept. of Labor
P.O. Box 94094
Baton Rouge, LA 70804
Phone : (504) 342-7692

MAINE
Mark Ayotte
Executive Director
Labor Relations Board
Dept. of Labor
State House Station # 90
Augusta, ME 04333
Phone : (207) 287-2015

MASSACHUSETTS
William J. Dalton
Chairman
Labor Relations Comm.
Executive Off. of Labor
100 Cambridge St., 16th Fl.
Boston, MA 02202
Phone : (617) 727-3505

MICHIGAN
Shlomo Sperka
Director
Bur. of Employment Relations
Dept. of Labor
1200 Sixth St., 14th Fl.
Detroit, MI 48226
Phone : (313) 256-3540

MINNESOTA
Lance Teachworth
Acting Commissioner
Bur. of Mediation Srvcs.
1380 Energy Ln., Ste. 2
St. Paul, MN 55108-5253
Phone : (612) 649-5421

MISSOURI
Francis R. Brady
Chairman
State Board of Mediation
Dept. of Labor & Ind. Rel.
3315 W. Truman Blvd.
P.O. Box 591
Jefferson City, MO 65102-0591
Phone : (314) 751-3614
Fax : (314) 751-0215

MONTANA
Robert R. Jensen
Administrator
Personnel Appeals Div.
Dept. of Labor & Industry
P.O. Box 201501
Helena, MT 59624
Phone : (406) 444-2723

NEBRASKA
Lawrence S. Primeau
Director
Div. of Personnel
Dept. of Administration Srvcs.
P.O. Box 94664
Lincoln, NE 68509-4905
Phone : (402) 471-2331

NEVADA
Tamera Barengo
Commissioner
Local Government, Employee Management & Rel. Board
2501 E. Sahara, Ste. 301
Las Vegas, NV 89158
Phone : (702) 486-4504

NEW HAMPSHIRE
Gregory Robbins
Chairman
Board of Conciliation & Arbitration
25 Maplewood Ave.
Portsmouth, NH 03801
Phone : (603) 436-3110

NEW JERSEY
John F. Tesauro
Executive Director
State Bd. of Mediation
Dept. of Labor
50 Park Pl.
Newark, NJ 07102-4301
Phone : (201) 648-2860

NEW MEXICO
Rudy J. Maestas
Director
Labor & Industrial Div.
1596 Pacheco St., Rm. 105
Santa Fe, NM 87501
Phone : (505) 827-6875
Fax : (505) 827-1664

NEW YORK*
Chair
Public Employee Relations Bd.
50 Wolf Rd.
Albany, NY 12205
Phone : (518) 457-2578

NORTH CAROLINA
Taylor McMillan
Director
Arbitration Div.
Dept. of Labor
4 W. Edenton St.
Raleigh, NC 27601
Phone : (919) 733-7495

NORTH DAKOTA
Craig Hagen
Commissioner
Dept. of Labor
State Capitol, 6th Fl.
600 E. Boulevard Ave.
Bismarck, ND 58505
Phone : (701) 328-2660
Fax : (701) 328-2031

OHIO
Sue Pohler
Chair
State Employment Relations Bd.
65 E. State St., 12th Fl.
Columbus, OH 43266-0336
Phone : (614) 644-8573
Fax : (614) 466-3074

OKLAHOMA
Brenda Reneau
Commissioner
Dept. of Labor
1315 Broadway Pl.
Oklahoma City, OK 73103
Phone : (405) 521-2461

OREGON
Daniel C. Ellis
Chairman
Employment Relations Bd.
528 Cottage St., NE
Salem, OR 97310
Phone : (503) 378-3807

PENNSYLVANIA
Mark A. Lamont
Director
Bur. of Mediation
Dept. of Labor & Industry
Labor & Ind. Bldg., Rm. 1610
Harrisburg, PA 17120
Phone : (717) 787-2803

RHODE ISLAND
William F. Tammelleo
Director
Workers Compensation Div.
Dept. of Labor
220 Elmwood Ave.
Providence, RI 02907
Phone : (401) 272-0700

SOUTH CAROLINA
Lewis Gossett
Director
Dept. of Labor, Licensing & Regulations
P.O. Box 11329
Columbia, SC 29211
Phone : (803) 734-9600

SOUTH DAKOTA*
Director
Div. of Labor & Management
Dept. of Labor
Kneip Bldg.
Pierre, SD 57501
Phone : (605) 773-3101

TENNESSEE
John Moffett
Assistant Commissioner
Labor Standards
Dept. of Labor
710 James Robertson Pkwy.
Nashville, TN 37243
Phone : (615) 741-2858

TEXAS
Jim Grametbauer
Director
Dept. of Labor Laws
Employment Comm.
3520 Executive Ctr. Dr., # 320
Austin, TX 78731
Phone : (512) 463-2222

UTAH
Anna Jensen
Director
Div. of Anti-Disc. & Labor
Industrial Comm.
160 E. 300 S.
Salt Lake City, UT 84111
Phone : (801) 530-6921

VERMONT
Tim Noonan
Executive Director
Labor Relations Bd.
13 Baldwin St.
Montpelier, VT 05602
Phone : (802) 828-2700

VIRGINIA
Theron J. Bell
Commissioner
Dept. of Labor & Industry
13 S. 13th St.
Richmond, VA 23219
Phone : (804) 786-2377

WASHINGTON
Meredith Wright Morton
Assistant Attorney General
Off. of the Attorney General
905 Plum St.
Olympia, WA 98504
Phone : (360) 459-6563

WEST VIRGINIA
Shelby Leary
Commissioner
Div. of Labor
State Capitol Complex, Bldg. 3
Charleston, WV 25305
Phone : (304) 558-7890

WISCONSIN
Henry Hempe
Chairman
Employment Relations Comm.
14 W. Mifflin St.
P.O. Box 7870
Madison, WI 53707
Phone : (608) 266-1381
Fax : (608) 266-6930

WYOMING
Mike Sullivan
Administrator
Div. of Labor Standards
Dept. of Employment
Herschler Bldg.
Cheyenne, WY 82002
Phone : (307) 777-7435

DISTRICT OF COLUMBIA
Debra McDowell
Director
Off. of Labor
441 4th St., NW, 2nd Fl.
Washington, DC 20001
Phone : (202) 724-4953

GUAM
Juan M. Taijito
Director
Dept. of Labor
P.O. Box 9970
Tamuning, GU 96911
Phone : (671) 646-4142
Fax : (671) 646-9004

NORTHERN MARIANA ISLANDS
Francisco M. Camacho
Director
Dept. of Labor
P.O. Box 10007
Saipan, MP 96950
Phone : (670) 664-2000
Fax : (670) 664-2020

PUERTO RICO
Samuel De La Rosa
Director
Bur. of Employment Security
Labor & Human Resources Dept.
505 Munoz Rivera Ave.
Hato Rey, PR 00918
Phone : (809) 721-0060

U.S. VIRGIN ISLANDS
Oran C. Roebuck
Chief Negotiator
Off. of Collective Bargaining
#8 GD Lyttons Fancy
St. Thomas, VI 00802
Phone : (809) 774-6450
Fax : (809) 779-6213

LATINO AFFAIRS

Represents and examines the concerns of Latin Americans.

CALIFORNIA
Wilbert Smith
Director
Off. of Community Relations
1400 Tenth St.
Sacramento, CA 95814
Phone : (916) 445-1114

FLORIDA
Mariela Fraser
Executive Director
Comm. on Hispanic Aff.
Exec. Off. of the Governor
LL 06, The Capitol
Tallahasse, FL 32399
Phone : (904) 488-8146

IDAHO
Gypsy S. Hall
Administrator
Comm. on Hispanic Affairs
5460 Franklin Rd. #B
Boise, ID 83705-1080
Phone : (208) 334-3776

ILLINOIS
Maria Balderas
Executive Assistant
Off. of the Governor
100 W. Randolph, 16th Fl.
Chicago, IL 60601
Phone : (312) 814-6709
Fax : (312) 814-5512

IOWA
Sylvia Tijerina
Administrator
Div. of Latino Affairs
Dept. of Human Rights
Lucas State Off. Bldg.
Des Moines, IA 50319
Phone : (515) 281-4080

KANSAS
Eva Pereira
Executive Director
Advisory Comm. on Hispanic Affairs
Dept. of Human Resources
117 SW Tenth Ave.
Topeka, KS 66612-2201
Phone : (913) 296-3465
Fax : (913) 296-8818

LOUISIANA
Sandra Alphonso
Administrator
Pan American Comm.
P.O. Box 94004
Baton Rouge, LA 70804
Phone : (504) 342-6900

MARYLAND
Jose Ruiz
Executive Director
Governor's Comm. on Hispanic Affairs
311 W. Saratoga St.
Baltimore, MD 21201
Phone : (410) 333-2532

MICHIGAN
Marylou Mason
Director
Comm. on Spanish Speaking Aff.
Dept. of Civil Rights
611 W. Ottawa
Lansing, MI 48933
Phone : (517) 373-8339

MONTANA
Ann MacIntyre
Administrator
Human Rights Div.
Dept. of Labor & Industry
616 Helena Ave., Ste. 302
Steamboat Block
Helena, MT 59624-1728
Phone : (406) 444-2884

NEBRASKA
Cecilia Olivarez Huerta
Executive Director
Mexican-American Comm.
P.O. Box 94965
Lincoln, NE 68509-4965
Phone : (402) 471-2791

NEW JERSEY
Alicia Diaz
Director
Center for Hispanic Policy
Dept. of Community Affairs
101 S. Broad St., CN800
Trenton, NJ 08625
Phone : (609) 984-3223

NEW YORK*
Governor's Off. of Hispanic Affairs
2 World Trade Ctr., 57th Fl.
New York, NY 10047
Phone : (212) 417-2266

OREGON
Celia Nunez-Brewster
Acting Director
Comm. on Hispanic Affairs
c/o State Police
400 Public Srvc. Bldg.
Salem, OR 97310
Phone : (503) 378-3725
Fax : (503) 378-8282

SOUTH CAROLINA
William C. Ham
Commissioner
Comm. on Human Affairs
P.O. Box 4490
Columbia, SC 29240
Phone : (803) 253-6336

VERMONT
Susan Sussman
Director
Human Rights Commission
6 Baldwin St.
Montpelier, VT 05633
Phone : (802) 828-2480
Fax : (802) 828-3522

VIRGINIA
Roxie Raines Kornegay
Director
Council on Human Rights
Washington Bldg., 12th Fl.
1100 Bank St.
Richmond, VA 23219
Phone : (804) 225-2292
Fax : (804) 225-3294

WASHINGTON
Martin G. Martinez
Director
State Comm. on Hispanic Affairs
P.O. Box 40924
Olympia, WA 98504
Phone : (360) 753-3159

LAW ENFORCEMENT

Conducts state-level criminal investigations.

ALABAMA
Gene Mitchell
Director
Dept. of Public Safety
500 Dexter Ave.
Montgomery, AL 36130
Phone : (334) 242-4394
Fax : (334) 242-0512

ALASKA
Ronald L. Otte
Commissioner
Dept. of Public Safety
P.O. Box 111200
Juneau, AK 99811-1200
Phone : (907) 465-4322
Fax : (907) 465-4362

ARIZONA
Joe Albo
Director
Dept. of Public Safety
2102 W. Encanto Blvd.
Phoenix, AZ 85009

ARKANSAS
John Bailey
Director
State Police
P.O. Box 5901
Little Rock, AR 72215
Phone : (501) 221-8200
Fax : (501) 224-4722
Phone : (602) 223-2000

CALIFORNIA
Daniel E. Lungren
Attorney General
1515 K St., Rm. 612
Sacramento, CA 95814
Phone : (916) 324-5437

COLORADO
Carl W. Whiteside
Director
Bureau of Investigation
Dept. of Public Safety
690 Kipling St.
Lakewood, CO 80215
Phone : (303) 239-4300
Fax : (303) 235-0568

CONNECTICUT
John M. Bailey
Chief State's Attorney
Div. of Criminal Justice
340 Quinnipiac St.
P.O. Box 5000
Wallingford, CT 06492
Phone : (203) 265-2373

DELAWARE
Alan D. Ellingsworth
Superintendent
State Police
State Police Headquarters
Dover, DE 19901
Phone : (302) 739-5911
Fax : (302) 739-5966

FLORIDA
Tim Moore
Commissioner
Dept. of Law Enforcement
P.O. Box 1489
Tallahassee, FL 32302
Phone : (904) 488-8771
Fax : (904) 488-2189

GEORGIA
Milton E. Nix Jr.
Director
Bureau of Investigtion
3121 Panthersville Rd.
Decatur, GA 30034
Phone : (404) 244-2501

HAWAII
Margery S. Bronster
Attorney General
425 Queen St.
Honolulu, HI 96813
Phone : (808) 586-1500
Fax : (808) 586-1239

IDAHO
Robert Sobba
Director
Alcohol Beverage Control Div.
Dept. of Law Enforcement
P.O. Box 55
Boise, ID 83707
Phone : (208) 334-3628

ILLINOIS
Terrence Gainer
Director
Dept. of State Police
103 State Armory
Springfield, IL 62706
Phone : (217) 782-4593
Fax : (217) 785-2821

INDIANA
Lloyd R. Jennings
Superintendent
State Police
IGC-North, 3rd Fl.
Indianapolis, IN 46204
Phone : (317) 232-8241

IOWA
Darwin Chapman
Director
Div. of Criminal Investigation
Dept. of Public Safety
Wallace State Off. Bldg.
Des Moines, IA 50319
Phone : (515) 281-6203

KANSAS
Larry Welch
Director
Bur. of Investigation
1620 SW Tyler
Topeka, KS 66612-1837
Phone : (913) 296-8200
Fax : (913) 296-6781

KENTUCKY
Jerry Lovitt
Commissioner
State Police
919 Versailles Rd.
Frankfort, KY 40601
Phone : (502) 695-6300

LOUISIANA
Jannitta Antoine
Deputy Secretary
Dept. of Public Safety & Corrections
P.O. Box 94304
Baton Rouge, LA 70804-9304
Phone : (504) 342-6744

MAINE
Andrew Ketterer
Attorney General
Dept. of Attorney General
State House Station # 6
Augusta, ME 04333
Phone : (207) 626-8800

MARYLAND
David Mitchell
Superintendent
State Police
State Police Headquarters
1201 Reisterstown Rd.
Baltimore, MD 21208
Phone : (301) 653-4219

MASSACHUSETTS
Charles Henderson
Commissioner
Div. of State Police
Dept. of Public Safety
470 Worcester Rd.
Framingham, MA 01701
Phone : (508) 820-2350

MICHIGAN
Mike Robinson
Director
Dept. of State Police
714 S. Harrison Rd.
East Lansing, MI 48823
Phone : (517) 336-6158
Fax : (517) 336-6255

MINNESOTA
Nicholas O'Hara
Superintendent
Bur. of Criminal Apprehension
Dept. of Public Safety
1246 University Ave.
St. Paul, MN 55104
Phone : (612) 642-0600

MISSISSIPPI
Jim Ingram
Commissioner
Dept. of Public Safety
Hwy. Patrol Bldg., I-55 N.
Jackson, MS 39216
Phone : (601) 987-1490

MISSOURI
Gary B. Kempker
Director
Dept. of Public Safety
Truman Bldg., Rm. 870
P.O. Box 749
Jefferson City, MO 65102
Phone : (314) 751-4905
Fax : (314) 751-5399

MONTANA
Mike Batista
Administrator
Law Enforcement Div.
Dept. of Justice
303 N. Roberts
Helena, MT 59620
Phone : (406) 444-3874

NEBRASKA
Ron Tussing
Superintendent
State Patrol
P.O. Box 94907
Lincoln, NE 68509-4907
Phone : (402) 471-4545

NEVADA
John Drew
Chief
Div. of Investigations
Dept. of Motor Veh. & Pub. Safety
555 Wright Way
Carson City, NV 89710
Phone : (702) 687-4412

NEW HAMPSHIRE
Lynn Presby
Director
Div. of State Police
Dept. of Safety
10 Hazen Dr.
Concord, NH 03305
Phone : (603) 271-2575

NEW JERSEY
Deborah Poritz
Attorney General
Office of the Attorney General
Dept. of Law & Public Safety
Hughes Justice Complex, CN081
Trenton, NJ 08625
Phone : (609) 292-8740

NEW MEXICO
Frank Taylor
Chief
State Police
P.O. Box 1628
Santa Fe, NM 87504
Phone : (505) 827-9003
Fax : (505) 827-3395

NEW YORK*
Superintendent
Div. of State Police
State Campus, Public Security Bldg.
Albany, NY 12226
Phone : (518) 457-6721

NORTH CAROLINA
Jim Coman
Director
State Bur. of Investigation
Dept. of Justice
3320 Garner Rd.
Raleigh, NC 27610-5698
Phone : (919) 662-4500

NORTH DAKOTA
Bill Broer
Director
Criminal Justice Div.
Off. of Attorney General
600 E. Boulevard Ave.
Bismarck, ND 58505
Phone : (701) 328-6180
Fax : (701) 328-5510

OHIO
Mike Quinn
Chief
Investigation & Identification
State Hwy. Patrol
660 E. Main St.
Columbus, OH 43205
Phone : (614) 466-3375
Fax : (614) 644-0652

OKLAHOMA
David McBride
Secretary of Safety & Security
Dept. of Public Safety
P.O. Box 11415
Oklahoma City, OK 73136
Phone : (405) 425-2424

OREGON
L.R. Howland
Superintendent
Dept. of Police
400 Public Service Bldg.
Salem, OR 97310
Phone : (503) 378-3720

PENNSYLVANIA
Paul Evanko
Commissioner
Pennsylvania State Police
1800 Elmerton Ave.
Harrisburg, PA 17110
Phone : (717) 783-5558

RHODE ISLAND
Edmund Culhane
Superintendent
Dept. of State Police
311 Danielson Pike
North Scituate, RI 02857
Phone : (401) 444-1111

SOUTH CAROLINA
Robert Stewart
Chief
Law Enforcement Div.
Broad River Rd.
P.O. Box 21398
Columbia, SC 29221
Phone : (803) 896-7136

SOUTH DAKOTA
Chuck Schamens
Director
Div. of Criminal Investigation
Off. of the Attorney General
500 E. Capitol Ave.
Pierre, SD 57501-5070
Phone : (605) 773-3332

TENNESSEE
Larry Wallace
Director
Bur. of Investigation
1148 Foster Ave.
Nashville, TN 37210-4406
Phone : (615) 741-0430

TEXAS
D.C. Jim Dozier
Executive Director
Comm. on Law Enforcement, Officer Standards & Educ.
1033 La Posada Dr., Ste. 240
Austin, TX 78752-3824
Phone : (512) 450-0188

UTAH
Douglas Bodrero
Commissioner
Dept. of Public Safety
4501 S. 2700 W.
Salt Lake City, UT 84119
Phone : (801) 965-4463

VERMONT
Nicholas Ruggiero
Commissioner
Div. of State Police
Dept. of Criminal Inv.
103 S. Main St.
Waterbury, VT 05671-2101
Phone : (802) 244-8718
Fax : (802) 244-1106

VIRGINIA
M. Wayne Huggins
Superintendent
Dept. of State Police
7700 Midlothian Tpke.
Richmond, VA 23235
Phone : (804) 674-2087
Fax : (804) 674-2132

WASHINGTON
Annette Sandberg
Chief
State Patrol
General Administration Bldg.
P.O. Box 42601
Olympia, WA 98504-2601
Phone : (360) 753-6540

WEST VIRGINIA
Thomas L. Kirk
Superintendent
Dept. of Public Safety
725 Jefferson Rd.
S. Charleston, WV 25309-1698
Phone : (304) 746-2111

WISCONSIN
Frank Meyers
State Fire Marshal
Div. of Criminal Investigation
Dept. of Justice
123 W. Washington, 7th Fl.
P.O. Box 7857
Madison, WI 53703
Phone : (608) 266-1671
Fax : (608) 267-2223

WYOMING
Tom Pagel
Director
Criminal Investigation Div.
Off. of the Attorney General
316 W. 22nd
Cheyenne, WY 82002
Phone : (307) 777-7181

DISTRICT OF COLUMBIA
Fred Thomas
Chief
Metropolitan Police Dept.
300 Indiana Ave., NW, Rm. 5080
Washington, DC 20001
Phone : (202) 727-4218

AMERICAN SAMOA
Fonoti D. Jessop
Commissioner
Dept. of Public Safety
American Samoa Government
Pago Pago, AS 96799
Phone : (684) 633-1111
Fax : (684) 633-5111

GUAM
Jack S. Shimizu
Chief of Police
Guam Police Dept.
P.O. Box 2950
Agana, GU 96910
Phone : (671) 472-8911
Fax : (671) 472-4036

NORTHERN MARIANA ISLANDS
Gregorio M. Camacho
Director
Dept. of Public Safety
Off. of the Governor
Saipan, MP 96950
Phone : (670) 234-6823

PUERTO RICO
Pedro R. Pierluisi
Attorney General
Dept. of Justice
P.O. Box 192
San Juan, PR 00904
Phone : (809) 724-7000
Fax : (809) 724-4770

U.S. VIRGIN ISLANDS
Ramon Davila
Commissioner
Police Dept.
Nisky Ctr., #6
St. Thomas, VI 00802
Phone : (809) 774-6400
Fax : (809) 774-4057

LAW LIBRARY

Legal resource for the state court of last resort.

ALABAMA
Timothy A. Lewis
Director
Supreme Court Law Library
300 Dexter Ave.
Montgomery, AL 36104-3741
Phone : (334) 242-4347
Fax : (334) 242-4484

ALASKA
Cynthia Petumenos
State Law Librarian
State Court Libraries
303 K St.
Anchorage, AK 99501-2084
Phone : (907) 264-0580
Fax : (907) 264-0733

ARKANSAS
Jacqueline Wright
Law Librarian
Supreme Court
Justice Bldg.
Little Rock, AR 72201
Phone : (501) 682-2147
Fax : (501) 682-6877

CALIFORNIA
Karen Toran
Law Librarian
Supreme Court
303 Second St., S. Tower
San Francisco, CA 94107
Phone : (415) 396-9439

COLORADO
Fran Campbell
Librarian
Supreme Court Law Library
State Judicial Bldg., # B112
2 E. 14th Ave.
Denver, CO 80203
Phone : (303) 861-1111

CONNECTICUT
Denise Jernigan
Head of Law & Legal Reference Unit
Dept. of Law
State Library
231 Capitol Ave.
Hartford, CT 06106
Phone : (203) 566-4601

DELAWARE
Rene Yucht
Librarian
New Castle County Law Library
Public Bldg.
1000 King St.
Wilmington, DE 19801
Phone : (302) 577-2437

Mary Dickson
Librarian
Law Library
Sussex County Superior Court
P.O. Box 717
Georgetown, DE 19947
Phone : (302) 856-5483

Aurora Gardner
Law Librarian
State Law Library in Kent County
38 The Green
Dover, DE 19901
Phone : (302) 739-5467

FLORIDA
Joan Cannon
Head Librarian
Supreme Court
Supreme Court Bldg.
500 S. Duval St.
Tallahassee, FL 32399-1927
Phone : (904) 488-1531

GEORGIA
Martha Lappe
State Law Librarian
Dept. of State Law
Judicial Bldg., 3rd Fl.
40 Mitchell St.
Atlanta, GA 30334
Phone : (404) 656-3468

HAWAII
Ann Koto
Law Librarian
Supreme Court Law Library
The Judiciary
P.O. Box 779
Honolulu, HI 96808
Phone : (808) 539-4964

IDAHO
Kris Everson
Deputy Librarian
Law Library
Supreme Court Bldg.
451 W. State St.
Boise, ID 83720
Phone : (208) 334-3317

ILLINOIS
Brenda Larison
Librarian
Supreme Court Library
Supreme Court Bldg.
Springfield, IL 62706
Phone : (217) 782-2424

INDIANA
Constance Matts
Law Librarian
Supreme Court Law Library
State House, Rm. 316
Indianapolis, IN 46204
Phone : (317) 232-2557

IOWA
Linda Robertson
Law Librarian
State Law Library
State Capitol Bldg.
Des Moines, IA 50319
Phone : (515) 281-5124

KANSAS
Fred Knecht
Law Librarian
Supreme Court Law Library
Kansas Judical Center
301 W. Tenth
Topeka, KS 66612-1507
Phone : (913) 296-3257

KENTUCKY
Sallie M. Howard
Librarian
State Law Library
700 Capitol Ave., Ste. 200
Frankfort, KY 40601-3489
Phone : (502) 564-4848

LOUISIANA
Carol Billings
Librarian
Supreme Court
301 Loyola Ave.
New Orleans, LA 70112
Phone : (504) 568-5705

MAINE
Lynn E. Randall
State Law Librarian
Law & Legis. Reference Library
State House Station # 43
Augusta, ME 04333
Phone : (207) 287-1600

MARYLAND
Michael S. Miller
Director
State Law Library
361 Rowe Blvd.
Annapolis, MD 21401
Phone : (410) 974-3395

MASSACHUSETTS
Gasper Caso
State Librarian
State Library
State House, Rm. 341
Boston, MA 02133
Phone : (617) 727-2592

MICHIGAN
Susan Adamczak
Director
Law Library Div.
Library of Michigan
P.O. Box 30012
Lansing, MI 48909
Phone : (517) 373-0630

MINNESOTA
Marvin R. Anderson
Librarian
State Law Library
117 University Ave.
St. Paul, MN 55155
Phone : (612) 296-2775

MISSISSIPPI
Mary Miller
State Librarian
Law Library
P.O. Box 1040
Jackson, MS 39215
Phone : (601) 359-3672

MISSOURI
Tyronne Allen
Librarian
Supreme Court Library
Supreme Court Bldg.
207 W. High St.
P.O. Box 448
Jefferson City, MO 65102
Phone : (314) 751-2636
Fax : (314) 751-2573
E-Mail: TALLEN@MAIL.MORE.NET

MONTANA
Judith Meadows
Librarian
Supreme Court
Justice Bldg.
215 N. Sanders
Helena, MT 59620
Phone : (406) 444-3660

NEBRASKA
Reta Johnson
Deputy State Librarian
State Library
State Capitol, 3rd Fl.
P.O. Box 98910
Lincoln, NE 68509
Phone : (402) 471-3189

NEVADA
Susan Southwick
Law Librarian
Law Library
Supreme Court
Supreme Court Bldg.
Carson City, NV 89710
Phone : (702) 687-8770

NEW HAMPSHIRE
Christine Swan
Law Librarian
State Law Library
Supreme Court Bldg.
Concord, NH 03301-6160
Phone : (603) 271-3777

NEW JERSEY
Louise Minervino
State Librarian
Div. of State Library
Dept. of Education
185 W. State St., CN520
Trenton, NJ 08625
Phone : (609) 292-6230

NEW MEXICO
Thaddeus Bejnar
Director
Supreme Court Law Library
237 Don Gaspar Ave.
P.O. Drawer L
Santa Fe, NM 87504
Phone : (505) 827-4850
Fax : (505) 827-4852

NEW YORK*
Director & Chief Law Librarian
Libraries & Records Mgt. Off.
State Unified Court System
Agency Bldg. 4, Empire St. Plz.
Albany, NY 12223
Phone : (518) 473-1196

NORTH CAROLINA
Louise Stafford
Librarian
Supreme Court Library
Justice Bldg., Rm. 500
2 W. Morgan St.
Raleigh, NC 27601-1400
Phone : (919) 733-3425

NORTH DAKOTA
Marcella Kramer
Acting Law Librarian
Supreme Court Law Library
Judicial Wing, 2nd Fl.
600 E. Boulevard Ave.
Bismarck, ND 58505-0530
Phone : (701) 328-2229
Fax : (701) 328-4480

OHIO
Paul S. Fu
Librarian
Supreme Court Law Library
30 E. Broad St., 4th Fl.
Columbus, OH 43266-0419
Phone : (614) 466-2044
Fax : (614) 466-1559

OKLAHOMA
Judith Clarke
Head Librarian
Law Reference Div.
Jan Eric Cartwright Memorial Library
200 NE 18th St.
Oklahoma City, OK 73105
Phone : (405) 521-2502

OREGON
Joe Stephens
Law Librarian
Supreme Court Library
Supreme Court Bldg.
Salem, OR 97310
Phone : (503) 986-5640
Fax : (503) 986-5560

PENNSYLVANIA
Alice Lubrecht
Acting Director
Library Services Div.
Dept. of Education
203 Forum Bldg.
P.O. Box 1601
Harrisburg, PA 17105-1601
Phone : (717) 783-5968

RHODE ISLAND
Kendall Svengalis
State Law Librarian
State Law Library
Providence County Courthouse
Providence, RI 02903
Phone : (401) 277-3275

SOUTH CAROLINA
Janet Myer
Librarian
Supreme Court Library
Supreme Court Bldg.
Columbia, SC 29201
Phone : (803) 734-1080

SOUTH DAKOTA
Sheri Anderson
Chief of Legal Research
Supreme Court
State Capitol, 1st Fl.
Pierre, SD 57501
Phone : (605) 773-3474

TENNESSEE
Donna Wair
Librarian
State Law Library
Supreme Court Bldg.
Nashville, TN 37243
Phone : (615) 741-2016

TEXAS
Kay Schlueter
Director
State Law Library
P.O. Box 12367
Austin, TX 78711
Phone : (512) 463-1722

UTAH
Nancy Long
Librarian
Supreme Court Law Library
125 State Capitol
Salt Lake City, UT 84114
Phone : (801) 538-1101

VERMONT
Sybil B. McShane
Librarian
Ref. & Law Info. Srvcs. Unit
Dept. of Libraries
109 State St.
Montpelier, VT 05609
Phone : (802) 828-3268
Fax : (802) 828-2199

VIRGINIA
Gail Warren
State Law Librarian
Supreme Court
100 N. Ninth St., 3rd. Fl.
Richmond, VA 23219
Phone : (804) 786-2075

WASHINGTON
Deborah Norwood
State Law Librarian
Law Library
Temple of Justice
P.O. Box 40751
Olympia, WA 98504-0751
Phone : (360) 357-2143

WEST VIRGINIA
Marjorie Price
Supreme Court Law Librarian
State Law Library
Supreme Court of Appeals
State Capitol, Rm. E-404
Charleston, WV 25305
Phone : (304) 558-2607

WISCONSIN
Marcia J. Koslov
Law Librarian
State Law Library
310 East, State Capitol
P.O. Box 7881
Madison, WI 53702
Phone : (608) 266-1424
Fax : (608) 267-2319

WYOMING
Kathy Carlson
State Law Librarian
Law Library
Supreme Court
Supreme Court Bldg.
Cheyenne, WY 82002
Phone : (307) 777-7509
Fax : (307) 777-7240

DISTRICT OF COLUMBIA
Harriet E. Rotter
Librarian
Court of Appeals
500 Indiana Ave., NW, Rm. 6085
Washington, DC 20001
Phone : (202) 879-2767

AMERICAN SAMOA*
Law Clerk
High Court
Pago Pago, AS 96799
Phone : (684) 633-1261
Fax : (684) 633-1318

NORTHERN MARIANA ISLANDS
John G. Moore
Recorder
Superior Court
P.O. Box 307 CK
Saipan, MP 96950
Phone : (670) 234-6401

PUERTO RICO
Ivette Torres
Director
Supreme Court Library
P.O. Box 2392
San Juan, PR 00903
Phone : (809) 723-3863

U.S. VIRGIN ISLANDS
Thomas Moore
Chief Judge
District Court
District Court Bldg.
St. Thomas, VI 00802
Phone : (809) 773-1130

LICENSING

Licenses and regulates the function of various professions in the state. Currently, state occupational and professional licensure boards are fully autonomous in 17 states. Some degree of centralization is in place among the remaining states. Since there are literally hundreds of autonomous boards in the states, it is the centralized agencies that are represented in this listing.

ALASKA
Catherine Reardon
Director
Div. of Occupational Licensing
Dept. of Commerce & Economic Dev.
P.O. Box 110806
Juneau, AK 99811-0806
Phone : (907) 465-2538
Fax : (907) 465-2974

CALIFORNIA
Majorie Berte
Director
Dept. of Consumer Affairs
400 R St., Rm. 1060
Sacramento, CA 95814-6213
Phone : (916) 445-4465

COLORADO
Joseph A. Garcia
Executive Director
Dept. of Regulatory Agencies
1560 Broadway, # 1550
Denver, CO 80203
Phone : (303) 894-7855

CONNECTICUT
Mark A. Shiffrin
Commission of Consumer Protection
Bur. of Licensing & Regulation
165 Capitol Ave.
Hartford, CT 06106
Phone : (203) 566-4999

DELAWARE
Carol Ellis
Director
Div. of Professional Reg.
Dept. of Administrative Srvcs.
P.O. Box 1401
Dover, DE 19903
Phone : (302) 739-4522
Fax : (302) 739-2711

FLORIDA
Richard T. Farrell
Secretary
Dept. of Business & Professional Regulation
1940 N. Monroe St., # 60
Tallahassee, FL 32399-0750
Phone : (904) 488-2252
Fax : (904) 487-9622

John Russi
Director
Div. of Licensing
Dept. of State
Crossland Bldg.
2520 N. Monroe St.
Tallahassee, FL 32303
Phone : (904) 488-6982

GEORGIA
William G. Miller Jr.
Joint Secretary
State Examining Bd.
Off. of Secretary of State
166 Pryor St., SW
Atlanta, GA 30303
Phone : (404) 656-3900

HAWAII
Kathryn Matayoshi
Director
Dept. of Commerce & Consumer Affairs
1010 Richards St.
Honolulu, HI 96813
Phone : (808) 586-2850

IDAHO
Carmen Westberg
Chief
Occupational Licenses
1109 Main St., Ste. 220
Boise, ID 83702-5642
Phone : (208) 334-3233

ILLINOIS
Nikki M. Zollar
Director
Dept. of Professional Regulation
320 W. Washington St., 3rd Fl.
Springfield, IL 62786
Phone : (217) 785-0822
Fax : (217) 782-7645

INDIANA
Gerald Quigley
Executive Director
Professional Licensing Agency
302 W. Washington St., #306
Indianapolis, IN 46204
Phone : (317) 232-3997

Sarah B. McCarty
Executive Director
Health Professions Bur.
One American Sq., Rm. 041
402 W. Washington St.
Indianapolis, IN 46204
Phone : (317) 232-2960

IOWA
K. Marie Thayer
Administrator
Professional Lic. & Regs. Div.
Dept. of Commerce
1918 SE Hulsizer
Ankeny, IA 50021
Phone : (515) 281-5602

KANSAS
Betty Rose
Executive Director
State Board of Tech. Professions
Landon State Off. Bldg., Ste. 507
Topeka, KS 66612-1257
Phone : (913) 296-3053

KENTUCKY
David L. Nicholas
Director
Occupations & Professions Div.
Dept. of Admin.
P.O. Box 456
Frankfort, KY 40602
Phone : (502) 564-3296

LOUISIANA
Lilly McCallister
Acting Director
Off. of Licensing & Regulation
Health & Human Resources Dept.
P.O. Box 3767
Baton Rouge, LA 70821
Phone : (504) 342-0138

MAINE
Geraldine Betts
Acting Director
Div. of Licensing & Enforcment
Dept. of Prof. & Fin. Reg.
State House Station #35
Augusta, ME 04330
Phone : (207) 582-8723

MARYLAND
Frank Stegman
Secretary
Dept. of Licensing & Regulation
501 St. Paul Pl.
Baltimore, MD 21202-2272
Phone : (301) 333-6200

MASSACHUSETTS
William Wood
Director
Div. of Registration
Executive Off. of Consumer Affairs
100 Cambridge St., Rm. 1520
Boston, MA 02202
Phone : (617) 727-3074

MICHIGAN
Kathy Wilber
Director
Dept. of Licensing & Reg.
P.O. Box 30018
Lansing, MI 48909
Phone : (517) 373-1870

MINNESOTA
Gary LaVasseur
Deputy Commissioner
Enforcement & Licensing
Dept. of Commerce
133 E. 7th St.
St. Paul, MN 55101
Phone : (612) 296-3528

MISSISSIPPI
Dick Molpus
Secretary of State
P.O. Box 136
Jackson, MS 39201
Phone : (601) 359-1350

MISSOURI
Randall J. Singer
Director
Div. of Professional Registration
Dept. of Economic Development
3605 Missouri Blvd., Box 1335
Jefferson City, MO 65102
Phone : (314) 751-1081
Fax : (314) 751-4176

MONTANA
Steve Meloy
Chief
Prof. & Occ. Licensing Bur.
Dept. of Commerce
111 N. Jackson, Lower Level
Helena, MT 59620
Phone : (406) 444-3737

NEBRASKA
Helen Meeks
Director
Bur. of Examining Bd.
Dept. of Health
P.O. Box 95007
Lincoln, NE 68509-5007
Phone : (402) 471-2115

NEW HAMPSHIRE
William Gardner
Secretary of State
204 State House
Concord, NH 03301
Phone : (603) 271-3242

NEW JERSEY
Mark S. Herr
Director
Div. of Consumer Affairs
Dept. of Law & Public Safety
124 Halsey St.
P.O. Box 45027
Newark, NJ 07101
Phone : (201)504-6200

NEW MEXICO
Robin Otten
Superintendent
Dept. of Regulation & Licensing
725 St. Michaels Dr.
P.O. Box 25101
Santa Fe, NM 87504
Phone : (505) 827-7199
Fax : (505) 827-7083

NEW YORK
Alexander F. Treadwell
Secretary of State
Dept. of State
162 Washington Ave.
Albany, NY 12231
Phone : (518) 474-0050

Executive Coordinator
State Boards for Professions
Dept. of State Ed.
Cul. Ed. Ctr., Rm. 3059A
Albany, NY 12230
Phone : (518) 486-1765

NORTH DAKOTA
Alvin A. Jaeger
Secretary of State
State Capitol, 1st Fl.
600 E. Boulevard Ave.
Bismarck, ND 58505-0500
Phone : (701) 328-2905
Fax : (701) 328-2992

PENNSYLVANIA
Dorothy Childress
Commissioner
Prof. & Occuptl. Affairs
Dept. of State
124 Pine St.
Harrisburg, PA 17101
Phone : (717) 783-7194

RHODE ISLAND
Russell J. Spaight
Administrator
Professional Regulation
Dept. of Health
75 Davis St.
Providence, RI 02908
Phone : (401) 277-2827

SOUTH CAROLINA
Lewis Gossett
Director
Dept. of Labor, Licensing & Regulations
P.O. Box 11329
Columbia, SC 29211
Phone : (803) 734-9600

SOUTH DAKOTA
Trish Kusser-Wendte
Director
Prof. & Occuptl. Licensing
Commerce & Regulations Dept.
910 E. Sioux Ave.
Pierre, SD 57501
Phone : (605) 773-3178

TENNESSEE
Carol Peeples Cook
Director, Regulatory Boards
Dept. of Commerce & Insurance
Volunteer Plaza
500 James Robertson Pkwy.
Nashville, TN 37243-0572
Phone : (615) 741-3449

Raymon White
Director
Health Related Boards
287 Plus Park Blvd.
Nashville, TN 37217
Phone : (615) 367-6220

TEXAS
Jack W. Garison
Executive Director
Dept. of Licensing & Regulation
P.O. Box 12157ÿ
Austin, TX 78711
Phone : (512) 463-3173

UTAH
David Robinson
Director
Div. of Occupational & Professional Licensing
160 E. 300 S.
Salt Lake City, UT 84111
Phone : (801) 530-6620

VERMONT
John D. Detore
Director
Off. of Professional Reg.
Off. of the Secretary of State
26 Terrace St.
P.O. Drawer 9
Montpelier, VT 05609-1106
Phone : (802) 828-2363
Fax : (802) 828-2496

VIRGINIA
Ray Allen Jr.
Director
Dept. of Profess. & Occupational Regulation
3600 W. Broad St.
Richmond, VA 23230
Phone : (804) 367-8519
Fax : (804) 367-9537

WASHINGTON
Kathy Baros Friedt
Director
Dept. of Licensing
Highways-Licensing Bldg.
1125 Washington St.
P.O. Box 9020
Olympia, WA 98504-9020
Phone : (360) 902-3600

WISCONSIN
Marlene A. Cummings
Secretary
Regulation & Licensing Dept.
1400 E. Washington
P.O. Box 8935
Madison, WI 53708-8935
Phone : (608) 266-8609
Fax : (608) 267-0644

WYOMING
Gary Stephenson
Director; Administrative Div.
Dept. of Commerce
2301 Central Ave.
Barrett Bldg., 3rd Fl.
Cheyenne, WY 82002
Phone : (307) 777-6300

DISTRICT OF COLUMBIA
Winnie Huston
Administrator
Occupational & Professional Licensing Admin., DCRA
614 H St., NW, Rm. 931
Washington, DC 20001
Phone : (202) 727-7480

GUAM
Joseph T. Duenas
Director
Dept. of Revenue & Taxation
378 Chalan San Antonio
Tamuning, GU 96911
Phone : (671) 647-5106
Fax : (671) 632-1040

NORTHERN MARIANA ISLANDS
Florence S. Bocago
Administrator
Bd. of Professional Licensing
Capitol Hill
Saipan, MP 96950
Phone : (670) 234-5897
Fax : (670) 234-6040

PUERTO RICO
Luis A. Isaac Sanchez
Director
Examiners Bd.
Dept. of State
Fortaleza 50
San Juan, PR 00901
Phone : (809) 722-2122

U.S. VIRGIN ISLANDS
Vera Falu
Commissioner
Dept. of Lic. & Cons. Aff.
Sub Base Bldg. 1, Rm. 205
St. Thomas, VI 00802
Phone : (809) 774-3130
Fax : (809) 776-0675

LIEUTENANT GOVERNOR

The statewide elected official who is next in line of succession to the governorship. In Maine, New Hampshire, New Jersey, Tennessee and West Virginia, the presidents (or speakers) of the Senate are next in line of succession to the governorship. In Tennessee, the speaker of the Senate bears the statutory title of lieutenant governor.

ALABAMA
Don Siegelman
Lieutenant Governor
State Capitol
Montgomery, AL 36130
Phone : (334) 242-7900
Fax : (334) 242-4666

ALASKA
Fran Ulmer
Lieutenant Governor
P.O. Box 110015
Juneau, AK 99811-0015
Phone : (907) 465-3520
Fax : (907) 465-5400

ARIZONA
Jane Dee Hull
Secretary of State
State Capitol, West Wing
1700 W. Washington, Ste. 700
Phoenix, AZ 85007-2808
Phone : (602) 542-4285
Fax : (602) 542-6172

ARKANSAS
Mike Huckabee
Lieutenant Governor
State Capitol, Rm. 270
Little Rock, AR 72201
Phone : (501) 682-2144
Fax : (501) 682-2894

CALIFORNIA
Gray Davis
Lieutenant Governor
State Capitol, Rm. 1114
Sacramento, CA 95814
Phone : (916) 445-8994

COLORADO
Gail Schoettler
Lieutenant Governor
130 State Capitol
Denver, CO 80203-1792
Phone : (303) 866-2087
Fax : (303) 866-5469

CONNECTICUT
M. Jodi Rell
Lieutenant Governor
State Capitol, Rm. 304
Hartford, CT 06106
Phone : (203) 566-2614
Fax : (203) 566-4792

DELAWARE
Ruth Ann Minner
Lieutenant Governor
Tatnall Bldg., 3rd Fl.
Dover, DE 19901
Phone : (302) 739-4151
Fax : (302) 577-3019

FLORIDA
Buddy MacKay
Lieutenant Governor
The State Capitol, PLO5
Tallahassee, FL 32399-0001
Phone : (904) 488-4711
Fax : (904) 922-2894

GEORGIA
Pierre Howard
Lieutenant Governor
240 State Capitol
Atlanta, GA 30334
Phone : (404) 656-5030

HAWAII
Mazie Hirono
Lieutenant Governor
State Capitol
P.O. Box 3226
Honolulu, HI 96801
Phone : (808) 586-0255
Fax : (808) 586-0231

IDAHO
C.L. Otter
Lieutenant Governor
State House #225
Boise, ID 83720
Phone : (208) 334-2200
Fax : (208) 334-3259

ILLINOIS
Bob Kustra
Lieutenant Governor
214 State Capitol Bldg.
Springfield, IL 62706
Phone : (217) 782-7884
Fax : (217) 524-6262

INDIANA
Frank L. O'Bannon
Lieutenant Governor
State Capitol, Rm. 333
Indianapolis, IN 46204
Phone : (317) 232-4545
Fax : (317) 232-4788

IOWA
Joy C. Corning
Lieutenant Governor
State Capitol, Rm. 9
Des Moines, IA 50319
Phone : (515) 281-3421
Fax : (515) 281-6611

KANSAS
Sheila Frahm
Lieutenant Governor
State House, 2nd Fl.
Topeka, KS 66612-1504
Phone : (913) 296-2213
Fax : (913) 296-5669

KENTUCKY
Paul E. Patton
Lieutenant Governor
State Capitol, Rm. 142
Frankfort, KY 40601
Phone : (502) 564-7562
Fax : (502) 564-5959

LOUISIANA
Melinda Schwegmann
Lieutenant Governor
Pentagon Court Barracks
P.O. Box 44243
Baton Rouge, LA 70804
Phone : (504) 342-7009
Fax : (504) 342-1949

MARYLAND
Kathleen Kennedy Townsend
Lieutenant Governor
State House
Annapolis, MD 21401
Phone : (410) 974-2804
Fax : (410) 974-5252

MASSACHUSETTS
Paul Cellucci
Lieutenant Governor
State House, Executive Office
Rm. 360
Boston, MA 02133
Phone : (617) 727-3600

MICHIGAN
Connie Binsfeld
Lieutenant Governor
P.O. Box 30026
5215 State Capitol Bldg.
Lansing, MI 48909
Phone : (517) 373-6800
Fax : (517) 335-6763

MINNESOTA
Joanne Benson
Lieutenant Governor
130 State Capitol
St. Paul, MN 55155
Phone : (612) 296-0078
Fax : (612) 296-2089

MISSISSIPPI
Eddie Briggs
Lieutenant Governor
New Capitol, Rm. 315
P.O. Box 1018
Jackson, MS 39215-1018
Phone : (601) 359-3200
Fax : (601) 359-3935

MISSOURI
Roger B. Wilson
Lieutenant Governor
State Capitol, Rm. 121
Jefferson City, MO 65101
Phone : (314) 751-4727
Fax : (314) 751-9422

MONTANA
Dennis Rehberg
Lieutenant Governor
Capitol Station, Rm. 207
Helena, MT 59620
Phone : (406) 444-5551
Fax : (406) 444-5529

NEBRASKA
Kim Robak
Lieutenant Governor
State Capitol, Rm. 2315
P.O. Box 94863
Lincoln, NE 68509-4863
Phone : (402) 471-2256
Fax : (402) 471-6031

NEVADA
Lonnie Hammargren
Lieutenant Governor
Capitol Complex
Carson City, NV 89710
Phone : (702) 687-3037
Fax : (702) 687-3420

NEW MEXICO
Walter Bradley
Lieutenant Governor
State Capitol, Rm. 417
Santa Fe, NM 87503
Phone : (505) 827-3050
Fax : (505) 827-3057

NEW YORK
Betsy McCaughey
Lieutenant Governor
Executive Chamber
State Capitol, Rm. 326
Albany, NY 12224
Phone : (518) 474-4623
Fax : (518) 473-2444

NORTH CAROLINA
Dennis A. Wicker
Lieutenant Governor
State Capitol
116 W. Jones St.
Raleigh, NC 27603-8006
Phone : (919) 733-7350
Fax : (919) 733-6595

NORTH DAKOTA
Rosemarie Myrdal
Lieutenant Governor
State Capitol
Bismarck, ND 58505
Phone : (701) 328-4222
Fax : (701) 328-2205

OHIO
Nancy Hollister
Lieutenant Governor
State Office Tower II
77 S. High St., 30th Floor
Columbus, OH 43215
Phone : (614) 466-3396

OKLAHOMA
Mary Fallin
Lieutenant Governor
State Capitol, Rm. 211
Oklahoma City, OK 73105
Phone : (405) 521-2161
Fax : (405) 525-2702

OREGON
Phil Keisling
Secretary of State
136 State Capitol
Salem, OR 97310
Phone : (503) 986-1500
Fax : (503) 373-7414

PENNSYLVANIA
Mark Schweiker
Lieutenant Governor
200 Main Capitol
Harrisburg, PA 17120-0002
Phone : (717) 787-3300
Fax : (717) 783-0150

RHODE ISLAND
Robert A. Weygand
Lieutenant Governor
State House, Rm. 317
Providence, RI 02903
Phone : (401) 277-2371
Fax : (401) 277-2012

SOUTH CAROLINA
Bob Peeler
Lieutenant Governor
State House
P.O. Box 142
Columbia, SC 29202
Phone : (803) 734-2080
Fax : (803) 734-2082

SOUTH DAKOTA
Carole Hillard
Lieutenant Governor
State Capitol
500 East Capitol
Pierre, SD 57501
Phone : (605) 773-3661
Fax : (605) 773-4711

TENNESSEE
John S. Wilder
Lieutenant Governor
One Legislative Plaza
Nashville, TN 37219
Phone : (615) 741-2368
Fax : (615) 741-9349

TEXAS
Bob Bullock
Lieutenant Governor
Capitol Station
P.O. Box 12068
Austin, TX 78711
Phone : (512) 463-0001
Fax : (512) 463-0039

UTAH
Olene S. Walker
Lieutenant Governor
203 State Capitol
Salt Lake City, UT 84114
Phone : (801) 538-1040
Fax : (801) 538-1557

VERMONT
Barbara Snelling
Lieutenant Governor
State House
Montpelier, VT 05633
Phone : (802) 828-2226
Fax : (802) 828-3198

VIRGINIA
Donald S. Beyer
Lieutanent Governor
Off. of the Lt. Governor
900 E. Main St., 14th Fl.
Richmond, VA 23219
Phone : (804) 786-2078
Fax : (804) 786-7514

WASHINGTON
Joel Pritchard
Lieutenant Governor
304 Legislative Bldg.
P.O. Box 40400
Olympia, WA 98504-0400
Phone : (360) 786-7700
Fax : (360) 786-7520

WISCONSIN
Scott McCallum
Lieutenant Governor
22 East State Capitol
Madison, WI 53702
Phone : (608) 266-3516
Fax : (608) 267-3571

WYOMING
Diana Ohman
Secretary of State
State Capitol
Cheyenne, WY 82002-0020
Phone : (307) 777-5333
Fax : (307) 777-6217

AMERICAN SAMOA
Tauese P. Sunia
Lieutenant Governor
Off. of the Governor
Pago Pago, AS 96799
Phone : (684) 633-4116
Fax : (684) 633-2269

GUAM
Madeleine L. Bordallo
Lieutenant Governor
Executive Chambers
P.O. Box 2950
Agana, GU 96910
Phone : (671) 472-9209
Fax : (671) 477-4826

NORTHERN MARIANA ISLANDS
Jesus Borja
Lieutenant Governor
Off. of the Governor
Capitol Hill
Saipan, MP 96950
Phone : (670) 322-5091
Fax : (670) 322-5096

PUERTO RICO
Baltasar C. Del Rio
Secretary of State
Dept. of State
P.O. Box 3271
San Juan, PR 00902-3271
Phone : (809) 723-4323
Fax : (809) 725-7302

U.S. VIRGIN ISLANDS
Kenneth E. Mapp
Lieutenant Governor
18 Kongens Gade
Charlotte Amalie
St. Thomas, VI 00802
Phone : (809) 774-2991
Fax : (809) 774-6953

LOBBY LAW ADMINISTRATION

Administers registration and reporting requirements for lobbyists.

ALASKA
Karen Boorman
Director
Public Offices Comm.
2221 E. Northern Lights Blvd., Rm. 128
Anchorage, AK 99508
Phone : (907) 276-4176

ARIZONA
Jane Dee Hull
Secretary of State
1700 W. Washington St., 7th Floor
Phoenix, AZ 85007
Phone : (602) 542-4285

ARKANSAS
Amanda Nixon White
Director
State Ethics Comm.
2020 W. Third St., Ste. 300
Little Rock, AR 72205
Phone : (501) 324-9600
Fax : (501) 324-9603

CALIFORNIA
Robert Steele
Chief
Political Reform Div.
Off. of the Secretary of State
1230 J St., Rm. 219
Sacramento, CA 95814
Phone : (916) 322-4885

COLORADO
Vikki Buckley
Secretary of State
Dept. of State
1560 Broadway, Ste. 200
Denver, CO 80202
Phone : (303) 894-2200
Fax : (303) 894-2242

CONNECTICUT
Alan S. Plofsky
Executive Director
State Ethics Comm.
97 Elm St.
Hartford, CT 06106
Phone : (203) 566-4472

DELAWARE
Marlynn Hedgecock
Administrator
Div. of Research
Legislative Council
Legislative Hall
Dover, DE 19901
Phone : (302) 739-5803

FLORIDA
Bonnie J. Williams
Executive Director
Commission on Ethics
P.O. Drawer 15709
Tallahassee, FL 32317-5709
Phone : (904) 488-7864
Fax : (904) 488-3077

Fred Breeze
Executive Director
Jt. Legislative Mgt. Cmte.
111 W. Madison, Rm. G-68
Tallahassee, FL 32399
Phone : (904) 922-4990
Fax : (904) 921-5345

GEORGIA
C. Theodore Lee
Executive Secretary
State Ethics Comm.
2082 E. Exchange Pl., Ste. 235
Tucker, GA 30084
Phone : (404) 414-3456

HAWAII
Daniel J. Mollway
Executive Director
State Ethics Comm.
Pacific Tower, Ste. 970
1001 Bishop St.
Honolulu, HI 96813
Phone : (808) 587-0460

ILLINOIS
George H. Ryan
Secretary of State
213 State House
Springfield, IL 62706
Phone : (217) 782-2201
Fax : (217) 785-0358

INDIANA
Robert J. Fair
Chairman
Lobby Registration Comm.
Ste. 1375S
115 W. Washington St.
Indianapolis, IN 46204-3420
Phone : (317) 232-9598

IOWA
John F. Dwyer
Secretary of the Senate
State Capitol
Des Moines, IA 50319
Phone : (515) 281-5307

Liz Isaacson
Chief Clerk of the House
State Capitol
Des Moines, IA 50319
Phone : (515) 281-5381

KANSAS
Ron Thornburgh
Secretary of State
Off. of the Secretary of State
State Capitol, 2nd Fl.
Topeka, KS 66612
Phone : (913) 296-2236

KENTUCKY
Chris Gorman
Attorney General
State Capitol, Rm. 116
Frankfort, KY 40601
Phone : (502) 564-7600

LOUISIANA
Alfred W. Speer
Clerk of the House
P.O. Box 94062
Baton Rouge, LA 70804
Phone : (504) 342-7259

MAINE
Constance Holmes
Registrar
Div. of Elections
Dept. of State
State House Station # 101
Augusta, ME 04333
Phone : (207) 287-6221

MARYLAND
John O'Donnell
Executive Director
State Ethics Comm.
300 E. Joppa Rd., Ste. 301
Towson, MD 21204
Phone : (410) 321-3636

MASSACHUSETTS
Mary Schwind
Director
Public Records
Off. of the Secretary of State
1 Ashburton Pl., Rm. 1719
Boston, MA 02108
Phone : (617) 727-2832
Fax : (617) 727-5914

MICHIGAN
Candice Miller
Secretary of State
Treasury Bldg., 1st Fl.
430 W. Allegan St.
Lansing, MI 48918
Phone : (517) 373-2510

MINNESOTA
Jeanne Olson
Executive Director
Ethical Practices Bd.
S. Centennial Bldg., 1st Fl.
658 Cedar St.
St. Paul, MN 55155
Phone : (612) 296-1720

MISSOURI
Marion Sinnett
Administrative Secretary
State Ethics Commission
221 Metro Dr.
Jefferson City, MO 65109
Phone : (314) 751-2020
Fax : (314) 526-4506

MONTANA
Ed Argenbright
Commissioner of Political Practices
1205 8th Ave.
Helena, MT 59620
Phone : (406) 444-2942

NEBRASKA
Dannie Trautwein
Director
Accountability & Disclosure Comm.
P.O. Box 95086
Lincoln, NE 68509
Phone : (402) 471-2522

NEVADA
Lorne J. Malkiewich
Director
Legislative Counsel Bur.
Capitol Complex
Rm. 143, Legis. Bldg.
Carson City, NV 89710
Phone : (702) 687-6800

NEW HAMPSHIRE
William Gardner
Secretary of State
204 State House
Concord, NH 03301
Phone : (603) 271-3242

NEW JERSEY
Frederick M. Herrmann
Executive Director
Election Law Enforcement Comm.
Dept. of Law & Public Safety
28 W. State St., 12th Fl.
CN-185
Trenton, NJ 08625-0185
Phone : (609) 292-8700

NEW MEXICO
Stephanie Gonzales
Secretary of State
State Capitol, Rm. 420
Santa Fe, NM 87503
Phone : (505) 827-3601
Fax : (505) 827-3634

NEW YORK*
Acting Executive Director
Temp. State Comm. on Lobbying
Mezzanine Level, Ste. 304
1 Commerce Plz.
Albany, NY 12210
Phone : (518) 474-7126

NORTH CAROLINA
Rufus L. Edmisten
Secretary of State
300 N. Salisbury St.
Raleigh, NC 27603-5909
Phone : (919) 733-5140

NORTH DAKOTA
Alvin A. Jaeger
Secretary of State
State Capitol, 1st Fl.
600 E. Boulevard Ave.
Bismarck, ND 58505-0500
Phone : (701) 328-2905
Fax : (701) 328-2205

OHIO
Tom Sherman
Executive Director
Joint Cmte. on Agency Rule Review
77 S. High St., 21st Fl.
Columbus, OH 43266
Phone : (614) 466-4086
Fax : (614) 644-9494

OKLAHOMA
Marilyn Hughes
Executive Director
Ethics Comm.
State Capitol Bldg., Rm. B-2A
Oklahoma City, OK 73105
Phone : (405) 521-3451

OREGON
L. Patrick Hearn
Executive Director
Govt. Standards & Practices Comm.
100 High St., SE, Ste. 220
Salem, OR 97310-1360
Phone : (503) 378-5105
Fax : (503) 373-1456

RHODE ISLAND
Barbara M. Leonard
Secretary of State
State House, Rm. 217
Providence, RI 02903
Phone : (401) 277-2357

SOUTH CAROLINA
Jim Miles
Secretary of State
Wade Hampton Bldg.
P.O. Box 11350
Columbia, SC 29211
Phone : (803) 734-2170

SOUTH DAKOTA
Joyce Hazeltine
Secretary of State
State Capitol, 2nd Fl.
Pierre, SD 57501
Phone : (605) 773-3537

TENNESSEE
Peggy Nance Catalano
Executive Director
Registry of Election Fin.
Off. of Secretary of State
James K. Polk Bldg.
Nashville, TN 37243
Phone : (615) 741-7959

TEXAS
Kristin Newkirk
Director
Div. of Disclosure Filings
Ethics Comm.
P.O. Box 12070
Austin, TX 78711
Phone : (512) 463-5800

VERMONT
Donald M. Hooper
Secretary of State
109 State St.
Montpelier, VT 05609-1101
Phone : (802) 828-2148
Fax : (802) 828-2496

VIRGINIA
Betsy Davis Beamer
Secretary of the Commonwealth
P.O. Box 2454
Richmond, VA 23201
Phone : (804) 786-2441
Fax : (804) 371-0017

WASHINGTON
Melissa Warheit
Executive Director
Public Disclosure Comm.
711 Capitol Way, Rm. 403
P.O. Box 40908
Olympia, WA 98504
Phone : (360) 753-1111

WEST VIRGINIA
Richard Alker
Executive Director
Ethics Commission
1207 Quarrier St.
Charleston, WV 25311
Phone : (304) 558-0664
Fax : (304) 558-2169

WISCONSIN
Marjorie Robb
Administrator
Div. of Government Records
Off. of Secretary of State
30 W. Mifflin, 9th & 10th Fl.
P.O. Box 7848
Madison, WI 53703
Phone : (608) 266-5503
Fax : (608) 267-6813

WYOMING
Richard H. Miller
Director
Legislative Services Off.
State Capitol, Rm. 202
Cheyenne, WY 82002
Phone : (307) 777-7881

DISTRICT OF COLUMBIA**
Robert A. Lane
Executive Director
Board of Elections & Ethics
Off. of Campaign Finance
2000 14th St., NW, Rm. 420
Washington, DC 20009
Phone : (202) 939-8710

NORTHERN MARIANA ISLANDS
Juan M. Diaz
Executive Director
Board of Elections
P.O. Box 470
Saipan, MP 96950
Phone : (670) 234-6481

Leo Lawrence LaMotte
Public Auditor
P.O. Box 1399
Saipan, MP 96950
Phone : (670) 234-6481
Fax : (670) 234-7812

PUERTO RICO
Scott E. Thomas
Director
Corporation Div.
Dept. of State
P.O. Box 3271
San Juan, PR 00904
Phone : (809) 722-2121

U.S. VIRGIN ISLANDS
Alva A. Swan Esq.
Attorney General
Dept. of Justice
GERS Complex
48B-50C Kronprin Gade
St. Thomas, VI 00802
Phone : (809) 774-5666
Fax : (809) 774-9710

LOCAL GOVERNMENT RELATIONS

Coordinates federal and state programs affecting local government, and informs state officials about local government needs.

ALABAMA
Martha McInnis
Chief
Science, Tech. & Energy
Dept. of Econ. & Comm. Affairs
401 Adams Ave., Suite 560
Montgomery, AL 36103
Phone : (334) 242-5292
Fax : (334) 242-5099

ALASKA
Jeff Smith
Director
Div. of Community & Rural Dev.
Dept. of Community & Regional Affairs
333 West Fourth Ave., Ste. 220
Anchorage, AK 99501
Phone : (907) 269-4500
Fax : (907) 269-4520

ARIZONA
Sara Goertzen
Director
Dept. of Commerce
3800 N. Central Ave., Suite 1500
Phoenix, AZ 85012
Phone : (602) 280-1306

CALIFORNIA
Lee Grissom
Director
Off. of Planning & Research
1400 10th St.
Sacramento, CA 95814
Phone : (916) 322-2318

COLORADO
Larry Kallenberger
Executive Director
Dept. of Local Affairs
1313 Sherman St., Rm. 518
Denver, CO 80203
Phone : (303) 866-2771

CONNECTICUT
Don Downes
Under Secretary
Intergovernmental Policy
Off. of Policy & Mgt.
80 Washington St.
Hartford, CT 06106
Phone : (203) 566-8072

DELAWARE
Edward J. Freel
Secretary of State
P.O. Box 898
Dover, DE 19903
Phone : (302) 739-4111
Fax : (302) 739-3811

FLORIDA
Charles Pattison
Director
Resource Planning & Mgt. Div.
Dept. of Community Affairs
2740 Centerview Dr.
Tallahassee, FL 32399-2100
Phone : (904) 488-2356

GEORGIA
Jim Higdon
Commissioner
Dept. of Community Affairs
Equitable Bldg., Ste. 1200
100 Peachtree St.
Atlanta, GA 30303
Phone : (404) 656-3836

ILLINOIS
Dennis R. Whetstone
Director
Dept. of Commerce & Community Affairs
620 E. Adams St., 3rd Fl.
Springfield, IL 62701
Phone : (217) 782-3233
Fax : (217) 524-0864

INDIANA
Ron Gyure
Executive Assistant
Off. of the Governor
206 State House
Indianapolis, IN 46204
Phone : (317) 232-1053

KANSAS
Ron Green
Director
Governmental & Constituent Srvcs.
Off. of the Governor
State Capitol, 2nd Fl.
Topeka, KS 66612-1590
Phone : (913) 296-3232
Fax : (913) 296-7973

KENTUCKY
Bruce Ferguson
Commissioner
Dept. of Local Government
1024 Capitol Centre Dr.
Frankfort, KY 40601
Phone : (502) 564-2382

MARYLAND
Rick Farraro
Director
Commercial & Government Assistance
100 Community Pl.
Crownsville, MD 21032
Phone : (410) 514-7201

MASSACHUSETTS
Mary L. Padula
Secretary
Executive Off. of Communities & Development
100 Cambridge St., Rm. 1804
Boston, MA 02202
Phone : (617) 727-7765

MICHIGAN
Chris DeRose
Deputy Director for Mgt.
Dept. of Mgt. & Budget
P.O. Box 30026
Lansing, MI 48909
Phone : (517) 373-6741

MINNESOTA
Linda Kohl
Commissioner
Strategic & Long Range Pl. Off
Centennial Off. Bldg., 3rd Fl.
658 Cedar St.
St. Paul, MN 55155
Phone : (612) 297-2325

MISSISSIPPI
Clovis Williams
Special Advisor
Educ. & Intergovtl. Relations
Off. of the Governor
P.O. Box 139
Jackson, MS 39205
Phone : (601) 359-3150

MISSOURI
Lois Pohl
Director, Intergovtl. Relations
Div. of General Services
Off. of Administration
Truman Bldg., Rm. 760
P.O. Box 809
Jefferson City, MO 65102
Phone : (314) 751-4834
Fax : (314) 751-7819

MONTANA
Dennis Rehberg
Lieutenant Governor
Capitol Station, Rm. 207
Helena, MT 59620
Phone : (406) 444-5551

NEBRASKA
Jenne Rodriguez
Director
Div. of Community Development
Dept. of Economic Development
P.O. Box 94666
Lincoln, NE 68509
Phone : (402) 471-3111

NEW HAMPSHIRE
Jeff Taylor
Director
Off. of State Planning
2 1/2 Beacon St.
Concord, NH 03301
Phone : (603) 271-2155

NEW JERSEY
Beth Gates
Director
Div. of Local Government Srvcs.
Dept. of Community Affairs
101 S. Broad St., CN-803
Trenton, NJ 08625
Phone : (609) 292-6613

NEW MEXICO
Walter Bradley
Lieutenant Governor
State Capitol Bldg., 4th Fl.
Santa Fe, NM 87503
Phone : (505) 827-3050

NEW YORK
Alexander F. Treadwell
Secretary of State
Dept. of State
162 Washington Ave.
Albany, NY 12231
Phone : (518) 474-0050

NORTH CAROLINA
Ann Lichtner
Acting Director
Intergovernmental Relations
Off. of the Governor
116 W. Jones St.
Raleigh, NC 27603-8003
Phone : (919) 733-5201

NORTH DAKOTA
Shirley Dykshoorn
Director
Intergovernmental Assistance
Off. of Mgt. & Budget
600 E. Boulevard Ave.
Bismarck, ND 58505-0170
Phone : (701) 328-2094
Fax : (701) 328-2308

OHIO
Nancy Hollister
Lieutenant Governor
77 S. High Street
Columbus, OH 43215
Phone : (614) 466-3396

OKLAHOMA
Linda Sponster
Director
Intergovernmental Affairs
440 S. Houston St., Ste. 304
Tulsa, OK 74127
Phone : (918) 581-2801

PENNSYLVANIA
William C. Bostic
Secretary
Dept. of Community Affairs
Rm. 317, Forum Bldg.
Harrisburg, PA 17120
Phone : (717) 787-7160

RHODE ISLAND
Paul Moore
Director
Intergovernmental Relations
State House, Rm. 111
Providence, RI 02903
Phone : (401) 277-2080

SOUTH CAROLINA
Foster M. Routh III
Director
Intergovernmental Relations
Off. of the Governor
P.O. Box 11369
Columbia, SC 29211
Phone : (803) 734-0434

SOUTH DAKOTA*
Assistant to the Chief of Staff
Off. of the Governor
State Capitol
Pierre, SD 57501
Phone : (605) 773-3661

TENNESSEE*
Director
Off. of State Planning
Off. of the Governor
State Capitol
Nashville, TN 37243
Phone : (615) 741-4131

TEXAS
Henry Flores
Executive Director
Dept. of Housing & Comm. Aff.
811 Barton Springs Rd.
P.O. Box 13166
Austin, TX 78711
Phone : (512) 475-3800

UTAH
Olene S. Walker
Lieutenant Governor
203 State Capitol Bldg.
Salt Lake City, UT 84114
Phone : (801) 538-1520

VERMONT
Elizabeth Mullikin Drake
Commissioner
Dept. of Housing & Comm. Aff.
Agcy. of Dev. & Community Aff.
109 State St.
Montpelier, VT 05602
Phone : (802) 828-3217
Fax : (802) 828-2928

VIRGINIA
David L. Caprara
Director
Dept. of Housing & Community Development
501 N. 2nd St., Jackson Center
Richmond, VA 23219
Phone : (804) 371-7000
Fax : (804) 371-7090

WASHINGTON
Laura Porter
Director
Governmental Relations
Community, Trade/ Economic Develop.
P.O. Box 48300
Olympia, WA 98504-8300
Phone : (360) 753-2227

WEST VIRGINIA
Judy Margolin
Senior Executive Assistant
Off. of the Governor
State Capitol
1900 Kanawha Blvd., E.
Charleston, WV 25305
Phone : (304) 558-3702

WISCONSIN
Terry W. Grosenheider
Administrator
Div. of Economic Development
Dept. of Development
123 W. Washington
P.O. Box 7970
Madison, WI 53703
Phone : (608) 266-9467
Fax : (608) 264-6151

WYOMING
Mary Kay Hill
Intergovernmental Affairs Coord.
Governor's Off.
State Capitol
Cheyenne, WY 82002
Phone : (307) 777-7435

DISTRICT OF COLUMBIA
Bernard Demczuk
Director
Off. of Intergovernmental Relations
441 4th St., NW, Rm. 10105
Washington, DC 20001
Phone : (202) 727-6265

Philip C. Smith
Director
Iowa Off. For State-Federal Relations
444 N. Capitol St., NW, Ste. 359
Washington, DC 20001
Phone : (202) 624-5442
Fax : (202) 624-8189

AMERICAN SAMOA
Matautia Tuiafono
Secretary
Off. of Samoan Affairs
American Samoa Government
Pago Pago, AS 96799
Phone : (684) 633-5201
Fax : (684) 633-5590

GUAM
Madeleine Z. Bordallo
Federal Programs/State Clearing House
Off. of the Lt. Governor
Executive Chambers, Adelup
Agana, GU 96910
Phone : (671) 475-9209
Fax : (671) 477-4826

NORTHERN MARIANA ISLANDS
Jose M. Taitano
Special Assistant for Admin.
Off. of the Governor
Capitol Hill
Saipan, MP 96950
Phone : (670) 322-5091

U.S. VIRGIN ISLANDS
Nellon Bowry
Director
Off. of Mgt. & Budget
#41 Norre Gade
Emancipation Garden Sta., 2nd Fl.
St. Thomas, VI 00802
Phone : (809) 774-0750
Fax : (809) 776-0069

LOTTERY

Administers the state lottery system.

ARIZONA
Ralph Decker
Executive Director
State Lottery
4740 E. University Dr.
Phoenix, AZ 85034
Phone : (602) 921-4400

CALIFORNIA
A. A. Pierce
Interim Director
Lottery Comm.
600 N. 10th St.
Sacramento, CA 95814
Phone : (916) 324-2025

COLORADO
George Turner
Director
Lottery Div.
Dept. of Revenue
201 W. Eighth St., Rm. 600
Pueblo, CO 81003
Phone : (719) 546-2400

CONNECTICUT
John B. Meskill
Executive Director
Div. of Special Revenue
Dept. of Revenue Srvcs.
55 Russell Rd.
Newington, CT 06111
Phone : (203) 566-2757

DELAWARE
Wayne Lemons
Director
State Lottery
Dept. of Finance
1575 McKee Rd., #102
Dover, DE 19904-1903
Phone : (302) 739-5291
Fax : (302) 739-6706

FLORIDA
Marcia Mann
Secretary
Dept. of the Lottery
250 Marriott Dr.
Tallahassee, FL 32399-4000
Phone : (904) 487-7728
Fax : (904) 487-7709

GEORGIA
Rebecca Paul
President
State Lottery Corp.
250 Williams St.
Atlanta, GA 30303
Phone : (404) 577-0600

IDAHO
Dennis Jackson
Director
State Lottery
1199 Shoreline Ln., Ste. 100
Boise, ID 83702
Phone : (208) 334-2600

ILLINOIS
Desiree Glapion Rogers
Director
State Lottery
201 E. Madison
Springfield, IL 62702
Phone : (217) 524-5259
Fax : (217) 524-5235

INDIANA
John Dillon, III
Director
State Lotteries
P.O. Box 6124
Indianapolis, IN 46206

IOWA
Edward J. Stanek II
Lottery Comm.
2015 Grand Ave.
Des Moines, IA 50312
Phone : (515) 281-7900
Phone : (317) 264-4800

KANSAS
Gregory P. Ziemak
Executive Director
Kansas Lottery
128 N. Kansas Ave.
Topeka, KS 66603-3638
Phone : (913) 296-5700
Fax : (913) 296-5712

KENTUCKY
Arthur L. Gleason Jr.
President & CEO
State Lottery Corp.
6040 Dutchman's Ln., Ste. 400
Louisville, KY 40205
Phone : (502) 473-2200

LOUISIANA
Bonnie Fussell
President
State Lottery Corp.
11200 Industriplex Blvd., Ste. 190
Baton Rouge, LA 70879
Phone : (504) 297-2000

MAINE
Eben B. Marsh
Director
Bur. of Alc. Bev. & Lottery Op.
Dept. of Admin. & Fin. Srvcs.
#8 State House Station
Augusta, ME 04333-0008
Phone : (207) 287-3721

MARYLAND
Lloyd Jones
Director
State Lottery Agency
6776 Reisterstown Rd.
Baltimore, MD 21215
Phone : (410) 764-5700

MASSACHUSETTS
Eric Turner
Director
Lottery Comm.
60 Columbian St.
Braintree, MA 02184
Phone : (617) 849-5555

MICHIGAN
Bill Martin
Commissioner
Bur. of State Lottery
101 E. Hillsdale St.
Lansing, MI 48913
Phone : (517) 335-5608

MINNESOTA
George Andersen
Director
Lottery Div.
State Lottery Comm.
2645 Long Lake Rd.
Roseville, MN 55113
Phone : (612) 635-8100

MISSOURI
James Scroggins
Administrative Director
Missouri Lottery
1823 Southridge Dr.
P.O. Box 1603
Jefferson City, MO 65102-1603
Phone : (314) 751-4050
Fax : (314) 751-5188

MONTANA
Charmaine Murphy
Director
State Lottery
Dept. of Commerce
2525 N. Montana
Helena, MT 59620
Phone : (406) 444-5825

NEBRASKA
M. Berri Balka
State Tax Commissioner
Dept. of Revenue
P.O. Box 94818
Lincoln, NE 68509-4818
Phone : (402) 471-5604

NEW HAMPSHIRE
James E. Wimsatt
Executive Director
Sweepstakes Comm.
Ft. Eddy Rd.
Concord, NH 03301
Phone : (603) 271-3391

NEW JERSEY
Virginia Haines
Executive Director
Div. of State Lottery
Dept. of the Treasury
Brunswick Ave., CN041
Trenton, NJ 08625
Phone : (609) 599-5900

NEW YORK*
Director
Div. of Lottery
1 Broadway Ctr.
P.O. Box 7500
Schenectady, NY 12301
Phone : (518) 288-3400

OHIO
William Howell
Executive Director
Lottery Comm.
Frank J. Lausche Bldg., 4th Fl
615 W. Superior Ave.
Cleveland, OH 44113
Phone : (216) 787-4333
Fax : (216) 787-3313

OREGON
Gary Weeks
Director
State Lottery
2767 22nd St., SE
Salem, OR 97310
Phone : (503) 373-0202
Fax : (503) 373-0248

PENNSYLVANIA
Charles W. Kline
Director
Bur. of Lotteries
Dept. of Revenue
2850 Turnpike Industrial Rd.
Middletown, PA 17057
Phone : (717) 986-4759

RHODE ISLAND
Peter J. O'Connell
Director
State Lottery
1425 Pontiac Ave.
Cranston, RI 02920
Phone : (401) 463-6500

SOUTH DAKOTA
Rodger Leonard
Executive Director
State Lottery
St. Charles Bldg.
Pierre, SD 57501
Phone : (605) 773-5770

TEXAS
Nora Linares
Lottery Commission
6937 North IH35
Austin, TX 78752-3221
Phone : (512) 323-3700
Fax : (512) 451-1586

VERMONT
Fred McGibney
Director
Lottery Commission
379 South Barre Rd.
P.O. Box 420
South Barre, VT 05670-0420
Phone : (802) 479-5686
Fax : (802) 479-4294

VIRGINIA
Penelope W. Kyle
Director
State Lottery Dept.
900 E. Main St., 13th Fl.
Richmond, VA 23219
Phone : (804) 692-7000
Fax : (804) 692-7102

WASHINGTON
Evelyn Yenson
Director
State Lottery
814 Fourth Ave.
P.O. Box 43000
Olympia, WA 98504-3000
Phone : (360) 753-1412

WEST VIRGINIA
Rich Boyle
Director
State Lottery Comm.
P.O. Box 2067
Charleston, WV 25327-2067

WISCONSIN
Donald Walsh
Acting Director
Lottery Div.
Gaming Comm.
1802 W. Beltine
P.O. Box 8941
Madison, WI 53713
Phone : (608) 267-4848
Fax : (608) 264-6644

DISTRICT OF COLUMBIA
Anthony Cooper
Executive Director
Lottery & Charitable Games Control Bd.
2101 M.L. King, Jr., Ave. SE
Washington, DC 20020
Phone : (202) 433-8011

Barbara Bell Clark
Chair
Lottery & Charitable Games Control Bd.
2101 M.L. King, Jr. Ave., SE
Washington, DC 20020
Phone : (202) 433-8006

NORTHERN MARIANA ISLANDS
Maria D. Cabrera
Secretary of Finance
Dept. of Finance & Accounting
P.O. Box 5234, CHRB
Saipan, MP 96950
Phone : (670) 664-1100
Fax : (670) 664-1115

PUERTO RICO
Luis Tovet
Director
Lottery Admin.
New San Juan Ctr.
Chardon Ave.
Hato Rey, PR 00919
Phone : (809) 759-8686

U.S. VIRGIN ISLANDS
Alec Dizon
Director of the Lottery
75-B Kronprindsens Gade
St. Thomas, VI 00802
Phone : (809) 774-2502
Fax : (809) 776-4730

MASS TRANSPORTATION

Develops the state's mass transportation policies.

ALASKA
Joseph L. Perkins
Commissioner
Dept. of Transportation & Public Facilities
3132 Channel Dr.
Juneau, AK 99801-7898
Phone : (907) 465-3900
Fax : (907) 586-8365

ARIZONA
Jay Klagge
Assistant Director
Intermodel Division
Dept. of Transportation
206 S. 17th Ave.
Phoenix, AZ 85007
Phone : (602) 255-7431

ARKANSAS
Dan Flowers
Director
Dept. of Highways & Transportation
P.O. Box 2261
Little Rock, AR 72203
Phone : (501) 569-2211
Fax : (501) 569-2400

CALIFORNIA
Brian Smith
Deputy Director
Transportation Planning
Dept. of Transportation
1120 N St.
Sacramento, CA 95814
Phone : (916) 445-7111

COLORADO
Guillermo Vidal
Executive Director
Dept. of Transportation
4201 E. Arkansas Ave., Rm. 262
Denver, CO 80222
Phone : (303) 757-9011
Fax : (303) 757-9656

CONNECTICUT
Erik Bergman
Deputy Commissioner
Public Transportation Bur.
Dept. of Transporation
2800 Berlin Tpke., Rm. 1344
Newington, CT 06131-7546
Phone : (203) 594-3000

DELAWARE
Anne P. Canby
Secretary
Transportation Authority
Transportation Admin. Bldg.
P.O. Box 778
Dover, DE 19903
Phone : (302) 739-4306
Fax : (302) 739-4329

FLORIDA
Nick Serianni
Director
Off. of Public Transportation
Dept. of Transportation
605 Suwannee St.
Tallahassee, FL 32399-0450
Phone : (904) 488-6721
Fax : (904) 488-5526

GEORGIA
Luke Cousins
Administrator
Off. of Intermodal Programs
Dept. of Transportation
276 Memorial Dr.
Atlanta, GA 30303
Phone : (404) 651-9201

HAWAII
Kazu Hayashida
Director
Dept. of Transportation
869 Punchbowl St.
Honolulu, HI 96813
Phone : (808) 587-2150
Fax : (808) 587-2167

IDAHO
Dwight Bower
Director
Dept. of Transportation
P.O. Box 7129
Boise, ID 83707
Phone : (208) 334-8800

ILLINOIS
Stephen E. Schindel
Director
Div. of Public Transportation
Dept. of Transportation
310 S. Michigan, Rm. 1608
Chicago, IL 60604
Phone : (312) 793-2111

INDIANA
Robert Shields
Chief
Transportation Planning
Dept. of Transportation
100 N. Senate Ave., N901
Indianapolis, IN 46204-2208

IOWA
Darrel Rensink
Director
Dept. of Transportation
800 Lincoln Way
Ames, IA 50010
Phone : (515) 239-1111
Fax : (515) 239-1639
Phone : (317) 232-2380

KENTUCKY
Don C. Kelly
Secretary
Transportation Cabinet
State Off. Bldg., 10th Fl.
Frankfort, KY 40601
Phone : (502) 564-4890

LOUISIANA
Carol Cranshaw
Administrator
Div. of Public Transportation
Dept. of Transportation & Development
P.O. Box 94245
Baton Rouge, LA 70804
Phone : (504) 379-1100

MAINE
Russell Spinney
Deputy Commissioner
Bur. of Transportation Srvcs.
Dept. of Transportation
State House Station # 16
Augusta, ME 04333
Phone : (207) 287-2841

MARYLAND
John Agro
Administrator
Mass Transit Administration
Dept. of Transportation
300 W. Lexington St.
Baltimore, MD 21201
Phone : (410) 288-8410

MASSACHUSETTS
John J. Haley
General Manager
Bay Transit Authority
Off. of Transportation & Construction
10 Park Plz., Rm. 3910
Boston, MA 02116
Phone : (617) 722-5176

MICHIGAN
Phil Kazmierski
Deputy Director
Bur. of Urban & Public Transportation
Dept. of Transportation
P.O. Box 30050
Lansing, MI 48909
Phone : (517) 373-2282

MINNESOTA
Robert Mairs
Chairman
Metropolitan Transit Comm.
560 Sixth Ave., N.
Minneapolis, MN 55411
Phone : (612) 349-7400

Jeff Hamiel
Executive Director
Metropolitan Airports Comm.
6040 28th Ave., S.
Minneapolis, MN 55450
Phone : (612) 726-1892

MINNESOTA — Cont.
James Denn
Commissioner
Dept. of Transportation
Transportation Bldg., 4th Fl.
John Ireland Blvd.
St. Paul, MN 55155
Phone : (612) 297-2930

MISSISSIPPI
Chester Smith
Director
Div. of Energy
Dept. of Economic & Community Dev.
510 George St., Ste. 301
Jackson, MS 39202
Phone : (601) 359-3449

MISSOURI
Phil Richeson
Director
Div. of Transit
Dept. of Highways & Transport.
Highway Bldg.
P.O. Box 270
Jefferson City, MO 65102
Phone : (314) 751-2523
Fax : (314) 526-4709

MONTANA
Patricia Saindon
Administrator
Transportation Planning Div.
Dept. of Transportation
2701 Prospect Ave.
Helena, MT 59620
Phone : (406) 444-3423

NEBRASKA
Tom Wais
Deputy Director
Planning Div.
Dept. of Roads
P.O. Box 94759
Lincoln, NE 68509-4759
Phone : (402) 479-4671

NEVADA
Tom Stephens
Director
Dept. of Transportation
1263 S. Stewart St.
Carson City, NV 89712
Phone : (702) 687-5440

NEW JERSEY
Frank Wilson
Commissioner
Dept. of Transportation
1035 Parkway Ave., CN600
Trenton, NJ 08625
Phone : (609) 530-3535

NEW MEXICO
David Torres
Director
Transportation Programs Div.
State Hwy. Dept.
604 W. San Mateo
Santa Fe, NM 87501
Phone : (505) 827-0410
Fax : (505) 827-0431

NEW YORK*
Commissioner
Dept. of Transportation
Campus, Bldg. 5
Albany, NY 12232
Phone : (518) 457-4422

NORTH CAROLINA
David King
Director
Div. of Public Transportation
Dept. of Transportation
One S. Wilmington St.
Raleigh, NC 27601-1494
Phone : (919) 733-4713
Fax : (919) 733-9150

NORTH DAKOTA
Duane Bentz
Planning Engineer
Planning Div.
Highway Dept.
608 E. Boulevard Ave.
Bismarck, ND 58505
Phone : (701) 328-2513
Fax : (701) 328-1404

OHIO
Carla Cefaratti
Deputy Director
Div. of Public Transportation
Dept. of Transportation
25 S. Front St., Rm. 716
Columbus, OH 43215
Phone : (614) 466-8969
Fax : (614) 466-1768

OKLAHOMA
Jack Crowley
Director
Dept. of Transportation
200 NE 21st St.
Oklahoma City, OK 73105
Phone : (405) 521-2631

OREGON
Joni Reid
Manager
Public Transit Section
Dept. of Transportation
131 Transportation Bldg.
Salem, OR 97310
Phone : (503) 989-3300

PENNSYLVANIA
Joseph Daversa
Director
Bur. of Public Transportation & Goods
1215 Transportation & Safety Bldg.
Harrisburg, PA 17120
Phone : (717) 787-3921

RHODE ISLAND
William H. Trevitt
General Manager
Public Transit Authority
265 Melrose St.
Providence, RI 02907
Phone : (401) 781-9400

SOUTH CAROLINA
Jerome Noble
Director
Div. of Public Transportion
Dept. of Transportation
955 Park St.
Columbia, SC 29202
Phone : (803) 737-1280

SOUTH DAKOTA
Richard Howard
Secretary
Dept. of Transportation
700 E. Broadway
Pierre, SD 57501
Phone : (605) 773-3265

TENNESSEE
Malcolm Baird
Director
Public Transportation & Aeronautics
Dept. of Transportation
700 James K. Polk Bldg.
Nashville, TN 37243
Phone : (615) 741-2849

TEXAS
Alvin R. Luedecke Jr.
State Transportation Planning
Department of Transportation
P.O. Box 5051
Austin, TX 78763
Phone : (512) 467-5911

UTAH
George F. Thompson
Engineer
Planning & Programming
Dept. of Transportation
4501 S. 2700 W.
Salt Lake City, UT 84119
Phone : (801) 965-4366

VERMONT
William S. Bruzzese
Director
Air, Rail & Transit Program
Agency of Transportation
133 State St.
Montpelier, VT 05633
Phone : (802) 828-2093
Fax : (802) 828-2829

VIRGINIA
David R. Gehr
Commissioner
Dept. of Transportation
1401 E. Broad St.
Richmond, VA 23219
Phone : (804) 786-2701
Fax : (804) 786-2940

WASHINGTON
James P. Toohey
Assistant Secretary
Transit, Research & Intermodal Planning
Dept. of Transport
P.O. Box 47400
Olympia, WA 98504-7400
Phone : (360) 705-7000

WEST VIRGINIA
Susan L. O'Connell
Director
Div. of Public Transit
Dept. of Transportation
Bldg. 5, Rm. 716
Charleston, WV 25305-0432
Phone : (304) 558-0428

WISCONSIN
John H. Evans
Administrator
Transportation Assistance Div.
Dept. of Transportation
4802 Sheboygan Ave., Rm. 701
P.O. Box 7914
Madison, WI 53705
Phone : (608) 267-7111
Fax : (608) 267-6748

WYOMING
Don Diller
Director
Dept. of Transportation
5300 Bishop Blvd.
Cheyenne, WY 82002
Phone : (307) 777-4484

DISTRICT OF COLUMBIA
Art Lawson
Administrator
Off. of Mass Transit
Dept. of Public Works
2000 14th St., NW, 6th Fl.
Washington, DC 20009
Phone : (202) 939-8050

GUAM
Tyrone J. Taitano
General Manager
Mass Transit Authority
236 E. O'Brien
P.O. Box 2950
Agana, GU 96910
Phone : (671) 475-4682
Fax : (671) 475-4600

NORTHERN MARIANA ISLANDS
Edward M. Deleon Guerrero
Secretary
Dept. of Public Works
Lower Base
P.O. Box 2950
Saipan, MP 96950
Phone : (670) 322-9482
Fax : (670) 322-3547

PUERTO RICO
Hector R. Rivera
President
Metropolitan Bus Authority
P.O. Box 195349
San Juan, PR 00919
Phone : (809) 767-7979
Fax : (809) 751-0527

U.S. VIRGIN ISLANDS
Ann Abramson
Acting Commissioner
Dept. of Public Works
No. 8 Sub Base
St. Thomas, VI 00802
Phone : (809) 776-4844
Fax : (809) 774-5869

MEDICAID

Administers the medical assistance program that finances medical care for income assistance recipients and other eligible medically needy persons.

ALABAMA
Gwen Williams
Commissioner
Medicaid Agency
P.O. Box 5624
Montgomery, AL 36103
Phone : (334) 242-5600
Fax : (334) 242-5097

ALASKA
Kim Busch
Director
Div. of Medical Assistance
Dept. of Health & Social Srvcs.
P.O. Box 110660
Juneau, AK 99811-0660
Phone : (907) 465-3355
Fax : (907) 465-2204

ARIZONA
Mabel Chen
Director
Health Care Cost Contm. System
801 E. Jefferson
Phoenix, AZ 85034
Phone : (602) 234-3655

ARKANSAS
Roy Hart
Deputy Director
Economic & Medical Srvcs. Div.
Dept. of Human Srvcs.
P.O. Box 1437, Slot 316
Little Rock, AR 72203
Phone : (501) 682-8375
Fax : (501) 682-8367

CALIFORNIA
Virgil J. Toney
Chief
Medi-Cal Operations Div.
Dept. of Health Srvcs.
P.O. Box 942732
Sacramento, CA 95814
Phone : (916) 657-1282

COLORADO
Richard C. Allen
Director
Div. of Health Plans & Med. Srvcs.
Health Care Policy & Finance
1575 Sherman, 4th Fl.
Denver, CO 80203
Phone : (303) 866-2859
Fax : (303) 866-2803

CONNECTICUT
David Parella
Director
Health Care Financing
Department of Social Services
25 Sigourney St., 8th Fl.
Hartford, CT 06106-5003
Phone : (203) 424-5167

DELAWARE
Philip P. Soule
Director
Div. of Social Srvcs.
Medicaid Unit
DHSS Main Campus
1901 N. Dupont Highway
New Castle, DE 19720
Phone : (302) 577-4353
Fax : (302) 577-4899

FLORIDA
Marshall E. Kelly
Director
Bureau of Medicaid
Agency for Health Care Admin.
1317 Winewood Blvd., Bldg. Six
Tallhassee, FL 32399-0700
Phone : (904) 488-3560
Fax : (904) 488-2520

GEORGIA
Marge Smith
Commissioner
Dept. of Medical Assistance
2 M.L. King, Jr. Dr., NE
Atlanta, GA 30334
Phone : (404) 656-4507

HAWAII
Winifred Odo
Administrator
Health Care Admin. Div.
Dept. of Human Services
P.O. Box 339
Honolulu, HI 96809
Phone : (808) 586-5391

IDAHO
Tresa Newman
Acting Administrator
Div. of Welfare
Dept. of Health & Welfare
450 W. State St.
P.O. Box 83720
Boise, ID 83720-0036
Phone : (208) 334-5747
Fax : (208) 334-0657

ILLINOIS
Robert W. Wright
Director
Dept. of Public Aid
100 S. Grand Ave., E.
Springfield, IL 62762
Phone : (217) 782-1200
Fax : (217) 524-7979

INDIANA
Jim Verdier
Assistant Secretary
Medicaid Policy & Planning
Family & Social Srvcs. Admin.
IGC-South, Rm. W341
Indianapolis, IN 46204
Phone : (317) 233-4455

IOWA
Donald L. Herman
Chief
Medical Srvcs. Div.
Dept. of Human Srvcs.
Hoover State Off. Bldg.
Des Moines, IA 50319
Phone : (515) 281-8621

KANSAS
Candace Shively
Acting Director
Medicaid Operations
Dept. of Social & Rehab. Srvcs.
Docking State Off. Bldg., 6th Fl.
Topeka, KS 66612-1570
Phone : (913) 296-3981
Fax : (913) 296-4813

KENTUCKY
Masten Childers
Commissioner
Dept. for Medicaid Srvcs.
Cabinet for Human Resources
275 E. Main St.
Frankfort, KY 40621
Phone : (502) 564-4321

LOUISIANA
Tom Collins
Director
Bur. of Health Srvcs. Finan.
Dept. of Health & Hospitals
P.O. Box 629
Baton Rouge, LA 70821
Phone : (504) 342-3891

MAINE
Francis Finnegan
Director
Bur. of Medical Services
Dept. of Human Services
State House Station # 11
Augusta, ME 04333
Phone : (207) 287-2546

MARYLAND
Martin Wasserman
Secretary
Dept. of Health & Mental Hygiene
201 W. Preston St., 5th Fl.
Baltimore, MD 21201
Phone : (410) 225-6505

MASSACHUSETTS
Joseph V. Gallant
Commissioner
Medical Assistance
Dept. of Public Welfare
600 Washington St.
Boston, MA 02111
Phone : (617) 348-8400

MICHIGAN
Vernon Smith
Director
Medical Services Admin.
Dept. of Social Services
P.O. Box 30037
Lansing, MI 48909
Phone : (517) 335-5001

MINNESOTA
Helen M. Yates
Assistant Commissioner
Health Care Admin.
Dept. of Human Services
444 Lafayette Rd.
St. Paul, MN 55155-3852
Phone : (612) 297-3374

MISSISSIPPI
Helen Weatherbee
Director
Div. of Medicaid
Off. of the Governor
239 N. Lamar St., Ste. 801
Jackson, MS 39215-1399
Phone : (601) 359-6050

MISSOURI
Donna Checkett
Director
Div. of Medical Services
Dept. of Social Services
615 Howerton Ct.
P.O. Box 6500
Jefferson City, MO 65102-6500
Phone : (314) 751-6922
Fax : (314) 751-6564

MONTANA
John Donwen
Administrator
Economic Assistance Div.
Dept. of Social & Rehab. Srvcs.
111 Sanders St.
Helena, MT 59601
Phone : (406) 444-2651

NEBRASKA
Robert Seiffert
Administrator
Medical Srvcs.
Dept. of Social Srvcs.
P.O. Box 95026
Lincoln, NE 68509
Phone : (402) 471-9718

NEVADA
April Townley
Deputy Administrator
Medicaid Div.
Dept. of Human Resources
2527 N. Carson St.
Carson City, NV 89710
Phone : (702) 687-4378

NEW HAMPSHIRE
Barry Bodell
Director
Div. of Welfare
Dept. of Health & Human Srvcs.
Hazen Dr.
Concord, NH 03301
Phone : (603) 271-4321

NEW JERSEY
William Waldman
Commissioner
Dept. of Human Srvcs.
222 S. Warren St., CN700
Trenton, NJ 08625
Phone : (609) 292-5360

NEW MEXICO
Bruce Weydemeyer
Chief
Medical Assistance Div.
Dept. of Human Services
P.O. Box 2348
Santa Fe, NM 87503
Phone : (505) 827-3100
Fax : (505) 827-3185

NEW YORK*
Commissioner
Dept. of Social Srvcs.
40 N. Pearl St.
Albany, NY 12243
Phone : (518) 474-9475

NORTH CAROLINA
Barbara D. Matula
Director
Div. of Medical Assistance
Dept. of Human Resources
1985 Umstead Dr.
Raleigh, NC 27603-2001
Phone : (919) 733-2060

NORTH DAKOTA
Betty L. Strecker
Director
Medical Srvcs. Div.
Dept. of Human Srvcs.
600 E. Boulevard Ave.
Bismarck, ND 58505-0250
Phone : (701) 328-2321
Fax : (701) 328-2359

OHIO
John J. Nichols
Chief
Bur. of Medical Assistance
Dept. of Human Services
30 E. Broad St., 31st Fl.
Columbus, OH 43215
Phone : (614) 466-2365
Fax : (614) 752-7701

OKLAHOMA
George Miller
Interim Director
Health & Human Srvcs.
Dept. of Human Srvcs.
P.O. Box 25352
Oklahoma City, OK 73125
Phone : (405) 521-2778

OREGON
Jean Thorne
Manager
Off. of Medical Asst. Program
Dept. of Human Resources
500 Summer St., NE
Salem, OR 97310-1014
Phone : (503) 945-5772
Fax : (503) 373-7689

PENNSYLVANIA
Richard Lee
Acting Deputy Secretary
Medical Assistance
Dept. of Public Welfare
P.O. Box 2675
Harrisburg, PA 17105-2675
Phone : (717) 787-1870

RHODE ISLAND
Robert J. Palumbo
Associate Director
Medical Services
Dept. of Mental Health & Rehab.
600 New London Ave.
Cranston, RI 02920
Phone : (401) 464-3575

SOUTH CAROLINA
Andy Laurent
Executive Director
Health & Human Services Finance Comm.
P.O. Box 8206
Columbia, SC 29202
Phone : (803) 253-6100

SOUTH DAKOTA
David Christensen
Director
Div. of Medical Services
Dept. of Social Services
Kneip Bldg.
Pierre, SD 57501
Phone : (605) 773-3495

TENNESSEE
Manny Martins
Director
Medicaid Admin.
Dept. of Health
729 Church St.
Nashville, TN 37247
Phone : (615) 741-0213

TEXAS
Burton Raiford
Commissioner
Dept. of Human Services
P.O. Box 149030
Austin, TX 78714
Phone : (512) 450-3011

UTAH
Rod Betit
Director
Div. of Health Care Financing
Dept. of Health
288 N. 1460 W.
Salt Lake City, UT 84116
Phone : (801) 538-6111

VERMONT
Kent Stoneman
Director
Medicaid Services Div.
Dept. of Social Welfare
103 S. Main St.
Waterbury, VT 05671-1201
Phone : (802) 241-2880
Fax : (802) 241-2830

VIRGINIA
Robert C. Metcalf
Director
Dept. of Medical Assistance Srvcs.
600 E. Broad St., Ste. 1300
Richmond, VA 23219
Phone : (804) 786-8099
Fax : (804) 371-4981

WASHINGTON
James Peterson
Director
Div. of Medical Assistance
Dept. of Social & Health Srvcs.
P.O. Box 45010
Olympia, WA 98504-5010
Phone : (360) 753-1777

WEST VIRGINIA
Gretchen Lewis
Secretary
Dept. of Health & Human Resources
Bldg. 3, Rm. 206
State Capitol Complex
Charleston, WV 25305
Phone : (304) 558-0684

WISCONSIN
Ann Haney
Administrator
Div. of Health
Dept. of Health & Soc. Srvcs.
1 W Wilson St., Room 218
Madison, WI 53703
Phone : (608) 266-1511
Fax : (608) 267-2832

WYOMING
Kenneth C. Kamis
Director
Medical Assistance
Health & Medical Services Div.
Hathaway Bldg.
Cheyenne, WY 82002
Phone : (307) 777-7531

DISTRICT OF COLUMBIA
David Coronado
Commissioner
Heatlh Care Finance
Dept. of Human Srvcs.
2100 M.L. King, Jr. Ave., SE
Washington, DC 20020-5732
Phone : (202) 727-0735

AMERICAN SAMOA
Bob E. Parks
CEO
Hospital Authority
LBJ Tropical Medical Center
American Samoa Government
Pago Pago, AS 96799
Phone : (684) 633-1222
Fax : (684) 633-1869

GUAM
Dennis Rodriguez
Director
Dept. of Public Health & Social Services
P.O. Box 2816
Agana, GU 96910
Phone : (671) 734-7102
Fax : (671) 734-5910

NORTHERN MARIANA ISLANDS
Angie V. Guerrero
Administrator
Medicaid Div.
Dept. of Pub. Health & Env. Srvcs.
P.O. Box 409
Saipan, MP 96950
Phone : (670) 234-8950

PUERTO RICO
Carmen Feliciano
Secretary
Dept. of Health
P.O. Box 70184
San Juan, PR 00936
Phone : (809) 250-7227
Fax : (809) 250-6547

U.S. VIRGIN ISLANDS
Aracelis B. Hendry
Assistant Commissioner
Dept. of Health
St. Croix Hospital
St. Croix, VI 00820
Phone : (809) 773-1311

MENTAL HEALTH AND RETARDATION

Administers the mental health services of the state and/or plans and coordinates programs for the mentally disabled.

ALABAMA
Emmett Poundstone
Commissioner
Dept. of Mental Health & Mental Retardation
200 Interstate Park
Montgomery, AL 36109
Phone : (334) 271-9239
Fax : (334) 271-2623

ALASKA
Mike Renfro
Director
Div. of Mental Health & Developmental Disabilities
Dept. of Health & Social Services
P.O. Box 110620
Juneau, AK 99811-0620
Phone : (907) 465-3370
Fax : (907) 465-2668

ARIZONA
Sam Thurmond
Assistant Director
Developmental Disabilities Div
Dept. of Economic Security
1789 W. Jefferson
Phoenix, AZ 85007
Phone : (602) 542-6853

ARKANSAS
Pamela Marshall
Director
Div. of Mental Health
Dept. of Human Srvcs.
4313 W. Markham
Little Rock, AR 72205
Phone : (501) 686-9165
Fax : (501) 686-9182

CALIFORNIA
Stephen Mayberg
Director
Dept. of Mental Health
1600 9th St.
Sacramento, CA 95814
Phone : (916) 654-2309

COLORADO
Charlie Allinson
Director
Dev. Disabilities Div.
Dept. of Human Srvcs.
3824 W. Princeton Cir.
Denver, CO 80236
Phone : (303) 762-4550
Fax : (303) 762-4300

CONNECTICUT
Linda Goldfarb
Acting Commissioner
Dept. of Mental Retardation
90 Pitkin St.
East Hartford, CT 06108
Phone : (203) 528-7141

Albert Solnit
Commissioner
Dept. of Mental Health
90 Washington St.
Hartford, CT 06106
Phone : (203) 566-3869

DELAWARE
William E. Love
Director
Div. of Mental Retardation
Dept. of Health & Social Srvcs.
Jesse Cooper Building
Dover, DE 19901
Phone : (302) 739-4452
Fax : (302) 739-3008

Thomas M. Fritz
Director
Div. of Alcoholism, Drug Abuse & Mental Health
1901 N. DuPont Hwy.
New Castle, DE 19720
Phone : (302) 577-4461

FLORIDA
Robert Constantine
Assistant Secretary
Dept. of Health & Rehabilitative Services
1317 Winewood Blvd.
Tallahassee, FL 32399-0700
Phone : (904) 488-8304

GEORGIA
Eddie Roland
Director
Dept. of Mental Health, Mental Retardation & Substance Abuse
2 Peachtree St., 4th Fl.
Atlanta, GA 30303
Phone : (404) 657-2250

HAWAII
Masura Oshiro
Deputy Director
Behavioral Health Srvcs. Admin.
Dept. of Health
1250 Punchbowl St.
Honolulu, HI 96813
Phone : (808) 586-4434

Lois Suenishi
Mental Retardation Administrator
Waimano Training School/Hospital
Dept. of Health
Pearl City, HI 96782
Phone : (808) 456-6255

IDAHO
Roy Sargeant
Bureau Chief
Bur. of Mental Health
P.O. Box 83720
Boise, ID 83720-0036
Phone : (208) 334-6500
Fax : (208) 334-6667

ILLINOIS
Ann Patla
Director
Dept. of Mental Health & Developmental Disabilities
401 Stratton Bldg.
Springfield, IL 62706
Phone : (217) 782-0009
Fax : (217) 524-0835

INDIANA
Patrick Sullivan
Director
Div. of Mental Health & Addictions
402 W. Washington St.
Indianapolis, IN 46204
Phone : (317) 232-7845

IOWA
Sally Titus Cunningham
Deputy Director
Dept. of Human Srvcs.
Hoover State Off. Bldg.
Des Moines, IA 50319
Phone : (515) 281-6360
Fax : (515) 281-4597

KANSAS
George Vega
Commissioner
Mental Health & Retardation
Dept. of Social & Rehab. Srvcs.
Docking State Off. Bldg., 5th Fl.
Topeka, KS 66612-1570
Phone : (913) 296-3773
Fax : (913) 296-6142

KENTUCKY
Elizabeth Rehm Wachtel
Commissioner
Mental Health & Retardation Srvcs. Dept.
275 E. Main St.
Frankfort, KY 40621
Phone : (502) 564-4527

LOUISIANA
Walter Shervington
Assistant Secretary
Off. of Mental Health
Dept. of Health & Hospitals
P.O. Box 629
Baton Rouge, LA 70821
Phone : (504) 342-9500

MAINE
Melodie Peet
Commissioner
Dept. of Mental Health & Mental Retardation
State House Station # 40
Augusta, ME 04333
Phone : (207) 287-4223

MARYLAND
Stuart Silver
Director
Mental Hygiene Admin.
Public of Health Services
201 W. Preston St., Rm. 416A
Baltimore, MD 21201
Phone : (410) 225-6611

Lois M. Meszaros
Director
Dev. Disabilities Admin.
Dept. of Health & Mental Hygiene
201 W. Preston St., 4th Fl.
Baltimore, MD 21201
Phone : (301) 225-5600

MASSACHUSETTS
Phillip Campbell
Commissioner
Dept. of Mental Retardation
160 N. Washington St.
Boston, MA 02114
Phone : (617) 727-5608

Eileen Elias
Commissioner
Dept. of Mental Health
Executive Off. of Human Srvcs.
25 Staniford St.
Boston, MA 02114
Phone : (617) 727-5500

MICHIGAN
James Haveman
Director
Dept. of Mental Health
300 S. Walnut, 6th Fl.
Lansing, MI 48913
Phone : (517) 373-3500
Fax : (517) 335-3090

MINNESOTA
Jim Stoebner
Assistant Commissioner
Comm. Mental Health & Soc. Srvcs.
Dept. of Human Srvcs.
444 Lafayette Rd.
St. Paul, MN 55155-3826
Phone : (612) 296-2710

MISSISSIPPI
Roger McMurtry
Director
Mental Retardation Div.
Dept. of Mental Health
1101 Robert E. Lee Bldg.
Jackson, MS 39201
Phone : (601) 359-1288

Randy Hendrix
Director
Dept. of Mental Health
1101 Robert E. Lee Bldg.
Jackson, MS 39201
Phone : (601) 359-1288

MISSOURI
Greg Kramer
Director
Div. of Mental Retardation and Developmental Disabilities
1706 E. Elm
P.O. Box 687
Jefferson City, MO 65102
Phone : (314) 751-4054
Fax : (314) 751-9207

MONTANA
Mike Hanshew
Administrator
Developmental Disabilities Div.
Dept. of Social & Rehab. Srvcs.
SRS Bldg., Rm. 305
Helena, MT 59620
Phone : (406) 444-2995

Dan Anderson
Administrator
Mental Health Div.
Dept. of Institutions
1539 11th Ave.
Helena, MT 59620
Phone : (406) 444-3969

NEBRASKA
Dale B. Johnson
Director
Dept. of Public Institutions
P.O. Box 94728
Lincoln, NE 68509
Phone : (402) 471-2851

Priscilla Henkelmann
Director
Off. of Community Mental Health
Dept. of Public Institutions
P.O. Box 94728
Lincoln, NE 68509
Phone : (402) 471-2851

NEVADA
Carlos Brandenburg
Administrator
Mental Hygiene & Retardation
Dept. of Human Resources
505 E. King St., Rm. 403
Carson City, NV 89710
Phone : (702) 687-5943

NEW HAMPSHIRE
Donald Shumway
Director
Div. of Mental Health & Developmental Srvcs.
105 Pleasant St.
Concord, NH 03301
Phone : (603) 271-5007

NEW JERSEY
Alan Kaufman
Director
Div. of Mental Health & Hosp.
Dept. of Human Services
Capitol Ctr., CN727
Trenton, NJ 08625
Phone : (609) 777-0700

NEW MEXICO
Javier Acebes
Director
Developmental Disabilities Div.
Dept. of Health
1190 St. Francis, 3rd Fl.
Santa Fe, NM 87502
Phone : (505) 827-2574
Fax : (505) 827-2595

NEW MEXICO — Cont.
Jack Callaghan
Director
Div. of Mental Health
Dept. of Health
P.O. Box 26110
Santa Fe, NM 87502
Phone : (505) 827-2644
Fax : (505) 827-2695

NEW YORK*
Commissioner
Off. of Mental Health
44 Holland Ave.
Albany, NY 12229
Phone : (518) 474-4403

NORTH CAROLINA
Michael S. Pedneau
Director
Mental Health, Retardation & Substance Abuse
Dept. of Human Resources
325 N. Salisbury St.
Raleigh, NC 27603
Phone : (919) 733-7011

NORTH DAKOTA
Samih A. Ismir
Director
Mental Health Div.
Dept. of Human Services
600 E. Boulevard Ave.
Bismarck, ND 58505
Phone : (701) 328-2766
Fax : (701) 328-2359

OHIO
Jerome C. Manuel
Director
Dept. of Mental Retardation & Developmental Disabilities
30 E. Broad St., 12th Fl.
Columbus, OH 43266-0415
Phone : (614) 466-5214
Fax : (614) 644-5013

Michael Hogan Ph.D.
Director
Dept. of Mental Health
30 E. Broad St., 8th Fl.
Columbus, OH 43266-0414
Phone : (614) 466-2337
Fax : (614) 752-9453

OKLAHOMA
Sharon Boehler
Commissioner
Dept. of Mental Health & Substance Abuse Srvcs.
P.O. Box 53277
Oklahoma City, OK 73152
Phone : (405) 271-8644

OREGON
Barry Kast
Administrator
Mental Health & Developmental Disabilities Srvcs. Div.
2575 Bittern St., NE
Salem, OR 97310
Phone : (503) 945-9499
Fax : (503) 378-3796

PENNSYLVANIA
Nancy R. Thaler
Deputy Secretary
Mental Retardation
Dept. of Public Welfare
Health & Welfare Bldg., Rm. 512
Harrisburg, PA 17120
Phone : (717) 787-3700

Ford S. Thompson Jr.
Deputy Secretary
Mental Health
Dept. of Public Welfare
Health & Welfare Bldg., Rm. 502
Harrisburg, PA 17120
Phone : (717) 787-6443

RHODE ISLAND
A. Kathryn Power
Director
Dept. of Mental Health, Retardation & Hospitals
600 New London Ave.
Cranston, RI 02920
Phone : (401) 464-3201

SOUTH CAROLINA
Philip S. Massey
Director
Dept. of Disabilities & Special Needs
P.O. Box 4706
Columbia, SC 29240
Phone : (803) 737-6444

SOUTH DAKOTA*
Acting Director
Div. of Mental Health
Dept. of Human Srvcs.
500 E. Capitol Ave.
Pierre, SD 57501
Phone : (605) 773-5990

Bill Podradsky
Secretary
Dept. of Human Srvcs.
Hillsview Plz.
500 E. Capitol Ave.
Pierre, SD 57501
Phone : (605) 773-5990

TENNESSEE
Marjorie Nell Cardwell
Commissioner
Dept. of Mental Health
710 James Robertson Pkwy.
Nashville, TN 37243
Phone : (615) 532-6500
Fax : (615) 532-6514

TEXAS
Karen F. Hale
Commissioner
Dept. of Mental Health & Mental Retardation
P.O. Box 12668, Capitol Station
Austin, TX 78711
Phone : (512) 465-4588

UTAH*
Director
Div. of Mental Health
Dept. of Human Srvcs.
120 N. 200 W., 4th Fl.
Salt Lake City, UT 84103
Phone : (801) 538-4270

VERMONT
William A. Dalton
Commissioner
Mental Health & Retardation
Agency of Human Services
103 S. Main St.
Waterbury, VT 05671-1601
Phone : (802) 241-2610
Fax : (802) 241-3052

VIRGINIA
Timothy A. Kelly
Commissioner
Dept. of Mental Health, Retrd. & Substance Abuse Srvcs.
109 Governor St.
Richmond, VA 23219
Phone : (804) 786-3921
Fax : (804) 371-6638

WASHINGTON
Lyle Quasim
Assistant Secretary
Health & Rehab. Srvcs.
Dept. of Social & Health Srvcs.
P.O. Box 45010
Olympia, WA 98504-5010
Phone : (360) 753-3327

WEST VIRGINIA
Gretchen Lewis
Secretary
Dept. of Health & Human Resources
Bldg. 3, Rm. 206
State Capitol Complex
Charleston, WV 25305
Phone : (304) 558-0684

WISCONSIN
Dennis Harkins
Director
Off. of Developmental Dis.
Dept. of Health & Social Srvcs.
1 W. Wilson, Room 418
P.O. Box 7851
Madison, WI 53703
Phone : (608) 266-0805
Fax : (608) 266-0036

WYOMING
Kenneth C. Kamis
Director
Dept. of Health
Hathaway Bldg.
Cheyenne, WY 82002
Phone : (307) 777-7656

DISTRICT OF COLUMBIA
Melvin Williams
Commissioner
Mental Health Srvcs.
Dept. of Human Srvcs.
2700 M.L. King, Jr. Ave., SE
Washington, DC 20032
Phone : (202) 673-7166

AMERICAN SAMOA
Fualaau Hanipale
Director & Coordinator
Child Abuse Comm.
Dept. of Human Resources
Pago Pago, AS 96799
Phone : (684) 633-4485

GUAM
Janette S. Tanos
Director
Mental Health & Substance Abuse Agency
790 Gov. Carlos G. Camacho Rd.
Tamuning, GU 96911
Phone : (671) 647-5400
Fax : (671) 649-6948

NORTHERN MARIANA ISLANDS
Cathy Clay
Mental Health Div.
Dept. of Pub Health & Env. Srvc.
P.O. Box 409
Saipan, MP 96950
Phone : (670) 234-8950

PUERTO RICO
Nestor Galarza
Assistant Secretary
Mental Health Care
Dept. of Mental Health
P.O. Box 9342
Santurce, PR 00908
Phone : (809) 781-5660

U.S. VIRGIN ISLANDS
Aracelis B. Hendry
Assistant Commissioner
Dept. of Health
St. Croix Hospital
St. Croix, VI 00820
Phone : (809) 773-1311

MINED LAND RECLAMATION

Responsible for ensuring the reclamation of mined lands.

ALABAMA
Randall Johnson
Director
Surface Mining Comm.
P.O. Box 2390
Jasper, AL 35502
Phone : (205) 221-4130
Fax : (205) 221-5077

ALASKA
Jules Tileston
Director
Div. of Mining & Water Mgt.
Dept. of Natural Resources
3601 C St., Ste. 800
Anchorage, AK 99503-5935
Phone : (907) 762-2163
Fax : (907) 563-1853

ARIZONA
M. Jean Hassell
State Land Commissioner
Dept. of State Land
1616 W. Adams St.
Phoenix, AZ 85007
Phone : (602) 542-4621

ARKANSAS
Floyd Durham
Chief
Mining & Reclamation Div.
Pollution Control & Ecology
P.O. Box 8913
Little Rock, AR 72219
Phone : (501) 562-7444
Fax : (501) 562-4632

CALIFORNIA
James F. Davis
State Geologist
Div. of Mines & Geology
Dept. of Conservation
801 K St., 12th Fl.
Sacramento, CA 95814-3533
Phone : (916) 445-1923

COLORADO
Mike Long
Director
Div. of Minerals & Geology
Dept. of Natural Resources
1313 Sherman St., Rm. 215
Denver, CO 80203
Phone : (303) 866-3567

FLORIDA
Joseph Bakker
Bureau Chief
Mine Reclamation Bur.
Dept. of Environmental Protection
2051 E. Dirac Dr., MS-715
Tallahassee, FL 32310-3760
Phone : (904) 488-8217

GEORGIA
J. Lewis Tinley
Program Manager
Land Protection
Dept. of Natural Resources
4244 International Pkwy.
Atlanta, GA 30354
Phone : (404) 656-7404

IDAHO
Scott Nichols
Reclamationist
Dept. of Lands
1215 W. State St.
Boise, ID 83720-7000
Phone : (208) 334-0261

ILLINOIS
Timothy J. Hickmann
Executive Director
Abandoned Mined Lands Reclamation Council
928 S. Spring
Springfield, IL 62704
Phone : (217) 782-0588
Fax : (217) 524-6674

Fred Bowman
Director
Dept. of Mines & Minerals
300 W. Jefferson, Ste. 300
Springfield, IL 62791-0137
Phone : (217) 782-3831
Fax : (217) 524-4819

INDIANA
Paul Ehret
Deputy Director
Bur. of Mine Reclamation
Dept. of Natural Resources
IGC-South, Rm. W256
Indianapolis, IN 46204
Phone : (317) 232-4020

IOWA
James B. Gulliford
Administrator
Div. of Soil Conservation
Dept. of Agriculture & Land
Wallace State Off. Bldg.
Des Moines, IA 50319
Phone : (515) 281-6146

KANSAS
Murray Balk
Chief
Surface Mining Section
Dept. of Health & Environment
P.O. Box 1418
Pittsburg, KS 66762-1418
Phone : (316) 231-8540
Fax : (316) 231-0753

KENTUCKY
Phillip J. Shepherd
Secretary
Natural Resources & Environmental Prot. Cabinet
Capital Plz. Tower
Frankfort, KY 40601
Phone : (502) 564-3350

LOUISIANA
Ernest Burguie'res
Assistant Secretary
Off. of Conservation
Dept. of Natural Resources
P.O. Box 94396
Baton Rouge, LA 70804
Phone : (504) 342-4503

MAINE
Michael Foley
Resource Administrator
Bureau of Geology
Maine Geological Survey
State House Station # 22
Augusta, ME 04333
Phone : (207) 287-2801

MARYLAND**
Tony Abar
Director
Bur. of Mines
Dept. of Natural Resources
160 S. Water St.
Frostburg, MD 21532-2145
Phone : (410) 689-6104

MICHIGAN
Rodger Whitener
Resource Specialist
Policy Proc. & Special Srvcs.
Geological Survey Div.
P.O. Box 30256
Lansing, MI 48909
Phone : (517) 334-6907

MINNESOTA
Arlo Knoll
Manager
Mined Land Reclamation
Minerals Div.
1525 3rd Ave., E.
Hibbing, MN 55746
Phone : (218) 262-6767

MISSISSIPPI
Kevin E. Cahill
Director
Mining & Reclamation Div.
Off. of Geology
P.O. Box 20307
Jackson, MS 39289-1307
Phone : (601) 961-5515

MISSOURI
Charlie Stiefermann
Director
Land Reclamation Program
Div. of Environmental Quality
Jefferson Bldg., Rm. 915
P.O. Box 176
Jefferson City, MO 65102
Phone : (314) 751-4041
Fax : (314) 751-0534

MONTANA
Gary Amestoy
Administrator
Reclamation Div.
Dept. of State Lands
P.O. Box 201601
Helena, MT 59620-1601
Phone : (406) 444-2074

NEBRASKA
Randolph Wood
Director
Dept. of Environmental Quality
P.O. Box 98922
Lincoln, NE 68509-8922
Phone : (402) 471-2186

NEVADA
Doug Zimmerman
Chief
Bur. of Mining Reg. & Reclam.
Div. of Environmental Protection
123 W. Nye Ln.
Carson City, NV 89710
Phone : (702) 687-4675
Fax : (702) 687-5856

NEW MEXICO
Kathleene Garland
Director
Mining and Minerals Div.
Dept. of Energy, Min. & Nat. Res.
2040 S. Pacheco
Santa Fe, NM 87505
Phone : (505) 827-5970
Fax : (505) 827-7195

NEW YORK*
Commissioner
Dept. of Environmental Conservation
50 Wolf Rd.
Albany, NY 12233
Phone : (518) 457-3446

NORTH CAROLINA
Tracy Davis
Mine Specialist
Land Quality Section
Div. of Land Resources
512 N. Salisbury St.
Raleigh, NC 27604
Phone : (919) 733-4574
Fax : (919) 733-2876

NORTH DAKOTA
Edward Englerth
Director
Reclamation Div.
Public Service Comm.
State Capitol Bldg., 12th Fl.
Bismarck, ND 58505
Phone : (701) 328-4096
Fax : (701) 328-2410

OHIO
Lisa Morris
Acting Chief
Div. of Reclamation
Dept. of Natural Resources
1855 Fountain Sq., Bldg. H-3
Columbus, OH 43224-1387
Phone : (614) 265-6638
Fax : (614) 262-6546

OKLAHOMA
James Hamm
Director
Dept. of Mines
4040 N. Lincoln Blvd., Ste. 107
Oklahoma City, OK 73105
Phone : (405) 521-3859

Bennie Cox
Director
Dept. of Mines
4040 N. Lincoln Blvd., Ste. 107
Oklahoma City, OK 73105
Phone : (405) 521-3859

OREGON
Gary W. Lynch
Supervisor
Off. of Rec. of Sur. Min. Land
Dept. of Geology & Mining
1536 Queen Ave., SE
Albany, OR 97321-6687
Phone : (503) 967-2039
Fax : (503) 967-2075

PENNSYLVANIA
Ernest F. Giovannitti
Director
Bur. of Mining & Reclamation
Dept. of Env. Resources
P.O. Box 2357
Harrisburg, PA 17105-2357
Phone : (717) 787-5103

SOUTH CAROLINA
Patrick T. Walker
Director
Div. of Mining & Reclamation
Bur. or Solid and Hazardous Waste Management, SC DHEC
2600 Bull St.
Columbia, SC 29201
Phone : (803) 896-4000

SOUTH DAKOTA
Robert Townsend
Administrator
Off. of Minerals & Mining
523 E. Capitol Ave.
Pierre, SD 57501
Phone : (605) 773-4201

TENNESSEE
Tim Eagle
Director
Div. of Land Reclamation
Dept. of Environment & Cons.
2700 Middlebrook Pk., Ste. 230
Knoxville, TN 37921
Phone : (615) 594-6203

TEXAS
Melvin Hodgkiss
Director
Surface Mining Div.
Railroad Comm.
Box 12967, Capitol Station
Austin, TX 78711
Phone : (512) 463-6901

UTAH
Lowell P. Braxton
Associate Director
Div. of Oil, Gas & Mining
Dept. of Natural Resources
3 Triad Ctr., Ste. 350
Salt Lake City, UT 84180-1203
Phone : (801) 538-5340

VERMONT
Barbara Ripley
Agency Natural Resources
103 S. Main St.
Waterbury, VT 05671-0301
Phone : (802) 241-3600
Fax : (802) 241-3281

VIRGINIA
O. Gene Dishner
Director
Dept. of Mines, Minerals, & Energy
202 9th St. Off. Bldg., 8th Fl.
Richmond, VA 23219
Phone : (804) 692-3200
Fax : (804) 692-3237

WASHINGTON
Ray Lasmanis
State Geologist
Div. of Geology & Earth Res.
Dept. of Natural Resources
P.O. Box 47001
Olympia, WA 98504-7001
Phone : (360) 902-1450

WEST VIRGINIA
John Ailes
Chief
Off. of Mining & Reclamation
Div. of Environmental Prot.
10 McJunkin Rd.
Nitro, WV 25143-2506
Phone : (304) 759-0510

WISCONSIN
Gordon H. Reinke
Chief
Mining Reclamation Section
Bur. of Solid & Haz. Waste
101 S. Webster, 3rd Fl.
P.O. Box 7921
Madison, WI 53703
Phone : (608) 266-2050
Fax : (608) 267-2768

WYOMING
Gary Beach
Director
Abandoned Mine Land Program
Dept. of Environmental Quality
122 W. 25th St.
Cheyenne, WY 82002
Phone : (307) 777-6191

GUAM
Michael W. Kuhlman
Director
Dept. of Agriculture
P.O. Box 2950
Agana, GU 96910
Phone : (671) 734-3942
Fax : (671) 734-6539

NORTHERN MARIANA ISLANDS
Benigno M. Sablan
Secretary
Dept. of Lands & Natural Resources
P.O. Box 10007
Saipan, MP 96950
Phone : (670) 322-9830
Fax : (670) 322-2633

PUERTO RICO
Pedro Gelabert Marquez
Secretary
Dept. of Natural Resources
P.O. Box 5887
San Juan, PR 00906
Phone : (809) 724-8774

MINING SAFETY

Responsible for ensuring the safety of miners.

ARIZONA
Douglas Martin
Director
Off. of Mine Inspector
1700 W. Washington, # 400
Phoenix, AZ 85007-2805
Phone : (602) 542-5971

ARKANSAS
James Salkeld
Director
Dept. of Labor
10421 W. Markham, Ste. 100
Little Rock, AR 72205
Phone : (501) 682-4500
Fax : (501) 682-4532

CALIFORNIA
John Howard
Chief
Div. of Occ. Safety & Health
455 Golden Gate Ave., Ste. 5202
San Francisco, CA 94102
Phone : (415) 703-4341

COLORADO
Joe Nugent
Chief Inspector
Mined Land Reclamation Div.
Dept. of Natural Resources
P.O. Box 1184
Idaho Springs, CO 80452
Phone : (303) 567-9122

FLORIDA
Joseph Bakker
Bureau Chief
Mine Reclamation Bur.
Dept. of Environmental Protection
2051 E. Dirac Dr., MS-715
Tallahassee, FL 32310-3760
Phone : (904) 488-8217

IDAHO
Mike Weaver
Mine Safety
Labor & Industrial Services
277 N. 6th
Boise, ID 83720
Phone : (208) 334-3950

ILLINOIS
Fred Bowman
Director
Dept. of Mines & Minerals
300 W. Jefferson, Ste. 300
Springfield, IL 62791-0137
Phone : (217) 782-3831
Fax : (217) 524-4819

INDIANA
Joe Batson
Director
Bur. of Mines & Mine Safety
Dept. of Labor
1615 William Street
Evansville, IN 47591
Phone : (812) 882-7242

KENTUCKY
Burl Scott
Commissioner
Dept. of Mines
P.O. Box 14080
Lexington, KY 40512
Phone : (606) 254-0367

LOUISIANA
Ernest Burguie'res
Assistant Secretary
Off. of Conservation
Dept. of Natural Resources
P.O. Box 94396
Baton Rouge, LA 70804
Phone : (504) 342-4503

MAINE
James McGowan
Director
Bur. of Labor Standards
Dept. of Labor
State House Station # 45
Augusta, ME 04333
Phone : (207) 624-6400

MARYLAND**
Tony Abar
Director
Bur. of Mines
Dept. of Natural Resources
160 S. Water St.
Frostburg, MD 21532-2145
Phone : (410) 689-6104

MASSACHUSETTS
Patricia Circone
Manager, Federal Grant Program
Div. of Occupational Hygiene
Dept. of Labor & Industries
100 Cambridge St., 11th Fl.
Boston, MA 02202
Phone : (617) 727-3454
Fax : (617) 727-8082

MINNESOTA
Rod Sando
Commissioner
Dept. of Natural Resources
500 Lafayette Rd.
St. Paul, MN 55155
Phone : (612) 296-2549

MISSOURI
Charlie Stiefermann
Director
Land Reclamation Program
Div. of Environmental Quality
Jefferson Bldg., Rm. 915
P.O. Box 176
Jefferson City, MO 65102
Phone : (314) 751-4041
Fax : (314) 751-0534

MONTANA
John Weida
Supervisor
Workers' Compensation Div.
Dept. of Labor
P.O. Box 1728
Helena, MT 59624
Phone : (406) 444-6530

NEBRASKA
Darrell Jensen
Director
Nebraska Safety Ctr.
W. Ctr., Univ. of Nebraska at Kearney
Kearney, NE 68849
Phone : (308) 865-8256

NEVADA
Norton J. Pickett
Administrator
Div. of Mine Inspection
Dept. of Industrial Relations
1380 S. Curry St.
Carson City, NV 89710
Phone : (702) 687-5243

NEW JERSEY
Leonard Katz
Asst. Commissioner
Div. of Workplace Standards
Dept. of Labor
John Fitch Plz., CN110
Trenton, NJ 08625
Phone : (609) 777-0249

NEW MEXICO
Desi Apodaca
New Mexico State Mine Inspector
Bureau of Mine Inspection
P.O. Box W105 NMIMT
Socorro, NM 87801
Phone : (505) 835-5460
Fax : (505) 835-5430

Kathleene Garland
Director
Mining and Minerals Div.
Dept. of Energy, Min. & Nat. Res.
2040 S. Pacheco
Santa Fe, NM 87505
Phone : (505) 827-5970
Fax : (505) 827-7195

NEW YORK*
Commissioner
Dept. of Labor
State Off. Bldg., State Campus
Albany, NY 12240
Phone : (518) 457-2741

NORTH CAROLINA
Charles H. Gardner
Director
Div. of Land Resources
Dept. of Environment, Health & Natural Resources
512 N. Salisbury St.
Raleigh, NC 27604-1148
Phone : (919) 733-3833
Fax : (919) 733-4407

NORTH DAKOTA
Wally Kalmbach
Director of Loss Prevention
Worker's Compensation Bur.
500 E. Front Ave.
Bismarck, ND 58504-5685
Phone : (701) 328-3886
Fax : (701) 328-3750

OHIO
Paul Kidney
Chief
Div. of Mines
Industrial Relations Dept.
2323 W. Fifth Ave.
Columbus, OH 43216
Phone : (614) 644-2234
Fax : (614) 728-1256

OKLAHOMA
Robert Brown
Director
Non-Coal Minerals Div.
Dept. of Health & Safety
4040 N. Lincoln Blvd., Ste. 107
Oklahoma City, OK 73105
Phone : (405) 521-3859

James Hamm
Director
Dept. of Mines
4040 N. Lincoln Blvd., Ste. 107
Oklahoma City, OK 73105
Phone : (405) 521-3859

Bob Springer
Oklahoma Conservation Comm.
2800 N. Lincoln Blvd., Ste. 160
Oklahoma City, OK 73105
Phone : (405) 521-3859

PENNSYLVANIA
Thomas Ward
Director
Bur. of Deep Mine Reclamation
Dept. of Env. Resources
104 Executive House, Box 2357
Harrisburg, PA 17120
Phone : (717) 787-1376

SOUTH CAROLINA
William M. Lybrand
Administrator
Occupational Safety & Health
Labor, Licensing & Reg. Dept.
P.O. Box 11329
Columbia, SC 29211
Phone : (803) 734-9644

SOUTH DAKOTA*
Director
Mine Safety Training
Dept. of Health
Foss Bldg.
Pierre, SD 57501
Phone : (605) 773-4201

TENNESSEE
Charles Green
Director
Mine Safety & Training
Dept. of Labor
P.O. Box 124
Caryville, TN 37714
Phone : (615) 562-4914

TEXAS
Melvin Hodgkiss
Director
Surface Mining Div.
Railroad Comm.
Box 12967, Capitol Station
Austin, TX 78711
Phone : (512) 463-6901

UTAH
James W. Carter
Director
Div. of Oil, Gas & Mining
Dept. of Natural Resources
3 Triad Ctr., Ste. 350
Salt Lake City, UT 84180-1230
Phone : (801) 538-5340

VERMONT
Barbara Ripley
Agency Natural Resources
103 S. Main St.
Waterbury, VT 05671-0301
Phone : (802) 241-3600
Fax : (802) 241-3281

VIRGINIA
O. Gene Dishner
Director
Dept. of Mines, Minerals & Energy
202 9th St. Off. Bldg., 8th Fl.
Richmond, VA 23219
Phone : (804) 692-3200
Fax : (804) 692-3237

WASHINGTON
Ray Lasmanis
State Geologist
Div. of Geology & Earth Res.
Dept. of Natural Resources
P.O. Box 47001
Olympia, WA 98504-7001
Phone : (360) 902-1450

WEST VIRGINIA
Stephen Webber
Director
Miners' Hlth., Safety & Training
Dept. of Energy
1615 Washington St., E.
Charleston, WV 25311
Phone : (304) 558-1425

WISCONSIN
Gordon E. Helmeid
Director
Bur. of Technical Services
Ind. Labor & Human Rel. Dept.
201 E. Washington
P.O. Box 7969
Madison, WI 53707
Phone : (608) 266-1818
Fax : (608) 267-0592

WYOMING
Donald G. Stauffenberg
State Inspector of Mines
Board of Mines
Dept. of Employment
P.O. Box 1094
Rock Springs, WY 82902
Phone : (307) 856-3470

MOTOR VEHICLE ADMINISTRATION

Issues and maintains all records related to motor vehicle registrations, operators' licenses and certificates of titles in the state.

ALABAMA
Ralph Eagerton
Interim Director
Motor Vehicle Div.
Dept. of Revenue
64 N. Union St.
Montgomery, AL 36130
Phone : (334) 242-1175
Fax : (334) 242-0550

Ralph Cottinghan
Chief
Driver License Div.
Dept. of Public Safety
500 Dexter Ave.
P.O. Box 1471
Montgomery, AL 36102
Phone : (205) 242-4240

ALASKA
Jay Dulany
Director
Div. of Motor Vehicles
Dept. of Public Safety
5700 E. Tudor Rd.
Anchorage, AK 99507-1225
Phone : (907) 269-5559
Fax : (907) 333-8615

ARIZONA
Thomas G. Schmitt
Director
Motor Vehicle Division
Dept. of Transportation
1801 W. Jefferson
Phoenix, AZ 85007
Phone : (602) 255-8152

ARKANSAS
John Theis
Commissioner
Revenue Div.
Dept. of Finance & Admin.
P.O. Box 1272
Little Rock, AR 72203
Phone : (501) 682-7000
Fax : (501) 682-7900

CALIFORNIA
Dorothy L. Hunter
Division Chief
Headquarters Operation
Dept. of Motor Vehicles
P.O. Box 932328
Sacramento, CA 94232-3280
Phone : (916) 657-6940

COLORADO
Dee Hartman
Director
Div. of Motor Vehicles
Dept. of Revenue
140 W. Sixth Ave.
Denver, CO 80204
Phone : (303) 572-5653
Fax : (303) 620-4962

CONNECTICUT
Michael W. Kozlowski
Commissioner
Dept. of Motor Vehicles
60 State St.
Wethersfield, CT 06109
Phone : (203) 566-2240

DELAWARE
Michael Shahan
Director
Div. of Motor Vehicles
Dept. of Public Safety
P.O. Box 698
Dover, DE 19903
Phone : (302) 739-4421
Fax : (302) 739-3152

FLORIDA
Charles Brantley
Director
Motor Vehicles Div.
Dept. of Hwy. Safety & Motor Vehicles
Neil Kirkman Bldg.
2900 Apalachee Pkwy.
Tallahassee, FL 32399-0500
Phone : (904) 488-4597

GEORGIA
Clint Moye
Director
Motor Vehicle Div.
Dept. of Revenue
270 Washington St., SW
Atlanta, GA 30334
Phone : (404) 656-4156

IDAHO
Dave Hiatt
Supervisor
Licensing Section
Dept. of Parks & Recreation
5657 Warm Springs Ave.
Boise, ID 83712-8752
Phone : (208) 327-7444

Douglas Kraemer
Chief
Motor Vehicle Bur.
Dept. of Transportation
3311 W. State St.
Boise, ID 83703
Phone : (208) 334-8606

ILLINOIS
George H. Ryan
Secretary of State
213 State House
Springfield, IL 62756
Phone : (217) 782-2201
Fax : (217) 785-0358

INDIANA
Gilbert L. Holmes
Commissioner
Bur. of Motor Vehicles
IGC-North, Rm. 401
Indianapolis, IN 46204
Phone : (317) 232-2800

IOWA
Shirley Andre
Director
Motor Vehicle Div.
Dept. of Transportation
P.O. Box 10382
Des Moines, IA 50306
Phone : (515) 237-3202

KANSAS
Betty McBride
Director
Division of Motor Vehicles
Department of Revenue
Docking State Off. Bldg., Rm. 162-S
Topeka, KS 66612
Phone : (913) 296-3601
Fax : (913) 296-3852

KENTUCKY
Norris Beckley
Commissioner
Dept. of Vehicle Regulation
Transportation Cabinet
State Off. Bldg.
Frankfort, KY 40601
Phone : (502) 564-4890

LOUISIANA
John Politz
Assistant Secretary
Off. of Motor Vehicles
Dept. of Pub. Safety & Corr.
P.O. Box 66614
Baton Rouge, LA 70896
Phone : (504) 925-6335

MAINE
Gregory Hanscom
Deputy Secretary of State
Div. of Motor Vehicles
Dept. of State
State House Station # 29
Augusta, ME 04333
Phone : (207) 287-2761

MARYLAND**
Marshall Rickert
Administrator
Motor Vehicle Admin.
6601 Ritchie Hwy., NE, Rm. 120
Glen Burnie, MD 21062
Phone : (410) 768-7274

MASSACHUSETTS
Jerold A. Gnazzo
Registrar
Registry of Motor Vehicles
1135 Tremont St.
Boston, MA 02120
Phone : (617) 351-2700
Fax : (617) 351-9971

MICHIGAN
Joseph Pawlowski
Director
Driver & Vehicle Records Bur.
Dept. of State
7064 Crowner Dr.
Lansing, MI 48918
Phone : (517) 322-1528

MINNESOTA
Katherine Burke Moore
Director
Driver & Vehicle Service Div.
Dept. of Public Safety
2nd Fl., Transportation Bldg.
St. Paul, MN 55155
Phone : (612) 296-2001

MISSISSIPPI
Eagle Day
Executive Director
Motor Vehicle Comm.
1755 Lelia Dr., Ste. 200
Jackson, MS 39216
Phone : (601) 987-3995

MISSOURI
Raymond Hune
Director
Div. of Motor Veh. & Driver Licen.
Dept. of Revenue
Truman Bldg., Rm. 470
P.O. Box 629
Jefferson City, MO 65105
Phone : (314) 751-4429
Fax : (314) 526-4774

MONTANA
Dean G. Roberts
Administrator
Motor Vehicle Div.
Dept. of Justice
303 N. Roberts
Helena, MT 59620
Phone : (406) 444-4536

NEBRASKA
Al Abramson
Director
Dept. of Motor Vehicles
301 Centennial Mall S.
P.O. Box 94789
Lincoln, NE 68509
Phone : (402) 471-3900

NEVADA
James Weller
Director
Motor Vehicles & Public Safety
555 Wright Way
Carson City, NV 89711
Phone : (702) 687-5375

NEW HAMPSHIRE
Robert Turner
Director
Div. of Motor Vehicles
Dept. of Safety
10 Hazen Dr.
Concord, NH 03301
Phone : (603) 271-2484

NEW JERSEY
C. Richard Karmin
Director
Div. of Motor Vehicle Srvcs.
Dept. of Law & Public Safety
225 S. State St., CN160
Trenton, NJ 08625
Phone : (609) 292-7500

NEW MEXICO
Gary Montoya
Director
Motor Vehicle Div.
Dept. of Taxation & Revenue
P.O. Box 1028
Santa Fe, NM 87504
Phone : (505) 827-2294
Fax : (505) 827-2397

NEW YORK*
Commissioner
Dept. of Motor Vehicles
Empire State Plz.
Albany, NY 12228
Phone : (518) 474-0841

NORTH CAROLINA
Alexander Killens
Commissioner
Div. of Motor Vehicles
Dept. of Transportation
1100 New Bern Ave.
Raleigh, NC 27697-0001
Phone : (919) 733-2403

NORTH DAKOTA
Keith Magnuson
Registrar
Vehicle Srvcs. Div.
Highway Bldg.
600 E. Boulevard Ave.
Bismarck, ND 58505
Phone : (701) 328-2581
Fax : (701) 328-4545

OHIO
Mitchell Brown
Registrar
Bur. of Motor Vehicles
Dept. of Highway Safety
4300 Kimberly Pky.
Columbus, OH 43232-0801
Phone : (614) 752-7500
Fax : (614) 752-7973

OKLAHOMA
Curt Byers
Head
Motor Vehicle Div.
Tax Commission
M.C. Conners Bldg.
Oklahoma City, OK 73105
Phone : (405) 521-2519

OREGON
Jane Hardy Cease
Administrator
Motor Vehicles Div.
Dept. of Transportation
1905 Lana Ave., NE
Salem, OR 97314
Phone : (503) 378-6997
Fax : (503) 945-5100

PENNSYLVANIA
John A. Pachuta
Director
Bur. of Motor Vehicles
Dept. of Transportation
104 Trans. & Safety Bldg.
Harrisburg, PA 17120
Phone : (717) 787-2304

RHODE ISLAND
Thomas Harrington
Deputy Director
Div. of Motor Vehicles
286 Main St.
Pawtucket, RI 02860-2908
Phone : (401) 277-6900

SOUTH CAROLINA
Milton W. Dufford
Director
Motor Vehicle Div.
Dept. of Revenue & Taxation
301 Gervais St.
Columbia, SC 29201
Phone : (803) 737-1135

SOUTH DAKOTA
Pamela Ice
Program Manager
Div. of Drivers Licensing
Dept. of Commerce & Regulation
Public Safety Bldg.
Pierre, SD 57501
Phone : (605) 773-5949

TENNESSEE
Ann Kohler
Director
Div. of Motor Vehicles
Dept. of Safety
1283 Airways Plz.
Nashville, TN 37243
Phone : (615) 741-3101

TEXAS
Brett Bray
Motor Vehicle Division
Dept. of Transportation
125 E. 11th St.
Austin, TX 78701
Phone : (512) 476-3587

UTAH
Rick L. Leimback
Director
Div. of Motor Vehicles
Tax Commission
1095 Motor Ave.
Salt Lake City, UT 84116
Phone : (801) 297-3536

VERMONT
Patricia McDonald

Commissioner
Dept. of Motor Vehicles
Agency of Transportation
133 State St.
Montpelier, VT 05602
Phone : (802) 828-2011
Fax : (802) 828-2170

VIRGINIA
Richard Holcomb
Commissioner
Dept. of Motor Vehicles
2300 W. Broad St.
Richmond, VA 23220
Phone : (804) 367-6606
Fax : (804) 367-6631

WASHINGTON
Jim Wadsworth
Assistant Director
Vehicle Services
Dept. of Licensing
P.O. Box 9020
Olympia, WA 98507-9020
Phone : (360) 902-3818

WEST VIRGINIA
Jane Cline
Commissioner
Div. of Motor Vehicles
1800 Washington St., E., Bldg. 3
Charleston, WV 25305
Phone : (304) 558-2723

WISCONSIN
Norbert K. Anderson
Administrator
Div. of Motor Vehicles
Dept. of Transportation
4802 Sheboygan Ave., Room 112
P.O. Box 7911
Madison, WI 53705
Phone : (608) 266-2233
Fax : (608) 267-6974

WYOMING
Ray Martin
Director
Field Services
Dept. of Revenue & Taxation
Herschler Bldg.
Cheyenne, WY 82002
Phone : (307) 777-5216

DISTRICT OF COLUMBIA
Gwen Mitchell
Administrator
Transportation Systems Admin.
Dept. of Public Works
65 K St., NE
Washington, DC 20002
Phone : (202) 727-1735

AMERICAN SAMOA
Fonoti D. Jessop
Commissioner
Dept. of Public Safety
American Samoa Government
Pago Pago, AS 96799
Phone : (684) 633-1111
Fax : (684) 633-5111

GUAM
Joseph T. Duenas
Director
Dept. of Revenue & Taxation
378 Chalan San Antonio
Tamuning, GU 96911
Phone : (671) 647-5107
Fax : (671) 472-2643

NORTHERN MARIANA ISLANDS
Matias A. Chargualaf
Chief
Motor Vehicle Div.
Public Safety Dept.
Off. of the Governor
Saipan, MP 96950
Phone : (670) 234-6921

PUERTO RICO
Carlos Pesquera
Secretary
Highways Authority & Trans.
P.O. Box 42007
Santurce, PR 00940-2007
Phone : (809) 723-1390

U.S. VIRGIN ISLANDS
Ramon Davila
Commissioner
Police Dept.
Nisky Ctr., #6
Veterans Dr.
St. Thomas, VI 00802
Phone : (809) 774-6400
Fax : (809) 774-4057

NATIVE AMERICAN AFFAIRS

Acts as a liaison between state and tribal officials and advances the concerns of Native Americans.

ALABAMA
Darla Graves
Executive Director
Indian Affairs Comm.
669 S. Lawrence St.
Montgomery, AL 36104
Phone : (334) 242-2831
Fax : (334) 242-3408

ARIZONA
Tony Machukay
Executive Director
Indian Affairs Commission
1645 W. Jefferson, Rm. 127
Phoenix, AZ 85007
Phone : (602) 542-3123

CALIFORNIA
Larry Myers
Executive Secretary
Native American Heritage Comm.
915 Capitol Mall, Rm. 288
Sacramento, CA 95814
Phone : (916) 322-7791

COLORADO
Gail Schoettler
Lt. Governor
130 State Capitol
Denver, CO 80203-1792
Phone : (303) 866-2087

CONNECTICUT
Edward Serabia
Indian Affairs Coordinator
Indian Affairs Council
165 Capitol Ave., Rm. 245
Hartford, CT 06106
Phone : (203) 566-5191

FLORIDA
Joe Quetone
Executive Director
Governors Council on Indian Affairs, Inc.
Off. of the Governor
1020 E. Lafayette St., Ste. 102
Tallahassee, FL 32301
Phone : (904) 488-0730

GEORGIA
Chip Morgan
Archaeologist
Historic Preservation
Dept. of Natural Resources
205 Butler St.
Atlanta, GA 30334
Phone : (404) 488-0730

ILLINOIS
Allan Grosboll
Senior Advisor for Special Projects
Office of the Governor
2 1/2 State House
Springfield, IL 62706
Phone : (217) 524-1395
Fax : (217) 524-1678

INDIANA
Thomas Montezuma
Chairman, Native American Council
Historic Pres. & Arch. Div.
Dept. of Natural Resources
IGC-South, Rm. W274
Indianapolis, IN 46204
Phone : (317) 232-1646

KANSAS
Brent Anderson
Counsel to the Governor
Off. of the Governor
State Capitol, 2nd Fl.
Topeka, KS 66612
Phone : (913) 296-3232
Fax : (913) 296-2158

KENTUCKY
Joan Taylor
Administrative Assistant
Off. of the Governor
Capitol Bldg., Rm. 157
Frankfort, KY 40601
Phone : (502) 564-2611

LOUISIANA
Connie Koury
Office of the Governor
Indian Affairs
P.O. Box 94004
Baton Rouge, LA 70804
Phone : (504) 342-0955

MAINE
Diana Scully
Indian Tribal-State Comm.
P.O. Box 87
Hallowell, ME 04347

MARYLAND**
Patricia L. King
Director
Comm. on Indian Affairs
Dept. of Housing & Comm. Dev.
100 Community Pl.
Crownsville, MD 21032
Phone : (410) 514-7600

MASSACHUSETTS
John Peters
Executive Director
Indian Affairs
One Ashburton Pl., Rm. 1004
Boston, MA 02108
Phone : (617) 727-6394

MICHIGAN
Bernard Bouschor
Chair
Indian Affairs
Civil Rights Comm.
611 W. Ottawa
Lansing, MI 48909
Phone : (517) 373-0654

MINNESOTA
Joseph Day
Executive Director
Indian Affairs Council
1819 Bemidji Ave.
Bemidji, MN 56601
Phone : (612) 643-3032

MONTANA
Kathleen Fleury
Coordinator
Off. of Indian Affairs
Dept. of Commerce
State Capitol Bldg., Rm. 202
Helena, MT 59620
Phone : (406) 444-3702

NEBRASKA
Stephen M. Provost
Interim Director
Indian Comm.
State Capitol, 6th Fl.
P.O. Box 94981
Lincoln, NE 68509
Phone : (402) 471-3475

NEVADA
Gerald Allen
Executive Director
Indian Comm.
3100 Mill St., Ste. 206
Reno, NV 89502
Phone : (702) 688-1347

NEW MEXICO
Regis Pecos
Executive Director
Off. of Indian Affairs
228 E. Palace Ave.
Santa Fe, NM 87503
Phone : (505) 827-6440
Fax : (505) 827-6445

NEW YORK*
Executive Director
Off. of Indian Relations
State Capitol
Albany, NY 12224
Phone : (518) 474-5412

NORTH CAROLINA
Gregory A. Richardson
Director
Commission of Indian Affairs
Dept. of Administration
217 W. Jones St.
Raleigh, NC 27603
Phone : (919) 733-5998
Fax : (919) 733-1207

NORTH DAKOTA
Deborah Painte
Executive Director
Indian Affairs Comm.
600 E. Boulevard Ave.
Bismarck, ND 58505
Phone : (701) 328-2428
Fax : (701) 328-3000

OKLAHOMA
Charles Gourd
Executive Director
Oklahoma Indian Affairs Comm.
4010 N. Lincoln Blvd., Ste. 200
Oklahoma City, OK 73105
Phone : (405) 521-3828

OREGON
Douglas Hutchinson
Executive Director
Legislative Comm. on Indian Srvcs.
454 State Capitol
Salem, OR 97310
Phone : (503) 986-1067

SOUTH CAROLINA
William C. Ham
Commissioner
Comm. on Human Affairs
P.O. Box 4490
Columbia, SC 29240
Phone : (803) 253-6336

SOUTH DAKOTA*
Coordinator
Indian Affairs Off.
Public Safety Bldg., 3rd Fl.
Pierre, SD 57501
Phone : (605) 773-3415

TENNESSEE
Lavina Butler
Director
Comm. on Indian Affairs
Dept. of Environment & Conservation
401 Church St.
Nashville, TN 37243
Phone : (615) 532-0745

UTAH
Wil Numkena
Director
Off. of Indian Affairs
324 S. State St., Ste. 103
Salt Lake City, UT 84111
Phone : (801) 538-8808

VERMONT
Janet Ancel
Legal Counsel
Off. of the Governor
109 State St.
Montpelier, VT 05609
Phone : (802) 828-3333
Fax : (802) 828-3339

VIRGINIA
Kay Coles James
Secretary
Div. of Health & Human Resources
Governor's Cabinet
622 9th St. Office Bldg.
Richmond, VA 23219
Phone : (804) 786-7765
Fax : (804) 371-6984

WASHINGTON
Jennifer Scott
Executive Director
Off. of Indian Affairs
P.O. Box 40909
Olympia, WA 98504-0909
Phone : (360) 753-2411

WISCONSIN*
Policy Advisor
Governor's Off.
Executive Off.
115 E. State Capitol
Madison, WI 53702
Phone : (608) 266-1212
Fax : (608) 267-8983

WYOMING
Gary Maier
Executive Director
Indian Affairs Council
Dept. of Health
115 N. 5th E.
Riverton, WY 82501
Phone : (307) 856-9828

NATURAL RESOURCES

Formulates and coordinates policies to protect, develop, utilize, restore and enhance the state's natural resources.

ALABAMA
Jim Martin
Commissioner
Dept. of Conservation & Natural Resources
64 N. Union St.
Montgomery, AL 36130
Phone : (334) 242-3486
Fax : (334) 242-3489

ALASKA
John T. Shively
Commissioner
Dept. of Natural Resources
400 Willoughby Ave.
Juneau, AK 99801-1796
Phone : (907) 465-2400
Fax : (907) 465-3886

ARIZONA
Robert E. Yount
Director
Natural Resources Div.
Dept. of State Land
1616 W. Adams
Phoenix, AZ 85007
Phone : (602) 542-4626

ARKANSAS
Barbara Heffington
Deputy Director
Dept. of Arkansas Heritage
1500 Tower Bldg.
323 Center St.
Little Rock, AR 72201-2623
Phone : (501) 324-9150
Fax : (501) 324-9154

CALIFORNIA
Douglas Wheeler
Secretary
Resources Agency
1416 9th St., Rm. 1311
Sacramento, CA 95814
Phone : (916) 653-5656

COLORADO
James S. Lochhead
Executive Director
Dept. of Natural Resources
1313 Sherman St., Rm. 718
Denver, CO 80203
Phone : (303) 866-3311

CONNECTICUT
Edward C. Parker
Chief
Bureau of Natural Resources
Dept. of Environmental Protection
79 Elm St.
Hartford, CT 06106
Phone : (203) 424-3001

DELAWARE
Christophe A.G. Tulou
Secretary
Dept. of Natural Resources & Environmental Control
P.O. Box 1401
Dover, DE 19903
Phone : (302) 739-4403
Fax : (302) 739-6242

FLORIDA
Virginia Wetherell
Secretary
Dept. of Env. Protection
3900 Commonwealth Bldg., MS-10
Tallahassee, FL 32399-3000
Phone : (904) 488-4805
Fax : (904) 488-7093

GEORGIA
Joe D. Tanner
Commissioner
Dept. of Natural Resources
205 Butler St., SW, Ste. 1252
Atlanta, GA 30334
Phone : (404) 656-3500

HAWAII
Michael Wilson
Chairman
Dept. of Land & Natural Resources
1151 Punchbowl St.
Honolulu, HI 96813
Phone : (808) 586-0400
Fax : (808) 587-0390

ILLINOIS
Brent Manning
Director
Dept. of Conservation
Lincoln Towers Plz., Rm. 425
524 S. Second St.
Springfield, IL 62701-1787
Phone : (217) 782-6302
Fax : (217) 785-9236

INDIANA
Patrick Ralston
Executive Director
Dept. of Natural Resources
IGC-South, Rm. W256
Indianapolis, IN 46204
Phone : (317) 232-4020
Fax : (317) 232-8036

IOWA
Larry L. Wilson
Director
Dept. of Natural Resources
Wallace State Off. Bldg.
Des Moines, IA 50319
Phone : (515) 281-5385
Fax : (515) 281-8895

KANSAS
Steve Williams
Secretary
Dept. of Wildlife & Parks
Landon State Off. Bldg.
Topeka, KS 66612
Phone : (913) 296-2281
Fax : (913) 296-6953

KENTUCKY
William H. Martin
Commissioner
Dept. of Natural Resources
Natural Resources & Environmental Protection Cabinet
107 Mero St.
Frankfort, KY 40601
Phone : (502) 564-2184

LOUISIANA
Jack McClanahan
Secretary
Dept. of Natural Resources
P.O. Box 94396
Baton Rouge, LA 70804-9396
Phone : (504) 342-4503

MAINE
Ronald Lovaglio
Commissioner
Environmental Protection Dept.
State House Station # 17
Augusta, ME 04333
Phone : (207) 289-2812

Ned Sullivan
Commissioner
Dept. of Conservation
State House Station # 22
Augusta, ME 04333
Phone : (207) 287-2211

MARYLAND**
Torrey C. Brown
Secretary
Dept. of Natural Resources
Tawes State Off. Bldg.
Annapolis, MD 21401
Phone : (410) 974-3041

MASSACHUSETTS
Thomas Powers
Acting Commissioner
Dept. of Environmental Protection
Executive Off. of Environmental Affairs
1 Winter St.
Boston, MA 02108
Phone : (617) 292-5856

MICHIGAN
Roland Harmes
Director
Dept. of Natural Resources
P.O. Box 30028
Lansing, MI 48909
Phone : (517) 373-2329
Fax : (517) 335-4242

MINNESOTA
Rod Sando
Commissioner
Dept. of Natural Resources
500 Lafayette Rd.
St. Paul, MN 55155
Phone : (612) 296-2549

MISSISSIPPI
J.I. Palmer Jr.
Executive Director
Dept. of Environmental Quality
P.O. Box 20305
Jackson, MS 39289
Phone : (601) 961-5000

MISSOURI
David A. Shorr
Director
Dept. of Natural Resources
Jefferson Bldg., 12th Fl.
P.O. Box 176
Jefferson City, MO 65102
Phone : (314) 751-4422
Fax : (314) 751-7627

MONTANA
Mark Simonich
Director
Dept. of Natural Resources & Conservation
1520 E. 6th Avenue
Helena, MT 59620
Phone : (406) 444-6699

NEBRASKA
Dayle E. Williamson
Executive Director
Natural Resources Comm.
301 Centennial Mall S.
P.O. Box 94876
Lincoln, NE 68509-4876
Phone : (402) 471-2081

NEVADA
Peter G. Morros
Director
Dept. of Conservation & Natural Resources
123 W. Nye Ln.
Carson City, NV 89710
Phone : (702) 687-4360

NEW HAMPSHIRE
William Bartlett
Commissioner
Dept. of Resources & Economic Development
P.O. Box 856
Concord, NH 03302-0856
Phone : (603) 271-2411

NEW JERSEY
Robert Shinn
Commissioner
Dept. of Environmental Protection
401 E. State St., CN402
Trenton, NJ 08625
Phone : (609) 292-3541

NEW MEXICO
Jennifer Salisbury
Cabinet Secretary
Dept. of Energy, Minerals & Natural Resources
2040 S. Pacheco
Santa Fe, NM 87505
Phone : (505) 827-5950
Fax : (505) 438-3855

NEW YORK*
Commissioner
Dept. of Environmental Conservation
50 Wolf Rd.
Albany, NY 12233
Phone : (518) 457-3446

NORTH CAROLINA
Jonathan B. Howes
Secretary
Div. of Environmental Mgt.
Dept. of Health & Nat. Res.
512 N. Salisbury St.
Raleigh, NC 27604-1148
Phone : (919) 715-4101
Fax : (919) 715-3060

NORTH DAKOTA
Micheal McKenna
Chief
Natural Resources Div.
Game & Fish Dept.
100 N. Bismarck Expy.
Bismarck, ND 58501-5095
Phone : (701) 328-6332
Fax : (701) 328-6352

OHIO
Donald Anderson
Director
Dept. of Natural Resources
Fountain Sq., Bldg. D
1930 Belcher Drive, Bldg. D3
Columbus, OH 43224-1387
Phone : (614) 265-6879
Fax : (614) 261-9601

OKLAHOMA
David Davies
Director
Dept. of Tourism & Recreation
500 Will Rogers Bldg.
Oklahoma City, OK 73105
Phone : (405) 521-2413

PENNSYLVANIA
James M. Seif
Secretary
Dept. of Environmental Resources
Market St. State Office Bldg., 16th Fl.
Harrisburg, PA 17120
Phone : (717) 787-2814

RHODE ISLAND
Timothy Keeney
Director
Dept. of Environmental Mgt.
9 Hayes St.
Providence, RI 02908-5003
Phone : (401) 277-2771

SOUTH CAROLINA
Beth Partlow
Legal Counsel
Off. of the Governor
P.O. Box 11369
Columbia, SC 29211
Phone : (803) 734-9842

SOUTH DAKOTA
John Cooper
Secretary
Dept. of Game, Fish & Parks
445 E. Capitol
Pierre, SD 57501
Phone : (605) 773-3718

TENNESSEE
Don Dills
Commissioner
Dept. of Environment & Conservation
L&C Tower, 21st Fl.
Nashville, TN 37243
Phone : (615) 532-0104
Fax : (615) 532-0120

TEXAS
Dan Pearson
Natural Resources Conservation Comm.
P.O. Box 13087
Austin, TX 78711
Phone : (512) 239-3900

UTAH
Ted Stewart
Executive Director
Dept. of Natural Resources
1636 W. North Temple, Ste. 316
Salt Lake City, UT 84116-3193
Phone : (801) 538-7200

VERMONT
Barbara Ripley
Commissioner
Agency of Natural Resources
103 S. Main St.
Waterbury, VT 05676
Phone : (802) 241-3600
Fax : (802) 241-3281

VIRGINIA
Becky Norton Dunlop
Secretary of Natural Resources
Governor's Cabinet
733 9th St. Off. Bldg.
Richmond, VA 23219
Phone : (804) 786-0044
Fax : (804) 371-8333

WASHINGTON
Jennifer Belcher
Commissioner of Public Lands
Dept. of Natural Resources
P.O. Box 47001
Olympia, WA 98504-7001
Phone : (360) 902-1000

WEST VIRGINIA
Chuck Felton
Director
Div. of Natural Resources
Commerce, Labor & Environmental Resources
Capitol Complex, Bldg. 3
Charleston, WV 25305
Phone : (304) 348-2754

WISCONSIN
George Meyer
Secretary
Dept. of Natural Resources
101 S. Webster, 5th Fl.
P.O. Box 7921
Madison, WI 53703
Phone : (608) 266-2121
Fax : (608) 267-3579

WYOMING
Mike Purcell
Director
Dept. of Natural Resources
Herschler Bldg., Rm. 4W
Cheyenne, WY 82002
Phone : (307) 777-7626

DISTRICT OF COLUMBIA
Ferial Bishop
Administrator
Environmental Regulation Admin.
Dept. of Consumer & Reg.ulatory Affairs
2100 M.L. King, Jr. Ave., Ste. 203
Washington, DC 20020
Phone : (202) 404-1136

GUAM
Michael W. Kuhlman
Director
Dept. of Agriculture
P.O. Box 2950
Agana, GU 96910
Phone : (671) 734-3942
Fax : (671) 734-6569

NORTHERN MARIANA ISLANDS
Benigno M. Sablan
Secretary
Dept. of Lands & Natural Resources
P.O. Box 10007
Saipan, MP 96950
Phone : (670) 322-9830
Fax : (670) 322-2633

PUERTO RICO
Pedro Gelabert Marquez
Secretary
Dept. of Natural Resources
P.O. Box 5887
San Juan, PR 00906
Phone : (809) 723-3090

U.S. VIRGIN ISLANDS
Beulah Dalmida-Smith
Commissioner
Dept. of Planning & Natural Resources
Nisky Ctr., Ste. 231
St. Thomas, VI 00802
Phone : (809) 774-3320
Fax : (809) 775-5706

OCCUPATIONAL SAFETY

Enforces safety standards for the protection of employees in places of employment.

ALABAMA
Mike Morgan
Commissioner
Dept. of Labor
1789 Congressman Dickinson Dr.
Montgomery, AL 36130
Phone : (334) 242-3460
Fax : (334) 242-3417

ALASKA
John Abshire
Director
Div. of Labor Standards & Safety
Dept. of Labor
P.O. Box 107021
Anchorage, AK 99510
Phone : (907) 269-4914
Fax : (907) 465-3584

ARIZONA
Larry J. Etchechury
Director
Industrial Comm.
P.O. Box 19070
Phoenix, AZ 85005-9070
Phone : (602) 542-4411

ARKANSAS
James Salkeld
Director
Dept. of Labor
10421 W. Markham, Ste. 100
Little Rock, AR 72205
Phone : (501) 682-4500
Fax : (501) 682-4532

CALIFORNIA
Lloyd W. Aubry Jr.
Director
Dept. of Industrial Relations
455 Golden Gate Ave.
San Francisco, CA 94102
Phone : (415) 703-4590

COLORADO
Jerry Waddles
Director
Risk Mgt. Div.
Dept. of Administration
225 E. 16th St., 6th Fl.
Denver, CO 80202
Phone : (303) 866-3848
Fax : (303) 894-2409

CONNECTICUT
Samuel Moore
Director
Occupational Safety & Health
Dept. of Labor
38 Wolcott Hill Rd.
Wethersfield, CT 06109
Phone : (203) 566-4550

DELAWARE
Karen Peterson
Director
Div. of Industrial Affairs
Dept. of Labor
820 N. French St.
Wilmington, DE 19801
Phone : (302) 577-2877
Fax : (302) 577-3750

FLORIDA*
Director
Div. of Safety
Dept. of Labor & Empl. Sec.
2002 Old St. Augustine Rd.
Tallahassee, FL 32399-0663
Phone : (904) 488-3044

GEORGIA
Marti Fullerton
Deputy Commissioner
Dept. of Labor
148 International Blvd., Ste. 600
Atlanta, GA 30303
Phone : (404) 656-3028

HAWAII
Jennifer Shishido
Administrator
Occuptl. Safety & Health Div.
Dept. of Labor & Ind. Rel.
830 Punchbowl St., Rm. 423
Honolulu, HI 96813
Phone : (808) 586-9116

IDAHO
Bob Purcell
Director
Labor & Industrial Srvcs.
277 N. Sixth St.
Boise, ID 83720
Phone : (208) 334-3950

ILLINOIS
Lenore Killim
Manager
Dept. of Labor
1 W. Old State Capitol Plz.
Springfield, IL 62706
Phone : (217) 782-9386

INDIANA
David Bear
Deputy Commissioner
Occupational Sfty. & Hlth. Admin.
Dept. of Labor
IGC-South, Rm. W195
Indianapolis, IN 46204
Phone : (317) 232-3325

IOWA
Mary L. Bryant
Administrator
Occupational Safety & Health
Dept. of Employment Srvcs.
1000 E. Grand
Des Moines, IA 50319
Phone : (515) 281-3606

KANSAS
Duane Guy
Director
Div. of Labor Management & Employment Standards
Dept. of Human Resources
512 SW 6th Ave.
Topeka, KS 66603-3174
Phone : (913) 296-7475
Fax : (913) 296-1775

KENTUCKY
Bill Riggs
Secretary
Labor Cabinet
1049 U.S. 127 S.
Frankfort, KY 40601
Phone : (502) 564-3070

LOUISIANA
Joseph Stone
Assistant Secretary
Dept. of Labor
P.O. Box 94094
Baton Rouge, LA 70804
Phone : (504) 342-7692

MAINE
James McGowan
Director
Bur. of Labor Standards
Dept. of Labor
State House Station # 45
Augusta, ME 04333
Phone : (207) 624-6400

MARYLAND**
Milton H. Saul
Assistant Commissioner
Occupational Safety & Health
Dept. of Licensing & Reg.
501 St. Paul Pl.
Baltimore, MD 21202-2272
Phone : (301) 333-4195

MASSACHUSETTS
Douglas Dewar
Acting Director
Div. of Industrial Safety
Dept. of Labor & Industries
100 Cambridge St.
Boston, MA 02202
Phone : (617) 727-3454

MICHIGAN
Douglas R. Earle
Director
Bur. of Safety & Regulation
Dept. of Labor
P.O. Box 30015
Lansing, MI 48909
Phone : (517) 322-1814

MINNESOTA
Robert Mairs
Osha Management Team
Dept. of Labor & Industry
443 Lafayette Rd.
St. Paul, MN 55155
Phone : (612) 296-2116

MISSISSIPPI
Brenda Diane Smith
Director
Occupational Safety & Health
Workers' Compensation Comm.
2096 N. State St., Ste. 201
Jackson, MS 39216
Phone : (601) 987-3981

MISSOURI
Colleen Baker
Director
Div. of Labor Standards
Dept. of Labor & Ind. Rel.
3315 W. Truman Blvd., Box 449
Jefferson City, MO 65102
Phone : (314) 751-3403
Fax : (314) 751-3721

MONTANA
John Maloney
Chief
Workers' Compensation Div.
Dept. of Labor
1805 Prospect
P.O. Box 8011
Helena, MT 59604-8011
Phone : (406) 444-6424

NEBRASKA
Gary Hirsch
Director
Labor & Safety Standards Div.
Dept. of Labor
P.O. Box 94600
Lincoln, NE 68509
Phone : (402) 471-4712

NEVADA
Ronald Swirczek
Administrator
Occupational Safety & Health
Dept. of Industrial Relations
1370 S. Curry St.
Carson City, NV 89710
Phone : (702) 687-5240
Fax : (702) 687-6305

NEW HAMPSHIRE
Diane Symonds
Commissioner
Dept. of Labor
95 Pleasant St.
Concord, NH 03301
Phone : (603) 271-3171

NEW JERSEY
Leonard Katz
Assistant Commissioner
Div. of Workplace Standards
Dept. of Labor
John Fitch Plz., CN110
Trenton, NJ 08625
Phone : (609) 777-0249

NEW MEXICO
Sam Rogers
Bureau Chief
Occuptl. Health & Safety Bur.
Dept. of Health
1190 St. Francis, Box 26110
Santa Fe, NM 87502-0968
Phone : (505) 827-4230
Fax : (505) 827-4422

NEW YORK*
Commissioner
Dept. of Labor
State Off. Bldg., State Campus
Albany, NY 12240
Phone : (518) 457-2741

NORTH CAROLINA
Harry E. Payne Jr.
Commissioner
Dept. of Labor
4 W. Edenton St.
Raleigh, NC 27601-1092
Phone : (919) 733-7166
Fax : (919) 733-6197

NORTH DAKOTA
Wally Kalmbach
Director of Loss Prevention
Worker's Compensation Bur.
500 E. Front Ave.
Bismarck, ND 58504-5685
Phone : (701) 328-3886
Fax : (701) 328-3750

OHIO
Lou Gergely
Superintendent
Div. of Safety & Hygiene
Industrial Comm.
246 N. High St.
Columbus, OH 43266-0564
Phone : (614) 752-4463
Fax : (614) 644-5707

OKLAHOMA
Jim Greenawalt
Supervisor
Safety Standards Div.
Dept. of Labor
1315 Broadway Pl.
Oklahoma City, OK 73103
Phone : (405) 523-1500

OREGON
John Pompei
Administrator
Occupational Safety & Health Admin.
160 Labor Industries Bldg.
350 Winter St., NE
Salem, OR 97310
Phone : (503) 378-3272

PENNSYLVANIA
Charles J. Sludden
Director
Occupational & Industrial Safety
Dept. of Labor & Industry
1529 Labor & Industry Bldg.
Harrisburg, PA 17120
Phone : (717) 787-3323

RHODE ISLAND
Steve Condrey
Occupational Safety & Health
Dept. of Labor
220 Elmwood Ave.
Providence, RI 02907
Phone : (401) 457-1800

SOUTH CAROLINA
William M. Lybrand
Administrator
Occupational Safety & Health
Labor, Licensing & Reg. Dept.
P.O. Box 11329
Columbia, SC 29211
Phone : (803) 734-9644

SOUTH DAKOTA*
Director
Div. of Labor & Mgt.
Dept. of Labor
Kneip Bldg.
Pierre, SD 57501
Phone : (605) 773-3101

TENNESSEE
Don Witt
Director
Occupational Safety
Dept. of Labor
501 Union Bldg.
Nashville, TN 37243-0659
Phone : (615) 741-2793

TEXAS
David Smith
Commissioner
Dept. of Health.
1100 W. 49th St.
Austin, TX 78756
Phone : (512) 458-7111

UTAH
Jay W. Bagley
Administrator
Occupational Safety & Health Div.
State Industrial Comm.
160 E. 300 S.
Salt Lake City, UT 84114
Phone : (801) 530-6898

VERMONT
Robert McLeod
Manager
Div. of Occupational Safety & Health Administration
Dept. of Labor & Industry
North Bldg., National Life
Montpelier, VT 05620
Phone : (802) 828-2765
Fax : (802) 828-2748

VIRGINIA
Theron J. Bell
Commissioner
Dept. of Labor & Industry
13 S. 13th St.
Richmond, VA 23219
Phone : (804) 786-2377

WASHINGTON
Nick Kirchoff
Assistant Director
Industrial Safety & Health
Dept. of Labor & Industries
P.O. Box 44600
Olympia, WA 98504-4600
Phone : (360) 902-5580

WEST VIRGINIA
Shelby Leary
Commissioner
Div. of Labor
State Capitol Complex, Bldg. 3
Charleston, WV 25305
Phone : (304) 558-7890

WISCONSIN
William M. Norem
Administrator
Div. of Safety & Bldgs.
Dept. of Ind. Labor & Hum. Relations
201 E. Washington, Rm. 103
P.O. Box 7969
Madison, WI 53703
Phone : (608) 266-3151
Fax : (608) 267-9566

WYOMING
Steve Foster
Administrator
Div. of Occupational Safety & Health Admin.
Dept. of Employment
Herschler Bldg.
Cheyenne, WY 82002
Phone : (307) 777-7700

DISTRICT OF COLUMBIA
Delores Gray
Associate Director
Occupational Safety & Health Off.
Dept. of Employment Services
950 Upshur St., NW
Washington, DC 20011
Phone : (202) 576-6339

GUAM
Juan M. Taijito
Director
Dept. of Labor
P.O. Box 9970
Tamuning, GU 96911
Phone : (671) 647-4142
Fax : (671) 646-9004

NORTHERN MARIANA ISLANDS
Francisco M. Camacho
Director
Dept. of Labor
P.O. Box 10007
Saipan, MP 96950
Phone : (670) 664-2000
Fax : (670) 664-2020

PUERTO RICO
Ceasar Almodova Machany
Secretary
Dept. of Labor & Human Resources
505 Munoz Rivera Ave.
Hato Rey, PR 00918
Phone : (809) 754-5353

U.S. VIRGIN ISLANDS
Lisa Harris-Moorhead
Commissioner
Dept. of Labor
P.O. Box 208
St. Thomas, VI 00802
Phone : (809) 776-3700
Fax : (809) 773-0094

OIL AND GAS REGULATION

Regulates the drilling, operation, maintenance and abandonment of oil and gas wells in the state.

ALABAMA
Ernest A. Mancini
State Geologist Director
State Geological Survey
Oil & Gas Board
P.O. Drawer O
Tuscaloosa, AL 35846-2852
Phone : (205) 349-2852
Fax : (205) 349-2861

ALASKA
James Eason
Director
Div. of Oil & Gas
Dept. of Natural Resources
3601 C St., Ste. 1380
Anchorage, AK 99503-5948
Phone : (907) 762-2547
Fax : (907) 562-3852

ARIZONA
Larry D. Fellows
Director & State Geologist
Geological Survey
845 N. Park Ave., Ste. 100
Tucson, AZ 85719
Phone : (602) 882-4795

ARKANSAS
William E. Wright
Director
Oil & Gas Comm.
P.O. Box 1472
Eldorado, AR 71731-1472
Phone : (501) 862-4965
Fax : (501) 862-8823

CALIFORNIA
William F. Guerard
Supervisor
Div. of Oil & Gas
Dept. of Conservation
801 K St., 20th Fl.
Sacramento, CA 95814
Phone : (916) 323-1777

COLORADO
Richard T. Griebling
Acting Director
Oil-Gas Conservation Comm.
Dept. of Natural Resources
1120 Lincoln St., Ste. 801
Denver, CO 80203-2136
Phone : (303) 894-2100
Fax : (303) 894-2109

CONNECTICUT
Reginald J. Smith
Chairman
Dept. of Public Utility Control
1 Central Park Plz.
New Britain, CT 06051
Phone : (203) 827-1553

DELAWARE
Christophe A.G. Tulou
Secretary
Dept. of Natural Resources & Environmental Control
P.O. Box 1401
Dover, DE 19903
Phone : (302) 739-4403
Fax : (302) 739-6242

FLORIDA
Mickey Watson
Director
Div. of Law Enforcement
Dept. of Environmental Protection
3900 Commonwealth Blvd., MS600
Tallahassee, FL 32399
Phone : (904) 488-5600

GEORGIA
William McLemore
State Geologist
Environmental Protection Div.
Dept. of Natural Resources
19 M.L. King, Jr. Dr., Rm. 400
Atlanta, GA 30334
Phone : (404) 656-3214

ILLINOIS
Fred Bowman
Director
Dept. of Mines & Minerals
300 W. Jefferson, Ste. 300
Springfield, IL 62791-0137
Phone : (217) 782-6791
Fax : (217) 524-4819

INDIANA
James Slutz
Director
Oil & Gas Div.
Dept. of Natural Resources
IGC-South, Rm. W293
Indianapolis, IN 46204
Phone : (317) 232-4055

IOWA
Allan Thoms
Chairman
State Utilities Bd.
Dept. of Commerce
Lucas State Off. Bldg.
Des Moines, IA 50319
Phone : (515) 281-5167

KANSAS
William R. Bryson
Administrator
Oil & Gas Conservation
Kansas Corporation Commission
1500 SW Arrowhead Rd.
Topeka, KS 66604-4027
Phone : (913) 271-3233
Fax : (913) 271-3354

KENTUCKY
Burl Scott
Commissioner
Dept. of Mines
P.O. Box 14080
Lexington, KY 40512
Phone : (606) 254-0367

LOUISIANA
Ernest Burguie'res
Assistant Secretary
Off. of Conservation
Dept. of Natural Resources
P.O. Box 94396
Baton Rouge, LA 70804
Phone : (504) 342-4503

MAINE
Alan M. Prysunka
Director
Oil & Hazardous Materials Bur.
Dept. of Env. Protection
State House Station # 17
Augusta, ME 04333
Phone : (207) 287-2651

MICHIGAN
R. Thomas Seagull
Chief & State Geologist
Geological Survey
Dept. of Natural Resources
735 E. Hazel St.
Lansing, MI 48917
Phone : (517) 334-6907

MINNESOTA
William C. Brice
Director
Minerals Div.
Dept. of Natural Resources
500 Lafayette Rd.
St. Paul, MN 55146
Phone : (612) 296-4807

MISSISSIPPI
W.R. Lewis
Supervisor
Oil & Gas Bd.
500 Greymont Ave., Ste. E
Jackson, MS 39202
Phone : (601) 354-7142

MISSOURI
Evan Kifer
Geologist
Underground Injection Control & Wellhead Prot. Unit
Dept. of Natural Resources
111 Fairgrounds Rd.
P.O. Box 250
Rolla, MO 65401
Phone : (314) 368-2168
Fax : (314) 368-2111

Oil and Gas Regulation

MONTANA*
Executive Secretary
Oil & Gas Conservation Div.
Dept. of Nat. Res. & Conservation
1520 E. 6th Ave.
Helena, MT 59620
Phone : (406) 444-6675

NEBRASKA
William H. Sydow
Director
Oil & Gas Conservation Comm.
P.O. Box 399
Sidney, NE 69162
Phone : (308) 254-4595

NEVADA
Russell A. Fields
Executive Director
Dept. of Minerals
400 W. King St., Ste. 106
Carson City, NV 89710
Phone : (702) 687-5050

NEW JERSEY
Nusha Wyner
Director
Div. of Gas
Bd. of Regulatory Commissioner
2 Gateway Ctr.
Newark, NJ 07102
Phone : (201) 648-2049

NEW MEXICO
William Lemay
Director
Oil Conservation Div.
Dept. of Energy, Min. & Natural Resources
2040 Pacheco St.
Santa Fe, NM 87505
Phone : (505) 827-7131
Fax : (505) 827-8177

NEW YORK*
Commissioner
Dept. of Environmental Conservation
50 Wolf Rd.
Albany, NY 12233
Phone : (518) 457-3446

NORTH CAROLINA
Charles H. Gardner
Director
Div. of Land Resources
Dept. of Environment, Health & Natural Resources
512 N. Salisbury St.
Raleigh, NC 27604-1148
Phone : (919) 733-3833
Fax : (919) 733-4407

NORTH DAKOTA
Wes Norton
Director
Oil & Gas Div.
State Industrial Comm.
600 E. Boulevard Ave.
Bismarck, ND 58505
Phone : (701) 328-2969
Fax : (701) 328-3682

OHIO
Don Mason
Chief
Div. of Oil & Gas
Dept. of Natural Resources
Fountain Sq., Bldg. A.
Columbus, OH 43224
Phone : (614) 265-6893
Fax : (614) 268-4316

OKLAHOMA
C. D. Davidson
Director
Oil & Gas Conservation Div.
Corporation Comm.
Jim Thorpe Bldg.
Oklahoma City, OK 73105
Phone : (405) 521-2302

OREGON
Donald A. Hull
State Geologist
Dept. of Geology & Mineral Industries
800 NE Oregon St.
Portland, OR 97232
Phone : (503) 731-4100
Fax : (503) 731-4066

PENNSYLVANIA
James Erb
Director
Bur. of Oil & Gas Regulation
Dept. of Environmental Res.
400 Market St., 5th Fl.
Rachael Carson State Office Bldg.
Harrisburg, PA 17120
Phone : (717) 783-9645

RHODE ISLAND
James J. Malachowski
Chairman
Public Utilities Comm.
100 Orange St.
Providence, RI 02903
Phone : (401) 277-3500

SOUTH CAROLINA
Rod W. Cherry
Director
Div. of Hydrology
Water Resources Comm.
1201 Main St., Ste. 1100
Columbia, SC 29201
Phone : (803) 737-0800

SOUTH DAKOTA
Curt Johnson
Commissioner
School & Public Lands
Capitol Bldg., 1st Fl.
Pierre, SD 57501
Phone : (605) 773-3303

TENNESSEE
Edward T. Luther
Director
Div. of Geology
Dept. of Environment & Conservation
401 Church St.
Nashville, TN 37243
Phone : (615) 532-1500

TEXAS
David Garlick
Assistant Director
Oil & Gas Div.
Railroad Comm.
P.O. Box 12967, Capitol Station
Austin, TX 78711
Phone : (512) 463-6893

UTAH
James W. Carter
Director
Div. of Oil, Gas & Mining
Dept. of Natural Resources
3 Triad Ctr., Ste. 350
Salt Lake City, UT 84180-1230
Phone : (801) 538-5340

VERMONT
Barbara Ripley
Commissioner
Agency Natural Resources
103 South Main St.
Waterbury, VT 05671-0301
Phone : (802) 241-3600
Fax : (802) 241-3281

VIRGINIA
Becky Norton Dunlop
Secretary of Natural Resources
Governor's Cabinet
733 9th St. Off. Bldg.
Richmond, VA 23219
Phone : (804) 786-0044
Fax : (804) 371-8333

WASHINGTON
R. Bruce Mackey
Manager
Div. of Lands & Minerals
Dept. of Natural Resources
P.O. Box 47001
Olympia, WA 98504-7001
Phone : (360) 902-1600

WEST VIRGINIA
Theodore Streit
Director
Oil & Gas Div.
Div. of Energy
10 McJunkin Rd.
Nitro, WV 25143
Phone : (304) 759-0516

WISCONSIN
William J. Morrissey
Director
Bur. of Petroleum Inspection
Dept. of Ind. Labor & Hum. Rel.
201 E. Washington, Rm. 103
P.O. Box 7969
Madison, WI 53703
Phone : (608) 267-3753
Fax : (608) 267-9566

WYOMING
Donald Basko
Director
Oil & Gas Conservation Comm.
P.O. Box 2640
Casper, WY 82602
Phone : (307) 234-7147

GUAM
Gil A. Shinohara
Acting Director
Dept. of Public Works
P.O. Box 2950
Agana, GU 96910
Phone : (671) 646-3101
Fax : (671) 649-6178

NORTHERN MARIANA ISLANDS
Nicolas M. Guerrero
Director
Dept. of Natural Resources
Off. of the Governor
Saipan, MP 96950
Phone : (670) 322-9830

OMBUDSMAN

Investigates citizens' complaints about the administrative acts of any state agency.

ALASKA
Stuart C. Hall
Ombudsman
P.O. Box 113000
Juneau, AK 99811-3000
Phone : (907) 465-4970
Fax : (907) 465-3330

CALIFORNIA
Kurt R. Sjobert
Auditor General
660 J St., Ste. 300
Sacramento, CA 95814
Phone : (916) 445-0255

COLORADO
Patricia Barela Rivera
Director
Citizens' Advocacy & Outreach
Off. of the Governor
127 State Capitol
Denver, CO 80203
Phone : (303) 866-2885
Fax : (303) 866-4824

DELAWARE
Judith Morris
Director
Constituent Relations
Off. of the Governor
820 N. French St.
Wilmington, DE 19801
Phone : (302) 577-3210
Fax : (302) 577-3118

FLORIDA
Richard Doran
Assistant Deputy
General Legal Srvcs.
Dept. of Legal Affairs
The Capitol, PL01
Tallahassee, FL 32399-1050
Phone : (904) 488-8253

HAWAII
Yen Lew
Ombudsman
Off. of Ombudsman
KeKuanaoa Bldg., 4th Fl.
465 S. King St.
Honolulu, HI 96813
Phone : (808) 587-0770

ILLINOIS
Martin Green
Director
Governor's Off. of Citizens' Assistance
222 S. College
Springfield, IL 62706
Phone : (217) 782-0244
Fax : (217) 524-4049

IOWA
William C. Angrick II
Citizens' Aide/ Ombudsman
215 E. 7th St.
Des Moines, IA 50309
Phone : (515) 281-3592
Fax : (515) 242-6007

KANSAS
Roselie Orr
Senior Constituent Srvcs. Liaison
Office of the Governor
State Capitol, 2nd Fl.
Topeka, KS 66612-1590
Phone : (913) 296-3232
Fax : (913) 296-7973

KENTUCKY
Charles Lambert
Ombudsman
Cabinet for Human Resources
275 E. Main St.
Frankfort, KY 40621
Phone : (502) 564-5497

LOUISIANA
Angie LaPlace
Attorney
Legal Div.
Off. of the Secretary of State
P.O. Box 94125
Baton Rouge, LA 70804-9125
Phone : (504) 342-2065

MASSACHUSETTS
Linda Stundis
Director
Governor's Off. of External Relations
State House, Rm. 111
Boston, MA 02133
Phone : (617) 727-6250

MICHIGAN
Margaret O'Riley
Business Ombudsman
Jobs Comm.
Victor Off. Ctr., 3rd Fl.
201 N. Washington Sq.
Lansing, MI 48913
Phone : (517) 373-6241
Fax : (517) 373-0314

MINNESOTA
Hubert H. Humphrey III
Attorney General
102 State Capitol
St. Paul, MN 55155
Phone : (612) 296-6196

MISSOURI
Mel Carnahan
Governor
State Capitol, Rm. 216
P.O. Box 720
Jefferson City, MO 65102
Phone : (314) 751-3222
Fax : (314) 751-1495

MONTANA
Myrna Omholt-Mason
Citizens' Advocate
Off. of the Governor
State Capitol
Helena, MT 59620
Phone : (406) 444-3468

NEBRASKA
Marshall Lux
State Ombudsman
State Capitol, 8th Fl.
P.O. Box 94712
Lincoln, NE 68509-4712
Phone : (402) 471-2035

NEVADA
Fred Schmidt
Consumer Advocate
Off. of the Attorney General
1802 N. Carson St., #234
Carson City, NV 89710
Phone : (702) 687-6300

NEW JERSEY
Susan L. Retsner
Public Defender
Dept. of Public Defender
25 Market St., 2nd Fl., N.
CN850
Trenton, NJ 08625
Phone : (609) 292-7087

NEW MEXICO
Nicolas Bradey
Ombudsman
Off. of the Lt. Governor
State Capitol Bldg.
Santa Fe, NM 87503
Phone : (505) 827-3050
Fax : (505) 827-3057

NEW YORK
Alexander F. Treadwell
Secretary of State
Dept. of State
162 Washington Ave.
Albany, NY 12231
Phone : (518) 474-0050

NORTH CAROLINA
Christie Barbee
Executive Director of Citizens Aff.
Off. of the Governor
116 W. Jones St.
Raleigh, NC 27603-8001
Phone : (919) 733-5017
Fax : (919) 733-2120

OREGON
Annabelle Jaramillo
Governor's Representative
Off. of the Governor
160 State Capitol
Salem, OR 97310
Phone : (503) 378-5116
Fax : (503) 378-6827

PENNSYLVANIA
Richard Maxwell
Director
Governor's Action Ctr.
402 Finance Bldg.
Harrisburg, PA 17120
Phone : (717) 783-1198

RHODE ISLAND
David Darlington
Director
Off. of the Governor
Constituent Affairs
State House
Providence, RI 02903
Phone : (401) 277-2080

SOUTH CAROLINA
William Jeff Bryson
State Ombudsman
Off. of the Governor
1205 Pendleton St.
Columbia, SC 29201
Phone : (803) 734-0457

SOUTH DAKOTA
Susan Stoneback
Special Asst. to the Governor
Constituent Services
Off. of the Governor
500 E. Capitol Ave.
Pierre, SD 57501
Phone : (605) 773-3661

TEXAS
Barry Lovelace
Director
Ombudsman Div.
Off. of the Governor
P.O. Box 12428, Capitol Station
Austin, TX 78711
Phone : (512) 463-5319

VERMONT
Joan Bagio
Public Information Officer
Governor's Information & Referral Off.
109 State St.
Montpelier, VT 05609
Phone : (802) 828-3333
Fax : (802) 828-3339

WASHINGTON
Christine O. Gregoire
Attorney General
P.O. Box 40100
Olympia, WA 98504-0100
Phone : (360) 753-6200

WISCONSIN
Policy Advisor
Governor's Office
115 East State Capitol
Madison, WI 53702
Phone : (608) 266-1212
Fax : (608) 267-8983

WYOMING*
Ombudsman
Off. of the Governor
State Capitol
Cheyenne, WY 82002
Phone : (307) 777-6417

NORTHERN MARIANA ISLANDS
David M. Cing
Ninth Commonwealth Legis.
Capitol Hill
Saipan, MP 96950
Phone : (670) 664-5501

PUERTO RICO
Adolfo De Castro
Ombudsman
P.O. Box 41088
Santurce, PR 00940
Phone : (809) 724-7373

U.S. VIRGIN ISLANDS
Ohanio Harris
St. Croix Administrator
Government House
1105 Kings St.
Christiansted
St. Croix, VI 00820-4976
Phone : (809) 773-1404
Fax : (809) 778-7978

James Dalmida
St. John Administrator
Government House
P.O. Box 488
Cruz Bay
St. John, VI 00830
Phone : (809) 776-6484
Fax : (809) 776-6992

Ruth N. Cruz
St. Croix Administrators
Government House
1105 Kings St.
Christiansted
St. Croix, VI 00820-4976
Phone : (809) 773-1404
Fax : (809) 778-7978

Levron Sarauw
St. Thomas Administrator
Government House
21-22 Kongens Gade
St. Thomas, VI 00802
Phone : (809) 774-0943
Fax : (809) 774-0151

PARKS AND RECREATION

Manages the state's parks, historical sites and recreational areas.

ALABAMA
Gary Leach
Director
Div. of Parks
Dept. of Conser. & Natural Resources
64 N. Union St., Rm. 718
Montgomery, AL 36130
Phone : (334) 242-3334
Fax : (334) 242-0999

ALASKA
Neil Johannsen
Director
Div. of Parks & Outdoor Recreation
Dept. of Natural Resources
3601 C St., Ste. 1200
Anchorage, AK 99503-5921
Phone : (907) 762-2600
Fax : (907) 762-2535

ARIZONA
Ken Travous
Executive Director
State Parks
800 W. Washington, Ste. 415
Phoenix, AZ 85007
Phone : (602) 542-4174

ARKANSAS
Richard Davies
Director
Dept. of Parks & Tourism
One Capitol Mall
Little Rock, AR 72201
Phone : (501) 682-2535
Fax : (501) 682-1364

CALIFORNIA
Donald W. Murphy
Director
Dept. of Parks & Recreation
P.O. Box 942896
Sacramento, CA 94296-0001
Phone : (916) 653-8380

COLORADO
Laurie Mathews
Director
Parks & Outdoor Recreation
Dept. of Natural Resources
1313 Sherman St., 6th Fl.
Denver, CO 80203
Phone : (303) 866-3437

CONNECTICUT
Richard Clifford
Bureau Chief
Parks & Forest Bur.
Dept. of Env. Protection
79 Elm St.
Hartford, CT 06106
Phone : (203) 566-3015

DELAWARE
Charles A. Salkin
Director
Div. of Parks & Recreation
Dept. of Nat. Res. & Env. Ctrl.
89 Kings Hwy.
Dover, DE 19901
Phone : (302) 739-4401
Fax : (302) 739-3817

FLORIDA
Fran P. Mainella
Director
Div. of Recreation & Parks
Dept. of Environmental Protection
3900 Commonwealth Blvd.
Tallahassee, FL 32399-3000
Phone : (904) 488-6131

GEORGIA
Lonice Barrett
Director
Parks, Rec. & Historic Sites
Dept. of Natural Resources
205 Butler St., SE, # 1352
Atlanta, GA 30334
Phone : (404) 656-2770

HAWAII
Ralston Nagata
Administrator
State Parks, Outdoor Rec. & Historic Sites Div.
1151 Punchbowl St.
Honolulu, HI 96813
Phone : (808) 587-0300

IDAHO
Yvonne Ferrell
Director
Dept. of Parks & Recreation
5657 Warm Springs Ave.
Boise, ID 83712-8752
Phone : (208) 327-7444

ILLINOIS
Brent Manning
Director
Dept. of Conservation
Lincoln Towers Plz., Rm. 425
524 S. Second St.
Springfield, IL 62701-1787
Phone : (217) 782-6302
Fax : (217) 785-9236

INDIANA
Gerald J. Pagac
Director
State Parks Div.
Dept. of Natural Resources
402 W. Washington, Rm. W298
Indianapolis, IN 46204
Phone : (317) 232-4124

IOWA
Michael E. Carrier
Administrator
Parks, Recreation & Preserves
Dept. of Natural Resources
Wallace State Off. Bldg.
Des Moines, IA 50319
Phone : (515) 281-5886

KANSAS
Steve Williams
Secretary
Dept. of Wildlife & Parks
Landon State Off. Bldg. Ste. 502
Topeka, KS 66612-1220
Phone : (913) 296-2281
Fax : (913) 296-6953

KENTUCKY
Mark A. Lovely
Commissioner
Parks Dept.
Tourism Cabinet
Capital Plz. Tower, 10th Fl.
Frankfort, KY 40601
Phone : (502) 564-2172

LOUISIANA
Jim Ball
Assistant Secretary
Off. of State Parks
Dept. of Culture, Rec. & Tourism
P.O. Box 44426
Baton Rouge, LA 70804-4426
Phone : (504) 342-8111

MAINE
Herbert Hartman
Acting Director
Bur. of Parks & Recreation
Dept. of Conservation
State House Station # 19
Augusta, ME 04333
Phone : (207) 287-3821

MARYLAND
Rick Barton
Director
Public Lands, Forestry, Forest & Parks
Dept. of Natural Resources
Tawes State Off. Bldg., Rm. E3
Annapolis, MD 21401
Phone : (410) 974-3771

MASSACHUSETTS
Todd Frederick
Director
Div. of Forests & Parks
Dept. of Environmental Mgt.
100 Cambridge St.
Boston, MA 02202
Phone : (617) 727-3180

Jane Connolly
Director
Recreational Facilities
Metropolitan District Comm.
20 Somerset St.
Boston, MA 02108
Phone : (617) 727-5215

MICHIGAN
O.J. Scherschligt
Chief
Parks & Division
Dept. of Natural Resources
P.O. Box 30028
Lansing, MI 48909
Phone : (517) 373-1270

MINNESOTA
Bill Morrissey
Director
Div. of Parks & Recreation
Dept. of Natural Resources
500 Lafayette Rd.
St. Paul, MN 55146
Phone : (612) 296-2270

MISSISSIPPI
Sam Polles
Director
Parks & Recreation
Dept. of Wildlife, Fish. & Parks
P.O. Box 451
Jackson, MS 39205
Phone : (601) 362-9212

MISSOURI
Douglas K. Eiken
Director
Div. of State Parks
Dept. of Natural Resources
101 Adams St.
P.O. Box 176
Jefferson City, MO 65102
Phone : (314) 751-9392
Fax : (314) 751-8656

MONTANA
Arnold Olsen
Administrator
Parks Div.
Dept. of Fish, Wildlife & Parks
1420 E. Sixth Ave.
Helena, MT 59620
Phone : (406) 444-3750

NEBRASKA
Rex Amack
Director
Game & Parks Comm.
2200 N. 33rd St.
P.O. Box 30370
Lincoln, NE 68503-0370
Phone : (402) 471-0641

NEVADA*
Administrator
Div. of State Parks
Dept. of Conserv. & Nat. Res.
123 W. Nye Ln.
Carson City, NV 89710
Phone : (702) 687-4384

NEW HAMPSHIRE
Wilbur F. LaPage
Director
Div. of Parks & Recreation
Dept. of Res. & Econ. Dev.
P.O. Box 856
Concord, NH 03302
Phone : (603) 271-3255

NEW JERSEY
Gregory A. Marshall
Director
Div. of Parks & Forestry
Dept. of Env. Protection
501 E. State St., CN404
Trenton, NJ 08625
Phone : (609) 292-2733

NEW MEXICO
Tom Trujillo
Director
Park & Recreation Div.
Dept. of Energy, Min. & Nat. Res.
P.O. Box 1147
Santa Fe, NM 87504-1147
Phone : (505) 827-7465
Fax : (505) 827-4001

NEW YORK*
Acting Commissioner
Off. of Parks, Recreation & Historic Preservation
Empire St. Plz., Agcy., Bldg. 1
Albany, NY 12238
Phone : (518) 474-0443

NORTH CAROLINA
Philip K. McKnelly
Director
Parks & Recreation Div.
Dept. of Environ Hlth/ Nat. Res
512 N. Salisbury St.
Raleigh, NC 27604-1148
Phone : (919) 733-4181
Fax : (919) 715-3085

NORTH DAKOTA
Doug Prchal
Director
Dept. of Parks & Recreation
P.O. Box 5521
Bismarck, ND 58502-5521
Phone : (701) 328-6190
Fax : (701) 328-5363

OHIO
Glenn Alexander
Chief
Div. of Parks & Recreation
Dept. of Natural Resources
1952 Belcher Dr., Bldg. C-3
Columbus, OH 43224
Phone : (614) 265-6511
Fax : (614) 261-8407

OKLAHOMA
Ed Cook
Secretary
Dept. of Tourism & Recreation
500 Will Rogers Bldg.
Oklahoma City, OK 73105
Phone : (405) 521-2413

OREGON
Robert Meinen
Director
Dept. of Parks & Recreation
1115 Commercial St. NE
Salem, OR 97310-1001
Phone : (503) 378-5019
Fax : (503) 378-6447

PENNSYLVANIA
Roger Fickes
Director
Bur. of State Parks
Dept. of Environmental Resources
Rachael Carson State Office Bldg. , 8th Fl.
Harrisburg, PA 17101
Phone : (717) 787-6640

RHODE ISLAND
William Hawkins
Chief
Div. of Parks & Recreation
Dept. of Environmental Mgt.
2321 Hartford
Johnston, RI 02919
Phone : (401) 277-2632

SOUTH CAROLINA
Grace McKown
Director
Dept. of Parks, Rec. & Tourism
1205 Pendleton St., Ste. 248
Columbia, SC 29201
Phone : (803) 734-0166

SOUTH DAKOTA
Doug Hofer
Director
Div. of Parks & Recreation
Dept. of Game, Fish & Parks
Anderson Bldg.
Pierre, SD 57501
Phone : (605) 773-3391

TENNESSEE
Dale Truett
Assistant Commissioner
State Parks
Dept. of Environment & Conservation
401 Church St.
Nashville, TN 37243
Phone : (615) 532-0025

TEXAS
Andrew S. Sansom
Executive Director
Dept. of Parks & Wildlife
4200 Smith School Rd.
Austin, TX 78744
Phone : (512) 389-4802

UTAH
Cortland Nelson
Director
Div. of Parks & Recreation
Dept. of Natural Resources
1636 W. North Temple, Rm. 116
Salt Lake City, UT 84116-3156
Phone : (801) 538-7362

VERMONT
Conrad Motyka
Commissioner
Dept. of Forests, Parks & Recreation
103 S. Main St.
Waterbury, VT 05676
Phone : (802) 241-3670
Fax : (802) 244-1481

VIRGINIA
H. Kirby Burch
Director
Dept. of Conservation & Recreation
203 Governor St., Ste. 203
Richmond, VA 23219
Phone : (804) 786-6124
Fax : (804) 786-6141

WASHINGTON
Cleve Pinnix
Director
State Parks & Recreation Comm.
7150 Cleanwater Ln.
P.O. Box 42650
Olympia, WA 98504-2650
Phone : (360) 902-8509

WEST VIRGINIA
Jim Lawrence
Commissioner
Div. of Tourism & Parks
Bldg. 6, Rm. 451
1900 Kanawha Blvd., E.
Charleston, WV 25305-0312
Phone : (304) 558-2764

WISCONSIN
David L. Weizenicker
Director
Bur. of Parks & Recreation
Dept. of Natural Resources
101 S. Webster
P.O. Box 7921
Madison, WI 53703
Phone : (608) 266-2181
Fax : (608) 267-3579

WYOMING
David Kathka
Director
Div. of Parks & Cultural Resources
Dept. of Commerce
Barrett Bldg.
Cheyenne, WY 82002
Phone : (307) 777-7013

DISTRICT OF COLUMBIA
Carol Lowe
Director
Dept. of Recreation & Parks
3149 16th St., NW, 2nd Fl.
Washington, DC 20010
Phone : (202) 673-7665

AMERICAN SAMOA
Tua Falemanu
Director
Dept. of Parks & Recreation
Pago Pago, AS 96799
Phone : (684) 699-9513
Fax : (684) 699-4427

GUAM
Austin J. "Sonny" Shelton
Director
Dept. of Parks & Recreation
490 Chalan Palasyo Rd.
Agana Heights, GU 96910
Phone : (671) 477-9620
Fax : (671) 472-9626

NORTHERN MARIANA ISLANDS
Anthony T. Benavente
Director
Parks & Recreation
Dept. of Lands & Natural Resources
P.O. Box 10007
Saipan, MP 96950
Phone : (670) 234-7405
Fax : (670) 234-6480

PUERTO RICO
Marimer Olazagasti
Secretary
Public Recreation & Parks Admin.
P.O. Box 3207
San Juan, PR 00904
Phone : (809) 721-2800
Fax : (809) 722-3382

U.S. VIRGIN ISLANDS
Ira Hobson
Commissioner
Dept. of Housing, Parks & Rec.
Property & Procurement, Bldg. #1
Sub Base, 2nd Fl., Rm. 206
St. Thomas, VI 00802
Phone : (809) 774-0255
Fax : (809) 774-4600

PAROLE AND PROBATION

Determines whether paroles should be granted or revoked and supervises adult parolees and probationers.

ALABAMA
William C. Young
Executive Director
Bd. of Pardons & Parole
500 Monroe St.
Montgomery, AL 36130
Phone : (334) 242-8700
Fax : (334) 242-1809

ALASKA
Richard Collum
Executive Director
Parole Board
Dept. of Corrections
P.O. Box 112000
Juneau, AK 99811-2000
Phone : (907) 465-3384
Fax : (907) 465-3110

ARIZONA
Duane Belcher
Chairman
Bd. of Pardons & Paroles
1645 W. Jefferson, Ste. 326
Phoenix, AZ 85007
Phone : (602) 542-5656

ARKANSAS
Mike Gaines
Chairman
Post Prison Transfer Board
P.O. Box 34085
Little Rock, AR 72203
Phone : (501) 682-3850
Fax : (501) 682-3860

CALIFORNIA
Jim Nielsen
Chairman
Bd. of Prison Terms
428 J St., Ste. 600
Sacramento, CA 95814-2329
Phone : (916) 322-6366

COLORADO
Larry E. Trujillo
Chair
Parole Board
1600 W. 24th St.
Pueblo, CO 81003
Phone : (719) 546-0141
Fax : (719) 546-0363

CONNECTICUT
Robert J. Bosco
Director
Dept. of Adult Probation
2275 Silas Deane Hwy.
Rocky Hill, CT 06067
Phone : (203) 563-5797

DELAWARE
Marlene Lichtenstadter
Chair
Bd. of Parole
Carvel State Off. Bldg.
820 N. French St.
Wilmington, DE 19801
Phone : (302) 577-3452

FLORIDA
Gene R. Hodges
Chairman
Parole Comm.
1309 Winewood Blvd.
Tallahassee, FL 32399
Phone : (904) 922-0000
Fax : (904) 488-7199

GEORGIA
J. Wayne Garner
Chairman
Board of Pardons & Paroles
2 M.L. King, Jr. Dr., SE
Atlanta, GA 30334
Phone : (404) 656-5651

HAWAII
Claudio Suyat
Chair
Paroling Authority
Dept. of Public Safety
250 S. King St., Rm. 400
Honolulu, HI 96813
Phone : (808) 587-1290

IDAHO
Olivia Craven
Deputy Director
Comm. for Pardons & Parole
Dept. of Corrections
1075 Park Blvd.
Boise, ID 83720
Phone : (208) 334-2520

ILLINOIS
James K. Williams
Chairman
Prisoner Review Board
319 E. Madison, Ste. A
Springfield, IL 62702
Phone : (217) 782-7273
Fax : (217) 524-0012

INDIANA
Joseph L. Smith, Sr.
Chairman
Parole Bd.
Dept. of Corrections
IGC-South, Rm. E321
Indianapolis, IN 46204
Phone : (317) 232-5737

IOWA
Jeanette Bucklew
Deputy Director
Community Based Corrections
Dept. of Corrections
914 Grand, # 250 Jewett Bldg.
Des Moines, IA 50319
Phone : (515) 281-4806

KANSAS
Micah Ross
Director
Kansas Parole Board
Landon State Off. Bldg., Rm. 452-S
Topeka, KS 66612-1220
Phone : (913) 296-3469
Fax : (913) 296-0759

KENTUCKY
Helen Howard-Hughes
Chairman
State Parole Bd.
Dept. of Corrections
State Off. Bldg., 5th Fl.
Frankfort, KY 40601
Phone : (502) 564-3620

LOUISIANA
Gretchen McCarstle
Executive Assistant
Board of Parole
Public Safety & Corrections
P.O. Box 94304
Baton Rouge, LA 70804-9304
Phone : (504) 342-6622

MAINE
Peter Tilton
Director
Div. of Parole & Probation
Dept. of Corrections
State House Station # 111
Augusta, ME 04333
Phone : (207) 287-4381

MARYLAND
Paul Davis
Chairman
Parole Comm.
6776 Reisterstown Rd., Ste. 307
Baltimore, MD 21215
Phone : (301) 764-4235

MASSACHUSETTS
Shelia Hubbard
Chairman
Parole Bd.
Executive Off. of Human Srvcs.
27/43 Wormwood St., Ste. 300
Boston, MA 02210-1606
Phone : (617) 727-3271

MICHIGAN
Gary Gabry
Chairman
Parole Board
Dept. of Corrections
P.O. Box 30003
Lansing, MI 48909
Phone : (517) 373-0270

MINNESOTA
Frank W. Wood
Commissioner
Dept. of Corrections
300 Bigelow Bldg.
450 N. Syndicate St.
St. Paul, MN 55104
Phone : (612) 642-0282

MISSISSIPPI
Steward Murphy
Chair
Parole Bd.
723 N. President St.
Jackson, MS 39202
Phone : (601) 354-6454

MISSOURI
Cranston Mitchell
Chairman
Board of Probation & Parole
Dept. of Corrections
117 Commerce Dr.
Jefferson City, MO 65109
Phone : (314) 751-8488
Fax : (314) 751-8501

MONTANA
Mike Ferriter
Chief
Community Corrections Bur.
Dept. of Corrections & Human Srvcs.
1539 11th Ave.
Helena, MT 59601
Phone : (406) 444-4912

NEBRASKA
Ronald L. Bartee
Chairperson
State Parole Board
P.O. Box 94754
Lincoln, NE 68509-4754
Phone : (402) 471-2156

NEVADA
Richard Wyett
Chief
Dept. of Parole & Probation
1100 E. Williams, Ste. 210
Carson City, NV 89710
Phone : (702) 687-5040

NEW HAMPSHIRE
Michael K. Brown
Director
Div. of Field Services
Dept. of Corrections
P.O. Box 769
Concord, NH 03302
Phone : (603) 271-3261

NEW JERSEY
Mary Disabato
Chairman
State Parole Board
Dept. of Corrections
Whittlesey Rd., CN 862
Trenton, NJ 08625
Phone : (609) 984-4587

NEW MEXICO
Alan Shuman
Director
Probation & Parole Div.
Dept. of Corrections
P.O. Box 27116
Santa Fe, NM 87502
Phone : (505) 827-8709
Fax : (505) 827-8801

NEW YORK*
Chairman
Bd. of Parole
97 Central Ave.
Albany, NY 12206
Phone : (518) 473-9548

Executive Director
Div. of Probation & Correctional Alternatives
Stuyvesant Plaza
Executive Park Tower
Albany, NY 12203
Phone : (518) 474-1210

NORTH CAROLINA
Theodis Beck
Director
Adult Probation & Parole
Dept. of Corrections
4000 Old Wake Forest Rd.
Raleigh, NC 27609
Phone : (919) 850-2900
Fax : (919) 850-2818

NORTH DAKOTA
Warren Emmer
Director
Parole & Probation Dept.
P.O. Box 5521
Bismarck, ND 58502-5521
Phone : (701) 328-6190
Fax : (701) 328-6651

OHIO
Reginald A. Wilkinson
Director
Dept. of Rehabilitation & Corrections
1050 Freeway Dr., N.
Columbus, OH 43229
Phone : (614) 752-1164
Fax : (614) 752-1171

OKLAHOMA
Ray Page
Executive Director
Pardon & Parole Bd.
4040 N. Lincoln Blvd., Ste. 219
Oklahoma City, OK 73105
Phone : (405) 427-8601

OREGON
Marva Fabien
Chairperson
Bd. of Parole & Post-Prison Supervision
2575 Center St., NE
Salem, OR 97310
Phone : (503) 945-9009
Fax : (503) 373-7558

PENNSYLVANIA
Allen Castor, Jr.
Chairman
Bd. of Probation & Parole
3101 N. Front St.
Harrisburg, PA 17120
Phone : (717) 787-5100

RHODE ISLAND
Kenneth Walker
Chairman
Parole Bd.
Dept. of Corrections
1 Center Place
Providence, RI 02903-1614
Phone : (401) 277-3262

SOUTH CAROLINA
Eddie Gunn
Executive Director
Probation, Parole & Pardon Srvcs.
2221 Devine St., #600
P.O. Box 50666
Columbia, SC 29250
Phone : (803) 734-9278

SOUTH DAKOTA
Dan Jacobson
Executive Director
State Penitentiary
Off. of Correctional Service
1600 North Dr.
Sioux Falls, SD 57101
Phone : (605) 339-6780

TENNESSEE
Charles M. Traughber
Chairman
Bd. of Paroles
404 James Robertson Pkwy.
Nashville, TN 37243
Phone : (615) 741-1673

TEXAS
Bob Owens
Director
Pardons & Paroles Div.
Dept. of Criminal Justice
P.O. Box 13084
Austin, TX 78711
Phone : (512) 406-5200

UTAH
Lane McCotter
Executive Director
Dept. of Corrections
6100 S. 300 E.
Murray, UT 84107
Phone : (801) 265-5500

VERMONT
Richard Turner
Director of Probation
Dept. of Corrections
Agency of Human Services
103 S. Main St.
Waterbury, VT 05671-1001
Phone : (802) 241-2263

Linda Shambo
Director
Parole Board
103 S. Main St.
Waterbury, VT 05671
Phone : (802) 241-2294
Fax : (802) 241-2565

VIRGINIA
John B. Metzger III
Chairman
Parole Board
6900 Atmore Dr.
Richmond, VA 23225
Phone : (804) 674-3081
Fax : (804) 674-3284

WASHINGTON
Kathryn S. Bail
Chair
Indeterminate Sentencing Review Bd.
4317 6th Ave., SE
P.O. Box 40907
Lacey, WA 98504-0907
Phone : (360) 493-9266

WEST VIRGINIA
Bruce Carter
Chairman
Board of Probation & Parole
Bldg. 4, Rm. 307
112 California Ave.
Charleston, WV 25305-0700
Phone : (304) 558-6366

WISCONSIN
Eurial Jordan
Secretary
Div. of Probation & Parole
149 E. Wilson, 2nd Fl.
Madison, WI 53703
Phone : (608) 266-7740
Fax : (608) 267-1739

WYOMING
Robert E. Ortega
Director
Dept. of Probation & Parole
5801 Osage
Cheyenne, WY 82002
Phone : (307) 777-7208

DISTRICT OF COLUMBIA
Margaret Quick
Chairman
Bd. of Parole
717 14th St., NW, Ste. 200
Washington, DC 20005
Phone : (202) 727-0074

AMERICAN SAMOA
Malaetasi Togafau
Attorney General
American Samoa Government
P.O. Box 7
Pago Pago, AS 96799
Phone : (684) 633-4163
Fax : (684) 633-1838

GUAM
Eduardo C. Bitanga
Director
Dept. of Corrections
P.O. Box 3236
Agana, GU 96911
Phone : (671) 734-2458
Fax : (671) 734-4490

NORTHERN MARIANA ISLANDS
Jesus C. Bermudes
Parole Officer
Board of Parole
Off. of the Governor
Saipan, MP 96950
Phone : (670) 234-4841
Fax : (670) 235-4840

PUERTO RICO
Nydia M. Cotto-Vives
President
Parole Bd.
P.O. Box 40945, Minillas Station
San Juan, PR 00940
Phone : (809) 759-7127

U.S. VIRGIN ISLANDS
Verne A. Hodge
Presiding Judge
Territorial Court
P.O. Box 70
St. Thomas, VI 00804
Phone : (809) 774-6680

Frits T. Lawaetz
Chairman
Parole Board
P.O. Box 2668
St. Thomas, VI 00802
Phone : (809) 774-4821
Fax : (809) 777-8263

PERSONNEL

Formulates, implements and enforces personnel management policies and procedures for the state.

ALABAMA
Halycon Ballard
Director
Dept. of State Personnel
64 N. Union St., Rm. 300
Montgomery, AL 36130
Phone : (334) 242-3389
Fax : (334) 242-3171

ALASKA
Beverly Reaume
Director
Div. of Personnel
Dept. of Administration
P.O. Box 110201
Juneau, AK 99811-0201
Phone : (907) 465-4430
Fax : (907) 465-2576

ARIZONA
William Bell
Assistant Director
Personnel Division
Dept. of Administration
1831 W. Jefferson, Rm. 100
Phoenix, AZ 85007
Phone : (602) 542-5482

ARKANSAS
Artee Williams
Administrator
Dept. of Finance & Admin.
201 DFA Bldg.
1509 W. 7th St.
Little Rock, AR 72201
Phone : (501) 682-1823
Fax : (501) 682-5094

CALIFORNIA
David J. Tirapelle
Director
Dept. of Personnel Admin.
1515 S. St., North Bldg., Ste. 400
Sacramento, CA 95814
Phone : (916) 322-5193

COLORADO
Shirley Harris
Executive Director
Dept. of Personnel
1313 Sherman St., Rm. 123
Denver, CO 80203
Phone : (303) 866-2321

CONNECTICUT
Thelma Ball
Employment Relations Manager
Department of Administrative Srvcs.
165 Capitol Ave., Rm. 403
Hartford, CT 06106
Phone : (203) 566-3081

Peter Allen
Chief
Labor Relations
Dept. of Administrative Srvcs.
165 Capitol Ave., Rm. 403
Hartford, CT 06106
Phone : (203) 566-3081

DELAWARE
Harriet Smith
Director
Off. of Personnel
Townsend Bldg.
P.O. Box 1401
Dover, DE 19903
Phone : (302) 739-4195
Fax : (302) 739-3000

FLORIDA
Patsy M. Barber
Div. of Personnel Mgt. Srvcs.
Dept. of Management Srvcs.
435 Carlton Bldg.
Tallahassee, FL 32399
Phone : (904) 922-5449

GEORGIA
Bobbie Jean Bennett
Commissioner
Georgia State Merit System
200 Piedmont Ave. SE, Ste. 502
Atlanta, GA 30334
Phone : (404) 656-2705

IDAHO
Dick Hutchison
Director
Idaho Personnel Comm.
700 W. State St.
Boise, ID 83720-2700
Phone : (208) 334-2263

ILLINOIS
Julie Moscardelli
Manager
Bur. of Personnel
Dept. of Central Mgt. Srvcs.
503 Stratton Off. Bldg.
Springfield, IL 62706
Phone : (217) 782-6191
Fax : (217) 524-0836

INDIANA
Jennifer Vigran
Director
State Personnel Dept.
402 W. Washington St.
IGCS, Rm. W161
Indianapolis, IN 46204
Phone : (317) 232-3059

IOWA
Linda Hanson
Director
Dept. of Personnel
Grimes State Off. Bldg.
E. 14th & Grand
Des Moines, IA 50319
Phone : (515) 281-3351
Fax : (515) 242-6450

KANSAS
William B. McGlasson
Acting Director
Div. of Personnel Services
Dept. of Admininstration
Landon State Off. Bldg., Rm. 951-S
Topeka, KS 66612-1251
Phone : (913) 296-4278
Fax : (913) 296-0756

KENTUCKY
Lowell W. Clark
Commissioner
Dept. of Personnel
200 Fairoaks, Suite 516
Frankfort, KY 40601
Phone : (502) 564-4460

LOUISIANA
Herbert Sumrall
Director, Civil Service Comm.
Personnel Management Div.
Dept. of Civil Service
P.O. Box 94111
Baton Rouge, LA 70804-9111
Phone : (504) 342-8272

MAINE
Nancy J. Kenniston
Director
Bur. of Human Resources
Dept. of Admin. & Financial Srvcs.
State House Station # 4
Augusta, ME 04333
Phone : (207) 287-3761

MARYLAND
Michael Knapp
Secretary
Dept. of Personnel
301 W. Preston St., Rm. 609
Baltimore, MD 21201
Phone : (301) 225-4715

MASSACHUSETTS
Robert C. Dumont
Personnel Administrator
Dept. of Personnel Admin.
Executive Off. for Admin. & Finance
One Ashburton Pl., Rm. 203
Boston, MA 02108
Phone : (617) 727-1556

MICHIGAN
Martha Bibbs
Director
Dept. of Civil Service
P.O. Box 30002
Lansing, MI 48909
Phone : (517) 373-3020

MINNESOTA
Bruce E. Johnson
Commissioner
Dept. of Employee Relations
200 Centennial Bldg.
658 Cedar St.
St. Paul, MN 55101
Phone : (612) 296-8366

MISSISSIPPI
J.K. Stringer, Jr.
Director
State Personnel Bd.
301 N. Lamar St., Ste. 100
Jackson, MS 39201
Phone : (601) 359-2704

MISSOURI
Lee Capps
Director
Div. of Personnel
Off. of Administration
Truman Bldg., Rm. 430
P.O. Box 388
Jefferson City, MO 65102
Phone : (314) 751-3053
Fax : (314) 751-8641

MONTANA
Linda King
Administrator
Public Empl. Retirement Div.
Dept. of Administration
1712 Ninth Ave.
Helena, MT 59620
Phone : (406) 444-3154

NEBRASKA
Joseph P. Foster
Director
Div. of Personnel
Dept. of Administration Srvcs.
P.O. Box 94664
Lincoln, NE 68509-4905
Phone : (402) 471-2332

NEVADA
Barbara Willis
Director
Dept. of Personnel
209 E. Musser St.
Carson City, NV 89710
Phone : (702) 687-4050

NEW HAMPSHIRE
Virginia Lamberton
Director
Div. of Personnel
25 Capitol St.
Concord, NH 03301
Phone : (603) 271-3261

NEW JERSEY
Linda M. Anselmini
Commissioner
Dept. of Personnel
3 Station Plz., CN 317
Trenton, NJ 08625
Phone : (609) 292-4144

NEW MEXICO
Jody Hooper
Director
State Personnel Off.
P.O. Box 26127
Santa Fe, NM 87505-0127
Phone : (505) 827-8120
Fax : (505) 827-8127

NEW YORK*
President
Dept. of Civil Services
State Campus, Bldg. 1
Albany, NY 12239
Phone : (518) 457-3701

NORTH CAROLINA
Ronald G. Penny
Director
Off. of State Personnel
Dept. of Admin.
116 W. Jones St.
Raleigh, NC 27603-8004
Phone : (919) 733-7108
Fax : (919) 733-0653

NORTH DAKOTA
Brian McClure
Director
Off. of Management & Budget
State Capitol, 1st Fl.
600 E. Boulevard Ave.
Bismarck, ND 58505-0120
Phone : (701) 328-3290
Fax : (701) 328-3000

OHIO
Steve Buehrer
Deputy Director
Div. of Personnel
Dept. of Admin. Srvcs.
30 E. Broad St., 28th Fl.
Columbus, OH 43215
Phone : (614) 466-3455
Fax : (614) 728-2785

OKLAHOMA
Oscar Jackson
Secretary of Human Resources
Off. of Personnel Mgt.
Jim Thorpe Bldg., Rm. G-80
Oklahoma City, OK 73105
Phone : (405) 521-2177

OREGON
Karen Roach
Administrator
Human Resources Mgt. Div.
Dept. of Admin. Srvcs.
155 Cottage St., NE
Salem, OR 97310
Phone : (503) 378-5419
Fax : (503) 373-7684

PENNSYLVANIA
Charles T. Sciotto
Deputy Secretary
Employee Relations
Off. of Administration
517 Finance Bldg.
Harrisburg, PA 17120
Phone : (717) 787-5545

RHODE ISLAND
Anthony A. Bucci
Personnel Administrator
Off. of Personnel Admin.
Dept. of Admin.
One Capitol Hill
Providence, RI 02908-5860
Phone : (401) 277-2160

SOUTH CAROLINA
Phyllis M. Mayes
Assistant Executive Director
Budget and Control Board
P.O. Box 12444
Columbia, SC 29211
Phone : (803) 737-0900

TENNESSEE
Susan R. Williams
Commissioner
Dept. of Personnel
James K. Polk Bldg., 2nd Fl.
Nashville, TN 37243-0635
Phone : (615) 741-2958
Fax : (615) 741-6985

TEXAS
Don McCanless
Acting Classification Director
State Auditor's Off.
206 E. 9th St., Ste. 1900
Austin, TX 78711
Phone : (512) 479-4700

UTAH
Karen Suzuki-Okabe
Executive Director
Dept. of Human Resources Mgt.
2120 State Office Bldg.
Salt Lake City, UT 84114
Phone : (801) 538-3080

VERMONT
Brian Searles
Commissioner
Dept. of Personnel
110 State St.
Montpelier, VT 05602
Phone : (802) 828-3491
Fax : (802) 828-3409

VIRGINIA
Charles E. James, Sr.
Director
Dept. of Personnel & Training
Monroe Bldg., 12th Fl.
101 N. 14th St.
Richmond, VA 23219
Phone : (804) 225-2237
Fax : (804) 371-7401

WASHINGTON
Dennis Karras
Director
Dept. of Personnel
521 Capitol Way, S.
P.O. Box 47500
Olympia, WA 98504
Phone : (360) 753-5368

WEST VIRGINIA
Steve Stephens
Director
Div. of Personnel
Bldg. 6, Rm. 416
1900 Kanawha Blvd., E.
Charleston, WV 25305
Phone : (304) 558-3950

WISCONSIN
Jon Litscher
Secretary
Dept. of Employment Relations
137 E. Wilson St.
P.O. Box 7855
Madison, WI 53707-7855
Phone : (608) 266-9820
Fax : (608) 267-1020

WYOMING
Mike Miller
Administrator
Personnel Div.
Dept. of Admin. & Information
2001 Capitol Ave.
Cheyenne, WY 82002-0060
Phone : (307) 777-6713

DISTRICT OF COLUMBIA
Larry King
Director
Off. of Personnel
441 4th St., NW, 3rd Fl.
Washington, DC 20001
Phone : (202) 727-6406

AMERICAN SAMOA
Sapini Siatu'u
Director
Dept. of Human Resources
American Samoa Government
Pago Pago, AS 96799
Phone : (684) 633-4485
Fax : (684) 633-1139

GUAM
John S. Salas
Director
Dept. of Administration
P.O. Box 884
Agana, GU 96910
Phone : (671) 475-1101
Fax : (671) 477-6788

NORTHERN MARIANA ISLANDS
Norbert S. Sablan
Personnel Officer
Civil Service Comm.
Personnel Management Off.
Off. of the Governor
Saipan, MP 96950
Phone : (670) 234-6958

PUERTO RICO
Oscar Ramos
Executive Director
Off. for Personnel Admin.
P.O. Box 8476
Santurce, PR 00940
Phone : (809) 721-4300

U.S. VIRGIN ISLANDS
Ellen Murraine
Director
Div. of Personnel
GERS Complex, 3rd Fl.
48B-50C Konprindsens Gade
St. Thomas, VI 00802
Phone : (809) 774-8588
Fax : (809) 774-6916

PLANNING

Formulates long-range, comprehensive plans for the orderly and coordinated growth of the state.

ALABAMA
Martha McInnis
Chief
Science, Tech. & Energy Div.
Dept. of Economic & Comm. Aff.
P.O. Box 5690
Montgomery, AL 36103
Phone : (334) 242-5290
Fax : (334) 242-0552

ARIZONA
Peter Burns
Director
Strategic Plan. & Budget Off.
1700 W. Washington, W. Wing
Phoenix, AZ 85007
Phone : (602) 542-5381

CALIFORNIA
Lee Grissom
Director
Off. of Planning & Research
1400 10th St., Ste. 156
Sacramento, CA 95814
Phone : (916) 322-2318

COLORADO
George DeLaney
Director
Off. of State Planning & Budgeting
111 State Capitol
Denver, CO 80203
Phone : (303) 866-3317
Fax : (303) 866-3044

CONNECTICUT
Susan Shimelman
Under Secretary
Policy Dev. & Planning Div.
Off. of Policy & Mgt.
80 Washington St.
Hartford, CT 06106
Phone : (203) 566-4298

DELAWARE
David S. Hugg III
Director
State Planning Office
Tatnall Building
Dover, DE 19901
Phone : (302) 739-3090

FLORIDA
Robert B. Bradley
Deputy Director
Off. of Planning & Budgeting
Executive Off. of the Governor
The Capitol, Rm. 1601
Tallahassee, FL 32399-0001
Phone : (904) 488-7810

GEORGIA
Henry M. Huckaby
Director
Off. of Planning & Budget
254 Washington St., SW, Ste. 614
Atlanta, GA 30334
Phone : (404) 656-3820

HAWAII
Gregory G.Y. Pai
Director
Off. of State Planning
Off. of the Governor
P.O. Box 3540
Honolulu, HI 96813
Phone : (808) 587-2833
Fax : (808) 587-2848

IDAHO
James V. Hawkins
Director
Dept. of Commerce
700 W. State St.
Boise, ID 83720
Phone : (208) 334-2470

ILLINOIS
Steven B. Schnorf
Director of Policy
Office of the Governor
2 1/2 State House
Springfield, IL 62706
Phone : (217) 782-1674
Fax : (217) 524-1678

INDIANA
Tom Sugar
Dir. of Planning & Communication
Off. of the Governor
State House, Rm. 206
Indianapolis, IN 46204
Phone : (317) 232-1687

IOWA
Dave Lyons
Director
Dept. of Economic Development
200 E. Grand
Des Moines, IA 50309
Phone : (515) 242-4814
Fax : (515) 242-4832

KENTUCKY
Mark Guilfoyle
State Budget Director
Governor's Office for Policy & Management
Capitol Annex, Rm. 283
Frankfort, KY 40601
Phone : (502) 564-7300

LOUISIANA
Joan M. Wharton
Director
Off. of State Planning
P.O. Box 94095
Baton Rouge, LA 70804
Phone : (504) 342-7000

MAINE
Evan Richert
Director
State Planning Off.
State House Station # 38
Augusta, ME 04333
Phone : (207) 287-3261

MARYLAND
Ronald Kreitner
Director
Off. of Planning Data
Dept. of Planning
301 W. Preston St.
Baltimore, MD 21201
Phone : (410) 225-4510

MASSACHUSETTS
Gloria C. Larson
Secretary
Executive Off. of Economic Affairs
1 Ashburton Pl., Rm. 2101
Boston, MA 02108
Phone : (617) 727-8380

MINNESOTA
Linda Kohl
Commissioner
Strategic & Long Range Planning Office
Centennial Off. Bldg., 3rd Fl.
658 Cedar St.
St. Paul, MN 55155
Phone : (612) 297-2325

MISSISSIPPI
Clinton Graham
Director
Off. of Budget & Fund Mgt.
Dept. of Finance & Admin.
P.O. Box 267
Jackson, MS 39203
Phone : (601) 359-3927

MISSOURI
Mark E. Ward
Deputy Commissioner
Div. of Budget & Planning
Office of Administration
State Capitol, Rm. 124
P.O. Box 809
Jefferson City, MO 65102
Phone : (314) 751-3925
Fax : (314) 526-4811

MONTANA
David Lewis
Director
Budget & Program Planning Off.
Capitol Station
Helena, MT 59620-0801
Phone : (406) 444-3616

NEBRASKA
Al Curtis
Executive Director
Comm. on Law Enforcement & Criminal Justice
P.O. Box 94946
Lincoln, NE 68509
Phone : (402) 471-2194

NEVADA
John P. Comeaux
Director
Dept. of Administration
209 E. Musser St., Rm. 200
Carson City, NV 89710
Phone : (702) 687-4065
Fax : (702) 687-3983

NEW HAMPSHIRE
Jeff Taylor
Director
Off. of State Planning
2 1/2 Beacon St.
Concord, NH 03301
Phone : (603) 271-2155

NEW JERSEY
Herbert Simmens
Director
Off. of State Planning
Dept. of the Treasury
33 W. State St., CN-204
Trenton, NJ 08625
Phone : (609) 292-7156

NEW YORK*
Commissioner
Dept. of Commerce
1 Commerce Plz.
Albany, NY 12245
Phone : (518) 474-4100

NORTH CAROLINA
Sheron K. Morgan
State Planning Officer
Off. of State Planning
116 W. Jones St.
Raleigh, NC 27603
Phone : (919) 733-4131

NORTH DAKOTA
Shirley Dykshoorn
Director
Intergovernmental Assistance
Off. of Mgt. & Budget
600 E. Boulevard Ave.
Bismarck, ND 58505-0170
Phone : (701) 328-2094
Fax : (701) 328-2308

OHIO
R. Gregory Browning
Director
Off. of Budget & Mgt.
30 E. Broad St., 34th Fl.
Columbus, OH 43266-0411
Phone : (614) 752-2577
Fax : (614) 466-5400

OREGON
Richard Benner
Director
Dept. of Land Conservation & Development
1175 Court St., NE
Salem, OR 97310
Phone : (503) 373-0060
Fax : (503) 362-6705

PENNSYLVANIA
Charles Zogby
Director
Governor's Policy Off.
Off. of the Governor
Rm. 238, Main Capitol Bldg.
Harrisburg, PA 17120
Phone : (717) 772-9005

RHODE ISLAND
Daniel Varin
Associate Director
Div. of Planning
One Capitol Hill, 4th Fl.
Providence, RI 02908-5873
Phone : (401) 277-1220

SOUTH CAROLINA
Phyllis M. Mayes
Assistant Executive Director
Budget and Control Board
P.O. Box 12444
Columbia, SC 29201
Phone : (803) 737-1390
Fax : (803) 734-2117

SOUTH DAKOTA
Curt Everson
Commissioner
Bur. of Finance & Mgt.
State Capitol, 2nd Fl.
500 E. Capitol Ave.
Pierre, SD 57501
Phone : (605) 773-3411

TENNESSEE*
Director
Off. of State Planning
Off. of the Governor
State Capitol
Nashville, TN 37243
Phone : (615) 741-4131

TEXAS
Albert Hawkins
Director
Governor's Off. of Budget & Planning
P.O. Box 12428, Capitol Station
Austin, TX 78711
Phone : (512) 463-1778

UTAH
Lynne Koga
Director
Off. of Planning & Budget
116 State Capitol
Salt Lake City, UT 84114
Phone : (801) 538-1562

VERMONT
Steve Condrey
Policy Research & Coordination
Executive Dept.
109 State St.
Montpelier, VT 05609
Phone : (802) 828-3326
Fax : (802) 828-3339

VIRGINIA
Robert Lauterberg
Director
Dept. of Planning & Budget
P.O. Box 1422
Richmond, VA 23211
Phone : (804) 786-5375

WASHINGTON
Ruta Fanning
Director
Off. of Financial Mgt.
300 Insurance Bldg.
P.O. Box 43113
Olympia, WA 98504
Phone : (360) 753-5459

WEST VIRGINIA
Charles Polan
Secretary
Dept. of Finance & Admin.
State Capitol, Rm. E119
1900 Kanawha Blvd., E.
Charleston, WV 25305
Phone : (304) 558-2300
Fax : (304) 558-2999

WISCONSIN
Richard G. Chandler
Administrator
State Exec. Budget & Planning
Dept. of Admin.
101 E Wilson, 10th Fl.
P.O. Box 7864
Madison, WI 53703
Phone : (608) 266-1035
Fax : (608) 266-7645

WYOMING
Cynthia M. Lummis
General Counsel
State Capitol Bldg.
Cheyenne, WY 82002
Phone : (307) 777-7831

DISTRICT OF COLUMBIA
Albert G. Dobbins
Director
Off. of Planning
415 12th St., N.W., Rm. 300
Washington, DC 20004
Phone : (202) 727-6492

AMERICAN SAMOA
Alfonso Pete Galeai
Director
Off. Of Economic Development Planning
Utulei
Pago Pago, AS 96799
Phone : (684) 633-5155
Fax : (684) 633-4195

GUAM
Michael Cruz
Chief Planner
Bureau of Planning
P.O. Box 2950
Agana, GU 96910
Phone : (671) 472-4201
Fax : (671) 477-1812

NORTHERN MARIANA ISLANDS
Evelyn J. Tenorio
Special Assistant for Planning
Off. of the Governor
Capitol Hill
P.O. Box 10007
Saipan, MP 96950
Phone : (670) 322-5091
Fax: (670) 322-5099

PUERTO RICO
Norma Burgos Andujar
President
Planning Board
Minillas Government Ctr.
Avenida De Diego
P.O. Box 41119
San Juan, PR 00940
Phone : (809) 723-6200

U.S. VIRGIN ISLANDS
Kenneth Belle
Assistant Commissioner
Div. of Planning
Dept. of Planning & Nat. Resources
Nisky Ctr., Ste. 231
St. Thomas, VI 00802
Phone : (809) 774-3320
Fax : (809) 775-5706

POST AUDIT

Audits the accounts of state offices to detemine whether financial transactions have been made in conformity with state laws.

ALABAMA
Ronald L. Jones
Chief Examiner
Dept. of Examiners of Public Accounts
50 N. Ripley St.
Montgomery, AL 36130
Phone : (334) 242-9200
Fax : (334) 242-1775

ALASKA
Randy Welker
Legislative Auditor
Div. of Legislative Audit
P.O. Box 113300
Juneau, AK 99811-3300
Phone : (907) 465-3830
Fax : (907) 465-2347

ARIZONA
Douglas Norton
Auditor General
2910 N. 44th St., Ste. 410
Phoenix, AZ 85018
Phone : (602) 553-0333
Fax : (602) 553-0051

ARKANSAS
Charles L. Robinson
Legislative Auditor
Div. of Legislative Audit
State Capitol, Rm. 172
Little Rock, AR 72201
Phone : (501) 682-1931
Fax : (501) 376-8723

CALIFORNIA
Enrique Farias
Chief
Financial & Performance Audits
Dept. of Finance
915 L St.
Sacramento, CA 95814-3701
Phone : (916) 322-2985

Kurt R. Sjobert
Auditor General
660 J St., Ste. 300
Sacramento, CA 95814
Phone : (916) 445-0255

COLORADO
Tim O'Brien
State Auditor
State Auditor's Off.
Legislative Services Bldg.
200 E. 14th Ave.
Denver, CO 80203
Phone : (303) 866-2051

CONNECTICUT
Robert Jaechle
Auditor of Public Accounts
State Capitol, Rm. 114
Hartford, CT 06106
Phone : (203) 566-2119

Kevin Johnston
Auditor of Public Accounts
State Capitol, Rm. 116
Hartford, CT 06106
Phone : (203) 566-5572

DELAWARE
R. Thomas Wagner Jr.
State Auditor
Townsend Bldg.
P.O. Box 1401
Dover, DE 19901
Phone : (302) 739-4241

FLORIDA
Charles L. Lester
Auditor General
P.O. Box 1735
Tallahassee, FL 32302
Phone : (904) 488-5534

GEORGIA
Claude Vickers
State Auditor
Dept. of Audits
254 Washington St., Rm. 214
Atlanta, GA 30334
Phone : (404) 656-2174

HAWAII
James Yamamura
Chief Auditor
Div. of Audit
Accounting & General Srvcs. Dept.
1151 Punchbowl St.
Honolulu, HI 96813
Phone : (808) 586-0360

Marion M. Higa
State Auditor
Office of the Auditor
465 S. King St., Rm. 500
Honolulu, HI 96813
Phone : (808) 587-0800

IDAHO
Larry R. Kirk
Supervisor
Legislative Audit
Legislative Services Off.
Statehouse
Boise, ID 83720
Phone : (208) 334-3540

ILLINOIS
William G. Holland
Auditor General
Off. of the Auditor General
740 E. Ash St.
Springfield, IL 62703-3154
Phone : (217) 782-6046
Fax : (217) 785-8222

INDIANA
Donald L. Euratte
State Examiner
IGC-South, Rm. E418
302 W. Washington St.
Indianapolis, IN 46204-2281
Phone : (317) 232-2524

IOWA
Richard D. Johnson
State Auditor
State Capitol
Des Moines, IA 50319
Phone : (515) 281-5834

KANSAS
Barbara J. Hinton
Auditor
Legis. Div. of Post Audit
Mercantile Bank Tower
800 SW Jackson, Ste. 1200
Topeka, KS 66612-2212
Phone : (913) 296-3792

KENTUCKY
Ben Chandler
Auditor of Public Accounts
Capitol Annex, Rm. 144
Frankfort, KY 40601
Phone : (502) 564-5841

LOUISIANA
Daniel G. Kyle
Legislative Auditor
Off. of Legislative Auditor
P.O. Box 94397
Baton Rouge, LA 70804
Phone : (504) 342-7237

MAINE
Rodney L. Scribner
State Auditor
State Off. Bldg.
State House Station # 66
Augusta, ME 04333-0066
Phone : (207) 287-2201

MARYLAND
Anthony J. Verdecchia
Director
Div. of Legislative Audits
Dept. of Fiscal Srvcs.
301 W. Preston St.
Baltimore, MD 21201
Phone : (301) 225-1400

MASSACHUSETTS
A. Joseph DeNucci
Auditor of Commonwealth
State House, Rm. 229
Boston, MA 02133
Phone : (617) 727-2075

MICHIGAN
Thomas McTavish
Auditor General
201 N. Washington Sq.
Lansing, MI 48913
Phone : (517) 334-8050

MINNESOTA
James R. Nobles
Legislative Auditor
Centennial Bldg., 1st Fl.
658 Cedar St.
St. Paul, MN 55155
Phone : (612) 296-4710

Judi Dutcher
State Auditor
525 Park St., # 400
St. Paul, MN 55103
Phone : (612) 296-2551

MISSISSIPPI
Steve Patterson
State Auditor
P.O. Box 956
Jackson, MS 39205
Phone : (601) 364-2888

MISSOURI
Margaret Kelly
State Auditor
State Capitol, Rm. 224
P.O. Box 869
Jefferson City, MO 65102
Phone : (314) 751-4824
Fax : (314) 751-6539

MONTANA
Scott Seacat
Legislative Auditor
Off. of Legislative Auditor
State Capitol, Rm. 135
Helena, MT 59620
Phone : (406) 444-3122

NEBRASKA
John A. Breslow
Auditor of Public Accounts
State Capitol, Rm. 2303
P.O. Box 94786
Lincoln, NE 68509-4786
Phone : (402) 471-2111

NEVADA
William Gary Crews
Legislative Auditor
Audit Div.
Legislative Counsel Bur.
Capitol Complex
Carson City, NV 89710
Phone : (702) 687-6815

NEW HAMPSHIRE
Michael L. Buckley
Director of Audits
Post Audit Div.
Off. of Legis. Budget Asst.
State House, Rm. 102
Concord, NH 03301
Phone : (603) 271-2785

NEW JERSEY
Betsy Pugh
Director
Off. of Mgt. & Budget
Dept. of Treasury
33 W. State St.
Trenton, NJ 08625
Phone : (609) 292-6746

NEW MEXICO
Robert E. Vigil
State Auditor
Off. of State Auditor
PERA Bldg., Rm. 302
Santa Fe, NM 87503
Phone : (505) 827-4740
Fax : (505) 827-4750

NEW YORK*
State Comptroller
Off. of the State Comptroller
A.E. Smith Off. Bldg., 6th Fl.
Albany, NY 12236
Phone : (518) 474-4040

NORTH CAROLINA
Ralph Campbell
State Auditor
Dept. of State Auditor
300 N. Salisbury St.
Raleigh, NC 27603
Phone : (919) 733-3217
Fax : (919) 733-8443

NORTH DAKOTA
Robert Peterson
State Auditor
Off. of State Auditor
State Capitol, 3rd Fl.
600 E. Boulevard Ave.
Bismarck, ND 58505
Phone : (701) 328-2241
Fax : (701) 328-3000

Chester E. Nelson, Jr.
Legis. Budget Analyst/ Auditor
Legislative Council
State Capitol, 2nd Fl.
600 E. Boulevard Ave.
Bismarck, ND 58505
Phone : (701) 328-2916
Fax : (701) 328-3615

OHIO
Jim Petro
State Auditor
88 E. Broad St., 5th Fl.
Columbus, OH 43266-0040
Phone : (614) 466-2813
Fax : (614) 466-4490

OKLAHOMA
Clifton Scott
Auditor & Inspector
100 State Capitol
Oklahoma City, OK 73105
Phone : (405) 521-3495

OREGON
Don Waggoner
Director of Audits
Public Srvc. Bldg.
255 Capitol St., NE, Ste. 500
Salem, OR 97310
Phone : (503) 378-3329
Fax : (503) 378-6767

PENNSYLVANIA
Barbara Hafer
Auditor General
229 Finance Bldg.
Harrisburg, PA 17120
Phone : (717) 787-2543

RHODE ISLAND
Christine M. Albuquerque
Chief of General Audit Section
Off. of Accounts & Control
Dept. of Administration
One Capitol Hill
Providence, RI 02908-5883
Phone : (401) 277-2271

Ernest Almonte
Auditor General
Off. of the Auditor General
180 Norwood Ave.
Cranston, RI 02905
Phone : (401) 277-2435

SOUTH CAROLINA
Edgar A. Vaughn, Jr.
State Auditor
State Auditor's Office
P.O. Box 11333
Columbia, SC 29211
Phone : (803) 253-4160

SOUTH DAKOTA
Maurice C. Christiansen
Auditor General
Dept. of Legislative Audit
435 S. Chapelle
Pierre, SD 57501
Phone : (605) 773-3595

TENNESSEE
William R. Snodgrass
Comptroller of the Treasury
State Capitol, 1st Fl.
Nashville, TN 37243
Phone : (615) 741-2501
Fax : (615) 741-7328

TEXAS
Lawrence F. Alwin
State Auditor
Off. of State Auditor
P.O. Box 12067
Austin, TX 78711
Phone : (512) 479-4700

UTAH
Wayne L. Welsh
Audit Manager
Off. of the Legislative Auditor General
State Capitol, Rm. 412
Salt Lake City, UT 84114
Phone : (801) 538-1033

Tom L. Allen
State Auditor
Off. of the State Auditor
211 State Capitol
Salt Lake City, UT 84114
Phone : (801) 538-1360

VERMONT
Edward S. Flanagan
Auditor of Accounts
132 State St.
Montpelier, VT 05602
Phone : (802) 828-2281

VIRGINIA
Walter J. Kucharski
Auditor of Public Accounts
Off. of the Auditor of Public Accounts
101 N. 14th St.
Richmond, VA 23219
Phone : (804) 225-3350
Fax : (804) 225-3357

WASHINGTON
Brian Sonntag
State Auditor
Off. of the State Auditor
Legislative Bldg.
P.O. Box 40021
Olympia, WA 98504-0021
Phone : (360) 753-5277

WEST VIRGINIA
Thedford Shanklin
Director
Post Audit Div.
Bldg. 5, Rm. 751-A
Capitol Complex
Charleston, WV 25305
Phone : (304) 348-2154

WISCONSIN
R. Dale Cattanach
State Auditor
Legislative Audit Bur.
131 W. Wilson St., Rm. 402
Madison, WI 53703
Phone : (608) 266-2818
Fax : (608) 267-0410

WYOMING
Dave Ferrari
State Auditor
State Capitol, Rm. 114
200 W. 24th St.
Cheyenne, WY 82002
Phone : (307) 777-7831

DISTRICT OF COLUMBIA
Otis H. Troupe
Auditor
Presidential Bldg., Rm. 210
415 12th St., NW
Washington, DC 20004
Phone : (202) 727-3600

AMERICAN SAMOA
Wendall Harwell
Territorial Auditor
Off. of the Governor
Pago Pago, AS 96799
Phone : (684) 633-5191

GUAM
Robert G.P. Cruz
Public Auditor
Off. of the Public Auditor
GCIC Bldg., Ste.706
414 W. Soledad Ave.
Agana, GU 96910
Phone : (671) 472-7949
Fax : (671) 472-7951

NORTHERN MARIANA ISLANDS
Leo Lawrence LaMotte
Public Auditor
P.O. Box 1399
Saipan, MP 96950
Phone : (670) 234-6481
Fax : (670) 234-7812

PUERTO RICO
Ileana Colon Carlo
Comptroller
P.O. Box 366069
San Juan, PR 00936-6069
Phone : (809) 754-3030
Fax : (809) 751-6768

U.S. VIRGIN ISLANDS
Steven G. van Beverhoudt
Inspector General
Bur. of Audit & Control
75 Kronprindsens Gade
St. Thomas, VI 00802
Phone : (809) 774-3388
Fax : (809) 774-6431

PRE-AUDIT

Approves or determines the legality of a proposed expenditure before payment is made.

ALABAMA
Robert L. Childree
Comptroller
Dept. of Finance
State House
Montgomery, AL 36130
Phone : (334) 242-7050
Fax : (334) 242-4458

ALASKA
Don Wannie
Director
Div. of Finance
Dept. of Administration
P.O. Box 110204
Juneau, AK 99811-0204
Phone : (907) 465-2240
Fax : (907) 465-2169

ARIZONA
Robert Rocha
State Comptroller
Dept. of Administration
1700 W. Washington, Rm. 290
Phoenix, AZ 85007
Phone : (602) 542-5406

ARKANSAS
Robert Whatley
Manager
Pre-Audit Div.
Dept. of Finance & Admin.
P.O. Box 3278
Little Rock, AR 72203
Phone : (501) 682-1915

CALIFORNIA
Kathleen Connell
Controller
300 Capitol Mall, 18th Fl.
P.O. Box 942850
Sacramento, CA 94250
Phone : (916) 445-2636

COLORADO
Clifford W. Hall
State Controller
Div. of Accounts & Control
Dept. of Admininstration
1525 Sherman St., Ste. 250
Denver, CO 80203
Phone : (303) 866-3281

CONNECTICUT
Nancy Wyman
Comptroller
55 Elm St.
Hartford, CT 06106
Phone : (203) 566-5565

DELAWARE
R. Thomas Wagner, Jr.
State Auditor
Townsend Bldg.
P.O. Box 1401
Dover, DE 19901
Phone : (302) 739-4241

FLORIDA
Larry H. Fuchs
Executive Director
Dept. of Revenue
102 Carlton Bldg.
Tallahassee, FL 32399-0100
Phone : (904) 488-5050
Fax : (904) 488-0024

GEORGIA
Claude Vickers
State Auditor
Dept. of Audits
254 Washington St., Rm. 214
Atlanta, GA 30334
Phone : (404) 656-2174

HAWAII
Wilbert Sakamoto
Accounting Division Chief
Dept. of Accounting & General Services
1151 Punchbowl St., Rm. 320
Honolulu, HI 96813
Phone : (808) 586-0600

IDAHO
J.D. Williams
State Auditor
700 W. State St., 5th Fl.
Boise, ID 83720
Phone : (208) 334-3100

ILLINOIS
Loleta A. Didrickson
Comptroller
201 State House
Springfield, IL 62706
Phone : (217) 782-6000
Fax : (217) 782-7561

INDIANA
Morris Wooden
State Auditor
Off. of the State Auditor
State House, Rm. 240
Indianapolis, IN 46204
Phone : (317) 232-3300

IOWA
Gerald D. Bair
Director
Dept. of Revenue & Finance
Hoover State Off. Bldg.
Des Moines, IA 50319
Phone : (515) 281-3204
Fax : (515) 242-6040

KANSAS
JoAnn Remp
Pre-Audit Unit Supervisor
Div. of Accounts & Reports
Dept. of Administration
Landon State Off. Bldg., Rm. 251-S
Topeka, KS 66612
Phone : (913) 296-2493
Fax : (913) 296-6841

KENTUCKY
Crit Luallen
Secretary
Finance & Admin. Cabinet
Capitol Annex, Rm. 383
Frankfort, KY 40601
Phone : (502) 564-4240

LOUISIANA
Raymond J. Laborde
Commissioner
Div. of Administration
Capitol Annex
P.O. Box 94095
Baton Rouge, LA 70804-9095
Phone : (504) 342-7000

MAINE
Carol Whitney
Controller
Bur. of Accounts & Control
Dept. of Admin. & Fin. Srvcs.
State House Station # 14
Augusta, ME 04333
Phone : (207) 626-8422

MARYLAND
Carol Soutar
Manager for Pre-Audits
General Accounting Div.
State Treasury Bldg., Rm. 200
Annapolis, MD 21404
Phone : (410) 974-3403

MASSACHUSETTS
William Kilmartin
Comptroller
Executive Off. for Administration & Finance
1 Ashburton Pl., Rm. 909
Boston, MA 02108
Phone : (617) 727-5000

MICHIGAN
Thomas McTavish
Auditor General
201 N. Washington Sq.
Lansing, MI 48913
Phone : (517) 334-8050

MINNESOTA
Rosalie Greeman
Assistant Commissioner
Accounting Srvcs. Div.
Dept. of Finance
400 Centennial Bldg.
St. Paul, MN 55155
Phone : (612) 296-1699

MISSOURI
James Carder
Director
Div. of Accounting
Off. of Administration
Truman Bldg., Rm. 560
P.O. Box 809
Jefferson City, MO 65102
Phone : (314) 751-2971
Fax : (314) 751-0159
E-Mail: JCARDER@MAIL.MORE.NET

NEBRASKA
Robert D. Luth
Administrator
Accounting Div.
Dept. of Administrative Srvcs.
1309 State Capitol, Box 94664
Lincoln, NE 68509-4664
Phone : (402) 471-2581

NEVADA
John P. Comeaux
Director
Dept. of Administration
209 E. Musser St., Rm. 200
Carson City, NV 89710
Phone : (702) 687-4065
Fax : (702) 687-3983

NEW HAMPSHIRE
Dayle J. Carroll
Comptroller
Div. of Accounting Srvcs.
Dept. of Admin. Srvcs.
25 Capitol St., Rm. 413
Concord, NH 03301
Phone : (603) 271-3190

NEW JERSEY
Betsy Pugh
Director
Off. of Mgt. & Budget
Dept. of Treasury
33 W. State St.
Trenton, NJ 08625
Phone : (609) 292-6746

NEW MEXICO
Anthony I. Armijo
Director
Financial Control Div.
Dept. of Finance & Admin.
Bataan Memorial Bldg., Rm. 166
Santa Fe, NM 87503
Phone : (505) 827-3689
Fax : (505) 827-3692

NEW YORK*
State Comptroller
Off. of the State Comptroller
A.E. Smith Off. Bldg., 6th Fl.
Albany, NY 12236
Phone : (518) 474-4040

NORTH CAROLINA
Ralph Campbell
State Auditor
Dept. of State Auditor
300 N. Salisbury St.
Raleigh, NC 27603
Phone : (919) 733-3217
Fax : (919) 733-8443

NORTH DAKOTA
Bud Walsh
Director of Accounting
Off. of Mgt. & Budget
State Capitol, 4th Fl.
600 E. Boulevard Ave.
Bismarck, ND 58505-0400
Phone : (701) 328-2682
Fax : (701) 328-3230

OHIO
Jim Petro
State Auditor
88 E. Broad St., 5th Fl.
Columbus, OH 43266-0040
Phone : (614) 466-2813
Fax : (614) 466-4490

OKLAHOMA
Jack E. White
Director
Off. of State Finance
122 State Capitol
Oklahoma City, OK 73105
Phone : (405) 521-2141

PENNSYLVANIA
Catherine Baker Knoll
State Treasurer
129 Finance Bldg.
Harrisburg, PA 17120
Phone : (717) 787-2465

RHODE ISLAND
Christine M. Albuquerque
Chief of General Audit Section
Off. of Accounts & Control
Dept. of Administration
One Capitol Hill
Providence, RI 02908-5883
Phone : (401) 277-2271

SOUTH CAROLINA
Earle E. Morris, Jr.
Comptroller General
Wade Hampton Off. Bldg.
P.O. Box 11228
Columbia, SC 29211
Phone : (803) 734-2121

SOUTH DAKOTA
Vernon L. Larson
State Auditor
500 E. Capitol Ave.
Pierre, SD 57501
Phone : (605) 773-3341
Fax : (605) 773-5929

TENNESSEE
Danny Creekmore
Chief of Accounts
Dept. of Finance & Admin.
206 John Sevier Bldg.
Nashville, TN 37243
Phone : (615) 741-0320

TEXAS
John Sharp
Comptroller
Public Accounts
P.O. Box 13528, Capitol Station
Austin, TX 78711
Phone : (512) 463-4000

UTAH
Gordon L. Crabtree
Director
Div. of Finance
Dept. of Administrative Srvcs.
2110 State Off. Bldg.
Salt Lake City, UT 84114
Phone : (801) 538-3020

VERMONT
Thomas Pelham
Commissioner
Dept. of Finance & Mgt.
Agency of Administration
109 State St.
Montpelier, VT 05602
Phone : (802) 828-2376
Fax : (802) 828-2428

VIRGINIA
William E. Landsidle
Comptroller
Dept. of Accounts
P.O. Box 6-N
Richmond, VA 23215
Phone : (804) 225-2109
Fax : (804) 371-8587

WASHINGTON
Daniel Grimm
State Treasurer
Legislative Bldg.
P.O. Box 40200
Olympia, WA 98504-0200
Phone : (360) 753-7130

WEST VIRGINIA
Charles Polan
Secretary
Dept. of Finance & Admin.
State Capitol, Rm. E119
1900 Kanawha Blvd., E.
Charleston, WV 25305
Phone : (304) 558-2300
Fax : (304) 558-2999

WISCONSIN
Jim Behrend
Chief, Audit Section
Bureau of Financial Operations
Dept. of Administration
101 E Wilson, 8th Fl.
P.O. Box 784
Madison, WI 53703
Phone : (608) 266-1694
Fax : (608) 266-7734

WYOMING
Dave Ferrari
State Auditor
State Capitol, Rm. 114
200 W. 24th St.
Cheyenne, WY 82002
Phone : (307) 777-7831

DISTRICT OF COLUMBIA
Robert Pohlman
Chief Financial Officer
Financial Mgt.
441 4th St., N.W., Ste. 1150
Washington, DC 20001
Phone : (202) 727-2476

Robert Reid
Controller
Off. of Deputy Mayor for Finance
415 12th St., N.W., Rm. 412
Washington, DC 20004
Phone : (202) 727-5116

GUAM
Joseph E. Rivera
Acting Director
Bur. of Budget & Mgt. Research
P.O. Box 2950
Agana, GU 96910
Phone : (671) 472-8931
Fax : (671) 472-2825

NORTHERN MARIANA ISLANDS
Maria D. Cabrera
Secretary
Dept. of Finance
P.O. Box 5234 CHRB
Saipan, MP 96950
Phone : (670) 664-1100
Fax : (670) 664-1115

PUERTO RICO
Manuel Diaz Saldana
Secretary
Dept. of Treasury
P.O. Box S-4515
San Juan, PR 00905
Phone : (809) 721-2020
Fax : (809) 723-6213

U.S. VIRGIN ISLANDS
Gwendolyn P. Adams
Commissioner
Dept. of Finance
76 Kronprindsens Gade
St. Thomas, VI 00802
Phone : (809) 774-4750
Fax : (809) 776-4028

PRESS SECRETARY

Individual who handles communications with the public, press conferences and news releases for the Governor.

ALABAMA
Donald J. Claxton
Press Secretary
Governor's Office
600 Dexter Ave.
Montgomery, AL 36130
Phone : (334) 242-7150
Fax: (334) 242-4407

ALASKA
Bob King
Press Secretary
Off. of the Governor
P.O. Box 110001
Juneau, AK 99811-0001
Phone : (907) 465-3500
Fax : (907) 465-3533

ARIZONA
Doug Cole
Press Secretary
Off. of the Governor
1700 W. Washington
Phoenix, AZ 85007
Phone : (602) 542-4331

ARKANSAS
Max Parker
Press Secretary
Off. of the Governor
State Capitol, Rm. 250
Little Rock, AR 72201
Phone : (501) 682-2345
Fax : (501) 682-3597

CALIFORNIA
Leslie Goodman
Director of
Communications
Off. of the Governor
State Capitol
Sacramento, CA 95814
Phone : (916) 445-4571

COLORADO
James Carpenter
Press Secretary
Off. of the Governor
127 State Capitol
Denver, CO 80203
Phone : (303) 866-4572
Fax : (303) 866-2003

CONNECTICUT
John Chapin
Press Secretary
Off. of the Governor
200 State Capitol
Hartford, CT 06106
Phone : (203) 566-4840

DELAWARE
Sheri Woodruff
Press Secretary
Off. of the Governor
820 N. French St.
Wilmington, DE 19901
Phone : (302) 577-3210
Fax : (302) 577-3188

FLORIDA
Joanne Miglino
Press Secretary
Executive Off. of the
Governor
The Capitol
Tallahassee, FL 32399
Phone : (904) 488-5394

GEORGIA
Rick Dent
Director of
Communication
Off. of the Governor
100 State Capitol
Atlanta, GA 30334
Phone : (404) 651-7774

HAWAII
Randy Obata
News Secretary
Off. of the Governor
State Capitol
Honolulu, HI 96813
Phone : (808) 586-0034
Fax : (808) 586-0006

IDAHO
Amy Kleiner
Press Secretary
Office of the Governor
Statehouse
Boise, ID 83720
Phone : (208) 334-2100

ILLINOIS
Mike Lawrence
Press Secretary
Off. of the Governor
205 State House
Springfield, IL 62706
Phone : (217) 782-7355
Fax : (217) 524-1676

INDIANA
Fred J. Nation
Press Secretary
Off. of the Governor
State House, Rm. 206
Indianapolis, IN 46204
Phone : (317) 232-4578

IOWA
Christina Martin
Press Secretary
Off. of the Governor
State Capitol
Des Moines, IA 50319
Phone : (515) 281-3150
Fax : (515) 281-6611

KANSAS
Mike Matson
Press Secretary
Off. of the Governor
State Capitol Bldg., 2nd Fl.
Topeka, KS 66612-1590
Phone : (913) 296-3232
Fax : (913) 296-2158

KENTUCKY
Joe Lilly
Press Secretary
Off. of the Governor
State Capitol, Rm. 100
Frankfort, KY 40601
Phone : (502) 564-2611

LOUISIANA
Kim Hunter
Press Secretary
Off. of the Governor
P.O. Box 94004
Baton Rouge, LA 70804
Phone : (504) 342-9037

MAINE
Dennis Bailey
Press Secretary
Off. of the Governor
State House Station #1
Augusta, ME 04333
Phone : (207) 287-3531
Fax : (207) 287-1034

MARYLAND
Dianna Rosborough
Press Secretary
Off. of the Governor
State House
Annapolis, MD 21401
Phone : (410) 974-2316

MASSACHUSETTS
Virginia Buckingham
Press Secretary
Press Off. of the Governor
State House, Rm. 265
Boston, MA 02133
Phone : (617) 727-2759

MICHIGAN
John Truscott
Press Secretary
Communications Div.
Off. of the Governor
P.O. Box 30013
Lansing, MI 48909
Phone : (517) 373-3400

MINNESOTA
Cyndy Brucato
Deputy Chief of Staff/
Comm. Dir.
Off. of the Governor
130 State Capitol
St. Paul, MN 55155
Phone : (612) 296-0017

MISSISSIPPI
Johnna Van
Press Secretary
Off. of the Governor
New Capitol
P.O. Box 139
Jackson, MS 39205
Phone : (601) 359-3100

MISSOURI
Chris Sifford
Director of Communications
Off. of the Governor
State Capitol, Rm. 218
P.O. Box 720
Jefferson City, MO 65102
Phone : (314) 751-3222
Fax : (314) 751-4458
E-Mail: CSIFFORD@SERVICES.MORE.NET

MONTANA
Rorie Hanrahan
Press Secretary
Off. of the Governor
Capitol Station
Helena, MT 59620-0801
Phone : (406) 444-3111

NEBRASKA
Diane Gonzolas
Director of Public Affairs
Off. of the Governor
State Capitol, 2nd Fl.
Lincoln, NE 68509-4848
Phone : (402) 471-2244

NEVADA
Richard Urey
Press Secretary
Off. of the Governor
Capitol Complex
Carson City, NV 89710
Phone : (702) 687-5670
Fax : (702) 687-4486

NEW HAMPSHIRE
Jim Rivers
Press Secretary
Off. of the Governor
State House, Rm. 208
Concord, NH 03301
Phone : (603) 271-2121

NEW JERSEY
Carl Golden
Director
Off. of Communications
Off. of the Governor
State House, CN-001
Trenton, NJ 08625
Phone : (609) 292-6000

NEW MEXICO
Diane Kinderwater
Press Secretary
Off. of the Governor
State Capitol
Santa Fe, NM 87503
Phone : (505) 827-3000
Fax : (505) 827-3026

NEW YORK*
Press Secretary
Executive Chamber
State Capitol, Rm. 201
Albany, NY 12224
Phone : (518) 474-8418

NORTH CAROLINA
Rachel Perry
Director
Press Office
Off. of the Governor
State Capitol
Raleigh, NC 27601-2905
Phone : (919) 733-5612
Fax : (919) 733-5166

NORTH DAKOTA
Rick Collin
Communicaitons Director
Off. of the Governor
State Capitol, 1st Fl.
600 E. Boulevard Ave.
Bismarck, ND 58505-0001
Phone : (701) 328-2000
Fax : (701) 328-2205

OHIO
Michael Dawson
Press Secretary
Off. of the Governor
77 S. High St., 30th Fl.
Columbus, OH 43266-0601
Phone : (614) 644-0957
Fax : (614) 644-0951

OKLAHOMA
Rick Buchanan
Press Secretary
Off. of the Governor
212 State Capitol Bldg.
Oklahoma City, OK 73105
Phone : (405) 521-2342
Fax : (405) 521-3353

OREGON
Robert Applegate
Communications Director
Off. of the Governor
254 State Capitol
Salem, OR 97310
Phone : (503) 378-6496
Fax : (503) 378-8970

PENNSYLVANIA
Tim Reeves
Press Secretary
Off. of the Governor
Main Capitol Bldg., Rm. 308
Harrisburg, PA 17120
Phone : (717) 783-1116

RHODE ISLAND
Jim Taricahi
Director of Communications
Off. of the Governor
State House
Providence, RI 02903
Phone : (401) 277-2080

SOUTH CAROLINA
Ginny Wolfe
Press Secretary
Off. of the Governor
State House
P.O. Box 11369
Columbia, SC 29211
Phone : (803) 734-9818

SOUTH DAKOTA
Jim Soyer
Press Secretary
Off. of the Governor
500 E. Capitol Ave.
Pierre, SD 57501
Phone : (605) 773-3212

TENNESSEE
Beth Fortune
Director of Communications
Off. of the Governor
State Capitol
Nashville, TN 37243-0001
Phone : (615) 741-3763
Fax : (615) 741-1416

TEXAS
Karen Hughes
Director
Communications
Office of the Governor
P.O. Box 12428, Capitol Station
Austin, TX 78711
Phone : (512) 463-1826

UTAH
Vicki Varela
Deputy for Public Affairs
Off. of the Governor
210 State Capitol
Salt Lake City, UT 84114
Phone : (801) 538-1000

VERMONT
Stephanie Carter
Press Secretary
Executive Dept.
109 State St.
Montpelier, VT 05602
Phone : (802) 828-3333
Fax : (802) 828-3339

VIRGINIA
Kenneth S. Stroupe, Jr.
Press Secretary
Office of the Governor
State Capitol
Richmond, VA 23219
Phone : (804) 786-2211
Fax : (804) 371-6433

WASHINGTON
Jordan Dey
Communications Director
Off. of the Governor
Legislative Bldg.
P.O. Box 40002
Olympia, WA 98504
Phone : (360) 753-6790

WEST VIRGINIA
Jill Wilson
Press Secretary
Off. of the Governor
1900 Kanawha Blvd., E.
Charleston, WV 25305
Phone : (304) 558-2000

WISCONSIN
Kevin Keane
Press Secretary
Off. of the Governor
115 East, State Capitol
Box 7863
Madison, WI 53702
Phone : (608) 266-1212
Fax : (608) 266-3970

WYOMING
Jimmy Orr
Press Secretary
Off. of the Governor
State Capitol
Cheyenne, WY 82002
Phone : (307) 777-7930

DISTRICT OF COLUMBIA
Raymone Bain
Press Secretary
Executive Off. of the Mayor
441 4th St., N.W., Ste. 1100
Washington, DC 20001
Phone : (202) 727-5011

AMERICAN SAMOA
Aleni Ripine
Chief of Staff
Off. of the Governor
Pago Pago, AS 96799
Phone : (684) 633-4116
Fax : (684) 633-2269

Press Secretary

GUAM
Patrick McMurtry
Communications Director
Off. of the Governor
P.O. Box 2950
Agana, GU 96910
Phone : (671) 475-9309
Fax : (671) 475-6462

NORTHERN MARIANA ISLANDS
John B. Joyner
Public Information Officer
Off. of the Governor
Saipan, MP 96950
Phone : (670) 322-5094

PUERTO RICO
Rafael Cerame
Press Secretary
Off. of the Governor
La Fortaleza
San Juan, PR 00901
Phone : (809) 721-7000
Fax : (809) 723-8191

U.S. VIRGIN ISLANDS
Leona Bryant
Press Secretary
Dir. Public Relations Off.
#38 Kongens Gade
St. Thomas, VI 00802
Phone : (809) 774-0294
Fax : (809) 774-4988

PRINTING

Central state entity responsible for supplying the printing needs of state government.

ALABAMA
Gerald W. Wilson
Acting Director
Div. of Printing & Pubs.
Dept. of Finance
660 Chisholm St.
Montgomery, AL 36130
Phone : (334) 242-2808
Fax : (334) 242-7974

ALASKA
Dugan Petty
Director
Div. of General Srvcs. & Sup.
Dept. of Administration
P.O. Box 110210
Juneau, AK 99811-0210
Phone : (907) 465-2250
Fax : (907) 465-2189

ARIZONA
Ed Boot
Assistant Director
General Services Division
Dept. of Admininistration
1700 W. Washington, Rm. 600
Phoenix, AZ 85007
Phone : (602) 542-1920

ARKANSAS
Edward Erxleben
Director
Off. of State Purchasing
Dept. of Finance & Admin.
P.O. Box 2940
Little Rock, AR 72203
Phone : (501) 324-9312
Fax : (501) 324-9311

CALIFORNIA
Celeste M. Cron
State Printer
Off. of State Printing
344 N. 7th St.
Sacramento, CA 95814
Phone : (916) 445-9110

COLORADO
Bob O'Lear
Manager
State Printing Plant
Central Services Div.
1001 E. 62nd Ave.
Denver, CO 80216
Phone : (303) 287-2057
Fax : (303) 287-1926

CONNECTICUT
John Wadsworth
Director
Div. of Prtng. & Mailing Srvcs.
Dept. of Administrative Srvcs.
165 Capitol Ave., Rm. 223
Hartford, CT 06106
Phone : (203) 566-3997

DELAWARE
Patrick T. Coates, Sr.
Director
Div. of Support Operations
Tudor Industrial Park
604 Otis Dr.
Dover, DE 19901
Phone : (302) 739-5371
Fax : (302) 739-3492

FLORIDA
George C. Banks
Director
Div. of Purchasing
Dept. of Management Srvcs.
2737 Centerview Dr.
Knight Bldg., Ste. 206
Tallahassee, FL 32399-0950
Phone : (904) 488-7303

GEORGIA
Linda Stephens
Printing Administrator
General Srvcs. Div.
Dept. of Admin. Srvcs.
200 Piedmont Ave., NE, # 422-W
Atlanta, GA 30303-1702
Phone : (404) 756-4646

HAWAII
Marilyn McAuley
Corrections Industries Administrator
State Corrections Industries
Dept. of Public Safety
99-902 Moanalua Hwy.
Aiea, HI 96701
Phone : (808) 486-4883

IDAHO
Bobbi Eckerle
Chief
Records Mgt. & Printing Srvcs.
5569 Kendall Ctr.
Boise, ID 83720
Phone : (208) 327-7471

ILLINOIS
Nicholas Whitlow
Superintendent
Div. of Printing
Dept. of Central Mgt. Srvcs.
425 S. 4th St.
Springfield, IL 62701
Phone : (217) 782-4561
Fax : (217) 785-1229

INDIANA
Jerry Handfield
Director
Comm. of Public Records
Div. of Central Printing
100 N. Senate Ave.
Indianapolis, IN 46202-3205
Phone : (317) 232-3373

IOWA
Kristi Little
Superintendent of Printing
Dept. of General Srvcs.
Grimes State Off. Bldg.
400 E. 14th St.
Des Moines, IA 50319
Phone : (515) 281-5050

KANSAS
Richard Gonzales
Director
Division of Printing
Dept. of Administration
201 NW MacVicar
Topeka, KS 66606-2499
Phone : (913) 296-3631

KENTUCKY
Pam Burns
Director
Div. of Printing
Finance & Admin. Cabinet
300 Myrtle Ave.
Frankfort, KY 40601
Phone : (502) 564-2670

LOUISIANA
Irene Babin
Director
Forms Mgt. & Print Shop
Div. of Administration
P.O. Box 94095
Baton Rouge, LA 70804
Phone : (504) 342-7000

MAINE
Richard Thompson
Director
Div. of Public Printing
State House Station # 9
Augusta, ME 04333
Phone : (207) 287-3521

MARYLAND**
Martin W. Walsh Jr.
Secretary
Dept. of General Srvcs.
301 W. Preston St., Rm. 1401
Baltimore, MD 21201
Phone : (410) 225-4960

MASSACHUSETTS
Ed Goba
Manager
Central Reproduction Off.
1 Ashburton Pl.
Boston, MA 02108
Phone : (617) 727-6232

MICHIGAN
Mark Armbrustmacher
Manager
Reproduction Srvcs. Section
Office Services Division
7461 Crowner Dr.
Lansing, MI 48913
Phone : (517) 322-1889

MINNESOTA
Kathi Lynch
Manager
Print Communications Div.
Dept. of Administration
117 Univ. Ave., Rm. 128A
St. Paul, MN 55155
Phone : (612) 296-3277

MISSISSIPPI
Bobby Green Lee
Director
Joint Legislative Operations
400 High St.
P.O. Box 1018
Jackson, MS 39215-1018
Phone : (601) 359-1580

MISSOURI
Gary Judd
Printing Services Manager
State Printing Center
Div. of General Services
Off. of Administration
2733 Merchants Dr.
Jefferson City, MO 65109
Phone : (314) 751-3307
Fax : (314) 751-8263

MONTANA
Gary Wolf
Chief
Bur. of Pubs. & Graphics
920 Front St.
Helena, MT 59620-0132
Phone : (406) 444-3053

NEBRASKA
Steve Condrey
Dept. of Administrative Srvcs.
P.O. Box 94847
Lincoln, NE 68509-4847
Phone : (402) 471-2826

NEVADA
Donald L. Bailey Sr.
State Printer
Printing Div.
Dept. of General Services
301 S. Stewart St.
Carson City, NV 89710
Phone : (702) 687-4860

NEW HAMPSHIRE
James Dufour
Administrator
Bur. of Graphic Srvcs.
12 Hills Ave.
Concord, NH 03301
Phone : (603) 271-3205

NEW JERSEY
George Davis
Manager
Printing Control Off.
Div. of Purchasing Property
135 W. Hanover St.
Trenton, NJ 08625
Phone : (609) 984-6234

NEW MEXICO*
State Printing Bur.
Dept. of General Srvcs.
P.O. Drawer 26110
Santa Fe, NM 87503
Phone : (505) 827-6265
Fax : (505) 827-6276

NEW YORK*
Chief, Offset Printing Machine Op.
Central Production Unit
Off. of General Srvcs.
State Campus, Bldg. 18
Albany, NY 12226
Phone : (518) 457-6593

NORTH CAROLINA
Medwick Byrd
State Printing Officer
Off. of State Printing
116 W. Jones St.
Raleigh, NC 27603-8002
Phone : (919) 733-5194

NORTH DAKOTA
Jim Kapp
Manager
Central Duplicating Srvcs.
Div. of Printing
Jud. Wing, Basement, St. Cap.
Bismarck, ND 58505
Phone : (701) 328-2772
Fax : (701) 328-3000

OHIO
Robert Schleppi
Administrator
Div. of Printing
Dept. of Administrative Srvcs.
4200 Surface Rd.
Columbus, OH 43228-1395
Phone : (614) 466-8334
Fax : (614) 644-5799

OKLAHOMA
Gerlinde Williams
Administrator
Central Printing Div.
2120 N.E. 36th St.
Oklahoma City, OK 73111
Phone : (405) 425-2714

OREGON
Jerry Wagner
State Printer
Printing Plant
Dept. of Admin. Srvc.
550 Airport Rd., SE
Salem, OR 97310
Phone : (503) 378-3397
Fax : (503) 373-7789

PENNSYLVANIA*
Director
Bur. of Pub. & Paperwork Mgt.
Dept. of General Srvcs.
1825 Stanley Dr.
Harrisburg, PA 17103
Phone : (717) 787-3707

SOUTH CAROLINA
Bunyan M. Cave
State Printing Officer
Info. Tech. Mgt. Off.
Div. of General Srvcs.
1201 Main St., Ste. 600
Columbia, SC 29201
Phone : (803) 737-0629

SOUTH DAKOTA
Donald L. Monge
Director
Div. of Central Duplicating
Dept. of Administration
500 E. Capitol Ave.
Pierre, SD 57501
Phone : (605) 773-3614

TENNESSEE
Leroy Richmond
Director of Printing
Dept. of General Srvcs.
Andrew Jackson Bldg.
Nashville, TN 37243-0450
Phone : (615) 741-1726
Fax : (615) 532-2311

TEXAS
John White
Purchaser
General Srvcs. Comm.
P.O. Box 13047
Austin, TX 78711
Phone : (512) 463-3373

UTAH
Mark Shaw
Director
Legislative Printing Off.
419 State Capitol
Salt Lake City, UT 84114
Phone : (801) 538-1103

VERMONT
Paul F. Ohlson
Commissioner
Dept. of General Services
133 State St.
Montpelier, VT 05602
Phone : (802) 828-3331
Fax : (802) 828-2327

VIRGINIA
Donald C. Williams
Director
Dept. of General Services
209 9th St. Off. Bldg.
Richmond, VA 23219
Phone : (804) 786-3311
Fax : (804) 371-8305

WASHINGTON
Leland Blankenship
Public Printer
Dept. of Printing
P.O. Box 47100
Olympia, WA 98504-0002
Phone : (360) 753-6820

WEST VIRGINIA
Scott Padon
Assistant Director
Operations Section
Div. of Purchasing
212 California Ave.
Charleston, WV 25305
Phone : (304) 558-3808

WISCONSIN
James Hoverson
Chief
Div. of Printing & Publication
Dept. of Administration
202 S. Thornton
P.O. Box 7840
Madison, WI 53703
Phone : (608) 266-9327
Fax : (608) 267-6933

WYOMING
Dan E. Cunningham
Manager
Central Printing
Dept. of Admin. &
Information
720 W. 18th St.
Cheyenne, WY 82002-0060
Phone : (307) 777-6564

DISTRICT OF COLUMBIA
Freeman M. Murray
Chief
Printing Div.
Dept. of Administrative
Srvcs.
809 Channing Pl., N.E.
Washington, DC 20018
Phone : (202) 576-6693

AMERICAN SAMOA
Fa'i Faaita
Director
Dept. of Administrative
Srvcs.
American Samoa Govt.
Pago Pago, AS 96799
Phone : (684) 633-4156
Fax : (684) 633-1841

PUERTO RICO*
Administrator
General Services Admin.
P.O. Box 7428
San Juan, PR 00916
Phone : (809) 721-7370
Fax : (809) 722-7965

U.S. VIRGIN ISLANDS
Lawrence Ottley
Director of Printing
Dept. of Property &
Procurement
Sub Base Bldg. # 1
St. Thomas, VI 00802
Phone : (809) 774-0828

PUBLIC BROADCASTING

Controls and supervises the use of television channels assigned for non-commercial, educational use.

ALABAMA
Judy Stone
Executive Director
Education Television Comm.
2112 11th Ave., N.
Birmingham, AL 35256
Phone : (205) 328-8756
Fax : (205) 251-2192

ALASKA
Douglas Samimi-Moore
Executive Director
State Public Broadcasting Comm.
Dept. of Administration
P.O. Box 110223
Juneau, AK 99811-0223
Phone : (907) 465-2846
Fax : (907) 465-2496

ARKANSAS
Susan Howarth
Director
Educational Television Comm.
Dept. of Education
350 S. Donaghey St.
Conway, AR 72032
Phone : (501) 682-2386
Fax : (501) 682-4122

CONNECTICUT
Joan S. Briggaman
Assistant Supt.
Instruction and Professional Development
165 Capitol Ave.
Hartford, CT 06106
Phone : (203) 566-8113

FLORIDA
Eric C. Smith
Director
Office of Telecommunications
Dept. of Education
325 W. Gaines St., Ste. 154
Tallahassee, FL 32399-0400
Phone : (904) 488-0940

GEORGIA
Werner Rogers
Executive Director
Public Television Comm.
1540 Stewart Ave., SW
Atlanta, GA 30310
Phone : (404) 756-4710

HAWAII
James B. Young
Executive Director
Public Broadcasting Authority
Commerce & Consumer Aff. Dept.
2350 Dole St.
Honolulu, HI 96822
Phone : (808) 955-7878

IDAHO
Jerold Garber
General Manager
Educational Public Broadcasting
State Board of Education
1910 University Dr.
Boise, ID 83725
Phone : (208) 385-3727

ILLINOIS
Joseph A. Spagnolo
Superintendent
State Board of Education
100 N. First St.
Springfield, IL 62777
Phone : (217) 782-2221
Fax : (217) 785-3972

IOWA
Davis Bolender
Director
State Public Television
P.O. Box 6450
Johnston, IA 50131
Phone : (515) 242-3150

KANSAS
Susan Seltsam
Secretary
Public Broadcasting Council
Landon State Off. Bldg., Rm. 751-S
Topeka, KS 66612-1275
Phone : (913) 296-3463

KENTUCKY
Virginia G. Fox
Executive Director
Educational Television Authority
600 Cooper Dr.
Lexington, KY 40502
Phone : (606) 233-3000

LOUISIANA
Beth Courtney
Executive Director
Educational Television Authority
7860 Anselmo Ln.
Baton Rouge, LA 70810
Phone : (504) 342-1370

MARYLAND
Raymond K.K. Ho
President
Public Broadcasting Comm.
Dept. of Education
11767 Owings Mills Blvd.
Owings Mills, MD 21117
Phone : (410) 581-4141

MASSACHUSETTS
Linda Beardsly
Associate Commissioner
Bur. of Curriculum Instruction & Technologies
1385 Hancock St.
Quincy, MA 02169
Phone : (617) 338-3300

MINNESOTA
Larry Freund
Acting Director
Admin. Srvcs. Div.
Dept. of Admin.
50 Sherburne Ave., 2nd Fl.
St. Paul, MN 55155
Phone : (612) 296-5857

MISSISSIPPI
Larry Miller
Executive Director
Mississippi Education Television
3825 Ridgewood Rd.
Jackson, MS 39211-6463
Phone : (601) 982-6565

MONTANA
Carl Hotvedt
Chief
Telecommunications Bur.
Dept. of Admin.
Mitchell Bldg., Rm. 21
Helena, MT 59620
Phone : (406) 444-2700

NEBRASKA
Herbert H. Schimek
Chairman
Education Television Comm.
1800 N. 33rd St.
P.O. Box 83111
Lincoln, NE 68501-3111
Phone : (402) 472-3611

NEW JERSEY
Elizabeth Christophers
Executive Director
Public Broadcasting Authority
Dept. of Commerce & Econ. Dev.
25 S. Stockton St., CN-777
Trenton, NJ 08625
Phone : (609) 777-5000

NEW YORK*
Commissioner
Dept. of Education
Education Bldg.
Albany, NY 12234
Phone : (518) 474-5844

NORTH DAKOTA
Joe Linnertz
Staff Director
Educational Telecom. Council
State Capitol, 11th Fl.
600 E. Boulevard Ave.
Bismarck, ND 58505
Phone : (701) 328-3216

OHIO
Dave L. Fornshell
Executive Director
Educational Broadcasting Network Comm.
2470 N. Star Rd.
Columbus, OH 43221
Phone : (614) 644-1714
Fax : (614) 644-3112

OKLAHOMA
Bob Allen
Executive Director
Educational Television Authority
7403 N. Kelly
Oklahoma City, OK 73113
Phone : (405) 848-8501

OREGON
Maynard E. Orme
Executive Director
State Public Broadcasting
7140 S.W. Macadam Ave.
Portland, OR 97219
Phone : (503) 293-1900
Fax : (503) 293-4000

PENNSYLVANIA
H. Sheldon Parker, Jr.
General Manager
Public TV Network Comm.
24 Northeast Dr.
Hershey, PA 17033
Phone : (717) 533-6010

RHODE ISLAND
Susan L. Farmer
General Manager
WSBE-TV Channel 36
Dept. of Education
50 Park Ln.
Providence, RI 02907-3124
Phone : (401) 277-3636

SOUTH CAROLINA
Henry J. Cauthen
President & General Manager
Educational Television Network
2712 Millwood Ave.
P.O. Drawer L
Columbia, SC 29250
Phone : (803) 737-3240

SOUTH DAKOTA
Don Checots
Executive Director
Public Broadcasting
Cherry & Dakota Sts.
P.O. Box 5000
Vermillion, SD 57069-5000
Phone : (605) 677-5861

TEXAS
Fred Brown
Program Director
Div. of Education Technology
State Education Agency
1701 N. Congress Ave.
Austin, TX 78701
Phone : (512) 463-9087

UTAH
Cecelia Foxley
Commissioner
Board of Regents
3 Triad Ctr., Ste. 550
Salt Lake City, UT 84180-1205
Phone : (801) 321-7103

VERMONT
Hope Green
Station Manager
State Educational Television
University of Vermont
88 Ethan Allen Ave.
Colchester, VT 05446
Phone : (802) 655-4800

VIRGINIA
Charles C. Livingston
Director
Dept. of Information Technology
Richmond Plaza Bldg., 3rd Fl.
1105 7th St.
Richmond, VA 23219
Phone : (804) 344-5500
Fax : (804) 344-5505

WASHINGTON
Gayle Pauley
Supervisor, Learning Resources
Supt. of Public Instruction
Old Capitol Bldg.
P.O. Box 47200
Olympia, WA 98504-7200
Phone : (360) 753-6723

WEST VIRGINIA*
Acting Executive Director
Educational Broadcasting Authority
600 Capitol St.
Charleston, WV 25301
Phone : (304) 348-3400

WISCONSIN
Glenn Davison
Executive Director
Television Network
Programs & Operations
Educational Communications Board
3319 W. Beltline Hwy.
Madison, WI 53713
Phone : (608) 264-9600
Fax : (608) 264-9664

WYOMING
Larry Stolz
Administrator, Div. of Telecomm.
Dept. of Admin. & Information
Emerson Bldg., Rm. B-1
2001 Capitol Ave.
Cheyenne, WY 82002
Phone : (307) 777-6410

DISTRICT OF COLUMBIA
Elizabeth Lawson
Executive Director
Off. of Cable Television
2217 14th St., NW
Washington, DC 20009
Phone : (202) 727-0424

AMERICAN SAMOA
Vaoita Savali
Director
Public Information
Pago Pago, AS 96799
Phone : (684) 633-4191
Fax : (684) 633-1044

GUAM
Geraldine Underwood
Acting General Manager
Educational Telecommunications Corp.
P.O. Box 21449
GMF, GU 96921
Phone : (671) 734-2207
Fax : (671) 734-5483

NORTHERN MARIANA ISLANDS
Timothy P. Villagomez
Executive Director
Commonwealth Utilities Corp.
Off. of the Governor
Lower Base
Saipan, MP 96950
Phone : (670) 322-4033
Fax : (670) 322-4323

PUERTO RICO
Jorge Inserni
General Administrator
Dept. of Education
P.O. Box 909
Hato Rey, PR 00919
Phone : (809) 763-3666

U.S. VIRGIN ISLANDS
Calvin Bastian
General Manager
Public Television Systems Board
P.O. Box 7879
St. Thomas, VI 00801
Phone : (809) 774-6255

PUBLIC DEFENDER

Represents indigent criminal defendants who desire to appeal their convictions to the state's intermediate appellate court or court of last resort.

ALASKA
John Salemi
Director
Public Defender Agency
Dept. of Administration
900 W. Fifth Ave., Ste. 200
Anchorage, AK 99501-2090
Phone : (907) 264-4400
Fax : (907) 269-5476

CALIFORNIA
Fern M. Laethem
Public Defender
Off. of State Public Defender
801 K St., Ste. 1000
Sacramento, CA 95814
Phone : (916) 322-2676

COLORADO
David F. Vela
State Public Defender
Judicial Dept.
110 16th St., Ste. 800
Denver, CO 80202
Phone : (303) 620-4888

CONNECTICUT
Gerard Smyth
Chief Public Defender
Off. of Chief Public Defender
1 Hartford Sq., W.
Hartford, CT 06106
Phone : (203) 566-5328

DELAWARE
Lawrence Sullivan
Public Defender
Carvel State Off. Bldg.
820 N. French St.
Wilmington, DE 19801
Phone : (302) 577-3230
Fax : (302) 577-3995

FLORIDA
Nancy Daniels
Public Defender
Leon Cty. Courthouse, 4th Fl.
301 S. Monroe St., Ste. 401
Tallahassee, FL 32301
Phone : (904) 488-2458

GEORGIA
Michael J. Bowers
Attorney General
Dept. of Law
40 Capitol Square
Atlanta, GA 30334-1300
Phone : (404) 656-4585
Fax : (404) 651-9148

HAWAII
Richard Pollack
Public Defender
Off. of Public Defender
Dept. of Budget & Finance
1130 N. Nimitz, Hwy., # A-135
Honolulu, HI 96817
Phone : (808) 586-2222

ILLINOIS
Ted Gottfried
State Appellate Defender
400 S. Ninth St. # 201
Springfield, IL 62701-1908
Phone : (217) 782-7203

INDIANA
Susan K. Carpenter
Public Defender
Off. of Public Defender
1 N. Capitol Ave., Ste. 800
Indianapolis, IN 46204-2026
Phone : (317) 232-2475

IOWA
William Wegman
Appellate Defender
Dept. of Inspections & Appeals
Lucas State Off. Bldg.
Des Moines, IA 50319
Phone : (515) 281-8841

KANSAS
Al Bandy
Public Defender
State Board of Indigent's Defense Services
Landon State Off. Bldg., Rm. 304
Topeka, KS 66612-1255
Phone : (913) 296-1833
Fax : (913) 296-7418

KENTUCKY
Allison Connelly
Public Advocate
Off. for Public Advocacy
Justice Cabinet
Swear Oaks Lane, Ste. 302
Frankfort, KY 40601
Phone : (502) 564-5213

LOUISIANA
Richard Ieyoub, Jr.
Attorney General
Dept. of Justice
P.O. Box 94005
Baton Rouge, LA 70804
Phone : (504) 342-7013

MARYLAND
Stephen E. Harris
Public Defender
Off. of Public Defender
201 St. Paul Pl.
Baltimore, MD 21202
Phone : (301) 333-4826

MASSACHUSETTS
William Leahy
Chief Counsel
Cmte. for Public Counsel Srvcs.
470 Atlantic Ave., Ste. 700
Boston, MA 02210
Phone : (617) 482-6212

MICHIGAN
James Neuhard
State Appellate Defender
Supreme Court
North Tower, 3rd Fl.
1200 Sixth Ave.
Detroit, MI 48226
Phone : (313) 256-2814

MINNESOTA
John Stewart
Public Defender
University of Minnesota
95 Law Ctr.
Minneapolis, MN 55455
Phone : (612) 625-5008

MISSOURI
J. Marty Robinson
Director
Off. of State Public Defender
231 E. Capitol
Jefferson City, MO 65101
Phone : (314) 526-5210
Fax : (314) 526-5213

NEVADA
James J. Jackson
State Public Defender
303 E. Procter St.
Carson City, NV 89710
Phone : (702) 687-4880

NEW MEXICO
Sammy Quintana
Chief Public Defender
Public Defender Dept.
301 N. Guadalupe St., # 101
Santa Fe, NM 87501-1852
Phone : (505) 827-3900
Fax : (505) 827-3999

NORTH CAROLINA
Tye Hunter
Appellate Defender
Off. of Appellate Defender
1905 Meredith Dr., #200
Durham, NC 27713-2287
Phone : (919) 733-9490

OHIO
David H. Bodiker
Public Defender
Public Defender Comm.
8 E. Long St.
Columbus, OH 43215
Phone : (614) 466-5394
Fax : (614) 644-9972

OKLAHOMA
Ronald Chance
Director
Appellate Public Defender System
1660 Cross Center
Norman, OK 73019
Phone : (405) 325-3168

OREGON
Sally L. Avera
Public Defender
603 Cheneketa St., NE
Salem, OR 97310
Phone : (503) 378-3349
Fax : (503) 375-9701

RHODE ISLAND
Richard M. Casparian
Public Defender
100 N. Main St., 4th Fl.
Providence, RI 02903-1311
Phone : (401) 277-3490

SOUTH CAROLINA
Daniel T. Stacey
Chief Attorney
Off. of Appellate Defense
1122 Lady St., Ste. 940
Columbia, SC 29201
Phone : (803) 734-1330

VERMONT
Robert Appel
Defender General
141 Main St.
State Off. Bldg.
Montpelier, VT 05620-3301
Phone : (802) 828-3168
Fax : (802) 828-3163

VIRGINIA
Overton P. Pollard
Executive Director
Public Defender Comm.
701 E. Franklin St., # 910
Richmond, VA 23219
Phone : (804) 225-3297

WEST VIRGINIA
John A. Rogers
Executive Director
Public Defender Srvcs.
Public Legal Srvcs. Council
1900 Kanawha Blvd., E.
Charleston, WV 25305
Phone : (304) 348-3905

WISCONSIN
Nicholas Chiarkas
Public Defender
131 W Washington Ave.
P.O. Box 7923
Madison, WI 53707
Phone : (608) 266-0087
Fax : (608) 267-0584

WYOMING
Sylvia Hackle
State Public Defender
Off. of State Public Defender
1712 Carey Ave.
Cheyenne, WY 82002
Phone : (307) 777-6498

DISTRICT OF COLUMBIA
Angela Jordan Davis
Director
Public Defender Service
451 Indiana Ave., NW, Rm. 219
Washington, DC 20001
Phone : (202) 628-1200

AMERICAN SAMOA
Soli Aumoeualogo
Public Defender
Off. of Public Defender
Pago Pago, AS 96799
Phone : (684) 633-1286
Fax : (684) 633-4745

GUAM
Harold F. Parker
Director
Public Defender Services Corp.
200 Juridicial Annex
110 W. O'Brien
Agana, GU 96910
Phone : (671) 475-3100
Fax : (671) 477-5844

NORTHERN MARIANA ISLANDS
Daniel DeRienzo
Public Defender
Off. of the Governor
Saipan, MP 96950
Phone : (670) 234-6215
Fax : (670) 234-1009

U.S. VIRGIN ISLANDS
Thurston McKelvin
Federal Public Defender
P.O. Box 3450
Christiansted
St. Croix, VI 00820
Phone : (809) 773-3585

PUBLIC LANDS

Manages state-owned lands.

ALABAMA
Jim Martin
Commissioner
Div. of Lands
Dept. of Conserv. & Natural Resources
64 N. Union St., Rm. 702
Montgomery, AL 36130
Phone : (334) 242-3486
Fax : (334) 242-3489

ALASKA
John T. Shively
Commissioner
Dept. of Natural Resources
400 Willoughby Ave.
Juneau, AK 99801-1796
Phone : (907) 465-2400
Fax : (907) 465-3886

ARIZONA
M. Jean Hassell
State Land Commissioner
Dept. of State Land
1616 W. Adams St.
Phoenix, AZ 85007
Phone : (602) 542-4621

ARKANSAS
Charlie Daniels
State Land Commissioner
State Capitol, Rm. 109
Little Rock, AR 72201
Phone : (501) 324-9222
Fax : (501) 324-9422

CALIFORNIA
Robert Hight
Executive Officer
State Lands Comm.
1807 13th St.
Sacramento, CA 95814
Phone : (916) 574-1800

COLORADO
James B. Cooley
Chair
State Land Bd.
Dept. of Natural Resources
1313 Sherman St., Rm. 215
Denver, CO 80203
Phone : (303) 866-3567
Fax : (303) 832-8106

CONNECTICUT
Charles Reed
Director
Land Acquisition & Mgt.
Dept. of Env. Protection
Hartford, CT 06106
Phone : (203) 424-3016

DELAWARE
Charles A. Salkin
Director
Div. of Parks & Recreation
Dept. of Nat. Res. & Env. Ctrl.
89 Kings Hwy.
Dover, DE 19901
Phone : (302) 739-4401
Fax : (302) 739-3817

FLORIDA
Pete Mallison
Director
Div. of State Lands
Dept. of Env. Protection
3900 Commonwealth Blvd.
Tallahassee, FL 32399
Phone : (904) 488-2725

GEORGIA
J. Ray Crawford Jr.
Executive Director
State Properties Comm.
1 M.L. King, Jr. Dr., Ste. 204
Atlanta, GA 30334
Phone : (404) 656-5602

HAWAII
Michael Wilson
Chairman
Dept. of Land & Natural Resources
1151 Punchbowl St
Honolulu, HI 96813
Phone : (808) 587-0390

IDAHO
Stan Hamilton
Director
Dept. of Lands
1215 State St.
Boise, ID 83720
Phone : (208) 334-0200

ILLINOIS
Brent Manning
Director
Dept. of Conservation
Lincoln Towers Plz., Rm. 425
524 S. Second St.
Springfield, IL 62701-1787
Phone : (217) 782-6302
Fax : (217) 785-9236

INDIANA
John T. Costello
Deputy Director
Dept. of Natural Resources
IGC-South, Rm. W256
Indianapolis, IN 46204
Phone : (317) 232-4020

IOWA
John Beamer
Bureau Chief
Land Acquisition & Land Mgt.
Dept. of Natural Resources
Wallace State Off. Bldg.
Des Moines, IA 50319
Phone : (515) 281-5634

KANSAS
John Bond
Supervisor
Public Land Section
Dept. of Wildlife & Parks
3300 SW 29th St.
Topeka, KS 66614
Phone : (913) 273-6740

KENTUCKY
John McMenama
Manager
Dept. of Facilities Mgt.
Finance & Admin. Cabinet
Bush Building, Wapping St.
Frankfort, KY 40601
Phone : (502) 564-2193

LOUISIANA
Glenn Kent
Acting Director
Div. of State Lands
Dept. of Natural Resources
P.O. Box 44124
Baton Rouge, LA 70804
Phone : (504) 342-4503

MAINE
Thomas Morrison
Acting Director
Bur. of Public Lands
Dept. of Conservation
State House Station # 22
Augusta, ME 04333
Phone : (207) 287-3061

MARYLAND**
Rick Barton
Director
Forest & Parks
Dept. of Natural Resources
Tawes State Off. Bldg., Rm. E3
Annapolis, MD 21401
Phone : (410) 974-3771

MASSACHUSETTS
Lark Palermo
Commissioner
Capitol Planning & Operations
Executive Off. for Admin. & Finance
1 Ashburton Pl., Rm. 1505
Boston, MA 02108
Phone : (617) 727-4050

MINNESOTA
Beverly Kroiss
Director
Real Estate Mgt. Div.
Dept. of Administration
50 Sherburne Ave., Rm. G-22
St. Paul, MN 55155
Phone : (612) 296-1896

MISSISSIPPI
Jim Nelson
Assistant Secretary of State
Dept. of Public Lands
Off. of the Secretary of State
P.O. Box 136
Jackson, MS 39205
Phone : (601) 359-6374

MISSOURI
Douglas K. Eiken
Director
Div. of State Parks
Dept. of Natural Resources
101 Adams St.
P.O. Box 176
Jefferson City, MO 65102
Phone : (314) 751-9392
Fax : (314) 751-8656

MONTANA
Bud Clinch
Director
Dept. of State Lands
1625 11th Ave.
Helena, MT 59620-1601
Phone : (406) 444-2074

NEBRASKA
Rex Amack
Director
Game & Parks Comm.
2200 N. 33rd St.
P.O. Box 30370
Lincoln, NE 68503-0370
Phone : (402) 471-5539

Richard R. LeBlanc
Executive Secretary
Educational Lands & Funds Bd.
555 N. Cotner Blvd.
Lincoln, NE 68505
Phone : (402) 471-2014

NEVADA
Pamela B. Wilcox
Administrator
Div. of State Lands
Capitol Complex, Rm. 118
333 W. Nye Lane
Carson City, NV 89710
Phone : (702) 687-4363

NEW HAMPSHIRE
John Sargent
Director
Forest & Lands Div.
Dept. of Res. & Economic Dev.
172 Pembroke Rd.
Concord, NH 03301
Phone : (603) 271-2214

NEW JERSEY
William E. Ward
Director
Off. of Real Property Mgt.
Dept. of Treasury
33 W. State St., CN226
Trenton, NJ 08625
Phone : (609) 292-9694

NEW MEXICO
Ray B. Powell
Commissioner
State Land Office
P.O. Box 1148
Santa Fe, NM 87504-1148
Phone : (505) 827-5760
Fax : (505) 827-5766

NEW YORK*
Commissioner
Dept. of Environmental Conservation
50 Wolf Rd.
Albany, NY 12233
Phone : (518) 457-3446

NORTH CAROLINA
Joe Henderson
Deputy Director
Off. of State Property
Dept. of Administration
116 W. Jones St
Raleigh, NC 27603-8003
Phone : (919) 733-4346

NORTH DAKOTA
Timothy Kingstad
Commissioner
Land Dept.
918 E. Divide Ave., Ste. 410
Bismarck, ND 58502-5523
Phone : (701) 328-2800
Fax : (701) 328-3650

OHIO
Wayne Warren
Chief
Real Estate Land Mgt.
Dept. of Natural Resources
Fountain Sq.
Columbus, OH 43224
Phone : (614) 265-6385
Fax : (614) 267-4764

OKLAHOMA
Carol Ford
Secretary
Land Off. Comm.
P.O. Box 26910
Oklahoma City, OK 73126
Phone : (405) 521-2757

OREGON
Gary Gustafson
Director
Div. of State Lands
775 Summer St., NE
Salem, OR 97310
Phone : (503) 378-3805
Fax : (503) 378-4844

PENNSYLVANIA
Roger Fickes
Director
Bur. of State Parks
Dept. of Environmental Res.
Rachel Carson State Office Bldg., 8th Fl.
Harrisburg, PA 17101
Phone : (717) 787-6640

RHODE ISLAND
Timothy Keeney
Director
Dept. of Environmental Mgt.
9 Hayes St.
Providence, RI 02908-5003
Phone : (401) 277-2771

SOUTH CAROLINA
Alton T. Loftis
Director of Property Mgt.
Div. of General Services
Budget & Control Board
1201 Main St.
Columbia, SC 29201
Phone : (803) 737-0790

SOUTH DAKOTA
Curt Johnson
Commissioner
School & Public Lands
Capitol Bldg., 1st Fl.
Pierre, SD 57501
Phone : (605) 773-3303

TENNESSEE
Don Dills
Commissioner
Dept. of Environment & Cons.
401 Church St.
Nashville, TN 37243
Phone : (615) 532-0104
Fax : (615) 532-0120

TEXAS
Garry Mauro
Commissioner
General Land Off.
Stephen F. Austin Bldg. Rm. 837
1700 N. Congress
Austin, TX 78701
Phone : (512) 463-3035

UTAH
Scott Hirschi
Director
State Lands & Forestry Div.
Dept. of Natural Resources
3 Triad Ctr., Ste. 400
Salt Lake City, UT 84180-1204
Phone : (801) 538-5508

VERMONT
Barbara Ripley
Secretary
Agency of Natural Resources
103 S. Main St.
Waterbury, VT 05676
Phone : (802) 244-7347
Fax : (802) 241-3281

VIRGINIA
Donald C. Williams
Director
Dept. of General Srvcs.
209 N. 9th St.
Richmond, VA 23219
Phone : (804) 786-3311
Fax : (804) 371-8305

WASHINGTON
Jennifer Belcher
Commissioner of Public Lands
Dept. of Natural Resources
P.O. Box 47001
Olympia, WA 98504-7001
Phone : (360) 902-1000

WEST VIRGINIA
James H. Jones
Real Estate Management
Dept. of Natural Resources
Bldg. 3, Rm. 669
Charleston, WV 25305
Phone : (304) 558-3225

WISCONSIN
Stephen E. Gauger
Secretary
Public Lands
P.O. Box 8943
Madison, WI 53708-8943
Phone : (608) 266-1370

WYOMING
Howard Schrinar
Commissioner
Public Lands
Herschler Bldg.
Cheyenne, WY 82002
Phone : (307) 777-6523

DISTRICT OF COLUMBIA
Kenneth Burnette
Acting Administrator
Real Property Administration
441 4th St., NW, Ste. 750
Washington, DC 20001
Phone : (202) 727-9775

GUAM
Joseph A. "Tony" Martinez
Director
Dept. of Land Management
P.O. Box 2950
Agana, GU 96910
Phone : (671) 475-5263
Fax : (671) 477-0883

NORTHERN MARIANA ISLANDS
William R. Concepcion
Executive Director
Public Land Corporation
P.O. Box 380
Saipan, MP 96950
Phone : (670) 322-6914

PUERTO RICO
Jose Figueroa
Executive Director
Land Authority
P.O. Box 363767
San Juan, PR 00036-3767
Phone : (809) 723-9090
Fax : (809) 725-4004

U.S. VIRGIN ISLANDS
Beulah Dalmida-Smith
Commissioner
Dept. of Planning & Natural Resources
Nisky Ctr., Ste. 231
St. Thomas, VI 00802
Phone : (809) 774-3320
Fax : (809) 775-5706

Alvin O. Davis
Commissioner
Dept. of Property & Procurement
Sub Base, Bldg., 1
St. Thomas, VI 00801
Phone : (809) 774-0828
Fax : (809) 774-9704

Gordon Finch
Executive Director
Port Authority
P.O. Box 1707
St. Thomas, VI 00802
Phone : (809) 774-1629
Fax : (809) 774-8062

PUBLIC LIBRARY DEVELOPMENT

Oversees the development of public libraries in the state and administers state and federal programs related to such libraries.

ALABAMA
Patricia L. Harris
Director
Public Library Srvc.
6030 Monticello Dr.
Montgomery, AL 36130
Phone : (334) 213-3900
Fax : (334) 213-3993

ALASKA
Karen R. Crane
Director
State Libraries & Archives
Dept. of Education
P.O. Box 110571
Juneau, AK 99811-0571
Phone : (907) 465-2910
Fax : (907) 465-2151

ARIZONA
Tony Miele
Library Extension Div.
Dept. of Library, Archives & Public Records
1700 W. Washington
Phoenix, AZ 85007
Phone : (602) 542-5841

ARKANSAS
John A. Murphy Jr.
State Librarian
State Library
Dept. of Education
One Capitol Mall
Little Rock, AR 72201
Phone : (501) 682-1526
Fax : (501) 682-1529

CALIFORNIA
Yolanda Cuesta
Bureau Chief
Library Development Service
P.O. Box 942837
Sacramento, CA 94237-0001
Phone : (916) 322-0372

COLORADO
Nancy Bolt
Asst. Commissioner
Dept. of Education
201 E. Colfax Ave.
Denver, CO 80203
Phone : (303) 866-6900
Fax : (303) 866-6940

CONNECTICUT
Patricia Owens
Director
Library Development Division
State Library
231 Capitol Ave.
Hartford, CT 06106
Phone : (203) 566-5607

DELAWARE
Tom W. Sloan
State Librarian
Div. of Libraries
Dept. of Community Affairs
43 S. duPont Hwy.
Dover, DE 19901
Phone : (302) 739-4748
Fax : (302) 739-6787

FLORIDA
George B. Wilkins
Director
Library & Info. Services
R.A. Gray Bldg.
500 S. Bronough St.
Tallahassee, FL 32399-0250
Phone : (904) 487-2651

GEORGIA
Bill Gambill
Assoc. State School Superintendent
Off. of State Schools & Special Srvcs.
205 Butler St., SW
Atlanta, GA 30334
Phone : (404) 656-2591

HAWAII
Bartholomew A. Kane
State Librarian
State Public Library System
Dept. of Education
465 S. King St., Rm. B-1
Honolulu, HI 96813
Phone : (808) 586-3704

IDAHO
Ann Joslin
Library Development Associate Director
State Library
325 W. State St.
Boise, ID 83702
Phone : (208) 334-2153

ILLINOIS
Bridget Lamont
Director
State Library
300 S. Second St.
Springfield, IL 62701
Phone : (217) 782-2994

INDIANA
C. Ray Ewick
Director
State Library
140 N. Senate Ave.
Indianapolis, IN 46204
Phone : (317) 232-3692

IOWA
Sharman B. Smith
State Librarian
State Library Div.
Dept. of Education
E. 12th & Grand
Des Moines, IA 50319
Phone : (515) 281-4105

KANSAS
Duane F. Johnson
State Librarian
State Library
State Capitol Bldg., 3rd Fl.
Topeka, KS 66612
Phone : (913) 296-3296
Fax : (913) 296-6650

KENTUCKY
James A. Nelson
State Librarian & Commissioner
Dept. of Library & Archives
Education & Humanities Cabinet
300 Coffee Tree Rd., Box 537
Frankfort, KY 40602
Phone : (502) 875-7000

LOUISIANA
Thomas F. Jaques
State Librarian
Off. of State Library
Dept. of Culture, Rec. & Tour.
P.O. Box 131
Baton Rouge, LA 70821
Phone : (504) 342-4923

MAINE
J. Gary Nichols
State Librarian
Bur. of Library Services
State House Station # 64
Augusta, ME 04333
Phone : (207) 287-5600

MARYLAND**
J. Maurice Travillian
Asst. State Superintendent
Div. of Library Dev. & Srvcs.
Dept. of Education
200 W. Baltimore St.
Baltimore, MD 21201
Phone : (410) 333-2113

MASSACHUSETTS
Keith Fields
Director
Board of Library Commissioners
648 Beacon St.
Boston, MA 02215
Phone : (617) 267-9400

MICHIGAN
James W. Fry
State Librarian
State Library
P.O. Box 30007
Lansing, MI 48909
Phone : (517) 373-1580

MINNESOTA
William G. Asp
Director
Off of Library Dev. & Srvcs.
Capitol Sq., Rm. 440
550 Cedar St.
St. Paul, MN 55101
Phone : (612) 296-2821

MISSISSIPPI
Jane Smith
Acting Director
State Library Comm.
1221 Ellis Ave.
P.O. Box 10700
Jackson, MS 39289-0700
Phone : (601) 359-1036

MISSOURI
Sara Ann Parker
State Librarian
State Library
600 W. Main
P.O. Box 387
Jefferson City, MO 65102-0387
Phone : (314) 751-3615
Fax : (314) 751-3612

MONTANA
Richard T. Miller, Jr.
State Librarian
State Library
1515 E. Sixth Ave.
Helena, MT 59620
Phone : (406) 444-3115

NEBRASKA
Rod Wagner
Director
State Library Comm.
1200 N St., Ste. 120
Lincoln, NE 68508-2023
Phone : (402) 471-2045

NEVADA
Joan G. Kerschner
Director
Museums, Library & Arts Dept.
100 Stewart St.
Carson City, NV 89710
Phone : (702) 687-8315

NEW HAMPSHIRE
Kendall F. Wiggin
State Librarian
State Library
Dept. of Cultural Affairs
20 Park St.
Concord, NH 03301-6303
Phone : (603) 271-2397

NEW JERSEY
Louise Minervino
State Librarian
Div. of State Library
Dept. of Education
185 W. State St., CN520
Trenton, NJ 08625
Phone : (609) 292-6201

NEW YORK*
Commissioner
Dept. of Education
Education Bldg.
Albany, NY 12234
Phone : (518) 474-5844

NORTH CAROLINA
John Welch
Acting Director
Div. of State Library
Dept. of Cultural Resources
109 E. Jones St.
Raleigh, NC 27601-2801
Phone : (919) 733-2570
Fax : (919) 733-8748

NORTH DAKOTA
William R. Strader
State Librarian
State Library
Liberty Memorial Bldg.
604 E. Boulevard Ave.
Bismarck, ND 58505
Phone : (701) 328-2717
Fax : (701) 328-2040

OHIO
Richard M. Cheski
State Librarian
State Library
65 S. Front St., Rm. 1206
Columbus, OH 43266-0334
Phone : (614) 644-6843
Fax : (614) 466-3594

OKLAHOMA
Robert L. Clark
Director
Dept. of Libraries
200 NE 18th St.
Oklahoma City, OK 73105
Phone : (405) 521-2502

OREGON
Jim Scheppke
State Librarian
State Library
State Library Bldg.
Salem, OR 97310
Phone : (503) 378-4367
Fax : (503) 588-7119

RHODE ISLAND
Barbara Weaver
Director
Dept. of State Library Srvcs.
State Library
300 Richmond St.
Providence, RI 02903
Phone : (401) 277-2726

SOUTH CAROLINA
James B. Johnson
Director
State Library
P.O. Box 11469
Columbia, SC 29211
Phone : (803) 734-8666

SOUTH DAKOTA
Jane Kolbe
State Librarian
State Library
State Library Bldg.
800 Governors Dr.
Pierre, SD 57501
Phone : (605) 773-3131

TENNESSEE
Edwin S. Gleaves
State Librarian & Archivist
State Library & Archives
403 Seventh Ave., N.
Nashville, TN 37243-0312
Phone : (615) 741-2451
Fax : (615) 741-6471

TEXAS
Edward Seidenberg
Director
Library Development Div.
Library & Archives Comm.
P.O. Box 12927
Austin, TX 78711
Phone : (512) 458-0100

UTAH
Amy Owen
Director
State Library
2150 S. 300 W., Ste. 16
Salt Lake City, UT 84115
Phone : (801) 466-5888

VERMONT
Patricia E. Klinck
State Librarian
Dept. of Libraries
109 State St.
Montpelier, VT 05609
Phone : (802) 828-3265
Fax : (802) 828-2199

VIRGINIA
Nolan T. Yelich
State Librarian
The Library of Virginia
11th St. at Capitol Sq.
Richmond, VA 23219
Phone : (804) 786-2332
Fax : (804) 786-5855

WASHINGTON
Nancy L. Zussy
State Librarian
State Library
State Library Bldg.
P.O. Box 42460
Olympia, WA 98504-2460
Phone : (360) 753-5590

Mary Moore
Chief
Library Planning & Dev. Div.
State Library
P.O. Box 42460
Olympia, WA 98504-2460
Phone : (360) 753-5590

WEST VIRGINIA
Frederick J. Glazer
Director
Library Comm.
Cultural Ctr.
Charleston, WV 25305
Phone : (304) 558-2041

WISCONSIN
Larry Nix
Director
Bur. for Library Development
Dept. of Public Instruction
125 S. Webster
P.O. Box 7841
Madison, WI 53707
Phone : (608) 266-7270
Fax : (608) 267-1052

WYOMING
Jerry Krois
Acting State Librarian
State Library
Dept. of Admin. & Information
Supreme Court & Library Bldg.
Cheyenne, WY 82002-0660
Phone : (307) 777-7281

DISTRICT OF COLUMBIA
Hardy R. Franklin
Director
Public Library
901 G St., NW, Ste. 400
Washington, DC 20001
Phone : (202) 727-1101

AMERICAN SAMOA
Emma F.C. Penn
Supervisor & Program Director
Off. of Library Srvcs.
Dept. of Education
P.O. Box 1329
Pago Pago, AS 96799
Phone : (684) 633-5869
Fax : (684) 633-4240

GUAM
Christine Scott-Smith
Territorial Librarian
Guam Public Library
P.O. Box 9008
Tamuning, GU 96911
Phone : (671) 472-6417
Fax : (671) 477-9777

NORTHERN MARIANA ISLANDS
Kim Lafferty
Director
Library Service
Public School System
Saipan, MP 96950
Phone : (670) 322-9827

PUERTO RICO
Lidia Santiago
Director
Public Library Div.
Dept. of Education
P.O. Box 759
Hato Rey, PR 00919
Phone : (809) 753-9191

U.S. VIRGIN ISLANDS
Jeannette B. Allis-Bastian
Director
Libraries, Archives & Museums
Dept. of Planning & Natural Resources
23 Dronningens Gade
St. Thomas, VI 00802
Phone : (809) 774-5715

PUBLIC UTILITY REGULATION

Supervises and regulates the electric, gas, telephone and water utilities in the state.

ALABAMA
Jim Sullivan
President
Public Service Comm.
P.O. Box 991
Montgomery, AL 36101-0991
Phone : (334) 242-5218
Fax : (334) 240-3134

ALASKA
Don Schroer
Chairman
Public Utilities Comm.
Commerce & Econ. Dev. Dept.
1016 W. 6th Ave.
Anchorage, AK 99501-1963
Phone : (907) 276-6222
Fax : (907) 276-0160

ARIZONA
James Matthews
Executive Secretary
Corporation Commission
1200 W. Washington St.
Phoenix, AZ 85007
Phone : (602) 542-3931

ARKANSAS
Sam Bratton
Chairman
Public Service Comm.
P.O. Box 400
Little Rock, AR 72203-0400
Phone : (501) 682-1453
Fax : (501) 682-5731

CALIFORNIA
Daniel Fessler
President
Public Utilities Comm.
505 Van Ness Ave., Rm. 5218
San Francisco, CA 94102
Phone : (415) 703-3707

COLORADO
Robert J. Hix
Chairman
Public Utilities Comm.
Dept. of Regulatory Agencies
1580 Logan St., Rm. 203
Denver, CO 80203
Phone : (303) 894-2000
Fax : (303) 894-2065

CONNECTICUT
Reginald J. Smith
Chairman
Dept. of Public Utility Control
1 Central Park Plz.
New Britain, CT 06051
Phone : (203) 827-1553

DELAWARE
Robert J. Kennedy
Director
Public Utilities Control
P.O. Box 457
Dover, DE 19903
Phone : (302) 739-4247

FLORIDA
William D. Talbott
Executive Director
Public Service Comm.
2540 Sumard Oak Blvd.
Tallahassee, FL 32399-0850
Phone : (904) 488-7181
Fax : (904) 487-0509

GEORGIA
Bob Durden
Chairman
Public Service Comm.
244 Washington St., SW
Atlanta, GA 30334
Phone : (404) 656-0555

HAWAII
Yukio Naito
Chairman
Public Utilities Comm.
Dept. of Budget & Finance
465 S. King St., Rm. 103
Honolulu, HI 96813
Phone : (808) 586-2057
Fax : (808) 586-2066

IDAHO
Ralph Nelson
Chairman
Public Utilities Comm.
472 W. Washington St.
Boise, ID 83702-5983
Phone : (208) 334-0300

ILLINOIS
Josephine Simmons
Executive Director
Commerce Comm.
P.O. Box 19280
Springfield, IL 62794-9280
Phone : (217) 785-7456
Fax : (217) 524-6859

INDIANA
Jack Mortell
Chairman
State Utility Regulatory Co.
302 W. Washington, Rm. E306
Indianapolis, IN 46204
Phone : (317) 232-2705

IOWA
Allan Thoms
Chairman
State Utilities Bd.
Dept. of Commerce
Lucas State Off. Bldg.
Des Moines, IA 50319
Phone : (515) 281-5167

KANSAS
Don Low
Director
Kansas Corporation Commission
1500 SW Arrowhead Rd.
Topeka, KS 66604-4027
Phone : (913) 271-3220
Fax : (913) 271-3354

KENTUCKY
Ed Overbey, Jr.
Chairman
Public Service Comm.
730 Schenkel Ln.
P.O. Box 615
Frankfort, KY 40601
Phone : (502) 564-7072

LOUISIANA
Marshall Brinkley
Secretary
Public Service Comm.
P.O. Box 91154
Baton Rouge, LA 70821-9154
Phone : (504) 342-2000

MAINE
Thomas Welch
Chairman
Public Utilities Comm.
State House Station # 18
Augusta, ME 04333
Phone : (207) 287-3831

MARYLAND*
Chairman
Off. of the Commissioners
Public Service Comm.
231 E. Baltimore St.
Baltimore, MD 21202
Phone : (301) 333-6071

MASSACHUSETTS
Kenneth Gordon
Chairman
Dept. of Public Utilities
Executive Off. of Consumer Affairs
100 Cambridge St.
Boston, MA 02202
Phone : (617) 727-3500

MICHIGAN
John G. Strand
Chairman
Public Service Comm.
Dept. of Commerce
6545 Mercantile Way
Lansing, MI 48909
Phone : (517) 334-6368

MINNESOTA
Burl Haar
Executive Secretary
Public Utilities Comm.
121 7th Pl. E., Ste. 350
St. Paul, MN 55101-2147
Phone : (612) 296-7526

MISSISSIPPI
Brian V. Ray
Executive Director
Public Service Comm.
P.O. Box 1174
Jackson, MS 39215
Phone : (601) 961-5432

MISSOURI
Allan Mueller
Chairman
Public Service Comm.
Dept. of Economic Development
Truman Bldg., Rm. 530
P.O. Box 360
Jefferson City, MO 65102
Phone : (314) 751-3234
Fax : (314) 751-9285

MONTANA
Bob Anderson
Chairman
Public Service Comm.
1701 Prospect Ave.
Helena, MT 59620
Phone : (406) 444-6199

NEBRASKA
Robert R. Logsdon
Executive Director
Public Service Comm.
P.O. Box 94927
Lincoln, NE 68509-4927
Phone : (402) 471-3101
Fax : (402) 471-0254

NEVADA
John Mendoza
Chairman
Public Service Comm.
727 Fairview Dr.
Carson City, NV 89710
Phone : (702) 687-4870

NEW HAMPSHIRE
Douglass L. Patch
Chairman
Public Utilities Comm.
8 Old Suncook St.
Concord, NH 03301
Phone : (603) 271-2431

NEW JERSEY
Herbert Pate
President
Bd. of Public Utilities
2 Gateway Ctr.
Newark, NJ 07102
Phone : (201) 648-2503

NEW MEXICO
Lawrence Ingram
Chairman
Public Service Comm.
224 E. Place Ave.
Santa Fe, NM 87501-2013
Phone : (505) 827-6940
Fax : (505) 827-6973

NEW YORK*
Chairman
Public Service Comm.
Agency Bldg. 3
Empire State Plz.
Albany, NY 12223
Phone : (518) 474-2530

NORTH CAROLINA
John E. Thomas
Chairman
Utilities Comm.
Dept. of Commerce
430 N. Salisbury St.
Raleigh, NC 27603-5900
Phone : (919) 733-4249
Fax : (919) 733-7300

NORTH DAKOTA
Leo Reinbold
President
Public Srvc. Comm.
State Capitol, 12th Fl.
600 E. Boulevard Ave.
Bismarck, ND 58505
Phone : (701) 328-2400
Fax : (701) 328-2410

OHIO
Craig Glazer
Chairman
Public Utilities Comm.
180 E. Broad St.
Columbus, OH 43266-0573
Phone : (614) 466-3204
Fax : (614) 466-7366

OKLAHOMA
Ed Apple
Commissioner
Oklahoma Corp. Comm.
Jim Thorpe Bldg.
Oklahoma City, OK 73105
Phone : (405) 521-2264

OREGON
Joan Smith
Chairman
Public Utility Comm.
550 Capitol St., NE
Salem, OR 97310-1380
Phone : (503) 378-6611
Fax : (503) 378-5505

PENNSYLVANIA
John M. Quain
Chairman
Public Utility Comm.
104 North Off. Bldg.
Harrisburg, PA 17120
Phone : (717) 787-1925

RHODE ISLAND
James J. Malachowski
Chairman
Public Utilities Comm.
100 Orange St.
Providence, RI 02903
Phone : (401) 277-3500

SOUTH CAROLINA
Charles W. Ballentine
Executive Director
Public Service Comm.
P.O. Drawer 11649
Columbia, SC 29211
Phone : (803) 737-5120

SOUTH DAKOTA
Ken Stofferman
Chair
Public Utilities Commission
State Capitol, 1st Fl.
Pierre, SD 57501
Phone : (605) 773-3201

TENNESSEE
Keith Bissell
Chairman
Public Service Comm.
460 James Robertson Pkwy.
Nashville, TN 37243
Phone : (615) 741-3668
Fax : (615) 741-5015

TEXAS
Brenda Jenkins
Director
Public Utility Comm.
7800 Shoal Creek Blvd.
Austin, TX 78757
Phone : (512) 458-0100

UTAH
Frank Johnson
Director
Div. of Public Utilities
Dept. of Commerce
160 E. 300 S.
Salt Lake City, UT 84111
Phone : (801) 530-6675

VERMONT
Richard Cowart
Chairman
Public Service Bd.
120 State St.
Montpelier, VT 05620-2701
Phone : (802) 828-2358
Fax : (802) 828-3351

VIRGINIA
Preston C. Shannon
Chairman
State Corporation Comm.
Tyler Bldg.
1300 E. Main St.
Richmond, VA 23219
Phone : (804) 371-9608
Fax : (804) 371-9376

WASHINGTON
Sharon Nelson
Chair
Utilities & Trans. Comm.
1300 S. Evergreen Park Dr., SW
P.O. Box 47250
Olympia, WA 98504-7250
Phone : (360) 753-6423

WEST VIRGINIA
Boyce Griffith
Chairman
Public Service Comm.
201 Brook St.
Charleston, WV 25301
Phone : (304) 340-0306

WISCONSIN
Cheryl Parrino
Chairman
Public Service Comm.
4802 Sheboygan
P.O. Box 7854
Madison, WI 53705
Phone : (608) 266-5481
Fax : (608) 266-3957

WYOMING
Bill Tucker
Chairman
Public Service Comm.
Herschler Bldg.
Cheyenne, WY 82002
Phone : (307) 777-7427

DISTRICT OF COLUMBIA
Howard Davenport
Chairman
Public Service Comm.
450 Fifth St., NW, 8th Fl.
Washington, DC 20001
Phone : (202) 626-5100

GUAM*
Chairman
Public Utilities Comm.
P.O. Box 862
Agana, GU 96910
Phone: (671) 472-3461

NORTHERN MARIANA ISLANDS
Timothy P. Villagomez
Executive Director
Commonwealth Utilities Corp.
Lower Base
Saipan, MP 96950
Phone : (670) 322-4033
Fax : (670) 322-4323

PUERTO RICO
Nydia Rodriguez
Executive Director
Aqueduct & Sewer Authority
Barrio Obrero Station
P.O. Box 7066
Santurce, PR 00916
Phone : (809) 758-5757

U.S. VIRGIN ISLANDS
Toya Andrews
Executive Director
Public Srvcs. Comm.
P.O. Box 40
St. Thomas, VI 00801
Phone : (809) 776-1291

PUBLIC WORKS

Umbrella agency responsible for supervision of public works divisions such as aeronautics, highways and water resources.

ARIZONA
Larry S. Bonine
Director
Dept. of Transportation
206 S. 17th Ave., Rm. 100A
Phoenix, AZ 85007
Phone : (602) 255-7011

CALIFORNIA
James W. Van Loben Sels
Director
Dept. of Transportation
1120 N St., Ste. 1100
Sacramento, CA 95814
Phone : (916) 654-5267

CONNECTICUT
Ted Anson
Commissioner
Dept. of Public Works
State Office Bldg.
Hartford, CT 06106
Phone : (203) 566-3360

FLORIDA
Virginia Wetherell
Secretary
Dept. of Env. Protection
3900 Commonwealth
Bldg., MS-10
Tallahassee, FL 32399
Phone : (904) 488-4805
Fax : (904) 921-4303

Ben Watts
Secretary
Dept. of Transportation
605 Suwannee St., MS 57
Tallahassee, FL 32399-0450
Phone : (904) 488-6721
Fax : (904) 488-5526

IDAHO
Larry Osgood
Administrator
Div. of Public Works
Dept. of Administration
502 N. Fourth
Boise, ID 83720
Phone : (208) 334-3647

ILLINOIS
Kirk Brown
Secretary
Dept. of Transportation
2300 S. Dirksen Pkwy.,
Rm. 025
Springfield, IL 62764
Phone : (217) 782-5597
Fax : (217) 782-6121

INDIANA
Don Perry
Director
Public Works Div.
Dept. of Administration
IGC-South, Rm. W467
Indianapolis, IN 46204
Phone : (317) 232-3001

KENTUCKY
Don C. Kelly
Secretary
Transportation Cabinet
State Off. Bldg., 10th Fl.
Frankfort, KY 40601
Phone : (502) 564-4890

LOUISIANA
Jude W.P. Patin
Secretary
Public Transportation
Section
Dept. of Transportation &
Dev.
P.O. Box 94245
Baton Rouge, LA 70804
Phone : (504) 379-1100

MASSACHUSETTS
James Kerasiotes
Secretary
Executive Off. of
Transportation
& Construction
10 Park Plz., Rm. 3170
Boston, MA 02116
Phone : (617) 973-7000

MINNESOTA
James Denn
Commissioner
Dept. of Transportation
Transportation Bldg.,
4th Fl.
John Ireland Blvd.
St. Paul, MN 55155
Phone : (612) 297-2930

NEBRASKA
Robert R. Logsdon
Executive Director
Public Service Comm.
P.O. Box 94927
Lincoln, NE 68509-4927
Phone : (402) 471-3101
Fax : (402) 471-0254

NEVADA
Eric Raecke
Public Works Board
Dept. of Administration
505 E. King St.
Kinkead Bldg., Rm. 301
Carson City, NV 89710
Phone : (702) 687-4870
Fax : (702) 687-3981

NEW HAMPSHIRE
Charles P. O'Leary Jr.
Commissioner
Dept. of Transportation
John O. Moeton Bldg.
P.O. Box 483
Concord, NH 03302
Phone : (603) 271-3734

NEW MEXICO
Tom C. Turney
State Engineer
101 Bataan Memorial Bldg.
P.O. Box 25102
Santa Fe, NM 87504
Phone : (505) 827-6175
Fax : (505) 827-6188

NEW MEXICO — Cont.
Pete Rahn
Secretary
Dept. of Highways &
Transportation
1120 Cerrillos Rd.
P.O. Box 1149
Santa Fe, NM 87504
Phone : (505) 827-5110
Fax : (505) 827-5469

NEW YORK*
Commissioner
Dept. of Transportation
Campus, Bldg. 5
Albany, NY 12232
Phone : (518) 457-4422

NORTH DAKOTA
Marshall W. Moore
Director
Dept. of Transportation
608 E. Boulevard Ave.
Bismarck, ND 58505-0700
Phone : (701) 328-2581
Fax : (701) 328-4545

OHIO
James Conrad
Director
Director's Office
Department of
Administrative Srvcs.
30 E. Broad St. 40th Fl.
Columbus, OH 43266
Phone : (614) 466-6511
Fax : (614) 644-8151

RHODE ISLAND
William Bundy
Director
Dept. of Transportation
210 State Off. Bldg.
Providence, RI 02903
Phone : (401) 277-2481

SOUTH DAKOTA
Richard Howard
Secretary
Dept. of Transportation
700 E. Broadway
Pierre, SD 57501
Phone : (605) 773-3265

TENNESSEE
Bruce Saltsman
Commissioner
Dept. of Transportation
James K. Polk Bldg., Ste. 700
Nashville, TN 37243
Phone : (615) 741-2848
Fax : (615) 741-2508

VERMONT
Patrick Garahan
Secretary
Agency of Transportation
133 State St.
Montpelier, VT 05602
Phone : (802) 828-2657
Fax : (802) 828-3522

VIRGINIA
Jerry W. Kilgore
Secretary of Public Safety
Governor's Cabinet
P.O. Box 1475
Richmond, VA 23212
Phone : (804) 786-5351

WASHINGTON
Sid Morrison
Secretary
Dept. of Transportation
P.O. Box 47400
Olympia, WA 98504-7400
Phone : (360) 705-7000

WEST VIRGINIA
Charles Miller
Secretary
Dept. of Transportation
Bldg. 5, Rm. A109
1900 Kanawha Blvd., E.
Charleston, WV 25302
Phone : (304) 558-0444

DISTRICT OF COLUMBIA
Larry King
Director
Dept. of Public Works
2000 14th St., NW
Washington, DC 20009
Phone : (202) 939-8000

AMERICAN SAMOA
Sam Puletasi
Director
Power Authority
Dept. of Public Works
American Samoa Government
Pago Pago, AS 96799
Phone : (684) 633-4141
Fax : (684) 633-5958

GUAM
Gil A. Shinohara
Acting Director
Dept. of Public Works
P.O. Box 2950
Agana, GU 96910
Phone : (671) 646-3101
Fax : (671) 649-6178

NORTHERN MARIANA ISLANDS
Edward M. Deleon Guerrero
Secretary
Dept. of Public Works
Lower Base
P.O. Box 2950
Saipan, MP 96950
Phone : (670) 322-9482
Fax : (670) 322-3547

U.S. VIRGIN ISLANDS
Ann Abramson
Acting Commissioner
Dept. of Public Works
No. 8 Sub Base
St. Thomas, VI 00802
Phone : (809) 776-4844
Fax : (809) 774-5869

PURCHASING

Central screening and acquisition point for supplies, equipment and/or services for state agencies.

ALABAMA
N. Kent Rose
Director
Div. of Purchasing
Alabama State House
11 S. Union St., Rm 200
Montgomery, AL 36130
Phone : (334) 242-7250
Fax : (334) 242-4419

ALASKA
Dugan Petty
Director
Div. of General Srvcs. & Sup.
Dept. of Administration
P.O. Box 110210
Juneau, AK 99811-0210
Phone : (907) 465-2250
Fax : (907) 465-2189

ARIZONA
Margaret E. McConnell
State Procurement Administrator
State Purchasing Office
Financial Services Division
1700 W. Washington
Phoenix, AZ 85007
Phone : (602) 542-5511

ARKANSAS
Edward Erxleben
Director
Off. of State Purchasing
Dept. of Finance & Admin.
P.O. Box 2940
Little Rock, AR 72203
Phone : (501) 324-9312
Fax : (501) 324-9311

CALIFORNIA
Peter G. Stamison
Acting Director
Off. of Procurement
Dept. of General Srvcs.
1823 14th St.
Sacramento, CA 95814
Phone : (916) 323-8289

COLORADO*
Director
State Buildings Div. & State Purchasing Div.
225 E. 16th Ave.
Denver, CO 80203-1613
Phone : (303) 866-6100
Fax : (303) 894-7445

CONNECTICUT
Peter W. Connolly
Administrative Manager of Purchases
Bureau of Business Services
460 Silver St.
Middletown, CT 06457
Phone : (203) 638-3267

DELAWARE
Robert McWilliams
Director
Div. of Purchasing
Gov. Bacon Health Ctr.
Delaware City, DE 19706
Phone : (302) 834-4550

FLORIDA
George C. Banks
Director
Div. of Purchasing
Dept. of Management Srvcs.
2737 Centerview Dr.
Knight Bldg., Ste. 206
Tallahassee, FL 32399-0950
Phone : (904) 488-7303

GEORGIA
Tom Bostick
Deputy Commissioner
Dept. of Administrative Srvs.
200 Piedmont Ave.
Atlanta, GA 30334-5514
Phone : (404) 656-5516

HAWAII
Robert J. Governs
Chief
Purchasing Supply Div.
Dept. of Acct. & General Srvcs.
1151 Punchbowl St.
Honolulu, HI 96810
Phone : (808) 586-0555

IDAHO
Gerry Silvester
Administrator
Div. of General Srvcs.
Dept. of Admin.
650 W. State St.
Boise, ID 83720
Phone : (208) 327-7325

ILLINOIS
Ted Curtis
Manager
Procurement Services Division
Central Management Services
801 Stratton Bldg.
Springfield, IL 62706
Phone : (217) 785-3868
Fax : (217) 782-5187

INDIANA
David Gragan
Acting Director
Div. of Procurement
Dept. of Admininistration
402 W. Washington, Rm. 468
Indianapolis, IN 46204
Phone : (317) 232-3032

IOWA
Ken Paulsen
Purchasing Div.
Dept. of General Srvcs.
Hoover State Off. Bldg.
Des Moines, IA 50319
Phone : (515) 281-6285

KANSAS
Leo Vogel
Acting Director
Div. of Purchases
Dept. of Administration
Landon State Off. Bldg., 1st Fl.
Topeka, KS 66612-1286
Phone : (913) 296-2376
Fax : (913) 296-7240

KENTUCKY
Don Speer
Commissioner
Dept. of Administration
Finance & Admin. Cabinet
Capitol Annex, Rm. 362
Frankfort, KY 40601
Phone : (502) 564-2317

LOUISIANA
Virgie LeBlanc
Director
Off. of State Purchasing
Div. of Administration
P.O. Box 94095
Baton Rouge, LA 70804
Phone : (504) 342-7000

MAINE
Richard Thompson
Director
Div. of Public Printing
State House Station # 9
Augusta, ME 04333
Phone : (207) 287-3521

MARYLAND**
Paul T. Harris
Chief
Purchasing Bur.
Dept. of General Srvcs.
301 W. Preston St.
Baltimore, MD 21201
Phone : (410) 225-4620

MASSACHUSETTS
Philmore Anderson III
Purchasing Agent
Procurement and General Srvcs.
1 Ashburton Pl., Rm. 1017
Boston, MA 02108
Phone : (617) 727-7500

MICHIGAN
George Boersma
Director, Off. of Purchasing
Dept. of Management & Budget
Mason Bldg., 2nd Fl.
P.O. Box 30026
Lansing, MI 48909
Phone : (517) 373-0300

MINNESOTA
John W. Haggerty
Director
Div. of Materials Management
112 Administration Bldg.
50 Sherburne Ave.
St. Paul, MN 55155
Phone : (612) 296-1442

MISSISSIPPI
Don Buffum
Director
Bur. of Purchasing
Off. of Purchasing & Travel
1504 Sillers Bldg.
Jackson, MS 39201
Phone : (601) 359-3409

MISSOURI
Joyce Murphy
Director
Div. of Purchasing
Off. of Administration
Truman Bldg., Rm. 580
P.O. Box 809
Jefferson City, MO 65102
Phone : (314) 751-3273
Fax : (314) 751-7276

MONTANA*
Bureau Chief
Purchasing Div.
Dept. of Administration
P.O. Box 200135
Helena, MT 59620-0135
Phone : (406) 444-2575

NEBRASKA
Barbara A. Lawson
Administrator
Material Div.
Dept. of Administrative Srvcs.
301 Centennial Mall S.
Lincoln, NE 68509
Phone : (402) 471-2401

NEVADA
Thomas Tatro
Director
Dept. of Administration
209 E. Musser St., 304
Carson City, NV 89710
Phone : (702) 687-4094

NEW HAMPSHIRE
Wayne Myer
Administrator
Bur. of Purchasing & Property
State House Annex, Rm. 102
Concord, NH 03301
Phone : (603) 271-2700

NEW JERSEY
Lana Sims
Director
Div. of Purchase & Property
Dept. of Treasury
33 W. State St., CN039
Trenton, NJ 08625
Phone : (609) 292-4886

NEW MEXICO
Les French
Director
Purchasing Div.
Dept. of General Srvcs.
P.O. Box 26110
1100 St. Francis Dr.
Santa Fe, NM 87503
Phone : (505) 827-0482
Fax : (505) 827-0499

NEW YORK*
Commissioner
Off. of General Srvcs.
Corning Tower Bldg., 41st Fl.
Empire State Plaza
Albany, NY 12242
Phone : (518) 474-5991

NORTH CAROLINA
J. Arthur Leaston
State Purchasing Officer
Div. of Purchase & Contract
Dept. of Administration
116 W. Jones St.
Raleigh, NC 27603-8002
Phone : (919) 733-3581

NORTH DAKOTA
Bud Walsh
Director of Accounting
Off. of Mgt. & Budget
State Capitol, 4th Fl.
600 E. Boulevard Ave.
Bismarck, ND 58505-0400
Phone : (701) 325-2682
Fax : (701) 328-3230

OHIO
Roger Grime
Deputy Director
Div. of Direct Services
Dept. of Administrative Srvcs.
4200 Surface Rd.
Columbus, OH 43228
Phone : (614) 644-8493
Fax : (614) 752-9299

OKLAHOMA
Ross Johnson
Director
Dept. of Central Services
Central Purchasing Div.
State Capitol, Rm B-4
Oklahoma City, OK 73105
Phone : (405) 521-2110

OREGON
Cam Birnie
Administrator
Transportation, Purchasing & Print Srvcs. Div.
Dept. of Admin. Srvcs.
1225 Ferry St., SE
Salem, OR 97310
Phone : (503) 378-4643
Fax : (503) 373-1626

PENNSYLVANIA
Jane Doyle
Director
Bur. of Purchases
Dept. of General Services
414 North Off. Bldg.
Harrisburg, PA 17125
Phone : (717) 787-4718

RHODE ISLAND
Peter S. Corr
Director
Div. of Central Procurement
One Capitol Hill
Providence, RI 02908
Phone : (401) 277-2321

SOUTH CAROLINA
Voigt Shealy
State Procurement Officer
Materials Management Div.
Dept. of General Services
1201 Main St., Ste. 600
Columbia, SC 29201
Phone : (803) 737-0600

SOUTH DAKOTA
Jeff Holcomb
Director
Purchasing Div.
Bur. of Administration
523 E. Capitol Ave.
Pierre, SD 57501
Phone : (605) 773-3420

TENNESSEE
Elsie C. Smith
Assistant Commissioner
Purchasing & Support Srvcs.
Dept. of General Srvcs.
C2-200 Central Srvcs. Bldg.
Nashville, TN 37243
Phone : (615) 741-5922

TEXAS
Pat Martin
Director of Purchasing
General Services Comm.
P.O. Box 13047, Capitol Station
Austin, TX 78711-3047
Phone : (512) 463-3445

UTAH
Douglas Richins
Director
Div. of Purchasing
Dept. of Administrative Srvcs.
3150 State Off. Bldg.
Salt Lake City, UT 84114
Phone : (801) 538-3026

VERMONT
Peter E. Noyes
Director
Div. of Purchasing
Dept. of General Srvcs.
133 State St.
Montpelier, VT 05633-7501
Phone : (802) 828-2211
Fax : (802) 828-2222

VIRGINIA
Donald C. Williams
Director
Dept. of General Srvcs.
209 9th St. Off. Bldg.
Richmond, VA 23219
Phone : (804) 786-3311
Fax : (804) 371-8305

WASHINGTON
Alan Kurimura
Assistant Director
Off of State Procurement
Dept. of General Admin.
P.O. Box 41017
Olympia, WA 98504-1017
Phone : (360) 753-6461

WEST VIRGINIA
Ron Riley
Director
Purchasing Div.
Dept. of Finance & Admin.
State Capitol Bldg., Rm. E-108
Charleston, WV 25305
Phone : (304) 558-2648

WISCONSIN
Jan Abrahamsen
Director
Bur. of Procurement
Dept. of Administration
101 E. Wilson, 6th Fl.
P.O. Box 7867
Madison, WI 53703
Phone : (608) 266-2605
Fax : (608) 267-0600

WYOMING
Mac Landen
Manager
Procurement Services Div.
Dept. of Admin. & Information
Emerson Bldg.
Cheyenne, WY 82002
Phone : (307) 777-6707

DISTRICT OF COLUMBIA
James Gaston
Director
Dept. of Administrative Srvcs.
441 4th St., NW, Ste. 700
Washington, DC 20001
Phone : (202) 727-1179

AMERICAN SAMOA
Laau Seui
Director
Federal-Surplus Property Agency
Off. of Materials Mgt.
Pago Pago, AS 96799
Phone : (684) 699-1170
Fax : (684) 699-2387

GUAM
John S. Salas
Director
Dept. of Admin.
P.O. Box 884
Agana, GU 96910
Phone : (671) 475-1101
Fax : (671) 477-6788

NORTHERN MARIANA ISLANDS
Edward B. Palacios
Director
Procurement & Supply Div.
Dept. of Finance
Lower Base
Saipan, MP 96950
Phone : (670) 664-1500
Fax : (670) 664-1515

PUERTO RICO*
Administrator
General Services Admin.
P.O. Box 7428
San Juan, PR 00916
Phone : (809) 721-7370
Fax : (809) 722-7965

U.S. VIRGIN ISLANDS
Alvin O. Davis
Commissioner
Dept. of Property & Procurement
Sub Base, Bldg., 1
St. Thomas, VI 00802
Phone : (809) 774-0828
Fax : (809) 774-9704

RAILROADS

Responsible for railroad programming and planning.

ALASKA
Robert S. Hatfield
President
State Railroad Corp.
P.O. Box 107500
Anchorage, AK 99510
Phone : (907) 265-2403
Fax : (907) 258-1456

ARIZONA
Harry A. Reed
Assistant Director
Transportation Planning Div.
Dept. of Transportation
206 S. 17th Ave.
Phoenix, AZ 85007
Phone : (602) 255-7431

ARKANSAS
Dan Flowers
Director
Dept. of Highways & Transportation
P.O. Box 2261
Little Rock, AR 72203
Phone : (501) 569-2211
Fax : (501) 569-2400

CALIFORNIA
Cindy McKim
Chief
Div. of Rail Srvcs.
Dept. of Transportation
P.O. Box 942874
Sacramento, CA 94274-0001
Phone : (916) 653-3060

COLORADO
Harvey Atchison
Director
Div. of Transportation Dev.
Dept. of Transportation
4201 E. Arkansas Ave., Rm. 212
Denver, CO 80222
Phone : (303) 757-9525
Fax : (303) 757-9656

CONNECTICUT
Lawrence J. Forbes
Rail Administrator
Off. of Rail Operations
Bur. of Public Transportation
2800 Berlin Tpke.
Newington, CT 06111
Phone : (203) 594-2900

DELAWARE
Anne P. Canby
Secretary
Transportation Authority
Transportation Admin. Bldg.
P.O. Box 778
Dover, DE 19903
Phone : (302) 739-4306

FLORIDA
Ysela Llort
Director
Div. of Planning
Dept. of Transportation
605 Suwannee St.
Tallahassee, FL 32399-0450
Phone : (904) 488-3329

Nick Serianni
Director
Off. of Public Transportation
Dept. of Transportation
605 Suwannee St.
Tallahassee, FL 32399-0450
Phone : (904) 488-5704

GEORGIA
Luke Cousins
Administrator
Off. of Intermodal Programs
Dept. of Transportation
276 Memorial Dr.
Atlanta, GA 30303
Phone : (404) 651-9201

IDAHO
Ron Kerr
Senior Transportation Planner
Transportation Planning & Programming
Dept. of Transportation
P.O. Box 7129
Boise, ID 83707-1129
Phone : (208) 334-8210

ILLINOIS
Merrill Travis
Chief
Bur. of Railroads
Dept. of Transportation
2300 S. Dirksen Pkwy., Rm. 307
Springfield, IL 62764
Phone : (217) 782-2835

INDIANA
Deborah Simmons
Div. Chief
Railroad Div.
Dept. of Transportation
IGC-North, Rm. N901
Indianapolis, IN 46204-2208
Phone : (723) 214-91

IOWA
Les Holland
Director
Rail & Water Div.
Dept. of Transportation
800 Lincoln Way
Ames, IA 50010
Phone : (515) 239-1646

KANSAS
John Schierman
Chief of Rail Affairs
Bur. of Rail Affairs
Dept. of Transportation
Thacher Bldg., 217 SE 4th St
Topeka, KS 66612
Phone : (913) 296-4286

KENTUCKY
Jerry Ross
Director
Multimodel Program
Dept. of Highways
State Off. Bldg. Annex., 3rd Fl.
Frankfort, KY 40601
Phone : (502) 564-7433

LOUISIANA
Carol Cranshaw
Administrator
Div. of Public Transportation
Dept. of Transportation & Dev.
P.O. Box 94245
Baton Rouge, LA 70804
Phone : (504) 379-1100

MAINE
Russell Spinney
Deputy Commissioner
Bur. of Transportation Srvcs.
Dept. of Transportation
State House Station # 16
Augusta, ME 04333
Phone : (207) 287-2841

MARYLAND**
John Agro
Administrator
Mass Transit Administration
Dept. of Transportation
300 W. Lexington St.
Baltimore, MD 21201
Phone : (410) 288-8410

MASSACHUSETTS
Brian Cristy
Director
Railway & Bus. Div.
Dept. of Public Utilities
100 Cambridge St., Rm. 1203
Boston, MA 02202
Phone : (617) 727-3541

MICHIGAN
Phil Kazmierski
Deputy Director
Bur. or Urban & Public Trans.
Dept. of Transportation
P.O. Box 30050
Lansing, MI 48909
Phone : (517) 373-2282

MINNESOTA
Cecil Selness
Director
Off. of Railroads & Waterways
Dept. of Transportation
Transportation Bldg.
St. Paul, MN 55155
Phone : (612) 296-4888

MISSISSIPPI
Mike Merry
Mgr. of Railroad Activities
Div. of Energy & Trans.
Dept. of Economic & Community Dev.
510 George St., Ste. 301
Jackson, MS 39202
Phone : (601) 359-6639

MISSOURI
Jack Hynes
Admin. of Railroads & Waterways
Transportation Division
Dept. of Highways & Trans.
Highway Bldg.
P.O. Box 270
Jefferson City, MO 65102
Phone : (314) 751-7476
Fax : (314) 526-4709

MONTANA
Patricia Saindon
Administrator
Transportation Planning Div.
Dept. of Transportation
2701 Prospect Ave.
Helena, MT 59620
Phone : (406) 444-3423

NEBRASKA
Tom Wais
Deputy Director
Planning Div.
Dept. of Roads
P.O. Box 94759
Lincoln, NE 68509-4759
Phone : (402) 479-4671

NEVADA
Thomas Fronapfel
Assistant Director
Planning Div.
Dept. of Transportation
1263 S. Stewart St.
Carson City, NV 89710
Phone : (702) 687-5440

NEW HAMPSHIRE
William H. Carpenter
Administrator
Railroad & Public Trans. Div.
Dept. of Public Works & Hwys.
P.O. Box 483
Concord, NH 03302
Phone : (603) 271-2468

NEW JERSEY
Frank Wilson
Commissioner
Dept. of Transportation
1035 Parkway Ave., CN600
Trenton, NJ 08625
Phone : (609) 530-3536

NEW MEXICO
Fred Friedman
Chief
Rail Inter-Modal Bureau
Hwy. & Transportation Dept.
1120 Cerrillos Rd.
Santa Fe, NM 87504-1149
Phone : (505) 827-3233
Fax : (505) 989-4983

NEW YORK*
Commissioner
Dept. of Transportation
Campus, Bldg. 5
Albany, NY 12232
Phone : (518) 457-4422

NORTH CAROLINA
David King
Director
Div. of Public Transportation
Dept. of Transportation
One S. Wilmington St.
Raleigh, NC 27601-1494
Phone : (919) 733-4713

NORTH DAKOTA
Mark Sebesta
Rail Planner
Highway Dept.
608 E. Boulevard Ave.
Bismarck, ND 58505-0700
Phone : (701) 328-4630
Fax : (701) 328-1404

OHIO
Jeff Honefanger
Deputy Director
Div. of Rail Transportation
Dept. of Transportation
25 S. Front St., Rm. 716
Columbus, OH 43266-0899
Phone : (614) 275-0137
Fax : (614) 466-1768

OKLAHOMA
R. J. Driskill
Planning Engineer
Dept. of Transportation
200 NE 21st St.
Oklahoma City, OK 73105
Phone : (405) 521-2927

OREGON
Bob Russell
Assistant Commissioner
Rail-Air Program
Public Utility Comm.
550 Capitol St., NE
Salem, OR 97310
Phone : (503) 378-6351
Fax : (503) 378-6880

PENNSYLVANIA
John E. Brown
Director
Bur. of Goods Movement
Dept. of Transportation
506 Trans. & Safety Bldg.
Harrisburg, PA 17120
Phone : (717) 783-8539

RHODE ISLAND
William Bundy
Director
Dept. of Transportation
210 State Off. Bldg.
Providence, RI 02903
Phone : (401) 277-2481

SOUTH CAROLINA
Robert W. Parhan
Director
Public Railways
Dept. of Commerce
P.O. Box 279
Charleston, SC 29402-0279
Phone : (803) 727-2067

SOUTH DAKOTA
Richard Howard
Secretary
Dept. of Transportation
700 E. Broadway
Pierre, SD 57501
Phone : (605) 773-3265

TENNESSEE
Gordon Smith
Director
Div. of Transportation
Public Service Comm.
460 James Robertson Pkwy.
Nashville, TN 37243
Phone : (615) 741-2974

TEXAS
Jerry Martin
Director
Trans./Gas Utilities Div.
Railroad Comm.
P.O. Box 12967, Capitol Station
Austin, TX 78711
Phone : (512) 463-7001

UTAH
John Quick
Planner
Div. of Policy & Systems Planning
Dept. of Transportation
4501 S. 2700 W.
Salt Lake City, UT 84119
Phone : (801) 965-4808

VERMONT
William S. Bruzzese
Director
Air, Rail & Transit Program
Agency of Transportation
133 State St.
Montpelier, VT 05633
Phone : (802) 828-2093
Fax : (802) 828-2829

VIRGINIA
Leo J. Beron
Director
Dept. of Rail & Public Transportation
1401 E. Broad St.
Richmond, VA 23219
Phone : (804) 786-1051
Fax : (804) 786-7286

WASHINGTON
Ken Uznanski
Manager, Rail Branch
Planning Research & Public Transportation
Dept. of Transportation
P.O. Box 47387
Olympia, WA 98504-7387
Phone : (360) 705-7901

WEST VIRGINIA
John Hedrick
Executive Director
Railroad Maintenance Authority
P.O. Box 470
Moorefield, WV 26836
Phone : (304) 538-2305

WISCONSIN
Paul Heitmann
Director
Bur. of Railroads & Harbors
Dept. of Transportation
4802 Sheboygan Ave.
P.O. Box 7916
Madison, WI 53703
Phone : (608) 266-7094
Fax : (608) 267-6748

WYOMING
John Lane
Statewide Planning Engineer
Dept. of Transportation
5300 Bishop Blvd.
Cheyenne, WY 82002
Phone : (307) 777-4180

RECORDS MANAGEMENT

Oversees and coordinates programs to ensure the efficiency, scheduling, storage and reproduction of state government records.

ALABAMA
Deborah Skaggs
Head
Records Mgt. Div.
Dept. of Archives & History
624 Washington Ave.
Montgomery, AL 36130
Phone : (334) 242-4441
Fax : (334) 240-3433

ALASKA
John Stewart
State Archivist
Libraries, Archives & Museums
Dept. of Education
141 Willoughby Ave.
Juneau, AK 99801-1720
Phone : (907) 465-2241
Fax : (907) 465-2465

ARIZONA
Martin Richelsoph
Records Management Officer
Dept. of Library, Archives & Public Records
1919 W. Jefferson
Phoenix, AZ 85007
Phone : (602) 542-3741

ARKANSAS
John L. Ferguson
State Historian
History Comm.
One Capitol Mall
Little Rock, AR 72201
Phone : (501) 682-6900

CALIFORNIA
P. K. Agarwal
Chief
Off. of Information Srvcs.
Dept. of General Srvcs.
1500 5th St., Ste. 116
Sacramento, CA 95814-5404
Phone : (916) 445-2294

COLORADO
Terry Ketelsen
Director
Archives & Public Records Div.
Dept. of Admin.
1313 Sherman St., Rm. 1B-20
Denver, CO 80203
Phone : (303) 866-2055

DELAWARE
Howard P. Lowell
Administrator
Delaware State Archives
Dept. of State, Hall of Records
Dover, DE 19901
Phone : (302) 739-5318
Fax : (302) 739-6710

FLORIDA
Jim Berberich
Chief
Bur. of Archives & Records Mgt.
Dept. of State
R.A. Gray Bldg.
Tallahassee, FL 32399-0250
Phone : (904) 487-2073

GEORGIA
Edward Weldon
Director
Dept. of Archives & History
330 Capitol Ave., SW
Atlanta, GA 30334
Phone : (404) 656-2358

IDAHO
Michelle Stone
Records Management Supervisor
Central Records Mgt. Unit
Dept. of Admin.
5327 Kendall
Boise, ID 83706
Phone : (208) 327-7060

ILLINOIS
John Daly
Director
State Archives & Records Div.
Archives Bldg.
Springfield, IL 62756
Phone : (217) 782-4682

INDIANA
F. Gerald Handfield Jr.
Director
Comm. on Public Records
IGC-South, Rm. W472
402 W. Washington
Indianapolis, IN 46204
Phone : (317) 232-3373

IOWA
Kristi Little
Superintendent of Printing
Dept. of General Srvcs.
Grimes State Off. Bldg.
400 E. 14th St.
Des Moines, IA 50319
Phone : (515) 281-5050

George Hendrickson
State Archivist
Dept. of Cultrual Affairs
Capitol Complex
Des Moines, IA 50319
Phone : (515) 281-3007

KANSAS
Patricia Michaelis
State Archivist
Library & Archives
State Historical Society
120 W. 10th St.
Topeka, KS 66612-1291
Phone : (913) 296-2624
Fax : (913) 296-1005

KENTUCKY
James A. Nelson
State Librarian & Commissioner
Dept. of Library & Archives
Education & Humanities Cabinet
300 Coffee Tree Rd., Box 537
Frankfort, KY 40602
Phone : (502) 875-7000

LOUISIANA
Donald J. Lemieux
Director
State Archives
State Archives Bldg.
3851 Essen Ln.
Baton Rouge, LA 70804-9125
Phone : (504) 922-1000

MAINE
Rebecca Wyke
Assistant Secretary of State & First Deputy
State House Station #148
Augusta, ME 04333
Phone : (207) 626-8406

MARYLAND**
William Taylor
State Records Administrator
State Records Mgt. Ctr.
Dept. of General Srvcs.
P.O. Box 275
Jessup, MD 20794
Phone : (301) 799-1930

MASSACHUSETTS
Albert H. Whitaker Jr.
Archivist
Off. of Secretary of State
220 Morrissey Blvd.
Boston, MA 02125
Phone : (617) 727-2816
Fax : (617) 727-8730

MICHIGAN
Robert Bassett
State Records Manager
Records & Mgt. Srvcs.
Dept. of Mgt. & Budget
P.O. Box 30026
Lansing, MI 48909
Phone : (517) 335-9130

MINNESOTA
Beverly Schuft
Assistant Commissioner
Information Policy Off.
Dept. of Admin.
658 Cedar St., Rm. 320
St. Paul, MN 55155
Phone : (612) 296-5320

MISSISSIPPI
Elbert R. Hillard
Director
Dept. of Archives & History
P.O. Box 571
Jackson, MS 39205
Phone : (601) 359-6881

MISSOURI
Stuart Dunkel
Director
Records Mgt. & Archives Srvcs.
Off. of Secretary of State
600 W. Main
P.O. Box 778
Jefferson City, MO 65102
Phone : (314) 751-4502
Fax : (314) 526-5327
E-Mail: SDUNKEL@MAIL.MORE.NET

MONTANA
Ed Eaton
State Records Manager
Records Mgt. Section
Secretary of State
1320 Bozeman St.
Helena, MT 59601
Phone : (406) 444-2716

NEBRASKA
William P. Ptacek
Director
Records Mgt. Div.
Secretary of State's Off.
P.O. Box 94921
Lincoln, NE 68509
Phone : (402) 471-2559

NEVADA
Guy Louis Rocha
Administrator
Div. of Archives & Records
State Library & Archives
100 Stewart St.
Carson City, NV 89710
Phone : (702) 687-8317

NEW HAMPSHIRE
Frank C. Mevers
Director & State Archivist
Records Mgt. & Archives
Dept. of State
71 S. Fruit St.
Concord, NH 03301
Phone : (603) 271-2236

NEW JERSEY
Karl J. Niederer
Director
Div. of Archives & Records Mgt.
Dept. of State
2300 Stuyvesant Ave., CN 307
Trenton, NJ 08625
Phone : (609) 530-3200

NEW MEXICO
Elaine Olah
Administrator
State Records Ctr. & Archives
404 Montezuma Ave.
Santa Fe, NM 87503
Phone : (505) 827-7332
Fax : (505) 827-7331

NEW YORK*
State Archivist
State Archives & Records Mgt.
Dept. of Education
10D45 Cultural Education Ctr.
Albany, NY 12230
Phone : (518) 474-1195

NORTH CAROLINA
William S. Price Jr.
Director
Div. of Archives & History
Dept. of Cultural Resources
109 E. Jones St.
Raleigh, NC 27601-2807
Phone : (919) 733-7305
Fax : (919) 733-8807

NORTH DAKOTA
Gerald Newborg
State Historical Society
Heritage Center
612 E. Boulevard
Bismarck, ND 58505-0830
Phone : (701) 328-2668
Fax : (701) 328-3710

OHIO
David R. Larson
State Records Administrator
Information Management Section
364 S. Fourth St.
Columbus, OH 43266-0583
Phone : (614) 752-0003
Fax : (614) 752-8883

OKLAHOMA
Louis Coleman
Chairman
Archives & Records Comm.
Dept. of Libraries
200 NE 18th St.
Oklahoma City, OK 73105
Phone : (405) 521-2502

OREGON
Roy C. Turnbaugh
State Archivist
Archives Div.
Off. of Secretary of State
800 Summer St., NE
Salem, OR 97310
Phone : (503) 373-0701
Fax : (503) 373-0953

PENNSYLVANIA*
Director
Bur. of Publications & Paperwork Mgt.
Dept. of General Srvcs.
1825 Stanley Dr.
Harrisburg, PA 17103
Phone : (717) 787-3707

RHODE ISLAND
Timothy Slavin
State Archivist
Off. of Secretary of State
337 Westminister St.
Providence, RI 02903
Phone : (401) 277-2353

SOUTH CAROLINA
George L. Vogt
Director
Dept. of Archives & History
1430 Senate St.
P.O. Box 11669
Columbia, SC 29211
Phone : (803) 734-8577

SOUTH DAKOTA
Rick Voorhes
Director
Records Mgt. Program
State Capitol
500 E. Capitol Ave.
Pierre, SD 57501-5075
Phone : (605) 773-3589

TENNESSEE
Chester Hughes
Director
Records Mgt. Div.
843 Cowan St.
Nashville, TN 37243-0555
Phone : (615) 741-1718

TEXAS
William Dyess
Director
Records Mgt. Div.
State Archives Comm.
4400 Shoal Creek Blvd.
Austin, TX 78756
Phone : (512) 454-2705

UTAH
Jeffery O. Johnson
Director of State Archives
State Archives & Records Srvc.
State Capitol, Archives Bldg.
Salt Lake City, UT 84114
Phone : (801) 538-3012

VERMONT
A. John Yacavone
Director
Central Srvcs. & Public Record
General Srvcs. Center
R.R. 2
Middlesex, VT 05633-7601
Phone : (802) 828-3700
Fax : (802) 828-3710

VIRGINIA
Nolan T. Yelich
State Librarian
The Library of Virginia
11th St. at Capitol Sq.
Richmond, VA 23219
Phone : (804) 786-2332
Fax : (804) 786-5855

WASHINGTON
David Owens
Acting State Archivist
Archives & Records Mgt. Div.
Off. of Secretary of State
P.O. Box 40238
Olympia, WA 98504-0238
Phone : (360) 753-5485

WEST VIRGINIA
Royce Chambers
Director
Information System Srvcs.
Div. of Finance & Admin.
Bldg. 6, Rm. 102
Charleston, WV 25305
Phone : (304) 558-8918

WISCONSIN
Steven B. Hirsch
Chief
Records Management Section
Dept. of Admin.
4622 University Ave., 10-A
Madison, WI 53705
Phone : (608) 266-2995
Fax : (608) 266-5050

WYOMING
David Kathka
Director
Div. of Parks & Cultural Res.
Dept. of Commerce
Barrett Bldg.
Cheyenne, WY 82002
Phone : (307) 777-7013

DISTRICT OF COLUMBIA
Phillip W. Ogilive
Public Records Administrator
Off. of Public Records
1323 Naylor Ct., NW
Washington, DC 20001-4225
Phone : (202) 727-2052

AMERICAN SAMOA
Sopo AhSue
Acting Archivist
Off. of the Governor
P.O. Box C
Pago Pago, AS 96799
Phone : (684) 633-1609
Fax : (684) 633-1841

GUAM
John S. Salas
Director
Dept of Admin.
P.O. Box 884
Agana, GU 96910
Phone : (671) 475-1101
Fax : (671) 477-6788

PUERTO RICO
Carmen Alicea Davila
Director
General Archives
Ponde de Leon # 500
Puerta de Tierra
San Juan, PR 00902
Phone : (809) 722-0331

U.S. VIRGIN ISLANDS
Jeannette B. Allis-Bastian
Director
Libraries, Archives & Museums
Dept. of Planning & Natural Resources
23 Dronningens Gade
St. Thomas, VI 00802
Phone : (809) 774-5715

RECYCLING

Responsible for promoting and implementing state oversight of municipal solid waste recycling, source reduction and recycling within state government and industry.

ALABAMA
Mike Forster
State Recycling Coordinator
Div. of Solid Waste
Dept. of Environmental Mgt.
1751 Congressman Dickinson Dr.
Montgomery, AL 36130
Phone : (334) 271-7700
Fax : (334) 270-5651

ALASKA
Glenn J. Miller
Program Manager
Solid Waste Program
Solid & Hazardous Waste Mgt. Sect.
410 W. Willoughby Ave.
Juneau, AK 99801
Phone : (907) 465-5050
Fax : (907) 465-5274

ARIZONA
Robert L. Munari
Deputy Director
Waste Programs Division
Dept. of Environmental Quality
3033 N. Central, 5th Fl.
Phoenix, AZ 85012
Phone : (602) 207-2300

ARKANSAS
Laura Mack
Chief
Solid Waste Div.
Pollution Control & Ecology
P.O. Box 8913
Little Rock, AR 72219
Phone : (501) 562-7444
Fax : (501) 562-4632

CALIFORNIA
Jane Irwin
Director
Recycling Div.
Dept. of Conservation
801 K St., MS20-58
Sacramento, CA 95814
Phone : (916) 323-3836

COLORADO
Glenn Mallory
Section Chief
Solid Waste & Incident Mgt.
Dept. of Public Health/ Environment
4300 Cherry Creek Dr., S.
Denver, CO 80222-1530
Phone : (303) 692-3300

CONNECTICUT
Richard Barlow
Chief
Bureau of Waste Management
Dept. of Environ. Protection
79 Elm St., 1st Fl.
Hartford, CT 06106
Phone : (203) 424-3004

DELAWARE
N.C. Vasuki
General Manager
Solid Waste Authority
P.O. Box 455
Dover, DE 19903
Phone : (302) 739-5361
Fax : (302) 739-4287

FLORIDA
William W. Hinkley
Chief
Solid & Hazardous Waste
Dept. of Environmental Protection
2600 Blairstone Rd.
Tallahassee, FL 32399-2400
Phone : (904) 488-0300

GEORGIA
Cindy Harden
Coordinator of Special Projects
Georgia Bldg. Authority
1 Martin Luther King, Jr. Dr.
Atlanta, GA 30334
Phone : (404) 656-3250

HAWAII
Clyde Morita
Coordinator
Litter Control Off.
Environmental Health Admin.
1250 Punchbowl St.
Honolulu, HI 96801
Phone : (808) 586-8400

ILLINOIS
Michael Collins
Director
Recycling & Waste Reduction
Dept. of Energy & Nat. Res.
320 W. Washington, 7th Fl.
Springfield, IL 62704
Phone : (217) 524-2993

INDIANA
Bruce Palin
Branch Chief
Solid Waste Mgt. Branch
Dept. of Environmental Mgt.
105 S. Meridian St., Box 6015
Indianapolis, IN 46225
Phone : (317) 232-8892

IOWA
Teresa Hay
Administrator
Waste Mgt. Authority
Wallace State Off. Bldg.
Des Moines, IA 50319
Phone : (515) 281-8489

KENTUCKY
Vicki Tettus
Branch Manager
Resource Conservation Section
Div. of Waste Mgt.
14 Reilly Rd.
Frankfort, KY 40601
Phone : (502) 564-6716

LOUISIANA
Michael Vince
Program Manager
Recycling Section
Off. of Solid & Haz. Waste
P.O. Box 82178
Baton Rouge, LA 70884
Phone : (504) 765-0249

MAINE
John S. Williams
Director
Waste Management Agency
Executive Dept.
State House Station # 154
Augusta, ME 04333
Phone : (207) 287-5300

MARYLAND**
Richard Collins
Director
Off. of Waste Minimization/Recycling
Hazardous & Solid Waste Management Admin.
2500 Broening Hwy.
Baltimore, MD 21224
Phone : (410) 799-1930

MASSACHUSETTS
Willa Kuh
Director
Div. of Solid Waste Mgt.
Dept. of Environmental Protection
1 Winter St.
Boston, MA 02108
Phone : (617) 292-5500

MICHIGAN
Larry Hartwig
Director
Bur. of Environmental Services
Div. of Commerce
116 W. Allegan
Lansing, MI 48909
Phone : (517) 373-2730
Fax : (517) 335-4729

MINNESOTA
Julie Ketchum
Environmental Specialist
Program Development Section
Pollution Control Agency
520 Lafayette Rd.
St. Paul, MN 55155
Phone : (612) 296-7395

MISSISSIPPI
Tom Whitten
Director
Waste Reduction & Minimization
Off. of Pollution Control
P.O. Box 10385
Jackson, MS 39289
Phone : (601) 961-5241

MISSOURI
Kathy Weinsaft
Director
Planning Unit/Solid Waste Mgt. Pro.
Dept. of Natural Resources
Jefferson Bldg., 10th Fl.
P.O. Box 176
Jefferson City, MO 65102
Phone : (314) 751-5401
Fax : (314) 526-3902

MONTANA
Roger Thorvilson
Acting Administrator
Superfund, Solid Waste/ Junk Vehicles
Solid & Hazardous Waste Bur.
Cogswell Bldg.
Helena, MT 59620
Phone : (406) 444-1430

NEBRASKA
Steve Danahy
State Recycling Coordinator
Materiel Div.
Dept. of Administrative Srvcs.
P.O. Box 94847
Lincoln, NE 68509-4847
Phone : (402) 471-2431

NEVADA
James P. Hawke
Director
Emergency Management
Motor Vehicle & Public Safety Dept.
2525 S. Carson
Carson City, NV 89710
Phone : (702) 687-4989

NEW HAMPSHIRE
Elizabeth Bedard
Coordinator
Governor's Recycling Program
Off. of State Planning
2 1/2 Beacon St.
Concord, NH 03301
Phone : (603) 271-1098

NEW JERSEY
Gary Sondermeyer
Assistant Director
Recycling & Planning Element
Div. of Solid & Hazardous Waste of Environmental Protection
401 E. State St., CN414
Trenton, NJ 08625
Phone : (609) 530-8115

NEW MEXICO
Gerald Silva
Bureau Chief
Solid Waste Bur.
Dept. of Environment
P.O. Box 26110
Santa Fe, NM 87504
Phone : (505) 827-2775
Fax : (505) 827-2902

NEW YORK*
Chief
Bur. of Waste Reduction & Recycling
Div. of Solid Waste
50 Wolf Rd.
Albany, NY 12233
Phone : (518) 457-7337

NORTH CAROLINA
Katherine Foote
Recycling Coordinator
Div. of Solid Waste Mgt.
3825 Barrett Dr.
Raleigh, NC 27609
Phone : (919) 571-4100

NORTH DAKOTA
Neil Knatterud
Director
Div. of Solid Waste Mgt.
Health & Consolidated Laboratories
P.O. Box 5520
Bismarck, ND 58502-5520
Phone : (701) 328-5166
Fax : (701) 328-5200

OHIO
Paul Baldridge
Acting Chief
Litter Prevention & Recycling Off.
Dept. of Natural Resources
Fountain Sq., Bldg. E
Columbus, OH 43224
Phone : (614) 265-6333
Fax : (614) 262-9387

OKLAHOMA
Kelly Dixon
Environmental Specialist
Solid Waste Mgt. Srvcs.
Dept. of Env. Health Srvcs.
P.O. Box 53551
Oklahoma City, OK 73152
Phone : (405) 271-7159

OREGON
Pat Vernon
Manager
Recycling Section
Dept. of Environmental Quality
811 SW Sixth Ave.
Portland, OR 97204
Phone : (503) 229-6165

PENNSYLVANIA
James P. Snyder
Director
Bur. of Waste Management
Dept. of Env. Resources
Market St. State Off. Bldg.
Harrisburg, PA 17101
Phone : (717) 787-9870

RHODE ISLAND
Thomas Wright
Executive Director
Solid Waste Management Corp.
260 W. Exchange St.
Providence, RI 02903
Phone : (401) 831-4440

SOUTH CAROLINA
Hartsill Truesdale
Chief
Bur. of Solid & Hazardous Waste Mgt.
Dept. of Health & Env. Control
2600 Bull St.
Columbia, SC 29201
Phone : (803) 896-4000

SOUTH DAKOTA
David Templeton
Office Administrator
Off. of Waste Mgt.
Dept. of Environmental & Natural Resources
523 E. Capitol Ave.
Pierre, SD 57501-3182
Phone : (605) 773-3153

TENNESSEE
Don Dills
Commissioner
Dept. of Environment & Conservation
401 Church St.
Nashville, TN 37243
Phone : (615) 532-0104

TEXAS
D.E. Balusek
Chief
Recycling & Waste Minimization Branch
Solid Waste Management
1100 W. 49th St.
Austin, TX 78756
Phone : (512) 458-7271

Ron Bond
Director, Municipal Solid Waste
Natural Resources Conservation
P.O. Box 13087
Austin, TX 78711-3087
Phone : (512) 908-6695

VERMONT
Andrea Cohen
Chief
Recycling & Conservation Section
Div. of Solid Waste Mgt.
103 S. Main St.
Waterbury, VT 05671-0407
Phone : (802) 241-3444
Fax : (802) 241-3273

VIRGINIA
Allen Lassister
Director
Div. of Litter Control & Recycling
Dept. of Waste Mgt.
101 N. 14th St., 11th Fl.
Richmond, VA 23219
Phone : (804) 225-2667

WASHINGTON
Jim Pendowski
Program Manager
Waste Reduction,
Recycling & Litter
Dept. of Ecology
P.O. Box 47600
Olympia, WA 98504-7600
Phone : (360) 407-6100

WEST VIRGINIA
Charles Jordan
Director
Solid Waste Mgt. Board
1615 Washington St., E.
Charleston, WV 25311-2126
Phone : (304) 558-0844

WISCONSIN
Catherine Cooper
Coordinator
Waste Reduction &
Recycling
Dept. of Natural Resources
101 S. Webster, 3rd Fl.
P.O. Box 7921
Madison, WI 53707
Phone : (608) 267-7566
Fax : (608) 267-2768

WYOMING
Dianna Gentry Hogle
Senior Analyst
Solid & Hazardous Waste
Div.
Dept. of Environmental
Quality
122 W. 25th St.
Cheyenne, WY 82002
Phone : (307) 777-7746

GUAM
Gil A. Shinohara
Acting Director
Dept. of Public Works
P.O. Box 2950
Agana, GU 96910
Phone : (671) 646-3101
Fax : (671) 649-6178

PUERTO RICO
Daniel Pagan Rosa
Executive Director
Solid Waste Management
Authority
P.O. Box 40285
San Juan, PR 00940
Phone : (809) 765-7575
Fax : (809) 753-2220

U.S. VIRGIN ISLANDS
Ann Abramson
Acting Commissioner
Dept. of Public Works
No. 8 Sub Base
St. Thomas, VI 00802
Phone : (809) 776-4844
Fax : (809) 774-5869

REPORTERS OF JUDICIAL DECISIONS

Responsible for the publication and dissemination of appellate judicial decisions in their jurisdiction.

ALABAMA
George Earl Smith
Alabama Appellate Courts
Judicial Bldg.
300 Dexter Ave.
Montgomery, AL 36104-3741
Phone : (205) 242-4621
Fax : (205) 220-4485

ALASKA
David Lampen
Supreme Court of Alaska
303 K St.
Anchorage, AK 95501
Phone : (907) 264-0607

ARIZONA
Noel Dessaint
Supreme Court of Arizona
201 W. Wing
State Capitol
Phoenix, AZ 85007
Phone : (602) 542-4536

ARKANSAS
Marlo M. Bush
Arkansas Supreme Court & Court of Appeals
Justice Bldg.
625 Marshall St.
Little Rock, AR 72201
Phone : (501) 682-6851
Fax : (501) 682-6877

CALIFORNIA
Ed Jessen
Supreme Court of California
303 Second St., Eighth Fl.
San Francisco, CA 94107
Phone : (415) 396-9555

COLORADO
Leo H. Smith
Colorado Court of Appeals
2 East 14th Ave.
Denver, CO 80203
Phone : (303) 837-3738
Fax : (303) 837-3702

CONNECTICUT
Emily Lebovitz
Supreme Court of Connecticut
Drawer N, Station A
Hartford, CT 06106
Phone : (203) 566-5877
Fax : (203) 566-6521

DELAWARE
Andrew T. Horsey
Supreme Court of Delaware
55 The Green
Supreme Court Bldg.
Dover, DE 19901
Phone : (302) 736-4155

FLORIDA
James J. Logue
Florida Supreme Court
Supreme Court Bldg.
500 S. Duval St.
Tallahassee, FL 32399-1925
Phone : (904) 488-7802

GEORGIA
Wm. Scott Henwood
Supreme Court & Court of Appeals
568 State Off. Annex
244 Washington St., SW
Atlanta, GA 30334
Phone : (404) 656-3460
Fax : (404) 656-2253

HAWAII
Betty J. Davis
Hawaii Supreme Court
P.O. Box 2560
Honolulu, HI 96804
Phone : (808) 539-4732

IDAHO
Frederick C. Lyon
Supreme Court of Idaho
451 W. State St.
Boise, ID 83720
Phone : (208) 334-2210

ILLINOIS
Brian Ervin
Illinois Supreme Court
Box 3456
Bloomington, IL 61702
Phone : (309) 827-8513

INDIANA
Duane Brown
217 State House
Indianapolis, IN 46204
Phone : (317) 232-1930

IOWA
R.K. Richardson
Supreme Court of Iowa
State House
Des Moines, IA 50319
Phone : (515) 281-5911

KANSAS
Richard D. Ross
Supreme Court and Court of Appeals
Kansas Judicial Center
301 W. 10th St., Rm. 354
Topeka, KS 66612-1507
Phone : (913) 296-3214
Fax : (913) 296-7076

KENTUCKY
Susan Stokley Clary
Supreme Court of Kentucky
Capitol Bldg., Rm. 235
Frankfort, KY 40601
Phone : (502) 564-4176
Fax : (502) 564-2665

LOUISIANA
Dorothy M. Goldstein
Supreme Court of Louisiana
301 Loyola Ave., Rm. 220
New Orleans, LA 70112
Phone : (504) 568-5707

MAINE
James C. Chute
142 Federal St.
P.O. Box 368
Portland, ME 04112
Phone : (207) 822-4146

MARYLAND
Alexander L. Cummings
Court of Appeals of Maryland
361 Rowe Blvd.
Annapolis, MD 21401
Phone : (410) 269-3539

MASSACHUSETTS
Charles Clifford Allen III
Supreme Judicial Court of MA
1407 New Court House
Boston, MA 02108
Phone : (617) 557-1196

MICHIGAN
William F. Haggerty
Supreme Court of Michigan
P.O. Box 30052
Lansing, MI 48909
Phone : (617) 557-1196

MINNESOTA
Diane Sobcinski
Minnesota Supreme Court & Court of Appeals
25 Constitution Ave.
245 Minnesota Judicial Center
St. Paul, MN 55155
Phone : (612) 296-8579

MISSISSIPPI
Steve Kirchmayr
Supreme Court of Mississippi
Box 117
Jackson, MS 39205
Phone : (601) 359-3697

MISSOURI
Mary E. McHaney
Supreme Court of Missouri
Supreme Court Bldg.
Jefferson City, MO 65102
Phone : (314) 751-4144

MONTANA
Shauna Thomas
Supreme Court of Montana
P.O. Box 749
Helena, MT 59624
Phone : (406) 449-8889
Fax : (406) 449-4083

NEBRASKA
Peggy Polacek
Nebraska Supreme Court & Court of Appeals
State Capitol, Rm. 1214
Lincoln, NE 68509
Phone : (402) 471-3010

NEVADA
Janette M. Bloom
Nevada Supreme Court
Capitol Complex
Carson City, NV 89710
Phone : (702) 687-5180
Fax : (702) 687-3155

NEW HAMPSHIRE
Howard J. Zibel
Supreme Court of New Hampshire
Noble Drive
Concord, NH 03301
Phone : (603) 271-2646
Fax : (603) 271-6630

NEW JERSEY
Stephen W. Townsend
Supreme Court of New Jersey
Box CN970
Trenton, NJ 08625
Phone : (609) 292-4837

NEW MEXICO
Kathleen Jo Gibson
Supreme Court of New Mexico
P.O. Box 848
Santa Fe, NM 87504-0848
Phone : (505) 827-4860
Fax : (505) 827-4837

NEW YORK
Frederick A. Muller
New York Court of Appeals
One Commerce Plaza, 17th Fl.
Albany, NY 12210
Phone : (518) 474-8211
Fax : (518) 463-6869

NORTH CAROLINA
Ralph A. White Jr.
Supreme Court of North Carolina
P.O. Box 803
Raleigh, NC 27602
Phone : (919) 733-3710

NORTH DAKOTA
Penny Miller
Supreme Court of North Dakota
State Capitol, 1st Fl.
Bismarck, ND 58505-0530
Phone : (701) 328-2221
Fax : (701) 328-4480

OHIO
Walter S. Kobalka
Supreme Court of Ohio
30 East Broad St., 2nd Fl.
Columbus, OH 43266-0419
Phone : (614) 466-4961

OKLAHOMA
James Patterson
Supreme Court of Oklahoma
State Capitol, Rm. 1
Oklahoma City, OK 73105
Phone : (405) 521-2163

OREGON
Mary Bauman
Supreme Court Bldg.
1163 State St.
Salem, OR 97310
Phone : (503) 378-2777
Fax : (503) 373-7536

PENNSYLVANIA
Marlene F. Lackman
Supreme Court of Pennsylvania
468 City Hall
Philadelphia, PA 19107
Phone : (215) 560-6370

RHODE ISLAND
Albert Cippolla
Supreme Court of Rhode Island
250 Benefit St.
Providence, RI 02903
Phone : (401) 277-3073

SOUTH CAROLINA
Thomas M. Neal III
South Carolina Supreme Court
P.O. Box 11330
Columbia, SC 29211
Phone : (803) 734-1080

SOUTH DAKOTA
Gloria J. Engel
Supreme Court of South Dakota
State Capitol
Pierre, SD 57501
Phone : (605) 773-3511

TEXAS
John T. Adams
Supreme Court of Texas
P.O. Box 12248
Capitol Station
Austin, TX 87811
Phone : (512) 463-1312

UTAH
Geoffrey J. Butler
Supreme Court of Utah
332 State Capitol
Salt Lake City, UT 84114
Phone : (801) 533-5071

VERMONT
Larry Abbott
Vermont Supreme Court
109 State St.
Montpelier, VT 05609-0801
Phone : (802) 828-3076
Fax : (802) 828-3457

VIRGINIA
Kent Sinclair
Supreme Court of Virginia
P.O. Box 5104
Charlottesville, VA 22905
Phone : (804) 924-4689
Fax : (804) 293-7564

WASHINGTON
Deborah Norwood
Supreme Court of Washington
Temple of Justice
P.O. Box 40929
Olympia, WA 98504-0929
Phone : (206) 357-2087
Fax : (206) 357-2099

WEST VIRGINIA
Darrell V. McGraw Jr.
West Virginia Supreme Court of Appeals
State Capitol, Rm. 26E
Charleston, WV 25305
Phone : (304) 558-2021
Fax : (304) 558-0140

WISCONSIN
Marilyn L. Graves
Wisconsin Supreme Court
231 East, State Capitol
P.O. Box 1688
Madison, WI 53701-1688
Phone : (608) 266-1880
Fax : (608) 267-0640

WYOMING
Jerrill D. Carter
Supreme Court of Wyoming
Supreme Court Bldg.
Cheyenne, WY 82002
Phone : (307) 777-7316

DISTRICT OF COLUMBIA
Frank D. Wagner
United States Supreme Court
1 First St., NE
Washington, DC 20543
Phone : (202) 479-3390
Fax : (202) 479-3240

William H. Ng
Court of Appeals, Rm. 6000
500 Indiana Ave., NW
Washington, DC 20001
Phone : (202) 879-2725

GUAM
Robert E. Leon Guerrero
Judiciary Bldg.
110 W. O'Brien Dr.
Agana, GU 96910
Phone : (671) 472-8956

NORTHERN MARIANA ISLANDS
Sam Thompson
NMI Supreme Court
P.O. Box 2165
Saipan, MP 96950
Phone : (670) 235-5890
Fax : (670) 234-5183

PUERTO RICO

Lourdes Diaz-Antonmattei
Supreme Court of Puerto Rico
Box 2392 - Supreme Court
San Juan, PR 00902-2392
Phone : (809) 723-4466

RETIREMENT (STATE EMPLOYEES)

Administers the retirement program for state employees other than teachers.

ALABAMA
David G. Bronner
Secretary/Treasurer
Retirement Systems
135 S. Union St.
Montgomery, AL 36130
Phone : (334) 832-4140
Fax : (334) 240-3032

ALASKA
Robert Stalnaker
Director
Div. of Retirement & Benefits
Dept. of Administration
P.O. Box 110203
Juneau, AK 99811-0203
Phone : (907) 465-4460
Fax : (907) 465-3086

ARIZONA
Leroy Gilbertson
Director
Retirement System
P.O. Box 33910
Phoenix, AZ 85067-3910
Phone : (602) 240-2050

ARKANSAS
Kie D. Hall
Director
Public Employees Retirement System
124 W. Capitol Ave.
Little Rock, AR 72201-3706
Phone : (501) 682-7800
Fax : (501) 682-5731

CALIFORNIA
Dale M. Hanson
Executive Officer
Public Employee Retirement System
400 P St.
Sacramento, CA 95814
Phone : (916) 326-3829

COLORADO
Robert J. Scott
Executive Director
Public Employees Retirement Association
1300 Logan St.
Denver, CO 80203
Phone : (303) 832-9550

CONNECTICUT
Steven Weinberger
Director
Retirement Div.
Off. of the Comptroller
55 Elm St.
Hartford, CT 06106
Phone : (203) 566-5639

DELAWARE
David Craik
Director, Pension Off.
Off. of the State Treasurer
Thomas Collins Bldg.
P.O. Box 1401
Dover, DE 19901
Phone : (302) 739-4208
Fax : (302) 739-6129

FLORIDA
Andrew J. McMullian III
Director, Div. of Retirement
Dept. of Mgt. Srvcs.
Cedars Exec. Ctr., Bldg. C
2639 N. Monroe St.
Tallahassee, FL 32399-1560
Phone : (904) 488-5541

GEORGIA
Rudolph Johnson
Director
Employees' Retirement System
2 Northside 75, Ste. 300
Atlanta, GA 30318
Phone : (404) 352-6411

HAWAII
Stanley Siu
Executive Secretary
Employees' Retirement System
Dept. of Budget & Finance
201 Merchant St., # 1400
Honolulu, HI 96813-2929
Phone : (808) 586-1700
Fax : (808) 586-1677

IDAHO
Alan H. Winkle
Director
Public Employee Retirement
820 Washington St.
Boise, ID 83720
Phone : (208) 334-3365

ILLINOIS
Michael L. Mory
Executive Secretary
State Retirement Systems
2101 S. Veteran Park Way
P.O. Box 19255
Springfield, IL 62794-9255
Phone : (217) 785-7444
Fax : (217) 785-7019

INDIANA
Phillip Smith
Director
Public Employees Retirement Fund
143 W. Market St., Ste. 602
Indianapolis, IN 46204
Phone : (317) 232-4138

IOWA
Greg Cusack
Chief Retirement Benefits Officer
Public Employees Retirement System
Dept. of Personnel
600 E. Court Ave.
Des Moines, IA 50306
Phone : (515) 281-0020

KANSAS
Meredith Williams
Executive Secretary
Public Employee Retirement System
400 SW 8th Ave., Ste. 200
Topeka, KS 66603-3295
Phone : (913) 296-6666
Fax : (913) 296-2422

KENTUCKY
Pamela Johnson
General Manager
Retirement Systems
1260 Louisville Rd.
Frankfort, KY 40601
Phone : (502) 564-4646

LOUISIANA
Mary L. Landrieu
State Treasurer
Dept. of Treasury
P.O. Box 44154
Baton Rouge, LA 70804-0154
Phone : (504) 342-0010

MAINE
Claude Perrier
Executive Director
State Retirement System
State House Station # 46
Augusta, ME 04333
Phone : (207) 287-3461

MARYLAND**
Margaret Bury
Acting Executive Director
Retirement & Pension Systems
State Retirement Agency
301 W. Preston St., Rm. 202
Baltimore, MD 21201
Phone : (410) 225-4051

MASSACHUSETTS
Francis McCauley
Executive Secretary
State Bd. of Retirement
Off. of Treasurer
1 Ashburton Pl.
Boston, MA 02108
Phone : (617) 367-7770

MICHIGAN
Brian White
Director
State Employees Retirement
Dept. of Mgt. & Budget
P.O. Box 30171
Lansing, MI 48909
Phone : (517) 322-6236

MINNESOTA
David Bergstrom
Executive Director
State Retirement System
175 W. Lafayette
Frontage Rd.
St. Paul, MN 55107-1425
Phone : (612) 296-2761

MISSISSIPPI
Milton G. Walker
Executive Secretary
Public Employees
Retirement System
429 Mississippi St.
Jackson, MS 39201-1005
Phone : (601) 359-3589

MISSOURI
Gary Findlay
Executive Director
State Employees'
Retirement System
906 Leslie Blvd.
P.O. Box 209
Jefferson City, MO 65102
Phone : (314) 751-2342
Fax : (314) 751-7182

MONTANA
Linda King
Administrator
Public Employees
Retirement Div.
Dept. of Administration
1712 Ninth Ave.
Helena, MT 59620
Phone : (406) 444-3154

NEBRASKA
James S. Cashin
Director
Public Employees
Retirement Systems
P.O. Box 94816
Lincoln, NE 68509-4816
Phone : (402) 471-2053

NEVADA
George Pyne
Executive Officer
Public Employee
Retirement System
693 W. Nye Ln.
Carson City, NV 89710
Phone : (702) 687-4200

NEW HAMPSHIRE
Harry M. Descoteau
Executive Secretary
Retirement System
54 Regional Dr.
Concord, NH 03301-8509
Phone : (603) 271-3351

NEW JERSEY
Margaret M. McMahon
Director
Div. of Pensions
Dept. of Treasury
1 State St. Sq., CN 295
Trenton, NJ 08625
Phone : (609) 292-7524

NEW MEXICO
Leo Griego
Executive Secretary
Public Employees'
Retirement Bd.
PERA Bldg.
P.O. Box 2123
Santa Fe, NM 87504
Phone : (505) 827-4700
Fax : (505) 827-4670

NEW YORK*
State Comptroller
Off. of the State
Comptroller
A.E. Smith Off. Bldg.,
6th Fl.
Albany, NY 12236
Phone : (518) 474-4040

NORTH CAROLINA
Dennis Ducker
Director
Retirement & Health
Benefits
Off. of Treasurer
325 N. Salisbury St.
Raleigh, NC 27603-1388
Phone : (919) 733-6555
Fax : (919) 733-9586

NORTH DAKOTA
Sparb Collins
Executive Director
Public Employees
Retirement System
P.O. Box 1214
Bismarck, ND 58502-1214
Phone : (701) 328-3900
Fax : (701) 328-3920

OHIO
Richard E. Schumacher
Executive Director
Public Employees
Retirement
System
277 E. Town St.
Columbus, OH 43215
Phone : (614) 466-2822
Fax : (614) 466-5837

OKLAHOMA
Rex Privett
Director
Public Employees
Retirement System
Jim Thorpe Bldg.
Oklahoma City, OK 73105
Phone : (405) 521-2381

OREGON
Fred McDonnal
Director
Public Employees
Retirement System
200 SW Market St., Ste. 700
Portland, OR 97207-0073
Phone : (503) 229-5824
Fax : (503) 222-5504

PENNSYLVANIA
John Brosius
Executive Director
State Employees'
Retirement
30 N. Third St.
Harrisburg, PA 17108-1147
Phone : (717) 787-6780

RHODE ISLAND
Joan Flaminio
Executive Director
Employee Retirement
System
40 Fountain St., 1st Fl.
Providence, RI 02903
Phone : (401) 277-2203

SOUTH CAROLINA
Purvis W. Collins
Director
Retirement System
State Budget & Control
Board
202 Arbor Lake Dr.
Columbia, SC 29223
Phone : (803) 737-6934

SOUTH DAKOTA
Al Asher
Administrator
State Retirement System
P.O. Box 1098
Pierre, SD 57501-1098
Phone : (605) 773-3731

TENNESSEE
Steve Curry
Director
Div. of Retirement
Dept. of Treasury
1329 Andrew Jackson Bldg.
Nashville, TN 37219
Phone : (615) 741-7063

TEXAS
Charles V. Travis
Executive Director
Employees Retirement
System
Box 13207, Capitol Station
Austin, TX 78711
Phone : (512) 476-6431

UTAH
Dee Williams
Executive Director
State Retirement Off.
540 E. 200 S.
Salt Lake City, UT 84102
Phone : (801) 366-7301

VERMONT
Deborah Fielder
Director of Retirement
Srvcs.
Retirement Div.
Off. of the Treasurer
133 State St.
Montpelier, VT 05633-6901
Phone : (802) 828-2305
Fax : (802) 828-2772

VIRGINIA
William H. Leighty
Director
VA Retirement Systems
1200 E. Main St.
Richmond, VA 23219
Phone : (804) 786-3831
Fax : (804) 371-0613

WASHINGTON
Sheryl Wilson
Director
Dept. of Retirement
Systems
1025 E. Union St.
P.O. Box 48380
Olympia, WA 98504-8380
Phone : (360) 753-5281

Retirement (State Employees)

WEST VIRGINIA
James L. Sims
Executive Secretary
Consolidated Public Retirement Bd.
1000 Capitol Complex, Bldg. 5
Charleston, WV 25305
Phone : (304) 558-3570

WISCONSIN
Eric Stansfield
Secretary
Dept. of Employee Trust Funds
201 E. Washington Ave., Rm. 166
P.O. Box 7931
Madison, WI 53703
Phone : (608) 266-3285
Fax : (608) 267-4549

WYOMING
Jerry Fox
Director
Retirement System Board
Herschler Bldg.
Cheyenne, WY 82002
Phone : (307) 777-7691

DISTRICT OF COLUMBIA
Robert Pohlman
Chief Financial Officer
Financial Mgt.
441 4th St., NW, Ste. 1150
Washington, DC 20001
Phone : (202) 727-2476

AMERICAN SAMOA
George Odom
Retirement Officer
Dept. of Human Resources
Pago Pago, AS 96799
Phone : (684) 633-5456
Fax : (684) 633-1460

GUAM
Michelle B. Santos
Director
Retirement Fund
P.O. Box 3-C
Agana, GU 96910
Phone : (671) 647-8700
Fax : (671) 477-3863

NORTHERN MARIANA ISLANDS
Edward H. Manglona
Administrator
Retirement Fund
P.O. Box 1247
Saipan, MP 96950
Phone : (670) 234-7228
Fax : (670) 234-9624

PUERTO RICO
Elba I. Medina
Administrator
Personnel Retirement Div.
P.O. Box 42003
San Juan, PR 00940-2003
Phone : (809) 754-4600
Fax : (809) 250-7251

U.S. VIRGIN ISLANDS
Lawrence Bryan
Acting Administrator
Government Employee Retirement System
GERS Bldg.
Charlotte Amalie
St. Thomas, VI 00802
Phone : (809) 776-7703
Fax : (809) 776-4499

RETIREMENT (TEACHERS)

Administers the retirement program for state's public school teachers.

ALABAMA
Donald Yancey
Division Head
Retirement Systems
135 S. Union St.
Montgomery, AL 36130
Phone : (334) 832-4140
Fax : (334) 240-3032

ALASKA
Robert Stalnaker
Director
Div. of Retirement & Benefits
Dept. of Administration
P.O. Box 110203
Juneau, AK 99811-0203
Phone : (907) 465-4460
Fax : (907) 465-3086

ARIZONA
Leroy Gilbertson
Director
Retirement System
P.O. Box 33910
Phoenix, AZ 85067-3910
Phone : (602) 240-2050

ARKANSAS
Bill Shirron
Executive Director
Teachers Retirement System
Education Bldg. W., Rm. 209
Little Rock, AR 72201
Phone : (501) 371-1517
Fax : (501) 682-2663

CALIFORNIA
James D. Mosman
Chief Executive Officer
Teachers Retirement System
7667 Folsom Blvd., Ste. 300
Sacramento, CA 95851

COLORADO
Robert J. Scott
Executive Director
Public Employees Retirement Association
1300 Logan St.
Denver, CO 80203
Phone : (303) 832-9550

CONNECTICUT
John R. Shears
Administrator
Teachers' Retirement Bd.
165 Capitol Ave., Rm. 202
Hartford, CT 06106
Phone : (203) 566-3242

DELAWARE
David Craik
Director, Pension Off.
Off. of the State Treasurer
Thomas Collins Bldg.
P.O. Box 1401
Dover, DE 19901
Phone : (302) 739-4208
Fax : (302) 739-6129

FLORIDA
Andrew J. McMullian III
Director
Div. of Retirement
Dept. of Mgt. Srvcs.
Cedars Exec. Ctr., Bldg. C
2639 N. Monroe St.
Tallahassee, FL 32399-1560
Phone : (904) 488-5541

GEORGIA
Gerald S. Gilbert
Executive Secretary-Treasurer
Teachers' Retirement System
2 Northside 75, Ste. 500
Atlanta, GA 30318
Phone : (404) 352-6500

HAWAII
Stanley Siu
Executive Secretary
Employees' Retirement System
Dept. of Budget & Finance
201 Merchant St., # 1400
Honolulu, HI 96813-2929
Phone : (808) 586-1700
Fax : (808) 586-1677

IDAHO
Alan H. Winkle
Director
Public Employee Retirement
820 Washington St.
Boise, ID 83720
Phone : (208) 334-3365

ILLINOIS
Robert Daniels
Executive Director
Teachers' Retirement System
2815 W. Washington St.
Springfield, IL 62794
Phone : (217) 753-0315
Fax : (217) 753-0967

INDIANA
Mary Pettersen
Executive Secretary
Teachers' Retirement Fund
150 W. Market St., Ste. 300
Indianapolis, IN 46204-2809
Phone : (317) 232-3869

IOWA
Greg Cusack
Chief Retirement Benefits Officer
Public Empl. Retirement Sys.
Dept. of Personnel
600 E. Court Ave.
Des Moines, IA 50306
Phone : (515) 281-0020

KANSAS
Meredith Williams
Executive Secretary
Public Empl. Retirement System
400 SW 8th Ave., Ste. 200
Topeka, KS 66603-3925
Phone : (913) 296-6666
Fax : (913) 296-2422

KENTUCKY
Pat N. Miller
Executive Secretary
Teachers' Retirement System
479 Versailles Rd.
Frankfort, KY 40601
Phone : (502) 573-5120

LOUISIANA
James Hadley
Secretary-Treasurer
Teachers Retirement System
801 United Plz. Blvd.
Baton Rouge, LA 70809
Phone : (504) 925-6446

MAINE
Claude Perrier
Executive Director
State Retirement System
State House Station # 46
Augusta, ME 04333
Phone : (207) 287-3461

MARYLAND**
Margaret Bury
Acting Executive Director
Retirement & Pension Systems
State Retirement Agency
301 W. Preston St., Rm. 202
Baltimore, MD 21201
Phone : (410) 225-4051

MASSACHUSETTS
Joseph Malone
Treasurer & Receiver General
1 Ashburton Place, 12th Fl.
Boston, MA 02108-1518
Phone : (617) 727-3900

MICHIGAN
Thomas W. Schaefer
Executive Director
School Employees Retirement
Dept. of Mgt. & Budget
P.O. Box 30026
Lansing, MI 48909
Phone : (517) 322-6000

MINNESOTA
Gary Austin
Executive Director
Teachers Retirement Assn.
Galary Bldg., Ste. 500
17 W. Exchange St.
St. Paul, MN 55102
Phone : (612) 296-2409

MISSISSIPPI
Milton G. Walker
Executive Secretary
Public Employees
Retirement System
429 Mississippi St.
Jackson, MS 39201-1005
Phone : (601) 359-3589

MISSOURI
M. Steve Yoakum
Executive Secretary
Public School Retirement
System of Missouri
701 W. Main
P.O. Box 268
Jefferson City, MO 65102
Phone : (314) 634-5290
Fax : (314) 634-7934

MONTANA
Dave L. Senn
Administrator
Teacher's Retirement Div.
Dept. of Administration
1500 Sixth Ave.
Helena, MT 59601
Phone : (406) 444-3134

NEBRASKA
James S. Cashin
Director
Public Employees
Retirement
Systems
P.O. Box 94816
Lincoln, NE 68509-4816
Phone : (402) 471-2053

NEVADA
George Pyne
Executive Officer
Public Employee
Retirement System
693 W. Nye Ln.
Carson City, NV 89710
Phone : (702) 687-4200

NEW HAMPSHIRE
Harry M. Descoteau
Executive Secretary
Retirement System
54 Regional Dr.
Concord, NH 03301-8509
Phone : (603) 271-3351

NEW JERSEY
Margaret M. McMahon
Director
Div. of Pensions
Dept. of Treasury
1 State St. Sq., CN 295
Trenton, NJ 08625
Phone : (609) 292-7524

NEW MEXICO
Frank Ready
Director
Educational Retirement
Bd.
Lamy Bldg.
P.O. Box 26129
Santa Fe, NM 87502-6129
Phone : (505) 827-8030
Fax : (505) 827-1855

NEW YORK*
Executive Director
Teachers' Retirement
System
10 Corporate Woods Dr.
Albany, NY 12211
Phone : (518) 447-2700

NORTH CAROLINA
Dennis Ducker
Director
Retirement & Health
Benefits
Off. of Treasurer
325 N. Salisbury St.
Raleigh, NC 27603-1388
Phone : (919) 733-6555
Fax : (919) 733-9586

NORTH DAKOTA
Scott Engmann
Executive Secretary
Teachers' Fund for
Retirement
P.O. Box 7100
Bismarck, ND 58507
Phone : (701) 328-4885
Fax : (701) 328-4897

OHIO
Herbert Dyer
Executive Director
State Teachers Retirement
275 E. Broad St.
Columbus, OH 43215
Phone : (614) 227-4090
Fax : (614) 227-5233

OKLAHOMA
Tom Beavers
Executive Secretary
Teachers Retirement
System
472 Oliver Hodge Bldg.
Oklahoma City, OK 73105
Phone : (405) 521-2387

PENNSYLVANIA
James Perry
Executive Director
School Employees'
Retirement
5 N. Fifth St., Rm. 317
Harrisburg, PA 17108
Phone : (717) 787-6780

RHODE ISLAND
Joan Flaminio
Executive Director
Employee Retirement
System
40 Fountain St., 1st Fl.
Providence, RI 02903
Phone : (401) 277-2203

SOUTH CAROLINA
Purvis W. Collins
Director
Retirement System
State Budget & Control
Board
202 Arbor Lake Dr.
Columbia, SC 29223
Phone : (803) 737-6934

SOUTH DAKOTA
Al Asher
Administrator
State Retirement System
P.O. Box 1098
Pierre, SD 57501-1098
Phone : (605) 773-3731

TENNESSEE
Steve Curry
Director
Div. of Retirement
Dept. of Treasury
1329 Andrew Jackson Bldg.
Nashville, TN 37219
Phone : (615) 741-7063

TEXAS
Wayne Blevins
Executive Secretary
Teachers' Retirement
System
1000 Red River St.
Austin, TX 78701
Phone : (512) 397-6400

UTAH
Dee Williams
Executive Director
State Retirement Off.
540 E. 200 S.
Salt Lake City, UT 84102
Phone : (801) 366-7301

VERMONT
Deborah Fielder
Director of Retirement
Srvcs.
Retirement Div.
Off. of the Treasurer
133 State St.
Montpelier, VT 05633-6901
Phone : (802) 828-2305
Fax : (802) 828-2772

VIRGINIA
William H. Leighty
Director
Supplemental Retirement
System
1200 E. Main St.
Richmond, VA 23219
Phone : (804) 786-3831
Fax : (804) 371-0613

WASHINGTON
Sheryl Wilson
Director
Dept. of Retirement
Systems
1025 E. Union St.
P.O. Box 48380
Olympia, WA 98504-8380
Phone : (360) 753-5281

WEST VIRGINIA
James L. Sims
Executive Secretary
Consolidated Public Retirement Bd.
1000 Capitol Complex, Bldg. 5
Charleston, WV 25305
Phone : (304) 558-3570

WISCONSIN
Eric Stansfield
Secretary
Dept. of Employee Trust Funds
201 E. Washington Ave., Rm. 166
P.O. Box 7931
Madison, WI 53703
Phone : (608) 266-3285
Fax : (608) 267-4549

WYOMING
Jerry Fox
Director
Retirement System Board
Herschler Bldg.
Cheyenne, WY 82002
Phone : (307) 777-7691

DISTRICT OF COLUMBIA
Jeanna Collins
Executive Director
Retirement Board
1400 L St., NW, Ste. 300
Washington, DC 20005
Phone : (202) 535-1271

GUAM
Michelle B. Santos
Director
Retirement Fund
P.O. Box 3-C
Agana, GU 96910
Phone : (671) 647-8700
Fax : (671) 477-3863

NORTHERN MARIANA ISLANDS
Edward H. Manglona
Administrator
Retirement Fund
P.O. Box 1247
Saipan, MP 96950
Phone : (670) 234-7228
Fax : (670) 234-9624

PUERTO RICO
Sonia Babilonia
President
Teachers Retirement System
P.O. Box 1879
Hato Rey, PR 00919
Phone : (809) 764-8611

U.S. VIRGIN ISLANDS
Lawrence Bryan
Acting Administrator
Govt. Empl. Retirement System
GERS Bldg.
Charlotte Amalie
St. Thomas, VI 00802
Phone : (809) 776-7703
Fax : (809) 776-4499

REVENUE

Administers state tax laws and the collection and processing of state taxes.

ALABAMA
Ralph Eagerton
Interim Commissioner
Dept. of Revenue
50 Ripley St., 4th Fl.
Montgomery, AL 36130
Phone : (334) 242-1175
Fax : (334) 242-0550

ALASKA
Wilson Condon
Commissioner
Dept. of Revenue
P.O. Box 110400
Juneau, AK 99811-0400
Phone : (907) 465-2300
Fax : (907) 465-2389

ARIZONA
Harold Scott
Director
Dept. of Revenue
1600 W. Monroe
Phoenix, AZ 85007
Phone : (602) 542-3572

ARKANSAS
John Theis
Commissioner
Revenue Div.
Dept. of Finance & Admin.
P.O. Box 1272
Little Rock, AR 72203
Phone : (501) 682-7000
Fax : (501) 682-7900

CALIFORNIA
Gerald Goldberg
Executive Officer
Franchise Tax Bd.
P.O. Box 1468
Sacramento, CA 95812-1468
Phone : (916) 369-4543

COLORADO
Renny Fagan
Executive Director
Dept. of Revenue
1375 Sherman St., Rm. 486
Denver, CO 80203
Phone : (303) 866-3091

CONNECTICUT
Gene Gavin
Commissioner
Dept. of Revenue Srvcs.
25 Sigourney St.
Hartford, CT 06106
Phone : (203) 297-5650

DELAWARE
William Remington
Director
Div. of Revenue
Dept. of Finance
820 N. French St.
Wilmington, DE 19801
Phone : (302) 577-3315
Fax : (302) 577-3689

FLORIDA
Larry H. Fuchs
Executive Director
Dept. of Revenue
102 Carlton Bldg.
Tallahassee, FL 32399-0100
Phone : (904) 488-5050
Fax : (904) 488-0024

GEORGIA
Marcus E. Collins
Commissioner
Dept. of Revenue
270 Washington St., SW
Atlanta, GA 30334
Phone : (404) 656-4015

HAWAII
Ray Kamikawa
Director
Dept. of Taxation
830 Punchbowl St., Ste. 221
Honolulu, HI 96813
Phone : (808) 587-1510
Fax : (808) 587-1438

IDAHO
Coleen Grant
Chairman
State Tax Comm.
700 W. State St.
Boise, ID 83722
Phone : (208) 334-7500

ILLINOIS
Raymond T. Wagner Jr.
Director
Dept. of Revenue
101 W. Jefferson St.,
Rm. 6SW
Springfield, IL 62794
Phone : (217) 785-2602
Fax : (217) 782-6337

Ken Zehnder
Deputy Director
Dept. of Revenue
101 W. Jefferson St.
Springfield, IL 62794
Phone : (217) 785-7570

INDIANA
Kenneth Miller
Commissioner
Dept. of Revenue
State Off. Bldg., Rm. 202
Indianapolis, IN 46204
Phone : (317) 232-8039

IOWA
Gerald D. Bair
Director
Dept. of Revenue &
Finance
Hoover State Off. Bldg.
Des Moines, IA 50319
Phone : (515) 281-3204
Fax : (515) 242-6040

KANSAS
John LaFaver
Secretary
Dept. of Revenue
Docking State Off. Bldg.,
2nd Fl.
Topeka, KS 66612
Phone : (913) 296-3909
Fax : (913) 296-7928

KENTUCKY
Kim Burse
Secretary
Revenue Cabinet
200 Fairoaks
Frankfort, KY 40601
Phone : (502) 564-3226

LOUISIANA
Ralph Slaughter
Secretary
Dept. of Revenue &
Taxation
P.O. Box 201
Baton Rouge, LA 70821
Phone : (504) 925-7680

MAINE
Brian Mahoney
Acting State Tax Assesor
Bur. of Taxation
Dept. of Finance
State House Station # 24
Augusta, ME 04333
Phone : (207) 287-2076

MARYLAND**
Louis L. Goldstein
Comptroller
Dept. of Budget & Fiscal
Plan.
Treasury Bldg., Rm. 121
P.O. Box 466
Annapolis, MD 21404
Phone : (410) 974-3801

MASSACHUSETTS
Mitchell Adams
Commissioner
Dept. of Revenue
Executive Off. for Admin.
& Finance
100 Cambridge St.,
Rm. 806
Boston, MA 02202
Phone : (617) 727-4201

MICHIGAN
Thomas Hoatlin
Commissioner of
Revenue
Bur. of Revenue
Dept. of Treasury
Treasury Bldg.
Lansing, MI 48909
Phone : (517) 373-3196

MINNESOTA
Matt Smith
Acting Commissioner
Dept. of Revenue
10 River Park Plz.
St. Paul, MN 55146-7100
Phone : (612) 296-3403

MISSISSIPPI
Ed Buelow
Chairman
State Tax Comm.
102 Woolfolk Bldg.
P.O. Box 22828
Jackson, MS 39205
Phone : (601) 359-1098

MISSOURI
Janette M. Lohman
Director
Dept. of Revenue
Truman Bldg., Rm. 670
P.O. Box 311
Jefferson City, MO 65105
Phone : (314) 751-4450
Fax : (314) 751-7150

MONTANA
Michael Robinson
Director
Dept. of Revenue
Sam Mitchell Bldg., Rm. 455
Helena, MT 59620
Phone : (406) 444-2460

NEBRASKA
M. Berri Balka
State Tax Commissioner
Dept. of Revenue
P.O. Box 94818
Lincoln, NE 68509-4818
Phone : (402) 471-5604

NEVADA
Michael Pitlock
Executive Director
Dept. of Taxation
1340 S. Curry St.
Carson City, NV 89710
Phone : (702) 687-5981

NEW HAMPSHIRE
Stanley R. Arnold
Commissioner
Dept. of Revenue Admin.
61 S. Spring St.
Concord, NH 03302
Phone : (603) 271-2191

NEW JERSEY
Richard D. Gardner
Director
Div. of Taxation
Dept. of Treasury
50 Barrack St., CN240
Trenton, NJ 08625-0067
Phone : (609) 292-5158

NEW MEXICO
John Chavez
Secretary
Dept. of Taxation & Revenue
Joseph Montoya Bldg.
Santa Fe, NM 87503
Phone : (505) 827-0341
Fax : (505) 827-0331

NEW YORK*
Commissioner
Dept. of Taxation & Finance
State Campus, Bldg. 9, Rm. 205
Albany, NY 12227
Phone : (518) 457-2244

NORTH CAROLINA
Janice Faulkner
Secretary
Dept. of Revenue
501 N. Wilmington St.
Raleigh, NC 27640
Phone : (919) 733-7211

NORTH DAKOTA
Robert E. Hanson
Commissioner
Tax Dept.
State Capitol, 8th Fl.
600 E. Boulevard Ave.
Bismarck, ND 58505-0599
Phone : (701) 328-2770
Fax : (701) 328-3700

OHIO
Roger W. Tracy
Commissioner
Dept. of Taxation
30 E. Broad St., 22nd Fl.
Columbus, OH 43215-0030
Phone : (614) 466-2166
Fax : (614) 466-6401

OKLAHOMA
Bob Anderson
Chairman
Tax Comm.
2501 N. Lincoln Blvd.
Oklahoma City, OK 73194
Phone : (405) 521-3115

OREGON
Richard A. Munn
Director
Dept. of Revenue
955 Center St., NE
Salem, OR 97310
Phone : (503) 945-8210
Fax : (503) 945-8738

PENNSYLVANIA
Robert A. Judge Sr.
Secretary
Dept. of Revenue
11th Fl., Strawberry Square
Harrisburg, PA 17120
Phone : (717) 783-3680

RHODE ISLAND
R. Gary Clark
Chief
Div. of Taxation
Dept. of Administration
One Capitol Hill
Providence, RI 02908
Phone : (401) 277-3050

SOUTH CAROLINA
Gregorie Frampton
Administrator
Dept. of Revenue & Taxation
301 Gervais St.
Columbia, SC 29201
Phone : (803) 737-9820

SOUTH DAKOTA
Julie Johnson
Secretary
Dept. of Revenue
700 Governors Dr.
Pierre, SD 57501
Phone : (605) 773-3311

TENNESSEE
Ruth Johnson
Commissioner
Dept. of Revenue
1200 Andrew Jackson Bldg.
Nashville, TN 37219
Phone : (615) 741-2461

TEXAS
John Sharp
Comptroller
Public Accounts
P.O. Box 13528, Capitol Station
Austin, TX 78711
Phone : (512) 463-4000

UTAH
Rodney G. Marrelli
Executive Director
State Tax Comm.
210 N. 1950 W.
Salt Lake City, UT 84134
Phone : (801) 297-3845

VERMONT
Elizabeth Anderson
Commissioner
Dept. of Taxes
Agency of Administration
109 State St.
Montpelier, VT 05602
Phone : (802) 828-2505
Fax : (802) 828-2701

VIRGINIA
Danny M. Payne
Tax Commissioner
Dept. of Taxation
2220 West Broad St.
Richmond, VA 23220
Phone : (804) 367-8005
Fax : (804) 367-0971

WASHINGTON
Len McComb
Director
Dept. of Revenue
General Administration Bldg.
P.O. Box 47450
Olympia, WA 98504-7450
Phone : (360) 753-5540

WEST VIRGINIA
James H. Paige III
Secretary
Dept. of Tax & Revenue
Bldg. 1, Rm. WW-300
1900 Kanawha Blvd., E.
Charleston, WV 25305
Phone : (304) 558-0211

WISCONSIN
Mark D. Bugher
Secretary
Dept. of Revenue
125 S. Webster
Madison, WI 53702
Phone : (608) 266-6466
Fax : (608) 266-5718

WYOMING
Johnnie Burton
Director
Dept. of Revenue
Herschler Bldg.
122 W. 25th St.
Cheyenne, WY 82002
Phone : (307) 777-5287

DISTRICT OF COLUMBIA
Lorraine Britton
Director
Dept. of Finance & Revenue
441 4th St., NW
Washington, DC 20001
Phone : (202) 727-6020

AMERICAN SAMOA
Siona McMoore
Manager
Revenue Div.
Dept. of Treasury
Pago Pago, AS 96799
Phone : (684) 633-5166
Fax : (684) 633-4100

GUAM
Joseph T. Duenas
Director
Dept. of Revenue & Taxation
375 Chalan San Antonio
Tamuning, GU 96911
Phone : (671) 647-5107
Fax : (671) 472-2643

NORTHERN MARIANA ISLANDS
John L. Evangelista
Chief
Revenue & Taxation Div.
Dept. of Finance & Accounting
P.O. Box 234, CHRB
Saipan, MP 96950
Phone : (670) 664-1000

PUERTO RICO
Ruben Guzman
Director
Income Tax Bur.
Dept. of Treasury
P.O. Box S-4515
San Juan, PR 00904
Phone : (809) 721-2020
Fax : (809) 722-6854

U.S. VIRGIN ISLANDS
Joanne Bozzuto Esq.
Director
Bur. of Internal Revenue
Lockharts Garden No. 1A
St. Thomas, VI 00802
Phone : (809) 774-4572
Fax : (809) 776-4037

SAVINGS & LOAN

Administers laws regulating the operation of savings and loan associations in the state.

ALABAMA
Kenneth McCartha
Acting Superintendent
Dept. of State Banking
101 S. Union St.
Montgomery, AL 36130
Phone : (334) 242-3452
Fax : (334) 242-3500

ALASKA
Willis Kirkpatrick
Director
Banking, Securities & Corps.
Dept. of Comm. & Economic Dev.
P.O. Box 110807
Juneau, AK 99811-0807
Phone : (907) 465-2521
Fax : (907) 465-2549

ARIZONA
Richard C. Houseworth
Supertintendent
Dept. of Banking
2910 N. 44th St., Ste. 310
Phoenix, AZ 85018
Phone : (602) 255-4421

ARKANSAS
Joe Madden Jr.
Commissioner
Dept. of Securities
201 E. Marham St., 3rd Fl.
Little Rock, AR 72201
Phone : (501) 324-9260
Fax : (501) 324-9268

CALIFORNIA
Keith Bishop
Commissioner
Dept. of Savings & Loan
300 S. Spring St., Ste. 16502
Los Angeles, CA 90012
Phone : (213) 897-8242

COLORADO
David L. Paul
Commissioner
Div. of Financial Srvcs.
Dept. of Regulatory Agencies
1560 Broadway, Rm. 1520
Denver, CO 80202
Phone : (303) 894-2336

CONNECTICUT
John P. Burke
Commissioner
Dept. of Banking
260 Constitution Plaza
Hartford, CT 06103
Phone : (203) 240-8100

DELAWARE
Timothy McTaggart
State Bank Commissioner
Dept. of State
P.O. Box 1401
Dover, DE 19903
Phone : (302) 577-3315
Fax : (302) 577-3689

FLORIDA
Patrick Robichaud
Financial Administrator
Div. of Banking
Dept. of Banking & Finance
The Capitol
Tallahassee, FL 32399-0350
Phone : (904) 488-9570

GEORGIA
Edward D. Dunn
Commissioner
Dept. of Banking & Finance
2990 Brandywine Rd., # 200
Atlanta, GA 30341
Phone : (404) 986-1633

HAWAII
Raymond Muraoka
Commissioner
Div. of Financial Institutions
Dept. of Comm. & Consumer Aff.
250 S. King St.
Honolulu, HI 96813
Phone : (808) 586-2820

IDAHO
Gavin Gee
Director
Dept. of Finance
700 W. State St.
Boise, ID 83720
Phone : (208) 334-3319

ILLINOIS
Jack Schaffer
Commissioner
Savings & Residential Finance
500 E. Monroe, # 800
Springfield, IL 62701-1509
Phone : (217) 782-1398
Fax : (217) 782-6170

INDIANA
Charles W. Phillips
Director
Dept. of Fin. Institutions
IGC-West, Rm. 066
402 W. Washington St.
Indianapolis, IN 46204
Phone : (317) 232-0010

IOWA
Jack Nystrom
Director
Dept. of Commerce
1918 SE Hulsizer
Ankeny, IA 50021
Phone : (515) 281-7401
Fax : (515) 281-7372

KANSAS
Frank D. Dunnick
Commissioner
Off. of the State Banking Commissioner
700 SW Jackson, Ste. 300
Topeka, KS 66603-3796
Phone : (913) 296-2266
Fax : (913) 296-0168

KENTUCKY
Edward J. Holmes
Acting Commissioner
Dept. of Financial Inst.
Public Prot. & Reg. Cabinet
477 Versailles Rd.
Frankfort, KY 40601
Phone : (502) 573-3390

LOUISIANA
Larry L. Murray
Assistant Secretary
Off. of Financial Institutions
Dept. of Economic Development
P.O. Box 94185
Baton Rouge, LA 70804-9185
Phone : (504) 925-4660

MAINE
H. Donald DeMatteis
Superintendent
Bur. of Banking
Dept. of Prof. & Fin. Reg.
State House Station # 36
Augusta, ME 04333
Phone : (207) 582-8713

MARYLAND**
Margie Muller
Banking Commissioner
Dept. of Licensing & Regulation
501 St. Paul Pl., 13th Fl.
Baltimore, MD 21202
Phone : (410) 333-6812

MASSACHUSETTS
Thomas J. Curry
Acting Commissioner
Div. of Banks
100 Cambridge St., Rm. 2004
Boston, MA 02202
Phone : (617) 727-3145

MICHIGAN
Darwyn P. Sanborn
Director
Div. of Corporate Reg. Srvcs.
Dept. of Commerce
P.O. Box 30224
Lansing, MI 48909
Phone : (517) 373-6940

MINNESOTA
James Miller
Deputy Commissioner
Div. of Financial Examinations
Dept. of Commerce
133 7th St., E.
St. Paul, MN 55101
Phone : (612) 296-2715

MISSISSIPPI
Joseph H. Neely
Director
Dept. of Banking & Consumer Finance
P.O. Drawer 23729
Jackson, MS 39225
Phone : (601) 359-1103

MISSOURI
Earl Manning
Commissioner of Finance
Dept. of Economic Development
Truman Bldg., Rm. 630
P.O. Box 716
Jefferson City, MO 65102
Phone : (314) 751-2545
Fax : (314) 751-9192

MONTANA
Donald W. Hutchinson
Commissioner
Financial Div.
Dept. of Commerce
1520 E. 6th Ave., Rm. 50
Helena, MT 59620
Phone : (406) 444-2091

NEBRASKA
James A. Hansen
Director
Dept. of Banking & Finance
1200 N. Street, Suite #300
Lincoln, NE 68509-5006
Phone : (402) 471-2171

NEVADA
L. Scott Walshaw
Commissioner
Div. of Financial Institutions
Dept. of Business & Industry
406 E. Second St.
Carson City, NV 89710
Phone : (702) 687-4259

NEW HAMPSHIRE
A. Roland Roberge
Commissioner
Dept. of Banking
169 Manchester St.
Concord, NH 03301
Phone : (603) 271-3561

NEW JERSEY
Elizabeth Randall
Director
Div. of Supervision
Dept. of Banking
20 W. State St., CN 040
Trenton, NJ 08625
Phone : (609) 292-3420

NEW MEXICO
William L. Verant
Director
Financial Institutions Div.
Dept. of Reg. & Licensing
P.O. Box 25101
Santa Fe, NM 87504
Phone : (505) 827-7100
Fax : (505) 827-7107

NEW YORK*
Superintendent
Dept. of Banking
2 Rector St.
New York, NY 10006
Phone : (212) 618-6557

NORTH CAROLINA
Robert Jacobsen
Administrator
Div. of Savings & Loan
Dept. of Commerce
1110 Navaho Dr., Ste. 301
Raleigh, NC 27609
Phone : (919) 850-2888

NORTH DAKOTA
Gary Preszler
Commissioner
Dept. of Banking & Fin. Inst.
State Capitol, 13th Fl.
600 E. Boulevard Ave.
Bismarck, ND 58505
Phone : (701) 328-2253
Fax : (701) 328-3000

OHIO
John Gayton
Acting Superintendent
Division of Savings & Loan Assn.
Department of Commerce
2 Nationwide Plaza., 6th Floor
Columbus, OH 43266
Phone : (614) 466-3723
Fax : (614) 466-5594

OKLAHOMA
Mick Thompson
Commissioner
Dept. of Banking
4100 N. Lincoln Blvd.
Oklahoma City, OK 73105
Phone : (405) 521-2782

OREGON
Cecil Monroe
Administrator
Finance & Corp. Securities Div
Dept. of Consumer & Bus. Srvcs.
305 Winter St., NE
Salem, OR 97310
Phone : (503) 378-4387
Fax : (503) 378-4178

PENNSYLVANIA
Richard C. Rishel
Secretary
Dept. of Banking
16th Fl., Harristown 2
Harrisburg, PA 17120
Phone : (717) 787-6991

RHODE ISLAND
Edward Pare Jr.
Associate Director
Banking Div.
Dept. of Business Regulation
233 Richmond St., Ste. 231
Providence, RI 02903
Phone : (401) 277-2405

SOUTH CAROLINA
Richard Eckstrom
State Treasurer
Wade Hampton Bldg., Rm. 120
P.O. Box 11778
Columbia, SC 29211
Phone : (803) 734-2688

SOUTH DAKOTA
Dick Duncan
Director
Div. of Banking & Finance
Dept. of Commerce & Regulation
105 N. Euclid
Pierre, SD 57501
Phone : (605) 773-3421

TENNESSEE
Roger Thomas
Assistant Commissioner
Div. of Loans
Financial Institutions Dept.
James K. Polk Bldg., 2nd Fl.
Nashville, TN 37243
Phone : (615) 741-3186

TEXAS
James L. Pledger
Commissioner
Savings & Loan Dept.
2601 N. Lamar Blvd., Ste. 201
Austin, TX 78705
Phone : (512) 475-1350

UTAH
G. Edward Leary
Commissioner
Dept. of Financial Institutions
324 S. State, Ste. 201
P.O. Box 89
Salt Lake City, UT 84110
Phone : (801) 538-8854

VERMONT
Elizabeth R. Costle
Commissioner
Dept. of Banking, Ins. & Sec.
89 State St.
Montpelier, VT 05620-3101
Phone : (802) 828-3301
Fax : (802) 828-3306

VIRGINIA
Preston C. Shannon
Chair
State Corporation Comm.
Tyler Bldg.
1300 E. Main St.
Richmond, VA 23219
Phone : (804) 371-9608
Fax : (804) 371-9376

WASHINGTON
G. R. Zachary
Supervisor
Div. of Savings & Loan Assns.
Dept. of Financial Institutions
P.O. Box 41203
Olympia, WA 98504
Phone : (360) 902-8701

WEST VIRGINIA
Sharon G. Bias
Commissioner
Div. of Banking
Bldg. 3, Rm. 311-A
1800 Washington St., E.
Charleston, WV 25305
Phone : (304) 558-2294

WISCONSIN
Harold Lee
Commissioner
Off. of Commissioner of Savings & Loans
4785 Hayes Rd., #202
Madison, WI 53704
Phone : (608) 242-2180
Fax : (608) 242-2187

WYOMING
Sue Mecca
Commissioner
Banking Div.
Dept. of Audit
Herschler Bldg., 3rd Fl.
Cheyenne, WY 82002
Phone : (307) 777-7797

DISTRICT OF COLUMBIA
Fe Morales Marks
Superintendent
Off. of Banking & Financial Institutions
1250 I St., NW, Rm. 1003
Washington, DC 20005
Phone : (202) 727-1563

GUAM
Joseph T. Duenas
Director
Dept. of Revenue & Taxation
378 Chalan San Antonio
Tanuming, GU 96911
Phone : (671) 647-5107
Fax : (671) 472-2643

NORTHERN MARIANA ISLANDS
Oscar C. Camacho
Special Asst. for Banking
Dept. of Commerce & Labor
Off. of the Governor
Saipan, MP 96950
Phone : (670) 322-4361

PUERTO RICO
Miquel A. Martinez
Director
Employees' Association
P.O. Box 364508
San Juan, PR 00936-4508
Phone : (809) 753-2100
Fax : (809) 763-8918

U.S. VIRGIN ISLANDS
Kenneth E. Mapp
Lt. Governor
#18 Kongens Gade
St. Thomas, VI 00802
Phone : (809) 774-2991
Fax : (809) 774-6953

SECRETARY OF STATE

Statewide official who performs a variety of electoral, registration, custodial, publication and legislative duties for the state.

ALABAMA
Jim Bennett
Secretary of State
State Capitol
600 Dexter Ave.
Montgomery, AL 36130
Phone : (205) 242-7200
Fax : (205) 242-3138

ALASKA
Fran Ulmer
Lt. Governor
P.O. Box 110015
Juneau, AK 99811-0015
Phone : (907) 465-3520
Fax : (907) 465-5400

ARIZONA
Jane Dee Hull
Secretary of State
1700 W. Washington St., Ste. 700
Phoenix, AZ 85007
Phone : (602) 542-0681
Fax : (602) 542-1575

ARKANSAS
Sharon Priest
Secretary of State
State Capitol, Rm. 256
Little Rock, AR 72201
Phone : (501) 682-1010
Fax : (501) 682-3510

CALIFORNIA
Bill Jones
Secretary of State
1500 11th St.
Sacramento, CA 95814
Phone : (916) 653-7244

COLORADO
Vikki Buckley
Secretary of State
1560 Broadway, Ste. 200
Denver, CO 80202
Phone : (303) 894-2200
Fax : (303) 894-2242

CONNECTICUT
Miles S. Rapoport
Secretary of State
State Capitol, Rm. 104
Hartford, CT 06106
Phone : (203) 566-2739
Fax : (203) 566-6318

DELAWARE
Edward J. Freel
Secretary of State
P.O. Box 898
Dover, DE 19903
Phone : (302) 739-4111
Fax : (302) 739-3811

FLORIDA
Sandra B. Mortham
Secretary of State
The Capitol
The Plaza Level, Rm. 2
Tallahassee, FL 32399-0250
Phone : (904) 922-0234
Fax : (904) 487-2214

GEORGIA
Max Cleland
Secretary of State
State Capitol, Rm. 214
Atlanta, GA 30334
Phone : (404) 656-2881
Fax : (404) 656-0513

HAWAII
Mazie Hirono
Lt. Governor
State Capitol, 5th Floor
235 S. Beretania St.
Honolulu, HI 96813
Phone : (808) 586-0255
Fax : (808) 586-0231

IDAHO
Pete T. Cenarrusa
Secretary of State
State Capitol, Rm. 203
Boise, ID 83720
Phone : (208) 334-2300
Fax : (208) 334-2282

ILLINOIS
George H. Ryan
Secretary of State
213 State Capitol
Springfield, IL 62706
Phone : (217) 782-2201
Fax : (217) 785-0358

INDIANA
Sue Ann Gilroy
State House, Rm. 201
Indianapolis, IN 46204
Phone : (317) 232-6531
Fax : (317) 233-3283

IOWA
Paul Pate
Secretary of State
State Capitol
Des Moines, IA 50319
Phone : (515) 281-5204
Fax : (515) 242-5952

KANSAS
Ron Thornburgh
Secretary of State
State Capitol, 2nd Fl.
Topeka, KS 66612
Phone : (913) 296-4575
Fax : (913) 296-4570

KENTUCKY
Bob Babbage
Secretary of State
State Capitol, Rm. 150
Frankfort, KY 40601
Phone : (502) 564-3490
Fax : (502) 564-5687

LOUISIANA
W. Fox McKeithen
Secretary of State
P.O. Box 94125
Baton Rouge, LA 70804
Phone : (504) 342-4479
Fax : (504) 342-5577

MAINE
G. William Diamond
Secretary of State
State House Station # 148
Augusta, ME 04333-0148
Phone : (207) 626-8400
Fax : (207) 287-8598

MARYLAND
John T. Willis
Secretary of State
State House
Annapolis, MD 21401
Phone : (410) 974-5521
Fax: (410) 974-5190

MASSACHUSETTS
William F. Galvin
Secretary of the Commonwealth
State House, Rm. 337
Boston, MA 02133
Phone : (617) 727-9180
Fax : (617) 742-4722

MICHIGAN
Candice Miller
Secretary of State
Treasury Bldg., 1st Fl.
430 W. Allegan St.
Lansing, MI 48918
Phone : (517) 373-2510
Fax : (517) 373-0727

MINNESOTA
Joan Growe
Secretary of State
180 State Off. Bldg.
100 Constitution Ave.
St. Paul, MN 55155
Phone : (612) 296-2079
Fax : (612) 297-5844

MISSISSIPPI
Dick Molpus
Secretary of State
401 Mississippi St.
P.O. Box 136
Jackson, MS 39205
Phone : (601) 359-1350
Fax : (601) 354-6243

MISSOURI
Rebecca Cook
Secretary of State
208 State Capitol
P.O. Box 778
Jefferson City, MO 65102
Phone : (314) 751-4595
Fax : (314) 526-4903

MONTANA
Mike Cooney
Secretary of State
State Capitol, Rm. 225
Helena, MT 59620
Phone : (406) 444-2034
Fax : (406) 444-3976

NEBRASKA
Scott Moore
Secretary of State
State Capitol, Rm. 2300
P.O. Box 94608
Lincoln, NE 68509
Phone : (402) 471-2554
Fax : (402) 471-6031

NEVADA
Dean Heller
Secretary of State
Capitol Complex
Carson City, NV 89710
Phone : (702) 687-5203
Fax : (702) 687-3471

NEW HAMPSHIRE
William Gardner
Secretary of State
204 State House
Concord, NH 03301
Phone : (603) 271-3242
Fax : (603) 271-6316

NEW JERSEY
Lonna R. Hooks
Secretary of State
CN-300
Trenton, NJ 08625
Phone : (609) 984-1900
Fax : (609) 292-7665

NEW MEXICO
Stephanie Gonzales
Secretary of State
State Capitol, Rm. 420
Santa Fe, NM 87503
Phone : (505) 827-3600
Fax : (505) 827-3634

NEW YORK
Alexander F. Treadwell
Secretary of State
162 Washington Ave.
Albany, NY 12231
Phone : (518) 474-0050
Fax : (518) 474-4765

NORTH CAROLINA
Rufus L. Edmisten
Secretary of State
300 N. Salisbury St.
Raleigh, NC 27603-5909
Phone : (919) 733-5140

NORTH DAKOTA
Alvin A. Jaeger
Secretary of State
State Capitol, 1st Fl.
600 E. Boulevard Ave.
Bismarck, ND 58505-0500
Phone : (701) 328-2900
Fax : (701) 328-2992

OHIO
Bob Taft
Secretary of State
14th Fl., 30 East Broad
Columbus, OH 43266-0418
Phone : (614) 466-2655
Fax : (614) 644-0649

OKLAHOMA
Tom Cole
Secretary of State
State Capitol Bldg., Ste. 101
Oklahoma City, OK 73105
Phone : (405) 521-3911

OREGON
Phil Keisling
Secretary of State
136 State Capitol
Salem, OR 97310
Phone : (503) 986-1523
Fax : (503) 373-7414

PENNSYLVANIA
Yvette Kane
Secretary of the
Commonwealth
Dept. of State
Rm. 302, North Capitol
Bldg.
Harrisburg, PA 17120
Phone : (717) 787-7630

RHODE ISLAND
James R. Langevin
Secretary of State
Rm. 218, State House
Providence, RI 02903
Phone : (401) 277-2357
Fax : (401) 277-1356

SOUTH CAROLINA
Jim Miles
Secretary of State
Wade Hampton Bldg.
P.O. Box 11350
Columbia, SC 29211
Phone : (803) 734-2170
Fax : (803) 734-2164

SOUTH DAKOTA
Joyce Hazeltine
Secretary of State
State Capitol, 2nd Fl.
Pierre, SD 57501
Phone : (605) 773-3537
Fax : (605) 773-6580

TENNESSEE
Riley Darnell
Secretary of State
1st. Fl., State Capitol
Nashville, TN 37243-0305
Phone : (615) 741-2819
Fax : (615) 741-5962

TEXAS
Anthony O. Garza
Secretary of State
Capitol Extension,
Ste. E1.804
P.O. Box 12697
Austin, TX 78711
Phone : (512) 463-5701
Fax : (512) 475-2761

UTAH
Olene S. Walker
Lt. Governor
203 State Capitol Bldg.
Salt Lake City, UT 84114
Phone : (801) 538-1520

VERMONT
James Milne
Secretary of State
109 State St.
Montpelier, VT 05609-1101
Phone : (802) 828-2148
Fax : (802) 828-2496

VIRGINIA
Betsy Davis Beamer
Secretary of the
Commonwealth
Office of the Secretary of
the Commonwealth
Old Finance Building,
1st Fl.
Richmond, VA 23201
Phone : (804) 786-2441
Fax : (804) 371-0017

WASHINGTON
Ralph Munro
Secretary of State
P.O. Box 40220
Olympia, WA 98504-0220
Phone : (360) 753-7121
Fax : (360) 586-5629

WEST VIRGINIA
Ken Hechler
Secretary of State
State Capitol, Rm. W-157K
1900 Kanawha Blvd., E.
Charleston, WV 25305
Phone : (304) 558-6000
Fax : (304) 558-0900

WISCONSIN
Douglas La Follette
Secretary of State
30 W. Mifflin St.,
9th & 10th Fl.
Madison, WI 53703
Phone : (608) 266-9975
Fax : (608) 267-6813

WYOMING
Diana J. Ohman
Secretary of State
State Capitol
Cheyenne, WY 82002
Phone : (307) 777-5333
Fax : (307) 777-6217

DISTRICT OF COLUMBIA
Marianne C. Niles
Secretary of Dist. of
Columbia
441 4th St., NW, Ste. 1130
Washington, DC 20004
Phone : (202) 727-6306
Fax : (202) 727-3582

AMERICAN SAMOA
Tauese P. Sunia
Lt. Governor
Off. of the Governor
Pago Pago, AS 96799
Phone : (684) 633-5201
Fax : (684) 633-2269

GUAM
Madeleine Bordallo
Lieutenant Governor
Executive Chambers
P.O. Box 2950
Agana, GU 96910
Phone : (671) 474-8931
Fax : (671) 477-4826

Secretary of State

PUERTO RICO
Baltasar C. Del Rio
Secretary of State
Dept. of State
P.O. Box 3271
San Juan, PR 00904
Phone : (809) 722-2121
Fax : (809) 725-7303

U.S. VIRGIN ISLANDS
Kenneth E. Mapp
Lt. Governor
18 Kongens Gade
St. Thomas, VI 00801
Phone : (809) 774-2991
Fax : (809) 774-6953

SECURITIES

Regulates the sale of securities and registers securities prior to public sale.

ALABAMA
Joseph Borg
Director
Securities Comm.
770 Washington St., Ste. 570
Montgomery, AL 36130
Phone : (334) 242-2984
Fax : (334) 242-0240

ALASKA
Willis Kirkpatrick
Director
Banking, Securities & Corps.
Dept. of Comm. & Economic Dev.
P.O. Box 110807
Juneau, AK 99811-0807
Phone : (907) 465-2521
Fax : (907) 465-2549

ARIZONA
Dee Riddell Harris
Director
Securities Division
Corporation Commission
1200 W. Washington
Phoenix, AZ 85007
Phone : (602) 542-4242

ARKANSAS
Joe Madden Jr.
Commissioner
Dept. of Securities
201 E. Marham St., 3rd Fl.
Little Rock, AR 72201
Phone : (501) 324-9260
Fax : (501) 324-9268

CALIFORNIA
Gary S. Mendoza
Commissioner
Dept. of Corporations
3700 Wilshire Blvd., Ste. 600
Los Angeles, CA 90010
Phone : (213) 736-3481

COLORADO
Philip Feigin
Commissioner
Securities Div.
Dept. of Regulatory Agencies
1580 Lincoln, Ste. 420
Denver, CO 80203
Phone : (303) 894-2320

CONNECTICUT
Ralph Lambiase
Director
Securities & Bus. Investments
Dept. of Banking
260 Constitution Plaza
Hartford, CT 06103
Phone : (203) 240-8299

DELAWARE
Edward J. Freel
Secretary of State
P.O. Box 898
Dover, DE 19903
Phone : (302) 739-4111

FLORIDA
Don Saxon
Director
Securities Div.
Dept. of Banking & Finance
The Capitol, LL22
Tallahassee, FL 32399
Phone : (904) 488-9805

GEORGIA
James Gullion
Director
Business Srvcs. & Regulations
Off. of Secretary of State
2 M.L. King, Jr. Dr., SE, 306
Atlanta, GA 30334
Phone : (404) 656-6478

HAWAII
Lynn Wakatsuki
Commissioner of Securities
Business Registration Div.
Dept. of Commerce & Cons. Aff.
1010 Richards St.
Honolulu, HI 96813
Phone : (808) 586-2737

IDAHO
Gavin Gee
Director
Dept. of Finance
700 W. State St.
Boise, ID 83720
Phone : (208) 334-3319

ILLINOIS
George H. Ryan
Secretary of State
213 State House
Springfield, IL 62706
Phone : (217) 782-2201
Fax : (217) 785-0358

INDIANA
Brad Skolnik
Commissioner
Securities Div.
302 W. Washington, Rm. E111
Indianapolis, IN 46204
Phone : (317) 232-6690

IOWA
Craig Goettsch
Superintendent
Securities Div.
Dept. of Commerce
Lucas State Off. Bldg.
Des Moines, IA 50319
Phone : (515) 281-4441

KANSAS
John Wine Jr.
Securities Commissioner
618 S. Kansas Ave., 2nd Fl.
Topeka, KS 66603-3804
Phone : (913) 296-3307
Fax : (913) 296-6872

KENTUCKY
Edward J. Holmes
Acting Commissioner
Dept. of Financial Inst.
Public Prot. & Reg. Cabinet
477 Versailles Rd.
Frankfort, KY 40601
Phone : (502) 573-3390

LOUISIANA
Mary L. Landrieu
State Treasurer
Dept. of Treasury
P.O. Box 44154
Baton Rouge, LA 70804-0154
Phone : (504) 342-0010

MAINE
H. Donald DeMatteis
Superintendent
Bur. of Banking
Dept. of Prof. & Fin. Reg.
State House Station # 36
Augusta, ME 04333
Phone : (207) 582-8713

MARYLAND**
Robert N. McDonald
Commissioner
Div. of Securities
Off. of Attorney General
200 St. Paul Pl.
Baltimore, MD 21202
Phone : (410) 576-6362

MASSACHUSETTS
Barry C. Guthary
Director
Securities Div.
Off. of Secretary of Commonwealth
1 Ashburton Pl., Rm. 1701
Boston, MA 02108
Phone : (617) 727-7190

MICHIGAN
Ronald Jones
Acting Director
Securities
Dept. of Commerce
6546 Mercantile Way
Lansing, MI 48909
Phone : (517) 334-6200

MINNESOTA
Patrick Nelson
Deputy Commissioner
Registration & Analysis Div.
Dept. of Commerce
133 7th St., E.
St. Paul, MN 55101
Phone : (612) 296-6325

MISSISSIPPI
Susan Shands
Assistant Secretary of State
Securities Div.
Off. of Secretary of State
P.O. Box 136
Jackson, MS 39205
Phone : (601) 359-6368

MISSOURI
June Striegel Doughty
Acting Commissioner of Securities
Off. of Secretary of State
600 W. Main
P.O. Box 778
Jefferson City, MO 65102
Phone : (314) 751-4704
Fax : (314) 526-3124

MONTANA
Mark O'Keefe
State Auditor, Comm. of Insurance
Commissioner of Securities
Securities Div.
Off. of State Auditor
P.O. Box 4009
Helena, MT 59604-4009
Phone : (406) 444-2040

NEBRASKA
James A. Hansen
Director
Dept. of Banking & Finance
1200 N. Street #300
Lincoln, NE 68509-5006
Phone : (402) 471-2171

NEVADA
Donald Reis
Deputy Secretary of State
Securities Div.
555 E. Washington Ave., Ste. 2700
Las Vegas, NV 89101
Phone : (702) 486-2440
Fax : (702) 486-2452

NEW HAMPSHIRE
Jeffrey R. Howard
Attorney General
25 Capitol St.
Concord, NH 03301
Phone : (603) 271-3655

NEW JERSEY
Mark Herr
Director
Div. of Consumer Affairs
P.O. Box 45027
Newark, NJ 07101
Phone : (201) 504-6200

NEW MEXICO
Michael Vargon
Deputy Director
Securities Div.
Dept. of Reg. & Licensing
P.O. Box 25101
725 St. Michael Dr.
Santa Fe, NM 87501
Phone : (505) 827-7140
Fax : (505) 984-0617

NORTH CAROLINA
Eugene Cella
Securities Administrator
Div. of Securities
Off. of Secretary of State
300 N. Salisbury St., Ste. 404
Raleigh, NC 27603
Phone : (919) 733-3924

NORTH DAKOTA
Calvin J. Hoovestol
Commissioner
Off. of Securities Comm.
State Capitol, 5th Fl.
600 E. Boulevard Ave.
Bismarck, ND 58505-0510
Phone : (701) 328-2910
Fax : (701) 255-3113

OHIO
Mark V. Holderman
Commissioner
Div. of Securities
Dept. of Commerce
2 Nationwide Plz., 3rd Fl.
Columbus, OH 43266
Phone : (614) 644-7381
Fax : (614) 466-3316

OKLAHOMA
Irving Faught
Administrator
Securities Comm.
621 N. Robinson, Ste. 200
Oklahoma City, OK 73152-6217
Phone : (405) 235-0230

OREGON
Cecil Monroe
Administrator
Div. of Fin. & Corp. Securities
Dept. of Consumer & Business Srvcs.
305 Winter St., NE
Salem, OR 97310
Phone : (503) 378-4387
Fax : (503) 378-4178

PENNSYLVANIA
Robert Lam
Chairman
Securities Comm.
1010 N. 7th St.
Harrisburg, PA 17102-1410
Phone : (717) 787-8061

RHODE ISLAND
Maria D'Alessandr Piccirilli
Associate Director & Superintendent of Securities
Securities Div.
Dept. of Business Regulation
233 Richmond St.
Providence, RI 02903
Phone : (401) 277-3048

SOUTH CAROLINA
Tracy Meyers
Deputy Securities Commissioner
Securities Div.
Off. of Secretary of State
P.O. Box 11350
Columbia, SC 29211
Phone : (803) 734-1089

SOUTH DAKOTA
Deborah Bollinger
Director
Div. of Securities
Dept. of Commerce & Reg.
910 E. Sioux Ave.
Pierre, SD 57501
Phone : (605) 773-4823

TENNESSEE
Kenneth McClellan
Assistant Commissioner
Securities Div.
Dept. of Commerce & Insurance
500 James Robertson Pkwy.
Nashville, TN 37243
Phone : (615) 741-2947

TEXAS
Denise Voigt Crawford
Commissioner
State Securities Bd.
P.O. Box 13167
Austin, TX 78711-3167
Phone : (512) 305-8300

UTAH
Mark J. Griffin
Director
Securities Div.
Dept. of Commerce
160 E. 300 S.
Salt Lake City, UT 84111
Phone : (801) 530-6607

VERMONT
Elizabeth R. Costle
Commissioner
Dept. of Banking, Ins. & Sec.
89 State St.
Montpelier, VT 05620-3101
Phone : (802) 828-3301
Fax : (802) 828-3306

VIRGINIA
Preston C. Shannon
Director
Securities Div.
State Corporation Comm.
1300 E. Main St.
Richmond, VA 23219
Phone : (804) 371-9608
Fax : (804) 371-9376

WASHINGTON
Arnold Stoehr
Administrator
Securities Div.
Dept. of Licensing
P.O. Box 9045
Olympia, WA 98507-9045
Phone : (360) 664-9070

WEST VIRGINIA
Glenn Nichols
Director
Securities Div.
Off. of State Auditor
Bldg. 1, Rm. W100
Charleston, WV 25305
Phone : (304) 558-2257

WISCONSIN
Dan Eastman
Commissioner of Securities
101 E. Wilson, 4th Fl.
P.O. Box 1768
Madison, WI 53703
Phone : (608) 266-3431
Fax : (608) 256-1259

WYOMING
Diana J. Ohman
Secretary of State
State Capitol
Cheyenne, WY 82002-0020
Phone : (307) 777-5333

DISTRICT OF COLUMBIA
Robert Pohlman
Chief Financial Officer
Financial Mgt.
441 4th St., NW, Ste. 1150
Washington, DC 20001
Phone : (202) 727-2476

GUAM
Joseph T. Duenas
Director
Dept. of Revenue & Taxation
378 Chalan San Antonio
Tamuning, GU 96911
Phone : (671) 647-5107
Fax : (671) 472-2643

NORTHERN MARIANA ISLANDS
Pedro Q. Dela Cruz
Secretary
Dept. of Commerce
P.O. Box 10007
Saipan, MP 96950
Phone : (670) 322-4361
Fax : (670) 322-4008

PUERTO RICO
Juan Antonio Garcia
Commissioner
Insurance Comm.
P.O. Box 8330
Santurce, PR 00910
Phone : (809) 722-8686
Fax : (809) 722-4400

U.S. VIRGIN ISLANDS
Kenneth E. Mapp
Lt. Governor
Off. of the Lt. Governor
#18 Kongens Circle
St. Thomas, VI 00802
Phone : (809) 774-2991
Fax: (809) 774-6953

SMALL & MINORITY BUSINESS ASSISTANCE

Provides assistance and information on financing and government procurement opportunities to small and minority business ventures.

ALABAMA
Jack Crittenden
Director
Minority Business Development Off.
11 South Union
Montgomery, AL 36130
Phone : (334) 242-2220
Fax : (334) 242-4419

ALASKA
Martin Richard
Director
Div. of Investments
Commerce & Economic Dev. Dept.
P.O. Box 34159
Juneau, AK 99803-4159
Phone : (907) 465-2510
Fax : (907) 465-2103

ARIZONA
Sara Goertzen
Director
Dept. of Commerce
3800 N. Central Ave., Suite 1500
Phoenix, AZ 85012
Phone : (602) 280-1306

ARKANSAS
James Hall
Director
Minority Bus. Development Div.
Industrial Development Comm.
One Capitol Mall, Rm. 4C-300
Little Rock, AR 72201
Phone : (501) 682-5060
Fax : (501) 682-7341

CALIFORNIA*
Executive Director
Off. of Small Business
Dept. of Commerce
801 K St., Ste. 1700
Sacramento, CA 95814
Phone : (916) 322-3596

COLORADO
Rick Garcia
State Director
Small Business Program Div.
Off. of Business Dev.
1625 Broadway, Ste. 1710
Denver, CO 80202
Phone : (303) 892-3840

Verneeda Moore
Director
Minority Business Off.
Off. of Business Development
1625 Broadway, Ste. 1710
Denver, CO 80202-4729
Phone : (303) 892-3840
Fax : (303) 892-3848

CONNECTICUT
Ginne-Rae LeGree
Minority and Small Contracters Set Aside Program
Dept. of Economic Development
865 Brook St.
Rocky Hill, CT 06067
Phone : (203) 258-4207

DELAWARE
Robert W. Coy Jr.
Director
Delaware Economic Dev. Off.
99 Kings Highway
P.O. Box 1401
Dover, DE 19903
Phone : (302) 739-4271
Fax : (302) 739-5749

FLORIDA
Laurise Thompson
Comm. on Minority Economic & Business Development
Executive Off. of the Governor
201 Knight, 2737 Centerview Dr.
Tallahassee, FL 32399-0950
Phone : (904) 487-4698
Fax : (904) 487-0132

GEORGIA
Hooper Wesley
Coordinator
Small & Minority Business
Dept. of Admin. Srvcs.
200 Piedmont Ave., Ste. 1302
Atlanta, GA 30334
Phone : (404) 656-6315

HAWAII
Seiji Naya
Director
Dept. of Business, Economic Development & Tourism
220 S. King St., # 1100
Honolulu, HI 96813
Phone : (808) 586-2359
Fax : (808) 586-2377

IDAHO
James V. Hawkins
Director
Dept. of Commerce
700 W. State St.
Boise, ID 83720
Phone : (208) 334-2470

ILLINOIS
Lori Thompson
Deputy Director
Business Development
Dept. of Commerce & Comm. Aff.
100 W. Randolph, Ste. 3-400
Chicago, IL 60601
Phone : (312) 814-2811

INDIANA
Addison Simpson
Deputy Commissioner
Minority Business Development
Dept. of Administration
IGC-South, Rm. W479
Indianapolis, IN 46204
Phone : (317) 232-3073

IOWA
Mike Miller
Chief
Business Finance Bur.
200 E. Grand
Des Moines, IA 50309
Phone : (515) 242-4827

KANSAS
Antonio Augusto
Director
Minority Business Division
Dept. of Commerce & Housing
700 SW Harrison Ave., Ste. 1300
Topeka, KS 66603-3712
Phone : (913) 296-5298
Fax : (913) 296-5055

KENTUCKY
Floyd C. Taylor
Director
Small & Minority Business Dev.
Cabinet for Economic Dev.
Capital Plaza Tower
Frankfort, KY 40601
Phone : (502) 564-4252

LOUISIANA
Henry J. Stamper
Executive Director
Minority & Women Enterprise
Dept. of Economic Development
P.O. Box 94185
Baton Rouge, LA 70804-9185
Phone : (504) 342-5373

MAINE
Tom McBrierty
Commissioner
Dept. of Economic & Community Development
State House Station # 59
Augusta, ME 04333
Phone : (207) 287-2656

MARYLAND**
Stanley W. Tucker
Executive Director
Small Business Development Financing Authority
217 E. Redwood St.
Baltimore, MD 21202
Phone : (301) 333-4270

MASSACHUSETTS*
Executive Director
State Off. of Minority & Women Business Assistance
100 Cambridge St., 13th Fl.
Boston, MA 02202
Phone : (617) 727-8692

MICHIGAN
Carolyn Upshaw-Royal
Director of Operations
Minority Bus. Enterprise Div.
Dept. of Commerce
P.O. Box 30225
Lansing, MI 48909
Phone : (517) 335-4720

MINNESOTA
Charles Schaffer
Director
Small Business Assistance
Dept. of Trade & Economic Dev.
500 Metro Sq.
121 E. Seventh Pl.
St. Paul, MN 55101
Phone : (612) 296-0617

MISSISSIPPI
Jay Moon
Deputy Director
Dept. of Economic & Community Development
P.O. Box 849
Jackson, MS 39205
Phone : (601) 359-3448

MISSOURI
Bernie Andrews
Director
Nat'l Business Dev. Programs
Div. of Comm. & Economic Dev.
Truman Bldg., Rm. 720
P.O. Box 118
Jefferson City, MO 65102
Phone : (314) 751-4241
Fax : (314) 751-7384

Bob Vaughan
Director of Existing Business
Div. of Comm. & Economic Dev.
Dept. of Economic Development
Truman Bldg., Rm. 720
P.O. Box 118
Jefferson City, MO 65102
Phone : (314) 751-0482
Fax : (314) 751-7384

Dora Serrano
Manager
Minority Business Dev. Section
Dept. of Economic Development
Truman Bldg., Rm. 680
P.O. Box 1157
Jefferson City, MO 65102
Phone : (314) 751-3237
Fax : (314) 751-7258

Kimberly Kayira
Minority Purchasing Coordinator
Div. of Purchasing
Off. of Administration
Truman Bldg., Rm. 430
P.O. Box 809
Jefferson City, MO 65102
Phone : (314) 751-2348
Fax : (314) 526-3576

MONTANA
Andy Poole
Administrator
Business Development Div.
Dept. of Commerce
1424 Ninth Ave.
Helena, MT 59620
Phone : (406) 444-3923

NEBRASKA
Maxine Moul
Director
Dept. of Economic Development
301 Centennial Mall S.
P.O. Box 94666
Lincoln, NE 68509-4666
Phone : (402) 471-3747

NEVADA
Helen Myers
Director
Off. of Small Business
Comm. on Econmic Development
3770 Howard Hughes Pky., # 295
Las Vegas, NV 89158
Phone : (702) 486-7282

NEW HAMPSHIRE
Norman Storrs
Director
Div. of Economic Development
P.O. Box 1856
Concord, NH 03302-1856
Phone : (603) 271-2341

NEW JERSEY
Gualberto Medina
Commissioner
Dept. of Commerce & Economic Development
20 W. State St., CN820
Trenton, NJ 08625
Phone : (609) 292-2444

NEW MEXICO
Les French
Director
Purchasing Div.
Dept. of General Srvcs.
P.O. Box 26110
Santa Fe, NM 87503
Phone : (505) 827-0472
Fax : (505) 827-0499

NEW YORK*
Executive Director
Div. of Min. & Women's Bus. Dev.
Dept. of Economic Development
One Commerce Plz.
Albany, NY 12245-0001
Phone : (518) 474-6346

NORTH CAROLINA
Scott Daugherty
Executive Director
Small Business Technology & Development Center
4509 Creedmoor Rd., Ste. 201
Raleigh, NC 27612
Phone : (919) 571-4154

NORTH DAKOTA
Charles W. Stroup
Director
Dept. of Economic Dev. & Finance
1833 E. Bismarck Expy.
Bismarck, ND 58504
Phone : (701) 328-5300
Fax : (701) 328-5320

OHIO
Karen Conrad
Director
Small & Developing Bus. Div.
Dept. of Development
P.O. Box 1001
Columbus, OH 43266-0101
Phone : (614) 644-5996
Fax : (614) 466-0829

OKLAHOMA
Pamela S. Bryan
Director
Small Business Div.
Dept. of Commerce
P.O. Box 26980
Oklahoma City, OK 73126-0980
Phone : (405) 843-9770

OREGON
Jesus Borboa
Certification Manager
Off. of Minority, Women & Emerging Small Business
Dept. of Consumer & Business Srvcs.
155 Cottage St., NE
Salem, OR 97310
Phone : (503) 378-5651

PENNSYLVANIA
Emily J. White
Director
Off. of Small Business
Dept. of Commerce
Forsum Bldg., Rm. 401
Harrisburg, PA 17120
Phone : (717) 783-8950

RHODE ISLAND
Charles Newton
Executive Coordinator
Div. of Business Development
Dept. of Economic Development
7 Jackson Walkway
Providence, RI 02903
Phone : (401) 277-2601

SOUTH CAROLINA
Cleve Thomas
Director
Small & Minority Business
Off. of the Governor
1205 Pendleton St., Rm. 437
Columbia, SC 29201
Phone : (803) 734-0657

SOUTH DAKOTA
Bonnie Untereiner
Commissioner
Governor's Off. of Economic Develoment
Capitol Lake Plz.
Pierre, SD 57501
Phone : (605) 773-5032

TENNESSEE
John Birdsong
Director
Off. of Minority Business
Econ. & Community Dev. Dept.
320 Sixth Ave., N.
Nashville, TN 37243
Phone : (615) 741-2545

TEXAS
Brenda Arnett
Executive Director
Dept. of Commerce
P.O. Box 12728, Capitol Station
Austin, TX 78711
Phone : (512) 472-5059

UTAH
Johnny Bryan
Director of Procurement
Div. of Economic Development
Dept. of Community & Economic Dev.
324 S. State, Ste. 504
Salt Lake City, UT 84111
Phone : (801) 538-8791

VERMONT
Avram Patt
Director
State Econ. Opportunity Off.
Agency of Human Services
103 S. Main St.
Waterbury, VT 05671
Phone : (802) 241-2450

VIRGINIA
James E. House
Director
Dept. of Minority Business Enterprise
Ninth St. Off. Bldg., 11th Fl.
Richmond, VA 23219
Phone : (804) 786-5560
Fax : (804) 371-7359

WASHINGTON
James A. Medina
Director
Off. of Min. & Women's Bus. Environment
406 S. Water
P.O. Box 41160
Olympia, WA 98504-1160
Phone : (360) 753-9693

WEST VIRGINIA
Hazel Kroesser
Director
Small Business Dev. Ctr.
Development Off.
1115 Virginia St. E.
Charleston, WV 25301
Phone : (304) 348-2960

WISCONSIN
H.H. Rothwell
Director
Bur. of Business & Industry Srvcs.
Dept. of Development
P.O. Box 7970
Madison, WI 53707-7970
Phone : (608) 267-9550
Fax : (608) 267-0479

Robert Wynn II
Director
Bur. of Minority Business Dev.
Dept. of Development
P.O. Box 7970
Madison, WI 53707
Phone : (608) 266-8380

WYOMING
George H. Gault
Director
Div. of Econ. & Comm. Dev.
Dept. of Commerce
2301 Central Ave., 4N
Cheyenne, WY 82002
Phone : (307) 777-6435

DISTRICT OF COLUMBIA
Charles Countee
Executive Director
Off. of Business & Economic Development
717 14th St., NW, 7th Fl.
Washington, DC 20005
Phone : (202) 727-6600

GUAM
Joseph T. Duenas
Director
Dept. of Revenue & Taxation
378 Chalan San Antonio
Tamuning, GU 96911
Phone : (671) 647-5107
Fax : (671) 472-2643

NORTHERN MARIANA ISLANDS
James H. Ripple
Executive Director
Commonwealth Development Authority
P.O. Box 2149
Saipan, MP 96950
Phone : (670) 234-7145

U.S. VIRGIN ISLANDS
Rhudel George
Director
Small Business Dev. Authority
14A Norre Gade
St. Thomas, VI 00804
Phone : (809) 776-3206

SOCIAL SERVICES

Responsible for the delivery of services to children, the blind, disabled and the elderly.

ALABAMA
P.L. Corley
Acting Commissioner
Dept. of Human Resources
50 N. Ripley St.
Montgomery, AL 36130
Phone : (334) 242-8395
Fax : (334) 242-0198

ALASKA
Karen Perdue
Commissioner
Dept. of Health & Social Srvcs.
P.O. Box 110601
Juneau, AK 99811-0601
Phone : (907) 465-3030
Fax : (907) 465-3068

ARIZONA
Linda Blessing
Director
Dept. of Economic Security
1717 W. Jefferson
Phoenix, AZ 85007
Phone : (602) 542-4791

ARKANSAS
Tom Dalton
Director
Dept. of Human Srvcs.
P.O. Box 1437, Slot 316
Little Rock, AR 72203
Phone : (501) 682-8650
Fax : (501) 682-6836

CALIFORNIA
Eloise Anderson
Director
Dept. of Social Services
744 P St., MS 17-11
Sacramento, CA 95814
Phone : (916) 657-2598

COLORADO
Karen Beye
Managing Director
Dept. of Human Srvcs.
1575 Sherman St.
Denver, CO 80203-1714
Phone : (303) 866-5700
Fax : (303) 866-4214

CONNECTICUT
Joyce Thomas
Commissioner
Social Services
25 Sigourney St.
Hartford, CT 06106
Phone : (203) 424-5008

DELAWARE
Carmen R. Nazario
Secretary
Dept. of Health & Social Srvcs.
1901 N. duPont Hwy.
New Castle, DE 19720
Phone : (302) 577-4500
Fax : (302) 577-4510

Thomas P. Eichler
Secretary
Dept. of Srvcs. for Children, Youth & Their Families
1825 Faulkland Rd.
Wilmington, DE 19805
Phone : (302) 633-2500

FLORIDA
Edward A. Feaver
Deputy Secretary
Dept. of Health & Rehabilitative Srvcs.
1317 Winewood Blvd.
Tallahassee, FL 32399-0700
Phone : (904) 487-1111
Fax : (904) 922-2993

GEORGIA
Michael Thurmond
Interim Director
Family & Children Srvcs.
Dept. of Human Resources
2 Peachtree St., 4th Fl.
Atlanta, GA 30303
Phone : (404) 657-5100

HAWAII
Susan Chandler
Director
Dept. of Human Services
1390 Miller St.
Honolulu, HI 96813
Phone : (808) 586-4997
Fax : (808) 586-4890

IDAHO
Roseanne Hardin
Administrator
Family & Community Srvcs.
Dept. of Health & Welfare
450 W. State St., 3rd Fl.
P.O. Box 83720
Boise, ID 83720-0036
Phone : (208) 334-5700
Fax : (208) 334-6699

ILLINOIS
Jess McDonald
Director
Dept. of Children & Family Srvcs.
406 E. Monroe St.
Springfield, IL 62701
Phone : (217) 785-0863
Fax : (217) 785-1052

INDIANA
Cheryl Sullivan
Secretary
Family & Social Srvcs. Admin.
402 W. Washington St., #341
Indianapolis, IN 46204
Phone : (317) 233-4690

IOWA
Sally Titus Cunningham
Deputy Director
Dept. of Human Srvcs.
Hoover State Off. Bldg.
Des Moines, IA 50319
Phone : (515) 281-6360

KANSAS
Rochelle Chronister
Secretary
Dept. of Social & Rehab. Srvcs.
Docking State Off. Bldg., 6th Fl.
Topeka, KS 66612-1570
Phone : (913) 296-3959
Fax : (913) 296-1158

KENTUCKY
Peggy Wallace
Commissioner
Dept. for Social Srvcs.
Cabinet for Human Resources
275 E. Main St.
Frankfort, KY 40621
Phone : (502) 564-4650

LOUISIANA
Gloria Bryant-Banks
Secretary
Executive Off.
Dept. of Social Services
P.O. Box 3776
Baton Rouge, LA 70821
Phone : (504) 342-0286

MAINE
Kevin Concannon
Commissioner
Dept. of Human Services
State House Station # 11
Augusta, ME 04333
Phone : (207) 287-2736

MARYLAND**
Diane Gordy
Executive Director
Social Services Administration
Dept. of Human Resources
311 W. Saratoga St.
Baltimore, MD 21201
Phone : (410) 333-0109

MASSACHUSETTS
Gerald Whitburn
Secretary
Executive Off. of Health & Human Srvcs.
1 Ashburton Pl., Rm. 1109
Boston, MA 02108
Phone : (617) 727-7600

MICHIGAN
Gerald Miller
Director
Dept. of Social Srvcs.
P.O. Box 30037
Lansing, MI 48909
Phone : (517) 373-2000
Fax : (517) 373-8471

MINNESOTA
Laura Skaff
Assistant Commissioner
Social Services Administration
Dept. of Human Services
444 Lafayette Rd.
St. Paul, MN 55155
Phone : (612) 297-8281

MISSISSIPPI
Ronnie McGinnis
Director
Div. of Grants
Dept. of Human Services
P.O. Box 352
Jackson, MS 39205
Phone : (601) 359-6701

MISSOURI
Gary Stangler
Director
Dept. of Social Services
Broadway Bldg., Rm. 240
P.O. Box 1527
Jefferson City, MO 65102
Phone : (314) 751-4815
Fax : (314) 751-3203

MONTANA
Peter Blouke
Director
Dept. of Social & Rehabilitation Services
111 Sanders St.
Helena, MT 59604
Phone : (406) 444-5622

NEBRASKA
Mary Dean Harvey
Director
Dept. of Social Services
P.O. Box 95206
Nebraska State Off. Bldg.
Lincoln, NE 68509-5026
Phone : (402) 471-3121

NEVADA
Charlotte Crawford
Acting Director
Dept. of Human Resources
505 E. King St., Rm. 600
Carson City, NV 89710
Phone : (702) 687-4400

NEW HAMPSHIRE
Terry Morton
Commissioner
Dept. of Health & Human Srvcs.
Hazen Dr.
Concord, NH 03301
Phone : (603) 271-4331

NEW JERSEY
William Waldman
Commissioner
Dept. of Human Srvcs.
222 S. Warren St., CN700
Trenton, NJ 08625
Phone : (609) 292-5360

NEW MEXICO
Heather Wilson
Director
Social Services Div.
Dept. of Children, Youth & Families
P.O. Drawer 5160
Santa Fe, NM 87502-5160
Phone : (505) 827-7810
Fax : (505) 827-4053

NEW YORK*
Commissioner
Dept. of Social Srvcs.
40 N. Pearl St.
Albany, NY 12243
Phone : (518) 474-9475

NORTH CAROLINA
Kevin FitzGerald
Director of Social Services
Dept. of Human Resources
325 N. Salisbury St.
Raleigh, NC 27603-5905
Phone : (919) 733-3055
Fax : (919) 715-3581

NORTH DAKOTA
Bud Wessman
Associate Director
Field Srvc. & Program Dev.
Dept. of Human Srvcs.
600 E. Boulevard Ave.
Bismarck, ND 58505-0250
Phone : (701) 328-2318
Fax : (701) 328-2359

OHIO
Arnold Tompkins
Director
Dept. of Human Services
30 E. Broad St., 32nd Fl.
Columbus, OH 43266-0423
Phone : (614) 466-6282
Fax : (614) 466-2815

OKLAHOMA
George Miller
Interim Director
Health & Human Srvcs.
Dept. of Human Srvcs.
P.O. Box 25352
Oklahoma City, OK 73125
Phone : (405) 521-2778

OREGON
Jean Thorne
Acting Director
Dept. of Human Resources
500 Summer St., NE, 4th Fl.
Salem, OR 97310-1012
Phone : (503) 945-5944
Fax : (503) 378-2897

PENNSYLVANIA
Ann V. Beitzel
Acting Deputy Secretary
Social Programs
Dept. of Public Welfare
P.O. Box 2675
Harrisburg, PA 17105
Phone : (717) 787-3438

RHODE ISLAND
Christie Ferguson
Director
Dept. of Human Services
600 New London Ave.
Cranston, RI 02920
Phone : (401) 464-2121

SOUTH CAROLINA
Jim Clark
Interim Commissioner
Dept. of Social Srvcs.
1535 Confederate Ave. Ext.
Columbia, SC 29202
Phone : (803) 734-5760

SOUTH DAKOTA
James Ellenbecker
Secretary
Dept. of Social Srvcs.
700 Governors Dr.
Pierre, SD 57501
Phone : (605) 773-3165

TENNESSEE*
Assistant Commissioner
Social Srvcs.
Dept. of Human Srvcs.
400 Deaderick St.
Nashville, TN 37243
Phone : (615) 741-5924

TEXAS
Burton Raiford
Commissioner
Dept. of Human Services
P.O. Box 149030
Austin, TX 78714
Phone : (512) 450-3011

UTAH
Kerry Steadman
Executive Director
Dept. of Human Srvcs.
120 N. 200 W., # 319
Salt Lake City, UT 84103
Phone : (801) 538-3998

VERMONT
William Young
Director
Dept. of Social & Rehabilitation Srvcs.
103 S. Main St.
Waterbury, VT 05671
Phone : (802) 241-2101

VIRGINIA
Carol Brunty
Commissioner
Dept. of Social Services
Theater Row Bldg.
730 East Broad St.
Richmond, VA 23229
Phone : (804) 692-1900
Fax : (804) 692-1949

WASHINGTON
Jean Soliz
Secretary
Dept. of Social & Health Srvcs.
P.O. Box 45010
Olympia, WA 98504-5010
Phone : (360) 753-7039

WEST VIRGINIA
Gretchen Lewis
Secretary
Dept. of Health & Human Resources
Bldg. 3, Rm. 206
State Capitol Complex
Charleston, WV 25305
Phone : (304) 558-0684

WISCONSIN
Gerald Whitburn
Secretary
Dept. of Health & Social Srvcs.
1 W Wilson St., Rm. 650
P.O. Box 7850
Madison, WI 53703
Phone : (608) 266-3681
Fax : (608) 266-7882

WYOMING
George Lovato
Director
Wyoming Dept. of Family Services
Hathaway Bldg., 3rd Fl.
2300 Capitol Ave.
Cheyenne, WY 82002-0490
Phone : (307) 777-5831

DISTRICT OF COLUMBIA
Clarice Dibble Walker
Commissioner
Comm. on Social Srvcs.
Dept. of Human Srvcs.
609 H. St., NE, 5th Fl.
Washington, DC 20002
Phone : (202) 727-5930

AMERICAN SAMOA
Sapini Siatu'u
Director
Dept. of Human Resources
Pago Pago, AS 96799
Phone : (684) 633-4485
Fax : (684) 633-1139

GUAM
Dennis Rodriguez
Director
Dept. of Public Health & Social Services
P.O. Box 2816
Agana, GU 96910
Phone : (671) 734-7102
Fax : (671) 734-5910

NORTHERN MARIANA ISLANDS
Eleanor S. Dela Cruz
Director
Dept. of Community & Cultural Affairs
Off. of the Governor
Saipan, MP 96950
Phone : (670) 233-3343

PUERTO RICO
Carmen Rodriquez de Rivera
Secretary
Dept. of Social Services
P.O. Box 11398
Santurce, PR 00910
Phone : (809) 722-7400
Fax : (809) 723-1223

U.S. VIRGIN ISLANDS
Catherine Mills
Commissioner
Dept. of Human Srvcs.
Knud Hansen Complex, Bldg. A
1303 Hospital Ground
St. Thomas, VI 00802
Phone : (809) 774-0930
Fax : (809) 774-3466

SOIL CONSERVATION

Coordinates programs to conserve and protect the state's soil.

ALABAMA
Jim Martin
Commissioner
Dept. of Conservation & Natural Resources
64 N. Union St.
Montgomery, AL 36130
Phone : (334) 242-3151
Fax : (334) 242-3489

ALASKA
John T. Shively
Commissioner
Dept. of Natural Resources
400 Willoughby Ave.
Juneau, AK 99801-1796
Phone : (907) 465-2400
Fax : (907) 465-3886

ARIZONA
Robert E. Yount
Director
Natural Resources Division
Dept. of State Land
1616 W. Adams
Phoenix, AZ 85007
Phone : (602) 542-4626

ARKANSAS
J. Randy Young
Director
Soil & Water Conservation Comm.
101 E. Capitol Ave. # 350
Little Rock, AR 72201
Phone : (501) 682-1611
Fax : (501) 682-3991

CALIFORNIA
Douglas Wheeler
Secretary
Resources Agency
1416 9th St., Rm. 1311
Sacramento, CA 95814
Phone : (916) 653-5656

COLORADO
Dan Parker
Director
Soil Conservation
Dept. of Natural Resources
1313 Sherman St., Rm. 219
Denver, CO 80203
Phone : (303) 866-3351
Fax : (303) 832-8106

CONNECTICUT
Allan Bennett
Executive Director
Council on Soil & Water Conservation
79 Elm St.
Hartford, CT 06106
Phone : (203) 424-3905

DELAWARE
Christophe A.G. Tulou
Secretary
Dept. of Natural Resources & Environmental Control
P.O. Box 1401
Dover, DE 19903
Phone : (302) 739-4403
Fax : (302) 739-6242

FLORIDA
Virginia Wetherell
Secretary
Dept. of Env. Protection
3900 Commonwealth Bldg., MS-10
Tallahassee, FL 32399
Phone : (904) 488-4805
Fax : (904) 921-4303

GEORGIA
F. Graham Liles
Executive Director
State Soil & Water Conservation Comm.
P.O. Box 8024
Athens, GA 30603
Phone : (404) 542-3065

HAWAII
Michael Wilson
Chairman
Dept. of Land & Natural Resources
1151 Punchbowl St.
Honolulu, HI 96813
Phone : (808) 586-0400
Fax : (808) 587-0390

IDAHO
Wayne R. Faude
Administrator
Soil Conservation Comm.
Dept. of Lands
1215 W. State St.
Boise, ID 83720
Phone : (208) 334-0210

ILLINOIS
Brent Manning
Director
Dept. of Conservation
Lincoln Towers Plz., Rm. 425
524 S. Second St.
Springfield, IL 62701-1787
Phone : (217) 785-0075
Fax : (217) 785-9236

INDIANA
Patrick Ralston
Executive Director
Dept. of Natural Resources
IGC-South, Rm. W256
Indianapolis, IN 46204
Phone : (317) 232-4020
Fax : (317) 232-8036

IOWA
James B. Gulliford
Administrator
Div. of Soil Conservation
Dept. of Agriculture & Land
Wallace State Off. Bldg.
Des Moines, IA 50319
Phone : (515) 281-6146

KANSAS
Kenneth F. Kerr
Secretary
Conservation Commission
109 SW 9th St., Ste. 500
Topeka, KS 66612-1299
Phone : (913) 296-3600
Fax : (913) 296-6172

KENTUCKY
William H. Martin
Commissioner
Dept. of Natural Resources
Natural Resources & Env. Protection
107 Mero St.
Frankfort, KY 40601
Phone : (502) 564-2184

LOUISIANA
Jack McClanahan
Secretary
Dept. of Natural Resources
P.O. Box 94396
Baton Rouge, LA 70804-9396
Phone : (504) 342-4503

MAINE
Ed McLaughlin
Commissioner
Dept. of Agriculture, Food & Rural Resources
State House Station # 28
Augusta, ME 04333
Phone : (207) 287-3871

MARYLAND**
Robert Davis
Chairman
Soil Conservation Cmte.
Dept. of Agriculture
50 Harry S. Truman Pkwy.
Annapolis, MD 21401
Phone : (410) 841-5863

MASSACHUSETTS
Thomas Powers
Acting Commissioner
Dept. of Environmental Protection
Executive Off. of Environmental Affairs
1 Winter St.
Boston, MA 02108
Phone : (617) 292-5856

MICHIGAN
Roland Harmes
Director
Dept. of Natural Resources
P.O. Box 30028
Lansing, MI 48909
Phone : (517) 373-2329
Fax : (517) 335-4242

MINNESOTA
Rod Sando
Commissioner
Dept. of Natural Resources
500 Lafayette Rd.
St. Paul, MN 55155
Phone : (612) 296-2549

MISSISSIPPI
Sam Polles
Director
Parks & Recreation
Dept. of Wildlife, Fisheries & Parks
P.O. Box 451
Jackson, MS 39205
Phone : (601) 362-9212

MISSOURI
David A. Shorr
Director
Dept. of Natural Resources
Jefferson Bldg., 12th Fl.
P.O. Box 176
Jefferson City, MO 65102
Phone : (314) 751-4422
Fax : (314) 751-7627

MONTANA
Mark Simonich
Director
Dept. of Natural Resources & Conservation
1520 E. 6th Avenue
Helena, MT 59620
Phone : (406) 444-6699

NEBRASKA
Dayle E. Williamson
Executive Director
Natural Resources Comm.
301 Centennial Mall S.
P.O. Box 94876
Lincoln, NE 68509-4876
Phone : (402) 471-2081

NEVADA
Peter G. Morros
Director
Dept. of Conservation & Natural Resources
123 W. Nye Ln.
Carson City, NV 89710
Phone : (702) 687-4360

NEW HAMPSHIRE
William Bartlett
Commissioner
Dept. of Resources & Economic Development
P.O. Box 856
Concord, NH 03302-0856
Phone : (603) 271-2411

NEW JERSEY
Samuel R. Race
Executive Secretary
Soil Conservation Cmte.
Dept. of Agriculture
John Fitch Plz., CN330
Trenton, NJ 08625
Phone : (609) 292-5540

NEW MEXICO
Ray Polasky
Chief
Soil & Water Conservation Bur.
Dept. of Energy, Mining & Natural Resources
P.O. Box 1948
Santa Fe, NM 87504
Phone : (505) 827-7860
Fax : (505) 827-3903

NEW YORK*
Commissioner
Dept. of Environmental Conservation
50 Wolf Rd.
Albany, NY 12233
Phone : (518) 457-3446

NORTH CAROLINA
Jonathan B. Howes
Secretary
Div. of Environmental Mgt.
Dept. of Health & Nat. Res.
512 N. Salisbury St.
Raleigh, NC 27604-1148
Phone : (919) 715-4101
Fax : (919) 715-3060

NORTH DAKOTA
Blake Vander Vorst
Executive Secretary
State Soil Conservation Cmte.
Transportation Bldg., 2nd Fl.
608 E. Boulevard Ave.
Bismarck, ND 58505-0700
Phone : (701) 328-2650
Fax : (701) 328-4143

OHIO
Lawrence G. Vance
Chief
Div. of Soil Conservation
Dept. of Natural Resources
Fountain Sq.
Columbus, OH 43224
Phone : (614) 265-6610
Fax : (614) 262-2064

OREGON
Richard Benner
Director
Dept. of Land Conservation & Development
1175 Court St., NE
Salem, OR 97310
Phone : (503) 373-0060
Fax : (503) 362-6705

PENNSYLVANIA
James M. Seif
Secretary
Dept. of Environmental Resources
Market St.
State Office Bldg., 16th Fl.
Harrisburg, PA 17120
Phone : (717) 787-2814

RHODE ISLAND
Janet Keller
Chief
Off. of Environmental Coordination
Dept. of Environmental Mgt.
83 Park St.
Providence, RI 02908
Phone : (401) 277-3434

SOUTH CAROLINA
Beth Partlow
Legal Counsel
Off. of the Governor
P.O. Box 11369
Columbia, SC 29211
Phone : (803) 734-9842

SOUTH DAKOTA
Dean Anderson
Secretary
Dept. of Agriculture
Foss Bldg.
523 E. Capitol
Pierre, SD 57501-3182
Phone : (605) 773-3375

TENNESSEE
Jim Nance
Director
Agriculture Resources
Dept. of Agriculture
Ellington Agriculture Ctr.
Nashville, TN 37204
Phone : (615) 360-0108

TEXAS
Robert G. Buckley
Executive Director
State Soil & Water Conservation Board
P.O. Box 658
Temple, TX 76503
Phone : (817) 773-2250

UTAH
Ted Stewart
Executive Director
Dept. of Natural Resources
1636 W. N. Temple, Ste. 316
Salt Lake City, UT 84116-3193
Phone : (801) 538-7200

VERMONT
Barbara Ripley
Secretary
Agency of Natural Resources
103 S. Main St.
Waterbury, VT 05676
Phone : (802) 241-3600
Fax : (802) 241-3281

VIRGINIA
H. Kirby Burch
Director
Dept. of Conservation & Recreation
203 Governor St., Ste. 203
Richmond, VA 23219
Phone : (804) 786-6124
Fax : (804) 786-6141

WASHINGTON
Jennifer Belcher
Commissioner of Public Lands
Dept. of Natural Resources
P.O. Box 47001
Olympia, WA 98504-7001
Phone : (360) 902-1000

WEST VIRGINIA
Lance E. Tabor
Executive Director
State Soil Conservation Cmte.
1900 Kanawha Blvd., E.
Charleston, WV 25305
Phone : (304) 558-2204

WISCONSIN
Lakshmi Sridharan
Chief
Solid Waste Mgt. Section
Dept. of Natural Resources
P.O. Box 7921
Madison, WI 53707
Phone : (608) 266-0520
Fax : (608) 267-2768

WYOMING
Don Christianson
Manager
Natural Resources Div.
Dept. of Agriculture
2219 Carey Ave.
Cheyenne, WY 82002
Phone : (307) 777-6576

DISTRICT OF COLUMBIA
Magnus Blanchette
Acting Chief, Soil Resources Branch
Housing & Environ. Reg. Admin.
Dept. of Consumer & Regulatory Affairs
614 H St., NW, Lower Level
Washington, DC 20001
Phone : (202) 727-7577

GUAM
Joseph C. Cruz
Administrator
Guam Environmental Protection Agency
IT&E Harmon Plz., D-107
130 Rojas St.
Harmon, GU 96911
Phone : (671) 646-8863
Fax : (671) 646-9402

NORTHERN MARIANA ISLANDS
Benigno M. Sablan
Secretary
Dept. of Lands & Natural Resources
P.O. Box 10007
Saipan, MP 96950
Phone : (670) 322-9830
Fax : (670) 322-2633

PUERTO RICO
Pedro Gelabert Marquez
Secretary
Dept. of Natural Resources
P.O. Box 5887
San Juan, PR 00906-5887
Phone : (809) 724-8774
Fax : (809) 723-4255

SOLID WASTE MANAGEMENT

Develops and maintains a comprehensive solid waste management program in the state.

ALABAMA
Russell Kelly
Chief
Solid Waste Branch
Dept. of Environmental Mgt.
1751 Cong. Dickinson Dr.
Montgomery, AL 36130
Phone : (334) 271-7771
Fax : (334) 279-3050

ALASKA
Glenn J. Miller
Program Manager
Solid Waste Program
Solid & Haz. Waste Mgt. Sect.
410 W. Willoughby Ave.
Juneau, AK 99801
Phone : (907) 465-5050
Fax : (907) 465-5274

ARIZONA
Stephen Johnson
Assistant Director
Off. of Waste Programs
Dept. of Environmental Quality
3033 N. Central Ave.
Phoenix, AZ 85012
Phone : (602) 207-2300

ARKANSAS
Larry Wilson
Deputy Director
Pollution Control & Ecology
P.O. Box 8913
Little Rock, AR 72219
Phone : (501) 562-7444
Fax : (501) 562-4632

CALIFORNIA*
Chairman
Integrated Waste Management Board
8800 Cal Center Dr.
Sacramento, CA 95826-3268
Phone : (916) 255-2182

COLORADO
Pam Harley
Chief
Solid Waste & Incident Mgt.
Haz. Materials & Waste Mgt.
4300 Cherry Creek Dr., S.
Denver, CO 80222-1530
Phone : (303) 692-3300
Fax : (303) 759-5355

CONNECTICUT
Richard Barlow
Chief
Bureau of Waste Management
Dept. of Env. Protection
79 Elm St., 1st Floor
Hartford, CT 06106
Phone : (203) 424-3366

DELAWARE
N.C. Vasuki
CEO
Delaware Solid Waste Authority
1128 S. Bradford St.
P.O. Box 455
Dover, DE 19903
Phone : (302) 739-5361
Fax : (302) 739-4287

FLORIDA
William W. Hinkley
Chief
Solid & Hazardous Waste
Dept. of Environmental Protection
2600 Blairstone Rd.
Tallahassee, FL 32399-2400
Phone : (904) 922-6104
Fax : (904) 488-0300

GEORGIA
James Dunbar
Program Manager
Env. Protection Div.
Dept. of Natural Resources
205 Butler St., Ste. 1152
Atlanta, GA 30334
Phone : (404) 656-2836

HAWAII
Gracelda Simmons
Acting Manager
Solid & Hazardous Waste Branch
Dept. of Health
1250 Punchbowl St.
Honolulu, HI 96801
Phone : (808) 586-4225

IDAHO
Joy Palmer
Planning & Evaluation
Div. of Environmental Quality
1410 N. Hilton, 3rd Fl.
Boise, ID 83706
Phone : (208) 334-5879

ILLINOIS
Michael Collins
Director
Recycling & Waste Reduction
Dept. of Energy & Nat. Res.
320 W. Washington, 7th Fl.
Springfield, IL 62704
Phone : (217) 524-2993

INDIANA
Bruce Palin
Branch Chief
Solid Waste Mgt. Branch
Dept. of Environmental Mgt.
105 S. Meridian St., Box 6015
Indianapolis, IN 46225
Phone : (317) 232-8892

IOWA
Peter Hamlin
Chief, Air Quality & Solid Waste Protection
Dept. of Natural Resources
900 E. Grand
Des Moines, IA 50319
Phone : (515) 281-8852

KANSAS
William Bider
Director
Bur. of Waste Management
Dept. of Health & Environment
Landon State Off. Bldg.
Topeka, KS 66612-1290
Phone : (913) 296-1600
Fax : (913) 296-1592

KENTUCKY
George Gilbert
Branch Manager
Solid Waste Branch
Div. of Waste Mgt.
14 Reilly Rd.
Frankfort, KY 40601
Phone : (502) 564-6716

LOUISIANA
William J. Mollere
Administrator
Division of Solid Waste
Office of Solid & Hazardous Waste
P.O. Box 82178
Baton Rouge, LA 70804-2178
Phone : (504) 765-0741

MAINE
John S. Williams
Director
Waste Management Agency
Executive Dept.
State House Station # 154
Augusta, ME 04333
Phone : (207) 287-5300

MARYLAND**
Barry Schmidt
Administrator
Solid Waste Program
Dept. of Environment
2500 Broening Hwy.
Baltimore, MD 21224
Phone : (301) 631-3318

MASSACHUSETTS
Willa Kuh
Director
Div. of Solid Waste Mgt.
Dept. of Environmental Protection
1 Winter St., 4th Fl.
Boston, MA 02108
Phone : (617) 292-5692

MICHIGAN
Jim Sygo
Chief
Waste Mgt. Div.
Dept. of Natural Resources
P.O. Box 30028
Lansing, MI 48909
Phone : (517) 373-2730

MINNESOTA
Jim Warner
Director
Groundwater & Solid Waste Div.
Pollution Control Agency
520 Lafayette Rd.
St. Paul, MN 55155
Phone : (612) 296-7777

MISSISSIPPI
Billy Warden
Environmental Scientist
Groundwater Div.
Off. of Pollution Control
P.O. Box 10385
Jackson, MS 39289
Phone : (601) 961-5047

MISSOURI
Harold T. Morton
Director
Solid Waste Mgt. Program
Dept. of Natural Resources
Jefferson Bldg., 10th Fl.
P.O. Box 176
Jefferson City, MO 65102
Phone : (314) 751-3176
Fax : (314) 526-3902

MONTANA
Roger Thorvilson
Acting Administrator
Superfund, Solid Waste/Junk Vehicles
Solid & Hazardous Waste Bur.
Cogswell Bldg.
Helena, MT 59620
Phone : (406) 444-1430

NEBRASKA
Joe Francis
Assistant Director
Air & Waste Mgt. Div.
Dept. of Environmental Quality
P.O. Box 98922
Lincoln, NE 68509
Phone : (402) 471-0001

NEVADA
Lew Dodigon
Administrator
Div. of Environmental Protection
123 W. Nye Ln.
Carson City, NV 89710
Phone : (702) 687-4670

NEW HAMPSHIRE
Richard S. Reed
Supervisor
Solid Waste Compliance Section
Waste Mgt. Div.
6 Hazen Dr.
Concord, NH 03301
Phone : (603) 271-2925

NEW JERSEY
Kenneth J. Hart
Director
Div. of Solid & Hazardous Waste Mgt.
Dept. of Environ. Protection
840 Bear Tavern Rd., CN414
Trenton, NJ 08625
Phone : (609) 530-8591

NEW MEXICO
Gerald Silva
Bureau Chief
Solid Waste Bur.
Dept. of Environment
P.O. Box 26110
Santa Fe, NM 87504
Phone : (505) 827-2775
Fax : (505) 827-2902

NEW YORK*
Commissioner
Dept. of Environmental Conservation
50 Wolf Rd.
Albany, NY 12233
Phone : (518) 457-3446

NORTH CAROLINA
Dexter Matthews
Chief
Div. of Solid Waste Mgt.
401 Oberlin Rd., Ste. 150
Raleigh, NC 27605-1350
Phone : (919) 733-0692
Fax : (919) 733-4810

NORTH DAKOTA
Neil Knatterud
Director
Div. of Solid Waste Mgt.
Health & Consolidated Labs.
P.O. Box 5520
Bismarck, ND 58502-5520
Phone : (701) 328-5166
Fax : (701) 328-5200

OHIO
Barbara Bridika
Chief
Solid & Haz. Waste Mgt. Div.
Environmental Protection
1800 Watermark Dr., Box 1049
Columbus, OH 43266-0149
Phone : (614) 644-3135
Fax : (614) 728-5315

OKLAHOMA
Fenton Rood
Chief
Solid Waste Mgt. Srvcs.
Environmental Health Srvcs.
P.O. Box 53551
Oklahoma City, OK 73152
Phone : (405) 271-7159

OREGON
Mary Wahl
Manager
Waste Mgt. & Cleanup Div.
Dept. of Environmental Quality
811 SW Sixth Ave.
Portland, OR 97204
Phone : (503) 229-5913
Fax : (503) 229-6977

PENNSYLVANIA
James P. Snyder
Director
Bur. of Waste Management
Dept. of Env. Resources
Market St. State Off. Bldg.
Harrisburg, PA 17101
Phone : (717) 787-9870

RHODE ISLAND
Ronald Gagnon
Acting Chief
Solid Waste Section
Air & Hazardous Materials Div.
291 Promenade St.
Providence, RI 02908
Phone : (401) 277-2797

SOUTH CAROLINA
Hartsill Truesdale
Chief
Bur. of Solid & Haz. Waste Mgt.
Dept. of Health & Env. Control
2600 Bull St.
Columbia, SC 29201
Phone : (803) 734-5200

SOUTH DAKOTA
David Templeton
Office Administrator
Off. of Waste Mgt.
Dept. of Env. & Natural Res.
523 E. Capitol Ave.
Pierre, SD 57501-3182
Phone : (615) 773-3153

TENNESSEE
Tom Tiesler
Director
Solid Waste Management
Dept. of Environment & Cons.
401 Church St.
Nashville, TN 37243
Phone : (615) 532-0780

TEXAS
Ron Bond
Director
Municipal Solid Waste
Natural Resources Conservation
P.O. Box 13087
Austin, TX 78711-3087
Phone : (512) 908-6695

UTAH
Dennis R. Downs
Director
Div. of Solid & Hazardous Waste
Dept. of Environmental Quality
P.O. Box 14880
Salt Lake City, UT 84114-4880
Phone : (801) 538-6775

VERMONT
Edward Leonard
Director
Div. of Solid Waste Mgt.
Dept. of Env. Conservation
103 S. Main St.
Waterbury, VT 05671-0407
Phone : (802) 241-3444
Fax : (802) 241-3273

VIRGINIA
Peter W. Schmidt
Director
Dept. of Environmental Quality
629 E. Main St.
Richmond, VA 23219
Phone : (804) 762-4020
Fax : (804) 762-4019

WASHINGTON
Tom Eaton
Program Manager
Solid & Hazardous Waste Section
Dept. of Ecology
P.O. Box 47600
Olympia, WA 98504-8711
Phone : (360) 407-6700

WEST VIRGINIA
Charles Jordan
Director
Solid Waste Mgt. Board
1615 Washington St., E.
Charleston, WV 25311-2126
Phone : (304) 558-0844

WISCONSIN
Paul Didier
Director
Bur. of Solid & Haz. Waste
Dept. of Natural Resources
P.O. Box 7921
Madison, WI 53707
Phone : (608) 266-1327
Fax : (608) 267-2768

WYOMING
David Finley
Administrator
Solid & Hazardous Waste Div.
Dept. of Environmental Quality
Herschler Bldg.
Cheyenne, WY 82002
Phone : (307) 777-7753

DISTRICT OF COLUMBIA
F. Clayton Dade
Administrator
Solid Waste Mgt.
Dept. of Public Works
2750 S. Capitol St., SE
Washington, DC 20003
Phone : (202) 767-8512

AMERICAN SAMOA
Abe Malae
Director
Power Authority
Dept. of Public Works
Pago Pago, AS 96799
Phone : (684) 644-5251
Fax : (684) 644-5001

GUAM
Joseph C. Cruz
Administrator
Environmental Protection Agency
IT&E Harmon Plz., D-107
130 Rojas St.
Harmon, GU 96911
Phone : (671) 646-8863
Fax : (671) 646-9402

NORTHERN MARIANA ISLANDS
Edward M. Deleon Guerrero
Secretary
Dept. of Public Works
P.O. Box 10007
Saipan, MP 96950
Phone : (670) 322-9482
Fax : (670) 322-3547

PUERTO RICO
Daniel Pagan Rosa
Executive Director
Solid Waste Mgt. Authority
P.O. Box 40285
San Juan, PR 00940
Phone : (809) 765-7575
Fax : (809) 753-2220

U.S. VIRGIN ISLANDS
Ann Abramson
Acting Commissioner
Dept. of Public Works
No. 8 Sub Base
St. Thomas, VI 00802
Phone : (809) 776-4844
Fax : (809) 774-5869

SPECIAL EDUCATION

Has jurisdiction over the education of exceptional and handicapped children.

ALABAMA
Kenneth Wilson
Assistant Superintendent
Special Education Srvcs. Div.
Dept. of Education
50 N. Ripley St.
Montgomery, AL 36130
Phone : (334) 242-8114
Fax : (334) 242-9708

ALASKA
Jim Rich
Administrator
Off. for Exceptional Children
Dept. of Education
801 W. 10th St.
Juneau, AK 99801-1894
Phone : (907) 465-2970

ARIZONA
Lisa Graham
Supt. of Public Instruction
Dept. of Education
1535 W. Jefferson
Phoenix, AZ 85007
Phone : (602) 542-5393

ARKANSAS
Diane Sydoriak
Associate Director
Special Education Section
Dept. of Education
Capitol Mall, Bldg. 4
Little Rock, AR 72201
Phone : (501) 682-4221
Fax : (501) 682-4313

CALIFORNIA
Dhyan Lal
Interim Director
Special Schools & Srvcs.
Dept. of Education
721 Capitol Mall, Rm. 616
Sacramento, CA 94244
Phone : (916) 657-2642

COLORADO
Fred Smokoski
Director
Div. of Special Education
Dept. of Education
201 E. Colfax Ave.
Denver, CO 80203
Phone : (303) 866-6694

CONNECTICUT
Tom B. Gillung
Chief
Bur. of Special Education & Pupil Personnel Srvcs.
P.O. Box 2219
Hartford, CT 06106
Phone : (203) 566-4383

DELAWARE
Martha Brooks
Team Leader
Exceptional Children Team
Townsend Bldg.
P.O. Box 1401
Dover, DE 19903
Phone : (302) 739-5471

FLORIDA
Bettye Weir
Bur. of Education for Exceptional Students
Dept. of Education
325 W. Gaines St., Ste. 614
Tallahassee, FL 32399-0400
Phone : (904) 488-1570

GEORGIA
Paulette Braggs
Special Education Director
Dept. of Education
205 Butler St., SW
Atlanta, GA 30334
Phone : (404) 656-3963

HAWAII
Margaret Donovan
Educational Specialist
Special Education Section
Dept. of Education
3430 Leahi Ave.
Honolulu, HI 96815
Phone : (808) 737-3720

IDAHO
Fred Balcom
Supervisor
Special Education
Dept. of Education
650 W. State St.
Boise, ID 83720
Phone : (208) 334-3940

ILLINOIS
Gail Liberman
Assistant Superintendent
Dept. of Specialized Education
State Board of Education
100 N. First St., Rm. E-216
Springfield, IL 62777
Phone : (217) 782-6601

INDIANA
Bob Marra
Director
Special Education Section
Dept. of Education
State House, 3rd Fl.
Indianapolis, IN 46204
Phone : (317) 232-0570

IOWA
J. Frank Vance
Bureau Chief
Bur. of Special Education
Grimes State Off. Bldg.
Des Moines, IA 50319
Phone : (515) 281-5471

KANSAS
Betty Weithers
Team Leader
Special Ed. Outcomes Team
State Board of Education
120 E. 10th St.
Topeka, KS 66612-1182
Phone : (913) 296-3869

KENTUCKY
Hal Hayden
Acting Director
Exceptional Children Srvc.
Dept. of Education
Capital Plaza Tower
Frankfort, KY 40601
Phone : (502) 564-4970

Johnny Grissom
Associate Commissioner
Off. of Special Instruct. Srvc .
Dept. of Education
Capital Plaza Tower, 8th Fl.
Frankfort, KY 40601
Phone : (502) 564-4970

LOUISIANA
Tama Luther
Acting Assistant Superintendent
Special Education Services
Dept. of Education
P.O. Box 94064
Baton Rouge, LA 70804-9064
Phone : (504) 342-3633

MAINE
Wayne Mowatt
Commissioner
Dept. of Education
State House Station # 23
Augusta, ME 04333
Phone : (207) 287-5802

MARYLAND**
Richard Steinke
Assistant State Superintendent
Div. of Special Education
Dept. of Education
200 W. Baltimore St.
Baltimore, MD 21201
Phone : (410) 333-2491

MASSACHUSETTS
Piedad F. Robertson
Secretary
Special Education Div.
Dept. of Education
1 Ashburton Pl., Rm. 1401
Boston, MA 02108
Phone : (617) 727-1313
Fax : (617) 727-5570

MICHIGAN
Richard Baldwin
Director
Off. of Special Education
Dept. of Education
P.O. Box 30008
Lansing, MI 48909
Phone : (517) 373-9433

MINNESOTA
Wayne Erickson
Manager
Unique Learner Needs Section
Dept. of Education
550 Cedar St., 7th Fl.
St. Paul, MN 55101
Phone : (612) 296-1793

Jim Sauter
Deputy Commissioner
Dept. of Education
550 Cedar St., 7th Fl.
St. Paul, MN 55101
Phone : (612) 297-3115

Gene Mammenga
Commissioner
Dept. of Education
550 Cedar St., 8th Fl.
St. Paul, MN 55101
Phone : (612) 296-2358

MISSISSIPPI
Carolyn Black
Director
Bureau of Special Srvcs.
Dept. of Education
P.O. Box 771
Jackson, MS 39205
Phone : (601) 359-3513

MISSOURI
Melodie Friededach
Coordinator of Sp. Ed.
Div. of Special Education
Dept. of Elementary & Sec. Ed.
P.O. Box 480
Jefferson City, MO 65102
Phone : (314) 751-2965
Fax : (314) 526-4404

MONTANA
Gail Gray
Assistant Superintendent
Off. of Public Instruction
1300 11th Ave.
Helena, MT 59620
Phone : (406) 444-2089

NEBRASKA
Gary Sherman
Administrator
Special Education Branch
Dept. of Education
P.O. Box 94987
Lincoln, NE 68509
Phone : (402) 471-2471

NEVADA
Gloria Dopf
Director
Special Education
Dept. of Education
400 W. King St.
Carson City, NV 89710
Phone : (702) 687-3140

NEW HAMPSHIRE
Elizabeth Twomey
Commissioner
Dept. of Education
101 Pleasant St.
Concord, NH 03301
Phone : (603) 271-3144

NEW JERSEY
Barbara Gantwerk
Director
Div. of Special Education
Dept. of Education
225 W. State St., CN500
Trenton, NJ 08625
Phone : (609) 292-0147

NEW MEXICO
Diego Gallegos
Director
Special Education Office
Dept. of Education
Education Bldg.
Santa Fe, NM 87501
Phone : (505) 827-6541
Fax : (505) 827-6791

NEW YORK*
Commissioner
Dept. of Education
Education Bldg.
Albany, NY 12234
Phone : (518) 474-5844

NORTH CAROLINA
E. Lowell Harris
Director
Exceptional Children
Dept. of Public Education
116 W. Edenton St.
Raleigh, NC 27603
Phone : (919) 715-1000

NORTH DAKOTA
Gary Gronberg
Director
Special Education Div.
Dept. of Public Instruction
State Capitol, 10th Fl.
Bismarck, ND 58505-0440
Phone : (701) 328-2277
Fax : (701) 328-2461

OHIO
John Herner
Director
Div. of Special Education
Dept. of Education
933 High St.
Worthington, OH 43085
Phone : (614) 466-2650
Fax : (614) 728-1097

OKLAHOMA
John Corpolongo
Director
Special Education Section
Dept. of Education
2500 N. Lincoln Blvd.
Oklahoma City, OK 73105
Phone : (405) 521-3351

OREGON
Karen Brazeau
Associate Superintendent
Div. of Special Student Srvcs.
Dept. of Education
PSB, 255 Capitol St., NE
Salem, OR 97310
Phone : (503) 378-3598

PENNSYLVANIA
Richard E. Price
Director
Bur. of Special Education
Dept. of Education
Harristown Bldg. # 2, 7th Fl.
Harrisburg, PA 17108
Phone : (717) 783-6913

RHODE ISLAND
Robert Pryhoda
Director
Off. of Special Needs
Dept. of Education
22 Hayes St.
Providence, RI 02903
Phone : (401) 277-3505

SOUTH CAROLINA
Luther W. Seabrook
Senior Exec. Asst. for Curriculum
State Dept. of Education
1429 Senate St.
Columbia, SC 29201
Phone : (803) 734-8396

SOUTH DAKOTA
Deborah Barnett
Director
Off. of Special Education
Div. of Education
Kneip Bldg.
Pierre, SD 57501
Phone : (605) 773-3678

TENNESSEE
Joseph Fisher
Assistant Commissioner
Special Education
Dept. of Education
102 Cordell Hull Bldg.
Nashville, TN 37247
Phone : (615) 741-2851

TEXAS
Jill Gray
Director
Dept. of Special Education
State Education Agency
1701 N. Congress Ave.
Austin, TX 78701
Phone : (512) 463-9474

UTAH
Stevan J. Kukic
Director
At Risk & Special Education
Off. of Education
250 E. 500 S.
Salt Lake City, UT 84111
Phone : (801) 538-7706

VERMONT
Dennis Kane
Manager
Special Education Unit
Dept. of Education
120 State St.
Montpelier, VT 05620
Phone : (802) 828-3141
Fax : (802) 828-3140

VIRGINIA
William C. Bosher, Jr.
Superintendent
Public Instruction
Dept. of Education
101 N. 14th St.
Richmond, VA 23219
Phone : (804) 225-2023
Fax : (804) 371-2099

WASHINGTON
Doug Gill
Administrator
Curriculum Instructional Supt. & Sp. Ed. Srvc., Pub. Inst.
Old Capitol Bldg., Box 47200
Olympia, WA 98504-7200
Phone : (360) 753-6733

WEST VIRGINIA
Keith Smith
Director
Div. of Instructional & Stdnt. Srvcs., Bldg. 6, Rm. 358
1900 Kanawha Blvd., E.
Charleston, WV 25302-0330
Phone : (304) 558-2691

WISCONSIN
Juanita S. Pawlisch
Asst. Superintendent
Div. for Learning Supp. Equ. & Adv.
Dept. of Public Instruction
125 S Webster
P.O. Box 7841
Madison, WI 53703
Phone : (608) 266-1649
Fax : (608) 267-1052

WYOMING
Margie Simineo
Unit Director
Special Education
Dept. of Education
Hathaway Bldg.
Cheyenne, WY 82002
Phone : (307) 777-7221

DISTRICT OF COLUMBIA
David V. Burkett
Assistant Superintendent
Webster School Special Ed.
Browne JHS
26th & Benning Rd., NE
Washington, DC 20002
Phone : (202) 724-4018

AMERICAN SAMOA
Tuato'o Tautalatasi
Director
Dept. of Education
American Samoa Government
Pago Pago, AS 96799
Phone : (684) 633-5237
Fax : (684) 633-4240

Jane French
Director
Dept. of Human Resources
Pago Pago, AS 96799
Phone : (684) 633-4485
Fax : (684) 633-4240

GUAM
Roland L.G. Taimanglo
Interim Director
Guam Public School System-DOE
P.O. Box DE
Agana, GU 96910
Phone : (671) 475-0457
Fax : (671) 472-5003

NORTHERN MARIANA ISLANDS
Barbara Rudy
Special Education Coordinator
Public School System
Lower Base
Saipan, MP 96950
Phone : (670) 322-9956
Fax : (670) 322-4057

PUERTO RICO
Damaris Ciunentes
Auxiliar Secretary
Special Education Section
Dept. of Education
P.O. Box 759
Hato Rey, PR 00918
Phone : (809) 758-4949

U.S. VIRGIN ISLANDS
James Cheek
Commissioner
Dept. of Education
44-46 Kongens Gade
St. Thomas, VI 00802
Phone : (809) 774-0100
Fax : (809) 774-4679

STATE DATA CENTER

Center that acts as an information clearinghouse for the Census Bureau and other data sources within the state.

ALABAMA
Annette Watters
Manager
State Data Ctr.
University of Alabama
P.O. Box 870221
Tuscaloosa, AL 35487
Phone : (205) 348-6191
Fax : (205) 348-2951

ALASKA
Kathryn Lizik
Coordinator
State Data Center
Dept. of Labor
P.O. Box 25501
Juneau, AK 99802-5501
Phone : (907) 465-4500
Fax : (907) 465-2107

ARIZONA
Betty Jeffries
Statistical Analyst
Dept. of Economic Security
1789 W. Jefferson (045Z)
Phoenix, AZ 85007
Phone : (602) 542-5984

ARKANSAS
Sarah Breshears
Division Chief
State Data Ctr.
Univ. of AR at Little Rock
2801 S. University
Little Rock, AR 72204
Phone : (501) 569-8530
Fax : (501) 569-8538

CALIFORNIA
Linda Gage
Chief
Demographic Research
Dept. of Finance
915 L St.
Sacramento, CA 95814
Phone : (916) 322-4651

COLORADO
Jim Westkott
State Demographer
Div. of Local Government
Dept. of Local Affairs
1313 Sherman St., Rm. 521
Denver, CO 80203
Phone : (303) 866-2156
Fax : (303) 866-4819

Rebecca Picaso
Information Officer
Div. of Local Government
Dept. of Local Affairs
1313 Sherman St., Rm. 521
Denver, CO 80203
Phone : (303) 866-2156

CONNECTICUT
Susan Shimelman
Undersecretary
Policy Dev. & Planning Div.
Off. of Policy & Mgt.
80 Washington St.
Hartford, CT 06106
Phone : (203) 566-4298

DELAWARE
Judy McKinney-Cherry
Manager
State Data Center
Development Off.
99 Kings Hwy.
P.O. Box 1401
Dover, DE 19903
Phone : (302) 739-4271
Fax : (302) 739-5749

FLORIDA
Ed Levine
Policy Coordinator
Off. of Planning & Budgeting
Executive Off. of the Governor
The Capitol
Tallahassee, FL 32399-0001
Phone : (904) 488-6955

GEORGIA
Marty Sik
Operational Support & Dev.
Off. of Planning & Budget
254 Washington St., Rm. 640
Atlanta, GA 30334
Phone : (404) 656-0911

HAWAII
Richard Y.P. Joun
Division Head
Res. & Economic Analysis Div.
Bus., Economic Dev. & Tourism
220 S. King St., 4th Fl.
Honolulu, HI 96813
Phone : (808) 586-2470

IDAHO
Alan Porter
Information Srvcs. Manager
Dept. of Commerce
700 W. State St.
Boise, ID 83720-2700
Phone : (208) 334-2470

ILLINOIS
Suzanne Ebetsch
State Data Ctr. Coordinator
Planning & Financial Analysis
Bur. of the Budget
605 Stratton Off. Bldg.
Springfield, IL 62706
Phone : (217) 782-3500

INDIANA
Larry Hathaway
Coordinator
State Data Center
State Library
140 N. Senate Ave.
Indianapolis, IN 46204
Phone : (317) 232-3732

IOWA
Beth Henning
Census Data Ctr. Coordinator
State Library
E. 12th & Grand
Des Moines, IA 50319
Phone : (515) 281-4350

KANSAS
Marc Galbraith
Director of Reference
Reference & Legis. Srvcs.
State Library
State Capitol Bldg., 3rd Fl.
Topeka, KS 66612-1593
Phone : (913) 296-3296
Fax : (913) 296-6650

KENTUCKY
Ron Crouch
Director, State Data Ctr.
Urban Research Institute
College of Urban & Public Aff.
Univ. of Louisville
Louisville, KY 40292
Phone : (502) 852-7990

LOUISIANA
Karen Patterson
State Demographer
Off. of Planning & Budget
Div. of Administration
P.O. Box 94095
Baton Rouge, LA 70804
Phone : (504) 342-7000

MAINE
Jean Martin
Census Data Ctr. Manager
Div. of Econ. Analysis & Res.
Dept. of Labor
20 Union St.
Augusta, ME 04330-6826
Phone : (207) 287-2271

MARYLAND**
Robert F. Dadd
Manager
State Data Ctr.
Off. of Planning
301 W. Preston St., Rm. 1101
Baltimore, MD 21201-2365
Phone : (301) 225-4450

MASSACHUSETTS
Stephen Colen
Director
Institute for Social & Economic Research
University of Massachusetts
128 Thompson Hall
Amherst, MA 01003
Phone : (413) 545-3460

MICHIGAN
Ching-li Wang
State Demographer
State Information Ctr.
Dept. of Mgt. & Budget
P.O. Box 30026
Lansing, MI 48909
Phone : (517) 373-7910

MINNESOTA
Tom Gillaspy
State Demographer
State Planning Agency
300 Centennial Off. Bldg.
658 Cedar St.
St. Paul, MN 55155
Phone : (612) 296-2557

MISSISSIPPI
Max Williams
Director
Center for Population Studies
Univ. of Mississippi
Bondurant Bldg., Rm. 3W
University, MS 38677
Phone : (601) 232-7288

MISSOURI
Kate Graf
Coordinator
State Census Data Center
State Library
600 W. Main St.
P.O. Box 387
Jefferson City, MO 65102
Phone : (314) 751-3615
Fax : (314) 526-1142

MONTANA
Patricia Roberts
Program Manager
Census & Economic Info. Ctr.
Dept. of Commerce
1424 Ninth Ave.
Helena, MT 59620
Phone : (406) 444-4393

NEBRASKA
Jerome Deichert
Manager
State Data Center
University of NE at Omaha
Peter Kiewit Con. Ctr., Rm. 232
Omaha, NE 68182
Phone : (402) 595-2311

NEVADA
Karen Kavanaugh
Director
Dept. of Information Srvcs.
505 E. King St.
Kinkead Bldg., Rm. 403
Carson City, NV 89710
Phone : (702) 687-4091
Fax : (702) 687-3846

NEW HAMPSHIRE
Thomas J. Duffy
Senior Planner
Off. of State Planning
2 1/2 Beacon St.
Concord, NH 03301
Phone : (603) 271-2155

NEW JERSEY
Connie O. Hughes
Assistant Director
Div. of Occ. & Demo. Research
Dept. of Labor
John Fitz Plz., CN 388
Trenton, NJ 08625-0388
Phone : (609) 984-2593

NEW MEXICO
Carol Selleck
Research Program Officer
Economic Development
Joseph M. Montoya Bldg.
1100 St. Francis Dr.
Santa Fe, NM 87503
Phone : (505) 827-0278
Fax : (505) 827-0328

NEW YORK*
Chief Demographer
Dept. of Economic Development
1 Commerce Plz.
Albany, NY 12245
Phone : (518) 474-6005

NORTH CAROLINA
Francine Stephenson
Manager
State Data Center
Off. of State Planning
116 W. Jones St.
Raleigh, NC 27603-8005
Phone : (919) 733-4131

NORTH DAKOTA
Richard Rathge
Coord., State Census Data Ctr.
Dept. of Agricultural Econ.
ND State University
P.O. Box 5636
Fargo, ND 58105
Phone : (701) 237-7980

OHIO
Steve Kelly
Office Manager
Data Users Center
Dept. of Development
P.O. Box 1001
Columbus, OH 43266-0101
Phone : (614) 466-7772
Fax : (614) 644-5167

OKLAHOMA
Karen Selland
Director
State Data Center
Dept. of Commerce
6601 Broadway Ext., Box 26980
Oklahoma City, OK 73116-8214
Phone : (405) 843-9770

OREGON
Ed Schafer
Director
Ctr. for Pop. Res. & Census
Portland State University
P.O. Box 751
Portland, OR 97207
Phone : (503) 725-3922

PENNSYLVANIA
Michael Behney
Director, State Data Center
Institute of State & Reg. Aff.
Pa. State Univ. at Harrisburg
777 W. Harrisburg Pike
Middletown, PA 17057-4898
Phone : (717) 948-6178

RHODE ISLAND
Richard Dearson
Principal Research Technician
Off. of Municipal Affairs
Dept. of Administration
One Capitol Hill
Providence, RI 02908-5873
Phone : (401) 277-2276

SOUTH CAROLINA
Mike MacFarlane
State Demographer
Div. of Research & Stat. Srvcs.
Budget & Control Board
Rembert C. Dennis Bldg., Rm. 425
Columbia, SC 29201
Phone : (803) 734-3788

SOUTH DAKOTA
DeVee E. Dykstra
Director, State Data Ctr.
Business Research Bur.
School of Bus., Univ. of SD
414 E. Clark
Vermillion, SD 57069
Phone : (605) 677-5287

TENNESSEE
Charles Brown
Director, State Data Center
State Planning Office
John Sevier State Off. Bldg.
500 Charlotte Ave., Ste. 307
Nashville, TN 37243
Phone : (615) 741-1676

TEXAS
Susan Tully
Senior Economist
State Data Ctr.
Dept. of Commerce
P.O. Box 12728
Austin, TX 78711
Phone : (512) 472-5059

UTAH
Julie Johnsson
Research Analyst
Off. of Planning & Budget
State Capitol, Rm. 116
Salt Lake City, UT 84114
Phone : (801) 538-1554

VERMONT
Steve Condrey
Off. of Policy Research
Executive Dept.
109 State St.
Montpelier, VT 05609
Phone : (802) 828-3326
Fax : (802) 828-3339

VIRGINIA
Kenneth A. Bolles
Commissioner
VA Employment Commission
703 E. Main St.
Richmond, VA 23219
Phone : (804) 786-3001
Fax : (804) 225-3923

WASHINGTON
Gary Robinson
Deputy Director
Forecasting Unit
Off. of Financial Mgt.
P.O. Box 43113
Olympia, WA 98504
Phone : (360) 586-2151

WEST VIRGINIA
Mary C. Harless
Gov. Off. of Comm. & Ind. Dev.
Bldg. 6, Rm. B504
1900 Kanawha Blvd., E.
Charleston, WV 25305
Phone : (304) 558-2234

WISCONSIN
Robert Naylor
Census Data Consultant
Demographic Srvcs. Ctr.
Dept. of Admin.
101 E Wilson, 6th Fl.
P.O. Box 7868
Madison, WI 53703
Phone : (608) 266-1927
Fax : (608) 267-6931

WYOMING
Steve Furtney
Administrator
Economic Analysis Div.
Dept. of Admin. & Information
Emerson Bldg.
Cheyenne, WY 82002
Phone : (307) 777-7221

DISTRICT OF COLUMBIA
Gan Ahuja
Data Analyst
Off. of Planning
415 12th St., NW, Ste. 500
Washington, DC 20004
Phone : (202) 727-6533

AMERICAN SAMOA
Alfonso Pete Galeai
Director
Off. Of Economic Development Planning
Utulei
Pago Pago, AS 96799
Phone : (684) 633-5155
Fax : (684) 633-4195

GUAM
Frank B. Agnon Jr.
Director
Dept. of Commerce
590 S. Marine Dr.
ITC Bldg., Ste. 601
Tamuning, GU 96911
Phone : (671) 646-6931
Fax : (671) 646-7242

NORTHERN MARIANA ISLANDS
John S. Borja
Chief of Statistics
Dept. of Commerce and Labor
Capitol Hill
Saipan, MP 96950
Phone : (670) 322-0874
Fax : (670) 322-4008

PUERTO RICO
Norma Burgos Andujar
Planning Board
Minillas Government Ctr.
Avenida De Diego
P.O. Box 41119
San Juan, PR 00940
Phone : (809) 723-6200
Fax : (809) 724-3270

U.S. VIRGIN ISLANDS
Laverne Ragster
Director
Caribbean Research Institute
Univ. of the Virgin Islands
Charlotte Amalie
St. Thomas, VI 00802
Phone : (809) 776-9200

STATE FAIR

Responsible for the annual state fair.

ALABAMA
Jerry Robinson
General Manager
State Fair Authority
P.O. Box 3800-B
Birmingham, AL 35205
Phone : (205) 786-8100
Fax : (205) 786-8222

ARIZONA
Gary Montgomery
Executive Director
Coliseum & Expo Center Board
1826 W. McDowell Rd.
Phoenix, AZ 85005
Phone : (602) 252-6771

ARKANSAS
Jim Pledger
General Manager
Livestock Show Assn.
2600 Howard St.
Little Rock, AR 72206
Phone : (501) 372-8341
Fax : (501) 372-4197

CALIFORNIA
Norbert Bartosik
General Manager
Exposition & State Fair
1600 Exposition Blvd.
Sacramento, CA 95815
Phone : (916) 263-3000

COLORADO
John McGuiness
Chairman
State Fair Authority
P.O. Box 233
Broomfield, CO 80038
Phone : (303) 466-6433

CONNECTICUT
Charlene Magdich
Correspondence Secretary
Association of Connecticut State Fairs
P.O. Box 563
Somers, CT 06071
Phone : (203) 491-2761

DELAWARE
Dennis Hazzard
General Manager
State Fair
P.O. Box 28
Harrington, DE 19952
Phone : (302) 398-3269

FLORIDA
Sharon Lybrand
Director
Off. of the Commissioner
Dept. of Agriculture & Consumer Srvcs.
The Capitol, PL10
Tallahassee, FL 32399-0810
Phone : (904) 488-3022

GEORGIA
Michael Froehlich
Executive Director
Agricultural Exposition Authority
P.O. Box 1367
Perry, GA 31069
Phone : (404) 987-2774

ILLINOIS
Joseph Saputo
State Fair Manager
State Fair
State Fairgrounds
Springfield, IL 62706
Phone : (217) 782-0770
Fax : (217) 782-9115

INDIANA
William H. Stinson
Executive Director
State Fair Comm.
Fairgrounds Admin. Bldg.
1202 E. 38th St.
Indianapolis, IN 46205
Phone : (317) 927-7501

IOWA
Marion Lucas
Secretary
State Fair Authority
State Capitol
Des Moines, IA 50319
Phone : (515) 262-3111

KANSAS
Robert Gottschalk
General Manager
Kansas State Fair
2000 N. Poplar
Hutchinson, KS 67502-5598
Phone : (316) 669-3600

KENTUCKY
Harold Workman
President
State Fair Bd.
Fair & Exposition Ctr.
P.O. Box 37130
Louisville, KY 40233
Phone : (502) 367-5100

MAINE
Ed McLaughlin
Commissioner
Dept. of Agriculture, Food & Rural Resources
State House Station # 28
Augusta, ME 04333
Phone : (207) 287-3871

MARYLAND**
Philip Brendel
Chairman
Agricultural Fair Bd.
Dept. of Agriculture
50 Harry S. Truman Pkwy.
Annapolis, MD 21401
Phone : (410) 841-5770

MASSACHUSETTS
Wayne McCary
President
Eastern States Exposition
1305 Memorial Ave.
West Springfiel, MA 01089
Phone : (413) 737-2443

MICHIGAN
John Hertel
Director
State Fair
Dept. of Agriculture
1120 W. State Fair Ave.
Detroit, MI 48203
Phone : (313) 256-1442

MINNESOTA
Michael D. Heffron
Secretary/General Manager
State Fair Grounds
Snelling Ave.
St. Paul, MN 55108
Phone : (612) 642-2200

MISSISSIPPI
Billy Orr
Executive Director
Fair & Coliseum Comm.
1207 Mississippi St.
Jackson, MS 39202
Phone : (601) 961-4000

MISSOURI
Bill Arthaud
Director
Missouri State Fair
Dept. of Agriculture
2503 West 16th St.
Sedalia, MO 65301
Phone : (816) 530-5600
Fax : (816) 530-5609

NEBRASKA
John Skold
Manager
State Fair Off.
Fairgrounds
P.O. Box 81223
Lincoln, NE 68501-1223
Phone : (402) 474-5371

NEW JERSEY
Richard Kuhn
Secretary-Treasurer
Agriculture Fair Assn.
Div. of Markets
Dept. of Agriculture, CN330
Trenton, NJ 08625
Phone : (609) 292-5566

NEW MEXICO
Sam Hancock
Manager
State Fair Comm.
P.O. Box 8546
Albuquerque, NM 87198
Phone : (505) 265-1791
Fax : (505) 266-7784

NEW YORK*
Commissioner
Dept. of Ag. & Markets
Capitol Plz.
1 Winners Cir.
Albany, NY 12235
Phone : (518) 457-4188

NORTH CAROLINA
Sam G. Rand
Manager
State Fair
Dept. of Agriculture
One W. Edenton St.
Raleigh, NC 27601-1094
Phone : (919) 733-2145

NORTH DAKOTA
Gerald Iverson
Manager
State Fair Assn.
P.O. Box 1796
Minot, ND 58702
Phone : (701) 857-7620

OHIO
Richard Frenette
General Manager
Expositions Ctr.
717 E. 17th Ave.
Columbus, OH 43211-2698
Phone : (614) 466-8386
Fax : (614) 644-4031

OKLAHOMA
Donald J. Hotz
President & General Manager
State Fair
500 Land Rush St.
P.O. Box 74943
Oklahoma City, OK 73147
Phone : (405) 948-6700

OREGON
Robert (Rusty) Vernon
Director
State Fair & Exposition Ctr.
2330 17th St., NE
Salem, OR 97310
Phone : (503) 378-3247
Fax : (503) 373-1788

PENNSYLVANIA
John K. Stark
Director
Bureau of Markets
Dept. of Agriculture
2301 N. Cameron St.
Harrisburg, PA 17110
Phone : (717) 787-6041

RHODE ISLAND
William Hawkins
Chief
Div. of Parks & Recreation
Dept. of Environmental Mgt.
2321 Hartford
Johnston, RI 02919
Phone : (401) 277-2632

SOUTH CAROLINA
Gary Goodman
Manager
State Fair
P.O. Box 393
Columbia, SC 29202
Phone : (803) 799-3387

SOUTH DAKOTA
Wallace Johnson
Chairman
State Fair Board
State Fairgrounds
Huron, SD 57350
Phone : (605) 352-1431

TENNESSEE
Tom Womack
Public Affairs
Dept. of Agriculture
Ellington Agricultural Ctr.
Nashville, TN 37204
Phone : (615) 360-0117

UTAH*
Director
Div. of Expositions
Dept. of Community & Economic Development
155 N. 1000 W.
Salt Lake City, UT 84116
Phone : (801) 538-8440

VERMONT
Jerome Kelley
Deputy Commissioner
Dept. of Agriculture
116 State St.
Montpelier, VT 05602
Phone : (802) 828-2416
Fax : (802) 828-2361

VIRGINIA
J. Carlton Courter III
Commissioner
Dept. of Agriculture & Consumer Services
1100 Bank St.
Richmond, VA 23219
Phone : (804) 786-3501
Fax : (804) 371-2945

WASHINGTON
Eric Herlburlt
Director
International Marketing Development
Dept. of Agriculture
P.O. Box 42560
Olympia, WA 98504-2560
Phone : (360) 902-1925

WEST VIRGINIA
Ed Rock
Manager
State Fair
P.O. Box 829
Lewisburg, WV 24901
Phone : (304) 645-1090

WISCONSIN
Rick Bjorklund
Director
State Fair Park Bd.
Dept. of Agriculture, Trade & Consumer Protection
State Fair Park
8100 W. Greenfield Ave.
West Allis, WI 53214
Phone : (414) 266-7000
Fax : (141) 266-7007

WYOMING
Dave Noble
Director
Div. of State Fair
Dept. of Agriculture
State Fairgrounds
Douglas, WY 82633
Phone : (307) 358-2398

DISTRICT OF COLUMBIA
Carol Lowe
Director
Dept. of Recreation & Parks
3149 16th St., NW, 2nd Fl.
Washington, DC 20010
Phone : (202) 673-7665

NORTHERN MARIANA ISLANDS
Benigno M. Sablan
Secretary
Dept. of Lands & Natural Resources
P.O. Box 10007
Saipan, MP 96950
Phone : (670) 322-9830
Fax : (670) 322-2633

U.S. VIRGIN ISLANDS
Anthony Olive
Commissioner
Dept. of Economic Development & Agriculture
P.O. Box 6400
St. Thomas, VI 00803
Phone : (809) 774-8784
Fax : (809) 774-4390

STATE LIBRARY

Serves the information and research needs of state executive and legislative branch officials.

ALABAMA
Patricia L. Harris
Director
Public Library Srvc.
6030 Monticello Dr.
Montgomery, AL 36130
Phone : (334) 213-3900
Fax : (334) 213-3993

ALASKA
Karen R. Crane
Director
State Libraries & Archives
Dept. of Education
P.O. Box 110571
Juneau, AK 99811-0571
Phone : (907) 465-2910
Fax : (907) 465-2151

ARKANSAS
John A. Murphy Jr.
State Librarian
State Library
Dept. of Education
One Capitol Mall
Little Rock, AR 72201
Phone : (501) 682-1526
Fax : (501) 682-1529

CALIFORNIA
Kevin Starr
State Librarian
State Library
914 Capitol Mall
Sacramento, CA 95814
Phone : (916) 654-0174

COLORADO
Nancy Bolt
Assistant Commissioner
Dept. of Education
201 E. Colfax Ave.
Denver, CO 80203
Phone : (303) 866-6900
Fax : (303) 866-6940

CONNECTICUT
Richard G. Akeroyd Jr.
State Librarian
State Library
231 Capitol Ave.
Hartford, CT 06106
Phone : (203) 566-4301

DELAWARE
Tom W. Sloan
State Librarian
Div. of Libraries
Dept. of State
43 S. duPont Hwy.
Dover, DE 19901
Phone : (302) 739-4748
Fax : (302) 739-6787

FLORIDA
Linda Fuchs
Director
Bur. of Library & Network Srvcs.
Dept. of State
R.A. Gray Bldg.
500 S. Bronough St.
Tallahassee, FL 32399-0250
Phone : (904) 487-2651

GEORGIA
Joe B. Forsee
Director
Div. of Public Library Svcs.
156 Trinity Ave., S.W.
Atlanta, GA 30303
Phone : (404) 656-2461

HAWAII
Bartholomew A. Kane
State Librarian
State Public Library System
Dept. of Education
465 S. King St., Rm. B-1
Honolulu, HI 96813
Phone : (808) 586-3704
Fax : (808) 586-3715

IDAHO
Charles A. Bolles
State Librarian
State Library
325 W. State Street
Boise, ID 83702
Phone : (208) 334-5124

ILLINOIS
Bridget Lamont
Director
State Library
300 S. Second St.
Springfield, IL 62701
Phone : (217) 782-2994

INDIANA
C. Ray Ewick
Director
State Library
140 N. Senate Ave.
Indianapolis, IN 46204
Phone : (317) 232-3692

IOWA
Sharman B. Smith
State Librarian
State Library Div.
Dept. of Education
E. 12th & Grand
Des Moines, IA 50319
Phone : (515) 281-4105

KANSAS
Duane F. Johnson
State Librarian
State Library
State Capitol Bldg., 3rd Fl.
Topeka, KS 66612
Phone : (913) 296-3296
Fax : (913) 296-6650

KENTUCKY
James A. Nelson
State Librarian & Commissioner
Dept. of Library & Archives
Education & Humanities Cabinet
300 Coffee Tree Rd., Box 537
Frankfort, KY 40602
Phone : (502) 875-7000

LOUISIANA
Thomas F. Jaques
State Librarian
Off. of State Library
Dept. of Culture, Recreation & Tourism
P.O. Box 131
Baton Rouge, LA 70821
Phone : (504) 342-4923

MAINE
J. Gary Nichols
State Librarian
Bur. of Library Services
State House Station # 64
Augusta, ME 04333
Phone : (207) 287-5600

MARYLAND**
J. Maurice Travillian
Asst. State Superintendent
Div. of Library Development & Srvcs.
Dept. of Education
200 W. Baltimore St.
Baltimore, MD 21201
Phone : (410) 333-2113

MASSACHUSETTS
Keith Fields
Director
Board of Library Commissioners
648 Beacon St.
Boston, MA 02215
Phone : (617) 267-9400

MICHIGAN
James W. Fry
State Librarian
State Library
P.O. Box 30007
Lansing, MI 48909
Phone : (517) 373-1580

MINNESOTA
William G. Asp
Director
Off of Library Dev. & Srvcs.
Capitol Sq., Rm. 440
550 Cedar St.
St. Paul, MN 55101
Phone : (612) 296-2821

MISSISSIPPI
Jane Smith
Acting Director
State Library Comm.
1221 Ellis Ave.
P.O. Box 10700
Jackson, MS 39289-0700
Phone : (601) 359-1036

MISSOURI
Sara Ann Parker
State Librarian
State Library
600 W. Main
P.O. Box 387
Jefferson City, MO 65102-0387
Phone : (314) 751-3615
Fax : (314) 751-3612

MONTANA
Richard T. Miller Jr.
State Librarian
State Library
1515 E. Sixth Ave.
Helena, MT 59620
Phone : (406) 444-3115

NEBRASKA
Rod Wagner
Director
State Library Comm.
1200 N St., Ste. 120
Lincoln, NE 68508-2023
Phone : (402) 471-2045

NEVADA
Joan G. Kerschner
Director
Museums, Library & Arts Dept.
100 Stewart St.
Carson City, NV 89710
Phone : (702) 687-8315

NEW HAMPSHIRE
Kendall F. Wiggin
State Librarian
State Library
Dept. of Cultural Affairs
20 Park St.
Concord, NH 03301-6303
Phone : (603) 271-2397

NEW JERSEY
Louise Minervino
State Librarian
Div. of State Library
Dept. of Education
185 W. State St., CN520
Trenton, NJ 08625
Phone : (609) 292-6200

NEW MEXICO
Karen Watkins
State Librarian
State Library
Off. of Cultural Affairs
325 Don Gaspar
Santa Fe, NM 87503
Phone : (505) 827-3804
Fax : (505) 827-3888

NEW YORK*
State Librarian
State Library
Cultural Education Ctr.
Empire State Plz.
Albany, NY 12230
Phone : (518) 474-5930

NORTH CAROLINA
Sandra Cooper
State Librarian
Div. of State Library
Dept. of Cultural Resources
109 E. Jones St.
Raleigh, NC 27601-2807
Phone : (919) 733-2570

NORTH DAKOTA
William R. Strader
State Librarian
State Library
Liberty Memorial Bldg.
604 E. Boulevard Ave.
Bismarck, ND 58505
Phone : (701) 328-2717
Fax : (701) 328-2040

OHIO
Richard M. Cheski
State Librarian
State Library
65 S. Front St., Rm. 1206
Columbus, OH 43266-0334
Phone : (614) 644-6843
Fax : (614) 466-3584

OKLAHOMA
Robert L. Clark
Director
Dept. of Libraries
200 NE 18th St.
Oklahoma City, OK 73105
Phone : (405) 521-2502

OREGON
Jim Scheppke
State Librarian
State Library
State Library Bldg.
Salem, OR 97310
Phone : (503) 378-4367
Fax : (503) 588-7119

PENNSYLVANIA
Sara Parker
Commissioner of Libraries
State Library
Dept. of Education
P.O. Box 1601
Harrisburg, PA 17105
Phone : (717) 787-2646

RHODE ISLAND
Barbara Weaver
Director
Dept. of State Library Srvcs.
State Library
300 Richmond St.
Providence, RI 02903
Phone : (401) 277-2726

SOUTH CAROLINA
James B. Johnson
Director
State Library
P.O. Box 11469
Columbia, SC 29211
Phone : (803) 734-8666

SOUTH DAKOTA
Jane Kolbe
State Librarian
State Library
State Library Bldg.
800 Governors Dr.
Pierre, SD 57501
Phone : (605) 773-3131

TENNESSEE
Edwin S. Gleaves
State Librarian & Archivist
State Library & Archives
403 Seventh Ave., N.
Nashville, TN 37243-0312
Phone : (615) 741-2451

TEXAS
William D. Gooch
Director & Librarian
State Library
P.O. Box 12927, Capitol Sta.
Austin, TX 78711
Phone : (512) 463-5460

UTAH
Amy Owen
Director
State Library
2150 S. 300 W., Ste. 16
Salt Lake City, UT 84115
Phone : (801) 466-5888

VERMONT
Patricia E. Klinck
State Librarian
Dept. of Libraries
109 State St.
Montpelier, VT 05609
Phone : (802) 828-3265
Fax : (802) 828-2199

VIRGINIA
Nolan T. Yelich
State Librarian
The Library of Virginia
11th St. at Capitol Sq.
Richmond, VA 23219
Phone : (804) 786-2332
Fax : (804) 786-5855

WASHINGTON
Nancy L. Zussy
State Librarian
State Library
State Library Bldg.
P.O. Box 42460
Olympia, WA 98504-2460
Phone : (360) 753-5590

WEST VIRGINIA
Frederick J. Glazer
Director
Library Comm.
Cultural Ctr.
Charleston, WV 25305
Phone : (304) 558-2041

WISCONSIN
Sally Drew
Assistant Superintendent
Div. of Library Services
Dept. of Public Instruction
125 S. Webster St.
P.O. Box 7841
Madison, WI 53707
Phone : (608) 266-2205
Fax : (608) 267-1052

WYOMING
Jerry Krois
Acting State Librarian
State Library
Dept. of Admin. & Information
Supreme Court & Library Bldg.
Cheyenne, WY 82002-0660
Phone : (307) 777-7281

DISTRICT OF COLUMBIA
Hardy R. Franklin
Director
Public Library
901 G St., NW, Ste. 400
Washington, DC 20001
Phone : (202) 727-1101

AMERICAN SAMOA
Emma F.C. Penn
Supervisor & Program Director
Off. of Library Srvcs.
Dept. of Education
P.O. Box 1329
Pago Pago, AS 96799
Phone : (684) 633-5869
Fax : (684) 633-4240

GUAM
Christine Scott-Smith
Territorial Librarian
Guam Public Library
P.O. Box 9008
Tamuning, GU 96911
Phone : (671) 472-6417
Fax : (671) 477-9777

NORTHERN MARIANA ISLANDS
Rita S. Camacho
Librarian
Dept. of Education
Saipan, MP 96950
Phone : (670) 322-6451
Fax : (670) 322-4056

PUERTO RICO
Lidia Santiago
Director
Public Library Div.
Dept. of Education
P.O. Box 759
Hato Rey, PR 00919
Phone : (809) 753-9191

U.S. VIRGIN ISLANDS
Jeannette B. Allis-Bastian
Director
Libraries, Archives & Museums
Dept. of Planning & Natural Resources
23 Dronningens Gade
St. Thomas, VI 00802
Phone : (809) 774-5715

STATE POLICE

Patrols the state's highways and enforces the motor vehicle laws of the state.

ALABAMA
Larry Ray
Chief
Highway Patrol Div.
Dept. of Public Safety
500 Dexter Ave.
Montgomery, AL 36130
Phone : (334) 242-4393
Fax : (334) 242-4385

ALASKA
Glenn G. Godfrey
Director
Div. of Alaska State Troopers
Dept. of Public Safety
5700 E. Tudor Rd.
Anchorage, AK 99507-1225
Phone : (907) 269-5641
Fax : (907) 337-2059

ARIZONA
Joe Albo
Director
Dept. of Public Safety
2102 W. Encanto Blvd.
Phoenix, AZ 85009
Phone : (602) 223-2000

ARKANSAS
John Bailey
Director
State Police
P.O. Box 5901
Little Rock, AR 72215
Phone : (501) 221-8200
Fax : (501) 224-4722

CALIFORNIA
Maurice J. Hannigan
Commissioner
Dept. of Hwy. Patrol
2555 First Ave.
Sacramento, CA 95818
Phone : (916) 657-7152

COLORADO
John Dempsey
Chief
Colorado State Patrol
Dept. of Public Safety
700 Kipling
Lakewood, CO 80215
Phone : (303) 239-4500

CONNECTICUT
Kenneth H. Kirschner
Commissioner
Dept. of Public Safety
P.O. Box 2794
Middletown, CT 06457-9294
Phone : (203) 685-8000

DELAWARE
Alan D. Ellingsworth
Superintendent
State Police
State Police Headquarters
Dover, DE 19901
Phone : (302) 739-5911
Fax : (302) 739-5966

FLORIDA
Ronald Grimming
Director
Highway Patrol
Hwy. Safety & Motor Veh. Dept.
Neil Kirkman Bldg.
2900 Apalachee Parkway
Tallahassee, FL 32399-0500
Phone : (904) 922-5319

GEORGIA
Sidney R. Miles
Commissioner
Dept. of Public Safety
959 E. Confederate Ave.
Atlanta, GA 30316
Phone : (404) 624-7710

IDAHO
Ronald L. Moore
Superintendent
State Police
Dept. of Law Enforcement
3311 W. State St.
Boise, ID 83704
Phone : (208) 884-7000

ILLINOIS
Terrence Gainer
Director
Dept. of State Police
103 State Armory
Springfield, IL 62706
Phone : (217) 782-4593
Fax : (217) 785-2821

INDIANA
Lloyd R. Jennings
Superintendent
State Police
IGC-North, 3rd Fl.
Indianapolis, IN 46204
Phone : (317) 232-8241

IOWA
Earl Usher
Chief
Iowa State Patrol
Dept. of Public Safety
Wallace State Off. Bldg.
Des Moines, IA 50319-0044
Phone : (515) 281-8392

KANSAS
Lonnie McCollum
Superintendent
Highway Patrol
122 S.W. Seventh St.
Topeka, KS 66603-3847
Phone : (913) 296-6800
Fax : (913) 296-5956

KENTUCKY
Jerry Lovitt
Commissioner
Dept. of State Police
Justice Cabinet
919 Versailles Rd.
Frankfort, KY 40601
Phone : (502) 695-6300

LOUISIANA
Paul W. Fontenot
Deputy Secretary
Dept. of Public Safety Services
P.O. Box 94304
Baton Rouge, LA 70804-9304
Phone : (504) 925-6117

MAINE
Alfred Skolfield
Chief
State Police
Dept. of Public Safety
State House Station # 42
Augusta, ME 04333
Phone : (207) 287-4478

MARYLAND**
Larry W. Tolliver
Superintendent
State Police
State Police Headquarters
1201 Reisterstown Rd.
Baltimore, MD 21208
Phone : (301) 653-4219

MASSACHUSETTS
Charles Henderson
Commissioner
Div. of State Police
Dept. of Public Safety
470 Worcester Rd.
Framingham, MA 01701
Phone : (508) 820-2350

MICHIGAN
Mike Robinson
Director
Dept. of State Police
714 S. Harrison Rd.
East Lansing, MI 48823
Phone : (517) 336-6158
Fax : (517) 336-6255

MINNESOTA
Michael Chabries
Chief
State Patrol Div.
Dept. of Public Safety
107 Transportation Bldg.
St. Paul, MN 55155
Phone : (612) 297-3935

MISSISSIPPI
Jim Ingram
Commissioner
Dept. of Public Safety
Hwy. Patrol Bldg., I-55 N.
Jackson, MS 39216
Phone : (601) 987-1490

MISSOURI
F.M. Mills
Superintendent
State Highway Patrol
Dept. of Public Safety
1510 E. Elm
P.O. Box 568
Jefferson City, MO 65102
Phone : (314) 751-3313
Fax : (314) 751-9419

MONTANA
Craig T. Reap
Chief Administrator
Highway Patrol Div.
Dept. of Justice
Scott Hart Bldg., 303 N. Roberts
Helena, MT 59620
Phone : (406) 444-7000

NEBRASKA
Ron Tussing
Superintendent
State Patrol
P.O. Box 94907
Lincoln, NE 68509-4907
Phone : (402) 471-4545

NEVADA
Paul Corbin
Chief
Highway Patrol Div.
Motor Vehicles/Public Safety
555 Wright Way
Carson City, NV 89711-0525
Phone : (702) 687-5300
Fax : (702) 687-3564

NEW HAMPSHIRE
Lynn Presby
Director
Div. of State Police
Dept. of Safety
10 Hazen Dr.
Concord, NH 03305
Phone : (603) 271-2575

NEW JERSEY
Col. Carl A. Williams
Superintendent
Div. of State Police
Dept. of Law & Public Safety
P.O. Box 7068
West Trenton, NJ 08625
Phone : (609) 882-2201

NEW MEXICO
Darren White
Secretary
State Police
P.O. Box 1628
Santa Fe, NM 87504
Phone : (505) 827-9003
Fax : (505) 827-3434

NEW YORK*
Superintendent
Div. of State Police
State Campus, Public Security Bldg.
Albany, NY 12226
Phone : (518) 457-6721

NORTH CAROLINA
Robert A. Barefoot
Chief
Highway Patrol
Crime Control & Public Safety
512 N. Salisbury St.
Raleigh, NC 27604-1159
Phone : (919) 733-7952

NORTH DAKOTA
James M. Hughes
Superintendent
Highway Patrol
Judicial Wing, State Capitol
600 E. Boulevard Ave.
Bismarck, ND 58505
Phone : (701) 328-2455
Fax : (701) 328-3000

OHIO
Warren H. Davies
Superintendent
State Highway Patrol
660 E. Main St.
Columbus, OH 43266-0562
Phone : (614) 466-2990
Fax : (614) 644-9749

OKLAHOMA
David McBride
Secretary of Safety & Security
Dept. of Public Safety
P.O. Box 11415
Oklahoma City, OK 73136
Phone : (405) 425-2424

OREGON
L.R. Howland
Superintendent
Dept. of Police
400 Public Service Bldg.
Salem, OR 97310
Phone : (503) 378-3720

PENNSYLVANIA
Paul Evanko
Commissioner
Pennsylvania State Police
1800 Elmerton Ave.
Harrisburg, PA 17110
Phone : (717) 783-5558

RHODE ISLAND
Edmund Culhane
Superintendent
Dept. of State Police
311 Danielson Pike
North Scituate, RI 02857
Phone : (401) 444-1111

SOUTH CAROLINA
James Caulder
Director
Highway Patrol
Dept. of Public Safety
5400 Broad River Rd.
Columbia, SC 29210
Phone : (803) 896-7844

SOUTH DAKOTA
Gene Abdallah
Director
Div. of Hwy. Patrol
320 N. Nicollet
Pierre, SD 57501
Phone : (605) 773-3105

TENNESSEE
Mike Greene
Commissioner
Dept. of Safety
1150 Foster Ave.
Nashville, TN 37249
Phone : (615) 251-5166

TEXAS
James R. Wilson
Director
Dept. of Public Safety
5805 N. Lamar Blvd.
Austin, TX 78773
Phone : (512) 465-2000

UTAH
Richard Greenwood
Superintendent
Highway Patrol
Dept. of Public Safety
4501 S. 2700, W.
Salt Lake City, UT 84119
Phone : (801) 965-4379

VERMONT
Lane Marshall
Director
State Police
Dept. of Public Safety
103 S. Main St.
Waterbury, VT 05671
Phone : (802) 244-7345
Fax : (802) 244-1106

VIRGINIA
M. Wayne Huggins
Superintendent
Dept. of State Police
7700 Midlothian Tpke.
Richmond, VA 23235
Phone : (804) 674-2087
Fax : (804) 674-2132

WASHINGTON
Annette Sandberg
Chief
State Patrol
General Administration Bldg.
P.O. Box 42601
Olympia, WA 98504-2601
Phone : (360) 753-6540

WEST VIRGINIA
Thomas L. Kirk
Superintendent
Dept. of Public Safety
725 Jefferson Rd.
South Charlesto, WV 25309-1698
Phone : (304) 746-2111

WISCONSIN
Steven D. Sell
Executive Director
Off. of Justice Assistance
Dept. of Administration
222 State St., 2nd Fl.
Madison, WI 53703
Phone : (608) 266-3323
Fax : (608) 266-6676

WYOMING
Everette Ayers
Director
Highway Patrol Div.
Transportation Dept.
5300 Bishop Blvd.
Cheyenne, WY 82002
Phone : (307) 777-4301

DISTRICT OF COLUMBIA
Fred Thomas
Chief
Metropolitan Police Dept.
300 Indiana Ave., N.W., Rm. 5080
Washington, DC 20001
Phone : (202) 727-4218

AMERICAN SAMOA
Fonoti D. Jessop
Commissioner
Dept. of Public Safety
Pago Pago, AS 96799
Phone : (684) 633-1115
Fax : (684) 633-5111

GUAM
Jack S. Shimizu
Chief of Police
Guam Police Dept.
287 W. O'Brien Dr.
Agana, GU 96910
Phone : (671) 472-8911
Fax : (671) 472-4036

NORTHERN MARIANA ISLANDS
Jose M. Castro
Commissioner
Public Safety Dept.
Saipan, MP 96950
Phone : (670) 234-6921
Fax : (670) 234-8531

PUERTO RICO
Pedro Toledo
Superintendent
State Police Department
Dept. of Police
G.P.O. Box 70166
San Juan, PR 00936
Phone : (809) 781-3406
Fax : (809) 781-0080

U.S. VIRGIN ISLANDS
Ramon Davila
Commissioner
Police Dept.
Nisky Ctr. #6
St. Thomas, VI 00802
Phone : (809) 774-6400
Fax : (809) 774-4057

SURPLUS PROPERTY

Establishes and promotes ways and means of acquiring and distributing equitable federal personal property to public agencies, etc.

ALABAMA
Robert Lunsford
Director
Dept. of Economic & Community Affairs
P.O. Box 5690
Montgomery, AL 36103
Phone : (334) 242-8672
Fax : (334) 242-5099

ALASKA
Dugan Petty
Director
Div. of General Srvcs. & Sup.
Dept. of Administration
P.O. Box 110210
Juneau, AK 99811-0210
Phone : (907) 465-2250
Fax : (907) 465-2189

ARIZONA
Randy Frost
Administrator
Surplus Property Div.
Dept. of Administration
1537 W. Jackson
Phoenix, AZ 85007
Phone : (602) 542-5720

ARKANSAS
Gerald Marlin
Manager
Federal Surplus Property
8700 Remount Rd.
North Little Ro, AR 72118
Phone : (501) 835-3111
Fax : (501) 834-5240

CALIFORNIA
Dale Garrett
Manager
Div. of Material Srvcs.
Dept. of General Srvcs.
4675 Watt Ave.
North Highlands, CA 95660
Phone : (916) 973-3742

COLORADO
Ron Bachali
Manager
Agency for Surplus Property
Dept. of Corrections
4200 Garfield
Denver, CO 80216
Phone : (303) 321-4012
Fax : (303) 320-1050

CONNECTICUT
Robert F. Granquist
Administrative Manager
Bureau of Business Services
Dept. of Administrative Srvcs.
340 Capitol Ave.
Hartford, CT 06106
Phone : (203) 566-7093

DELAWARE
Ronald A. Anderson
Administrator
Surplus Property Program
Div. of Purchasing
P.O. Box 299
Delaware City, DE 19706
Phone : (302) 836-7640

FLORIDA
Chris Butterworth
Chief
Bureau of Federal Property Assit.
Dept. of Management Srvcs.
Ste. 206, Knight Bldg.
Tallahassee, FL 32399-0950
Phone : (904) 488-3524
Fax : (904) 922-6149

GEORGIA
Alonzo Spurley
Administrator
Dept. of Administrative Srvcs.
General Srvcs. Div.
1050 Murphy Ave., SE, Ste. 1A
Atlanta, GA 30310
Phone : (404) 756-4800

HAWAII
Craig Kuraoka
Manager
Surplus Property Branch
Dept. of Acctng & Gen. Srvc.
729 Kakoi St.
Honolulu, HI 96819
Phone : (808) 831-6757

IDAHO
Dennis Talbot
Manager
Bur. of Federal Surplus Property
Dept. of Administration
3204 E. Amity Rd.
Boise, ID 83705
Phone : (208) 334-3477

ILLINOIS
Michael S. Schwartz
Director
Dept. of Central Mgt. Srvcs.
715 Stratton Off. Bldg.
Springfield, IL 62706
Phone : (217) 782-2141
Fax : (217) 524-1880

INDIANA
Faye Johnson
Director
State Surplus Property
545 W. McCarty Street
Indianapolis, IN 46225
Phone : (317) 232-1365

IOWA
Janet E. Phipps
Director
Dept. of General Srvcs.
Hoover State Off. Bldg.
Des Moines, IA 50319
Phone : (515) 281-3196
Fax : (515) 242-5974

KANSAS
Lenny Ewell
Director
Correctional Industries Admin.
Dept. of Corrections
900 SW Jackson, 4th Fl.
Topeka, KS 66612
Phone : (913) 296-0460
Fax : (913) 296-0759

KENTUCKY
Crit Luallen
Secretary
Finance & Admin. Cabinet
Capitol Annex, Rm. 383
Frankfort, KY 40601
Phone : (502) 564-4240

LOUISIANA
Louis Amedee
Director
Property Assistance Agency
Division of Administration
P.O. Box 94095
Baton Rouge, LA 70804-9095
Phone : (504) 342-6890

MAINE
Richard Thompson
Director
Federal Surplus Property
Div. of Purchases
State House Station # 9
Augusta, ME 04333
Phone : (207) 287-3521

MARYLAND**
Avon J. Evans
Director
State Agency for Surplus Property
P.O. Box 1039
Jessup, MD 20794-1039
Phone : (301) 799-0440

MASSACHUSETTS
Frank Kelly
Director
Surplus Property Div.
Executive Off. for Admin. & Finance
One Ashburton Pl.
Boston, MA 02108
Phone : (617) 727-2920

MINNESOTA
John W. Haggerty
Director
Div. of Materials Management
112 Administration Bldg.
50 Sherburne Ave.
St. Paul, MN 55155
Phone : (612) 296-1442

MISSISSIPPI
Jim Majure
Director
Off. of Surplus Property
P.O. Box 5788
Jackson, MS 39288
Phone : (601) 939-2050

MISSOURI
Robert Taylor
Manager
State Surplus Property
Div. of Purchasing
117 N. Riverside Dr.
P.O. Box 1310
Jefferson City, MO 65102
Phone : (314) 751-3415
Fax : (314) 751-1264

NEBRASKA
Gary Bechtold
Manager
Surplus Property Div.
Dept. of Administrative Srvcs.
5001 S. 14th St.
Lincoln, NE 68509-4901
Phone : (402) 479-4890

NEVADA
Thomas Tatro
Director
Dept. of Administration
209 E. Musser St., 304
Carson City, NV 89710
Phone : (702) 687-4094

NEW HAMPSHIRE
Patrick Duffy
Commissioner
Dept. of Administrative Srvcs.
25 Capitol St.
Concord, NH 03301
Phone : (603) 271-3201

NEW JERSEY
Stephen M. Sylvester
Administrator
Unclaimed Property Admin.
Dept. of Treasury
50 Barrack St., CN214
Trenton, NJ 08625
Phone : (609) 292-8822

NEW MEXICO
Les French
Director
Purchasing Div.
Dept. of General Srvcs.
P.O. Box 26110
Santa Fe, NM 87503
Phone : (505) 827-0472
Fax : (505) 827-0499

NEW YORK*
Commissioner
Off. of General Srvcs.
Corning Tower Bldg., 41st Fl.
Empire State Plaza
Albany, NY 12242
Phone : (518) 474-5991

NORTH CAROLINA
John T. Massey Jr.
Federal Property Officer
Federal Surplus Property
Dept. of Administration
1950 Garner Rd.
Raleigh, NC 27610-3926
Phone : (919) 733-3885

NORTH DAKOTA
Bud Walsh
Director of Accounting
Off. of Mgt. & Budget
State Capitol, 4th Fl.
600 E. Boulevard Ave.
Bismarck, ND 58505-0400
Phone : (701) 328-2682
Fax : (701) 328-3230

OKLAHOMA
Jim Lyons
Director
Surplus Property
6137 N. Drexel Blvd.
Oklahoma City, OK 73111
Phone : (405) 843-1996

OREGON
Skip Morton
Manager
State Surplus Property
Dept. of Admin. Srvcs.
1655 Salem Industrial Dr., NE
Salem, OR 97310
Phone : (503) 378-4714
Fax : (503) 378-8558

PENNSYLVANIA
Ronald E. Wolf
Director
Bur. of Supp. & Surplus Operations
Dept. of General Services
22nd & Forster Sts.
Harrisburg, PA 17105
Phone : (717) 787-5940

SOUTH CAROLINA
Ron Cathey
Interim Director
Surplus Property
Budget & Control Board
1441 Boston Ave.
West Columbia, SC 29169
Phone : (803) 822-5490

SOUTH DAKOTA
Tom D. Geraets
Commissioner
Bur. of Administration
500 E. Capitol Ave.
Pierre, SD 57501
Phone : (605) 773-3688

TENNESSEE
Larry Haynes
Commissioner
Dept. of General Srvcs.
Tennessee Towers, 9th Fl.
Nashville, TN 37243
Phone : (615) 741-9263

TEXAS
Dan Bremer
Surplus Property Program
General Srvcs. Comm.
P.O. Box 13047, Capitol Station
Austin, TX 78711-3047
Phone : (512) 463-3035

UTAH
Michael Seely
Program Manager
State Div. of Surplus Property
Dept. of Administrative Srvcs.
522 S. 700 W.
Salt Lake City, UT 84104
Phone : (801) 533-5885

VERMONT
Peter E. Noyes
Director
Div. of Purchasing
Dept. of General Srvcs.
133 State St.
Montpelier, VT 05633-7501
Phone : (802) 828-3394

VIRGINIA
Donald C. Williams
Director
Dept. of General Srvcs.
209 9th St. Off. Bldg.
Richmond, VA 23219
Phone : (804) 786-3311
Fax : (804) 371-8305

WASHINGTON
Michael Levenson
Assistant Director
Div. of Commodity Redist.
Dept. of Gen. Admin.
2805 C. St., SW
Auburn, WA 98001-7401
Phone : (360) 931-3959

WEST VIRGINIA
Kenneth O. Frye
Director
Surplus Property Div.
Div. of Finance & Admin.
2700 Charles Ave.
Dunbar, WV 25064
Phone : (304) 766-2666

WISCONSIN
James Johnson
Administrator
Div. of State Agency Srvcs.
Dept. of Admin.
101 E. Wilson
P.O. Box 7867
Madison, WI 53707
Phone : (608) 266-1011
Fax : (608) 264-9500

WYOMING
Ellen Stephenson
Warehouse Manager
Procurement Services Div.
Dept. of Admin. & Information
2405 Westland Rd.
Cheyenne, WY 82002
Phone : (307) 777-7901

DISTRICT OF COLUMBIA
James Gaston
Director
Dept. of Administrative Srvcs.
441 4th St., NW, Ste. 700
Washington, DC 20001
Phone : (202) 727-1179

AMERICAN SAMOA
Laau Seui
Director
Federal-Surplus Property Agency
Off. of Materials Mgt.
Pago Pago, AS 96799
Phone : (684) 699-1170
Fax : (684) 699-2387

GUAM
John S. Salas
Director
Dept. of Admin.
P.O. Box 884
Agana, GU 96910
Phone : (671) 475-1101
Fax : (671) 477-6788

NORTHERN MARIANA ISLANDS
Edward B. Palacios
Director
Procurement & Supply Div.
Dept. of Finance
Lower Base
Saipan, MP 96950
Phone : (670) 664-1500
Fax : (670) 664-1515

PUERTO RICO
Carlos Soler Aquino
Administrator
General Services Admin.
P.O. Box 7428
San Juan, PR 00916
Phone : (809) 721-7370
Fax : (809) 722-7965

U.S. VIRGIN ISLANDS
Alvin O. Davis
Commissioner
Dept. of Property & Procurement
Sub Base, Bldg. 1
St. Thomas, VI 00801
Phone : (809) 774-0828
Fax : (809) 774-9704

TELECOMMUNICATIONS

Responsible for communications planning and organizing a statewide plan for total communications, especially with local government on emergency matters.

ALASKA
Mark Badger
Director
Div. of Information Srvcs.
Dept. of Administration
P.O. Box 110206
Juneau, AK 99811-0206
Phone : (907) 465-2220
Fax : (907) 465-3450

ARIZONA
Larry Beauchat
Telecommunications Manager
Information Services Div.
Dept. of Administration
1616 W. Adams St.
Phoenix, AZ 85007
Phone : (602) 542-5791

ARKANSAS
Ken Hall
Deputy Director
Telecommunications Div.
Dept. of Computer Srvcs.
10802 Exec. Ctr. Dr., Ste.310
Little Rock, AR 72211
Phone : (501) 682-4080
Fax : (501) 682-4310

COLORADO
Robert Tolman
Director
Div. of Telecommunications
Dept. of Administration
2452 W. Second Ave., Ste. 19
Denver, CO 80223
Phone : (303) 866-2341

CONNECTICUT
John Bennet
Executive Director
Off. of Info. & Technology
Off. of Policy & Mgt.
80 Washington St.
Hartford, CT 06106
Phone : (203) 566-1234

DELAWARE
Peter A. LaVenia
Director
Telecommunications Mgt. Off.
Barratt Bldg., Ste. 108
801 Silver Lake Blvd., Box 370
Dover, DE 19901
Phone : (302) 739-9693

FLORIDA
Glenn W. Mayne
Director
Div. of Communications
Dept. of General Srvcs.
2737 Centerview Dr.
Tallahassee, FL 32399-0950
Phone : (904) 488-3595

GEORGIA
George A. Christenberry Jr.
Director
Telecommunications Div.
Dept. of Adm. Srvcs.
200 Piedmont Ave., SE, # 1402
Atlanta, GA 30334-5540
Phone : (404) 656-1744

HAWAII
Thomas I. Yamashiro
Administrator
Information & Comm. Srvcs.
Dept. of Budget & Finance
P.O. Box 150
Honolulu, HI 96816
Phone : (808) 586-1930

IDAHO
Pamela Ahrens
Director
Dept. of Admin.
650 W. State St., Rm. 100
Boise, ID 83720
Phone : (208) 334-3382

ILLINOIS
Walt Erchinger
Chief, Telecommunications
Communications Services Div.
Dept. of Central Management
120 W. Jefferson St.
Springfield, IL 62702
Phone : (217) 782-4140
Fax : (217) 524-0755

INDIANA
Dawn J. Hahm
Senior Manager, Comm. Srvcs.
Information Srvcs. Div.
Dept. of Administration
IGC-North, Rm. N551
Indianapolis, IN 46204
Phone : (317) 232-4629

IOWA
Kathleen Williams
Administrator
Div. of Communications
Dept. of General Srvcs.
Hoover State Office Bldg.
Des Moines, IA 50319
Phone : (515) 281-3336

KANSAS
Don Heiman
Director
Div. of Information Systems & Communications (DISC)
Dept. of Administration
Landon State Off. Bldg., Rm. 751-S
Topeka, KS 66612-1275
Phone : (913) 296-3343
Fax : (913) 296-1168

KENTUCKY
J. Paul Warnecke
Director, Telecommunications Div.
Dept. of Facilities Mgt.
Finance & Admin. Cabinet
100 Fair Oaks Ln., Ste. 102
Frankfort, KY 40601-1109
Phone : (502) 564-5266

LOUISIANA
Allen Doescher
Assistant Commissioner
Tech. Srvcs. & Communications
Div. of Administration
P.O. Box 94095
Baton Rouge, LA 70804-9095
Phone : (504) 342-7105

MAINE
Carl Weston
Director
Div. of Telecommunications
397 Water St.
Gardiner, ME 04345
Phone : (207) 582-8884

MARYLAND**
John C. White
Assistant Secretary
Off. of Telecommunications Mgt.
Dept. of General Srvcs.
301 W. Preston St., Rm. 1400
Baltimore, MD 21201
Phone : (410) 225-4650

MASSACHUSETTS
Pat Fennesey
Director
Bur. of Network Srvcs.
Off. of Mgt. & Information Systems
1 Ashburton Pl., Rm. 1115
Boston, MA 02108
Phone : (617) 973-0815

MICHIGAN
Richard Boyd
Director
Telecommunications Div.
Dept. of Mgt. & Budget
P.O. Box 30026
Lansing, MI 48909
Phone : (517) 373-0785

MINNESOTA
Jack Ries
Telecommunication Manager
Div. of Business Technologies
Dept. of Administration
658 Cedar St.
St. Paul, MN 55155
Phone : (612) 296-6191

MISSISSIPPI
Gene Miller
Director
Bur. of Telecommunications
301 N. Lamar St., Ste. 508
Jackson, MS 39201
Phone : (601) 359-1395

MISSOURI
James Schutt
Director
Div. of Data Proc. & Telecomm.
Off. of Administration
Truman Bldg., Rm. 280
P.O. Box 809
Jefferson City, MO 65102
Phone : (314) 751-3338
Fax : (314) 751-3299
E-Mail: JSCHUTT@MAIL.MORE.NET

MONTANA
Anthony Herbert
Assistant Administrator
Information Srvcs.
Dept. of Administration
Mitchell Bldg., Rm. 221
Helena, MT 59620
Phone : (406) 444-2700

NEBRASKA
William Miller
Director
Div. of Communications
Dept. of Administrative Srvcs.
State Capitol Bldg., Rm. 1315
Lincoln, NE 68509
Phone : (402) 471-2761

NEVADA
Karen Kavanaugh
Director
Dept. of Information Srvcs.
505 E. King St.
Kinkead Bldg., Rm. 403
Carson City, NV 89710
Phone : (702) 687-4091
Fax : (702) 687-3846

NEW HAMPSHIRE
Dennis LeClerc
Supervisor
Off. of Information Tech. Mgt.
4 Hazen Dr.
Concord, NH 03301
Phone : (603) 271-3148

NEW JERSEY
Lou Jensen
Director
Off. of Telecomm. & Info. Sys.
200 Woolverton Ave., CN216
Trenton, NJ 08625
Phone : (609) 777-3858

NEW MEXICO
John Dawson
Deputy Director
Off. of Communications
Dept. of General Srvcs.
715 Alta Vista
Santa Fe, NM 87501
Phone : (505) 827-2183
Fax : (505) 827-0222

NEW YORK*
Director
Office of General Services
Corning Tower, 27th Fl.
Empire State Plz.
Albany, NY 12242
Phone : (518) 474-5575

Chief
Bur. of Intercity Srvcs.
Div. of Telecommunications
Corning Tower, 27th Fl.
Albany, NY 12242
Phone : (518) 473-3943

NORTH CAROLINA
Jim Broadwell
Director
State Telecommunications Srvcs.
3700 Old Wake Forest Rd.
Raleigh, NC 27609
Phone : (919) 981-5210
Fax : (919) 850-2827

NORTH DAKOTA
Marvin A. Fettig
Telecommunications Analyst
Information Srvcs. Div.
600 E. Boulevard Ave.
Bismarck, ND 58505
Phone : (701) 328-3190
Fax : (701) 328-3000

OHIO
Timothy D. Steiner
Telecommunications Administrator
Div. of Computer Srvcs.
Dept. of Administrative Srvcs.
30 E. Broad St., 39th Fl.
Columbus, OH 43266
Phone : (614) 466-0747
Fax : (614) 466-8159

OKLAHOMA
Ray Penrod
Chief/Communications Operations
Information Srvcs. Div.
Off. of State Finance
State Capitol Bldg., Rm. 4F
Oklahoma City, OK 73105
Phone : (405) 521-3309

OREGON
Tim Johnston
Manager
Telecommunications Srvcs.
Dept. of Admin. Srvcs.
1225 Ferry St., SE
Salem, OR 97310
Phone : (503) 373-7211
Fax : (503) 378-8333

PENNSYLVANIA
Joseph S. Connovitch
Director
Off. of Administration
Bur. of Automated Tech. Mgt.
2221 Forster St., Rm. G-13
Harrisburg, PA 17105
Phone : (717) 787-9106

RHODE ISLAND
Everett Travisono
Chief
Off. of General Srvcs.
Dept. of Administration
One Capitol Hill
Providence, RI 02908-5851
Phone : (401) 277-6200

SOUTH CAROLINA
Ted Lightle
Director
Div. of Info. Resource Mgt.
Budget & Control Board
1201 Main St., Ste. 930
Columbia, SC 29201
Phone : (803) 737-0077

SOUTH DAKOTA
Steve Linstrom
Director
Information Processing Srvcs.
Bur. of Administration
700 Governor Dr.
Pierre, SD 57501
Phone : (605) 773-3416

TENNESSEE
Norris Hoover
Director
Off. of Information Resources
Dept. of Finance & Admin.
598 James Robertson Pkwy., Fl. 3
Nashville, TN 37243-0560
Phone : (615) 741-7278

TEXAS
Donna Gessner
Planning & Design
Telecommunications Srvcs. Div.
General Services Comm.
P.O. Box 13047, Capitol Station
Austin, TX 78711-3047
Phone : (512) 463-3471

UTAH
Leon Miller
Director
Div. of Information Technical Srvcs.
Dept. of Administrative Srvcs.
6000 State Off. Bldg.
Salt Lake City, UT 84114
Phone : (801) 538-3476

VERMONT
Hale Irwin
Director
Telecommunications Div.
Dept. of General Srvcs.
149 State St.
Montpelier, VT 05620-3701
Phone : (802) 828-2204
Fax : (802) 828-2221

VIRGINIA
Charles C. Livingston
Director
Div. of Telecommunications
Dept. of Information Technology
110 S. 7th St., 3rd Fl.
Richmond, VA 23219
Phone : (804) 344-5500
Fax : (804) 344-5505

WASHINGTON
John M. Anderson
Assistant Dir. of Telecommun. Div.
Dept. of Information Srvcs.
512 - 12th Ave., SE
P.O. Box 42440
Olympia, WA 98504-2440
Phone : (360) 902-3333

WEST VIRGINIA
Matthew Brown
Manager, Div. of Telecommunications
Dept. of Administration
Bldg. 6, Rm. B163
1900 Kanawha Blvd., E.
Charleston, WV 25305
Phone : (304) 558-5980

WISCONSIN
Kathy Hertz
Director
Bur. of Info. & Telecomm.
Dept. of Admin.
101 E. Wilson, 8th Fl.
P.O. Box 7844
Madison, WI 53703
Phone : (608) 267-0627
Fax : (608) 266-2164

WYOMING
Larry Stolz
Administrator, Div. of Telecommunications
Dept. of Admin. & Information
Emerson Bldg., Rm. B-1
2001 Capitol Ave.
Cheyenne, WY 82002
Phone : (307) 777-6410

DISTRICT OF COLUMBIA
Gary Muren
Administrator
Info. Resources Mgt. Admin.
Dept. of Admin. Srvcs.
441 4th St., NW, Rm. 750
Washington, DC 20001
Phone : (202) 727-2277

AMERICAN SAMOA
Aleki Sene
Director
Off. of Communications
P.O. Box M
Pago Pago, AS 96799
Phone : (684) 633-1121
Fax : (684) 633-9032

GUAM
Juan B. Rosario
Director
Civil Defense
Emergency Services Off.
P.O. Box 2877
Agana, GU 96910
Phone : (671) 477-9841
Fax : (671) 477-3727

NORTHERN MARIANA ISLANDS
Joaquin I. Pangelinan
Special Assistant for Admin.
Off. of the Governor
P.O. Box 10007
Saipan, MP 96950
Phone : (670) 322-5091
Fax : (670) 322-5099

PUERTO RICO
Carlos Soler
Administrator
General Services Admin.
P.O. Box 7428
San Juan, PR 00916
Phone : (809) 721-7370
Fax : (809) 722-7965

U.S. VIRGIN ISLANDS
Kirk Grybowksi
Director
VITEMA
3-4 King St.
St. Croix, VI 00820
Phone : (809) 778-4916

TEXTBOOK APPROVAL

Recommends textbooks for public elementary and secondary schools.

ALABAMA
Barry Buford
State Textbook Coordinator
Dept. of Education
50 N. Ripley St.
Montgomery, AL 36130
Phone : (334) 242-9718
Fax : (334) 242-9708

ARIZONA
Lisa Graham
Supt. of Public Instruction
Dept. of Education
1535 W. Jefferson
Phoenix, AZ 85007
Phone : (602) 542-5393

ARKANSAS
Sue McKenzie
Coordinator
Instructional Materials
Dept. of Education
Education Bldg.
Little Rock, AR 72201
Phone : (501) 682-4593
Fax : (501) 682-4898

CALIFORNIA
Delaine Eastin
Acting Superintendent
Public Instruction
Dept. of Education
721 Capitol Mall, Rm. 524
Sacramento, CA 95814
Phone : (916) 657-2451

COLORADO
William Randall
Commissioner
Dept. of Education
201 E. Colfax
Denver, CO 80203-1715
Phone : (303) 866-6600

CONNECTICUT
Abigail Hughes
Bur. of Certification & Professional Dev.
Dept. of Education
165 Capitol Ave.
Hartford, CT 06106
Phone : (203) 566-8113

DELAWARE
Carol O. Mayhew
Team Leader
Curr., Inst. & Prof. Dev.
Dept. of Public Instruction
Townsend Bldg.
Dover, DE 19901
Phone : (302) 739-4647
Fax : (302) 739-4483

FLORIDA
Phillip Goldhagen
Administrator
Instructional TV, Radio & Ed. Products Dist.
Dept. of Education
325 W. Gaines St., Rm. 444
Tallahassee, FL 32399
Phone : (904) 488-1701

GEORGIA
Gerold Pace
Director
Dept. of Education
205 Butler St., SW, Rm. 2054
Atlanta, GA 30334
Phone : (404) 656-2418

HAWAII
Liberato Viduya
Assistant Superintendent
Off. of Instructional Srvcs.
Dept. of Education
1390 Miller St., Rm. 316
Honolulu, HI 96813
Phone : (808) 586-3446

IDAHO
Anne C. Fox
Superintendent of Public Instruction
Dept. of Education
650 W. State St.
Boise, ID 83720
Phone : (208) 334-3300

ILLINOIS
Bob Hardy
Textbooks & Scholarships
State Board of Education
100 N. First St., Rm. W-265
Springfield, IL 62777
Phone : (217) 782-9374

INDIANA
Suellen Reed
Superintendent
Dept. of Education
State House, Rm. 227
Indianapolis, IN 46204
Phone : (317) 232-6610

IOWA
Marcus Haack
Chief
Bureau of Instruction & Curriculum
Dept. Of Education
Grimes State Off. Bldg.
Des Moines, IA 50319
Phone : (515) 281-8141

KANSAS
Lee Droegemueller
Commissioner
State Board of Education
120 E. Tenth St.
Topeka, KS 66612-1182
Phone : (913) 296-3201
Fax : (913) 296-7933

KENTUCKY
Thomas C. Boysen
Commissioner
Dept. of Education
Ed. & Humanities Cabinet
Capital Plaza Tower
Frankfort, KY 40601
Phone : (502) 564-4770

LOUISIANA
Raymond Arveson
Superintendent
Dept. of Education
P.O. Box 94064
Baton Rouge, LA 70804
Phone : (504) 342-3602

MARYLAND**
Lorraine Costella
Assistant Superintendent
Div. of Instruction
Dept. of Education
200 W. Baltimore St.
Baltimore, MD 21201
Phone : (410) 666-2328

MICHIGAN
Ted Beck
Director
Training, Curr. & Approv. Prog.
Dept. of Education
P.O. Box 30008
Lansing, MI 48909
Phone : (517) 373-6325

MINNESOTA
Linda Powell
Commissioner
Dept. of Education
550 Cedar St., 8th Fl.
St. Paul, MN 55101
Phone : (612) 296-2358

MISSISSIPPI
Bob Tom Johnson
Executive Director
Div. of Textbooks
Dept. of Education
P.O. Box 771
Jackson, MS 39205
Phone : (601) 359-2791

MISSOURI
Fred Linhardt
Director
Vocational Planning & Evaluation
Dept. of Elem. & Secondary Education
Jefferson Bldg., 5th Fl.
P.O. Box 480
Jefferson City, MO 65102
Phone : (314) 751-8465
Fax : (314) 526-4261

NEBRASKA
Ann Masters
Curriculum Instr. Prog. Improvement
Dept. of Education
P.O. Box 94987
Lincoln, NE 68509-4987
Phone : (402) 471-4816

NEW MEXICO
Mary Jane Vinella
Director
Instructional Materials Div.
Dept. of Education
Education Bldg.
120 S. Fed. Pl., Rm. 206
Santa Fe, NM 87501
Phone : (505) 827-1801
Fax : (505) 827-1826

NEW YORK*
Commissioner
Dept. of Education
Education Bldg.
Albany, NY 12234
Phone : (518) 474-5844

NORTH CAROLINA
Travis Twiford
Chair
Textbook Comm.
Dept. of Public Instruction
301 N. Wilmington St.
Monroe, NC 27601-2825
Phone : (919) 715-1000

NORTH DAKOTA
Wayne G. Sanstead
Superintendent
Dept. of Public Instruction
State Capitol, 11th Fl.
600 E. Boulevard Ave.
Bismarck, ND 58505-0440
Phone : (701) 328-2260
Fax : (701) 328-2461

OKLAHOMA
Barbara Spriestersbach
Executive Director
Dept. of Education
2500 N. Lincoln Blvd.
Oklahoma City, OK 73105
Phone : (405) 521-3456

OREGON
Mary Jean Katz
Specialist
State Instructional Materials Srvcs.
Dept. of Education
255 Capitol St., NE
Salem, OR 97310
Phone : (503) 378-8004
Fax : (503) 373-7968

PENNSYLVANIA
Donald L. Clark
Director
Bur. of Curriculum Instruction
Dept. of Education
333 Market St., 8th Fl.
Harrisburg, PA 17126-0333
Phone : (717) 787-8913

RHODE ISLAND
Peter McWalters
Commissioner
Dept. of Education
22 Hayes St.
Providence, RI 02908
Phone : (401) 277-2031

SOUTH CAROLINA
Luther W. Seabrook
Senior Exec. Asst. for Curriculum
State Dept. of Education
1429 Senate St.
Columbia, SC 29201
Phone : (803) 734-8396

SOUTH DAKOTA
John Bonaiuto
Secretary
Dept. of Education & Cultural Affairs
700 Governors Dr.
Pierre, SD 57501-2291
Phone : (605) 773-3243

TENNESSEE
Larry Gregory
Director
Instructional Resources
Dept. of Education
130 Cordell Hull Bldg.
Nashville, TN 37247
Phone : (615) 741-3379

TEXAS
Ira Nell Turman
Director
Textbook Div.
Education Agency
1701 N. Congress Ave.
Austin, TX 78701
Phone : (512) 463-9601

UTAH
Bruce Griffin
Associate Supt. of Education
Curriculum & Instruction
Off. of Education
250 E. Fifth S.
Salt Lake City, UT 84111
Phone : (801) 538-7762

VERMONT
Douglas R. Walker
Director
Teaching & Learning Div.
Dept. of Education
120 State St.
Montpelier, VT 05620
Phone : (802) 828-3135
Fax : (802) 828-3140

VIRGINIA
William C. Bosher, Jr.
Superintendent
Dept. of Education
Monroe Bldg., 25th Fl.
101 N. 14th St.
Richmond, VA 23219
Phone : (804) 225-2023
Fax : (804) 371-2099

WASHINGTON
David Moberly
Assistant Superintendent
School & Agency Operations
Off. of Supt. of Public Instruction
P.O. Box 47200
Olympia, WA 98504-7200
Phone : (360) 753-6742

WEST VIRGINIA
Ed Moran
Director
Off. of Instructional Srvcs.
Dept. of Education
Bldg. 6, Rm. 358
Charleston, WV 25305-0330
Phone : (304) 558-2702

WISCONSIN
Arnold Chandler
Assistant Superintendent
Div. for Instructional Srvcs.
Dept. of Public Instruction
125 S. Webster
P.O. Box 7841
Madison, WI 53703
Phone : (608) 266-3361
Fax : (608) 267-1052

AMERICAN SAMOA
Tautalatasi Tuato'o
Director
Dept. of Education
American Samoan Government
Pago Pago, AS 96799
Phone : (684) 633-5237
Fax : (684) 633-4240

NORTHERN MARIANA ISLANDS
Rita A. Sablan
Deputy Commissioner of Instruction
Public School System
P.O. Box 1370 CK
Saipan, MP 96950
Phone : (670) 322-6453
Fax : (670) 322-4056

PUERTO RICO
Franciso Rodriquez
Director
Textbook Approval
Dept. of Education
P.O. Box 190759
San Juan, PR 00919-0759
Phone : (809) 754-8610
Fax : (809) 753-7926

U.S. VIRGIN ISLANDS
Liston Davis
Supt. of Schools STT/STJ
Dept. of Education
44-46 Kongens Gade
St. Thomas, VI 00802
Phone : (809) 774-3725
Fax : (809) 774-4917

TOURISM

Coordinates promotional and advertising program for the tourism industry in the state.

ALABAMA
Aubrey Miller
Director
Dept. of Tourism & Travel
401 Adams Ave., Ste. 126
Montgomery, AL 36104
Phone : (334) 242-4169
Fax : (334) 242-4554

ALASKA
Mary Pignalberi
Director
Div. of Tourism
Dept. of Commerce & Econ. Dev.
P.O. Box 110801
Juneau, AK 99811-0801
Phone : (907) 465-2010
Fax : (907) 465-2287

ARIZONA
Greg W. Gilstrap
Director
Off. of Tourism
1100 W. Washington
Phoenix, AZ 85007
Phone : (602) 542-8687

ARKANSAS
Joe Rice
Director
Tourism Div.
Dept. of Parks & Tourism
One Capitol Mall
Little Rock, AR 72201
Phone : (501) 682-1088
Fax : (501) 682-1364

CALIFORNIA
John Poimiroo
Director
Off. of Tourism
801 K St., Ste. 1600
Sacramento, CA 95814
Phone : (916) 322-2881

COLORADO
Rich Meredith
Director
Travel & Tourism Authority
5500 Greenwood Plaza Blvd., #200
Englewood, CO 80111
Phone : (303) 770-8087
Fax : (303) 770-8410

CONNECTICUT
Arthur H. Diedrick
Exofficio Chairman
Tourism Div.
Dept. of Economic Development
865 Brook St.
Rocky Hill, CT 06067
Phone : (203) 258-4286

DELAWARE
Gigi Windley
Director
Delaware Economic Development Off.
P.O. Box 1401
Dover, DE 19901
Phone : (302) 736-4271
Fax : (302) 739-5749

FLORIDA
Richard B. Kenney
Director
Div. of Tourism
Dept. of Commerce
Collins Bldg., Rm. 511
107 W. Gaines St.
Tallahassee, FL 32399-2000
Phone : (904) 488-5607
Fax : (904) 922-9150

GEORGIA
Hanna M. Ledford
Deputy Commissioner
Tourist Div.
Industry, Trade & Tourism
285 Peachtree Ctr. Ave., # 1000
Atlanta, GA 30303
Phone : (404) 656-3556

HAWAII
Seiji Naya
Director
Dept. of Business, Economic Development & Tourism
220 S. King St., # 1100
Honolulu, HI 96813
Phone : (808) 586-2359
Fax : (808) 586-2377

IDAHO
Carl G. Wilgus
Administrator
Tourism Dev.
Dept. of Commerce
700 W. State St.
Boise, ID 83720
Phone : (208) 334-2470

ILLINOIS
Dennis R. Whetstone
Director
Dept. of Commerce & Community Affairs
620 E. Adams St., 3rd Fl.
Springfield, IL 62701
Phone : (217) 782-3233
Fax : (217) 524-0864

INDIANA
John Goss
Director
Tourism Development
Dept. of Commerce
1 N. Capitol
Indianapolis, IN 46204
Phone : (317) 232-8870

IOWA
David K. Reynolds
Administrator
Div. of Tourism & Visitors
Dept. of Economic Development
200 E. Grand
Des Moines, IA 50309
Phone : (515) 242-4705

KANSAS
Norine Kruse
Division Director
Travel, Tourism & Film Services
Dept. of Commerce & Housing
700 SW Harrison Ave., Ste. 1300
Topeka, KS 66612-3712
Phone : (913) 296-2009
Fax : (913) 296-5055

KENTUCKY
Greg Ginter
Secretary
Tourism Cabinet
Capital Plaza Tower, 24th Fl.
Frankfort, KY 40601
Phone : (502) 564-4270

LOUISIANA
Alfred F. Trappey II
Assistant Secretary
Off. of Tourism
Dept. of Culture, Recreation & Tourism
P.O. Box 94291
Baton Rouge, LA 70804
Phone : (504) 342-8125

MAINE
Hilary Sinclair
Director
Div. of Tourism
Dept. of Econ. & Commun. Dev.
State House Station # 59
Augusta, ME 04333
Phone : (207) 287-5711

MARYLAND**
George Williams
Director
Off. of Tourism & Promotion
Dept. of Econ. & Emplymt. Dev.
217 E. Redwood St.
Baltimore, MD 21202
Phone : (410) 333-6611

MASSACHUSETTS
Abbie Goodman
Director
Travel & Tourism
Executive Off. of Economic Affairs
100 Cambridge St., 13th Fl.
Boston, MA 02202
Phone: (617) 727-3201

MICHIGAN
Thomas Altemus
Director
Travel Bur.
Dept. of Commerce
333 S. Capitol Ave.
Lansing, MI 48909
Phone: (517) 335-1879

MINNESOTA
Henry R. Todd
Director
Off. of Tourism
100 Metro Sq. Bldg.
121 7th Pl., E.
St. Paul, MN 55101
Phone: (612) 296-2755

MISSISSIPPI
George Smith
Director
Div. of Tourism
Dept. of Econ. & Commun. Dev.
P.O. Box 849
Jackson, MS 39205
Phone: (601) 359-3449

MISSOURI
Marjorie Beenders
Director
Division of Tourism
Dept. of Economic Development
Truman Bldg., Rm. 290
P.O. Box 1055
Jefferson City, MO 65102
Phone: (314) 526-5900
Fax: (314) 751-5160

MONTANA
Matthew T. Cohn
Chief Administrator
Promotion Bureau
Dept. of Commerce
1424 Ninth Ave.
Helena, MT 59620
Phone: (406) 444-2654

NEBRASKA
Peggy Briggs
Director
Div. of Travel & Tourism
Dept. of Economic Development
P.O. Box 94666
Lincoln, NE 68509
Phone: (402) 471-3794

NEVADA
Thomas G. Tait
Executive Director
Comm. on Tourism
5151 S. Carson St.
Carson City, NV 89710
Phone: (702) 687-4322

NEW HAMPSHIRE
Chris Jennings
Director
Vacation Travel Promotion Off.
Dept. of Resources & Econ. Dev.
172 Pembroke Rd.
Concord, NH 03301
Phone: (603) 271-2665

NEW JERSEY
Linda Conlin
Director
Div. of Travel & Tourism
Dept. of Commerce & Econ. Dev.
20 W. State St., CN826
Trenton, NJ 08625
Phone: (609) 292-2470

NEW MEXICO
John Garcia
Secretary
Tourism Div.
1100 St. Francis Dr.
Santa Fe, NM 87503
Phone: (505) 827-0291
Fax: (505) 827-7402

NEW YORK*
Commissioner
Dept. of Commerce
1 Commerce Plz.
Albany, NY 12245
Phone: (518) 474-4100

NORTH CAROLINA
Dick Trammell
Director
Travel Development Div.
Dept. of Commerce
430 N. Salisbury St.
Raleigh, NC 27603
Phone: (919) 733-4171
Fax: (919) 733-8582

NORTH DAKOTA
Kevin Cramer
Director of Tourism
Dept. of Parks & Recreation
Liberty Memorial Bldg.
604 E. Boulevard Ave.
Bismarck, ND 58505-0662
Phone: (701) 328-2525
Fax: (701) 328-4878

OHIO
George Zimmerman
Deputy Director
Off. of Travel & Tourism
Dept. of Development
30 E. Broad St., 25th Fl.
Columbus, OH 43266
Phone: (614) 466-8844
Fax: (614) 466-6744

OKLAHOMA
David Davies
Director
Dept. of Tourism & Recreation
500 Will Rogers Bldg.
Oklahoma City, OK 73105
Phone: (405) 521-2413

OREGON
Joe D'Alessandro
Manager
Tourism Div.
Dept. of Economic Development
775 Summer St.
Salem, OR 97310
Phone: (503) 986-0000
Fax: (503) 986-0001

PENNSYLVANIA
Thomas B. Hagen
Secretary
Dept. of Commerce
433 Forum Bldg.
Harrisburg, PA 17120
Phone: (717) 783-3003

RHODE ISLAND
David C. DePetrillo
Director of Tourism
Dept. of Economic Development
7 Jackson Walkway
Providence, RI 02903
Phone: (401) 277-2601

SOUTH CAROLINA
Marion M. Edmonds
Director
Div. of Tourism
Dept. of Parks, Recreation & Tourism
1205 Pendleton St.
Columbia, SC 29201
Phone: (803) 734-0135

SOUTH DAKOTA
Patty VanGerpen
Secretary
Dept. of Tourism
Capitol Lake Plz.
Pierre, SD 57501
Phone: (605) 773-3301

TENNESSEE
John Wade
Commissioner
Dept. of Tourist Development
320 Sixth Ave., N.
Nashville, TN 37243
Phone: (615) 741-9001
Fax: (615) 532-0477

TEXAS
Dianne Galaviz
Director of Tourism
Dept. of Commerce
P.O. Box 12728
Austin, TX 78711
Phone: (512) 936-0197

UTAH
Dean Reeder
Director
Div. of Travel Development
Dept. of Community & Economic Development
Council Hall/Capitol Hill
Salt Lake City, UT 84114
Phone: (801) 538-1370

VERMONT
Barbara R. Maynes
Commissioner
Travel Div.
Agcy. of Dev. &
Community Aff.
134 State St.
Montpelier, VT 05602
Phone : (802) 828-3236
Fax : (802) 828-3233

VIRGINIA
Wayne L. Sterling
Director
Dept. of Economic
Development
West Tower-19th Fl.
901 E. Byrd St.
Richmond, VA 23219
Phone : (804) 371-8106
Fax : (804) 371-8112

WASHINGTON
John Savich
Director
Tourism Development
Dept. of Trade &
Economic Development
P.O. Box 42500
Olympia, WA 98504-2500
Phone : (360) 753-5795

WEST VIRGINIA
Jim Lawerence
Commissioner
Div. of Tourism & Parks
Bldg. 6, Rm. 451
1900 Kanawha Blvd., E.
Charleston, WV 25305-0312
Phone : (304) 558-2764

WISCONSIN
Richard Speros
Administrator
Div. of Tourism
Development
Dept. of Development
123 W Washington
P.O. Box 7970
Madison, WI 53703
Phone : (608) 266-2345
Fax : (608) 266-3403

WYOMING
Gene Bryan
Director
Tourism Div.
Dept. of Commerce
I-25 at College Dr.
Cheyenne, WY 82002
Phone : (307) 777-7777

DISTRICT OF COLUMBIA
George Demarest
General Manager
Washington Convention
Ctr.
900 Ninth St., NW
Washington, DC 20004
Phone : (202) 789-1600

Ann Pina
Acting Director
Off. Of Tourism &
Promotions
1212 New York Ave., NW,
Ste. 200
Washington, DC 20005
Phone : (202) 727-4511

Daniel Mobley
Executive Director
DC Visitors & Convention
Association
1212 New York Ave., NW,
Ste. 600
Washington, DC 20005
Phone : (202) 789-7000

Neville Waters
Director
Cmte. to Promote
Washington
1212 New York Ave.,
NW,# 200
Washington, DC 20005
Phone : (202) 724-4091

AMERICAN SAMOA
Sinira L. Fuimaouo
Director
Off. of Tourism
Pago Pago, AS 96799
Phone : (684) 633-1092
Fax : (684) 633-1094

GUAM
James E. Nelson
General Manager
Guam Visitors Bureau
401 Pace San Vitores
Tumon, GU 96911
Phone : (671) 646-5278
Fax : (671) 646-8861

NORTHERN MARIANA ISLANDS
Anicia A. Tomoleane
Managing Director
Visitors Bureau
P.O. Box 861
Saipan, MP 96950
Phone : (670) 234-8325
Fax : (670) 234-3596

PUERTO RICO
Luis Fortuno
Director
Tourism Co.
P.O. Box 4435
San Juan, PR 00903
Phone : (809) 721-2400
Fax : (809) 722-6238

U.S. VIRGIN ISLANDS
David Edgell
Acting Director of Tourism
Dept. of Economic
Development &
Agriculture
P.O. Box 6400
St. Thomas, VI 00802
Phone : (809) 774-8784
Fax : (809) 774-4390

TRAINING AND DEVELOPMENT

Responsible for the training and development of state employees.

ALABAMA
Sharleen Smith
Manager of Training
Training Div.
State Personnel
64 N. Union
Montgomery, AL 36130
Phone : (334) 242-3389
Fax : (334) 240-3171

ALASKA
Phyllis Schmidt
Chief, EEO Section
Div. of Personnel
Dept. of Administration
P.O. Box 240488
Anchorage, AK 99524-0488
Phone : (907) 562-5294
Fax : (907) 562-0470

ARIZONA
Frank Liu
Manager
Employment & Training
Dept. of Admininstration
1831 Jefferson
Phoenix, AZ 85007
Phone : (602) 542-5642

ARKANSAS
Carol H. Philpott
Director
Inter-Agency Training Program
Dept. of Finance & Admin.
P.O. Box 3278
Little Rock, AR 72203
Phone : (501) 682-2252
Fax : (501) 682-5094

CALIFORNIA
Patricia Pavone
Division Chief
Training & Development Div.
Dept. of Personnel Admin.
1515 S St.
Sacramento, CA 95814
Phone : (916) 324-9371

COLORADO
Jerry Davies
Director
Technical & Consulting Srvcs.
Dept. of Personnel
1313 Sherman St., Rm. 115
Denver, CO 80203
Phone : (303) 866-2438
Fax : (303) 866-2021

CONNECTICUT
Ernest Magler
Director
Personnel Dev. & Training
Dept. of Administrative Srvcs.
1380 Asylum Ave.
Hartford, CT 06105
Phone : (203) 566-8115

DELAWARE
Joe Hickey
Manager
State Personnel Office
Employee Development
820 N. French St., 6th Fl.
Wilmington, DE 19801
Phone : (302) 577-3950
Fax : (302) 577-3996

FLORIDA
Patsy M. Barber
Div. of Personnel Mgt. Srvcs.
Dept. of Management Services
435 Carlton Bldg.
Tallahassee, FL 32399
Phone : (904) 922-5449

GEORGIA
John Thompson
Director
Training & Organizational Dev.
Merit System of Personnel Admin.
900 South Tower, 1 CNN Ctr.
Atlanta, GA 30303
Phone : (404) 656-2734

HAWAII
Vernon Von
Chief
Training & Safety Div.
Dept. of Personnel Srvcs.
830 Punchbowl St., Rm. 412
Honolulu, HI 96816
Phone : (808) 587-1057

IDAHO
Connie Pratt
Training Officer
Personnel Comm.
700 W. State St.
Boise, ID 83720
Phone : (208) 334-3346

ILLINOIS
Julie Moscardelli
Manager
Bur. of Personnel
Dept. of Central Mgt. Srvcs.
503 Stratton Off. Bldg.
Springfield, IL 62706
Phone : (217) 782-6191
Fax : (217) 524-0836

INDIANA
John Galloway
Training Director
Training Div.
Dept. of Personnel
402 W. Washington, Rm. W-161
Indianapolis, IN 46204
Phone : (317) 232-3007

IOWA
Sallie Nostwich
Administrative Assistant
Personnel Development Seminars
Dept. of Personnel
Grimes State Off. Bldg.
Des Moines, IA 50319
Phone : (515) 281-6382

KANSAS
Sandra Lassley
Director
Training
Dept. of Human Resources
512 SW 6th Ave.
Topeka, KS 66603-3174
Phone : (913) 296-6673
Fax : (913) 296-8177

KENTUCKY
John Brock
Executive Director
Governmental Services Center
Kentucky State University
Academic Srvcs. Bldg., 4th Fl.
Frankfort, KY 40601
Phone : (502) 564-8170

LOUISIANA
Sam Breen
Administrator
Comprehensive Public Training Program
Div. of Administration
P.O. Box 94095
Baton Rouge, LA 70804
Phone : (504) 342-7000

MAINE
Elaine Trubee
Director
State Training & Development Program
Dept. of Admin. & Financial Srvcs.
State House Station # 4
Augusta, ME 04333
Phone : (207) 287-4400

MARYLAND**
Jeanne M. Zarnoch
Director
Employee Srvcs. & Work Force Quality
Dept. of Personnel
301 W. Preston St., Rm. 608
Baltimore, MD 21201
Phone : (410) 225-4943

MASSACHUSETTS
Mary O'Neil
Director
Bur. of Human Resource Development
Dept. of Personnel Admin.
1 Ashburton Pl., Rm. 519
Boston, MA 02108
Phone : (617) 727-7801

MICHIGAN
Marvin S. Ray
Director
Personnel Development Div.
Dept. of Civil Service
400 S. Pine
Lansing, MI 48909
Phone : (517) 373-2853

MINNESOTA
Linda See
Manager
Training & Development Div.
Dept. of Employee Relations
658 Cedar St.
St. Paul, MN 55155
Phone : (612) 296-2380

MISSISSIPPI
Marianne Gaudin
Division Director
Training Div.
State Personnel Bd.
301 N. Lamar, Ste. 100
Jackson, MS 39201
Phone : (601) 359-2781

MISSOURI
Terry McAdams
Sect. Mgr. for Empl. Dev.
Div. of Personnel
Off. of Administration
Truman Bldg., Rm. 430
P.O. Box 388
Jefferson City, MO 65102
Phone : (314) 751-4514
Fax : (314) 751-8641

MONTANA
John Moore
Director
Professional Development Ctr.
Mitchell Bldg., Ste. 130
Helena, MT 59620
Phone : (406) 444-3871

NEBRASKA
William Wood
Acting Director
Div. of Personnel
Dept. of Administration Srvcs.
P.O. Box 94664
Lincoln, NE 68509-4905
Phone : (402) 471-2075
Fax : (402) 471-3754

NEVADA
John Hastings
Training Manager
Personnel Division
Western Nevada Commun. College
Stewart Facility, Rm. 216
Carson City, NV 89701
Phone : (702) 687-4120

NEW HAMPSHIRE
Peter Gamache
Training Director
Div. of Personnel
State House Annex
25 Capitol St.
Concord, NH 03301
Phone : (603) 271-2833

NEW JERSEY
Edward J. Mount
Asst. Commissioner
Div. of Administrative Srvcs.
Dept. of Labor
John Fitch Plz., CN385
Trenton, NJ 08525
Phone : (609) 292-2000

NEW MEXICO
Tommy Thomas
Director
Human Resources Development Div.
State Personnel Office
2041 S. Pacheco St., Ste. 1
Santa Fe, NM 87501
Phone : (505) 827-6299
Fax : (505) 827-6263

NEW YORK*
Director
Off. of Employee Relations
Agency Bldg. 2, 12th Fl.
Empire State Plz.
Albany, NY 12223-0001
Phone : (518) 474-6988

President
Dept. of Civil Services
State Campus, Bldg. 1
Albany, NY 12239
Phone : (518) 457-3701

NORTH CAROLINA
James A. Savage
Director
Personnel Development Ctr.
101 W. Peace St.
Raleigh, NC 27603
Phone : (919) 733-8343
Fax : (919) 733-0653

NORTH DAKOTA
Linda Jensen
Director of Training
Central Personnel Div.
Capitol Bldg., 14th Fl.
Bismarck, ND 58505-0120
Phone : (701) 328-3290
Fax : (701) 328-3000

OHIO
Caryl Rice
Administrator
Training & Education Programs
Dept. of Administrative Srvcs.
30 E. Broad St., 28th Fl.
Columbus, OH 43215
Phone : (614) 644-6332
Fax : (614) 466-6061

OKLAHOMA
Larry Fisher
Assistant Administrator
Human Resource Dev. Div.
2101 N. Lincoln Blvd.
Oklahoma City, OK 73105
Phone : (405) 521-3083

OREGON
Vicki Nakashima
Manager
Training Recruitment & Career Srvcs.
155 Cottage St., NE
Salem, OR 97310
Phone : (503) 378-3844
Fax : (503) 373-7684

PENNSYLVANIA
Bette H. Williams
Manager
Employee Training & Dev.
Training & Development Div.
512 Finance Bldg.
Harrisburg, PA 17120
Phone : (717) 787-3679

RHODE ISLAND
Robert G. Tetreault
Associate Director
Administration & Personnel
Off. of Training
One Capitol Hill
Providence, RI 02908
Phone : (401) 277-2155

SOUTH CAROLINA
Karen Kuehner
Manager
Staff Development & Training
Div. of Human Resource Mgt.
1205 Main St., Ste. 1000
Columbia, SC 29201
Phone : (803) 737-0930

SOUTH DAKOTA
Ellen Zeller
Director
Classification & Training
Bur. of Personnel
Capitol Bldg.
Pierre, SD 57501
Phone : (605) 773-3148

TENNESSEE
Ron Gibson
Director
Training Div.
Dept. of Personnel
James K. Polk Bldg., 2nd Fl.
Nashville, TN 37243
Phone : (615) 741-5546

TEXAS
Barry Bales
Director
State Management Development Center
P.O. Box 12428
Austin, TX 78711
Phone : (512) 463-1901

UTAH
James N. West
Director
Employment, Staff & Training
Dept. of Human Resource Mgt.
2120 State Off. Bldg.
Salt Lake City, UT 84114
Phone : (801) 538-3075

VERMONT
Nancy Simoes
Director
State Human Resources
Dept. of Personnel
146 State St.
P.O. Drawer 20
Montpelier, VT 05620
Phone : (802) 828-3541
Fax : (802) 828-3409

VIRGINIA
Charles E. James Sr.
Director
Dept. of Personnel & Training
101 N. 14th St.
Richmond, VA 23219
Phone : (804) 225-2237
Fax : (804) 371-7401

WASHINGTON
Scott Turner
Assistant Director
Div. of Human Resources Development
Dept. of Personnel
P.O. Box 47500
Olympia, WA 98504-7500
Phone : (360) 586-1342

WEST VIRGINIA
Willard Max Farley
Assistant Director of Personnel
Civil Service System
1900 Washington St., W.
Charleston, WV 25305
Phone : (304) 558-3950

WISCONSIN
Arely Gonnering
Administrator
Div. of Affirmative Action
Dept. of Employment Relations
137 E. Wilson
Madison, WI 53702
Phone : (608) 266-5709
Fax : (608) 267-1020

WYOMING
Jody Warder
Div. Director
Training & Development
Dept. of Admin. & Information
2001 Capitol Ave.
Cheyenne, WY 82002
Phone : (307) 777-6723

AMERICAN SAMOA
Sapini Siatu'u
Director
Dept. of Human Resources
Pago Pago, AS 96799
Phone : (684) 633-4485
Fax : (684) 633-1139

GUAM
John S. Salas
Director
Dept. of Administration
P.O. Box 884
Agana, GU 96910
Phone : (671) 475-1101
Fax : (671) 477-6788

NORTHERN MARIANA ISLANDS
Norbert S. Sablan
Personnel Officer
Civil Service Comm.
Personnel Management Off.
Off. of the Governor
Saipan, MP 96950
Phone : (670) 234-6958

PUERTO RICO
Aura Gonzalez
Director
Central Off. for Personnel Admin.
P.O. Box 8476
San Juan, PR 00910-8476
Phone : (809) 721-4300
Fax : (809) 722-3390

U.S. VIRGIN ISLANDS
Yvonne Bowsky
Div. of Personnel
GERS Complex
Charlotte Amalie
St. Thomas, VI 00802
Phone : (809) 774-8588

TRANSPORTATION

Umbrella agency of transportation responsible for planning, designing, constructing and maintaining public transportation services and facilities throughout the state.

ALABAMA
Jimmy Butts
Director
Highway Dept.
1409 Coliseum Blvd.
Montgomery, AL 36130
Phone : (334) 242-6311
Fax : (334) 262-8041

ALASKA
Joseph L. Perkins
Commissioner
Dept. of Transportation & Public Facilities
3132 Channel Dr.
Juneau, AK 99801-7898
Phone : (907) 465-3900
Fax : (907) 586-8365

ARIZONA
Larry S. Bonine
Director
Dept. of Transportation
206 S. 17th Ave., Rm. 100A
Phoenix, AZ 85007
Phone : (602) 255-7011

ARKANSAS
Dan Flowers
Director
Dept. of Highways & Transportation
P.O. Box 2261
Little Rock, AR 72203
Phone : (501) 569-2211
Fax : (501) 569-2400

CALIFORNIA
James W. Van Loben Sels
Director
Dept. of Transportation
1120 N St., Ste. 1100
Sacramento, CA 95814
Phone : (916) 654-5267

COLORADO
Guillermo Vidal
Executive Director
Dept. of Transportation
4201 E. Arkansas Ave., Rm. 262
Denver, CO 80222
Phone : (303) 757-9011
Fax : (303) 757-9656

CONNECTICUT
J. William Burns
Commissioner
Dept. of Transportation
2800 Berlin Tpke.
Newington, CT 06111
Phone : (203) 594-3000

DELAWARE
Anne P. Canby
Secretary
Dept. of Transportation
Transportation Admin. Bldg.
P.O. Box 778
Dover, DE 19903
Phone : (302) 739-4303
Fax : (302) 739-4329

FLORIDA
Frank Carlile
Assistant Secretary
Transportation Policy
Dept. of Transportation
605 Suwannee St.
Tallahassee, FL 32399-0450
Phone : (904) 488-8261

GEORGIA
Wayne Shackelford
Commissioner
Dept. of Transportation
2 Capitol Sq.
Atlanta, GA 30334
Phone : (404) 656-5206

HAWAII
Kazu Hayashida
Director
Dept. of Transportation
869 Punchbowl St.
Honolulu, HI 96813
Phone : (808) 587-2150
Fax : (808) 587-2167

IDAHO
Dwight Bower
Director
Dept. of Transportation
P.O. Box 7129
Boise, ID 83707
Phone : (208) 334-8800

ILLINOIS
Kirk Brown
Secretary
Dept. of Transportation
2300 S. Dirksen Pkwy., Rm. 025
Springfield, IL 62764
Phone : (217) 782-3053
Fax : (217) 782-6121

INDIANA
Stanley C. Smith
Commissioner
Dept. of Transportation
IGC-North, Rm. N755
Indianapolis, IN 46204
Phone : (317) 232-5525

IOWA
Darrel Rensink
Director
Dept. of Transportation
800 Lincoln Way
Ames, IA 50010
Phone : (515) 239-1111
Fax : (515) 239-1639

KANSAS
Dean Carlson
Secretary
Dept. of Transportation
Docking State Off. Bldg., 7th Fl.
Topeka, KS 66612-1568
Phone : (913) 296-3566
Fax : (913) 296-1095

KENTUCKY
Don C. Kelly
Secretary
Transportation Cabinet
State Off. Bldg., 10th Fl.
Frankfort, KY 40601
Phone : (502) 564-4890

LOUISIANA
Jude W.P. Patin
Secretary
Public Transportation Section
Dept. of Transportation & Development
P.O. Box 94245
Baton Rouge, LA 70804
Phone : (504) 379-1100

MAINE
John Melrose
Commissioner
Dept. of Transportation
State House Station # 16
Augusta, ME 04333
Phone : (207) 287-2551

MARYLAND
David L. Winstead
Secretary
Dept. of Transportation
P.O. Box 8755
Baltimore, MD 21240
Phone : (410) 859-7600

MASSACHUSETTS
James Kerasiotes
Secretary
Executive Off. of Transportation & Construction
10 Park Plz., Rm. 3170
Boston, MA 02116
Phone : (617) 973-7849

MICHIGAN
Patrick Nowak
Director
Dept. of Transportation
P.O. Box 30050
Lansing, MI 48909
Phone : (517) 373-2114
Fax : (517) 373-6457

MINNESOTA
James Denn
Commissioner
Dept. of Transportation
Transportation Bldg., 4th Fl.
John Ireland Blvd.
St. Paul, MN 55155
Phone : (612) 297-2930

MISSISSIPPI
Chester Smith
Director
Div. of Energy
Dept. of Economic & Community Dev.
510 George St., Ste. 301
Jackson, MS 39202
Phone : (601) 359-3449

MISSOURI
Joe Mickes
Chief Engineer
Dept. of Highways & Transportation
Highway Bldg.
P.O. Box 270
Jefferson City, MO 65102
Phone : (314) 751-4622
Fax : (314) 526-5419

MONTANA
Patricia Saindon
Administrator
Transportation Planning Div.
Dept. of Transportation
2701 Prospect Ave.
Helena, MT 59620
Phone : (406) 444-3423

NEBRASKA
Allan L. Abbott
Director
Dept. of Roads
P.O. Box 94759
Lincoln, NE 68509-4759
Phone : (402) 479-4615

NEVADA
Tom Stephens
Director
Dept. of Transportation
1263 S. Stewart St.
Carson City, NV 89712
Phone : (702) 687-5440

NEW HAMPSHIRE
Charles P. O'Leary Jr.
Commissioner
Dept. of Transportation
John O. Moeton Bldg.
P.O. Box 483
Concord, NH 03302
Phone : (603) 271-3734

NEW JERSEY
Frank J. Wilson
Commissioner
Dept. of Transportation
1035 Parkway Ave., CN601
Trenton, NJ 08625
Phone : (609) 530-3535

NEW MEXICO
Pete Rahn
Secretary
Dept. of Highways & Transportation
1120 Cerrillos Rd.
Santa Fe, NM 87504-1149
Phone : (505) 827-5110
Fax : (505) 827-3214

NEW YORK*
Commissioner
Dept. of Transportation
Campus, Bldg. 5
Albany, NY 12232
Phone : (518) 457-4422

NORTH CAROLINA
Sam Hunt
Secretary
Dept. of Transportation
One S. Wilmington St.
Raleigh, NC 27601-1494
Phone : (919) 733-2520
Fax : (919) 733-9150

NORTH DAKOTA
Marshall W. Moore
Director
Dept. of Transportation
608 E. Boulevard Ave.
Bismarck, ND 58505-0700
Phone : (701) 328-2581
Fax : (701) 328-4545

OHIO
Jerry Wray
Director
Dept. of Transportation
25 S. Front St., 7th Fl.
Columbus, OH 43215
Phone : (614) 466-2335
Fax : (614) 644-0587

OKLAHOMA
Neal McCaleb
Secretary
Dept. of Transportation
3500 Martin Luther King Blvd.
Oklahoma City, OK 73111
Phone : (405) 425-3601

OREGON
Don Forbes
Director
Dept. of Transportation
135 Transportation Bldg.
Salem, OR 97310
Phone : (503) 986-3200
Fax : (503) 986-3446

PENNSYLVANIA
Bradley Mallory
Secretary
Dept. of Transportation
Transportation & Safety Bldg., Rm. 1200
Harrisburg, PA 17120
Phone : (717) 787-5574

RHODE ISLAND
William Bundy
Director
Dept. of Transportation
210 State Off. Bldg.
Providence, RI 02903
Phone : (401) 277-2481

SOUTH CAROLINA
Buck Limehouse
Director
Dept. of Transportation
955 Park St.
P.O. Box 191
Columbia, SC 29202
Phone : (803) 737-1300

SOUTH DAKOTA
Richard Howard
Secretary
Dept. of Transportation
700 E. Broadway
Pierre, SD 57501
Phone : (605) 773-3265

TENNESSEE
Bruce Saltsman
Commissioner
Dept. of Transportation
700 James K. Polk Bldg.
Nashville, TN 37243
Phone : (615) 741-2848
Fax : (615) 741-2508

TEXAS
William G. Burnett
Executive Director
Dept. of Transportation
11th & Brazos St.
Austin, TX 78701
Phone : (512) 465-7346

UTAH
Craig Zwick
Director
Dept. of Transportation
4501 S. 2700 W.
Salt Lake City, UT 84119
Phone : (801) 965-4113

VERMONT
Patrick Garahan
Secretary
Agency of Transportation
133 State St.
Montpelier, VT 05602
Phone : (802) 828-2657
Fax : (802) 828-3522

VIRGINIA
David R. Gehr
Commissioner
Dept. of Transportation
1401 E. Broad St.
Richmond, VA 23219
Phone : (804) 786-2701
Fax : (804) 786-2940

WASHINGTON
Sid Morrison
Secretary
Dept. of Transportation
P.O. Box 47400
Olympia, WA 98504-7400
Phone : (360) 705-7000

WEST VIRGINIA
Charles Miller
Secretary
Dept. of Transportation
Bldg. 5, Rm. A109
1900 Kanawha Blvd., E.
Charleston, WV 25302
Phone : (304) 558-0444

WISCONSIN
Charles Thompson
Secretary
Dept. of Transportation
4802 Sheboygan Ave.
P.O. Box 7910
Madison, WI 53707
Phone : (608) 266-1113
Fax : (608) 266-9912

WYOMING
Don Diller
Director
Dept. of Transportation
5300 Bishop Blvd.
Cheyenne, WY 82002
Phone : (307) 777-4484

DISTRICT OF COLUMBIA**
Betty Hager Francis
Director
Dept. of Public Works
2000 14th St., NW
Washington, DC 20009
Phone : (202) 939-8000

AMERICAN SAMOA
Sila Poasa
Director
Dept. of Port Admin.
Pago Pago, AS 96799
Phone : (684) 633-4251
Fax : (684) 633-5281

GUAM
Gil A. Shinohara
Director
Dept. of Public Works
P.O. Box 2950
Agana, GU 96910
Phone : (671) 646-3101
Fax : (671) 649-6178

NORTHERN MARIANA ISLANDS
Edward M. Deleon Guerrero
Secretary
Dept. of Public Works
Lower Base
P.O. Box 2950
Saipan, MP 96950
Phone : (670) 322-9482
Fax : (670) 322-3547

U.S. VIRGIN ISLANDS
Ann Abramson
Acting Commissioner
Dept. of Public Works
No. 8 Sub Base
St. Thomas, VI 00802
Phone : (809) 776-4844
Fax : (809) 774-5869

TREASURER

The custodian of all state funds and securities belonging to or held in trust by the state.

ALABAMA
Lucy Baxley
State Treasurer
State Capitol, Room S-106
600 Dexter Ave.
Montgomery, AL 36130
Phone : (334) 242-7500
Fax : (334) 242-7592

ALASKA
William M. Howe
Deputy Commissioner
Alaska Dept. of Revenue
PO Box 110405
Juneau, AK 99811
Phone : (907) 465-4880
Fax : (907) 465-2389

ARIZONA
Tony West
State Treasurer
106 State Capitol
1700 West Washington
Phoenix, AZ 85007
Phone : (602) 542-1463
Fax : (602) 258-6627

ARKANSAS
Jimmie Lou Fisher
State Treasurer
220 State Capitol Bldg.
Little Rock, AR 72201
Phone : (501) 682-5888
Fax : (501) 682-3820

CALIFORNIA
Matthew K. Fong
State Treasurer
915 Capitol Mall, Rm. 110
Sacramento, CA 95814
Phone : (916) 653-2995
Fax : (916) 653-3125

COLORADO
Bill Owens
State Treasuerer
140 State Capitol
Denver, CO 80203
Phone : (303) 866-2441
Fax : (303) 866-2123

CONNECTICUT
Christopher B. Burnham
State Treasurer
55 Elm St.
Hartford, CT 06106
Phone : (203) 566-5050
Fax : (203) 566-8820

DELAWARE
Janet C. Rzewnicki
State Treasurer
Thomas Collins Bldg.
P.O. Box 1401
Dover, DE 19903
Phone : (302) 739-3382
Fax : (302) 739-5635

FLORIDA
Bill Nelson
Treasurer & Insurance Commissioner
Dept. of Insurance
The Capitol, PL-11
Tallahassee, FL 32399-0300
Phone : (904) 922-3100
Fax : (904) 488-0699

GEORGIA
Steven N. McCoy
Director
Off. of Treasury & Fiscal Srvcs.
200 Piedmont Ave., SE
1202 W. Tower
Atlanta, GA 30334
Phone : (404) 651-8971
Fax : (404) 656-9048

HAWAII
Earl I. Anzai
Director of Finance
Dept. of Budget and Finance
P.O. Box 150
Honolulu, HI 96810-0150
Phone : (808) 586-1518
Fax : (808) 586-1976

IDAHO
Lydia Justice Edwards
State Treasurer
P.O. Box 83720
102 State Capitol
Boise, ID 83720-0091
Phone : (208) 334-3200
Fax : (208) 334-2543

ILLINOIS
Judy Baar Topinka
State Treasurer
219 State House
Springfield, IL 62706
Phone : (217) 782-2211
Fax : (217) 785-2777

INDIANA
Joyce Brinkman
State Treasurer
242 State House
Indianapolis, IN 46204
Phone : (317) 232-6386
Fax : (317) 232-5656

IOWA
Michael L. Fitzgerald
State Treasurer
State Capitol Bldg.
Des Moines, IA 50319
Phone : (515) 281-5368
Fax : (515) 281-7562

KANSAS
Sally Thompson
State Treasurer
900 SW Jackson, Ste. 201
Topeka, KS 66612-1235
Phone : (913) 296-3171
Fax : (913) 296-7950

KENTUCKY
Frances Jones Mills
State Treasurer
Capitol Annex, Rm. 183
Frankfort, KY 40601
Phone : (502) 564-4722
Fax : (502) 564-6545

LOUISIANA
Mary L. Landrieu
State Treasurer
P.O. Box 44154
Baton Rouge, LA 70804
Phone : (504) 342-0010
Fax : (504) 342-0046

MAINE
Samuel Shapiro
State Treasurer
Dept. of Treasury
State Off. Bldg.
Augusta, ME 04333
Phone : (207) 289-2771
Fax : (207) 287-2367

MARYLAND
Lucille Maurer
State Treasurer
80 Calvert St.
109 Goldstein Bldg.
Annapolis, MD 21401
Phone : (410) 974-3542
Fax : (410) 974-3530

MASSACHUSETTS
Joseph Malone
Treasurer & Receiver General
State House, Rm. 227
Boston, MA 02133
Phone : (617) 367-6900
Fax : (617) 248-0372

MICHIGAN
Douglas B. Roberts
Treasurer
Treasury Bldg.
430 W. Allegan St.
Lansing, MI 48922
Phone : (517) 373-3223
Fax : (517) 335-1785

MINNESOTA
Michael A. McGrath
State Treasurer
303 Administration Bldg.
50 Sherburne Ave.
St. Paul, MN 55155
Phone : (612) 296-7091
Fax : (612) 296-8615

MISSISSIPPI
Marshall G. Bennett
State Treasurer
404 Walter Sillers Bldg.
P.O. Box 138
Jackson, MS 39205
Phone : (601) 359-3600
Fax : (601) 359-2001

MISSOURI
Bob Holden
State Treasurer
State Capitol, Rm. 229
P.O. Box 210
Jefferson City, MO 65102
Phone : (314) 751-2411
Fax : (314) 751-9443

MONTANA
Lois A. Menzies
Director
Ex Officio State Treasurer
Dept. of Administration
155 Mitchell Bldg.
Helena, MT 59620
Phone : (406) 444-2032
Fax : (406) 444-2812

NEBRASKA
David E. Heineman
State Treasurer
P.O. Box 94788
2001 State Capitol Bldg.
Lincoln, NE 68504
Phone : (402) 471-2455
Fax : (402) 471-4390

NEVADA
Robert L. Seale
State Treasurer
Capitol Complex
Carson City, NV 89710
Phone : (702) 687-5200
Fax : (702) 687-5532

NEW HAMPSHIRE
Georgie A. Thomas
State Treasurer
121 State House Annex
Concord, NH 03301-6399
Phone : (603) 271-2621
Fax : (603) 271-3922

NEW JERSEY
Brian W. Clymer
State Treasurer
State House, CN002
125 W. State St.
Trenton, NJ 08625
Phone : (609) 292-5031
Fax : (609) 292-6145

NEW MEXICO
Michael A. Montoya
State Treasurer
P.O. Box 608
130 South Capitol St.
Santa Fe, NM 87504
Phone : (505) 827-6400
Fax : (505) 827-6395

NEW YORK*
Deputy Commissioner & Treasurer
Dept. of Taxation & Finance
P.O. Box 7002
Albany, NY 12225
Phone : (518) 474-4250
Fax : (518) 428-5165

NORTH CAROLINA
Harlan E. Boyles
State Treasurer
325 N. Salisbury St.
Raleigh, NC 27603-1388
Phone : (919) 733-3951
Fax : (919) 733-9586

NORTH DAKOTA
Kathi Gilmore
State Treasurer
State Capitol, 3rd Fl.
600 E. Boulevard Ave.
Bismarck, ND 58505-0600
Phone : (701) 328-2643
Fax : (701) 328-3002

OHIO
J. Kenneth Blackwell
Treasurer of State
30 E. Broad St., 9th Fl.
Columbus, OH 43266-0421
Phone : (614) 466-2057
Fax : (614) 644-7313

OKLAHOMA
Robert Butkin
State Treasurer
2300 North Lincoln
217 State Capitol
Oklahoma City, OK 73105
Phone : (405) 521-3191
Fax : (405) 521-4994

OREGON
Jim Hill
State Treasurer
159 State Capitol
Salem, OR 97310-0840
Phone : (503) 378-4329
Fax : (503) 373-7051

PENNSYLVANIA
Catherine Baker Knoll
State Treasurer
129 Finance Bldg.
Harrisburg, PA 17120
Phone : (717) 787-2465
Fax : (717) 783-9760
E-Mail: CBKnoll@patreas0.cmic.state.pa.

RHODE ISLAND
Nancy J. Mayer
General Treasurer
102 State House
Providence, RI 02903
Phone : (401) 277-2397
Fax : (401) 277-6140

SOUTH CAROLINA
Richard Eckstrom
State Treasurer
118 Wade Hampton Office Bldg.
Columbia, SC 29201
Phone : (803) 734-2688
Fax : (803) 734-2039

SOUTH DAKOTA
Richard Butler
State Treasurer
500 East Capitol
Pierre, SD 57501-5070
Phone : (605) 773-3378
Fax : (605) 773-3115

TENNESSEE
Stephen D. Adams
State Treasurer
State Capitol
Nashville, TN 37243-0225
Phone : (615) 741-2956
Fax : (615) 741-7328

TEXAS
Martha Whitehead
State Treasurer
State Treasury Bldg.
P.O. Box 12608, Capitol Station
Austin, TX 78711-2608
Phone : (512) 463-6000
Fax : (512) 463-6315

UTAH
Edward T. Alter
State Treasurer
215 State Capitol
Salt Lake City, UT 84114
Phone : (801) 538-1042
Fax : (801) 538-1465

VERMONT
James H. Douglas
State Treasurer
133 State St.
Montpelier, VT 05633-6200
Phone : (802) 828-2301
Fax : (802) 828-2772

VIRGINIA
Ronald L. Tillett
State Treasurer
P.O. Box 1879
Richmond, VA 23215-1879
Phone : (804) 371-6013
Fax : (804) 225-3187

WASHINGTON
Daniel Grimm
State Treasurer
Legislative Bldg.
P.O. Box 40200
Olympia, WA 98504-0200
Phone : (206) 753-7139
Fax : (206) 753-6147

WEST VIRGINIA
Larrie Bailey
State Treasurer
145 E. Wing, The Capitol
1900 Kanawha Blvd., E.
Charleston, WV 25305
Phone : (304) 343-4000
Fax : (304) 346-6602

WISCONSIN
Jack C. Voight
State Treasurer
101 E. Wilson St., 5th Fl.
PO Box 7871
Madison, WI 53707-7871
Phone : (608) 266-1714
Fax : (608) 266-2647

WYOMING
Stan Smith
State Treasurer
State Capitol
Cheyenne, WY 82002
Phone : (307) 777-7408
Fax : (307) 632-3701

DISTRICT OF COLUMBIA
Maria Day-Marshall
Treasurer
One Judiciary Square
441 Fourth St., NW, Ste. 360
Washington, DC 20001
Phone : (202) 727-6055
Fax : (202) 727-6049

AMERICAN SAMOA
Aitofele Sunia
Treasurer
Dept. of the Treasury
Government of American Samoa
Pago Pago, AS 96799
Phone : (684) 633-4155

GUAM
John S. Salas
Director
Dept. of Administration
P.O. Box 884
Agana, GU 96910
Phone : (671) 475-1101
Fax : (671) 477-6788

NORTHERN MARIANA ISLANDS
Dolores S. Guerrero
Treasurer
Dept. of Finance
Off. of Governor
Saipan, MP 96950
Phone : (670) 664-1300
Fax : (670) 664-1115

PUERTO RICO
Manuel Diaz Saldana
Secretary of the Treasury
Intendente Ramirez Bldg.
Paseo Covadonga
San Juan, PR 00901
Phone : (809) 729-0916
Fax : (809) 723-2838

U.S. VIRGIN ISLANDS
Bernice A. Turnbull
Acting Director, Treasury
Dept. of Finance
#76 Kronprindsens Gade
Charlotte Amalie, VI 00801-2515
Phone : (809) 774-4114

UNCLAIMED PROPERTY

Responsible for the marshaling, administration and disposition of unclaimed or abandoned property.

ALASKA
Larry E. Meyers
Director
Div. of Income & Excise Audit
Dept. of Revenue
550 W. Seventh Ave.
Anchorage, AK 99501-3556
Phone : (907) 276-5364
Fax : (907) 269-6644

ARIZONA
Harold Scott
Director
Dept. of Revenue
1600 W. Monroe
Phoenix, AZ 85007
Phone : (602) 542-3572

ARKANSAS
Gus Wingfield
State Auditor
State Capitol, Rm. 230
Little Rock, AR 72201
Phone : (501) 682-6030
Fax : (501) 682-2521

CALIFORNIA
Barbara Reagan
Chief
Div. of Unclaimed Property
Off. of the Controller
300 Capitol Mall, Ste. 801
Sacramento, CA 95814
Phone : (916) 323-2843

COLORADO
Bill Owens
State Treasurer
Dept. of Treasury
140 State Capitol Bldg.
Denver, CO 80203
Phone : (303) 866-2441
Fax : (303) 866-2123

CONNECTICUT
Christopher B. Burnham
Treasurer
Off. of the Treasurer
55 Elm St.
Hartford, CT 06106-1773
Phone : (203) 566-5050

FLORIDA
Linda G. Dilworth
Division of Finance
Dept. of Banking & Finance
The Capitol, LL 22
Tallahassee, FL 32399-0350
Phone : (904) 488-0545

GEORGIA
Kay Powell
Administrative Specialist
Dept. of Revenue
270 Washington St.
Atlanta, GA 30334
Phone : (404) 656-4240

HAWAII
Earl I. Anzai
Director
Dept. of Budget & Finance
P.O. Box 150
Honolulu, HI 96810
Phone : (808) 586-1518
Fax : (808) 586-1976

IDAHO
Del Byers
Chief
Unclaimed Property Div.
State Tax Comm.
700 W. State St.
Boise, ID 83722
Phone : (208) 334-7598

ILLINOIS
Frank C. Casillas
Director
Dept. of Financial Institutions
500 Iles Park Pl.
Springfield, IL 62718
Phone : (217) 782-2831
Fax : (217) 785-6999

INDIANA
Gretchen Thomas
Director
Div. of Unclaimed Property
Off. of Attorney General
State House, Rm. 219
Indianapolis, IN 46204
Phone : (317) 232-6348

IOWA
Michael L. Fitzgerald
State Treasurer
State Capitol Bldg.
Des Moines, IA 50319
Phone : (515) 281-5368

KANSAS
Sally Thompson
State Treasurer
900 SW Jackson, Ste. 201
Topeka, KS 66612-1235
Phone : (913) 296-3171
Fax : (913) 296-7950

KENTUCKY
Crit Luallen
Secretary
Finance & Admin. Cabinet
Capitol Annex, Rm. 383
Frankfort, KY 40601
Phone : (502) 564-4240
Fax : (502) 564-6785

LOUISIANA
Benjamin Spann
Director
Unclaimed Property Unit
Dept. of Revenue & Taxation
P.O. Box 91010
Baton Rouge, LA 70821
Phone : (504) 925-7407

MAINE
Samuel Shapiro
State Treasurer
Dept. of Treasury
State Off. Bldg.
Augusta, ME 04333
Phone : (207) 287-2771

MARYLAND**
Ronald La Martina
Manager
Unclaimed Property Div.
Comptrollers Off.
301 W. Preston St.
Baltimore, MD 21201
Phone : (301) 225-1700

MASSACHUSETTS
Frank Kelly
Director
Surplus Property Div.
Executive Off. for Admin. & Finance
1 Ashburton Pl.
Boston, MA 02108
Phone : (617) 727-2920

MINNESOTA
Sandy MacKenthun
Supervisor
Department of Commerce
135 E. 7th Street
St. Paul, MN 55101
Phone : (612) 296-2568
Fax : (612) 296-8591

MISSOURI
William Johnson
Director
Unclaimed Property Division
Off. of State Treasurer
Truman Bldg., Rm. 770
P.O. Box 1272
Jefferson City, MO 65102
Phone : (314) 751-0840
Fax : (314) 526-6027

NEBRASKA
David E. Heineman
State Treasurer
P.O. Box 94788
Lincoln, NE 68509
Phone : (402) 471-2455

NEVADA
Constance Longero
Administrator
Unclaimed Property Div.
Dept. of Business & Industry
2601 E. Sahara Ave.
Las Vegas, NV 89158
Phone : (702) 486-4140
Fax : (702) 486-4177

NEW JERSEY
Stephen M. Sylvester
Administrator
Unclaimed Property Admin.
Dept. of Treasury
50 Barrack St., CN214
Trenton, NJ 08625
Phone : (609) 292-8822

NEW MEXICO
Cathy Clay
Section Supervisor
Special Tax Programs
Dept. of Taxation & Revenue
Manuel Lujan Off. Bldg.
Santa Fe, NM 87503
Phone : (505) 827-0760
Fax : (505) 827-1759

NEW YORK*
State Comptroller
Off. of the State Comptroller
A.E. Smith Off. Bldg., 6th Fl.
Albany, NY 12236
Phone : (518) 474-4040

NORTH CAROLINA
Marvin K. Dorman
State Budget Officer
Off. of State Budget
116 W. Jones St.
Raleigh, NC 27603-8005
Phone : (919) 733-7061
Fax : (919) 733-0640

NORTH DAKOTA
Valerie Jundt
Deputy Administrator
Unclaimed Property Div.
Dept. of State Land
918 E. Divide Ave., Ste. 410
Bismarck, ND 58502-5523
Phone : (701) 328-2805
Fax : (701) 328-3650

OHIO
Jessie T. Baker
Acting Chief
Div. of Unclaimed Funds
Dept. of Commerce
77 High St., 20th Fl.
Columbus, OH 43266-0545
Phone : (614) 644-6226
Fax : (614) 752-5078

OKLAHOMA
Randy Ross
Director
Business Tax Div.
Tax Comm.
2501 N. Lincoln Blvd.
Oklahoma City, OK 73105
Phone : (405) 521-3796

PENNSYLVANIA*
Deputy Secretary for Admin.
Dept. of Revenue
Strawberry Sq., 11th Fl.
Harrisburg, PA 17127
Phone : (717) 783-3682

RHODE ISLAND
Richard Coffey
Supervisor
Div. of Unclaimed Property
Dept. of the Treasury
40 Fountain St.
Providence, RI 02903
Phone : (401) 277-2397

SOUTH CAROLINA
Voigt Shealy
State Procurement Officer
Materials Management Div.
Dept. of General Services
1201 Main St., Ste. 600
Columbia, SC 29201
Phone : (803) 737-0600

SOUTH DAKOTA
Richard Butler
State Treasurer
Unclaimed Property
Off. of State Treasurer
500 E. Capitol Ave.
Pierre, SD 57501
Phone : (605) 773-3378

TENNESSEE
Stephen D. Adams
State Treasurer
State Capitol
Nashville, TN 37243
Phone : (615) 741-2957
Fax : (615) 741-7328

TEXAS
Martha Whitehead
State Treasurer
Dept. of the Treasury
P.O. Box 12608, Capitol Station
Austin, TX 78711
Phone : (512) 463-6000

UTAH
Lorin P. Nielsen
Deputy State Treasurer
Div. of Unclaimed Property
341 S. Main
Salt Lake City, UT 84114
Phone : (801) 533-4101

VERMONT
James H. Douglas
Treasurer
State Administration Bldg.
133 State St.
Montpelier, VT 05633-6200
Phone : (802) 828-2301
Fax : (802) 828-2772

VIRGINIA
Ronald L. Tillett
State Treasurer
Dept. of the Treasury
Monroe Bldg., 3rd Fl.
101 N. 14th St.
Richmond, VA 23219
Phone : (804) 371-6013
Fax : (804) 225-3187

WASHINGTON
Gary O'Neil
Assistant Director
Misc.. Tax/Unclaimed Property Section
Dept. of Revenue
P.O. Box 47450
Olympia, WA 98504-7450
Phone : (360) 753-2871

WEST VIRGINIA
Dwight Smith
Director
Unclaimed Property
Off. of the Treasurer
200 Morris St.
Charleston, WV 25301-1821
Phone : (304) 343-4000

WISCONSIN
Jack C. Voight
State Treasurer
101 E. Wilson St.
P.O. Box 7871
Madison, WI 53707
Phone : (608) 266-1714
Fax : (608) 266-2647

WYOMING
Nancy Sutton
Director
Unclaimed Property Div.
Off. of the State Treasurer
State Capitol
Cheyenne, WY 82002
Phone : (307) 777-7408

DISTRICT OF COLUMBIA
Wanda Moorman
Administrator
Material Management Admin.
613 G St., NW, Rm. 1014
Washington, DC 20001
Phone : (202) 727-0252

GUAM
Joseph A. "Tony" Martinez
Director
Dept. of Land Management
P.O. Box 2950
Agana, GU 96910
Phone : (671) 475-5263
Fax : (671) 477-0883

NORTHERN MARIANA ISLANDS
Joaquin I. Pangelinan
Special Assistant for Admin.
Off. of the Governor
P.O. Box 10007
Saipan, MP 96950
Phone : (670) 322-5091
Fax : (670) 322-5099

U.S. VIRGIN ISLANDS
Kenneth E. Mapp
Lt. Governor
#18 Kongens Gade
St. Thomas, VI 00802
Phone : (809) 774-2991
Fax : (809) 774-6953

UNEMPLOYMENT INSURANCE

Administers the unemployment insurance program in the state.

ALABAMA
Dottie Cieszynski
Director
Dept. of Industrial Relations
649 Monroe St.
Montgomery, AL 36131
Phone : (334) 242-8990
Fax : (334) 242-3960

ALASKA
Rebecca Nance
Director
Employment Security Div.
Dept. of Labor
P.O. Box 25509
Juneau, AK 99802-1149
Phone : (907) 465-2711
Fax : (907) 465-4537

ARIZONA
Linda Blessing
Director
Dept. of Economic Security
1717 W. Jefferson
Phoenix, AZ 85007
Phone : (602) 542-4791

ARKANSAS
Phil Price
Director
Employment Security Div.
Dept. of Labor
Capitol Mall
Little Rock, AR 72201
Phone : (501) 682-2121
Fax : (501) 682-3713

CALIFORNIA
Al Lee
Chief Deputy Director
Dept. of Employment Dev.
800 Capitol Mall, Rm. 5000
Sacramento, CA 95814
Phone : (916) 654-8210

COLORADO
Robert Hale
Director
Employment & Training Div.
Dept. of Labor & Employment
600 Grant St., 8th Fl.
Denver, CO 80203
Phone : (303) 620-4718
Fax : (303) 620-4714

CONNECTICUT
Alice Carrier
Director
Operational Support
Dept. of Labor
200 Folly Brook Blvd.
Wethersfield, CT 06109
Phone : (203) 566-4288

DELAWARE
W. Thomas MacPherson
Director
Unemployment Insurance Div.
Dept. of Labor
University Plaza
Newark, DE 19711
Phone : (302) 368-6730
Fax : (302) 368-6748

FLORIDA
Kenneth Holmes
Assistant Director
Div. of Unemployment Compen.
Dept. of Labor & Employment Security
201 Caldwell Bldg.
Tallahassee, FL 32399
Phone : (904) 921-3889

GEORGIA
Tom Lowe
Assistant Commissioner
Unemployment Insurance Div.
Dept. of Labor
148 International Blvd., Rm. 718
Atlanta, GA 30303
Phone : (404) 656-3050

HAWAII
Douglas Odo
Administrator
Unemployment Insurance Div.
Dept. of Labor & Ind. Rel.
830 Punchbowl St., Rm. 325
Honolulu, HI 96813
Phone : (808) 586-9069

IDAHO
Tom Johnson
Administrator
Unemployment Insurance Div.
Dept. of Employment
317 Main St.
Boise, ID 83735
Phone : (208) 334-6466

ILLINOIS
Lynn Doherty
Director
Dept. of Employment Security
401 S. State St., 6th Fl.
Chicago, IL 60605
Phone : (312) 793-9274
Fax : (312) 793-9834

INDIANA
Jerry Haver
Commissioner
Workforce Development
10 N. Senate
Indianapolis, IN 46204
Phone : (317) 233-5661

IOWA
William J. Yost
Division Chief
Div. of Job Srvcs.
Dept. of Employment Srvcs.
1000 E. Grand Ave.
Des Moines, IA 50319
Phone : (515) 281-5526

KANSAS
Gard Adkins
Director
Employment Security Systems Inst.
Dept. of Human Resources
1309 S. Topeka Blvd.
Topeka, KS 66612-1894
Phone : (913) 296-2118
Fax : (913) 296-2119

KENTUCKY
Marcia Morgan
Director
Div. of Unemployment Insurance
Cabinet for Human Resources
275 E. Main St.
Frankfort, KY 40621
Phone : (502) 564-2900

LOUISIANA
Lowry Lacy
Assistant Secretary
Off. of Employment
Dept. of Labor
P.O. Box 94094
Baton Rouge, LA 70804
Phone : (504) 342-3013

MAINE
Gail Thayer
Director
Bur. of Employment Security
Dept. of Labor
State House Station # 55
Augusta, ME 04333
Phone : (207) 287-3377

MARYLAND**
Tom Wendel
Executive Director
Unemployment Insurance Admin.
Dept. of Economic & Employment Dev.
110 N. Eutaw St., Rm. 501
Baltimore, MD 21201
Phone : (410) 333-5711

MASSACHUSETTS
Nils L. Nordberg
Commissioner
Dept. of Employment & Training
Charles F. Hurley Bldg.
19 Staniford St., 3rd Fl.
Boston, MA 02114
Phone : (617) 626-6600

MICHIGAN
Robert Edwards
Director
Employment Security Comm.
Dept. of Labor
7310 Woodward Ave.
Detroit, MI 48202
Phone : (313) 876-5000

MINNESOTA
Gary Sorensen
Assistant Commissioner
Job Srvc. & Unemploy. Ins. Div.
Dept. of Jobs & Training
390 N. Robert St.
St. Paul, MN 55101
Phone : (612) 296-1692

MISSISSIPPI
Tom Lord
Director
Employment Security Comm.
Dept of Equal Empl. Opp.
P.O. Box 1699
Jackson, MS 39215
Phone : (601) 354-8711

MISSOURI
Marilyn Hutcherson
Assistant Director
Unemployment Insurance Operations
Dept. of Labor & Ind. Rel.
421 E. Dunklin
P.O. Box 59
Jefferson City, MO 65104
Phone : (314) 751-3643
Fax : (314) 751-4554

MONTANA
Laurie Ekanger
Director
Dept. of Labor & Industry
P.O. Box 1728
Helena, MT 59624
Phone : (406) 444-3555

NEBRASKA
Allan Amsberry
Director
Unemployment Insurance Div.
Dept. of Labor
P.O. Box 94600
Lincoln, NE 68509
Phone : (402) 475-9979

NEVADA
Stanley P. Jones
Administrator
Div. of Employment Security
Emplymt., Trng. & Rehab. Dept.
500 E. Third St.
Carson City, NV 89713
Phone : (702) 687-4635

NEW HAMPSHIRE
John J. Ratoff
Commissioner
Dept. of Employment Security
32 S. Main St.
Concord, NH 03301
Phone : (603) 224-3311

NEW JERSEY
Michael Malloy
Director
Div. of Field Operations
Dept. of Labor
John Fitch Plz., Fl. 10, CN058
Trenton, NJ 08625
Phone : (609) 292-2460

NEW MEXICO
Jimmy Sanchez
Chief
Unemployment Insurance Bur.
Dept. of Labor
P.O. Box 1928
Albuquerque, NM 87103
Phone : (505) 841-8657
Fax : (505) 841-9053

NEW YORK*
Commissioner
Dept. of Labor
State Off. Bldg., State Campus
Albany, NY 12240
Phone : (518) 457-2741

NORTH CAROLINA
Ann Duncan
Chair
Employment Security Comm.
Dept. of Commerce
700 Wade Ave.
Raleigh, NC 27605-1167
Phone : (919) 733-7546

NORTH DAKOTA
John Welder
Director
Job Insurance Div.
P.O. Box 1537
Bismarck, ND 58502-1537
Phone : (701) 328-2833
Fax : (701) 328-2728

OHIO
Debra Bowland
Administrator
Bur. of Employment Srvcs.
145 S. Front St.
Columbus, OH 43216
Phone : (614) 466-8032
Fax : (614) 466-5025

OKLAHOMA
Wayne Winn
Executive Director
Employment Security Comm.
200 Will Rogers Bldg.
Oklahoma City, OK 73105
Phone : (405) 557-7200

OREGON
Roger Auerbach
Acting Director
Employment Dept.
875 Union St., NE
Salem, OR 97311
Phone : (503) 373-7298

PENNSYLVANIA
James Weaver
Deputy Secretary
Employment Security & Job Training
Dept. of Labor & Industry
Labor & Industry Bldg., Rm. 1708
Harrisburg, PA 17120
Phone : (717) 787-1745

RHODE ISLAND
Thomas Morrisey
Associate Director for Benefits
Dept. of Employment & Training
101 Friendship St.
Providence, RI 02903
Phone : (401) 277-3649

SOUTH CAROLINA
Robert E. David
Executive Director
Employment Security Comm.
P.O. Box 995
Columbia, SC 29202
Phone : (803) 737-2617

SOUTH DAKOTA
Donald Kattke
Director
Div. of Unemployment Insurance
Dept. of Labor
607 N. Fourth St., Box 1700
Aberdeen, SD 57401
Phone : (605) 622-2340

TENNESSEE
Bill Stokes
Commissioner
Dept. of Employment Security
Volunteer Plz., 12th Fl.
500 James Robertson Pkwy.
Nashville, TN 37243
Phone : (615) 741-2131
Fax : (615) 741-3203

TEXAS
William Grossenbacher
Administrator
Employment Comm.
101 E. 15th St.
Austin, TX 78778
Phone : (512) 463-2222

UTAH
Terry Burns
Director
Dept. of Employment Security
140 E. Broadway
Salt Lake City, UT 84111
Phone : (801) 536-7423

VERMONT
Thomas Douse
Director
Unemployment Insurance Div.
Dept. of Employment & Training Admin.
P.O. Box 488
Montpelier, VT 05601
Phone : (802) 828-4100

VIRGINIA
Kenneth A. Bolles
Commissioner
Virginia Employment Commission
703 E. Main St.
Richmond, VA 23219
Phone : (804) 786-3001
Fax : (804) 225-3923

WASHINGTON
Vernon Stoner
Commissioner
Dept. of Employment Security
212 Maple Park
P.O. Box 49046
Olympia, WA 98504-9046
Phone : (360) 753-5116

WEST VIRGINIA
Andrew N. Richardson
Commissioner
Div. of Worker's Compensation
P.O. Box 3151
Charleston, WV 25332
Phone : (304) 558-2630

WISCONSIN
Michael Corry
Administrator
Unemployment Compensation Div.
Dept. of Ind. Labor & Human Relations
201 E. Washington, Rm. 371X
P.O. Box 7903
Madison, WI 53703
Phone : (608) 266-7074
Fax : (608) 267-0593

WYOMING
Beth Nelson
Unemployment Ins. Administrator
Unemployment Compensation Div.
Dept. of Employment
P.O. Box 2760
Casper, WY 82602
Phone : (307) 235-3200

DISTRICT OF COLUMBIA
Bruce Eanet
Associate Director
Unemployment Compensation Off.
Dept. of Employment Services
500 C St., NW, Rm. 515
Washington, DC 20001
Phone : (202) 639-1163

GUAM
Juan M. Taijito
Director
Dept. of Labor
P.O. Box 9970, ITC Bldg.
Tamuning, GU 96911
Phone : (671) 647-4142
Fax : (671) 646-9004

NORTHERN MARIANA ISLANDS*
Personnel Officer
Civil Service Comm.
Personnel Management Off.
Off. of the Governor
Saipan, MP 96950
Phone : (670) 234-6958

PUERTO RICO
Ednidia Padilla
Director
Bur. of Employment Security
Dept. of Labor & Human Res.
505 Munoz Rivera Ave.
Hato Rey, PR 00918
Phone : (809) 754-5375
Fax : (809) 763-2227

U.S. VIRGIN ISLANDS
Lisa Harris-Moorhead
Commissioner
Dept. of Labor
P.O. Box 208
St. Thomas, VI 00802
Phone : (809) 776-3700
Fax : (809) 773-0094

VETERANS AFFAIRS

Provides services and information to the state's veterans, their dependents and survivors.

ALABAMA
Frank D. Wilkes
Director
Dept. of Veterans Affairs
770 Washington Ave., Ste. 530
Montgomery, AL 36130
Phone : (334) 242-5077
Fax : (334) 242-5102

ALASKA
Jake Lestenkof
Adjutant General
Dept. of Military & Vet. Aff.
P.O. Box 5800
Fort Richardson, AK 99505-5800
Phone : (907) 428-6003
Fax : (907) 428-6019

ARIZONA
Norman O. Gallion
Director
Veterans' Service Comm.
3225 N. Central, Ste. 910
Phoenix, AZ 85012
Phone : (602) 255-4713

ARKANSAS
Nick Bacon
Director
Dept. of Veterans Affairs
c/o VA Regional Off.
P.O. Box 1280
North Little Ro, AR 72115
Phone : (501) 370-3820
Fax : (501) 370-3829

CALIFORNIA
Jay R. Vargas
Director
Dept. of Veterans Affairs
1227 O St., Ste. 300
Sacramento, CA 95814
Phone : (916) 653-2158

COLORADO
Richard Ceresko
Director
Veteran Affairs Div.
Dept. of Human Srvcs.
789 Sherman St., #460
Denver, CO 80203
Phone : (303) 894-0838

CONNECTICUT
Eugene A. Migliaro, Jr.
Commissioner
Dept. of Veterans Affairs
287 West St.
Rocky Hill, CT 06067
Phone : (203) 721-5890

Sharon R. Wood
Hospital Administrator
Veterans Home & Hospital Comm.
287 West St.
Rocky Hill, CT 06067
Phone : (203) 529-2571

DELAWARE
Antonio Davila
Executive Secretary
Comm. of Veterans Affairs
Dept. of State
P.O. Box 1401
Dover, DE 19903
Phone : (302) 739-2792
Fax : (800) 344-9900

FLORIDA
Earl G. Peck
Executive Director
Dept. of Veterans' Affairs
P.O. Box 31003
St. Petersburg, FL 33731
Phone : (813) 898-4443
Fax : (813) 893-2497

GEORGIA
Pete Wheeler
Commissioner
Dept. of Veterans Srvcs.
Veterans Memorial Bldg., Ste. 970
Atlanta, GA 30334
Phone : (404) 656-2300

HAWAII
Robert Viduya
Director
Off. of Veterans Srvcs.
Dept. of Defense
733 Bishop St., Ste. 1270
Honolulu, HI 96813
Phone : (808) 587-3010
Fax : (808) 587-3009

IDAHO
Gary Bermeosolo
Administrator
Div. of Veterans Affairs
Dept. of Health & Welfare
P.O. Box 7765
Boise, ID 83707
Phone : (208) 334-5000

ILLINOIS
Robert E. Foster
Director
Dept. of Veterans Affairs
833 S. Spring St.
Springfield, IL 62794
Phone : (217) 785-6641
Fax : (217) 524-0344

INDIANA
Gerald Bole
Director
Dept. of Veterans Affairs
302 W. Washington St., Rm. E120
Indianapolis, IN 46204
Phone : (317) 232-3920

IOWA
Randy Brown
Administrator
Div. of Veterans Affairs
Dept. of Public Defense
7700 NW Beaver Dr.
Johnston, IA 50131
Phone : (515) 242-5333

KANSAS
Stan Teasley
Executive Director
Comm. on Veterans' Affairs
700 SW Jackson St., Rm. 701
Topeka, KS 66603-3743
Phone : (913) 296-3976
Fax : (913) 296-1462

KENTUCKY
Robert Dezarn
Military Affairs
Boone National Guard
100 Minutemen Pkwy.
Frankfort, KY 40601-6168
Phone : (502) 564-8600

LOUISIANA
Ernie P. Broussard
Executive Director
Veterans Affairs Comm.
Off. of the Governor
P.O. Box 94095
Baton Rouge, LA 70804
Phone : (504) 342-5863

MAINE
Earl L. Adams
Commissioner/Adjutant General
Dept. of Defense & Veterans Srvcs.
#33 State House Station
Augusta, ME 04333-0033
Phone : (207) 626-4225

MARYLAND**
Tom Bratten
Director
Veterans' Comm.
31 Hopkins Plz., Rm. 110
Baltimore, MD 21201
Phone : (410) 333-4428

MASSACHUSETTS
Thomas Hudner
Commissioner
Off. of Veterans Srvcs.
100 Cambridge St., Rm. 1002
Boston, MA 02202
Phone : (617) 727-3570

MICHIGAN
Jack G. Devine
Director
Veterans' Trust Fund
Dept. of Mgt. & Budget
P.O. Box 30026
Lansing, MI 48909
Phone : (517) 373-3130

MINNESOTA
Bernie Melter
Commissioner
Dept. of Veterans Affairs
Veterans Bldg.
20 W. 12th St.
St. Paul, MN 55155
Phone : (612) 296-2783

MISSISSIPPI
Jack Stephens
Executive Secretary
Veterans Affairs Bd.
4607 Lindberg Dr.
Jackson, MS 39209
Phone: (601) 354-7205

MISSOURI
Robert Buckner
Executive Director
Missouri Veterans' Commission
Dept. of Public Safety
1719 Southridge Dr.
P.O. Drawer 147
Jefferson City, MO 65102
Phone: (314) 751-3779
Fax: (314) 751-6836

MONTANA
James F. Jacobson
Administrator
Veteran's Affairs Div.
Dept. of Military Affairs
P.O. Box 4789
Helena, MT 59604-4789
Phone: (406) 444-6926

NEBRASKA
Jonathan F. Sweet
Director
Dept. of Veterans' Affairs
State Off. Bldg., 4th Fl.
P.O. Box 95083
Lincoln, NE 68509
Phone: (402) 471-2458

NEVADA
Randy Day
Commissioner
Comm. for Veterans Affairs
1201 Terminal Way, # 108
Reno, NV 89520
Phone: (702) 688-1155

NEW HAMPSHIRE
Conrad V. Moran
Director
State Veterans Council
359 Lincoln St.
Manchester, NH 03103
Phone: (603) 624-9230

NEW JERSEY
Paul J. Glazar
Adjutant General
Dept. of Military & Veterans' Affairs
Eggert Crossing Rd., CN340
Trenton, NJ 08625-0340
Phone: (609) 530-6957

NEW MEXICO
Michael D'Arco
Director
Veterans Service Comm.
P.O. Box 2324
Santa Fe, NM 87504
Phone: (505) 827-6300
Fax: (505) 827-6372

NEW YORK*
Director
Div. of Veterans' Affairs
Corning Tower, # 28
Albany, NY 12223
Phone: (518) 474-3725

NORTH CAROLINA
Charles F. Smith
Asst. Secretary
Div. of Veterans' Affairs
Dept. of Administration
325 N. Salisbury St., # 1065
Raleigh, NC 27603-1388
Phone: (919) 733-3851

NORTH DAKOTA
Ray Harkenma
Commissioner
Dept. of Veteran's Affairs
1411 32nd St., South
Fargo, ND 58106
Phone: (701) 239-7165
Fax: (701) 239-7165

OHIO
Dave Alstadt
Administrator
Veterans Affairs
Off. of the Governor
77 S. High
Columbus, OH 43266
Phone: (614) 644-0898
Fax: (614) 466-9354

OKLAHOMA
Richard P. Heuckendorf
Executive Director
Dept. of Veterans Affairs
2311 N. Central
Oklahoma City, OK 73152
Phone: (405) 521-3684
Fax: (405) 521-6533

OREGON
Jon Mangis
Director
Dept. of Veterans' Affairs
700 Summer St., NE
Salem, OR 97310
Phone: (503) 373-2388

PENNSYLVANIA
James MacVay
Adjutant General
Dept. of Military Affairs
Ft. Indiantown Gap
Annville, PA 17003
Phone: (717) 861-8500

RHODE ISLAND
David Foehr
Chief
Veterans' Home
Dept. of Social & Rehabilitative Srvcs.
600 New London Ave.
Cranston, RI 02920
Phone: (401) 253-8000

SOUTH CAROLINA
G. Stoney Wages
Director
Div. of Veterans' Affairs
Off. of the Governor
1205 Pendleton St., Ste. 226
Columbia, SC 29201
Phone: (803) 734-0200
Fax: (803) 734-0197

SOUTH DAKOTA
Dennis Foell
Director
Veterans Div.
Military & Veterans' Affairs Dept.
500 E. Capitol Ave.
Pierre, SD 57501
Phone: (605) 773-4981

TENNESSEE
Fred Tucker
Commissioner
Dept. of Veterans' Affairs
215 Eighth Ave., N.
Nashville, TN 37243
Phone: (615) 741-2345

TEXAS
Douglas K. Brown
Executive Director
Veterans Commission
P.O. Box 12277, Capitol Station
Austin, TX 78711
Phone: (512) 463-5538

VERMONT
Aline Boisjoli
Director
Veterans' Affairs
120 State St.
Montpelier, VT 05620
Phone: (802) 828-3380

VIRGINIA
Donald W. Duncan
Director
Poff Federal Bldg., Rm. 1012
270 Franklin Rd., SW
Roanoke, VA 24011-2215
Phone: (703) 857-7104
Fax: (703) 857-7573

WASHINGTON
Beau Bergeron
Director
Dept. of Veteran Affairs
505 E. Union
P.O. Box 41150
Olympia, WA 98504
Phone: (360) 753-5586

WEST VIRGINIA
Gail Harper
Director
Veterans' Affairs
1321 Plaza E., # 101
Charleston, WV 25301
Phone: (304) 558-3661

WISCONSIN
Ray Boland
Secretary
Dept. of Veterans' Affairs
30 W. Mifflin
P.O. Box 7843
Madison, WI 53707
Phone: (608) 266-1311
Fax: (608) 267-0403

WYOMING
Ted Sherar
Chairman
Council for Veterans' Affairs
Dept. of Employment
1819 Park Ave.
Cheyenne, WY 82007
Phone: (307) 682-8389

DISTRICT OF COLUMBIA
Cleveland Jordan
Chief
Off. of Veterans' Affairs
Dept. of Human Services
941 N. Capitol, NE, Rm. 1211-F
Washington, DC 20002
Phone: (202) 727-0328

AMERICAN SAMOA
Elmer Nakiso
Officer
Veterans' Affairs
Off. of the Governor
Pago Pago, AS 96799
Phone : (684) 633-4206
Fax : (684) 633-2269

GUAM
John Blaz
Administrator
Off. of Veterans Affairs
P.O. Box 3279
Agana, GU 96910
Phone : (671) 475-4222

NORTHERN MARIANA ISLANDS
Joseph M. Palacios
Director
Div. of Veterans' Affairs
Dept. of Commun. & Cult. Aff.
Off. of the Governor
Saipan, MP 96950
Phone : (670) 233-3475
Fax : (670) 235-9001

PUERTO RICO
Roberto Gonzalez Vazquez
Director
Off. of Veterans' Affairs
P.O. Box 11737
San Juan, PR 00910-1737
Phone : (809) 758-5760
Fax : (809) 758-5788

U.S. VIRGIN ISLANDS
Lawrence Bastian
Director
Veterans Affairs
No. 13A Estate Richmond
Christiansted
St. Croix, VI 00820
Phone : (809) 775-3498
Fax : (809) 778-7978

VETERINARIAN

Responsible for the prevention, control and eradication of transmissible diseases of domestic animals and poultry.

ALABAMA
J. Lee Alley
State Veterinarian
Dept. of Agriculture & Ind.
1445 Federal Dr.
P.O. Box 3336
Montgomery, AL 36193
Phone : (334) 242-2647
Fax : (334) 240-3135

ALASKA
Berton Gore
State Veterinarian
Div. of Environmental Health
Dept. of Environmental Conservation
500 S. Alaska, Ste. A
Palmer, AK 99645
Phone : (907) 745-3236
Fax : (907) 745-8125

ARIZONA
William Allen
Associate Director
Animal Services Div.
Dept. of Agriculture
1688 W. Adams St.
Phoenix, AZ 85007
Phone : (602) 542-4373

ARKANSAS
Jack Gibson
Director
Livestock & Poultry Comm.
P.O. Box 5497
Little Rock, AR 72215
Phone : (501) 324-9193
Fax : (501) 225-9727

CALIFORNIA
Kenneth Tomazin
Chief
Bur. of Animal Health
Dept. of Food & Agriculture
1220 N St., Rm. A-107
Sacramento, CA 95814
Phone : (916) 654-0881

COLORADO
Jerry Bohlender
State Veterinarian
Animal Industry Div.
Dept. of Agriculture
700 Kipling, Rm. 1100
Lakewood, CO 80215
Phone : (303) 239-4161
Fax : (303) 239-4164

CONNECTICUT
Jack Meister
State Veterinarian
Livestock Div.
Dept. of Agriculture
165 Capitol Ave.
Hartford, CT 06106
Phone : (203) 566-4616

DELAWARE
H. Wesley Towers Jr.
State Veterinarian
Div. of Consumer Protection
Dept. of Agriculture
2320 S. duPont Hwy.
Dover, DE 19901
Phone : (302) 739-4811
Fax : (302) 697-6287

FLORIDA
W. E. Pace
State Veterinarian/Director
Div. of Animal Industry
Dept. of Agriculture & Consumer Srvcs.
Mayo Bldg.
Tallahassee, FL 32399-0800
Phone : (904) 488-7747

GEORGIA
John A. Cobb
State Veterinarian
Dept. of Agriculture
Capitol Sq.
Atlanta, GA 30334
Phone : (404) 656-3671

HAWAII
Calvin W.S. Lum
Administrator/State Veterinarian
Animal Industry Div.
Dept. of Agriculture
99-762 Moanalua Rd.
Aiea, HI 96701
Phone : (808) 487-5765

IDAHO
Bob Hillman
Administrator
Div. of Animal Industries
Dept. of Agriculture
2270 Old Penitentiary Rd.
Boise, ID 83707
Phone : (208) 334-3256

ILLINOIS
Richard Hull
State Veterinarian
Div. of Animal Industries
Dept. of Agriculture
P.O. Box 19281
Springfield, IL 62794
Phone : (217) 782-4944

INDIANA
Bret Marsh
State Veterinarian
Animal Health Board
805 Beachway Dr., Ste. 50
Indianapolis, IN 46224
Phone : (317) 232-1344

IOWA
Walter Felker
Bureau Chief
Div. of Animal Industry
Dept. of Agriculture
Wallace State Off. Bldg.
Des Moines, IA 50319
Phone : (515) 281-5305

KANSAS
George Teagarden
Livestock Commissioner
Animal Health Dept.
712 Kansas Ave., Ste. 4B
Topeka, KS 66603-3808
Phone : (913) 296-2326
Fax : (913) 296-1765

KENTUCKY
Don Notter
State Veterinarian
Dept. of Agriculture
100 Fairoaks Lane, Ste. 252
Frankfort, KY 40601
Phone : (502) 564-3956

LOUISIANA
Clyde Raby
Assistant Commissioner
Off. of Animal Health
Dept. of Agriculture
P.O. Box 631
Baton Rouge, LA 70821
Phone : (504) 922-1251

MAINE
David Dineen
Director
Div. of Poultry & Livestock
Dept. of Agriculture, Food & Rural Resources
State House Station # 28
Augusta, ME 04333
Phone : (207) 287-3701

MARYLAND**
Jack K. Grigor
Public Health Veterinarian
Dept. of Health & Mental Hygiene
201 W. Preston St., 3rd Fl.
Baltimore, MD 21201
Phone : (410) 225-6711

MASSACHUSETTS
Peter Mcardle
State Veterinarian
Dept. of Food & Agriculture
100 Cambridge St.
Boston, MA 02202
Phone : (617) 727-3018

MICHIGAN
Michael Chaddock
Veterinarian
Animal Health Div.
Dept. of Agriculture
P.O. Box 30017
Lansing, MI 48909
Phone : (517) 373-1077

MINNESOTA
Thomas J. Hagerty
Executive Secretary
Bd. of Animal Health
90 W. Plato Blvd., Rm. 119
St. Paul, MN 55107
Phone : (612) 296-2942

MISSISSIPPI
Harvey F. McCrory
State Veterinarian
Animal Health & Veterinary Diagnostic Laboratory
2531 N. West St.
Jackson, MS 39202
Phone : (601) 324-9380

MISSOURI
F. Thomas Satalowich
Director
Bureau of Veterinary Public Health
Dept. of Health
1730 E. Elm
P.O. Box 570
Jefferson City, MO 65102
Phone : (314) 751-6136
Fax : (314) 751-6010

John W. Hunt Jr.
State Veterinarian
Div. of Animal Health
Dept. of Agriculture
1616 Missouri Blvd.
P.O. Box 630
Jefferson City, MO 65102
Phone : (314) 751-3377
Fax : (314) 751-6919

MONTANA
Clarence Siroky
State Veterinarian
Animal Health Div.
Dept. of Livestock
P.O. Box 202001
Helena, MT 59620-2001
Phone : (406) 444-2043

MONTANA — Cont.
Donald Ferlicka
State Veterinarian
Animal Health Div.
Dept. of Livestock
301 Roberts, Scott Hart Bldg.
Helena, MT 59620
Phone : (406) 444-2043

NEBRASKA
Larry Williams
State Veterinarian
Dept. of Agriculture
P.O. Box 94947
Lincoln, NE 68509
Phone : (402) 471-2351

NEVADA
Jack N. Armstrong
Chief
Div. of Animal Industry
Dept. of Agriculture
P.O. Box 11100
Reno, NV 89510
Phone : (702) 688-1180

NEW HAMPSHIRE
Clifford W. McGinnis
State Veterinarian
Dept. of Agriculture
P.O. Box 2042
Concord, NH 03302
Phone : (603) 271-2404

NEW JERSEY
Ernest W. Zirkle
Director
Div. of Animal Health
Dept. of Agriculture
John Fitch Plz., CN330
Trenton, NJ 08625
Phone : (609) 292-3965

NEW MEXICO
Joe B. Baker
Director
NM Board of Veterinary Medicine
1650 University Blvd., NE, Ste. 400-C
Albuquerque, NM 87102
Phone : (505) 841-9112
Fax : (505) 841-9113

NEW YORK*
Commissioner
Dept. of Ag. & Markets
Capitol Plz.
1 Winners Cir.
Albany, NY 12235
Phone : (518) 457-4188

NORTH CAROLINA
George Edwards
Director
Veterinary Div.
Dept. of Agriculture
One W. Edenton St.
Raleigh, NC 27601
Phone : (919) 733-7601

NORTH DAKOTA
Robert J. Velure
State Veterinarian
State Bd. of Animal Health
600 E. Boulevard Ave.
Bismarck, ND 58505-0390
Phone : (701) 328-2654
Fax : (701) 328-3000

OHIO
David Galuer
Acting Chief
Div. of Animal Industry
Dept. of Agriculture
65 S. Front St., Rm. 608
Columbus, OH 43266
Phone : (614) 728-6200
Fax : (614) 728-6310

OREGON
Leroy Coffman
State Veternarian
Animal Health Program
Dept. of Agriculture
635 Capitol St., NE
Salem, OR 97310
Phone : (503) 378-4710
Fax : (503) 378-6525

PENNSYLVANIA
Max A. Van Buskirk Jr.
Director
Bur. of Animal Industry
Dept. of Agriculture
2301 N. Cameron St., Rm. 408
Harrisburg, PA 17110
Phone : (717) 783-5301

RHODE ISLAND
Susan Littlefield
Public Health Veterinarian
Agriculture & Marketing Div.
Dept. of Environmental Mgt.
22 Hayes St.
Providence, RI 02903
Phone : (401) 277-2781

SOUTH CAROLINA
Jones W. Bryan
State Veterinarian
Div. of Livestock-Poultry
Dept. of Health
P.O. Box 102406
Columbia, SC 29224-2406
Phone : (803) 788-2260

SOUTH DAKOTA
Sam Holland
State Veterinarian
Livestock Sanitary Bd.
Dept. of Agriculture
411 S. Fort St.
Pierre, SD 57501
Phone : (605) 773-3321

TENNESSEE
John R. Ragan
Veterinarian
Div. of Animal Industries
Dept. of Agriculture
P.O. Box 40627, Melrose Station
Nashville, TN 37204
Phone : (615) 360-0120

TEXAS
Terry Beals
Executive Director
Animal Health Comm.
P.O. Box 12966, Capitol Station
Austin, TX 78711
Phone : (512) 719-0700

UTAH
Michael Marshall
Veterinarian
Div. of Animal Industry
Dept. of Agriculture
350 N. Redwood Rd.
Salt Lake City, UT 84116
Phone : (801) 538-7160

VERMONT
Samuel Hutchins III
State Veterinarian
Dept. of Agriculture
116 State St.
P.O. Drawer 20
Montpelier, VT 05620
Phone : (802) 828-2426
Fax : (802) 828-2361

VIRGINIA
J. Carlton Courter III
Commissioner
Dept. of Agriculture & Consumer Services
1100 Bank St.
Richmond, VA 23219
Phone : (804) 786-3501
Fax : (804) 371-2945

WASHINGTON
Robert Mead
State Veterinarian
Dept. of Agriculture
P.O. Box 42577
Olympia, WA 98504-2577
Phone : (360) 902-1881

WEST VIRGINIA
Lewis P. Thomas
Director
Animal Health Div.
Dept. of Agriculture
State Capitol
Charleston, WV 25305
Phone : (304) 558-2214

WISCONSIN
Dennis J. Carr
Administrator
Div. of Animal Health
Dept. of Agriculture, Trade & Consumer Protection
2811 Agriculture Dr.
P.O. Box 8911
Madison, WI 53708
Phone : (608) 244-4872
Fax : (608) 224-4871

WYOMING
Don Bosman
State Veterinarian
Livestock Board
Herschler Bldg.
122 W. 25th St.
Cheyenne, WY 82002
Phone : (307) 777-7515

DISTRICT OF COLUMBIA
Richard Levinson
Administrator
Preventive Health Srvc. Admin.
Dept. of Human Srvcs.
1660 L St., NW, Rm. 815
Washington, DC 20036
Phone : (202) 673-6741

AMERICAN SAMOA
Talitua Uele
Veterinarian
Dept. of Agriculture
Pago Pago, AS 96799
Phone : (684) 699-1497
Fax : (684) 699-4031

GUAM
Michael W. Kuhlman
Director
Dept. of Agriculture
P.O. Box 2950
Agana, GU 96910
Phone : (671) 734-3942
Fax : (671) 734-6569

NORTHERN MARIANA ISLANDS
George M. Moses
Director
Animal Health & Industry Div.
Dept. of Natural Resources
Off. of the Governor
Saipan, MP 96950
Phone : (670) 234-6169

U.S. VIRGIN ISLANDS
Anthony Olive
Commissioner
Dept. of Economic Development & Agriculture
P.O. Box 6400
St. Thomas, VI 00803
Phone : (809) 774-8784
Fax : (809) 774-4390

VITAL STATISTICS

Maintains a statewide file of birth, death, marriage and divorce records, and issues certified copies of those records.

ALABAMA
Dorothy Harshbarger
State Registrar
Ctr. for Health Statistics
Dept. of Public Health
572 E. Patton Ave.
Montgomery, AL 36111
Phone : (334) 613-5300
Fax : (334) 240-3097

ALASKA
Al Zangri
Chief
Bur. of Vital Statistics
Dept. of Health & Social Srvcs.
P.O. Box 110675
Juneau, AK 99811-0675
Phone : (907) 465-3393
Fax : (907) 465-3618

ARIZONA
Renee Gaudino
Assistant State Registrar
Off. of Vital Records
Dept. of Health Services
2727 W. Glendale Ave.
Phoenix, AZ 85051
Phone : (602) 255-2501

ARKANSAS
Henry C. Robinson
Registrar
Vital Records Div.
Dept. of Health
4815 W. Markham St.
Little Rock, AR 72205
Phone : (501) 661-2371
Fax : (501) 661-2601

CALIFORNIA
Michael Davis
Chief
Vital Statistics Branch
Dept. of Health Srvcs.
P.O. Box 730241
Sacramento, CA 94244
Phone : (916) 445-1719

COLORADO
Joseph Carney
Director
Health Policy Div.
Dept. of Health
4300 Cherry Creek Dr., S.
Denver, CO 80222
Phone : (303) 692-2248
Fax : (303) 782-4883

CONNECTICUT
John N. Boccaccio
Registrar of Vital Records
Dept. of Health Services
150 Washington St.
Hartford, CT 06106
Phone : (203) 566-3238

DELAWARE
Michael L. Richards
Vital Statistics Off.
Div. of Public Health
P.O. Box 637
Dover, DE 19903
Phone : (302) 739-4701

Donald L. Berry
Health Planning & Resources Mgt.
Delaware Health & Social Srvcs.
Jesse Cooper Bldg.
Federal & Water Sts.
Dover, DE 19901
Phone : (302) 739-4776

FLORIDA
Ken Jones
Acting Chief
Off. of Vital Statistics
Dept. of Health & Rehab. Srvcs.
P.O. Box 210
Jacksonville, FL 32231
Phone : (904) 359-6970

GEORGIA
Michael Lavoie
Director
Vital Records Div.
Dept. of Human Resources
47 Trinity Ave., SW
Atlanta, GA 30334
Phone : (404) 656-4750

HAWAII
Alvin R. Onaka
Acting Chief
Research & Statistics Off.
Dept. of Health
1250 Punchbowl St.
Honolulu, HI 96813
Phone : (808) 586-4526

IDAHO
Jane Smith
State Registrar & Chief
Ctr. for Health Statistics
Dept. of Health & Welfare
450 W. State St.
P.O. Box 83720
Boise, ID 83720-0036
Phone : (208) 334-5976
Fax : (208) 334-0685

ILLINOIS
Steven Perry
Chief
Div. of Vital Records
Dept. of Public Health
605 W. Jefferson
Springfield, IL 62761
Phone : (217) 782-6554

INDIANA
Edward Lutz
Registrar
Vital Records Section
Dept. of Health
Rm. 332 W.
P.O. Box 1964
Indianapolis, IN 46206-1964
Phone : (317) 383-0695
Fax : (317) 383-6489

IOWA
Jill France
Bureau Chief
Vital Records & Statistics
Dept. of Public Health
Lucas State Off. Bldg.
Des Moines, IA 50319
Phone : (515) 281-6762

KANSAS
Charlene Satzler
Director
Off. of Vital Statistics
Dept. of Health & Environ.
Landon State Off. Bldg., 1st Fl.
Topeka, KS 66612-1290
Phone : (913) 296-1414
Fax : (913) 296-8075

KENTUCKY
Ken Fiser
Assistant Director
Div. of Vital Rec. & Hlth. Dev.
Cabinet for Human Resources
Dev. of State & Local Health Admin.
275 E. Main St.
Frankfort, KY 40621
Phone : (502) 564-4212

LOUISIANA
William Barlow
Director of Vital Statistics
Off. of Preventive & Public Health Services
P.O. Box 60630
New Orleans, LA 70160
Phone : (504) 586-8353

MAINE
Ellen Naor
Director
Div. of Vital Records & Stats.
Dept. of Human Services
State House Station # 11
Augusta, ME 04333
Phone : (207) 624-5445

MARYLAND**
Joan Dodson
Deputy Chief
Div. of Vital Records
Dept. of Health & Mental Hyg.
4201 Patterson Ave.
Baltimore, MD 21215
Phone : (410) 764-3028

MASSACHUSETTS
Elaine Trudeau
Registrar
Vital Statistics
Dept. of Public Health
150 Tremont St.
Boston, MA 02111
Phone : (617) 727-2700

MICHIGAN
George Van Amburg
State Registrar
Vital & Health Statistics
Dept. of Public Health
P.O. Box 30195
Lansing, MI 48909
Phone : (517) 335-8676

MINNESOTA
Frederick King
State Registrar
Vital Records Srvcs. Section
Dept. of Health
717 Delaware St., SE
Minneapolis, MN 55440
Phone : (612) 623-5121

MISSISSIPPI
David Lohrisch
State Registrar
Vital Records
Dept. of Health
2423 N. State St.
Jackson, MS 39216
Phone : (601) 960-7982

MISSOURI
Gary L. Shipley
Vital Records Administrator
Bur. of Vital Records
Dept. of Health
1730 E. Elm
P.O. Box 570
Jefferson City, MO 65102
Phone : (314) 751-6383
Fax : (314) 751-6010

MONTANA
Sam H. Sperry
Chief
Vital Statistics Bur.
Dept. of Health & Env. Science
Cogswell Bldg.
Helena, MT 59620
Phone : (406) 444-2614

NEBRASKA
Stanley Cooper
Director
Bur. of Vital Statistics
Dept. of Health
P.O. Box 95007
Lincoln, NE 68509
Phone : (402) 471-2871

NEVADA
William Moell
Manager
State Off. of Vital Records
Dept. of Human Resources
505 E. King St.
Carson City, NV 89710
Phone : (702) 687-4740

NEW HAMPSHIRE
Patrick Duffy
Commissioner
Dept. of Administrative Srvcs.
25 Capitol St.
Concord, NH 03301
Phone : (603) 271-3201

Frank Novak
Acting Director
Bur. of Vital Records & Health Statistics
Dept. of Health & Welfare
Hazen Dr.
Concord, NH 03301
Phone : (603) 271-4651

NEW JERSEY
Charles Karkut
Registrar
Vital Statistics
Dept. of Health
S. Warren & Market Sts., CN370
Trenton, NJ 08625
Phone : (609) 292-4087

NEW MEXICO
Betty Hileman
Chief
Vital Statistics Bureau
Dept. of Health
1190 St. Francis Dr.
Santa Fe, NM 87503
Phone : (505) 827-0121
Fax : (505) 827-1751

NEW YORK*
Director
Vital Records
Dept. of Health
733 Broadway
Albany, NY 12207
Phone : (518) 474-3055

NORTH CAROLINA
A. Torrey McLean
Head
Vital Records Branch
Dept. of Human Resources
225 N. McDowell St.
Raleigh, NC 27603-5902
Phone : (919) 733-3000
Fax : (919) 733-1611

NORTH DAKOTA
Beverly Wittman
Data Processing Coordinator
Vital Records
Dept. of Health
600 E. Boulevard Ave.
Bismarck, ND 58505-0200
Phone : (701) 328-2360
Fax : (701) 328-4727

OHIO
John Conner
Chief
Div. of Vital Statistics
Dept. of Health
65 S. Front St., Rm. G-20
Columbus, OH 43266
Phone : (614) 466-2533
Fax : (614) 644-7740

OKLAHOMA
Roger Pirrong
Director
Vital Records Div.
Dept. of Health
1000 NE 10th St.
Oklahoma City, OK 73152
Phone : (405) 271-4040

OREGON
Edward J. Johnson II
State Registrar
Ctr. for Health Statistics
Dept. of Human Resources
800 NE Oregon St.
Portland, OR 97201
Phone : (503) 731-4109
Fax : (503) 731-4084

PENNSYLVANIA
Charles L. Hardester
Chief
Div. of Vital Statistics
Dept. of Health
P.O. Box 1528
New Castle, PA 16103
Phone : (412) 656-3100

RHODE ISLAND
Edward J. Martin
Chief
Vital Statistics
Dept. of Health
75 Davis St.
Providence, RI 02908
Phone : (401) 277-2812

SOUTH CAROLINA
Murray B. Hudson
Director
Vital Records & Public Health
Health & Environmental Control
2600 Bull St.
Columbia, SC 29201
Phone : (803) 734-4810

SOUTH DAKOTA
Barbara Smith
Secretary
Dept. of Health
445 E. Capitol Ave.
Pierre, SD 57501
Phone : (605) 773-3361

TENNESSEE
Paula Taylor
Director
Div. of Vital Records
Dept. of Health
Cordell Hull Bldg.
Nashville, TN 37247
Phone : (615) 532-2600

TEXAS
Richard Bays
Chief
Bur. of Vital Statistics
Dept. of Health
1100 W. 49th St.
Austin, TX 78756
Phone : (512) 458-7111

UTAH
John E. Brockert
Director
Bur. of Health Statistics
Dept. of Health
288 N. 1460 W.
P.O. Box 16700
Salt Lake City, UT 84116
Phone : (801) 538-6360

VERMONT
Linda Davis
Supervisor
Vital Records Div.
Dept. of Health
P.O. Box 70
Burlington, VT 05402
Phone : (802) 863-7275
Fax : (802) 865-7701

VIRGINIA
Russell E. Booker
Director
Div. of Vital Records
Dept. of Health
900 Ridge Top Rd.
Richmond, VA 23229-6732
Phone : (804) 786-6202

WASHINGTON
Elizabeth Ward
Director
Center for Health Statistics
Dept. of Health
P.O. Box 47814
Olympia, WA 98504-7814
Phone : (360) 753-5936

WEST VIRGINIA
Charles Bailey
Director
Vital Registration Off.
Bur. of Public Health
Bldg. 3, Rm. 516
Charleston, WV 25305
Phone : (304) 558-2931

WISCONSIN
Raymond Nashold
Director
Ctr. for Health Statistics
Dept. of Health & Social Srvcs.
1 W. Wilson, Room 172
P.O. Box 309
Madison, WI 53703
Phone : (608) 266-1939
Fax : (608) 267-2832

WYOMING
Lucinda McCaffrey
Deputy State Registrar
Vital Records
Dept. of Health
Hathaway Bldg.
Cheyenne, WY 82002
Phone : (307) 777-7591

DISTRICT OF COLUMBIA
Carl W. Wilson
Chief
Research & Statistics Div.
Dept. of Human Services
425 I St., NW, Rm. 3001
Washington, DC 20001
Phone : (202) 727-0682

AMERICAN SAMOA
Mereane Tagoai
Manager
Vital Statistics
Dept. of Health
Pago Pago, AS 96799
Phone : (684) 633-1222
Fax : (684) 633-1869

GUAM
Dennis Rodriguez
Director
Dept. of Public Health & Social Services
P.O. Box 2816
Agana, GU 96910
Phone : (671) 734-7102
Fax : (671) 734-5910

NORTHERN MARIANA ISLANDS
John G. Moore
Recorder
Superior Court
P.O. Box 307 CK
Saipan, MP 96950
Phone : (670) 234-6401
Fax : (670) 234-8010

PUERTO RICO
Carmen Ayende
Director
Demographic Registry
Dept. of Health
Fernandez Juncos Station
San Juan, PR 00910
Phone : (809) 726-1027

U.S. VIRGIN ISLANDS
Natalie George-McDowell
Commissioner
Dept. of Health
48 Sugar Estate
St. Thomas Hospital
St. Thomas, VI 00802
Phone : (809) 776-8311
Fax : (809) 777-4001

VOCATIONAL EDUCATION

Administers public vocational education programs which provide individuals with marketable skills.

ALABAMA
Stephen Franks
Director
Vocational Education Div.
Dept. of Education
50 N. Ripley St.
Montgomery, AL 36130
Phone : (334) 242-9111
Fax : (334) 242-9708

ALASKA
Ed Obie
Administrator
Adult & Vocational Education
Dept. of Education
801 W. 10th St., Ste. 200
Juneau, AK 99801-1894
Phone : (907) 465-8726

ARIZONA
Richard Condit
Assoc. Supt/ State Director
Voc., Technological & Adult Ed
Dept. of Education
1535 W. Jefferson
Phoenix, AZ 85007
Phone : (602) 542-5343

ARKANSAS
Lonnie McNatt
Director
Div. of Voc. & Technical Educ.
Dept. of Education
Education Bldg., W.
Little Rock, AR 72201
Phone : (501) 682-1500
Fax : (501) 682-1509

CALIFORNIA
Susan Reese
State Director/Assoc. Supt.
Div. of Vocational Education
Dept. of Education
721 Capitol Mall, 4th Fl.
Sacramento, CA 95814
Phone : (916) 657-2532

COLORADO
Jerome F. Wartgow
President
Occupational Education Systems
Dept. of Higher Education
1391 Speer Blvd., Ste. 600
Denver, CO 80204
Phone : (303) 620-4000

CONNECTICUT
Juan Lopez
Superintendent
Voc. & Technical School System
Dept. of Education
25 Industrial Park Rd.
Middletown, CT 06457
Phone : (203) 638-4010

DELAWARE
Lewis L. Atkinson III
Team Leader
Vocational Education
Dept. of Public Instruction
Townsend Bldg.
Dover, DE 19901
Phone : (302) 739-4638

FLORIDA
Joseph Stephens
Acting Director
Div. of Applied Technology & Adult Education
Dept. of Education
1114 B Florida Education Center
Tallahassee, FL 32399
Phone : (904) 488-8961

GEORGIA
Gail Fletcher
Director
Council on Vocational Education
254 Washington St., 4th Fl.
Atlanta, GA 30334
Phone : (404) 656-7782

HAWAII
Alan R. Kohan
Acting State Director
Off. for Vocational Education
1633 Bachman Pl.
Sinclair Annex 1, Rm. 4
Honolulu, HI 96822-2489
Phone : (808) 956-7461

IDAHO
Trudy Anderson
State Administrator
Div. of Vocational Education
P.O. Box 83720
Boise, ID 83720-0095
Phone : (208) 334-3216

ILLINOIS
Joseph A. Spagnolo
Superintendent
State Board of Education
100 N. First St.
Springfield, IL 62777
Phone : (217) 782-2221
Fax : (217) 785-3972

INDIANA
Patty Shutt
Director
Vocational Education Section
Dept. of Education
State House, 4th Fl.
Indianapolis, IN 46204
Phone : (317) 232-9184

IOWA
Roger Foelske
Chief
Bur. of Technical & Voc. Educ.
Dept. of Education
Grimes State Off. Bldg.
Des Moines, IA 50319
Phone : (515) 281-4702

KANSAS
David L. DePue
Executive Director
State Council on Vocational Ed.
1020 S. Kansas Ave., Ste. 250
Topeka, KS 66612-1300
Phone : (913) 296-2451
Fax : (913) 296-0622

KENTUCKY
Kyle Parker
Commissioner
Dept. for Adult & Tech. Educ.
Workforce Development Cabinet
Capital Plaza Tower, 3rd Fl.
Frankfort, KY 40601
Phone : (504) 564-4286

Thomas C. Boysen
Commissioner
Dept. of Education
Ed. & Humanities Cabinet
Capital Plaza Tower
Frankfort, KY 40601
Phone : (502) 564-4770

LOUISIANA
Chris Strother
Assistant Superintendent
Off. of Vocational Programs
Dept. of Education
P.O. Box 94064
Baton Rouge, LA 70804
Phone : (504) 342-3523

MAINE
Mary Majorowicz
Associate Commissioner
Bur. of Vocational Education
Dept. of Education
State House Station # 23
Augusta, ME 04333
Phone : (207) 287-5113

MARYLAND**
Katharine M. Oliver
Assistant State Superintendent
Div. of Career & Technology Ed
Dept. of Education
200 W. Baltimore St.
Baltimore, MD 21201
Phone: (410) 333-2075

MASSACHUSETTS
Marsha Mitnacht
Acting Director
School to Employment Srvcs.
Dept. of Education
1385 Hancock St.
Quincy, MA 02169
Phone: (617) 388-3300

MICHIGAN
William Wiesgerber
Acting Director
Career & Technical Ed. Srvcs.
Dept. of Education
P.O. Box 30009
Lansing, MI 48909
Phone: (517) 373-3373

MINNESOTA
Carole Johnson
Chancellor
State Bd. of Tech. Colleges
Capitol Sq. Bldg., Ste. 300
550 Cedar St.
St. Paul, MN 55101
Phone: (612) 296-3995

MISSISSIPPI
Elwyn G. Wheat
Associate State Superintendent
Voc., Technical & Adult Ed.
Dept. of Education
P.O. Box 771
Jackson, MS 39205
Phone: (601) 359-3088

MISSOURI
Robert Robison
Coordinator of Voc. Education
Div. of Voc. & Adult Education
Dept. of Elem. & Secondary Ed.
Jefferson Bldg., 5th Fl.
P.O. Box 480
Jefferson City, MO 65102
Phone: (314) 751-3500
Fax: (314) 526-4261

MONTANA
Jim Burns
Division Administrator
Off. of Public Instruction
Dept. of Vocational Ed. Srvc.
1300 11th Ave.
Helena, MT 59601
Phone: (406) 444-2413

NEBRASKA
Dick Campbell
Program Manager of Vocational Technology
Dept. of Education
P.O. Box 94987
Lincoln, NE 68509
Phone: (402) 471-2783

NEVADA
Michael Raponi
Director
Occupational & Continuing Ed.
Dept. of Education
400 W. King St.
Carson City, NV 89710
Phone: (702) 687-3100

NEW HAMPSHIRE
G. William Porter
Director
Vocational-Technical Srvcs.
Dept. of Education
10 Pleasant St.
Concord, NH 03301
Phone: (603) 271-3454

NEW JERSEY
Thomas A. Henry
Assistant Commissioner
Div. of Vocational Education
Dept. of Education
225 W. State St., CN500
Trenton, NJ 08625
Phone: (609) 292-6340

NEW MEXICO
Betty L. Campbell
Assistant Superintendent
Vocational Technical Unit
Dept. of Education
300 Don Gasper
Santa Fe, NM 87503
Phone: (505) 827-6512
Fax: (505) 827-4041

NEW YORK*
Commissioner
Dept. of Education
Education Bldg.
Albany, NY 12234
Phone: (518) 474-5844

NORTH CAROLINA
Robin Britt
Secretary
Dept. of Human Resources
101 Blair Dr.
Raleigh, NC 27603
Phone: (919) 733-4534

NORTH DAKOTA
Reuben Guenthner
Director of Vocational Ed.
State Capitol Bldg., 15th Fl.
600 E. Boulevard Ave.
Bismarck, ND 58505
Phone: (701) 328-3180
Fax: (701) 328-1255

OHIO
Vicki Melvin
Acting Director
Vocational & Career Education
Dept. of Education
65 S. Front St., Rm. 907
Columbus, OH 43266
Phone: (614) 466-3430
Fax: (614) 644-5702

OKLAHOMA
Roy Peters
Director
Dept. of Vocational-Technical Education
1500 W. Seventh Ave.
Stillwater, OK 74074
Phone: (405) 377-2000

OREGON
J.D. Hoye
Associate Superintendent
Professional Technical Education
Dept. of Education
255 Capitol NE
Salem, OR 97310
Phone: (503) 378-2337

PENNSYLVANIA
Ferman B. Moody
Director
Bur. of Vocational Education
Dept. of Education
333 Market St.
Harrisburg, PA 17126
Phone: (717) 787-5530

RHODE ISLAND
Frank M. Santoro
Deputy Assistant Commissioner
Vocational-Technical Education
Dept. of Education
22 Hayes St.
Providence, RI 02908
Phone: (401) 277-2691

SOUTH CAROLINA
Anne L. Matthews
Director
Off. of Occupational Education
State Dept. of Education
904 Rutledge Bldg.
Columbia, SC 29201
Phone: (803) 734-8410

SOUTH DAKOTA
Larry Zikmund
Director
Voc. & Technical Educ. Div.
Dept. of Ed. & Cultural Aff.
Kneip Bldg.
Pierre, SD 57501
Phone: (605) 773-4527

TENNESSEE
Becky Kent
Executive Director
Div. of Vocational Education
Dept. of Education
Gateway Plaza Bldg., 4th Fl.
Nashville, TN 37243-0383
Phone: (615) 532-2800

TEXAS
Robert Gordon
Director
Vocational Programs
Education Agency
1701 N. Congress Ave.
Austin, TX 78701
Phone : (512) 463-9692

UTAH
Bill Gibson
Director
Dept. of Vocational Rehab.
309 E. 100 S.
Salt Lake City, UT 84111
Phone : (801) 533-9393

VERMONT
Gerard Asselin
External Manager
Career & Lifelong Learning Div
Dept. of Education
120 State St.
Montpelier, VT 05620
Phone : (802) 828-3101
Fax : (802) 828-3140

VIRGINIA
William C. Bosher, Jr.
Superintendent of Public Instruction
Dept. of Education
101 N. 14th St.
Richmond, VA 23219
Phone : (804) 225-2023
Fax : (804) 371-2099

WASHINGTON
Ellen O'Brien Saunders
Executive Director
Workforce Training & Ed. Cord. Bd.
Airdustrial Park, Bldg. 17
P.O. Box 43105
Olympia, WA 98504-3105
Phone : (360) 753-5662

WEST VIRGINIA
Saundra Randolph Perry
Executive Director
Vocational, Technical, & Occupational Education
1018 Kanawha Blvd. E., Rm. 109
Charleston, WV 25301
Phone : (304) 558-2411

WISCONSIN
Dwight York
Director
Bd. of Vocational, Technical & Adult Education
310 Price Place
P.O. Box 7874
Madison, WI 53705
Phone : (608) 266-1207
Fax : (608) 266-1690

WYOMING
Gayle Lain
Executive Director
Vocational Programs
6106 Yellowstone Rd., Ste. A
Cheyenne, WY 82009
Phone : (307) 634-5707

DISTRICT OF COLUMBIA
Cynthia Ball
Assistant Superintendent
Div. of Career Education
Public Schools
415 12th St., N.W., Rm. 904
Washington, DC 20004
Phone : (202) 724-4178

AMERICAN SAMOA
Dave Kulberg
Director
Vocational Education
Dept. of Education
Pago Pago, AS 96799
Phone : (684) 633-5237
Fax : (684) 633-4240

GUAM
John Cruz
President
Community College
P.O. Box 23069
GMF, GU 96921
Phone : (671) 734-4311
Fax : (671) 734-5238

NORTHERN MARIANA ISLANDS
Patrick Tellei
Director
Vocational Education
Public School System
P.O. Box 1370 CK
Saipan, MP 96950
Phone : (670) 322-6451
Fax : (670) 322-4056

PUERTO RICO
Alenidia Falcon
Assistant Secretary
Vocational School
Dept. of Education
P.O. Box 759
Hato Rey, PR 00919
Phone : (809) 753-9128

U.S. VIRGIN ISLANDS
James Cheek
Commissioner
Dept. of Education
44-46 Kongens Gade
St. Thomas, VI 00802
Phone : (809) 774-0100
Fax : (809) 774-4679

VOCATIONAL REHABILITATION

Assists and encourages handicapped persons to find suitable employment through training programs.

ALABAMA
Lamona H. Lucas
Commissioner
Dept. of Rehabilitation Srvcs.
2129 E. South Blvd.
Montgomery, AL 36111
Phone : (334) 281-8780
Fax : (334) 281-1973

ALASKA
Keith Anderson
Director
Vocational Rehabilitation
Dept. of Education
801 W. 10th St., Ste. 200
Juneau, AK 99801-1894
Phone : (907) 465-2814
Fax : (907) 465-2856

ARIZONA
James B. Griffith
Assistant Director
Employment & Rehabilitation Srvc. Div.
Dept. of Economic Security
1789 W. Washington
Phoenix, AZ 85007
Phone : (602) 542-4910

ARKANSAS
Bobby Simpson
Deputy Director
VoTech Education Div.
Dept. of Education
P.O. Box 3781
Little Rock, AR 72203
Phone : (501) 682-6709
Fax : (501) 682-1509

CALIFORNIA
Brenda Premo
Director
Dept. of Rehabilitation
830 K St. Mall, Rm. 322
Sacramento, CA 95814
Phone : (916) 445-3971

COLORADO
Diana Huerta
Manager
Rehab. Field Srvcs. Div.
Dept. of Human Srvcs.
110 16th St., 2nd Fl.
Denver, CO 80203
Phone : (303) 620-4156
Fax : (303) 620-4189

CONNECTICUT
John Halliday
Bureau of Rehabilitative Services
Department of Social Services
10 Griffen Rd. N.
Windsor, CT 06095
Phone : (203) 298-2000

DELAWARE
Michelle P. Pointer
Director
Vocational Rehabilitation Div.
Dept. of Labor
321 E. 11th St., 4th Fl.
Wilmington, DE 19801
Phone : (302) 577-2850
Fax : (302) 577-2855

FLORIDA
Tamara Bibb Allen
Director
Div. of Vocational Rehab.
Dept. of Labor & Employment Security
1709A Mahan Dr.
Tallahassee, FL 32308
Phone : (904) 488-6210

GEORGIA
Yvonne Johnson
Director
Div. of Rehabilitative Srvcs.
Dept. of Human Resources
2 Peachtree St., 23rd Fl.
Atlanta, GA 30303
Phone : (404) 657-3000

HAWAII
Neal Shim
Administrator
Vocational Rehab. & Srvcs. for Blind
Dept. of Human Srvcs.
1000 Bishop, Rm. 605
Honolulu, HI 96813
Phone : (808) 586-5366

IDAHO
George Pelletier
Administrator
Vocational Rehabilitation Div.
State Board of Education
650 W. State St.
Boise, ID 83720
Phone : (208) 334-3390

ILLINOIS
Audrey McCrimon
Director
Dept. of Rehabilitative Srvcs.
623 E. Adams St.
Springfield, IL 62705
Phone : (217) 785-0169
Fax : (217) 785-5753

INDIANA
Suellen Jackson-Boner
Executive Director
Governor's Planning Council for People with Disabilities
143 W. Market, Ste. 404
Indianapolis, IN 46204
Phone : (317) 232-7773

IOWA
Marge Knudsen
Administrator
Voc. Rehabilitative Srcvs.
Dept. of Education
510 E. 12th St.
Des Moines, IA 50319
Phone : (515) 281-6731

KANSAS
Glen Yancey
Acting Director
Vocational Rehab. & Srvcs. for the Blind
Dept. of Social & Rehab. Srvcs.
300 SW Oakley, W. Hall
Topeka, KS 66606-2807
Phone : (913) 296-4424
Fax : (913) 296-1359

KENTUCKY
Salvatore Serraglio
Commissioner
Dept. of Vocational Rehab.
Capital Plaza Tower, 9th Fl.
Frankfort, KY 40601
Phone : (502) 564-4566

LOUISIANA
Gloria Bryant-Banks
Secretary
Executive Off.
Dept. of Social Services
P.O. Box 3776
Baton Rouge, LA 70821
Phone : (504) 342-0286

MAINE
Pamela Tetley
Director
Bur. of Rehabilitation
Dept. of Education
State House Station # 11
Augusta, ME 04333
Phone : (207) 624-5300

MASSACHUSETTS
Elmer C. Bartels
Commissioner
Rehabilitation Comm.
27-43 Wormwood St.
Ft. Point Pl.
Boston, MA 02210
Phone : (617) 727-2172

MICHIGAN
Peter Griswold
Rehabilitation Director
Michigan Jobs Commission
Victor Office Center
201 Washington Square
Lansing, MI 48913
Phone : (517) 373-3391

MINNESOTA
Norena Hale
Assistant Commissioner
Div. of Rehabilitative Srvcs.
Dept. of Jobs & Training
390 N. Robert St.
St. Paul, MN 55101
Phone : (612) 296-1822

MISSISSIPPI
Nell C. Carney
Dept. of Rehabilitation Srvcs.
P.O. Box 1698
Jackson, MS 39215-1698
Phone : (601) 936-0200

MISSOURI
Don L. Gann
Assistant Commissioner
Div. of Vocational Rehab.
Dept. of Elem. & Secondary Ed.
2401 E. McCarty St.
Jefferson City, MO 65101
Phone : (314) 751-3251
Fax : (314) 751-1441

MONTANA
Joe A. Mathews
Administrator
Rehabilitative Services Div.
Dept. of Social & Rehab. Srvcs.
111 Sanders St.
Helena, MT 59601
Phone : (406) 444-2590

NEBRASKA
Margaret Hoffmann
Interim Director
Rehabilitation Services Div.
Dept. of Education
P.O. Box 94987
Lincoln, NE 68509
Phone : (402) 471-3645

NEVADA
Steven Shaw
Administrator
Rehabilitation Div.
Dept. of Human Resources
505 E. King St.
Carson City, NV 89710
Phone : (702) 687-4440

NEW HAMPSHIRE
Paul K. Leather
Director
Bur. of Vocational Rehab.
Dept. of Education
78 Regional Dr., Bldg. 2
Concord, NH 03301
Phone : (603) 271-3471

NEW JERSEY
Thomas G. Jennings
Director
Dept. of Labor
Div. of Vocational Rehab. Srvcs.
CN 398
Trenton, NJ 08625-0398
Phone : (609) 292-5987

NEW MEXICO
Terry Brigance
Director
Div. of Vocational Rehab.
Dept. of Education
435 St. Michaels Dr., # D
Santa Fe, NM 87503
Phone : (505) 827-3500
Fax : (505) 827-3746

NEW YORK*
Deputy Commissioner
Off. of Voc. & Ed. Srvcs. for Individuals with Dis.
1 Commerce Pl., Rm. 1606
Albany, NY 12234
Phone : (518) 474-2714

Thomas Sobol
Commissioner
Dept. of Education
Education Bldg.
Albany, NY 12234
Phone : (518) 474-5844

NORTH CAROLINA
Claude A. Myer
Director
Vocational Rehab. Srvcs. Div.
Dept. of Human Resources
805 Ruggles Dr.
Raleigh, NC 27603
Phone : (919) 733-3364

NORTH DAKOTA
Gene Hysjulien
Associate Director
Vocational Rehabilitation
Dept. of Human Srvcs.
400 E. Broadway Ave., Ste. 303
Bismarck, ND 58501
Phone : (701) 328-3999
Fax : (701) 328-3976

OHIO
Robert Rabe
Administrator
Rehabilitation Services Comm.
P.O. Box 359001
W. Worthington, OH 43235
Phone : (614) 438-1210
Fax : (614) 438-1257

OKLAHOMA
George Miller
Interim Director
Health & Human Srvcs.
Dept. of Human Srvcs.
P.O. Box 25352
Oklahoma City, OK 73125
Phone : (405) 521-2778

OREGON
Joil Southwell
Administrator
Div. of Vocational Rehab.
Dept. of Human Resources
500 Summer St., NE
Salem, OR 97310
Phone : (503) 945-6201
Fax : (503) 378-3318

PENNSYLVANIA
Gilbert Selders
Executive Director
Off. of Rehabilitation
Dept. of Labor & Industry
1300 Labor & Industry Bldg.
Harrisburg, PA 17120
Phone : (717) 787-5244

RHODE ISLAND
William Messore
Administrator
Vocational Rehabilitation
Dept. of Human Srvcs.
40 Fountain St.
Providence, RI 02903
Phone : (401) 421-7005

SOUTH CAROLINA
P. Charles LaRosa Jr.
Commissioner
Dept. of Vocational Rehab.
1410 Boston Ave.
P.O. Box 15
West Columbia, SC 29171-0015
Phone : (803) 822-4300

SOUTH DAKOTA
Bill Podradsky
Secretary
Dept. of Human Srvcs.
Hillsview Plz.
500 E. Capitol Ave.
Pierre, SD 57501
Phone : (605) 773-5990

TENNESSEE*
Assistant Commissioner
Div. of Rehabilitation Srvcs.
Dept. of Human Srvcs.
400 Deaderick St., 15th Fl.
Nashville, TN 37248
Phone : (675) 741-2019

TEXAS
Will Reece
Executive Director
Council on Workforce & Economic Competitiveness
P.O. Box 2241
Austin, TX 78768-2241
Phone : (512) 707-8222

UTAH
Judy Ann Buffmire
Director
Rehabilitation Srvcs. Div.
Off. of Education
250 E. Fifth S.
Salt Lake City, UT 84111
Phone : (801) 538-7545

VERMONT
Diane Dalmasse
Director
Vocational Rehabilitation Div.
Dept. of Social & Rehab. Srvcs.
103 S. Main, 2nd Fl.
Waterbury, VT 05671
Phone : (802) 241-2186

VIRGINIA
Ronald C. Gordan
Commissioner
Dept. of Rehabilitative Services
8004 Franklin Farms Dr., #K300
Richmond, VA 23288-0001
Phone : (804) 662-7010
Fax : (804) 662-9532

WASHINGTON
Joyce Walker
Assistant Director
Vocational Rehab. Section
Dept. of Labor & Industries
P.O. Box 44000
Olympia, WA 98504-4000
Phone : (360) 902-4477

WEST VIRGINIA
William Dearien
Director
Rehabilitation Srvcs.
State Capitol
Charleston, WV 25305
Phone : (304) 776-4671

WISCONSIN
Judy Norman-Nunnery
Administrator
Div. of Vocational Rehab.
Dept. of Health & Social Srvcs.
1 W. Wilson, Room 850
P.O. Box 7852
Madison, WI 53703
Phone : (608) 266-1281
Fax : (608) 267-3657

WYOMING
Gary Child
Administrator
Vocational Rehabilitation Div.
Dept. of Employment
122 W. 25th St.
Herschler Bldg.
Cheyenne, WY 82002
Phone : (307) 777-7341

DISTRICT OF COLUMBIA
Ruth Hill
Administrator
Rehabilitation Services Admin.
Dept. of Human Services
605 G St., NW, Rm. 1111
Washington, DC 20001
Phone : (202) 727-3227

AMERICAN SAMOA
Alfonso Pete Galeai
Director
Off. Of Economic Development Planning
Utulei
Pago Pago, AS 96799
Phone : (684) 633-5155
Fax : (684) 633-4197

GUAM
Joseph Artero-Cameron
Acting Director
Dept. of Vocational Rehabilitation
Harmon Industrial Park
122 Harmon Plz., B201
Harmon, GU 96911
Phone : (671) 646-9468
Fax : (671) 649-7672

NORTHERN MARIANA ISLANDS
Patricia T. Conley
Director
Vocational Rehabilitation Div.
Dept. of Public Health & Environmental Srvcs.
Saipan, MP 96950
Phone : (670) 664-6537
Fax : (670) 322-6536

PUERTO RICO
Elia Moliveras
Assistant Secretary
Vocational Rehabilitation
Dept. of Social Services
P.O. Box 1118
Santurce, PR 00919-1118
Phone : (809) 725-1792
Fax : (809) 721-6286

U.S. VIRGIN ISLANDS
Sedonie Halbert
Administrator
Div. of Disab. & Rehab. Srvcs.
Dept. of Human Srvcs.
Knud Hansen Complex, Bldg. A
1303 Hospital Ground
St. Thomas, VI 00802
Phone : (809) 774-0930
Fax : (809) 774-3466

WATER QUALITY

Responsible for water quality protection programs in the state.

ALABAMA
James McIndoe
Chief
Water Quality Branch
Water Div.
1751 Congressman Dickinson Dr.
Montgomery, AL 36130
Phone : (334) 271-7826
Fax : (334) 279-3051

ALASKA
Doug Redburn
Coordinator
Off. of Water Quality Mgt.
Div. of Environmental Quality
410 Willoughby Ave., Ste. 105
Juneau, AK 99801-1795
Phone : (907) 465-5300
Fax : (907) 465-5274

ARIZONA
Brian Munson
Assistant Director
Off. of Water Qualtiy
Dept. of Environmental Quality
3033 N. Central Ave.
Phoenix, AZ 85012
Phone : (602) 207-2300

ARKANSAS
William Keith
Manager
Planning Branch, Water Div.
Pollution Control & Ecology
P.O. Box 8913
Little Rock, AR 72219
Phone : (501) 562-7444
Fax : (501) 562-4632

CALIFORNIA
Jesse Diaz
Chief
Div. of Water Quality
Water Resources Control Bd.
P.O. Box 944213
Sacramento, CA 94244
Phone : (916) 657-0756

COLORADO
J. David Holm
Director
Water Quality Control Div.
Dept. of Health
4300 Cherry Crk. Dr., S.
Denver, CO 80220
Phone : (303) 692-3500
Fax : (303) 782-0390

CONNECTICUT
Karl J. Wagener
Executive Director
Council on Environmental Quality
Dept. of Env. Protection
79 Elm St., 3rd Floor
Hartford, CT 06106
Phone : (203) 424-4000

DELAWARE
John Schneider
Program Manager
Watershed Mgt.
Dept. of Nat. Res. & Environmental Control
P.O. Box 1401
Dover, DE 19903
Phone : (302) 739-5726
Fax : (302) 739-6140

FLORIDA
Richard M. Harvey
Director
Division of Water Facilities
Dept. of Env. Protection
2600 Blairstone Rd., MS 3500
Tallahassee, FL 32399-2400
Phone : (904) 487-1855
Fax : (904) 921-4303

GEORGIA
William M. Winn
Program Manager
Environmental Protection Div.
Dept. of Natural Resources
205 Butler St., Ste. 1152
Atlanta, GA 30334
Phone : (404) 656-4905

HAWAII
Denis Lau
Chief
Clean Water Branch
Dept. of Health
500 Ala Moana Blvd., Ste. 250A
Honolulu, HI 96813
Phone : (808) 586-4309

IDAHO
Larry L. Koenig
Bureau Chief
Monitoring & Technical Support
Div. of Environmental Quality
1410 N. Hilton St.
Boise, ID 83706
Phone : (208) 334-5860

ILLINOIS
Jim Park
Manager
Water Pollution Control Div.
2200 Churchill Rd.
Springfield, IL 62706
Phone : (217) 782-1654

INDIANA
John L. Winters Jr.
Branch Chief
Water Quality Survey & Standards Branch
Dept. of Environmental Mgt.
P.O. Box 6015
Indianapolis, IN 46206-6015
Phone : (317) 243-5028

IOWA
Jack Riesen
Supervisor
Water Resource Section
Wallace State Off. Bldg.
Des Moines, IA 50319
Phone : (515) 281-8941

KANSAS
Karl Mueldener
Director
Bureau of Water
Dept. of Health & Environment
Forbes Field, Bldg. 240
Topeka, KS 66620-0001
Phone : (913) 296-5500
Fax : (913) 296-5509

KENTUCKY
Terry Anderson
Manager
Water Quality Branch
Div. of Water
14 Reilly Rd.
Frankfort, KY 40601
Phone : (502) 564-3410

LOUISIANA
Dale Givens
Assistant Secretary
Off. of Water Resources
Dept. of Environmental Quality
P.O. Box 82215
Baton Rouge, LA 70884
Phone : (504) 765-0634

MAINE
Martha Kirkpatrick
Director
Land & Water Quality Control
Dept. of Env. Protection
State House Station # 17
Augusta, ME 04333
Phone : (207) 287-3901

MARYLAND**
Mary Jo Garreis
Administrator
Water Quality Program
Dept. of the Environment
Tawes State Off. Bldg.
Annapolis, MD 21401
Phone : (410) 841-5724

MASSACHUSETTS
Yvette DePeiza
Manager
Water Quality Control
Div. of Water Supply
1 Winter St., 9th Fl.
Boston, MA 02108
Phone : (617) 292-5857

MICHIGAN
Jim Bredin
Director
Great Lakes Off.
Dept. of Natural Resources
P.O. Box 30028
Lansing, MI 48909
Phone : (517) 373-3588

MINNESOTA
Patricia Burke
Director
Water Quality Div.
Pollution Control Agency
520 Lafayette Rd.
St. Paul, MN 55155
Phone : (612) 296-7202

MISSISSIPPI
Barry Royals
Chief
Surface Water Branch
Off. of Pollution Control
P.O. Box 10385
Jackson, MS 39208
Phone : (601) 961-5102

MISSOURI
Edwin Knight
Director
Water Pollution Control Prog.
Div. of Environmental Quality
Dept. of Natural Resources
P.O. Box 176
Jefferson City, MO 65102
Phone : (314) 751-1300
Fax : (314) 751-9396
E-Mail: EKNIGHT@MAIL.MORE.NET

MONTANA
Jim Melstad
Supervisor
Drinking Water Program
Water Quality Bur.
Cogswell Bldg.
Helena, MT 59620
Phone : (406) 444-2406

NEBRASKA
Patrick Rice
Chief
Water Quality Division
Dept. of Environmental Control
P.O. Box 98922
Lincoln, NE 68509
Phone : (402) 471-2186
Fax : (402) 471-2909

NEVADA
Lew Dodgion
Administrator
Div. of Environmental Protection
123 W. Nye Ln.
Carson City, NV 89710
Phone : (702) 687-4670

NEW HAMPSHIRE
Raymond Carter
Administrator
Water Quality & Permit Compliance Bureau
Dept. of Water Supply & Pollution Control
6 Hazen Dr.
Concord, NH 03301
Phone : (603) 271-3503

NEW JERSEY
James Mumman
Administrator
Water & Technical Programs
401 E. State St., CN029
Trenton, NJ 08625
Phone : (609) 292-1623

NEW MEXICO
Marcy Leavitt
Director
Groundwater Bur.
Dept. of Environment
P.O. Box 26110
Santa Fe, NM 87504
Phone : (505) 827-2918
Fax : (505) 827-2965

NEW YORK*
Commissioner
Dept. of Environmental Conservation
50 Wolf Rd.
Albany, NY 12233
Phone : (518) 457-3446

NORTH CAROLINA
Steve Tedder
Section Chief
Water Quality Section
Div. of Environmental Mgt.
P.O. Box 27687
Raleigh, NC 27611
Phone : (919) 733-5083
Fax : (919) 733-2496

NORTH DAKOTA
Dennis Fewless
Director
Div. of Water Quality
Dept. of State Health
1200 Missouri Ave.
Bismarck, ND 58502
Phone : (701) 328-5210
Fax : (701) 328-5200

OHIO
Seim Amragy
Manager
Water Quality Modeling Section
Div. of Water Quality Planning
P.O. Box 1049
Columbus, OH 43266
Phone : (614) 644-2884
Fax : (614) 644-2329

OKLAHOMA
Dave O. Dillon
Chief
Water Quality Div.
Water Resources Bd.
P.O. Box 150
Oklahoma City, OK 73152
Phone : (405) 231-2500

OREGON
Michael Downs
Administrator
Div. of Water Quality
Dept. of Environmental Quality
811 SW Sixth Ave.
Portland, OR 97204
Phone : (503) 229-5324

PENNSYLVANIA
Daniel B. Drawbaugh
Director
Water Quality Mgt.
Dept. of Environmental Res.
Market St., State Off. Bldg.
Harrisburg, PA 17101
Phone : (717) 787-2666

RHODE ISLAND
Edward Szymanski
Associate Director
Water Quality Mgt.
Div. of Groundwater
291 Promenade St.
Providence, RI 02908
Phone : (401) 277-2234

SOUTH CAROLINA
Russell W. Sherer
Chief
Div. of Water Pollution Control
Dept. of Health & Environmental Control
2600 Bull St.
Columbia, SC 29201
Phone : (803) 734-5300

SOUTH DAKOTA
Steve Pirner
Director
Div. of Environmental Regulation
Dept. of Water & Natural Resources
523 E. Capitol, Joe Foss Bldg.
Pierre, SD 57501
Phone : (605) 773-3151

TENNESSEE
Paul Davis
Director
Tech. & Admin. Srvc. Section
Div. of Water Pollution Control
401 Church St.
Nashville, TN 37243
Phone : (615) 532-0625

TEXAS
Dan Pearson
Executive Director
Natural Resources Conservation Comm.
P.O. Box 13087, Capitol Station
Austin, TX 78711
Phone : (512) 463-7791

UTAH
Don A. Ostler
Director
Water Quality Mgt. Section
Bur. of Water Pollution Control
288 N. 1460 W.
P.O. Box 144870
Salt Lake City, UT 84116
Phone : (801) 538-6047

VERMONT
David L. Clough
Director
Div. of Water Quality
Dept. of Environ. Conservation
103 S. Main St.
Waterbury, VT 05676
Phone : (802) 241-3770
Fax : (802) 241-3287

VIRGINIA
Peter W. Schmidt
Director
Dept. of Environmental Quality
629 E. Main St.
Richmond, VA 23219
Phone : (804) 762-4020
Fax : (804) 762-4019

WASHINGTON
Michael T. Llewelyn
Program Manager
Water Quality Program
Dept. of Ecology
P.O. Box 47600
Olympia, WA 98504-7600
Phone : (360) 407-6400

WEST VIRGINIA
Mark A. Scott
Chief
Off. of Water Resources
Dept. of Environmental Protection
1201 Greenbrier St.
Charleston, WV 25311
Phone : (304) 558-2107

WISCONSIN
Mary Jo Kopecky
Director
Bur. of Waste Water Mgt.
Dept. of Natural Resources
101 S. Webster, 2nd Fl.
P.O. Box 7921
Madison, WI 53707
Phone : (608) 267-7694
Fax : (608) 267-3579

WYOMING
William Garland
Administrator
Water Quality Div.
Dept. of Environmental Quality
122 W. 25th St.
Cheyenne, WY 82002
Phone : (307) 777-7072

DISTRICT OF COLUMBIA
Edward M. Scott
Administrator
Water & Sewer Utility Admin.
Dept. of Public Works
5000 Overlook Ave., SW
Washington, DC 20032
Phone : (202) 767-7651

AMERICAN SAMOA
Togipa Tausaga
Executive Secretary
Environmental Quality Comm.
Off. of the Governor
Pago Pago, AS 96799
Phone : (684) 633-2304
Fax : (684) 633-5801

GUAM
Joseph C. Cruz
Administrator
Environmental Protection Agency
130 Rojas St., Ste. D-107
Harmon, GU 96911
Phone : (671) 646-8863
Fax : (671) 646-9402

NORTHERN MARIANA ISLANDS
Juan I. Castro
Director
Environmental Quality Div.
Dept. of Public Health & Environmental Srvcs.
P.O. Box 409
Saipan, MP 96950
Phone : (670) 234-1011
Fax : (670) 234-1003

PUERTO RICO
Lusinia Giyoty
President
Environmental Quality Bd.
P.O. Box 11488
San Juan, PR 00910-1488
Phone : (809) 767-8057
Fax : (809) 766-2483

U.S. VIRGIN ISLANDS
Benjamin Nazario
Director
Environmental Protection Div.
Dept. of Planning & Natural Resources
Nisky Ctr., Ste. 231
St. Thomas, VI 00802
Phone : (809) 774-3320

WATER RESOURCES

Responsible for water conservation, development, use and planning in the state.

ALABAMA
Charles Horn
Chief
Water Quality Branch
Water Div.
1751 Congressman Dickinson Dr.
Montgomery, AL 36130
Phone : (334) 271-7823
Fax : (334) 279-3051

ALASKA
Jules Tileston
Director
Div. of Mining & Water Mgt.
Dept. of Natural Resources
3601 C St., Ste. 800
Anchorage, AK 99503-5935
Phone : (907) 762-2163
Fax : (907) 745-7112

ARIZONA
Rita P. Pearson
Director
Dept. of Water Resources
15 S. 15th Ave.
Phoenix, AZ 85007
Phone : (602) 417-2410

ARKANSAS
William Keith
Manager
Planning Branch, Water Div.
Pollution Control & Ecology
P.O. Box 8913
Little Rock, AR 72219
Phone : (501) 562-7444
Fax : (501) 562-4632

CALIFORNIA
Kathlin R. Johnson
Principal Engineer
State Water Project Planning Branch
Dept. of Water Resources
1416 Ninth St., Rm. 252-18
Sacramento, CA 95814
Phone : (916) 653-6636

COLORADO
Hal D. Simpson
State Engineer
Div. of Water Resources
Dept. of Natural Resources
1313 Sherman St., Rm. 818
Denver, CO 80203
Phone : (303) 866-3581

CONNECTICUT
Robert Smith
Chief
Bureau of Water Management
Dept. of Environmental Protection
79 Elm St., 1st Floor
Hartford, CT 06106
Phone : (203) 424-3004

DELAWARE
Gerald L. Esposito
Director
Div. of Water
Dept. of Nat. Res. & Env. Control
P.O. Box 1401
Dover, DE 19901
Phone : (302) 739-4860

FLORIDA
Don Berryhill
Bureau Chief
Local Govt. Waste Water Finance Assistance
Dept. of Environ. Protection
2600 Blairstone Rd.
Tallahassee, FL 32399
Phone : (904) 488-8163

GEORGIA
Nolton G. Johnson
Branch Chief
Environ. Protection Div.
Dept. of Natural Resources
205 Butler St., Rm. 1066
Atlanta, GA 30334
Phone : (404) 656-6328

HAWAII
Rae M. Loui
Deputy Director
Div. of Water Resource Mgt.
Land & Natural Resources Dept.
1151 Punchbowl St.
Honolulu, HI 96813
Phone : (808) 587-0393
Fax : (808) 587-0390

IDAHO
Karl Dreher
Director
Dept. of Water Resources
1301 N. Orchard St.
Boise, ID 83720
Phone : (208) 327-7910

ILLINOIS
Donald R. Vonnahme
Director
Div. of Water Resources
Dept. of Transportation
2300 S. Dirksen Pkwy.
Springfield, IL 62764
Phone : (217) 782-0690

INDIANA
John Simpson
Director
Div. of Water
Dept. of Natural Resources
402 W. Washington
Indianapolis, IN 46204

IOWA
Dennis Alt
Supervisor
Water Supply Section
Surface & Groundwater Protection Bureau
Wallace State Off. Bldg.
Des Moines, IA 50319
Phone : (515) 281-8998

KANSAS
David Pope
Director
Div. of Water Resources
Dept. of Agriculture
901 S. Kansas Ave., 2nd Fl.
Topeka, KS 66612-1283
Phone : (913) 296-3717
Fax : (913) 296-1176

KENTUCKY
Pam Wood
Supervisor
Water Quality Mgt. Section
Dept. for Env. Protection
14 Reilly Rd., Ft. Boone Plz.
Frankfort, KY 40601
Phone : (502) 564-3410

Terry Anderson
Manager
Water Quality Branch
Div. of Water
18 Reilly Rd.
Frankfort, KY 40601
Phone : (502) 564-3410

LOUISIANA
Dale Givens
Assistant Secretary
Off. of Water Resources
Dept. of Environmental Quality
P.O. Box 82215
Baton Rouge, LA 70884
Phone : (504) 765-0634

MAINE
Martha Kirkpatrick
Director
Land & Water Quality Control
Dept. of Env. Protection
State House Station # 17
Augusta, ME 04333
Phone : (207) 287-3901

MARYLAND**
Robert D. Miller
Director
Water Resources Admin.
Dept. of Natural Resources
Tawes State Off. Bldg.
Annapolis, MD 21401
Phone : (410) 974-3846

MASSACHUSETTS
Mike Rapacz
Program Manager
Groundwater
Div. of Water Supply
1 Winter St., 9th Fl.
Boston, MA 02108
Phone : (617) 292-5952

MICHIGAN
Frank Baldwin
Chief
Compliance & Enforcement Section
Div. of Surface Water Quality
P.O. Box 30273
Lansing, MI 48909
Phone : (517) 373-4624

MINNESOTA
Kent Lokkesmoe
Director
Div. of Waters
Dept. of Natural Resources
500 Lafayette Rd.
St. Paul, MN 55155
Phone : (612) 296-4810

MISSISSIPPI
James Spencer
Director
Hydrologic Inventory & Reporting
Bureau of Land & Water Resources
P.O. Box 10385
Jackson, MS 39289
Phone : (601) 354-7110

MISSOURI
Steve McIntosh
Program Director
Water Resources Program
Div. of Geology & Land Survey
Dept. of Natural Resources
P.O. Box 176
Jefferson City, MO 65102
Phone : (314) 751-2867
Fax : (314) 751-8475

MONTANA
Richard Moy
Supervisor
Water Planning Section
Water Management Bureau
1520 E. 6th Ave
Helena, MT 59620
Phone : (406) 444-6606

NEBRASKA
J. Michael Jess
Director
Dept. of Water Resources
P.O. Box 94676
Lincoln, NE 68509-4676
Phone : (402) 471-2363

NEVADA
Michael Turnipseed
State Engineer
Div. of Water Resources
123 W. Nye Ln.
Carson City, NV 89710
Phone : (702) 687-4380

NEW HAMPSHIRE
Ken Stern
Chief Engineer
Water Resources Div.
64 N. Main St.
P.O. Box 2008
Concord, NH 03302
Phone : (603) 271-3406

NEW JERSEY
James Mumman
Administrator
Water & Technical Programs
401 E. State St., CN029
Trenton, NJ 08625
Phone : (609) 292-1623

NEW MEXICO
Tom C. Turney
State Engineer
101 Bataan Memorial Bldg.
P.O. Box 25102
Santa Fe, NM 87504
Phone : (505) 827-6175
Fax : (505) 827-6188

NEW YORK*
Director
Bur. of Water Resources
Dept. of Environmental Conservation
50 Wolf Rd., Rm. 302
Albany, NY 12233
Phone : (518) 457-8681

NORTH CAROLINA
John Morris
Director
Div. of Water Resources
Dept. of Environment, Health & Natural Resources
P.O. Box 27687
Raleigh, NC 27611
Phone : (919) 733-4064

NORTH DAKOTA
David Sprynczynatyk
State Engineer
Water Comm.
State Off. Bldg.
900 E. Boulevard Ave.
Bismarck, ND 58505-0187
Phone : (701) 328-4940
Fax : (701) 328-3696

OHIO
Gail Hesse
Manager
Environ. Planning & Review Section
Div. of Water Quality Planning
P.O. Box 1049
Columbus, OH 43266
Phone : (614) 644-2146
Fax : (614) 644-2329

OKLAHOMA
Walid Maher
Chief
Planning & Development Div.
Water Resources Bd.
P.O. Box 150
Oklahoma City, OK 73152
Phone : (405) 231-2500

OREGON
Martha Pagel
Director
Dept. of Water Resources
158 12th St., NE
Salem, OR 97310
Phone : (503) 378-3739
Fax : (503) 378-8130

PENNSYLVANIA
Glenn E. Maurer
Director
Community Env. Control Bur.
Dept. of Environmental Res.
P.O. Box 2357
Harrisburg, PA 17105
Phone : (717) 787-9035

RHODE ISLAND
Alicia M. Good
Chief
Div. of Water Resources
Dept. of Environmental Mgt.
291 Promenade St.
Providence, RI 02908
Phone : (401) 277-3961

SOUTH CAROLINA
Alfred H. Vang
Deputy Director
Water Resources Div.
1201 Main St., Ste. 1100
Columbia, SC 29201
Phone : (803) 737-0800

SOUTH DAKOTA
Tim Bjorke
Natural Resources Admin.
Facilities Mgt. Off.
Dept. of Environmental & Natural Resources
Foss Bldg.
Pierre, SD 57501
Phone : (605) 773-4216

TENNESSEE
W. David Draughon Jr.
Director
Div. of Water Supply
Dept. of Environment & Conservation
401 Church St.
Nashville, TN 37247
Phone : (615) 532-0191

TEXAS
Dan Pearson
Executive Director
Natural Resources Conservation Comm.
P.O. Box 13087, Capitol Station
Austin, TX 78711
Phone : (512) 463-7791

UTAH
D. Larry Anderson
Director
Div. of Water Resources
Dept. of Natural Resources
1636 W. North Temple, Ste. 310
Salt Lake City, UT 84116
Phone : (801) 538-7250

VERMONT
David L. Clough
Director
Div. of Water Quality
Dept. of Environmental Conservation
103 S. Main St.
Waterbury, VT 05676
Phone : (802) 241-3770
Fax : (802) 241-3287

VIRGINIA
Peter W. Schmidt
Director
Dept. of Environmental Quality
629 E. Main St.
Richmond, VA 23219
Phone : (804) 762-4020
Fax : (804) 762-4019

WASHINGTON
Hedia Adelsman
Manager
Water Resources Program
Dept. of Ecology
P.O. Box 47600
Olympia, WA 98504-7600
Phone : (360) 407-6602

WEST VIRGINIA
Mark A. Scott
Chief
Off. of Water Resources
Dept. of Environmental Protection
1201 Greenbrier St.
Charleston, WV 25311
Phone : (304) 558-2107

WISCONSIN
Charles Ledin
Chief
Water Resource Planning & Policy
Bur. of Water Resource Mgt.
101 S. Webster, 2nd Fl.
P.O. Box 7921
Madison, WI 53703
Phone : (608) 267-7610
Fax : (608) 267-2800

WYOMING
Mike Purcell
Director
Dept. of Natural Resources
Herschler Bldg., Rm. 4W
122 W. 25th St.
Cheyenne, WY 82002
Phone : (307) 777-7626

AMERICAN SAMOA
Abe Malae
Director
Power Authority
Dept. of Public Works
Pago Pago, AS 96799
Phone : (684) 644-5251
Fax : (684) 644-5005

GUAM
Joseph C. Cruz
Administrator
Environmental Proteciton Agency
130 Rojas St., Ste. D-107
Harmon, GU 96911
Phone : (671) 646-8863
Fax : (671) 646-9402

NORTHERN MARIANA ISLANDS
Timothy P. Villagomez
Executive Director
Commonwealth Utilities Corp.
Off. of the Governor
Lower Base
Saipan, MP 96950
Phone : (670) 322-4033
Fax : (670) 322-4323

PUERTO RICO
Emilio Colon
Executive Director
Aqueduct & Sewer Authority
P.O. Box 7066
San Juan, PR 00916-7066
Phone : (809) 756-2492
Fax : (809) 763-5222

U.S. VIRGIN ISLANDS
Benjamin Nazario
Director
Environmental Protection Div.
Dept. of Planning & Natural Resources
Nisky Ctr., Ste. 231
St. Thomas, VI 00802
Phone : (809) 774-3320

WEIGHTS & MEASURES

Inspects commercially-used measuring and weighing devices.

ALABAMA
Don E. Stagg
Director
Div. of Weights & Measures
Agriculture & Industries Dept.
P.O. Box 3336
Montgomery, AL 36193
Phone : (334) 242-2614
Fax : (334) 240-3435

ALASKA
Edward Moses
Director
Div. of Measurement Standards
Dept. of Commerce & Economic Development
12050 Industry Way
Anchorage, AK 99515-3512
Phone : (907) 345-7750
Fax : (907) 345-6835

ARIZONA
John U. Hays
Director
Dept. of Weights & Measures
9535 E. Doubletree Ranch Rd.
Scottsdale, AZ 85258-5539
Phone : (602) 255-5211

ARKANSAS
Mike Hile
Acting Director
Bur. of Standards
State Plant Board
4603 W. 61st St.
Little Rock, AR 72209
Phone : (501) 324-9680
Fax : (501) 562-7605

CALIFORNIA
Darrell A. Guensler
Director
Measurement Standards Div.
Dept. of Food & Agriculture
8500 Fruitridge Rd.
Sacramento, CA 95826
Phone : (916) 387-4241

COLORADO
David Wallace
Chief
Measurement Standards Section
Dept. of Agriculture
3125 Wyandot
Denver, CO 80211
Phone : (303) 866-2845

CONNECTICUT
Allan Nelson
Chief
Weights & Measures Div.
Dept. of Consumer Protection
165 Capitol Ave.
Hartford, CT 06106
Phone : (203) 566-4778

DELAWARE
Bill Lagemann
Supervisor, Weights & Measures
Div. of Consumer Protection
Dept. of Agriculture
2320 S. duPont Hwy.
Dover, DE 19901
Phone : (302) 739-4811
Fax : (302) 697-6287

FLORIDA
Don Farmer
Director
Div. of Standards
Agriculture & Consumer Srvcs. Dept.
3125 Conner Blvd.
Tallahassee, FL 32399-1650
Phone : (904) 488-0645

GEORGIA
Bill Truby
Admin. Assistant to the Commissioner
Fuel & Measure Standards Div.
Dept. of Agriculture
321 Agriculture Bldg.
Atlanta, GA 30334
Phone : (404) 656-3605

HAWAII
James Maka
Administrator
Div. of Measurement Standards
Dept. of Agriculture
725 Ilalo St.
Honolulu, HI 96813
Phone : (808) 586-0870

IDAHO
Glen H. Jex
Chief
Bur. of Weights & Measures
Dept. of Agriculture
2216 Kellogg Ln.
Boise, ID 83712
Phone : (208) 334-2345

ILLINOIS
Sidney Colbrook
Program Manager
Weights & Measures Bur.
Div. of Consumer Srvcs.
P.O. Box 19281
Springfield, IL 62794
Phone : (217) 782-3817

INDIANA
Sharon Rhoades
Director
Div. of Weights & Measures
State Bd. of Health
1330 W. Michigan St., Rm. 136
Indianapolis, IN 46206
Phone : (317) 383-6350

IOWA
Jerry Bane
Chief
Weights & Measures Bur.
Ag. & Land Stewardship Dept.
Wallace State Off. Bldg.
Des Moines, IA 50319
Phone : (515) 281-5716

KANSAS
DeVern Phillips
State Sealer
Div. of Inspection-Weights & Measures
Dept. of Agriculture
2016 SW 37th St.
Topeka, KS 66611-2570
Phone : (913) 267-4641
Fax : (913) 267-2518

KENTUCKY
Vicki Searcy
Director
Div. of Weights & Measures
Dept. of Agriculture
106 W. Second St.
Frankfort, KY 40601
Phone : (502) 564-4870

LOUISIANA
Bob Odom
Commissioner
Dept. of Agriculture & Forestry
P.O. Box 631
Baton Rouge, LA 70821-0631
Phone : (504) 922-1234

MAINE
Ed McLaughlin
Commissioner
Dept. of Agriculture, Food & Rural Resources
State House Station # 28
Augusta, ME 04333
Phone : (207) 287-3871

MARYLAND**
Louis E. Straub
Chief
Weights & Measures Section
Dept. of Agriculture
50 Harry S. Truman Pkwy.
Annapolis, MD 21401
Phone : (301) 841-5790

MASSACHUSETTS
Donald B. Falvey
Director
Div. of Standards
Executive Off. of Consumer Affairs
One Ashburton Pl., Rm. 1115
Boston, MA 02108
Phone : (617) 727-3480

MICHIGAN
E.C. Heffron
Director
Food Div.
Dept. of Agriculture
Ottawa Bldg., 4th Fl.
Lansing, MI 48909
Phone : (517) 373-1060

MINNESOTA
Michael Blacik
Director
Weights & Measures Div.
Dept. of Public Srvc.
2277 Hwy. 36
Minneapolis, MN 55113
Phone : (612) 341-7200

MISSISSIPPI
Bill Eldridge
Director
Weights & Measures Div.
Agriculture & Commerce Dept.
P.O. Box 1609
Jackson, MS 39215-1609
Phone : (601) 354-7080

MISSOURI
Roy Humphreys
Director
Div. of Weights & Measures
Dept. of Agriculture
1616 Missouri Blvd.
P.O. Box 630
Jefferson City, MO 65102
Phone : (314) 751-4278
Fax : (314) 751-0281

MONTANA
W. James Kembel
Administrator
Div. of Public Safety
Dept. of Commerce
1424 Ninth Ave.
Helena, MT 59620
Phone : (406) 444-3934

NEBRASKA
Steve Malone
Director
Weights & Measures Div.
Dept. of Agriculture
P.O. Box 94947
Lincoln, NE 68509-4947
Phone : (402) 471-4292

NEVADA
William McCrea
Supervisor
Div. of Agriculture
Weight & Measures Section
350 Capitol Hill Ave.
Reno, NV 89502
Phone : (702) 688-1180
Fax : (702) 688-1178

NEW HAMPSHIRE
Michael F. Greiner
Supervisor
Bur. of Weights & Measures
Dept. of Agriculture
P.O. Box 2042
Concord, NH 03302-2042
Phone : (603) 271-3700

NEW JERSEY
Mark Herr
Director
Div. of Consumer Affairs
Dept. of Law & Public Safety
124 Halsey St.
Newark, NJ 07102
Phone : (201) 504-6200

NEW MEXICO
Frank A. DuBois
Director
Dept. of Agriculture
New Mexico State University
P.O. Box 30005, Dept. 3189
Las Cruces, NM 88003
Phone : (505) 646-3007
Fax : (505) 646-8120

NEW YORK*
Commissioner
Dept. of Ag. & Markets
Capitol Plz.
1 Winners Cir.
Albany, NY 12235
Phone : (518) 457-4188

NORTH CAROLINA
N. David Smith
Director
Standards Div.
Dept. of Agriculture
1 W. Edenton St.
Raleigh, NC 27601-1094
Phone : (919) 733-3313

NORTH DAKOTA
Allan Moch
Director, Testing & Safety
Public Service Comm.
State Capitol, 13th Fl.
600 E. Boulevard Ave.
Bismarck, ND 58505
Phone : (701) 328-2400
Fax : (701) 328-2410

OHIO
Jim Truex
Acting Chief
Div. of Weights & Measures
Dept. of Agriculture
8995 E. Main St.
Reynoldsburg, OH 43068
Phone : (614) 866-6200
Fax : (614) 728-6424

OKLAHOMA
Sue Cannon
Director of Weights & Measures
Agricultural Laboratory Div.
Dept. of Agriculture
2800 N. Lincoln
Oklahoma City, OK 73105
Phone : (405) 521-3864

OREGON
Kendrick J. Simila
Administrator
Measurement Standards Div.
Dept. of Agriculture
635 Capitol St., NE
Salem, OR 97310
Phone : (503) 373-0964
Fax : (503) 378-6525

PENNSYLVANIA
Neil Cashman
Director
Bur. of Ride & Measurement Standards
Dept. of Agriculture
2301 Cameron St., Rm. 206
Harrisburg, PA 17110
Phone : (717) 787-6772

RHODE ISLAND
William F. Tammelleo
Director
Workers Compensation Div.
Dept. of Labor
220 Elmwood Ave.
Providence, RI 02907
Phone : (401) 272-0700

SOUTH CAROLINA
Carol P. Fulmer
Assistant Commissioner
Consumer Service Div.
Dept. of Agriculture
P.O. Box 11280
Columbia, SC 29211
Phone : (803) 737-2080

SOUTH DAKOTA
Michael Mehlhaff
Director
Div. of Comm. Insp. & Regulations
Dept. of Commerce & Regulations
118 W. Capitol Ave.
Pierre, SD 57501
Phone : (605) 773-3697

TENNESSEE
Bob Williams
Supervisor
Weights & Measures
Dept. of Agriculture
Box 40627, Melrose Station
Nashville, TN 37204
Phone : (615) 360-0144

TEXAS
Rick Perry
Commissioner
Dept. of Agriculture
P.O. Box 12847
Capitol Station
Austin, TX 78711
Phone : (512) 463-7476

UTAH
Kyle R. Stephens
Director
Div. of Regulatory Srvcs.
Dept. of Agriculture
350 N. Redwood Rd.
Salt Lake City, UT 84116
Phone : (801) 538-7150

VERMONT
Bruce Martel
Supervisor of Consumer Assurance
Weights & Measures Off.
Dept. of Agriculture
116 State St.
P.O. Drawer 20
Montpelier, VT 05620-2901
Phone : (802) 244-4510
Fax : (802) 241-3008

VIRGINIA
J. Carlton Courter, III
Commissioner
Dept. of Agriculture & Consumer Srvcs.
1100 Bank St.
Richmond, VA 23219
Phone : (804) 786-3501
Fax : (804) 371-2945

WASHINGTON
Bob Arrington
Program Manager
Weights & Measures Section
Dept. of Agriculture
1111 Washington St.
P.O. Box 42560
Olympia, WA 98504-2560
Phone : (360) 902-1857

WEST VIRGINIA
Karl H. Angell
Director
Weights & Measures Section
Div. of Labor
570 W. McCorkle Ave.
St. Albans, WV 25177
Phone : (304) 722-0606

WISCONSIN
Patricia Allen
Administrator
Trade & Consumer Protection Div.
Agriculture, Trade & Consumer Protection
2811 Agriculture Dr.
P.O. Box 8911
Madison, WI 53708
Phone : (608) 224-4970
Fax : (608) 224-4939

WYOMING
Victor Gerber
APSM Compliance Officer
Weights & Measures Div.
Dept. of Agriculture
1510 E. Fifth St.
Cheyenne, WY 82002
Phone : (307) 777-6586

DISTRICT OF COLUMBIA
Catherine Williams
Administrator
Business Regulation Admin.
Consumer & Regulatory Affairs
614 H St., NW, Rm. 621
Washington, DC 20001
Phone : (202) 727-7247

AMERICAN SAMOA
Arthur Young
Manager
Weights & Measures
Dept. of Administrative Srvcs.
Pago Pago, AS 96799
Phone : (684) 633-1663
Fax : (684) 633-1838

GUAM
Joseph T. Duenas
Director
Dept. of Revenue & Taxation
378 Chalan San Antonio
Tamuning, GU 96911
Phone : (671) 647-5107
Fax : (671) 472-2643

NORTHERN MARIANA ISLANDS
Pedro Q. Dela Cruz
Director
Dept. of Commerce
P.O. Box 10007
Saipan, MP 96950
Phone : (670) 322-4361
Fax : (670) 322-4008

PUERTO RICO
Jose A. Alicea
Secretary
Consumer Affairs Dept.
P.O. Box 41059
San Juan, PR 00940-1059
Phone : (809) 722-7555
Fax : (809) 726-6570

U.S. VIRGIN ISLANDS
Vera Falu
Commissioner
Dept. of Licensing & Consumer Affairs, Property & Procurement
Sub Base Bldg. 1, Rm. 205
St. Thomas, VI 00802
Phone : (809) 774-3130
Fax : (809) 776-0675

WELFARE

Administers the delivery of financial and medical benefits to low-income families and individuals.

ALABAMA
P. L. Corley
Acting Commissioner
Dept. of Human Resources
50 N. Ripley St.
Montgomery, AL 36130
Phone : (334) 242-8395
Fax : (334) 242-0198

ALASKA
Jan Hansen
Director
Div. of Public Assistance
Dept. of Health & Social Srvcs.
P.O. Box 110640
Juneau, AK 99811-0640
Phone : (907) 465-3347
Fax : (907) 463-5154

ARIZONA
Julie Vaughn
Assistant Director
Div. of Family Support
Dept. of Economic Security
P.O. Box 40458 (021A)
Phoenix, AZ 85007
Phone : (602) 274-7846

ARKANSAS
Tom Dalton
Director
Dept. of Human Srvcs.
P.O. Box 1437, Slot 316
Little Rock, AR 72203
Phone : (501) 682-8650
Fax : (501) 682-6836

CALIFORNIA
Eloise Anderson
Director
Dept. of Social Services
744 P St., MS 17-11
Sacramento, CA 95814
Phone : (916) 657-2598

COLORADO
Karen Beye
Managing Director
Dept. of Human Srvcs.
1575 Sherman St.
Denver, CO 80203-1714
Phone : (303) 866-5700
Fax : (303) 866-4214

CONNECTICUT
Joyce Thomas
Commissioner
Dept. of Social Services
25 Sigourney St.
Hartford, CT 06106
Phone : (203) 424-5008

DELAWARE
Elaine Archangelo
Director
Div. of Social Srvcs.
P.O. Box 906
New Castle, DE 19720
Phone : (302) 577-4400
Fax : (302) 577-4405

FLORIDA
Linda G. Dilworth
Assistant Secretary
Economic Srvcs. Program Off.
Dept. of Health & Rehabilitation Srvcs.
1317 Winewood Blvd.
Tallahassee, FL 32399-0700
Phone : (904) 488-3271

GEORGIA
Michael Thurmond
Interim Director
Family & Children Srvcs.
Dept. of Human Resources
2 Peachtree St., 4th Fl.
Atlanta, GA 30303
Phone : (404) 657-5100

HAWAII
Judy Nakano
Administrator
Public Welfare Div.
Dept. of Human Srvcs.
1390 Miller St.
Honolulu, HI 96813
Phone : (808) 586-8048

IDAHO
Jean Phillips
Administrator
Div. of Welfare
Dept. of Health & Welfare
450 W. State St.
Boise, ID 83720
Phone : (208) 334-5747

ILLINOIS
Robert W. Wright
Director
Dept. of Public Aid
100 S. Grand Ave., E.
Springfield, IL 62762
Phone : (217) 782-1200
Fax : (217) 524-7979

INDIANA
James Hmurovich
Director
Div. of Families & Children
Family & Social Srvcs. Admin.
IGC-South, Rm. W392
Indianapolis, IN 46204
Phone : (317) 232-4705

IOWA
Doug Howard
Chief
Bur. of Economic Assistance
Dept. of Human Srvcs.
Hoover State Off. Bldg.
Des Moines, IA 50319
Phone : (515) 281-8629

KANSAS
Candace Shively
Acting Director
Income Support & Medical Srvcs.
Dept. of Social & Rehabilitation Srvcs.
Docking State Off. Bldg., 6th Fl.
Topeka, KS 66612-1570
Phone : (913) 296-3981
Fax : (913) 296-4813

KENTUCKY
John Clayton
Commissioner
Dept. for Social Insurance
Cabinet for Human Resources
275 E. Main St.
Frankfort, KY 40621
Phone : (502) 564-3703

LOUISIANA
Howard Prejean
Assistant Secretary
Off. of Family Support
Dept. of Social Services
P.O. Box 3776
Baton Rouge, LA 70821
Phone : (504) 342-3947

MAINE
Judy Williams
Acting Director
Bur. of Income Maintenance
Dept. of Human Services
State House Station # 11
Augusta, ME 04333
Phone : (207) 287-2826

MARYLAND**
Diane Gordy
Executive Director
Social Services Administration
Dept. of Human Resources
311 W. Saratoga St.
Baltimore, MD 21201
Phone : (410) 333-0109

MASSACHUSETTS
Joseph V. Gallant
Commissioner
Dept. of Public Welfare
600 Washington St., 6th Fl.
Boston, MA 02111
Phone : (617) 348-8400

MICHIGAN
Gerald Miller
Director
Dept. of Social Srvcs.
P.O. Box 30037
Lansing, MI 48909
Phone : (517) 373-2000
Fax : (517) 373-8471

MINNESOTA
Ann Sessoms
Director
Assistance Payments
444 Lafayette Rd.
St. Paul, MN 55101
Phone : (612) 296-0978

MISSOURI
Carmen Schulze
Director
Div. of Family Services
Dept. of Social Services
615 Howerton Ct.
P.O. Box 88
Jefferson City, MO 65103
Phone : (314) 751-4247
Fax : (314) 751-8949

MONTANA
Peter Blouke
Director
Dept. of Social & Rehabilitation Services
111 Sanders St.
Helena, MT 59604
Phone : (406) 444-5622

NEBRASKA
Mary Dean Harvey
Director
Dept. of Social Services
P.O. Box 95206
Nebraska State Off. Bldg.
Lincoln, NE 68509-5026
Phone : (402) 471-3121

NEVADA
Myla Florence
Administrator
Welfare Div.
Dept. of Human Resources
2527 N. Carson St.
Carson City, NV 89710
Phone : (702) 687-4128

NEW HAMPSHIRE
Lloyd W. Peterson
Acting Director
Div. of Welfare
Dept. of Health & Human Srvcs.
Hazen Dr.
Concord, NH 03301
Phone : (603) 271-4321

NEW JERSEY
Karen Highsmith
Director
Div. of Family Development
Dept. of Human Services
Quakerbridge Rd., CN716
Trenton, NJ 08625
Phone : (609) 588-2401

NEW MEXICO
Scott Chamberlin
Chief
Financial Assistance Bur.
Dept. of Human Services
P.O. Box 2348
Santa Fe, NM 87503
Phone : (505) 827-7254
Fax : (505) 827-7203

NEW YORK*
Commissioner
Dept. of Social Srvcs.
40 N. Pearl St.
Albany, NY 12243
Phone : (518) 474-9475

NORTH CAROLINA
Robin Britt
Secretary
Dept. of Human Resources
101 Blair Dr.
Raleigh, NC 27603
Phone : (919) 733-4534

NORTH DAKOTA
Henry C. Wessman
Executive Director
Dept. of Human Services
State Capitol, Judicial Wing
600 E. Boulevard Ave.
Bismarck, ND 58505
Phone : (701) 328-2358
Fax : (701) 328-2359

OHIO
Arnold Tompkins
Director
Dept. of Human Services
30 E. Broad St., 32nd Fl.
Columbus, OH 43266-0142
Phone : (614) 466-6282
Fax : (614) 466-2815

OKLAHOMA
George Miller
Interim Director
Health & Human Srvcs.
Dept. of Human Srvcs.
P.O. Box 25352
Oklahoma City, OK 73125
Phone : (405) 521-2778

OREGON
Stephen Minnich
Administrator
Adult & Family Srvcs. Div.
Dept. of Human Resources
500 Summer St., NE
Salem, OR 97310
Phone : (503) 945-5600
Fax : (503) 373-7492

PENNSYLVANIA
Feather Houstoun
Secretary
Dept. of Public Welfare
Rm. 333, Health & Welfare Bldg.
Harrisburg, PA 17120
Phone : (717) 787-2600

RHODE ISLAND
John D. Bamford
Associate Director
Social & Economic Srvcs.
Dept. of Human Srvcs.
600 New London Ave.
Cranston, RI 02920
Phone : (401) 461-1000

SOUTH CAROLINA
Jim Clark
Commissioner
Dept. of Social Srvcs.
1535 Confederate Ave. Ext.
Columbia, SC 29202
Phone : (803) 734-5760

SOUTH DAKOTA
James Ellenbecker
Secretary
Dept. of Social Srvcs.
700 Governors Dr.
Pierre, SD 57501
Phone : (605) 773-3165

TENNESSEE
Linda Rudolph
Commissioner
Dept. of Human Services
400 Deadrick St.
Nashville, TN 37243
Phone : (615) 741-3241
Fax : (615) 741-4165

TEXAS
Burton Raiford
Commissioner
Dept. of Human Services
P.O. Box 149030
Austin, TX 78714
Phone : (512) 450-3011

UTAH
Cindy Haag
Director
Off. of Assistance Payments
Dept. of Human Srvcs.
120 N. 200 W., 3rd Fl.
Salt Lake City, UT 84103
Phone : (801) 374-7843

VERMONT
Martha B. Kitchel
Commissioner
Dept. of Social Welfare
Agency of Human Services
103 S. Main St.
Waterbury, VT 05671
Phone : (802) 241-2853
Fax : (802) 241-2830

VIRGINIA
Carol Brunty
Commissioner
Dept. of Social Services
Theater Row Building
730 E. Broad St.
Richmond, VA 23219
Phone : (804) 692-1900
Fax : (804) 692-1949

WASHINGTON
Jean Soliz
Secretary
Dept. of Social & Health Srvcs.
P.O. Box 45010
Olympia, WA 98504-5010
Phone : (360) 753-7039

WEST VIRGINIA
Gretchen Lewis
Secretary
Dept. of Health & Human Resources
Bldg. 3, Rm. 206
State Capitol Complex
Charleston, WV 25305
Phone : (304) 558-0684

WISCONSIN
Gerald Born
Administrator
Div. of Community Srvcs.
1 W. Wilson, Room 550
P.O. Box 7851
Madison, WI 53703
Phone : (608) 266-2701
Fax : (608) 267-4549

WYOMING
George Lovato
Director
Wyoming Dept. of Family Services
Hathaway Bldg., 3rd Fl.
2300 Capitol Ave.
Cheyenne, WY 82002-0490
Phone : (307) 777-5831

DISTRICT OF COLUMBIA
James D. Butts
Administrator
Income Maintenance Admin.
Dept. of Human Services
645 H St., NE, 5th Fl.
Washington, DC 20002
Phone : (202) 724-5506

GUAM
Dennis Rodriguez
Director
Dept. of Public Health & Social Services
P.O. Box 2816
Agana, GU 96910
Phone : (671) 734-7102
Fax : (671) 734-5910

NORTHERN MARIANA ISLANDS
Eleanor S. Dela Cruz
Director
Dept. of Community & Cultural Affairs
Off. of the Governor
Saipan, MP 96950
Phone : (670) 233-3343

PUERTO RICO
Carmen Rodriquez de Rivera
Secretary
Dept. of Social Services
P.O. Box 11398
Santurce, PR 00910-1398
Phone : (809) 722-7400
Fax : (809) 723-1223

U.S. VIRGIN ISLANDS
Kathleen Richards
Administrator
Div. of Financial Programs
Dept. of Human Srvcs.
Knud Hansen Complex, Bldg. A
1303 Hospital Ground
St. Thomas, VI 00802
Phone : (809) 774-2399
Fax : (809) 774-3466

WELLNESS

Administers state employee programs designed to improve employee health; to lower employee health benefit costs, absenteeism and turnover; to prevent premature death; and to increase employee morale.

ARIZONA
Maryann Knight
Benefits Manager
Div. of Personnel
Dept. of Administration
1831 W. Jefferson
Phoenix, AZ 85007
Phone : (602) 542-5250

CALIFORNIA
Patricia Pavone
Division Chief
Training & Development Div.
Dept. of Personnel Admin.
1515 S St.
Sacramento, CA 95814
Phone : (916) 324-9371

COLORADO
Betty J. Crist
Wellness Coordinator
Div. of Risk Management
Dept. of Administration
225 E. 16th Ave., 6th Fl.
Denver, CO 80203
Phone : (303) 866-3848
Fax : (303) 894-2409

DELAWARE
Carmen R. Nazario
Secretary
Dept. of Health & Social Srvcs.
1901 N. duPont Hwy.
New Castle, DE 19720
Phone : (302) 577-4500
Fax : (302) 577-4510

GEORGIA
Bobbie Jean Bennett
Director
Georgia State Merit System
200 Piedmont Ave., SW, Ste. 502
Atlanta, GA 30334-5100
Phone : (404) 656-2705

HAWAII
Charlene S.W. Young
Deputy Director
Health Promotion & Disease Prev. Admin., Dept. of Health
1250 Punchbowl St.
Honolulu, HI 96813
Phone : (808) 586-4438

IDAHO
Barbara R. Porter
Administrator
Internal Operations
Dept. of Admin.
650 W. State St.
Boise, ID 83720
Phone : (208) 334-3389

ILLINOIS
Vicki Alewelt
Health Coordinator
Dept. of Public Health
525 W. Jefferson St.
Springfield, IL 62761
Phone : (217) 524-6817

INDIANA
Louise Polansky
Executive Assistant
Div. of Mental Health
Family & Social Srvcs. Admin.
402 E. Washington St.
Indianapolis, IN 46204-2739
Phone : (317) 232-7863

IOWA
Phyllis Watson
Training Officer, Employment & Training
Dept. of Personnel
Grimes State Off. Bldg.
E. 14th & Grand
Des Moines, IA 50319
Phone : (515) 281-8856

KENTUCKY
Julie True
Director
Div. of Employee Srvcs.
Dept. of Personnel
200 Fairoaks, Suite 529
Frankfort, KY 40601
Phone : (502) 564-7911

MAINE
Frank Johnson
Director
State Employee Health
Dept. of Administration
State House Station # 122
Augusta, ME 04333
Phone : (207) 287-4515

MARYLAND**
Libby Lewandowkis
Wellness Director
Dept. of Personnel
301 W. Preston St., 6th Fl.
Baltimore, MD 21201
Phone : (410) 225-4945

MASSACHUSETTS
David Mulligan
Commissioner
Dept. of Public Health
150 Tremont St.
Boston, MA 02111
Phone : (617) 727-0201

MICHIGAN
Don Alsbro
Health Instructor
Lake Michigan College
2755 E. Napier Ave.
Benton Harbor, MI 49022
Phone : (616) 927-3571

MINNESOTA
Keith Tvedten
Director
Employee Assistance
Dept. of Administration
205 Aurora Ave.
St. Paul, MN 55103
Phone : (612) 296-0765

MISSOURI
Tom Vansaghi
Executive Director
Gov's Council on Physical Fitness & Health
Truman Bldg., Rm. 760
P.O. Box 809
Jefferson City, MO 65102
Phone : (314) 751-0915
Fax : (314) 751-7819

MONTANA
Jeanette Schmidt
Employee Benefits Bur.
Dept. of Administration
Sam Mitchell Bldg., Rm. 130
Helena, MT 59620
Phone : (406) 444-3947

NEBRASKA
Michael G. Heyl
Wellness Coordinator
Dept. of Health
P.O. Box 95007
Lincoln, NE 68509
Phone : (402) 471-2101

NEVADA
Lindley Steere
E.A.P. Counselor
Employee Assistance Program
Dept. of Personnel
675 Fairview Dr., Ste. 221
Carson City, NV 89710
Phone : (702) 687-3869

NEW JERSEY
John Hennessy
Supervisor
Medical Services Bur.
State Police
P.O. Box 7068
West Trenton, NJ 08628
Phone : (609) 882-2000, Ext. 2630

NEW MEXICO
Lydia Pendley
Bureau Chief
Off. of Health Promotion
Dept. of Health
1190 St. Francis
P.O. Box 26110
Santa Fe, NM 87502
Phone : (505) 827-2389
Fax : (505) 827-2329

NEW YORK*
Off. of Employee Relations
Agency Bldg. 2, 12th Fl.
Empire State Plz.
Albany, NY 12223-0001
Phone : (518) 474-6988

NORTH CAROLINA
Barbara Coward
Administrator
State Personnel Comm.
Off. of State Personnel
116 W. Jones St.
Raleigh, NC 27603
Phone : (919) 733-7112

NORTH DAKOTA
Kathy Allen
Benefits Planner
Pub. Employees
Retirement System
P.O. Box 1214
Bismarck, ND 58502
Phone : (710) 328-3900
Fax : (701) 328-3920

OKLAHOMA
Oscar Jackson
Secretary of Human
Resources
Off. of Personnel Mgt.
Jim Thorpe Bldg.,
Rm. G-80
Oklahoma City, OK 73105
Phone : (405) 521-2177

SOUTH CAROLINA
Joan McGee
Coordinator
Div. of Insurance Srvcs.
Budget & Control Board
1201 Main St.
Columbia, SC 29201
Phone : (803) 734-0578

TENNESSEE
Regina Ranish
Employee Health Group
Insurance
Dept. of Finance & Admin.
Andrew Jackson Bldg.
Nashville, TN 37243
Phone : (615) 741-8675

TEXAS
Nolan Bewley
Personnel Director
Employment Comm.
101 E. 15th St.
Austin, TX 78701
Phone : (512) 463-2222

VERMONT
Cathryn Callaghan
Director
State Employee Wellness
Dept. of Personnel
110 State St.
Montpelier, VT 05602
Phone : (802) 828-3455
Fax : (802) 828-3409

VIRGINIA
Anthony Graziano
Director
State & Local Health
Benefits Program
101 N. 14th St.
Richmond, VA 23219
Phone : (804) 371-7931

WISCONSIN
Chet Bradley
Health Education
Consultant
Dept. of Public Instruction
125 S. Webster
Madison, WI 53703
Phone : (608) 266-7032
Fax : (608) 267-1052

WYOMING
Ward Gates
Chairman
Governor's Council on
Physical Therapy
Univ. of Wyoming
Box 3196, University
Station
Laramie, WY 82071
Phone : (307) 777-7930

GUAM
Carl Gutierrez
Governor
Executive Chambers
P.O. Box 2950
Agana, GU 96910
Phone : (671) 472-8931
Fax : (671) 477-4826

NORTHERN MARIANA ISLANDS*
Personnel Officer
Civil Service Comm.
Personnel Management
Off.
Off. of the Governor
Saipan, MP 96950
Phone : (670) 234-6958

WOMEN

Responsible for reporting on employment practices and social and economic considerations influencing the status of women, and tracking state laws that affect their civil and political rights.

ALASKA*
Off. of the Governor
3601 C St., Ste. 742
Anchorage, AK 99503
Phone : (907) 561-4227

ARIZONA
Harriett Barnes
Director
Governor's Off. for Women
1700 W. Washington, 4th Fl.
Phoenix, AZ 85007
Phone : (602) 542-1761

CALIFORNIA
Pat Towner
Executive Director
Comm. on the Status of Women
1303 J St., Ste. 400
Sacramento, CA 95814-2900
Phone : (916) 445-3173

CONNECTICUT
Leslie Brett
Executive Director
Permanent Comm. on the Status of Women
90 Washington St.
Hartford, CT 06106
Phone : (203) 566-5702

DELAWARE
Romona S. Fullman
Executive Director
Comm. for Women
Carvel State Off. Bldg.
820 N. French St.
Wilmington, DE 19801
Phone : (302) 577-3879
Fax : (302) 577-2735

FLORIDA
Sandi Beare
Executive Director
Comm. on the Status of Women
Dept. of Legal Affairs
Off. of the Attorney General
The Capitol
Tallahassee, FL 32399-1050
Phone : (904) 922-0252

HAWAII
Pamela Ferguson-Brey
Executive Director
Comm. on the Status of Women
Dept. of Human Srvcs.
335 Merchant St., Rm. 253
Honolulu, HI 96813
Phone : (808) 586-5758

IDAHO
Carolyn Beaver
Chair
Comm. on Women's Programs
Towers Bldg., 10th Fl.
450 W. State St.
Boise, ID 83720
Phone : (208) 334-4673

ILLINOIS
Karen Loeb
Assistant Chief of Staff
Office of the Governor
2 1/2 State House
Springfield, IL 62706
Phone : (217) 785-8652
Fax : (217) 524-1678

INDIANA
Ann Nobles
Chairperson
Comm. for Women
IGC-South, Rm. N103
Indianapolis, IN 46204
Phone : (317) 276-0313

IOWA
Charlotte Nelson
Administrator
Comm. on the Status of Women
Dept. of Human Rights
Lucas State Off. Bldg., 1st Fl.
Des Moines, IA 50319
Phone : (515) 281-4467

KENTUCKY
Marsha Weinstein
Executive Director
Comm. on Women
614A Shelby St.
Frankfort, KY 40601
Phone : (502) 564-6643

LOUISIANA
Bobbette Apple
Director
Off. of Women's Services
Off. of the Governor
P.O. Box 94095
Baton Rouge, LA 70804-9095
Phone : (504) 922-0960

MARYLAND**
Phyllis B. Trickett
Chairwoman
Maryland Comm. for Women
311 W. Saratoga St.
Baltimore, MD 21201
Phone : (301) 333-4810

MASSACHUSETTS
Mary-Lee King
Chief Policy Advisor
Off. of the Governor
State House, Rm. 360
Boston, MA 02133
Phone : (617) 727-9173

MICHIGAN
Sharon Miller
Executive Director
Michigan Women's Commission
611 W. Ottawa St., 3rd Fl.
Lansing, MI 48933
Phone : (517) 373-2884

MINNESOTA
Aviva Breen
Executive Director
Comm. on the Economic Status of Women
85 State Off. Bldg.
St. Paul, MN 55155
Phone : (612) 296-8590

MISSOURI
Sue P. McDaniel
Executive Director
Missouri Womens' Council
Dept. of Economic Development
1442 Aaron Ct., Ste. E.
P.O. Box 1684
Jefferson City, MO 65102
Phone : (314) 751-0810
Fax : (314) 751-8835

MONTANA
Patricia Haffey
Director
Staff Support
Council on Women & Employment
Off. of Gov., State Capitol
Helena, MT 59620
Phone : (406) 444-3111

NEBRASKA
Rose Meile
Executive Director
Comm. on Status of Women
P.O. Box 94985
Lincoln, NE 68509-4985
Phone : (402) 471-2039

NEW HAMPSHIRE
Katherine Pedrone
Chair
Comm. on the Status of Women
16 State House Annex
Concord, NH 03301
Phone : (603) 271-2660

NEW JERSEY
Linda B. Bowker
Director
Div. on Women
Dept. of Community Affairs
101 S. Broad St., CN 801
Trenton, NJ 08625
Phone : (609) 292-8840

NEW MEXICO
Yolanda Roybal
Acting Executive Director
Comm. on the Status of Women
4001 Indian School Rd., Ste. 220
Albuquerque, NM 87110
Phone : (505) 827-4662
Fax : (505) 841-4665

NEW YORK*
Director
Women's Div.
State Capitol
Albany, NY 12224
Phone : (518) 474-3612

NORTH CAROLINA
Juanita Bryant
Director
Council on Status for Women
Dept. of Administration
526 N. Wilmington St.
Raleigh, NC 27604-1199
Phone : (919) 733-2455
Fax : (919) 733-2464

NORTH DAKOTA
Tara S. Holt
Chair
Comm. on the Status of Women
204 N. 4th St.
Bismarck, ND 58501-4004
Phone : (701) 258-2251

OHIO
Carol Porter
Director
Women's Div.
Bur. of Employment Services
145 S. Front St., 6th Fl.
Columbus, OH 43266-0556
Phone : (614) 466-4496
Fax : (614) 466-5025

OKLAHOMA
Linda Sponster
Director
Intergovernmental Affairs
440 S. Houston St., Ste. 304
Tulsa, OK 74127
Phone : (918) 581-2801

OREGON
Laurie Wimmer
Executive Director
Comm. for Women
PSU Smith Ctr., Rm. M315
P.O. Box 751
Portland, OR 97207
Phone : (503) 725-5889
Fax : (503) 725-5889

PENNSYLVANIA
Karen S. Fleisher
Director
Commission for Women
Office of the Governor
209 Finance Bldg.
Harrisburg, PA 17120
Phone : (717) 787-8128

Rosemary Thompson-McAvoy
Director
Commission for Women
Office of the Governor
209 Finance Bldg.
Harrisburg, PA 17120
Phone : (717) 787-8128

RHODE ISLAND
Mary Deibler
Executive Director
Advisory Comm. on Women
W. Exchange Ctr.
Providence, RI 02903
Phone : (401) 277-6105

SOUTH CAROLINA
Mary Waters
Director
Div. on Women
Off. of the Governor
2221 Devine St., Ste. 408
Columbia, SC 29205
Phone : (803) 734-9144

TEXAS
Lynn Leverty
Director
Comm. on Women
Off. of the Governor
Box 12428, Capitol Station
Austin, TX 78711
Phone : (512) 475-2615

UTAH
Bonnie Studdert
Chair
Comm. on Women & Children
1124 State Office Bldg.
Salt Lake City, UT 84114
Phone : (801) 538-1736
Fax : (801) 538-3562

VERMONT
Sara Lee
Executive Director
Governor's Comm. on the Status of Women
126 State St.
Montpelier, VT 05633-6801
Phone : (802) 828-2851
Fax : (802) 828-2930

VIRGINIA
Kay Coles James
Secretary
Div. of Health & Human Res.
Governor's Cabinet
622 9th St. Office Bldg.
Richmond, VA 23219
Phone : (804) 786-7765
Fax : (804) 371-6984

WASHINGTON
Rachel LeMieux
Chair
Interagency Cmte. on the Status of Employed Women
P.O. Box 47450
Olympia, WA 98504-7450
Phone : (360) 753-5540

WEST VIRGINIA
Adrienne Worthy
Executive Director
Women's Comm.
Bldg. 6, Rm. 637
Charleston, WV 25305
Phone : (304) 348-0070

WISCONSIN
Eileen DeGrand-Mershart
Chair
16 N. Carroll St., Ste 720
Madison, WI 53702
Phone : (608) 266-2219

WYOMING*
Executive Director
Council for Women's Issues
Dept. of Employment
820 Park
Worland, WY 82401
Phone : (307) 777-6070

DISTRICT OF COLUMBIA
Annette J. Samuels
Executive Director
Comm. for Women
2000 14th St., NW, 3rd Fl.
Washington, DC 20009
Phone : (202) 939-8083

GUAM
Zeny Custodio
Executive Director
Bureau of Women's Affairs
P.O. Box 2950
Agana, GU 96910
Phone : (671) 472-8931
Fax : (671) 477-4826

NORTHERN MARIANA ISLANDS
Remedio R. Sablan
Special Assistant
Women's Affairs
P.O. Box 10007
Saipan, MP 96950
Phone : (670) 322-5090

PUERTO RICO
Albita Rivera
Executive Director
Women's Affairs Comm.
P.O. Box 11382
San Juan, PR 00910-1382
Phone : (809) 722-2907
Fax : (809) 723-3611

U.S. VIRGIN ISLANDS
Edith L. Bornn
Chair
Comm. on the Status of Women
P.O. Box 1500
St. Thomas, VI 00802
Phone : (809) 774-1400

WORKERS COMPENSATION

Administers laws providing insurance and compensation for workers for job-related illness, injury or death.

ALABAMA
Frank Willett
Administrator
Workers Compensation Div.
Dept. of Industrial Relations
602 Madison Ave.
Montgomery, AL 36130
Phone : (334) 242-2868
Fax : (334) 261-3143

ALASKA
Paul Grossi
Director
Div. of Workers' Compensation
Dept. of Labor
P.O. Box 25512
Juneau, AK 99802
Phone : (907) 465-2790
Fax : (907) 465-2797

ARIZONA
Jerry LeCompte
President
State Compensation Fund
3031 N. Second St.
Phoenix, AZ 85012
Phone : (602) 631-2000

ARKANSAS
James Daniel
Chairman
Workers' Compensation Comm.
Justice Bldg., 2nd Fl.
Little Rock, AR 72201
Phone : (501) 682-3930
Fax : (501) 682-2777

CALIFORNIA
Lloyd W. Aubry, Jr.
Director
Dept. of Industrial Relations
455 Golden Gate Ave.
San Francisco, CA 94102
Phone : (415) 703-4590

COLORADO
John J. Donlon
Executive Director
Dept. of Labor & Employment
1515 Arapahoe St., Tower 2, Ste. 400
Denver, CO 80202-2117
Phone : (303) 620-4717
Fax : (303) 620-4714

CONNECTICUT
Jesse M. Frankl
Chairman
Workers Compensation Comm.
21 Oak St., 4th Floor
Hartford, CT 06106
Phone : (203) 493-1500
Fax : (203) 247-1361

DELAWARE
Karen Peterson
Director
Div. of Industrial Affairs
Dept. of Labor
820 N. French St.
Wilmington, DE 19801
Phone : (302) 577-2884
Fax : (302) 577-3750

FLORIDA
Ann Clayton
Director
Div. of Workers' Compensation
Dept. of Labor & Emp. Security
301 Forest Bldg.
Tallahassee, FL 32399
Phone : (904) 488-2514

GEORGIA
Mr. Harrill Dawkins
Chairman
State Bd. of Workers Compensation
1 CNN Ctr., Ste. 1000
Atlanta, GA 30303
Phone: (404) 656-2034

HAWAII
Gary S. Hamada
Administrator
Disability Compensation Div.
Dept. of Labor & Ind. Rel.
830 Punchbowl St.
Honolulu, HI 96813
Phone : (808) 586-9151

IDAHO
Steve Lord
Chairman
State Industrial Comm.
317 Main
Boise, ID 83720-6000
Phone : (208) 334-6000

ILLINOIS
Robert Malooly
Chairman
State Industrial Comm.
100 W. Randolph St., Ste. 8-272
Chicago, IL 60601
Phone : (312) 814-5559
Fax : (312) 814-6523

INDIANA
G. Terrence Coriden
Director
Violent Crime Compensation Div.
Worker's Compensation Bd.
402 W. Washington St., Rm. W196
Indianapolis, IN 46204
Phone : (317) 232-3808

IOWA
Byron Orton
Commissioner
Industrial Services Div.
Dept. of Employment Srvcs.
1000 E. Grand
Des Moines, IA 50319
Phone : (515) 281-5934

KANSAS
George Gomez
Director
Div. of Workers Compensation
Dept. of Human Resources
800 SW Jackson, Ste. 600
Topeka, KS 66612-1227
Phone : (913) 296-3441
Fax : (913) 296-0839

KENTUCKY
J. Patrick Abell
Chairman
Workers' Compensation Board
Dept. of Workers Claims
403 Wapping St., Bush Bldg.
Frankfort, KY 40601
Phone : (502) 564-5550

LOUISIANA
Joseph Stone
Assistant Secretary
Dept. of Labor
P.O. Box 94094
Baton Rouge, LA 70804
Phone : (504) 342-7692

MAINE
Jim McGowan
Director
Workers' Compensation Comm.
State House Station # 27
Augusta, ME 04333
Phone : (207) 287-3751

MARYLAND**
Charles J. Krysiak
Chairman
Workers' Compensation Comm.
6 N. Liberty St., Rm. 940
Baltimore, MD 21201
Phone : (410) 333-4775

MASSACHUSETTS
James Campbell
Commissioner
Industrial Accident Bd.
600 Washington St., 7th Fl.
Boston, MA 02111
Phone: (617) 727-4900

MICHIGAN
Jack F. Wheatley
Director
Bur. of Workers' Compensation
Dept. of Labor
P.O. Box 30016
Lansing, MI 48909
Phone: (517) 373-3480

MINNESOTA
Kevin Wilkins
Acting Assistant Commissioner
Workers Compensation Div.
Dept. of Labor & Industry
443 Lafayette Rd.
St. Paul, MN 55155
Phone: (612) 296-6490

MISSISSIPPI
Claire Porter
Chairman
Workers' Compensation Comm.
1428 Lakeland Dr.
Jackson, MS 39216
Phone: (601) 987-4204

MISSOURI
JoAnn Karll
Director
Div. of Workers' Compensation
Dept. of Labor & Ind. Rel.
3315 W. Truman Blvd.
P.O. Box 58
Jefferson City, MO 65102
Phone: (314) 751-4231
Fax: (314) 526-4960

MONTANA
Carl Swanson
President
State Compensation & Mutual Fund Insurance
5 S. Last Chance Gulch
Helena, MT 59601
Phone: (406) 444-6518

NEBRASKA
Ben Novicoff
Presiding Judge
Worker's Compensation Court
P.O. Box 98908
Lincoln, NE 68509
Phone: (402) 471-2568

NEVADA
Doug Dirks
General Manager
State Industrial Insurance System
515 E. Musser St.
Carson City, NV 89714
Phone: (702) 687-5284

NEW HAMPSHIRE
Katherine Bargar
Director
Workmen's Compensation Div.
State Off. Park S.
95 Pleasant St.
Concord, NH 03301
Phone: (603) 271-3174

NEW JERSEY
Paul A. Kapalko
Director
Div. of Workers' Compensation
Dept. of Labor
John Fitch Plz., CN381
Trenton, NJ 08625
Phone: (609) 292-2414

NEW MEXICO
Stephen W. Kennedy
Director
Workmen's Compensation Admin.
1820 Randolph, SE
Albuquerque, NM 87106
Phone: (505) 841-6000
Fax: (505) 841-6009

NEW YORK*
Chairman
Executive Off.
Workers Compensation Bd.
180 Livingston St.
Brooklyn, NY 11248
Phone: (718) 802-6666

NORTH CAROLINA
James J. Booker
Chairman
Industrial Comm.
Dept. of Commerce
430 N. Salisbury St.
Raleigh, NC 27603
Phone: (919) 733-4820

NORTH DAKOTA
Randy Hoffman
Acting Director
Worker's Compensation Bur.
500 E. Front Ave.
Bismarck, ND 58504-5685
Phone: (701) 328-3800
Fax: (701) 328-3820

OHIO
Wes Trimble
Director
Workers' Compensation Bur.
246 N. High St.
Columbus, OH 43266
Phone: (614) 466-1935

OKLAHOMA
Marsha Davis
Administrator
Workers' Compensation Committee
1915 N. Stiles
Oklahoma City, OK 73105
Phone: (405) 557-7600

OREGON
Sara Harmon
Administrator
Workers' Compensation Div.
Consumer & Business Srvcs.
Labor & Industries Bldg.
Salem, OR 97310
Phone: (503) 945-7881

PENNSYLVANIA
Richard Himler
Director
Bur. of Workers' Compensation
Dept. of Labor & Industry
1171 S. Cameron St.
Harrisburg, PA 17104-2501
Phone: (717) 783-5421

RHODE ISLAND
Dennis Revens
Administrator
Workers' Compensation Comm.
One Dorrance Plz.
Providence, RI 02903
Phone: (401) 277-3097

SOUTH CAROLINA
Michael Grant Lefever
Executive Director
Workers Compensation Comm.
P.O. Box 1715
Columbia, SC 29202
Phone: (803) 737-5744

SOUTH DAKOTA*
Director
Div. of Labor & Mgt.
Dept. of Labor
Kneip Bldg.
Pierre, SD 57501
Phone: (605) 773-3101

TENNESSEE
Dena Pobin
Director
Workers Compensation
Dept. of Labor
501 Union Bldg.
Nashville, TN 37243
Phone: (615) 741-2395

TEXAS
Todd Brown
Executive Director
Workers' Compensation Comm.
200 E. Riverside Dr.
Austin, TX 78704
Phone: (512) 448-7900

UTAH
Stephen M. Hadley
Chairman
State Industrial Comm.
State of Utah
Salt Lake City, UT 84114
Phone: (801) 538-6800

VERMONT
Mary S. Hooper
Commissioner
Dept. of Labor & Industry
National Life Bldg.
Drawer 20
Montpelier, VT 05620-3401
Phone: (802) 828-2286
Fax: (802) 828-2195

VIRGINIA
Lawrence D. Tarr
Chairman
Workers' Compensation Comm.
1000 DMV Dr.
Richmond, VA 23220-2036
Phone : (804) 367-8666
Fax : (804) 367-9740

WASHINGTON
Mark Brown
Director
Dept. of Labor & Industries
P.O. Box 44000
Olympia, WA 98504
Phone : (360) 902-4200

WEST VIRGINIA
Andrew N. Richardson
Commissioner
Div. of Worker's Compensation
P.O. Box 3151
Charleston, WV 25332
Phone : (304) 558-2630

WISCONSIN
Greg Frigo
Administrator
Div. of Workers' Compensation
Dept. of Industrial Labor & Human Relations
201 E. Washington, Rm. 161
P.O. Box 7901
Madison, WI 53703
Phone : (608) 266-1340
Fax : (608) 267-0394

WYOMING
Dennis Guilford
Administrator
Workers' Compensation Div.
Dept. of Employment
122 W. 25th St.
Cheyenne, WY 82002
Phone : (307) 777-6750

DISTRICT OF COLUMBIA
Denise Wilson Taylor
Associate Director
Off. of Workers Compensation
Dept. of Employment Services
1200 Upshur St., NW, 3rd Fl.
Washington, DC 20011
Phone : (202) 576-6265

AMERICAN SAMOA
Fai Faita
Chairman
Workmen's Compensation Comm.
Legal Affairs
Pago Pago, AS 96799
Phone : (684) 633-5520
Fax : (684) 633-1841

GUAM
Juan M. Taijito
Director
Dept. of Labor
P.O. Box 9970
Tamuning, GU 96911
Phone : (671) 647-4142
Fax : (671) 646-9004

NORTHERN MARIANA ISLANDS
Luis S. Camacho
Director of Personnel
Personnel Mgt. Off.
Off. of the Governor
Saipan, MP 96950
Phone : (670) 234-6958
Fax : (670) 234-1013

PUERTO RICO
Oscar Ramos
Administrator
State Insurance Fund
P.O. Box 365028
San Juan, PR 00936-5028
Phone : (809) 793-5959
Fax : (809) 793-7735

U.S. VIRGIN ISLANDS
Lisa Harris-Moorhead
Commissioner
Dept. of Labor
P.O. Box 890
St. Croix, VI 00820
Phone : (809) 776-3700
Fax : (809) 773-0094

Notes

Notes